## SAP PRESS Books: Always on hand

Print or e-book, Kindle or iPad, workplace or airplane: Choose where and how to read your SAP PRESS books! You can now get all our titles as e-books, too:

- ► By download and online access
- ► For all popular devices
- ► And, of course, DRM-free

Convinced? Then go to **www.sap-press.com** and get your e-book today.

# Implementing SAP HANA®

# SAP PRESS

SAP PRESS is a joint initiative of SAP and Galileo Press. The know-how offered by SAP specialists combined with the expertise of the Galileo Press publishing house offers the reader expert books in the field. SAP PRESS features first-hand information and expert advice, and provides useful skills for professional decision-making.

SAP PRESS offers a variety of books on technical and business-related topics for the SAP user. For further information, please visit our website: *www.sap-press.com*.

Dr. Berg and Penny Silvia
SAP HANA: An Introduction (2nd Edition)
2013, 527 pp., hardcover
ISBN 978-1-59229-865-5

Thorsten Schneider, Eric Westenberger, and Hermann Gahm
ABAP Development for SAP HANA
2014, approx. 530 pp., hardcover
ISBN 978-1-59229-859-4

Xavier Hacking and Jeroen van der A
Getting Started with SAP BusinessObjects Design Studio
2014, approx. 450 pp., hardcover
ISBN 978-1-59229-895-2

Christian Ah-Soon, Didier Mazoué, and Pierpaolo Vezzosi
SAP BusinessObjects BI Universes: The Comprehensive Guide
2014, approx. 700 pp., hardcover
ISBN 978-1-59229-901-0

Jonathan Haun, Chris Hickman, Don Loden, and Roy Wells

# Implementing SAP HANA®

**Galileo Press**

Bonn • Boston

Galileo Press is named after the Italian physicist, mathematician, and philosopher Galileo Galilei (1564–1642). He is known as one of the founders of modern science and an advocate of our contemporary, heliocentric worldview. His words *Eppur si muove* (And yet it moves) have become legendary. The Galileo Press logo depicts Jupiter orbited by the four Galilean moons, which were discovered by Galileo in 1610.

**Editor** Emily Nicholls
**Acquisitions Editor** Kelly Grace Weaver
**Copyeditor** Julie McNamee
**Cover Design** Graham Geary
**Photo Credit** iStockphoto.com/11728654/© kevinjeon00
**Layout Design** Vera Brauner
**Production** Kelly O'Callaghan
**Typesetting** Publishers' Design and Production Services, Inc.
**Printed and bound in** the United States of America, on paper from sustainable sources

ISBN 978-1-59229-856-3
© 2013 by Galileo Press Inc., Boston (MA)
1st edition 2013

**Library of Congress Cataloging-in-Publication Data**
Loden, Don.
Implementing SAP HANA / Don Loden, Jonathan Haun, Chris Hickman, and Roy Wells. — 1st edition.
pages cm
ISBN-13: 978-1-59229-856-3 (print)
ISBN-10: 1-59229-856-7 (print)
ISBN-13: 978-1-59229-857-0 (E-book)
ISBN-13: 978-1-59229-858-7 (print and E-book) 1. Database management. 2. Business enterprises—Data processing.
3. SAP HANA (Electronic resource) I. Haun, Jonathan. II. Hickman, Chris. III. Wells, Roy. IV. Title.
QA76.9.D3L638 2013
005.74—dc23
2013026265

# Contents at a Glance

# Dear Reader,

Do not be deceived. Writing your first book is not nearly as easy as Jonathan Haun, Chris Hickman, Don Loden, and Roy Wells make it look.

From project proposal to proofs, the author team behind *Implementing SAP HANA* sailed through the editorial process, seemingly without breaking a sweat. They clairvoyantly dodged many common author pitfalls through transparent communication, faithfulness to the writing schedule, and good humor. Given a few pointers early in the game, these four took my suggestions in stride and extended the logic to yet unwritten chapters (which, of course, they delivered in flawless condition).

Coordinating and assembling an over 800-page book about a dynamic topic can be a challenge, but the team seamlessly executed its vision for the project. They brought contributor Hillary Bliss on board to add to their collective expertise, they knew when to sacrifice target page count for comprehensive coverage, and—most importantly—they demonstrated a keen sense of what information you, their reader, would need. I think you'll be very pleased with the depth of coverage in these pages.

If I could clone them, I would. Until technology catches up with me, I suppose I must content myself with writing a glowing note of praise for Jonathan, Chris, Don, and Roy's work—and encourage you to weigh in, too. Is the approach taken in *Implementing SAP HANA* helpful to you? Are there other topics that merit additional coverage? Visit our website at *www.sap-press.com* and share your feedback about *Implementing SAP HANA*.

**Emily Nicholls**
Editor, SAP PRESS

Galileo Press
Boston, MA

*emily.nicholls@galileo-press.com*
*www.sap-press.com*

# Contents

## 8  Security in SAP BusinessObjects BI and SAP HANA ............... 521

## PART III  Integrating SAP BusinessObjects BI with SAP HANA

## Appendices ................................................................................................ 815

# Preface

As a powerful, new technology with a lot of hype, SAP HANA is often misunderstood. Many believe that they can simply place their data into SAP HANA, and all of their business intelligence (BI) problems will disappear. However, the technology alone is not a magic bullet; there is indeed a methodology behind an implementation of SAP HANA, and other software tools are needed to complement such a solution and fully leverage its substantial benefits.

## Purpose

This book was written with the goal of educating readers about implementing an SAP HANA solution. Specifically, we focus on delivering BI solutions using SAP HANA as a data warehouse platform. We begin with an overview of SAP HANA and all of the ways organizations can implement BI solutions using SAP HANA. We then walk you through a specific solution that harnesses the power of SAP Data Services and SAP BusinessObjects to complete an end-to-end BI solution.

## Who Should Read This Book

This book will help an organization's project teams and technology consultants, as well as anyone looking for a one-stop guide to implementing SAP HANA from a BI perspective. Note that this book is not intended to teach basic BI concepts, and we try to always focus on specific SAP HANA implementation knowledge. We also address specific functionality not often discussed in standard SAP documentation or training materials. The book goes well beyond the typical SAP HANA sales cycle conversation.

Before reading this book, we recommend the following prerequisites:

- General knowledge of data warehousing concepts
- Familiarity with BI tools and constructs

► Foundational knowledge of traditional database provisioning, multidimensional modeling, and reporting technologies

This book strives to offer a uniquely real-world perspective to follow the academic sections of each chapter. Each chapter is structured to offer background and theory around the technology. The theory is then followed with a case study—the story of the fictitious AdventureWorks Cycle Company—to show a "real-world" example of the topics covered in the book. You can download the data used for the AdventureWorks Cycle Company case study from this book's website at *http://www.sap-press.com/products/ Implementing-SAP-HANA.html*. Our goal is to provide you with a unique perspective of how these solutions have worked in the field based on real customer engagements.

## Structure of This Book

The book is structured into three parts. The first part covers how data is stored, conformed, cleaned, and physically modeled in SAP HANA using SAP Data Services. The second part of the book covers the unique multidimensional modeling capabilities built into SAP HANA. We also cover the use of predictive analysis within SAP HANA and the basics of integrating data security with established technologies. The third and final part of the book covers consuming data from SAP HANA using the various reporting and visualization tools found in the SAP BusinessObjects suite. These parts are explained in more detail in the following sections.

### Part I: Data Modeling and Provisioning

#### Chapter 1: SAP HANA, SAP BusinessObjects Business Intelligence, and SAP Data Services

An implementation of SAP HANA isn't just an implementation of SAP HANA—it also requires other products, such as SAP BusinessObjects BI and SAP Data Services. By explaining how these three products work together in a successful SAP HANA implementation, we'll lay the foundation for the entire book.

#### Chapter 2: Storing Data in SAP HANA

This chapter takes a deep dive into data storage in SAP HANA and answers several key questions: How is data stored? What type of data models perform best on SAP HANA and why? The goal is to give an understanding of how data is stored in memory in order to provision data most effectively.

### Chapter 3: Preprovisioning Data with SAP Data Services

Before provisioning or data loading can occur, you must first perform source system analysis to see what aspects of the data need repair. Learn how to provide high-quality data as a base for SAP HANA using SAP Data Services.

### Chapter 4: Provisioning Your Data

This chapter explains the design and build of the data loading process for SAP HANA. For standalone SAP HANA, you must load your data, and this can be done via SAP Data Services or replication, which we outline here.

### Chapter 5: Loading Your Data

In most enterprise deployments, both batch processing and real-time processing are necessary to meet business objectives, and in this chapter, we provide an in-depth overview of the various options for loading data into SAP HANA tables using both.

## Part II: Multidimensional Modeling in SAP HANA

### Chapter 6: Modeling Data for Analytic Consumption in SAP HANA

We explore the components of the multidimensional modeling capabilities that are built-in to SAP HANA. The chapter also discusses the differences between traditional data modeling and modeling multidimensional views in SAP HANA.

### Chapter 7: Integrating Predictive Analytics with SAP HANA

This chapter discusses the various tools and methodologies for integrating predictive analytics within the SAP HANA platform and SAP BusinessObjects tools. Many organizations need to tap into insights within their operational data, and SAP has developed several tools that integrate with SAP HANA to run predictive algorithms on very large data sets.

### Chapter 8: Security in SAP BusinessObjects BI and SAP HANA

This chapter discusses ways of integrating the security among the SAP Business-Objects BI platform, SAP HANA, and well-established security platforms. We discuss the processes for provisioning accounts, leveraging Single Sign-On (SSO), and using analytic privileges to secure data. For many organizations, deploying a comprehensive security model with SAP BusinessObjects and SAP HANA is a key step in delivering an end-to-end solution.

## Part III: Integrating SAP BusinessObjects BI with SAP HANA

### Chapter 9: SAP BusinessObjects Universe Design

This chapter provides an in-depth look at the two semantic layers built into SAP BusinessObjects. You'll gain a basic understanding of the tools and how they are used to provide access to data within SAP HANA. We conclude the chapter with two case studies that walk you through the processes of developing universes on SAP HANA tables and analytic views.

### Chapter 10: Professionally Authored Dashboards Powered by SAP HANA

This chapter focuses on both SAP BusinessObjects Dashboards and SAP Business-Objects Design Studio (the intended successor to SAP BusinessObjects Dashboards). It gives users an overview of the types of dashboards that qualify as professionally authored, discusses the two SAP products available to generate dashboards, and outlines the process for connecting dashboards to SAP HANA with a case study.

### Chapter 11: Data Exploration and Self-Service Analytics with SAP HANA

This chapter covers the major activities of connecting SAP BusinessObjects Explorer and SAP Lumira to SAP HANA. It discusses the technical aspects of both solutions and their benefits when paired with SAP HANA. From the perspective of SAP BusinessObjects Explorer, we discuss how the solution can be a quick and easy way to deploy both Internet browser-based and mobile data analysis for a sales force. The chapter concludes with a case study for developing an SAP BusinessObjects Explorer information space for sales data.

### Chapter 12: SAP BusinessObjects Web Intelligence Powered by SAP HANA

This chapter provides an in-depth overview of how SAP BusinessObjects Web Intelligence can interact with data from SAP HANA. It discusses the various features of SAP BusinessObjects Web Intelligence and the types of reporting that are common within organizations. It also covers the various ways that users can access and share analytics created within SAP BusinessObjects Web Intelligence, concluding with a case study.

## Chapter 13: SAP Crystal Reports Powered by SAP HANA

This chapter provides an in-depth overview of how SAP Crystal Reports can interact with data within SAP HANA. We discuss the two versions of SAP Crystal Reports that are available in SAP BusinessObjects BI, and which tool should be used within an organization. We also explain the various ways that users can access and share reports and analytics created in SAP Crystal Reports. We conclude with a case study on how an accounting department can leverage financial data with SAP HANA using SAP Crystal Reports.

# Acknowledgments

We would like to dedicate this book to our families and loved ones for their support and understanding during the endless hours and many weekends that were committed to the completion of this project. To Lauren Loden, Parks Loden, Samantha Haun, Addison Haun, Mason Haun, Curry Bordelon, Adam Bordelon, and Jennifer Wells: Without your thoughtfulness and support, this book would not have been possible.

We would also like to thank our customers for trusting us with their SAP HANA initiatives. Without these experiences from the field, this book would not be possible.

We would also like to recognize Decision First Technologies and show our appreciation to co-owners Scott Golden and Taylor Courtnay. Without their support and the use of their SAP HANA environments in the Decision First Technologies SAP HANA Center of Excellence, most of the content of this book could not have been created.

Special thanks to Hillary Bliss for her knowledge of and esteemed expertise with the SAP Predictive Analysis product and her track record on the subject. Her guidance and input on predictive analysis, statistics, and modeling made the level of depth possible and offered far more valuable content for the reader.

Finally, our sincere and utmost thanks go to everyone at Galileo Press, especially to Kelly G. Weaver and Emily Nicholls, for their patience, dedication, and guidance in helping us through this process and seeing this dream become reality.

# PART I
# Data Modeling and Provisioning

*An implementation of SAP HANA isn't just an implementation of SAP HANA—it also requires other products such as SAP BusinessObjects BI and SAP Data Services. By explaining how these three products work together in a successful SAP HANA implementation, we'll lay the foundation for the entire book.*

# 1 SAP HANA, SAP BusinessObjects Business Intelligence, and SAP Data Services

SAP HANA is an exciting new technology from SAP. When conversations about SAP HANA are initiated, mystique often surrounds the discussion. This mystique is often related to the multiple ways that SAP HANA can be implemented within an organization as well as its hardware and software features. To help clarify any misconceptions, this book will introduce you to a specific SAP HANA business intelligence (BI) solution that can be implemented by any organization, regardless of its data sources or requirements: an implementation of SAP HANA that uses SAP Data Services and SAP BusinessObjects.

However, before we venture too deep into this particular solution, we first aim to fortify your general knowledge of SAP HANA in the first part of this chapter. We start by describing SAP HANA itself by exploring both its software and hardware aspects (Section 1.1) and then by guiding you through the various ways that SAP HANA can be used as a BI appliance (Section 1.2). For a glimpse of the future, we'll also briefly discuss how SAP HANA can be used with SAP Business Suite applications (Section 1.3)—in particular, how SAP Business Suite powered by SAP HANA might change the traditional concepts of a BI solution.

The second half of this chapter discusses the aspects of an implementation of SAP HANA using both SAP Data Services and SAP BusinessObjects Enterprise. Our hope is that you'll gain insight into how these three components make up the core solution that is discussed within this book. We start by helping you understand why SAP BusinessObjects and SAP Data Services are needed in an SAP HANA implementation (Section 1.4). We then guide you through the traditional Enterprise Information

Management (EIM) process to introduce you to SAP Data Services and the ways it can benefit an SAP HANA implementation (Section 1.5). We then walk through a traditional BI landscape running SAP BusinessObjects to help you understand how it exposes the power of SAP HANA to an organization's users (Section 1.6). In Section 1.7, we discuss the overall solution architecture to show how each component functions within the overall solution architecture.

## 1.1   What Is SAP HANA?

In short, there's no single statement that can fully describe what SAP HANA is. Some consider SAP HANA just another database, while others consider it an analytics appliance. The truth is that SAP HANA is more than just a database and more than just an analytics appliance. SAP HANA is the next-generation data appliance. It can serve as many things throughout an organization. To be more precise, it can facilitate many solutions throughout an organization. This includes both solutions where SAP HANA is used to manage data for an application and instances where it's used to process BI queries.

However, even these descriptions do not fully describe SAP HANA. To understand SAP HANA better and to answer this question, we must first examine both the software layers and hardware layers of SAP HANA.

At the software layer, some components of SAP HANA act as a database, while others facilitate multidimensional models. In fact, there are also parts that act as an application server, a predictive analytics engine, and even an online transaction processes engine. Let's not forget that it can also act as an unstructured data processor and full-text search engine.

At a high level, Figure 1.1 depicts the software features and layers of the SAP HANA appliance that allow it to facilitate more than just standard relational data queries. The SAP HANA in-memory database layer contains multiple query processing engines such as the calculation engine, OLAP engine, row engine, and join engine. This layer also contains the row and columnar store database tables. There are also engines designed to specifically manage text processing and text search. The SAP HANA software appliance layer, which includes the SAP HANA in-memory database layer, also includes the web application server (XS Engine), a scripting engine, and management services. These layers build upon each other to form the SAP HANA appliance.

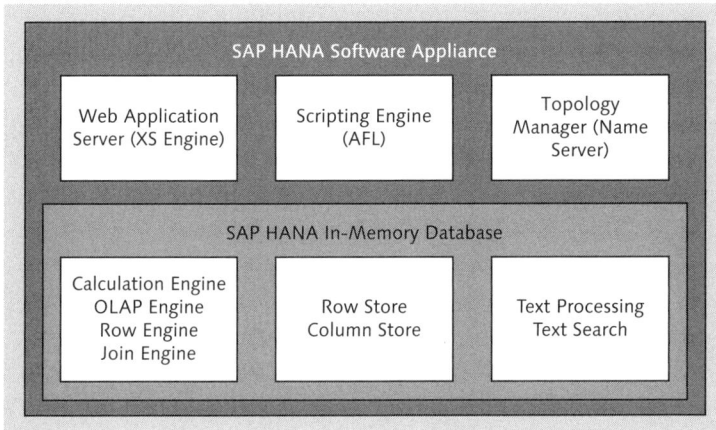

**Figure 1.1** A High-Level Overview of the SAP HANA Software Appliance Layers

SAP HANA incorporates columnar tables to aid in the processing of analytic queries. Columnar tables use a special type of storage mechanism that results in two advantages.

The first advantage centers on its ability to facilitate analytic queries. These queries typically incorporate the use of grouping, ranking, sorting, and aggregating. Columnar tables are perfect candidates to facilitate these queries because the process of storing data in a columnar store effectively creates indexes that describe the location of each unique value in the column. In addition, a columnar store provides a better mechanism for querying large quantities of data because data is quickly pinpointed in each column without the need to scan every row in the table. In general, this reduces the amount of CPU time that is required to pinpoint data in a table and increases the response time of queries.

The second advantage of a columnar table is that it effectively compresses the data stored in each column of the table. Identical values in each column are replaced with smaller surrogates that require less storage than the original values. If we account for this process on each column, the total storage for the entire table can be reduced as much as 20×, but in reality, there is no set number for describing the amount of compression that a table will experience; the amount of compression that a table yields depends largely on how many times values are repeated in a column and the type of data that exists in the column. In general terms, SAP agrees that you'll experience anywhere from 3× to 7× compression. However, there can be a plus or minus factor at both ends of this expectation.

With that said, compression is an important component of the SAP HANA appliance and is significant in today's implementations. Despite all of the hardware advancements over the past 20 years, an individual server is still limited to only 1 to 4 terabytes (TB) of *random access memory* (RAM) depending on the vendor. Most certified SAP HANA hardware vendors currently only scale a multinode appliance to about 16 TB of RAM where each server node has between 512 GB and 1 TB of RAM. IBM currently has a certified appliance cluster that scales to 56 TB of total RAM. With compression, the top systems are able to accommodate anywhere from 56 TB of data to 196 TB data given a compression of 7×.

Therefore, compression is an extremely important benefit of the columnar store; without it, most large enterprises would not be able to implement SAP HANA because their data needs would exceed the limitations of the hardware.

However, we can also expect the amount of RAM supported on an SAP HANA server to increase significantly over the next few years. There are rumors that some hardware vendors are working on technologies that would allow a single logical server node to incorporate 16 TB of RAM or more in the near future. If this rumor is true, SAP HANA multinode implementations might one day be able to accommodate over a petabyte of RAM.

---

**SAP HANA Sizing**

Compression contributes a great deal to making SAP HANA a reality. In general, the sizing requirements for SAP HANA can be obtained using the equation *(SD × 2) / CF*. SD represents the uncompressed size of the source data. CF represents the compression factor expected within SAP HANA.

Pay close attention to the equation, though. Notice that the SD is multiplied by a factor of 2 before it's divided by the CF. Within the SAP engines, we need about 50% of the available RAM to manage the computation of data. This leaves the remaining 50% for data storage, code, and other items.

There is also a difference in the sizing requirements for SAP NetWeaver BW on SAP HANA compared to SAP HANA native solutions. This is mostly due to the abundance of row store tables that are needed in an SAP NetWeaver BW on SAP HANA implementation. However, there are other factors to consider as well.

The CF, or compression factor, can vary depending on the structure of the data. Columns that have more repeated values will compress better than columns with a majority of unique values.

SAP has provided several documents and tools to help you determine the correct size SAP HANA appliance. Please refer to the following links for additional information.

---

- SAP HANA Sizing Note 15149: *https://service.sap.com/sap/support/notes/1514966*
- Quick Sizer tool for SAP HANA: *http://service.sap.com/sap/bc/bsp/spn/quicksizer/main. do?sap-language=en&bsp-language=en*
- Quick Sizer for Beginners Guide: *http://service.sap.com/~sapidb/ 011000358700000523272005*
- Links to sizing: *http://help.sap.com/hana_platform#section7*

Within the SAP HANA software layers are unique query processing engines that are well optimized to retrieve columnar or row data stored in-memory using parallel processing:

- The *OLAP engine* processes basic analytic queries. These queries are often defined by an underlying physical or logical data model where the tables, when joined, produce a star schema. In data modeling terms, you can identify a star schema when one or more conformed dimensions are joined to one or more facts.

- The *calculation engine* processes complex queries or choreographs basic logical data modeling.

- The *join engine* processes standard SQL queries. The join engine is best described as the engine to process the standard select, from, and where SQL statements that have become an industry standard.

- The *row engine* processes complex SQL query logic, row store tables, or logic that is recursive in nature.

Each engine is well optimized because they are accessing data that is stored in RAM. However, each engine also has a unique ability to process different types of queries. As a result, their capabilities and performance will vary.

The hardware components of SAP HANA are also fundamentally important in understanding what SAP HANA is. With SAP HANA, data is stored in *dynamic random-access memory* (DRAM) and within the *central processing unit* (CPU) cache. This allows the software to deliver exceptional performance because data is stored close to the CPU. Traditional databases store and access data on disk drives that are architecturally further away from the CPU and slower in accessing data for a variety of technical reasons.

Each server is also configured with 20 or more CPU cores and 2 or more CPU sockets so that the software can process multiple requests concurrently. For example, when data is stored in a column store, the software can reduce the processing of each column of data into one or more parallel requests. Because there are multiple CPU cores available, each request can be processed by one or more CPU cores in parallel. The net result is more data being processed at the same time for an individual query.

The SAP HANA hardware appliance also incorporates high-speed NAND flash disks and magnetic disks to manage its two persistent storage layers. Because DRAM is volatile or erased when the server loses power, it's important that the data in DRAM be backed up to a nonvolatile storage layers both automatically and periodically. The SAP HANA appliance manages these periodic snapshots of memory to disk automatically. It incorporates a fast storage layer to manage database logging. Typically, the logging layer is managed on Solid State Disk (SSD) arrays or NAND flash cards like those developed by the company Fusion-io. It also incorporates a magnetic disk array layer to house the snapshots of the row or columnar data.

SAP HANA is *ACID compliant*—a term that describes a database that has *atomicity*, *consistency*, *isolation*, and *durability*. ACID compliance guarantees that each database transaction is reliable, even if the server loses power.

Although SAP HANA does rely on traditional disk-based storage, data is stored and accessed in DRAM first. However, data is also simultaneously preserved in persistent nonvolatile disks to provide ACID compliance and data integrity.

Figure 1.2 depicts an overview of the hardware features and layers of a single-node SAP HANA appliance. Data is stored in-memory and close to the CPU for faster processing. The SAP HANA software also makes precise use of the CPU cache to bring frequently accessed data even closer to the CPU. The storage layer is used in conjunction with DRAM to provide ACID compliance and data integrity.

SAP HANA can run on a single server, or it can be scaled out to run on multiple servers that act as a single instance. It acts as a single appliance when scaled over multiple nodes, giving users a single point of access. When distributed on multiple nodes, the core software engines are active on each node and used to manage the distributed data in-memory.

In the multinode or scale-out SAP HANA appliance, all nodes share a single logical persistent storage layer. This ensures that the in-memory data on each node is written to the same shared persistent storage when it performs its regular in-memory data snapshots and backups. Figure 1.3 depicts the SAP HANA appliance running as a single instance distributed over multiple nodes. Note that SAP HANA is ACID-compliant even when it's scaled to multiple nodes.

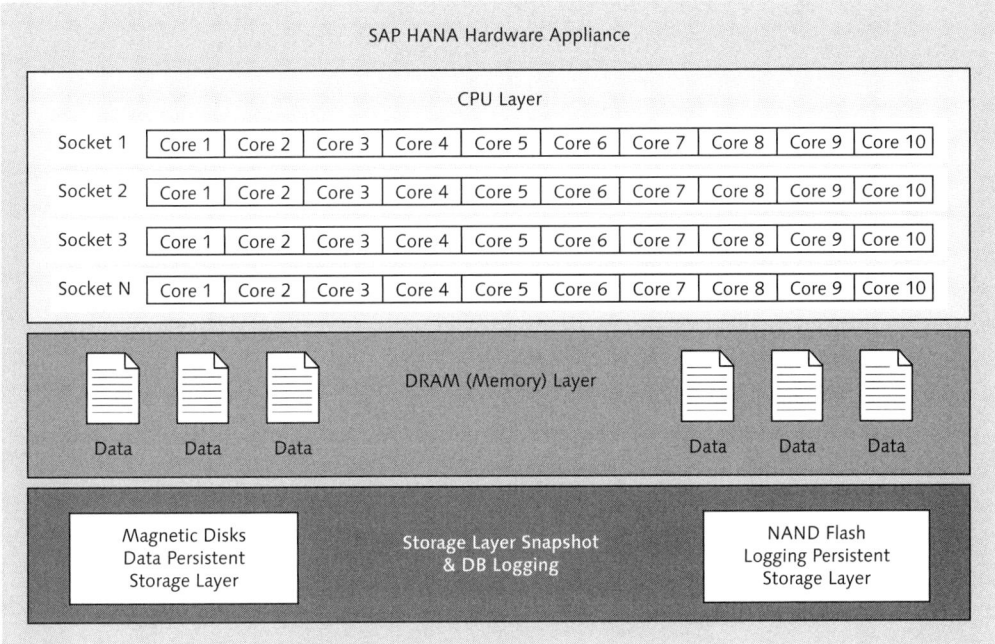

**Figure 1.2** A Single-Node SAP HANA Hardware Appliance

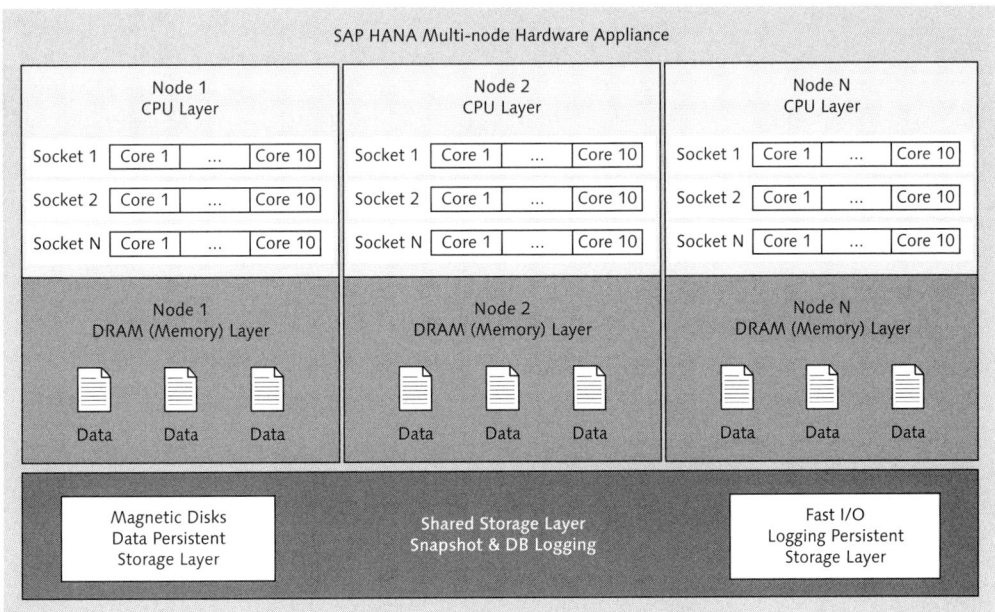

**Figure 1.3** The SAP HANA Scale-Out Appliance with One or More Nodes

## SAP HANA Hardware Vendors

A variety of server hardware vendors provide certified systems to run SAP HANA. Each hardware vendor is required to undergo a strenuous certification processes to ensure that its hardware platform meets or exceeds the standards set by SAP. Because the SAP HANA software was developed to take advantage of the Intel Nehalem EX or Intel Westmere EX E7 processors, it can't be installed on all servers that are currently available, so not every server from every vendor qualifies. For a complete listing of certified servers by vendor, refer to the SAP HANA Product Availability Matrix (PAM) at *http://www.saphana.com/docs/DOC-2382* for more details.

The available persistent storage technologies vary from vendor to vendor, and the selection is even more diverse when we study the different configurations that vendors choose in the scale-out SAP HANA scenarios. For example, IBM, Dell, Cisco, and Huawei have configurations that use an SSD array for logging. These same vendors and other vendors have also chosen to incorporate Fusion-io cards for logging. In scale-out scenarios, vendors might choose different technologies to provide a shared storage layer. For example, IBM uses the General Parallel File System (GPFS) to logically share the local storage of each node while presenting it as a single shared storage layer to each node. Cisco uses Multi-Path File System (MPFS) or EXT3 with an EMC Storage Area Network (SAN) storage array. Cisco also offers an option with NetApp storage arrays that uses NFS to share the storage layer. Hewlett-Packard has chosen to use a Network File System (NFS) with its EVA Storage array. Some vendors choose to use standard rack-mountable servers while others incorporate the use of blade technology. For example, both Cisco and Hewlett-Packard offer scale-out SAP HANA appliances that use their blade technology.

A thorough discussion on the differences between hardware vendors is beyond the scope of this book, but remember that because each hardware vendor is able to take liberties in designing the storage layers, CPU models, and server chassis, you should give careful consideration to these factors when choosing a hardware vendor. Although each vendor must meet the standards established by SAP, not every hardware solution is the same.

At its heart, SAP HANA is built from the ground up to manage, store, and process data in-memory while leveraging multiple CPU cores and the CPU cache. It's a fusion of both software and hardware that was designed to take advantage of today's server hardware capabilities. If SAP were to attempt to deliver technology such as SAP HANA just 20 years ago, it would have found the task to be both technically difficult and cost prohibitive. The cost of DRAM per megabyte has decreased more than 250 times during the past 20 years. During the same time period, the speed and capacity of networks, CPUs, motherboards, and disk drives have increased substantially. SAP recognized this trend and designed SAP HANA to be the true next-generation data appliance.

Traditional database vendors are in a position that limits their ability to quickly adapt to modern hardware because they still need to support legacy technologies designed when hardware was significantly more limited compared to today. Most database vendors are also restricted by the costs and risks associated with redesigning their database software to take advantage of today's hardware. This isn't to say that other database vendors won't *try* to make the transition, but rather an indication that it will be difficult for them to make the transition without requiring their customers to make renewed investments in their legacy database technologies.

The net result of this fusion between hardware and software is a platform that can process queries 1,000 times faster than the traditional magnetic disk-based database. Speed alone doesn't justify SAP HANA, nor does it create an instant value proposition. There are other components of the SAP HANA platform that also add value. Some of those components are built directly into the SAP HANA appliance while others work closely with SAP HANA to deliver solutions and value for an organization. SAP has made a considered effort to incorporate other technologies into the SAP HANA appliance landscape. An SAP HANA instance contains a web application server that allows developers to not only move the data closer to the CPU but to also move web application code closer to the CPU and data. In addition, SAP has incorporated predictive analytics, multidimensional models, and row store tables in the SAP HANA platform. When you consider all of the capabilities internal to the SAP appliance, you'll find that it's more than just a database.

In addition to the components built directly into SAP HANA, there are other technologies that SAP HANA incorporates to deliver an end-to-end solution. As we continue throughout this chapter, we'll discuss the different solutions that are built upon the SAP HANA appliance foundation and how they are used to deliver SAP HANA solutions. However, the core of this book is based on a solution that incorporates the use of two specific tools originating from the SAP BusinessObjects acquisition. Although there are multiple ways to implement SAP HANA, this book focuses on one solution that uses both SAP BusinessObjects and SAP Data Services to deliver an end-to-end BI platform and solution.

## 1.2 Business Intelligence Solutions with SAP HANA

While this book largely focuses on an implementation of SAP HANA that uses SAP Data Services and SAP BusinessObjects, there are several other ways to implement SAP HANA within the BI landscape.

---

**What Is SAP BusinessObjects and SAP Data Services?**

SAP BusinessObjects represents the core platform and tool sets that are used to analyze, secure, and visualize data. It's comprised of a server platform that can be configured to secure, distribute, and manage BI content within an organization. It also supports multiple reporting and visualization tools that are capable of facilitating multiple BI requirements.

SAP Data Services represents the core platform and tool sets that are used to extract, transform, and load data. It also contains several data quality tools to help organizations manage their data quality. SAP Data Services is data source-agnostic, meaning that it can connect to both SAP and non-SAP data sources. It can also target both SAP and non-SAP data sources during the load process.

---

This decision by no means represents the preferred or recommended way to implement SAP HANA but rather expresses one of many options that are currently available. From the perspective of the authors, we have more than ten years of experience each implementing solutions with SAP BusinessObjects and SAP Data Services. This is in part why we chose to focus on such a solution.

However, it's important that we discuss the full range of solutions that are currently available for organizations that are looking to implement BI solutions based on SAP HANA. At a high level, organizations can choose either to implement SAP NetWeaver BW powered by SAP HANA or to implement SAP HANA natively. With SAP HANA native, there are multiple ways to implement solutions on SAP HANA. Each solution that is discussed in Section 1.2.1 and Section 1.2.2 has its own unique set of benefits, components, and use cases. With this knowledge, you should gain a better understanding of SAP HANA and the different ways it can be implemented before we dive into implementing it with SAP BusinessObjects BI and SAP Data Services in later chapters.

### 1.2.1 SAP NetWeaver Business Warehouse 7.3 Powered by SAP HANA

SAP NetWeaver Business Warehouse (SAP NetWeaver BW) is a BI solution that was designed by SAP to facilitate reporting, analytics, data security, master data management, and general data warehouse principles. It's predominantly for use with data generated in the SAP Business Suite applications, but solutions are available that provide support for third-party data as well. SAP NetWeaver BW is comprised of a software layer and an underlying *relational database management system* (RDBMS).

Historically, SAP NetWeaver BW performed many of its functions in the software layer while agnostically using the underlying RDBMS to store the data. This decision was largely based on the need for SAP NetWeaver BW to support multiple vendor RDBMSs. As the use of SAP NetWeaver BW became more prominent, and the volumes of data it stored began to increase, the application layer component of SAP NetWeaver BW became a hindrance to its scalability. SAP's initial attempt to solve this problem was found in a solution called the *SAP NetWeaver BW Accelerator* (BWA). While this solution solved many of the scalability and performance issues associated with querying SAP NetWeaver BW, it was largely focused on fixing the response times of queries. Architecturally, it didn't solve all of the fundamental issues associated with SAP NetWeaver BW. For example, the SAP NetWeaver BW application layer was still predominantly used for extracting, transforming, and loading (ETL) data. For many organizations, the inefficacies of the ETL processes in the SAP NetWeaver BW application layer were not solved with BWA.

In response to the need to better respond to customer's requirements, SAP developed SAP HANA. Initially, SAP HANA was used alongside SAP NetWeaver BW much like BWA. Data was moved from SAP NetWeaver BW InfoProviders into SAP HANA for faster query response times. Much like the BWA solution, using SAP HANA in this capacity didn't solve the fundamental issues associated with the SAP NetWeaver BW ETL processes.

In November 2011, SAP officially released SAP NetWeaver Business Warehouse 7.3 powered by SAP HANA. While SAP HANA and BWA were already usable solutions for SAP NetWeaver BW, the release of SAP NetWeaver Business Warehouse 7.3 powered by SAP HANA fundamentally changed the way that SAP NetWeaver BW interacted with the underlying RDBMS. With its release, SAP began the process of integrating the software layer of SAP NetWeaver BW with the underlying RDBMS of SAP HANA.

Here, SAP HANA serves as the underlying RMDS of SAP NetWeaver BW. Given the powerful features of SAP HANA, this marriage was destined to resolve many of the historical performance and scalability issues associated with SAP NetWeaver BW running on legacy RDBMS. SAP NetWeaver BW powered by SAP HANA simultaneously solves the issues associated with both the SAP NetWeaver BW ETL processes and the SAP NetWeaver BW querying processes.

In addition to the overall performance gains, SAP NetWeaver BW powered by SAP HANA also incorporates many changes to the application layer. Many of the traditional software features of SAP NetWeaver BW are now pushed to SAP HANA for processing. As a result, many traditional SAP NetWeaver BW functions are accelerated throughout the complete SAP NetWeaver BW development lifecycle. This is truly the first step in leveraging SAP HANA and SAP NetWeaver BW as the preferred data warehouse for SAP Business Suite applications. Figure 1.4 illustrates a high-level depiction of the architecture for SAP NetWeaver BW powered by SAP HANA.

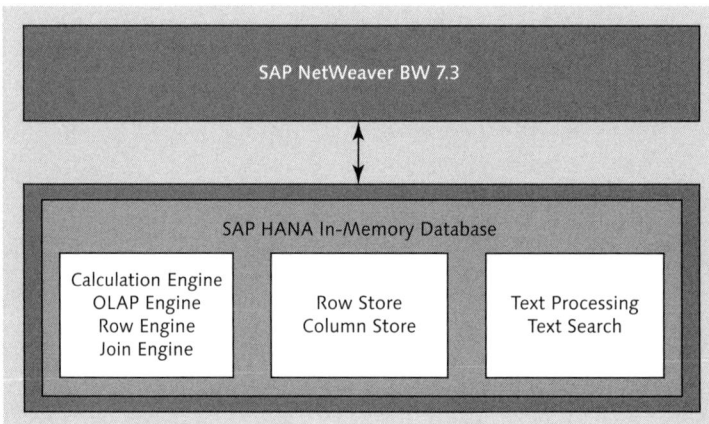

**Figure 1.4**  SAP NetWeaver BW 7.3 Powered by SAP HANA

For organizations that currently run SAP NetWeaver BW with a third-party RDBMS, SAP NetWeaver BW powered by SAP HANA will be an easy transition. Because SAP NetWeaver BW is still the primary software interface, very few changes have been made to the current development tools and processes in version 7.3. That is, while it contains several SAP HANA-specific optimizations, all development and administrative tasks continue to be performed using the SAP GUI or the existing BI tool sets associated with SAP NetWeaver BW.

To implement SAP NetWeaver BW powered by SAP HANA, your organization needs to create a new SAP NetWeaver BW powered by SAP HANA environment and then migrate its existing SAP NetWeaver BW environment to the new landscape—that is, you can't simply do an in-place upgrade of your existing architecture to support SAP HANA. Based on firsthand experience, the process is very straightforward.

Let's examine some of the reasons that an organization would implement SAP NetWeaver BW powered by SAP HANA:

- ▶ **Minimal changes**
  The most compelling reason to implement SAP NetWeaver BW powered by SAP HANA is based on the fact that there are very few changes required for an organization to adopt this SAP HANA solution. Of course, this is assuming the company is currently running SAP NetWeaver BW. The SAP NetWeaver BW application layer continues to be the primary point of contact with this solution. Unlike solutions that replicate SAP NetWeaver BW or SAP Business Suite data to SAP HANA, SAP NetWeaver BW powered by SAP HANA results in a minimal learning curve in its adoption. Developers don't need to use the SAP HANA development tools or models to adopt this solution. In addition, this solution leverages all of the historical development investments associated with the legacy SAP NetWeaver BW environment.

- ▶ **Faster load times**
  Due to enhanced integration between the SAP NetWeaver BW application layer and the overall power of the SAP HANA appliance, organizations can expect a significant boost in load times and the overall ETL process.

- ▶ **Faster query response times**
  Due to the enhanced integration between the SAP NetWeaver BW application and the overall power of the SAP HANA appliance, organizations can expect a significant boost in BI query response times. Based on firsthand experience, SAP NetWeaver BW powered by SAP HANA can result in a 70 to 100 times faster query response time for BI queries in SAP Business Explorer (BEx) and in SAP BusinessObjects 4.0.

- ▶ **Integration with SAP Business Suite applications**
  Because SAP NetWeaver BW is delivered with prebuilt content and direct integration with SAP Business Suite applications, SAP NetWeaver BW powered by SAP HANA will also have these same benefits. Again, this solution merely changes the underlying RDBMS that operates SAP NetWeaver BW. All remaining SAP NetWeaver BW powered by SAP HANA enhancements are minimal and easy to adopt.

▶ **Reduced storage footprint**
With SAP NetWeaver BW powered by SAP HANA, there are several optional application layer enhancements that allow developers to reduce the overall storage footprint of SAP NetWeaver BW by moving legacy operations from the application layer to the SAP HANA platform. In addition, some InfoCubes can be replaced with direct reporting on SAP NetWeaver BW powered by SAP HANA in-memory optimized DataStore Objects (DSOs).

▶ **Reduced reliance on the application layer**
With SAP NetWeaver BW powered by SAP HANA, there are several operational steps that can be pushed directly to the SAP HANA engines for processing. This reduces the number of round trips between the application layer and RDBMS layers that were associated with traditional SAP NetWeaver BW systems. The end result is faster development cycles and load times.

▶ **Near-line storage**
SAP NetWeaver BW offers the ability to directly integrate an independent storage tier into the SAP NetWeaver BW landscape. While SAP HANA offers in-memory data processing, it's not always the most cost-effective medium to store legacy or infrequently accessed data. Near-line storage offers organizations an option to store select data in a storage system that incorporates the benefits of the Sybase IQ columnar store database. Near-line storage uses cost-effective disks to store the data.

▶ **Expected future enhancements**
While there are no guarantees as to what future enhancements will look like for SAP NetWeaver BW powered by SAP HANA, there have been several rumors that future versions will further remove the dependencies on the SAP NetWeaver BW application layer and move more processing to the SAP HANA appliance. In addition, many of the persistent steps associated with legacy SAP NetWeaver BW processes will likely be removed. If the rumors turn out to be true, the SAP NetWeaver BW application layer will eventually serve as a logical modeling tool, and data will only need to be stored once within an SAP HANA table.

### 1.2.2 SAP HANA Native

Solutions that use SAP HANA native are fundamentally different from SAP NetWeaver BW powered by SAP HANA. SAP HANA native represents solutions that provision and access data within SAP HANA directly. After the data is provisioned within SAP

HANA, the multidimensional modeling views can be created to express the data in a business-centric multidimensional model. SAP BusinessObjects can then be used to access the data using its powerful reports, dashboards, and visualization tools.

When SAP HANA was first introduced, SAP devised several solutions that allowed data to be replicated or batch loaded into SAP HANA from SAP NetWeaver BW, third-party data sources, or SAP Business Suite applications. As we'll discover, SAP HANA native solutions continue to add value to organizations for a variety of reasons.

SAP HANA native solutions require an organization to use the tools and processes within SAP HANA such as its multidimensional models, columnar tables, and other supported SAP provisioning tools to facilitate analytics and reporting. An organization's resource will also need to become knowledgeable in the methods for provisioning, modeling, and managing data that will be stored directly in SAP HANA. Although many organizations implement SAP Business Suite applications to run their business, not everyone does. Many of the legacy SAP BusinessObjects customers fall into this category. Many organizations support both SAP Business Suite applications and third-party applications within their organization while other organizations use systems that have no association with SAP. To that end, SAP NetWeaver BW isn't always the most appropriate choice when implementing SAP HANA. Fortunately, SAP HANA native solutions offer several viable alternatives. Later in this section, we'll discuss these different SAP HANA native provisioning solutions, but before we discuss these solutions, let's compare and contrast SAP HANA native to SAP NetWeaver BW powered by SAP HANA. This comparison will give you further insight into the distinctions.

Solutions running with SAP HANA native offer organizations the opportunity to directly leverage SAP HANA without any additional software layer to impede data access. Granted, independent software tools are used to provision and interact with SAP HANA natively. However, this isn't exactly the same methodology that SAP NetWeaver BW uses. With SAP NetWeaver BW powered by SAP HANA, query and reporting tools access the SAP NetWeaver BW software layer and then broker requests to SAP HANA. Figure 1.5 depicts, at a high level, the overall process flow of using SAP BusinessObjects to access SAP NetWeaver BW powered by SAP HANA. As you can see, SAP NetWeaver BW brokers requests to SAP HANA.

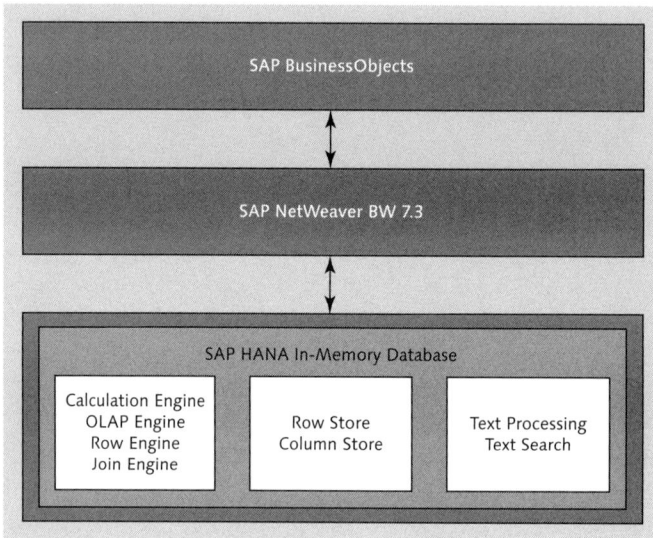

**Figure 1.5** Query and Analysis Tools Accessing SAP HANA via SAP NetWeaver BW When Running SAP NetWeaver BW Powered by SAP HANA

With SAP HANA native solutions, query and reporting tools interact directly with the SAP HANA engines instead of through SAP NetWeaver BW. Our firsthand experience has been that accessing data directly within SAP HANA currently offers a slightly faster experience than accessing data through the SAP NetWeaver BW layer. Figure 1.6 depicts, at a high level, the way that that SAP BusinessObjects interacts directly with SAP HANA native.

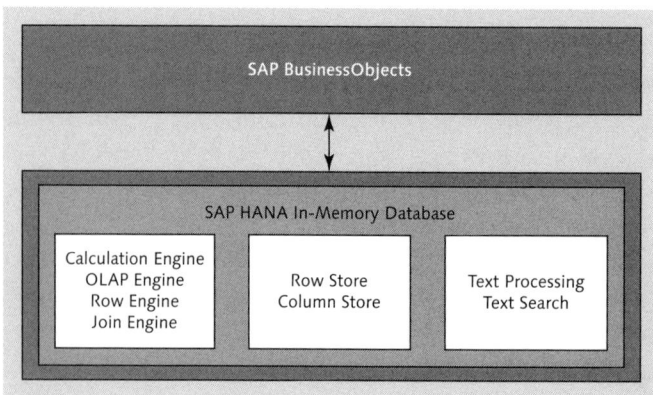

**Figure 1.6** Query and Analysis Tools Accessing SAP HANA Directly in an SAP HANA Native Implementation

Figure 1.5 and Figure 1.6 depict the current state of the two integrations. However, as the integration between SAP HANA and SAP NetWeaver BW matures, you should expect SAP NetWeaver BW solutions to offer more direct access to SAP HANA. In the near future, SAP will likely enhance SAP NetWeaver BW to better leverage the SAP HANA platform natively. Also, in the current versions of SAP NetWeaver BW powered by SAP HANA, organizations can import SAP NetWeaver BW metadata into SAP HANA. The process automatically creates a calculation view or analytic view that can be accessed natively by SAP BusinessObjects. While this feature has not fully matured, it does indicate that SAP is moving in this direction.

Now that we've compared SAP NetWeaver BW powered by SAP HANA to SAP HANA native, it's time to better understand the reasons that organizations would choose to implement SAP HANA native solutions. As it pertains to the core subject of this book, we'll be discussing a solution that uses SAP Data Services and SAP BusinessObjects to manage an SAP HANA native solution. Therefore, it's important that we establish the compelling reasons an organizations would choose to implement SAP HANA native.

We can cite five specific reasons that an organization would choose to implement SAP HANA native. Individually, they might not provide a compelling justification. However, if you find that your needs match more than one of the reasons listed, you'll likely find SAP HANA native to be an appropriate solution.

▶ **Third-party data**

In the context of this book, third-party data refers to data that is generated and stored using applications which have no association to SAP Business Suite. While SAP dominates the overall market share with its SAP Business Suite applications, Forbes reported in May 2013 that it still only accounts for about 25% of the overall ERP market share. To this regard, there are more overall applications generating data than those developed by SAP.

It's our opinion that SAP NetWeaver BW isn't the appropriate solution to manage mass amounts of third-party data. This is especially true when organizations predominantly use non-SAP systems to run their business. This isn't to say that it can't manage third-party data, but rather to express the opinion that there are better solutions available within the SAP portfolio.

If an organization wants to leverage SAP HANA, the amount of third-party data the company chooses to load into SAP HANA has a direct bearing on which solution the company should choose. SAP HANA native solutions support tools that are well-equipped to manage data from third-party sources. At the same time, SAP NetWeaver BW is better equipped to manage data from SAP systems. Third-party data alone should not be the deciding factor, but it does play an important role in making the right decision.

▶ **Custom solutions**
When organizations require a custom information management or BI solution, they will find that both SAP HANA native and its accompanying tools offer a great deal of flexibility.

The SAP HANA platform has several embedded scripting languages, a web application server, and support for industry standard connectivity. This makes SAP HANA an ideal development platform for custom solutions. SAP HANA also supports several data source-agnostic extraction and loading tools that further enhance the flexibility of a custom solution.

▶ **Native performance**
Because SAP HANA native solutions directly leverage the SAP HANA engines and platform, the performance of such solutions will be unimpeded by additional software layers.

▶ **Real-time replication**
When an organization needs a platform that supports both real-time data replication and real-time analytical modeling, SAP HANA native will prove to be the best solution.

▶ **Complex transformations**
When the source data requires complex transformation, data cleansing, and complex data merging, an SAP HANA native and SAP Data Services solution will provide the most flexibility and capability.

To further understand SAP HANA native, we need to first examine all of the methods that are used to provision the data it will manage. Before we can create meaningful reports and analytics, we must first decide how best to extract data and load it into SAP HANA. SAP currently support four main provisioning solutions for SAP HANA native: SAP Landscape Transformation (SLT), Direct Extract Connector (DXC), SAP Data Services, and SAP HANA Studio. Let's take a closer look at each of these.

### SAP Landscape Transformation

SAP Landscape Transformation (SLT) is one way that an organization can choose to implement SAP HANA. The key technology behind SLT is its ability to perform real-time log-based replication of data from both an SAP Business Suite application or from a third-party source.

SLT can also process data in batch mode, but it's more appropriately used to provision data within SAP HANA in real-time mode. Organizations will benefit from SLT when they need to create analytics using data that has near zero latency. With the goal of SLT centered on the concept of real time, there is little room for complex transformations of the data within the SLT engines. This is where SAP HANA plays an important role in an overall SLT solution. As you'll discover in later chapters, SAP HANA has the capability to transform basic raw data into multidimensional or analytic models in real time as well.

Figure 1.7 depicts the SLT provisioning processes at a high level. Logs and database triggers are created within the source system. As data is inserted, updated, or deleted within the source, triggers are executed to populate the logging table with the details of these operations. The SLT server monitors the source logs and replicates the source system changes to a mirrored table in the SAP HANA appliance. SLT can make a few changes to the data as it's transferred, but the changes are limited to basic filtering and a few linear functions. The end result is a mirror or near-mirror copy of the source system's data and tables. After the data lies in SAP HANA, multidimensional models can be created to further transform and calculate the data.

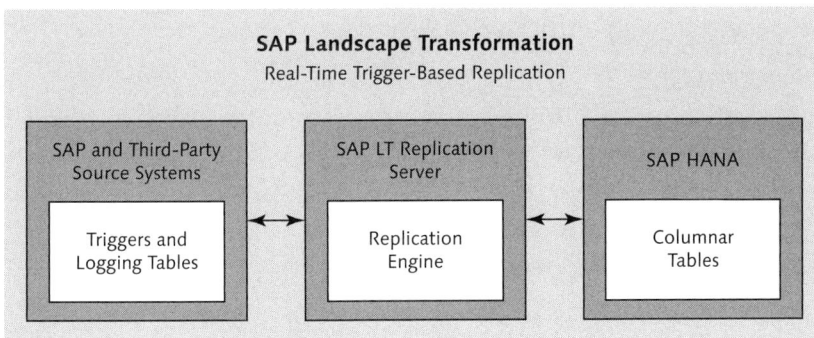

**Figure 1.7** Replicating Data from an SAP System or Third-Party Database into SAP HANA in Real Time

SLT supports replication from many popular third-party RDBMs such as Microsoft SQL Server, Oracle Enterprise Edition, IBM DB2, and SAP Max DB. This is in addition to its support of the SAP Business Suite applications. This makes SLT an ideal solution for organizations that need to deliver real-time analytics.

Because an implementation of SAP HANA has many possible solutions, let's take a look at the main reasons an organizations would choose to implement SAP HANA with SLT:

▶ **Real-time access to data**
Many organizations have a legitimate need to provide data to decision makers in real time. The use cases are vast and vary from one industry to the next. While the organization as a whole might not need all of its data in real time, an organizations might have one or more processes that can only be successful when data is provided in an actionable and real-time way. In these cases, SLT will prove to be a successful tool that complements the capabilities of SAP HANA.

▶ **SAP HANA Live**
SAP HANA Live represents a set of rapid development code and applications that can be imported into SAP HANA. It consists of various SAP HANA analytic models, views, and applications designed to support replicated data from SAP Business Suite applications. The code is prebuilt by SAP to accommodate basic reporting and analytic needs. SAP BusinessObjects is then used to analyze and visualize the data. It can also be customized to meet the specific needs of the organization. For many organizations, these packages will help streamline their implementation of SAP HANA and SLT. In general, it will reduce the time and resources required to implement such a solution.

▶ **Reduced complexity**
For some organizations, SLT will simplify the overall BI processes by eliminating many of the traditional barriers associated with a rigid ETL process. Data is moved from the source to SAP HANA using an incremental and automatic process. The SAP HANA platform is then leveraged to convert the raw data into a logic multidimensional model. This can prove to be a very simple and agile process for many organizations.

▶ **Increased flexibility**
Because the data isn't persisted beyond the initial SLT provisioning step, organizations will find that an SLT and SAP HANA solution are very flexible. SAP HANA's multidimensional models are logical, meaning that they don't move the data into subsequent tables. Traditional ETL processes sometimes require that data be moved from one table to the next as it undergoes its transformation

process. This often requires a very long and complex development lifecycle that can impact an organization's ability to react to changing requirements and business rules. SLT and SAP HANA remove these barriers because only code and logical changes are required. There is also little need to physically move data within the SAP HANA platform, which also increases the flexibility.

In addition to these benefits, we recommend that you consider a few other items before deciding on SLT. This isn't to say that SLT is an inappropriate means of managing data, but rather to expose common issues that can make SLT difficult to implement.

▶ **Data quality**
One of the most compelling reasons to be cautious of SLT is based on the quality and governance of the source data. Data is effectively replicated from the source "as is." Within an SLT and SAP HANA solution, there are very few effective mechanisms to clean and manage bad data. The old adage of "garbage in, garbage out" is a very real concern with an SLT-based solution. To be effective, the source data must be tightly governed independent of SLT.

▶ **Complex transformations**
Depending on the state of the source system data, there is a chance that SLT and SAP HANA will be unable to properly transform complex data into meaningful analytics. In subsequent chapters, we'll discuss these concepts in more detail. However, as this stage, we must anticipate that there will be some limitations associated with the processing of data using a combination of SLT and SAP HANA.

▶ **Multiple sources**
SLT and SAP HANA have a limited ability to work with data that originates from multiple sources. Take, for example, an organization that has four subsidiaries. If each subsidiary has its own product master table, it will be difficult to merge, conform, and de-duplicate this data in real time.

▶ **Diversity of data sources**
Given these points, take a moment to fully grasp all of the data sources that an organization can have. Using SLT to provision SAP HANA alone isn't a replacement for a data warehouse. On the achievable side, SLT and SAP HANA do an excellent job of replicating and presenting a focused subset of an organization's data to end users because SLT supports a limited list of data sources. On the cautious side, SLT and SAP HANA will likely fail in acting as a substitute for a

traditional central store of the organization's data or a data warehouse. Organizations will find that ETL tools such as SAP Data Services are much better at obtaining and managing data from a variety of sources.

As with all technology, not all rules are black and white. Organizations could choose to replicate data into SAP HANA in real time and then leverage SAP HANA's scripting code to address many of these concerns. There's more to an SAP HANA appliance than its capability to deliver data through its multidimensional modeling views. SAP HANA supports a higher level of programing through its SQLScript, stored procedures, and other coding languages. When you combine these capabilities with the hardware and software capabilities of SAP HANA, there are few technical barriers within the SAP HANA platform. Organizations could also look at hybrid solutions that leverage all of the provisioning methods supported by SAP HANA. For example, transactional tables could be replicated into SAP HANA using SLT in real time. At the same time, descriptive tables could be managed using traditional ETL-based tools that better manage complex transformations. The SAP HANA multidimensional models could then be used to conform these tables into a comprehensive logic model.

SLT is an excellent means of replicating a focused set of data from a supported SAP and non-SAP source in real time. SAP HANA provides logical modeling tools that can convert raw data into multidimensional models in real time as well.

Let's keep exploring other SAP solutions for provisioning data within SAP HANA.

**Direct Extract Connect**

Direct Extract Connect (DXC) is another solution that can to be leveraged to move data from an SAP Business Suite application directly to SAP HANA. Because it interacts directly with the SAP HANA appliance, it too is considered an SAP HANA native solution. DXC uses the same *SAP Business Content DataSource Extractors* that are found in SAP NetWeaver BW to move data into SAP HANA. DXC extracts the data from the SAP source in batch mode on a scheduled and reoccurring basis. DXC has limited transformation capabilities, but it's ranked in the same class as many ETL tools.

Figure 1.8 depicts the DXC extraction processes at a high level. Starting with SAP NetWeaver version 7.0, SAP NetWeaver BW is embedded in the standard application stack. While this stack isn't used to run all of the features of SAP NetWeaver BW, a limited set of its components can be leveraged to provision data directly into SAP

HANA. In essence, DXC uses the same extraction process that is found in a stand-alone SAP NetWeaver BW stack. However, DXC redirects the extracted data directly into the SAP HANA system. DXC creates an in-memory DSO (IMDSO) within the SAP HANA system. The IMDSO consists of a series of SAP HANA columnar tables. Note that the embedded SAP NetWeaver BW modules can't be used to model the extracted data. Within the SAP HANA appliance, multidimensional models should be created based on these columnar tables to serve as the primary modeling tools.

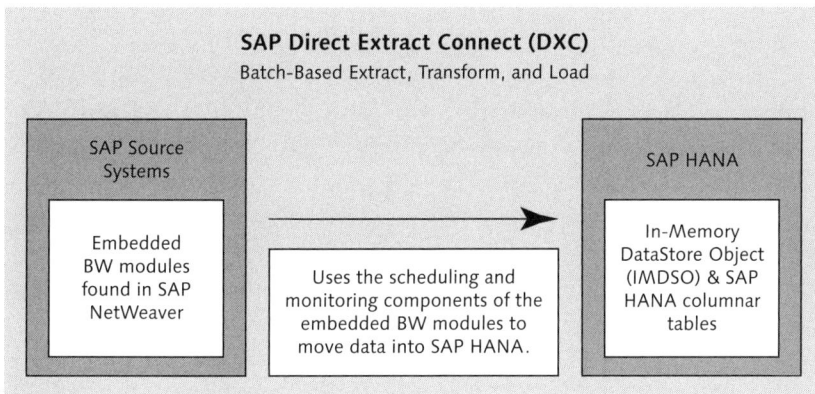

**SAP Direct Extract Connect (DXC)**
Batch-Based Extract, Transform, and Load

SAP Source Systems

Embedded BW modules found in SAP NetWeaver

Uses the scheduling and monitoring components of the embedded BW modules to move data into SAP HANA.

SAP HANA

In-Memory DataStore Object (IMDSO) & SAP HANA columnar tables

**Figure 1.8** *Moving Data from an SAP Application to SAP HANA Using the DXC Extractors*

Because the DXC modules run directly within the SAP source system, the overall architecture of the DXC solution is simplified. There is no need to maintain and run an intermediary server to broker the movement of data. This is an ideal solution for organizations or hosting companies that need a simplified architecture capable of moving data from an SAP source to an SAP HANA target.

For many tables in the SAP source system, DXC offers a very simple mechanism to extract only changed data—the *delta load process* or *change data capture process*. In fact, this is the same technology that is used by SAP NetWeaver BW to extract data from the SAP source. Organizations will also find this to be an added benefit of the DXC solution.

The DXC extraction process is very different from those used in the SLT solution because the data is moved on a scheduled basis in batch. However, after the data is provisioned within SAP HANA, DXC also relies on the multidimensional models or other SAP HANA code to transform the data. DXC transfers the data from the SAP source to a special web dispatcher service or XML processor that is embedded in the SAP web application server or XS Engine. It's also important to understand that not all data sources found in SAP sources can be managed with DXC.

Be mindful that DXC can fall victim to many of the same limitations described within the SLT section of this chapter. However, the extractors used by the DXC process contain code that facilitates some of the most common transformations. We should also reiterate that the DXC only supports SAP applications as a data source.

> **Additional References**
>
> For more information on the SAP DXC setup, implementation, and other limitations, refer to the ETL-based *Data Acquisition by SAP HANA Direct Extractor Connection* guide found within the SAP Service Marketplace. You can also refer to SAP Note 1665602 to obtain additional details by going to *https://service.sap.com/sap/support/notes/1665602*.

### SAP Data Services (ETL)

Now let's turn our attention to the solution that we discuss throughout the core of this book: SAP Data Services.

The core technology behind SAP Data Services is based on a product originally named ActaWorks. In 2002, the organization Business Objects acquired Acta Technologies and enhanced the product that is now commonly referred to as Data Integrator. When SAP acquired Business Objects, the product was renamed to SAP Data Services.

Although the name has changed, the core technology behind SAP Data Services has not. SAP Data Services is a data source-agnostic ETL tool. Its primary purpose is based on an organization's need to manage, centralize, and govern data that exists in one or more data sources. It's capable of extracting data from almost every commonly used data source. After the data is extracted, it's then cleansed, transformed, and merged into the desired data model. Its final feat is then to load the data into one or more databases or formats.

Figure 1.9 shows the ETL process as managed by SAP Data Services.

SAP Data Services and other ETL tools have traditionally been used to manage several common data processes within an organization and integrate data between source systems.

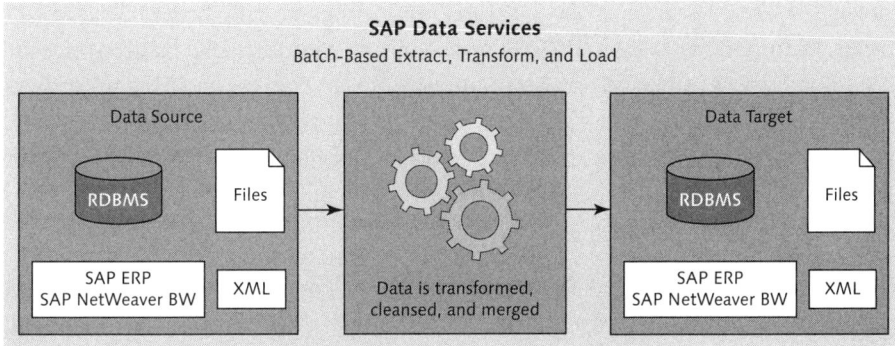

**Figure 1.9**  The ETL Process of SAP Data Services

Take, for example, a large enterprise that has acquired another organization. Let's assume that both organizations managed their business by collecting data using software applications. After the two entities are legally combined, there will be a need to migrate one organization's customer data into the other organization's existing applications. Because SAP Data Services is capable of extracting, transforming, and loading the data, it will serve as an ideal tool to manage this process.

SAP Data Services can also be used to create a comprehensive central store of data or a data warehouse. For that data to be useful, it must be conformed into a clean, denormalized, and relational series of data tables. SAP Data Services can also be used to create data marts or datastores that are well optimized for multidimensional analysis. Finally, SAP Data Services provides several data quality tools to help organizations track, manage, clean, and identify problems within their data.

---

**The Data Warehouse versus the Data Mart**

A *data warehouse* describes a system of database tables and their relationships that encompasses all relevant information within an organization. All information is organized by business constructs or terms rather than the source fields or tables. The information, obtained from multiple sources, is conformed into business concepts and relationships.

A *data mart* describes a similar system of database tables and their relationships. However, it's generally focused on a subset of data. It's typically well optimized for multidimensional analysis. Its source can be the data warehouse or staged data from various sources. In short, a data mart is a better source for reporting and analytics.

---

Because SAP Data Services is the ideal tool to manage an ETL process, it too can serve as an important tool in an SAP HANA native solution. SAP Data Services is maintained by SAP, so its integration with SAP HANA and other SAP applications is very sound. However, its legacy capabilities also mean that it integrates well with third-party applications and data sources. This makes SAP Data Services an ideal tool to manage both SAP and third-party data that needs to be moved into an SAP HANA native solution.

From a technology standpoint, SAP Data Services use a massively parallel processing engine that makes excellent use of RAM and multiple CPU cores when processing data. These technology features result in a tool that isn't only capable of managing data but also managing data while achieving outstanding throughput. It supports x86 64-bit servers running the Windows, AIX, Linux, or Solaris operating systems. Because it supports these commonly used operating systems, most organizations will find it easy to implement within their unique environment.

From a software standpoint, SAP Data Services uses an intuitive graphical user interface (GUI) to manage and develop the ETL processes. This interface is also very mindful of an organization's need to leverage metadata; several UI features allow data managers to quickly identify the relationships between data processing elements. There are even tools that give data managers a comprehensive view of the data lineage and impact analysis. This is all possible because SAP Data Services makes excellent use of the source, transformation, and target metadata. In subsequent chapters, we'll discuss this interface in more detail, but for now, it's important to understand its basic capabilities.

In the context of this book, we'll thoroughly discuss a solution that uses SAP Data Services to provision data within SAP HANA, and we'll continue our discussion of SAP Data Services in Chapters 2-5. SAP Data Services can load data into either SAP HANA columnar or row tables. Figure 1.10 depicts the process flow of this solution. Data is retrieved from one or more types of sources. It's then transformed into a data model that bests suits the analytic and performance requirements of the organization. The model is then loaded into an SAP HANA columnar table.

After the data is physically stored in SAP HANA, Chapter 6 will walk you through the processes of designing a logical multidimensional model within SAP HANA. These models will act as views that can serve as the basis for end-user consumption of the data. You can then connect the SAP BusinessObjects platform using either the SAP HANA base columnar tables or the SAP HANA multidimensional models to deliver stunning reports and visualizations.

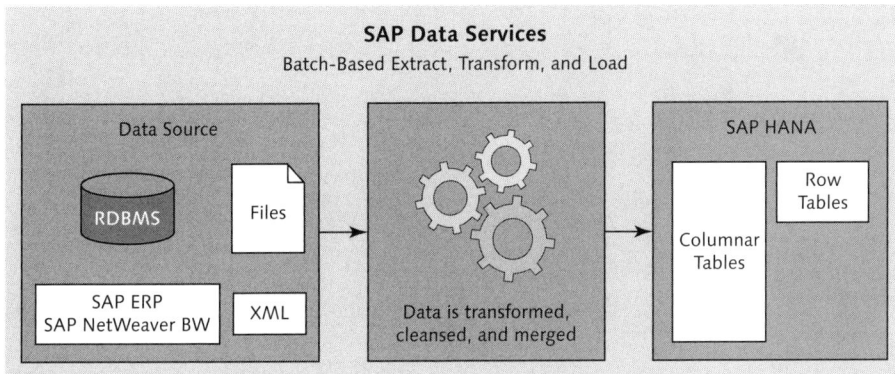

**Figure 1.10** The Process Flow of Moving Data from an Agnostic Data Source to SAP HANA Using SAP Data Services

### SAP HANA Studio

The final option for provisioning data within SAP HANA native involves the use of SAP HANA Studio, which is the development and administration tool for SAP HANA. It can be run from the SAP HANA server or on a separate computer.

With SAP HANA Studio, there are options that allow you to import flat files into an SAP HANA table in supported formats (.csv, .xls, and .xlsx). When importing the flat file, the UI allows you to either create a new target table based on the source flat file metadata or to use an existing table that has the required data types and columns.

This feature is intended for quick proof-of-concept projects that only need the data to be loaded on a limited basis. The process is entirely manual, and subsequent imports will always append to the existing data set. It offers no transformation, delta load, or direct-from-database import options. However, it's an option whereby you can provision data within SAP HANA. Figure 1.11 depicts the workflow of the file import process. An administrator collects the needed files. Using the SAP HANA Studio application, the administrator launches the file import wizard and imports the file data directly into either a columnar or row store table.

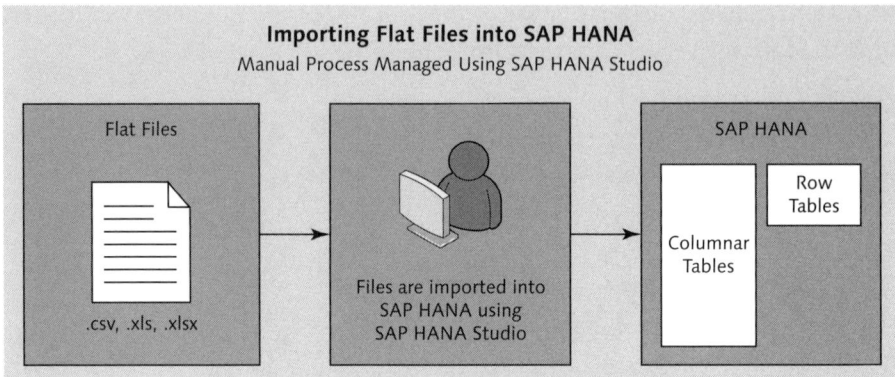

**Figure 1.11** Importing Flat Files into SAP HANA Using SAP HANA Studio

---

**Additional Resources**

For more information pertaining to the process and steps required to import flat files into SAP HANA, we recommend that you watch the video located on the main SAP HANA website at *http://www.saphana.com/docs/DOC-2191*.

---

There are multiple ways to provision data within SAP HANA. Each option has a unique and appropriate use case. One or more of the described methods can be used together to provide a hybrid SAP HANA native solution. SAP Data Services is the ideal provisioning method when designing a data mart or data warehouse hosted in an SAP HANA native solution. SLT is the ideal solution for replicating data that requires real-time analysis. DXC is a viable solution that can quickly and easily move SAP application data into SAP HANA on a recurring basis. When data needs to be quickly imported into SAP HANA for temporary analysis, SAP HANA Studio can be used to import flat files.

## 1.3    Running the SAP Business Suite on SAP HANA

Although the primary focus of this book is on using SAP HANA as a BI appliance, it's important that we also discuss the evolution of SAP HANA as the engine for SAP Business Suite applications.

Tens of thousands of organizations use SAP Business Suite applications to run and operate their businesses. In terms of BI, these applications are the machines that produce the data that inevitably supports the analysis of data. Traditionally these applications used a standard RDBMS to store and process the data inputs that were generated by an organization's operations. In 2013, SAP announced its support for SAP HANA as the engine to replace the standard RDBMS.

With the power of SAP HANA, several lines of business processes can now be enhanced, in the form of both processing speed and the scripting capabilities of SAP HANA. Business processes that require the analysis of mass amounts of data can now be managed in seconds. Complex procedural processing can also be enhanced in the same manner. Statistical calculations can be performed within SAP HANA without the need to marshal data into third-party applications.

While SAP Business Suite on SAP HANA is a relatively new technology, the future possibilities for this solution are very intriguing. In the very near future, SAP Business Suite on SAP HANA will likely be able to accommodate both business process automation and BI within a single platform. This will inevitably lead to a revolution where data will stay in source system, and reporting and analytic functions will be performed directly against the source. In terms of real-time data access, this will prove to be the ideal solution. For those that have been involved in the BI field for the past few decades, this is a reversal of well-established best practices.

As it stands today, this dream is has not fully realized, but SAP appears to be moving in that direction. It will be very interesting to see how successful such implementations will be as there are still several unanswered questions as to how SAP HANA will evolve to accommodate this desire.

**Addition Reference**

For more information about SAP Business Suite powered by SAP HANA, we recommend that you visit *http://www.saphana.com/community/learn/solutions/sap-business-suite-on-hana*.

Now that we've discussed the current BI solutions available for use with SAP HANA, it's time that will focus on the core solution of this book. As we've discussed, there are several ways to leverage SAP HANA as a BI appliance. You can choose to run SAP NetWeaver BW powered by SAP HANA or one of the four native SAP HANA provisioning methods that are currently available. It's hard to say that any one solution is the "right choice" for an organization—the diversity of available solutions is a product of the diversity that exists around an organization's requirements—but we now turn our focus to implementing SAP HANA using SAP Data Services and SAP BusinessObjects.

To better understand this solution, we first provide you with a view of a traditional BI implementation with SAP BusinessObjects and SAP Data Services. There are two aspects to a traditional SAP BusinessObjects BI implementation:

▸ **An organization's requirement to manage its data**
Traditionally speaking, this process involved the creation of a data warehouse or data mart. If we assume that data can only be useful when it's organized and correct, we must then allow it to be conformed and cleaned. This is where SAP Data Services plays a key role.

▸ **An organization's requirement to provide access to its data**
Decision makers need tools that allow them to visualize and analyze their data. This is where SAP BusinessObjects plays a key role. The SAP BusinessObjects platform is home to multiple features and tools, all of which were designed with the idea of presenting data to data consumers.

## 1.4    Traditional EIM with Data Services

Let's begin our traditional data loading conversation with a high-level overview of the data management process. In many ways, getting data into SAP HANA is more than simply moving data into SAP HANA tables—you need to develop a strategy and a series of rules that help you manage the process on a recurring basis. When designing a data warehouse or data mart, these strategies and rules are critical to the success of the implementation.

There are multiple aspects to an implementation of a data warehouse or data mart. In all, we refer to this solution and its tool sets, processes, and methodologies as *Enterprise Information Management* (EIM). You use the tools to help manage the process, but there are other aspects of an EIM implementation that must be implemented outside the control of software. At a high level, there are four main aspects to the EIM process: the alignment of IT resources with the business, analysis of the data sources, development of a data model, and the loading or provisioning of the data. As you'll see, there are aspects of the EIM processes that aren't simply managed with tools such as SAP Data Services.

### 1.4.1    Align IT with the Business

The most important step of an EIM implementation—and, unfortunately, the one that is most often overlooked—is the alignment of IT and the business community. In some ways, this step gets skipped because IT tends to lead these projects and because this step isn't strictly a technical process. In reality, this step involves strong management, teamwork, and leadership.

The goal of the alignment is twofold. First, IT needs to fully understand the data analysis requirements of the business community. This helps IT to identify the source of the information and any gaps that exists in obtaining the data. It also helps IT understand the needs of the business when architecting the EIM solution. Second, the business needs to take ownership of the data. This helps the business understand that IT can't solve all data issues with IT resources alone. Sometimes the data simply needs to be entered into the frontend systems better. This is where leadership and management on the business side play a key role.

Far too often, IT leads an EIM project at the behest of the business community, which then fails to be properly involved in the process. This typically leads to a failed project for a variety of reasons. It's difficult for an IT resource to fully grasp the daily operations, challenges, and goals of the business community. At the same time, the business community doesn't always fully understand the technology, data, and challenges that the IT resources have to manage. This is why it's important that the two sides work together as a properly aligned team.

When the business community takes ownership of the process and works directly with IT resources, we typically see the project end in success. The business community begins to understand that the full lifecycle of the data must be governed and not simply collected, and IT must thoroughly understand what the business community needs and how to solve the business requirements. If the alignment is successful, the organization will discover that the foundation for strong data governance process is formed.

SAP HANA is capable of many technical wonders, but it relies on traditional tools and processes to obtain data. When implementing SAP HANA with SAP Business-Objects and SAP Data Services, aligning the business community with IT is critical.

### 1.4.2 Source System Analysis

After IT and the business are aligned, it's time for the two sides to fully analyze both the source data and the processes that help form the source data. IT resources generally profile the data or collect statistics about source data. SAP Data Services contains tools to help automate this process and to collect the data. IT resources then identify the relationships between the data sources as it helps them identify gaps in the data. Based on the results of the data profiling, the business owners then analyze their business processes to help IT understand the gaps. In some cases, these gaps must be solved with a change in the business process. In other cases, IT resources can fill the gaps using the technology at their disposal.

In the context of an SAP HANA implementation, SAP Data Services provides several tools that help with source system analysis. Other add-ons to SAP Data Services such as SAP Information Steward can also be used to help with this step. Without proper source system analysis, it will be hard for an implementation of SAP HANA to be successful. Understanding the state of the data and where it exists is very important. Without this step, the benefits native to SAP HANA will be overshadowed by the lack of coherent data.

### 1.4.3 Develop a Data Model

Before you can load data into SAP HANA, you have to develop a data model. In a data mart or data warehouse, the data model describes the relationships between the various data elements in the form of database tables and technical diagrams. A data model is comprised of both *dimensions* and *facts*. Dimensions are tables that are used to describe or characterize a transaction. Fact tables are used to store transactions. A typical fact table contains keys that link back to one or more dimensions. Dimensions are often conformed to link to one or more fact tables. A proper data model is based on the need to conform the various dimensions to one or more fact tables. However, as we'll demonstrate in subsequent chapters, the traditional data model approach might need to be updated because of the ways that SAP HANA stores data.

In subsequent chapters of this book, the components of the data model are discussed in more detail. At this point, it's only important to understand that developing a data model is an important step in implementing SAP HANA with SAP Data Services and SAP BusinessObjects.

### 1.4.4 Load the Data

With sound business community support and an understanding of the source data, IT resources are now ready to move data into SAP HANA. Using SAP Data Services, data is obtained from the various sources, staged into SAP HANA or another RDBMS, and then transformed into the prescribed data model within SAP HANA.

In subsequent chapters, we'll dive deeper into this phase of the SAP HANA implementation by exposing the capabilities of SAP Data Services. At this point, it's important that you understand that the full lifecycle of an EIM process is composed of more than just provisioning data.

## 1.5  Traditional Business Intelligence with SAP Business-Objects

In the traditional BI landscape, SAP BusinessObjects is the quintessential platform for managing the presentation and analysis of data stored in SAP HANA. On its own, SAP HANA can't properly present data to the business community—it needs the SAP BusinessObjects platform to form a proper BI solution. In other words, you need SAP BusinessObjects to properly implement SAP HANA.

In the SAP landscape, SAP BusinessObjects has become the de facto standard reporting and analytics tool for all SAP systems and applications. Based on its legacy support for third-party data sources, it's also capable of working with most enterprise data sources found within an organization.

The SAP BusinessObjects platform possess multiple reporting tools such as SAP Crystal Reports, SAP BusinessObjects Web Intelligence, SAP BusinessObjects Analysis edition for Microsoft Office, SAP BusinessObjects Analysis edition for OLAP, and SAP Predictive Analysis. It contains dashboard tools such as SAP BusinessObjects Dashboards and SAP BusinessObjects Design Studio. It offers a new breed of BI self-service tools such as SAP BusinessObjects Explorer and SAP Lumira, and multiple mobile-enabled versions of these tools.

The SAP BusinessObjects platform contains multiple features that are essential to all BI implementations, such as the capability to properly secure the data, serve up analytical content, distribute the content, and integrate the content with existing systems.

We use the term "platform" to describe SAP BusinessObjects because it's more than just a single application or service. It's comprised of multiple layers and processes that can be scaled to meet the needs of any size organization. It's capable of pushing BI content to the users as well as providing them with mechanisms to interact directly with the data.

Before we venture further into the book, let's establish a few high-level concepts surrounding the SAP BusinessObjects solution. These concepts are important because they highlight the fact that SAP BusinessObjects is more than a single tool. These concepts also introduce you to many of the topics that will be discussed through this book and how they facilitate a proper implantation of SAP HANA.

SAP BusinessObjects is a portfolio of applications and solutions. Within this portfolio, there are four main concepts and solutions: the semantic layer, ad hoc reporting, self-service BI, and IT-delivered content.

### 1.5.1 The Semantic Layer or Universe

The semantic layer, within the SAP BusinessObjects platform, is a metadata rich data access layer. It's mostly commonly referred to as the *universe*. A semantic layer is a logic layer that sits between the data source and the data consumer. It's designed to provide an intuitive, central, and secure point of access to a supported data source. This layer shields the report developer from the common complexities of querying data by presenting data in business terms as opposed to crude technical terms. In many ways, it's similar to the InfoCubes that are found in SAP NetWeaver BW. However, the universe or semantic layer is a logical layer, which means that no data is physically stored in the universe.

In the SAP BusinessObjects platform, all but a handful of tools access data through the universe. When implementing SAP HANA, you'll discover that the universe is needed to provide access to the data that is stored within SAP HANA in some cases. You'll also discover that some tools can bypass the universe and interact directly with SAP HANA. It's important that you have a basic understanding of the universe as we guide you through the remaining components of the solution. In subsequent chapters, we'll discuss the universe in more detail. In addition, we'll provide you with instructions for connecting the universe to SAP HANA.

## 1.5.2  Ad Hoc Reporting

The term ad hoc reporting has somewhat been redefined in recent years. In the legacy Business Objects landscape, ad hoc reporting referred to tools that empowered users to create their own reports and to analyze data. Before the existence of ad hoc reporting tools, the report design process was largely managed by IT developers. This was in part due to the complexity of such reporting tools. Business Objects designed Web Intelligence and Desktop Intelligence with the goal of empowering nontechnical users to interact with data. In recent years, new tools have evolved in the SAP BusinessObjects portfolio to further simplify the data analysis process for nontechnical users, although SAP BusinessObjects Web Intelligence continues to be a powerful ad hoc reporting tool for many technical and nontechnical report developers.

In the context of an SAP HANA implementation, most organizations will find ad hoc reporting tools to be a valuable solution. In many ways, ad hoc reporting tools possess more power and features than many of the more recent self-service alternatives. SAP BusinessObjects Web Intelligence will likely be a critical part of your SAP HANA implementation.

## 1.5.3  Self-Service BI

Self-service BI or self-service analytics is a relatively new term used to describe tools within the SAP BusinessObjects platform. They are derived from the fundamental ideas of ad hoc reporting tools, but they focus more on the delivery of information to the business community.

In the traditional ad hoc reporting landscape, data needs to be consolidated, standardized, and secured before it can be consumed, which requires significant time and resources to implement (see Section 1.4 and Section 1.5 of this chapter). In the meantime, the business community is forced to wait for the solution to be developed. For many in the business community, this isn't acceptable. However, at the same time, we can't disregard the reasons that a proper EIM and BI process are needed. In some ways, we're then left with a paradoxical situation with few alternatives.

Self-services BI tools are designed with the goal of allowing users to consume data and analytics quickly, without barriers. Tools such as SAP Lumira are built on a foundation that allows the average user to quickly merge, transform, and then share data within the SAP HANA or SAP BusinessObjects platform. Other tools such as SAP BusinessObjects Explorer are built on a foundation that allows the user to effortlessly search and explore open-ended data sets without the need to leverage an IT resource. Both tools can also be used in tandem to empower the user community because they define BI content without a reliance on IT developers, and both tools also have a stunning visualization layer that can produce analytics in the form of charts and graphs.

Developing a self-service BI solution can be a challenge for most organizations. While it's essential for users to gain access to their data quickly, it's also essential that they produce accurate, consistent, and secure results. Based on our experience, we find that self-service BI plays an important role in allowing users to form a hypothesis and then test their theory. In a BI solution, such tools can provide a very cost-effective alternative to the established EIM and BI process. This is especially true when the business users only need a one-time answer to a BI-related question. If the user community finds that their solution provides value, it can then be implemented under the guise of the standard EIM and BI process. With these goals in mind, organizations will find a proper avenue to implement self-service BI tools.

In the context of SAP HANA, the self-service BI tools within the SAP Business-Objects platform are capable of directly leveraging its power and performance. SAP Lumira can query and write data directly from and to SAP HANA. SAP Business-Objects Explorer can bypass its native engines and use the SAP HANA platform engines to explore millions and even billions of detailed records. Based on the need for self-service BI, this combination can prove to be a powerful solution. In subsequent chapters, we'll discuss these self-service BI tools under the concept of data exploration and self-service analytics.

### 1.5.4 IT-Developed Content

While ad hoc reporting and self-service BI tools are essential to an SAP HANA implementation and solution, you'll find that business communities' requirements often exceed the capabilities of such tools. This is where tools such as SAP Crystal Reports, SAP Dashboards, and SAP BusinessObjects Design Studio play an important role. IT-developed content refers to content that can only be developed by an experienced and skilled professional resource. When pixel-perfect reports need to be developed, SAP Crystal Reports will prove to be the ideal tool. When highly formatted and interactive dashboards are required, SAP BusinessObjects Dashboards and SAP BusinessObjects Design Studio will prove to be the ideal solution. Although SAP BusinessObjects Web Intelligence was mentioned in the ad hoc reporting section, it too can serve as an ideal tool for IT resources when an organization's requirements exceed the capabilities of the average business user.

When implementing SAP HANA with SAP BusinessObjects, you must understand that a skilled technical resource will often be required to develop content to the business communities' specifications. In the ideal world, an IT resource would only need to set up the environment and then push content development entirely to the business community. However, you'll often find that some BI needs can only be developed by IT. In subsequent chapters, we'll discuss IT-developed content under the concept of SAP Crystal Reports and professionally authored dashboards.

## 1.6    Solution Architectural Overview

So before we dive into the details of an SAP HANA implementation with SAP BusinessObjects and SAP Data Services, we should discuss the product versions and basic architecture that will be covered within this book and give you an overview of each product's core architecture to help you better understand the solution.

### 1.6.1    SAP Data Services 4.1

SAP Data Services is responsible for managing the ETL aspects of an SAP HANA native solution. In this book, we reference SAP Data Services version 4.1, which is comprised of four main layers. There is the web application server layer and the tools it hosts. There is the SAP Data Services *job server* and the *information platform services* layer. SAP Data Services also uses several RDBMS repositories to manage the platform and developed code. Finally there are several management and development desktop tools. Figure 1.12 depicts these layers at a high level. We'll now discuss each layer in more detail.

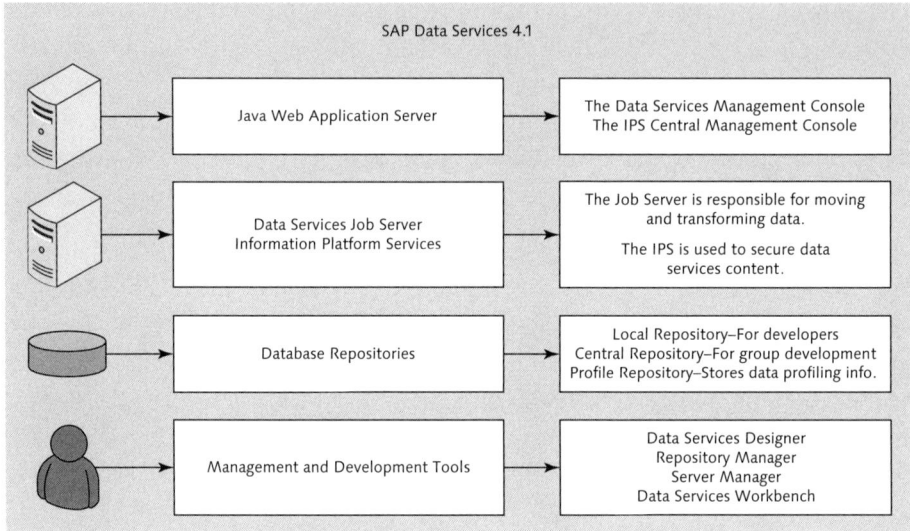

**Figure 1.12** Components of the SAP Data Services 4.1 Platform

### The Java Web Application Server

The default installation of SAP Data Services includes Apache Tomcat to serve as the SAP Web Application Server for Java. The main web applications that are managed at this layer include the SAP Data Services *Management Console* and the *Central Management Console*. Both tools are used, in one form or another, to manage application access, security, or ETL jobs. The Java web application server can be installed with the services found in other layers of the platform, or it can be deployed on a dedicated server. These tools can also be deployed to an existing SAP BusinessObjects Java application server or to a number of supported third-party Java application servers.

> **Additional References**
>
> A thorough discussion of the installation and configuration of SAP Data Services is beyond the scope of this book, so we recommend that you refer to the installation documentation located on the SAP Help portal at *http://help.sap.com/bods#section2*.

### The Job Server and Information Platform Services

The job server is used to process the ETL code. Specifically, it's responsible for the read, transformation, and write processes that are orchestrated within the

ETL code. The job server process runs under the main operating system process named `al_jobservice`. Multiple child processes, with the name of `al_engine`, will be generated by this process depending on the level of parallel execution defined in the ETL code. This is important to understand when deploying your SAP Data Services architecture because you need to make sure to include a sufficient number of CPUs and RAM on the job server host to accommodate the parallel processing. It's also possible to cluster the job servers across multiple hosts to facilitate the appropriate level of scalability.

The *information platform services* (IPS) package is a scaled-down version of the SAP BusinessObjects Enterprise platform. It doesn't have to be explicitly deployed in the SAP Data Services architecture as it's possible to use an existing SAP Business-Objects Enterprise platform to service as its replacement. However, in our experience, most organizations choose to separate their SAP Data Services platform from their existing SAP BusinessObjects platform by using the IPS. The IPS contains many of the core services found in the SAP BusinessObjects platform. This includes the SAP BusinessObjects *central management service* (CMS) and the *file repository services* (FRS). As a result, a dedicated CMS database and audit schema is needed to facilitate the requirements of the IPS. There are other core services available as well. The IPS can either be deployed on the same host with the job server, or it can be deployed to a dedicated host.

**The Database Repositories**

Several database repositories are required to facilitate the use of SAP Data Services. There are three main types of repositories. One or more *local repositories* are required to facilitate individual developers and job execution. A *profile repository* is needed to hosts the statically results of data profiling requests. The *central repository* will serve as the main software versioning and team development repository within the platform. ETL code can be versioned, checked in, and checked out using this repository. It's ideal for environments where multiple developers are responsible for managing the code.

Your SAP Data Services environment will require one or more database schemas to host each repository. When using the IPS, a CMS and audit repository will also be required. All repositories are typically hosted on a dedicated RDBMS to provide peak performance and scalability. However, the default installation of SAP Data Services and IPS will provide you with an option to install a local RDBMS.

**The Management and Development Tools**

Several management and developer desktop tools are included in the SAP Data Services platform. Five main tools will be used:

▶ **Data Services Designer**
The Data Services Designer and its GUI are used by developers to create the ETL code. It can also be used to manage data profiling requests, metadata, job execution, and the central repository. In subsequent chapters, we'll discuss this tool in more detail.

▶ **Data Services Server Manager**
The Data Services Server Manager is executed using either a command line interface (CLI) or a GUI, depending on the operating system selected. It's responsible for the configuration of the job server. This includes the ability to associate a repository with a job server, the ability to configure clustering, the ability to configure email server integration, and many of the job server-related tasks. For more information on the role of this tool, please consult the SAP Data Services documentation.

▶ **Data Services Repository Manager**
The Data Services Repository Manager is responsible for the creation of a local repository, central repository, or profiler repository. It, too, is either a CLI tool or GUI tool depending on the operating system. Before a repository can be used by any layer of the SAP Data Service platform, it must be set up using the Data Services Repository Manager.

▶ **Data Services Workbench**
The Data Services Workbench is a new tool that will eventually supplement or replace the Data Services Designer client. In its current state, it can be used to quickly batch replicate data into SAP HANA or other RDBMS targets.

▶ **Data Services License Manager**
The Data Services License Manager is used to add, edit, or delete the current license key. It's either run as a CLI or GUI depending on the operating system selected.

Understanding the key components and layers of the SAP Data Services platform is important when implementing SAP HANA and SAP Data Services. In subsequent chapters, we'll provide you with additional information that will further enhance your understanding of the SAP Data Services platform.

## 1.6.2 SAP BusinessObjects 4.x

SAP BusinessObjects version 4.0 and 4.1 are used to describe the applicable features and components throughout this book. In the version 4.0 stack, Support Pack 5 Patch 5 was used. In the version 4.1 stack, Support Pack 0 Patch 1 was used. Because the SAP BusinessObjects platform is used to manage and facilitate end-user functions such as reporting, visualization, and analysis in an implementation of SAP HANA native, we want to give you an overview of the SAP BusinessObjects platform as it pertains to the overall solution.

The SAP BusinessObjects architecture is comprised of four main layers: the Java web application server layer, the server architecture layer, the database repositories layer, and the management and development tools layer. The server architecture layer is further divided into three main sublayers. Figure 1.13 depicts the four main platform layers found in the SAP BusinessObjects architecture.

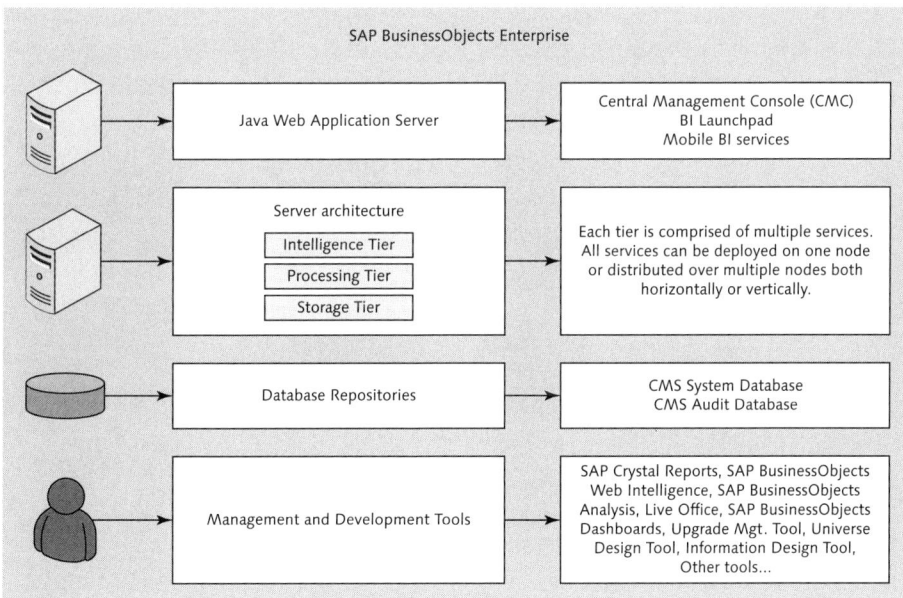

**Figure 1.13** Components of the SAP BusinessObjects 4.x Platform

### The Java Web Application Server

The default installation of SAP BusinessObjects 4.x includes Apache Tomcat to serve as the Java web application server. However, SAP provides support for several additional mainstream Java applications servers. The main web applications that are managed at this layer include the *SAP BusinessObjects BI Launchpad* and the *SAP BusinessObjects Central Management Console* (CMC). This layer also hosts the web services servlet, RESTful APIs, and a few other management functions as well. It can be installed with the remaining layers of the platform, but most often it's hosted on a dedicated host. This layer can also be clustered using a supported IP load balancer or proxy server.

In the SAP BusinessObjects architecture, the SAP BusinessObjects BI Launchpad is the main point of contact for most BI consumers. Depending on the number of expected users, it can manage several concurrent sessions. Therefore, it's an important layer in the overall SAP BusinessObjects platform.

**The Server Architecture Layer**

The server architecture layer is comprised of three main sublayers: the intelligence tier that represents the core services used to manage the platform (including the CMS, the lifecycle management service, the platform search service, the monitoring service, the SAP BusinessObjects Explorer Master services, and other administrative services); the processing tier layer that represents the services used to process, schedule, and render reports and visualizations (including the adaptive job services, the adaptive processing services, the SAP Crystal Reports services, the SAP BusinessObjects Web Intelligence services, and the SAP BusinessObjects Explorer services); and the storage tier that represents the services used to store and cache content and data (including FRS, the cache for the various processing services, and the SAP BusinessObjects Explorer data).

By default, these services are installed to a single host or node. However, it's recommended that they be distributed both horizontally and vertically to achieve proper performance. You must also ensure that your storage tier services have sufficient storage to manage all of the content and data within the platform. In some cases, components of the storage tier will need to be shared between hosts. This is especially true when deploying a clustered SAP BusinessObjects environment.

**Additional References**

For additional information pertaining to the installation and sizing of SAP BusinessObjects, look for the *SAP BusinessObjects BI Sizing Companion Guide* and the *Business Intelligence Platform Installation Guide* that is appropriate for your operating system.

**The Database Repositories**

SAP BusinessObjects uses two key database repositories to manage the platform. The first repository is the central management server repository, which stores content metadata, security information, system information, and other platform-specific data. The second repository is used to store the audit history. This information can be used to track user activities and configuration changes within the system.

The default installation of SAP BusinessObjects includes a local database server that will manage these repositories. However, it's generally advised that these repositories run on a supported database server that is independent of your SAP BusinessObjects deployment.

**The Management and Development Tool**

Multiple management and development client tools are available within the SAP BusinessObjects platform that run on the desktop, as opposed to within the Java Application Server. Therefore, it's important that we identify the main tools discussed in this book and provide a brief description of their use. Please keep in mind that there are other client and management tools in the platform, but they aren't within the scope of this book.

▶ **Universe Designer**
The Universe Designer is the legacy developer tool used to create an SAP Business-Objects universe. It creates universe files that end in the .UNV extension.

▶ **Information Design Tool (IDT)**
The IDT is new in the SAP BusinessObjects 4.x platform. It's used to create universes as well. IT creates universe files that end in the .UNX extension.

▶ **Web Intelligence Desktop**
Web Intelligence Desktop is a full client desktop version of SAP BusinessObjects Web Intelligence. The SAP BusinessObjects Web Intelligence client can also be run in the client browser using the Java Web Application Server layer.

▶ **SAP Crystal Reports 2011/2013**
SAP Crystal Reports 2011 and 2013 is the legacy Crystal Reports developer tool. It's used to create SAP Crystal Reports.

▶ **SAP Crystal Reports for Enterprise**
SAP Crystal Reports for Enterprise is new in the SAP BusinessObjects 4.x

platform. It's used to create SAP Crystal Reports. We expect it to be the eventual replacement for SAP Crystal Reports 2011/2013.

▶ **SAP BusinessObjects Dashboards 4.x**
Dashboards 4.x is a full client desktop application that is used to develop dashboards.

▶ **SAP Lumira**
SAP Lumira is a full client desktop application used to develop self-service analytics.

▶ **SAP BusinessObjects Design Studio**
SAP BusinessObjects Design Studio is a full client application that is used to design dashboards. It's best suited to connect directly to SAP HANA or SAP NetWeaver BW when OLAP-style navigation is required.

▶ **QaaWS Designer**
Query as a Web Service (QaaWS) Designer is used to create web service-based connections within the SAP BusinessObjects platform.

### 1.6.3 SAP HANA 1.0 SPS5

When we reference SAP HANA in this book, we're talking about the features and functionality of version 56, which includes SPS 5, to describe the features and functionality. As discussed, SAP HANA is the backbone of this solution. Data is loaded into SAP HANA using SAP Data Services. It's then consumed using the tools and features of the SAP BusinessObjects platform. Figure 1.14 depicts this solution at a high level. As you'll learn in subsequent chapters, SAP HANA Studio is the primary client tool used to administer the SAP HANA appliance as well as develop SAP HANA-specific content.

When implementing the SAP HANA solution that is discussed within this book, it's important to understand the different types of human resources that are required for its implementation and administration. Figure 1.14 also depicts the areas where different resource types will be required. To properly manage the ETL process with SAP Data Services, an experienced ETL developer is required. This resource should also have specific SAP Data Services experience. To properly manage the SAP HANA components, an experienced SAP HANA modeler and SAP HANA database administrator are required. Finally, an experienced SAP BusinessObjects developer and administrator should also be selected.

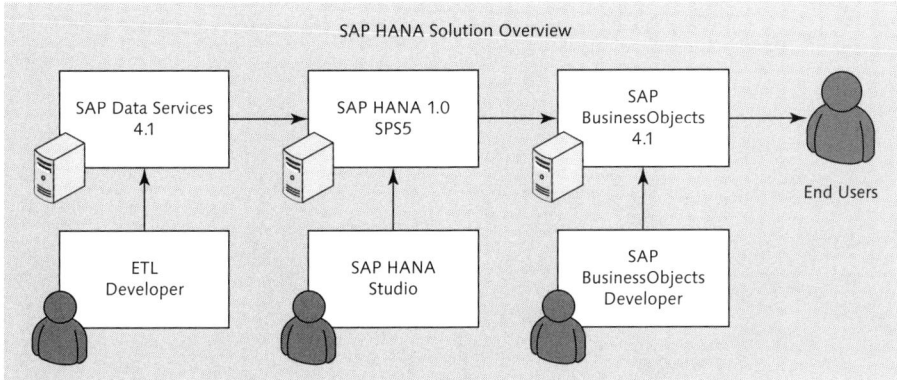

**Figure 1.14** An Overview of the SAP HANA Solution Discussed within This Book

## 1.7 Summary

SAP HANA is more than just a database—it's a next-generation data management platform. It can be characterized and also implemented in many ways. SAP has developed many ways to implement SAP HANA. As a result, organizations that have heavily invested in SAP applications will find multiple ways to leverage SAP HANA in their BI landscape. At the same time, organizations with little or no investment in SAP applications will also find that there are multiple ways to implement SAP HANA.

As you've discovered in this chapter, an implementation of SAP HANA requires more than just SAP HANA. You need to identify the best means to provision SAP HANA or load data into SAP HANA. Although there are multiple ways to provision SAP HANA, this book explores how to leverage SAP Data Services to provision data within SAP HANA.

In subsequent chapters, we'll also discuss the different components and parts within SAP HANA. These components are used to manage the data and to produce multidimensional models of the data. We'll also discuss the different ways SAP BusinessObjects is then used to access the data stored in SAP HANA. In the end, you should have a thorough understanding of what it takes to implement SAP HANA with SAP Data Service and SAP BusinessObjects.

*This chapter helps you understand how data is stored most effectively in memory so you can get the best results in both compression and performance.*

# 2    Storing Data in SAP HANA

In this chapter, we'll go into great detail on how data is stored in SAP HANA. Understanding data storage in SAP HANA is an important foundation because data storage differs from traditional database management systems in a number of ways. First, we'll start with on overview of data storage in SAP HANA to highlight these differences, and then we'll move into all of the components that make this possible (Section 2.1 and Section 2.2, respectively). We'll then discuss physical data modeling for SAP HANA in Section 2.3 to draw clear differences between traditional database systems and techniques and tools that are available in SAP HANA, and why it makes sense to actually "think backwards" about a data model in certain cases. The chapter ends in Section 2.4 with a case study for data modeling using our sample organization, AdventureWorks Cycle Company.

Let's begin by exploring SAP HANA data storage.

## 2.1    How Is Data Stored in SAP HANA?

Storing data in SAP HANA is quite different from a traditional disk-based database. The first and most obvious point is that SAP HANA is a *relational database management system* (RDBMS) where data is stored entirely in memory instead of relational data being stored entirely on spinning disks.

Storing data entirely in memory was once a revolutionary concept that first had its detractors making statements such as, "Data for an entire application or data warehouse structure would never all fit into memory." In fact it was such an unconventional idea that it took some time to gain ground. However, many leading vendors now have in-memory solutions and are touting both the in-memory platform and stance for the same reason SAP sought to use this strategy in the first place—unbelievable performance. Data loaded into SAP HANA and consumed by external applications performs at a speed that is unbelievable—almost as if the data were staged for a demonstration. The response times are just simply too fast.

---

**SAP HANA Real-World Performance: Exhibit A**

In our lab at Decision First Technologies, we took data from a customer paired with the SQL produced by an SAP BusinessObjects Web Intelligence report and placed the supporting data in SAP HANA. We then witnessed the following about the original query against SQL Server:

▶ We took the underlying query provided by the SAP BusinessObjects report and ran this query at the command line against the SQL Server database.

▶ The original SQL Server-based SAP BusinessObjects query runtime: over one hour.

The query was tuned and the data optimized in the SQL Server database, but the query was frankly quite complex and the data volume was large. The report was critical to the customer's business, so over one hour of runtime was simply too long to wait for the data.

As a proof of concept, we moved the data to SAP HANA for the customer, used the same exact SQL from the SAP Web Intelligence report, and the following occurred:

▶ We did not tune the database tables or structures for SAP HANA; we merely ported the data from SQL Server to SAP HANA.

▶ We did not tune the query. This was simply just a "copy and paste" exercise.

▶ The new SAP HANA query runtime: 4 seconds.

Although we did absolutely nothing to the data or the report, the runtime was immediate. Needless to say, this was a compelling story for the customer, even before we invoked the modeling techniques that exploit the storage and engine processes in SAP HANA (we'll discuss these later in this chapter).

---

The example in the preceding box is a real-world result that this particular customer would benefit from immediately just by simply porting its data to SAP HANA. These are the incredible performance benefits of in-memory computing that SAP has not been shy about touting—and rightfully so.

However, as with any great software platform, a developer must consider the needs of the platform and embrace techniques that envelop all of its strengths. This is where a gap has existed in the discussion of SAP HANA. SAP HANA simply performs so well that it allows some sloppiness in the design and still performs at an incredible pace. It's our belief that this sloppiness can be avoided by merely taking a step back and catering the pillars of the development effort to the needs and special characteristics native to the SAP HANA platform. As you weigh design considerations at the onset of the project, begin by considering how you want to store the data in the architecture that is unique to SAP HANA.

### 2.1.1   The Spinning Disk Problem

Spinning disks have been a performance bottleneck ever since they were introduced. The closer the disk is to the CPU, the faster data is rendered, searched, sorted, and processed; in SAP HANA, you take the physically spinning disk completely out of the equation to fully maximize this realization. Take, for instance, the process flow of information in a typical system and database:

▶ Data is collected from an application via a user input from a screen or form.

▶ Data is passed to the database in a process known as an input/output (or I/O) transfer of information.

▶ Data may be written or read from a cache in memory on the database server.

▶ Data is finally stored on a spinning disk.

I/O transfers performed without the use of a cache can take much longer intervals of time to process. Factors that contribute to extra time include physical disk platter spinning rates, time needed to move mechanical components of the drive heads to read the disk platter, and numerous other factors that are inherent to this disk-based process and add additional latency. This is a rather archaic process that hasn't changed greatly since the onset of computing. Conventional database systems try to improve on this by targeting specific systems that provide disk caching controllers.

*Caching data* is a method used to speed this process of data access from a spinning disk, and all of the major database vendors work closely with the disk manufacturers to tune the needs and specific requirements of the database I/O processing needs. In most cases, the database vendors seek to exploit caching techniques to limit that final disk interaction as much as possible. This is simply to avoid the native issues present with disk seek and write times by using the various optimizations of the caching controllers. This is all to try to work around the slowness of the disk whose performance may only be maximized so far.

### 2.1.2   Technologies Used to Combat the Problem

Many technologies that we rely on today were invented to work around the inherent slowness caused by the disk. Take, for instance, *online analytical processing* (OLAP) technologies (which enable faster read performance by physically restructuring the data), or *online transaction processing* (OLTP) technologies (whose goal is to make writing data to disk as fast as possible), and finally column storage technologies (whose goal is compression to both minimize store and increase the speed of access to the data). The important thing to keep in mind is that all of these technologies at their core were designed around the spinning disk and its native challenges.

### OLTP Storage Methods

An OLTP or relational database stores data in a normalized fashion at its core. Data is normalized to reduce redundant data and data storage patterns to optimize precious disk space and make the writing of that data to disk as fast as possible. Without techniques to minimize the storage factor, relational databases by nature will use lots of space to store these redundant values. Consider Figure 2.1, which shows a typical normalized RDBMS table structure that's been designed to reduce redundant data storage.

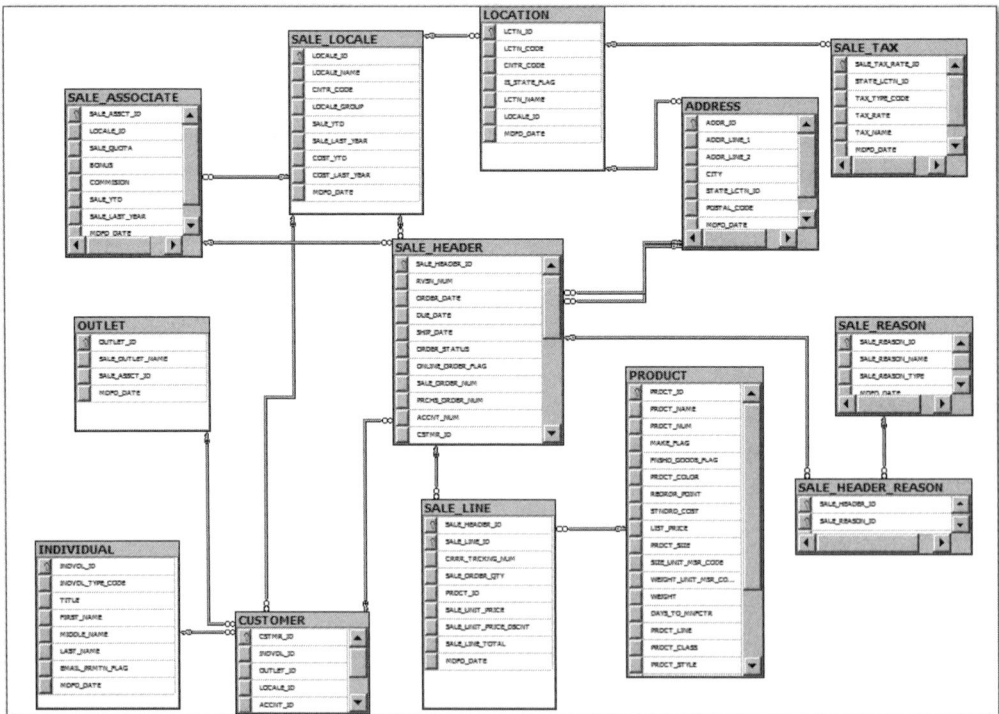

**Figure 2.1**  Normalized RDBMS Table Structure

Data is normalized or reduced into multiple tables so that repeating values are removed into multiple tables to store repeating values once and contain a pointer to those repeating values. For example, in Figure 2.1, SALE_HEADER records are normalized into their own table instead of just storing the columns into the SALE_HEADER table. This concept is the pinnacle of an OLTP system. This is simply the design principal on which OLTP systems are based.

There is nothing wrong with this design for inserting or storing data in *conventional* RDBMS systems. In fact, for this purpose, it's quite good. (There is a reason for this methodology being the way the world stores its data!) However, there is one fundamental problem with this system: *getting data out*.

Retrieving data or getting data out of an OLTP system requires multiple joins and combinations of various related tables. This is expensive in terms of processing in these database designs. Often, reporting in these systems is certainly an after-thought. It is problems like this one—combined with the slowness and natural speed impediment—that many technologies evolve to solve. Techniques such as OLAP technologies were invented to solve this problem.

## OLAP Storage Methods

OLAP data storage methods were conceived to combat slowness caused by both data access to disk and the way that data was stored in conventional relational databases, as just described. Technologies such as OLAP data storage physically store the data in a different way because traversing a relational database on disk isn't exactly the fastest solution for reading or retrieving data. Figure 2.2 shows this alternative data storage in an OLAP database, in a typical "star" schema (named so because of the shape the related tables resemble).

In an OLAP database, data is organized into concepts called *facts* and *dimensions*. The facts and dimensions are just standard tables, but their names denote what they store. Facts are the heart of the star schema or dimensional data model. For example, FACT_SALE is the fact table in Figure 2.2. Fact tables store all of the measures or values that will be used as metrics to measure or describe facts about a business concept. Fact tables may also contain foreign keys to the date dimension tables to allow pivoting or complex date metrics. Fact tables will be arranged with differing granularities. Fact tables could have a high granularity and be at an aggregate level, aggregating measures by calendar week or a product line, for instance, or a fact table could be at the lowest level of granularity: a transaction line from a source system or combined source systems. Fact tables also contain foreign keys that refer back to dimension tables by the primary key of the dimension table. A fact will be the "many" side of the relationship.

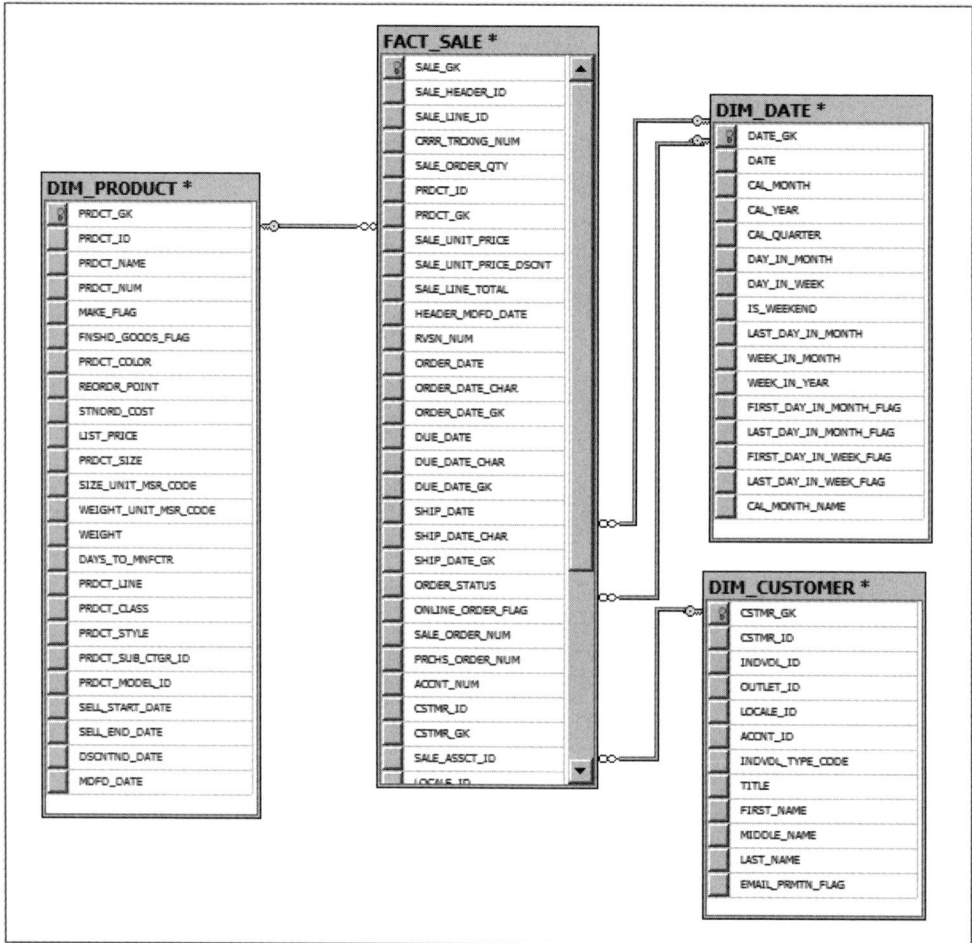

**Figure 2.2** Data Stored in an OLAP Database

Dimension tables are the ancillary tables prefixed with "DIM_" in Figure 2.2. Dimension tables are somewhat the opposite of fact tables because dimensions contain descriptions of the measures in the form of accompanying text to describe the data set for analysis by labeling the data, or the dimensions will often be used to query or filter the data quickly. In Figure 2.2, the DIM_CUSTOMER table provides details about customer data or attributes and is used to filter and query sales from the prospect of customer data. The same can be said for DIM_PRODUCT.

This is a dramatic solution because an entirely different table structure had to be established and created. If the modeling task symbolized in Figure 2.2 isn't enough, another element adds to the complexity: A batch-based process is created out of necessity.

A batch-based process is needed to both load and transform the data from the OLTP normalized data structure into the denormalized OLAP structure needed for fast querying. That batch process is typically called *extract, transform, and load* (ETL). An ETL process physically transforms the data to conform to this OLAP storage method.

---

**Typical ETL Process Workflow**

▶ After data is extracted from one or multiple source systems, the data then loads to a staging database where multiple transformations occur.

▶ Staging is a key layer where the data loses the mark of the source system and is standardized into business concepts.

▶ Data is loaded into the data warehouse tables and finalized into an OLAP structure to allow for both high-performing reads and flexibility in analytical methods and ad hoc data access.

---

SAP's solution for ETL data integration is SAP Data Services. SAP Data Services is a fully functional ETL and data quality solution that makes building very complex processes relatively straightforward. SAP Data Services is used to extract and transform data through complex transforms with many powerful built-in functions. Because it's the primary means to provision non-SAP data into SAP HANA, SAP Data Services plays a pivotal role in setting up data models and data storage the right way for maximum performance in SAP HANA. We'll discuss this tool's capabilities at length later in this book.

OLAP data structures like those shown in Figure 2.2 are the focus and primary use case of ad hoc analytical tools such as SAP BusinessObjects Business Intelligence (SAP BusinessObjects BI). The OLAP or star schema structure allows the tool to be quite flexible with the data in terms of drilling if hierarchies exist in the data or if using a date dimension (in the preceding example, this is DIM_DATE) to not only search and sort but to effortlessly provide running calculations or more complex date-based aggregations. Analytic activities like these would be quite difficult to address in a fully normalized OLTP system. Certainly, this data storage and system design eases the burden placed by the slowness of the platform as well as adding nice features for analytics.

## Columnar Data Storage Technologies

One final data storage technology that is worth considering is the *columnar database architecture*, which is predominantly used in SAP HANA. Columnar databases also take on the problem of working around the slowness of the disk by changing the way that data is stored on the disk. We'll walk through the SAP HANA specifics later in this chapter, but it's important to have a basic understanding of columnar architectures now.

Columnar databases have been around for quite some time, and the concept was certainly not invented with SAP HANA. Rather, this was a design methodology that was integrated into SAP HANA for the unique features and data storage aspects that a columnar database brings to the data storage equation. Columnar databases still use tables to store data as logical components, but the way that the data is laid out on the disk differs considerably from standard row store tables. Data values are gathered and stored in columns instead of rows. A very simple example is a product table with colors and product descriptions. In Figure 2.3, the data is stored in rows as it's represented in the logical tables in the database.

```
1, Dinner Plate , Blue  , SK001
2, Saucer          , White , SK002
3, Dinner Plate , White , SK003
4, Dinner Plate , Red   , SK004
```

**Figure 2.3** Data Storage in Rows in a Table

Data is organized into rows in the physical storage of the data on disk. This is a great design for OLTP systems and is the standard for most of the world's data. So data in a column store table would be arranged quite differently on the disk. Data is arranged by the columns of the data in Figure 2.4.

```
1,2,3,4;
Dinner Plate, Saucer;
Blue, White, Red;
SK001, SK002, SK003, SK004;
```

**Figure 2.4** Data Stored as Columns in a Columnar Store Table

Notice that the repeating values are only stored once to minimize the physical "footprint" of the data on the disk.

> **Important**
>
> Note that column store tables can still be relational tables and data. The relational concept still applies to columnar store tables, but the difference lies in the way the data is arranged on the disk.

Columnar databases have traditionally been used for OLAP applications where reads are very important because data can be read much more efficiently from this type of storage structure. Data is read and presented quickly to a consuming application or report. Other challenges can arrive when inserting data into disk-based column store tables. For example, UPDATE operations are quite expensive for column store data structures compared to their row store cousins.

> **Inserts in Disk-Based Column Store Tables**
>
> We recently ported data for a data warehouse OLAP structure in our lab at Decision First from SQL Server to SAP Sybase IQ to take advantage of the superior compression and read technology available in columnar Sybase IQ tables. However, we did notice some considerations that should be made in this port. These considerations are somewhat alleviated by the in-memory storage in SAP HANA, but they are still worth considering as these are in the domain of a column-based database.
>
> - SELECT statements or reads are much faster than with a conventional row-based database. The data then loads to a staging database where multiple transformations occur.
> - Using BULK INSERT uploading data was considerably faster and should be used whenever possible, especially with large record sets.
> - UPDATES or MERGE target operations are considerably slower than a conventional row-based database.
> - DELETE inserts are faster when updates are needed.
>
> The main takeaway is that SELECT SQL statements or reading data for operations such as a report do not need to be altered too much, but the ETL process will most likely require INSERTS, UPDATES, and DELETES to be altered, especially for delta or change-based loads.

For reasons like these, porting an existing structure to a columnar form—while not an insurmountable task—certainly has more considerations than simply moving the data over to a different platform. As mentioned, SAP HANA mitigates some of these issues by memory being so much faster. In a sense, SAP HANA masks some of these issues, but you should still consider them when you're porting very large existing data warehouse structures that require some type of ETL process with most often non-SAP data.

**Solutions Used by SAP HANA**

We've discussed OLTP, OLAP, and columnar data storage methods and the reasons why these were introduced, and SAP HANA is unique in the sense that it can be a bit of a chameleon. SAP HANA can act as any of these platforms by first physically storing data in both row and column fashions; however, even more than that, it can also act as an OLAP structure and even process data by interpreting multidimensional expressions or MDX query language. It also has a common and conventional SQL interface.

In essence, SAP takes advantage of the best of all of these platforms natively. This adaptable nature has been great for SAP, as it allows SAP HANA to quickly and seamlessly be addressed under many conventional applications. If a multidimensional cube-based application such as SAP NetWeaver Business Warehouse (SAP NetWeaver BW) or SAP Business Planning and Consolidation (SAP BPC) needs MDX to interface data, then no problem. SAP HANA has an interface layer to behave just like a cube to the application. Most applications in the world interact with a database via SQL, and SAP HANA is just as comfortable interfacing as SQL.

It's important to note that most of these technologies were invented to combat the slowness of disk-based data access. But SAP HANA is different. Even though it can masquerade as any of these technologies, it's taking on the performance problems directly. Instead of working around the issues of the platform, SAP HANA simply changes the platform altogether. It skips the disk, and data is stored directly in memory close to the CPU where it will perform better. The fact that SAP HANA works natively as any of these technologies was merely a product-related strategy to foster adoption of SAP HANA as a platform capable of replacing existing underlying database technologies while offering developers new and exciting ways to both access and model data. We'll cover both accessing and modeling data in later chapters of this book.

SAP HANA goes even further by rethinking the developer's platform by moving the various data processing layers in an application so that a developer must re-envision what is trying to be achieved. It's truly a revolutionary platform. Now, that we've covered all of the technologies supported by SAP HANA, we can move into the actual data storage components to lay the foundation for how data is stored in SAP HANA.

## 2.2 SAP HANA Data Storage Components

To begin using SAP HANA, you must first load or provision your data into SAP HANA, but to do this, you need a *persistent layer of data storage*. This persistent layer (also known as a persistent model) is made up of basic data storage and organizational components that are actually quite common concepts to database-savvy professionals.

The first two organizational components are schemas and users. From there, the components start to diverge and take on a much more SAP HANA-specific dialect: *row store tables* and *column store tables*.

To set up a persistence model in SAP HANA, follow these steps:

1. Create a schema by defining the schema and maintaining the definition in the repository.
2. Create a table by defining the table in SAP HANA Studio and maintaining the table definition in the repository.
3. Create a view by defining the view and maintaining the view in the repository.
4. Import table content or data by defining the data-provisioning rules that enable importing data from comma-separated values using the SAP HANA Extended Application Services (SAP HANA XS) table-import feature. You can use this method or use SAP Data Services as the means to import data into SAP HANA.

SAP Data Services allows data to also be transformed on the way into the import into SAP HANA. An import is certainly one way to provision data into SAP HANA, but SAP Data Services is available with a runtime license with SAP HANA and provides so many options with transformations that it's an obvious choice.

Let's wade further into these organizational components. All of the storage components mentioned in this chapter are found in the SAP HANA Studio under the Administration and Modeling perspective.

### 2.2.1 Schemas and Users

Recall that SAP HANA has many conventional components that will make database administrators and database developers quickly feel at home. These are mostly organizational components that facilitate administration tasks. In this section, we'll discuss schemas and users.

At a very high level, a *user* is used to connect and authenticate to SAP HANA, and a *schema* is used to group and classify various database objects such as tables or views. Because these aren't new concepts for SAP HANA, we'll limit the detail to what is required to provide a foundation for further discussion of SAP HANA-specific topics and for the building of the physical database-level objects for the case study examples.

### Schemas

Schemas are similar concepts that exist in other conventional database platforms. Most database platforms use schemas as a subdividing tool, and SAP HANA is no exception. In SAP HANA, schemas are used to divide the larger database installation into multiple subdatabases to organize the database objects into logical groupings. You use schemas to logically group together objects such as tables, views, and stored procedures. A schema in SAP HANA is essentially a database within the larger database or catalog.

Figure 2.5 shows the BOOK_USER schema in SAP HANA, from which all of the case study examples in this book will be crafted.

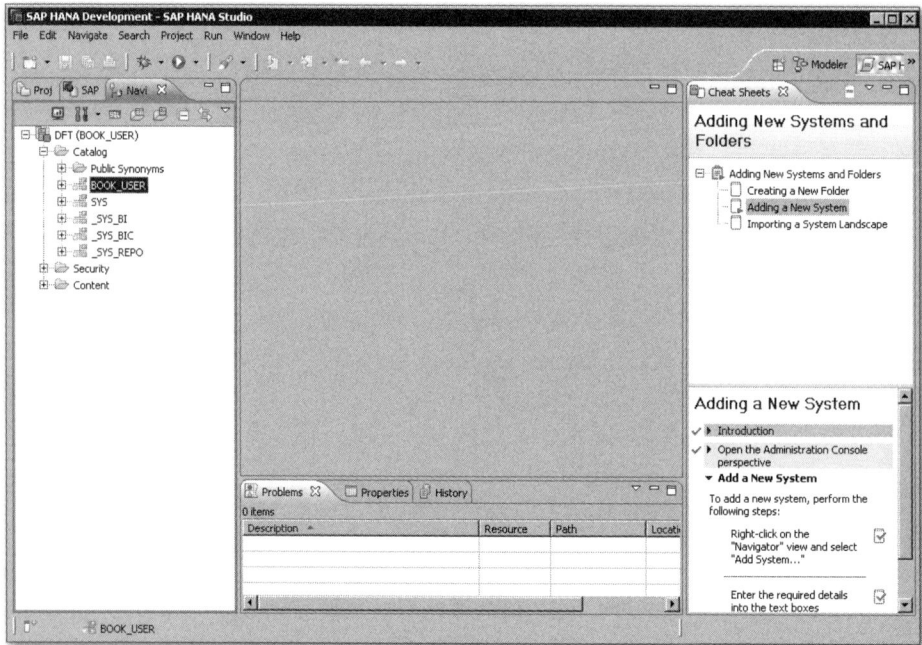

**Figure 2.5** The BOOK_USER Schema in SAP HANA

The BOOK_USER schema is the only *user-defined* schema that is visible. The rest of the schemas visible in the figure—SYS, _SYS_BI, _SYS_BIC, and _SYS_REPO—are all default *system-generated* schemas.

## Users and User Authentication

SAP HANA users are no different from users in any other conventional database in the sense that if you want to work in SAP HANA, you must have a user name to log in to the system. After logging into SAP HANA, your user must have privileges to perform certain tasks. Much like schemas, users will feel quite standard in concept to most savvy database administrators.

SAP HANA also supports the concept of a *role*, which is a superset of privileges. Roles are granted to database users and inherit the privileges assigned to the role the user belongs to.

When SAP HANA is installed, a database user called SYSTEM is created as the default admin user. This user has superior system-level privileges to create users, access system tables, and so on. As a best practice, you should not use the system user for normal administration activities or assign roles to this user. Use the SYSTEM user to create databases users with roles with the minimum set of responsibilities to perform the user's duties.

> **Operating System Administrator User**
>
> Aside from the SYSTEM database user, it's also important to note that an operating system administrator user (<sid>adm) is also created on the SAP HANA system upon installation. This user exists to provide a context or linkage to the base operating system in SAP HANA.
>
> This user has unlimited access to all local system resources and owns all SAP HANA files and all operating system processes. Within SAP HANA Studio, this user's credentials are required to perform advanced operations such as stopping or starting a database process or executing a recovery. This isn't to be confused with a database user because the (<sid>adm) user is only concerned with the operating system on the SAP HANA machine.

Users in SAP HANA exist only as database users to map to the privileges discussed earlier, and for internal authentication, this is the only means available. When you must authenticate with external sources, you can use two methods: Kerberos network authentication protocol or Security Assertion Markup Language (SAML).

**Additional References**

For additional information about establishing Kerberos or SAML, consult the *SAP HANA Administration Guide*.

**User Authorization**

Establishing the identity of a user occurs when the database user is created. The database user is then authenticated either at the database level or through one of two external authentication methods described earlier. After that authentication has occurred, the user has one last hurdle to pass to confirm that the authenticated user has the rights or privileges to perform the task. This process is called *authorization*.

Authorization is a simple concept that isn't specific to SAP HANA; authorization contains various privileges that are grouped into privilege types:

▶ **System privilege**
SQL privileges control various activities in the system. Examples are creating schemas, users, or roles.

▶ **SQL privilege**
SQL privileges are used to access and alter database objects. Examples are `SELECT`, `CREATE`, `DROP`, or `ALTER` table scripts and commands.

▶ **Analytic privilege**
Analytic privileges are used to restrict access to information models, specifically analytic views, attribute views, and calculation views. These are synonymous with SAP BusinessObjects row-level security, and these concepts will be shown in great detail in later chapters.

▶ **Package privilege**
Package privileges restrict the ability to use packages in the repository of the SAP HANA database. Packages contain the design-time objects of the analytic views, attribute views, and calculation views. This is where the work is done to create and craft changes to these objects.

▶ **SAP HANA XS privileges**
These privileges are supported for external client access to an SAP HANA application. Rights or privileges are granted through `GRANT_APPLICATION_PRIVILEGE` or `REVOKE_APPLICATION_PRIVILEGE` commands. These privileges must be managed through procedures and can't be managed through SAP HANA Studio.

As shown in Figure 2.6, you can use tabs to control the SQL PRIVILEGES, ANALYTICS PRIVILEGES, SYSTEM PRIVILEGES, and PACKAGE PRIVILEGES. SAP HANA XS privileges are managed via procedures or commands.

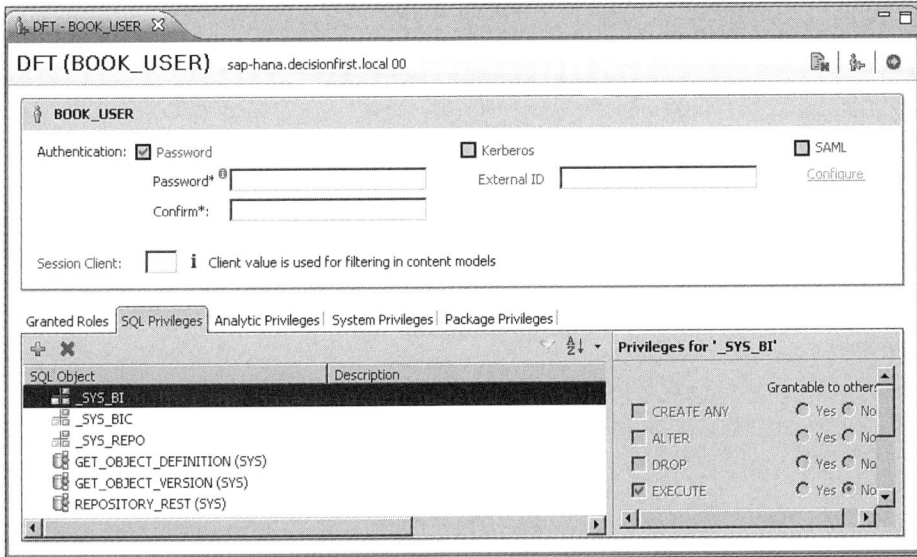

**Figure 2.6**  User Privileges for the BOOK_USER User Managed in SAP HANA Studio

## User Roles

Roles are tools that system administrators use to make tasks such as user provisioning and user maintenance much easier. For example, assigning privileges directly to each user of a large group would make maintenance quite time-consuming and tedious. Roles are the best way to grant complex and reusable hierarchies of user privileges. You can find roles in SAP HANA Studio in the NAVIGATOR window pane on the left side of Figure 2.7.

---

**User Roles Use Case Scenario**

Let's take a marketing department within an organization with 20 associates as an example.

The 20 associates all need to share the same data in SAP HANA with very similar data access privileges. The administrator could assign privileges directly to each user. This method would work fine and be completely functional in SAP HANA. However, if the department is quite volatile and often has new users entering and exiting the group, then each time the administrator needs to alter or add a user, he must compare the user's privileges with the rest of the group of 20.

This would be very difficult to keep in synch and prone to error. So in this case, it would make much more sense to add a custom Marketing role with all of the right privileges for the group. Then, when users are added or deleted, the users are simply added and deleted from the role.

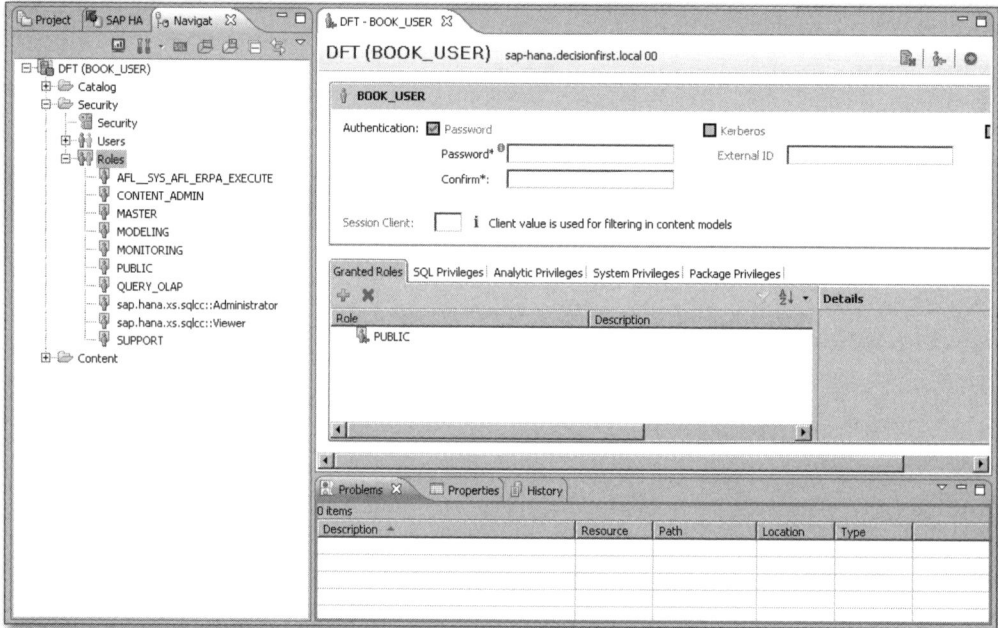

**Figure 2.7**  Roles in SAP HANA Studio under the Navigator Pane

As we've seen, roles offer tremendous flexibility and can be structured in various ways. Roles may contain any combination of system, object, package, analytic, or application privileges. It's this flexibility that makes roles so powerful. Roles can also extend the capabilities of other roles.

It's also important to note that roles may be modeled as design-time objects stored in the SAP HANA repository or they may be based on SQL statements at application runtime. Modeling roles as design-time objects can be advantageous because they may move between systems such as from development to production—and runtime objects can't. Also, runtime roles are associated with the user that is running the SQL statement. This might cause multiple problems because database users are associated with individuals who may or may not always be present in the SAP HANA system.

In short, when managing users in SAP HANA, always use roles. (We recommend using design-time roles as your first choice.) There are many ways to take advantage of using roles. Roles will give you much less anxiety in terms of management and a much more consistent user access level across the system.

We've discussed many different data storage components in SAP HANA; so far, all of these components have been fairly conventional in terms of most database platforms coverage as well. In fact, none of them—neither schemas, users, authorization, nor roles—have been unique to SAP HANA.

Next, we'll discuss column store tables and row store tables; on their own, these are also not unique to SAP HANA. Instead, one characteristic that makes SAP HANA unique is that it can offer a platform to house both column and row store tables! This offers tremendous flexibility to the platform in terms of multiple development and data storage options for both application and database developers.

### 2.2.2 Column Store Tables

Because SAP HANA is optimized or tuned for storing data in columns over data in rows, you should use *column store tables* whenever possible. Reading data is much faster in column-based tables; from a data storage perspective, columnar storage and compression are two of SAP HANA's best offerings. In a column store table, data simply compresses at higher rates.

As discussed earlier in this chapter, columnar storage allows repeating values to be expressed only once in storage, which allows the physical storage required to "compress." In SAP HANA, this compression is due to run-length encoding or the storage of sorted data where there is a high probability of two or more values being stored contiguously or in the same spatial locale. Run-length encoding counts the repeating values as the same value, which is achieved by storing the original column as a two column list.

This sophisticated system of reducing redundancy is an important concept of column-based storage for financial reasons. SAP HANA is licensed and priced by memory blocks, so the more memory you need to store your data, the more expensive your SAP HANA solution will be. However, pricing and cost are only one side of the equation.

Compression is also an important aspect of high-performing queries in SAP HANA. When data is compressed, it can be loaded into the CPU cache faster. The limiting factor is the distance between memory and the CPU cache, and this performance gain will exceed the additional computing needed to decompress the data. One factor that enables compression is run-length encoding, which stores values as a two-column list, while repeated values are stored only once in one column with another column as an index or pointer to the repetitious storage. One would think this would cause a latency in performance, but the two-column list's equality check on the index column is based on a higher performing integer value for the equality comparison—which is why proper compression can considerably speed aggregate operations or table scans. These are the operations that stand to benefit the most from compressed data in SAP HANA.

It's easy to create a table as a column store table in SAP HANA. To create a column store table, just use the Administration Console perspective in SAP HANA Studio (as shown in Figure 2.8), and select COLUMN STORE under the TYPE menu. Now you have a column store table that is ready for use!

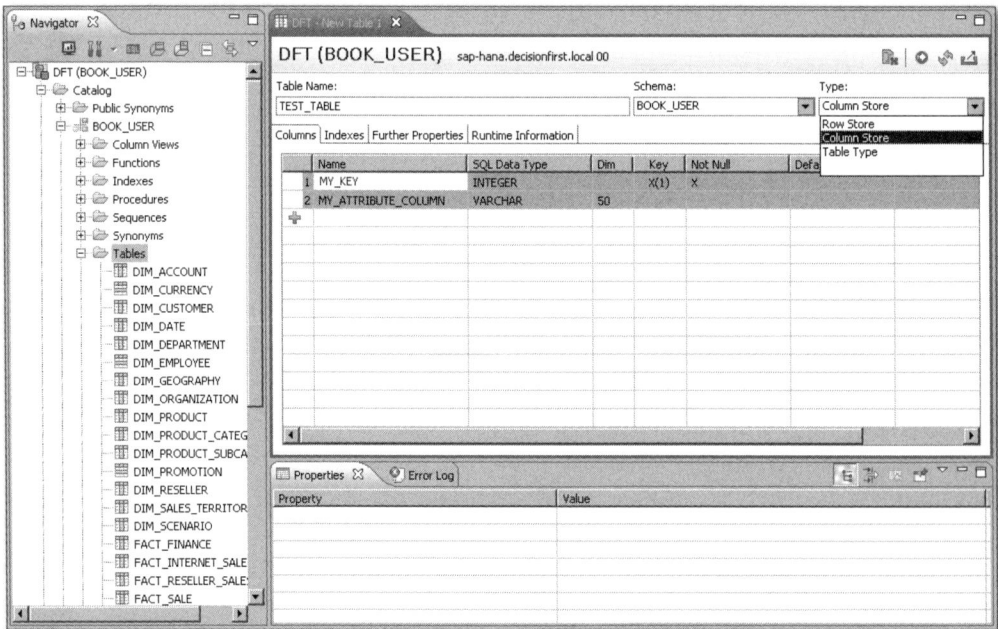

**Figure 2.8** Create a Column Store Table

When you're deciding between a row or column store table, consider how the data is going to be used. For example, column store tables are a good choice because some features such as partitioning are only available to column-based tables. So if partitioning is required in your application, then your decision of whether to use column- or row-based tables has already been made.

You should also weigh column-based storage in terms of updates and inserts. Bulk updates, or bulk operations in general, perform well against large tables with column storage. Column store tables are great choices for large tables with lots of read-based operations or SELECT statements—especially when you're performing aggregate operations. A number of aggregate functions exist natively in the column engine. Consider the list of SAP HANA functions that are available as native column functions by using column engine expressions as arguments. Thus, columnar tables will simply perform better because of being able to use functions built directly into this column engine rather than having to switch the processing and physically move the data to the row engine.

The following functions use column engine expressions as arguments:

▶ Numeric functions: TO_DECIMAL, TO_NUMBER, TO_BIGINT, TO_REAL, TO_DOUBLE, TO_CHAR, TO_NCHAR, TO_DATE, TO_TIMESTAMP, and BINTOHEX/HEXTOBIN.

▶ String functions: LTRIM, RTRIM, TRIM, LENGTH, SUBSTR, INSTR, and LOWER, UPPER.

▶ Date and time functions: WEEKDAY, DAYS_BETWEEN, SECONDS_BETWEEN, ADD_DAYS, UTCTOLOCAL, LOCALTOUTC, ISOWEEK, and QUARTER.

▶ Mathematical functions: LN, LOG, EXP, POWER, SQRT, SIN, COS, TAN, ASIN, ACOS, ATAN, SINH, COSH, FLOOR, and CEIL.

▶ Logic driving functions: NULLIF, NVL, NVL2, and COALESCE.

▶ Date extract function: EXTRACT ( YEAR /MONTH FROM <column engine expression> )*.

Three more specific advantages to column store tables will never be achieved in row store tables. The first of these advantages is that columnar storage with proper compression eliminates the need for additional indexing. The columnar scans of the column store tables, especially for run-length encoded tables, allow very high-performing reads. In most cases, these reads are fast enough that an index, with its additional overhead of metadata in terms of both storage and maintenance, is simply not necessary. It's basically an obsolete concept for a column store table in many cases. Without having a need to index, SAP HANA not only gains storage due to compression, but you also don't need to account for extra storage space or time in terms of jobs and scheduled offline tasks necessary to maintain indexes to speed data retrieval as you would in a conventional database. In a sense, you're actually gaining performance while simplifying the physical model due to not having to maintain separate index structures.

The second advantage is that the nature of the column store structure makes parallelization possible; that is, data is already vertically partitioned into columns. With that partitioned structure of divided columns, SAP HANA easily allows parallel operations to be assigned to multiple cores on the CPU. This way multiple columns can be searched and aggregated at the same time by different cores. The portioning that requires extra thought and maintenance—much like the indexing structures— is both redundant and unnecessary with column store tables and column engine processing in SAP HANA.

The final advantage is the elimination of physical aggregate data structures. Traditional BI applications and designs often call for aggregation in the database models at the presentation layer simply to deal with reporting or retrieving data against large and cumbersome record sets. This is often to work around the fact that the platform and disk-based data access will bind I/O operations and simply prove negative performance implications when performing complex aggregations or queries across larger data sets. To solve this problem in a traditional RDBMS, data will be physically persisted into aggregate tables that "roll up" the data to a higher level of granularity.

In Figure 2.9, we see an example of an aggregate table where transactional level sales data has been aggregated to raise the granularity of the data to records totaled by period, year, and product. This table would need to be created for analysis in a traditional RDBMS if the sales transaction table contained lots of history, and the analysis was mostly done at the year level of granularity. This would eliminate the performance problem while still addressing the reporting need.

| | PERIOD | YEAR | PRODUCT | PERIOD_QTY | PERIOD_SOLD... |
|---|---|---|---|---|---|
| ▶ | 1 | 2013 | BLUE WAGON | 25 | 250.00 |
| | 2 | 2013 | RED WAGON | 30 | 300.00 |
| | 12 | 2012 | RED WAGON | 20 | 200.00 |
| ✳ | *NULL* | *NULL* | *NULL* | *NULL* | *NULL* |

**Figure 2.9**  Example of an Aggregate Table

Deriving this aggregate table is relatively straightforward; it's just a SUM of the quantity and amount column in the transactional source. This means that

```
Select PERIOD, YEAR, PRODUCT, QTY, SOLD_AMT From Table_A
```

would become

```
Select PERIOD, YEAR, PRODUCT, SUM(QTY), SUM(SOLD_AMT)
From Table_A
Group By PERIOD, YEAR, PRODUCT
```

This is a very simple example; the logic from moving from transactional granularity to an aggregate by product isn't terribly difficult to derive or design. However, you would need an ETL process to physically transform the structure and move the data over to this new structure. So even with this one simple example, we've added quite a bit of complexity in terms of more data and more processes to be maintained.

On top of this complexity, this model introduces another problem: inherent latency. The data in the aggregate will never be real time because the aggregate will either be handled by an ETL process (by definition, a batch-based process) or by the database layer (which may introduce concurrency issues with updates in terms of locking operations that could potentially block reads during rebuilds). So the important point to take away about a column store table in SAP HANA operating using column engine native functions is that *it isn't necessary!*

This layer can be completely removed. SAP HANA can scan the data and perform the aggregate simple or complex at runtime in memory with similar speeds as a conventional architecture performing against aggregates. This is all happening in real time against the base transaction-level data where there is no need to have a latent batch-based process. When you have this level of performance natively, you simply don't need these additional layers. Because the data has not persisted, storage needs and cost actually diminish with the support of these column store structures in SAP HANA.

This is a very simple example, but you can see how this might grow as the needs for multiple views of aggregated data produce more duplicated redundant data with more processes to maintain. By removing these layers, you dramatically simplify the data model, thus simplifying the interaction of querying the data. With this one layered model, there is no need to hop from reading an aggregate view of the data to reading the base transactional view of the data. You use the same SQL from the clause and base statement and add in function calls when necessary. This type of simplification is a major benefit of using SAP HANA and one of the ways SAP HANA is transforming the data landscape.

### 2.2.3    Row Store Tables

Row store tables are exactly as they sound. Data is stored in memory but in a row fashion. Because these tables at the base storage level are very similar to traditional databases structures and constructs found in conventional databases, we won't go into the level of detail in this book to discuss row base-level components and data storage methodology as we did with column store tables.

However, one item to pay particular attention to with row store tables is that there is virtually no additional compression available by using a row store table. So, what is a proper use case for a row store table?

Column store tables clearly offer many benefits from data compression to tuning options to pure speed that is otherwise unobtainable with conventional row storage. It's pretty obvious from all of the examples discussed that column store tables are the first choice for developers when considering how to physically lay out data in SAP HANA. So why would you ever choose to use a row store table? There certainly are reasons to use a row store table, which is why row store tables and a row engine to process the requests are included in the SAP HANA platform.

Row store tables were included in the SAP HANA platform to first and foremost offer the ability for SAP HANA to be used as a valid and suitable OLTP platform. SAP has announced that the SAP Business Suite is certified to run on SAP HANA, which was a huge announcement solidifying and proving the fact that SAP HANA was tested and ready to support a very large and very complex application base. A large part of enabling that possibility is that row store tables and a row engine exist to process row-by-row data access requests.

> **Why Use Row Store Tables?**
>
> In short, use a row store table if you're developing a transactional interactive system such as a row-based system or an OLTP design. Row store tables will suit this purpose well.
>
> In other words:
>
> ▶ If your table will be used mostly for getting data in through a user input driven design, then use a row store table.
> ▶ If your table will mostly be used for retrieval or aggregate-based operations, then use a column store table.

The backbone of any OLTP system that involves data entry is rapid row-by-row access to complete or mostly complete records. These aren't cases where one SQL statement is returning, parsing, and aggregating millions of records on just a few columns. An OLTP design requires one customer record to be looked up and written into the application layer quickly in real time while a sales transaction is being established in the system. This response time needs to be instantaneous, and, in most cases, the entire row of the record is needed to satisfy the application.

This type of data access is effectively the complete opposite of the OLAP style of churning through complex data sets to group, sort, and aggregate on just a few columns. Needs like this necessitated SAP to include both platforms and engines. This inclusion of both sides (both row and column) of the data processing house truly makes SAP HANA unique, and presenting a viable row store option fosters rapid adoption of SAP HANA as much more than a valid BI or OLAP serving platform. By serving the row needs, SAP HANA is the new, remarkable, multifaceted platform built and scaled to handle complex and sizable applications such as the SAP Business Suite.

It's easy to create a table as a row store table in SAP HANA Studio. The process is much like the one outlined earlier to create a column store table. Just use the Administration Console perspective, and select ROW STORE under the TYPE menu, as shown in Figure 2.10. After performing this step, you now have a row store table that is ready to use.

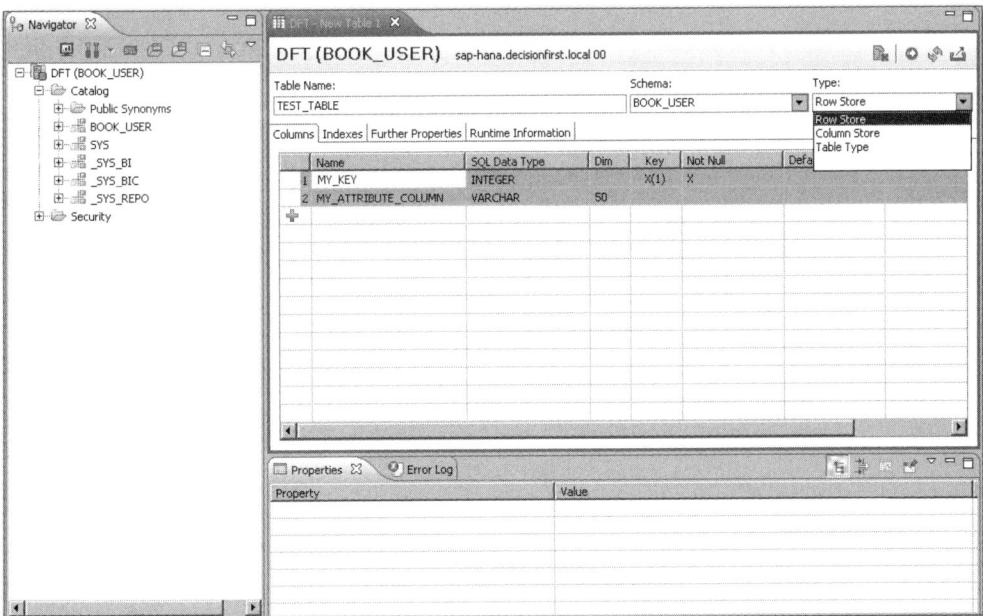

**Figure 2.10** Row Store Table in SAP HANA Studio

### 2.2.4 Use Cases for Both Row and Column Store Tables

Because they are primarily suited for most tasks in SAP HANA, column store tables are generally the reflexive first choice for an application developer. However, as shown earlier, row stores certainly have their place for developers as well. We've assembled the following list as a good comparison for when to use row-based storage versus column-based storage.

The following are scenarios for column-based storage:

- Tables are very large in size, and bulk operations will be used against the data.
  - Data warehouse tables fit into this category.
  - Historical tables with large record sets are another example.
- Data is primarily staged for reads or SELECT statements.
  - Data warehouse tables or data mart tables for BI reporting.
  - Application-based tables that will serve as the basis for reports or "getting data out."
- Aggregate functions will be used on a small number of columns with each SELECT or read operation.
- Table will be searched by values in one or a few columns.
- Table will be used to perform operations that require scanning the entire set of data, such as average calculations.
  - Searches like this are quite slow even with proper indexing in conventional or row-based structures.
  - The columnar constructs of SAP HANA are quite good at this type of analysis.
- High compression can be achieved by large tables that contain columns with few distinct values in relation to the record count.
- Complex aggregations or calculations will be needed often on one or a few columns in the table.

The following are scenarios for row-based storage:

- Table is relatively small in size or record count, making low compression rates less of an issue.

▶ Table will be used for returning one record quite often. A classic use case for this is an OLTP application table. This is probably the most important point and will ultimately be the best overall use case.

▶ Row store tables in SAP HANA will be the backbone of the OLTP application base.

▶ Aggregations aren't required.

▶ Writing data one record at a time is required.

▶ Fast searching isn't required.

When considering these criteria, you'll notice clear patterns that emerge regarding which type of data is best for each storage method. If your application requires record-by-record OLTP-style data interaction, then you'll need to use row-based tables. Be cautious with these tables because when they become large, they offer virtually no compression. This will bloat the licensed memory required to store the data. Column-based storage is best used for applications that have many complex read-based or `SELECT` operations such as OLAP or data warehousing structures. Column-based table structures compress nicely, and properly modeled physical data structures will take advantage of all of the sophisticated functions that are only available to column store tables.

## 2.3    Physical Data Modeling in SAP HANA

When considering modeling data for SAP HANA, we'll limit our discussion to modeling the data needed to fuel and power the column store tables and engine for maximum performance and processing. To examine row store data modeling in this book would overlap too much with conventional data modeling books because modeling data in a row store table follows a conventional normalized playbook. The column store tables and the compression that is offered in the SAP HANA platform are what expand this playbook into something that exists outside of the conventional normalized data constructs.

The SAP HANA data modeling playbook offers ideas that initially seem contrary to conventional data logic and wisdom. However, this is with good reason. It's only when considering the SAP HANA platform and storage paradigm as discussed in detail earlier in this chapter (Section 2.2.2) that these ideas begin to converge, resonate, and ultimately become conventional.

### 2.3.1   Comparing Data Modeling Techniques

To compare and contrast data modeling techniques for SAP HANA, it's valuable to first start with a basic understanding of legacy relational data modeling techniques and then finish by comparing how those modeling techniques are modified to best exploit SAP HANA's unique data structures and capabilities.

Many of the concepts and even physical structures translate over to SAP HANA directly from the conventional legacy OLAP counterparts. However, some distinctions specific to SAP HANA emerge. We'll explore these distinctions in detail; these will drive the focus and the discussion to draw attention to the techniques to exploit SAP HANA for maximum performance benefit.

**Legacy Relational OLAP modeling**

Legacy relational OLAP modeling is the backbone of traditional SAP BusinessObjects InfoView reporting with non-SAP data. As we described earlier in the context of the spinning disk problem, data is arranged into a series of tables of both facts and dimensions for performance for reporting but also to organize data effectively into data marts. A *data mart* is a collection of one or more relational OLAP fact tables and dimensions that are unified in purpose. For this chapter, we'll use two example data marts: the first for sales data and the second for financial data.

Both structures are simplistic in nature; it's plain to see that the focal point of the design resides around speed of access to the data. The fact table in each case contains fields that are used for measuring data. Usually amounts or counts will be used as attributes in a fact table. The other fields present in a fact table will be foreign key fields related to a primary key field in a dimension.

This series of one-to-many relationships of dimensions to facts gives expansive querying abilities to the dimensions that will, in many cases, search, sort, and pivot the data effectively. The dimensions are used to describe the facts and grant a means for actively querying the facts.

It's important to remember that all of these tables are just regular database tables. Fact tables will always be the 'heart' of the dimensional data model. Dimensions can also be conformed or shared across multiple fact tables or data marts. Conforming dimensions, which is the overlap of tables, is a common practice in relational OLAP data models. Dimensions are usually conformed because there is no need to store the table more than once, as they will be used across data marts. These conformed dimensions are logically represented in a logical data model of each mart, but the data is only physically persisted in one table to reduce storage.

Figure 2.11 shows an example for a financial data mart. In this mart you have ACCOUNT, DATE (TIME), DEPARTMENT, SCENARIO, and some type of ORGANIZATION structure dimensions—all relating to a simple FACT table containing the AMOUNT values. The data is modeled into these tables because these subjects of data are commonly used concepts for financial applications. The DATE dimension allows for flexible time-based reporting, and this dimension will be conformed across the next data mart shown in Figure 2.12: the sales data mart.

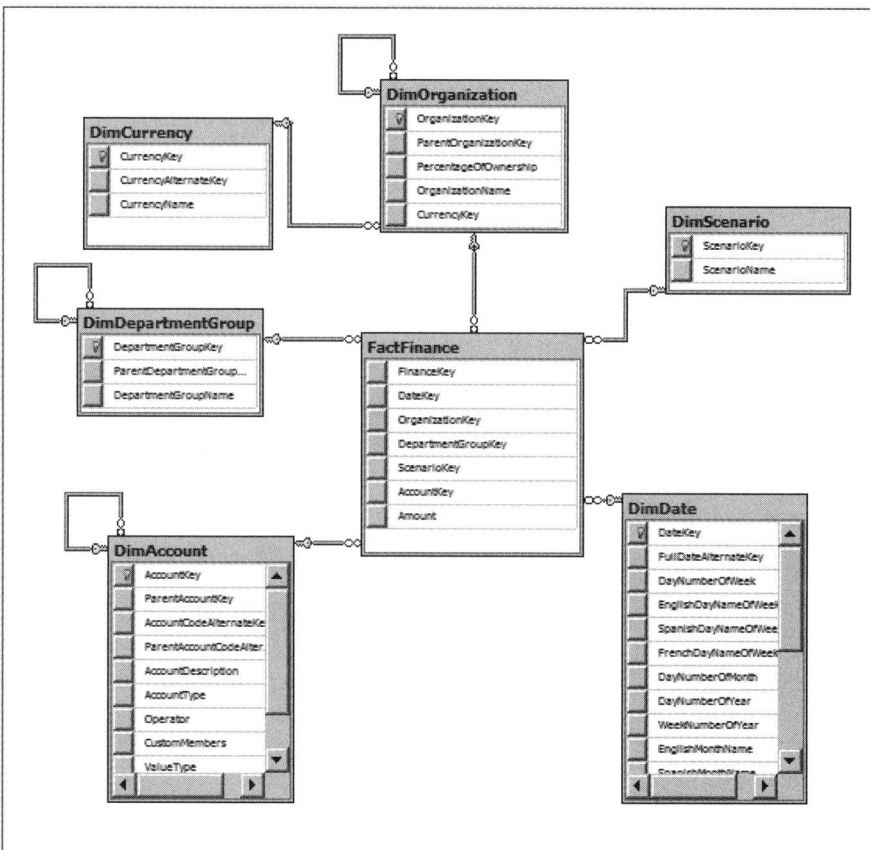

**Figure 2.11** Typical Relational OLAP Data Model for a Financial Data Mart

In a typical sales data mart, you have dimensions such as PRODUCT, DATE (TIME), CUSTOMER, CURRENCY, and some type of ORGANIZATION (TERRITORY in this case)—all relating to a simple FACT table containing the AMOUNT values. The DATE dimension is used for the same flexible time reporting principles outlined in the financial data mart, but all of the other dimensions represent subjects that are needed for sales analysis and reporting.

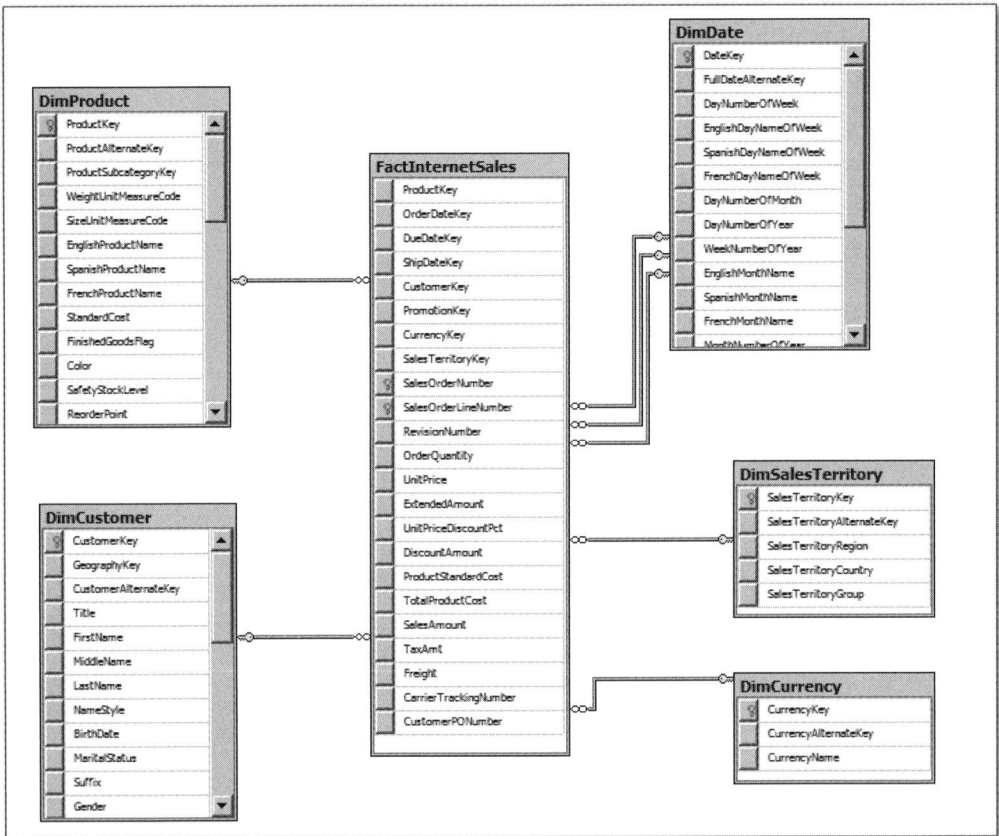

**Figure 2.12**  Typical Relational OLAP Data Model for a Sales Data Mart

Notice that the DATE dimension and the CURRENCY dimension are repeated or shared across the two data marts. Physically, at the database level, the tables aren't repeated; there is only one DIMCURRENCY table and one DIMDATE table, and so it's merely a logical repetition for organizational purposes. This repetition is a perfect example of a conformed dimension. We'll use conformed dimensions while building out the examples in the case study in this chapter (Section 2.4) to save on table space for the data marts in SAP HANA.

Recall that the data marts are segregated in terms of the data that they measure and describe. Considering Figure 2.11 and Figure 2.12, it's easy to see why there are two different data marts. There is little similarity in respect to the fact tables between these two data marts. The finance data mart simply has one amount field and all of the dimensional foreign keys. This allows quick pivoting and aggregations of the amount data by any of the dimensions. The sales data mart contains more complex facts because there are many more facets of a sale to measure, but the important point to note is that all sales measures are centrally located in the fact table so that all of the dimensional pivoting, querying, and sorting is done effortlessly across any or all of the dimensions. This is the primary concept that is central to a relational OLAP model.

The other concept central to a data mart is the grain of the data that is stored in the fact table or tables that make up the data mart. The grain of the data—sometimes known as the granularity of the data mart—is specific to the logical key structure of the fact table. The logical key structure is the single attribute (or combination of attributes) that makes the row of data in the fact unique.

Take, for example, the sales data mart in Figure 2.12. The FACTINTERNETSALES table has two primary key columns that make a composite key, or a combined logical key: SALESORDERNUMBER and SALESORDERLINENUMBER. Data in this example is stored at the line level of the transaction; this is the lowest level of granularity, as this is at the line item of the sale. However, data is often repeated and stored in other fact tables at a higher level of granularity such as by calendar week or product. This preaggregation or materialized aggregation is often necessary as a performance boost or method to realize a performance gain when the database platform runs out of tuning capabilities.

In this example, the fact table is at the line level, though it also contains header information in a denormalized fashion. *Denormalizing data* is merely the process of optimizing the data for reads by grouping redundant attributes together into one structure, rather than splitting the redundant attributes into multiple normalized tables. In an OLTP-normalized model, both the header level data and the line level data would be in two separate tables. Denormalizing occurs to ensure that one read from the FACTINTERNETSALES table obtains the necessary data rather than reading two tables and reconstructing the data logically in the database engine with a join. This principle of denormalizing is crucial to optimizing performance in an OLAP model.

SAP HANA takes this principle of denormalizing data further to a level that at first seems contrary to performance and storage considerations; however, upon closer inspection, we find that in many cases, denormalized data performs much faster in a column store table in SAP HANA using native column store functions than a normalized table structure in SAP HANA. In a normalized design, in many cases, SAP HANA may need to use the slower row engine to join the data. So even though this may seem counterintuitive at first, it's a core principle that will make an already fast SAP HANA system even faster!

---

**Key Points about Data Marts**

▶ Fact tables are the central element or "heart" of the data mart.

▶ Fact tables are surrounded by dimension tables.

▶ Fact tables contain only the measures and foreign keys back to the dimension tables.

▶ Dimension tables describe the facts.

▶ Denormalizing data or materializing aggregated data are techniques that are often used to boost performance when performance gains are no longer available from the database platform.

---

### SAP HANA Relational OLAP Modeling

The baseline for relational OLAP modeling in SAP HANA is exactly what we've just described. It is best practice to lay out a solid relational OLAP model as a starting point for running BI operations against SAP HANA, but then a major deviation occurs: *further denormalizing*.

In SAP HANA, joins are sometimes more costly than one read against a compressed column store data set containing the columns needed for any and all aggregate operations. Because SAP HANA has some pretty sophisticated built-in functions available in the column engine, we recommend that you "flatten" or denormalize dimensional columns into the facts where you have data between two tables that has high cardinality, or a high degree of uniqueness within the column. This way, there is one read against the table that is used to get all of the data that you need. We'll go further into detail around denormalizing techniques a little bit later in this chapter.

It's true that SAP HANA can render hierarchies against denormalized or flattened data natively, but to maximize reusability in the SAP HANA analytic model, we still recommend that you keep the core attributes of a dimension in a true dimensional structure residing in a separate table. This way, if attributes from one dimension are all that is needed for an attribute view, for example, then there is less work needed if a change needs to occur in the base tables columns. This allows for greater reusability when the base data is distributed in a more standard fashion.

Another technique that works well in an SAP HANA relational OLAP data model is to add aggregate columns directly into the fact tables rather than only storing the components of aggregations. For example, if you often multiply quantity by price to store an extended price in a fact table, consider storing the extended price as a calculation. The calculation will happen just as fast as if you stored the calculated value in a separate column. Storing the calculation is also always faster than reassembling the calculation at runtime in either the column or row engine. The final benefit of not storing the calculated data is that there is no redundant data occupying valuable space in memory in the SAP HANA database.

Of course, keep in mind that after you have calculated columns stored in SAP HANA tables, you'll need to explicitly state the columns when you need to insert data to avoid inadvertently setting the calculated columns by mistake.

Table 2.1 shows a scenario where you have a simple example of a conventional query and table storage structure that stores the components of quantity and price as a stored, calculated value in the faster query block. This is unnecessary with SAP HANA because the calculation can be stored instead of a value that needs updates. This speeds the query because the calculation happens in real time and is always updated.

| Scenario | SQL Needed |
|---|---|
| Conventional | select * <br> from my_table <br> where quantity * price = 100; |
| Faster query | `select *` <br> `from` my_table <br> `where` extended price = 100; |
| Supporting DDL for calculated extended_price column | `alter table` fact_sale <br> `add` (extended_price `decimal`(10,2) <br> GENERATED ALWAYS <br> AS quantity * price); |

**Table 2.1** Calculated Column for a"Faster" Query

Paying attention to dates is also important for dimensional modeling in SAP HANA. For best practice much like the denormalizing examples listed earlier, keep a date or time dimension separated from your facts for drilling or range-based date manipulatives, just as with a standard dimensional model. However, SAP HANA offers some sophisticated built-in date extraction functions. These will be shown in detail later in the analytic modeling sections, but it's important to note that dates should be stored in your fact tables with "sister" `varchar(8)` columns. You'll notice in the case study at the end of this chapter that for each date column listed in the FACT_INTERNET_SALES table for each of the date fields, there are both `datefieldnameKEY` columns present as well as `datfieldname_CHAR` columns. The second column is simply a `varchar(8)` representation of the date, needed to fuel the built-in date functions in SAP HANA.

As an example value for both types of date fields, '2013-01-01 00:00:00' in your table would also be stored in a `varchar(8)` column ('20130101') to take advantage of the built-in date extraction functions present in SAP HANA (covered in the analytic modeling sections of this book).

A final item worth considering when you're constructing your data model in SAP HANA is the fact that you must ensure data type support for all of your aggregate operations.

Take a simple example of a numeric column with a data type `Decimal(8,4)` containing a value 1111.1111. If this number is multiplied by 10, you'll have a value of 11110.1111. This value will now be out of range in the base column of the SAP HANA table. You must always store your data at the greatest precision required for the max operation that will occur on that data.

This requires some thinking in advance about the types of calculations that will occur on the data you're using, even while choosing data types upfront for your tables. Please keep in mind that the maximum declaration that is currently allowed is a `Decimal(34,4)`. So no matter what you're going to use, if you're sticking with a `DECIMAL` data type, then this is the maximum value allowed. A best practice to avoid this behavior is to just simply convert all decimal columns to float to handle overflow for division operations ratios; this will always avoid overflow issues because SAP HANA doesn't handle the conversion automatically.

> **Key Points about SAP HANA-Specific Data Marts:**
>
> ▶ As with SAP HANA nonspecific data marts, fact tables are the central element or "heart" of the data mart.
>
> ▶ As with SAP HANA nonspecific data marts, fact tables are surrounded by dimension tables.
>
> ▶ As with SAP HANA nonspecific data marts, fact tables contain the measures and foreign keys back to the dimension tables but also specific denormalized attributes where cardinality is high between tables.
>
> ▶ SAP HANA data marts also contain a time dimension, but have dates stored both as date values and character data types for specific SAP HANA functions to realize further performance from SAP HANA.
>
> ▶ Denormalizing data to extremes that would cripple a conventional database often perform best in SAP HANA.
>
> ▶ Materializing aggregated data is simply not necessary with SAP HANA as performance is quite considerable in column store tables and in the column engine.
>
> ▶ Numeric types that will be used in aggregate calculations require particular attention. You must cover the size of the resulting value from a calculation in the base numeric column. Remember that `decimal(34,4)` is the maximum decimal type allowed.

### 2.3.2 Denormalized Data in SAP HANA

In column store tables, denormalized data is something that you should always find in some area of a dimensional data model in SAP HANA. Recall our recommendation that you flatten or denormalize dimensional columns into the facts where you have data between two tables that has high cardinality or a high degree of uniqueness within the column. This is because joining data from a dimension with high cardinality is often more costly in terms of performance than just storing the attributes from the dimension that will be used often for querying or aggregations directly into the fact.

Two important principles are addressed by denormalizing data in SAP HANA: First, avoid the join in the engine and (most times) stay entirely in the column engine, where processing is much faster. Second, the penalty for the redundant data from a storage perspective isn't too severe because the column store table will only store the values that repeat once anyway due to the nature of compression in the column store table. Normalization is something that typically occurs in a relational database to increase performance and decrease storage, however in columnar tables in SAP HANA, this idea is turned on its head because compression helps with both the speed of access and limiting the extra footprint of the data in memory.

### 2.3.3 Techniques for Denormalizing Data in SAP HANA

Now that we've discussed why you should store denormalized data in SAP HANA column store tables, we'll now explain how to do it.

Take, for instance, a product dimension and a sales fact table. These tables are often used together in SQL queries for reporting. Maybe you want to filter on attributes such as color, class, or style, or you need to see standard cost as an aggregated value to be used in calculations such as price or sold quantity. These are combinations that will occur quite often in typical sales analysis scenarios. Product data will have a high degree of uniqueness or cardinality as well because data is often stored at a SKU or UPC level. A record in the product dimension will be a record of unique product attributes and is the perfect candidate for denormalizing aspects of the dimension into the fact.

To start, you must identify the attributes in the table that will be the subject of querying, filtering, or aggregations. For this example, we selected the highlighted attributes from the DIM_PRODUCT table shown in Figure 2.13 to store as denormalized attributes in the fact table.

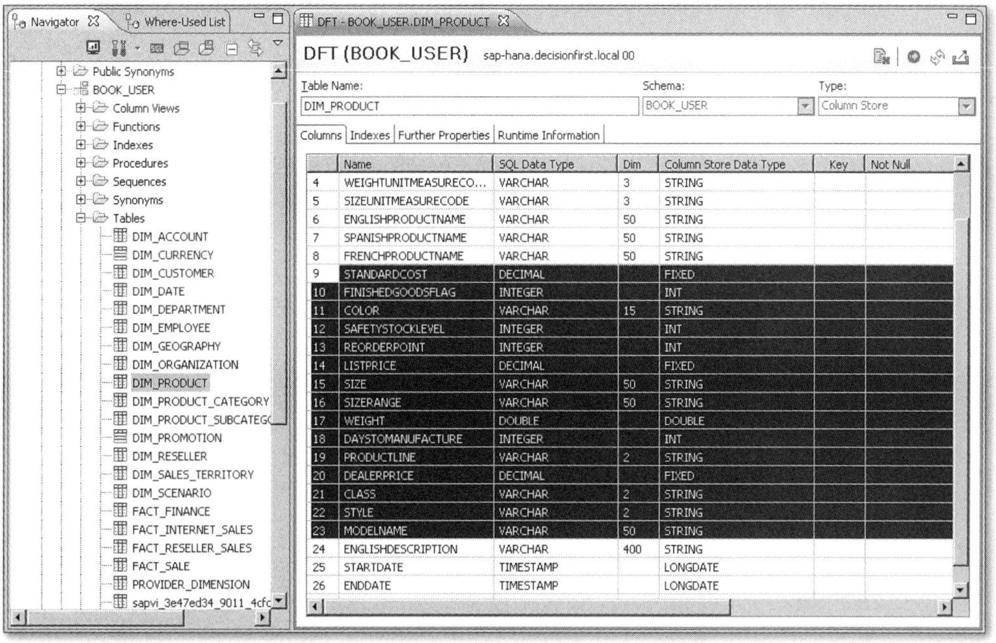

**Figure 2.13** Columns from DIM_PRODUCT Added to Reduce Frequent Joins

To create the columns in the FACT_INTERNET_SALES table, you'll now need to write an ALTER TABLE SQL statement to add the new columns. Listing 2.1 shows an example of the ALTER TABLE statement that will be used to add the columns to the FACT_INTERNET_SALES table.

**SQL Used to Add the Columns to the Fact Table: FACT_INTERNET_SALES**

```
-- Add DIM_Product columns to FACT_INTERNET_SALES
-- due to high cardinality.
-- Don Loden
-- 02.15.2013
```

```
alter table fact_internet_sales add
  (
  "DIM_PRD__STANDARDCOST" DECIMAL(19,4) CS_FIXED null,
  "DIM_PRD__FINISHEDGOODSFLAG" INTEGER CS_INT null,
  "DIM_PRD__COLOR" VARCHAR(15) null,
  "DIM_PRD__SAFETYSTOCKLEVEL" INTEGER CS_INT null,
  "DIM_PRD__REORDERPOINT" INTEGER CS_INT null,
```

```
"DIM_PRD__LISTPRICE" DECIMAL(19,4) CS_FIXED null,
"DIM_PRD__SIZE" VARCHAR(50) null,
"DIM_PRD__SIZERANGE" VARCHAR(50) null,
"DIM_PRD__WEIGHT" DOUBLE CS_DOUBLE null,
"DIM_PRD__DAYSTOMANUFACTURE" INTEGER CS_INT null,
"DIM_PRD__PRODUCTLINE" VARCHAR(2) null,
"DIM_PRD__DEALERPRICE" DECIMAL(19,4) CS_FIXED null,
"DIM_PRD__CLASS" VARCHAR(2) null,
"DIM_PRD__STYLE" VARCHAR(2) null,
"DIM_PRD__MODELNAME" VARCHAR(50) null
);
```

**Listing 2.1** SQL Data Definition Language (DDL) Used to Create FACT_INTERNET_SALES

See in Figure 2.14 what the FACT_INTERNET_SALES table looks like after executing the SQL to add the columns. All of the denormalized columns are ready for use in the fact table. Notice that the columns were not removed from DIM_PRODUCT to foster reusability and ease maintenance for analytic modeling, as you'll see later in the book.

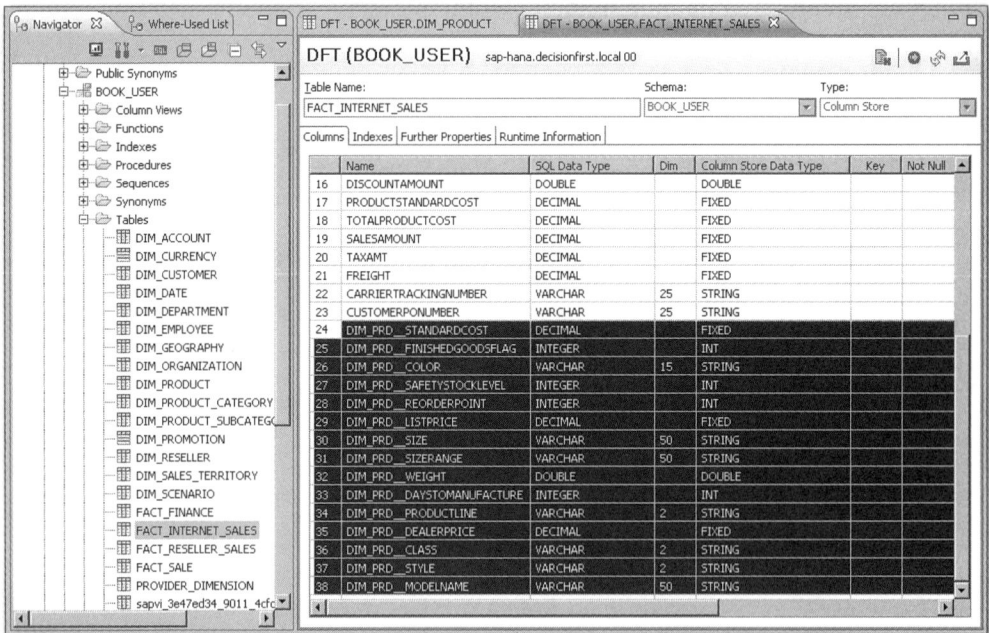

**Figure 2.14** FACT_INTERNET_SALES Table after Replicating the Columns from DIM_PRODUCT

## 2.4 Case Study: Modeling Data for an SAP HANA Project

To illustrate various presentation options and use cases, we've created a case study to follow a project from the ground up by starting with the data model, then provisioning the data, creating the analytic model, and finally fully realizing the BI capabilities with the consumption of the data using the SAP BusinessObjects BI tools. To perform all of these actions, we'll be using the sample Microsoft Adventure-Works data model for a fictitious company called AdventureWorks Cycle Company. We chose this data and model because it's a readily available sample schema with data that is familiar to many developers.

Currently, this SAP HANA system is a blank slate containing nothing but a bare install. So first you'll need to create a schema to house and organize the tables that you'll create. Then you'll finally create the tables and model them to illustrate best practices in an SAP HANA data model.

### 2.4.1 Create a Schema for the Data Mart

Before you can begin building tables in SAP HANA Studio using SQL or using a tool such as SAP Data Services, you need a schema created to house and organize your tables. To create the schema in SAP HANA, you must have a user created that can authenticate to SAP HANA. For all of the connections in the case study for this book, you'll be using the user BOOK_USER.

To create the schema using BOOK_USER, perform the following steps:

1. Open SAP HANA Studio, and connect using the BOOK_USER user, as shown in Figure 2.15.

   If you're currently connected as a different user and need to change the user, you may do so in the popup menu. Get to this menu by right-clicking on your connected SAP HANA system.

2. Open the SAP HANA Development perspective.

3. Open the Project Explorer view.

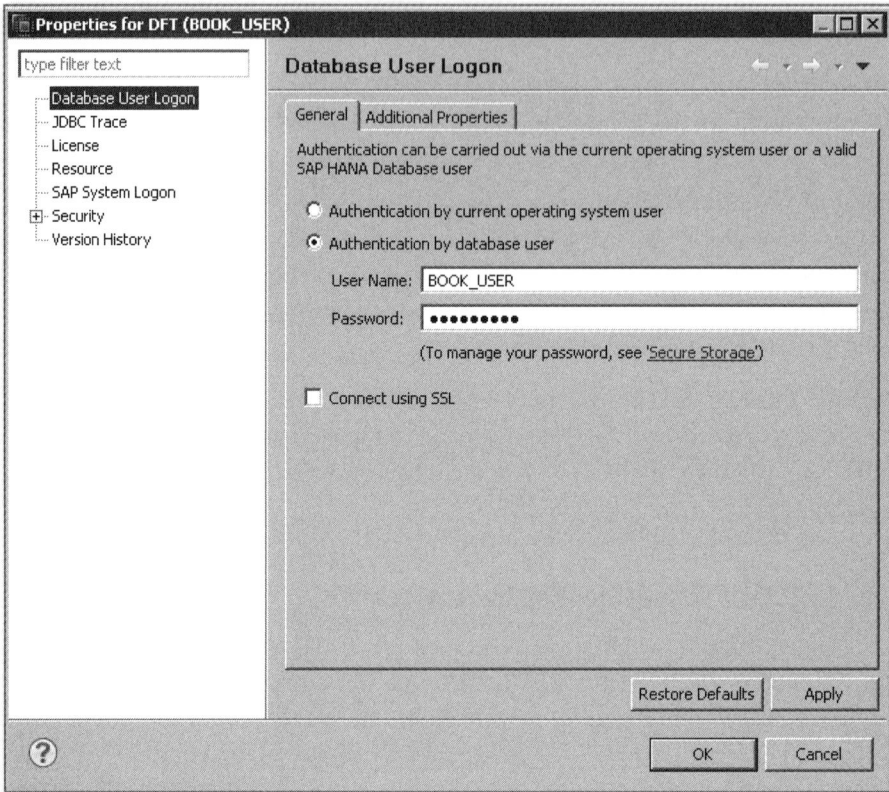

**Figure 2.15** Choosing a User Name to Sign In

4. Browse in the Project Workspace to the folder where you want to create your schema definition file, and right-click the folder. A menu pops up with a field where you can specify the name of the schema. For our example, use "BOOK_USER.hdbschema". Then choose FINISH to save the schema.

> **Caution!**
>
> If you want your schema to be a design-time object, then you'll need to create the schema as a file to be saved in the repository.

5. Define the schema name by opening up the file you just created in the previous step by inserting this code: `schema_name = "BOOK_USER";`.

6. Save and activate the schema file.

▶ Commit the schema to the repository by right-clicking the BOOK_USER schema and choosing TEAM • COMMIT.

▶ Activate the schema by right-clicking the BOOK_USER schema.

▶ Choose TEAM • COMMIT.

By performing these steps, you've now both created and activated a schema in SAP HANA, as shown in Figure 2.16. This schema is ready for use. In the next section of the case study, you'll begin to create the column store tables. These tables will be the foundation of all of the rest of the examples in this book.

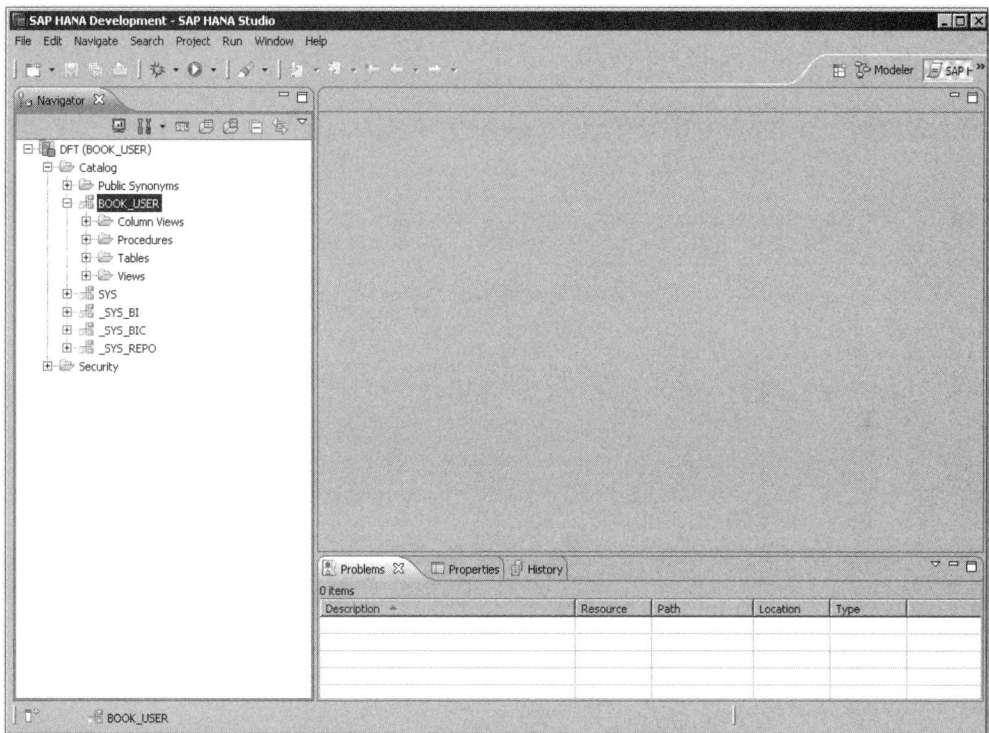

**Figure 2.16**  Finished Schema Ready for Use in SAP HANA

## 2.4.2  Create the Fact Table and Dimension Tables in SAP HANA

To create the fact and dimension tables in SAP HANA, we'll show a few different ways in this book, especially during the data provisioning sections using the unique features of SAP Data Services. However, for this chapter, and to focus on creating the tables and the underlying model of the tables, you'll create the tables using SQL in the SAP HANA Studio.

To create the tables using SQL in the SAP HANA Studio, perform the following steps:

1. Open SAP HANA Studio, and connect using the BOOK_USER user.

2. Open the Modeler perspective.

3. Open the Project Explorer view.

4. Browse in the Project Workspace to select the tables folder under the BOOK_USER schema that you created an earlier (shown in Figure 2.16).

5. Click on the SQL button illustrated by the arrow in Figure 2.17.

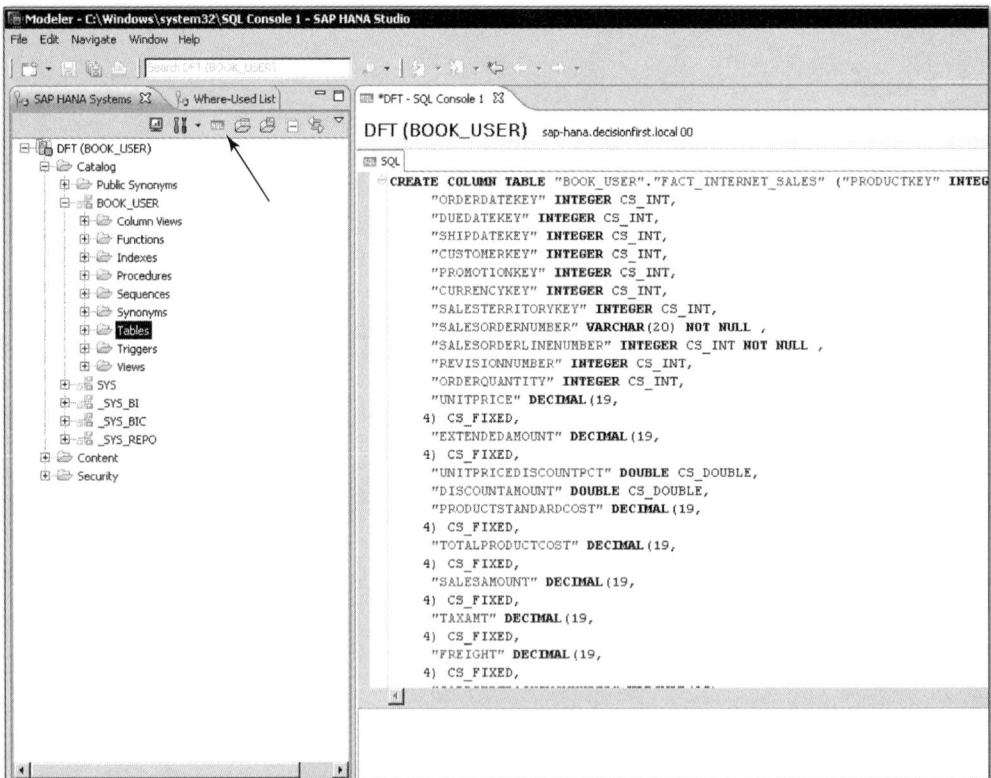

**Figure 2.17** Opening the SQL Editor for the Current Session to Create the Tables

6. Type each of the following SQL statements—Listing 2.2 for FACT_INTERNET_ SALES, Listing 2.3 for DIM_PRODUCT, Listing 2.4 for DIM_CUSTOMER, and Listing 2.5 for DIM_DATE into the SQL Editor, as shown in Figure 2.17.

Listing 2.2 is the main fact table with Internet sales measures. The only things differentiating this fact table from a standard fact table are the extra `varchar()` date columns for SAP HANA functions and denormalized columns from product dimension.

```
CREATE COLUMN TABLE "BOOK_USER"."FACT_INTERNET_SALES" ("PRODUCTKEY"
INTEGER CS_INT,
    "ORDERDATEKEY" INTEGER CS_INT,
    "ORDERDATE_CHAR" VARCHAR(8), --SUPPORTS HANA DATE FUNCTIONS
    "DUEDATEKEY" INTEGER CS_INT,
    "DUEDATE_CHAR" VARCHAR(8), --SUPPORTS HANA DATE FUNCTIONS
    "SHIPDATEKEY" INTEGER CS_INT,
    "SHIPDATE_CHAR" VARCHAR(8), --SUPPORTS HANA DATE FUNTIONS
"CUSTOMERKEY" INTEGER CS_INT,
    "PROMOTIONKEY" INTEGER CS_INT,
    "CURRENCYKEY" INTEGER CS_INT,
    "SALESTERRITORYKEY" INTEGER CS_INT,
    "SALESORDERNUMBER" VARCHAR(20) NOT NULL ,
    "SALESORDERLINENUMBER" INTEGER CS_INT NOT NULL ,
    "REVISIONNUMBER" INTEGER CS_INT,
    "ORDERQUANTITY" INTEGER CS_INT,
    "UNITPRICE" DECIMAL(19,
   4) CS_FIXED,
    "EXTENDEDAMOUNT" DECIMAL(19,
   4) CS_FIXED,
    "UNITPRICEDISCOUNTPCT" DOUBLE CS_DOUBLE,
    "DISCOUNTAMOUNT" DOUBLE CS_DOUBLE,
    "PRODUCTSTANDARDCOST" DECIMAL(19,
   4) CS_FIXED,
    "TOTALPRODUCTCOST" DECIMAL(19,
   4) CS_FIXED,
    "SALESAMOUNT" DECIMAL(19,
   4) CS_FIXED,
    "TAXAMT" DECIMAL(19,
   4) CS_FIXED,
    "FREIGHT" DECIMAL(19,
   4) CS_FIXED,
    "CARRIERTRACKINGNUMBER" VARCHAR(25),
    "CUSTOMERPONUMBER" VARCHAR(25),
```

```
    "DIM_PRD__STANDARDCOST" DECIMAL(19,
  4) CS_FIXED,
    "DIM_PRD__FINISHEDGOODSFLAG" INTEGER CS_INT,
    "DIM_PRD__COLOR" VARCHAR(15),
    "DIM_PRD__SAFETYSTOCKLEVEL" INTEGER CS_INT,
    "DIM_PRD__REORDERPOINT" INTEGER CS_INT,
    "DIM_PRD__LISTPRICE" DECIMAL(19,
  4) CS_FIXED,
    "DIM_PRD__SIZE" VARCHAR(50),
    "DIM_PRD__SIZERANGE" VARCHAR(50),
    "DIM_PRD__WEIGHT" DOUBLE CS_DOUBLE,
    "DIM_PRD__DAYSTOMANUFACTURE" INTEGER CS_INT,
    "DIM_PRD__PRODUCTLINE" VARCHAR(2),
    "DIM_PRD__DEALERPRICE" DECIMAL(19,
  4) CS_FIXED,
    "DIM_PRD__CLASS" VARCHAR(2),
    "DIM_PRD__STYLE" VARCHAR(2),
    "DIM_PRD__MODELNAME" VARCHAR(50),
    PRIMARY KEY ("SALESORDERNUMBER",
    "SALESORDERLINENUMBER"))
```

**Listing 2.2** SQL DDL (Fact Table) for FACT_INTERNET_SALES

The standard product dimension describes product-level attributes. Notice that certain columns have been repeated in the fact table in Listing 2.3, yet they still exist here for reusability in the SAP HANA analytic model.

```
CREATE COLUMN TABLE "BOOK_USER"."DIM_PRODUCT" ("PRODUCTKEY" INTEGER
CS_INT NOT NULL ,
    "PRODUCTALTERNATEKEY" VARCHAR(25),
    "PRODUCTSUBCATEGORYKEY" INTEGER CS_INT,
    "WEIGHTUNITMEASURECODE" VARCHAR(3),
    "SIZEUNITMEASURECODE" VARCHAR(3),
    "ENGLISHPRODUCTNAME" VARCHAR(50),
    "SPANISHPRODUCTNAME" VARCHAR(50),
    "FRENCHPRODUCTNAME" VARCHAR(50),
    "STANDARDCOST" DECIMAL(19,
  4) CS_FIXED,
    "FINISHEDGOODSFLAG" INTEGER CS_INT,
    "COLOR" VARCHAR(15),
    "SAFETYSTOCKLEVEL" INTEGER CS_INT,
    "REORDERPOINT" INTEGER CS_INT,
  "LISTPRICE" DECIMAL(19,
```

```
   4) CS_FIXED,
    "SIZE" VARCHAR(50),
    "SIZERANGE" VARCHAR(50),
    "WEIGHT" DOUBLE CS_DOUBLE,
    "DAYSTOMANUFACTURE" INTEGER CS_INT,
    "PRODUCTLINE" VARCHAR(2),
    "DEALERPRICE" DECIMAL(19,
   4) CS_FIXED,
    "CLASS" VARCHAR(2),
    "STYLE" VARCHAR(2),
    "MODELNAME" VARCHAR(50),
    "ENGLISHDESCRIPTION" VARCHAR(400),
    "STARTDATE" LONGDATE CS_LONGDATE,
    "ENDDATE" LONGDATE CS_LONGDATE,
    "STATUS" VARCHAR(7),
    PRIMARY KEY ("PRODUCTKEY"))
```

**Listing 2.3** SQL DDL (Dimension Table) for DIM_PRODUCT

This standard customer dimension table describes customer-level attributes
(Listing 2.4). The CUSTOMERKEY field has a foreign key that relates this table to
the fact table.

```
CREATE COLUMN TABLE "BOOK_USER"."DIM_CUSTOMER" ("CUSTOMERKEY" INTEGER
CS_INT NOT NULL ,
    "GEOGRAPHYKEY" INTEGER CS_INT,
    "CUSTOMERALTERNATEKEY" VARCHAR(15),
    "TITLE" VARCHAR(8),
    "FIRSTNAME" VARCHAR(50),
    "MIDDLENAME" VARCHAR(50),
    "LASTNAME" VARCHAR(50),
    "NAMESTYLE" INTEGER CS_INT,
    "BIRTHDATE" DAYDATE CS_DAYDATE,
    "MARITALSTATUS" VARCHAR(1),
    "SUFFIX" VARCHAR(10),
    "GENDER" VARCHAR(1),
    "EMAILADDRESS" VARCHAR(50),
    "YEARLYINCOME" DECIMAL(19,
   4) CS_FIXED,
    "TOTALCHILDREN" INTEGER CS_INT,
    "NUMBERCHILDRENATHOME" INTEGER CS_INT,
    "ENGLISHEDUCATION" VARCHAR(40),
    "SPANISHEDUCATION" VARCHAR(40),
```

```
    "FRENCHEDUCATION" VARCHAR(40),
    "ENGLISHOCCUPATION" VARCHAR(100),
    "SPANISHOCCUPATION" VARCHAR(100),
    "FRENCHOCCUPATION" VARCHAR(100),
    "HOUSEOWNERFLAG" VARCHAR(1),
    "NUMBERCARSOWNED" INTEGER CS_INT,
    "ADDRESSLINE1" VARCHAR(120),
    "ADDRESSLINE2" VARCHAR(120),
    "PHONE" VARCHAR(20),
    "DATEFIRSTPURCHASE" DAYDATE CS_DAYDATE,
    "COMMUTEDISTANCE" VARCHAR(15),
    PRIMARY KEY ("CUSTOMERKEY"))
```

**Listing 2.4** SQL DDL (Dimension Table) for DIM_CUSTOMER

The standard time dimension describes date attributes (Listing 2.5). The `DATEKEY` field has a foreign key that relates this table to the fact table on multiple date attributes. The basic concept is that the date dimension will be related back on any date column in the fact table to allow for flexibility on any type of date- or time-based reporting.

```
CREATE COLUMN TABLE "BOOK_USER"."DIM_DATE" ("DATEKEY" INTEGER CS_INT
NOT NULL ,
    "FULLDATEALTERNATEKEY" DAYDATE CS_DAYDATE,
    "DAYNUMBEROFWEEK" INTEGER CS_INT,
    "ENGLISHDAYNAMEOFWEEK" VARCHAR(10),
    "SPANISHDAYNAMEOFWEEK" VARCHAR(10),
    "FRENCHDAYNAMEOFWEEK" VARCHAR(10),
    "DAYNUMBEROFMONTH" INTEGER CS_INT,
    "DAYNUMBEROFYEAR" INTEGER CS_INT,
    "WEEKNUMBEROFYEAR" INTEGER CS_INT,
    "ENGLISHMONTHNAME" VARCHAR(10),
    "SPANISHMONTHNAME" VARCHAR(10),
    "FRENCHMONTHNAME" VARCHAR(10),
    "MONTHNUMBEROFYEAR" INTEGER CS_INT,
    "CALENDARQUARTER" INTEGER CS_INT,
    "CALENDARQUARTERYEAR" VARCHAR(8),
    "CALENDARYEAR" INTEGER CS_INT,
    "CALENDARYEARMONTH" VARCHAR(15),
    "CALENDARYEARWEEK" VARCHAR(20),
    "CALENDARSEMESTER" INTEGER CS_INT,
    "FISCALQUARTER" INTEGER CS_INT,
    "FISCALYEAR" INTEGER CS_INT,
```

```
    "FISCALSEMESTER" INTEGER CS_INT,
    PRIMARY KEY ("DATEKEY"))
```

**Listing 2.5** SQL DDL (Dimension Table) for DIM_DATE

7. Press ⏷F8 to execute the queries.

After executing all four SQL statements, you have one fact table and three dimension tables. These tables form the core of the data mart that will be used in the subsequent sections of the case study, and this data set will remain the base data for all of the examples present in this book for continuity. You'll also notice a financial structure consisting of the following data mart tables:

- ▸ FACT_FINANCE
- ▸ DIM_CURRENCY
- ▸ DIM_ORGANIZATION
- ▸ DIM_SCENARIO
- ▸ DIM_DATE
- ▸ DIM_ACCOUNT
- ▸ DIM_DEPARTMENT_GROUP

Note that DIM_DATE is a conformed dimension across the financial mart and the sales mart. DIM_DATE references the same table that was created in this section.

These financial data mart tables are created in the same manner as the sales data mart. The descriptions were only given to limit redundant descriptions for the case study. Now that all tables have been modeled and created, in the next chapter we'll move into the case study section that provisions data into the tables and populates data into our SAP HANA instance.

## 2.5    Summary

SAP HANA is a tremendously powerful and flexible platform, in part because it truly has the ability to act as a chameleon and masquerade as multiple platforms. SAP HANA is unique in the sense that it can easily replace many of these platforms quickly as it shares the common conventionally approved language for data access: SQL. This makes SAP HANA a plug-and-play fit for replacing the data and analytic architecture for many applications with a far more sophisticated and well-thought-out development platform. The fact that SAP HANA also can interpret MDX queries natively speaks to the same rapid integration and replacement of conventional cube-based technologies.

Native support for MDX was one reason it was no surprise that SAP undertook the task of moving SAP NetWeaver BW to SAP HANA so quickly. For an application such as SAP NetWeaver BW, moving to SAP HANA was merely another database port. This ease of movement and transport goes a long way toward SAP's "no disruption" model. Finally, now that the SAP Business Suite is certified to run on SAP HANA, the sky is the limit in terms of possibilities on a mature and robust platform that really does do it all.

Now that you have an understanding of how SAP HANA stores data and what is needed for high-performing data in SAP HANA, we can now look toward the data provisioning process. We call out the word "process" because you shouldn't just simply load your data into SAP HANA. Before you provision data into SAP HANA, there are some things that need to be addressed with a thorough preprovisioning process. We'll examine this preprovisioning in process in detail in Chapter 3.

*Before provisioning or data loading can occur, you must first perform source system analysis to see what aspects of the data need repair. Learn how to provide high-quality data as a base for SAP HANA using SAP Data Services.*

# 3 Preprovisioning Data with SAP Data Services

SAP HANA is immensely powerful and offers tremendous possibilities to your organization, but any system is only as good as the quality of its data. In this chapter, we'll explore the profiling tools that SAP Data Services provides as a platform in Section 3.2 to analyze the source, and then we'll conclude with setting up a mapping document in Section 3.3.4 to illustrate logic and use as a communication tool with the business users on how data will be loaded and what you plan to do with the data before loading it into SAP HANA.

We'll also discuss the steps that you simply must complete before you provision data into SAP HANA. Having spent lots of time, effort, and money on your SAP HANA investment, you don't want to load just any data into this blank and now pristine system; instead, the detailed source system analysis steps and tasks will help you closely examine the data and avoid costly mistakes. This SSA will show you the real story behind your data and help you ensure that you're not just loading "fast trash" into SAP HANA.

## 3.1 Source System Analysis

You may find yourself wondering exactly what *source system analysis* (SSA) is. Quite simply, SSA is taking a hard, detailed look at a source to really see the story behind the data.

SSA typically begins with data profiling using a profiling tool or even just SQL against the base database tables. Using findings uncovered in the profiling effort, you can dig deeper into the source to uncover data realities. These realities are sometimes painful, in that they may prove or disprove stated facts or beliefs about how data is stored and represented across the enterprise.

This seems like a fairly simple concept, but SSA is very empowering for a development cycle of an SAP HANA implementation: At the core, SSA gets to the real story of what is going on with data in the enterprise, making it a very necessary step in your SAP HANA journey.

---

**How SSA Impacted One Organization**

During site visits, we often hear, "That's not possible with our data..." or "Our systems don't do that...," which are often disproven empirically by profiling and analyzing the source data in detail. Although these lessons are sometimes painful for the business users, they are important for realizing a design that will truly deliver and meet functional expectations even when the data doesn't!

Once on an engagement, we were working with a customer and performing detailed SSA on a source that was to be used for budgeting data. After SSA, we determined that the way the accounting was being performed through classifications in the financial system was violating a core business rule, resulting in improper accounting practices and actually costing the company a great deal of money—all simply due to the way the system was set up. The data had always been behaving this way, and the business users had no idea until SSA was performed!

---

At a high level, SSA starts with data profiling with a profiling tool. In this book, we'll explore the built-in features of SAP Data Services because a runtime license of SAP Data Services is included with standalone SAP HANA. Many column profile attributes are available that save time in a development effort. Consider all of the following column metrics that are available with a simple column profile in SAP Data Services, as shown in Figure 3.1. Some are simple, such as MIN and MAX, while others are complex, such as the patterns of data on the far right.

---

**Note**

SAP Data Services 4.1 was generally available at the time of writing (summer 2013), so all SAP Data Services screenshots were taken from that version.

---

Some measures are available in SQL, but all of these were created at the press of a button in SAP Data Services! Column profiling in SAP Data Services results in valuable time savings for an SAP HANA initiative. Using a tool like this gives you a quick view into your source data to begin the journey of SSA.

| | Min | Min count | Max | Max count | Average | Median | Min string | Max string | Average st | Median st | Distincts | Nulls | Nulls % | Zeros | Zeros % | Blanks | Blanks % | Patterns |
|---|---|---|---|---|---|---|---|---|---|---|---|---|---|---|---|---|---|---|
| item | 000100031 | 1 | ess-0001203 | 1 | n/a | 26447 | 1 | 30 | 6 | 7 | 63309 | 0 | 0% | n/a | n/a | 0 | 0% | 168 |
| description | #10 HOSE | 1 | track drive | 1 | n/a | LOCK BAR | 2 | 40 | 22 | 24 | 45388 | 28 | 0.04% | n/a | n/a | 0 | 0% | 27665 |
| qty_allocjob | 0 | 62006 | 581 | 1 | 0.180304 | 0 | n/a | n/a | n/a | n/a | 85 | 0 | 0% | 62006 | 97.94% | n/a | n/a | n/a |
| u_m | BOX | 1 | YRD | 4 | n/a | EA | 1 | 3 | 2 | 2 | 22 | 0 | 0% | n/a | n/a | 0 | 0% | 3 |
| lead_time | 0 | 13509 | 745 | 1 | 19.91202 | 20 | n/a | n/a | n/a | n/a | 75 | 0 | 0% | 13509 | 21.33% | n/a | n/a | n/a |
| lot_size | 1 | 63290 | 25 | 1 | 1.001406 | 1 | n/a | n/a | n/a | n/a | 8 | 0 | 0% | 0 | 0% | n/a | n/a | n/a |
| qty_used_ytd | -16 | 1 | 156550 | 1 | 33.70335 | 0 | n/a | n/a | n/a | n/a | 893 | 0 | 0% | 56292 | 88.91% | n/a | n/a | n/a |
| qty_mfg_ytd | 0 | 62658 | 949 | 1 | 0.321281 | 0 | n/a | n/a | n/a | n/a | 108 | 0 | 0% | 62658 | 98.97% | n/a | n/a | n/a |
| abc_code | A | 1763 | C | 57156 | n/a | C | 1 | 1 | 1 | 1 | 3 | 0 | 0% | n/a | n/a | 0 | 0% | 1 |
| drawing_nbr | !! SEE NOT | 1 | see notes | 1 | n/a | <Blank> | 1 | 25 | 2 | 2 | 4017 | 42803 | 67.60% | n/a | n/a | 0 | 0% | 191 |
| product_code | ATTACH | 25 | k | 1 | n/a | ISP | 1 | 10 | 3 | 3 | 161 | 0 | 0% | n/a | n/a | 0 | 0% | 24 |
| p_m_t_code | M | 6782 | T | 54 | n/a | P | 1 | 1 | 1 | 1 | 3 | 0 | 0% | n/a | n/a | 0 | 0% | 1 |
| cost_method | F | 60745 | S | 2564 | n/a | F | 1 | 1 | 1 | 1 | 2 | 0 | 0% | n/a | n/a | 0 | 0% | 1 |
| lst_lot_size | 0 | 63309 | 0 | 63309 | 0 | 0 | n/a | n/a | n/a | n/a | 1 | 0 | 0% | 63309 | 100.00% | n/a | n/a | n/a |
| unit_cost | 0 | 13176 | 411273.11 | 1 | 1283.086 | 9.887 | n/a | n/a | n/a | n/a | 28648 | 91 | 0.14% | 13176 | 20.81% | n/a | n/a | n/a |
| lst_u_cost | 0 | 29181 | 411273.11 | 1 | 1193.318 | 0.54 | n/a | n/a | n/a | n/a | 18599 | 0 | 0% | 29181 | 46.09% | n/a | n/a | n/a |
| avg_u_cost | 0 | 29277 | 411273.11 | 1 | 1158.309 | 0.511 | n/a | n/a | n/a | n/a | 21534 | 0 | 0% | 29277 | 46.24% | n/a | n/a | n/a |
| job | 2 | 1 | 32837 | 1 | n/a | <Blank> | 10 | 10 | 10 | 10 | 13294 | 50016 | 79.00% | n/a | n/a | 0 | 0% | 5 |
| suffix | 0 | 63309 | 0 | 63309 | 0 | 0 | n/a | n/a | n/a | n/a | 1 | 0 | 0% | 63309 | 100.00% | n/a | n/a | n/a |
| stocked | 0 | 6684 | 1 | 56625 | 0.894423 | 1 | n/a | n/a | n/a | n/a | 2 | 0 | 0% | 6684 | 10.55% | n/a | n/a | n/a |
| matl_type | F | 7 | T | 12 | n/a | M | 1 | 1 | 1 | 1 | 4 | 0 | 0% | n/a | n/a | 0 | 0% | 1 |
| family_code | BA | 10 | TT | 5 | n/a | <Blank> | 2 | 2 | 2 | 2 | 49 | 59016 | 93.21% | n/a | n/a | 0 | 0% | 1 |
| low_level | 0 | 37618 | 8 | 37 | 0.859183 | 0 | n/a | n/a | n/a | n/a | 9 | 0 | 0% | 37618 | 59.41% | n/a | n/a | n/a |
| last_inv | 1991.05.0 | 1 | 2009.07.24 0 | 1 | n/a | 1900.01.0 | n/a | n/a | n/a | n/a | 2496 | 38302 | 60.50% | n/a | n/a | n/a | n/a | n/a |
| days_supply | 0 | 4 | 563 | 1 | 8.457139 | 1 | n/a | n/a | n/a | n/a | 22 | 0 | 0% | 4 | 0% | n/a | n/a | n/a |
| order_min | 0 | 49845 | 1000000 | 2 | 33.24851 | 0 | n/a | n/a | n/a | n/a | 60 | 0 | 0% | 49845 | 78.73% | n/a | n/a | n/a |
| order_mult | 0 | 51444 | 4901 | 1 | 0.748108 | 0 | n/a | n/a | n/a | n/a | 39 | 0 | 0% | 51444 | 81.25% | n/a | n/a | n/a |
| plan_code | .TS | 2 | VS | 871 | n/a | MS | 1 | 3 | 2 | 2 | 127 | 9418 | 14.87% | n/a | n/a | 0 | 0% | 7 |

**Figure 3.1**  Column Profile Results from SAP Data Services

After examining the profiling results of the tool, the analyst will use SQL to dig deeper and explore patterns in the data. This is done to see how to design the logic or the extract, transform, and load (ETL) code that will guide the data through the business rules and into the reporting structures that have been modeled in SAP HANA.

Before the coding can begin, you'll use mapping documents for two reasons: first as a conversation piece to start a dialogue with the business users on how the rules will be realized in ETL code, and second as a guide or "map" for the ETL developer to actually write the code to finally deliver the design. We'll go into great detail about all of these facets in this chapter.

### 3.1.1  Why Perform SSA?

So why perform SSA? The answer is as simple as the task itself: SSA tells you what you need to code. ETL development generally requires transforming the data from its source form to whatever format is required by a presentation layer. That presentation layer might be a business intelligence (BI) design with a data mart that will be consumed by BI tools, like the ones featured in the case study sections of this book, or might be something as different as a data migration. Regardless of the target, you're starting with a source (or multiple sources) and have to transform the data to prepare the data for the target. The rules of the business lead you to the target design, but there is still another side of the story: the source. The development effort revolves around blending the needs of both sides, and the only way that you'll acquaint yourself with the source is by analyzing with proper SSA. Considering what you find in the source compared with what is needed in the target leads you down the path of what to code.

Another positive result of proper SSA is that it allows the developer to establish all use cases at once. Instead of just going straight to code, you take the time to plan and to analyze all of the permutations and scenarios that actually exist in the data at the beginning of the process. This is a key step because if you just jump straight into the code, you'll certainly achieve addressing the use case in front of you, but you may miss all of the things that aren't readily present on first glance. SSA allows a break in this process cycle to create code that is more holistic and causes you to consider the whole picture of the development effort, rather than just exploring the immediate and obvious use cases that are brought to light by the business or development effort.

Mapping everything that you need to accomplish is very important for constructing modular code. You can accomplish this by thinking in terms of objects. Using an object-oriented approach and thinking in generic use cases to solve allows for reusability and ensures that your code is smarter—that is, more modular. This is necessary when you're writing object-oriented code because it avoids multiple cycles of refactoring and wasting valuable time in an SAP HANA development effort.

This may seem somewhat counterintuitive—as though time is being wasted analyzing a source and mapping logical definitions or diagrams—and may prompt your team to wonder why it's necessary to perform SSA and mapping when you already know what you need to code. If it seems that just coding the use case as you see it would be much faster, consider the following example.

### SSA and Mapping Example

A client had two systems that were going to be loaded from the same source into two different targets. The landing schemas for the data were the same column layout but with two different target database platforms. One target was MySQL; these tables contained fully spelled-out names such as CUSTOMER. The other target was an IBM DB2 operational datastore whose table names were limited to eight characters. In this example, the CUSTOMER table in MySQL was equivalent to the CUST table in DB2. The other caveat is that the business logic was the same, but some of the data for DB2 required special logic to handle nulls and special characters in the ETL code.

The coding was straightforward, and we knew that we needed to address those two scenarios, but rather than going straight to the code and hoping for the best, we took the time to profile the data to get a full view of the source. We found no fewer than four more scenarios that would have created trouble in DB2!

By profiling, we were able to see what was needed at the beginning of the process rather than taking the "faster" approach and just coding before detailed examination. We were able to write good code once rather than quick code four more times!

### 3.1.2    What Can Be Achieved by Analyzing a Source?

Much can be gained from analyzing a source both in terms of ultimate time savings in a development effort, as well as just delivering better data to SAP HANA or a better ETL development cycle.

One thing that we always try to do during SSA is to disprove business logic, not to be skeptical or cynical, but to use the business rules as the standard that the data should pass. We're effectively looking for the data to fail any of the rules. Although this seems pessimistic, it's a very good approach that is both simple and concise. Generally, you want to try to look for holes or gaps in the data. These could be as simple as gaps where a nonnull column in the source is null in the database. Gaps happen often when application-based constraints are used. Application-based constraints are tidy from an application development perspective because they are all managed in the same layer of code and not distributed between the database and the application layer. However, because it's up to the developer to implement them consistently and properly in the database, the data that application-based constraints leave can be quite messy.

You can take even this simple example further by profiling business logic across sources or platforms. If you're merging two systems from different departments or possibly different physical instances in a global organization, the data can be even messier because application-level rules enforcement may not even be possible across platforms. By analyzing the source system using a profiling tool that separates itself from the data connections, such as SAP Data Services, which is equipped with metadata capabilities, you have the power to perform this cross-platform analysis to look for patterns and sequences that would not be possible otherwise.

After seeing what is possible by analyzing a source and what can be achieved, it's easy to see why this step is very importing on your data's journey to SAP HANA.

Always remember that SAP HANA is an incredible platform, but, like any system, it's only as good as its underlying data.

### 3.1.3   Avoiding "Fast Trash" in SAP HANA

Recall the old saying, "Garbage in, garbage out." This axiom certainly holds true for SAP HANA. SAP HANA is very fast and is a great solution for analyzing vast amounts of data in real time. Because complex queries or logic can be achieved on the fly in real time, there is truly no need to stage data as with traditional systems. All of this leads to the fact that speed isn't the only consideration with SAP HANA! But if you start with garbage data and then load it into SAP via ETL-based replication in SAP Data Services (as in the case study sections of this book) or with SAP Landscape Transformation (SLT) from SAP ERP, the net result will be the same: You'll merely have fast trash!

Data quality has always been a very important concept, but it may be more important than ever with SAP HANA. If SAP HANA forms the base platform of your BI or decision support system, you'll encounter any quality issues more quickly, and this could be quite costly. It's simply more important that data be correct and of high quality before it gets to SAP HANA as this will be a core platform for the organization.

Much dialogue revolves around the speed and the way that SAP HANA will alter the IT landscape, and there are multiple case studies available to prove this and lay credibility to this claim. However, SAP HANA's real measure of success in an organization will be if the information contained is useful, but without quality data in SAP, this will be impossible. It would all be just speeds and feeds—but you would never get the right answer at any speed.

Now that we've examined why SSA is necessary in an SAP HANA development cycle and what benefits can be gained from properly analyzing a source, let's explore some of the SSA tools and techniques present in SAP Data Services to provide you with the robust profiling tools needed to accomplish proper SSA.

## 3.2   SSA Techniques in SAP Data Services

SAP Data Services offers a comprehensive set of ad hoc profiling tools with no need for customization. To analyze a multitude of options right out of the box, SAP Data Services ships with two types of profiling:

▶ **Column profiling**

This type of profiling lets you profile individual column attributes. Measures include minimum, maximum, distinct values, or the amount of nulls. Pattern distribution is also available to allow a quick look into all of the patterns present in a source table column.

▶ **Relationship profiling**

This type of profiling lets you see how data is related across multiple tables.

Profiling in SAP Data Services is of an ad hoc nature. Ad hoc profiling, as described in this chapter, is more for a developer to leverage within a development cycle. This type of profiling should not be confused with the more complex profiling that is available in SAP Information Steward (another product in SAP's information management product portfolio designed to support passive data governance). SAP Information Steward's Data Insight module allows for scheduled profiling over time so you can gain a more holistic view of the state of your data. In comparison, the column profiling in SAP Data Services is a development tool rather than a tool for data stewards to measure the quality of the data. The key differences are really both the focus of the audience and the time dimension introduced by SAP Information Steward.

SAP Data Services is quite flexible and operates on the concept of *metadata*. Metadata is simply data providing information about other data. In this sense, any data being analyzed is actually just an array of columns and rows. This segregation from a source or SQL connection allows SAP Data Services to profile databases, tables, flat files, and application connections in exactly the same way. The following are the different connection options for SAP Data Services profiling:

▶ Databases

   ▶ Attunity Connector for mainframe databases

   ▶ DB2

   ▶ Oracle

   ▶ SQL Server

   ▶ Sybase IQ

   ▶ Teradata

▶ Applications

   ▶ JDE One World

- ▸ JDE World

- ▸ Oracle applications

- ▸ PeopleSoft

- ▸ SAP applications

- ▸ Siebel

▸ Flat files

As you can see from this list, SAP Data Services offers many built-in connections to jump-start developers' profiling efforts. For this chapter, our focus will be on SAP Data Services column and relationship profiling for developers. We'll limit the scope of the profiling to database tables, but do keep in mind that the examples in this chapter relate directly to these other source types as they are all just metadata to SAP Data Services. To perform our profiling tasks for loading SAP HANA, we'll be using the SAP Data Services Designer client application, as this is where you run profiling tasks in SAP Data Services. To launch the SAP Data Services Designer, begin at the START menu on the client computer where SAP Data Services is installed, and perform the following steps:

1. Click the START button.

2. Select SAP Data Services from the START menu.

3. Select SAP DATA SERVICES DESIGNER from the SAP DATA SERVICES START MENU group. The SAP BUSINESSOBJECTS DATA SERVICES REPOSITORY LOGIN menu pops up, as shown in Figure 3.2.

4. Log in to SAP Data Services with a user name set up to use a local repository by clicking the LOG ON button; the repositories available to the user appear in the white dialog box. Enter the "Administrator" login to access the DS_RA_DEMO local repository in Figure 3.2.

5. Click OK to connect to the SAP Data Services local repository. The SAP DATA SERVICES DESIGNER opens, as shown in Figure 3.3.

Now that the SAP DATA SERVICES DESIGNER is open and ready for use, let's set our focus and begin our profiling journey with column profiling.

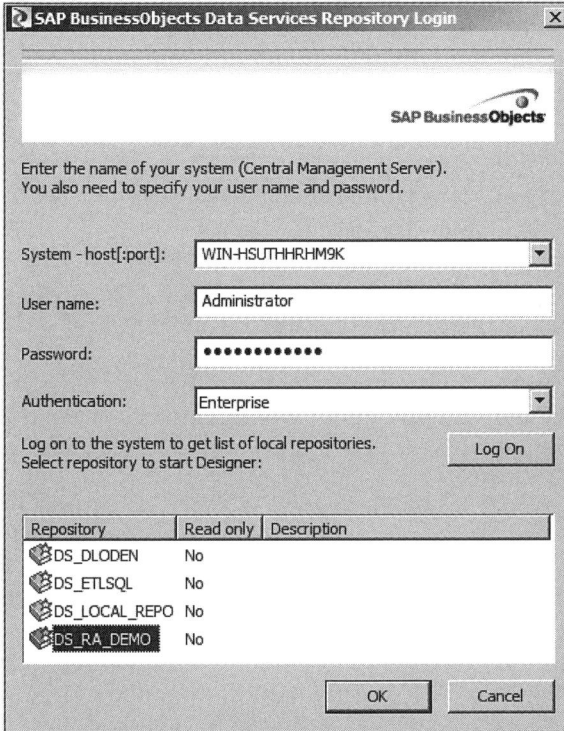

**Figure 3.2** SAP Data Services Repository Login Screen

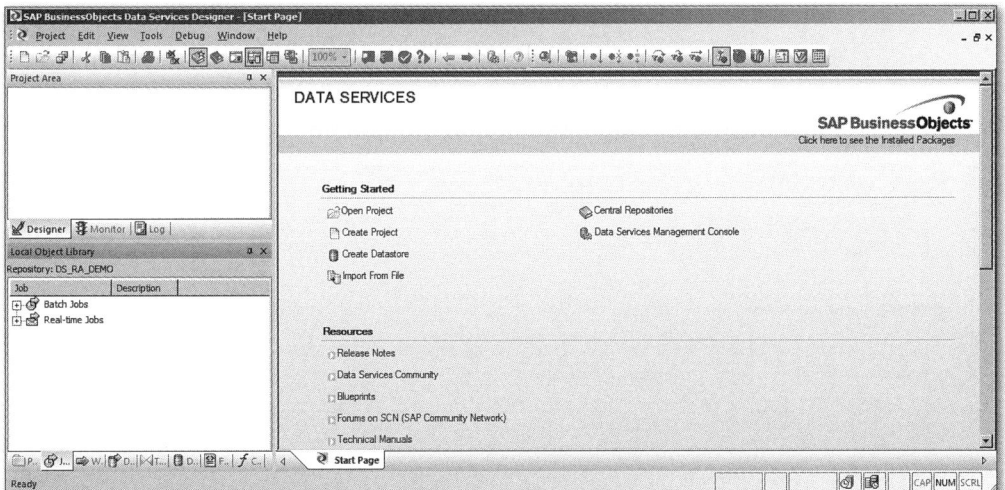

**Figure 3.3** SAP Data Services Designer Client Application Ready for Use

### 3.2.1  Column Profiling

Column profiling in SAP Data Services is exactly as it sounds: You profile the data present in the columns of a table.

This process is very simple. You instantiate a profile task from the SAP Data Services Designer and run the task interactively. After the profiling task completes, you'll have both profiling results and data at your disposal.

There are two types of column profiles: basic and advanced. We'll explore both types in detail in this section of the chapter. Before discovering the details of each type of column profile, let's discuss how to submit a column profile request.

To submit a column profile request in the SAP Data Services Designer, perform the following steps:

1. Locate the local object library in the bottom-left corner of the SAP Data Services Designer.
2. Navigate to the Data Stores tab of the local object library.
3. Expand the datastore containing the table that you want to profile.
4. Right-click the table in the local object library to produce the popup menu shown in Figure 3.4.

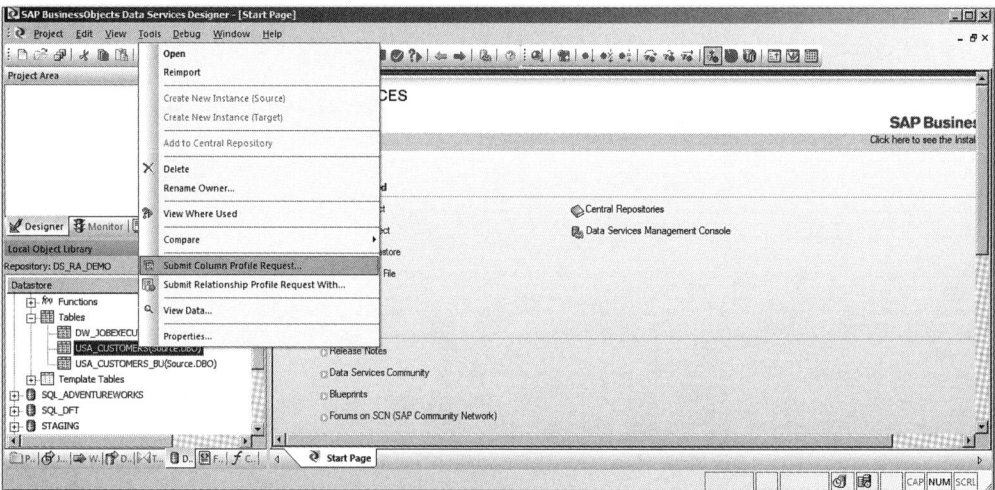

**Figure 3.4**  Accessing the Table to Profile

5. Select the SUBMIT COLUMN PROFILE REQUEST option from the popup menu. The SUBMIT COLUMN PROFILE REQUEST dialog box appears as shown in Figure 3.5. This dialog box allows you to select which columns you want to use to submit detailed profile requests. This is an optional selection because detailed profiling is resource intensive and care should be used when selecting this option.

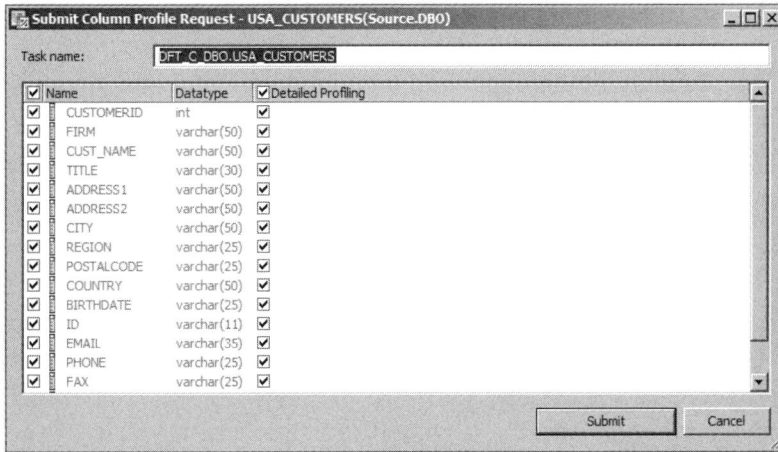

**Figure 3.5** Selecting the Columns for Detailed Profiling

6. In the PROFILER SERVER MONITOR dialog box that appears as shown in Figure 3.6, multiple columns are present:

   ▶ NAME: Name of the profile task.

   ▶ TYPE: Type of profiling task being executed (either column or relationship profile task).

   ▶ STATUS: Current status indicator field of the profile task (either RUNNING or DONE).

   ▶ TIMESTAMP: Date and time when the profiling task was submitted.

   ▶ SOURCE: Source table or datastore connection that the profiling task was run against.

7. After the profiling task is done, the STATUS will change to DONE in the PROFILER SERVER MONITOR dialog box. You may need to refresh the dialog box by clicking the REFRESH button to see the status reflect DONE, as it doesn't always refresh automatically.

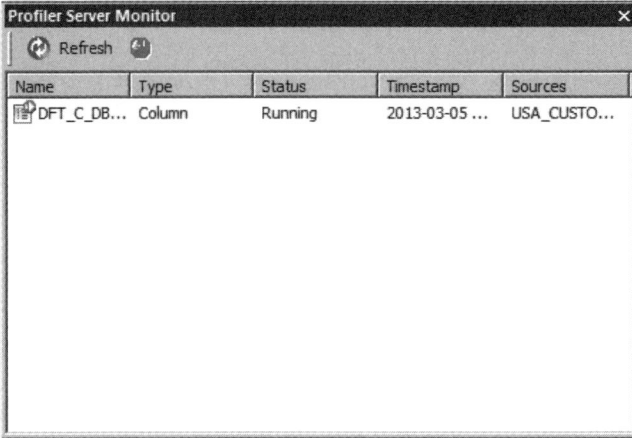

**Figure 3.6** Column Profile Task Running in SAP Data Services

Now you can see the results of the column profile by right-clicking the table in the local object library and selecting the VIEW DATA option from the popup menu shown previously in Figure 3.4. Figure 3.7 shows the VIEW DATA dialog box that appears displaying the profile results. The pattern data in the right window pane illustrates all of the patterns of data in the ADDRESS1 field from the USA_CUS-TOMERS table. It's clear to see that many patterns are available for analysis, and this display can be used to quickly toggle between viewing other patterns and the example data of the patterns in the bottom window pane. This profile data was all produced simply using the built-in column profiling task in SAP Data Services with just a few clicks! This is the true power of the column profiling task.

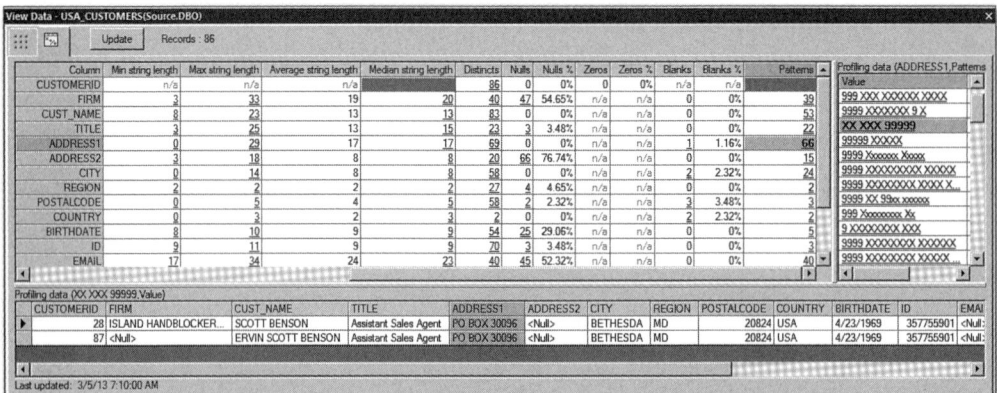

**Figure 3.7** Column Profile Results Showing Patterns in the ADDRESS1 Field

Pattern profile attributes are quite handy tools, but notice all of the other elements available from this profiling task. You can quickly see and examine the data of NULL values, MIN values, MAX values, and numerous other measures. These types of data elements and the quick quantifications are great tools for starting the dialogue with the organization about what types of issues may be present in the data and what type of rules will be necessary to clean up data quality issues on the way into SAP HANA. Because we've now covered how to run both a basic and advanced profile task, we won't go into more detail on what options are covered with each of these types of profiling tasks.

**Basic Column Profiling**

As mentioned earlier, column profiling is divided into two groups of attributes: basic and advanced.

Let's explore the basic column profiling attributes in detail:

▶ **Min**
The minimum value present for this column.

▶ **Min count**
The number of rows that contain the minimum column value.

▶ **Max**
The maximum value present for this column.

▶ **Max count**
The number of rows that contain the maximum column value.

▶ **Average**
The average value for the column. This is only present for numeric columns and will be blank for all nonnumeric columns.

▶ **Min string length**
The shortest string value in the column. This is only present for character columns and will be blank for all noncharacter columns.

▶ **Max string length**
The longest string value in the column. This is only present for character columns and will be blank for all noncharacter columns.

▶ **Average string length**
The average length string value in the column. This is only present for character columns and will be blank for all noncharacter columns.

- **Nulls**
  The number of NULL values in this column.

- **Nulls %**
  The percentage of rows that contain a NULL value in this column.

- **Zeros**
  The number of zero values (0) in this column.

- **Zeros %**
  The percentage of rows that contain a zero (0) value in this column.

- **Blanks**
  The percentage of rows that contain a blank value (" ") in this column. This is only present for character columns and will be blank for all noncharacter columns.

- **Blanks %**
  The percentage of rows that contain a blank (" ") value in this column.

Basic column profiling attributes are simple measures of quality that are mostly derived by the profiling engine via SQL statements. So why use the profiling tool to derive these when they are available via SQL? Two reasons come to mind. The first is for the simplicity and the convenience offered in the profiling task that offers a repeatable outcome. With just a few clicks and a submission, you can run the same set of measures against any table, providing a baseline set of quality measures for a table or series of tables. The second reason is the flexibility present by using metadata in SAP Data Services to run this same set of measures against database tables or application connects.

In short, the true power of the tool lies in its ability to work with any type of platform or database. Basic column profiling is usually just a start, and most often you'll choose to perform advanced column profiling as well against a source table.

### Advanced Column Profiling

Advanced column profiling offers additional attributes over the basic column profile attributes, such as the following:

- **Median**
  The median value of this column.

- **Median string**
  The string length of the median value for this column. This is only present for character columns and will be blank for all noncharacter columns.

▶ **Distincts**
The number of distinct values in this column.

▶ **Distincts %**
The percentage of rows that contain distinct values for this column.

▶ **Patterns**
The number of different patterns available in this column. Numeric, nonnumeric, uppercase characters, lowercase characters, and spacing are all signified and measured in the profile results.

▶ **Patterns %**
The percentage of rows that contain patterns for this column.

These attributes are particularly useful on tables with a large number of `varchar()` columns. This is the typical scenario when you choose to employ advanced column profiling.

Consider the patterns of ADDRESS1 data shown earlier in Figure 3.7. After seeing the patterns as well as the sample data exposed in the ADDRESS1 field, you can make a few assumptions about the coding tasks that will be required. You can see via the patterns that there are P.O. box values as well as street addresses. These are two distinct postal types; a P.O. box is a postal type, and a street address is a mailing address.

Consider a business rule example involving a manufacturer that makes a hazardous good. These goods are only available for delivery at a mailing address, so a postal address type is nondeliverable, requiring some kind of modification in the ETL code. This is a very simple example of how a quick profile task can isolate issues that require modifications and display all of the scenarios in the data that show differences that need to be handled. Examples like these demonstrate the power of the advance profile task.

So why wouldn't you run advanced profile tasks with every profile, especially because there are more options and tables generally have at least one `varchar()` column that would benefit from this type of analysis? The answer is the simple fact that an advanced profile tasks is a much more expensive operation in terms of performance and processing. The processing task is much more resource-intensive on the SAP Data Services job server, and the advanced profile task runs longer. So, you must weigh the benefit of obtaining the additional character-based attributes from an advanced column profile over the performance and processing expense.

Note that when you're running these expensive profiles, you must be cognizant of what is occurring on the SAP Data Services job server. For example, if you're running an ETL job, you don't want to kick off an advanced profile task against a large table. If the ETL job is processing a large amount of data or has long-running resource-intensive operations, then you'll probably overrun the capabilities of the SAP Data Services job server. So be cautious what is running on the job server before submitting the profiling tasks.

### 3.2.2 Relationship Profiling

Relationship profiling is important because it allows relationships to be examined and tested against two tables. This is useful if you want to see orphan records or examine whether parent-child applications are supported in the data behind the application. Great examples of this are sales headers and sales detail records; you expect to always have a header record that corresponds to the detail record because an application typically has this flow when transactions are being created.

This relationship test can be pretty easily established across multiple tables either in one database or using some sort of database linking method in SQL. To perform this operation with SQL, you combine an outer join and look for NULL values in the outer source table. The SQL looks like this:

```
SELECT
  C.*
FROM
  ChildTable C
LEFT JOIN MasterTable M
  ON M.ID = C.MasterID
WHERE
  M.ID IS NULL
```

This task is further complicated if the tables are across multiple sources. For example, you need a customer record to create a sale in any application. However, consider what happens if you're combining two application sources into a data mart. A customer exists in a point of sales system housed in an SQL Server database and is related to sales records that are stored in this SQL Server source, but what if the business has an online point of sales system hosted in a different platform and server? The business rule is still valid because the business still should only sell to valid customer records, but the customers in IBM DB2 are difficult to compare to either customers or sales in SQL server. The only way to perform a logical relationship test across platforms is with a profiling tool such as SAP Data Services.

Recall that SAP Data Services operates on the concept of metadata, which frees you from the confines of a source. Logical comparisons and profiles still need to be drawn as relationships across systems because business rules aren't concerned with the physical implementations of various systems. These rules operate at a logical level. Checks like these are important before coding begins when combining sources. Otherwise, assumptions are made on how data should work; if coding develops directly from these assumptions, it can lead to some very costly course corrections.

Now that we've discussed why relationship profiles are important we'll discuss running a relationship profile task in the SAP Data Services Designer.

To submit a relationship profile request in the SAP Data Services Designer, follow these steps:

1. Locate the local object library in the bottom-left corner of the SAP DATA SERVICES DESIGNER page.

2. Navigate to the datastores tab of the local object library.

3. Expand the datastore containing the table that you want to profile.

4. Right-click the table in the local object library to produce the popup menu shown in Figure 3.8.

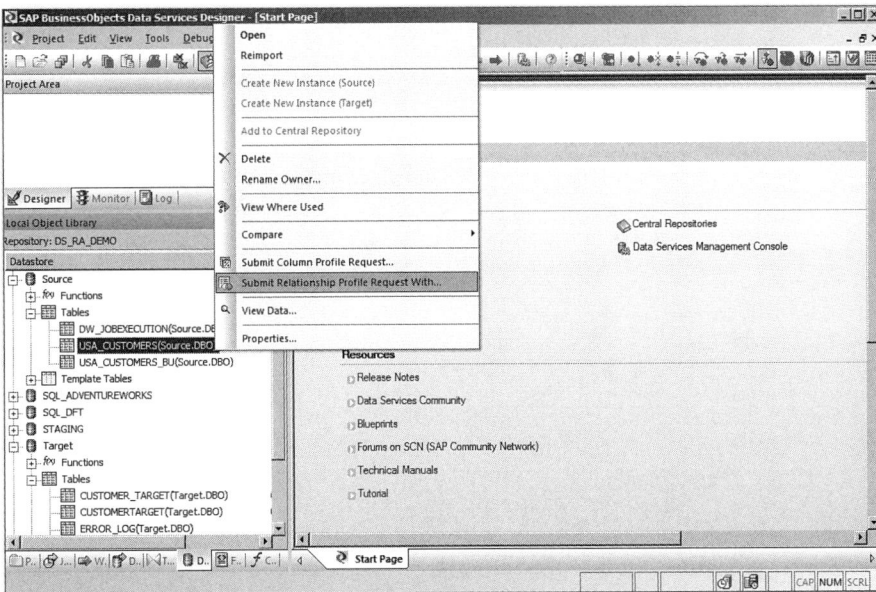

**Figure 3.8** Right-Clicking on the Source Table to Select Submit Relationship Profile Request

5. Select the SUBMIT RELATIONSHIP PROFILE REQUEST option from the popup menu.

6. The SUBMIT RELATIONSHIP PROFILE REQUEST dialog box appears as shown in Figure 3.9. This dialog box allows you to select which columns you want to relate for the relationship profile requests. This is laid out as two tables that appear side by side that you join with lines just as in other conventional database graphical tools. You may relate one or more columns by dragging lines between the two tables.

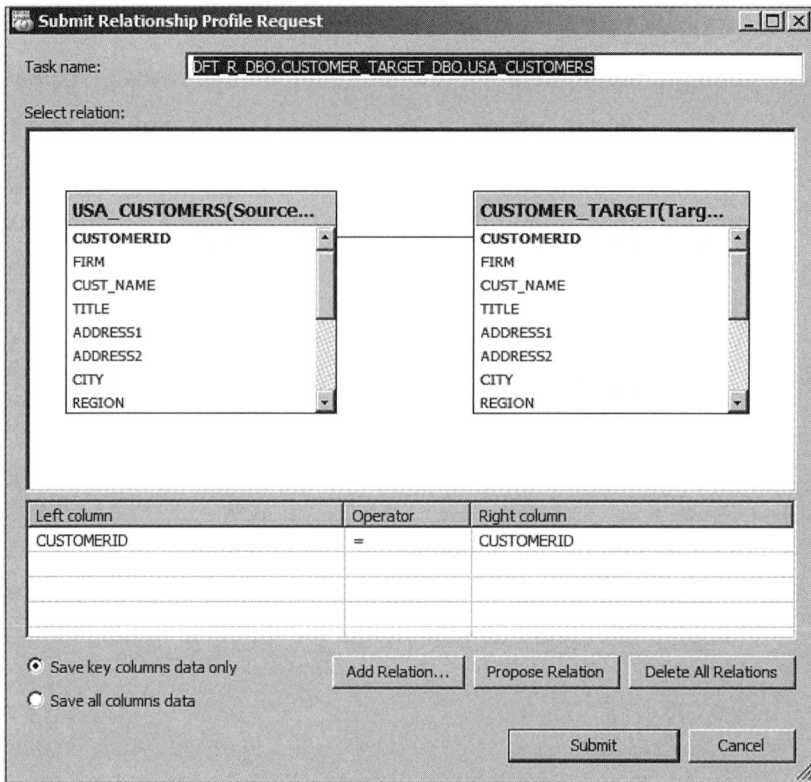

**Figure 3.9** Define Relationship Profile Request in SAP Data Services

7. After you've defined the relationships, click SUBMIT to submit the relationship profile request. The PROFILER SERVER MONITOR dialog box appears, as shown in Figure 3.10. Notice the line present now to signify that a relationship profile request is running.

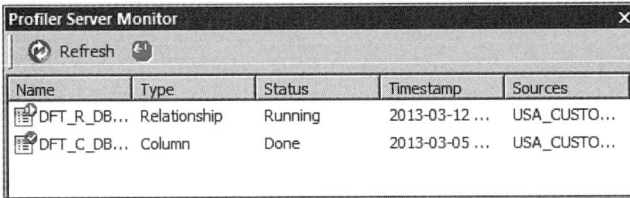

**Figure 3.10**  Profiler Server Monitor Screen Illustrating a Running Relationship Profile Task

8. After the profiling task is done, the status will change to DONE in the PROFILER SERVER MONITOR dialog box (see Figure 3.10). You may need to refresh the dialog box by clicking the REFRESH button to see the status reflect DONE because it doesn't always refresh automatically.

After the profiler task is complete, you may view the results in the VIEW DATA screen shown in Figure 3.11 by right-clicking the table in the local object library and selecting the VIEW DATA option.

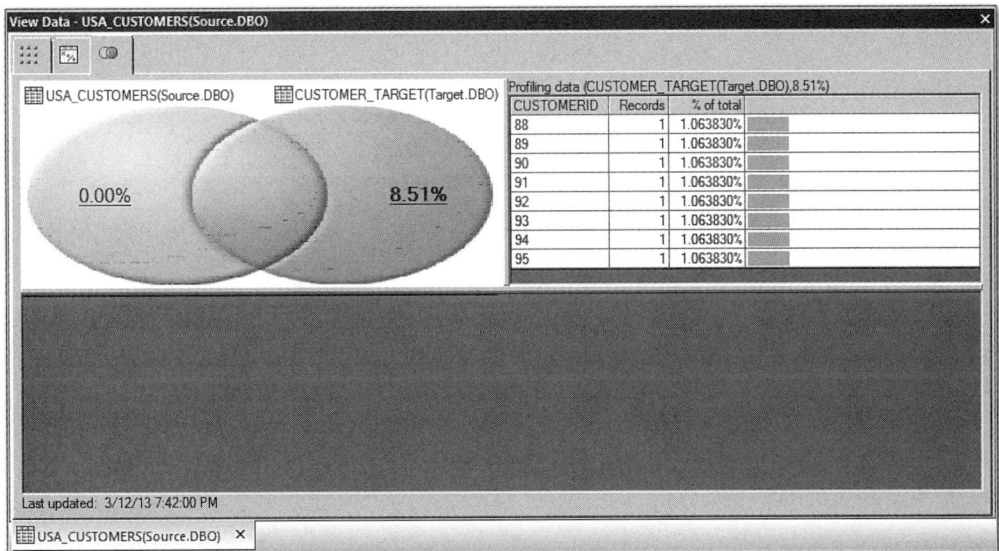

**Figure 3.11**  Relationship Profiles in SAP Data Services

This perfect example shows that all customers are contained in the USA_CUSTOMERS table, but only a portion are referenced in the target table. We loaded this table so that only a subset of records are used in the target—8.51%, to be exact. You can view the results graphically in the window pane on the right, and when you select the CUSTOMERID line in the right pane, the example data shows through in the gray area below. The important thing to note is that the value of 0.00% for USA_CUSTOMERS indicates that there are no orphan customer records present in the target that don't exist in the source.

After examining the profiling tools available in SAP Data Services and running both column and relationship profile tasks, you now have a great deal of information about the data that you'll load into SAP HANA. You know that you have some null columns that defy business rules and, in the customer example, you have a relationship that conforms to what you expect. So now what?

## 3.3 SSA: Beyond Tools and Profiling

Now it's time to actually look into the data at a deeper level. The profiling that we've shown with SAP Data Services happens quite rapidly. As you can see with the examples in this chapter, profiling is a point-and-click exercise—you pick the table, select the options you want to profile, and start the task. This happens very fast and now we're ready to begin the next step of SSA: the dialogue with the business users.

To facilitate conversation with the business users, we often put together an SSA document in Microsoft Word with the following components:

▶ **Table name**
Name of the table, which is usually the fully qualified physical name of the table.

▶ **Description**
Description of the logical use of the table.

▶ **Record count**
Count of records at the time of the profile snapshot.

▶ **Profile results**
Reference to the name of the spreadsheet that is typically used to save the profile results from SAP Data Services.

▶ **Recommendations**
Overall summary of your review of the profile results and data in the table with your understanding of the business rules.

▶ **Primary key columns**
Listing of the primary key columns in the table.

The following elements also appear and repeat for each column in the table in the document:

▸ **Column name**
Column name in the table.

▸ **Column data type**
Data type for the column in the table.

▸ **Column foreign key**
Yes or No value to note whether the column is used as a foreign key in the table.

▸ **Column text description of business rule**
Text description of the business rule of the column and how it's used in the table.

▸ **SQL text for evaluating the business rule**
SQL that was used to evaluate the business rule (blank if no SQL was used).

▸ **Column recommendations**
Your judgment and recommendations of how the data conforms to the business rules and what needs to be done in the source or in the ETL process to correct the data.

Equipped with an SSA document like the one described here, you're ready to have a full discussion with examples of the source data in detail. It's very important to have all of this detail because you'll have many of these discussions with nontechnical functional users. These users are key to arriving at conclusions about why a source is behaving a certain way, so it's important to have as much information as possible to effectively communicate what you're seeing in a source.

When creating this document, let the profiling results be your guide. Returning to the example of NULL values that exist in a nonnullable column, you use the null violation to fill in the COLUMN TEXT DESCRIPTION OF A BUSINESS RULE and COLUMN RECOMMENDATIONS sections of the document to open a conversation with the business users. Even an example as simple as this often leads to research into the system that can uncover things as far as legacy code missteps that have always been present in custom systems or simply a configuration step that was missed in an SAP source.

Note that no matter what issues are found in the profile task or the deeper inspection of the source, the result will be additional research for functional resources as well as the resulting business decisions of how to handle the errors. Having an

SSA document is an important tool to share the full story of the source data with the business users.

It's best practice to correct the source when possible. We advocate handling errors in the ETL process only if you're constrained from making changes in the source system. Let the document created from this list be the guide for the discussion with the business and functional resources to deal with the issues encountered in SSA, and strive to use the document to channel the discussion to correct issues in the source before the ETL. If that isn't possible, then use the column recommendations to describe how to handle the rule violations in the ETL process. It's paramount that these be handled before moving the data into the pristine SAP HANA environment.

Reviewing sources often involves digging into the tables that you profiled with ad hoc SQL to look beyond the profile task. After further review of the data with SQL, don't be surprised if one rule violation leads to another. It's often the case from our experience that the closer you look at a source, the more problems you'll find. This isn't an easy journey and quite often it leads to some startling realizations for the business users. However this is an incredibly important step in the SAP HANA development journey. Reassure the business users that all of the issues found and handled now will lead to a better SAP HANA system. Remember, the profile results are the starting point, and a thorough SSA is where patterns emerge and you begin to see the true color of the source.

### 3.3.1 Establishing Patterns

Patterns are important when performing SSA. When looking at a source, try to look for all of the patterns present in the data. Searching for patterns is one place where you need to step beyond the established business rules to see things that haven't been disclosed. This is both an art and a science, but we'll explore some techniques that make this process easier and repeatable.

The first way to look for patterns is to search for actual patterns present in the data fields. Start with the address field example cited earlier in Figure 3.7. This example illustrated an address pattern present in a text field using the pattern attribute of the column profile. The pattern attribute in the column profile is a good starting point for assimilating all of the patterns that exist in text fields, but you need to look more broadly into the data as well. Take nulls, for example. An easy pattern to spot is if a column is entirely null. This is very straightforward because the column was never used in the source system, and the result is obvious. What if the column was 70% percent null? At that point, you use SQL to determine if there was a date correlation to when the NULL values began occurring. Was it a particular point in time? Maybe something occurred in the application after a date exposed by a date column in the table or after an ID range maximum value? These are the type of behavior patterns that can become quite useful.

This is the inquisitive approach that is necessary to dig into the source as you should. The answers that you're looking to uncover with this type of analysis are whether the column's use changed over time, which is another type of pattern but not one that is exposed by a simple snapshot profile. Multiple profiles are needed over time, or you will most likely combine the profile results from SAP Data Services with ad hoc SQL against date columns to establish your own patterns.

Another pattern that often develops is *field misuse*, which occurs when a field, or column in a table, is used for a misleading purpose based on the name of the field in the table. With custom-developed systems, we've seen many cases where, for lack of an available field, a developer often just uses a field for a purpose that had nothing to do with the field name. Another example you'll encounter is where an application has generic fields of varying data types that are used for a variety of reasons.

*Field overuse*, which occurs when one field is used for multiple purposes, is another potential that should also be discussed. We often see this in code fields, where one code field is used for multiple purposes or in combination with another field. Sometimes we see that multicharacter fields contain multiple code values at a specific string position of the field. This positional reference is then used in combination with the character value that the code should signify. We often see these in legacy mainframe systems where techniques like these were used to save storage and to use every byte.

These are all examples of patterns that need to be documented and discussed with the business users. Patterns like these will lead you to questions—but not answers—on the first pass.

These are all problematic examples from an ETL or BI design, but from our experience, you'll encounter these often in source systems. Patterns are crucial for true understanding of a source. Without thorough SSA, patterns will be missed and data misinterpreted further, extending the cycle of poor data quality into SAP HANA.

### 3.3.2 Looking Across Sources

So far, we've described SSA as looking into a single source, but there may be times when you need to combine multiple sources. Whenever you're striving to combine multiple sources into an OLAP design for a data mart, you'll certainly need to use a profiling tool such as SAP Data Services because SQL won't take you across multiple source tables. You can use SAP Data Services relationship profiling as a tool to see and measure logical relationships across source systems and platforms.

We recommend that you use column profiling with datastore configurations to quickly run baseline profile results across multiple sources, as shown previously in Figure 3.11. You can see where sales records don't have customers, or even whether there was supposed to be an employee attached to a sales transaction no matter the platform. These are simple scenarios that won't be handled with SQL.

Think about the employee example. If the human resources system with employee information is hosted in the cloud, but the online point-of-sale system is in an Oracle database, you'll never be able to write SQL to see if a relationship exists even if you have the same field Employee_ID in both the human resources system and the online point-of-sales table. The only way to accomplish this is with a relationship profile in SAP Data Services. Concepts like these and tools to accomplish this type of analysis are really important for combining data from multiple sources.

### 3.3.3 Treating Disparate Systems as One

Treating multiple sources as one is always a challenge. By definition, most BI and data mart efforts combine multiple sources into the final OLAP data mart target. This is a challenge because when you're developing these targets, you strive to combine data from multiple sources that was never meant to be combined. This is where the business rules are very important because they serve as the guide that "knits" together the various systems into one story to build a comprehensive reporting solution about the business and not the various systems.

To do this effectively, you must look across sources and let the business rules be your guide. Metadata can help you do this but not without powerful tools to help profile the data across the sources. Without a tool such as SAP Data Services, you'll get lost in the weeds of one particular source and have a hard time seeing the larger picture available.

Without metadata, this would be very difficult, especially with stock SQL because this only hits one source. Stock SQL keeps you at the database level, which, by definition, keeps you in the application, diminishing the ability to see relationships that should or should not exist between systems. Without metadata, you'll never truly be able to break out of the sources to see what the business needs. It's simply necessary for combining sources into SAP HANA.

### 3.3.4 Mapping Your Data

Now that you've profiled your data and exhausted the source via thorough SSA, you'll need to begin the mapping process. Mapping your data is simply a logical exercise to "precode" the ETL code before you even open SAP Data Services. You perform mapping by creating a mapping document (usually in Microsoft Excel, like the one shown in Figure 3.12) and using a TARGET section to illustrate the target table fields. A SOURCE section illustrates the fields that you're reading from in the source table. A TRANSFORMATION column shows any special logic or transformations that have occurred in the ETL process.

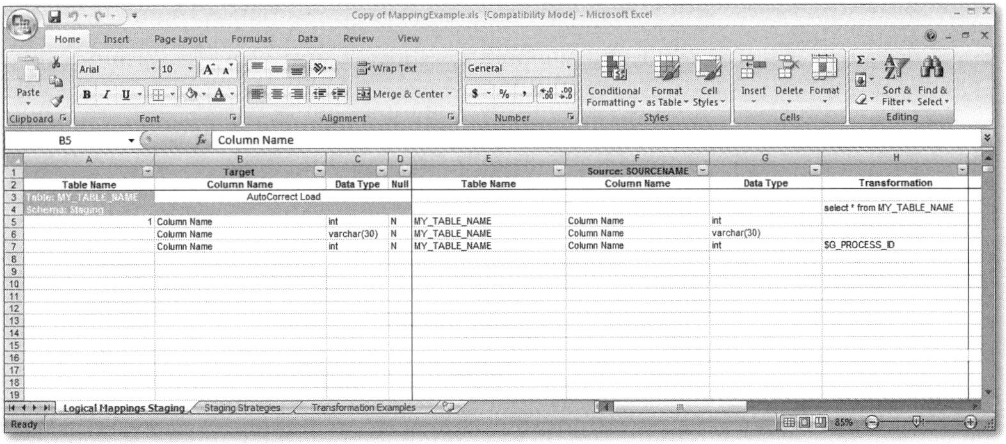

**Figure 3.12** Sample Mapping Document

You may be wondering why to bother with mapping because SAP Data Services is such an easy-to-use graphical tool. The first reason is simple: It's easier, faster, and cheaper to create a complete mapping document that you can throw away rather than throwing away code in SAP Data Services. If it seems counterintuitive at first, bear in mind that you'll actually save time in your SAP HANA development effort by spending the time to fully map your sources.

The second reason to use a mapping document and mapping process in your SAP HANA project is that the mapping document serves as a wonderful conversation piece to force a dialogue with the business users or functional consultants. The mapping document is the culmination of all of your research and SSA. It's a product of your interpretations of conversations with the business users and is a final result that explicitly communicates what is going into SAP HANA and how you'll be doing it. This Excel platform provides an easily digestible format for a nontechnical audience to review some rather technical things. As the last step before coding begins, this mapping phase is important to get correct the first time.

One final, often-overlooked topic should be discussed: whether to use a style in the mapping document that favors a straightforward English descriptive style or a syntactically correct style of language. Take a simple `UPPER()` function used to convert a field to uppercase. A syntactically correct style reads `UPPER(myFieldName)`. If you used an English descriptive style, then the mapping document reads `Convert myFieldName to upper case`.

This is specifically regarding the transformations section of the mapping document seen in column H in Figure 3.12. Although this may not seem like a large distinction, consider that both your development team and nontechnical audience will use this mapping document. Table 3.1 shows scenarios where each mapping document style works.

| Mapping Document Style | When to Use |
| --- | --- |
| English descriptive style | ▶ Small development team is used. <br> ▶ Very technical and senior developers are present. <br> ▶ Lots of interaction occurs with the business users. <br> ▶ The business users make up the main audience for the document. |
| Syntactically correct | ▶ Many developers are involved to keep the code consistent. <br> ▶ Junior developers are present in the project. <br> ▶ The business users review the document but with the help of the architect. <br> ▶ The developers make up the main audience of the document, and the purpose is to keep the code uniform and succinct. |

**Table 3.1** Mapping Document Style Comparison

## 3.4    Summary

In this chapter, we've discussed many steps and tasks that are needed before you provision data into SAP HANA. We covered the importance of proper profiling, followed by in-depth SSA, and finally creating a mapping document to ensure that you're getting it all right before loading into SAP HANA.

SAP HANA is an immensely powerful platform, but it will only be really useful with high-quality data. Speed is only helpful if the information is worth discovering. Profiling your sources is important because it saves time and money. A really good option with SAP HANA is to use SAP Data Services for your profiling tasks because you get a runtime license for an enterprise class data integration tool complete with enterprise class profiling and SSA capabilities.

Preprovisioning data is one step in the process that you don't want to skip. Remember that profiling is only the start of your SSA journey. You must perform thorough SSA to expose the issues to correct and then use a mapping document to guide your code through the issues. Not performing proper SSA upfront in the process can lead to costly mistakes in your development cycle. Performing proper SSA shows you the real story behind your data, and ensures that you're not just loading "fast trash" into SAP HANA. It's only after this step that you're ready to begin the process to provision your data into SAP HANA, which is the subject of the next chapter.

*Let's talk about how to design and build the data loading process for SAP HANA, which you need to do for the standalone SAP HANA. This can be done via SAP Data Services and replication.*

# 4    Provisioning Your Data

SAP Data Services has been SAP HANA's singular solution for non-SAP data since SAP HANA's inception, and it remains the only fully integrated extract, transform, and load (ETL) solution where SAP HANA's native API is exposed. With this capability, SAP Data Services is in a unique position to take advantage of options such as the sophisticated bulk loading functionality in SAP HANA natively. This allows for incredibly fast loads of very large datasets directly into memory into SAP HANA. SAP Data Services can create both columnar and row tables at runtime with a unique template table functionality. SAP Data Services has leveraged this functionality for years with almost all of the conventional database vendors, so SAP HANA is a natural extension of this functionality.

The purpose of this chapter is to take a deep dive into SAP Data Services to see what it can offer to a data provisioning effort. In Section 4.1, we examine how SAP Data Services is the right choice to load data into SAP HANA and create tables at runtime, and we also explore the wide palate of SAP Data Services tools, functions, and transforms that are ready and poised to enrich data on the way into SAP HANA. We'll begin by reviewing the concept of metadata and its role in SAP Data Services, followed by the various aspects of SAP Data Services in detail in Section 4.1.2 through Section 4.1.8. We then turn our attention to the SAP Data Services 4.1 Workbench in Section 4.2 and data provisioning within real-time replication in Section 4.3.

## 4.1    Understanding SAP Data Services

SAP HANA customers that purchase SAP HANA in a standalone configuration are quite fortunate because they receive a runtime license of SAP Data Services, which is SAP's premier ETL solution in its information management portfolio.

SAP Data Services has a long track record of providing a quality Enterprise Information Management (EIM) platform for both data integration and data quality, and the product is often a leader in various independent resource polls such as Gartner's Magic Quadrant. We've used SAP Data Services successfully during many efforts in numerous verticals on projects that range from small departmental efforts to enterprise-wide ETL and data quality efforts for the largest of global organizations. SAP Data Services is truly an enterprise class product that is bundled with standalone SAP HANA, so it makes perfect sense to leverage this great tool. The heart of the SAP Data Services deployment is the SAP Data Services Designer client where all of the ETL code is crafted, as shown in Figure 4.1.

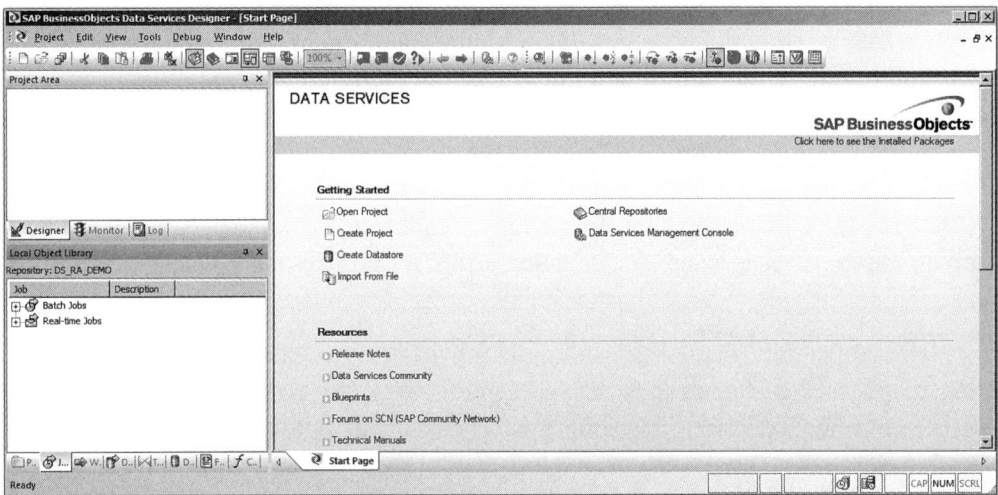

**Figure 4.1** SAP Data Services Designer Client Application

Before you can provision data with SAP Data Services, you must walk through the various aspects of the tool and explore all of the facets and features present to successfully provision data into SAP HANA. The next eight sections cover the following aspects of SAP Data Services:

- Metadata
- Datastores
- Jobs
- Workflows
- Data flows

- Custom functions and scripts
- File formats
- Real-time jobs

### 4.1.1    Metadata

Recall from Chapter 3 that SAP Data Services is quite flexible and operates on the concept of *metadata*. Metadata is simply data providing information about other data. In this sense, any data being analyzed is actually just an array of columns and rows. This segregation from a source or SQL connection allows SAP Data Services to connect to databases, tables, flat files, and application connections, as well as interact with these connections in exactly the same way. This is an important concept for SAP Data Services because a developer only needs to understand and master one interface. SAP Data Services acts as an insulating layer to the developer, and, after a developer has mastered the SAP Data Services functions, transforms, and platform, these concepts are applicable to connecting to any source database.

The development platform in SAP Data Services offers uniformity across sources, which is important for both ETL and for SAP HANA because a developer will often be asked to combine multiple sources of data into SAP HANA. For SAP Data Services, these various sources and source platforms are all simply connections of arrays of data. SAP Data Services presents the developer merely with rows and columns of data that need to be handled with all of the various functionalities within the tool. SAP Data Services doing the actual heavy lifting under the surface connections, but automatically converts all of the native SAP Data Services functions available to the SQL syntax of the native database connections.

Consider an example where an SAP Data Services UPPER() function is used on a varchar() column such as a FIRST_NAME field. That function that exists in the data flow depicted in Figure 4.2 is actually converted to the SQL depicted in Figure 4.3.

This is the SQL that is presented to the database, and this functionality (known as *push down*) allows SAP Data Services to effectively push the operations or "heavy lifting" down to the source or target databases. Here, the developer only needs to master this one interface to the data and doesn't have to know the specifics of the syntax of the function in the source database. SAP Data Services takes care of the conversion in the OPTIMIZED SQL window shown in Figure 4.3.

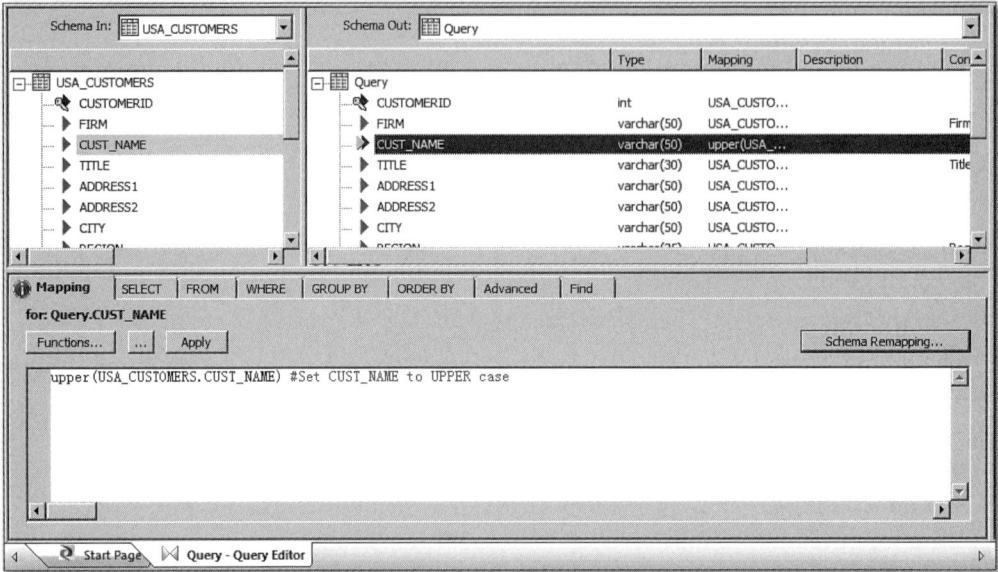

**Figure 4.2**  UPPER() Function in SAP Data Services Query Transform

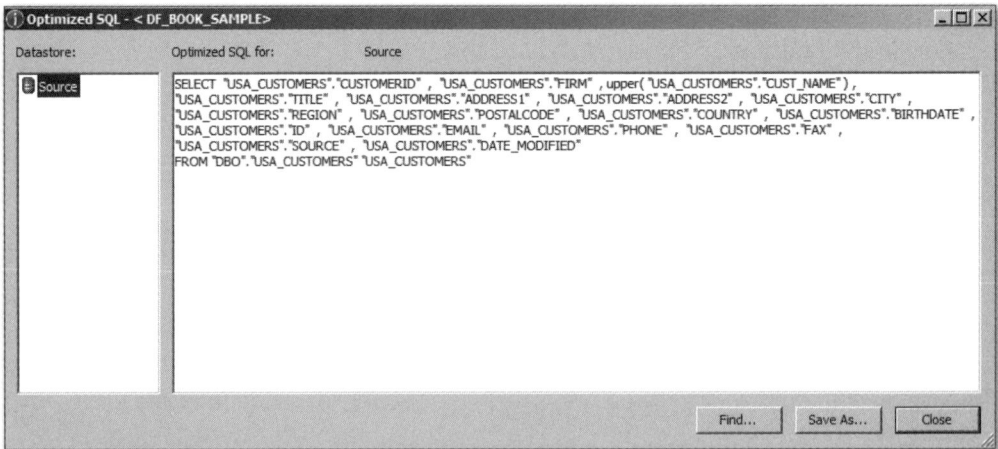

**Figure 4.3**  Optimized SQL Push Down to Database via Metadata

In this example, the source database SQL Server happened to have the same syntax as SAP Data Services for the upper function: upper(). However, this is often not the case and is especially true across database platforms. If a developer were combining two sources, and the syntax were different in the two database platforms, the SAP Data Services syntax in Figure 4.2 would still be the same. However, depending on the source database connection, SAP Data Services would handle the difference in the SQL to each of the varying sources! This is a great benefit that metadata brings to a development effort, and this allows true standardization for a team.

## 4.1.2 Datastores

Datastores are the physical realization of the metadata connection layer in SAP Data Services; they provide the layer of abstraction from the actual database and application connections. Datastores are connections to databases or applications from SAP Data Services that are fully configurable. These configurations can be made directly to database tables or through software adapters. Datastore configurations allow SAP Data Services to access metadata from a database or application and read from or write to that database or application while the SAP Data Services is executing a job.

> **Note**
>
> Note that datastores don't store or hold data! They are merely a description of the connection, not the actual data stored in the table. These connections are made in the SAP Data Services Designer application.

Creating a datastore is the first step in any development effort because a connection must be made to a source and to a target. The connection parameters, such as DATABASE SERVER NAME, DATABASE NAME, and PASSWORD to access the database are set in the EDIT DATASTORE configuration screen shown in Figure 4.4.

Table 4.1 describes the connection parameters range from SAP Data Services settings. These are SAP Data Services settings that detail the connection to the source or target database. Keep in mind that when you're establishing a datastore, you can't go back and change the first four configuration settings (shown with an asterisk in Table 4.1) after you've specified them, so make sure you choose these settings wisely.

This is one reason that it's a good idea to name the datastore after what it will be used for. If this will be the only source for your job, then you can simply call it "Source." If this is a source that will be used to load or read human resources data, you may want to call it "HUMAN_RESOURCES." Try to avoid names that are closely linked with a database or application platform because these tend to change over time. It's a best practice to keep a datastore name generic and descriptive of the task at hand.

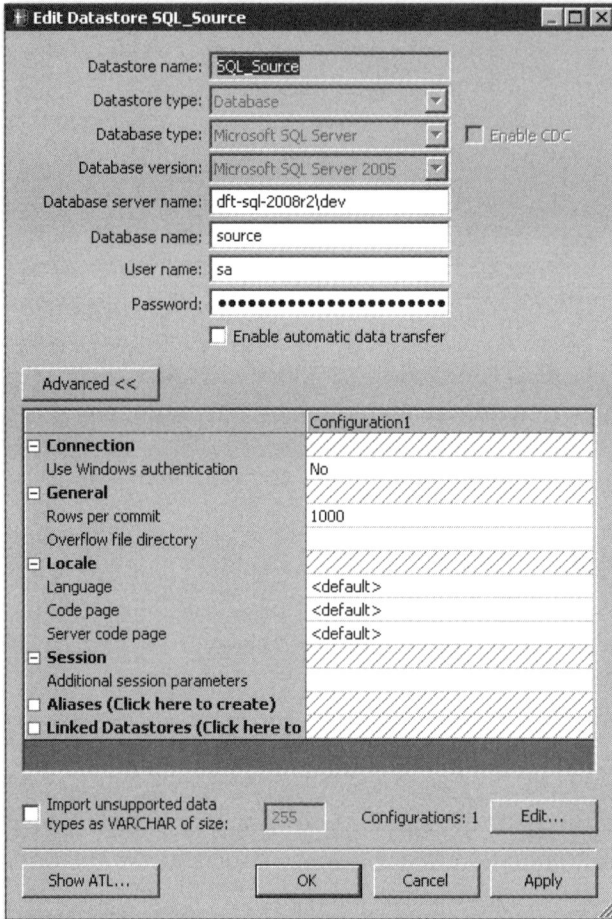

**Figure 4.4** Edit Datastore Connection Parameters

| Datastore Configuration Property | Description |
| --- | --- |
| DATASTORE NAME* | Logical name of the datastore that will be used in SAP Data Services |
| DATASTORE TYPE* | Type of the datastore that you're creating |
| DATABASE TYPE* | Type of the database that you're connecting |

**Table 4.1** Datastore Configuration Properties

| Datastore Configuration Property | Description |
| --- | --- |
| DATABASE VERSION* | Version of the database that you're connecting |
| DATABASE SERVER NAME | Logical name of the database server |
| DATABASE NAME | Logical name of the database that you're connecting |
| USER NAME | Database user that will be used to establish the connection |
| PASSWORD | Database password that will be used to establish the connection |

**Table 4.1** Datastore Configuration Properties (Cont.)

Another point that is important to note is that these settings can be replicated across multiple configurations. A configuration allows the same datastore to connect to different databases or even different servers! You can create multiple configurations for a datastore, which allows you to plan ahead for different environments for your datastore as well as limiting the level of effort when migrating jobs.

For example, you can add a set of configurations (DEV, TEST, and PROD) to the same datastore name. These connection settings stay with the datastore during export or import. You can group any set of datastore configurations into a system configuration. When you're running or scheduling a job, you can select a system configuration, and thus, the set of datastore configurations for your current environment. This way you can change connections at will both during unit testing and when you're scheduling a job; the net result is a very easy way to test code against multiple environments on multiple platforms. These system configurations can also have specific applications for an SAP HANA provisioning task.

Figure 4.5 shows an example of a datastore that has a DEV, TEST, and PROD configuration. Note that even though this example has all configurations pointing to the same Microsoft SQL Server database, that needn't always be the case. These connections could be to any database, providing the schemas for the tables are the same. The datastore configurations are a very powerful component for enabling metadata in SAP Data Services.

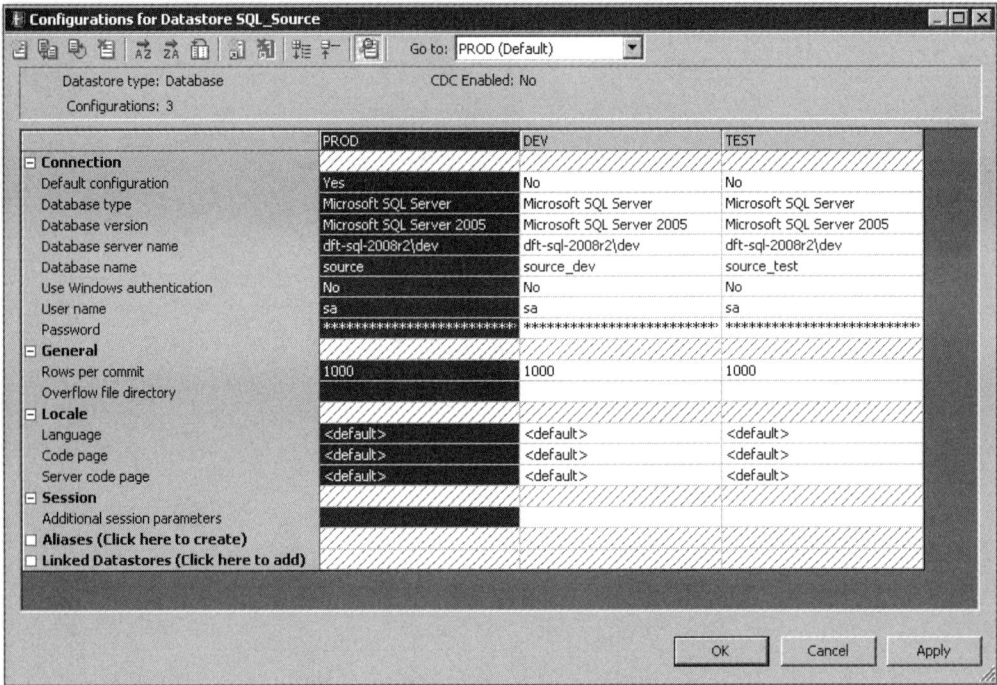

**Figure 4.5** Multiple Datastore Configurations: PROD, DEV, and TEST

### Provisioning Data in SAP HANA Using System Configurations

Most business intelligence (BI) initiatives using SAP HANA provision data from multiple sources into a reporting structure, which involves setting up multiple source environments. This is the precise scenario where you want to use multiple datastore configurations as shown in Figure 4.5. These configurations allow easy switching from environment to environment and enables you to use the same code with minimal modifications.

Instead of a connection for DEV, TEST, and PROD, you might see a connection for customer data from an SQL Server point-of-sales system as well as a DB2 customer source from a mainframe enterprise resource planning (ERP) source table. As long as the customer source columns are the same, you can switch the connection at runtime from one connection to the next and use the same code to read the data. This is a very easy way to move between sources for an SAP HANA data load.

Datastores provide this important layer of isolation between objects in SAP Data Services. As mentioned earlier, datastores merely facilitate connections underlying source or target objects in SAP Data Services. To enable SAP Data Services to act on a connection and actually execute or perform an operation of work, you need to invoke an SAP Data Services job. We discuss jobs in detail in the next section of this chapter.

### 4.1.3    Jobs

A *job* is the only executable element in SAP Data Services. Without a job to execute in SAP Data Services, a datastore can't do anything. Because a datastore is just a connection to a database, it stands to reason that a datastore with nothing to invoke action is just metadata describing a connection. This is where a job takes over and controls the execution or the actions in SAP Data Services.

Jobs are found in the SAP Data Services Designer under the JOBS tab in the LOCAL OBJECT LIBRARY, as highlighted in the bottom left of Figure 4.6.

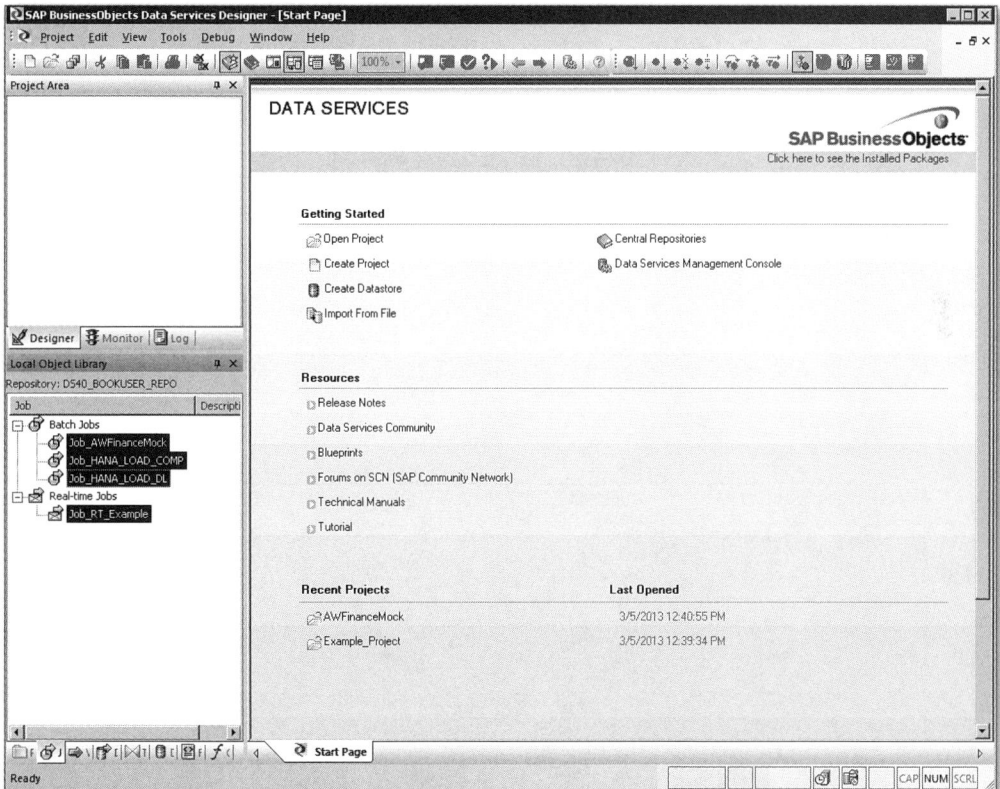

**Figure 4.6**    Batch and Real-Time Jobs in Designer

Batch jobs operate on a schedule and run at specified intervals of time dictated by the schedule. A schedule is just another object in SAP Data Services, so one job can have multiple schedules with different parameters for connections and variables. Batch jobs are used the predominantly to load the data into SAP HANA for the next chapter of this book.

Proper batch job form is illustrated in Figure 4.7. Best practices dictate that a batch job contain a `Try` and a `Catch` block object (see the Try and End objects at the beginning and end in Figure 4.7). The Try and Catch blocks capture errors both at the application and the database level and control process flow and interpretation of the errors.

Inside the Try and Catch are the script objects. The script objects are shown in Figure 4.7 as `SCR_START_JOB` and `SCR_END_JOB`, respectively. These script objects do things such as set variable values by both literal declarations and return values from database tables. The `SCR_END_JOB` script is used to finalize variable values and is used most often to signify the end of the job.

Finally, the workflow icon in the center with the blue arrow is what contains the working elements of the job: the data flow. These are discussed in great detail in the upcoming Section 4.1.4 and Section 4.1.5.

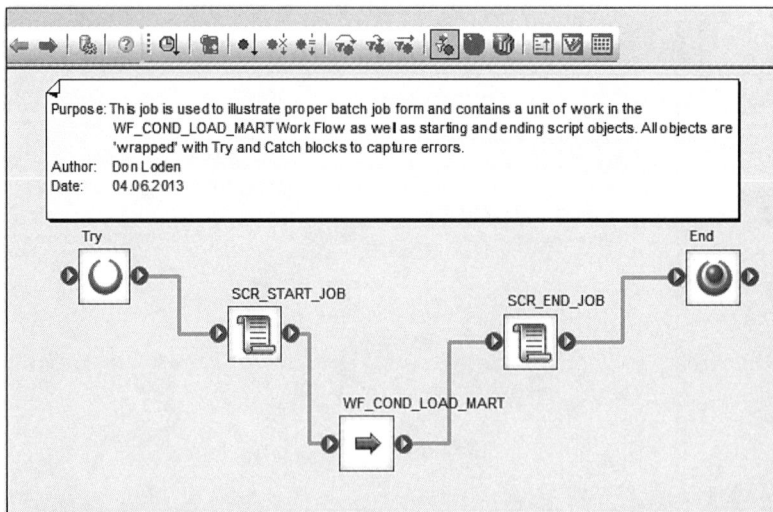

**Figure 4.7** Proper Batch Job Form in Designer

Jobs can also be run in real time; by definition, this doesn't require a schedule. Real-time jobs are created in the SAP Data Services Designer application just as a batch job; however, they are always waiting and ready to respond to web services. They act as stateless objects, where an application passing data in the form of a generic XML web services gets a response back with the output of the real-time job. Real-time jobs look very similar to their batch counterparts. An example of a real-time job is shown in Figure 4.8.

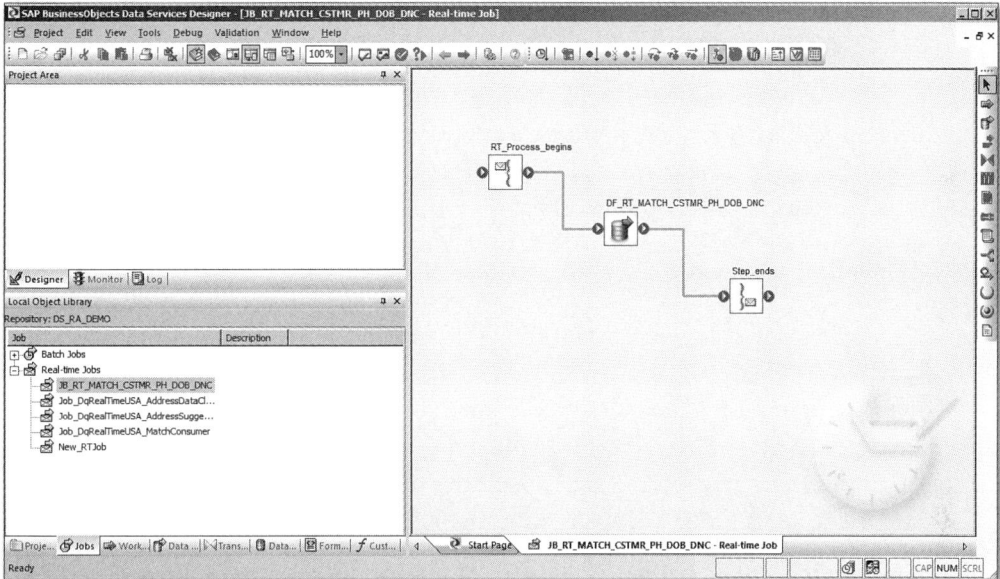

**Figure 4.8**  Real-Time Job Example in Designer

This type of functionality and interaction is used by applications ranging from the SAP Business Suite to SAP Customer Relationship Management (SAP CRM) and SAP NetWeaver Master Data Management (SAP MDM) mostly for data enhancements such as address cleansing or matching records. It's important to note that using this functionality isn't limited to SAP applications. This functionality may be extended to any application that can pass XML web services!

The only real difference in terms of what is seen in the SAP Data Services Designer application is the two icons surrounding the unit of work in the middle. These are placeholder icons that show this is a real-time job. They are placed in the real-time job by SAP Data Services upon creation, and they are nonconfigurable objects. Real-time jobs are also very important for provisioning data into SAP HANA because they can be used for real-time replication of data when the data needs alterations of some sort on the way into SAP HANA. Real-time jobs are discussed in great detail in Section 4.1.8 in this chapter.

In Figure 4.7 and Figure 4.8, we've shown and exemplified where the work happens in SAP Data Services jobs by referencing workflows and data flows. Next, let's discuss these components in detail. We begin the next section with workflows and follow with data flows.

## 4.1.4 Workflows

A *workflow* is a grouping mechanism that controls the flow of work in the job. Because it doesn't actually perform work on its own, its name may seem puzzling. It's a container object that SAP Data Services can use to layer any of the work tasks in any order possible. So, a workflow is really just an organizational component in an SAP Data Services job. The best way to think of a workflow is similar to a folder in Microsoft Windows.

Although it may not seem like workflows do very much, they actually perform some very powerful tasks in SAP Data Services. They allow parallel or series operations with some unique recovery options. Workflows also extend the object-oriented nature of SAP Data Services by extending the reusability of objects in certain cases. All of these features expand the capabilities of SAP Data Services with some very important items for SAP HANA conversions.

The first of these we'll discuss is the parallel capabilities of workflows.

### Parallel Execution

Workflows allow a developer to run objects or work in parallel with one another. In the example in Figure 4.9, these workflows control the work of loading the dimension tables. This is a perfect example of *parallel* operations, which occur when multiple units of work happen at the same time in an SAP Data Service job. In this example, account, employee, or customer data are all independent with no relation to each other, and because there are no database or data dependencies on any of the tables that are being loaded, the loads can run in parallel.

By running all three data loads for DIM_ACCOUNT, DIM_CUSTOMER, and DIM_EMPLOYEE in parallel, the runtime is shortened dramatically. Let's assume for this example that loading DIM_CUSTOMER takes the longest because the organization sees more changes in customer data per day over DIM_EMPLOYEE or DIM_ACCOUNT data. So in this example, assume that DIM_CUSTOMER has a runtime of 15 minutes while DIM_ACCOUNT and DIM_EMPLOYEE have runtimes of 5 minutes and 10 minutes, respectively. See the details in Table 4.2.

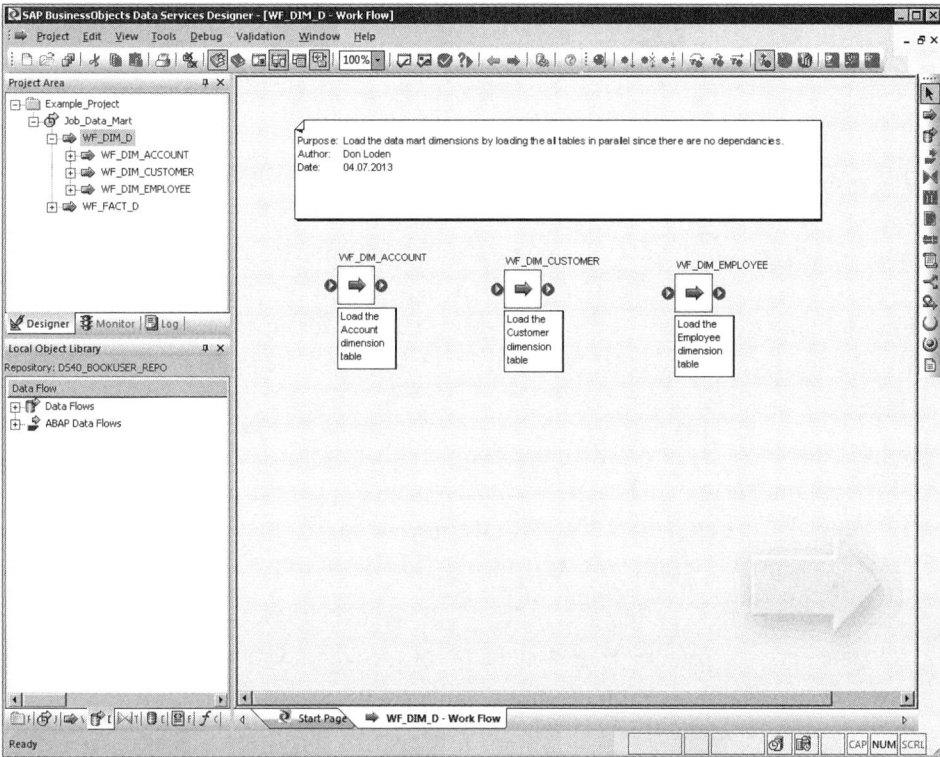

**Figure 4.9**  Workflows in Parallel in Designer

| | Parallel Time | Series Time |
|---|---|---|
| Table Loaded | Runtime | Runtime |
| DIM_ACCOUNT | 5 minutes | 5 minutes |
| DIM_CUSTOMER | 15 minutes | 15 minutes |
| DIM_EMPLOYEE | 10 minutes | 10 minutes |
| = Time Net | 15 minutes | 30 minutes |

**Table 4.2**  Runtime Cut in Half with Parallel Operations

With running the three tables in a series, you have a runtime of 30 minutes because each unit of work that loads each table must complete before the next begins. If you run the units of work that load each table in parallel, you now have a longer running operation that covers the other shorter running operations. SAP Data Services is a multithreaded application that can take advantage of this parallelization. As long as the underlying database source and target can handle the requests and the throughput, then this is a great scenario with a much better performing outcome. By running the data in parallel for all three tables, you've now cut the runtime for all three tables in half!

This principle is very import for loading data into SAP HANA because you'll be loading very large volumes of data from your sources. Operations have long running load times, so the first thing you should consider for tuning an SAP HANA application is what operations can be run in parallel by examining the dependencies present in the data. This covers a very important process for getting data into SAP HANA and is great until something causes a failure and the job screeches to a halt.

Recovery is always an important consideration. However, now with parallel work being done, recovery is a little more complex than it if performing the work in a linear fashion. Fortunately, SAP Data Services not only performs checkpoint recovery, but it also has some nice recovery features to handle these types of situations. These situations exist more often in an SAP HANA environment requiring parallel loads to cope with extreme amounts of data.

SAP Data Services offers a robust checkpoint recovery system that is fairly intelligent. *Checkpoint recovery* monitors the job execution and keeps track of which units of work complete successfully and which don't. If any unit of work doesn't complete successfully, then the job can recover the data by reprocessing the step upon the next execution of the job. This feature is enabled by running the job with recovery enabled. To do this, you run the job from SAP Data Services Designer by right-clicking the job and choosing EXECUTE in the project window, as shown in Figure 4.10.

This brings up the EXECUTION PROPERTIES window in the SAP Data Services Designer application. This window is used for many things, but if you want to enable checkpoint recovery for an SAP Data Services job at runtime, all you need to do is select the ENABLE RECOVERY checkbox, as shown in Figure 4.11.

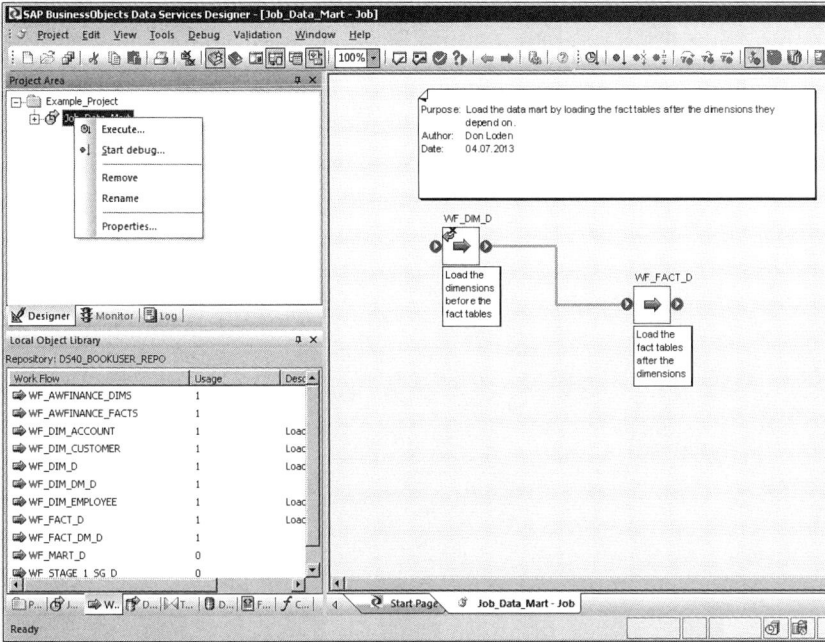

**Figure 4.10**  Executing a Job from Designer

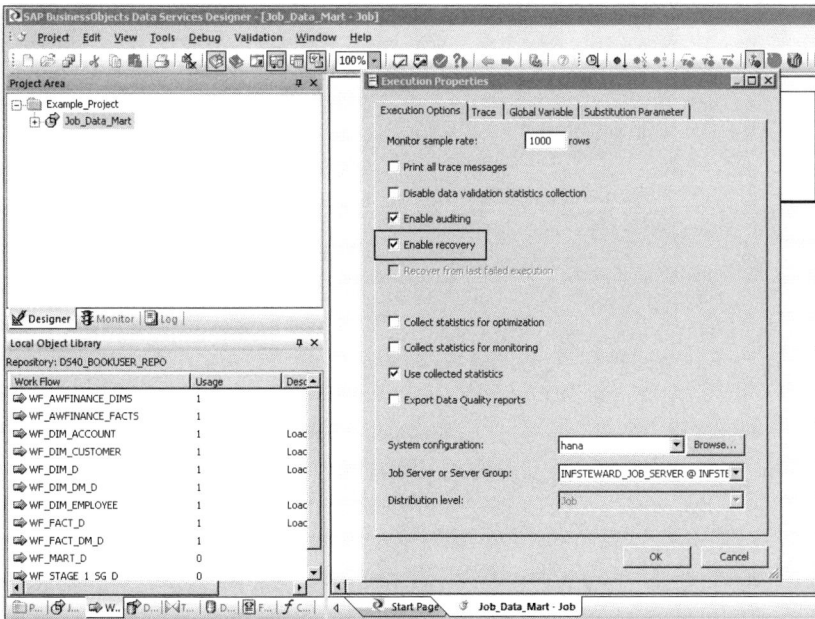

**Figure 4.11**  Enabling Checkpoint Recovery

This great feature works quite well when data is loaded in a singular stream. However, other challenges are introduced when you're loading data in parallel. Parallel data loads become a bit more complicated. If the tables in Figure 4.9 had a downstream dependency in the job, and you needed to ensure that loading these tables was always concluded concurrently, then you could set the workflows to recover as a unit, as shown in Figure 4.12.

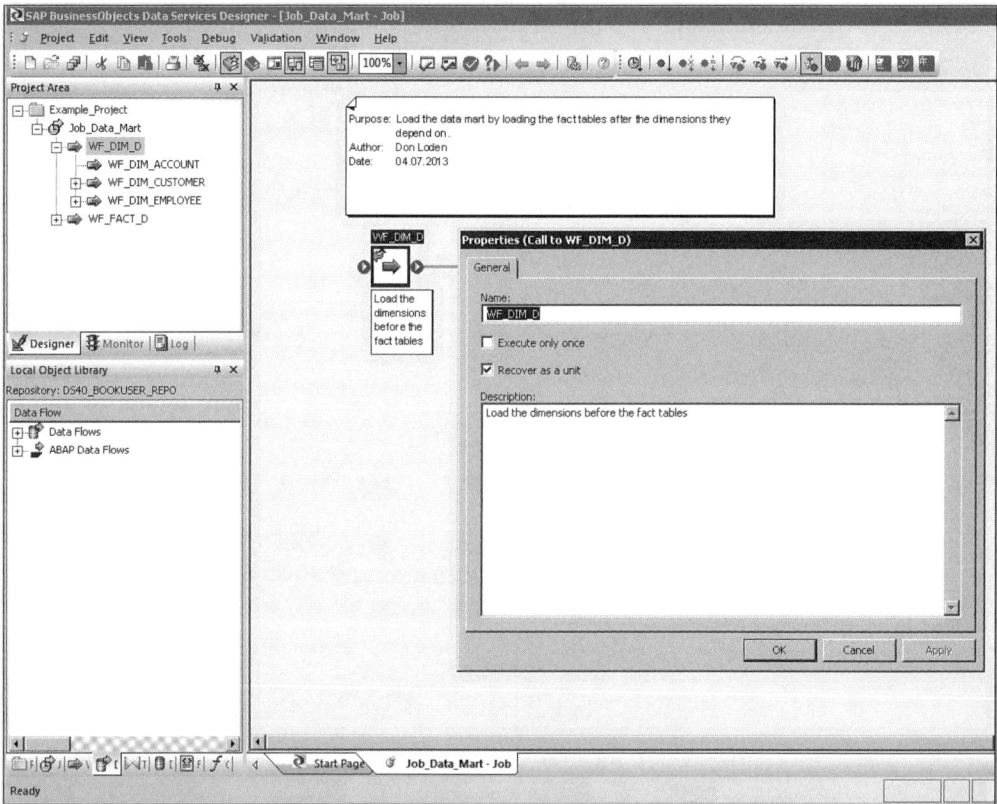

**Figure 4.12**  Properties of Workflow Illustrating Recovery as a Unit

Recovering as a unit overrides the checkpoint recovery for any of the workflows that had finished and causes them to reprocess in the event of a failure. Sometimes this can be dangerous, such as if the data within the tables need to be treated as a unit. If a dependency like this exists in your data, you need to create the parallel workflow to recover as a unit. When this is established, the recovery will behave as illustrated in Table 4.3.

| Tables Loaded in Parallel | Runtime | Failed Status | Checkpoint Recovery Only | Recover as a Unit Enabled |
|---|---|---|---|---|
| DIM_ACCOUNT | 5 minutes | Success | Skip | Reprocess |
| DIM_CUSTOMER | 15 minutes | Fail | Reprocess | Reprocess |
| DIM_EMPLOYEE | 10 minutes | Success | Skip | Reprocess |

**Table 4.3** Recovery Processing Comparing Checkpoint Only to Recover as a Unit

This works well, and there is one more level of granularity for this type of a recovery scenario. You can still have all of the workflows recover as a unit, but in cases where you need the workflow to execute only once, you can use the checkbox shown in Figure 4.12. This situation usually exists where processing triggers are involved either in this job or outside the context of the SAP Data Services job.

---

**Example of Executing Only Once**

The situation arises (albeit infrequently) where you may only process the operations in a workflow once, even on recovery. We typically see this when you need to trigger behavior in another application via depositing a file or writing to a database table.

If you have a business rule stating that a process can run only once per month, and you encountered a job failure, you don't want to retrigger the processing again with an SAP Data Services job recovery. Instead, use the EXECUTE ONLY ONCE option to force the recovery to skip the operation on recovery. This allows a much greater degree of control on what is recovered, processed, or skipped in a complex recovery situation.

---

**Series Execution**

Series execution is the most common design in SAP Data Services workflows. This design allows workflows or operations to run sequentially or in a series. One operation has to complete before the next can begin. Although this has a negative performance impact, it's a great option when dependencies arise in the data. In these types of situations, the data elements or workflows are often building blocks of logic where step one must be completed before step two can start.

An example of this is shown in Figure 4.13 where the workflow WF_DIM_D builds the dimensions in the data mart in SAP HANA and workflow WF_FACT_D builds the facts in SAP HANA.

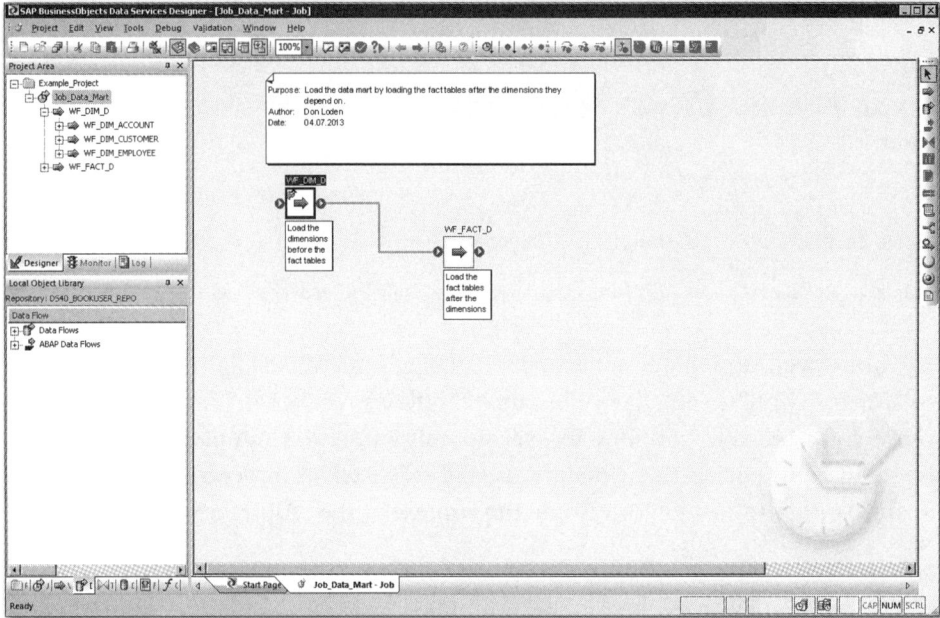

**Figure 4.13**  Workflows in Series in the Designer

By definition, you need to build the fact tables that are in the second workflow after the dimension tables because they depend on the dimensions in terms of the key structure. Fact tables always have foreign keys that reference a primary key field of a dimension table.

Consider the data example in Figure 4.14 that supports the SAP Data Services code example in Figure 4.13. To have a record in FACT_SALE, you need a product record in DIM_PRODUCT to sell. Please notice as well that the WF_DIM_D has the green icon arrow in Figure 4.13 to recover as a unit, as just discussed. All of the dimension tables may be built in parallel because there are no dependencies present, but you may want to recover all tables together in the event of a failure.

FACT_SALE records in our SAP HANA data mart are all measures of the sales of products and customers stored at a certain level of granularity organized by a date dimension table. So, for this model to work, you have to create the primary keys in the dimension tables in the SAP Data Services job before those values can be looked up or assigned as foreign key references in the FACT_SALE table. This is the perfect example of why you need to take a hit in terms of load performance to simply meet the constraints that arise in your data model while loading SAP HANA with SAP Data Services.

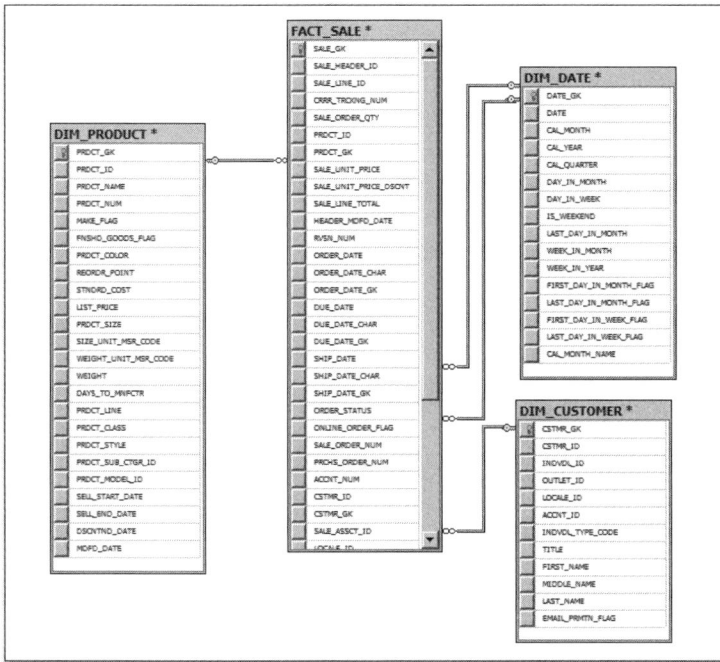

**FACT_SALE ***
- SALE_GK
- SALE_HEADER_ID
- SALE_LINE_ID
- CRRR_TRCKNG_NUM
- SALE_ORDER_QTY
- PRDCT_ID
- PRDCT_GK
- SALE_UNIT_PRICE
- SALE_UNIT_PRICE_DSCNT
- SALE_LINE_TOTAL
- HEADER_MDFO_DATE
- RVSN_NUM
- ORDER_DATE
- ORDER_DATE_CHAR
- ORDER_DATE_GK
- DUE_DATE
- DUE_DATE_CHAR
- DUE_DATE_GK
- SHIP_DATE
- SHIP_DATE_CHAR
- SHIP_DATE_GK
- ORDER_STATUS
- ONLINE_ORDER_FLAG
- SALE_ORDER_NUM
- PRCHS_ORDER_NUM
- ACCNT_NUM
- CSTMR_ID
- CSTMR_GK
- SALE_ASSCT_ID
- LOCALE_ID

**DIM_PRODUCT ***
- PRDCT_GK
- PRDCT_ID
- PRDCT_NAME
- PRDCT_NUM
- MAKE_FLAG
- FNSHD_GOODS_FLAG
- PRDCT_COLOR
- REORDR_POINT
- STNDRD_COST
- LIST_PRICE
- PRDCT_SIZE
- SIZE_UNIT_MSR_CODE
- WEIGHT_UNIT_MSR_CODE
- WEIGHT
- DAYS_TO_MNFCTR
- PRDCT_LINE
- PRDCT_CLASS
- PRDCT_STYLE
- PRDCT_SUB_CTGR_ID
- PRDCT_MODEL_ID
- SELL_START_DATE
- SELL_END_DATE
- DSCNTND_DATE
- MDFO_DATE

**DIM_DATE ***
- DATE_GK
- DATE
- CAL_MONTH
- CAL_YEAR
- CAL_QUARTER
- DAY_IN_MONTH
- DAY_IN_WEEK
- IS_WEEKEND
- LAST_DAY_IN_MONTH
- WEEK_IN_MONTH
- WEEK_IN_YEAR
- FIRST_DAY_IN_MONTH_FLAG
- LAST_DAY_IN_MONTH_FLAG
- FIRST_DAY_IN_WEEK_FLAG
- LAST_DAY_IN_WEEK_FLAG
- CAL_MONTH_NAME

**DIM_CUSTOMER ***
- CSTMR_GK
- CSTMR_ID
- INDVDL_ID
- OUTLET_ID
- LOCALE_ID
- ACCNT_ID
- INDVDL_TYPE_CODE
- TITLE
- FIRST_NAME
- MIDDLE_NAME
- LAST_NAME
- EMAIL_PRMTN_FLAG

**Figure 4.14** Dimensional Data Mart Model Illustrating Data Dependencies

To summarize, any time there is a dependency present in your job, you must design the workflows to operate in series; if there is no logical dependency, then use parallel workflow designs because these operate with the highest level of efficiency and perform at the maximum level for fast loads into SAP HANA.

Series and parallel execution are two important design considerations when using workflows in an SAP Data Services job. These are the classic use cases for these container objects in SAP Data Services. However, there is one often overlooked yet important function that a workflow provides in an SAP Data Services job: reusability.

## Reusability

SAP Data Services is, at its core, an object-oriented tool. We've already examined the SAP Data Services constructs—datastores, jobs, and workflows are all objects in SAP Data Services. This will continue throughout this chapter as we examine the rest of the objects used to provision your data into SAP HANA. But if these objects are reusable, the SAP Data Services reusability concept applies. Table 4.4 shows a concise list of reusable and single-use objects in SAP Data Services.

| SAP Data Services Object | Object State |
|---|---|
| Workflow | Reusable |
| Data flow | Reusable |
| Query transform | Single use |
| Template table | Single use |
| Template XML | Single use |
| Script | Single use |
| Conditional | Single use |
| Try | Single use |
| Catch | Single use |
| Annotation | Single use |

**Table 4.4** SAP Data Services Objects and Reusability State

A single-use object is just as it sounds: an object that may only be used once.

In contrast, a reusable object is an object that may be used multiple times, but only one instance of that object is stored in the repository. The rest of the times that reusable object is stored, only the pointer to the object is referenced in the code, so any of the changes made to that object need to happen only once at the base level of that object. In a single-use object, any changes made to that object need to be replicated wherever the object is used. This often shows up with a script because the script's functionality often needs to be replicated in various points in an SAP Data Services job, but the script is only a single-use object. This often requires copy and pasting the contents of a script to another single use script.

Consider the moderately complex script in Figure 4.15. Copying and pasting single-use objects works fine until a change needs to be made to the underlying logic of the script. This isn't something that you want to have to go back and change later in many places and attempt synchronicity. This forces the developer to always go back to each script and change the logic in each of the places. There is an easy way to reconcile this issue and transform the single-use script into a reusable object: envelop the script in a workflow!

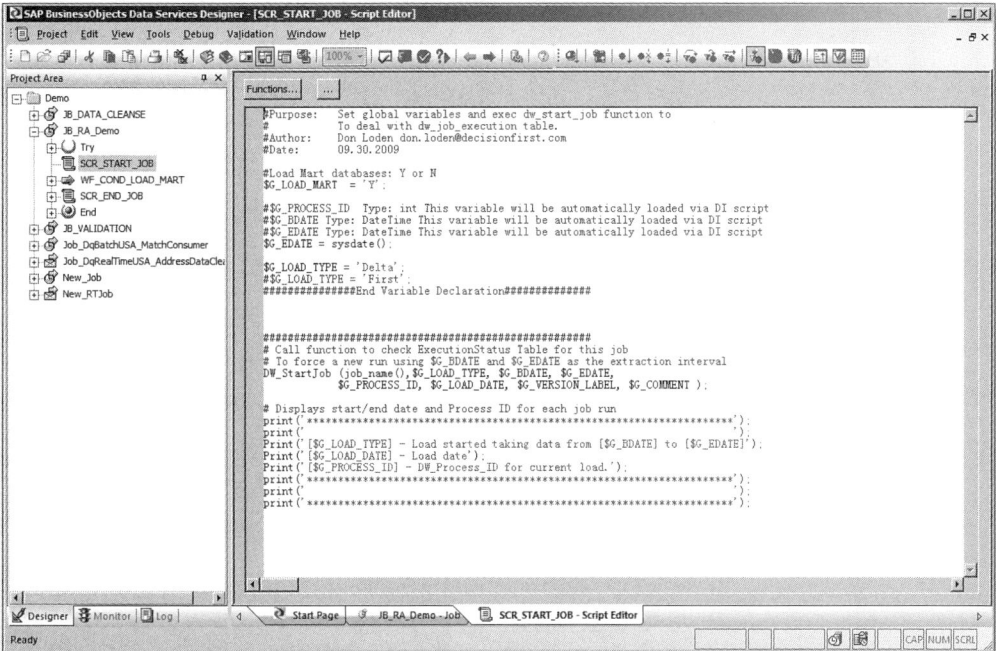

**Figure 4.15** Single-Use Script Object in Designer

By doing this, you're changing the properties of the script by simply adding this script to the workflow (a reusable object). You can now treat the contents of the script as one object. If the script needs to be reused, you may now drag and drop the workflow wherever it's needed in the job. For the example in Figure 4.15, where the script had been used multiple times, if the script is in the workflow, you only need to make changes in one place. You change the original script in the workflow, and the workflow acts as a pointer and cascades all changes wherever you used the workflow.

This extension of object-oriented reusability is a huge but often overlooked benefit to using workflows in SAP Data Services because it's not only a time savings but also results in more modular designs that are resilient to change.

Workflows are powerful objects in terms of reusability, controlling series or parallel execution, and extending recovery. Workflows certainly have a very important place in SAP Data Services jobs; however, they still don't perform any work. Work and logical operations are actually performed at the data flow level in SAP Data Services, so let's turn our attention there next.

### 4.1.5 Data Flows

Data flows in SAP Data Services are the basic units of work. Data flows occur when data is moved from the source to your SAP HANA target tables. Data flows are where data (or even entire sets of data) is transformed at the column level. In short, data flows are where all of the action resides and the transformation logic in an SAP Data Services job happens.

This is accomplished by an extensive set of built-in *functions* and built-in *transforms*. A function operates on a column, and a transform operates on an entire row of data, however, both significantly transform the data output. Properly designed data flows are comprised of both functions and transforms, and when used appropriately, they create a powerful canvas of data manipulation for loading SAP HANA. Properly designed data flows not only transform the data but also need to be constructed in a certain order to make the best use of SAP Data Services. An example of a properly constructed data flow is shown in Figure 4.16.

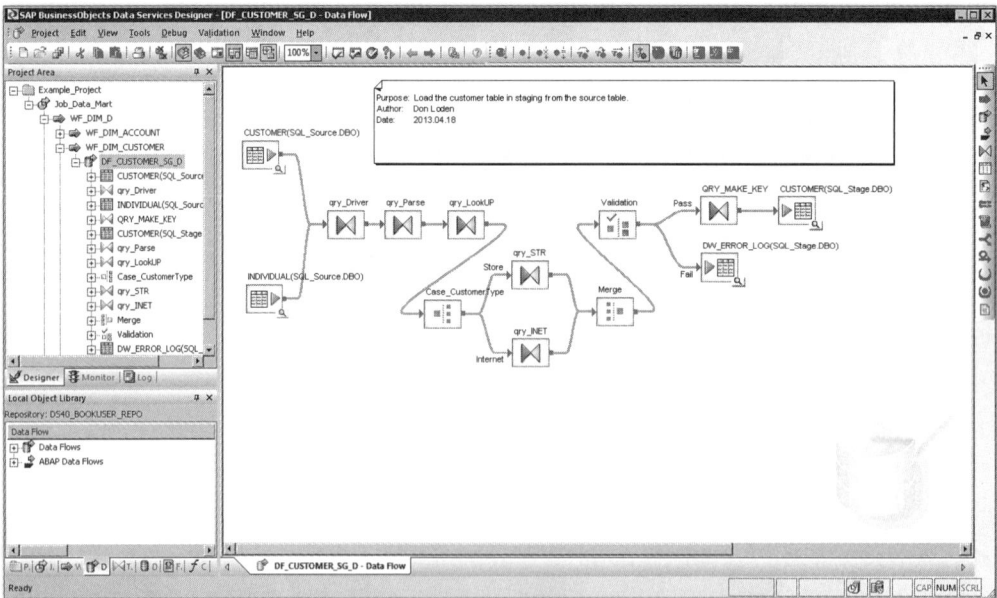

**Figure 4.16**  Customer Data Flow Illustrating All Stages of Processing

Having order in the data flow helps not only with delivering the logic in the data flow but also with the performance of the data flow and the job as a whole. This order results in dividing the data flow into various processing stages.

**Processing Stages**

The data flow is moving and transforming data at its core, so it makes sense to divide the work into meaningful sections segregated by the logical operations contained. This is doubly beneficial because it both makes the data flow easier to understand in terms of objectives and typically boosts performance.

A well-constructed data flow can be separated into five main stages, which are shown in Figure 4.16:

▶ **Driver stage**
Limits the record set by pushing down all joins or restrictions to the source database.

▶ **Parsing stage**
Parses the data using SAP Data Services functions or transforms. Some of this happens in the SAP Data Services job server engine.

▶ **Lookup stage**
Looks up values for denormalization purposes or other means. This happens more often for the SAP HANA target because further denormalization is required for good base data designs (as described in Chapter 2).

▶ **Business rules validation stage**
Validates all of the work performed in the data flow against the business rules that guide the data flow. Determines whether the flow performed the work it needed to perform.

▶ **Loading data stage**
Loads the SAP HANA tables. The tables are bulk loaded (in most cases) and, in some cases, they are created in SAP HANA. Both column store and row store tables can be created with SAP Data Services.

As shown in this list, the first stage of a properly constructed data flow is the *driver stage*, which constitutes a very important step in data flow design. This stage limits your data set with your first Query transform. Most often, data flows in an SAP HANA replication job do not process all of the data from the source with each run. The SAP Data Services job is usually constructed in such a way that it gathers only changed records to replicate over changed records. This is shown in great detail in the next chapter, but at a high level, we'll do this by using the first Query transform to drive down the record set that SAP Data Services processes in the data flow by limiting the data with a range-based WHERE clause. Figure 4.17 illustrates the driver stage, with the first Query transform highlighted with an annotation.

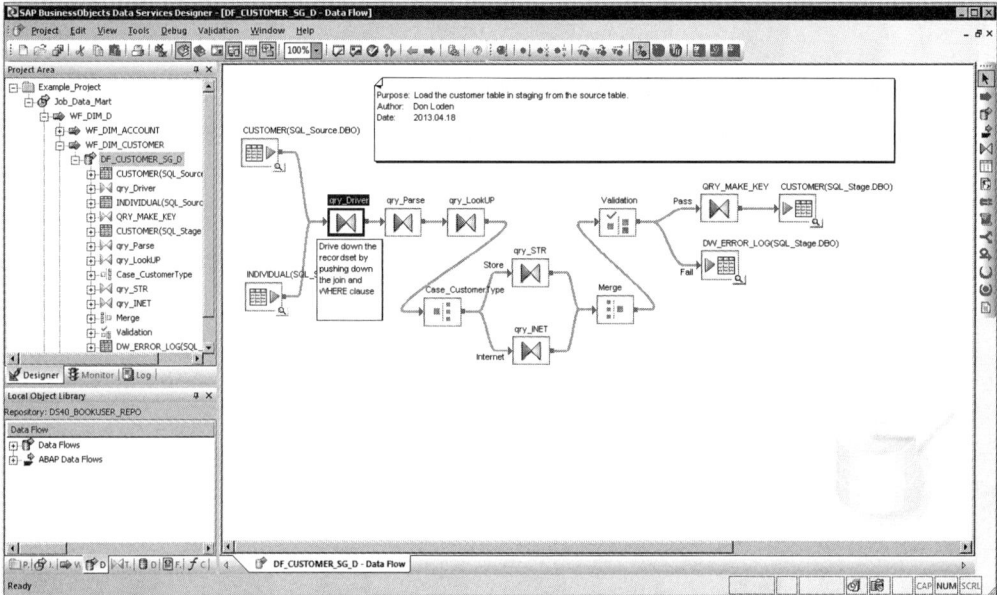

**Figure 4.17** Use the First Query Transform as the Driver Stage

In this example, qry_Driver is used to push down a join between the CUSTOMER and INDIVIDUAL tables. This pushes down all possible operations, including the expensive WHERE clause and any joins to the source database. The database is much more efficient because the join happens natively in the database as well as the WHERE clause to limit the data set. Then, the resulting set is rendered into SAP Data Services for further transformation in the next section of the code. SAP Data Services is designed with the intent of stratifying the work load between the database server and the SAP Data Services job engine, and it's this stratification that must be leveraged to create data flows using best practices.

The *parsing stage* is the next stage to occur in the data flow. Parsing usually occurs in the job server using built-in SAP Data Services transforms and functions, so you want to make sure that this occurs after the driver stage drives down the amount of data to process. The parsing stage is shown in Figure 4.18 with the `qry_Parse Query` transform highlighted.

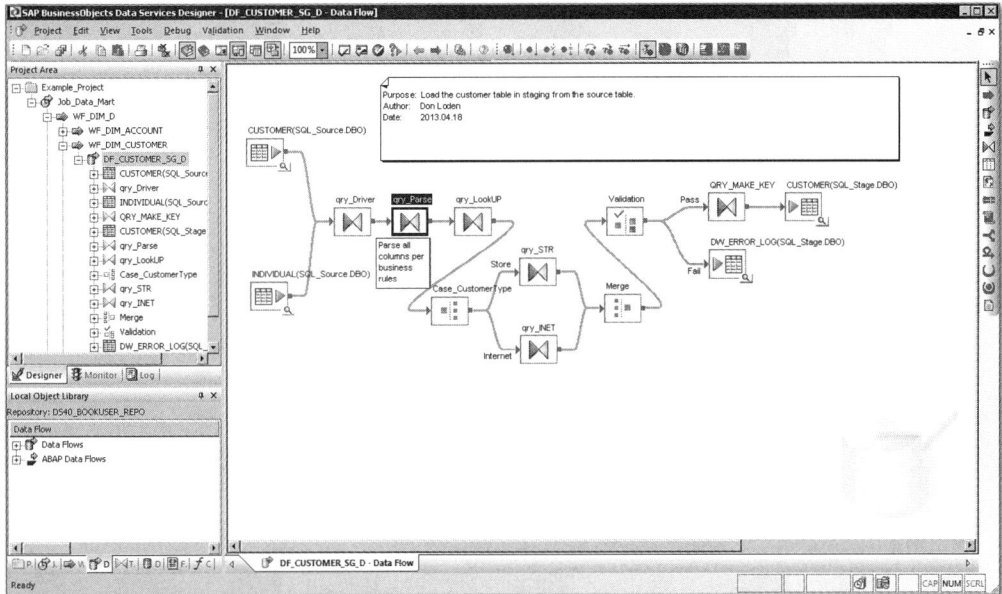

**Figure 4.18** The Parsing Stage Parses Data per Business Rules

This stage may do things that are as simple as using an `UPPPER()` function to convert all customer names to uppercase due to business rules, or as complex as if-then type logic—using a `DECODE()` function or `IFTHENELSE()`. Some of these operations can be pushed down to the database if there is an equivalent function in the database that SAP Data Services can translate, whereas other operations will occur in the job server engine if no equivalent function exists in the database. This is why it's so important to ensure the record set is as small as possible before invoking expensive operations in the SAP Data Services job engine. Having a smaller record set to process in the engine becomes really important in the next stage: the lookup stage.

The *lookup stage* happens almost entirely in the SAP Data Services job server engine, so it follows both the driver stage and the parsing stage. Figure 4.19 shows an example of the lookup stage in the data flow occurring after the `qry_Driver` and `qry_Parse`.

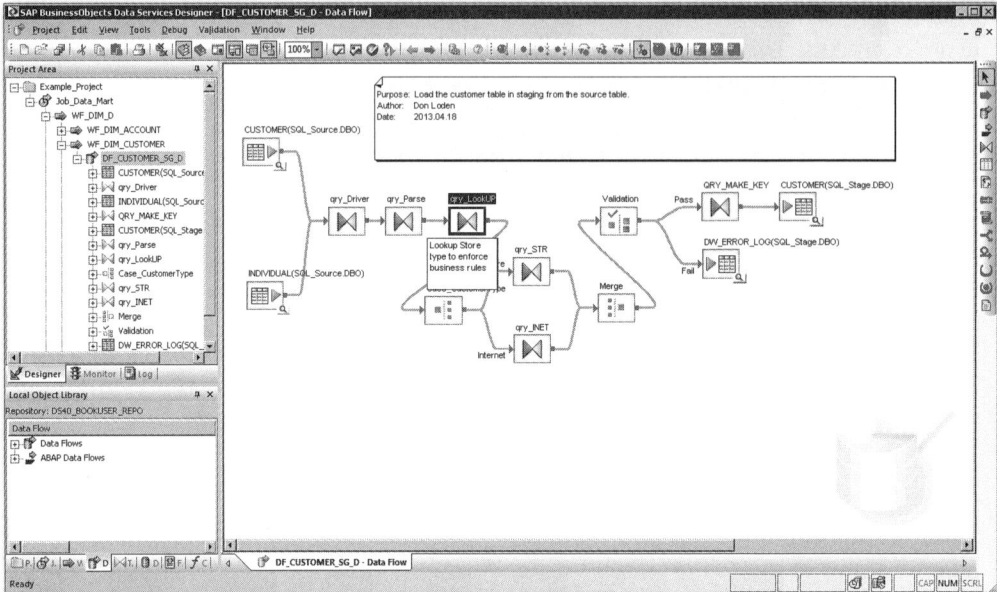

**Figure 4.19** Lookup Stage in the Data Flow

Although lookups are expensive in terms of processing, they can be very powerful tools when used effectively. They are great tools for denormalizing data from normalized reference tables in OLTP systems where data is highly normalized.

Take, for example, a customer record where you need to know whether the customer is an online or in-store customer for reporting. In the source system, this information appears in two tables: CUSTOMER and CUSTOMER_TYPE. This need to be denormalized into a simple CUSTOMER_TYPE column in the customer table in SAP HANA to avoid the join cost (as discussed in Chapter 2). To do this efficiently, you use SAP Data Services to look up the value either as an in-line outer join or using `lookup_ext()` functions for more tailored results. Using this function, you can pick `Max` and `Min` values if the source CUSTOMER_TYPE table contains history records. Figure 4.20 shows an example of the `lookup_ext()` in action.

Notice how custom SQL is also an option for limiting a result set in `lookup_ext()` by clicking the CUSTOM SQL button in the bottom-right corner of the screen. If you use custom SQL, then you can limit the comparison result set of the `Lookup` transform by typing in the SQL directly "covers" all of the fields that are selected in the `Condition:` section as well as the `Output:` section in Figure 4.20. Using this feature for the example in Figure 4.20 would look like the following:

```
SELECT CUSTOMERTYPE, CUSTOMERTYPEDESC
FROM CUSTOMER_TYPE
WHERE CUSTOMERTYPEDESC = 'Online'
```

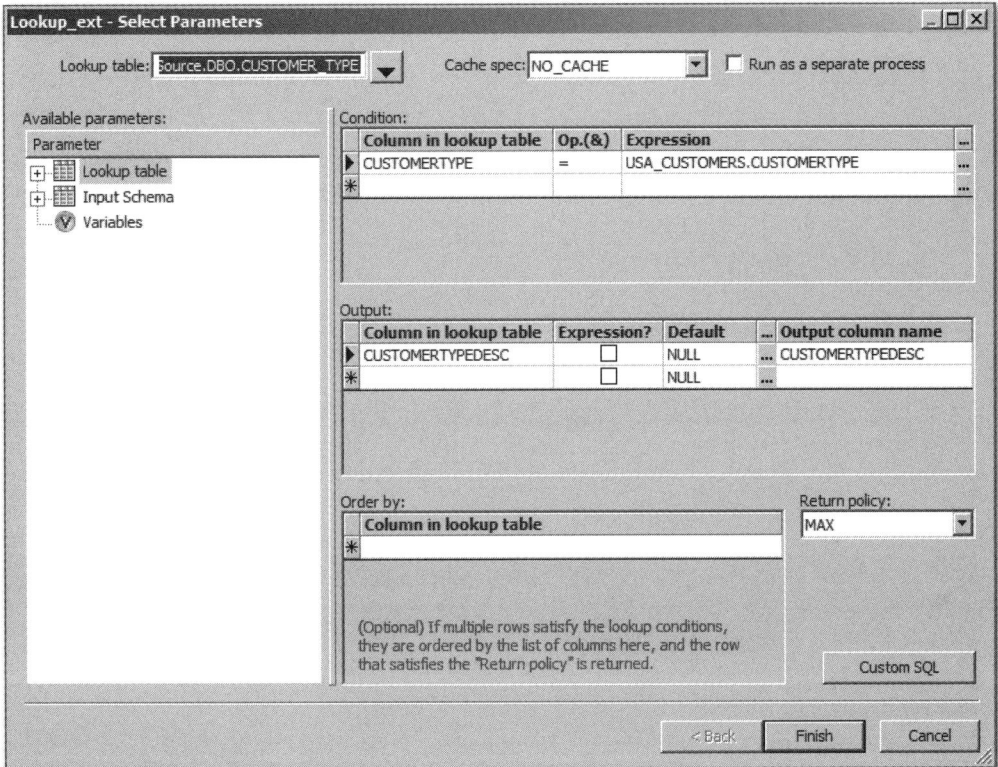

**Figure 4.20** Lookup_ext Function Used to Denormalize Data for SAP HANA

This feature really is used if there is a `WHERE` clause that limits the set of data for the comparison. This example would not improve any performance because CUS-TOMER_TYPE is quite a small table, but if the table had millions of records, this feature can be quite a performance boost.

An exciting new feature in SAP Data Services 4.1 allows lookups to be pushed down to the source database in certain occasions:

- ▶ Only in `no_cache` mode
- ▶ Only if the database can access source and lookup tables
- ▶ Only with "=" conditions
- ▶ Only if upstream functions and transforms don't prevent joins

Because this is such a limited list of scenarios, we still recommend that these stages be followed as a general rule with lookups coming after both the driver and parsing stages to perform lookups after data is limited and parsed. The key is to always limit the result set before evoking expensive operations in the job engine, but with the new pushdown features, it's worth noting when to deviate from the norm. If the lookup meets all of the preceding conditions, then put it upfront in the process at the driver stage. If all conditions are met, then the lookup will push down to the source database as an inline `SELECT` statement, as shown in Figure 4.21.

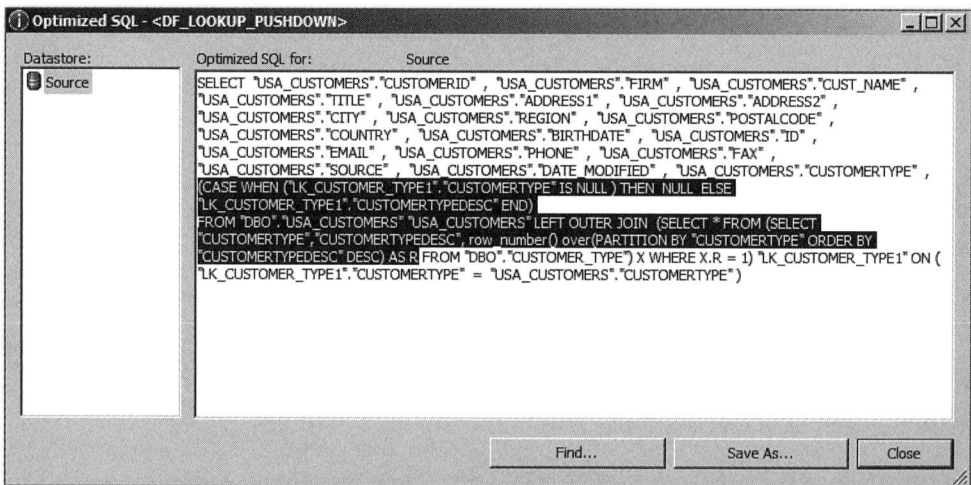

**Figure 4.21** Lookup_ext SQL Pushed Down to the Source Database

Now after all work has been performed in the driver, parsing, and lookup stages, you can validate the work that performed on the load on the way to SAP HANA with the business rules validation stage.

In the business rules validation stage, you validate your data using transforms such as `Validation`, `Case Logic`, and `Error Trapping`. All of these techniques are used to perform a series of logical tests to ensure that the records were transformed according to the business rules. This is shown in Figure 4.22 in the highlighted transforms: `Case_CustomerType`, `qry_STR`, `qry_INET`, `Merge`, and `Validation`.

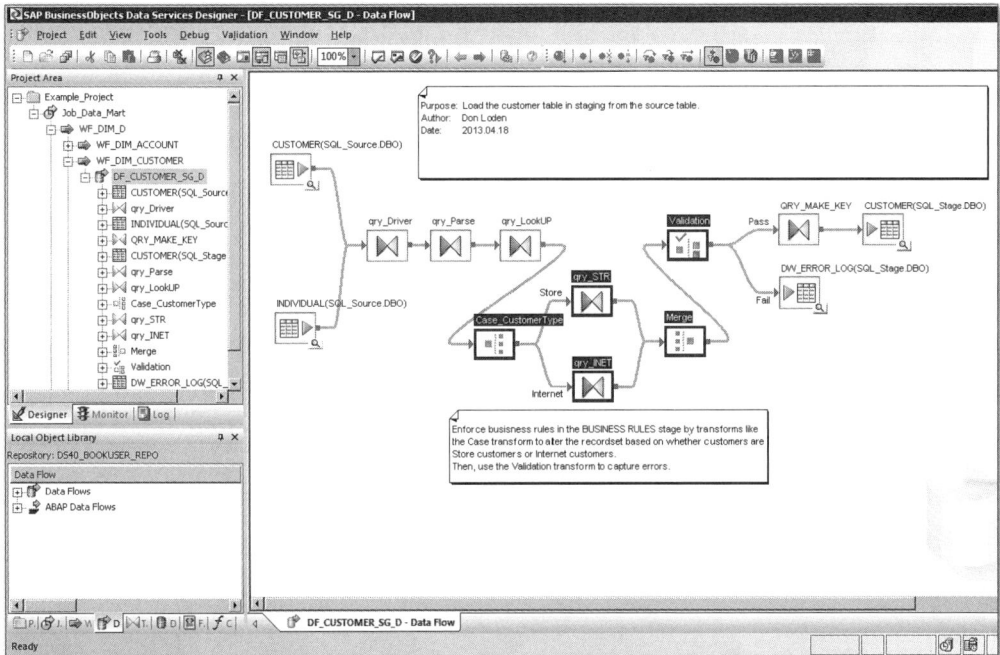

**Figure 4.22** Using Validation Logic in the Business Rules Validation Stage

The `Case_CustomerType` transform is used to split the processing between customers that were either Internet customers or customers that purchased products inside the store. The `qry_STR` transform allows special transformations to occur to store customers, and the `qry_INET Query` transform allows special transformations to occur to Internet customers. This all is merged back together in the `Merge` transform, which is like a `UNION ALL` in SQL. Then, the `Validation` transform evaluates and captures statistics around whether the data passed or failed the business rules throughout the data flow. This provides metrics around the data processed because the `Validation` transform captures both pass and fail statistics and metrics around the processing. All of this occurs just because the `Validation` transform is used.

`Validation` provides statistics of errors that are automatically collected in the metadata reports that are viewed in the SAP Data Services Management Console.

To access the metadata reports that are collected in the system automatically anytime a `Validation` transform is used, open the SAP Data Services Management Console, and click on METADATA REPORTS. The reports are a great tool to capture this extra metadata without any additional development, but to ensure that validation efforts are not lost in the metadata reports, always give your validations meaningful names while setting up the transforms. These reports are somewhat generic—and without proper naming conventions all of your work will just be lumped together and difficult to read—so ensure that the validation results will be readable by using proper segregation.

The final stage of the data flow is to load the table structures in SAP HANA. SAP Data Services can load both row and column store tables in SAP HANA when using a regular loader. When using the bulk loader, the default tables used are column store tables. The bulk loader options are shown in Figure 4.23, and the regular loader options are shown in Figure 4.24.

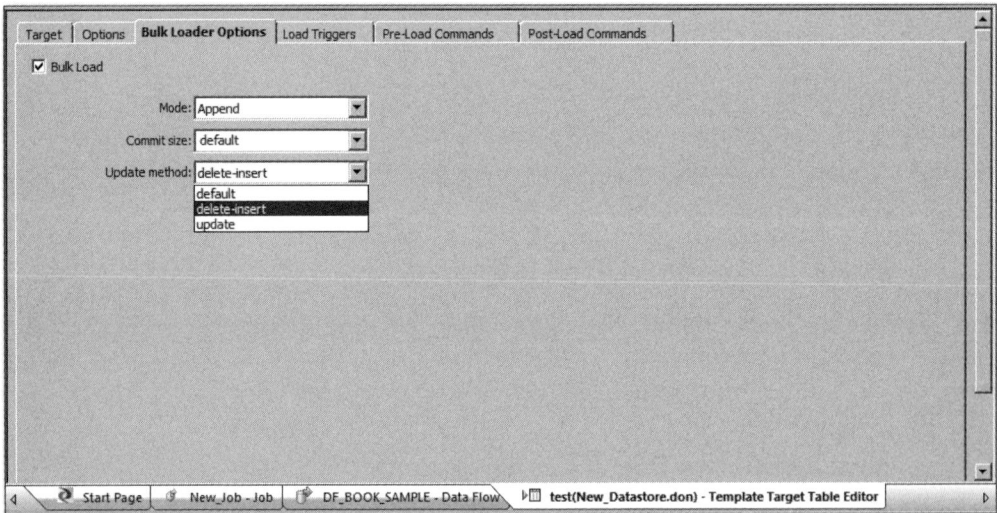

**Figure 4.23**  Bulk Loader Options in an SAP HANA Target Table

Notice that there are not many controls in the bulk loader options. Because you're using the SAP HANA bulk load API, all controls go to SAP HANA, and this is a very streamlined process without many controls because it's focused on the highest performance possible. Regular loaders offer somewhat diminished performance but many more options for controlling how data is loaded into a table.

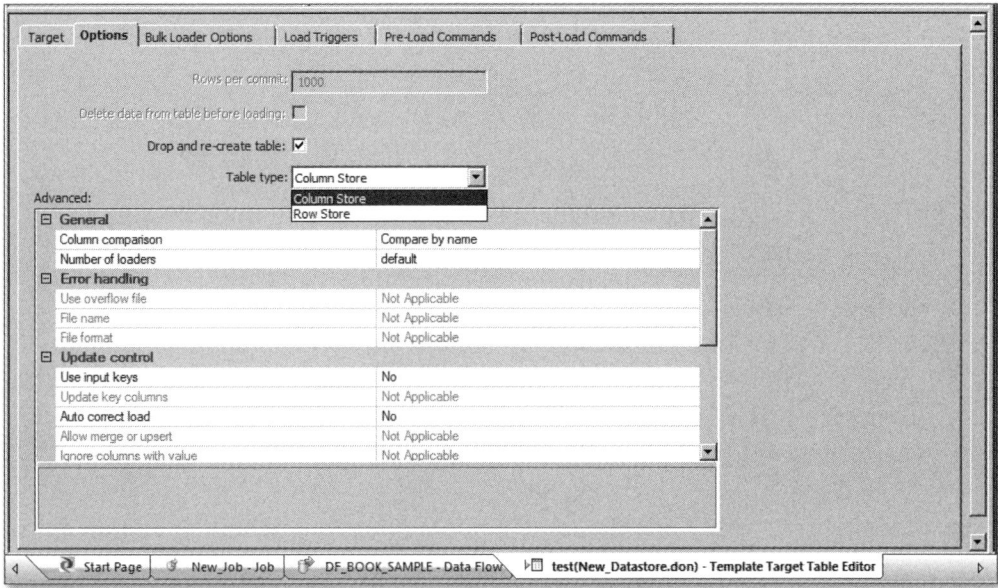

**Figure 4.24** Regular Loader Options in an SAP HANA Target Table

For instance, in the UPDATE CONTROL section shown in Figure 4.24, you can set the AUTO CORRECT LOAD feature to YES. Just this simple property setting causes SAP Data Services to change the behavior of the target table loader. Instead of just sending INSERT SQL statements as it would with the AUTO CORRECT LOAD set to No, the setting produces INSERT/UPDATE pairs to test the target table to see if the records have already been loaded. Either the INSERT or UPDATE will be successful.

SAP Data Services even goes a step further by pushing down an SQL MERGE operation to the target database if that functionality is supported in the database platform. This technique is very powerful for jobs designed around the concept of a *delta,* which processes only changed data, and for the concept of recovery. The comparison of the data can be achieved by using either the native primary key of the table, or a comparison key field can be established by the software, so that a key isn't necessary.

Another important feature is the ERROR HANDLING section. You can use an overflow file to trap records that fail database constraints or data type mismatch issues. You can either write the SQL that failed or the actual data values. We find that the SQL is quite useful for troubleshooting because this allows you to run the statements individually against the target database on a native SQL client for the database for better debugging and troubleshooting database errors on loading.

The final aspect to note about the SAP HANA table loaders are the fact that they can create either row store or column store tables. This simplifies the development process because the developer only needs the final result set of the data flow to produce the table structures in SAP HANA. This is performed by using the drop and re-create table functionality of a `Template Table` transform. The DROP AND RE-CREATE TABLE checkbox is shown in Figure 4.24, earlier in this section.

You can find the `Template Table` transform on the tool palate on the right side of the workspace, as shown in Figure 4.25. To implement a template table in a data flow, just click the icon the arrow is pointing to and drop the template table where you want in the data flow. This is a great time-saving feature that allows the developer to stay in one tool to create both the logic of the data flow and table structure for SAP HANA.

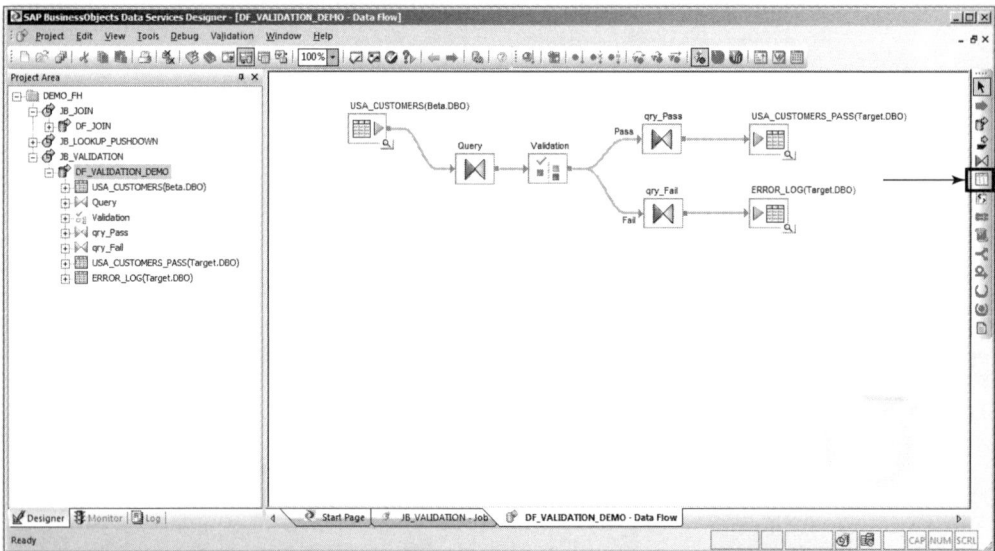

**Figure 4.25** Where to Find the Template Table in Designer

After exploring all of the processing stages of a data flow it's clear that many things may be accomplished in a single data flow. One of the most important is the ability to create complex logic. Creating complex logic is easy in SAP Data Services, and this is generally accomplished by using the powerful transforms that SAP Data Services contains. We explore these transforms in great detail in the next section of this chapter.

### Transforms

Transforms operate on data sets by receiving incoming data, transforming that data, and finally producing one or many output sets. Transforms are different from functions because they operate on sets of data or entire records where functions operate on columns within a record. SAP Data Services is packed with many powerful built-in transforms that are available from the LOCAL OBJECT LIBRARY on the TRANSFORMS tab shown in Figure 4.26.

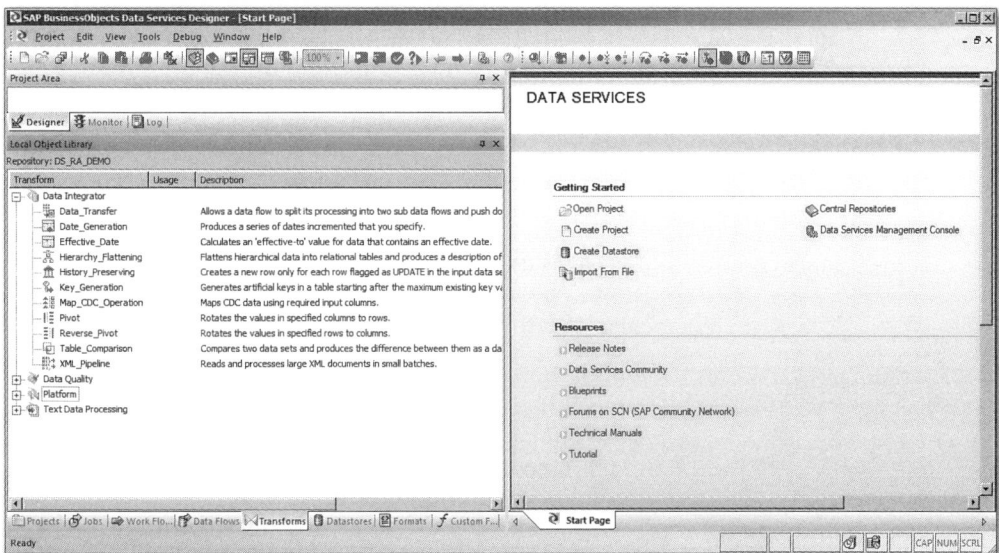

**Figure 4.26** Transforms Tab in Designer with the Data Integrator Node Open

Transforms in the TRANSFORMS tab are broken into four sections: DATA INTEGRATOR, DATA QUALITY, PLATFORM, and TEXT DATA PROCESSING. The upcoming tables provide a comprehensive list of all available built-in transforms and their descriptions by section. Data Integrator transforms (Table 4.5) are available with the full SAP Data Services licensing or the Data Integrator licensing, while Data Quality transforms (Table 4.6) are available with the full SAP Data Services licensing or the Data Quality Management licensing. Platform transforms (Table 4.7) are always included with the product, and Text Data Processing transforms (Table 4.8) require a separate license. If you don't have licensing for the transforms, the top-level nodes of DATA INTEGRATOR, DATA QUALITY, PLATFORM, and TEXT DATA PROCESSING will be visible, but none of the transforms in Table 4.5 will be available.

| Transform Name | Description |
|---|---|
| Data_Transfer | Splits data flow processing between two subdata flows to allow for better push down for resource-intensive operations. This is very useful for tuning data flows. |
| Date_Generation | Generates a date column as a baseline date for a user-specified range of dates. |
| Effective_Date | Generates an effective date column based on the specified primary key of the record. |
| Hierarchy_Flattening | Flattens nested relational data model (NRDM) data into relational tables. Useful for transforming XML data hierarchies into parent-child relational tables in SAP HANA. |
| History_Preserving | Converts records flagged by the software as UPDATEs to INSERTs to preserve original values. An effective date is also specified. Useful for creating slowly changing dimension. |
| Key_Generation | Generates new key values for a source. Most often used for creating a surrogate key in a data mart or data warehouse when you combine data from multiple sources. |
| Map_CDC_Operation | Sorts data from an input table and maps output data after resolving before and after UPDATE images. Commonly used to support Oracle changed-data capture (CDC) but can be used for other database CDC support if the input requirements are met. |
| Pivot | Pivots the data set from columns to rows. Opposite operation of a reverse pivot. |
| Reverse_Pivot | Pivots the data set from rows to columns. Opposite operation of a pivot. |
| Table_Comparison | Compares an input data set to a target data set and produces the difference between them with the output records flagged as INSERTs or UPDATEs. |
| XML_Pipeline | Processes large XML input sets in small batches. |

**Table 4.5** Data Integrator Transforms and Descriptions

| Transform Name | Description |
|---|---|
| Associate | Combines the result sets of two or more Match transforms or two or more Associate transforms to find matches across match sets. |
| Country_ID | Parses input data and identifies the country associated with the record. |
| Data_Cleanse | Identifies and parses name, title, firm, phone number, Social Security information, dates, and email addresses. Data_Cleanse transforms enhance the input data by providing gender and first names; generate match standards; and convert sources to standard formats. |
| DSF2_Walk_Sequencer | Adds delivery sequence information to data that can be used with presorting software to quality for walk-sequencing discounts. |
| Geocoder | Uses geographic location of input data to assign latitude and longitude data. |
| Global_Address_Cleanse | Identifies, parses, validates, and corrects global address data such as primary number, name, and type, as well as directional and secondary data. |
| Global_Suggestion_List | Compares input addresses to provide suggestions for possible matching addresses. Can be used for a "did you mean 'x' address?" |
| Match | Identifies matching records based on input sets using a complex mulidimensional algorithm. Outputs unique ID, best record, and grouping data. |
| USA_Regulatory_Address_Cleanse | Identifies, parses, standardizes, and corrects USA addresses according to the US Coding Accuracy Support System (CASS). |
| User_Defined | Completely customizable transform using Python code. Can process records individually or as sets of data. |

**Table 4.6** Data Quality Transforms and Descriptions

| Transform Name | Description |
|---|---|
| Case | Splits data in a data flow into separated output branches of data based on input records that qualify specific conditions. |
| Map_Operation | Allows control over changing any SQL operation to any other SQL operation of a record against a target table. For example, INSERT statements can be changed to UPDATE statements. |
| Merge | Performs a UNION for all of two or more input streams of identical data in a data flow. |
| Query | Controls the read operations from one or more source tables. Similar to a SELECT statement. |
| Row_Generation | Generates a row of data identified by a single incrementing integer column. Useful for creating test sets of data for a target table. |
| SQL | Executes the SQL specified in a free-text field in the transform. Blindly pushes down whatever free-form SQL is entered. |
| Validation | Controls and measures how well an input set performs against business rules or logic. Captures and measures pass and fail statistics around the data processed. |
| XML_MAP | Handles complex levels of nesting present in input data. This is a finely tuned NRDM transform. |

**Table 4.7**  Platform Transforms and Descriptions

| Transform Name | Description |
|---|---|
| Entity_Extraction | Extracts entities and facts from any free-form text input source set. |

**Table 4.8**  Text Data Processing Transforms and Descriptions

Depending on the licensing of SAP Data Services, there are many built-in transforms that are great time-saving aids to any development task in SAP HANA. Many of these transforms were designed around data mart activities and create proper functioning star schemas as outlined in Chapter 2 of this book. We highlight some of the more useful transforms in this section by examine the top five Data Integrator and Platform transforms in terms of usefulness from a BI perspective for SAP HANA.

### The Query Transform

The Query transform is the heart of a data flow. It's singularly the most used transform in SAP Data Services. The Query transform performs all portions of the SELECT statement to prepare a read of data against a source table. The Query transform controls the SELECT, FROM, WHERE, and ORDER BY clauses. Functions can be called against columns from source tables. Tables can be joined, and these joins pushed can be down to source databases to return a unified record set. Also, complex WHERE clauses can be invoked to limit or push down the WHERE clause to the source database. The Query transform is incredibly important for controlling the push down of operations, so understanding its intricacies are important for proper data flow construction. The SELECT portion of the Query transform is housed in the MAPPING tab of the Query transform shown in Figure 4.27.

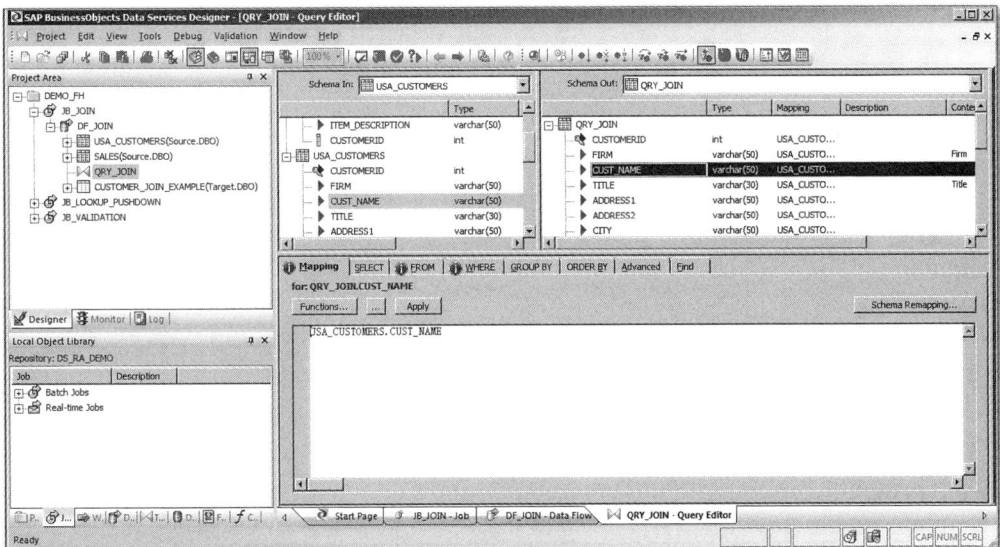

**Figure 4.27** SELECT Portion of SQL Read in the Mapping Tab of the Query Transform

In the MAPPING tab of the Query transform, a field can be straight mapped where the field CUST_NAME is just read from the source table. This produces the SQL in Listing 4.1.

```
SELECT  "USA_CUSTOMERS"."CUSTOMERID"  ,  "USA_CUSTOMERS"."FIRM"
,  "USA_CUSTOMERS"."CUST_NAME"  ,  "USA_CUSTOMERS"."TITLE"  ,
"USA_CUSTOMERS"."ADDRESS1"  ,  "USA_CUSTOMERS"."ADDRESS2"  ,
"USA_CUSTOMERS"."CITY"  ,  "USA_CUSTOMERS"."REGION"  ,  "USA_
CUSTOMERS"."POSTALCODE"  ,  "USA_CUSTOMERS"."COUNTRY"  ,  "USA_
CUSTOMERS"."BIRTHDATE"  ,  "USA_CUSTOMERS"."ID"  ,  "USA_
CUSTOMERS"."EMAIL"  ,  "USA_CUSTOMERS"."PHONE"  ,  "USA_
CUSTOMERS"."FAX"  ,  "USA_CUSTOMERS"."SOURCE"  ,  "USA_
CUSTOMERS"."DATE_MODIFIED"  ,  "USA_CUSTOMERS"."CUSTOMERTYPE"  ,
"SALES"."AMOUNT"  ,  "SALES"."ITEM_DESCRIPTION"
FROM "DBO"."USA_CUSTOMERS" "USA_CUSTOMERS" INNER JOIN "DBO"."SALES"
"SALES" ON ( "USA_CUSTOMERS"."CUSTOMERID"  =  "SALES"."CUSTOMERID" )

WHERE ( "USA_CUSTOMERS"."DATE_MODIFIED"  >= '2013.05.05 00:00:00') and
( "USA_CUSTOMERS"."DATE_MODIFIED"  <= '2013.05.11 00:00:00')
```
**Listing 4.1** SQL Pushed Down from the Query Transform

Notice that the SELECT portion of the SQL displayed in the USA_CUSTOMERS.CUST_NAME field is just straight mapped with no functions applied. However, if you chose to include any functions due to business rule necessity, then they would be included in the SELECT portion of this SQL statement.

Notice the FROM clause of the SQL in Listing 4.1 and the join on the USA_CUSTOMERS table and the SALES table. This portion of the SQL is handled in the FROM tab of the Query transform as shown in Figure 4.28.

In the FROM tab of the Query transform, simple joins between two tables, such as this example, can be constructed. However, you can fashion very complex joins with mixed types: INNER joins can now be mixed with OUTER joins. The entire join specifications happen in the JOIN PAIRS section of the tab, as displayed in Figure 4.27.

The WHERE clause of the SQL produced happens in the WHERE tab of the Query transform. This is shown as a simple date range example, but the WHERE can be as complex as necessary to satisfy business rules. The WHERE tab is depicted in Figure 4.29, and the WHERE clause text is simply typed into the tab in Designer.

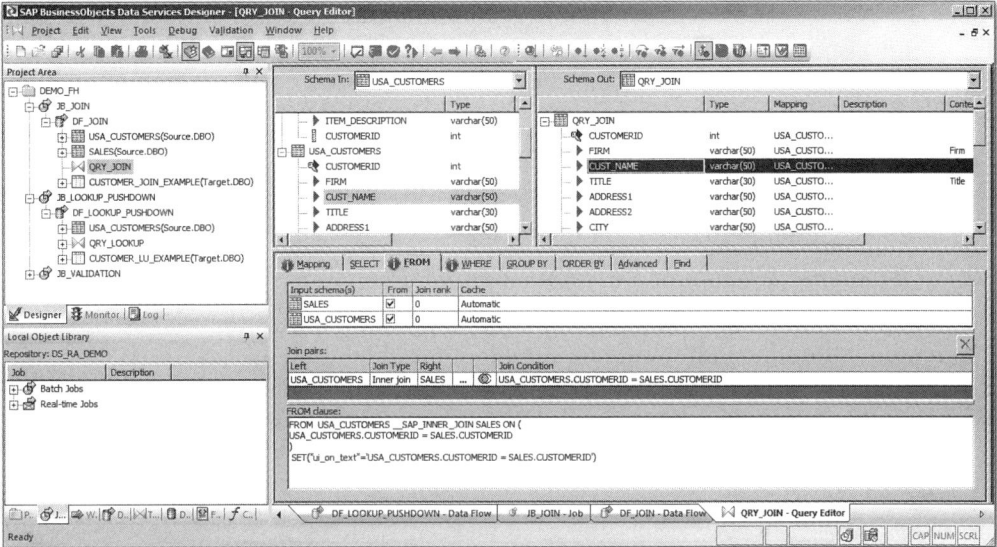

**Figure 4.28** FROM Clause Tab in the Query Transform

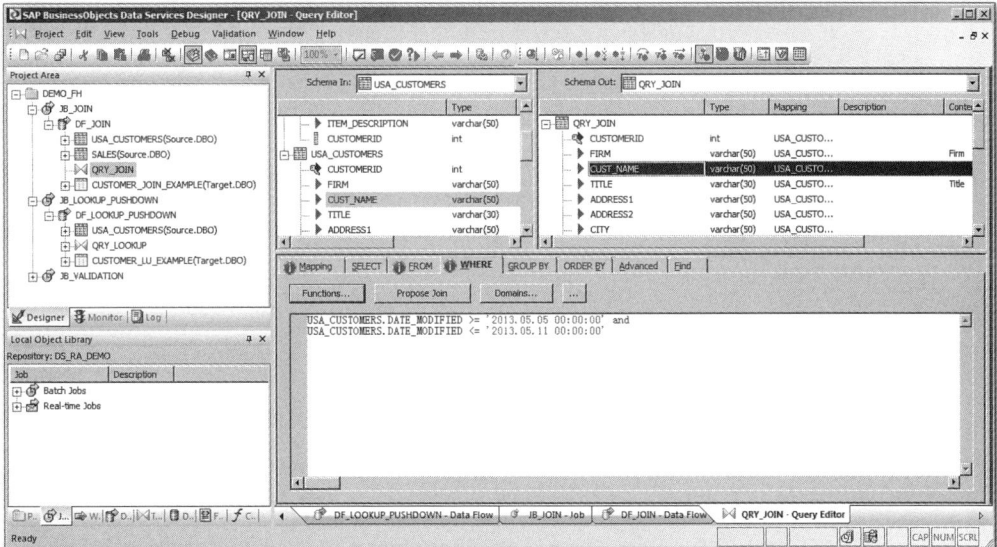

**Figure 4.29** WHERE Clause Tab in the Query Transform

You've seen how complex or simple SQL can be created using a `Query` transform in the SAP Data Services Designer. It can't be overstated that this transform is simply the most used transform in SAP Data Services, and it will be used extensively to design the read operations against your sources for loading data into SAP HANA. However, there are still four more transforms that make development much easier and faster for getting data into SAP HANA. The next of these transforms is the Table_Comparison transform.

### Table_Comparison Transform

Isolating changed data is very important for a number of reasons in ETL development, and developing for SAP HANA is no different. This can be easily accomplished by using a Table_Comparison transform to isolate changed records in a table, as shown in Figure 4.30.

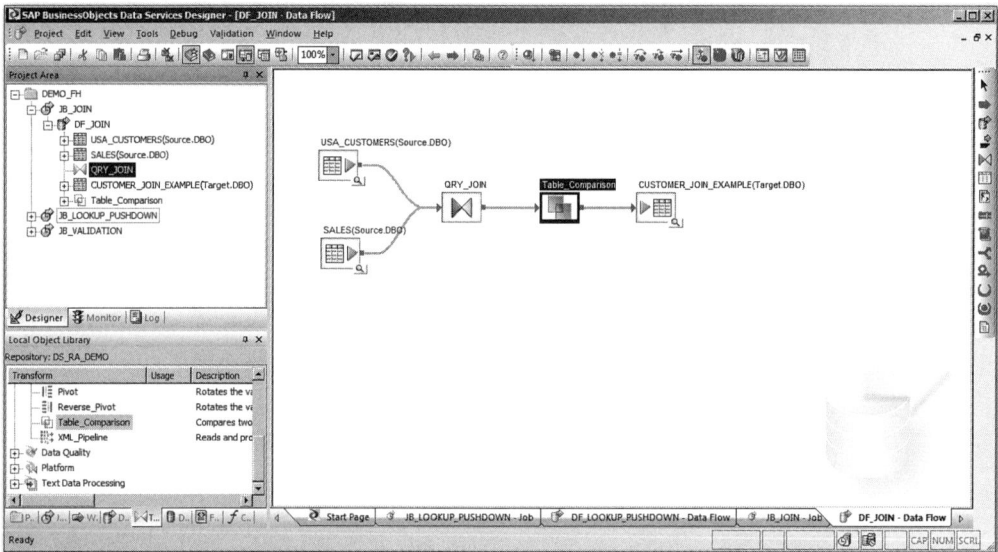

**Figure 4.30** Table_Comparison Transform to Isolate Changed Data from the Target

Data may change in a source, and the volume of that data loading to SAP HANA may be quite large, so it can be important to your cutover strategy to process only changed data.

Another situation where detecting changes are important is for recovery operations. If the SAP Data Services job fails, the data flow quits in mid-processing, and if the data flow isn't intelligent enough to know what records already exist in the target table, then the flow fails on recovery due to duplicate INSERTs. Situations like these are perfect examples of when to use a Table_Comparison transform.

A Table_Comparison transform is a drag-and-drop transform that detects whether records exist in a specified table by comparing key fields as well as nonkey fields. If a record exists and is unchanged from the input record, then no record is sent to the target SAP HANA table. If the record isn't found in the target table, then an INSERT SQL statement is produced to insert the record into the target table. If the record exists in the target table, and the record has changed, then an UPDATE statement is produced for the target table.

You need to set a few options after dropping the transform into the data flow. Set the comparison table to the proper table to compare in the TABLE NAME field; the example table in Figure 4.31 is the CUSTOMER_JOIN_EXAMPLE table. Then specify the input primary key field and the columns to compare in the fields: INPUT PRIMARY KEY COLUMNS and COMPARE COLUMNS, respectively.

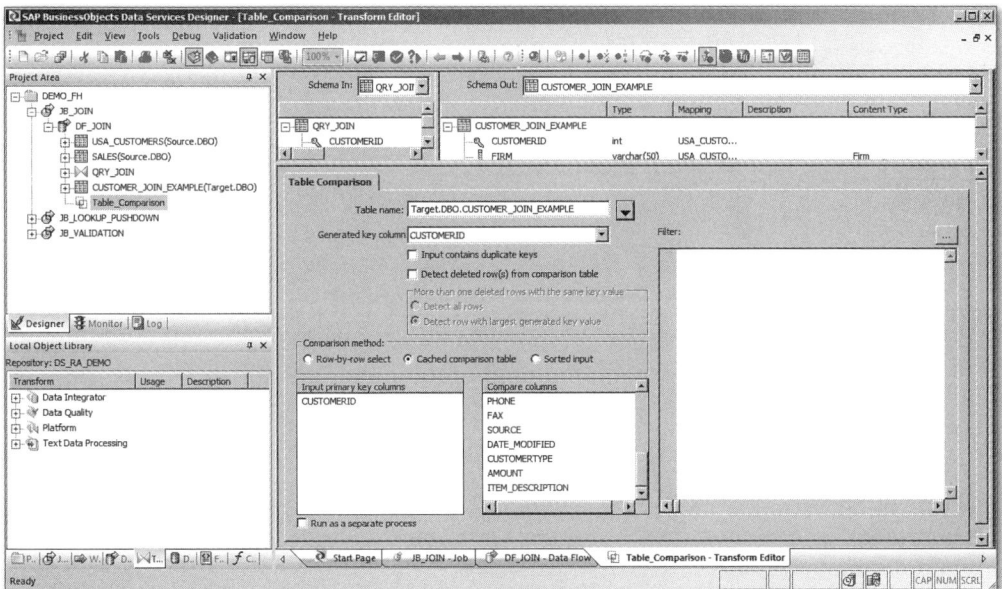

**Figure 4.31** Table_Comparison Transform Options in Designer

The `Table_Comparison` transform is now ready for use. This is a very useful transform for CDC operations and is generally one of the last transforms used before the target table. If you need to perform different operations on a record set based on the data contained in the record set, then use a `Case` transform.

### Case Transform

A `Case` transform is another very useful transform for splitting processing tasks based on decision logic. For example, business logic may call for value substitutions only when certain conditions are met for certain fields. This would be a perfect example of when to use a `Case` transform.

Take the example data flow in Figure 4.32. This data flow uses the `Case` transform to specify different values for an Internet customer over a customer that came into a retail store.

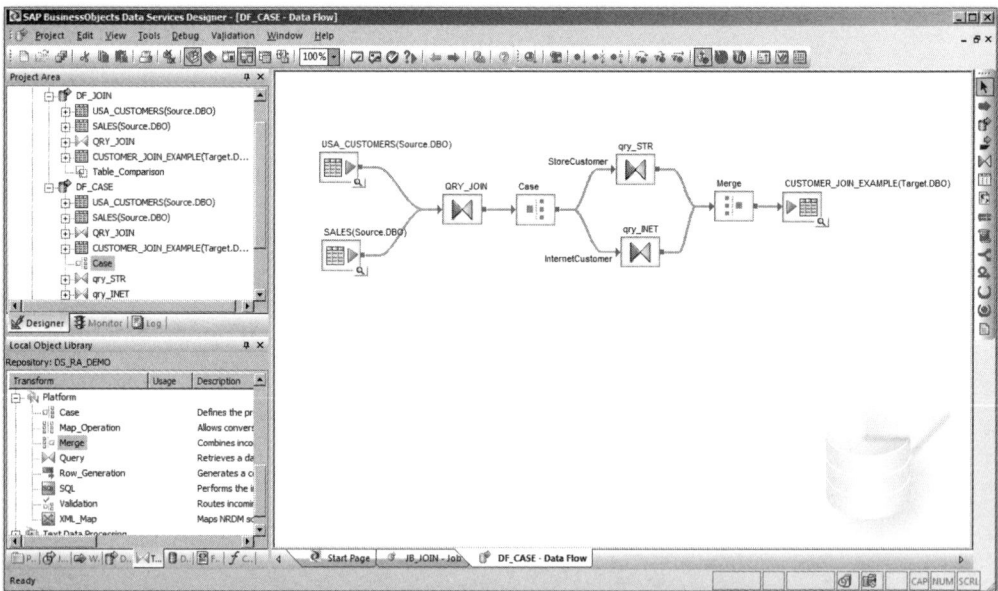

**Figure 4.32** Use a Case Transform for Independent Conditional Logic in Designer

The `Case` transform tests a CUSTOMER_TYPE field and splits the processing of the data into two streams: one for a CUSTOMER_TYPE value of 'Store' and another for a CUSTOMER_TYPE value of 'Internet'. Different values are then substituted in the two `Query` transforms: `qry_STR` for store values and `qry_INET` for Internet values. See how the `Case` transform is configured in Figure 4.33.

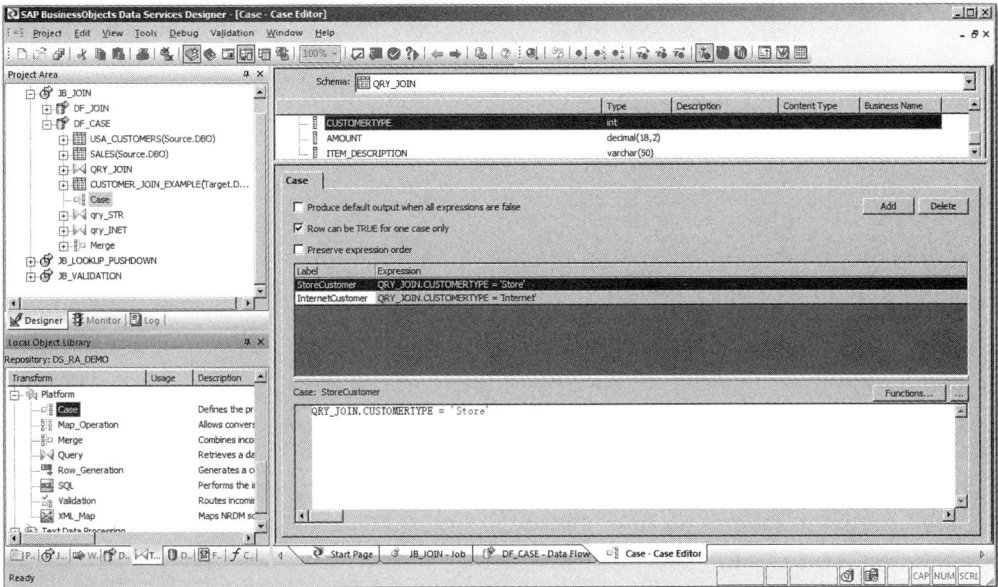

**Figure 4.33**  Configure the Case Transform in Designer

So far, we have basic to advanced SQL read processing with the `Query` transform, complex CDC target comparison processing with the `Table_Comparison` transform, and conditional logic handled within the data flow with the `Case` transform. These are all powerful complex transforms, and all are used to detect conditions in data. There is another very simple but powerful transform you can use if you know what you want to do with your data, and this is especially important for performance, which is vital for loading data into SAP HANA: the `Map_Operation`.

### Map_Operation Transform

The `Map_Operation` transform is deceptively simple — it only has five fields on INPUT ROW TYPE and OUTPUT ROW TYPE as illustrated in Figure 4.34.

The following choices are available for the OUTPUT ROW TYPE for each of the five fields:

▶ NORMAL
Sets the operation of a record back to NORMAL or just as the record was read.

189

▶ Update
Sets the operation of the output record to an UPDATE SQL statement.

▶ Insert
Sets the operation of the output record to an INSERT SQL statement.

▶ Delete
Sets the operation of the output record to a DELETE SQL statement.

▶ Discard
Sets the operation of the output so that no statement or output is produced. In essence, the row accomplishes nothing on the target table.

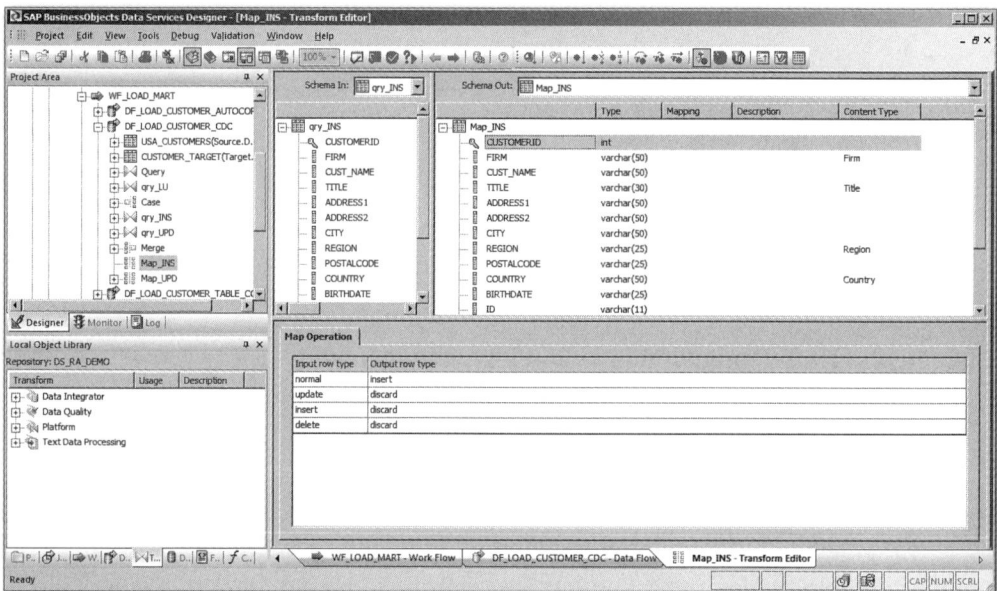

**Figure 4.34** Limited Configuration Settings of the Map_Operation Transform

This is such a simple transform that it may seem strange to mention its use as one of the top five transforms. The reason is simple: performance on loads. Performance is very important for an SAP HANA data conversion. If your code has already done the work to detect how to handle a target record, then just use this transform to set the output operations appropriately. This transform usually is used in conjunction with a Case transform and a Merge transform, as shown in Figure 4.35.

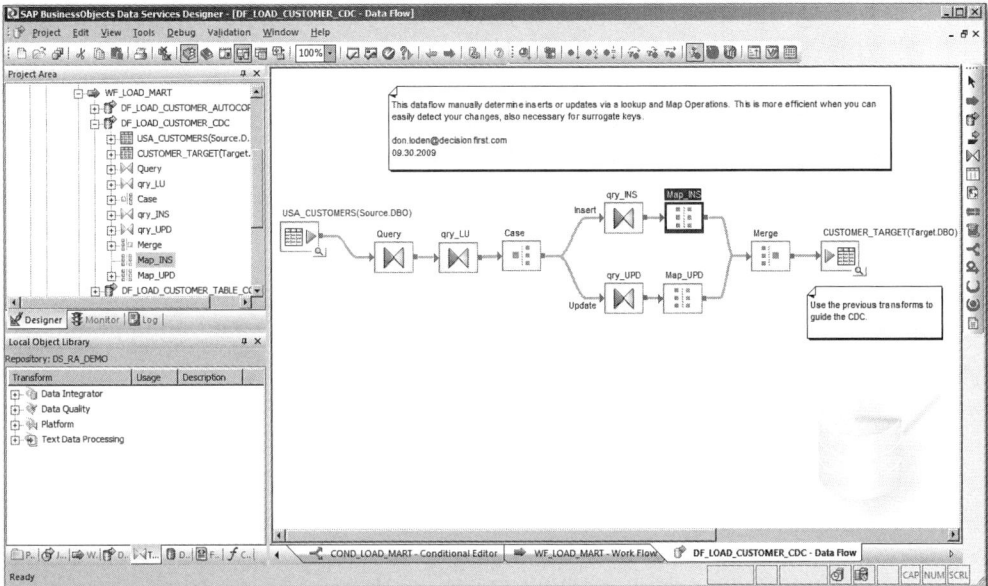

**Figure 4.35** Map_Operation Transform Used to Create Both INSERT and UPDATE Statements

The `Case` transform splits the processing after determining, in this case, the inserts and the updates. Then, the `Map_Operations` transform is used to convert the SQL statements to both `INSERT` and `UPDATE` statements in this example. After this, the `Merge` transform performs a `UNION` operation to merge the data streams back together before the target. Even with this simple example, you cut the workload in half from a typical autocorrect load operation and still maintain the recovery. You've already determined what to issue against the target table, so the autocorrect operation makes twice the work with no gain because it always issues both inserts and updates.

We've discussed the means to handle quite a bit of commonly processed logic with the first four commonly used transforms, but after you've performed all of the transformations, you need to ensure that your code did what you anticipated before you load your data to SAP HANA. To do this, we recommend the `Valida-tion` transform.

*Validation Transform*

The `Validation` transform simply validates your ETL code against your business rules to determine if the transformations were successful and performed the appropriate business logic. However, the `Validation` transform also captures statistics that can be used to report and measure your success or failure. Just by using the `Validation` transform, you'll gather metrics through built-in reports on percentages of success or failure. All of this is accomplished by merely inserting the `Validation` transform and making a few simple configurations. You insert the transform by placing it in a data flow from the PLATFORM node of the TRANSFORMS tab, as shown in Figure 4.36.

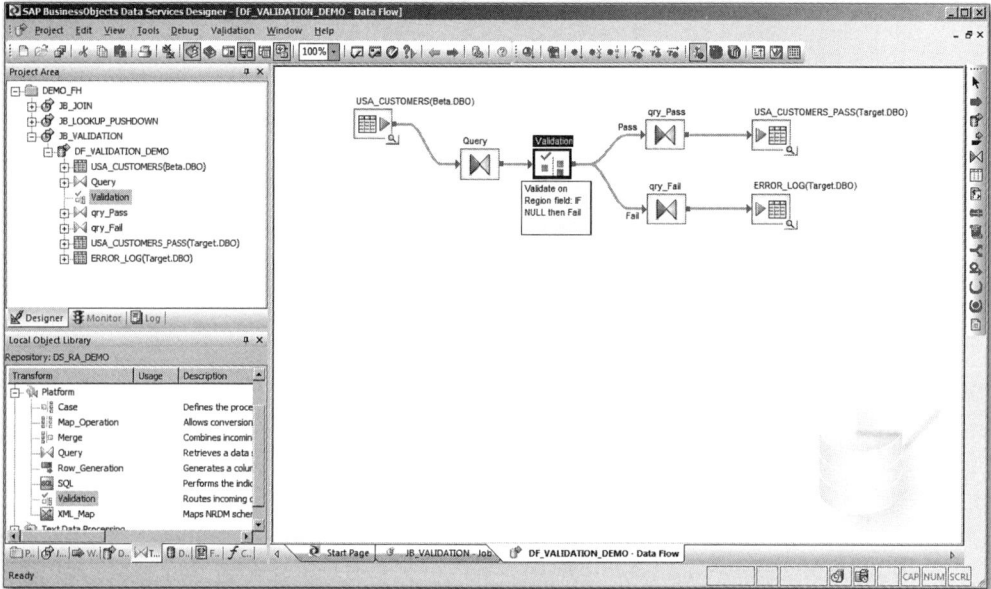

**Figure 4.36**   Use the Validation Transform to Check Rules and Gather Statistics

Then, double-click the `Validation` transform as shown in Figure 4.36 to set the configuration of what field(s) you want to validate. You accomplish the configuration by using the controls shown in Figure 4.37. This example is quite simple—you're validating whether the field REGION is not null. If the field is NULL, it will fail the condition, and the record will be sent to both output paths: the USA_CUS-TOMER_PASS table as well as the ERROR_LOG table.

You can easily configure this to only send to the failure path (ERROR_LOG), by selecting a different option for the ACTION ON FAIL field. Click the EDIT button in Figure 4.37 to get to the RULE EDITOR screen, as shown in Figure 4.38.

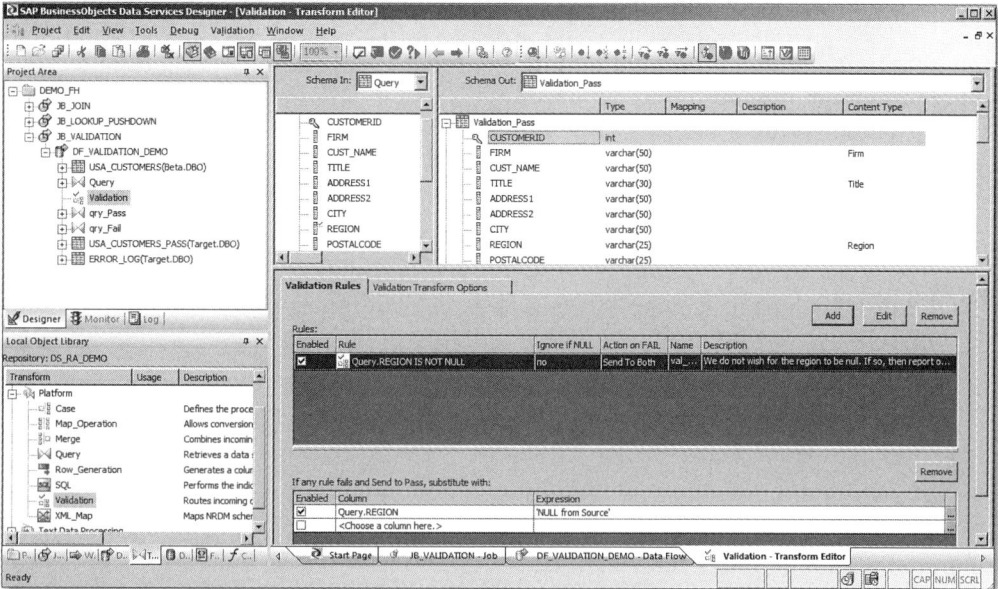

**Figure 4.37** Inside the Validation Transform Configuration

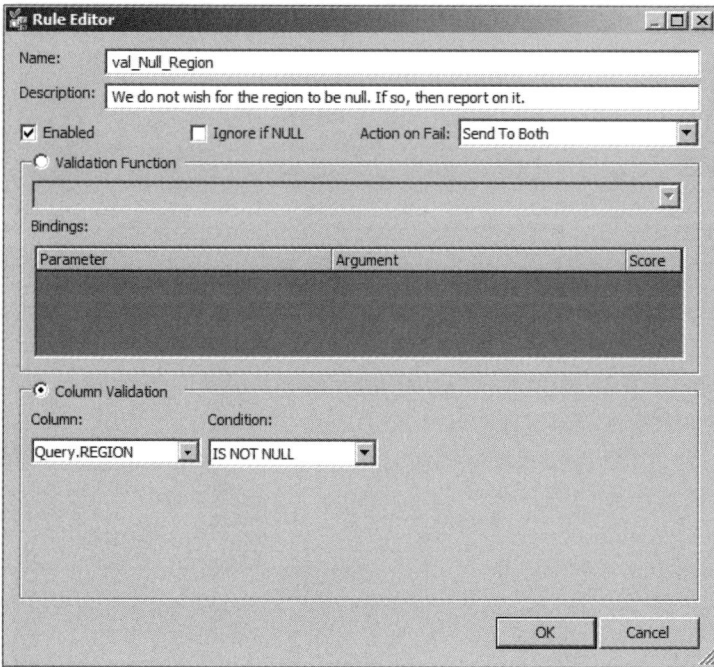

**Figure 4.38** Setting Your Comparison Expression in the Validation Transform

This is where all configurations for the field validations take place. You can validate as many fields as you want with as many complex validations as possible. This screen allows validations to be configured in the COLUMN VALIDATION section of this form if you create the validation rules within the `Validation` transform. SAP Data Services also allows for this transform to capitalize on custom validation functions that are written with SAP Data Services. Another option for consuming custom validation functions is the unique capability to allow the sharing of validation rules with SAP Information Steward. This requires a separate license because SAP Information Steward is a separate product, but this is certainly something to keep in mind because you can use validation functions that are created with this product as well. This allows for a modular rules-sharing capability where an ETL developer for an SAP HANA migration can leverage existing business rules validation functions or SAP Information Steward functions created and approved by business users.

We've covered what we consider to be the top five Data Integrator and Platform transforms, but there are two very important Data Quality transforms that are also worth noting for their importance for cleansing, standardizing, and matching data on the way into SAP HANA: `Data_Cleanse` and `Match`. The Data Quality transforms are not included with the runtime license of out-of-the-box SAP HANA but can be added as an additional license purchase. We include them in this chapter to show the powerful capabilities and use cases of the transforms and to support the case for quality data in SAP HANA because remember—the last thing you want to do in SAP HANA is replicate "fast trash".

### Data_Cleanse Transform

The `Data_Cleanse` transform is the first step in any data quality process for SAP HANA because it takes an input record and first breaks it into all of the record's individual logical components and then evaluates and enhances those components. Then, the `Data_Cleanse` transform gives an additional option of adding enhancements to the content of the data. These enhancements range from cleansing address values to comparing proper addresses or person or firm names to their standardized components. Cleansing records is more than just parsing the data with a substring and replacing functions. The `Data_Cleanse` transforms operates on the concept of breaking a record down to evaluate the data to its standard form.

Consider the following example of cleansing a customer record to its standard forms to correct customer name discrepancies before sending it to SAP HANA. Figure 4.39 shows customer data that needs to be cleansed to fix name variations; to provide standard names for SAP HANA, you insert a `Data_Cleanse` transform labeled the `EnglishNorthAmerican_Data_Cleanse` transform in Figure 4.39.

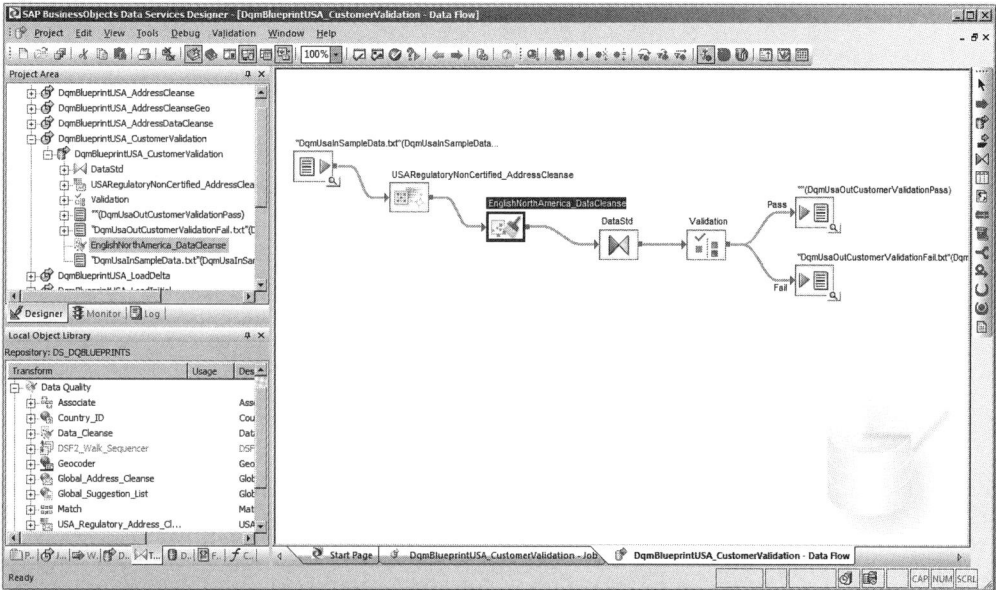

**Figure 4.39** Data_Cleanse Transform Highlighted to Standardize Customer Data

This transform requires configuring both input fields to break down to their standard forms for cleansing opportunities as well as selecting the fields from the `Data_Cleanse` transform's output that enhances the record by appending the cleansed fields onto the record. The configuration or "mapping" of the input fields is shown in Figure 4.40, and this is simply a mapping of the input fields from the previous transform to the transform input fields of the `Data_Cleanse` transform.

In this example, Table 4.9 shows the input field level mappings. The field being fed to the transform is on the right side in the INPUT SCHEMA COLUMN NAME column, and the `Data_Cleanse` transform field type mapping is in the left column labeled TRANSFORM INPUT FIELD NAME.

| Transform Input Field Name | Input Schema Column Name |
|---|---|
| FIRM_LINE1 | ORGANIZATION |
| MULTILINE1 | MISCELLANEOUS1 |
| MULTILINE2 | MISCELLANEOUS2 |
| NAME_LINE1 | NAME |

**Table 4.9**  Data_Cleanse Transform Field Level Input Mappings

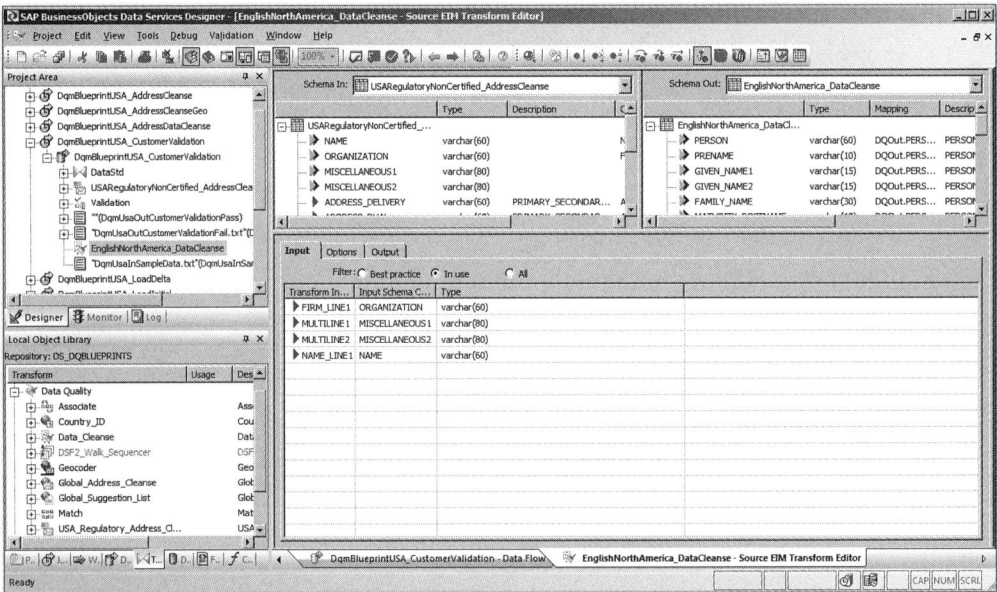

**Figure 4.40**  Configuring the Input Field Values of the Data_Cleanse Transform

After you've mapped the input fields, they are ready for the transform to break them down to their standard forms and evaluate the contents of the input fields. For example, the miscellaneous fields are treated as multiline information and examined as first names, last names, and both first and last names in one field. The NAME_LINE1 field is looking for customer name-specific values, and the FIRM_LINE1 field is looking for business names in any form. All of these values are evaluated against a data cleansing package for proper (language-specific) values for both person and firm data. Then, the output of this complex processing is returned from the output configuration of the transform that is shown in Figure 4.41.

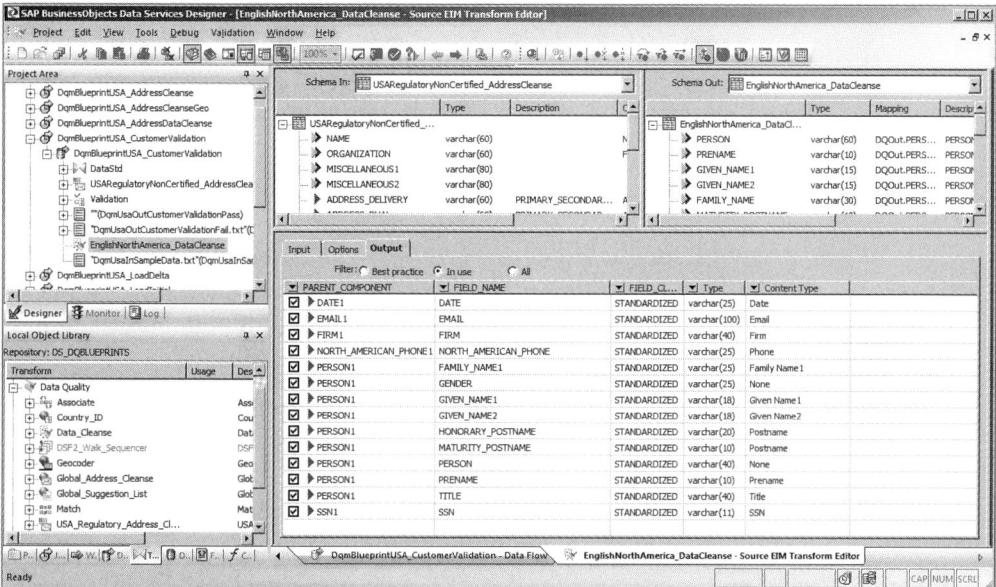

**Figure 4.41** Selecting the Output Enhanced (Standardized) Fields from the Data_Cleanse Transform

Upon selecting the `Data_Cleanse` transform's output fields, you want to return to the record set. The record is enhanced by the addition of these cleansed fields. No field contents in the OUTPUT tab of Figure 4.41 were available to the record before the `Data_Cleanse` transform was used. This content of enhanced fields was returned from using the `Data_Cleanse` transform and the complex processing of the data in SAP Data Services, but these are the kind of quality enhancements that are so important for avoiding "fast trash" data in SAP HANA. Now that data has been effectively cleansed, the data is ready for complex matching that can be invoked by the `Match` transform.

### Match Transform

The `Match` transform is incredibly powerful and does just what it states in the name: performs matching operations on data that is passed in as input values. This transform is used to deduplicate data on the way into SAP HANA.

For example, if you're combining multiple customer source data to use for reporting in SAP HANA, you can use the `Match` transform to expose and group duplicate records to have a best customer record as a single record. That record can be related to all of the individual customer records that make up that customer. Without data quality processing, this would not be possible in the SAP HANA calculation engine. In SAP HANA, you can see any type of calculation on the base repetitious customer records but never know that the customers were the same customer! This is why cleansing and matching are incredibly important in SAP HANA; not only are you getting quality data in SAP HANA and avoiding fast trash, but also with matching you can see a full 360-degree view of your customer data!

It's important to note that much like the `Data_Cleanse` transform just chronicled, the `Match` transform is much more than just a lookup type match or a series of simple outer joins. The `Match` transform uses a complex multidimensional algorithm to perform the matching. In the example shown in Figure 4.42, you can see that the highlighted `Match` transform (NAMEADDRESS_BATCHMATCH) is ready to receive both person and firm data for the preceding DATASTD query transform.

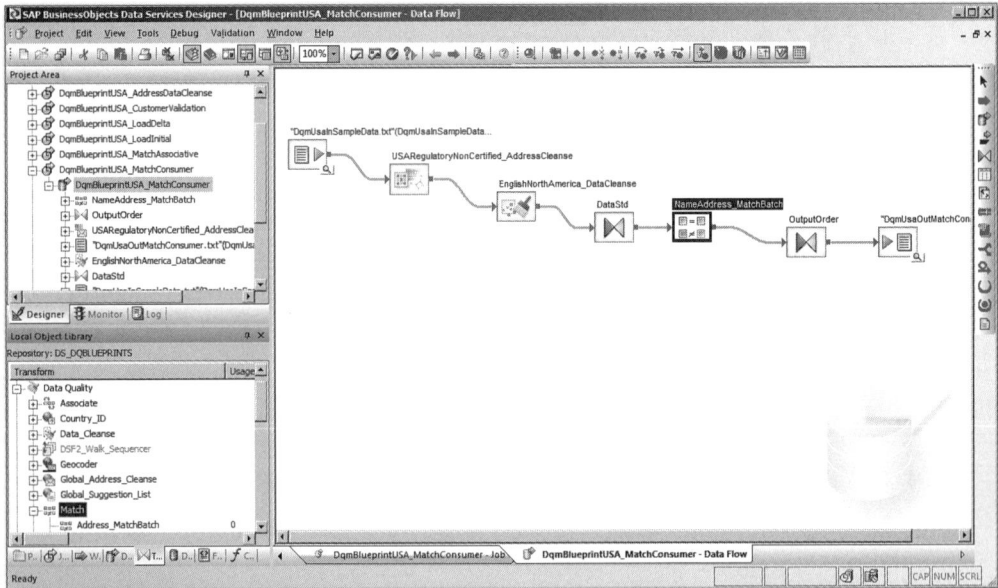

**Figure 4.42** Match Transform Ready for Person and Firm Data

Notice that the data has been standardized using the `EnglishNorthAmerica_Data-Cleanse` transform right before the `Query` transform. This is the same `Data_Cleanse` transform from the previous section of this chapter, and cleansing data before matching is always a best practice. When you match, you want standardized input data fed to the `Match` transform, and the most efficient way to do that is to use the `Data_Cleanse` transform. After the data is cleansed and standardized, you use the `Match` transform to evaluate the person and firm input fields shown in Figure 4.43 for consideration of matching in the transform.

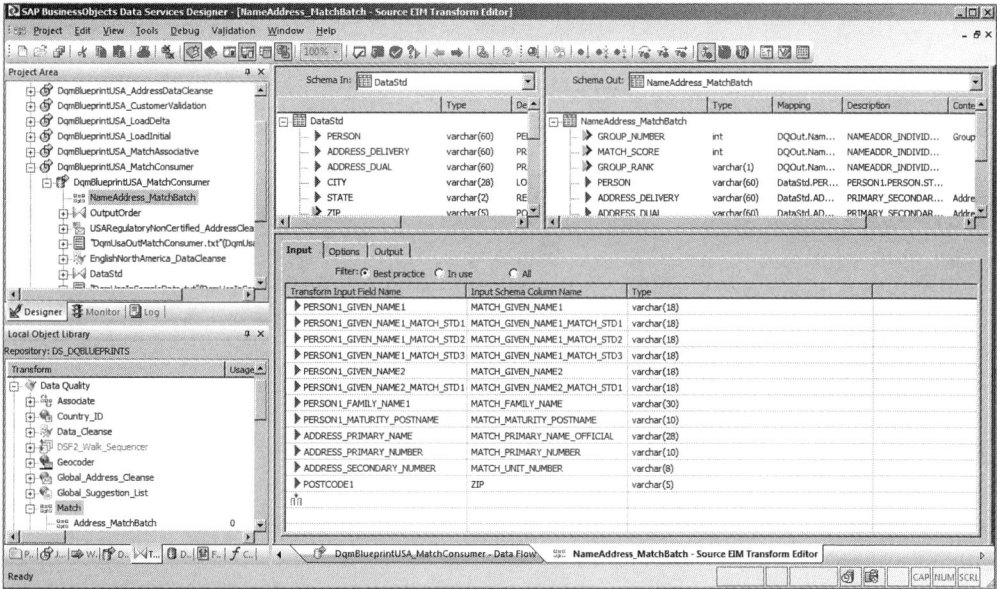

**Figure 4.43**  All of the Specified Input Fields for Matching Consideration

The `Match` transform uses these fields to see if the records score high enough in the processing steps to be individually considered a match based on each field's merit, and then the composite scoring of all of the fields in consideration are merged. A total score of all fields matching is used to determine if the record is a matching record. The matching transform in this example is just matching on all candidate records that are fed from the `DataStd` transform, however, you can also compare matches against an entirely different record set. This offers a great degree of flexibility. To configure the matching scores and `Match` transform behavior, use the MATCH EDITOR form in Figure 4.44 exposed on the OPTIONS tab, which is the middle tab shown in Figure 4.43.

This MATCH EDITOR form is elegantly simple yet quite powerful. This is where you specify the MATCH SCORE and NO MATCH SCORE to determine the threshold for whether or not the field scores as a matching element. The CONTRIBUTION gives the weight as a percentage of the total composite match score of the record. If the record's score is high enough, then the record is a match and grouped into a match group for the output of the transform. Let's establish definitions for each of the criteria fields shown in Figure 4.44 for more clarification:

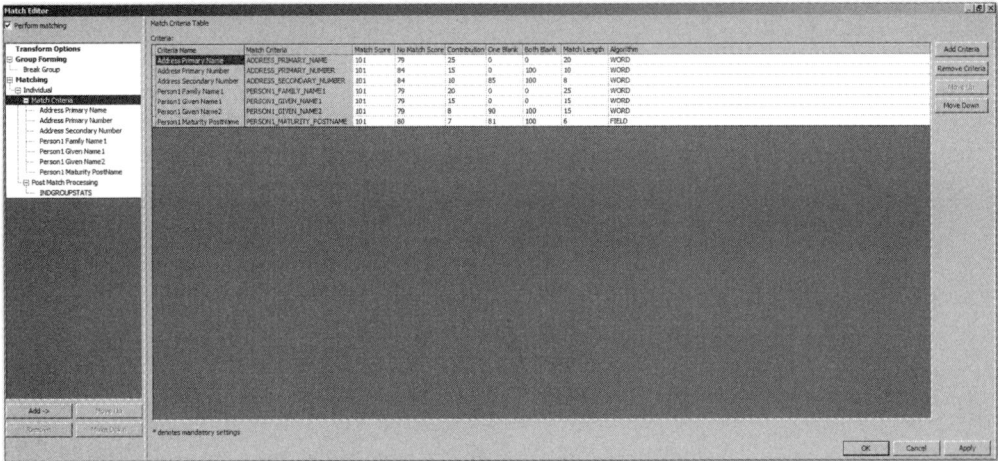

**Figure 4.44** The Matching Options Overview

▶ MATCH SCORE
If the field is above this value, the field is considered a match. If the value is set to 101, then all fields are considered, even if they aren't matches.

▶ NO MATCH SCORE
If the field is below this value, the field isn't considered a match. A -1 value forces the consideration of every field whether or not they are matches, if desired.

▶ CONTRIBUTION
This is the percentage of the field, and it's the maximum contribution weight of the field based on the matching score of the field. All contribution values specified must add up to 100%.

▶ ONE BLANK
This makes a decision on whether to use the field or ignore it in the scoring based on blanks or nulls on *one* side of the field's comparison.

▶ BOTH BLANK
This makes a decision on whether to use the field or ignore it in the scoring based on blanks or nulls on *both* sides of the field's comparison.

▶ MATCH LENGTH

This is the length of the string that is considered for the match.

▶ ALGORITHM

This is the algorithm used for matching in the transform. Can be word similarity, field similarity, geo proximity, numeric difference, or numeric percent difference based on the input field's data type.

All of these configuration settings are considered for the match; then the `Match` transform enhances the input data much like the `Data_Cleanse` transform, discussed earlier, by appending additional fields onto the output record. These additional fields are shown in Figure 4.45.

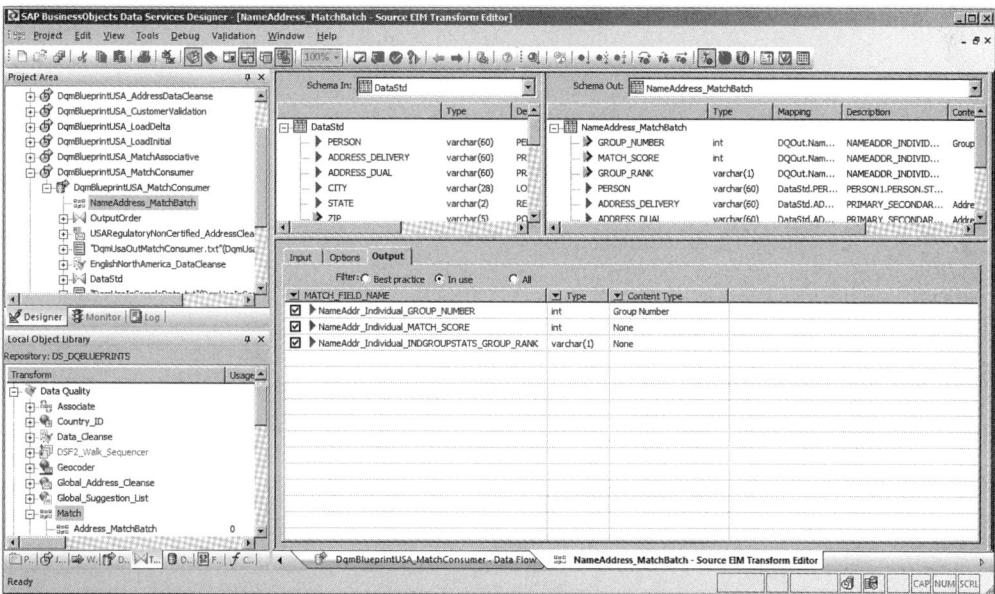

**Figure 4.45** Matching Output Fields: Scores, Groups, and Ranks

The output fields in this example that get appended onto the record are NAME-ADDR_INDIVIDUAL_GROUP_NUMBER, NAMEADDR_INDIVIDUAL_MATCH_SCORE, and NAMEADDR_INDIVIDUAL_INDGROUPSTATS_GROUP_RANK. These values are simply the group number for the match to be used as an identifier to cluster matching records together, the score each record received as a composite for all of the comparisons, and the ranking of the match groups, respectively. These fields can be used in numerous ways to associate records and provide relationships on records that would have never been seen before.

It's easy to see why data quality transforms are important to consider for SAP HANA because this type of processing is simply not available in SAP HANA. SAP HANA contains numerous built-in and calculation abilities, but it's absolutely lacking certain functionality to truly reach the pinnacle of quality data in SAP HANA. This is why the combination of SAP HANA calculation engine processing with the proper data preparation with SAP Data Services makes for a completely unique solution of reaching answers at never seen before speed—on correct and complete data. While the transforms are the "heart" of SAP Data Services and provide tremendous power on working through data and data quality issues, there are also a number of built-in functions present in SAP Data Services.

**Built-in Functions**

Like many software tools, SAP Data Services provides a set of built-in functions. Functions in SAP Data Services differ from transforms in that functions operate on columns specifically rather than transforms that operate on entire sets of data. In SAP Data Services, database and application functions, custom functions, and most built-in functions can be executed in parallel within the transforms in which they are used, but you also have the ability to run resource-intensive functions, such as `lookup_ext` (lookup function) and `count_distinct` (aggregate function), as a separate subdata flow that uses separate resources (both memory and computer) from each other. Built-in functions save development time and resources, and SAP Data Services contains a large library of built-in functionality.

SAP Data Services boasts 130 built-in functions that are ready for use. Although this is far too many to review in detail in this text, there are complete descriptions within the SAP Data Services technical manual supplied with the product. The technical manual provides a complete definition as well as great examples of how to use each function within data flows and syntax examples. This is a very useful resource to an SAP HANA developer who may be unfamiliar with the function syntax. We'll discuss how the functions are grouped logically in the technical manuals as well as show an example of how the functions are used inside a query transform.

The 130 built-in functions in SAP Data Services are grouped into 14 function categories. The categories are shown in Figure 4.46 in the SELECT FUNCTION dialog box and are described in Table 4.10.

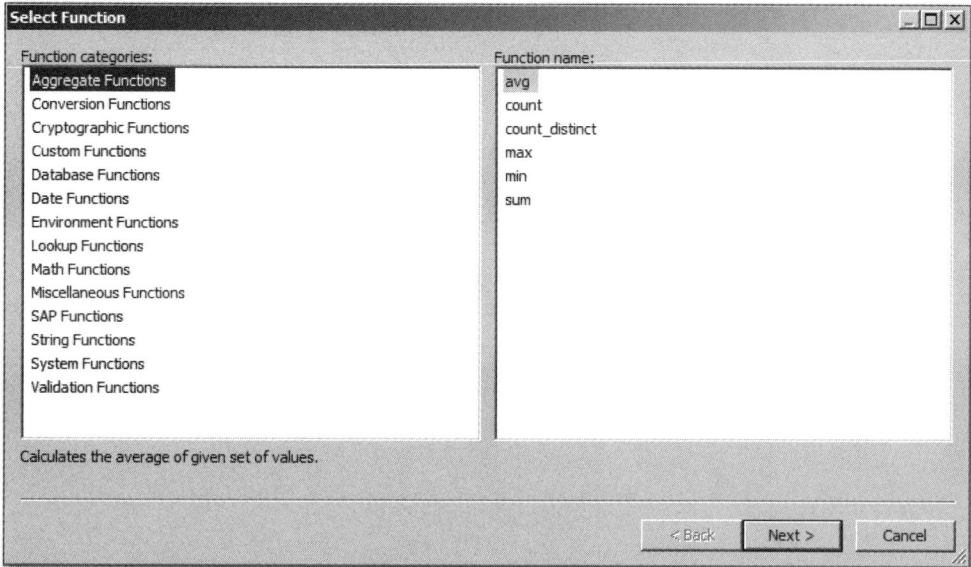

**Figure 4.46** Fourteen Groups of Built-In Functions in Designer

| Function Group Name | Description |
| --- | --- |
| Aggregate Functions | Aggregation operations such as average, sum, and count. |
| Conversion Functions | Convert between data types, for example, dates to text, numeric to text, varchar to long, and long to varchar. |
| Cryptographic Functions | Encryption and decryption functions. |
| Custom Functions | Developer-built custom functions and all GUI parameters just like any other built-in function. |
| Database Functions | Database functions such as the SQL function to call explicit SQL statements, total rows of a table, and key generation to generate keys for a database table. |
| Date Functions | Numerous date manipulation functions. |
| Environment Functions | Functions specific to the SAP Data Services environment and development platform. |
| Lookup Functions | Complex lookup functions allowing lookups to return values from any datastore connection. |
| Math Functions | Numerous mathematical functions. |

**Table 4.10** SAP Data Services Built-In Function Groups

| Function Group Name | Description |
|---|---|
| Miscellaneous Functions | Function grouping for a variety of useful functions that don't fit into any of the categories. |
| SAP Functions | SAP application-specific functions. |
| String Functions | Numerous string manipulation functions. |
| System Functions | System functions such as executing external programs and sending email. |
| Validation Functions | Functions to validate data and field contents; all have a Boolean return. |

**Table 4.10**  SAP Data Services Built-In Function Groups (Cont.)

SAP Data Services contains many functions to aid development and speed the task of realizing data flows and complex job logic. Table 4.10 is just a starting point to explore all of the functions that are available to the developer. However, the way that the functions are used in SAP Data Services data flows is the same no matter the function. To use the UPPER() function to convert a name field to uppercase, follow these steps:

1. Navigate to the column in the output schema of the Query transform where you want to use a function, as shown in Figure 4.47.

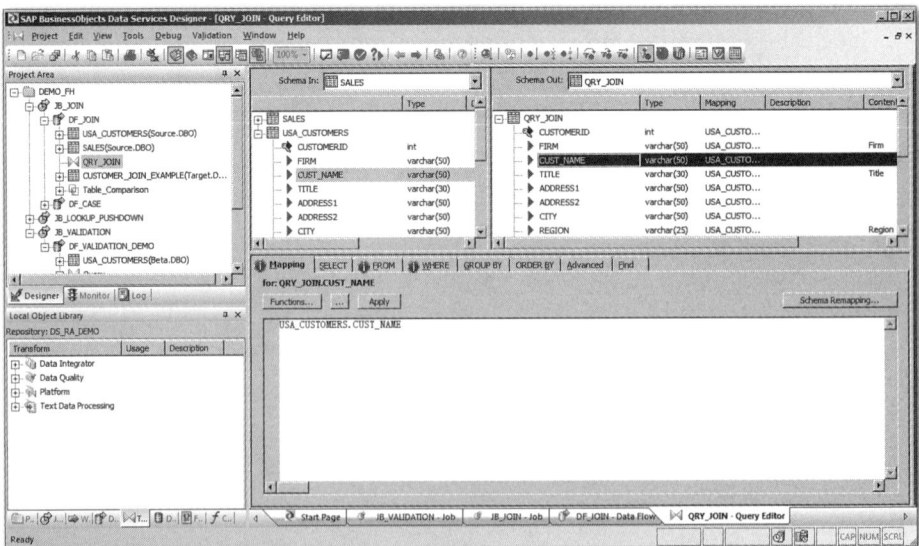

**Figure 4.47**  CUST_NAME Field Ready for the UPPER() Function

2. Click the FUNCTIONS button in Figure 4.47 to show the dialog box to select the UPPER function under STRING FUNCTIONS (Figure 4.48).

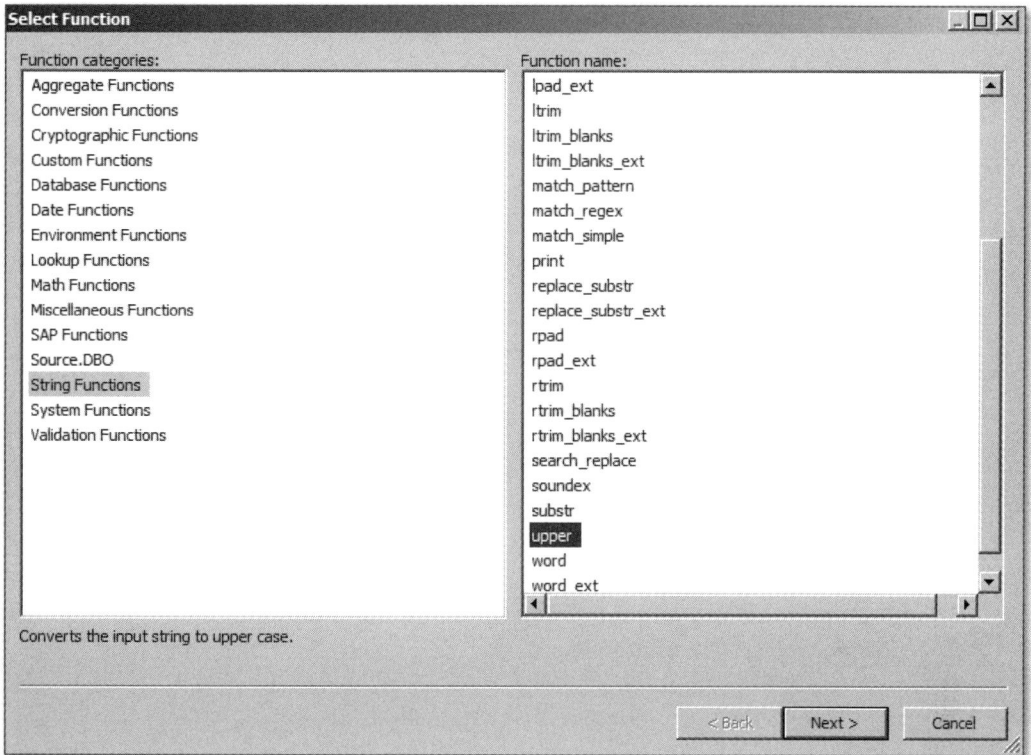

**Figure 4.48**   Select Function Dialog Box to Choose the UPPER Function

3. Click NEXT after selecting the UPPER function.

4. The DEFINE INPUT PARAMETER(S) dialog box appears, as shown in Figure 4.49. Fill in the INPUT STRING field. You may leave the INPUT LOCALE field blank because it's optional.

5. Click FINISH in the INPUT PARAMETERS dialog box to go back to the output schema of the CUST_NAME field and the fully realized function in Figure 4.50.

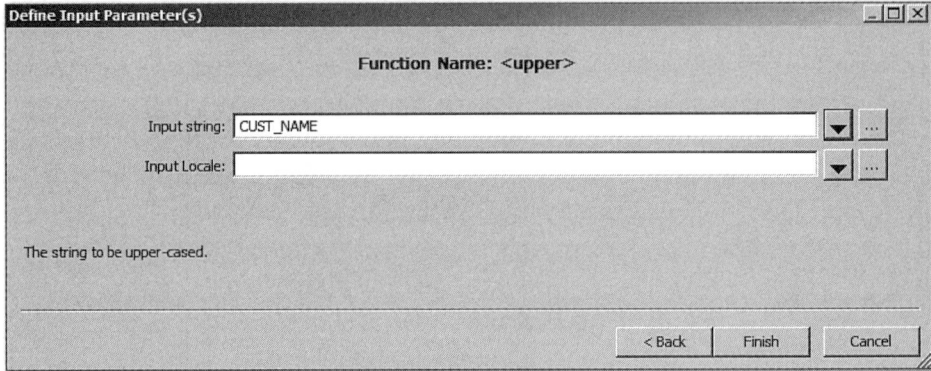

**Figure 4.49**   Using Define Input Parameters Input String Field to Map the UPPER Function

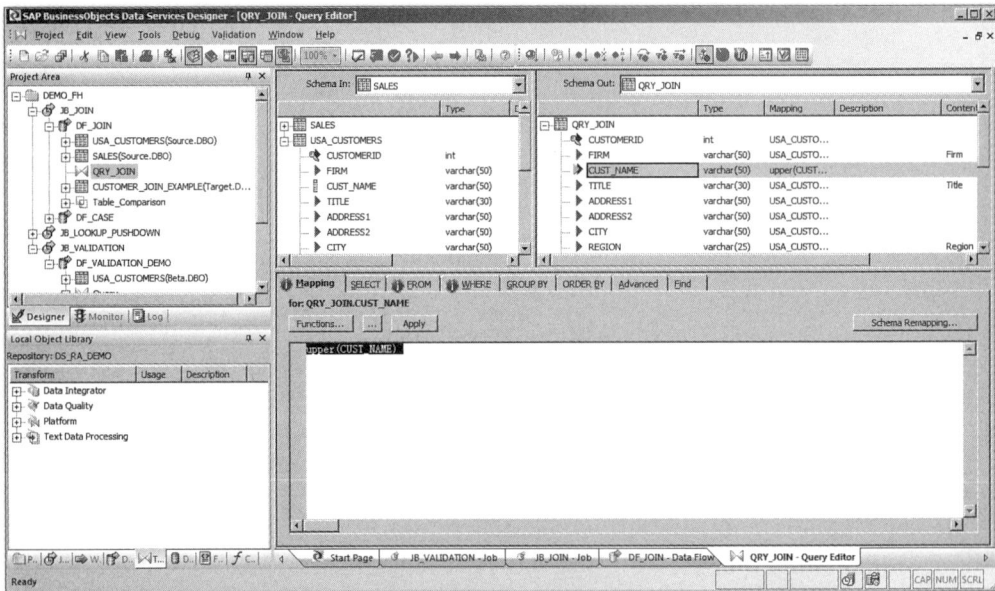

**Figure 4.50**   Fully Realized Upper Function in Designer

This is a very simple function example, but it's a great example of how to use the built-in function GUI. This GUI is available for any of the functions in SAP Data Services regardless of whether they are built-in functions or custom functions that a developer creates. This way, the development team preparing the data for SAP HANA only needs to be familiar with one function syntax and interface in SAP Data Services rather than understanding the functions present in all of the source databases from the legacy systems that are combined in SAP HANA. After examining the built-in functions, it's clear that it's easy to accomplish many things with them, but sometimes logic for SAP HANA data provisioning is either too complex or out of scope for built-in functions. Fortunately, SAP Data Services allows you to create your own custom functions, as we'll discuss in the next section.

### 4.1.6  Custom Functions and Scripts

Custom functions are exactly as they sound SAP Data Services allows a developer to create custom functions for reusing logic by placing that logic into a custom function container object. This allows any SAP Data Services developer to use this custom function just as you would any of the built-in functions covered in the previous section complete with a GUI "wrapper" for the parameters of the custom function.

This is really useful when you have a complex task or logic that needs to be used repeatedly by a team. The idea is to first create the function, and then any member of the team can use the code anywhere in the SAP Data Services jobs.

One use case that we see often is a complex job initialize script to control the change data capture behavior of a source. These initialize functions can be somewhat complex, and most batch jobs that are running as *delta* jobs (or jobs that process only changed data) require some type of initialize function to control variables that set date ranges or processing ranges with a beginning and ending value to select changed data. A function, such as this initialize function, is created in a custom function SMART EDITOR window shown in Figure 4.51.

The Smart Editor allows a developer to free-form code any type of logical operation that is necessary in an SAP Data Services job for provisioning into SAP HANA. The function logic looks complex, and it certainly can be! The real benefit is the reusability of the complex logic by other developers on the team that don't have to know (or even care!) about the inner workings of the function. From their perspective, the function is just a screen of input parameters as shown in Figure 4.49. This distribution of duties in the SAP HANA project makes sure that the complex logic is correct and lends itself to a team with varying levels of development experience.

To create a new custom function and find the SMART EDITOR screen, browse to the FUNCTIONS tab in the LOCAL OBJECT LIBRARY in the bottom-left corner of Designer and right-click CUSTOM FUNCTIONS. Then, select NEW from the popup window, as shown in Figure 4.52.

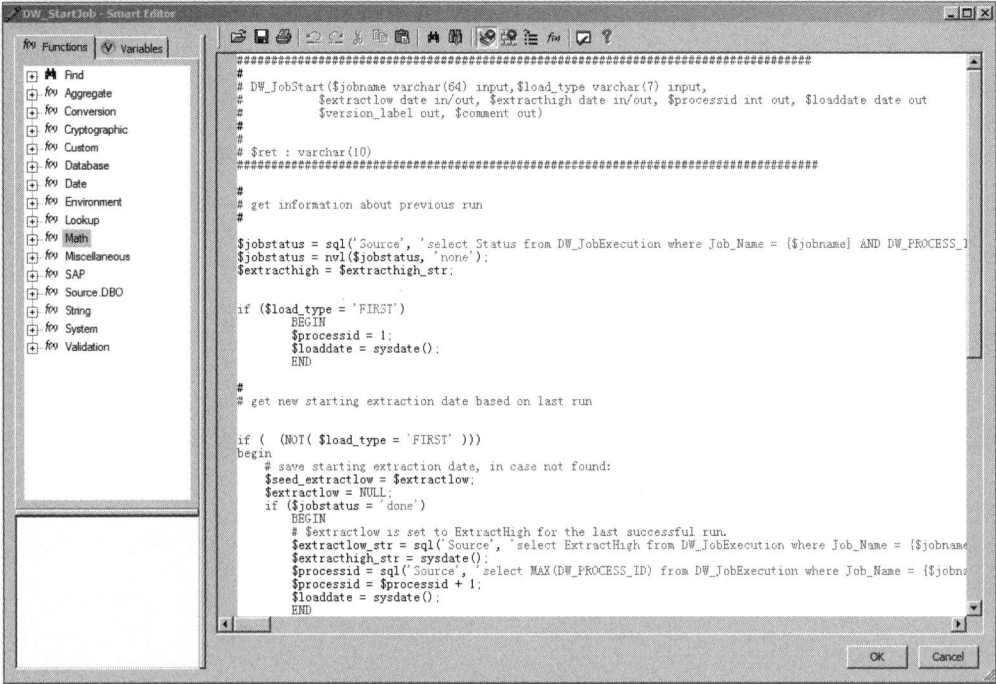

**Figure 4.51** Custom Function Smart Editor in Designer

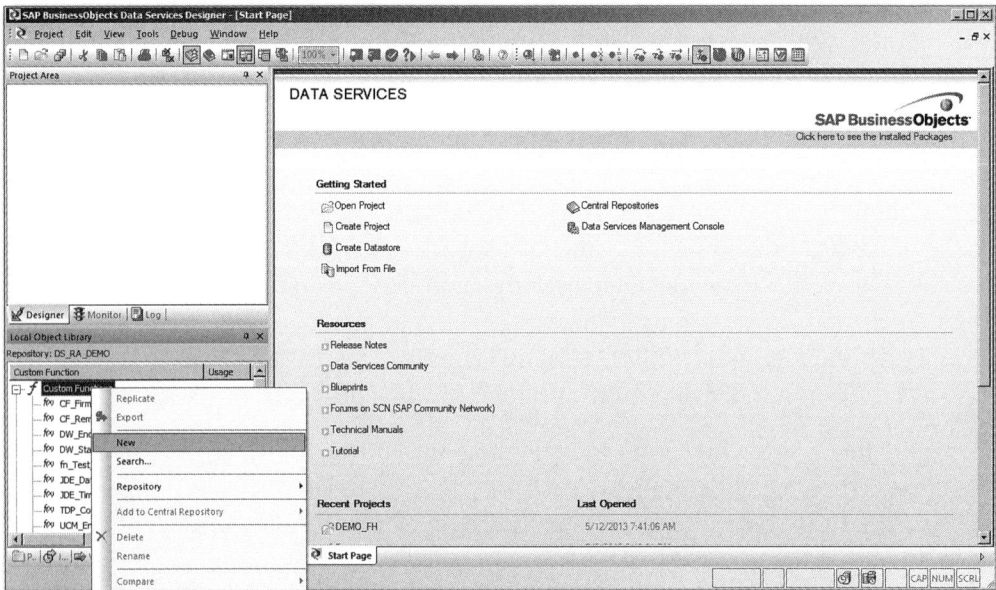

**Figure 4.52** Context Menu for Creating a New Function

You then use the Smart Editor to write whatever function is needed for the task. After you have the function crafted, you can use your new function. We've already seen that functions can be called from within Query transforms, but this example of an initialize function wouldn't make sense in that context. A function in a column of a Query transform is called once for every record, or iteratively. By definition, you only want to call an initialize function once at the beginning of an SAP Data Services job. To accomplish this singular call, you need to use a script object.

A *script object* is a single-use object that is a free-form text type tool in SAP Data Services. Recall that script use cases occur when you want to call or perform steps only once. A script reads left to right, top to bottom, and performs whatever functions are called in the order that the script sees them. Scripts are highlighted in Figure 4.53; the arrow on the right shows where the script control is located.

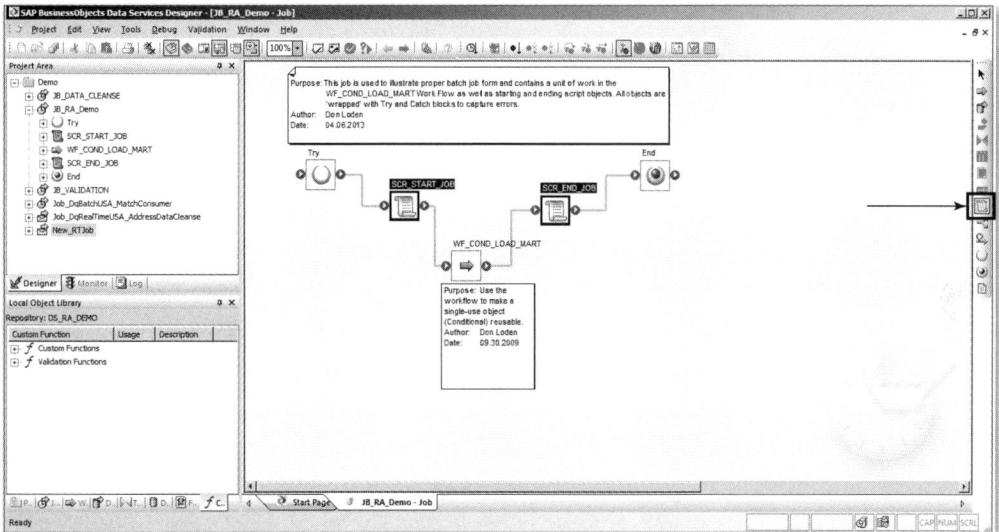

**Figure 4.53** Where to Find Script Controls in Designer

The script is used to bind variables that are used as input parameters to control logic in the job. For example, the initialize script referenced in the previous examples would be placed in the script to be called only once but also the variable assignments would happen in the script. Both the script function call (which is highlighted) and the variable assignments (both in the highlight and the text above) are shown in Figure 4.54. Variables are preceded with "$" and are needed in this format by SAP Data Services.

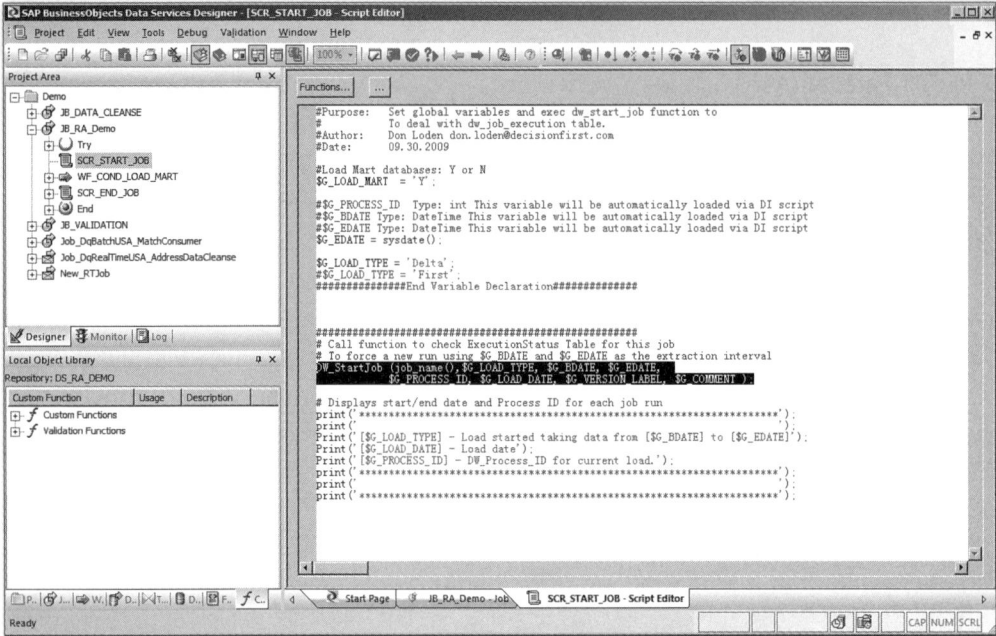

**Figure 4.54**  SCR_START_JOB Script Object Contents Calling a Custom Function

This way, when the script is finished executing, the custom function has performed its work and figured out the beginning and ending date values to pull the data as cited earlier in Figure 4.51. Then, the values of the upper- and lower bound date are assigned to variables in the script shown in the highlighted text in Figure 4.54.

We've exhausted most of the SAP Data Services controls for logic in your SAP HANA data journey at this point. You've seen how there are numerous built-in functions and transforms that save time and developer effort and handle both simple and complex transformations. Then, when you need to take logical operations beyond what is included with SAP Data Services, you can use custom functions and scripts. However, with all of these examples, we've been connecting to source database tables. There may come a time when you need to load data from text files into SAP HANA, or you might need to combine the file data with data from database tables. This is certainly possible with SAP Data Services, but you need to use a file format.

### 4.1.7  File Formats

A *file format* is much like a datastore connection, which was covered in Section 4.1.2, except that it connects to flat files of varying types. A file format object is a multiuse object that connects to a flat file and acts as a metadata wrapper to define both the connection and characteristics of the particular file. You can find the flat file object by browsing to the FORMAT tab in the LOCAL OBJECT LIBRARY in the bottom-right corner of Designer and expanding the FLAT FILES node, as shown in Figure 4.55.

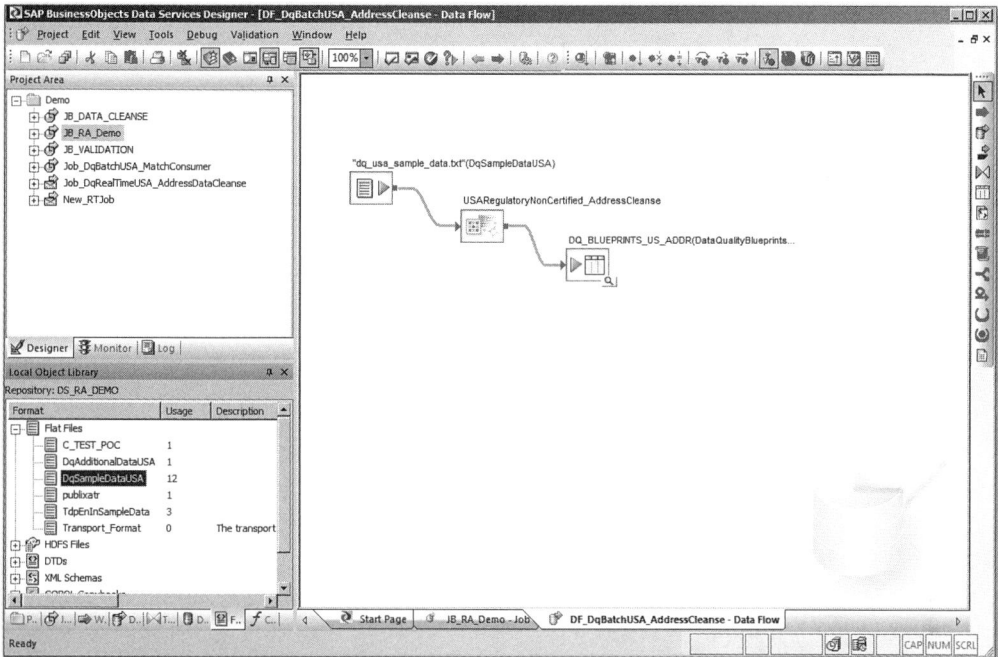

**Figure 4.55**  Flat File as a Source Object in a Data Flow in Designer

We've been presented with this scenario numerous times where a business receives a data feed as a file from a vendor or a customer, and that data must be merged into a BI data mart structure for reporting. This is the same challenge for SAP HANA as it is for other traditional legacy database platforms. Fortunately, the file format object makes this task simple, and the flat file object ensures that this task is repeatable as well. To create a new flat file object, right-click on the FLAT FILE node, and select NEW from the popup menu. This brings you to the FILE FORMAT EDITOR, as shown in Figure 4.56.

The FILE FORMAT EDITOR allows for almost any imaginable combination of options for dealing with flat file connections and characteristics. Essentially the editor is broken into three sections. The left side, or properties/values section, allows settings of various fields to drive flat-file behavior in SAP Data Services in everything from connections to delimiters. The upper-right side of the editor (the column attributes section) shows the column definitions, and the lower-right side (the data preview section) shows the data preview when data is available from the connection. If no data is available, the text No DATA appears, as shown in Figure 4.56.

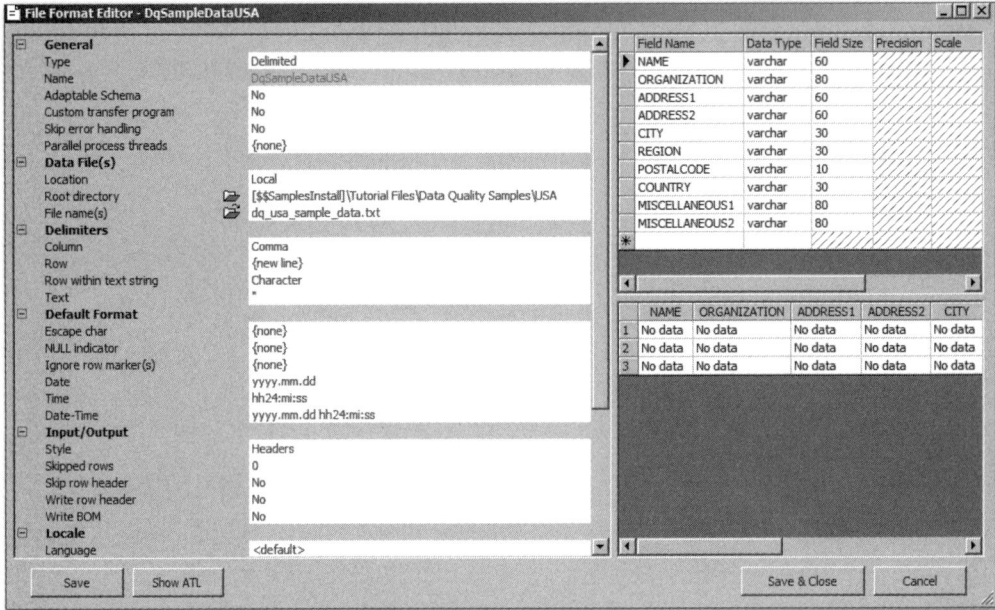

**Figure 4.56**  Configuring the Flat File Form in the File Format Editor in Designer

There are more options in this object than we'll cover in this chapter, but to ensure that all functionality is covered, we'll review the sections of fields present in the object. These sections are outlined in Table 4.11.

| Flat File Editor Section Name | Description |
| --- | --- |
| GENERAL | Set options such as whether the file is delimited or fixed width and whether to process the data in parallel. |
| DATA FILES | Specify the connection to the flat file. |
| DELIMITERS | Configure the type and style of the delimiter if the file is a delimited type file. |

**Table 4.11**  Flat File Option Groups

| Flat File Editor Section Name | Description |
|---|---|
| DEFAULT FORMAT | Specify escape characters or NULL indicators and date formatting. |
| INPUT/OUTPUT | Configure whether or not to skip rows or use the row header as the column headers. |
| CUSTOM TRANSFER | Specify custom transfer protocols, if used. |
| LOCALE | Set language and code page settings for file interpretation. |
| ERROR HANDLING | Handle all records that don't meet the definitions of the file. Determine what happens if data fails the read of the flat file object. |

**Table 4.11**  Flat File Option Groups (Cont.)

As you can see, you can deal with about any option for file-based connections with this object in SAP Data Services. This makes reading files quite simple. It's important to note that many of these field settings shown in Figure 4.56 can also be bound to variables, which dramatically increases the reusable nature of this connection. Take for instance a situation where you are always presented with the same data structure, but the file name or location for the connection is different. In this scenario, you bind the LOCATION field, ROOT DIRECTORY field, and FILE NAME(S) field (all shown in Figure 4.56) to variables to create a reusable object. This simplifies development and makes maintenance much easier.

Another important aspect of the flat file object in SAP Data Services is the fact that it acts as a metadata level object and allows the same abstraction layer for flat files as is present for datastores against database tables. The flat file object connects the software to the flat file data; however, to SAP Data Services, the data that is being processed in the data flow isn't different from data from any type of database table. This abstraction layer and the ability to manage transformations on any type of data the same way is a great strength of the tool.

This simplicity of management and the power of the transformations make SAP Data Services the obvious choice for batch loads into SAP HANA. This is great for loading data in batch, but what about transforming data in real time? SAP Data Services provides this capability as well, but you need to use a real-time job to accomplish this.

### 4.1.8 Real-Time Jobs

SAP Data Services offers a real-time jobs platform that allows complex transformations to happen in real time from any source application that can produce a web service output. This means that any application that can produce a web service for consumption can be echoed into SAP HANA. This echo can be a direct replication of data, but more than likely, it will consist of complex transformations. Many times, these complex transformations are not just around business rules that create uniform data or get data into better structures for performance as we've discussed before. Sometimes data quality needs to be addressed on the way into SAP HANA. For instance, addresses may need to be corrected using complex data quality algorithms, or customers or vendors may need to be standardized or deduplicated before loading to SAP HANA.

Real-time jobs in SAP Data Services are *stateless* application constructs. This means that all of the logic and functionality is encapsulated within the SAP Data Services real-time job. This way, another application doesn't have to have any knowledge of what is going to happen in the SAP Data Services real-time job. As a high-level example, a source application produces a web service in an XML format that an SAP Data Services exports to a URL that is hosted on the SAP Data Services job server. This process invokes the SAP Data Services real-time job to process the data, and the data is output to SAP HANA. An example of a real-time job is depicted in Figure 4.57.

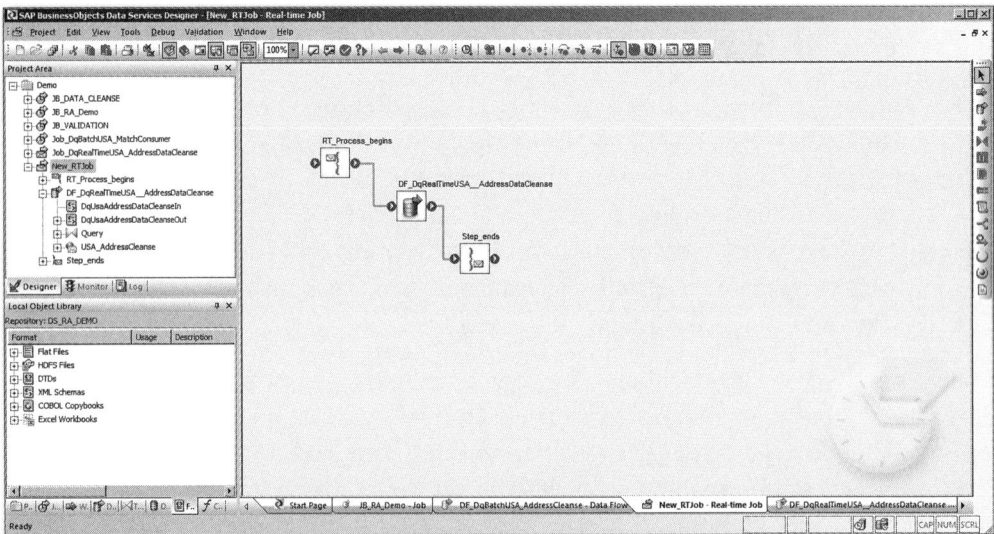

**Figure 4.57** Real-Time Job Illustrated in Designer

This is a very different scenario from a batch job as we've outlined previously. Batch jobs are scheduled and executed at specific time intervals. With a real-time job, there is really nothing to execute, and the job just responds to, consumes, and processes the records as they are ready. Many times, real-time jobs do have a data quality focus, but these jobs can be used with SAP HANA anytime data needs to be significantly transformed and replicated in real time from a source application. An example of a real-time data flow that processes data from a web service is shown in Figure 4.58.

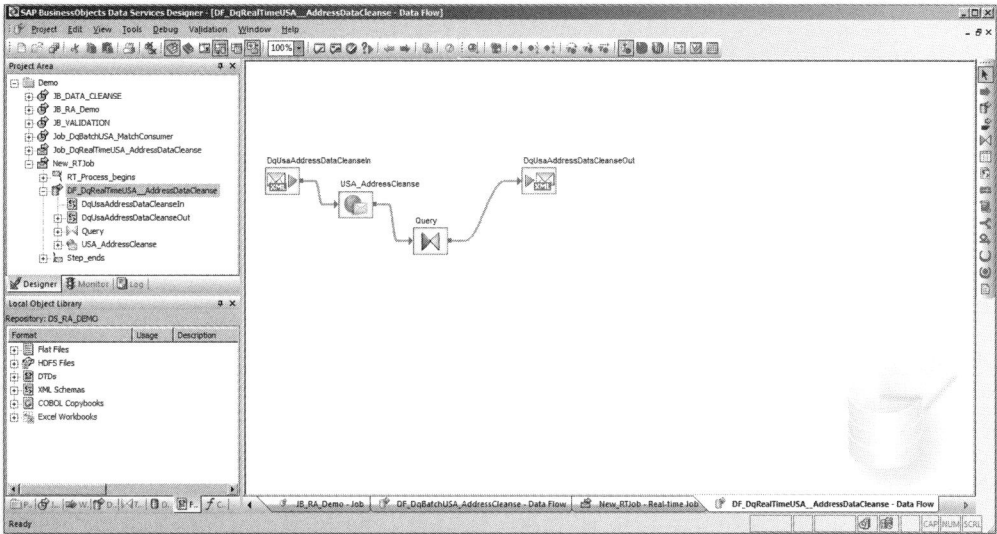

**Figure 4.58**  Real-Time Job Using XML Web Services as Source and Target Objects

Real-time jobs are great solutions for SAP HANA when data needs to be seen immediately, but you should never use them to load large amounts of data. They work best when data is trickled out of an application record by record. If large amounts of data need to be consumed at one time, then a batch job is a much better method to transport data.

## 4.2    SAP Data Services 4.1 Workbench

We've discussed the SAP Data Services Designer at length in this chapter. Designer is the client development environment that has been demonstrated in most of the images in this book up until this point; however, with SAP Data Services 4.1, SAP offers a next-generation client tool. This new client tool is called the SAP Data Services Workbench, as shown in Figure 4.59.

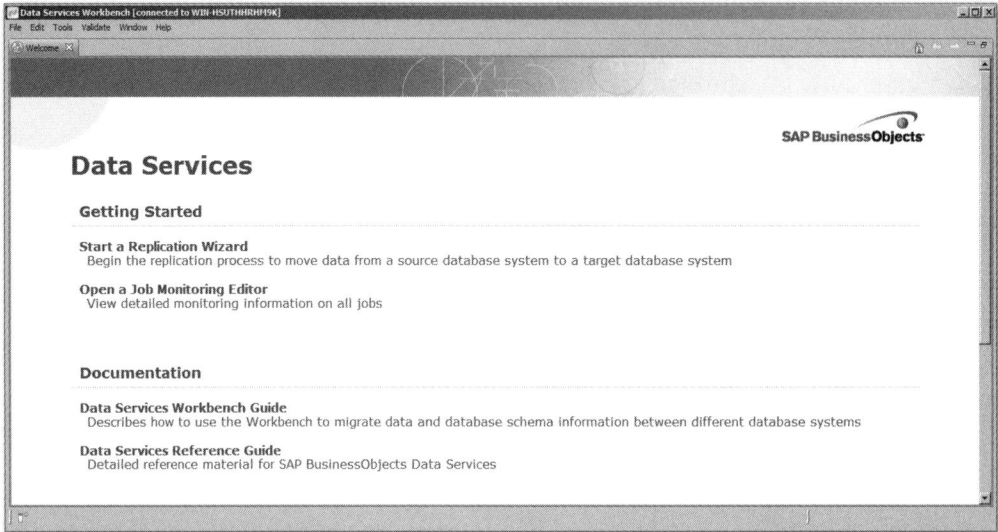

**Figure 4.59**   SAP Data Services Workbench: Welcome Screen

The Workbench is very different from the SAP Data Services Designer client. The most striking difference is the fact that it's an Eclipse-developed client application, so it looks more modern and confirms to the current SAP BusinessObjects and SAP HANA Eclipse look and feel. This is a dramatic departure for SAP, and much work has been poured into this client tool. This is the first iteration of the Workbench, and while it contains some core functionality, by no means, does it replicate all of SAP Data Services Designer in this version. SAP has made it clear that this will be the client tool of the future, but for now, there are still some compelling use cases and reasons where using the Workbench makes sense even with its limited functionality.

We discuss these in detail in this section of the chapter, but before examining specific features, let's examine the Workbench Job Monitoring Editor, which is the SAP Data Services Designer client of the future (see Figure 4.60).

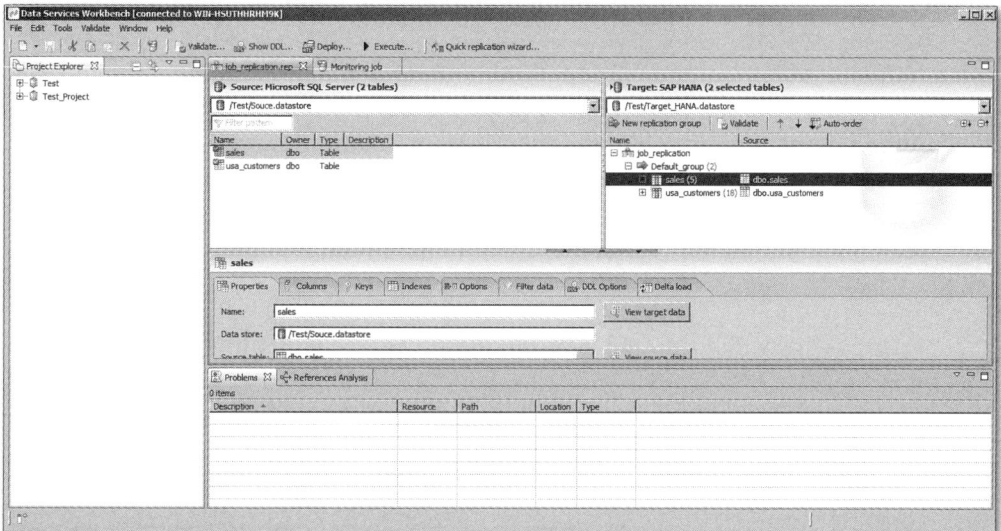

**Figure 4.60** Workbench Job Monitoring Editor

This client has a very different look and feel, but with this view, you're looking at a job with two connections in the source SQL Server database and two tables in the target SAP HANA system. The section in Figure 4.60 marked SALES will change as a context-sensitive screen pane after clicking on different sections of the TARGET pane. For instance, if you click on the SALES table section, the bottom section will reflect the context of the SALES load in terms of target tables, Data Definition Language (DDL) to create the target table in SAP HANA, and so on. The same happens if you click the USA_CUSTOMERS table.

Another major leap forward in functionality is the fact that the SAP Data Services Workbench doesn't require a constant database connection. With the Workbench, you can actively work in an offline mode. This is a great enhancement for those who have worked with the SAP Data Services Designer application because it requires a constant repository database connection. After getting past the look and feel and the fact that this application is useful in scenarios without a network connection, it does become apparent that many features are missing with the 4.1 release. To examine the use cases for the current functionality, we'll discuss what features are supported and which are currently unsupported.

### 4.2.1   Supported Features

As mentioned earlier, SAP Data Services Workbench is a limited feature set for 4.1. The focus of this release is certainly geared toward porting data or data migrations. Almost all of the advanced transforms are currently missing from the SAP Data Services Workbench in this release. Those will follow in future releases. So if you need to connect to multiple sources and port data as-is directly into SAP HANA, then the SAP Data Services Workbench is built for this task.

The current use case for the SAP Data Services Workbench is if a customer has an existing data warehouse and wants to move the data without (many) transformations to SAP HANA, copying both the metadata (table structures, indexes, etc.) and the data. This is possible with SAP Data Services 4.0, but this is a complicated task involving setting up many data flows, workflows, jobs, and datastores. You also have to create the tables and indexes before loading the data. The SAP Data Services Workbench alleviates the work and heavy lifting to build large numbers of data flows, just for simple source-to-target mapping where little to no transformation is required. In many cases, the coding process also requires manual effort to handle loading changed data. The Workbench offers a brand new interface where a user can use a wizard interface to perform the following steps:

1. Select a source system connection.
2. Select tables to be copied.
3. Select a target system connection.
4. Execute and monitor the progress of the load.

This is a very simplistic point of view and presentation to a user that makes a complicated task quite easy. You are able to turn on/off creation of indexes for one or many tables, you can use the native bulk loaders of the target systems that are supported (SAP HANA, Sybase IQ, Teradata). You can also examine the SQL DDL before it executes to ensure you approve of the creation syntax. You can create column-based or row-based tables in SAP HANA just as with the SAP Data Services Designer. Finally, you can port all of the code that is created with the Workbench to Designer to support all custom functions, built-in transforms, and functions that are currently not supported but will be in future releases. With the limitations in SAP Data Services Workbench 4.1, this is the best practice from our experience.

It's no accident that this is the main focus, and this tool was delivered at the time SAP HANA is becoming more mainstream. SAP realized that while SAP Data Services is a great enterprise-class ETL tool, sometimes complex transformations are not immediately necessary. This is when the Workbench shines. When you need to port data directly with minimal to no transformations, use the Workbench. There is even a wizard to make this task very easy—reducing it to a matter of a few steps and clicks. This wizard is called the Job Replication Wizard. This feature will be examined in great detail in the next section where we discuss porting data into SAP HANA.

## 4.2.2    Porting Data

Figure 4.61 shows the first step in the QUICK REPLICATION WIZARD welcome screen: assigning a name to your project. This name corresponds to the name of the SAP Data Services job that will be created by the wizard.

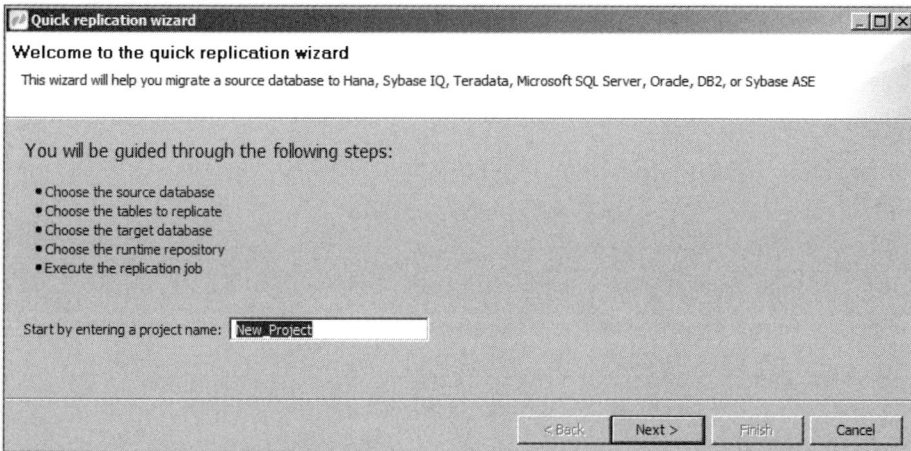

**Figure 4.61**   Step 1: Assign a Job Name

The next step is to specify the source database CREDENTIALS and source database CONNECTION information, as shown in Figure 4.62.

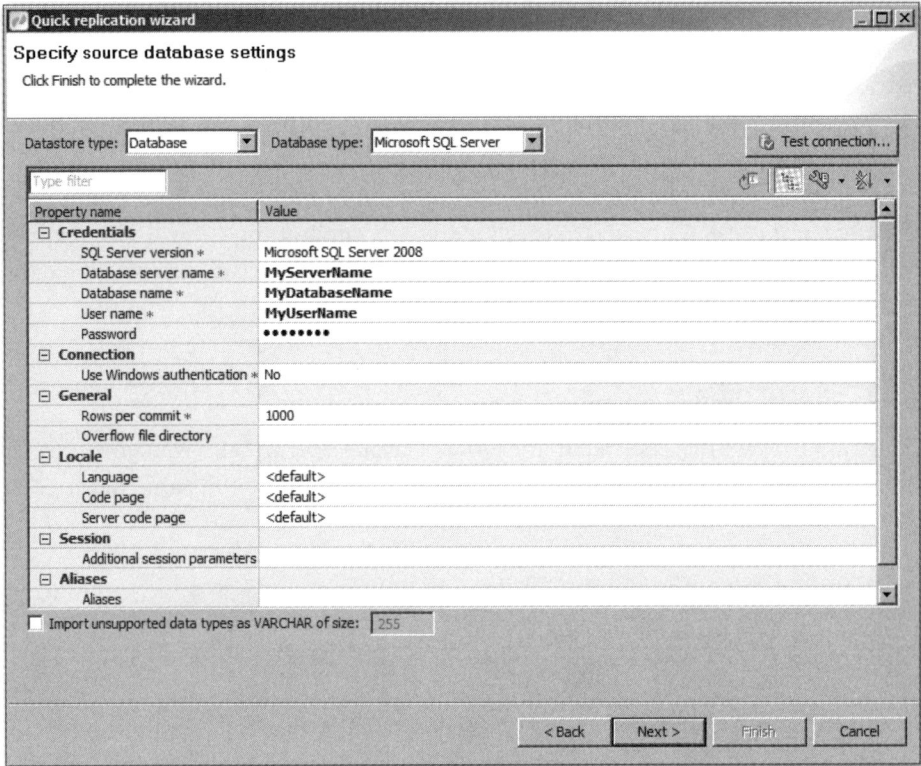

**Figure 4.62**  Step 2: Create a Source Database Connection

Currently, many different sources are supported as connections for the SAP Data Services Workbench in version 4.1, as chronicled in Table 4.12.

| Source Name | Source Type |
|---|---|
| Attunity Connector | Database |
| HP Neoview | Database |
| IBM DB2 | Database |
| SAP HANA | Database |
| Informix | Database |
| Microsoft SQL Server | Database |
| MySQL | Database |
| Netezza | Database |

**Table 4.12**  Source Database Types Supported in Workbench 4.1

| Source Name | Source Type |
|---|---|
| ODBC | Database |
| Oracle | Database |
| Sybase ASE | Database |
| Sybase IQ | Database |
| Teradata | Database |
| SAP Applications | Application |
| SAP NetWeaver BW | Application |

**Table 4.12** Source Database Types Supported in Workbench 4.1 (Cont.)

The next step in the process is to select the tables that you want to move into SAP HANA. The screen to perform this task is shown in Figure 4.63.

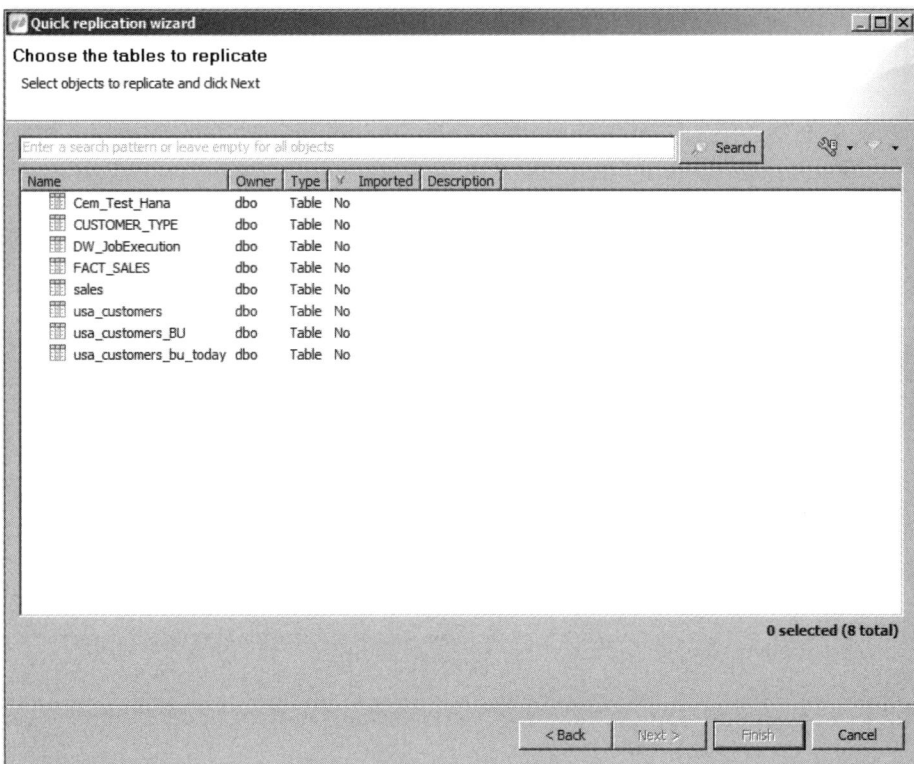

**Figure 4.63** Step 3: Select Tables to Replicate into SAP HANA

The next step is to select your target system and specify the CREDENTIALS and CONNECTION information as shown in Figure 4.64. At the time of publication, in version 4.1, you can specify SAP HANA, Sybase IQ, and Teradata. More target systems will be allowed in later patches and releases.

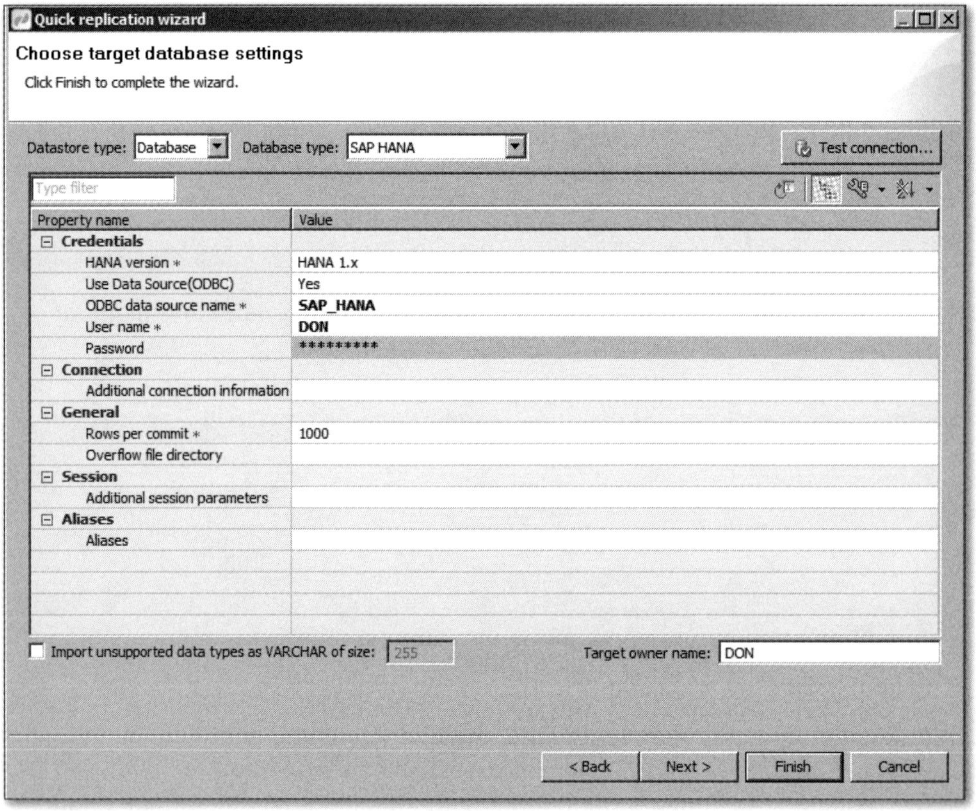

**Figure 4.64**  Step 4: Specify SAP HANA Target System

Now you're ready either to execute the job and monitor the results from the Workbench, or to uncheck the EXECUTE REPLICATION JOB NOW checkbox to simply save the finished project (see Figure 4.65). This is helpful if you may require further currently unsupported transformations in the future. This needs to be done in the SAP Data Services Designer as outlined with the tools earlier in this chapter.

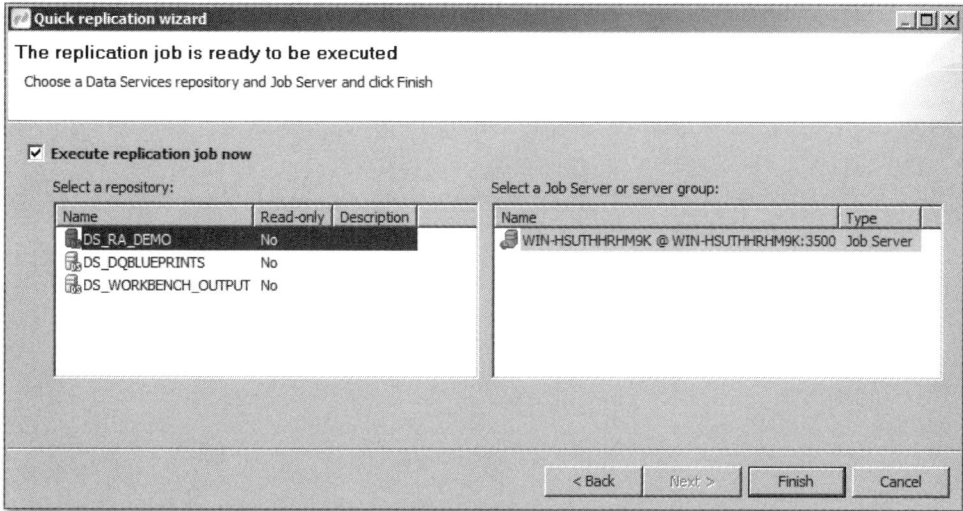

**Figure 4.65** Step 5: Confirm Execution or Just Save Code

### 4.2.3 Options for Data Flow and Job Modification

If you do need to modify this code, then you can do so by transporting the project that you just created using the Quick Replication Wizard to an SAP Data Services repository. This is both quick and easy to do, but keep in mind that this porting to Designer is currently a one-way street. After you port the code, you can't go back into the Workbench! So be cautious when you do move the code over to Designer to ensure that you've received the maximum benefit of the rapid deployment that the Workbench has to offer before you do any more advanced development options with the additional transforms that SAP Data Services Designer offers.

The example of the ported SAP Data Services NEW_PROJECT is found in Figure 4.66. This code is just like any that we've examined up to this point and can be modified using any of the advanced functionality available in the SAP Data Services Designer.

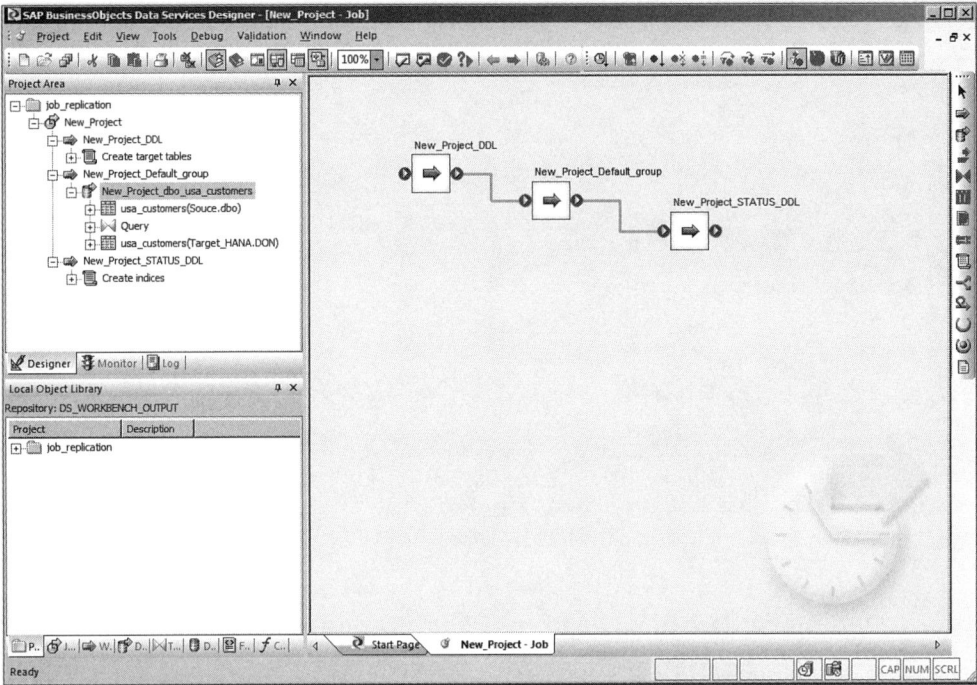

**Figure 4.66** Resulting SAP Data Services Job from the Workbench Replication Wizard

## 4.3 Data Provisioning via Real-Time Replication

We've discussed the concept of replication of data into SAP HANA in many ways so far, but all have involved transferring data via a batch method. A batch-based method is just a port of the data at some specified interval of time. So what if your use case involves moving the data into SAP HANA in real time as it's created in the source systems? This can be accomplished with multiple means. Some of these methods are heavily touted by SAP, and others are often overlooked, but we'll provide an overview of all methods to perform real-time replication of data into SAP HANA.

### 4.3.1 Benefits of Real-Time Replication

Real-time data replication from a source system is inherently more complex than batch-based replication. There are many more points to consider besides just running a job at specified intervals. One additional complexity that comes to mind is that if data is echoed in real time, how are you sure that you're getting a complete transaction? There are many questions like this that are simply not an issue with batch loads. So why is real-time processing worth the effort? Sometimes it's because the business case requires real time.

Some data is just too volatile to wait. This is especially true if the reporting is more operational in nature. With real-time replication, changes occur and are reflected in real time from the sources when the changes are occurring in the sources. Real-time replication is certainly important, and it does have its proper placed in a standalone SAP HANA project.

## 4.3.2 Methods for Real-Time Replication

There are two primary methods for real-time replication in an SAP HANA implementation. The first is SAP Data Services, and the second is *SAP Landscape Transformation* (SLT). There are certainly times and places for each, and depending on the sources to replicate, your use case may require both. Both have their own unique strengths and challenges. We explore each in this section.

### SAP Data Services ETL-Based Method (ETL and DQ)

Using SAP Data Services ETL processes to denormalize, load, and create data structures in SAP HANA is what we've discussed at length in this chapter. We've covered batch jobs, but as mentioned in Section 4.1.8, SAP Data Services also has a real-time capability. The majority of the transforms and functions are available as well as all of the powerful data quality transforms. Cleansing data and matching records in real time is a classic use of SAP Data Services real-time jobs, and this is no different for replicating data into SAP HANA.

There are three primary situations in which to use SAP Data Services for your real-time replication choice:

▶ When you need to replicate data from multiple sources into SAP HANA in real time

▶ When you need to substantially transform the data in real-time

▶ When your source data, from one or many sources, has systemic data quality issues

When you have data coming from multiple sources that requires significant transformations, the SAP Data Services real-time capabilities will likely be required.

SAP Data Services allows you to design a complex ETL job that reads data from multiple sources while building the interdependency across platforms. This ensures the conformity of the data or that the data is properly merged. It's worth noting that this type of design won't be easy to code in SAP Data Services. The job that you design will be both complex and difficult to design. However, if real-time data exchange is required, then SAP Data Services is more than capable of managing the merger of data.

When the structure or form of the source data requires substantial transformation and real-time replication, SAP Data Services will prove to be the ideal solution. Data can be consumed and then transformed using the standard transforms available in the SAP Data Services suite. This occurs in real time, just before the records are provisioned within SAP HANA.

In terms of data quality, SAP Data Services contains multiple tools and options to help you clean data in real time. Developers can use both real-time matching and cleansing to standardize data while it is being provisioned within SAP HANA. The idea is that as the data is going into SAP HANA, data is being both corrected and enhanced. Therefore, with real-time data quality, you're not only avoiding "fast trash" in SAP HANA, but you're also doing it in real time as records are being created in the source(s).

**SAP Landscape Transformation**

We introduced the provisioning of data using SLT log-based replication in Chapter 1. Recall that it's an excellent real-time replication tool for either SAP Business Suite application data or for data found in supported third-party sources. There are, however, differences in the capabilities of SLT when compared to that of SAP Data Services. In general, the differences are centered on either tool's capability to transform the data as it's being replicated. In addition, the tools interface with the source using different mechanisms.

SLT provides a few basic transformation capabilities, such as filtering rows and performing in-line changes to rows. For example, you can develop an SLT job that limits sales transactions that are set to a status of complete. At the same time, you can concatenate the customer's first and last names into a new file. While this is an excellent feature of SLT, organizations often find the need to perform more complex transformations on applicable source data. In these cases, the SAP Data Services real-time capabilities will likely be required to facilitate the organization's needs.

When SLT uses an SAP Business Suite application as its source, the relationships between source tables are often very sound. This is due to the constraints that are placed in the source system that prevent incomplete or nonrelated data from being captured. With that said, various pieces of information being entered are often misspelled or inconsistent. In terms of third-party sources, there is no guarantee that the information will have sound referential integrity or quality. To that end, SLT simply replicates the data into SAP HANA based on the source system's structures and quality. When the quality of your data is in question, and there is a need to purify that data as it's replicated, the real-time features of SAP Data Services are required.

It's also important to understand the ways that either SLT or SAP Data Services interface with source system data. SLT uses remote function calls (RFCs) to interface with SAP Business Suite application data. SLT can also use direct to database connections to interface with third-party data. In Chapter 1, we discussed how SLT creates logging tables in the source to help it keep track of data changes. In contrast, the SAP Data Services real-time replication interface requires that the initial communication of data changes be via web service calls. These calls are made using the W3C XML Schema Standards. In short, the source application or data source needs to send SAP Data Services a message, via web service call, to initiate the replication of data. The data can then be transferred using either web services to transfer a data block or by using a standard batch SAP Data Services job to connect using ODBC or native middleware. If the data source doesn't support or can't provide a web services mechanism, SLT will likely be required. This also implies that SAP Data Services won't be able to easily replicate data from SAP Business Suite applications in real time. Therefore, real-time replication through SAP Data Services will likely be most appropriate for third-party data sources or custom interfaces that are integrated with SAP Business Suite applications.

### 4.3.3 Challenges of Denormalizing Data in Real Time

Many challenges arise with real-time data replication. Simply put, doing real-time data exchange is tough. The main challenge arises when data needs to be altered in quality attributes or modified in structure in real time—both of which are often the case when creating BI structures. SAP Data Services can meet those needs, but be warned that the jobs created will have to contain quite a bit of intelligence coded into the effort. True real-time will be a challenge because most of the SAP Data Services job will either not need to run or the job, will need to be coded into subject areas of the SAP HANA BI target, and those subjects are only called or invoked when data is changed in the source.

For instance, if there is a customer dimension in the SAP HANA target but that customer dimension is being fed by two different sources, then any time those sources change customer data, the real-time "Customer" subject of the SAP HANA job is invoked to process and replicate the data into SAP HANA. The customer SAP Data Services job as a bonus can also contain cleansing and matching operations to repair the data on the way into SAP HANA. The job(s) in SAP Data Services can either designed as a smart "subject" as described earlier or one massive job that is holistic in nature. The holistic job has to be very smart with knowledge of what types of data to process. You can see how this might get quite complex very quickly. The tools are certainly available with SAP Data Services and SLT, but you need to assess the business needs and requirements to ascertain what the best fit is from an implementation perspective.

## 4.4    Summary

In this chapter, we've examined all of the methods and tools available to provision data into SAP HANA using SAP Data Services. There are certainly a variety of options for provisioning, and the choice of which to use often depends on the level of transformation needed for SAP HANA as well as the number of sources and source complexity. That transformation can be in structure to offer better storage and performance operations for SAP HANA, for data quality when data from the sources is suspect, or finally when multiple sources need to be combined for analysis. All of these scenarios are great for SAP Data Services because the built-in capabilities make these types of efforts much easier to achieve. However, if you have a single source of data such as SAP ERP and the quality is good, then other supported SAP HANA provisioning methods, discussed in Chapter 1, may prove to be good options as well. The thing to remember is that no matter your data or use case, SAP has a good provisioning solution and toolset to tackle the job.

Now that we've provided a solid overview of all the methods of provisioning data into SAP HANA using SAP Data Services, we can now move on to loading data into SAP HANA, covered in the next chapter.

*In most enterprise deployments, both batch and real-time processing will be necessary to meet business objectives. In this chapter, we provide an in-depth overview of the various options for loading data into SAP HANA tables using both batch and real-time data processing.*

# 5    Loading Your Data

In the previous chapter, we discussed all of the data provisioning processes that are acceptable to prepare to load data into SAP HANA, so now we'll turn our attention to the loading process and examine it in detail. In Section 5.1 and Section 5.2, respectively, we'll discuss batch loading and real-time loading and conclude with a detailed case study section to build basic dimension and fact table structures in SAP HANA that will be used for the next sections of the book for consumption by the various SAP business intelligence (BI) tools.

We'll start our discussions in Section 5.1 with loading data into SAP HANA in batch, which is the method that is used most often to combine multiple sources of data into a common BI structure for SAP HANA. In Section 5.2, we'll move on to real-time data loading, which is required by some use cases. After covering both batch and real-time jobs, we'll examine various ways to trigger data loads in Section 5.3. The case studies in Section 5.4 and Section 5.5 will reflect both batch and real-time data loads, respectively, and act as concrete illustration points to begin our journey from design to realization in SAP HANA.

However, before we can begin building the structures with the case study sections of this chapter, let's review the concepts of batch and real-time loads to ensure that you have the proper foundation to begin.

## 5.1    Loading Data in Batch

Batch data loading is probably the single most important way to get large amounts of data into SAP HANA. It's used very often, so we'll cover this process in detail. We'll start by describing the process and the proper structure for a batch job, and then complete our study with the methods available to batch load data into SAP HANA using SAP Data Services.

### 5.1.1 What Is Batch Data Loading?

*Batch data loading* is loading data from an executed process on a scheduled basis. This is the most common way to load data warehouses, and SAP HANA is no exception to this process. Data is often loaded in batch to establish the basic BI data structure.

> **Note**
>
> All batch loading in this chapter is supported and illustrated using SAP Data Services, which is bundled with SAP HANA as the best means of integrating third-party (non-SAP) data, as was discussed in Chapter 4 (Section 4.1.3).

Batch data loading is generally accomplished using an SAP Data Services job that contains four distinct steps:

1. **Initialize**
   Initialize aspects of the job by setting variables and controlling comparison logic to control loading delta records or changed data.

2. **Staging**
   Stage data to isolate sources and present data with surrogacy while denormalizing aspects for performance and storage in SAP HANA.

3. **Mart**
   Load the data into SAP HANA in structures designed for high-performing BI needs.

4. **End**
   Close logical operators to ensure that the process is ready to begin again when the next batch is called.

These steps aren't mandatory constructs for SAP Data Services to function or even create a batch job, but this is the best-practice workflow we recommend, developed over years of development cycles. Each of these steps corresponds to workflows in Figure 5.1 and Table 5.1.

| Job Step Name | Workflow Name |
|---|---|
| Initialize | WF_START_JOB |
| Staging | WF_STAGE_SG_D |
| Mart | WF_MART_D |
| End | WF_END_JOB |

**Table 5.1**  SAP Data Services Job Steps and Workflow Examples

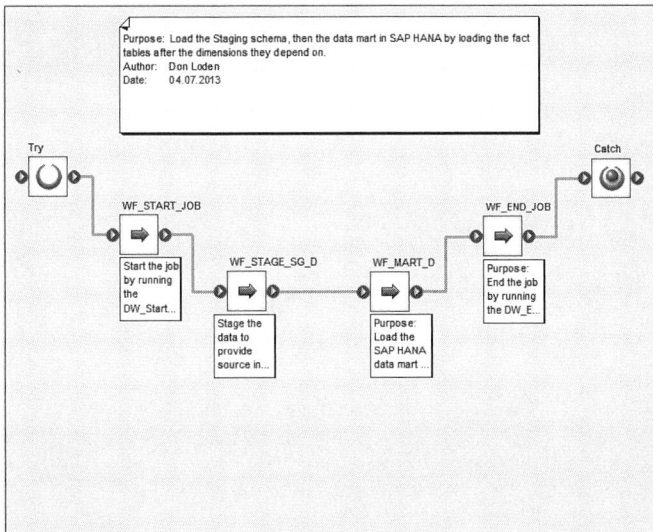

**Figure 5.1**  Typical SAP Data Services Batch Job to Load SAP HANA

You'll notice that there are two more objects present in Figure 5.1: the `Try` and the `Catch` objects. These are objects designed to catch errors and perform different activities based on the errors that are trapped. We'll explore these objects in greater detail in Section 5.4.

Let's explore each of these steps in detail to see how a proper batch job is constructed in SAP Data Services to load a data mart in SAP HANA.

## Initialization

The initialization stage is depicted in Figure 5.1 by WF_SCR_JOB, and this work-flow typically contains only one object: a script. The initialization script, which is shown in Figure 5.2, performs many tasks such as setting variables to drive certain behaviors in the job. The most important variables set controls that load the data by helping select only changed records from the source.

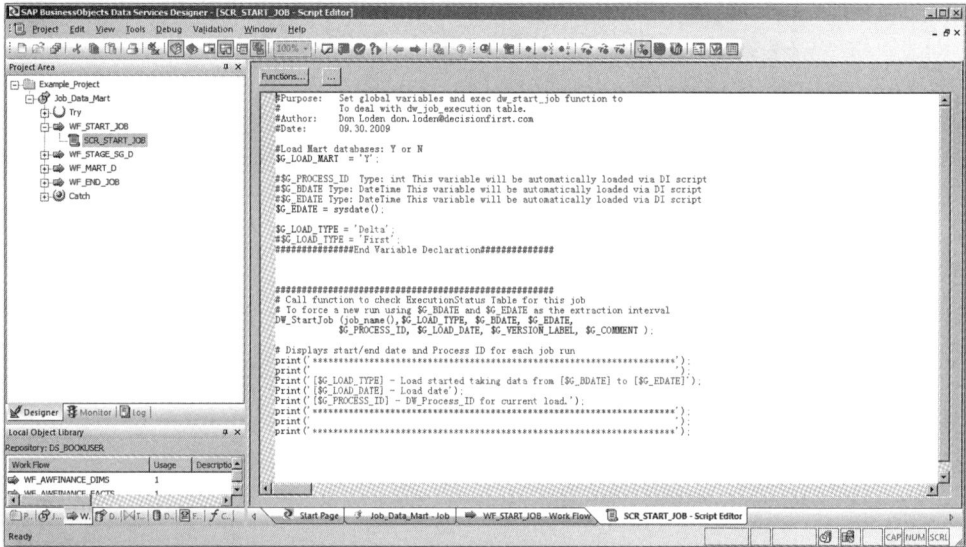

**Figure 5.2**  Initialization Script Containing the DW_StartJob Function

The initialization script shown in Figure 5.2 is contained inside the initialize workflow (WF_START_JOB), which is depicted in SAP Data Services batch job in Figure 5.1. This script sets many variables, but the most important variables are the ones that the DW_StartJob sets by calling this custom function. (For more details on custom functions, please reference Chapter 4, Section 4.1.6.) This function sets the beginning and ending date values and marks those to a DW_JobExecution table to control and bind the beginning and ending date values to a process ID or execution counter value. This way those beginning and ending dates are used to drive the extract or read of the data from the source system.

Let's take a look at the example of a DW_JobExecution table shown in Figure 5.3.

| Job_Name | DW_Process_id | Load_Type | Status | ExtractLow | ExtractHigh | Load_Date | Remark | Version_Label | DW_Procid_Start | DW_Procid_End |
|---|---|---|---|---|---|---|---|---|---|---|
| JB_RA_Demo | 1 | Delta | done | 1900-01-01 00:00:00.000 | 2009-10-23 19:25:15.000 | 2009-10-28 19:19:38.000 | | | 0 | 0 |
| JB_RA_Demo | 2 | Delta | done | 2009-10-23 19:25:15.000 | 2012-09-26 10:52:00.000 | 2012-09-26 10:52:00.323 | | | 0 | 0 |
| JB_RA_Demo | 3 | Delta | done | 2012-09-26 10:52:00.000 | 2013-02-27 14:35:19.000 | 2013-02-27 14:35:19.743 | | | 0 | 0 |
| JB_RA_Demo | 4 | Delta | started | 2013-02-27 14:35:19.000 | 2013-04-08 12:29:52.000 | 2013-04-08 12:29:52.630 | | | 0 | 0 |
| NULL | NULL | NULL | NULL | NULL | NULL | NULL | NULL | NULL | NULL | NULL |

**Figure 5.3**  Typical Job Execution Table in a Staging Schema

In Figure 5.3, the process ID is represented by the DW_Process_ID column and is a simple incrementing integer value. The beginning and ending date range that actually drive setting the variables are the ExtractLow and ExtractHigh columns. These are date-time data type columns with precision down to the millisecond. This way, with the overlap from record to record, there is no chance of missing any data or any time series. The Job_Name column controls which job the records belong because there may be runs from many different jobs in this Job_Execution table.

The final column that is really important is the Status column, which controls the recovery of the job by having two distinct values: Started and Done. Started tells the DW_StartJob function to reuse the variables in the record to recover a run and reprocess the same date ranges of data in the WHERE clauses of all of the data flows present in the job. If the value is Done, a new record is created with a process ID value, incremented by one in the new record. The new record also contains the ExtractLow value set to the ExtractHigh value of the previous record, and the ExtractHigh value of the new record is a time stamp of the SAP Data Services job server time at the time of the run. The DW_StartJob function shown in Figure 5.2 is intelligent enough to contain all of this logic, and it uses the Job_Execution table in Figure 5.3 to record the return values.

The Job_Execution table typically exists in a staging database or schema, which may or may not exist in SAP HANA. We'll discuss the reasons for this shortly, but for now, just note that the job execution table exists in staging because it's one of the vital logical components that will control the source based change data capture (CDC) aspects of our SAP HANA job.

Now let's explore more details about the staging step of the SAP Data Services job.

## Staging

The staging step of the SAP Data Services job is used for all of the heavy transformations that are often needed to go from a source system to support high-performance

SAP HANA application designs. It's true that while SAP HANA outperforms traditional databases with just a mere port of the data with no transformations, recall from Chapter 2 that when data is stored to maximize SAP HANA's strengths, both better data storage compression and better performance are realized. Figure 5.4 shows the flow of data from multiple sources to staging where most transformations occur, and then finally to the data mart in SAP HANA where data will be consumed by users.

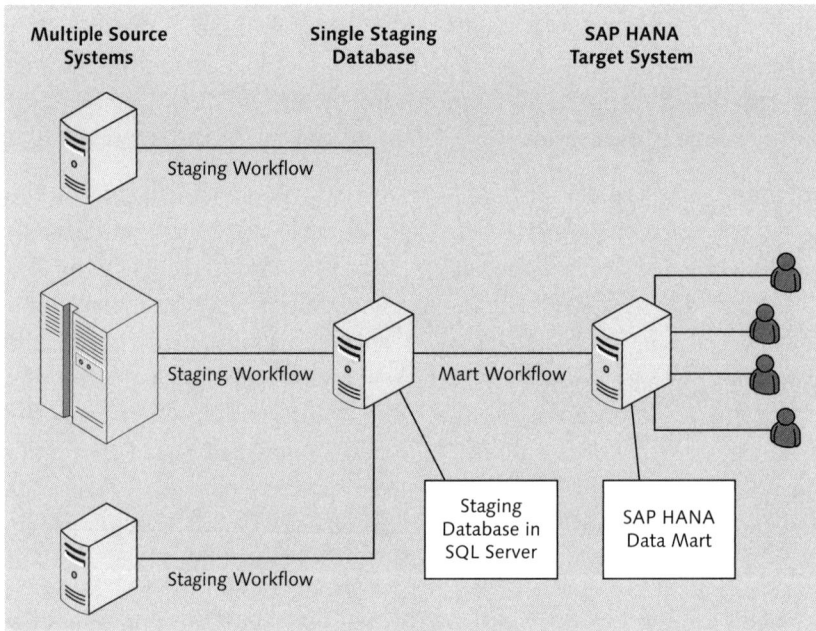

**Figure 5.4** SAP HANA Data Mart Load Layout

The coding process in SAP Data Services Designer is also divided into meaningful logical sections when developing the staging code. These sections not only make for more readable code, but the code that is produced is easier to translate and share with other developers when it's organized logically. This organization also allows for the ordering of objects that need to come first in the data load process for SAP HANA. For instance, staging operations to prepare customer data for loading into a customer dimension in SAP HANA has to come first and run before the load of the data mart in SAP HANA. This process of segmentation and organization is shown in Figure 5.5.

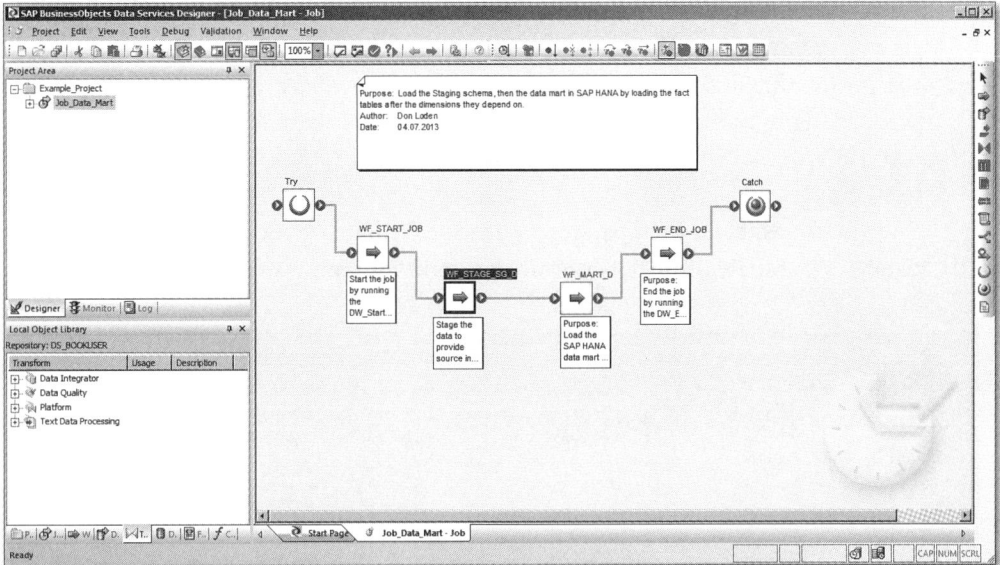

**Figure 5.5**  Staging Workflow Highlighted in Designer

The workflow WF_STAGE_SG_D is loaded before the data mart workflow WF_
MART_D, which performs the load into SAP HANA. Workflows in SAP Data Services
provide this level of both organization and order of execution.

*Data compression* is a key factor for maximizing the data that you can store in SAP
HANA, as SAP HANA is licensed by storage size in memory. Because performance
is the end goal for using SAP HANA in the first place, it makes sense to want to
maximize both of these aspects in SAP HANA. All of the transformations that will
occur in staging support these goals but because staging is essentially a layer where
work is performed to achieve these goals, it should only exist in SAP HANA if
needed to overcome a performance burden. This staging section is shown as the
workflow WF_STAGE_SG_D in Figure 5.5.

Staging is also the primary place for combining multiple sources of data and providing surrogacy over the sources by shifting the primary key duties of the database
tables to surrogate key columns in the tables. Though we won't load multiple
sources of data in the case study sections of the chapter, we'll cover creating surrogate keys within the SAP Data Services ETL code to illustrate the concept. This
concept is central to data warehousing, whether the data is sourced from one
system or many systems.

Another point worth mentioning about staging data for SAP HANA is the fact that staging databases or schemas are often crafted outside of SAP HANA. The simple reason for this is that SAP HANA's speed and power comes at a price and that price escalates as more data is stored. Consequently, we recommend that you use SAP HANA to solve performance problems, which typically arise and are seen in user-facing roles. In this respect, a staging database is often not the best use of SAP HANA, as this is a preparatory stage for the data. A good example of a staging database in Microsoft SQL Server is shown in Figure 5.6.

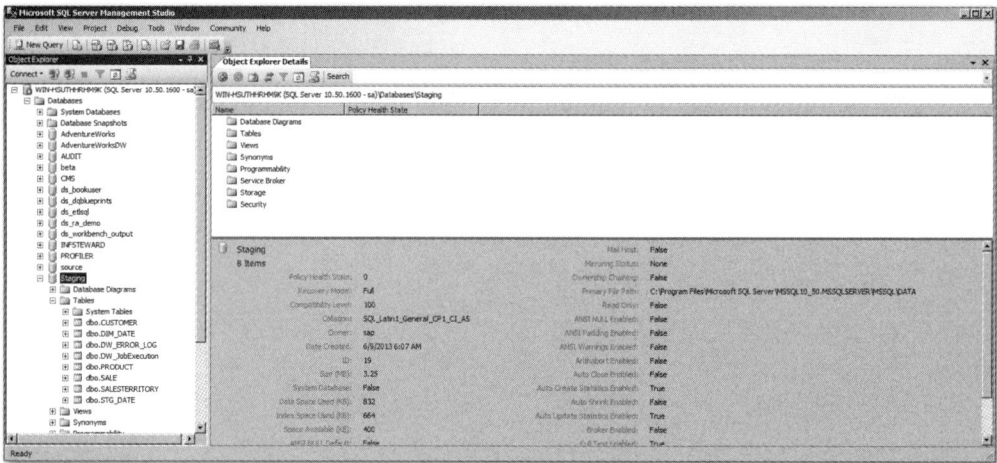

**Figure 5.6** Staging Database in SQL Server

The only processes and tools to touch the system are ETL tools or system-generated devices. One exception is if the ETL process itself is performing poorly enough to get the data ready in time for presenting to the users with the SAP BusinessObjects BI reporting or exploration tools. Then, you can use the power of SAP HANA for those long-running processes to make sure that the service level agreements for data delivery are met. However, this is a unique scenario, and we more often find only the user-facing data elements and tables in SAP HANA. These user-facing tables are generally created and/or loaded with data in the mart step of the job, which we'll examine in the next section of this chapter.

**Mart**

The mart step is what actually builds the data mart tables and loads the data into SAP HANA. This schema contains the data model necessary to support all of the reporting needs from the various SAP BusinessObjects BI tools as well as the foundation to build attribute views, analytic views, and calculation views. The data mart target tables are shown in the BOOK_USER schema in Figure 5.7.

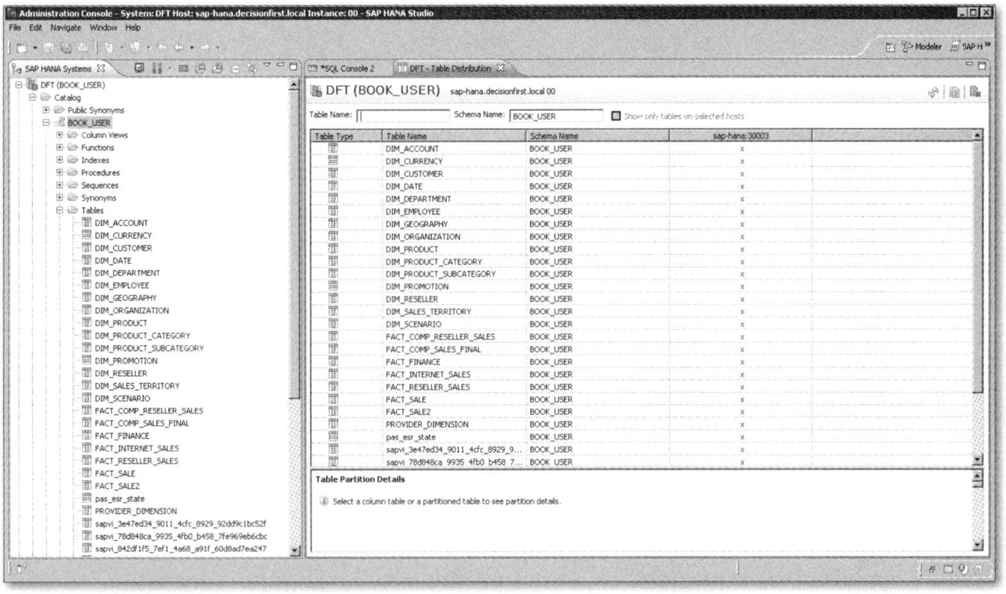

**Figure 5.7** SAP HANA Data Mart Target Tables

This step is segregated from the staging load to provide insulation from the schema in SAP HANA because this will be the user-facing data layer. Data will be consumed out of SAP HANA tables listed in Figure 5.7 using the SAP BusinessObjects BI tools to present the data, so it makes sense to segregate this layer from staging to offer more freedom for development.

For instance, later you may need to alter the logic of the creation and population of the data to present to SAP HANA. If the data structures are contained within one schema, then reporting will be affected with the changes as they are made in the BOOK_USER schema. But if staging is separated into a separate database or even data platform, then the changes can be made in the staging database/schema as well as the SAP Data Services code without ever affecting reports until an appropriate time for the disruption, such as after business hours.

The workflow in SAP Data Services that actually builds the data mart is shown in Figure 5.8.

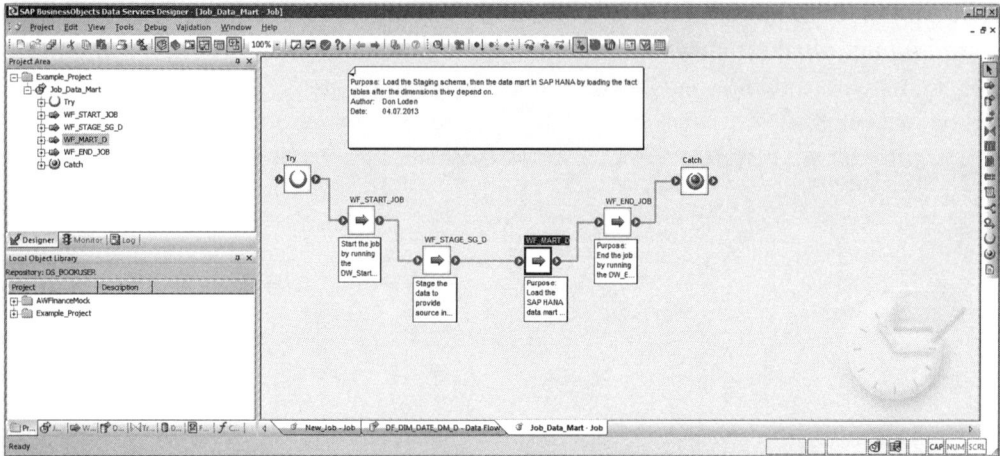

**Figure 5.8** Workflow to Build the SAP HANA Data Mart in Designer

As shown in Figure 5.8, the code in SAP Data Services for the data mart is segregated as well from the staging code. The code that loads the staging schema runs in the previous workflow, and this separation allows a split between processing the logic of staging and the data mart load to SAP HANA so that you can easily divorce both environments as needed.

After the SAP HANA data mart is loaded, then there is one final task needed to close the loop or effectively end the job: the end script.

### End Script

The end script step of the SAP Data Services job is the final step in a batch data load in SAP HANA. The sole purpose of this step in the batch data load is to finish tasks that the initialization section of the batch job started. For instance, earlier in this chapter, we illustrated that there is a `DW_StartJob` function that sets variables for `ExtractLow` and `ExtractHigh` dates for the CDC date comparisons against multiple sources. This function sets the STATUS in the DW_JobExecution table (refer to Figure 5.3) to STARTED as the job commences and clears this step.

After the job's successful execution of the staging and mart workflows, the end script then closes the loop by setting the STATUS value in the job execution table to DONE. This essentially tells the job upon next execution that all was successful from the last run and not to try to recover anything. The `DW_EndJob` function is shown in Figure 5.9.

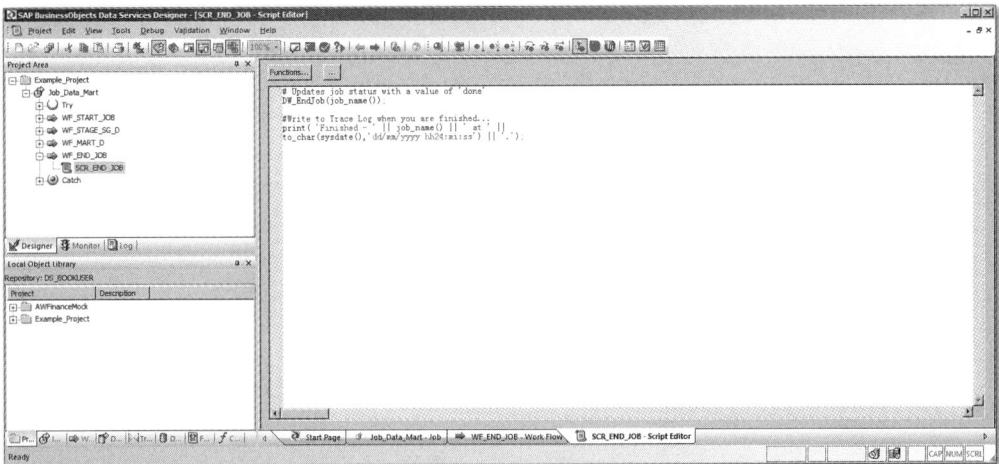

**Figure 5.9** End Script Call in Designer

The end script also returns any variable statuses back to a state of ready if needed and also may call post-load operations such as triggering reports to run in SAP BusinessObjects BI via executables or file triggers. These types of tasks or clean-up operations are common for the end script step of a batch job.

These four steps have taken you through the batch data load process and how a typical batch data load job for SAP HANA is constructed in SAP Data Services. We'll now explore methods for batch loading data into SAP HANA. The job structure is constant, but you have options for data comparison and loading only changed data via CDC operations. We'll explore these in detail in the next section.

### 5.1.2 Methods for Batch Loading Data

There are many methods for loading data in batches into SAP HANA using SAP Data Services. In the remainder of this section, we'll focus on the following three main methods:

- Truncate and reload
- Target-based CDC
- Source-based CDC

The primary distinction between these three methods is derived from whether you care about capturing changes within the batch load. If you care about changes, or are forced to care about changes because the reload of the source data sets won't be possible in the time frame of your load window of time, then you'll need to perform some sort of change data capture (CDC) operation. This involves the second two options. If you're able to reload the entire data set in the load time, then the first method will suffice.

In the past, with traditional database architectures and technologies, you always needed some sort of CDC operation to overcome performance issues. However, that isn't always the case with SAP HANA. SAP HANA can bulk load data incredibly fast, making it good not only for reads but, with the proper tuning and parallelization, also for the writes, so now CDC isn't as important as it used to be.

Let's investigate each of these methods and discuss use cases for when each should be used.

**Truncate and Reload**

Truncate and reload is exactly as it sounds: The target table in SAP HANA is truncated and then reloaded. Data is pulled from a target, and the transformations occur in the ETL process in SAP Data Services; however, before data is loaded into the target table, the target in SAP HANA is truncated, thus clearing the target table of data so that all records can be extremely fast inserts. This is the easiest method to support in terms of maintenance and recovery from failures.

Figure 5.10 shows the two ways that you can perform this method in SAP Data Services and achieve the same result. With the first method, data is cleared before the ETL process begins in SAP Data Services. This usually occurs with the initialization step of the batch load process. The SAP Data Services workflow is as follows:

1. Initialization script clears all necessary target tables in one sweep.

2. ETL processing within SAP Data Services workflows and data flows occurs.

3. Tables are loaded as bulk inserts in each of the data flows clear their respective processing tasks.

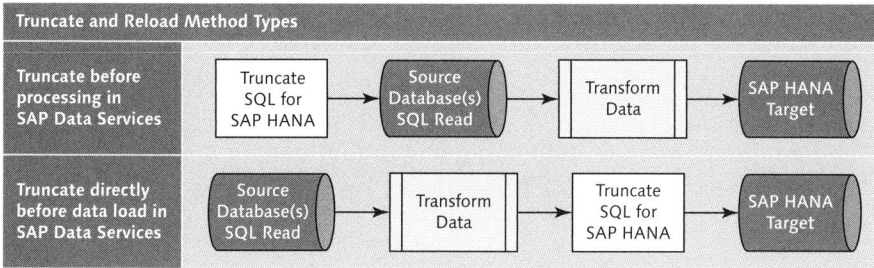

**Figure 5.10**  Two Types of Truncate and Reload in SAP Data Services

The second method is a little different and allows a more granular control at the SAP Data Services data flow level. In this example, the SAP HANA target table truncation actually occurs within the SAP Data Services data flows, which are scattered throughout the job. This is handled with the target table screen option shown in Figure 5.11.

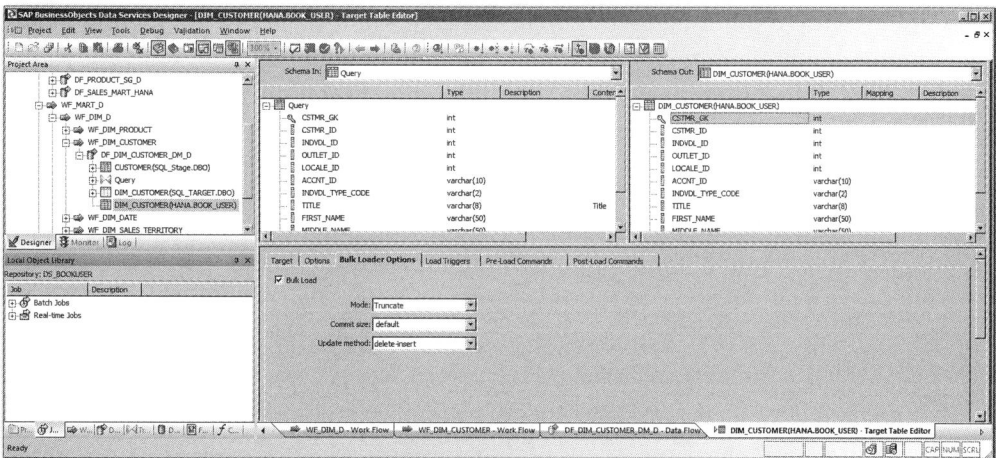

**Figure 5.11**  SAP HANA Bulk Loader Options in Designer

This method is typically reserved for small sources resulting in small data loads in data warehousing with traditional architectures. Even with the bulk loading capabilities of most mainstream traditional database platforms, the performance of this method will always be a hindrance that outweighs the benefits of the ease of maintenance.

This isn't always the case with SAP HANA. There are many situations when, with proper parallelization, you can increase the speed at which SAP Data Services produces inserts for SAP HANA, removing the speed problem as an obstacle. This is a departure from traditional data warehousing, which has always relied on CDC. This will handle far more cases than a traditional data warehouse. However, there are times some sort of CDC operation is necessary; we discuss options and methods for CDC next.

**Target-Based CDC**

In many cases, even with SAP HANA, you might need to focus on a subset of the data. Focusing on changed data is a great way to process only what you need to process, but even with the power of SAP HANA, this will be a realization under really tight data load windows or time lines.

SAP Data Services offers many options of target-based CDC. In our opinion, the Table_Comparison transform offers one of the best means of target-based comparison for your SAP Data Services batch job to load SAP HANA, if you don't need to perform changes in the data based on certain fields. In other words, if you're merely detecting changes and writing the same nonkey attribute fields no matter whether it's an insert or an update, then a Table_Comparison transform is the most efficient and simplest operation.

Recall from Chapter 4, Section 4.1.5, that Table_Comparison transforms allow for a rapid implementation of target-based CDC. The interface is drag and drop, and the comparison is as easy as specifying the fields that you want to compare against either your SAP HANA target system or your staging database to the source data that you're channeling through the data flow. The Table_Comparison transform is shown in the product staging data flow in Figure 5.12.

The Table_Comparison transform in this example is comparing input data from the read of the source database in the Query transform to the target staging table called PRODUCT. Each record is compared on the fields that are specified in Figure 5.13, and this captures whether records are inserts, updates, or deletes by specifying the columns to compare in the COMPARE COLUMNS window pane.

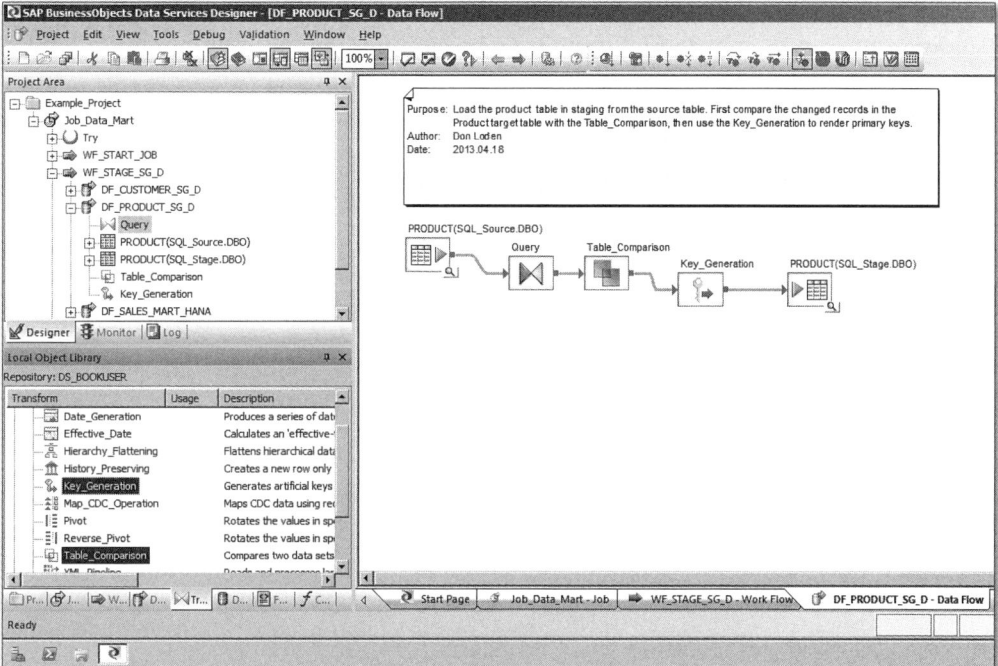

**Figure 5.12**  Table_Comparison Transform in Designer

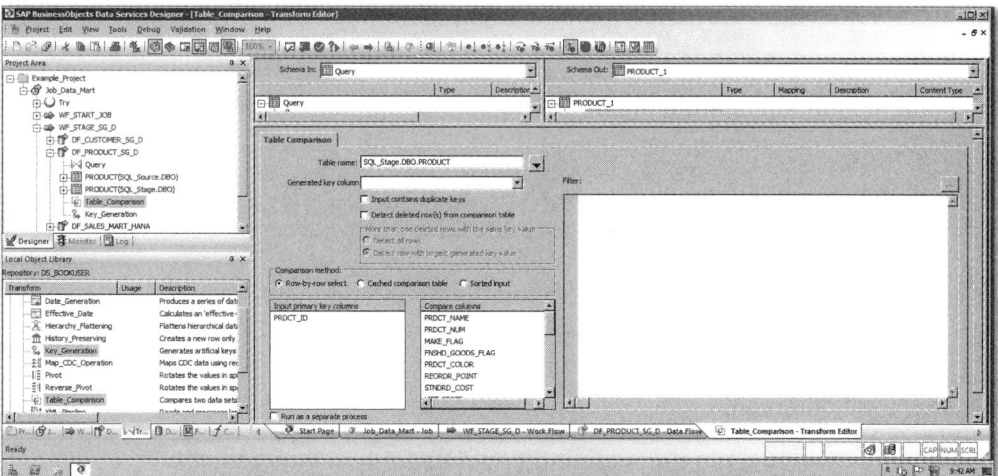

**Figure 5.13**  Table_Comparison Options and Columns to Compare in Designer

This way, after data has cleared the `Table_Comparison` transform, SAP Data Services has enough information about the data to provide guidance to the target table on whether to insert, update, or delete the records from the target table. If no data has changed, the records will merely be discarded so that no actions occur against the target. This is very effective in comparing target tables to incoming record sets, but the processing is somewhat expensive in terms of performance.

To avoid unnecessary processing, it's best to only select records that have changed from the source using source-based CDC techniques. Let's look at these now.

### Source-Based CDC

In most data warehousing scenarios, you'll have some tables that require CDC; we discussed some techniques available in SAP Data Services to handle target-based CDC in the previous section. This target-based CDC is almost always combined with source-based CDC to ensure that you're not trying to compare all of the data from the source with the target in staging or SAP HANA. You only want to focus on the changes that occurred in the source since the last time that data was processed. This is usually performed by comparing a date column or a process ID indication column. In this example, a modified date is used in a source to the date range of a job execution run. This date comparison is achieved by a using the `Query` transform's `WHERE` clause to supply the date range for comparison to the source table. This is shown in the WHERE clause tab depicted in Figure 5.14.

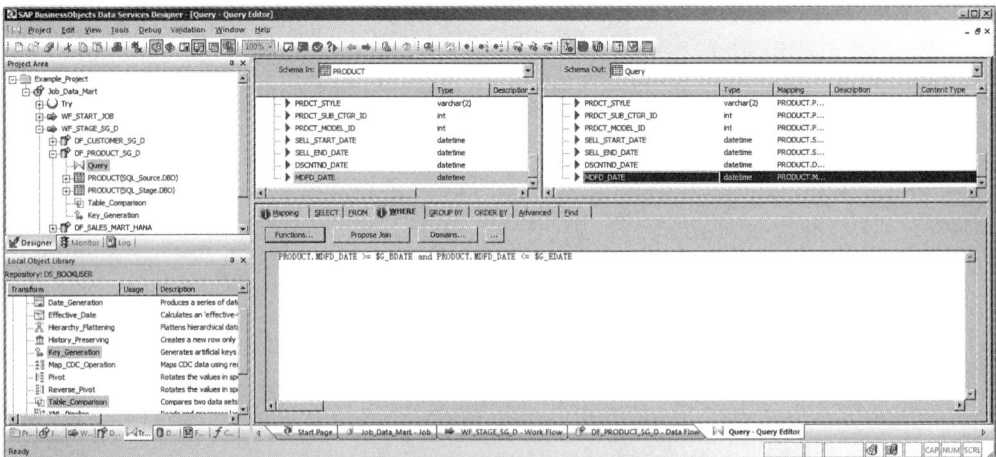

**Figure 5.14**  Where Clause in the Query Transform in Designer

Using dates is typical because most source applications use this concept of a date to mark when the record was inserted or updated. The PRODUCT.MDFD_DATE (or modified date field) is used to capture a range of records from the source PRODUCT table that has been modified since the last run. The run range of dates are controlled using two variables: one for the lower bound date $G_BDATE and one for the upper bound date $G_EDATE. These date values are assigned via the initialize section of the batch job (Initialization). This is done by the DW_JobExecution function returning the $G_BDATE and $G_EDATE variables from the DW_JOBEXECUTION table, which is shown in Figure 5.15.

> **Note**
>
> Make sure that you can trust your dates by performing proper source system analysis, which we covered in Chapter 3. This is crucial for using the modified date effectively and actually picking up all changed records.
>
> Don't just assume that dates are good and accurate. Make sure they are up to the task before you stake your SAP Data Services code to load SAP HANA on them!

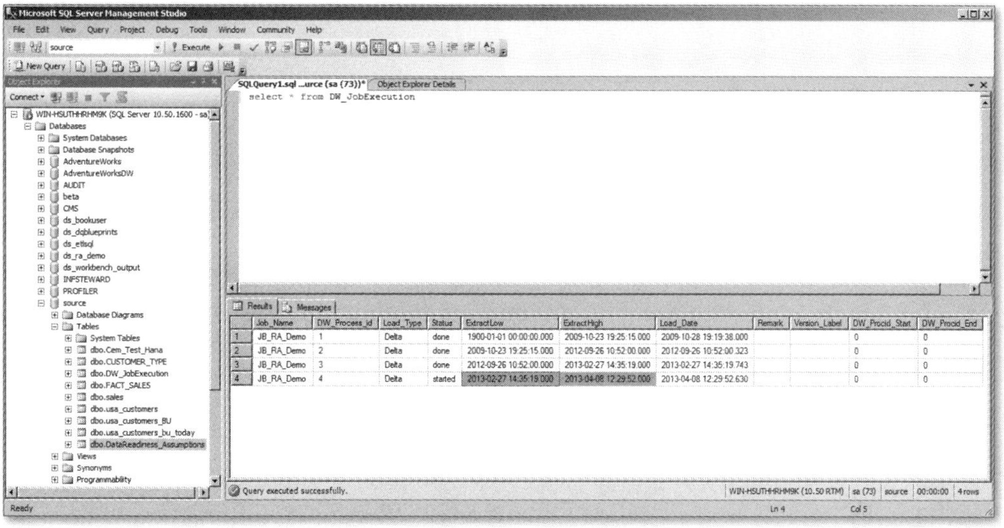

**Figure 5.15** DW_JobExecution Table's Upper and Lower Bound Dates

This `Query` transform returns only the changed records from the source, and these records process throughout the rest of the data flow and the SAP Data Services job. In most CDC situations for loading data into SAP HANA, there will be a combination of both source-based and target-based CDC. This ensures that the batch jobs perform as efficiently as possible and don't overprocess records that don't need to be touched.

But what if you need data echoed and transformed in real time from a source application? This can also be accomplished in SAP Data Services by using real-time jobs.

## 5.2 Loading Data in Real Time

We discussed real-time data provisioning in Chapter 4, Section 4.3, and the scenarios when it would be used. In this section, we'll focus on real-time data loading complete with heavy transformations to the data.

### 5.2.1 What Is Real-Time Loading?

Let's briefly revisit the concept of batch loading, which loads data and handles transformations in sets of data. For a batch operation, a transaction may be as few as 10 records or as many as 10 million records. All of the records contained in the batch load into SAP HANA need to be treated as a transaction or a unit.

In contrast, real-time loading into SAP HANA, simply put, is echoing data into SAP HANA *as changes occur*, record by record, in a source. SAP Data Services is the best method to accomplish this functionality, with its massive library of transforms and functions to accomplish varied output formats, cleansing, and standardization.

### 5.2.2 SAP Data Services for Real-Time Loading

Let's consider a scenario where an online application creates a customer record, and you want to load that record in SAP HANA immediately as it's created online. The business requirement is that the sales group needs to see customer changes as they occur because research has proven that the sale is more effective knowing up-to-the-second customer information. However, there is one issue: The customer list in SAP HANA has already been cleansed and standardized to build a concise list of customers for reporting. The BI application already has a great customer list for the customer dimension that is used for precise and complex reporting. The last thing that you want to do is to see customer records for a rogue application pollute that list.

Fortunately, you can use SAP Data Services to cleanse the customer data from the application and match the record against your list in SAP HANA. This ensures that you meet the requirement and keep fast trash out of SAP HANA. An example real-time job depicting the scenario of immediately reflected customer changes is shown in Figure 5.16.

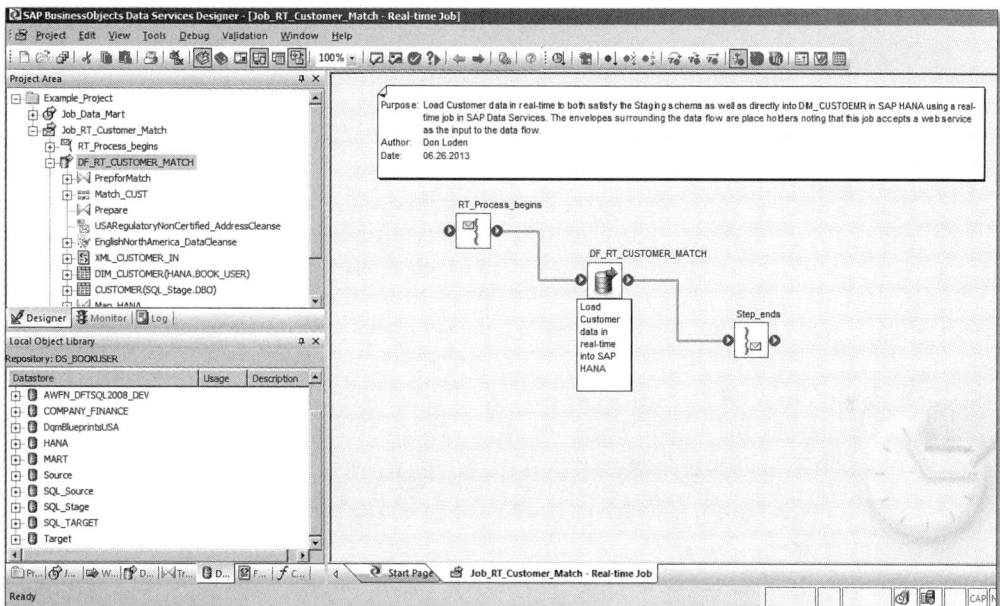

**Figure 5.16**  Real-Time Job in Designer to Load SAP HANA

This real-time job takes a web service input, signified in Figure 5.16 by the envelope icons that surround the data flow. (However, note that these icons have no meaning or use other than to illustrate a place holder to show that this is a real-time job.) The data flow DF_RT_CUSTOMER_MATCH is just a standard data flow that can be used in any batch or real-time job. This data flow is shown in Figure 5.17.

The data flow takes web services as input records and then uses a `Query` transform to flatten the hierarchical XML data. That flattened data is fed to an address cleansing transform to cleanse customer address attributes from the web application that won't be used for output to the customer staging or customer dimension tables. Rather, the address data will be used as supplementary input information along with the cleansed customer fields in the `Data_Cleanse` transform to achieve a better matching result.

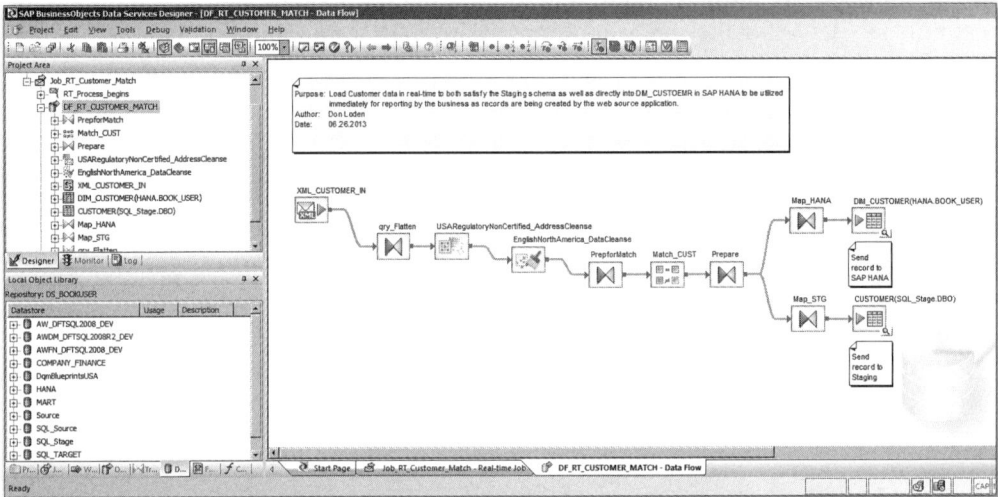

**Figure 5.17**  Real-Time Data Flow to Load SAP HANA as Data Is Created in the Source

After the customer-specific attributes are cleansed with the `Data_Cleanse` transform, then matching takes place in the `Matching` transform using both the cleansed customer and address components. The cleansing process is important because you want to standardize not only the record elements to prepare for the match against the data in SAP HANA but also the incoming data to the same standards and specifications that the SAP HANA `DIM_CUSTOMER` data has already been cleansed. After matches have occurred, the elements that you care to load into the respective customer staging table and the SAP HANA-specific table are prepared and finalized by the remaining `Query` transforms just before the target tables.

Table 5.2 shows this process in more detail down to the data flow element name, the respective element type, and the description of what task each object is responsible for performing.

| Data Flow Element Name | Element Type | Description |
|---|---|---|
| `XML_CUSTOMER_IN` | XML message source object | This is the XML message source from the source application. This message is in a hierarchical data format that consists of both the elements of the data as well as the structure and data types to describe the data. SAP Data Services supports W3C standards. |
| `qry_Flatten` | `Query` transform | The `Query` transform is used to un-nest or flatten the hierarchy that is present in the XML data. The data must be in a flat table. A flat table consists of only rows and columns and not relationships to other objects or constructs. |
| `USA_Regulatory NonCertified_ AddressCleanse` | USA address cleanse transform | The address cleanse transform was described in Chapter 4, Section 4.1.5. This transform is used to both parse and correct the address elements coming from the web source application. After the address is cleansed and standardized, it's ready for use in further processing of the data flow. |
| `EnglishNorth American_ DataCleanse` | Data cleanse transform | The data cleanse transform (described in Chapter 4, Section 4.1.5) cleanses the customer-specific attributes by using the SAP-supplied person- and firm-supporting software to both parse, standardize, and correct missing or incorrect person names or firm names. This transform is also used to note the standard form of a name and provide match standard name suggestions (e.g., William could be considered as Bill or Billy). This yields a better match result. |

**Table 5.2** Details of the Specific Objects in the Real-Time Data Flow

| Data Flow Element Name | Element Type | Description |
|---|---|---|
| PrepForMatch | Query transform | This Query transform organizes all of the fields that will be considered for the Match transform into a concise order and format that will be used for matching. |
| Match_CUST | Match transform | This is where the matching occurs. The Match transform (described in Chapter 4, Section 4.1.5) performs a complex match using a multidimensional algorithm. |
| | | Comparison fields are presented in a specified order, and each field has dozens of options that can be specified that all present possibilities of matches rendered as scores at the element level. These individual elements are aggregated up to a whole number that must meet a user-specified threshold to be considered a match at the record level. If the record is deemed a match, it's placed into a group with its respective matching record and given a score that can be used for later processing. |
| Prepare | Query transform | This Query transform prepares the output by selecting only the fields that are needed to satisfy both output tables. Because the schema and columns are different between SAP HANA and staging, this Query transform must contain all of the columns to satisfy both. |
| Map_HANA | Query transform | This Query transform selects only the columns that are specific to SAP HANA DIM_CUSTOMER for the insert or update. |

**Table 5.2** Details of the Specific Objects in the Real-Time Data Flow (Cont.)

| Data Flow Element Name | Element Type | Description |
|---|---|---|
| Map_STG | Query transform | This Query transform selects only the columns that are specific to the staging CUSTOMER for the insert or update. |
| DIM_CUSTOMER | Target table: SAP HANA | Target table in SAP HANA: DIM_CUSTOMER. We're using the Auto_Correct option shown in Chapter 4, Section 4.1.5, to determine whether the record is an insert or an update to the target SAP HANA table. |
| CUSTOMER | Target table: staging | Target table in staging: CUSTOMER. We're using the Auto_Correct option shown in Chapter 4, Section 4.1.5, to determine whether the record is an insert or an update to the target staging table in SQL Server. |

**Table 5.2**  Details of the Specific Objects in the Real-Time Data Flow (Cont.)

**Note**

*W3C standards* define the standard that XML schemas should maintain and define. Various vendors have their own methods and flavors, but these standards make up the basic components of XML structures. SAP Data Services supports these; more information on these standards can be found at the W3C website: *www.w3.org/XML/Schema.*

The data flow is complex but not too extreme when broken down to its individual elements. The important thing to note here is that this real-time data loading example with SAP Data Services is the perfect example of what is possible in terms of complex transformations that could never be accomplished with SAP HANA multidimensional modeling. Multidimensional modeling can handle complex aggregations, but we're maintaining and creating master data in SAP HANA with our complex cleansing and matching process. This is the type of data quality operation that will ensure that our data in SAP HANA is trustworthy as well as not contributing to "fast trash" in SAP HANA.

This is a great example of supplementing the batch load process that we've detailed in this chapter with real-time information in SAP HANA that includes complex transformations. Both batch and real-time loading must work together in a fully realized deployment of native SAP HANA. A real-time job requires no trigger as you've seen in this example. The real-time job is merely listening for data. However, for batch loads to be successful in performing a data load to SAP HANA, they must be triggered. Triggers are needed because without an instigating force, the batch job will lie dormant forever. In earlier discussions in Section 5.1.1, we covered how to code the batch job to perform logical operations. Now, it's time to cover the various ways to instigate or trigger the batch jobs into action, which we'll cover in the next section.

## 5.3    Methods to Trigger Data Loads

Real-time data loading using SAP Data Services happens in mature SAP HANA deployments, but batch loading data using SAP Data Services happens in almost every SAP HANA deployment that we've experienced. For these batch jobs to run, they must be executed.

This is a fundamental difference in SAP Data Services batch jobs and SAP Data Services real-time jobs. While real-time jobs are in a waiting status "listening" for web service requests as records are presented and then echoing transformed data as the process and the data flow require to the targets, batch loads require an instigating force to perform their tasks. Instigating forces can come in the form of a schedule, execution command, or a web service. We'll detail each of these methods in the following sections of this chapter.

### 5.3.1    SAP Data Services Scheduling

SAP Data Services scheduling of batch jobs is probably the most typical way to instigate a batch job in SAP Data Services. This is the method that is shipped with the product and supported by the documentation as the primary means. It's handled with two different methods in the Enterprise Information Management (EIM) landscape: the SAP Data Services scheduler and the SAP BusinessObjects BI scheduler.

### SAP Data Services Scheduler

The SAP Data Services scheduler is the traditional means to schedule batch jobs in SAP Data Services. It's found in the Data Services Management Console web tier application, as shown in Figure 5.18.

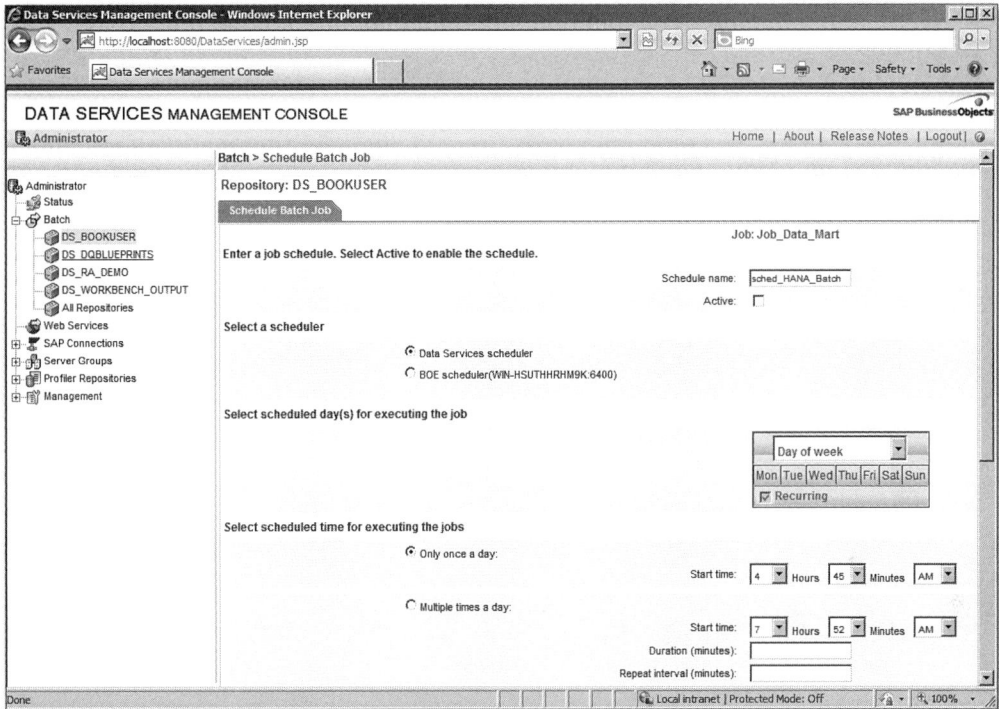

**Figure 5.18**  SAP Data Services Scheduler in the Management Console

This very simple, very flexible scheduler application allows scheduling by the day of the week, days in the month, within a certain time range, as well as numerous other options shown in Figure 5.19. We normally see it used the majority of the time for controlling the load times of batch SAP HANA loads.

The SAP Data Services scheduler also supports one job having multiple schedules. This can be useful if you have to run the same job numerous times throughout the day, such as to pick up data and load to SAP HANA every 15 minutes. This is easily accomplished with one batch job and a schedule to run every 15 minutes. If you need the job to execute in a smarter fashion, you can create multiple schedules and bind different variables to the schedules to force different batch job behavior at different times, as variable assignments can be stored with the schedules as well as with the jobs. This flexibility offers a number of possibilities for instigating jobs.

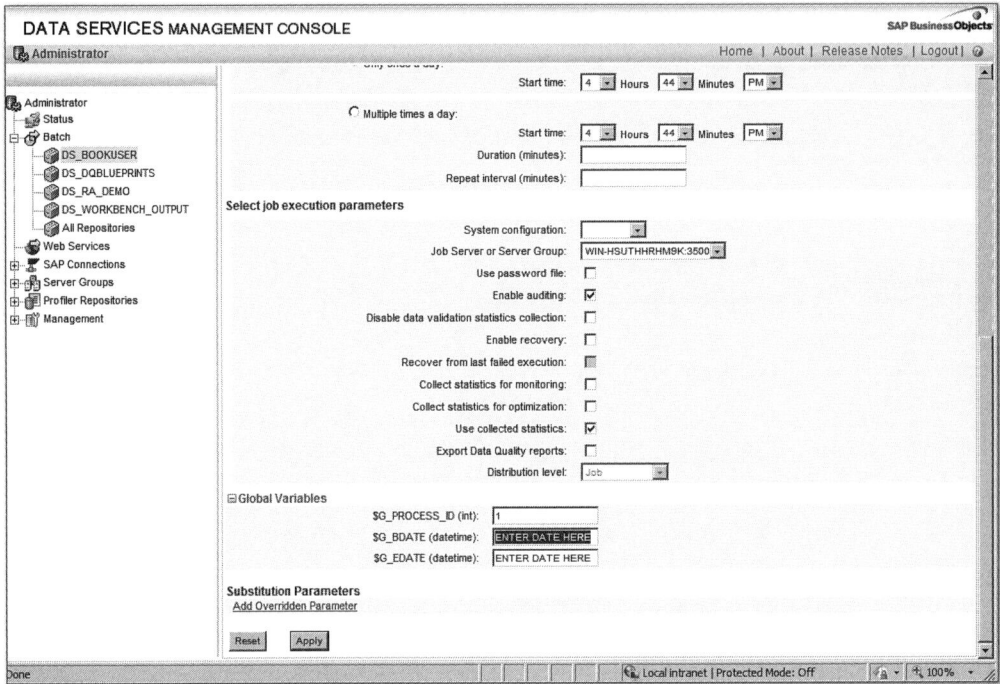

**Figure 5.19** Date Variable Examples Assigned on a Schedule

### SAP BusinessObjects BI Scheduler

SAP Data Services offers another option for scheduling batch jobs natively if you don't want to use the SAP Data Services scheduler: The SAP BusinessObjects BI scheduler. This is a great option if you're using SAP BusinessObjects BI for your reporting out of SAP HANA, as well as the rest of your enterprise. The SAP BusinessObjects BI scheduler is wrapped within the SAP BusinessObjects BI Central Management Console (CMC), which is shown in Figure 5.20.

If you're using SAP BusinessObjects BI for this purpose, you'll already have lots of scheduled tasks to run reports in place; it makes sense to avoid spreading the scheduling tasks to process on the SAP Data Services system because the SAP

BusinessObjects BI system can be the central processing point for all of your enterprise's scheduled report tasks.

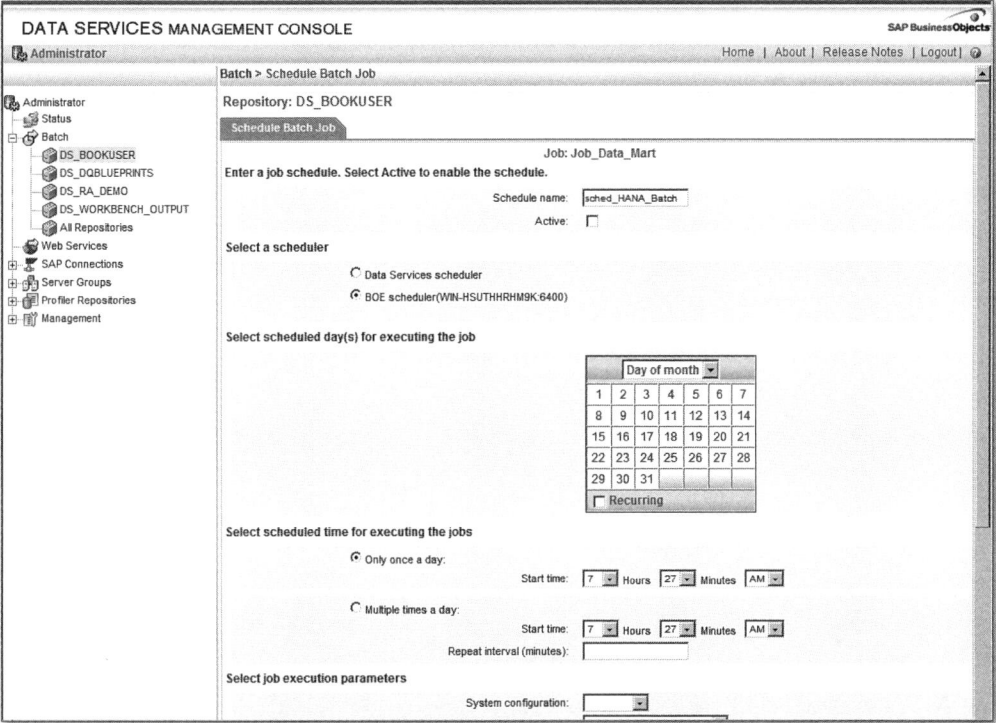

**Figure 5.20**  The Easy-to-Use SAP BusinessObjects BI Scheduler

Using the SAP BusinessObjects BI scheduler is as easy as selecting the BOE SCHEDULER radio button shown in Figure 5.20. After clicking the radio button, the scheduled task will run in SAP BusinessObjects BI.

These are two great options that are native to SAP Data Services. However, there are two third-party scheduling options that are worth noting: integration via web services and third-party scheduling.

## 5.3.2    Integration via Web Services

Organizations use web services for a variety of purposes—everything from data exchange between applications on different platforms to stateless process execution.

We've already discussed SAP Data Services real-time jobs and data flows fostering stateless real-time data exchange, but SAP Data Services batch jobs can also be triggered via web services!

This process isn't as straightforward, but it can certainly be accomplished if required by the needs of an organization. Figure 5.21 shows a real-time job calling a batch job that is instigated by a web service from an external application.

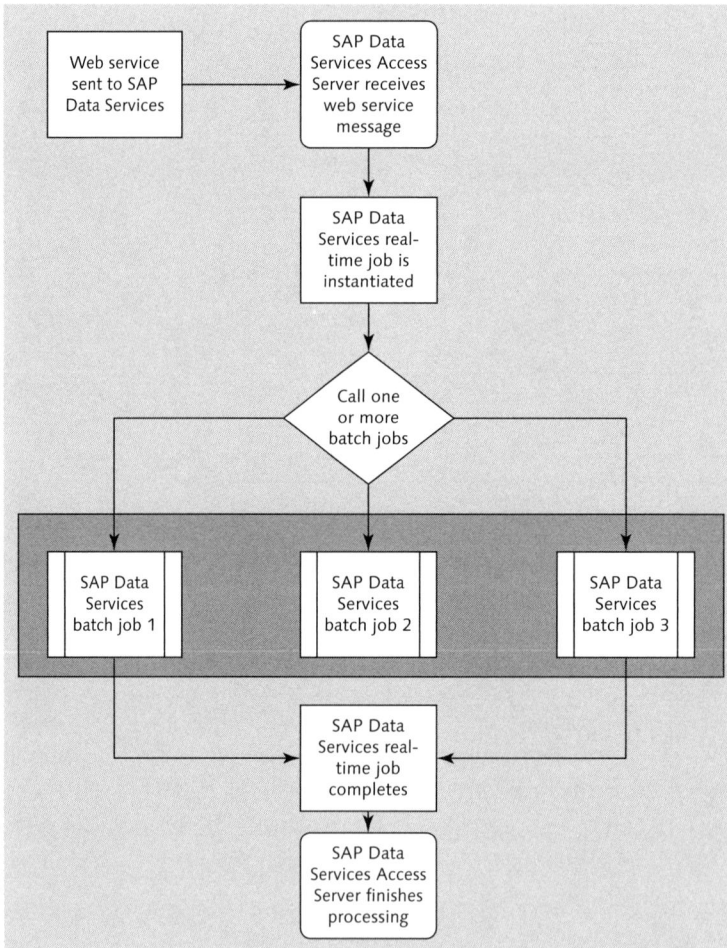

**Figure 5.21** Web Services Triggering Multiple SAP Data Services Batch Jobs

Let's walk through this workflow process step by step:

1. A web service from an external application is sent to the SAP Data Services Access Server, which is always listening for web service requests.

2. The Access Server processing starts, and the web services specified real-time job starts.

3. The SAP Data Services real-time job is configured to call another batch job instead of move data in data flows or workflows. This is performed by an `exec()` function in a script object. The example in Figure 5.21 calls three batch jobs, but this number can vary depending on what is needed.

4. The batch jobs start execution.

5. All batch jobs finish execution.

6. The real-time job finishes execution.

7. The application server finishes processing and returns the web service response of completion back to the source application.

This example is reasonably complicated, but it shows further options of knitting the SAP Data Services loading SAP HANA processing into the operational landscape. This is especially useful to organizations that don't want to manage multiple scheduling systems.

### 5.3.3    Integration via Execution Commands

Much of the functionality of the previous section (Section 5.3.2) detailed running a batch job from another batch job in SAP Data Services. This is because a batch job can be exposed as an executable object by creating an execution command in the Management Console in SAP Data Services, as shown in Figure 5.22, by clicking the ACTION column value EXPORT EXECUTION COMMAND.

After clicking EXPORT EXECUTION COMMAND, a screen appears that allows you to set many different options for job execution (see Figure 5.23). It's a more limited set of options than when you schedule a batch job in SAP Data Services, but you can still bind variables and run different configurations that connect to different sources to load SAP HANA. There is great flexibility when performing this function.

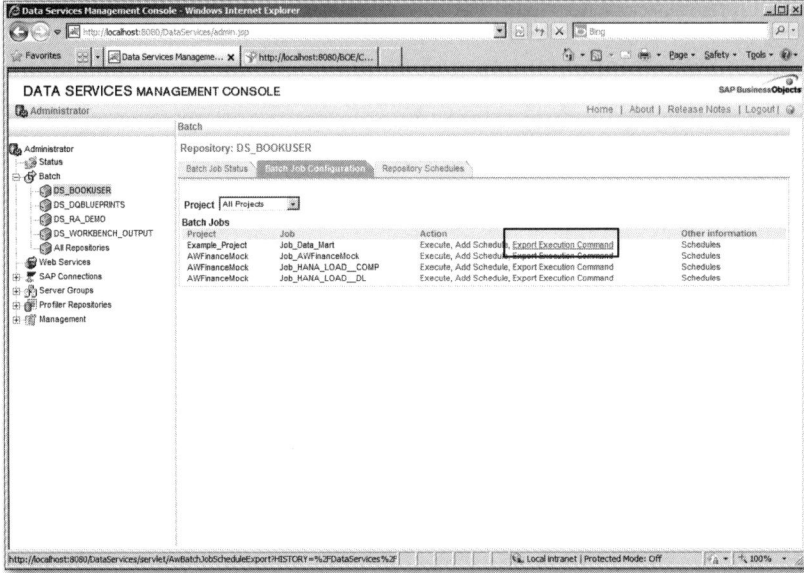

**Figure 5.22**  The Export Execution Command

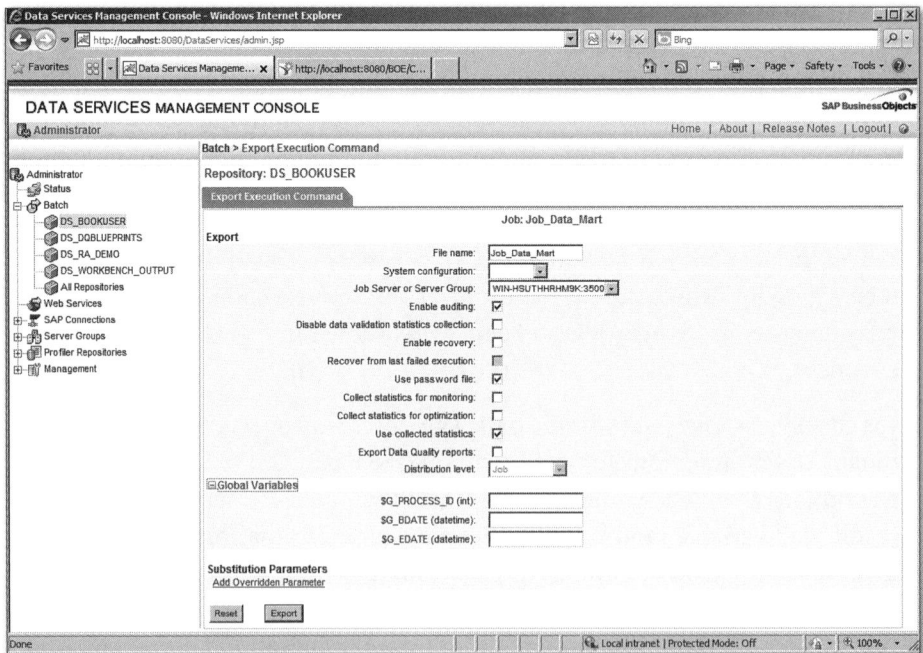

**Figure 5.23**  Execution Command Properties

When you click the EXPORT button to export the execution command, two files are produced containing execution properties in a batch (.bat) file and instructions in a text file (.txt).

> **Batch File Contents**
>
> E:\PROGRA~1\SAPBUS~1\DATASE~1/BIN/AL_RWJ~1.EXE  "C:\PROGRAMDATA\ SAP BUSINESSOBJECTS\DATA SERVICES/LOG/WIN-HSUTHHRHM9K/" -W "INET:WIN-HSUTHHRHM9K:3500" -C "C:\PROGRAMDATA\SAP BUSINESSOBJECTS\DATA SERVICES/ LOG/JOB_DATA_MART.TXT"

> **Text File Contents**
>
> -PLOCALEUTF8 -R"DS_BOOKUSER.TXT" -G"4D57CCC2_BFF5_481B_A7A8_A7B123F164A5" -T5 -T14 -LOCALEGV -GV"$G_PROCESS_ID=MTAwMA;$G_BDATE=JzIwMTMuMDYuMDU GMDA6MDA6M" -GV"DAN;" -CTBATCH -CMWIN-HSUTHHRHM9K -CAADMINISTRATOR -CJWIN-HSUTHHRHM9K -CP3500

These files work together. The batch file is the executable component, and the text file supplies the supplementary instructions to guide the batch file to all of the values that you specified in the Export Execution Command process.

So when you need to call an SAP Data Services batch job, you just execute the batch file produced by this process, and the job executes with all of the logic, variables, and system configurations that have been specified in the execution command. This makes for a very simple but smart execution process.

## 5.3.4 Third-Party Scheduler

Many organizations have integrated scheduling into a third-party application that handles all job and task scheduling opportunities for the organization. SAP has made allowances with this with SAP Data Services so that loading SAP HANA can be scheduled using the same mechanisms. Essentially, this is all done with the Export Execution Command functionality that was just chronicled in the previous section. The workflow is as follows and is shown in Figure 5.24:

1. Create your batch job to load SAP HANA.

2. Export an execution command of your completed SAP Data Services batch job that loads SAP HANA. This will export both the batch file and instruction file.

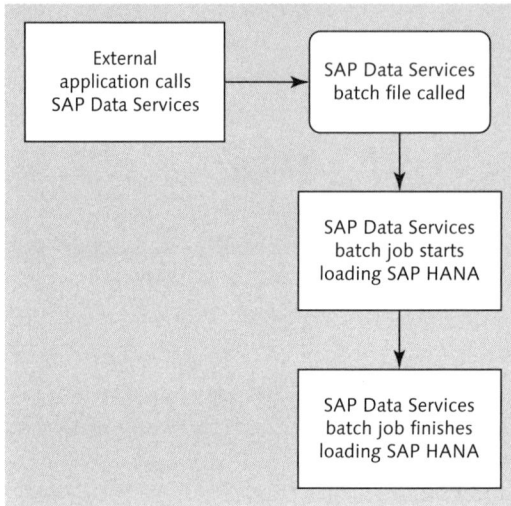

**Figure 5.24**  External Application Calling SAP Data Services Batch Job

3. Ensure that your third-party scheduling application has permissions to the directory on the SAP Data Services server where this file is stored.

4. Integrate a command-line call to the batch file from your scheduling application via a UNC path: \\SAPDATASERVICESSERVER\INSTALLATIONDIRECTORY\BATCH-FILE.BAT.

5. Schedule your task in your third-party application.

Let's walk through two case studies—one each for loading data in batches (Section 5.4) and in real time (Section 5.5).

## 5.4    Case Study: Loading Data in Batch

The AdventureWorks Cycle Company has recently implemented a new BI platform based on SAP HANA, SAP Data Services, and SAP BusinessObjects BI. Using SAP Data Services, its BI resources were able to successfully extract, translate, and load the supporting Internet sales dimension and fact tables into an SAP HANA schema using a batch approach.

This section of the chapter outlines this process and cites specific examples of the build of the SAP Data Services job, the transformations contained in the job, and the mechanisms to build the tables in SAP HANA.

This first case study details the batch job that loads and creates the following tables in SAP HANA:

► DIM_Product

► DIM_Customer

► DIM_Sales_Territory

► DIM_Date

► FACT_Internet_Sales_Retail

To create these tables, you'll construct a batch job in SAP Data Services that first loads a staging database as described in Chapter 4 per best practices and then loads these tables.

For the purpose of our examples in the batch job case study, the staging database is in Microsoft SQL Server 2008R2. Any number of database platforms can be used, but we wanted to select a staging database platform that is readily available to customers and most likely in their enterprise.

### 5.4.1 Structure the Job

The first step is to structure the SAP Data Services job, which is shown in Figure 5.25. Recall that this job is comprised of four steps:

- Initialization
- Staging
- Mart
- End

We'll walk through these workflows, which are surrounded by `Try` and `Catch` objects that capture and respond to processing errors for recovery purposes. Later, we'll uncover the details of the staging load as well as details of each of the dimension and fact tables.

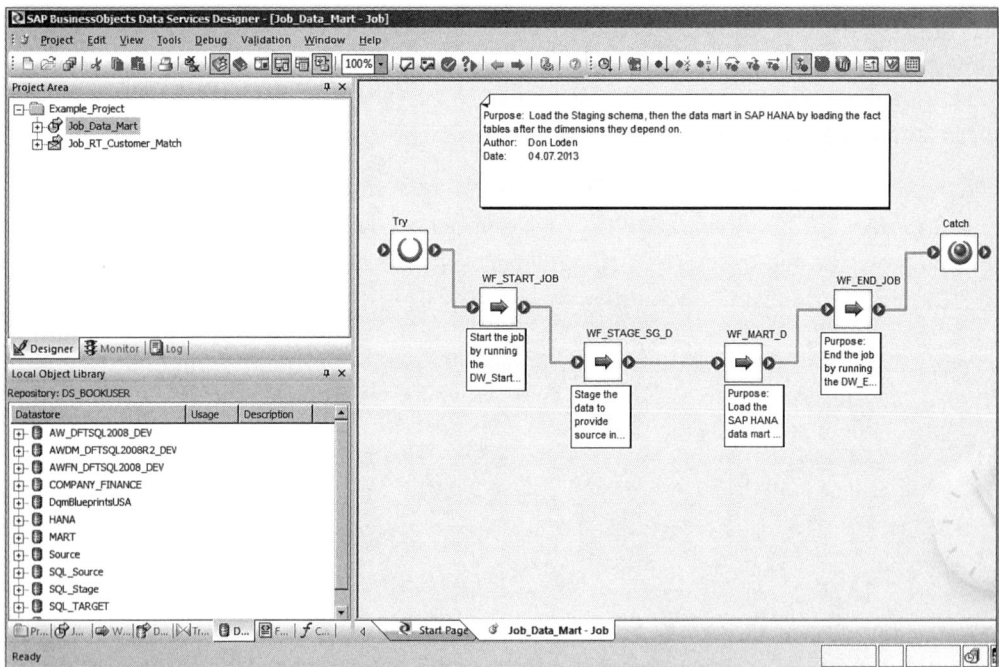

**Figure 5.25** SAP Data Services Job That Loads SAP HANA

## 5.4.2 Try/Catch Block

The `Try` and `Catch` objects shown in Figure 5.25 that wrap the workflows are generally referred to as a block. This block of objects performs all of the error trapping, halts to the job, and notifications to the users in the event of a problem. The `Try` object is just a placeholder object for noting that error trapping has begun for all workflows or data flows placed after the `Try`. The `Catch` object has all of the design-making power; this object can trap many types of errors, as shown in Figure 5.26.

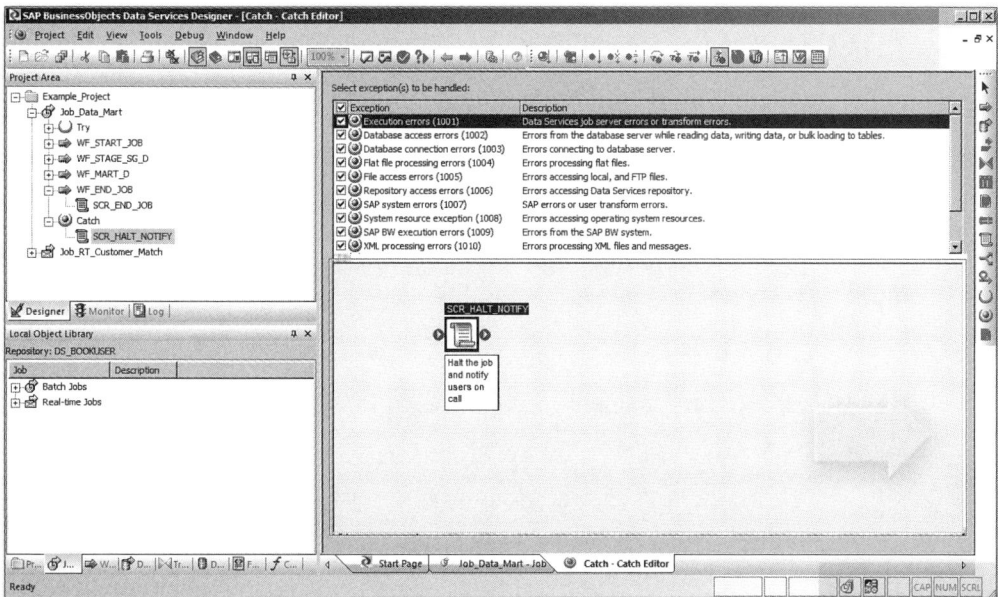

**Figure 5.26**   Inside the Catch Block: Script to Halt and Email Users

Any of the errors shown in Figure 5.26 will cause SAP Data Services to execute the code contained in the script object SCR_HALT_NOTIFY. This script object contains the code provided in Listing 5.1 that will both halt the job and send out an email notification to any specified user that there is a problem.

```
#### HALT THE JOB ###
#
#Raise Exception for the log and to denote failure for recoverability.
raise_exception(job_name( ) || ' terminated due to error');

##### Email users
#
```

```
#First parameter is the list of emails
#Second is the email subject
#Third is text for the email body
#Fourth and fifth are line counts of how much of the SAP Data Services
logs to include
#
smtp_to('don.loden@decisionfirst.com','SAPHANA_Mart_Job Failed',
'SAPHANA_Mart_Job Failed.', 10, 10);
```

**Listing 5.1** Halt the Job in the Event of an Error

### 5.4.3 Initialization

After clearing the `Try` and entering the `Try/Catch` block section of the code, you now enter the initialization stage of the SAP Data Services code. The initialization phase is pretty simplistic because this workflow (WF_START_JOB) only contains one object: SCR_START_JOB. SCR_START_JOB's function is twofold: to set the variables that will control the logic of the job and to execute the `DW_StartJob` function to control the `ExtractLow` and `ExtractHigh` dates for source-based CDC operations. The SCR_START_JOB script object is shown in Figure 5.27.

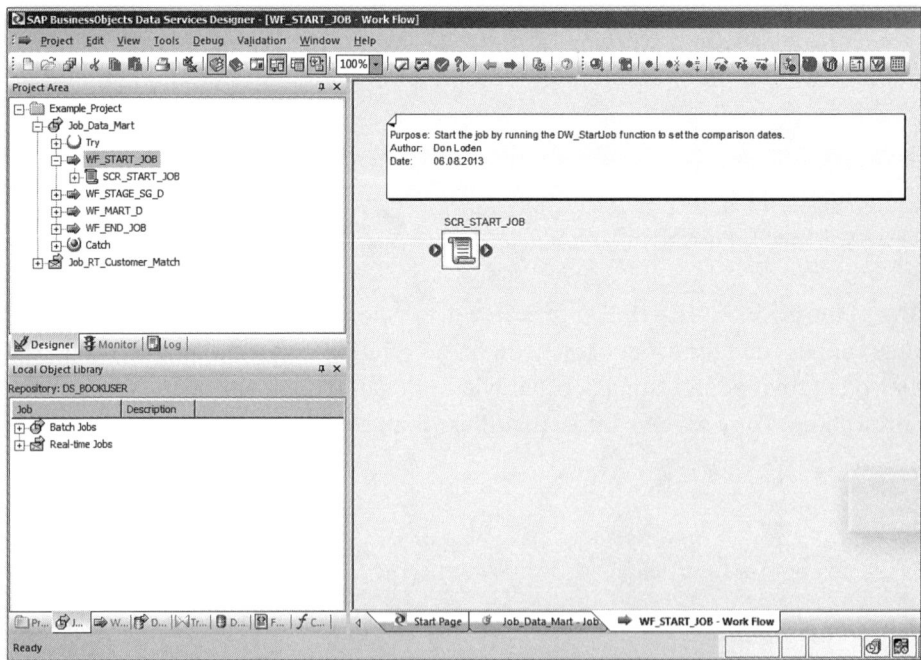

**Figure 5.27** SCR_START_JOB Contained within the Workflow WF_START_JOB

The script contains the code shown in Listing 5.2.

```
#Purpose:   Set global variables and exec
# dw_start_job function to
# deal with dw_job_execution table.
#Author: Don Loden don.loden@decisionfirst.com
#Date:    09.30.2012

#Load Mart databases: Y or N
$G_LOAD_MART  = 'Y';

#$G_PROCESS_ID  Type: int This variable will be automatically loaded
via DI script
#$G_BDATE Type: DateTime This variable will be automatically loaded via
DI script
#$G_EDATE Type: DateTime This variable will be automatically loaded via
DI script
$G_EDATE = sysdate();

$G_LOAD_TYPE = 'Delta';
#$G_LOAD_TYPE = 'First';
###############End Variable Declaration#############

# Call function to check ExecutionStatus Table for this job
# To force a new run using $G_BDATE and $G_EDATE as the extraction
interval
DW_StartJob (job_name(),$G_LOAD_TYPE, $G_BDATE, $G_EDATE,
        $G_PROCESS_ID, $G_LOAD_DATE, $G_VERSION_LABEL, $G_COMMENT );

# Displays start/end date and Process ID for each job run
print('*****************************************');
print('                          ');
Print('[$G_LOAD_TYPE] - Load started taking data from [$G_BDATE] to
[$G_EDATE]');
Print('[$G_LOAD_DATE] - Load date');
Print('[$G_PROCESS_ID] - DW_Process_ID for current load.');
print('*****************************************');
print('
   ');
print('*****************************************');
```

**Listing 5.2** Code to Set Variables and Call DW_StartJob in the Script

### 5.4.4  Staging Workflow

After clearing the initialization stage of the job, it's time for the real work to begin in the staging stage of the SAP Data Services batch job. This structuring the job step performs many tasks, including the following important ones:

- Surrogate keys
- Source independence
- Data standardization
- CDC against the source
- Transformations for denormalization for SAP HANA

> **Important**
>
> We're only loading a single source in this batch job into SAP HANA, but the examples of surrogacy still hold true whether you have one data source for SAP HANA or ten.

The staging workflow (WF_STAGE_SG_D) is depicted in Figure 5.28. This workflow performs all of the tasks previously mentioned to properly prepare data for high performance in SAP HANA.

You start the journey to SAP HANA by creating surrogate keys in staging as described in Section 5.1.1 to divorce the data source constraints from the key structures needed for SAP HANA. This will be done in staging, which is used to build the tables and provide independence from the source system database constraints; this make no sense when multiple sources are combined in SAP HANA. We'll examine this in detail and show how this process is executed in each of the four staging table builds. These fields result in a naming convention shift from "_ID" to "_GK". Fields ending with ID will be the native source primary keys, where GK stands for generated key. GK fields are the surrogate keys that encompass all source relationships.

*Source independence* will also be shown in staging by using a column to identify where records are coming from as they make their way to SAP HANA. This is particularly important when there are multiple sources, but in any data mart or data warehouse construct, it is best practice to include these columns. Because you never know when you'll encounter more sources, it's always prudent to plan ahead and assume that you'll have them. The source column for staging and SAP HANA is the same among all of the tables and is called DW_SOURCE.

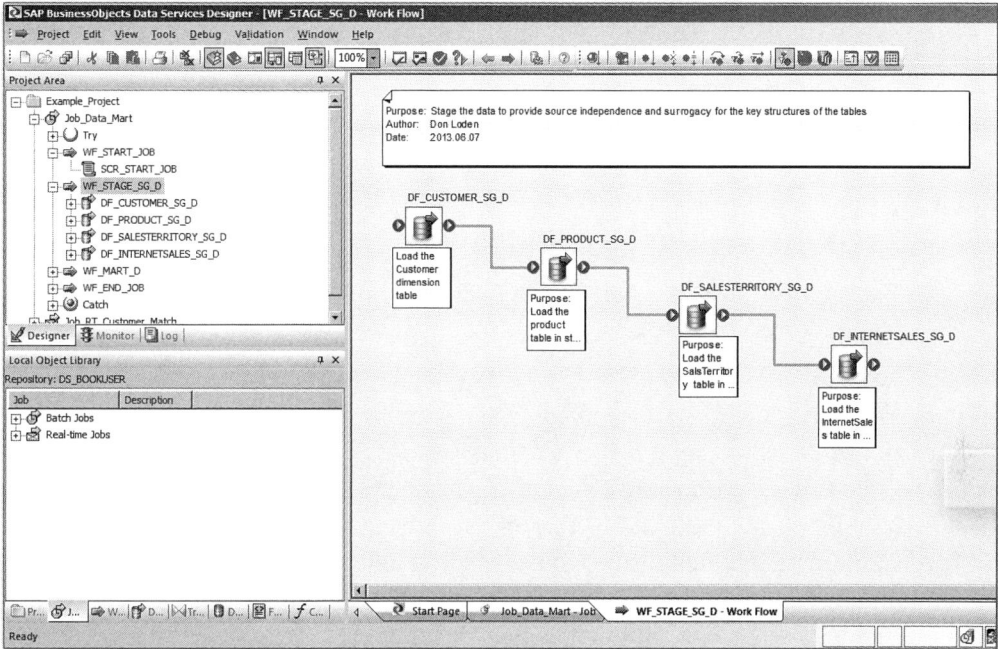

**Figure 5.28** Staging Workflow that Will Prepare Data for SAP HANA

*Data standardization* is another theme that remains central throughout the staging process. You're taking data from a transactional source system in this case study and standardizing it for use in SAP HANA. Again, because there is only one source, this isn't as crucial, yet it's still important that standards are followed so that reports from SAP HANA consume data of high quality. There isn't one specific example of this, but this theme remains constant throughout the staging transformation layer of the SAP Data Services batch job.

Source-based CDC is something else that is also quite prevalent in staging. In these examples, assume that you're not performing an initial load from the Adventure-Works transactional system with every batch data load. You'll use the concepts discussed earlier of driving data with a range of modified date values from the respective source tables. This will be performed by using variables for an ExtractLow date as well as an ExtractHigh date in the WHERE clause of our various data flows in the staging level of the SAP Data Services batch job.

Finally, we'll illustrate denormalization into one staging table that will be used to load a fact table in SAP HANA, which we discussed in Chapter 1 and Chapter 2. This concept is crucial for maximum performance of SAP HANA, especially across two tables with high cardinality, such as for the sales header and sales detail source tables. There are other cases of mild denormalization for the dimension table loads in staging, but this fact sales table, called Internet Sales in Staging, is the classic SAP HANA denormalization example as referenced in the earlier chapters in this book.

Now, let's discuss the details of the next four table builds—Customer, Product, Sales Territory, and Internet Sales.

### Customer

The CUSTOMER staging table is the first staging table build that we'll explore, and it's also the most complicated of the staging tables because there were unique requirements around CUSTOMER for the AdventureWorks Cycle Company. For instance, certain values needed to be substituted depending on customer type; also an alternative method of performing target-based CDC is required. With these extra requirements, the data flow becomes quite complex, as you can see in Figure 5.29.

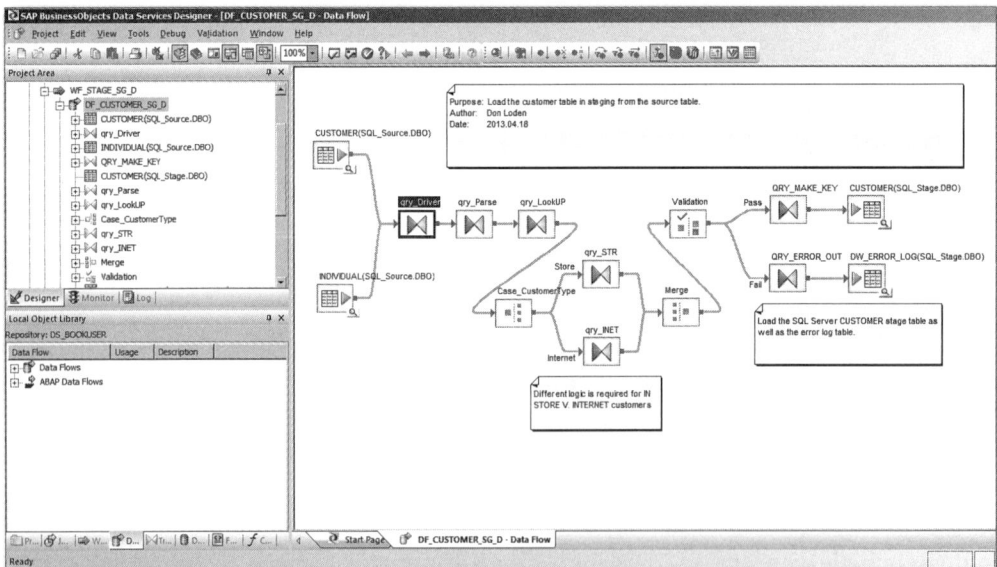

**Figure 5.29** Driver Stage of the Staging CUSTOMER Build

This example covers all stages of data flow, which were discussed in Chapter 4, Section 4.1.5:

- Driver stage
- Parsing stage
- Lookup stage
- Business rules validation stage

These sections are exemplified in the build of this data flow starting with the driver stage shown as QRY_DRIVER in Figure 5.30. This shows a properly constructed join that will be pushed down to the source database. Figure 5.31 depicts the WHERE clause using two variables $G_BDATE and $G_EDATE; these two variables obtain their values from the DW_JobExecution function in the Initialization subsection of Section 5.1.1 of this chapter, and is used throughout the remaining staging table driver sections.

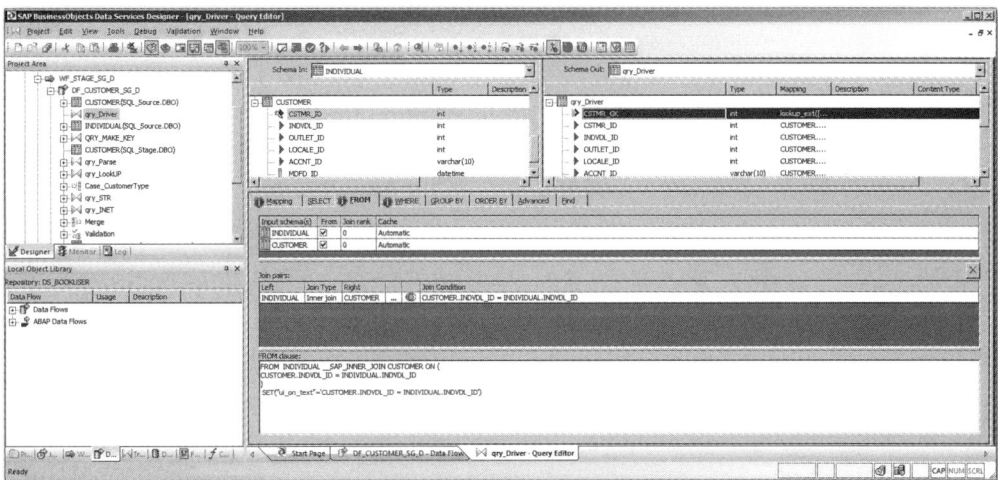

**Figure 5.30** Join that Will Be Pushed Down to the Source Tables

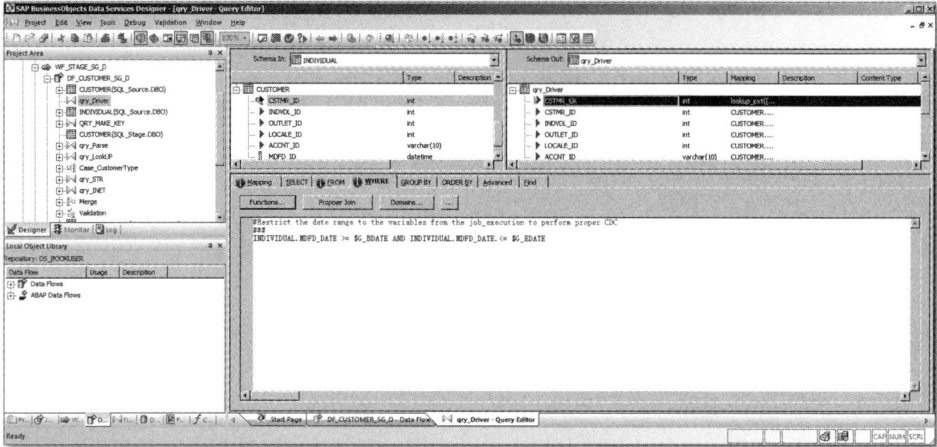

**Figure 5.31** CDC WHERE Clause to Only Capture Changed Data from the Source

One last item makes the CUSTOMER build's driver section unique. To show an alternative method of target-based CDC in this CUSTOMER load, a `lookup_ext` function was included to return the primary key values from the CUSTOMER table if they exist. This is shown in Figure 5.32.

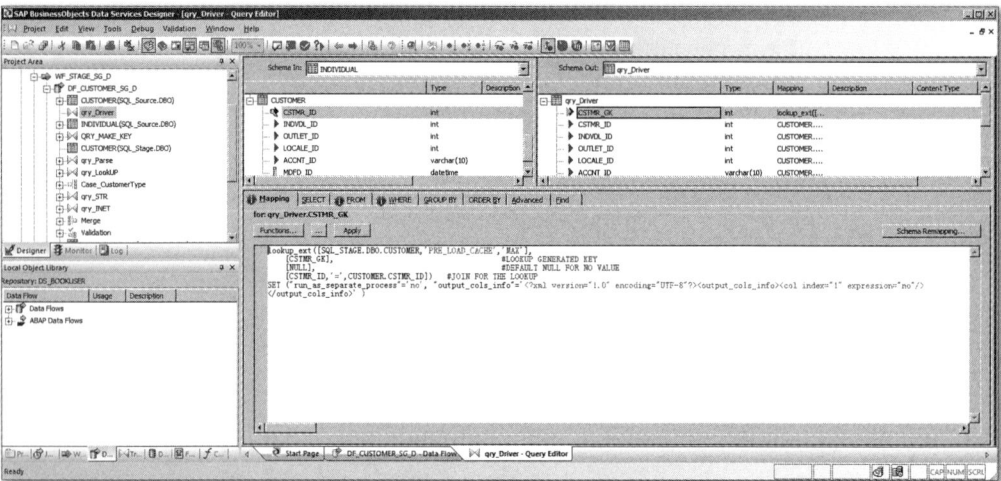

**Figure 5.32** Lookup_Ext Function Syntax Performed Inline

If the value exists then, the GK (CUSTOMER primary key) value will be returned. Otherwise, a NULL value will be returned. This NULL will be handled in the parsing section of the data flow.

The lookup syntax isn't trivial, so it may be best to code it in the SAP Data Services GUI that is shown in Figure 5.33. Both of these methods perform the same task, so developers are able to pick whichever method they desire.

Next we'll explore the parsing stage of the CUSTOMER staging data flow per business rules. This is shown in qry_Parse in Figure 5.34. This occurs after the record set is driven down with the source-based CDC performed in the driver stage.

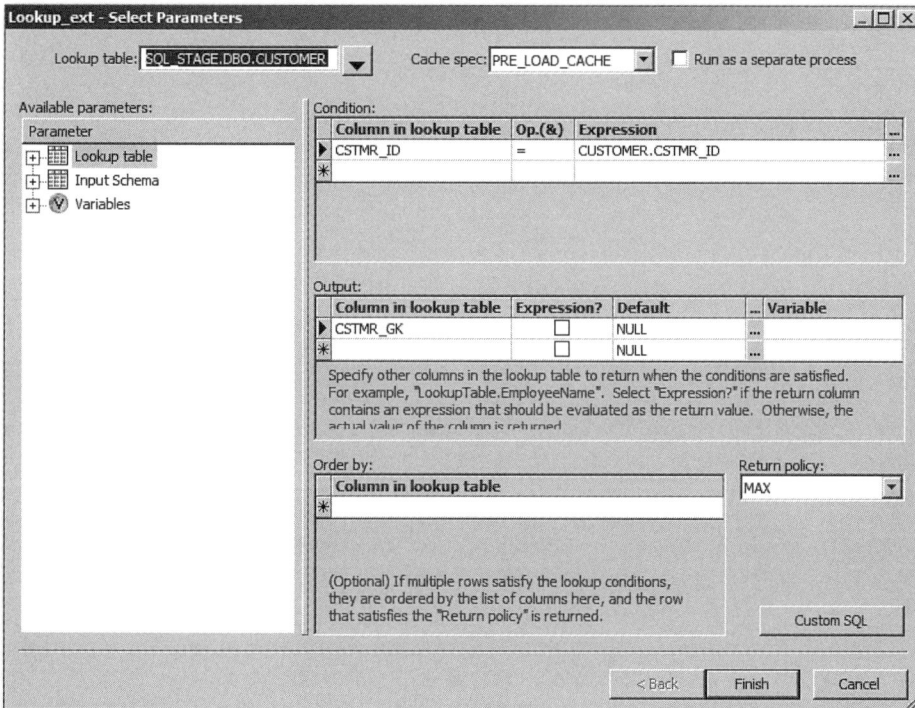

**Figure 5.33** Options in the GUI for the Customer_GK lookup_ext Function

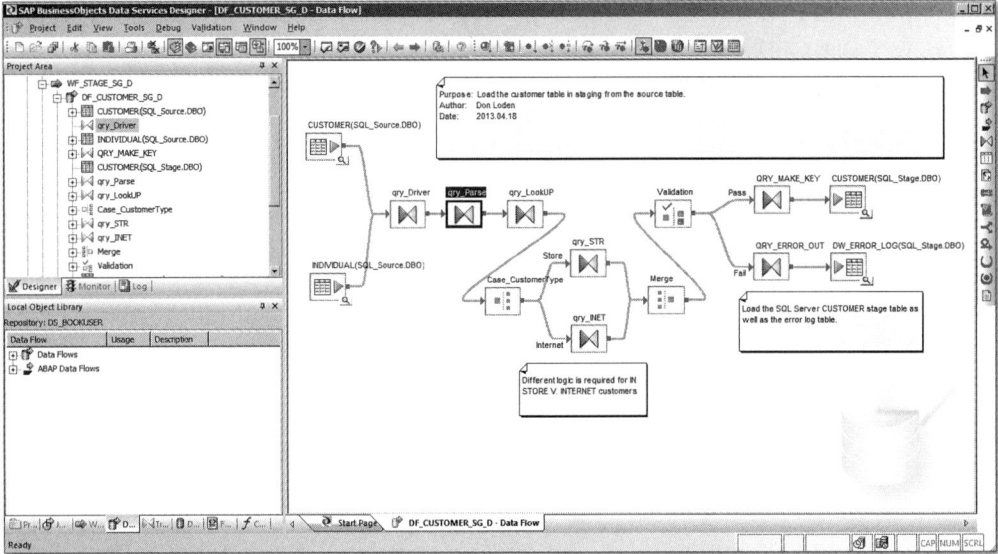

**Figure 5.34** Parsing Stage of the Staging CUSTOMER Build

This parsing stage of the CUSTOMER build is actually quite simple in that the only values that need to be parsed are the NULL GK values returned by the lookup_ext function in the previously covered driver stage. This is accomplished by an NVL() function that replaces NULL values with any specified values, as shown in Figure 5.35.

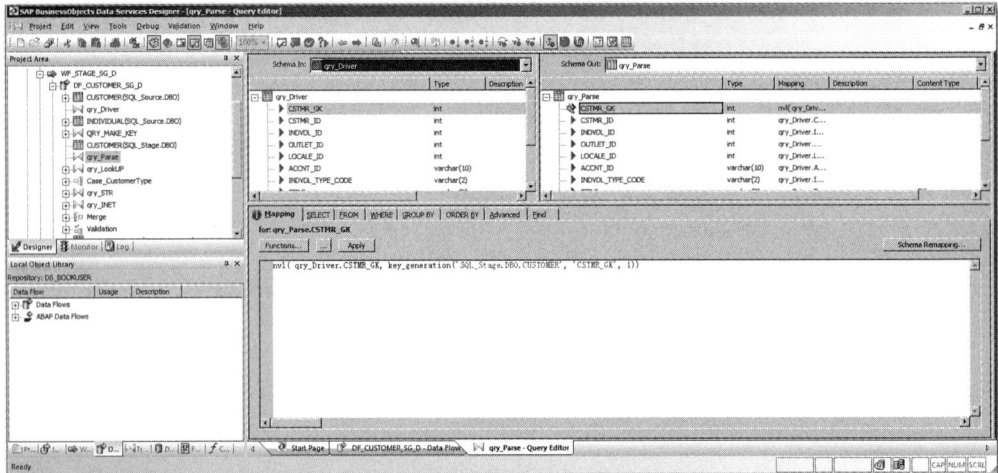

**Figure 5.35** NVL() Function Produces Key Values for New Records

This function works with `lookup_ext` to produce primary key values for new records. If you didn't do this, new records or inserts would fail the lookup and have a `NULL` value because they wouldn't be found in the CUSTOMER target table. Thus, you team the `NVL()` function with a `Key_Generation` function to produce the necessary key values. This is an alternative method to the `Table_Comparison` transform that you'll use for the remaining staging tables.

**NVL() + Key_Generation Function Syntax**

```
nvl( qry_Driver.CSTMR_GK, key_generation('SQL_Stage.DBO.CUSTOMER',
'CSTMR_GK', 1))
```

After the parsing stage of the CUSTOMER staging data flow finishes, it's time to begin the lookup stage. This is the `qry_Lookup` shown in Figure 5.36.

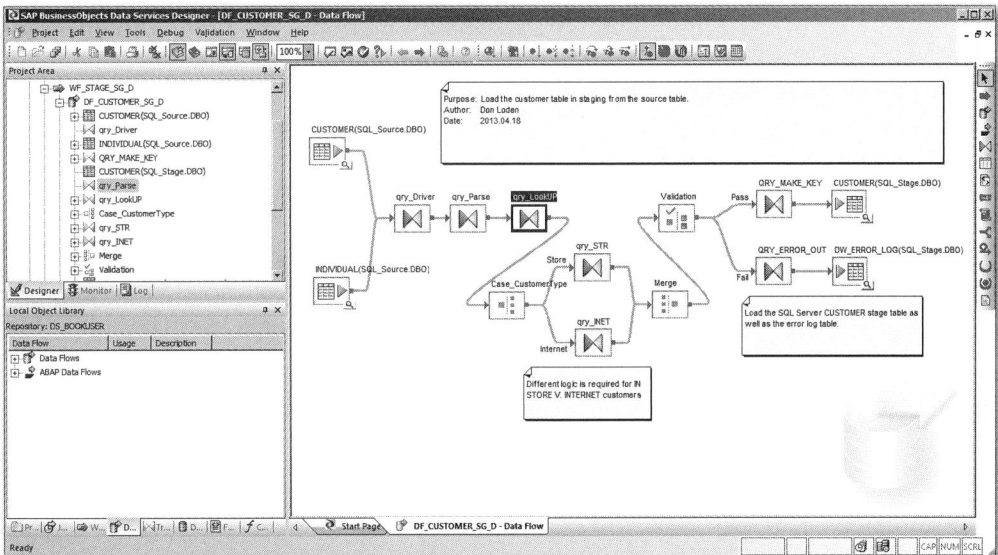

**Figure 5.36** Lookup Stage of the Staging CUSTOMER Build

In terms of performance, lookups are expensive and consequently should be limited to this stage of the data flow where possible. The target-based CDC operation illustrated earlier is one exception, as parsing needed to occur after that lookup to replace `NULL` values with newly created primary key values using the `NVL` function.

You'll use the lookups in this section to drive business logic by looking up whether a customer is an Internet customer or came in and purchased a bicycle in a store.

Lookups can be performed in-line as you saw earlier in this section with the difficult-to-read syntax, but they also may be inserted as function calls. This is the case for the ONLINE_ORDER_FLAG field that you need to return from the SALES_HEADER table from the source system. The function call method is shown in Figure 5.37; the lookup_ext function in the GUI is shown in Figure 5.38.

Figure 5.37  Lookup_ext Functions Inserted as Function Calls Not Inline

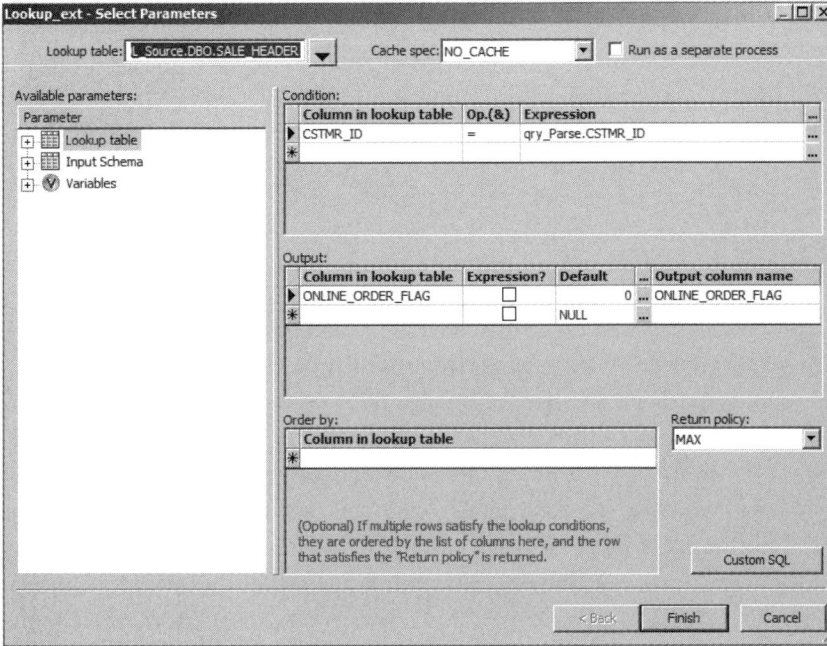

**Figure 5.38** Lookup_ext to Return ONLINE_ORDER_FLAG Field

A final item in the lookup stage is assigning two very important columns to the CUSTOMER table: a source indictor column (DW_SOURCE) and a process ID column (DW_PROCESS_ID). These are shown in Figure 5.39.

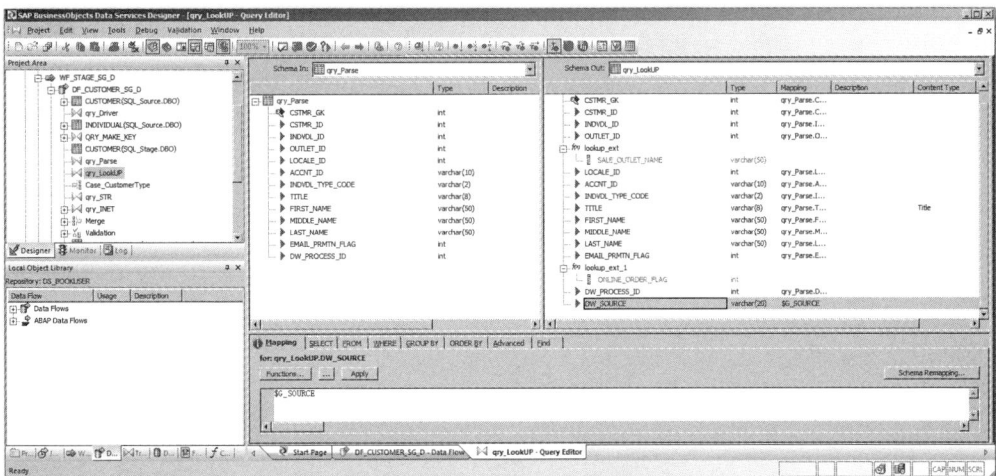

**Figure 5.39** Setting the Source Field with a Variable for Flexibility

The DW_SOURCE column acts as an identifier to tell the users where the records came from. Of course, because we only have one source, this isn't as important for our case study example, but data warehousing applications in SAP HANA frequently combine multiple sources, so this column always should be used. Notice that a variable $G_SOURCE is used to set this column. This is done for code flexibility so that this method can be used everywhere to avoid hard-coding source values in the data flow. This best practice makes the data flow modular and allows for greater reuse.

The other column that is set in a similar manner with a variable is the DW_PRO-CESS_ID column. This is a crucial column that exists in every table in staging as well as SAP HANA because it serves an important purpose. This is the ID value, which is a numeric value that signifies the number of the execution or job run. So, when the job runs, all of the data that is produced by the date range from the source system is stamped with this value. This concept provides a platform for recovery. You can recover the job; dates have been removed from the equation because with our Process ID value, the transaction is just that ID. The ID transaction of today may have pulled 50,000 customers, but it's still execution number 1,000 in the DW_PROCESS_ID column. This allows you to recover as a unit should a failure occur. Process ID also plays a very important role in the mart batch job section of the code for loading to SAP HANA, which we'll cover in a later section of this chapter.

Now that you've used the `lookup_ext` functions to know which ones are Internet customers and which are in-store customers, you can use a combination of `Case`, `Query`, and `Merge` transforms to perform the field substitutions needed to fulfill the business requirements shown in Figure 5.40.

First, you need to use the `Case` transform to act upon the values returned from the lookup. You'll use the `Case` transform to drive the data into one query transform or another. If the ONLINE_ORDER flag is 0, then guide the records to the `qry_STR` transform, or if you know the customer must be an Internet customer, you can also we'll drive the records to the `qry_STR`. The options in the CASE tab to guide the data in this manner are shown in Figure 5.41.

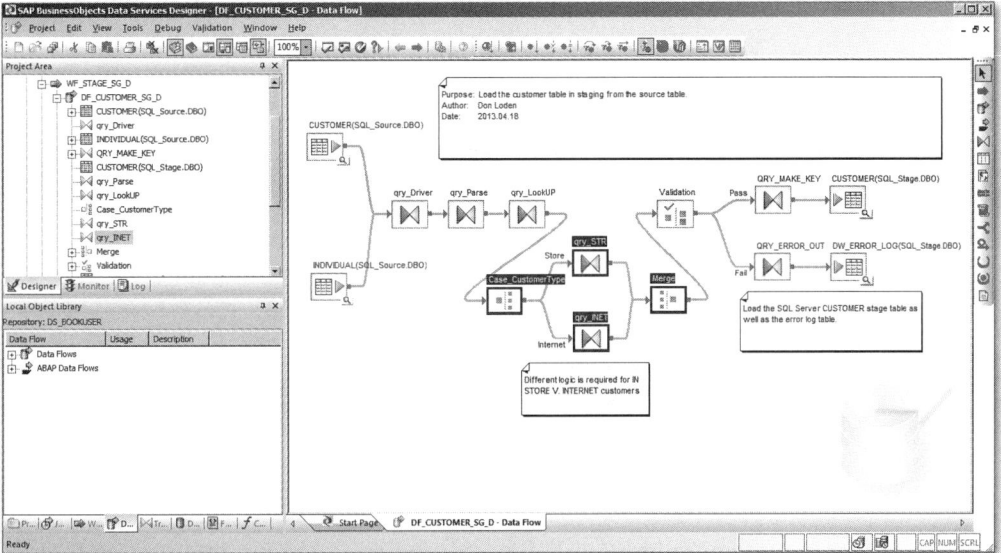

**Figure 5.40** Complex Case Logic and Merging the Staging CUSTOMER Build

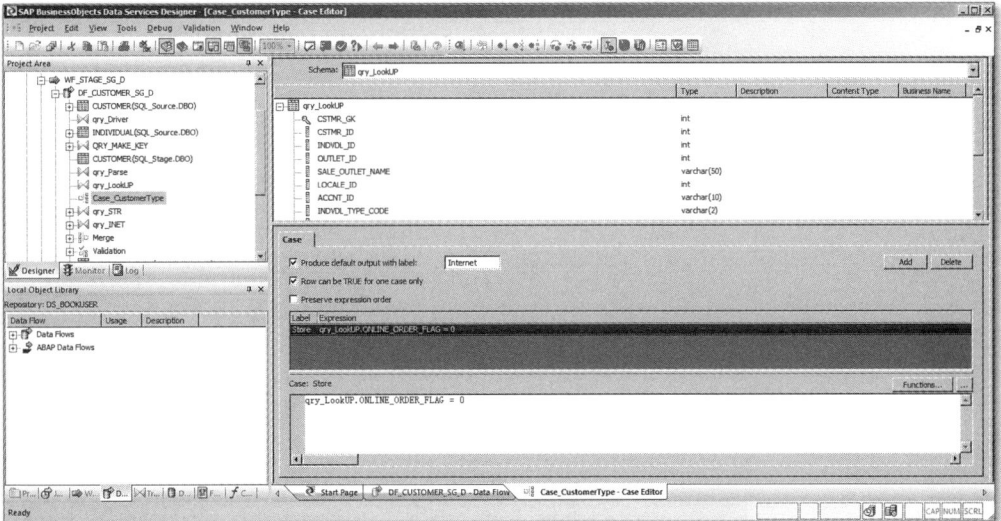

**Figure 5.41** Case Transform Options That Drive the Flow of Data

After the data has been driven into the appropriate `Query` transform, the value substitutions will occur as shown in Figure 5.42 and Figure 5.43, showing brick-and-mortar and Internet settings, respectively.

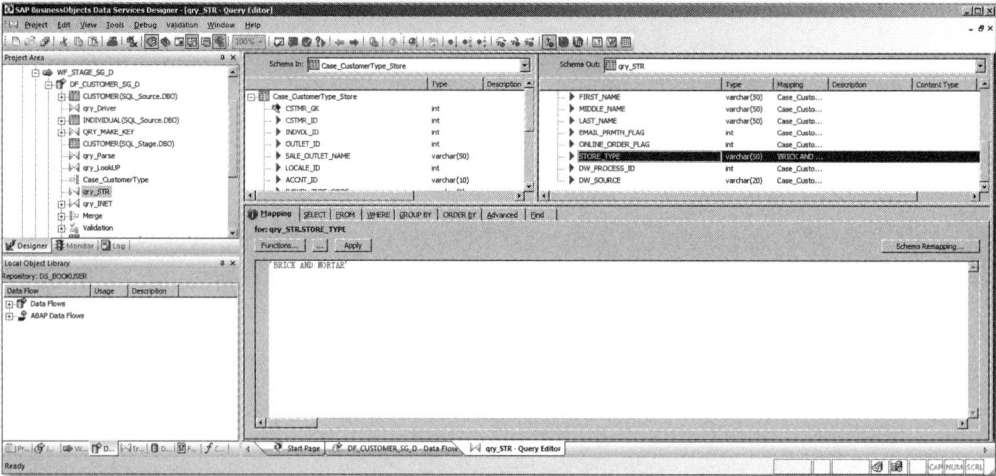

**Figure 5.42**  Setting the Brick-and-Mortar Value

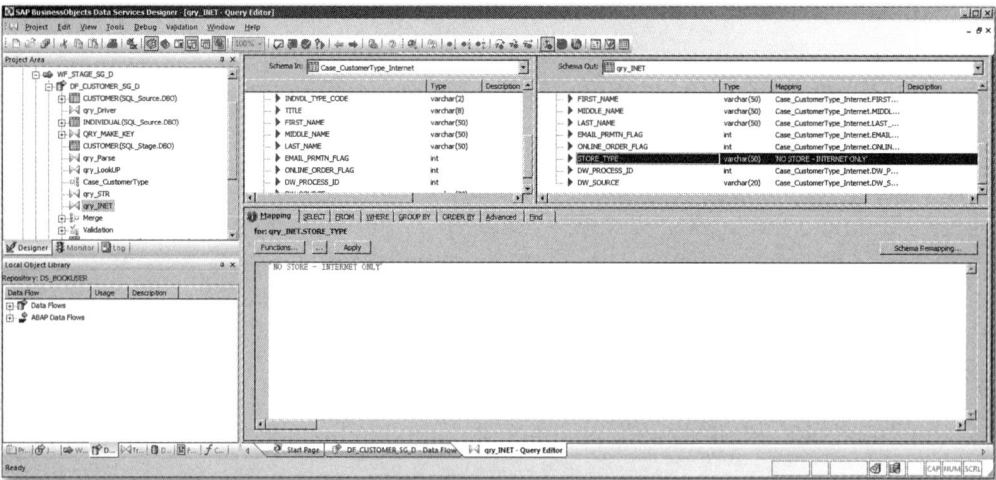

**Figure 5.43**  Setting the Internet Store Value

The record sets, which are identical in structure, are merged back together using a `Merge` transform as shown in Figure 5.44.

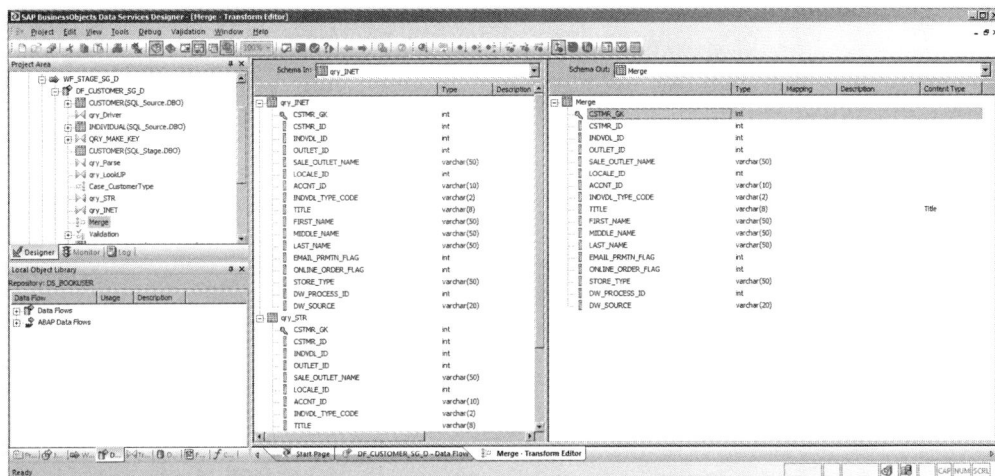

**Figure 5.44**  Merging the Two Record Sets Back Together

This is a very simple demonstration of case logic, but a good example of how `Case`, `Query`, and `Merge` transforms work together. The important thing to keep in mind is that this is where you perform value substitutions, even with complex logic such as lookups or decode functions. The complexity doesn't matter, but the field's structure is important.

> **Note**
>
> For the merge to be performed, the field names and order in both `Query` transforms must be identical.

Now that all of the transformations from the CUSTOMER data flow have been performed, and the data is almost ready to write to the staging CUSTOMER table, you need to validate your work in the validation stage shown in Figure 5.45.

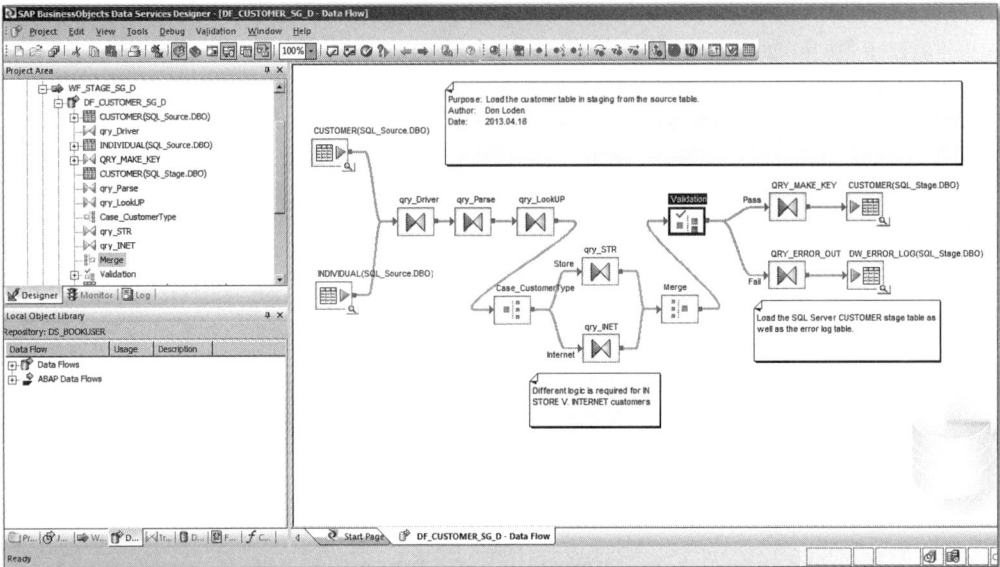

**Figure 5.45** Validation Stage of the Staging CUSTOMER Build

The validation stage is a combination of the Validation transform and the DW_ ERROR_LOG table. This section of the code captures failures of the business rules that need enforcement posttransformations. Common examples include primary and foreign key (orphan records) enforcement across sources, but you can really measure any fields.

In this case, the Validation transform measures both orphans and custom transformations recently produced with the case logic, specifically the following:

▶ Ensuring Internet versus in-store values were set correctly

▶ Checking for customer orphan records

▶ Checking for individual orphan records

▶ Checking for outlet orphan records

The validation property settings to produce this result are shown in Figure 5.46.

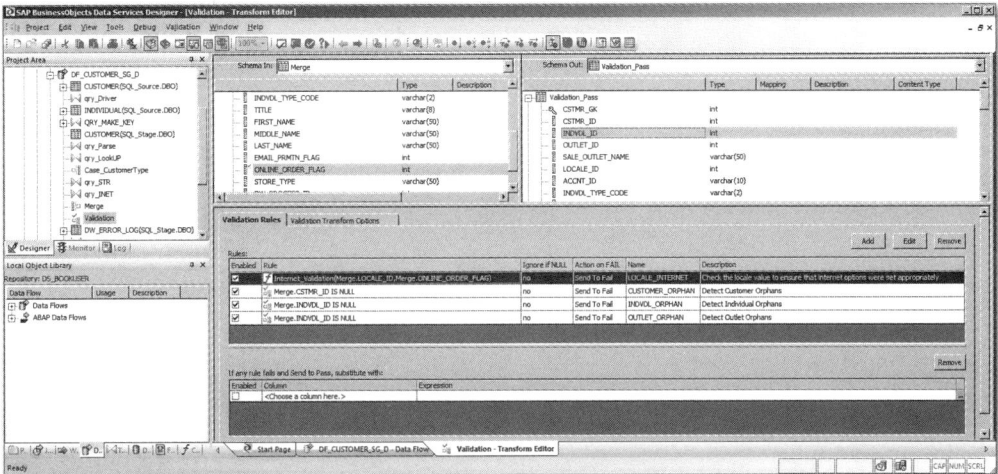

**Figure 5.46** Details of the Validation Transform

> **Note**
>
> Notice the validation function in comparison to the field validations. This validation function can also come from SAP Information Steward.

If all of the logic tests in the `Validation` transform succeed, then the record is sent to the CUSTOMER target through the QRY_MAKE_KEY transform, as shown in Figure 5.47.

Then, the records will be written to the CUSTOMER table using the Auto Correct Load functionality described in Chapter 4. The Auto Correct Load functionality provides insert records if the record isn't detected in the target table and update records if the record is detected in the target. As you see in Figure 5.48, this is easily accomplished with the selected property field.

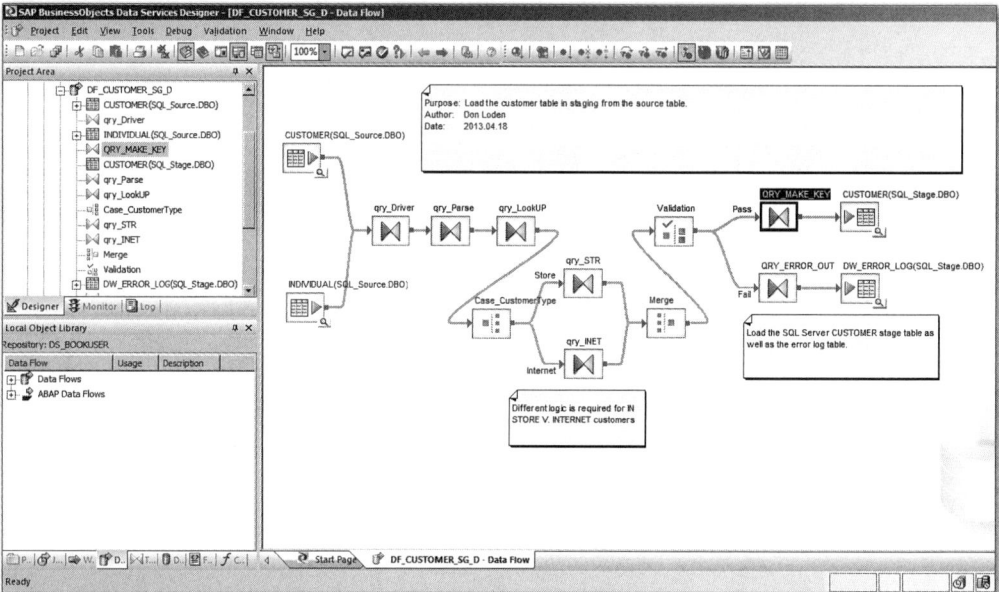

**Figure 5.47** Final Query Transform Aligns the Output Field Names with the CUSTOMER Table

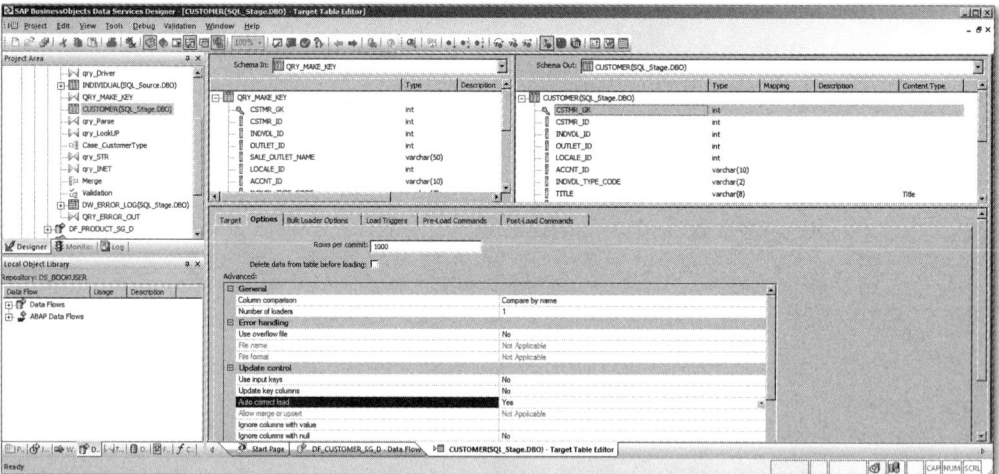

**Figure 5.48** Auto Correct Load Option Set for CUSTOMER Table on the GK Field

The update occurs against the CSTMR_GK field because this is the primary key field with the primary key icon in Figure 5.48. If you need this functionality against a table that doesn't have any keys, you can use the USE INPUT KEYS setting after declaring one or more fields as a key in the previous `Query` transform.

In the event that records did not meet the conditions of the `Validation` transform, then they are routed to the `QRY_ERROR_OUT` transform as shown in Figure 5.49.

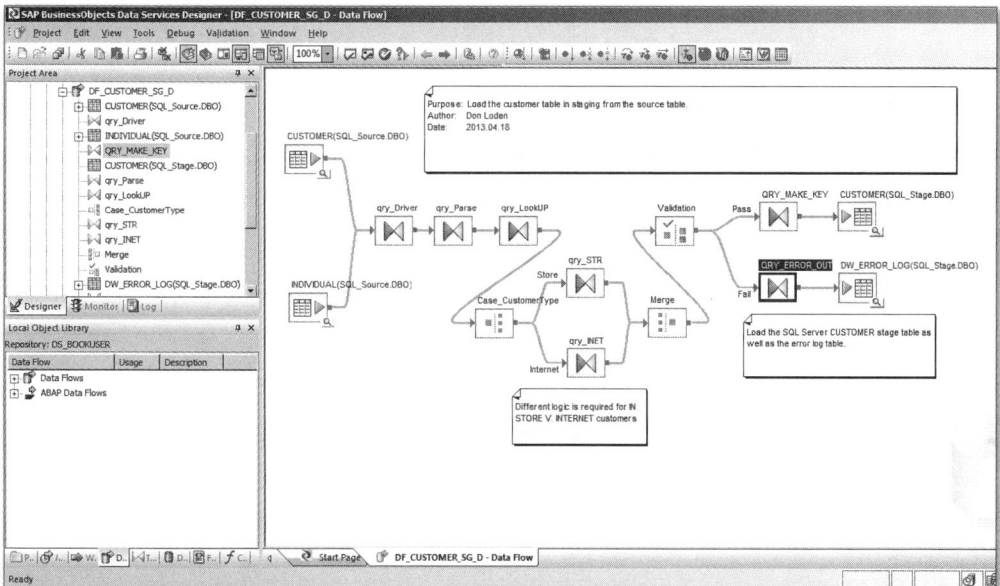

**Figure 5.49**  Error Trapping Stage of the Staging CUSTOMER Build

This error trapping logic is something that you *can't* do in SAP HANA. This is something that can only occur in SAP Data Services. With a properly constructed SAP Data Services batch load job, you can perform complex error substitutions, as shown in Figure 5.50.

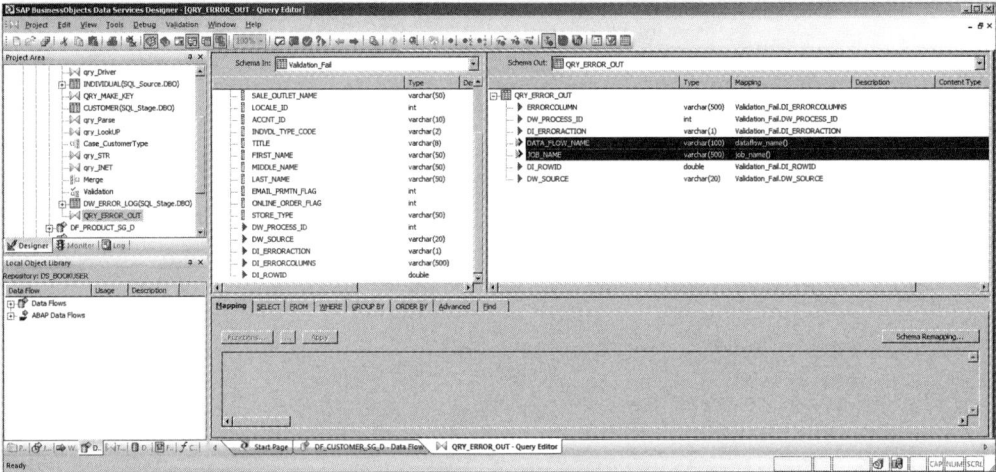

**Figure 5.50** Specific Fields Routed to Error Log Table

You're capturing both data errors and statistics that SAP Data Services captures about the processing. This is a great deal of information that—because you're putting the data into a table—will be easy to report using one of the SAP BusinessObjects tools. After the Query transform, you'll use the AUTO CORRECT LOAD property setting to control the inserts and updates in the target table, as shown in Figure 5.51.

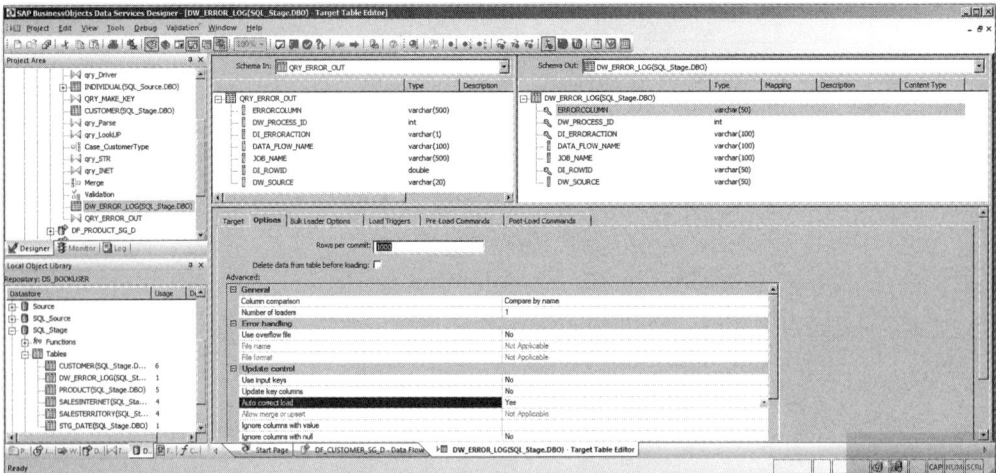

**Figure 5.51** Auto Correct Load Property Set for Error Log Table

This completes the CUSTOMER staging table, so let's move on to the next table in staging: PRODUCT.

### Product

In comparison to the complexity of the CUSTOMER table, the PRODUCT staging data flow is quite simple. The data in the table from the source was already quite good for reporting, and the business rules didn't require any further transformations past the typical data warehousing constructs detailed in the CUSTOMER section. Note the relative simplicity of the data flow in Figure 5.52.

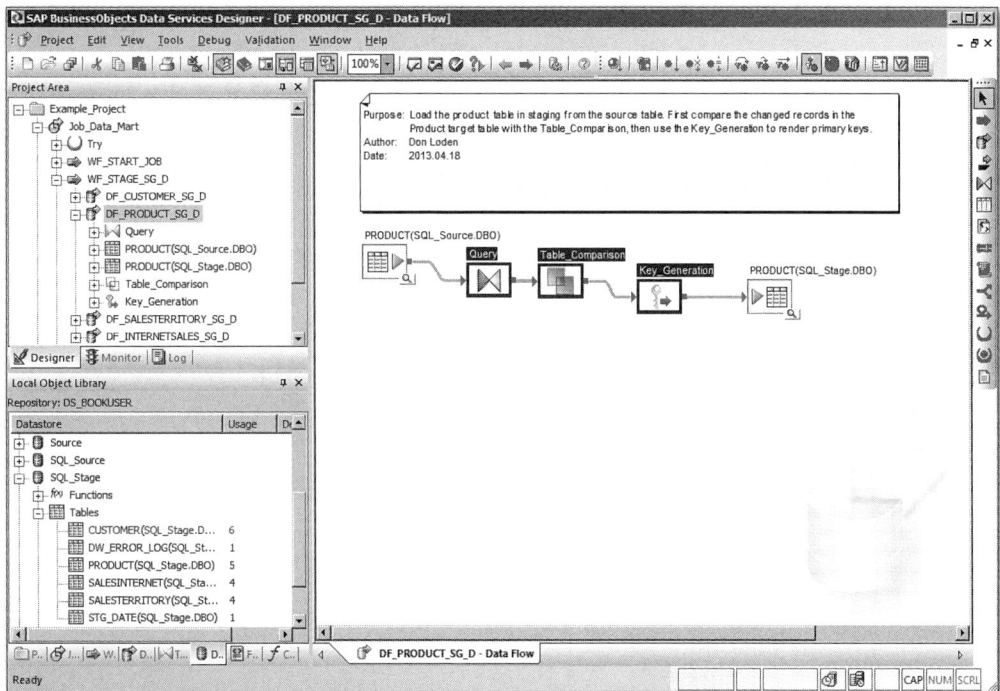

**Figure 5.52** Simplicity of Product Load with Unique CDC Mechanisms

The data flow and the introduction of the `Table_Comparison` transform are simple. You'll see how this transform takes the place of many of the transforms that you used in the CUSTOMER flow, as the `Table_Comparison` transform is quite powerful. However, before exploring the capabilities of the `Table_Comparison`, let's look at the first `Query` transform to see that the same `$G_BDate` and `$G_EDate` variable values and `WHERE` clause are used in Figure 5.53.

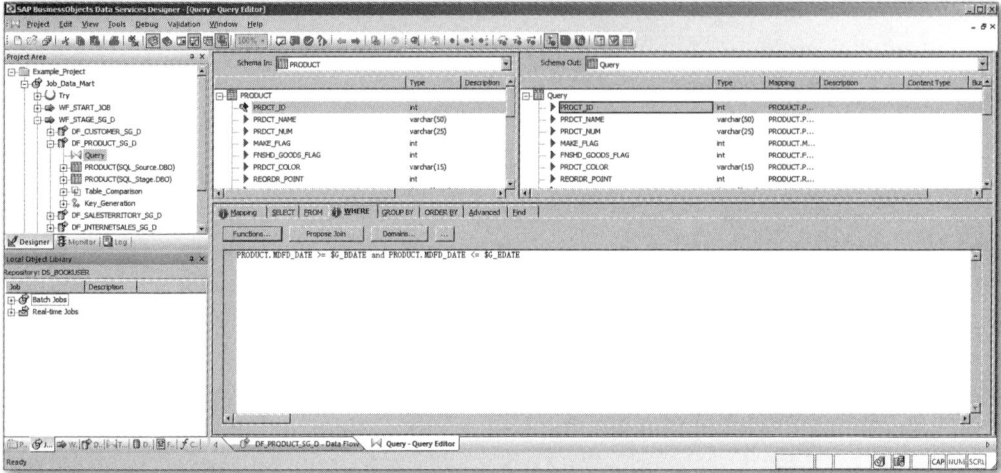

**Figure 5.53** Driver Stage of the Product Load Showing the Source-Based CDC

The WHERE clause is exactly the same because you still want to process only changed data from the source that is marked with a modified date (MDFD_DATE). However, not many transformations are occurring in the schema out right-hand section because the Table_Comparison transform handles many of the operations that require the use of other transforms. It should also be noted that the GK will be handled later by a different method, but first you must deal with the target CDC and handle the update controls of the target using the options in Figure 5.54.

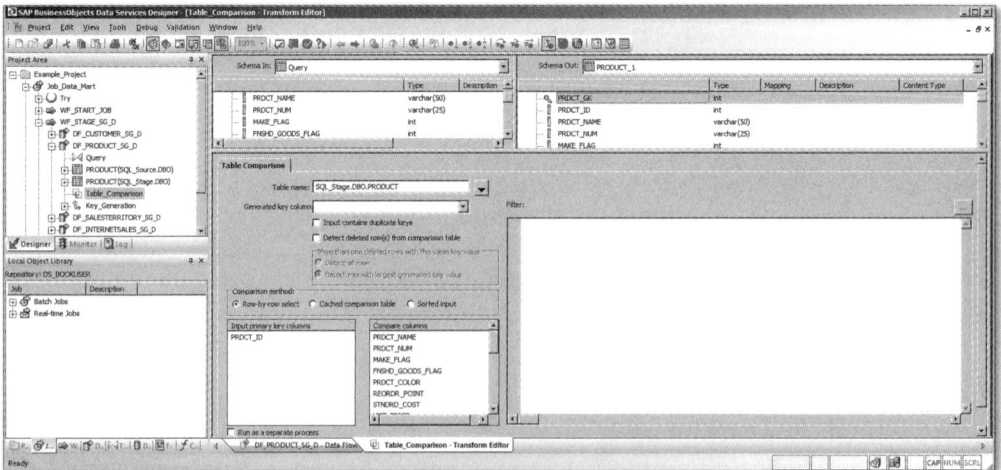

**Figure 5.54** Table_Comparison Transform to Provide the Target-Based CDC

The PRDCT_ID is used in the INPUT PRIMARY KEY COLUMNS box in the screen, and all of the attribute fields selected in the COMPARE COLUMNS box are used to compare the fields from the Query transform in the data flow with the PRODUCT target table. If the record is found using these comparison columns, the output of the Table_Comparison transform produces an UPDATE SQL statement. If the record isn't found, then an INSERT SQL statement is produced.

This sounds much like Auto Correct Load, but there is one important difference: If there is no change in a record, the table comparison discards the record as not to touch the target table in the event of no net change. The Auto Correct Load setting always produces an update and "touch" of the target with every record. The Table_Comparison won't do this.

After the Table_Comparison is finished handling all of the CDC duties, use a Key_ Generation transform, as shown in Figure 5.55.

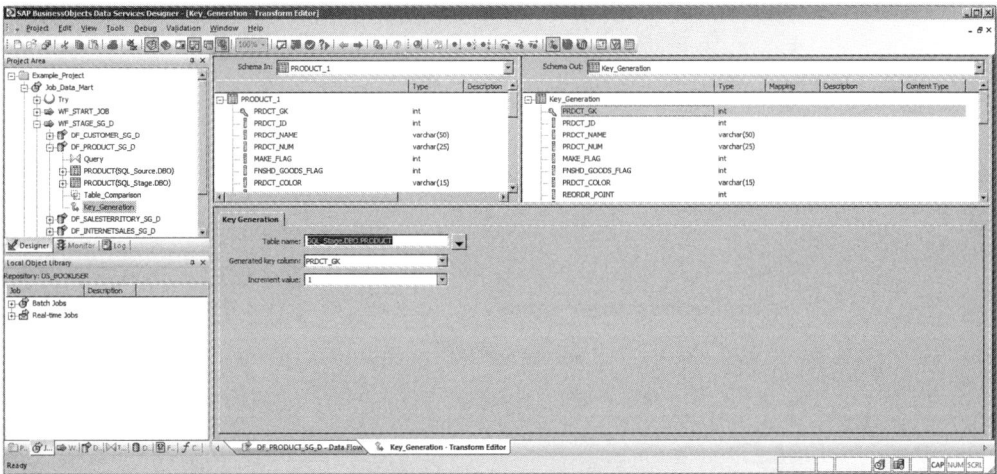

**Figure 5.55**  Key_Generation Function Creating the GK Column

The Key_Generation transform is quite simple. You merely point the transform to the target table and set the field you want to cast the key values against. Then the final property is the level to increment the value. The default value is 1, and this is typically what is required.

> **Note**
>
> The `Key_Generation` transform is a direct equivalent of the `Key_Generation` function that you used in the CUSTOMER data flow. This is simply another way to accomplish the same task and typically is used with the `Table_Comparison` due to the output row types that the `Table_Comparison` produces.

The final step of loading the table is to take a look at the options present in the PRODUCT table. Note that all options are default, and AUTO CORRECT LOAD is set to No. Because the `Table_Comparison` has performed all of the heavy lifting and figured out exactly what is needed for the target load, no loader options are required, and the data is ready as is (see Figure 5.56).

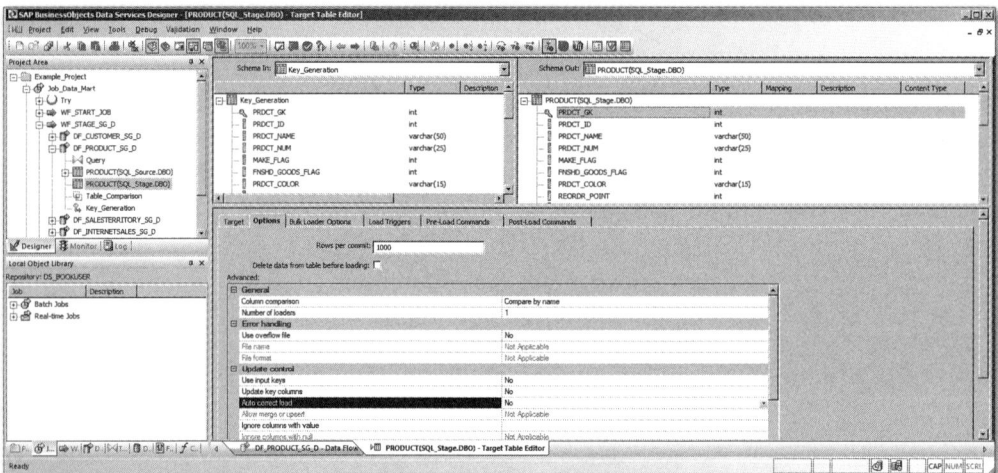

**Figure 5.56** Default Target Table Options with No Auto Correct Load

With PRODUCT complete, you're now ready to focus on loading the SALES-TERRITORY table.

### Sales Territory

The SALESTERRITORY table is much like the PRODUCT table. This simple table is shown in Figure 5.57.

`Table_Comparison` and `Key_Generation` transforms are used for the target-based CDC comparisons just like in the PRODUCT flow. Also, you'll again always use the MDFD_DATE field to focus only on reading the changed records into the data flow for processing. Notice that the WHERE clause tab in Figure 5.58 is very similar to PRODUCT. There aren't any transformations in the schema out section of the `Query` transform.

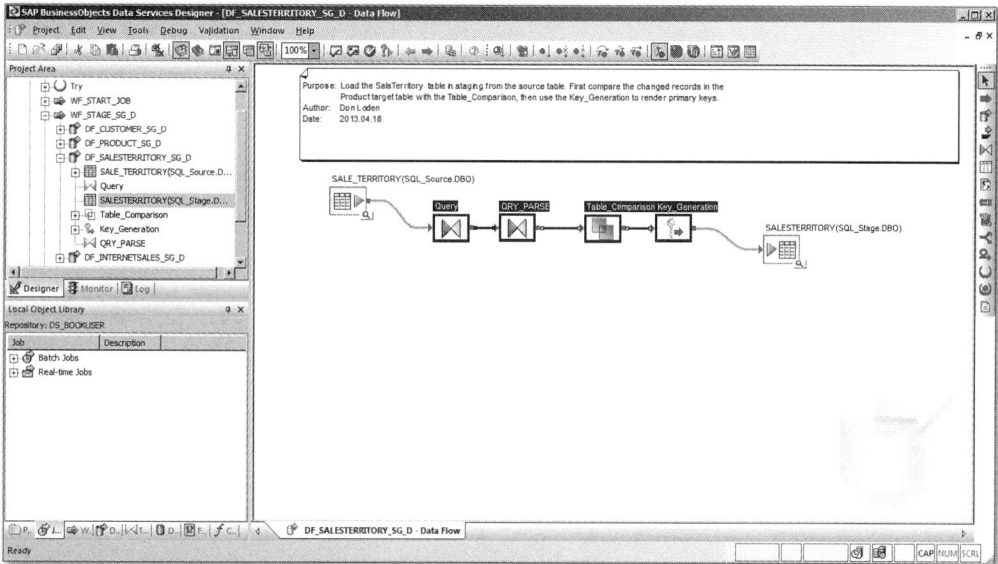

**Figure 5.57** Sales Territory Using Table_Comparison for CDC

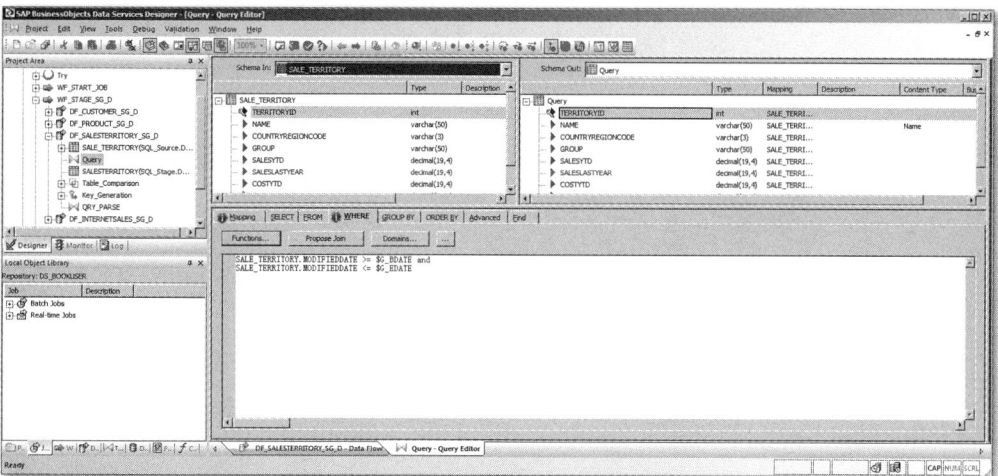

**Figure 5.58** Source-Based CDC in the Driver Stage Query Transform

An additional `Query` transform is required in Figure 5.59 to map some of the fields to fields that have different names in the target table of SALESTERRITORY. It's critical to perform this before the `Table_Comparison` in Figure 5.60.

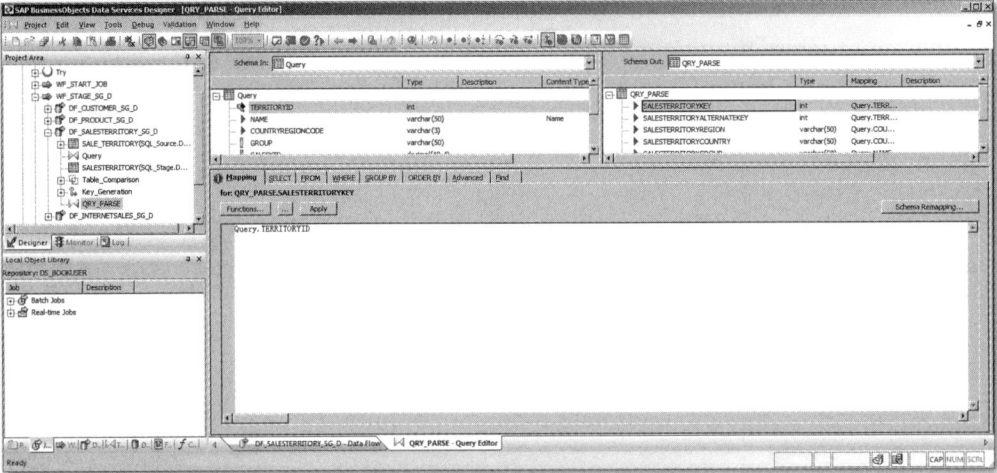

**Figure 5.59** The Parsing Stage Query Transform Remapping Field Names

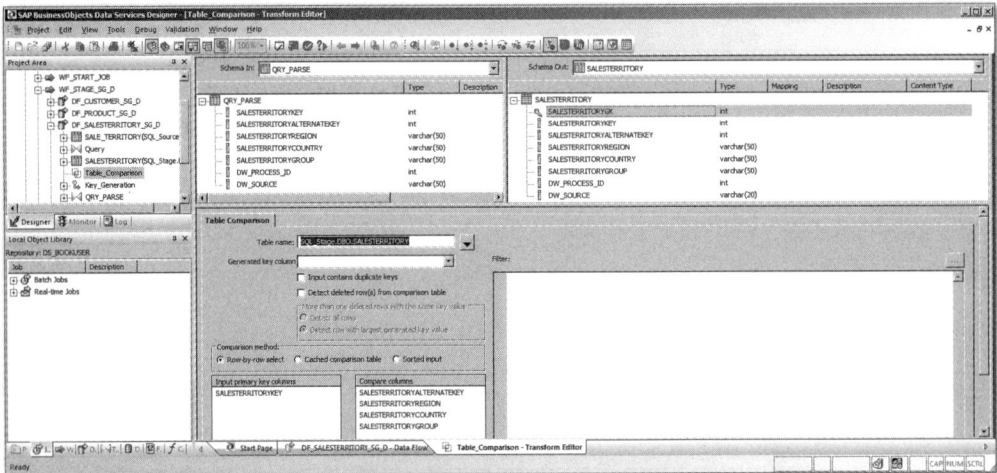

**Figure 5.60** Table_Comparison Options to Perform the Target-Based CDC

Then, after the CDC operations are handled by the `Table_Comparison`, use the KEY_ GENERATION function in Figure 5.61 to assign the GK field for SALESTERRITORY.

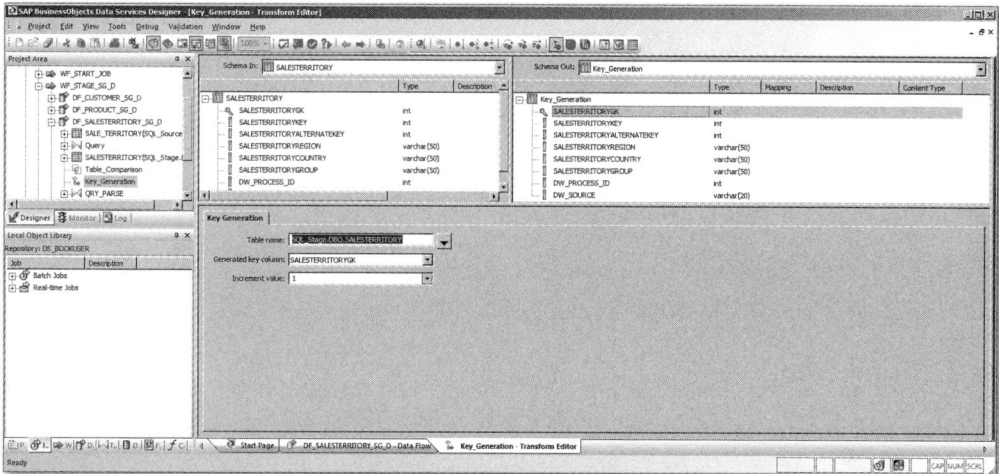

**Figure 5.61** Key_Generation Function Creating the GK Column

Finally, the target table is loaded just as PRODUCT was with no options; for example, there is no AUTO CORRECT LOAD property set. All target table options are the defaults shown in Figure 5.62. They are simply not needed with the `Table_ Comparison` transform.

### Internet Sales

All of the staging tables that will form all of the dimension tables in SAP HANA are now complete with the finalization of SALESTERRITORY. It's now time to construct the table that will form the baseline of one of the central tables for this book: FACT_INTERNET_SALES. FACT_INTERNET_SALES will derive directly from the staging table INTERNET_SALES, so we'll go into great detail on how this table is constructed.

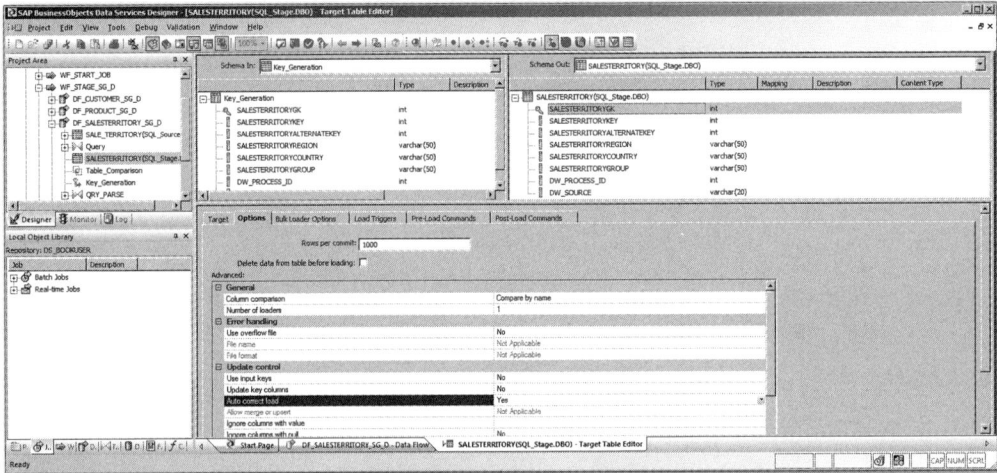

**Figure 5.62** Default Target Table Options

> **Note**
>
> Another fact table will be mentioned quite often in the SAP BusinessObjects BI case study sections is FACT_RESELLER_SALES. We won't cover the build of this fact table because it would be redundant after the coverage of the INTERNETSALES table.

The first thing to note of importance is that we'll do something quite different with INTERNET SALES that is specific for SAP HANA. In a traditional data warehouse on a traditional hardware and database platform, you would construct two fact tables: one for header and one for detail. For SAP HANA, that isn't the case; you denormalize the two tables into one table called SALESINTERNET. This causes the header values to repeat.

In a traditional structure, this would be bad both in terms of data storage and performance, but due to the topics covered in Chapter 2 of this book on columnar table data storage, compression, and run length encoding, this isn't a problem for SAP HANA—in fact, it's preferable. You'll achieve better performance as well as have no penalty in terms of data storage. For these reasons, you'll denormalize the data in the data flow depicted in Figure 5.63.

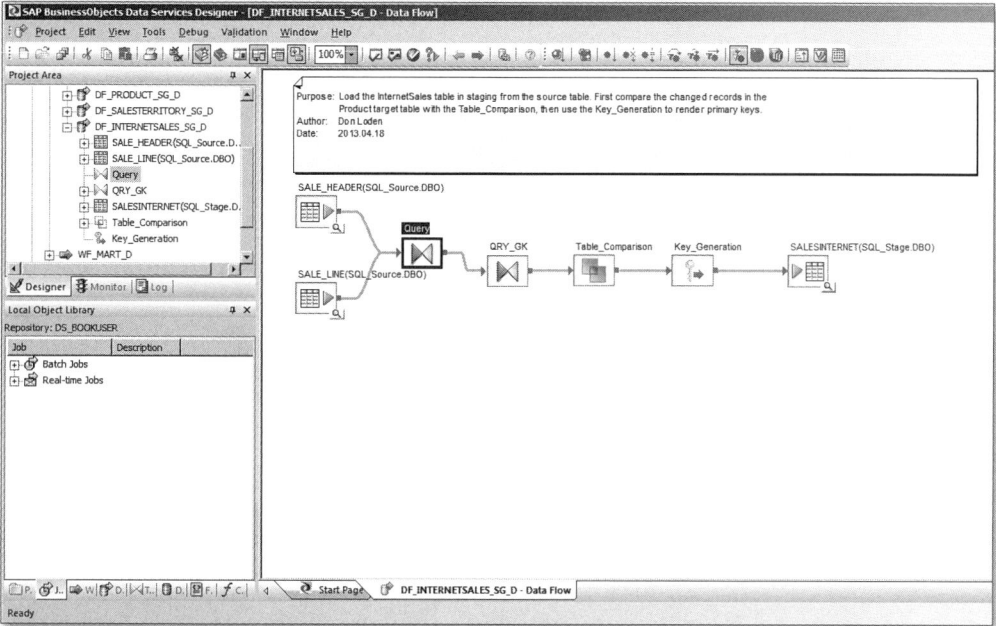

**Figure 5.63** Combining Header and Detail Tables to Denormalize for SAP HANA

Notice in Figure 5.63 that two source tables—SALE_HEADER and SALE_LINE— are joined to combine the results. The first `Query` transform contains the join to combine tables and is shown in Figure 5.64.

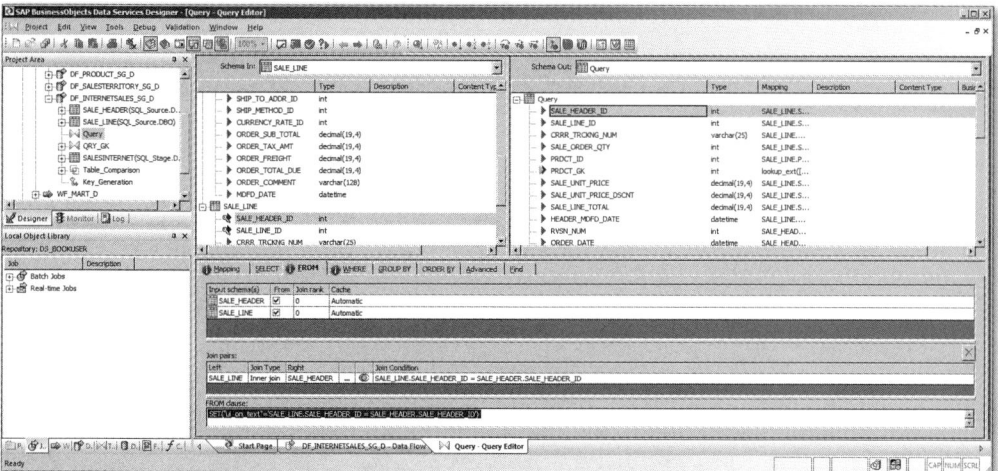

**Figure 5.64** Join to Be Pushed Down to the Source Database

The same WHERE clause is used in Query to produce only changed records from the source system (see Figure 5.65).

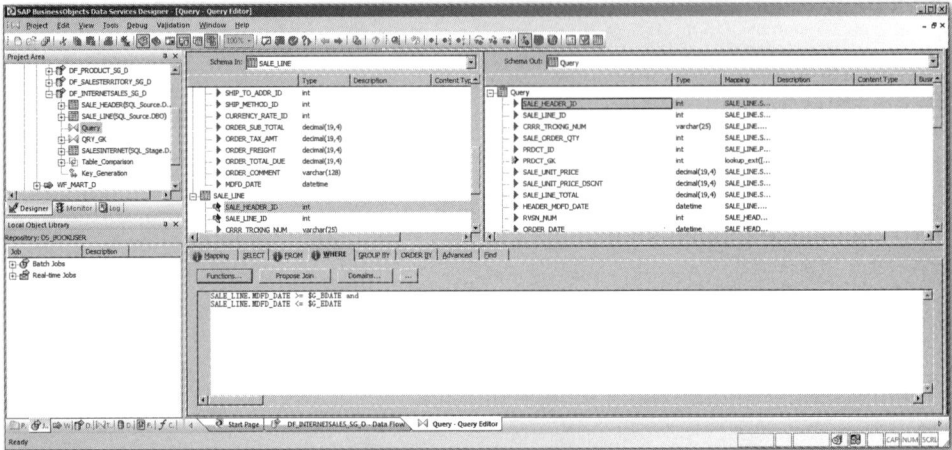

**Figure 5.65** Driver Stage WHERE Clause to Perform the Source-Based CDC

You'll then use a Lookup_ext() function (much like before) to look up the GK values in the target tables to see if the record exists or not. There is one difference with the SALESINTERNET table: Because this will be the basis for a fact table, it will be the center of the star in the star schema. This means that you'll need foreign key relationships for all of the related dimension tables—which is precisely what all of the lookup_ext() functions are performing in Figure 5.66.

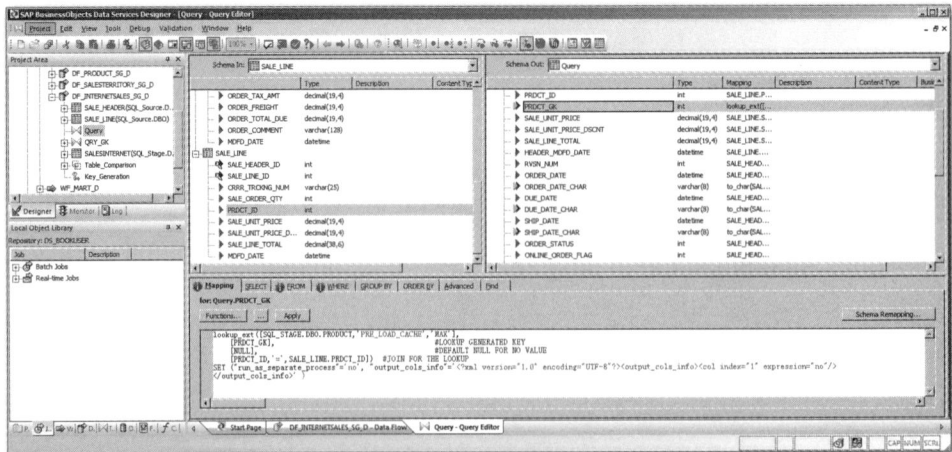

**Figure 5.66** Lookup_Ext Example to Provide the Foreign Key Values for Sales-Based Tables

Now that you've handled the foreign keys, you can assign the DW_PROCESS_ID and DW_SOURCE columns in Figure 5.67.

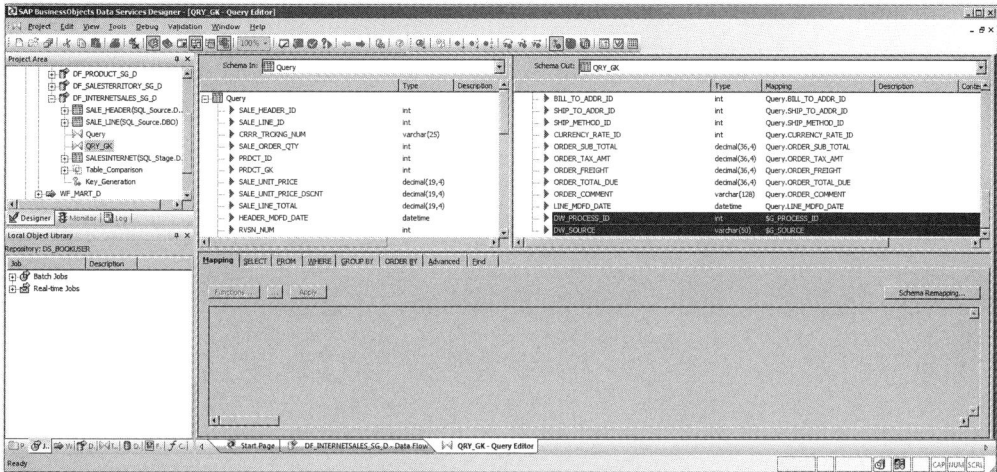

**Figure 5.67** Assigning the Source and DW_Process_ID Values

The `Table_Comparison` then provides all of the target-based CDC operations on SALESINTERNET as before for all of the base dimension tables in Figure 5.68.

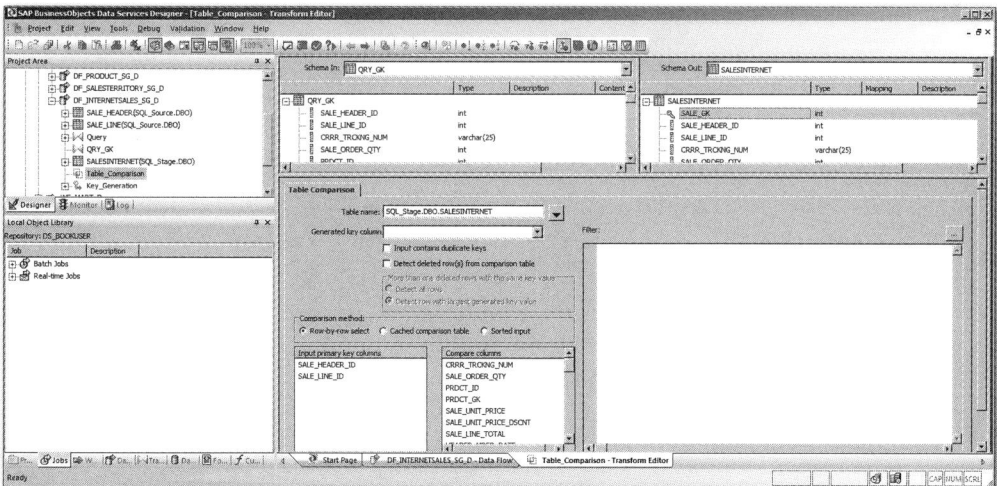

**Figure 5.68** Table_Comparison Transform to Provide the Target-Based CDC

Then, the `Key_Generation` transform performs its work by assembling the GK values for the SALESINTERNET table's primary key in Figure 5.69.

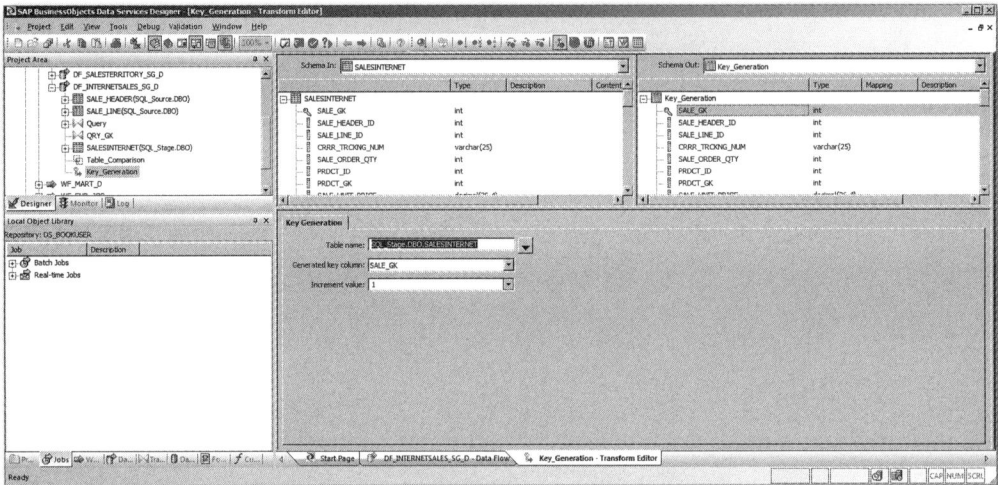

**Figure 5.69**  Key_Generation Function Creating the GK Column

Finally, the SALESINTERNET target table options are generic because the `Table_Comparison` transform has handled the rest as shown in Figure 5.70.

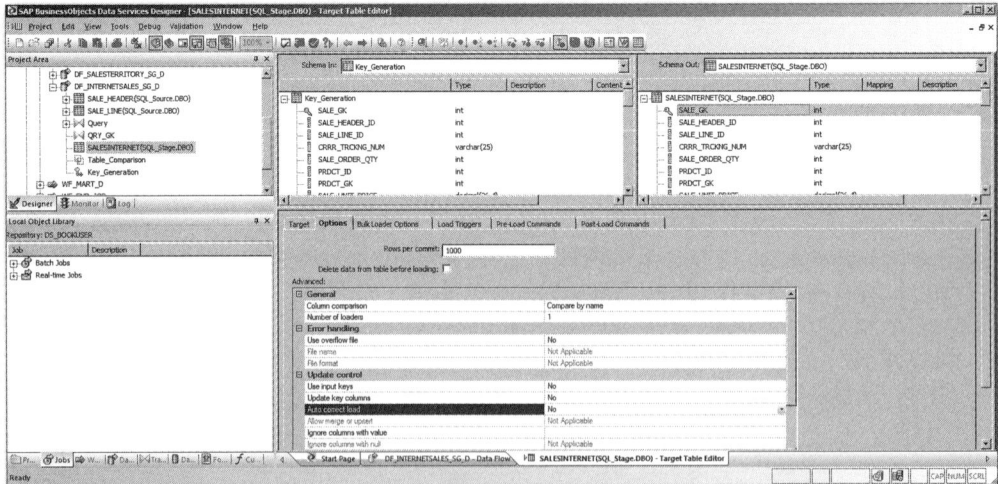

**Figure 5.70**  Default Target Table Options with No Auto Correct Load

This completes the loading process of the various staging tables. You're now ready to begin loading data into SAP HANA. Because data has been properly prepared per best practices, the data flows that load SAP HANA are actually quite simple. All of the more complex logic has been performed in staging, so you're now ready to load SAP HANA.

## 5.4.5 Build Dimension Tables in SAP HANA

The data mart workflow used to load SAP HANA is depicted in Figure 5.71. As you'll see in this section, this flow is somewhat different from the staging flows.

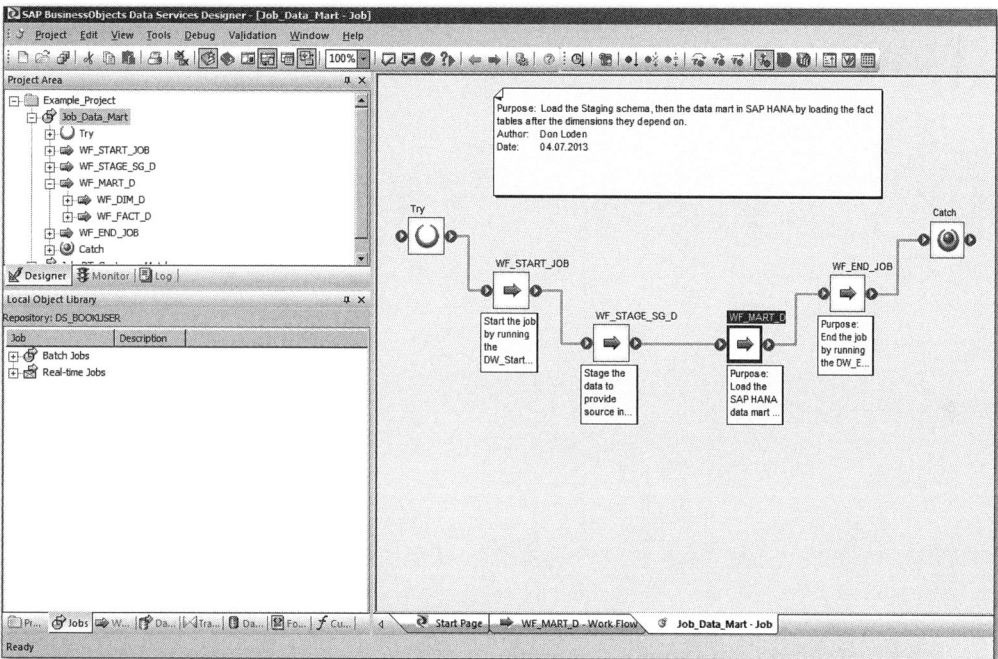

**Figure 5.71** Mart Workflow That Loads Data into SAP HANA

Order is very important at a higher level for the build of the tables in SAP HANA. Dimension tables must be loaded before the fact tables are loaded, as shown in Figure 5.72. The workflows are used to organize the parallel load of the dimension tables in Figure 5.73.

> **Note**
>
> Parallel loading of SAP HANA is important for extreme performance. It's possible because all of the order and dependencies were met by the organization of the staging load. All primary keys and foreign keys are intact and ready to process into SAP HANA as fast as possible.

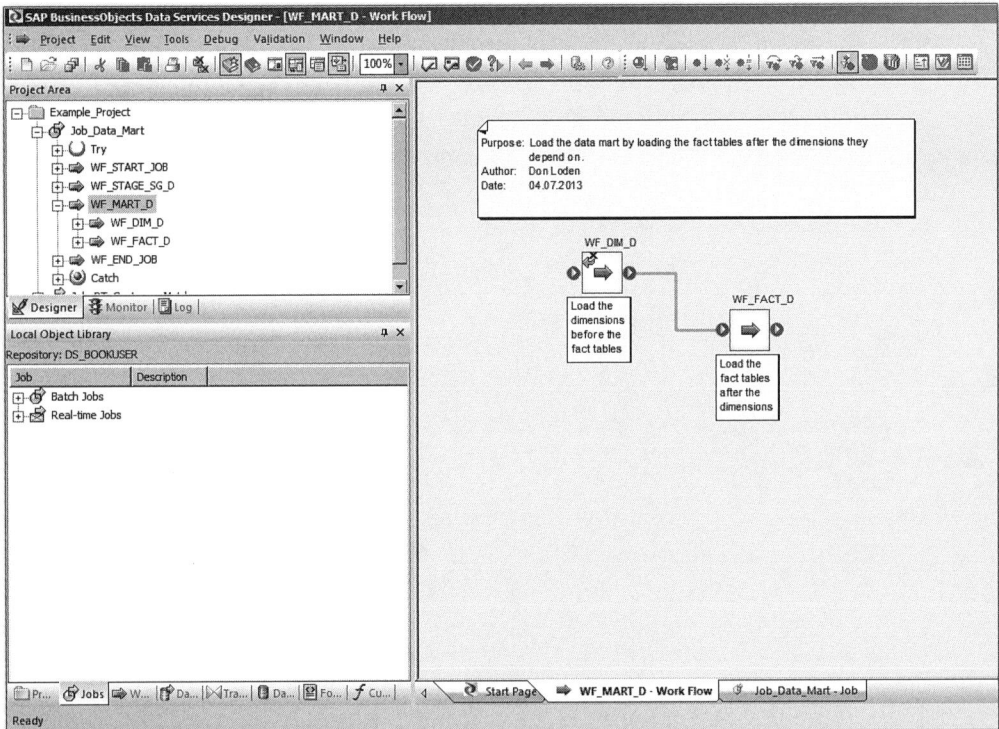

**Figure 5.72** Mart Workflow Detailed with Dimension and Fact Builds

You need to load data into SAP HANA in a certain order, which is dictated by the data via dependencies. For instance, dimensions need to be loaded before facts because they will be referenced in the fact loads. Hence, load data in the following order:

1. Dimension tables: All tables will be loaded in parallel.

2. Fact table: Load this in order because the foreign keys must reference values that already exist in the dimension tables.

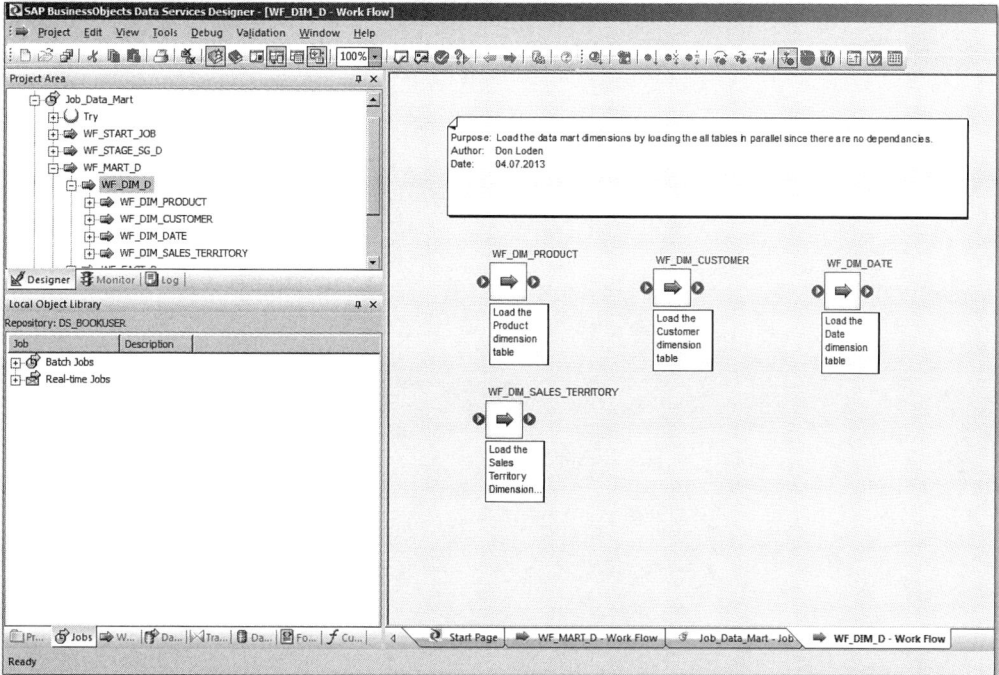

**Figure 5.73** Contents of the Dimension Workflows within the Mart Workflow

With a basic understanding of the order of execution of the dimensions and fact table, you can start the build process with the production dimension DIM_PRODUCT.

## DIM_Product

Upon first glance at the DIM_PRODUCT data flow in Figure 5.74, you discover that the data flow is simple. This flow is intentionally even simpler than the simplest data flows in staging. The reason for the simplicity is that these flows should load SAP HANA as fast as possible.

CDC is important for loading into SAP HANA, but you can't perform this operation by using date comparisons because staging contains many different sources with many different modified dates. This is where the concept of the DW_PROCESS_ID column takes effect. You use this to insulate the CDC processing from the needs and requirements of any of the source-modified date columns. The idea is that whatever was loaded or "touched" in staging should be moved to the data mart in SAP HANA by a very simple WHERE clause, as shown in Figure 5.75.

299

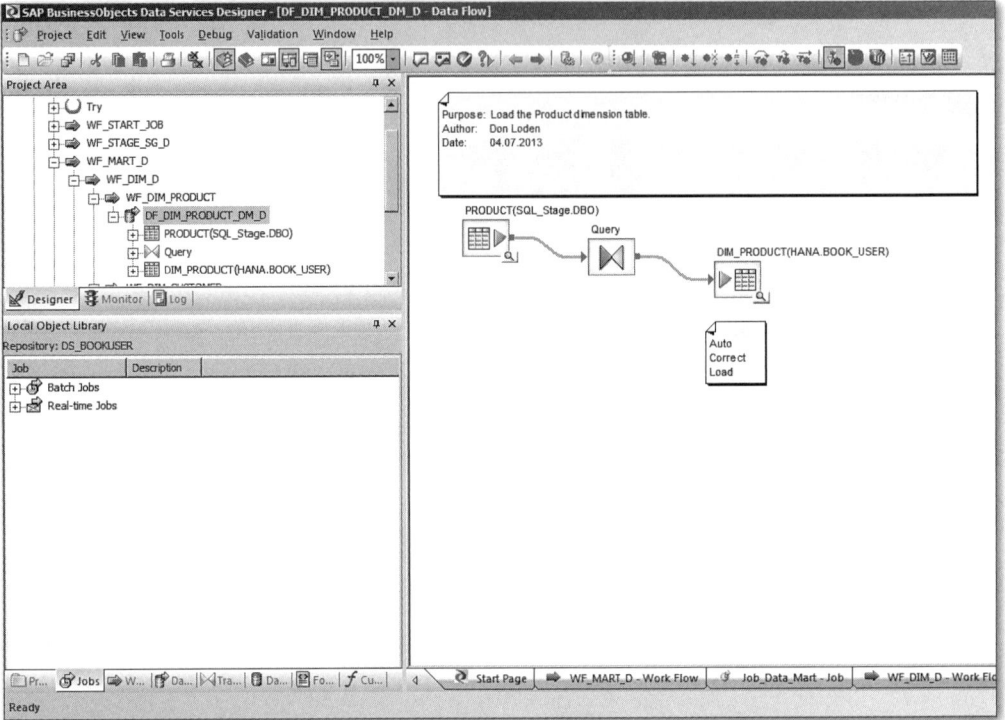

**Figure 5.74** Data Flow to Load DIM_PRODUCT in SAP HANA

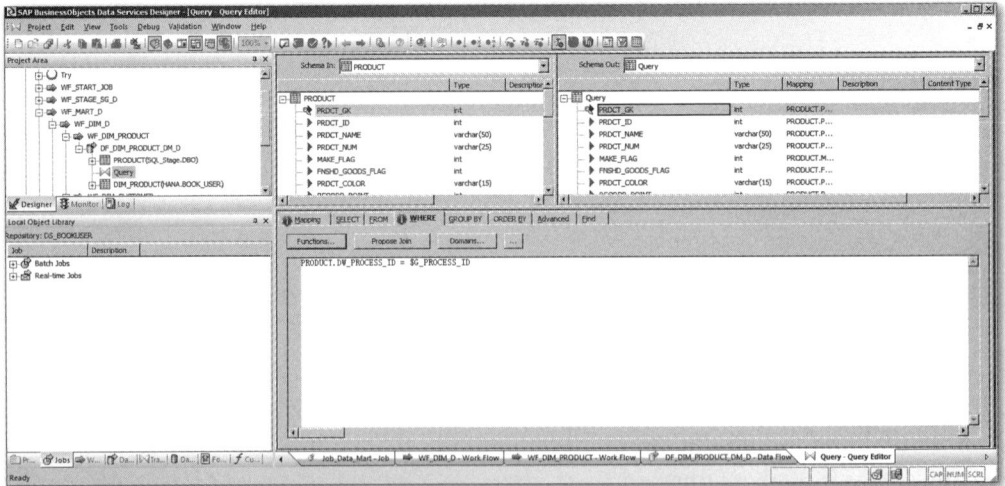

**Figure 5.75** Source CDC from Staging Handled via a Process ID Comparison

Best practices are to perform all of the transformations in staging, so after this, no transformations are present in the `Query` transform. Staging is complete, so you're essentially just moving the data in its current state to SAP HANA. You'll be using similar options for the target tables for the target-based CDC such as Auto correct load, as shown in Figure 5.76.

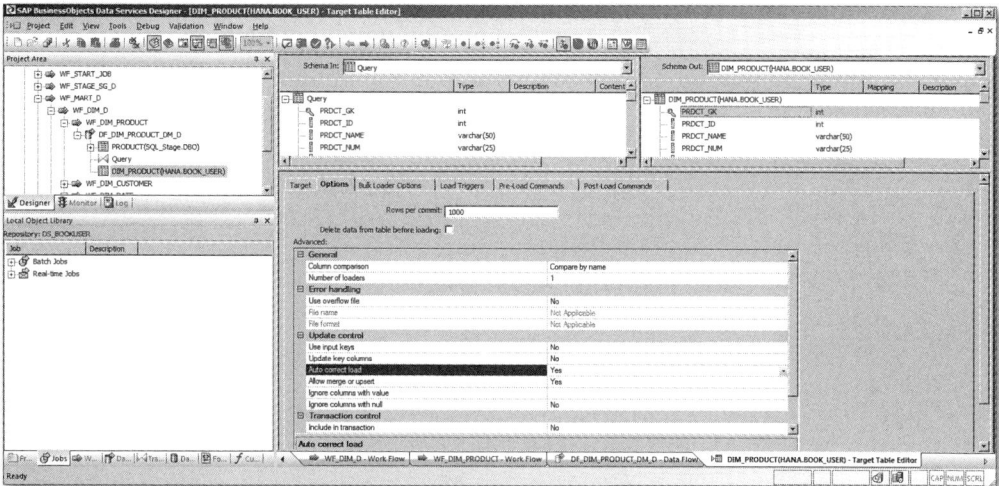

**Figure 5.76** Auto Correct Load Option in the DIM_PRODUCT Table

This is because you're loading small amounts of changed data in this example, so the inefficiency of Auto Correct Load won't hurt the performance objectives, but it will make recovery quite simple.

> **Note**
>
> Many target options exist in SAP Data Services for SAP HANA load performance. We detailed bulk loading options in Chapter 4 that can be used in the right use case.
>
> This example in the case study focuses on small data sets narrowed by a date range in the source. If large data is required, then you have to employ a different approach using the bulk loader capabilities in SAP HANA.

### DIM_Customer

DIM_CUSTOMER is much like DIM_PRODUCT in that it's simple and requires no transformations. Auto Correct Load is used as well against the DIM_PRODUCT target table. The only piece of logic that is distinctive is the DW_PROCESS_ID comparison against the product table. Aside from comparing against a different table, all of this functionality works the same way as in the DIM_PRODUCT table, so we won't go to that same level of detail in DIM_CUSTOMER. The data flow for DIM_CUSTOMER is shown for reference in Figure 5.77.

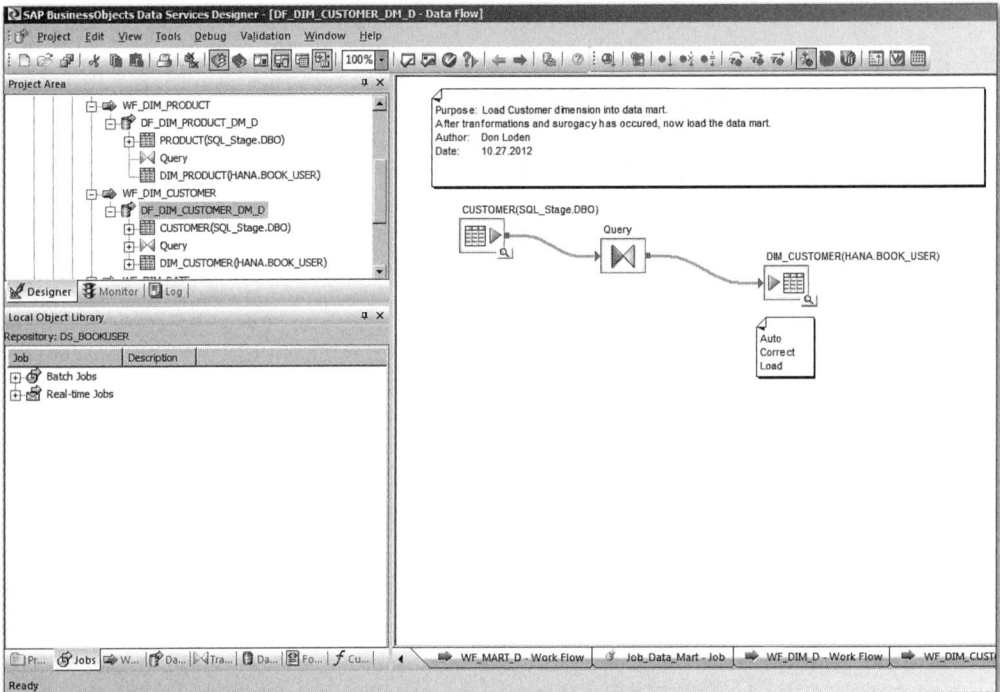

**Figure 5.77**  Data Flow to Load DIM_CUSTOMER in SAP HANA

### DIM_Sales_Territory

Again, DIM_SALES_TERRITORY is much like DIM_PRODUCT and DIM_CUS-TOMER; it, too, is simple and requires no transformations. Auto correct load is used as well against the DIM_SALES_TERRITORY target table. The only piece of logic that is distinctive is the DW_PROCESS_ID comparison against the product table. All functionality works the same way as in the DIM_PRODUCT and DIM_CUSTOER tables, so we won't go to that same level of detail in DIM_SALES_TERRITORY. The data flow for DIM_SALES_TERRITORY is shown for reference in Figure 5.78.

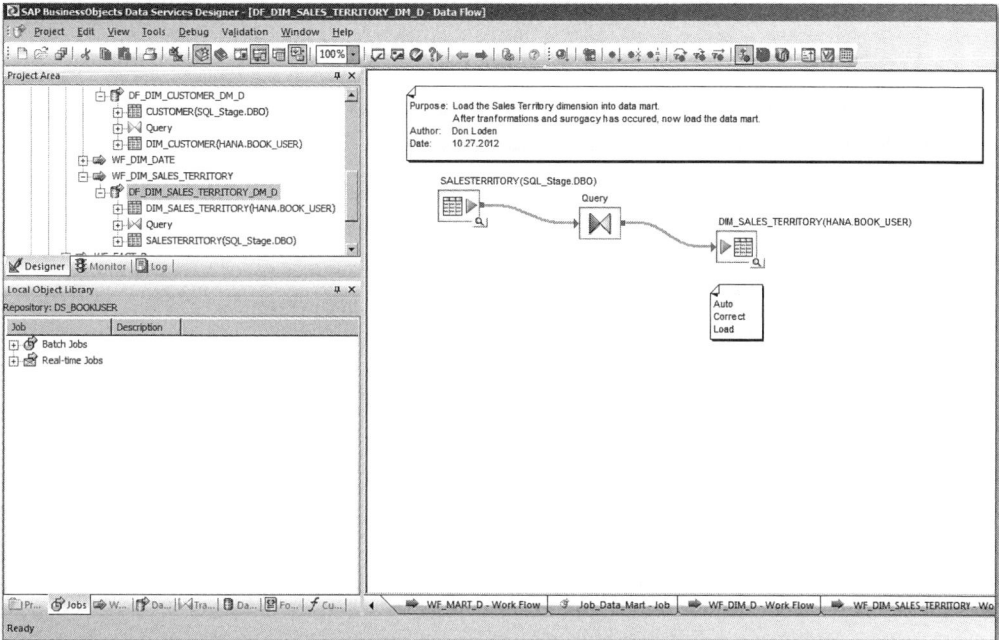

**Figure 5.78** Data Flow to Load DIM_SALESTERRITORY in SAP HANA

## DIM_Date

The DIM_DATE data flow is somewhat unique for a few different reasons:

▶ It has no source table. DF_DIM_DATE_DM_D is sourced from a `Date_Generation` transform that only produces a generated date.

▶ All of the columns that are generated from the `Date_Generation` transform are entirely manufactured from transformations within the data flow.

▶ This data flow primarily constructs the date dimension table DIM_DATE in the SAP HANA data mart, but it also writes back to a date table in staging that possibly can be used for other ETL processing and transformation needs in staging.

The DIM_DATE table in SAP HANA is the foundational table for the date reporting and visualization operations that will be shown in subsequent sections of the case study. We'll show its build here. The data flow that builds DIM_DATE is shown in Figure 5.79.

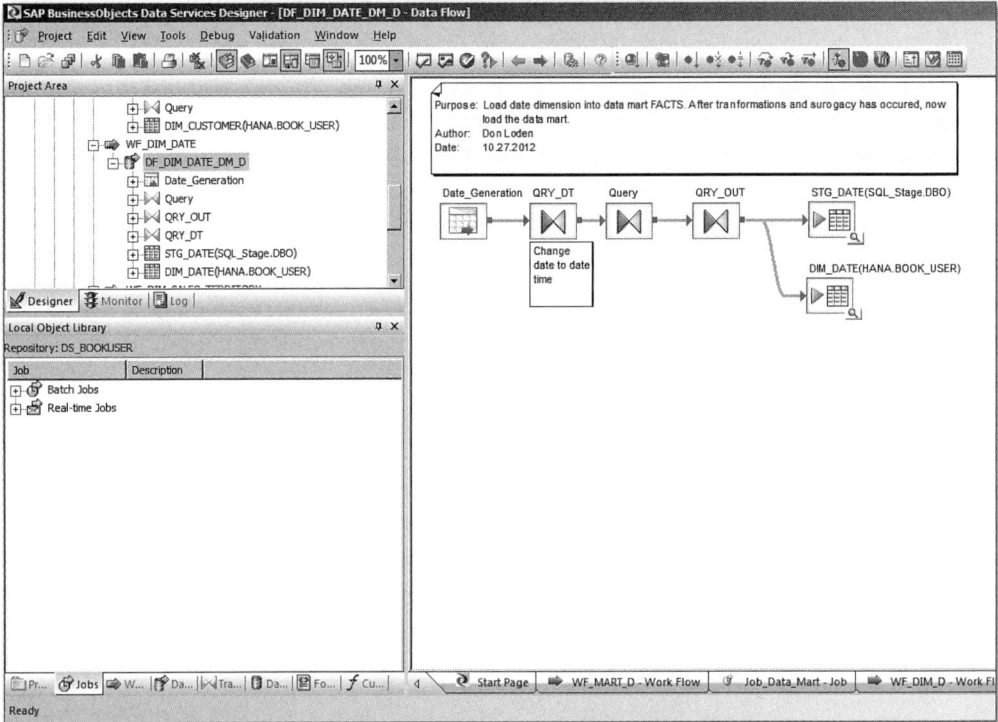

**Figure 5.79** Data Flow to Load DIM_DATE in SAP HANA

Notice the difference in the data source for the data flow in Figure 5.79. Recall that this is an SAP Data Services transform! There is no true data source—just a transform that is quite flexible in terms of generating dates from a specified range. These options that control this behavior are shown in Figure 5.80.

This transform looks and is quite simple; there aren't many options to set, and it only produces a generated date column to read.

So what makes it so special? The answer is that with all of the date functions present in SAP Data Services, you can use this column as the baseline to create sophisticated date dimension tables. Consider all of the columns that are being derived in Figure 5.81.

Although this is a pretty simple date dimension, there are quite a few columns.

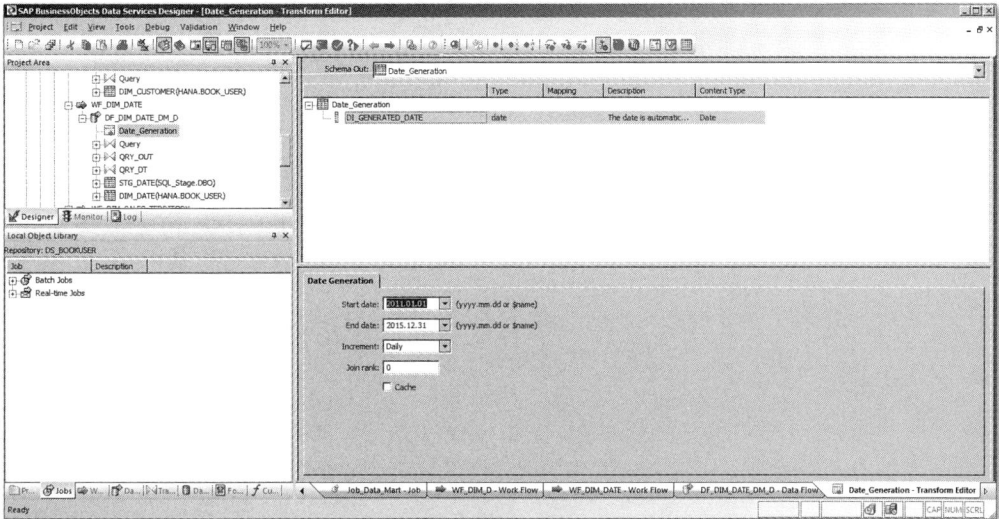

**Figure 5.80** Date_Generation Transform Detailed with Options

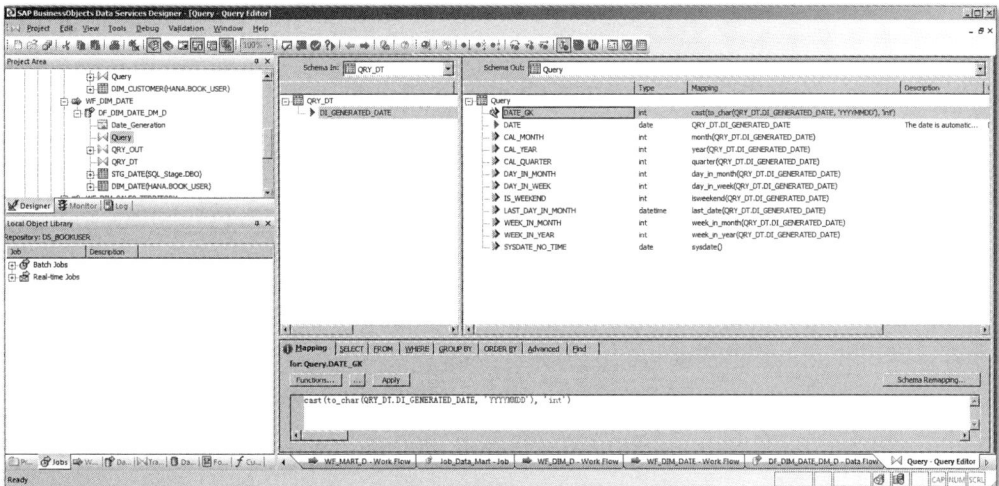

**Figure 5.81** Various Date Functions and Parsing to Create Date Metrics

We've used this technique hundreds of times in real-world examples to create almost any date metric imaginable. The built-in functions can be combined in just about any way possible, but we wanted to keep the example simple for the AdventureWorks Cycle Company to demonstrate the basic possibilities. Consider Table 5.3 to see the syntax of the various functions in detail.

| Column | Function | Syntax | Description |
|---|---|---|---|
| DATE_GK | CAST() and TO_CHAR() | `cast(to_char(QRY_DT.DI_GENERATED_DATE, 'YYYYMMDD'), 'int')` | Creates the GK value in the format of YYYYMMDD to make the value a more usable. |
| CAL_MONTH | MONTH() | `month(QRY_DT.DI_GENERATED_DATE)` | Integer of the month number of the calendar year. |
| CAL_YEAR | YEAR() | `year(QRY_DT.DI_GENERATED_DATE)` | Integer of the year number of the calendar year. |
| CAL_QUARTER | QUARTER() | `quarter(QRY_DT.DI_GENERATED_DATE)` | Integer of the quarter number of the calendar year. |
| DAY_IN_MONTH | DAY_IN_MONTH() | `day_in_month(QRY_DT.DI_GENERATED_DATE)` | Integer of the day of the calendar month. |
| DAY_IN_WEEK | DAY_IN_WEEK() | `day_in_week(QRY_DT.DI_GENERATED_DATE)` | Integer of the day of the week. |
| IS_WEEKEND | ISWEEKEND() | `isweekend(QRY_DT.DI_GENERATED_DATE)` | Flag for whether the day of the week falls on a weekend. Value of 1 for the weekend days and 0 for weekdays. |
| LAST_DAY_IN_MONTH | LAST_DATE() | `last_date(QRY_DT.DI_GENERATED_DATE)` | Date value of the last day of the month. Useful for setting flag values. |
| WEEK_IN_MONTH | WEEK_IN_MONTH() | `week_in_month(QRY_DT.DI_GENERATED_DATE)` | Integer of the number of the week in a calendar month. |
| WEEK_IN_YEAR | WEEK_IN_YEAR() | `week_in_year(QRY_DT.DI_GENERATED_DATE)` | Integer of the number of the week in a calendar year. |
| SYSDATE_NO_TIME | SYSDATE() | `sysdate()` | Returns a date time value of the system date. This column was cast in the data flow into a date data type truncate the time. |

**Table 5.3**  Details of the Various Date Functions and Definitions for Usage

As you can see, there are many ways to derive useful date information, and this is only a small fraction of what is possible. Sometimes it's necessary to break out of the stock function returns and build upon a value that is produced by the function, and Figure 5.82 shows this in the building of date flags (see the boxed sections in the figure). The date flags will be used to signify the first and last days of the month and week and to sum operations in the SAP HANA mart tables.

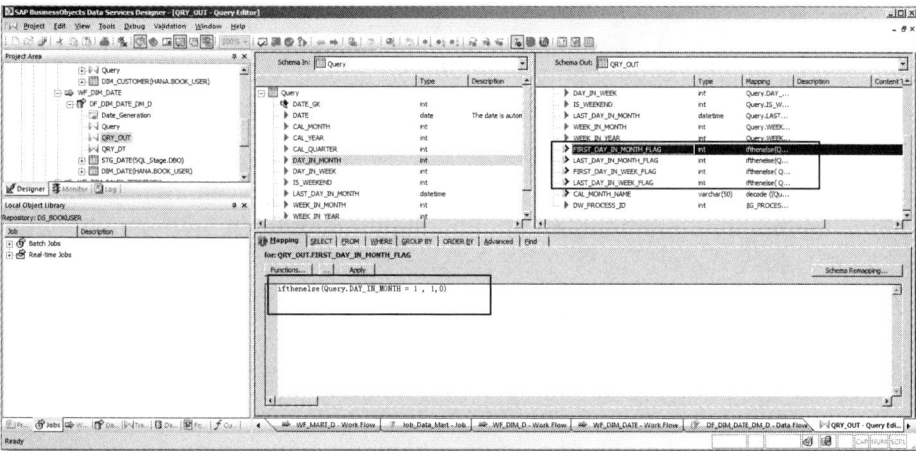

**Figure 5.82** Date Flag Construction in the QRY_OUT Transform

Consider Table 5.4 for a more detailed view of the syntax of the functions:

| Column | Function | Syntax | Description |
|---|---|---|---|
| FIRST_DAY _IN_MONTH _FLAG | IFTHENELSE() | ifthenelse(Query.DAY_ IN_MONTH = 1 , 1,0) | Flag the first day of the calendar month as a 1, otherwise zero. |
| LAST_DAY _IN_MONTH _FLAG | IFTHENELSE() | ifthenelse(Query."DATE" = Query.LAST_DAY_IN_ MONTH, 1,0) | Flag the last day of the calendar month as a 1, otherwise zero. |
| FIRST_DAY _IN_WEEK _FLAG | IFTHENELSE() | ifthenelse( Query.DAY_ IN_WEEK = 1,1,0) | Flag the first day of the calendar week as a 1, otherwise zero. |
| LAST_DAY _IN_WEEK _FLAG | IFTHENELSE() | ifthenelse( Query.DAY_ IN_WEEK = 1,1,0) | Flag the last day of the calendar week as a 1, otherwise zero. |

**Table 5.4** DIM_Date SAP Data Services Date Functions and Column Definitions

Staging is now complete, and all of the dimensions are in place in SAP HANA. We've taken the time to ensure all logical dependencies are met by running all flows in order and in sequence and performing staging. We could take some performance liberties in the dimension builds in the data mart in SAP HANA by running the work in parallel. With all of this accomplished, we're now ready to build the final table in the data mart: FACT_INTERNET_SALES.

### 5.4.6 Build Fact Table

The fact table, like many of the dimension tables, isn't a very complex build in the SAP HANA data mart. All of the denormalization transformations were completed in the staging INTERNETSALES data flow (Internet Sales), so the movement of the data into SAP HANA follows the precedent of the dimensions and is quite simple. The workflow that houses the data flow to build the table FACT_INTERNET_SALES is housed within the WF_FACT_D workflow and runs after all of the dimensions are built in parallel in WF_DIM_D (see Figure 5.83).

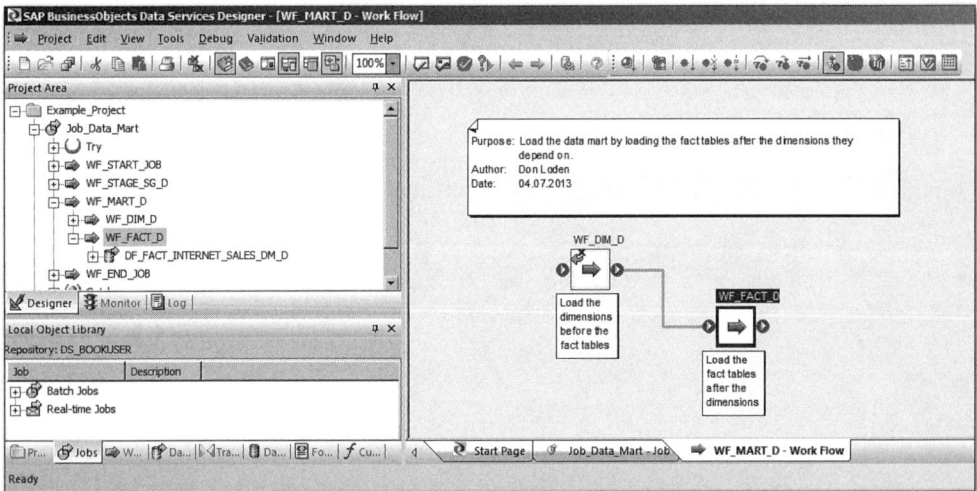

**Figure 5.83**  Workflow to Build the FACT_INTERNET_SALES_RETAIL Table

**FACT_Internet_Sales_Retail**

There is only one table and hence one data flow in the WF_MART_D workflow that contains the data flow FACT_INTERNET_SALES_DM_D. As mentioned earlier, this data flow is quite simple, as shown in Figure 5.84.

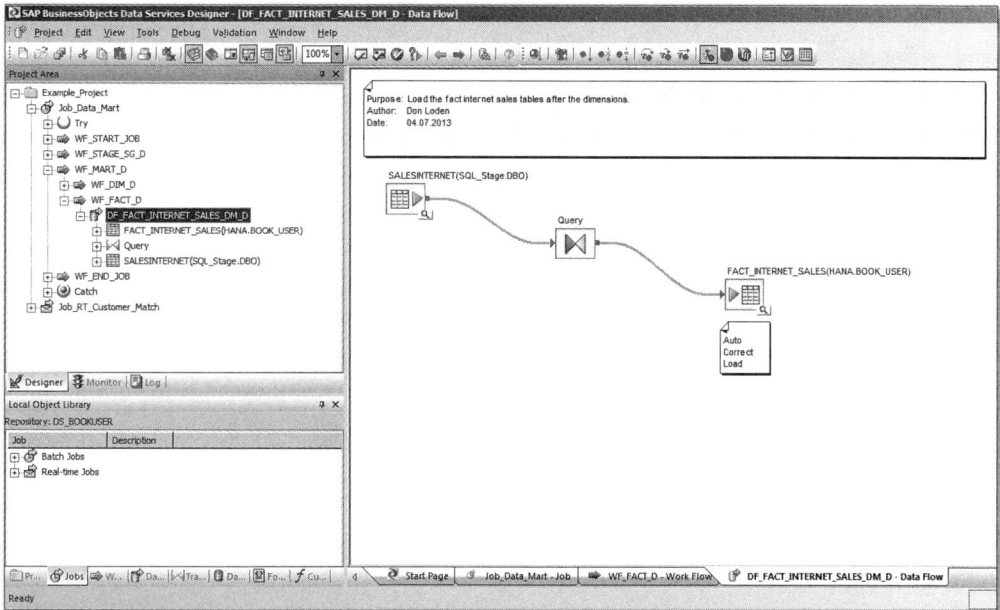

**Figure 5.84**  Data Flow to Construct FACT_INTERNET_SALES in SAP HANA

There is a read from the staging table INTERNETSALES that was previously denormalized and then standardized to SAP HANA best practices for data modeling as described in Chapter 2, so all that is left to do is to perform the source-based CDC on DW_PROCESS_ID in the WHERE clause, as shown in Figure 5.85.

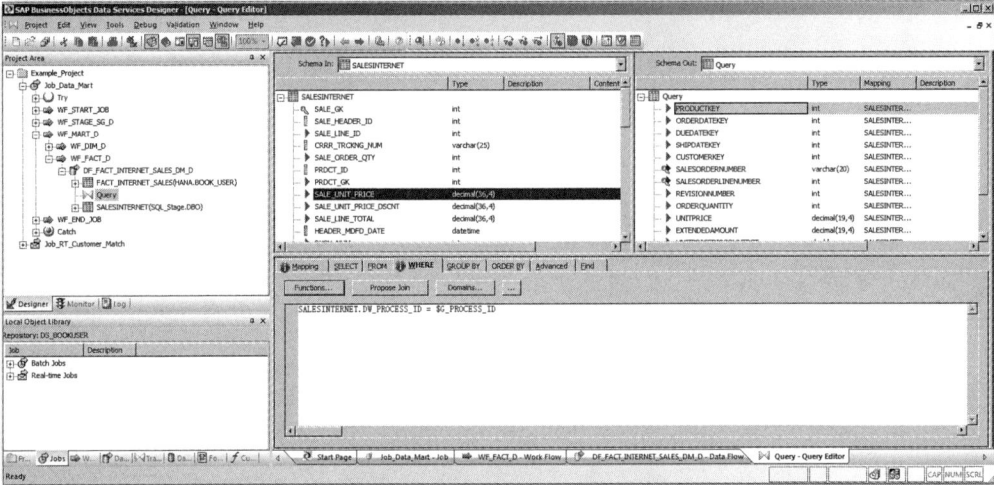

**Figure 5.85**  Source CDC from Staging Handled via Process ID Comparison

Now, you're merely left to write data to the FACT_INTERNET_SALES table using the AUTO CORRECT LOAD approach that was described earlier in this chapter and shown in Figure 5.86.

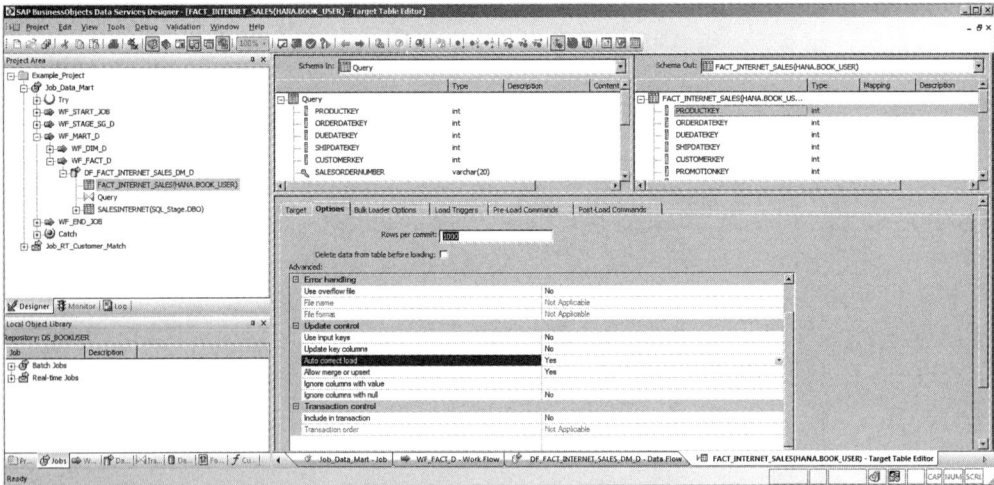

**Figure 5.86**  Auto Correct Load Options in the FACT_INTERNET_SALES Table

With the entire list of the data mart tables in SAP HANA now loaded, you're almost finished with the batch job to load the data mart. There is only one task left to complete. You started the load process in the installation phase; now to close the loop that you opened in the DW_JobExecution table, you run the end script as described next.

### 5.4.7 End Script

The end script section of the job is as simple as the initialize script section of the job, and they have mutually exclusive purposes. The initialize script starts the load process by creating the DW_JobExecution record and setting the STATUS value to STARTED. The end script simply sets the value of the STATUS field in the DW_JobExecution record to DONE to begin again with the next run. The workflow and script object are shown in Figure 5.87 and Figure 5.88, respectively.

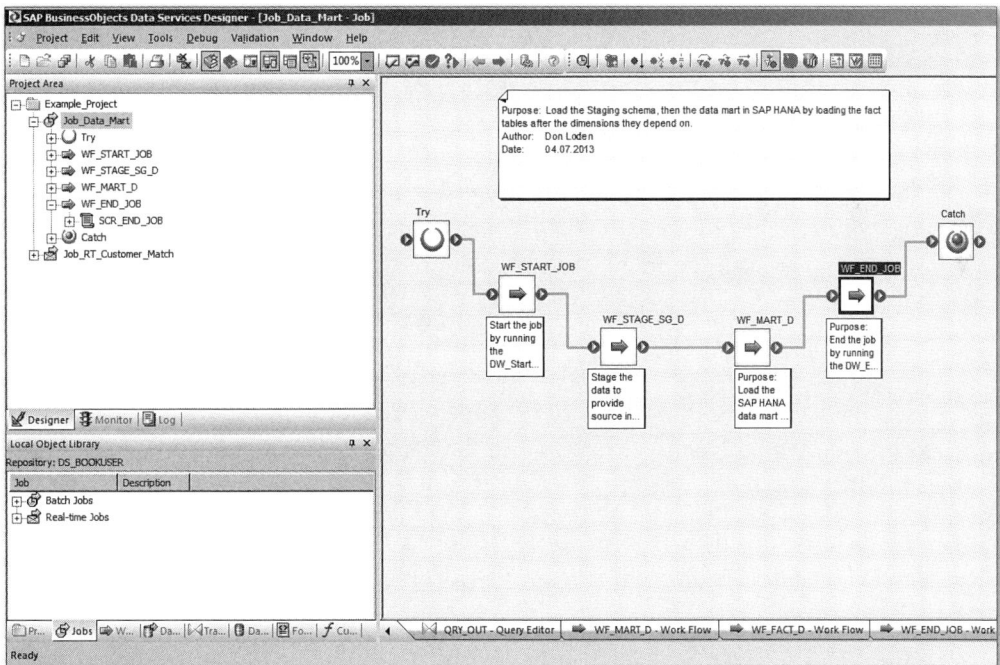

**Figure 5.87** End Script Workflow to End the Job

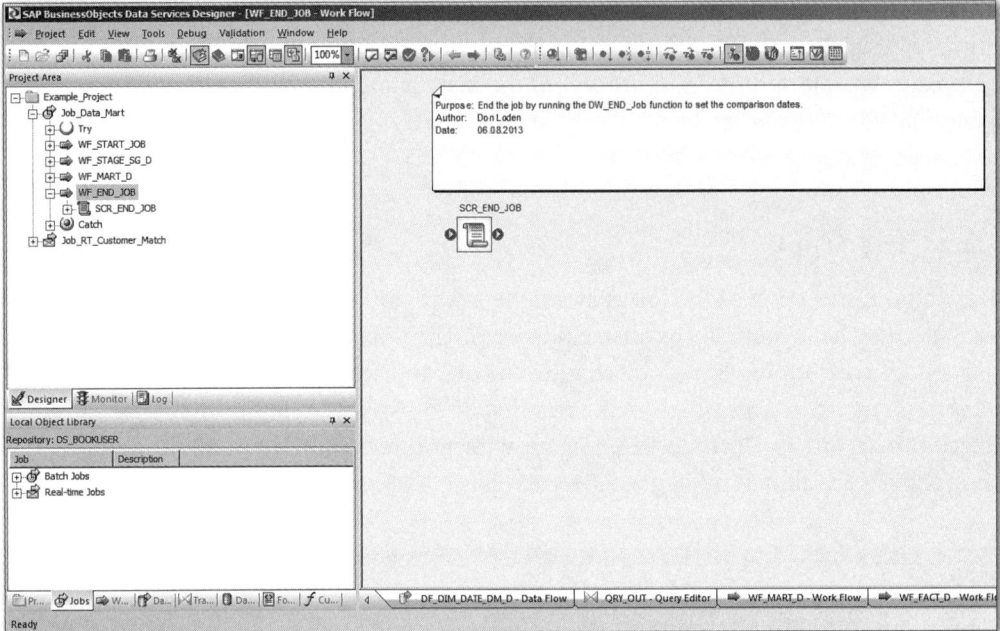

**Figure 5.88**  End Script Object within the Workflow

The idea is quite simple. By placing the end script at the end of the job, no further logic needs to be built into the function or the call of the function. If the job makes it to the end to call the script, then it's complete. If there were a problem with the job, then the `Try Catch` block would have caught the error and halted the job. The job would have never made it to the end script to "close the loop" and set the STATUS field in the DW_JobExecution to DONE. Because the loop would have remained open with the DW_JobExecution value set to STARTED, then the next run of the job would have recovered all of the variable values and reprocessed them until it completed.

This is how the end script section of code works together with the initialization section of code. It's only with these two working together that you can ensure that all of your data made it successfully to SAP HANA.

The contents of the end script are as follows:

```
# Updates job status with a value of 'done'
DW_EndJob(job_name());
```

```
#Write to Trace Log when you are finished...
print( 'Finished - ' || job_name() || ' at ' ||
to_char(sysdate(),'dd/mm/yyyy hh24:mi:ss') || '.');
```

## 5.5    Case Study: Loading Data in Real Time

Data has now been loaded in batch in SAP HANA, and the process has worked well for the AdventureWorks Cycle Company. The batch process that was coded and designed in the first case study (Section 5.4) runs once a day, and this has met the majority of the business needs. The analysts at AdventureWorks are able to access data with speeds never seen before.

However, upon further analysis of both business and supporting data needs, the BI team determined that certain aspects of sales data needed to be loaded in real time to support the analysis of Internet sales transactions.

Particularly, sales attributes and customer attributes need to be refreshed as sales transactions are entered in the online sales system. This would allow the sales associates to have up-to-the-minute customer and sales transactional information in SAP HANA as a supplement to the data mart data that is being loaded once a day in batch. Data can easily be triggered as web services, as this is a native communication platform of the company's web-based sales system. As these web services are rendered, portions of the data are loaded into SAP HANA to support the sales staff with changed data throughout the day. This met the business need for up-to-the-second sales information, but didn't necessitate an entire refresh of the data warehouse during the day in real time. This is how the AdventureWorks Cycle Company was able to meet their needs but not disrupt their batch load or design of the batch-based system for data loading and transformation.

In this section, we'll review the design process and the build of the real-time data flows for the sales data and how the AdventureWorks team was able to reuse certain aspects of the SAP Data Services data flows. This section won't go into nearly the detail of Section 5.4, as real-time loads are merely a subset of the batch load.

When designing a real-time solution to meet stated business needs, the IT team at AdventureWorks constructed two different components:

▶ A new real-time job

▶ A new batch job exposed as an executable

The real-time job is a web services-triggered job that is very similar to the customer master data cleansing job described earlier in this chapter (Section 5.2.2). The job is similar in how it's called, but its purpose is very different. This real-time job is just an execution mechanism that can be called from a generic web service from the AdventureWorks online sales system. The job is quite simple, as shown in Figure 5.89.

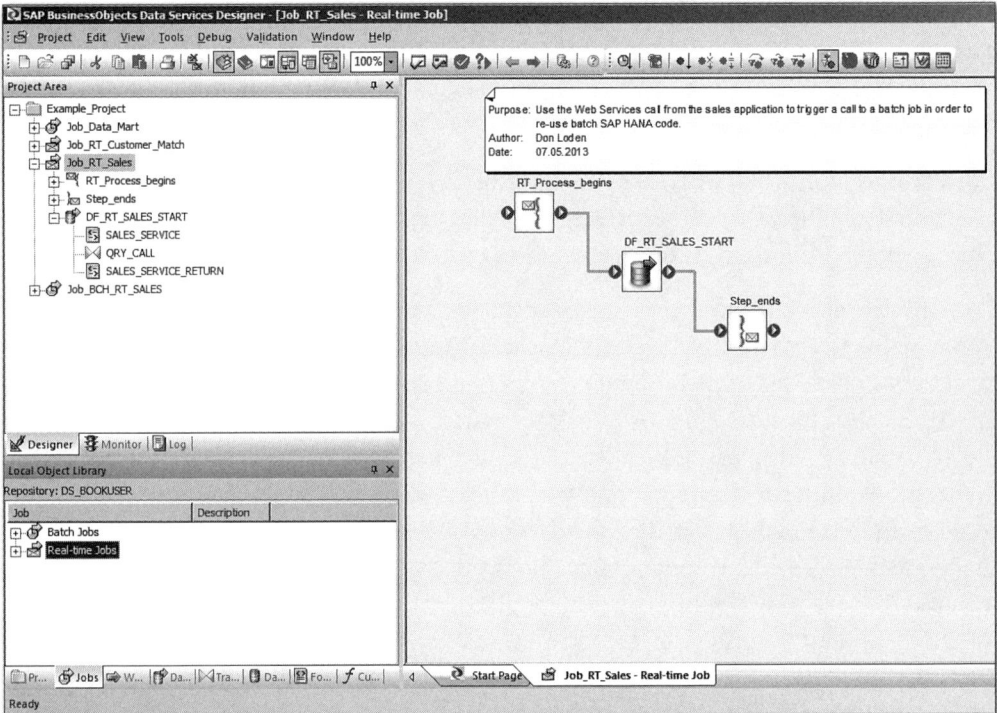

**Figure 5.89** Real-Time Sales Job Acting as an Execution Object for a Batch Job

This real-time job is only the first step in the process to load the customer and sales data into SAP HANA, but to see why, you have to open the data flow DF_RT_SALES_START, shown in Figure 5.90.

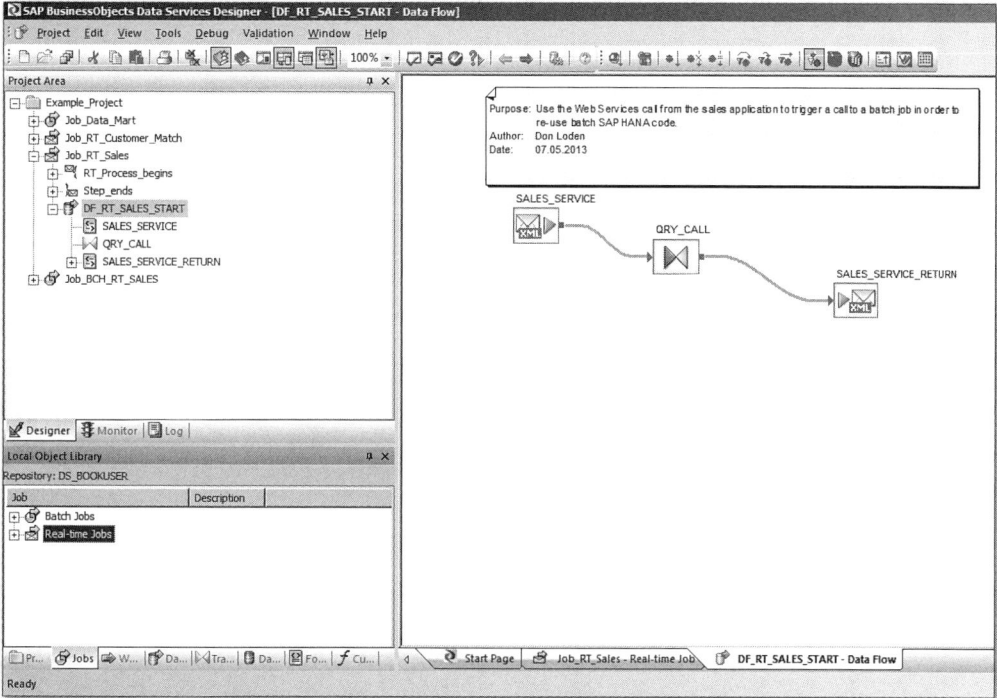

**Figure 5.90**   Contents of the Real-Time Sales Start Data Flow

Everything looks quite similar to earlier examples with a web service call coming from the online sales application. The XML message request to represent this in Figure 5.90 is called SALES_SERVICE. After that, there is only one Query transform, but its usage isn't for data transformations.

You'll use the Query transform to call another SAP Data Services job. To do this, you'll use a very flexible SAP Data Services exec() function. This function is capable of triggering .exe or .bat files from anywhere that the SAP Data Services service user has rights to see. To keep this example simple, a batch file is executed that launches the SAP Data Services batch file, which is stored on the local job server, as shown in Figure 5.91.

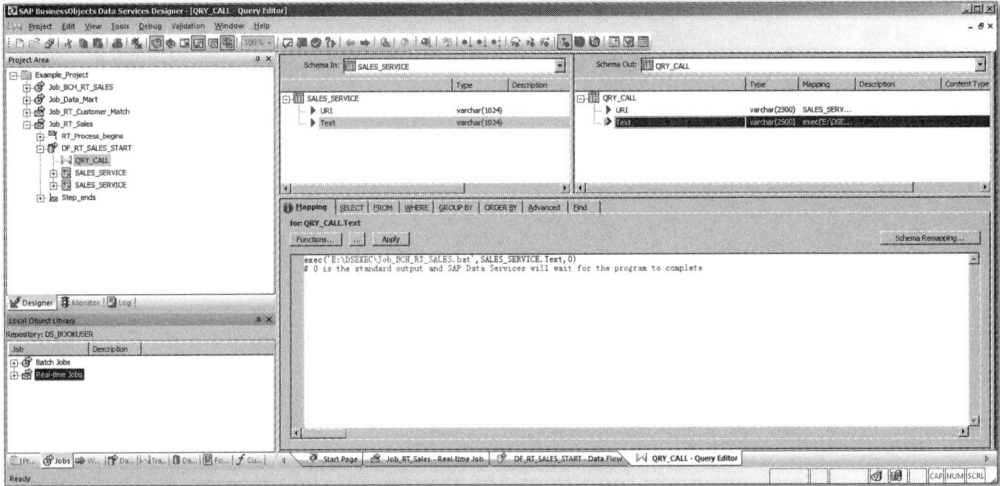

**Figure 5.91** Exec Function Call in the Query Transform

The `exec` function calls the batch file that starts the SAP Data Services batch job with the first parameter, and arguments can be passed with the second parameter. This example passes the XML message text as the argument because it's formatted appropriately. If additional formatting were needed for the string, you could perform the string transformations using other built-in SAP Data Services functions. The third parameter is the output of the function. Choose the output option of 0, as this is the standard output.

This option also forces the SAP Data Services real-time job to wait for the execution of the batch file/SAP Data Services batch job to complete, making the real-time job act as a wrapper for the call to the executable to instantiate the SAP Data Services batch job. The real-time job won't report success or failure back to the web-based sales system supplying the call until the SAP Data Services batch job processing is complete. The following is the entire syntax to call the batch job:

```
exec('E:\DSEXEC\Job_BCH_RT_SALES.bat',SALES_SERVICE.Text,0)
# 0 is the standard output, and SAP Data Services will wait for the
program to complete
```

**Additional Resources**

For more information on all of the output and processing options available, consult the SAP Data Services reference manual *sbo411_ds_reference_en.pdf* that you can download from *https://help.sap.com/*.

Create the batch file that is called by this `exec()` function by exporting an execution command of an SAP Data Services batch job that was detailed earlier in this chapter in Section 5.3.3. After the process to create the execution command is complete, both the .bat file and .txt instructions file are produced, and they have been moved to the local job server directory E:\DSEXEC (see Figure 5.92).

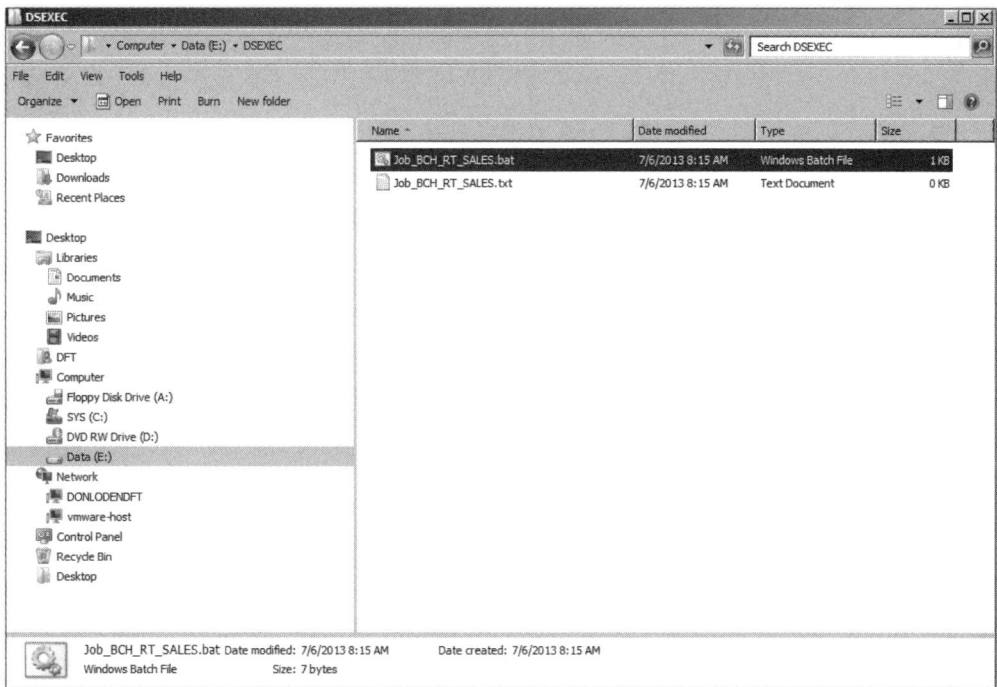

**Figure 5.92** Batch File for Execution and Text File for Instructions in the DSEXEC Folder

These two files have all of the components needed to call the batch job that has been created to reuse existing SAP HANA and staging data flows for the following tables that were created in the first case study:

- Staging.CUSTOMER

- HANA.BOOK_USER.DIM_CUSTOMER

- Staging.INTERNETSALES

- HANA.BOOK_USER.FACT_INTERNET_SALES

The batch job is called JOB_BCH_RT_SALES (see Figure 5.93) and is a pared-down version of the batch job created in the previous case study.

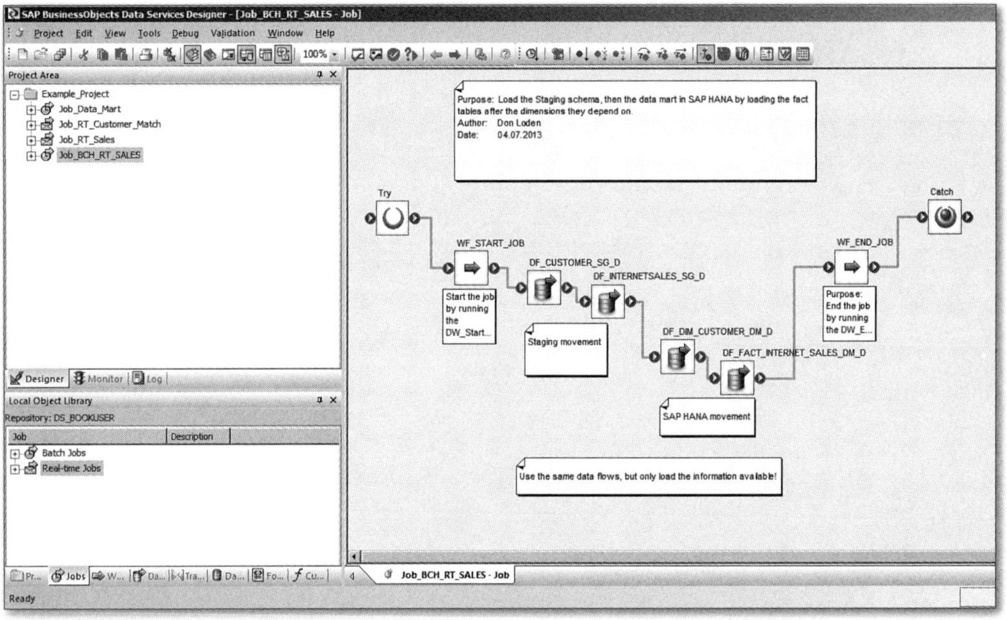

**Figure 5.93** Batch Job Constructed Fully Reusing Data Mart Build Elements

This job reuses the data flows as well as the scripts, so there is no need to walk through the job in its entirety. By reusing SAP Data Services, you've successfully met the needs of the business for real-time data with reusing 100% of the data flows created to move the data into SAP HANA! This means that when a change happens from the business for a table or column, you'll only need to make that change in one place, as the object is the same for both real-time and batch.

This is a perfect example of harnessing the power of best practices in object-oriented code design with SAP Data Services. Because we won't walk through the entire job in this section due to the redundancy of the data flows, we've provided Table 5.5, which lists the first case study sections where the build of the job elements occurs.

| Real-Time Job Element | Batch Job Section |
|---|---|
| WF_START_JOB | Section 5.4.3, Initialization |
| DF_CUSTOMER_SG_D | Section 5.4.4, Staging Workflow: Customer |
| DF_INTERNETSALES_SG_D | Section 5.4.4, Staging Workflow: Internet Sales |
| DF_DIM_CUSTOMER_DM_D | Section 5.4.5, Build Dimension Tables in SAP HANA: DIM_Customer |
| DF_FACT_INTERNET _SALES_DM_D | Section 5.4.6, Build Fact Table: FACT_Internet_Sales_Retail |
| WF_END_JOB | Section 5.4.7, End Script |

**Table 5.5** SAP Data Services Real-Time Job Components

## 5.6 Summary

Now that data has been loaded into SAP HANA, you have the data foundation. You've successfully set the stage for a data platform that can be loaded in a variety of different ways as well as provided the properly designed data tables for the SAP HANA data mart. Data is modeled into a best-practice, denormalized structure in columnar tables that are still heavily based on a traditional star schema. This approach will both unleash the power of SAP HANA's performance as well as exploit the capabilities of the SAP BusinessObjects BI suite of tools.

You're now ready to explore the data in the next section of this book. You'll leave the data layer and move into some of the most exciting elements that SAP HANA has to offer in multidimensional modeling.

SAP HANA's unique multidimensional modeling capabilities are where SAP HANA really shines, and these are the capabilities most often reviewed and highlighted in all commonplace discourse from SAP. Multidimensional modeling brings to SAP HANA a revolutionary development platform. However, this platform can only be fully realized by a properly prepared and constructed data foundation layer. Because you now have this foundation, you're ready to examine the multidimensional modeling capabilities in SAP HANA.

# PART II
# Multidimensional Modeling in SAP HANA

*Explore the multidimensional models capabilities that are built-in to SAP HANA.*

# 6 Modeling Data for Analytic Consumption in SAP HANA

In previous chapters, we discussed in length the ability of SAP Data Services to manage and combine data from multiple sources. The combined data was then stored in a data model that was both comprehensive and optimized for providing fast access to the data. We also discussed the importance of data quality and how SAP Data Services can be used to manage data quality. This chapter focuses on the role SAP HANA plays in producing quality multidimensional models and how you can use them to create value for your organization and users of the SAP Business-Objects reporting tools.

The true value of data to an organization comes in many forms. It can be measured through its depth, its quality, and its ability to effectively explain occurrences within an organization. There is no doubt that businesses and organizations have accumulated vast amounts of data with the emergence of information systems and software applications that manage their daily operations. However, to truly assign value to data, it must be structured and organized in a way that is intuitive and easy to understand. In addition, the data must be able to quickly, accurately, and securely answer the questions that are posed by analysts, managers, and executives. In this regard, the goal of multidimensional modeling is just that—to help facilitate the answering of questions that bring insight and value to the questioner.

SAP HANA was designed with this very principle in mind. It's capable of storing data in a platform that was designed to provide secure and easy access to a wealth of data. In addition, it has built-in mechanisms to facilitate intuitive and easily understood multidimensional data models. Many SAP HANA marketers refer to it as an analytics platform and not just a database because SAP HANA can do much more than simply store data. Among other qualities, it has multidimensional modeling capabilities built directly into its core; these were developed to organize data into categories or structures that can explain the movement of processes or transactions throughout time or across the hierarchy of facets that characterize the attributes of each data record.

Before we begin our coverage of SAP HANA's multidimensional capabilities, let's review the basics of the *multidimensional model*. The foundation of the multidimensional model is the *transaction*. Transactions are stored in rows that contain multiple columns. Each column represents a characteristic of the row. As multiple rows are stacked together, these columns begin to form common groups. The groups are then capable of providing dimensionality to the rows. In traditional online analytical processing (OLAP), these groups are called *dimensions*. Dimensions are then paired with *measures* to explain how often, when, or where dimensional values are expressed. Dimensions and measures can be attributed to *hierarchies* that highlight both the macro and micro perspectives of aggregated data. Hierarchies also contain paths that can be followed to help properly explain the results of aggregated data.

The basic multidimensional model illustrated in Figure 6.1 shows the basic relationships between dimensions and transactions. This logical relationship between dimensions and transactions is commonly referred to as the *star schema*. Dimensions are derived from each Internet sales transaction and are grouped into logical areas such as customers, dates, products, and shipping addresses. Measures are derived from the Internet sales transactions by aggregating items such as sales amount, tax amount, and quantity sold.

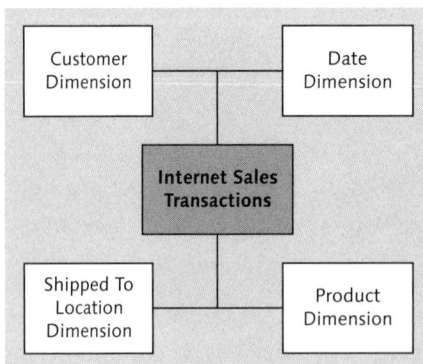

**Figure 6.1**  Internet Sales Multidimensional Model Diagram

Each dimension is comprised of one or more attributes that can be used for sorting, grouping, or filtering. The attributes of a dimension are derived from the transaction and other master data sources both internal and external to an organization. In Figure 6.2, you can see that attributes such as age, name, and gender are all components of customers. After these attributes are combined with the Internet sales transaction's measures, you can easily answer basic questions, such as "Which age group places the most orders over the Internet?" You can also combine attributes from other dimensions with the customer dimension to answer more complex questions, such as "What were the top products sold last year by country?"

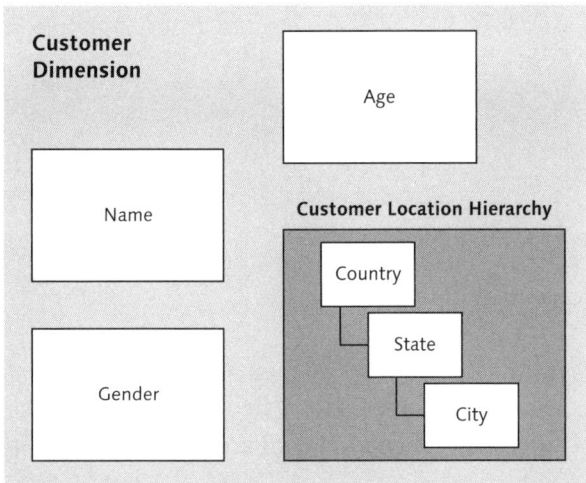

**Figure 6.2**  Attributes and Hierarchies in a Customer Dimension

Dimensions are also the basis for deriving hierarchies. A hierarchy can be defined from the customer's country, state, and city as shown in Figure 6.2. Hierarchies are derived from the natural parent-child relationships that exist in the attributes of a dimension. For example, the relationship among country, state, and city is naturally derived from the customer's address. Based on the hierarchy in Figure 6.2, a sales manager can easily identify the top country for sales, drill into the states to find the top state, and finally drill into city to identify the top city.

Hierarchies are also used to provide a concentric set of roll-up levels or subtotaling levels in reporting tools. Hierarchies based on dates can, for example, provide subtotals for the year, month, and week, as shown in the calendar date hierarchy in Figure 6.3. Dimensions can contain one or more hierarchies; in Figure 6.3, the two hierarchies are the Retail Date Hierarchy and the Calendar Date Hierarchy.

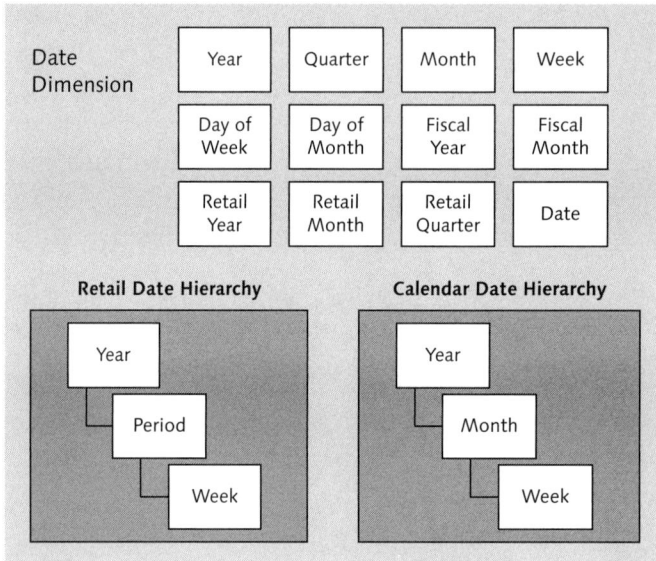

**Figure 6.3** Attributes and Hierarchies in a Date Dimension

Although hierarchies aren't required in dimensions, they are a key feature of multidimensional analysis based on many of the reasons stated previously. Dimensions that don't contain hierarchies are considered flat but are still very useful in grouping, filtering, and sorting data.

With the basic building blocks in a multidimensional model, simple and complex questions can be answered. Developers create multidimensional models to define relationships between transactions and their attributes. These relationships create a new set of information about the data that is commonly referred to as *metadata*. Dimension names, attribute names, and their long text descriptions are also considered metadata. All of this metadata is stored in the model and used to describe both the relationships between attributes and additional information to help consumers locate and use the appropriate attributes.

Many OLAP tools on the market use these basic components and the actual supporting data to create a proprietary storage medium called a *cube*. The cube is a combination of both the source data and the defined metadata. When both the data and metadata are stored in this special database, it's widely referred to as *multidimensional OLAP (MOLAP)* storage. MOLAP is preferred in most products because it contains special indexes or aggregated data to help optimize the performance of queries executed against the multidimensional model.

Many tools on the market also support *relational OLAP* storage (ROLAP). ROLAP is similar to MOLAP, but only the metadata is stored in the cube, while the actual source data remains in the supporting relational database. ROLAP is preferred either in situations where the time required to create or update the cube is extensive or in situations where real-time access to the data is required.

In comparison to MOLAP, ROLAP is generally slower at answering queries with traditional relational databases and cubes. This isn't true in every circumstance, but when large quantities of data are concerned, MOLAP almost always produces faster results. Traditionally speaking, ROLAP is slower largely based on the inefficiencies of the underlying relational databases. As you'll discover in this chapter, SAP HANA uses a storage mechanism similar to ROLAP. However, SAP HANA's underlying columnar in-memory relational database is exceptionally fast, making ROLAP storage a viable solution for multidimensional analysis. In short, the SAP HANA appliance has the unique capability to offer the benefits of both MOLAP and ROLAP in a single platform.

The usefulness of a multidimensional model depends largely on the quality of the source data, the definition of the model, and the tools that are used to access it. So, in this chapter, we'll discuss the components of the SAP HANA analytic models and how they can be used to add value to analytics.

In the previous chapters, we used SAP Data Services to produce both quality data and meaningful data models. As you'll discover in this chapter, the data models that are produced using SAP Data Services play a very important role in aiding the SAP HANA models. This is true even when we consider the multidimensional capabilities of SAP HANA. In subsequent chapters, we'll discuss the role that SAP BusinessObjects plays in designing visual analytics based on either the columnar tables or multidimensional model. For the multidimensional model to provide value, the reporting and analytic tools that access the models must be able to use its metadata to produce quality results. Quality tools should provide consumers the ability to slice, dice, drill, roll up, and pivot the data. In addition, the tools must facilitate the answering of both simple and complex questions.

> **The Role of SAP HANA Models**
>
> Before venturing too deep into this chapter, it's important for you to understand the role of SAP HANA models in the overall context of the SAP BusinessObjects Business Intelligence (SAP BusinessObjects BI) platform and solution we describe in this book.
>
> In Chapters 1 through 5 we introduced you to SAP Data Services. This chapter introduces you to the concepts and steps required to create analytic models. In subsequent chapters, we'll discuss the role that SAP BusinessObjects plays in managing the tools that users use to access the data stored in SAP HANA using the models discussed in this chapter.
>
> Again, SAP Data Services serves as the engine to consolidate, clean, manage, and load data from one or more sources into the SAP HANA columnar tables. SAP Data Services is also required, at times, to denormalize or restructure the source data when SAP HANA cannot or should not. After the data is stored in the SAP HANA columnar tables, special views can be created to express the data in a multidimensional model. The models themselves can't answer questions or visualize the data without a tool to analyze, explore, or generate reports. This is a job for SAP BusinessObjects, which provides the tools necessary to access either the multidimensional models or columnar tables in SAP HANA.

Let's begin this high-level overview of the multidimensional modeling capabilities of SAP HANA by walking through the main components of the models using SAP HANA Studio. You'll discover the role that *schemas*, *tables*, *attribute views*, *analytic views*, *calculation views*, and *analytic privileges* serve in developing models using SAP HANA Studio in Section 6.1. We then explore the benefits that organizations can realize with respect to SAP HANA and its modeling capabilities in Section 6.2. From a best practices standpoint, we then differentiate between data modeling and analytic modeling (Section 6.3). In conclusion, we walk through the processes of designing both a simple multidimensional model and a complex model in Section 6.4 and Section 6.5, respectively.

## 6.1    SAP HANA Modeling Main Components

In this section, we'll explore the basic tools and components of the SAP HANA multidimensional models. When explaining the basic components of the multidimensional model in the introduction to this chapter, we used terms such as dimensions, hierarchies, measures, and cubes. SAP HANA has incorporated many of these same basic components into its multidimensional modeling tools, but

SAP has chosen to name its basic components a little differently. While the names might not be the same, the principles and features are identical, if not very similar.

### 6.1.1 SAP HANA Studio

The first step in creating multidimensional models in SAP HANA requires the installation and configuration of SAP HANA Studio. SAP HANA Studio is a client tool that is installed on an SAP HANA developer or administrator's workstation. It's built on the Java-based Eclipse 3.6 platform.

Whether you're installing SAP HANA Studio or upgrading SAP HANA Studio, we recommend that the installed version match that of the SAP HANA appliance that is used for development. Each patch version of SAP HANA Studio supports either a full installation or an update of an existing SAP HANA Studio installation. As a result, only one download and installation is required for the first installation to support the appropriate version of the SAP HANA appliance that is being used. From an operating system standpoint, SAP HANA Studio Version 45 (SPS5) supports the operating systems listed in Table 6.1.

| Supported Operating Systems | Version |
|---|---|
| Windows XP | 32 bit and 64 bit |
| Windows Vista | 32 bit and 64 bit |
| Windows 7 | 32 bit and 64 bit |
| SUSE Linux 11 x86 | 64 bit |

**Table 6.1**  Supported Operating Systems for SAP HANA Studio

Because SAP HANA Studio runs in a Java Virtual Machine (JVM), the Java 1.6 or 1.7 Java Runtime Environment (JRE) must be installed prior to the SAP HANA Studio installation. If you plan to install the 32-bit version of SAP HANA Studio, you must download and install the 32-bit version of the JRE. If you plan to use the 64-bit version of SAP HANA Studio, you must download and install the 64-bit version of the JRE.

> **Additional References**
>
> The installation of SAP HANA Studio is beyond the scope of this book. For more informa-
> tion on the installation of SAP HANA Studio, please download the *SAP HANA Database:*
> *Studio Installation Guide* from *http://help.sap.com/hana_appliance#section2*.
>
> In addition, the installation instructions for installing a JVM are beyond the scope of
> this book. For more information on installing the Oracle JRE, please visit *www.java.com*.

SAP HANA Studio provides several *perspectives* depending on the nature of the work that you're attempting to complete. Perspectives are essentially a set of predefined layouts or views for the Eclipse *workbench*. The workbench is effectively a user's local space in SAP HANA Studio. To access a perspective in the SAP HANA Studio, select WINDOW • OPEN PERSPECTIVE • OTHER from the FILE menu bar. As of SAP HANA Studio version 45 (SPS5), the perspectives shown in Figure 6.4 can be used.

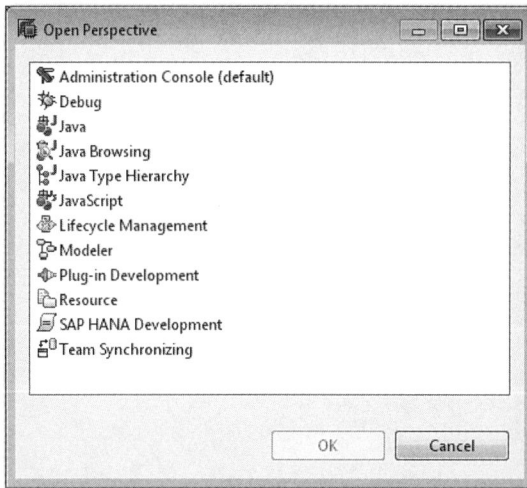

**Figure 6.4** The SAP HANA Studio Open Perspective Window

Perspectives are simply predefined or custom collections of views within the SAP HANA Studio Eclipse workspace. Each view provides one or more operations spe-cific to SAP HANA administration, SAP HANA modeling, or other supported SAP HANA features. SAP HANA Studio includes the SAP HANA Development, Modeler, Debug, and Administration Console perspectives by default; these are listed in Table 6.2, along with a description of when you should use them. The other listed perspectives in Figure 6.4 are standard to the Eclipse workspace.

| Perspective | Best Use |
|---|---|
| Modeler | The Modeler perspective is best used for the management and development of the SAP HANA multidimensional models. This perspective also provides many of the same views of the Administration Console perspective, but primarily it contains the views specific to development. The Modeler perspective contains a handy QUICK LAUNCH screen that lists the main components of modeling with a brief description of their uses. In addition, the QUICK LAUNCH screen allows you to create or manage various aspects of the SAP HANA models. |
| Administration Console | The Administration Console perspective contains the basic views that are needed to administer the SAP HANA appliance. This perspective doesn't contain the main views to aid in the development of modeling content. Administrative tasks include creating users, creating roles, managing system settings, and executing Structured Query Language (SQL) statements. It's best used by SAP HANA appliance administrators. |
| SAP HANA Development | The SAP HANA Development perspective contains many of the same features or views found in the Modeler perspective. However, this perspective also contains support for the SAP HANA repository and SAP HANA Extended Application Services (SAP HANA XS) projects. This perspective is best used by more advanced or experienced SAP HANA developers. It doesn't include access to the convenient QUICK LAUNCH screen. |
| Debug | The Debug perspective is used to debug JavaScript and SQL script code. This perspective is best used by more advanced or experienced SAP HANA application developers. |

**Table 6.2** SAP HANA Studio Perspectives

From this point forward, we'll primarily focus on the Modeler perspective. This perspective contains all of the features necessary to explain the components of SAP HANA models. When the Modeler perspective is active, there are two main areas that can be used to create the components of the SAP HANA multidimensional models. The first is the *Navigator view*, which is located on the far-left side of the perspective. Figure 6.5 shows an example NAVIGATOR view in SAP HANA Studio.

You'll also see the QUICK LAUNCH welcome screen located to the right in the Modeler perspective, which is discussed in more detail shortly.

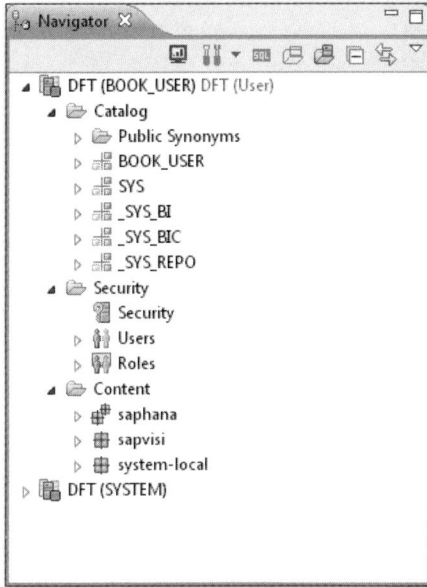

**Figure 6.5** The Navigator View in the SAP HANA Modeler Perspective

The NAVIGATOR view contains one or more hierarchies that each start with the system objects. The system object contains the connection details for a defined SAP HANA appliance and an associated user account. To log on to SAP HANA and develop content, you must first define a system by right-clicking anywhere in the NAVIGATOR view and choosing ADD SYSTEM.

To define a system, you need to know the following information:

▶ The SAP HANA appliance host name

▶ The SAP HANA appliance system number

▶ The user name and password to access the SAP HANA appliance

After the system is defined, a view appears similar to that previously shown in Figure 6.5. There are three main areas listed under each system in the NAVIGATOR view:

▶ CATALOG
The CATALOG provides access to the PUBLIC SYNONYMS (links to system

procedures) and the database schemas. We'll discuss schemas in more detail in Section 6.1.2.

▶ SECURITY

The SECURITY area is used primarily by administrators to manage access to the SAP HANA appliance. From a developer's standpoint, this area is used to grant permissions to other users or roles that might want to access their content.

▶ CONTENT

The CONTENT area is used predominantly during the multidimensional model development lifecycle to create and manage the main components of SAP HANA modeling. In the CONTENT view, you find a hierarchy of objects specific to SAP HANA modeling. We'll discuss these objects in more detail throughout the remainder of this chapter.

As mentioned earlier, there is a second area that you can use to create the SAP HANA multidimensional models. Located on the right side of the Modeler perspective is the QUICK LAUNCH view. Figure 6.6 shows what you typically see in this view.

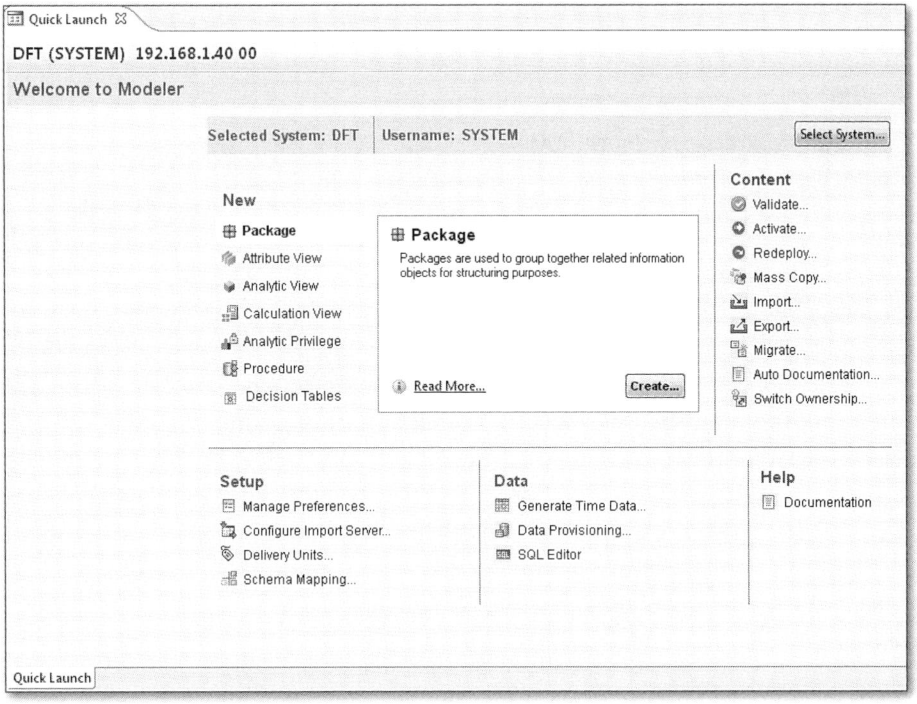

**Figure 6.6** The Quick Launch Modeler Welcome Screen

The Quick Launch view contains five main sections. Each section contains one or more links that launch functions or wizards specific to an SAP HANA development task.

► New

Contains links to create the various components of the SAP HANA multidimensional models. As each item is selected, a helpful message is displayed to the right that includes a summary of the objects purpose, a Read More link, and a button to launch a wizard to create the selected object.

► Content

Contains links to various development-related tasks. After the link is clicked, a wizard appears to guide you through the selected task.

► Setup

Contains links to tools that can set up specific functions such as promotion of content or the importing of schema DDL from third-party databases.

► Data

Contains links to tasks specific to the importing of data using SAP Landscape Transformation (SLT) or Sybase replication, the creation of the SAP HANA built-in date-time table, or the launching of the SAP HANA Studio SQL Editor.

► Help

Contains a link to the SAP HANA documentation area on *http://help.sap.com/hana.*

Many of the links in the Content, Setup, and Data areas are only available through the Quick Launch view. However, many of the options under the New area are also available in the content Navigator view discussed earlier. As you use SAP HANA Studio, the availability of each function and its location will become more apparent. The majority of the multidimensional modeling takes place in the content Navigator view after you become more familiar with the components of the SAP HANA models. For new developers, the Quick Launch view provides basic help as they start the development process. As we discuss the remaining components of SAP HANA modeling throughout this chapter, we delve into more detail about the options for creating each object type.

In summary, SAP HANA Studio is a desktop application that is used to administer the SAP HANA appliance as well as develop multidimensional models. Three main perspectives available in SAP HANA Studio offer a view specific to either administrators or developers. Developers can create each component of the multidimensional model using either the content Navigator view or the modeler Quick Launch view in the Modeler perspective. In the subsequent sections, we'll discuss in more detail the options and processes for creating each component of the multidimensional model.

## 6.1.2    Schemas

While the schema isn't a direct component of the multidimensional modeling features in SAP HANA, it's a vital component of the overall process. Schemas are logic storage containers in a relational database; they are often referred to as subdatabases within a relational database management system (RDBMS). They are used to logically store key database components such as tables, views, procedures, functions, triggers, and other items that we'll discuss shortly. Developers can manage schemas from the Modeler perspective in the CATALOG section of the NAVIGATOR view.

Figure 6.7 contains a fully expanded view of the CATALOG section where schemas are managed in SAP HANA. The schema BOOK_USER contains several subfolders that each represent a specific component type that will be logically stored in a schema. As each user account is created in SAP HANA, a schema is automatically created for that user bearing the name of the user. The schema BOOK_USER was generated when the user account BOOK_USER was created by the database administrator (DBA). SAP HANA also contains several default system schemas. As shown in Figure 6.7, the SYS and _SYS_REPO schemas are used by the SAP HANA appliance for managing repository content, multidimensional metadata, and other content essential to the operation of SAP HANA. In general, any schema that is prefixed with _SYS can be considered a system-managed schema.

From the perspective of multidimensional modeling, the TABLES component in a schema is essential to the overall design process. Once expanded, the TABLES component lists the row or columnar tables associated with the schema. Tables defined as the columnar type are used directly by the multidimensional models.

Recall from earlier chapters that SAP HANA tables are also used to manage the relational data that is loaded and stored in the SAP HANA appliance with SAP Data Services. As we continue through this chapter, we'll illustrate how the main components of SAP HANA's multidimensional models are based on the tables stored in one or more schemas. In essence, tables are the key components where data is logically stored and organized in SAP HANA. Without tables, the multidimensional models in SAP HANA would not be able provide data results to users querying the models.

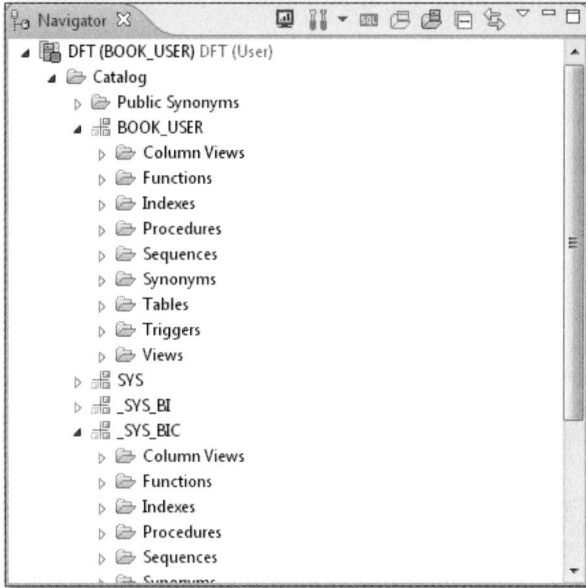

**Figure 6.7**  The Catalog Section in the Navigator View and Modeler Perspective

As mentioned earlier, the schema contains several components that are listed beneath it on the screen. Some of these components can be used directly by the multidimensional models. The components that are listed under a schema vary by perspective. The Administrative perspective contains all possible components, while the Modeler perspective only lists those components related to modeling. Table 6.3 outlines each component that is available from the Modeler perspective and its relationship to the SAP HANA multidimensional models.

| Schema Component | Relationship to Multidimensional Models |
|---|---|
| TABLES | Tables are the physical components that store data in SAP HANA. They can be defined as either row or columnar type. Tables are a fundamental component of the SAP models. Many of the SAP HANA modeling components directly reference one or more tables. |

**Table 6.3**  Objects Created in a Schema (When in Modeler Perspective)

| Schema Component | Relationship to Multidimensional Models |
|---|---|
| VIEWS | Views are logical objects that can be developed to act as a virtual table. Views are compiled using simple or complex SQL statements that can join, filter, sort, or rank data from one or more tables or views. Views can't be used directly in the multidimensional modeling components, but they can be used in procedures that are referenced by calculation views. |
| PROCEDURES | Procedures allow for the development of complex transactional SQL code that is appropriate when the basic use of table joins and filtering isn't sufficient to properly express a result set. Procedures use the SAP HANA SQL and R languages and support higher levels of application style programming. In the context of the multidimensional models, procedures can only be used indirectly in SAP HANA calculation views. |
| COLUMN VIEWS | Column views are a special type of view unique to SAP HANA. In general, they act as virtual database tables, but they have characteristics that are different from tables or views. In the _SYS_BIC schema, they provide multidimensional model metadata to external reporting or visualization tools. |
| | Column views should not be confused with database SQL views. Unlike database views, column views don't contain any complied SQL SELECT statements or transactional SQL code. They are compiled using a coding language specific to SAP HANA. |
| | Column views are also created with procedures that return a result set when executed. Procedural columns views can be used by SAP HANA calculation views or other external reporting tools and act as virtual tables. |

**Table 6.3**  Objects Created in a Schema (When in Modeler Perspective) (Cont.)

Tables in a schema are used by the multidimensional models as the source for all data, making them an important component of the overall process. Procedures in a schema can also be used by the multidimensional models but in a more limited capacity. As we'll discuss in more detail, tables can be used directly within the components of the SAP HANA multidimensional models such as the attribute views, analytic views, and calculation views. In addition, procedures can be used in calculation views in situations where more complex data processing or complex calculations are required. In the next few sections, we'll discuss the role of attribute views, analytic views, and calculation views in more detail.

> **SAP HANA Schema Security and SQL Privileges**
>
> Each component in a schema can be secured based on SAP HANA SQL privileges. SAP HANA users and roles can be granted a variety of SQL privileges by an administrator or by the schema owner. Privileges can be granted to an entire schema or to one or more tables, views, procedures, or column views in a schema. When a new user schema is created, only the owner of the schema has access to grant SQL privileges to the schema or schema components.
>
> This is an important concept in the overall SAP HANA multidimensional modeling process. As each component of the multidimensional model is committed to the SAP HANA repository, the _SYS_REPO system user manages the request. The _SYS_REPO user is responsible for creating column views under the _SYS_BIC system schema and updating runtime information in the _SYS_REPO and _SYS_BI system schema tables. In addition to managing metadata from the multidimensional models, the _SYS_REPO system user is also responsible for establishing the SQL privileges necessary for the models to access the underlying data in the schema tables.
>
> Every multidimensional model in SAP HANA is based on one or more tables in a schema. For the _SYS_REPO system user to properly establish the security for a model, the owner of the referenced schema must assign the SELECT and *grantable to others* privilege to the _SYS_REPO user. If stored procedures are used in the models, the EXECUTE and *grantable to others* privilege must also be given to the _SYS_REPO user as well. Therefore, if an administrator creates a new schema with the intent of using the schema in the SAP HANA models, he must log in as the schema owner and assign the SELECT and EXECUTE including *grantable to others* privilege to the _SYS_REPO user.

### 6.1.3 Packages

Packages are another key component of the SAP HANA multidimensional models. Each component of the multidimensional model must be stored in a user-defined package. These are the parent objects of each modeling component that is developed in SAP HANA Studio. Packages can have subpackages, which facilitate arrangement in a logical hierarchal order. As a result, package privileges can be established to limit other SAP HANA Studio users or developers from viewing, editing, activating, or maintaining packages and their child objects. The package hierarchy also allows developers and administrators to arrange packages and their child objects in a logical order that facilitates reusability and promotes a logical organization for a shared development environment. Packages can also be arranged into delivery units that are used to transport modeling content from one SAP HANA system to another.

To access packages in SAP HANA Studio, choose the Modeler perspective by selecting WINDOWS • OPEN PERSPECTIVE • MODELER. As shown in Figure 6.8 on the left side of the Modeler perspective is the NAVIGATOR view. Expand the CONTENT folder to view existing packages or right-click the CONTENT folder and select NEW to create a new package. To modify a package, right-click an existing package and choose EDIT.

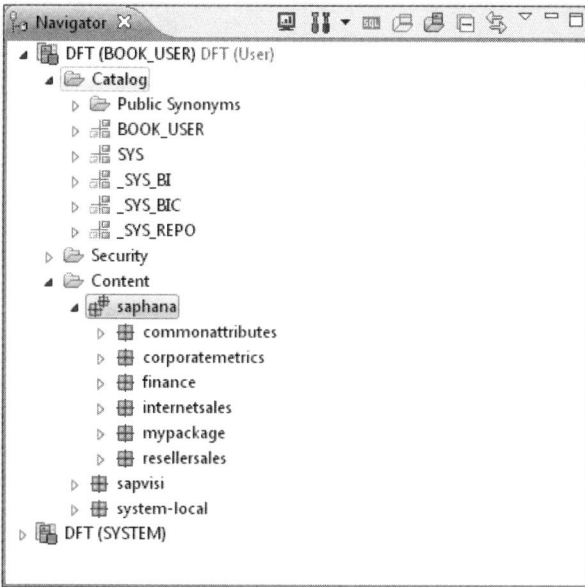

**Figure 6.8** The SAP HANA Package Hierarchy

As an alternative to using the NAVIGATOR view, you can also use the Modeler perspective QUICK LAUNCH view to create a new package. To create packages this way, choose the Modeler perspective by selecting WINDOWS • OPEN PERSPECTIVE • MODELER. The QUICK LAUNCH view should now appear as the prominent window or view as shown in Figure 6.9. In the QUICK LAUNCH view, click the PACKAGE icon and click the CREATE button located in the white box that appears to the right. A wizard appears to walk you through the processes of creating a package.

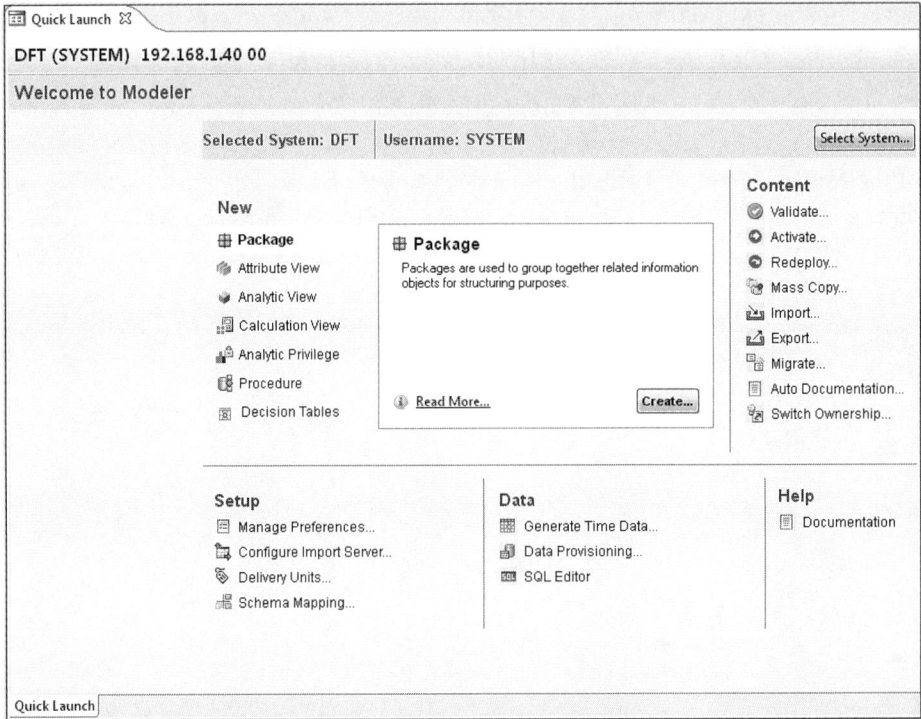

**Figure 6.9** Use the Modeler Welcome View to Create a Package

Table 6.4 outlines the properties that can be established when creating a package or modifying an existing package.

| Package Property | Description of Property |
|---|---|
| NAME | The NAME field reflects the name of the package. Each package name must be unique in its respective level. A subpackage can have the same name of its parent, but it can't have the same name of its sibling. Subpackage names are created by appending a "." and the subpackage name to the parent. Each subsequent subpackage will be prefixed with a ".", for example, `acme.department.finance.gl`.<br><br>Only the following characters are allowed: lowercase letters (a-z), numbers (0-9), hyphen (-), and up to nine nonconsecutive periods (.) |

**Table 6.4** Available Properties When Creating or Editing a Package

| Package Property | Description of Property |
|---|---|
| DESCRIPTION | The DESCRIPTION field should be used to fully explain the purpose of the package. It can also be used to provide useful metadata to users and developers. |
| DELIVERY UNIT | The DELIVERY UNIT is a special object that allows one or more packages to be grouped into a common unit for exportation or migration to another SAP HANA system. Packages that contain dependencies to each other should be grouped together. |
| STRUCTURAL | The STRUCTURAL option allows you to configure a package so that it can only contain subpackages. If the option is set to YES, then only a subpackage can be created in the package. If the option is set to NO, then the package can contain subpackages and modeling objects as well. This option is best used to prevent you from creating modeling content in a designated package. |
| ORIGINAL LANGUAGE | The ORIGINAL LANGUAGE field defines the language of the package |
| PERSON RESPONSIBLE | The PERSON RESPONSIBLE field reflects SAP HANA user account that is responsible for the package. |
| LOGON LOCALE | The locale that is established when defining the SAP HANA system within SAP HANA Studio. Generally the LOGON LOCALE and ORIGINAL LANGUAGE properties should be the same during the development process. |

**Table 6.4**  Available Properties When Creating or Editing a Package (Cont.)

After a package has been created, developers or administrators can't change the name of the package. Therefore, it's important that you thoroughly develop a proper naming convention and package hierarchy before creating any multidimensional modeling components. This step is especially important before external reporting tools, such as SAP BusinessObjects, begin using the content.

Packages play an important role in helping developers and administrators organize, secure, and distribute each component of the SAP HANA multidimensional model. Before developers can create and maintain components of the model, a package must be created, and the appropriate privileges must be granted to the developer's user account or role. As we discuss the remaining components of the SAP HANA models in the subsequent sections of this chapter, it's important to understand that a package is the starting point of the process.

## SAP HANA Package Security and Package Privileges

SAP HANA platform users who require development access to the multidimensional models need to be assigned roles or privileges to access a package or their child components in the SAP HANA appliance. By default, members of the modeling role and content_admin role have full access to the root package or top-level package. In most cases, it's recommended that these default roles are never assigned to a user and that custom roles be established by the organization. With that said, each package that is created is automatically considered a child of the root package. Therefore, each child package automatically inherits the privileges established for the root package. If an SAP HANA user is created and not assigned the modeling or Content Admin role, a system administrator must grant that user the appropriate access to the packages the user manages or needs to review in SAP HANA Studio.

Because the modeling or Content Admin roles effectively grant administrative rights to all packages, these roles should only be used for users that require full access to all packages. To delegate access to packages, an SAP HANA administrator must explicitly assign package privileges to each nonadministrative user or create specialized roles for these users.

The following privileges are available for packages:

▶ **REPO.READ**
Grants the ability for the user or role to view the selected package or modeling content.

▶ **REPO.EDIT_NATIVE_OBJECTS**
Grants the ability for the user or role to modify the modeling content in a package. This privilege doesn't grant access to edit a package.

▶ **REPO.ACTIVATE_NATIVE_OBJECTS**
Grants the ability for the user or role to activate or reactivate modeling components in a package.

▶ **REPO.MAINTAIN_NATIVE_PACKAGES**
Grants the ability for the user or role to modify, edit, or create a package or subpackage.

## Additional References

A thorough discussion on the topic of SAP HANA privileges is beyond the scope of this book. For additional information concerning package security, please consult the following SAP HANA documentation available at *http://help.sap.com/hana_appliance*:

▶ SAP HANA Developer Guide
▶ SAP HANA Security Guide

### 6.1.4    Attribute Views

As we discussed in the introduction of this chapter, dimensions are an important component of multidimensional modeling. They contain one or more values that are used to describe a transaction or quantifiable measure. In many cases, the combination of values in a dimension forms a hierarchy that can be used to provide drilling, aggregation levels, or navigation paths.

In the example shown in Figure 6.10, there are five columns of data. The first column, PRODUCT ID, represents the *primary key* of the table and is used predominantly to join to other tables in the model. The remaining columns are used to describe an attribute of the product ID. In this case, the PRODUCT NAME and PRODUCT NUMBER will likely be unique values just like the PRODUCT ID, but the PRODUCT COLOR and PRODUCT LINE values will have duplicate values. Because these values repeat from record to record, a natural hierarchy can be defined based on the values in these columns. In our example, a PRODUCT LINE, PRODUCT COLOR, and PRODUCT NAME hierarchy can be defined based on the three columns, meaning that the top level of the hierarchy is the PRODUCT LINE, followed by PRODUCT COLOR, and finally PRODUCT NAME.

| Product ID | Product Name | Product Number | Product Color | Product Line |
|---|---|---|---|---|
| 989 | Mountain-500 Black, 40 | BK-M18B-40 | Black | M |
| 990 | Mountain-500 Black, 42 | BK-M18B-42 | Black | M |
| 991 | Mountain-500 Black, 44 | BK-M18B-44 | Black | M |
| 992 | Mountain-500 Black, 48 | BK-M18B-48 | Black | M |
| 993 | Mountain-500 Black, 52 | BK-M18B-52 | Black | M |
| 984 | Mountain-500 Silver, 40 | BK-M18S-40 | Silver | M |
| 985 | Mountain-500 Silver, 42 | BK-M18S-42 | Silver | M |
| 986 | Mountain-500 Silver, 44 | BK-M18S-44 | Silver | M |
| 987 | Mountain-500 Silver, 48 | BK-M18S-48 | Silver | M |
| 988 | Mountain-500 Silver, 52 | BK-M18S-52 | Silver | M |
| 980 | Mountain-400-W Silver, 38 | BK-M38S-38 | Silver | M |
| 981 | Mountain-400-W Silver, 40 | BK-M38S-40 | Silver | M |
| 982 | Mountain-400-W Silver, 42 | BK-M38S-42 | Silver | M |
| 983 | Mountain-400-W Silver, 46 | BK-M38S-46 | Silver | M |

**Figure 6.10**    Example Product Dimension Columnar Table in an SAP HANA Schema

> **What's in a Name?**
>
> SAP HANA uses the term *attribute view* to describe the traditional multidimensional modeling term *dimension*. Attribute view is one of three types of *information views* that are available in the SAP HANA platform. From this point forward, we'll refer to dimensions as attribute views.

Attribute views are the logical modeling components in SAP HANA that allow you to define attributes and hierarchies to describe a series of transactions or quantifiable measures in a set of data. Based on the example data set in Figure 6.10, imagine that this table was joined with another table that contained sales transactions. For each transaction, you can use the products table to identify which product was sold. In addition, you can use the PRODUCT COLOR and PRODUCT LINE columns to identify its product color and line. You can use filters and aggregates to identify the number of Mountain-500 Black, 40 products that were sold and the amount of revenue they generated. You can also use the PRODUCT COLOR column to identify the most popular colors by product line. By definition, attribute views can be considered the modeling component that is used to describe a series of transactions or measures.

**Creating an Attribute View**

To create an attribute view in the SAP HANA Studio client, use the Modeler perspective by selecting WINDOWS • OPEN PERSPECTIVE • MODELER from the FILE menu bar. When the Modeler perspective is activated, there are two options for creating an attribute view:

▶ **Quick Launch view**
Select the ATTRIBUTE VIEW icon, and click the CREATE button located in the white box that appears to the right. This launches a wizard that walks you through the processes of defining an attribute view.

▶ **Navigator view**
In the NAVIGATOR view, expand the CONTENT folder to view the packages. If no packages are present, create a package to store the attribute view. Right-click the appropriate nonstructural package, and choose NEW • ATTRIBUTE VIEW. This launches a wizard allowing you to define a new attribute view.

Both options result in the appearance of a wizard (see Figure 6.11). Table 6.5 outlines the six main properties that must be defined in the wizard.

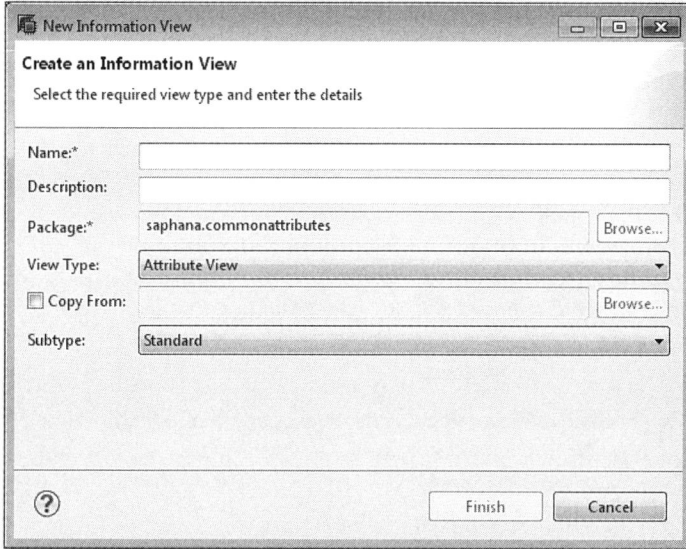

**Figure 6.11**   The New Attribute View Wizard Window

| Property | Purpose |
|----------|---------|
| NAME | The name of the attribute view. |
| | This is a required property that can't be changed after the attribute view is saved and activated. It's important to establish a standard attribute view naming convention before starting a development project in SAP HANA. Only the alphabet characters Aa-Zz, numbers 0-9, and underscore (_) are allowed in the name. |
| DESCRIPTION | The description of the attribute view. |
| | This property can contain a free-text description of the attribute view and should be used to add additional metadata to the view or a thorough description that other developers can use to identify the purpose of the attribute view. |
| PACKAGE | The package that the attribute view will be assigned to. |
| | Only nonstructural packages can be used as the parent object for an attribute view. If using the QUICK LAUNCH view to create the attribute view, a package must be selected. If using the NAVIGATOR view, the package that was right-clicked will automatically be selected. |

**Table 6.5**   Main Properties of an Attribute View and Their Purpose

| Property | Purpose |
|---|---|
| VIEW TYPE | The view type that allows you to identify the *information view* as either an ATTRIBUTE VIEW or ANALYTIC VIEW. |
| | This can be confusing depending on the workflow that was selected to create the attribute view. While you might assume that the workflow only creates an attribute view, the wizard allows you to select another modeling component called an analytic view. We'll discuss analytic views in more detail in subsequent sections of this chapter. Assuming that you intend to create an attribute view, select the default selection of ATTRIBUTE VIEW from the dropdown. |
| COPY FROM | Checkbox that allows you to effectively copy the definition of an existing attribute view to create a new attribute view based on an existing attribute view. |
| | After an attribute is copied, the new copy will have no association with any existing attribute views. |
| SUBTYPE | The subtype that can be defined with each attribute view. |
| | The following list describes each of the three subtypes: |
| | ▶ STANDARD: Standard attributes are those that you use when intending to define each facet of the attribute. This includes the various table joins, output columns, filters, calculated columns, and hierarchies. |
| | ▶ TIME: Choosing the time-based attribute subtype invokes the wizard to automatically generate a date- and time-based attribute view. The attribute view will be based on the system tables starting with M_TIME_DIMENSION* that are found in the _SYS_BI schema. |
| | ▶ DERIVED: A derived attribute is an attribute view that is based on an existing attribute view. However, this isn't the same as the COPY FROM option listed in this table. A derived attribute is simply an alias of an existing attribute. Any changes made to the master attribute view are automatically implemented in the derived attribute. Derived attributes are used in situations where an attribute view must be joined to an analytic view foundation more than once. |

**Table 6.5**  Main Properties of an Attribute View and Their Purpose (Cont.)

**The Attribute View Designer Interface**

A standard attribute view is comprised of two main nodes; the *Data Foundation node* and the *Semantics node*. After successfully creating an attribute view using the wizard, you'll see a design window similar to that in Figure 6.12. On the far left side of the design window are two nodes that can be selected to invoke their respective properties. Clicking the DATA FOUNDATION node invokes all necessary panes to manage the attribute view foundation. Clicking the SEMANTICS node invokes the necessary panes to manage the Semantics options for the attribute view.

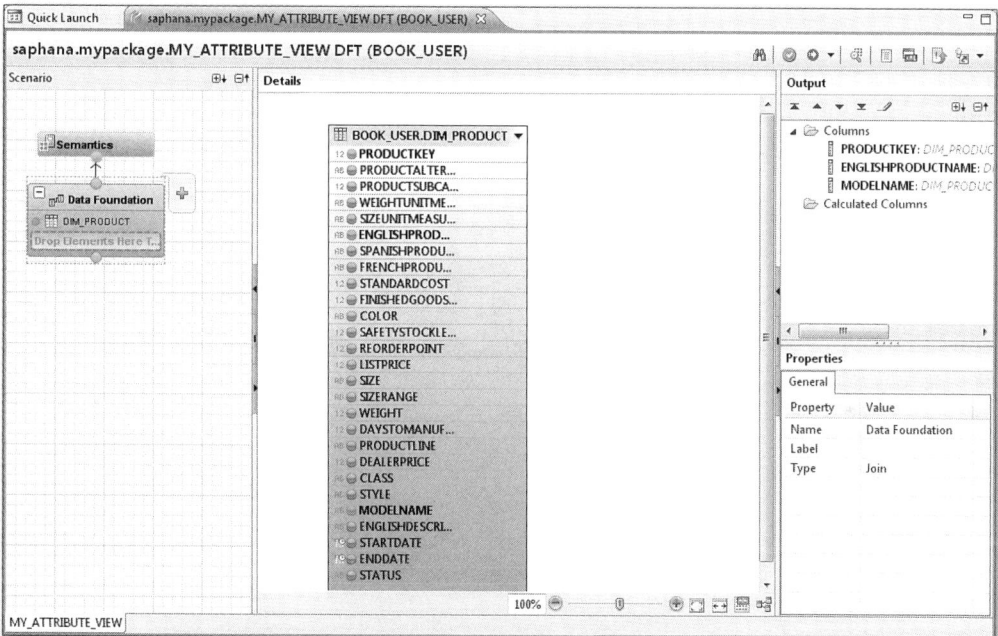

**Figure 6.12** The Data Foundation and Semantics Nodes of an Attribute View

**The Data Foundation Node**

The *Data Foundation* node is used to define the relationship between two or more tables and for defining output columns, filters, and calculated columns. An attribute view can be based on one or more tables. It can also be modeled based on the joining of two or more tables in a fashion that is very similar to joining tables in SQL. In SQL, you join two or more tables to produce a more complete set of results. For example, you can join a customer table to an address table to produce a single result set that contains both a customer's name and address. You can incorporate a similar technique in an attribute view.

The amount of joining that is required in an attribute view depends greatly on the physical structure of the underlying tables or the overall structure of the data model that is stored in the source schema. In the context of this book, we generally try to reduce the number of joins in an SAP HANA attribute view by using the powerful SAP Data Services engine to model a table that is fully denormalized. In short, we do most of the modeling and denormalization in SAP Data Services before we prevision the table in SAP HANA. This methodology not only simplifies the processes of creating an attribute view but also increases the overall performance of the model by eliminating expensive table joins.

When joining two or more tables in the Data Foundation node of an attribute view, you can use one of the five types of joins outlined in Table 6.6.

| Join Type | Description |
|---|---|
| Inner | When joining two tables by using the inner join option, the values in the adjoining columns from both tables are evaluated. The resulting data set will be limited to only those records where the adjoining columns match. If the values don't match in either column, their associated records are effectively filtered from the results. The inner join is always evaluated, even when there are no output columns associated with one table or the other. |
| | It's best to use an inner join when the referential integrity of the adjoining column is known to be sound. |
| Left outer | When joining two tables by using the left outer join option, all values in the leftmost table are evaluated and compared to those in the rightmost table. The resulting data set will contain all records from the leftmost table and only those that match the adjoining columns in the rightmost table. If no match is found in the rightmost table, NULL values will be returned for any output columns associated with the rightmost table. |
| | The left outer join is best used when values in the leftmost table are known to not always have a match in the rightmost table. |

**Table 6.6** Supported Join Types between Tables in the Attribute View Data Foundation

| Join Type | Description |
|-----------|-------------|
| Right outer | When joining two tables using the right outer join option, all values in the rightmost table are evaluated and compared to those in the leftmost table. The resulting data set will contain all records from the rightmost table and only those that match the adjoining columns in the leftmost table. If no match is found in the leftmost table, NULL values will be returned for any output columns associated with the leftmost table. |
| | The right outer join is best used when values in the rightmost table are known to not always have a match in the left most table. |
| Referential | The referential join type is the default join type in any SAP HANA modeling component. Referential joins are similar to inner joins in that the values in the adjoining columns, from both tables can be evaluated. The resulting data set will be limited to only those records where the adjoining columns match. However, if a query fails to reference columns in both tables, only the tables that contain the requested columns will be included in the results. This will effectively remove the unreferenced table from the join equation and eliminate the need to perform any expensive matching between the two tables. Referential joins can be called smart joins because they automatically remove unnecessary join processes from the SAP HANA engines. Referential joins can lead to issues, however. Tables that don't have sound referential integrity can produce unpredictable results. Given that the inner joins are only evaluated when a query references columns in each table, an orphaned value in either table can lead to the inclusion or conversely the exclusion of records. |
| | Therefore, it's best to use the referential join only when adjoining values exists in both tables. In terms of this book, you should use SAP Data Services to validate the date and referential integrity before you provision the tables in an SAP HANA schema. |

**Table 6.6** Supported Join Types between Tables in the Attribute View Data Foundation (Cont.)

| Join Type | Description |
|---|---|
| Text | A text join is unique to SAP HANA. Text joins allow you to join two tables where one contains characteristics, and the other contains the characteristic in a specific language. They were developed specifically to work with SAP ERP tables and the SPRAS fields to provide automatic translation of characteristics or columns. |
| | Text joins act as inner joins, meaning that they will restrict the results based on matching records. There is also a special dynamic language parameter that is defined in the join definition. This parameter is automatically processed with the join to filter the language table, producing a record where the specified column will return text in a specific language. This parameter is evaluated based on the locale of the user querying the attribute. In short, text joins are used to provide automatic multilanguage support in query results for attributes. |

**Table 6.6** Supported Join Types between Tables in the Attribute View Data Foundation (Cont.)

You can also define calculated columns and filters in the attribute view Data Foundation node. Calculated columns are those that are derived on the basis of one or more existing output columns in our foundation tables. Calculated columns can be developed using the standard SAP HANA SQL syntax and functions.

For example, you can create a calculated column that concatenates a customer's last name and first name into a single string. You can also create a calculated column that derives a customer's current age in years based on the customer's birthday and today's date. Again, the use of calculated columns depends greatly on the needs to further transform or derive data stored in the source table. If you're using SAP Data Services to provision your tables in SAP HANA, you can perform the same calculation in your SAP Data Services code and further simplify the attribute view design. In many ways, using SAP Data Services to generate the calculated columns will be beneficial. Calculated columns have the potential to move the processing of queries from the SAP HANA OLAP Engine and into the SAP HANA Calculation Engine. In Chapter 9, we'll discuss these engines in more detail, but for this chapter, it's important to understand that calculated columns can have an effect on the performance of queries so they should be used with caution.

You can also filter tables in an attribute view foundation. Filtering is another modeling technique that can be used to limit the records that are returned from an attribute view. There are a wide range of reasons that you might want to filter the attribute view, including the need to denormalize the data to the need to remove null records from the table. Regardless of the reason, it's important to understand that you can create filters to restrict the data set in an attribute view. In the context of this book, we generally use SAP Data Services to filter the data before provisioning the table in SAP HANA. However, there are legitimate reasons that the filtering should only be implemented in the attribute view based on the way in which it will be used.

The goal of an attribute view is to produce a result set that contains a key column and one or more attributes columns to describe the key column. In the attribute view foundation, it's the developer's responsibility to identify the columns that will be used for output and those that will represent key columns.

It's important to understand the role of the key columns when designing an attribute view. The key columns are used to join an attribute view to the analytic view foundation. We'll discuss the role of the analytic view foundation in more detail in subsequent sections of this chapter. However, you should define a key column if you intend to use the attribute in an SAP HANA model. The key column should be assigned to one or more columns that represent the uniqueness in your foundation table.

Key columns are important as they relate to creating measures and other aggregates in the overall model. If you join an attribute view to an analytic foundation, and the adjoining column isn't unique in the attribute view, there is a possibility that any resulting aggregation will be overstated. This is similar to the typical SQL traps that are created when joining two tables and aggregating their results. If there are two identical product ID values in the PRODUCT ID field, any records in the transaction table that reference them in the attribute view will be repeated and overstated. If you're not careful in this regard, the reliability of your model might come into question. Therefore, it's important that you not only define the key column in your attribute view but that you also profile the results to ensure that each column is unique. In the context of this book, we generally validate that each key column is unique during the processes of provisioning tables using SAP Data Services. This further simplifies the process of creating an attribute view and also increases the overall reliability of the model.

In addition to defining output columns and key columns in our attribute view foundation, you can also configure columns using the properties described in Table 6.7.

| Property | Description |
|---|---|
| NAME | This is the technical name of the output column.<br><br>This generally matches the name of the source column, but it can be changed to make it more intuitive. |
| LABEL | This is an alternative name for the column.<br><br>This is a secondary field that can be used to further enhance the attribute view's overall metadata. Generally, it's used to create a more user friendly and longer text version of the output column name. |
| KEY ATTRIBUTE | If set to YES, the column is defined as a key attribute or key column. If set to NO, the column is considered a standard output column. |
| DRILL DOWN ENABLED | This property can be used to indicate that the object is a member of a drill group. It also affects the presentation or organization of attributes in some reporting tools such as SAP BusinessObjects Analysis for OLAP. In general, only reporting or visualization tools that support this property can use it. |
| LABEL COLUMN | This property allows you to define a surrogate column to be used in place of the actual column. For example, the PRODUCT KEY column can be configured to always display the product SKU text.<br><br>Using a label column is preferred when the selected OUTPUT column values have no meaning to the user consuming the model's data. |
| HIDDEN | This property allows you to define a column in the output of the model but suppress it from being used by the user consuming the models data.<br><br>It's best used in situations where the column needs to be used for calculations but needs to be suppressed from output. |
| HIERARCHY ACTIVE | External tools that are designed to interpret the hierarchies from your SAP HANA model use this property to determine if the member is available in the hierarchy. |

**Table 6.7** Output Column Properties in an Attribute View Foundation

## The Semantic Node

The second main node of the attribute view is the Semantics node, which is used to manage the output columns identified in the foundation and any hierarchies that need to be defined in the attribute view. Figure 6.13 shows an example of the column and hierarchy view that will be visible after selecting the SEMANTICS node in the attribute view management view.

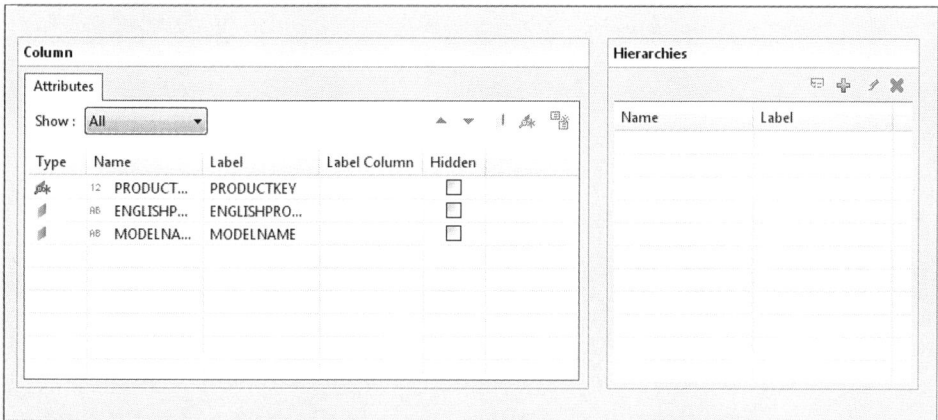

**Figure 6.13**  The Column and Hierarchy Management Windows after Selecting the Semantics Node

The column configuration pane is shown on the left side of Figure 6.13. In the column section of the SEMANTICS node view, you can specify the column type. The column TYPE field allows you to specify whether the column is a key attribute or standard attribute. A similar option was available in the DATA FOUNDATION node as well, only it was set using a TRUE/FALSE dropdown.

There are also options for specifying the LABEL column and a checkbox to indicate if the objects should be HIDDEN. Again, these are the same options that were available in the DATA FOUNDATION node and described in Table 6.6. The SEMANTICS view appears to provide you with a more intuitive and graphical alternative of setting these properties.

## Creating Hierarchies

The HIERARCHIES design pane is shown on the right side of Figure 6.13. You can use this pane to create or define hierarchies in your attribute view. To create a new hierarchy, select the plus sign icon on the icon bar. A new window appears that allows you to define the properties for the hierarchy (see Figure 6.14).

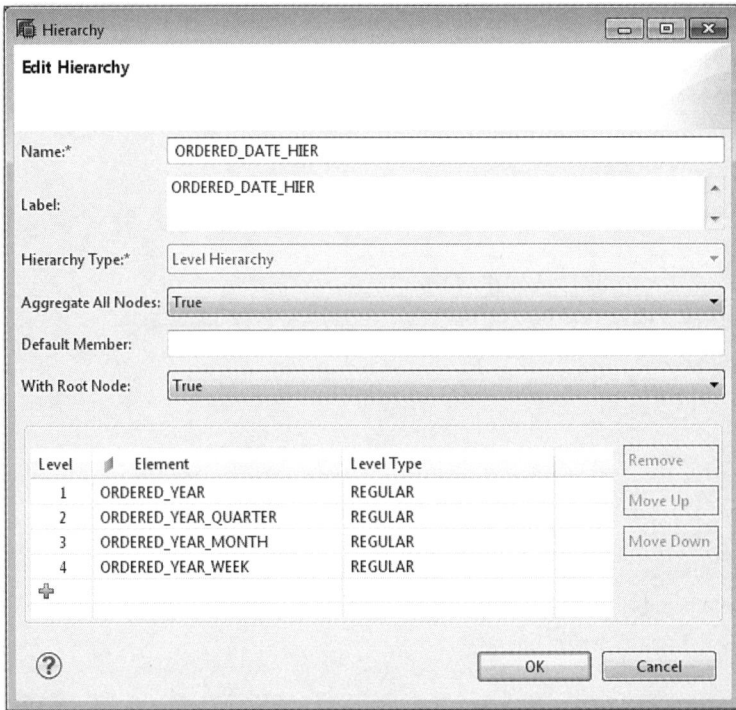

**Figure 6.14** Hierarchy Configuration Window

Table 6.8 outlines the seven main areas that can be defined in reference to the hierarchy.

| Property | Description |
|---|---|
| NAME | The technical name of the hierarchy. |
| | This is a mandatory field, but it can be changed at any time. |
| LABEL | An alternative name for the hierarchy. |
| | This is a secondary field that can be used to further enhance the attribute view's overall metadata. Generally, it's used to create a more user-friendly and longer text version of the hierarchy name. |

**Table 6.8** Hierarchy Configuration Window Properties

| Property | Description |
|---|---|
| HIERARCHY TYPE | Two types of hierarchies are available.<br><br>▶ LEVEL HIERARCHY: This hierarchy can be derived from one or more output columns. It's assumed that there is a natural order to the values in a column selected for this type of hierarchy. For example, Year, Quarter, Month, Week, and Day can be used to derive a calendar date hierarchy.<br><br>▶ PARENT-CHILD HIERARCHY: This hierarchy can be derived by a recursive self-join in the Data Foundation table. For example, the employee foundation table might contain a column that contains the employee's supervisor. A supervisor might have multiple employees in the same table. SAP HANA can generate a hierarchy by recursively joining the table to itself until a flattened parent-child relationship is established.<br><br>It's important to note that after a hierarchy type is established, it can't be changed. |
| AGGREGATE ALL NODES | Specifies whether each level of the node should include its own measure value in any aggregate.<br><br>If set to TRUE, the value of the parent is aggregated with the values of the child members. If set to FALSE, the child values are aggregated independently of the parent level. This won't affect the overall results of the model because only the SAP HANA multidimensional expression (MDX) engine will interpret this value. |
| DEFAULT MEMBER | Currently not defined by SAP. |
| WITH ROOT NODE | In instances where your hierarchy doesn't have a root node, setting this option to TRUE will create one. |
| NODE STYLE | Defines the composition of the hierarchy level name.<br><br>Because hierarchy level names needs to be unique, these options allow you to define three different options to achieve this uniqueness:<br><br>▶ LEVEL NAME: The unique node value is composed of the level name and node value, for example, "[Level 1].[USA]".<br><br>▶ NAME ONLY: The unique node value is composed of the node value only, for example, "USA".<br><br>▶ NAME PATH: The unique node value is composed by the result node name and the names of all ancestors apart from the (single physical) root node, for example, "[USA].[GEORGIA]". |

**Table 6.8**  Hierarchy Configuration Window Properties (Cont.)

| Property | Description |
|---|---|
| HIERARCHY LEVELS | Allows you to define the parent-child relationships between the columns in the hierarchy. |
| | With level hierarchies, one or more columns can be defined to represent the natural hierarchy that can occur in an attribute view foundation. The columns should be placed in logical order based on the relationship of the values in the selected columns. With a parent-child hierarchy, only the parent and child columns are available for selection. SAP HANA then parses these columns recursively to produce a hierarchy. Both columns and calculated columns can be defined as hierarchy levels. |

**Table 6.8** Hierarchy Configuration Window Properties (Cont.)

| Previewing a Hierarchy in SAP HANA Studio |
|---|
| It's important to note that there is no OLAP style interface in SAP HANA Studio to preview or see a hierarchy in action. However, you can query the column view that is created in the _SYS_BIC schema after the attribute view is saved and activated in the repository. This column view returns a fully flattened tabular representation of the hierarchy. |
| This is an excellent way to troubleshoot hierarchy parsing issues when querying the raw hierarchy level data defined by its column view. If there are design issues with the hierarchy definition, queries against this column view will fail to execute. |
| You can find this column view in the _SYS_BIC schema using the naming convention PACKAGE.SUBPACKAGE/ATTRIBUTE_NAME/HIER/HIERARCHY_NAME. |

### Saving and Activating the Attribute View

After defining all of the options in both the Data Foundation and Semantics nodes of an attribute view, it is standard practice for the attribute view to be saved and activated in the repository. Before the attribute view can be previewed or rendered usable in the model, you need to save and activate the attribute view. As we discuss the remaining components of SAP HANA modeling, you'll discover that they need to be saved and activated as well.

There are two ways to save and activate or save and validate an attribute view. The first option is to locate the green icon on the top right of the attribute view design window. Hover the mouse over the icon that contains a white arrow pointing to the right. The hover text should read, SAVE AND ACTIVATE. Click the icon to initiate the save and activate process. The second option for saving and activating the attribute view is to right-click the attribute view in the NAVIGATOR window, and choose the SAVE AND ACTIVATE option.

In either case, a job log window or tab appears to display the status and outcome of the activate process. If the process completes successfully, the job action name will remain black with black text. If there are any errors, the job action name will turn red. You can double-click the job action name to reveal the job details and review details of the activate process.

There is also an option to allow you to save and validate the attribute view. The SAVE AND VALIDATE option can be executed in a similar fashion. However, its icon is green with a white checkmark. This option only validates that the code is correct and doesn't make the attribute view available for use.

Attribute views are effectively the dimensions of the SAP HANA multidimensional models. It's quite common for there to be dozens if not more attribute views in a package. The number of attribute views that are needed for a project depends greatly on the type of data that is being modeled. Attribute view are used to describe a transaction or quantifiable records in a table. In SAP HANA, an attribute view can be comprised of one or more joined tables to produce a single logical modeling objects. You can use joins, filters, and calculated columns to produce a logical dimension. In subsequent sections of this chapter, we'll discuss how attribute views are combined with analytic views to produce the complete multidimensional model.

---

**Security Required for Viewing the Results of an Information View**

When attribute views or any of the information views in SAP HANA are saved and activated, one or more column views are created in the _SYS_BIC schema. For you to query column views in the _SYS_BIC schema, you must have the correct SQL privileges and analytic privileges.

At a minimum, you need the SELECT and EXECUTE privilege on the _SYS_BIC schema. If you're using the built-in time data attributes, you also need the SELECT privilege on the _SYS_BI schema. In addition to these SQL privileges, you also need analytic privileges to view the application data in an information view.

Developers require elevated privileges to develop, save, and activate information views. For reference, view the privilege setup on the default MODELER role to determine the rights required to develop information views.

Because a thorough discussion on the topic of SAP HANA privileges is beyond the scope of this book, we recommend that you consult the following SAP HANA documentation available at *http://help.sap.com/hana_appliance*:

---

▸ SAP HANA Developer Guide

▸ SAP HANA Security Guide

We also recommend that you search for SAP HANA security topics on the SAP Community Network (SCN) at *http://scn.sap.com*.

### 6.1.5 Analytic Views

As we've already discussed in this chapter, attribute views are the modeling components used to describe a transaction or other quantifiable data in a table. But before you can match attribute views to a transaction table, the transaction table must be configured in an analytic view. Analytic views are the second type of information view available in the SAP HANA platform. Analytic views are the SAP HANA multidimensional modeling components that are used to define both measures and the relationship between their attributes. Measures are defined by aggregating quantifiable columns in a table. For example, if you have a sales transaction table that contains a column for quantity sold, you can define a measure on that table that will summarize all values in the table. If you were to summarize all of the rows in the table for quantity sold, you would have the grand total of all transactions in the table.

However, to add value to this measure, you need to assign characteristics to the measure to produce dimensionality or subtotals. For example, you can add a product attribute view to the measure to allow the consumer to see the quantity sold per product. You can also add a sale date attribute view to this measure to show both the quantity of products that were sold and the days, weeks, months, or years in which they were sold. You can add a customer attribute view to the measure to see the number of products sold by customer region as well.

We hope you're now beginning to visualize the potential that adding dimensionality to a set of quantifiable transactions can achieve. With SAP HANA, the analytic view can be best described as the modeling component that allows you to define both measures and their relationships between one or more attributes. Technically speaking, the primary goal is to define the logical star schema depicted at the beginning of this chapter in Figure 6.1.

**Creating an Analytic View**

There are two ways to create an analytic view in SAP HANA Studio. As with attribute views, you can use either the NAVIGATOR view or the QUICK LAUNCH view.

To create an analytic view using the QUICK LAUNCH view, open the Modeler perspective by selecting WINDOWS • OPEN PERSPECTIVE • MODELER from the FILE menu bar. On the right side of the screen we should now see the QUICK LAUNCH window similar to what is displayed in Figure 6.15. Select ANALYTIC VIEW, and click the CREATE button located in the white box that appears to the right. This launches a wizard that walks through the processes of defining an analytic view.

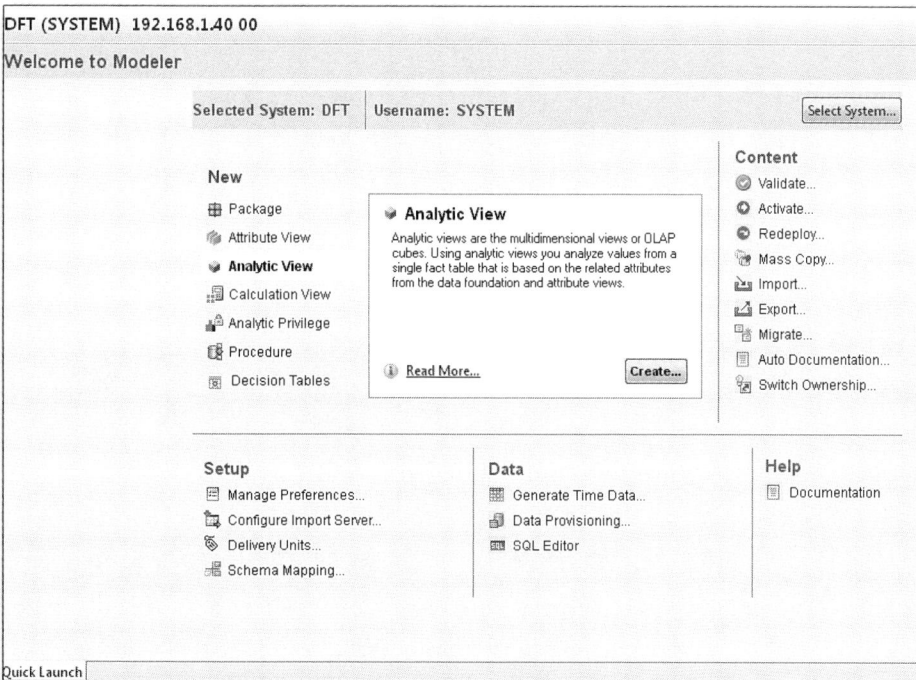

**Figure 6.15** Creating an Analytic View in SAP HANA Studio

The second option for creating an analytic view is to use the Navigator view located on the left side of the Modeler perspective. In the Navigator view, expand the Content folder to view the packages. If no packages are present, create a package to store the analytic view. Right-click the appropriate nonstructural package, and choose New • Analytic View. This launches a wizard enabling you to define a new analytic view as shown in Figure 6.16. You'll define the five main properties in the wizard outlined in Table 6.9.

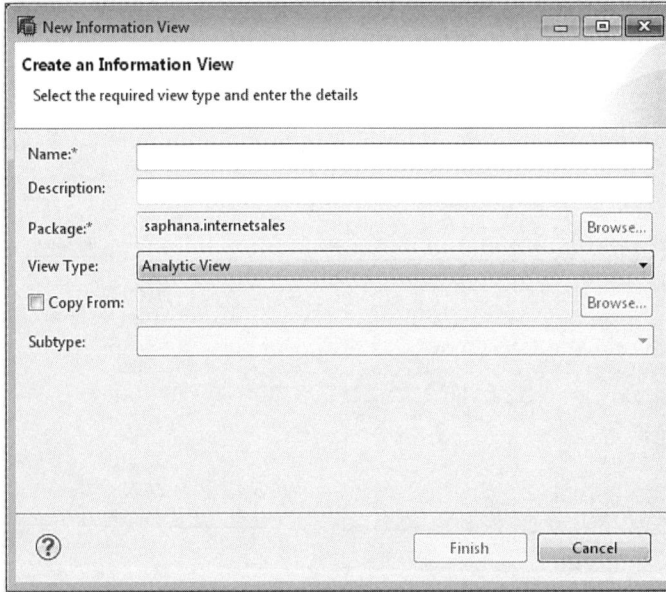

**Figure 6.16** The New Analytic View Wizard Window

| Property | Purpose |
|---|---|
| NAME | The name of the analytic view. |
|  | This is a required property that can't be changed after the analytic view is saved and activated. It's important to establish a standard analytic view naming convention before starting a development project in SAP HANA. Only the alphabet characters Aa-Zz, numbers 0-9, and underscore (_) are allowed in the name. |

**Table 6.9** Main Properties of an Analytic View and Their Purposes

| Property | Purpose |
|---|---|
| DESCRIPTION | The description of the analytic view. |
| | This property can contain a free-text description of the analytic view and should be used to add additional metadata to the view or a thorough description that other developers can use to identify the purpose of the analytic view. |
| PACKAGE | The package that the analytic view will be assigned to. |
| | Only nonstructural packages can be used as the parent object for an analytic view. If you're using the QUICK LAUNCH view to create the analytic view, a package must be selected. If using the NAVIGATOR view, the package that was right-clicked will automatically be selected. |
| VIEW TYPE | The view type that allows you to identify the information view as either an attribute view or analytic view. |
| | This can be confusing depending on the workflow that was selected to create the analytic view. While you might assume that the workflow only creates an analytic view, the wizard allows you to select either an ANALYTIC VIEW or ATTRIBUTE VIEW. Assuming that you intend to create an analytic view, select the default selection of ANALYTIC VIEW from the dropdown menu. |
| COPY FROM | Checkbox that allows you to effectively copy the definition of an existing analytic view to create a new analytic view based on an existing analytic view. After an analytic view is copied, the new copy will have no association with any existing analytic views. |
| SUBTYPE | Currently not defined by SAP. |
| | As of SAP HANA version 45 (SPS5), analytic views don't have a subtype. |

**Table 6.9** Main Properties of an Analytic View and Their Purposes (Cont.)

## The Analytic View Designer Interface

An analytic view is comprised of three main nodes; the DATA FOUNDATION node, LOGICAL JOIN node, and the SEMANTICS node. After successfully creating an attribute view using the wizard, you should see a design window similar to that shown in Figure 6.17. As you click on each node found on the left side of the analytic view user interface (UI), a different set of panes will appear to the right side. Each set of panes is unique to the selected node.

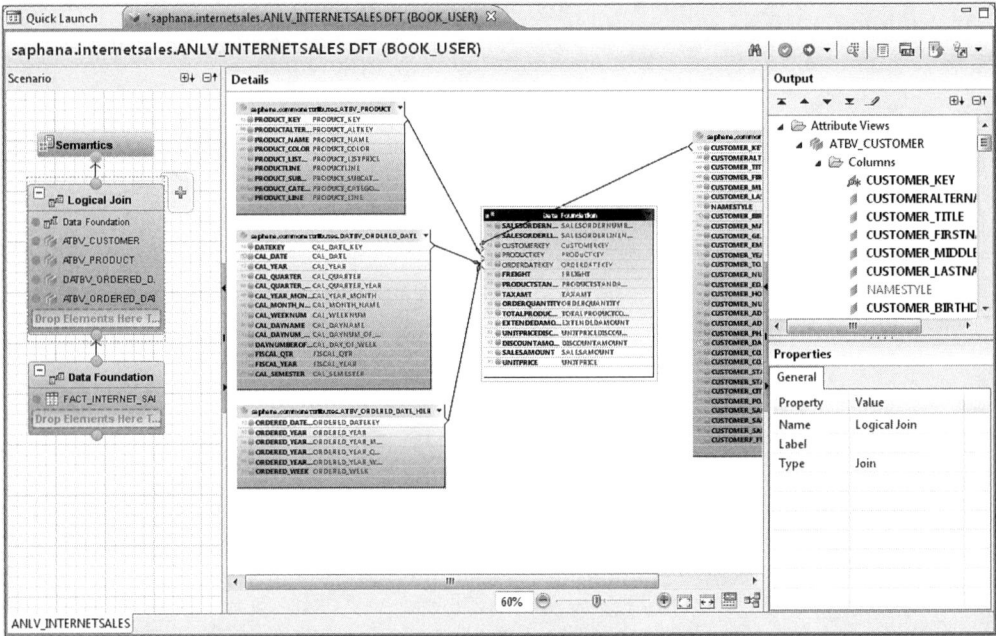

**Figure 6.17**  Three Main Nodes of an Analytic View

As mentioned earlier, the main purpose of the analytic view is to allow you to define both measures and their relationships between attributes. However, before you can define a measure, you must identify the transaction table where they are stored.

### The Data Foundation Node

The DATA FOUNDATION node, in an analytic view, is the area in which you define these base tables. Figure 6.18 shows an example screenshot of the DATA FOUNDATION node UI. Similar to attribute views, you can define one or more tables in the analytic view foundation. If you have more than one table, the tables need to be joined in a manner similar to joining tables in SQL. Technically speaking, you can join your transaction table in this node to other column tables that contain attributes. However, these attributes won't be reusable with other analytic views, and you can't define hierarchies in an analytic view. Therefore, it's best to build attribute views for the purpose of reusability and hierarchies.

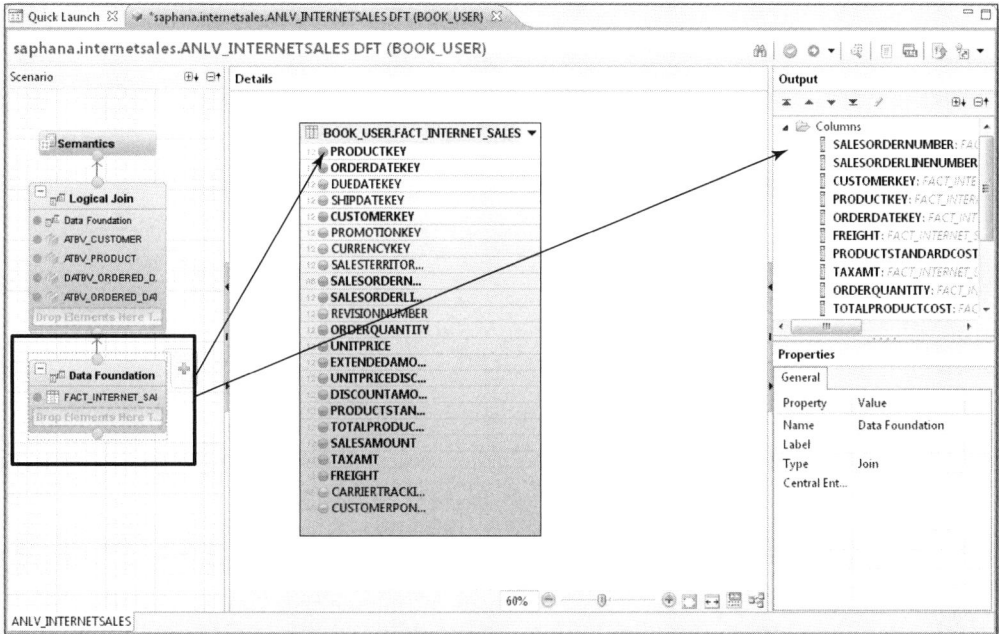

**Figure 6.18**  The Data Foundation Node User Interface

**Joining Multiple Transaction Tables in the Analytic View Foundation**

While it's possible to join multiple transaction or fact tables in the analytic view foundation, you should make note of three items:

▶ Make sure that the cardinality isn't adversely affected when you join two or more transaction tables in this node. If the adjoining columns produce duplicate measureable rows, the resulting aggregation will be overstated. This will lead to incorrect results in the model. As we'll discuss shortly, calculation views are capable of solving aggregation issues like this. However, you'll need to define an individual analytic view for each transaction or fact table to solve this problem with a calculation view.

> ▸ If you join two or more large transaction tables in the analytic view foundation, the model's performance will likely be affected. In many cases, the cost of joining the two multimillion row tables will slow the response of the query. We recommend that you use the powerful SAP Data Services engine to model all required data into a single fact or transaction table before it's provisioned into an SAP HANA schema. This will eliminate the need for the SAP HANA engines to join the two tables and likely will increase the performance of the query.
>
> ▸ Each attribute view can only be joined to one physical table in the Data Foundation.

In addition to managing the foundation table, the DATA FOUNDATION node is also used to identify the output columns that will be used in the LOGICAL JOIN and SEMANTICS nodes. The columns that are specified for output in this node are represented in a logical table in the subsequent node. Effectively, you use the Data Foundation node to physically join one or more tables and to specify each column that will be needed throughout the remaining nodes of the analytic view.

**The Logical Join Node**

The LOGICAL JOIN node, in an analytic view, is the area in which you define the logical joins between existing attribute views and the analytic view Data Foundation output columns. In addition, additional output columns can be defined in the LOGICAL JOIN node to further enhance the model. The joins are logical because only the output columns of the analytic Data Foundation table are joined to one or more existing attribute views. At this stage, you're not joining physical tables.

To join an attribute view to the analytic view Data Foundation table, you must add one or more existing attribute views to the LOGICAL JOIN node detail section. As shown in Figure 6.19 in the DETAILS pane, we've joined an attribute view to the OUTPUT columns defined in the DATA FOUNDATION node. While both objects appear to be tables, they are in fact only a logical representation of either the attribute view you designed in Section 6.1.4 or the outputs defined in the analytic view DATA FOUNDATION node.

Once added, you can define the join relationship between the attribute view and analytic DATA FOUNDATION table using the attribute view's key column and one or more OUTPUT columns defined in the analytic view DATA FOUNDATION node. As with the attribute view, there are six supported join types, which are listed in Table 6.10.

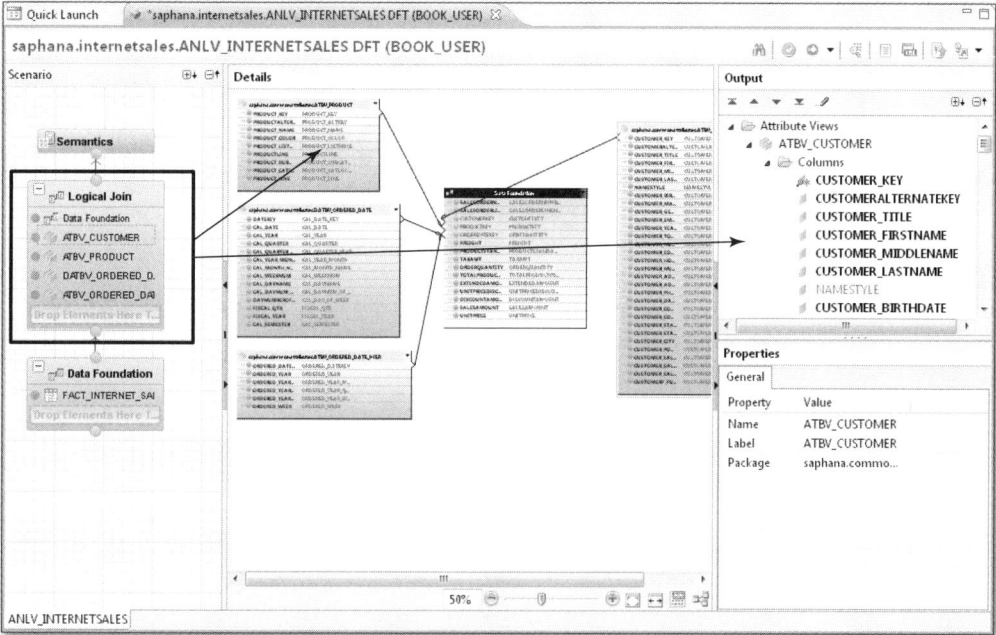

**Figure 6.19**  The Logical Join Node

| Join Type | Description |
|-----------|-------------|
| Inner join | When joining attribute views to the analytic Data Foundation table using the inner join option, the values in the adjoining columns from both logical tables are evaluated. The resulting data set is limited to only those records where the adjoining columns match. If the values don't match in either column, their associated records are effectively filtered from the results. The inner join is always evaluated between the two logical tables even if values from the attribute view aren't selected during the query process. |
| Left outer | When joining attribute views to the analytic Data Foundation table using the left outer join option, all values in the Data Foundation table are evaluated and compared to those in the attribute view. The resulting data set contains all records from the Data Foundation table and only those that match the adjoining columns in the attribute view. If no match is found in the attribute view, NULL values are returned for any output columns associated with the attribute view.

The left outer join is best used when values in the Data Foundation table are known to not always have a match in the attribute view. |

**Table 6.10**  The Supported Join Types between an Analytic View Data Foundation Table and an Attribute View

| Join Type | Description |
|-----------|-------------|
| Right outer | When joining attribute views to the analytic Data Foundation table using the right outer join option, all values in the attribute view are evaluated and compared to those in the Data Foundation table. The resulting data set contains all records from the attribute view and only those that match the adjoining columns in the Data Foundation table. If no match is found in the Data Foundation table, NULL values are returned for any output columns associated with the Data Foundation table. |
| | The right outer join is best used when all values in the attribute view must be returned even when there are no associated transactions in the Data Foundation table. |
| Referential | The referential join type is the default join type in any SAP HANA modeling component. Referential joins are similar to inner joins in that the values in the adjoining columns, from both logic tables, can be evaluated. The resulting data set is limited to only those records where the adjoining columns match. |
| | However, if a query fails to reference columns in an attribute view, only the attribute views that contain the requested columns are included in the join calculation. This effectively removes the unreferenced attribute view from the join equation and eliminates the need to perform any expensive matching between the two logical tables. Referential joins can be called smart joins because they automatically remove unnecessary join processes from the SAP HANA engines. |
| | Referential joins can lead to issues, however. Logical tables that don't have sound referential integrity can produce unpredictable results. Given that the inner joins are only evaluated when a query references columns in both logical tables, an orphaned value in either table can lead to the inclusion or conversely the exclusion of records or aggregated results. Therefore, it's best to use the referential join only when the adjoining values exist in both tables. In terms of this book, we recommend that you use SAP Data Services to validate the date and referential integrity before the tables are provisioned in an SAP HANA schema. |

**Table 6.10** The Supported Join Types between an Analytic View Data Foundation Table and an Attribute View (Cont.)

| Join Type | Description |
|---|---|
| Text | Text joins are unique to SAP HANA. They are special join types that allow you to join two tables where one contains characteristics, and the other contains the characteristic in a specific language. Text joins were developed specifically to work with SAP ERP tables and the SPRAS fields to provide automatic translation of characteristics or columns. Text joins act as an inner join, meaning that they restrict the results based on matching records. |
| | There is also a special dynamic language parameter in the join definition. This parameter is automatically processed with the join to filter the language table, producing a record where the specified column returns text in a specific language. This parameter is evaluated based on the locale of the user querying the attribute. In short, text joins are used to provide automatic multilanguage support in query results for attributes. |
| Temporal | Temporal joins are only available when joining an analytic view foundation to attribute views. It's a special referential join type that allows you to define a series of join conditions where the attribute value is time dependent on the record in the analytic foundation table. A temporal column from the Data Foundation table is compared to a From Column and To Column in that attribute view to return an attribute value that is time dependent. There are also temporal conditions that can be defined in this join type to manipulate how the between join is executed. |

**Table 6.10** The Supported Join Types between an Analytic View Data Foundation Table and an Attribute View (Cont.)

In addition to creating joins, you can also define calculated columns, restricted columns, and input parameters in the LOGICAL JOIN node. Each item that is created in the Logical Join node will be available as an output column. As we'll discuss shortly, each output column can then be defined as a measure or private attribute in the model. In addition to the logical output columns, all columns from the adjoined attribute views will also be available as a shared output column. This includes the calculated columns and the hierarchies that were defined in the attribute view. You can't make changes to an attribute view in the Logical Join node, but you can see each supported item in the OUTPUT pane by expanding the attribute view folder.

*Calculated columns* in the LOGICAL JOIN node are similar to those that can be created in the attribute view. The calculated columns can be developed using the SAP HANA SQL syntax and functions. However, in the LOGICAL JOIN node, you can define calculations that incorporate columns from one or more attribute views. These cross-attribute view calculations allow for more sophisticated calculations to be performed. For example, you can define a flag value that indicates customers in a particular region that purchased products from a particular product line. This type of calculated column evaluates values in both the customer attribute view and products attribute view.

As with attribute views, the use of calculated columns can negatively affect the performance of the final model. In many cases, the use of calculated columns forces the model to be processed in the SAP HANA Calculation Engine. The use of this engine can slow the processing of the query. As we recommended before, it's best to define calculated columns using SAP Data Services, when possible. Admittedly, there are some calculations that can only be defined in an SAP HANA information view. In these cases, it's important to know that the impact of calculated columns will likely invoke the use of the SAP HANA Calculation Engine. In Chapter 9, we'll discuss the role of the SAP HANA Calculation Engine in more detail.

*Restricted columns* can be used to create conditional aggregates. For example, a restricted column can be developed to return the sales amount when the ordered year is equal to 2010. Later, in the SEMANTICS node, you can convert this into a measure so that only transactions that were ordered in 2010 are summarized in this column. The conditions in a restricted column are built using a graphical user interface (GUI) and dropdown lists. Neither complex formula language nor SAP HANA SQL code can be used to derive restricted measures; therefore, they are limited to basic filtering criteria. However, restricted measures provide faster processing compared to measures executed on calculated columns.

*Input parameters* can be used to define a runtime parameter or a list of values for a runtime parameter. An input parameter can be defined in all three nodes of an analytic view. The node you choose to create the input parameter within has no bearing on how it functions or how it's used. On their own, input parameters have little bearing on the overall analytic view. They must be used in a calculated column as a placeholder for a runtime value before they will have an effect on the model results. For example, you might define a formula in a calculated column to multiply the sales amount times a user-provided percentage. Input parameters aren't used for filtering. As we'll discuss shortly, you can use variables for dynamic runtime filtering, a feature that greatly enhances the usability of any model.

In the context of an analytic view, parameters can be defined as one of the five types outlined in Table 6.11.

| Input Parameter Type | Description |
|---|---|
| Direct | A direct input parameter can be used to provide a runtime value to the model for calculation purposes. It's also used in the processes of converting currencies at runtime. It's best used in instances where a single static value is used to manipulate the output of a column. |
| Column | A column-based parameter derives its list of values from an existing column in the model. It's best used when an input parameter requires a large list of possible input values, and these values can be derived from an existing column in the model. |
| Derived from table | A derived from table parameter derives its list of values from an existing column found in a table. The values doesn't need to be in the model and can be derived from any existing table in a schema. It's best used when an input parameter requires a large list of possible input values, and these values can be derived from an existing table in the database. |
| Static list | A static list parameter derives its list from a user-defined list stored in the parameter. If the values in the list require updating, you have to modify the list and reactive the model. It's best used when an input parameter requires a large list of possible input values, and these values can't be derived from an existing table or attribute. |

**Table 6.11** Types of Input Parameters in an Analytic View

**The Semantic Node**

The final node of the analytic view is the *Semantics node*. In the SEMANTICS node, you can define both local and shared output columns. Figure 6.20 shows the SEMANTICS node UI. LOCAL output columns are those that were created in the LOGICAL JOIN node. SHARED output columns are those that are automatically included with the adjoined attribute views.

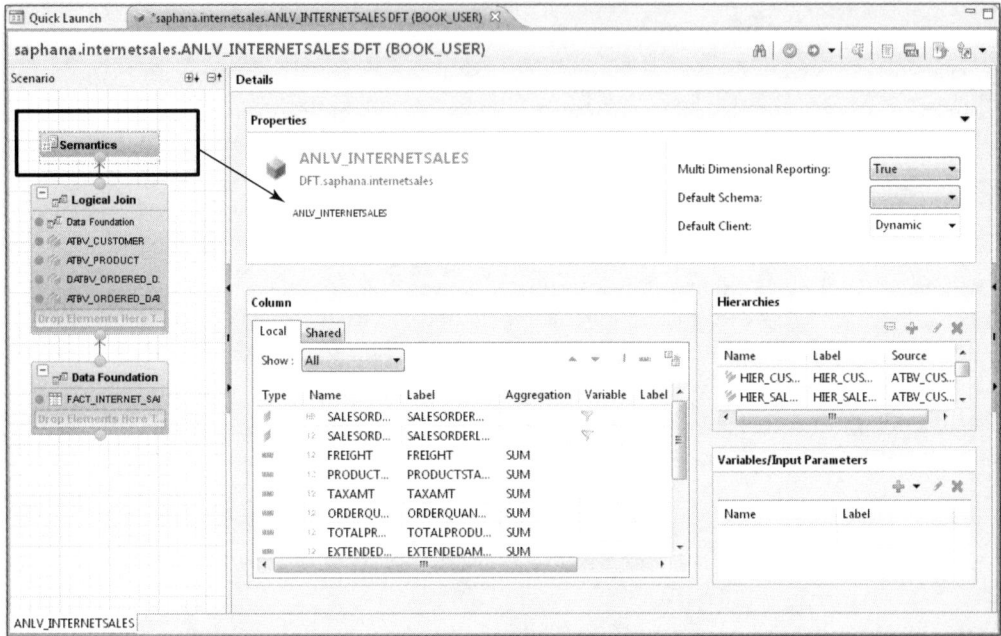

**Figure 6.20** The Semantics Node and the Local and Shared Columns Configuration Window

In the COLUMN pane there are two tabs. The first tab is labeled LOCAL. The LOCAL tab is used to define each output column in the analytic view. Output columns can either be defined as an attribute or measure type. To change the output column type, click the cell in the TYPE column and a dropdown list appear.

To define a column as a measure, choose the MEASURE type. Measures are the output columns that will be aggregated in the model. SAP HANA only support the SUM, MIN, MAX, and COUNT aggregation functions in an analytic view.

To change the aggregation function, click the cell in the AGGREGATION column and a dropdown appears containing a list of the available aggregation functions. The SUM, MIN, and MAX aggregates can only be defined for numeric output columns. The COUNT function can be used with any column type.

In the LOCAL tab of the COLUMN pane, you can also configure the output column as an attribute type. Attributes defined in the LOCAL column tab were referred to as private attributes in previous revisions of SAP HANA. As of SAP HANA version 45 (SPS5), they are simply called local attributes.

*Local attributes* are the values in the Data Foundation table, which can be used to describe each transaction. They are similar to the attributes found in an attribute view, but they are defined explicitly in the analytic view and based on the Data Foundation table. They can't be reused in other analytic views without being explicitly defined in that analytic view.

Depending on the SAP Data Services data modeling strategy, it's possible that the fact or transaction table will contain several local attributes. As mentioned during the SAP Data Services discussions, joins are very expensive in a columnar store database. Therefore, it's sometimes better to include attributes in the fact or transaction table versus storing them in a separate dimension table. This isn't a strict rule, but rather a suggestion that can sometime increase the performance of the overall analytic view.

You can configure a LABEL COLUMN to serve as a surrogate value for any local attribute. To configure an attribute column's LABEL COLUMN, simple click the cell in the LABEL COLUMN and a dropdown list appears containing existing output columns that will serve as a substitute.

Finally, you can also define a variable for any attribute type output column. Variables are created in the SEMANTICS node and can be used to create runtime filters.

For both measures and attributes, you can configure each output column as HIDDEN. Hidden output columns can be used in the model for processing but will be excluded from the analytic view results. There is also a LABEL column that can be used to provide an alternative name for any output column. This column should not be confused with the LABEL COLUMN column. LABEL COLUMN columns are based on other columns in the model; they change the columns output. However, a label is a static value that is used to name the column, and it has no effect on the column's output values.

The second tab in the COLUMN pane is labeled SHARED. The SHARED tab contains a listing of all columns associated with attribute views defined in the analytic view model. You can configure three options for each column in the SHARED tab:

▶ **Change the name of the attributes or columns**
To change the name, click in the desired cell of the NAME column, and enter a new name.

▶ **Associate a variable with one or more columns**
Variables can be used to create a runtime filter and prompt a list of values for

the analytic view. To associate a variable to a column, click the desired cell in the VARIABLE column. A dropdown list appears allowing you to select an existing variable. As we'll discuss shortly, variables are defined in a separate pane found in the SEMANTICS node.

▶ **Hide a column from the final model**
The HIDDEN column contains a checkbox. Any column that has this boxed checked will be hidden from the results of the analytic view. However, the column can be used in the model for processing.

In the SEMANTICS node of an analytic view, you can also define variables and input parameters. The ability to create input parameters in this node is redundant. You can also create the same input parameters in the LOGICAL JOIN node and DATA FOUNDATION node. The types of input parameters that are listed in Table 6.11 also pertain to input parameters created in this node.

Variables, on the other hand, can only be defined in the SEMANTICS node. On the far right side of the SEMANTICS node interface is a pane labeled VARIABLES/INPUT PARAMETERS. On the menu bar in this pane, there is a plus sign and a dropdown arrow. To create a variable, select the plus sign icon. Note that clicking the down arrow to the right of the plus sign allow you to choose between a variable and an input parameter.

The primary purpose of a variable is to filter rows based on a runtime parameter. Variables are associated with an existing attribute to define a pick list or list of values. They are also assigned to an attribute for filtering purposes. When creating variables, a wizard will appear. In this wizard there are eight different configuration options, as outlined in Table 6.12.

| Option | Description |
|--------|-------------|
| NAME | The name of the variable is presented to the user during runtime. It's best to name a variable so those users understand its purpose at runtime. The variable name can't contain spaces or certain special characters. Only the alphabet characters Aa-Zz, numbers 0-9, and underscore (_) are allowed in the name, for example, Select_A_Product_For_Filtering. |
| LABEL | The label can be used to provide a free text description of the variable. This metadata can be used to fully describe the purpose of the variable. |

**Table 6.12** Configuration Options for a Variable Defined in an Analytic View

| Option | Description |
|---|---|
| ATTRIBUTE | This is the associated attribute that contains the values that will populate the pick list or list of values for the variable at runtime. This doesn't assign the variable to the attribute for filtering. |
| SELECTION TYPE | The type of filter or operator that will be used to restrict the rows of data at runtime. The following selection types are supported in a variable:<br><br>▶ Single value: Used when only a single value is required. This assumes the use of the operator equal (=), and the operator can't be changed.<br><br>▶ Range: Used when the selected value operator needs to be defined at runtime. This assumes the use of the operators "=", "between", "<", ">", "<=", ">=", "is null", or "isn't null".<br><br>▶ Interval: Used when all values that exists between a specified starting and ending value are required. This assumes the use of the "between" operator, and the operator can't be changed. |
| MULTIPLE ENTRY | The MULTIPLE ENTRY checkbox allows you to specify whether a variable can be used multiple times at runtime. For example, a user can select products sold in year 2010 and products sold between 2006 and 2008. Each entry is assumed as an OR condition. |
| DEFAULT VALUE | This is the default value for the variable. If a variable is often used with a particular value, you can configure this value and store it with the variable. At runtime, the variable is automatically prepopulated with this default value. |
| IS MANDATORY | The IS MANDATORY checkbox allows you to require a value for the configured variable at runtime. In short, this prevents the value from remaining blank. |
| ATTRIBUTE ASSIGNMENT | This is the attribute assigned to the variable for filtering purposes. A variable can be assigned to one or more attributes for filtering at runtime. |

**Table 6.12** Configuration Options for a Variable Defined in an Analytic View (Cont.)

### Saving and Activating the Analytic View

It's standard practice to save and activate the analytic view in the repository after defining all of the options in an analytic view. The same is true for attribute views as well. Before the analytic view can be previewed or rendered usable in the model, you need to save and activate it. There are two ways to save and active or save and validate an analytic view.

The first option is to locate the green icon on the top right of the analytic view design window. Hover the mouse over the icon that contains a white arrow pointing to the right. The hover text should read SAVE AND ACTIVATE. Click the icon to initiate the save and activate process. The second option to save and activate the analytic view is to right-click the analytic view in the NAVIGATOR window and choose the SAVE AND ACTIVATE option. In either case, a JOB LOG window or tab should appear to display the status and outcome of the activate process. If the process completes successfully, the job action name remains black with black text. If there are any errors, the job action name turns red. You can double-click the job action name to reveal the job details and review details of the activate process. There is also an option that allows you to save and validate the analytic view. The SAVE AND VALIDATE option can be executed in a similar fashion. However, its icon is green with a white checkmark. This option only validates that the code is correct and doesn't mark the analytic view available for use.

After saving and activating the analytic view, a complete multidimensional model is available for external consumption. We'll discuss other components of the SAP HANA multidimensional models shortly, but the analytic view is the core of any model. That analytic view is a combination of attribute views and transactions tables that contain quantifiable columns. The attribute views are used to describe the *what, how, when, where,* and *why* characteristics of each transaction. Because analytic views allow for the definition of measures, you can aggregate the quantifiable columns to any level defined in an attribute view or local attribute column.

You've now taken the first steps in assigning real value to the data that is being stored in the underlying SAP HANA tables. The remaining modeling components can be used to expand upon the capabilities of the analytic view. As we'll discuss, they can provide scenarios where more advanced calculations are required. In addition, there are components to aid in the implementation of data level security.

### 6.1.6 Calculation Views

In cases where more advanced processing or advanced data mining is required, SAP HANA provides *calculation views*. In contrast to calculation views, attribute views and analytic views can be thought of as the simplest form of an information view in the SAP HANA platform.

Attribute views are, in some ways, a reusable type of information view whose primary purpose is to characterize a transaction or measurable values. They can be associated with one or more analytic views or reused from one model to the next. For example, a products attribute view could be associated with both sales transactions and inventory transactions.

Analytic views are used primarily to associate a transaction table with one or more attribute views. The role of either of these information views are relegated to managing simple joins, calculations, and filters. For perspective, it isn't possible to accurately model both sales transactions and inventory transactions in the same analytic view. Doing so subjects the model to incorrect aggregations. Imagine that a product has been sold 10 times and contains 20 movements in and out of inventory. If you join the inventory, sales, and products tables together in a single analytic view Data Foundation table, the resulting data set contains 200 records for the example product. Any aggregations defined against this Data Foundation table is overinflated for both the sales transactions and inventory movements. As a result, an analytic view is somewhat limited to a single class of transactions in its Data Foundation. This doesn't mean that you can only use one table in the analytic view Data Foundation node, but it *does* indicate that the results of any joining in the Data Foundation node should only represent one class of transactions.

With that said, SAP HANA does contain an information view that facilitates the processing of complex aggregations and calculations. *Calculation views* can be used, in many cases, to model these complex aggregations into a comprehensive and accurate data set.

Calculation views are used in situations where an analytic view or attribute view are unable to properly express a calculation or when business requirements dictate a more advanced layering of processing logic. Calculation views can't be used to physical manipulate data because they are considered read-only views. A calculation view can be used to express the same functionality as an analytic view, but they are more appropriately used in situations where an analytic view is unable to facilitate a desired query.

Previously, we discussed how an analytic view should be limited to a single class of transactions. Attempting to join sales transactions and inventory movements into the same foundation results in incorrect results. This is one of many scenarios where a calculation view can be developed to solve a common aggregation issue. Calculation views can solve this problem by first aggregating the sales transactions and products to produce a product summary. You can then produce a similar summary using products and inventory movements. Finally, you can then combine the results of both summaries using the product attributes as the merger point. Because both results were aggregated independently and then combined post-aggregation, the final results will be calculated correctly. For purposes of data mining, calculation views can be used to identify correlations, intersections, trends, and other common mining tasks.

### Creating a Calculation View

There are two way to create a calculation view in SAP HANA Studio. As with other information views, you can use either the Navigator view or the Quick Launch view.

To create a calculation view using the Quick Launch view, open the Modeler perspective by selecting Windows • Open Perspective • Modeler from the File menu bar. On the right side of the window, the Quick Launch window appears (see Figure 6.21). In the Quick Launch view, select the Calculation View button, and then click the Create button located in the white box that appears to the right. This launches a wizard that walks you through the processes of defining a calculation view.

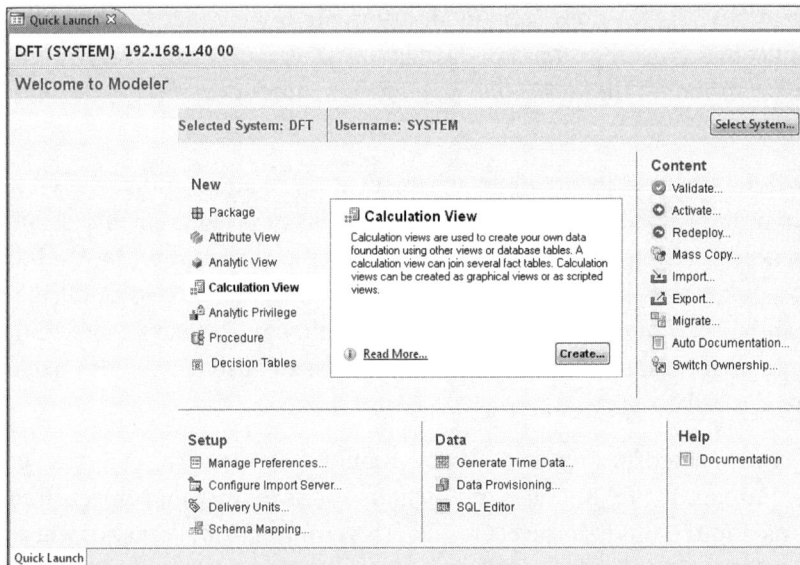

**Figure 6.21**  Creating a Calculation View in the Quick Launch View

The second option for creating a calculation view is to use the NAVIGATOR view located on the left side of the Modeler perspective. In the NAVIGATOR view, expand the CONTENT folder to view the packages. If no packages are present, create a package to store the calculation view. Right-click the appropriate nonstructural package, and choose NEW • CALCULATION VIEW. This launches a wizard allowing you to define a new calculation view.

Figure 6.22 shows the wizard that is launched as a result of both methods.

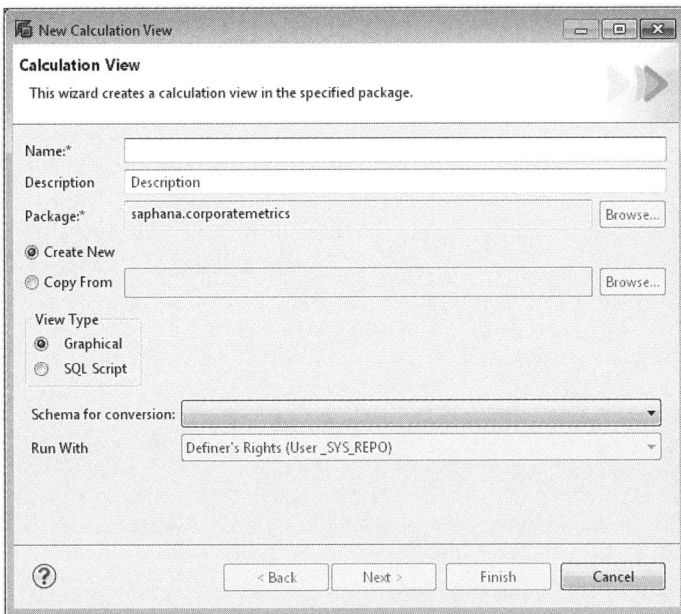

**Figure 6.22**   The New Calculation View Wizard Window

The CALCULATION VIEW wizard window offers you 10 options to be configured or selected, as outlined in Table 6.13.

| Property | Description |
|---|---|
| NAME | The name of the calculation view. |
| | This is a required property that can't be changed after the calculation view is saved and activated. It's important to establish a standard calculation view naming convention before starting a development project in SAP HANA. Only the alphabet characters Aa-Zz, numbers 0-9, and underscore (_) are allowed in the name. |
| DESCRIPTION | The description of the calculation view. |
| | This property can contain a free-text description of the calculation view and should be used to add additional metadata to the view or a thorough description that other developers can use to identify the purpose of the calculation view. |
| PACKAGE | The package that the calculation view will be assigned to. |
| | Only nonstructural packages can be used as the parent object for a calculation view. If you're using the QUICK LAUNCH view to create the calculation view, you must select a package. If using the NAVIGATOR view, the package that was right-clicked is automatically selected. |
| CREATE NEW | Choose the CREATE NEW option when developing a new calculation view. This option allows you to define the calculation view from scratch. |
| COPY FROM | Choose the COPY FROM option when there is a need to create a new calculation view that is a copy of an existing calculation view. Select the BROWSE button to select an existing calculation view. All content from the source calculation view is copied into the new view. |
| VIEW TYPE - GRAPHICAL | Choose the VIEW TYPE – GRAPHICAL option to create a calculation view using graphical objects and workflows. This option doesn't require you to use SQL code or the SAP HANA Calculation Engine functions. |
| VIEW TYPE – SQLSCRIPT | Choose the VIEW TYPE – SQLSCRIPT option to create a calculation view using SQLscript code or SAP HANA Calculation Engine functions. This option should be used by experienced developers that need to define complex calculations and by developers with a thorough understanding of the SAP HANA Calculation Engine functions. |

**Table 6.13** Calculation View Configuration Options

| Property | Description |
|---|---|
| SCHEMA FOR CONVERSION | The list of schemas that can be used to convert values to facilitate the currency conversion process. |
| | Only schemas with currency related tables display in this list. Currency conversion tables must be defined independently of the calculation view. This option is only available when defining graphical-based calculation views. |
| DEFAULT SCHEMA | The list of schemas defined in the SAP HANA platform. |
| | This option is used exclusively with SQL script-based calculation views. Once defined, all SQL code in the calculation view assumes the selected schema. This option is best used when you want to develop SQL code without the need to fully qualify tables with a schema name. |
| RUN WITH | The privileges that will be used when users execute the final calculation view. |
| | Graphical type views are always executed with the definer's rights or _SYS_REPO. SQL script-based calculation views can be executed with either the definer's rights or the invoker's rights. In either case, the designer's rights are those of the _SYS_REPO system user. |

**Table 6.13** Calculation View Configuration Options (Cont.)

Calculation views essentially allow you to choreograph the movement of data sets through a gauntlet of logical transformations, until the desired result set is produced. In some ways, calculation views can be used to transform data similar to the ways in which SAP Data Services can transform data.

As we'll discuss later in this chapter, calculation views contain fewer transformations than SAP Data Services. They can be defined using a GUI or using scripts. However, in either case, the general workflow is the same. Figure 6.23 contains a workflow diagram that illustrates an example calculation view's workflow.

In the example workflow in Figure 6.23, five major steps and components are used to transform two analytic views into a single comprehensive information view. For this example, we'll assume that the goal of the calculation view is to produce a combined information view that displays the product, year, and month attributes. In addition, we'll associate two measures representing the quantity sold and quantity of products returned. If we assume that returned products are a KPI, this information view can be used to identify products that are defective or unsatisfactory.

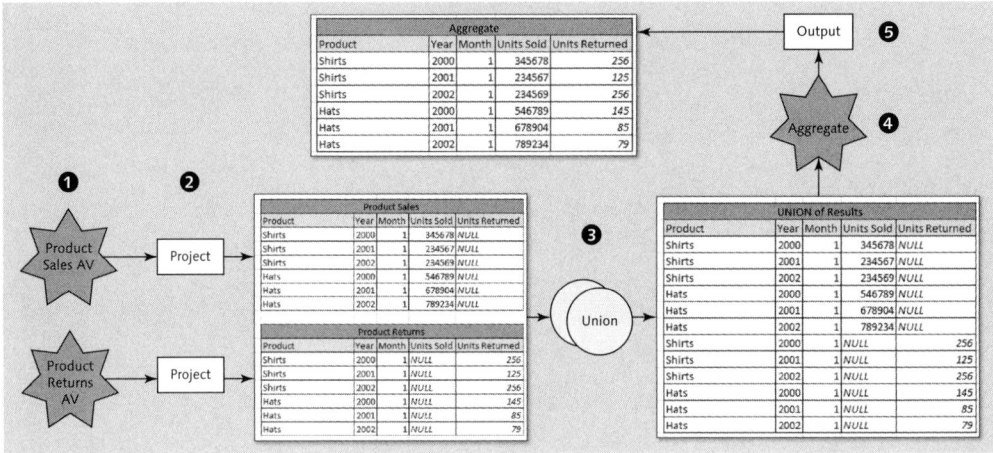

**Figure 6.23** Example of a Calculation View Workflow

Let's walk through the steps now:

❶ Using an existing "products sold" analytic view and a "products returned" analytic view, obtain the needed attributes and measures from each view.

❷ Using the *project* transformation, select the desired components from each analytic view. If you assume that each analytic view contains several attributes and measures, then projecting the results to the needed components can increase the performance of the overall calculation view. In addition, you can use the *project* transformation to add new calculated columns or to add filters. (We'll discuss all of the features of the project transformation shortly.)

❸ Using the *union* transformation, combine the two projected analytic views into a single logical result set. This transformation works similar to the SQL function union. At this point, the results have not been fully combined. There will be records for the products returned and the products sold.

❹ Using the *aggregation* transformation, fully combine the results of each analytic view. This aggregation transformation works similar to the SQL GROUP BY function. Because you're aggregating the two measures against the three attribute columns, rows for products that were sold are combined with rows of products sold.

❺ The final output is a comprehensive result set that contains a row for each product, year, month, quantity sold, and quantity returned. You can define each output column as either an attribute or measure in the output transformation.

### Defining a Graphical Calculation View

As mentioned before, SAP HANA supports the development of calculation views using either a GUI or custom-developed scripts. Each interface has different options and capabilities. The GUI is the easiest for a developer to use. As its name suggests, all of the development in this interface is conducted by placing objects on a canvas and using drag-and-drop principles to connect and choreograph their relationships.

Figure 6.24 contains an example of the graphical calculation view design window. The TOOLS PALETTE pane appears on the left side, and the DETAILS and OUTPUT panes appear on the right. The panes on the right side contain properties that will appear depending on the object that is selected from the TOOLS PALETTE. In some cases, objects also contain a secondary OUTPUT pane, allowing you to manage the logical output of the transformation.

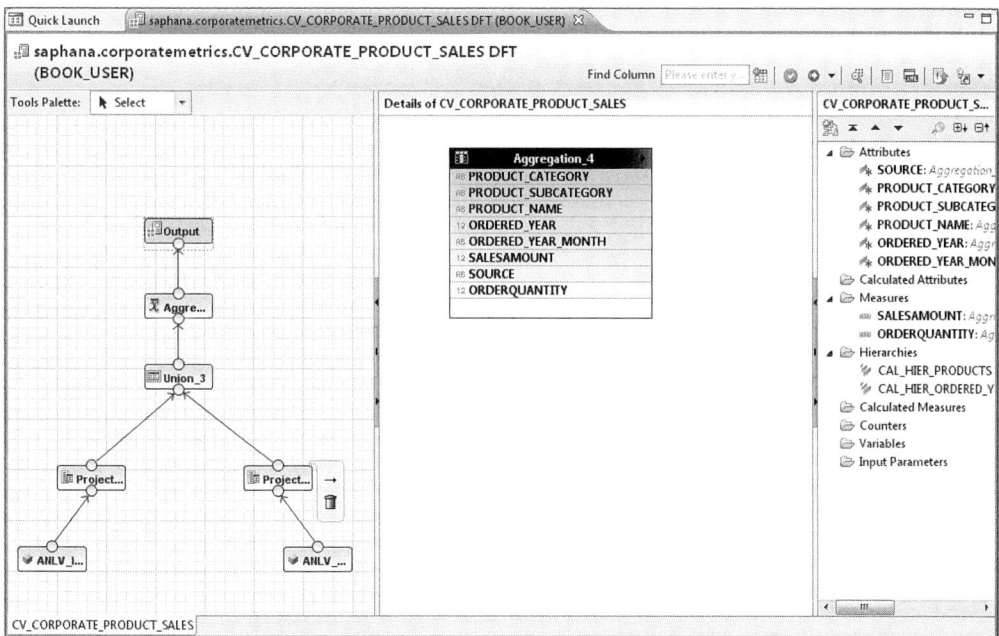

**Figure 6.24**  A Calculation View Design Window in the Graphical User Interface

The TOOLS PALETTE is the main graphical design window in the calculation view design screen. Various data sources and transformations can be added to the TOOLS PALETTE pane. Lines can be created to connect objects and to express their workflow of transformation. The starting point of a calculation view begins with the addition of data sources to the TOOLS PALETTE pane. One or more analytic views, attribute views, stored procedure column views, or tables can be considered a data source for a calculation view.

After the data sources are added to the TOOLS PALETTE, five additional transformations can also be added to the TOOLS PALETTE pane. Each transformation has a unique purpose, which is outlined in Table 6.14. Also note that the SELECT option shown in the TOOLS PALETTE dropdown list isn't a transformation, but it must be selected for you to use the drag-and-drop functionality in the TOOLS PALETTE pane.

| Transformation | Description |
|---|---|
| Join | The *join* transformation enables you to query one or more supported data sources to generate a new logical result set. After the object is added to the TOOLS PALETTE and selected, the DETAILS and OUTPUT panes appear to the right. The DETAILS pane allows you to graphically join data sources connected to the join transformation. |
| | You also select one or more data source columns in the DETAIL pane and assign them as output columns. The OUTPUT pane allows you to specify the output column name and to generate calculated columns. Finally, you can select existing input parameters or create new input parameters. |
| Project | The *project* transformation allows you to manipulate a supported data source to generate a new logical result set. The manipulations include the ability to select a subset of columns from the source, create calculated columns, define filters, and define input parameters. After the object is added to the TOOLS PALETTE and selected, the DETAILS and OUTPUT panes appear to the right. Select one or more data source columns in the DETAIL pane and assign them as output columns. The OUTPUT pane allows you to specify the output column name and to generate calculated columns. You can select existing input parameters, defined in any connected analytic views, or create new input parameters and define filters to limit the results of the connected data source. |

**Table 6.14** Graphical Transformations Supported in a Calculation View

| Transformation | Description |
|---|---|
| Union | The *union* transformation allows you to merge two or more data source into a single logical result set. The merger doesn't combine rows but simply stacks them one on top of the other. After the object is added to the Tools Palette and selected, the Details pane appears to the right. The Details pane allows you to graphically connect columns from each data source to a common target column. Columns from the source are placed in the target area using standard drag-and-drop techniques. The connection points are used by the union transform to identify which columns should be aligned when the two data sources are combined. The combined columns must share the same data type and precision. Any column that isn't linked to a target column will output a NULL value for the unassigned data source. |
| Aggregate | The aggregate transformation allows you to summarize measureable columns into groups of attributes. The functionality is similar to using a GROUP BY statement in an SQL statement. The transform support the aggregation functions SUM, MIN, and MAX. |
| Output | The output transformation is required for each calculation view. It's the final step in the workflow of supported transformations. Output columns from the connected transformation or table are configured as either attributes or measures. You can also create additional hierarchies, calculated attributes, counters, variables, and input parameters based on the connected source. |

**Table 6.14**  Graphical Transformations Supported in a Calculation View (Cont.)

Using the Tools Palette GUI and standard drag-and-drop principles, you can design a workflow that connects both data sources and transformations together to produce a comprehensive result set. Typically, these workflows are designed from the bottom up.

In the Tools Palette on the left side of Figure 6.25, you can see an example in which two analytic views are being transformed into a single logical data set. The workflow starts with two analytic views at the bottom of the Tools Palette pane; each view has a connection to a separate projection transform. The results of each project transform are then combined using a union transform. The results of the union transform are then aggregated to produce a summary. In the final output transform, the summarized results are converted into attributes, measures, and hierarchies.

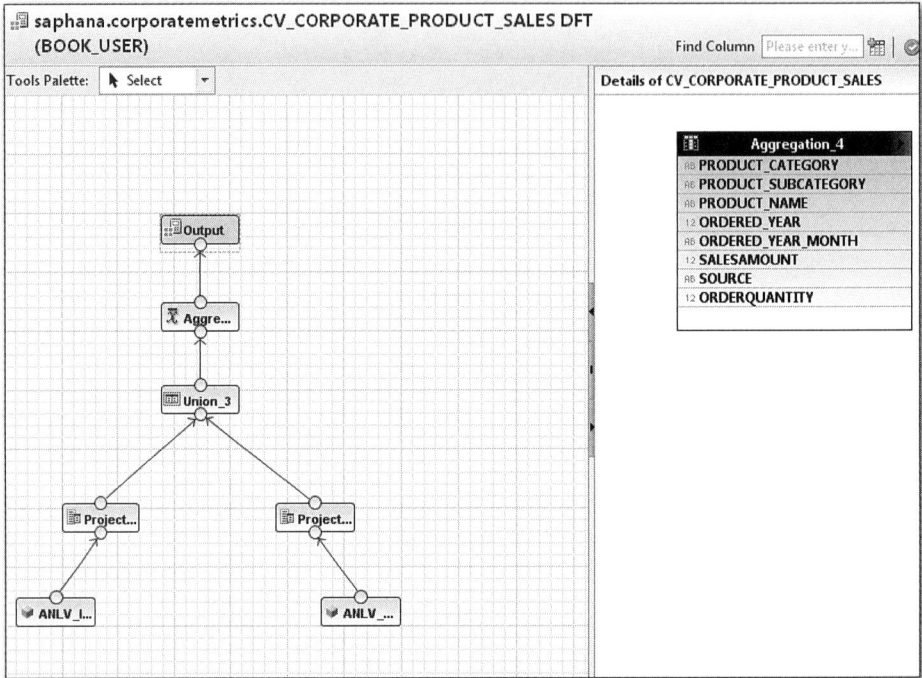

**Figure 6.25** Calculation View Workflow

Objects in the Tools Palette are connected by dragging the small circle located on the top or bottom of the object to the small circle located on the adjoining object. Each line represents the movement of a logical data set from one object to the next. Lines connected on the bottom of the object are considered the incoming connection. Lines protruding from the top of the object are considered the outgoing connection. The assumption is that the incoming data is changed, using the supported logic of the transformation, and then passed along to the next object for additional transformation or final output.

Objects can be connected in a variety of configurations, but they should be connected in the most logical order. For example, the join and union transformations typically contain two or more incoming connections and a single outgoing connection. However, you can create two or more outgoing connections for many of the objects as well. While you can output more than one logical data set, all branches of the workflow must inevitably coincide with a single output transform. In other words, all objects and workflows must eventually connect to a single output transform. Therefore, the most logical workflow is one that performs the least amount of necessary transformation and calculation, while producing the desired output. After the workflow is completed, the calculation view can be saved and activated to allow consumers to query the results.

The final step of a calculation view is the configuration of the output transform. The output transform is designed to allow you to configure the calculation view using features similar to both analytic view and attribute views. When selecting the output transform in the TOOL PALETTE pane, two additional panes appear to the right. Figure 6.25, shown earlier, contains an example of these two panes. In the DETAILS panes, you right-click each column in the virtual table and configure them as either an attributes or as measures. In the pane furthest to the right, the columns are displayed in either the ATTRIBUTES or MEASURES sections. In total, there are eight objects that can be created in this pane, as outlined in Table 6.15.

| Object | Description |
|---|---|
| Attributes | Attributes are the columns that will be used for grouping, sorting, filtering, and ranking the results of the calculation view. They incorporate many of the features described in the sections pertaining to attribute view columns, but they are defined explicitly in the calculation view. |
| | Attribute are assigned to this pane by right-clicking COLUMN in the details pane virtual table and selecting ADD AS ATTRIBUTE. |
| Calculated attributes | Calculated attributes are columns that are derived from one or more attribute columns in the calculation view. They are designed using the SAP HANA SQL syntax. They incorporate many of the features described in the sections pertaining to attribute view calculated columns, but they are defined explicitly in the calculation view. |
| | Calculated attributes are assigned to this pane by right-clicking the calculated attribute section and selecting NEW. |
| Measures | Measures represent the columns that will be summarized or aggregated in the calculation view. Calculation view measures support the SUM, MIN, and MAX aggregation functions. They incorporate many of the same features that were described in the sections pertaining to analytic view measures. |
| | Measures are assigned to this pane by right-clicking COLUMN in the DETAILS pane virtual table and selecting ADD AS MEASURE. |

**Table 6.15**  Output Column Types to Define in a Calculation View's Output Transform

| Object | Description |
| --- | --- |
| Hierarchies | Hierarchies can be created directly in a calculation view. They are designed using one or more of the attributes defined in the calculation view. Unlike attribute views, hierarchies in a calculation view can span columns that exist naturally in desperate attribute views. |
| | Hierarchies are assigned to this pane by right-clicking the HIERARCHIES section and selecting either a parent-child or level hierarchy. |
| Calculated measures | Calculated measures can be created directly in the output transform of a calculation view. As their name implies, calculated measures can be used to formulate new measure values using the SAP HANA SQL syntax, existing attributes, and existing measures that are defined in the calculation view. |
| | Calculated measures are assigned to this pane by right-clicking the CALCULATED MEASURES section and selecting NEW. |
| Counters | Counter can be used to create a count distinct aggregate and measure. They are based on attributes defined in the calculation view. At this time, only a count distinct and a single attribute can be configured in each counter's options. |
| | Counters are assigned to this pane by right-clicking the COUNTERS section and selecting NEW. |
| Variables | As with analytic views, variables can be used to create a runtime filter and prompt list of values for the calculation view. They can be configured using the same options listed previously in Table 6.12 in Section 6.1.4. |
| | Variables are assigned to this pane by right-clicking the VARIABLES section and selecting NEW. |
| Input parameters | Input parameters can be used to define a runtime parameter or a list of values for a runtime parameter. Input parameters can be used in calculated columns and calculated measures to facilitate runtime manipulation of the data. They can be defined in multiple calculation view transforms as well. In addition, input parameters can be inherited from source analytic views used in the definition of the calculation view. |
| | Input parameters can be assigned in the join, projection, aggregation, and output transforms. In all areas, they are assigned by right-clicking the INPUT PARAMETERS section and choosing NEW. There is also an option to manage the inherited input parameters labeled MANAGE MAPPINGS. |

**Table 6.15**  Output Column Types to Define in a Calculation View's Output Transform (Cont.)

After the calculation view is activated, SAP HANA converts the graphical workflow of the transformation into highly optimized code that maximizes the use of the hardware capabilities of the SAP HANA appliance. Calculation views should not be confused with stored procedures in the SAP HANA appliance. Although both mechanisms are capable of transforming data to produce robust analytics, stored procedure logic is generally more expensive to execute than calculation view logic. Stored procedures rely heavily on orchestration logic and procedural SQL statements. They can be characterized by the use of costly row-by-row operations that evaluate records in a loop. They can also be characterized by the need to calculate data in a series of rigid steps. Calculation views incorporate a different technique in the processing of data. If designed correctly, calculation views use declarative logic to minimize the cost of processing data. They work more efficiently analyzing data in sets, using logic that can be parallelized in the SAP HANA engines. Calculation views can be characterized by their ability to efficiently process multiple calculations at the same time. Because of this, calculation views are ideal for producing complex analytical models, which are based on high-cardinality tables, each possessing complex relationships to other tables. With that said, calculation views invoke the use of the SAP HANA Calculation Engine. In situations where the query can be satisfied using the standard star schema analytic view, calculation views aren't recommended.

**Defining a Script-Based Calculation View**

Calculation views can also be composed using scripting language for situations where the GUI has limitations or complex procedure logic is required. Script-based calculation views can be defined using standard SAP HANA SQL statements or by using a special *SQLScript* language and *CE_functions*. The CE_ functions are the preferred choice for developers when creating SQLScript-based calculation views. CE_ functions are directly executed in the SAP HANA Calculation Engine and can be better optimized for parallel execution by the SAP HANA engine. Script-based calculation views can contain a mixture of either standard SQL statements or CE_ functions. However, we don't recommend that you mix these scripting languages in the same calculation view because, in many cases, intermixing can have an adverse effect on the calculation view's performance.

Figure 6.26 shows an example of the script-based calculation view design window. The SCENARIO pane appears on the left side, the DETAILS pane containing the scripting interface appears in the center, and the input parameters, output parameters, and output columns generated for the script appear on the far right side. The output columns aren't automatically generated from the script so you must define them manually.

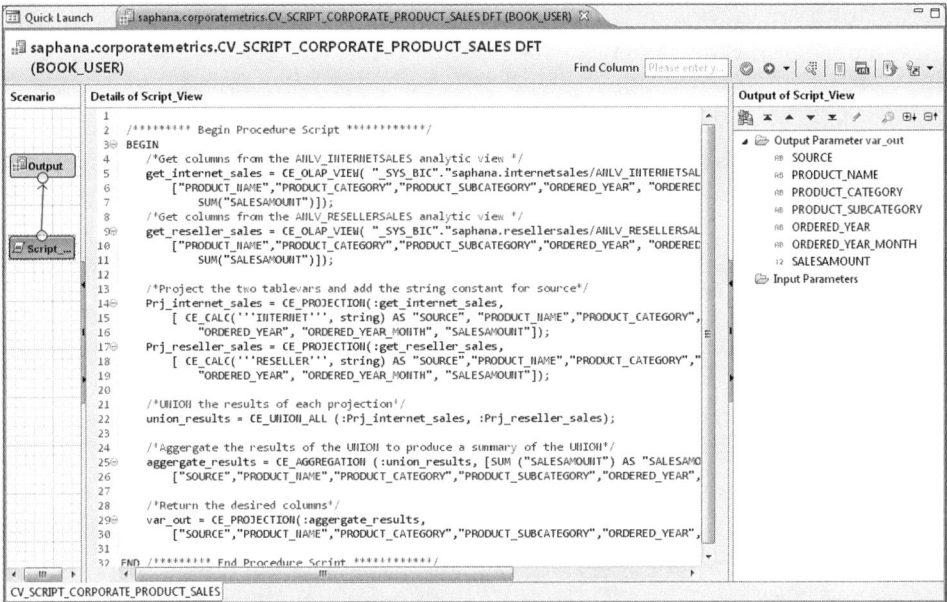

**Figure 6.26**  An Example of a Script-Based Calculation View

The SCENARIO pane only contain two nodes:

▶ The SCRIPT node is used when writing the script and defining input and output parameters.

▶ The OUTPUT node is used to define attributes, measures, hierarchies, variables, and additional input parameters based on the output of the script.

To activate a node, click on the node object, and its properties panes will appear to the right side.

The scripting process is conducted using many of the same principles we discussed regarding the graphical calculation view design process. The goal of the script is to choreograph the movement of a data set through a series of transformations until the desired results are produced. While the methodology may be the same, the process is implemented using a specific code language and not graphical objects.

In comparison to the GUI, the scripting interface is considerably more complex. However, increased complexity brings more control and features. For example, the scripting interface can accommodate situations where stored procedures are needed to transform data sets or predictive analysis functions need to be used in the calculation view.

To help you better understand script-based calculation views, let's review the example workflow that was shown earlier in Figure 6.23. The graphical calculation view combined both Internet sales and reseller sales into a single result set. Because the Internet sales and reseller sales transactions were maintained in two separate transaction tables, we were unable to develop a sole analytic view to properly query and aggregate the combined sales transactions. Using a graphical calculation view, we were able to orchestrate the processing of data and solve the issues related to aggregating results from two different transaction tables.

Listing 6.1 contains an example calculation view script. The script is the equivalent of the graphical example displayed in Figure 6.25. The exact semantics of the SAP HANA SQLScript language are beyond the scope of this book, but we offer this example to illustrate how a calculation view can be devised using handwritten SAP HANA SQLScript code. In addition, this example script incorporates the use of the highly optimized CE_ functions. CE_ functions are a faster alternative to standard SQL statements or stored procedure logic.

```
/********* Begin Procedure Script ************/
 BEGIN
/**Step 1**/
/**Get columns from the ANLV_INTERNETSALES analytic view **/
get_internet_sales = CE_OLAP_VIEW( "_SYS_BIC"."saphana.internetsales/
ANLV_INTERNETSALES/olap",["PRODUCT_NAME","PRODUCT_CATEGORY","PRODUCT_
SUBCATEGORY","ORDERED_YEAR", "ORDERED_YEAR_MONTH",SUM("SALESAMOUNT")]);
/**Get columns from the ANLV_RESELLERSALES analytic view **/
get_reseller_sales = CE_OLAP_VIEW( "_SYS_BIC"."saphana.
resellersales/ANLV_RESELLERSALES/olap",["PRODUCT_NAME","PRODUCT_
CATEGORY", "PRODUCT_SUBCATEGORY", "ORDERED_YEAR", "ORDERED_YEAR_
MONTH",SUM("SALESAMOUNT")]);

/**Step 2**/
/**Project the two results to add the string constant for source**/
Prj_internet_sales = CE_PROJECTION( :get_internet_sales,  [ CE_CALC(
'''INTERNET''', string) AS "SOURCE",  "PRODUCT_NAME",  "PRODUCT_
CATEGORY", "PRODUCT_SUBCATEGORY", "ORDERED_YEAR", "ORDERED_YEAR_MONTH",
```

```
"SALESAMOUNT"]);
Prj_reseller_sales = CE_PROJECTION( :get_reseller_sales, [ CE_
CALC('''RESELLER''', string) AS "SOURCE", "PRODUCT_NAME", "PRODUCT_
CATEGORY", "PRODUCT_SUBCATEGORY", "ORDERED_YEAR", "ORDERED_YEAR_MONTH",
"SALESAMOUNT"]);

/**Step 3**/
/**UNION the results of each projection**/
union_results = CE_UNION_ALL (:Prj_internet_sales, :Prj_reseller_
sales);

/**Step 4**/
/**Aggregate the results of the UNION to produce a summary**/
aggergate_results = CE_AGGREGATION (:union_results, [SUM
("SALESAMOUNT") AS "SALESAMOUNT"], ["SOURCE", "PRODUCT_NAME", "PRODUCT_
CATEGORY", "PRODUCT_SUBCATEGORY", "ORDERED_YEAR", "ORDERED_YEAR_
MONTH"]);

/**Step 5**/
/**Return the desired columns**/
 var_out = CE_PROJECTION(:aggergate_results, ["SOURCE", "PRODUCT_NAME",
"PRODUCT_CATEGORY", "PRODUCT_SUBCATEGORY", "ORDERED_YEAR", "ORDERED_
YEAR_MONTH", "SALESAMOUNT"]);

END
/********* End Procedure Script ************/
```

**Listing 6.1** Example SAP HANA SQLScript that Incorporates CE_ Functions

---

**Additional References**

As stated, the semantics of the SAP HANA SQLScript is beyond the scope of this book. For more information on the SAP HANA SQLScript language and a complete listing of the available CE_ functions, please review the SAP HANA SQLScript reference guide found at *http://help.sap.com/hana_appliance#section5*.

---

Calculation views are powerful information views that allow you to solve complex aggregation problems or to perform complex data-mining tasks. In simple terms, they allow for the orchestration of a data set for the purpose of complex analytical analysis. Calculation views add value to the SAP HANA platform by allowing you to formulate queries where standard multidimensional analysis can't accommodate your requirements.

### 6.1.7    Analytic Privileges

*Analytic privileges* are another important component of the SAP HANA modeling processes. Note that analytic privileges aren't information views. They don't manage any relationships between tables, nor do they provide mechanisms to solve complex calculations.

Instead, analytic privileges are used to either grant or restrict access to data in an SAP HANA information view. Before consumers or external tools can query an information model, they must first authenticate with the SAP HANA system. The SAP HANA system challenges any query or management attempt and forces the challenger to provide valid credentials. The SAP HANA system uses this authentication process to establish a security layer that can grant or deny access to objects such as tables, schemas, packages, procedures, and views. It can also be used to control user access to administrative tasks or predefined system privileges. In general terms, this is referred to as authorization. In short, the user must first authenticate with the SAP HANA system. After they authenticate, the SAP HANA system will contain a list of authorizations that dictate what the user can do in the SAP HANA system.

In addition to user accounts, SAP HANA also uses *roles*. Roles are security objects that can be assigned privileges in the same way that user accounts can be assigned privileges. Roles can also be assigned to one or more users or other existing roles. In some ways, roles are a type of user group. When a role is assigned to a user or existing roles, the user or role inherits all of the privileges of the assigned role. Most administrators find it easier to assign new user accounts to established roles than to manage each account individually.

SAP HANA also contains an additional layer of security that can be incorporated directly into information views and used to impose data-level restrictions or runtime filters. These dynamic data-level restrictions are used to filter access to rows of data. In general terms, we refer to this as row-level security. In SAP HANA, we refer to this as analytic privileges. Analytic privileges are a collection of runtime filters that can be assigned to one or more users or roles. Analytic privileges contain a collection of one or more specific information view filters that are applied to any associated user or role. Each user or role must be assigned an analytic privilege to query and subsequently view results from an information view. If a user doesn't have an assigned analytic privilege for a given information view, the user cannot access the data within it. This is true for any role associated with a user as well. In short, all information views are assumed fully restricted by default, and users must be explicitly assigned one or more analytic privileges before they can access the data in a model.

For dynamic data-level filters to be useful, it's assumed that each SAP HANA consumer has his own unique user account. For example, if a shared user account were assigned to 10 regional managers, each using the same user account and password, there would be no way to distinguish one regional manager from another. To solve this problem, each regional manager can be assigned a unique user account. After each regional manager has an account, you can develop specific analytic privileges to restrict each manager's access to their assigned region.

There are two ways to create analytic privileges in SAP HANA. This process should be very familiar to you, as it's shared with other modeling components. Again, you can use either the NAVIGATOR view or the QUICK LAUNCH view.

To create an analytic privilege using the QUICK LAUNCH view, open the Modeler perspective by selecting WINDOWS • OPEN PERSPECTIVE • MODELER from the FILE menu bar. In the Quick Launch view (see Figure 6.27), select the ANALYTIC PRIVILEGES button, and click the CREATE button to the right. This launches a wizard that walks you through the processes of defining an analytic privilege.

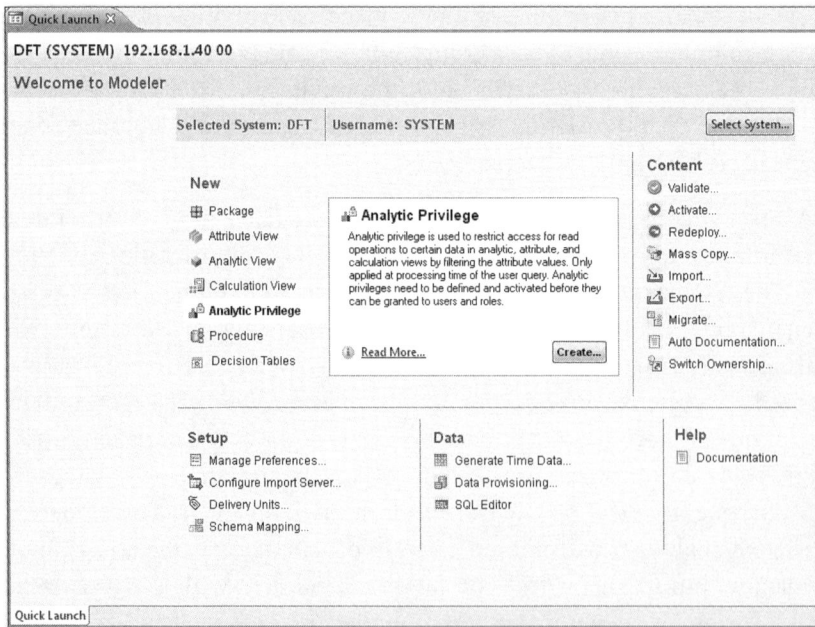

**Figure 6.27** Creating Analytic Privileges in the Quick Launch View

As before, the second option for creating an analytic privilege is to use the NAVI-GATOR view located on the left side of the Modeler perspective. In the NAVIGATOR view, you expand the CONTENT folder to view the packages. If no packages are present, create a package to store the analytic privilege. Right-click the appropriate nonstructural package, and choose NEW • ANALYTIC PRIVILEGE. This launches a wizard allowing you to define a new analytic privilege. When creating an analytic privilege, the NEW ANALYTIC PRIVILEGE wizard shown in Figure 6.28 appears.

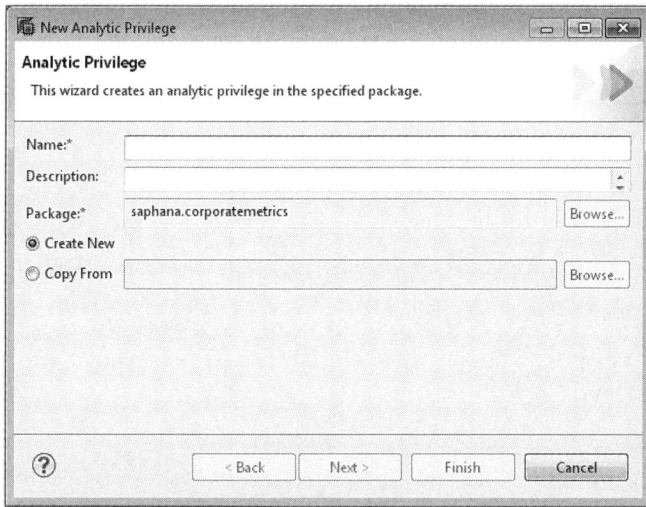

**Figure 6.28**   The New Analytic Privilege Wizard Window

Table 6.16 outlines the five options that can be configured or selected in this wizard.

| Property | Description |
| --- | --- |
| NAME | The name of the analytic privilege. |
| | This is a required property that can't be changed after the analytic privilege is saved and activated. It's important to establish a standard analytic privilege naming convention before starting a development project in SAP HANA. Only the alphabet characters Aa-Zz, numbers 0-9, and underscore (_) are allowed in the name. |

**Table 6.16**   Options to Configure When Creating an Analytic Privilege

| Property | Description |
|---|---|
| DESCRIPTION | The description of the analytic privilege. |
|  | This property can contain a free-text description of the analytic privilege and should be used to add additional metadata to the analytic privilege or a thorough description that other developers can use to identify the purpose of the analytic privilege. |
| PACKAGE | The package that the analytic privilege will be assigned to. |
|  | Only nonstructural packages can be used as the parent object for an analytic privilege. If you're using the QUICK LAUNCH view to create the analytic privilege, you must select a package. If using the NAVIGATOR view, the package that was right-clicked is automatically selected. |
| CREATE NEW | Choose the CREATE NEW option when developing a new analytic privilege to define the analytic privilege from scratch. |
| COPY FROM | Choose the COPY FROM option when you need to create a new analytic privilege that is a copy of an existing analytic privilege. Select the BROWSE button to select an existing analytic privilege. All content from the source analytic privilege is copied into the new analytic privilege. |

**Table 6.16** Options to Configure When Creating an Analytic Privilege (Cont.)

Analytic privileges are defined by identifying and configuring just a few options. An information view, attribute, and restriction can be set up for each analytic privilege. There is also an option to apply the restriction to all information models or information views. After completing the NEW ANALYTIC PRIVILEGE wizard, a design window similar to the one shown in Figure 6.29 appears, in which these main options can be configured.

Not all panes require configuration in the analytic privilege design window. Carefully consider which are necessary when configuring analytic privilege options. Table 6.17 outlines each of the four main options that can be configured.

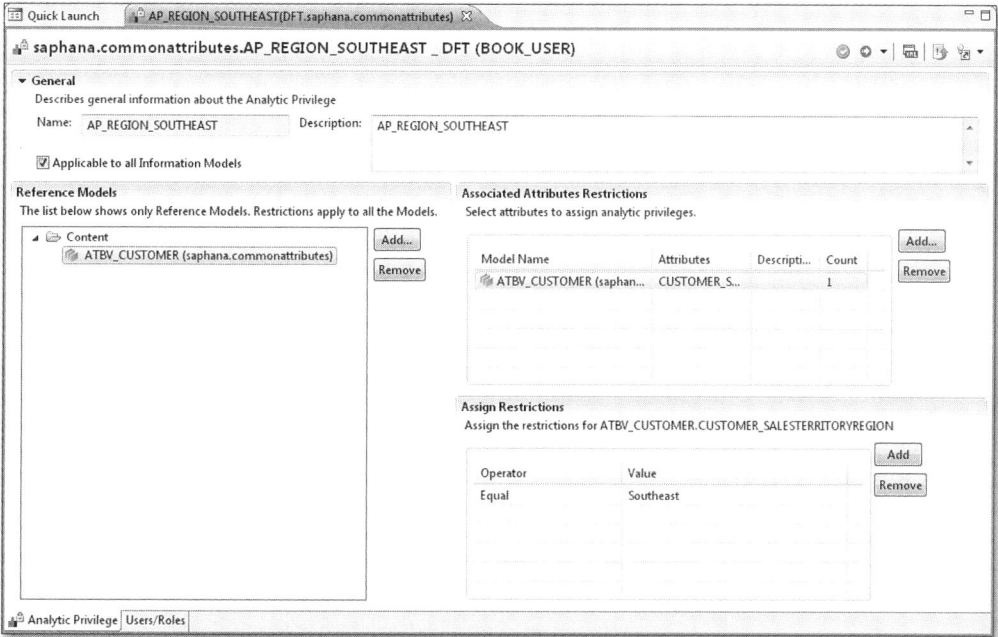

**Figure 6.29** An Example Analytic Privilege Design Window

| Option | Description |
|---|---|
| REFERENCE MODELS | Using the ADD and REMOVE buttons to the right of the REFERENCE MODEL pane, you can associate one or more information views to the analytic privilege. Attribute views, analytic views, and calculation views can be added to the list.<br><br>Items in this list are the basis for defining access to the data. Access can be either granted or restricted. If no restrictions are defined, the consumer is assumed full access to the data. If restrictions are defined, the consumer is assumed access based on the defined filters.<br><br>If users or roles have multiple analytic privileges defined for the same information view, the least restrictive option will take precedence. Analytic privileges are combined using an OR operator, meaning either can be true. |

**Table 6.17** Analytic Privilege Design Window Configuration Options

| Option | Description |
|---|---|
| ASSOCIATED ATTRIBUTE RESTRICTIONS | Using the ADD and REMOVE buttons located on the right of the ASSOCIATED ATTRIBUTE RESTRICTIONS pane, you can select one or more attributes or columns based on the information views that were defined in the REFERENCE MODEL pane. |
| | When assigning multiple attributes or columns, the combined restrictions use an AND operator internally to restrict the information view. This implies that all defined attribute or column restrictions conditions must be true. |
| | This is an optional setting. If no attributes or columns are specified in this section, the analytic privilege grants full access to the associated information views. |
| ASSIGN RESTRICTIONS | Using the ADD and REMOVE buttons to the right of the assign restrictions pane, you can define one or more restrictions for the column that is highlighted in the ASSOCIATED ATTRIBUTE RESTRICTIONS pane. |
| | When assigning multiple restrictions to the same attribute or column, the restrictions use an OR operator internally to filter the attributes or columns. This implies that each individually defined restriction can be true without affecting the other. Separate restrictions are defined for each column in the ASSOCIATED ATTRIBUTE RESTRICTIONS pane. To define a restriction, you must select each attribute or column individually in the associated attribute restrictions pane and subsequently define its restrictions. |
| | Restrictions can be defined using the following operators: |
| | ▶ Equal (=) |
| | ▶ Between (<>) |
| | ▶ Greater than (>) |
| | ▶ Greater than or equal (>=) |
| | ▶ Less than (<) |
| | ▶ Less than or equal (<=) |
| | ▶ Contains Pattern (like) |
| | ▶ Is Null |
| | ▶ Is Not Null |

**Table 6.17**  Analytic Privilege Design Window Configuration Options (Cont.)

| Option | Description |
|---|---|
| | For each selected attribute or column, a list of values pane can be invoked, in the VALUE column, allowing you to select or search from all values associated with the attribute. |
| | This is an optional setting. If no attributes, columns, or restrictions are specified, the analytic privilege returns all rows for the associated information view. |
| APPLICABLE TO ALL INFORMATION MODELS | This checkbox is used to determine how the privileges should be applied to information views. Place a checkmark in the box to enable this option. If checked, the analytic privilege will apply to all information views that reference the specified information view. If unchecked, the analytic privilege will only be valid for each information view explicitly listed in the reference model pane. |

**Table 6.17** Analytic Privilege Design Window Configuration Options (Cont.)

SAP HANA has a special system-generated analytic privilege named _SYS_BI_CP_ALL. If this privilege is assigned to a user or role, SAP HANA assumes that the associated users or roles have full access to all information views. By default, the MODELER, CONTENT_ADMIN, and MASTER roles are assigned this analytic privilege. Analytic privileges are required for every user in the SAP HANA system, assuming they require access to an information view's data. If a user or a user's role doesn't have any analytic privileges assigned, the user will be unable to query any information view stored in the _SYS_BIC schema. If a user or user's role has the _SYS_BI_CP_ALL analytic privilege, the user will be able to see all data even when assigned other more restrictive analytic privileges. Therefore, the _SYS_BI_CP_ALL analytic privilege should not be assigned to users that need specific restrictions for data security purposes.

---

**Effective Analytic Privileges**

To help you quickly identify the effective analytic privileges assigned to a user, there is a database view stored in the SYS schema called EFFECTIVE_PRIVILEGES. Using the following example query, administrators can quickly identify the effective analytic privileges assigned to a user:

```
SELECT * FROM "SYS"."EFFECTIVE_PRIVILEGES" WHERE USER_NAME = 'BOOK_USER'
AND OBJECT_TYPE = 'ANALYTICALPRIVILEGE'
```

The administrator simply replaces the 'BOOK_USER' string literal in the WHERE clause with the user name to review (for example, USER_NAME = '<your user>').

As we have alluded to, it's possible to create an analytic privilege that has no defined attributes or restrictions. When defining an analytic privilege, any information views listed in the REFERENCE MODELS pane are assumed unrestricted unless a restriction is defined. If a user or role is assigned such an analytic privilege, the user will have access to all of the data for the referenced models or information views. If a more restrictive analytic privilege is also assigned to the same user to role, the least restrictive analytic privilege will effectively take precedence. When multiple analytic privileges are assigned to the same user or role, they are internally executed as OR restrictions. This implies that either condition can be true. For example, if one analytic privilege grants access to the entire attribute in an information view, and another restricts access to a single attribute view record, the associated user or role will have access to the entire data set and virtually ignore the restrictions.

In summary, analytic privileges are used to grant and deny access to the data that is being modeled within SAP HANA. Each user or role of SAP HANA must be assigned an analytic privilege to gain access to an information view's application data. Some of the default roles in SAP HANA have been granted full access to all information views. If a user account isn't a member of these roles, they must be explicitly assigned access to each information view. Each analytic privilege can be configured to grant or deny access to one or more information views. Analytic privileges add value to multidimensional models by allowing organizations to selectively grant access to data and not just to modeling objects. Without analytic privileges, developers and administrators would need to develop multiple versions of each information view, each having specific filters. This would lead to a proliferation of content and an inflexible solution.

## 6.2 Benefits of SAP HANA Modeling

In the previous section of this chapter, we discussed the main components of SAP HANA's multidimensional models, detailing the purpose of each component and the various options that are available for each item. In this section, we'll discuss the benefits that the models offer to business users or other consumers of the models. In addition, we'll cover the benefits that SAP HANA offers to an IT department in terms of solution and management. In some cases, the benefits are based on the capabilities of the platform in conjunction with the SAP HANA modeling capabilities.

## 6.2.1 Business Benefits

If we truly believe that the purpose of business intelligence (BI) is to transform raw data into meaningful and informative decision-making tools, we must provide users and other consumers of the data a capable platform and solution. This book discusses the use of SAP Data Services, SAP HANA, and SAP BusinessObjects to outline the components of a complete BI solution.

SAP HANA is at the center of this solution. It's not just a database—it's a decision making platform. SAP HANA has many of the same characteristics of a database, but it also has many unique features that are centered on the best practices of BI. In total, these unique features deliver a solution that adds value to organizations, including those that aren't conducting commercial business. SAP HANA's benefits are universal for many departments and organizations. For example, government agencies, nonprofits, medical research firms, customer service companies, accounting firms, manufacturing companies, and other entities can gain value from SAP HANA.

This section discusses the five main benefits that the SAP HANA platform provides to the direct end users of an SAP HANA platform: simple and complex analytics, operational data, metadata, centralized business logic, and data processing.

### Simple and Complex Analytics

A staple of any sound BI platform is the ability to facilitate both simple and complex data analysis tasks. Organizations need a means to measure and analyze trends, KPIs, leading indicators, lagging indicators, and goals. They also need a sound platform that can facilitate predictive analysis, statistical analysis, and multidimensional analysis.

Through the use of information views, SAP HANA can facilitate all of these tasks while delivering value to its users in a single platform. On its own, SAP HANA is simply the engine to facilitate these needs. In the context of this book, both SAP BusinessObjects and SAP Data Services play a key role in the overall solution as well. SAP Data Services is responsible for managing the structure and quality of the data. SAP BusinessObjects provides the tools that users use to visualize and analyze the data. To this regard, SAP HANA is the core engine that facilitates both simple and complex analysis. As we'll discuss shortly, SAP HANA supports multiple query languages and statistical libraries that transform it from an ordinary database into an extraordinary analytics platform.

**Operational Data**

Organizations use BI not only to analyze data but to also to bolster operations, business processes, and real-time performance management. Many organizations use data for their day-to-day operations. Operational reporting is one of the most common and legacy forms of BI. As opposed to generating analytics, operational reporting is more focused on the detailed transactions that are occurring throughout the day or the transactions that occurred in the recent past. For example, an inventory manager can use a listing of currently open orders to understand the impact fulfilling those orders would have on his current inventory and staff. In addition, a customer support center manager can see the number of calls currently in the call queue, allowing him to add additional capacity. In general terms, operational reporting focuses on the here and now and less on the historical or long term. The supporting data is often obtained directly from online transaction processes (OLTP) sources.

SAP HANA has several features that facilitate operational reporting needs for organizations. Real-time access to data is something that many organizations require. It can be used to provide knowledge where immediate action is required. It adds benefits to organizations that need to react to information before it becomes unusable. The SAP HANA platform includes support for real-time data replication through the use of the SAP LT Replication server and SAP Sybase Replication Server. Though both of these technologies are beyond the scope of this book, it's worth noting that SAP HANA has a solution for either trigger-based replication or log-based replication.

SAP Data Services has two options for this as well: replicate batch data from a source on a near real-time basis or replicate data in real time using web services and XML messages. In general terms, this is called *ETL-based replication*. When you couple these real-time capabilities with the capabilities of the SAP HANA multidimensional models and scripting languages, organizations have a viable solution to leverage data in real time.

In situations where analytical processing isn't needed, data can be accessed directly from the base SAP HANA tables using SQL statements or the SAP HANA SQLScript language. In short, using the multidimensional models isn't a requirement for data access in the SAP HANA platform. As we've established, SAP HANA can support both analytical and operational needs in the same platform. This adds value to most organizations because a single platform can be used to facilitate either need.

**Metadata**

Metadata is often referred to as information about information. Organizations can amass large volumes of data from the multitude of systems they use to manage their day-to-day operations. As we've already established, this vast quantity of data will add value to an organization after it has been messaged into a solution that is intuitive and easy to understand.

SAP HANA can facilitate the benefits of metadata through its multidimensional models. The data relationships, hierarchies, attribute names, measures, and attribute descriptions are all components of metadata. Metadata can be used to provide consumers and external applications with information about the data stored in SAP HANA. This in turn adds value to the data because it makes the data easier to analyze and understand.

**Centralized Business Logic**

All sound BI solutions are centered on the need to provide consumers a single version of the truth. Without this single version of the truth, organizations will find it difficult to make the correct strategic decisions, largely due to lack of faith in the data or lack of access to a central repository of information. For data to bring value to an organization, the data must be readily available and trusted.

SAP Data Services is the starting point for providing a single version of the truth. Data is extracted, translated, cleansed, and loaded into tables that create a single source for quality information. SAP HANA adds value to this data by providing a central repository of metadata, calculations, and data relationships in the form of its multidimensional models. Poorly implemented BI strategies often focus on department or subsidiary level solutions where each is the master of the data they manage. This typically creates a scenario where each unit establishes disjointed master data repositories and subjective business rules to govern their analytical calculations. In these situations, it's often impossible for executives to find a single source and version of the truth. SAP Data Services and SAP HANA can solve this problem through sound data governance and through the proper implementation of each tool.

**Data Processing**

Throughout this chapter, we've focused largely on the components of SAP HANA's multidimensional models and how they deliver value to organizations. While these items are a very important aspect of SAP HANA's capabilities, we must also remember that SAP HANA is a powerful platform for processing data. SAP HANA is a fusion of both software and hardware. The software is highly optimized to take advantage of modern hardware capabilities such as in-memory storage, multicore central processing units, 10 GB Ethernet networks, and NAND flash storage disks.

Because of this marriage between software and hardware, data processing is accelerated in the SAP HANA platform. The exact technical details of how this marriage works is beyond the scope of this book. However, organizations will find that SAP HANA is capable of managing billions of rows of data, complex calculations, and operational data at incredible speeds. Consumers will find tremendous benefit in the response times that SAP HANA offers compared to traditional magnet disk-based platforms.

### 6.2.2 Technology Benefits

In addition to the benefits that SAP HANA provides to organizations as a whole, there are also several technology benefits SAP HANA can offer as a solution. SAP HANA is unique in that it offers several capabilities in a single platform.

We've established that SAP HANA is more than just a database and how it benefits the needs of an organization, so let's examine four specific technical reasons this is true: OLAP analysis with MDX; relational analysis with SQL; integration with Predictive Analysis Library (PAL), Business Function Library (BFL), and R language; and aggregate table elimination.

**OLAP Analysis with MDX**

SAP HANA provides support for the multidimensional expression language (MDX). MDX is a well-established query language that has been used by organizations and analysts for decades. It's a specific language designed to support data that is stored in OLAP cubes. Its unique qualities make it ideal for querying multidimensional models.

From a technology perspective, SAP HANA has incorporated the support of MDX directly within its platform. After a multidimensional model is activated in SAP HANA, users can query the model using the MDX language with tools that support the SAP HANA Object Linking and Embedding Database for OLAP (OLE DB for

OLAP) driver. Because MDX is a well-known query language, organizations will find it easy to adopt SAP HANA.

With SAP HANA, there is no need to load data into a cube. The multidimensional models of SAP HANA always access their data directly from columnar tables in a schema. This technical benefit can help with the overall load times associated with the solution. Data only needs to be replicated or batch loaded into SAP HANA columnar tables. After data is loaded into the tables, any of the associated models are usable. This benefit can reduce organizations' overall daily data processing times.

> **The SAP HANA OLE DB FOR OLAP, ODBC, and JDBC Drivers**
>
> For an application to access data in a given database, it needs to speak the language of that database. If we assume that each database has its own unique set of features and options, we must also assume that each database speaks its own language. However, if every database and application on the market today spoke its own language, it would be incredibly difficult for applications and database to communicate with each other. To solve this problem, many database and application venders adopted the use of standard drivers or application programing interfaces (API) to facilitate the communications between applications and databases. These drivers act as an interpreter, allowing supporting applications to communicate using a universal language.
>
> SAP HANA supports the Open Database Connectivity (ODBC), Java Database Connectivity (JDBC), and Object Linking and Embedding Database for OLAP connectivity (OLE DB for OLAP). Because SAP HANA supports these industry-standard drivers, application vendors and BI developers will find it easier to communicate with SAP HANA.

### Relational Analysis with SQL

SAP HANA provides support for SQL. SQL is also a well-established query language that has been used by organizations and analysts. SQL was designed to support access to data that is stored in an RDBMS. SQL has a standard structure that has been adopted by many RDBMS vendors. As a result, many analysts, developers, and DBAs have SQL coding experience. Knowledge from one vendor's RDBMS can be easily applied to another system. Because SAP HANA supports the use of SQL, organizations will find it easy to adopt SAP HANA. SAP HANA provides support for SQL using the industry standard ODBC or JDBC drivers.

> **Quick Tip: Using SQL to Access the SAP HANA Models**
>
> The multidimensional models in SAP HANA can be queried using SQL. In the _SYS_BIC schema, every active information view has one or more corresponding column views. These column views can be queried using standard SQL SELECT statements. Column views associated with OLAP-based analytic views can be queried using SQL, but each SQL statement must aggregate a measure column and must also contain a GROUP BY clause. This is a unique characteristic of SAP HANA in that OLAP-style sources can actually be queried using standard SQL statements.

### Integration with PAL, BFL, and R

SAP HANA has built-in Predictive Analysis Library (PAL) functions, Business Function Library (BFL) functions, and support for the open-source R statistical languages.

Because these languages and functions are directly integrated into the SAP HANA platform, there is no need to extract the data from SAP HANA to perform the desired analysis. While there are several vendors that support these libraries and functions, most of them require that the data be extracted from an RDBMS and placed into an application layer for processing. These processes can lead to several performance bottlenecks and also increase the complexity of the BI architecture. Because they are integrated directly into the SAP HANA platform, the data can be processed using the hardware and software benefits of SAP HANA. This will substantially increase the performance of such advanced calculations while allowing organizations to react quickly. In addition, the data will remain in the SAP HANA system during processing, reducing the footprint of the BI architecture required to support these types of calculations.

In subsequent chapters, we'll discuss this capability in more detail. For now, though, we'll only advise that this direct integration, coupled with the power of SAP HANA, can greatly benefit an organization based on the previously mentioned benefits.

### Aggregate Table Elimination

Due to the hardware and software benefits of the SAP HANA platform, large quantities of data can be processed without the need to create aggregate tables. When large quantities of data are stored in a traditional RDBMS, aggregate tables are often created to help reduce the overall impact that analytic queries tend to have on large tables and indexes. SAP HANA doesn't need to maintain aggregate tables to achieve faster query-response times. As a result, the overall data load and data storage footprint is reduced.

Aggregate tables also have the tendency to remove valuable attributes from the data. The process of aggregating results into smaller tables requires that detailed transactions or rows be substituted for summaries. In many cases, this process can reduce the effectiveness of the data being analyzed and lead to incorrect analysis. SAP HANA can provide organizations the full value of their data due to its overall architecture and design.

### Embedded Application Server

With the release of SAP HANA SPS5, there is now an embedded application server in the SAP HANA landscape. The *SAP HANA Extended Application Services* or *XS Engine* is an application and web server that is directly embedded into the SAP HANA platform. This application server allows you to directly embed applications into the SAP HANA platform. Because these services are embedded directly in the SAP HANA landscape, you can develop code that directly leverages the SAP HANA database without transferring data between the database and application tiers. This advantage enables you to define HTML5-based and JavaScript-based visualization applications that can directly leverage the information views, stored procedures, and columnar tables in the SAP HANA platform. Because the application code in the XS Engine is running on the same landscape as the SAP HANA appliance, you can push more work to the SAP HANA engines for processes.

In addition to these technical performance capabilities, you'll also find it beneficial that the development workbench for the XS Engine is directly embedded in SAP HANA Studio. This is advantageous because the full development lifecycle can be managed in a single tool. You can create the information views, stored procedures, HTML5, JavaScript code, and other dependent coding parts with a single tool. In addition, SAP HANA Studio SPS5 supports the use of a central code repository that facilitates standard lifecycle management, versioning, and the transportation of code between environments.

**Additional References**

A complete listing of the capabilities and features of the SAP HANA XS development platform is beyond the scope of this book. For more information on SAP HANA XS, visit *http://scn.sap.com/* and search for "SAP HANA Extended Application Services."

> You can find additional development information on the SAP HANA appliance software site at *http://help.sap.com/hana_appliance*.

## 6.3    Methods for Modeling Analytics in SAP HANA

Up to this point, this chapter has focused largely on the tools and options used to model analytics in SAP HANA. We'll now take a moment to examine the capabilities of SAP HANA modeling in the context of how data can be stored in the SAP HANA tables and fields. We'll discuss normalized and denormalized data, which are the two main types of data that can exist in SAP HANA. In addition, we'll discuss the effects that each format can have on the SAP HANA system.

With any RDBMS, there are specific database field and table design techniques that application developers use to eliminate data storage redundancy. These design techniques are also used to optimize the processes that application code uses to insert and update data in a database. This design technique is referred to as *database normalization,* and it's often incorporated into the data model design of databases used for OLTP. On the other hand, BI applications often work better when accessing data that has undergone a *denormalization* process. This denormalization process can be incorporated directly into the data model design of data warehouses or data marts, but it can also be accomplished on the fly using RDBMS stored procedures, scripts, or functions. At their core, both of these data modeling techniques are mutually exclusive concepts. Normalized data models work best with OLTP applications, whereas denormalized data is better suited for BI applications. With the SAP HANA appliance, either data model scenario can exist in its tables. Therefore, it's important that we discuss the challenges and benefits associated with both modeling techniques. Section 6.3 explores the issues associated with modeling normalized data in SAP HANA. We also differentiate the terms *data modeling* and *analytic modeling*. In conclusion, we discuss the specific solutions SAP HANA offers for managing normalized data.

### What Is Online Transaction Processing (OLTP)?

OLTP is often used to describe applications, systems, or databases that are used for transactional data input and retrieval. Most organizations use software applications to facilitate their daily operations by tracking occurrences or transactions. These transactions are then stored in a database for future reference. For example, a sales agent records all of the details of a telephone sales order into an ordering system. This data can later be retrieved by the shipping department to fulfill the order. The data can also be periodically updated with an order status that allows the customer to view the status over the Internet and receive email notifications until the order is shipped. With this in mind, the primary purposes of an OLTP application and database is to manage each transaction.

### 6.3.1 Modeling and the Challenges Associated with Normalized Data

In this section we define normalized and denormalized data. In addition, we discuss the difference between the logical denormalization and the physical denormalization of data. These terms and concepts are important for SAP HANA information view developers to understand because it relates to the capabilities and scalability of such solutions.

Database normalization is an issue inherent to data that is replicated into SAP HANA from an OLTP system in its native format. The SAP HANA platform, coupled with SAP Data Services, SLT, or Sybase replication services, has the capability of processing data in real time or near real time. When data is replicated into SAP HANA, without any further transformation, it will likely be replicated in its native normalized formats or in the format that the business application uses. In the preceding chapters of this book, we discussed in detail the role that SAP Data Services can play in not only replicating the data from one or more sources but also in transforming data from a normalized structure into a star schema (legacy relational OLAP model) or modified star schema denormalized structure (SAP HANA relational OLAP model) (see Chapter 2). While real-time replication isn't a topic of this book, it's important to understand the scenarios in which normalized data is replicated into SAP HANA. It's also important that we discuss the impact that normalized data can have on the SAP HANA platform.

While database normalization is an optimal field and table design technique for applications, it presents several challenges to BI solutions that focus on multidimensional modeling. Database normalization techniques typically encourage table and field design techniques that force individual attributes into their own table. For example, a customer table might contain the customer's first and last name, but the address, city, state, and country fields exist as only foreign key fields referencing other tables that contain the address, city, state, and country information. In other scenarios, a customer's attributes might be stored in a table where each attribute is represented by a separate record in the database. For example, the customer's contact information might exist in a customer contact table, where each phone number is stored as an individual row. In a fully denormalized structure, the same customer information will exist as a single row with each telephone number attribute stored as a column in the row. To query the normalized structure, you must join multiple tables and possibly pivot the contact information using complex scripts to eliminate future cardinality issues. In contrast, to query the denormalized structure, the query need only reference a single table. In general, there are five areas where normalized data can be challenging in a multidimensional model, as described below.

Keep in mind that normalized data must be denormalized before it can be presented to users in a physical or logical start schema. When you create multidimensional models in SAP HANA, you're effectively transforming data into a logical start schema. There are some instances where normalized data can be a challenge when devising a logical star schema or multidimensional model on the fly in SAP HANA.

▶ **Excessive joins**
Normalized data stores related attributes in multiple tables. When creating multidimensional models, these attributes often need to be combined together in a single attribute view to support hierarchies and to make the attributes more intuitive for users. The process of combining these attributes is often achieved using table joins. The table joining processes aren't very challenging unless the cardinality between the tables creates duplicate rows for each distinct attribute. These duplicate rows can create aggregation issues when joined to the analytic view Data Foundation table. Excessive joining can also lead to performance issues in the SAP HANA multidimensional models.

▶ **Data pivots**
Normalized data can often be stored so that each attribute is stored as a separate record. In contrast, a denormalized structure stores each attribute as a separate column. In an attribute view, this scenario creates cardinality issues and subsequent aggregation issues for the model. However, if the data is transformed from multiple rows into a single row with multiple columns, the issue can be eliminated. This type of transformation is often referred to as a data pivot. While the concept of pivoting data is easily understood, the coding required to achieve the transformation in an attribute view is very difficult. In terms of an SAP HANA attribute view, there aren't many options for solving this problem on the fly. Technically speaking, this type of transformation can be achieved in a stored procedure and subsequently incorporated into a calculation view. However, the

use of stored procedures in calculation views can lead to both performance and scalability issues.

▶ **Audit history**

In OLTP application databases, you'll often find situations where an application keeps track of transaction changes by recording each attribute change as a separate record. For example, a customer table might contain multiple records for the same customer, where each record represents a small change to a column in that record. This is a common technique used in applications where an audit trail is required for each data change. However, in its native format, this too can create a cardinality issue in an SAP HANA attribute view. To solve the problem, SAP HANA developers need to logically reduce the table to a single record for each unique attribute. In many cases, this can be solved with a simple filter. However, in other cases, there is insufficient information in the table to identify the correct record for the attribute view. In the more complex scenarios, this situation will have to be solved in a calculation view and stored procedure. However, the use of stored procedures in calculation views can lead to both performance and scalability issues.

▶ **Multiple sources**

Many organizations will have multiple systems for managing their daily operations. In some cases, these systems can overlap in terms of product, customer, or other types of attribute and analytical information. When replicating normalized data into an SAP HANA schema, from two or more sources, there are times when the data needs to be merged from each source to form a single comprehensive information view. While one could argue that this issue isn't directly the result of normalized data, developers will find it difficult to model data from multiple sources into a single comprehensive information view. This is especially true when the data is replicated in a normalized format. SAP HANA calculation views provide limited options for merging data and deduplicating attributes, but there are cases where stored procedures will again be required to properly merge and transform the data. However, the use of stored procedures in calculation views can lead to both performance and scalability issues.

▶ **Hierarchical data**

Hierarchical data is often stored in a normalized relational database table in a format that is problematic for reporting. For example, an employee table might contain a self-referential column for the employee's manager. This self-referential column will contain a reference to another record in the same table. In some situations, this self-referencing can lead to a complex matrix of parent-child relationships where parent records can have parent records themselves. As these parent-child relationships are formed, levels are also formed. Application designers prefer the normalized approach to storing hierarchical data because there are no limits to the number of levels that can be stored in the table. However, from a BI standpoint, developers often need to flatten this data into a single record to prevent cardinality issues and subsequent aggregation issues. SAP HANA attribute views contain options allowing this data to be represented in an attribute hierarchy. However, there are few options to flatten this data into columns in an attribute view. Stored procedures can be developed to flatten the data and then incorporated into a calculation view, but there are both performance and scalability issues associated with the use of stored procedures.

In the context of BI applications and RDBMS, two main methodologies for denormalizing normalized data into a star schema have arisen: logically or physically. In either case, BI developers need to logically or physically restructure normalized data into a star schema when creating multidimensional models.

The process of logically or physically modeling the structure of data to support multidimensional queries is referred to as data *denormalization*. Logically redesigning the structure implies that the process is accomplished using stored procedures, scripts, or views where the physical source structure is never permanently manifested into a persistent and reusable structure. Physical denormalization implies that the process is accomplished by extracting, transforming, and loading the data into a new set of well-defined permanent tables.

Physical denormalization is the processes that best describes traditional data modeling—the use of SAP Data Services and ETL-based loading of SAP HANA where well-defined dimension and fact tables are transformed in a star schema. With physical denormalization, the major workload is only executed once per batch ETL job. Subsequent queries to the physical denormalized tables result in little or no workload because the excessive joins and other complex transformations have already been completed and permanently stored in the table. In contrast, direct replication of data, followed by the use of SQL statements, information views, or stored procedures best describes the *logical denormalization* of data. Logical denormalization also implies that the denormalization work is repeated each time the information is queried from the model.

If we assume that logical denormalization results in complex and repetitive work, we must also assume that the work is executed at a higher overall CPU and memory cost in the SAP HANA landscape. In database terms, high-cost denormalization can affect the overall performance of the database or the individual execution time of any given query. Work is required each time the model is queried and is repeated each time the same model is queried. Add to this that multiple users can access these models at the same time, and the cost of logical denormalization can accrue exponentially. Also remember that your total SAP HANA license cost can increase when excessive amounts of RAM are required to manage all of the computations of logical denormalization. This is because the RAM used for computation is included in the cost of each SAP HANA license unit.

Logical denormalization isn't unique to SAP HANA. Since the invention of the relational database, organizations have struggled with this issue. Some organizations will use complex scripts and procedures to denormalize their data on the fly while others will choose to build physical denormalized tables in a data mart or warehouse. In most cases, the physical denormalization approach proves to be the most economical. This is largely based on the limitations of legacy relational databases. With SAP HANA, this might not be the case. Both physical and logical denormalization may prove to be viable because of the power of the SAP HANA platform. However, it's our opinion that physical denormalization is the most sustainable and scalable methodology for SAP HANA. This isn't necessarily based on the need to maximize the performance of the SAP HANA models. There are other issues that need to be considered as well. Data quality, master data management, the centralization of business rules, the need for advanced functions, the limitations of SAP HANA scripts, and data governance practices are all examples where physical denormalization using SAP Data Services provides advantages.

It's also wise to remember that SAP HANA can be used to manage data from any source, not just data from SAP applications. SAP has solutions such as SAP HANA Live that focus on real-time replication and logical denormalization. Because SAP HANA is powerful, this solution works well for SAP application data. However, not all source data is structured and managed like the data in an SAP application. Therefore, physical denormalization is often a better option for third-party data sources.

Normalized data can create many challenges when designing multidimensional models. In SAP HANA, there are two options for denormalizing data to facilitate multidimensional modeling. You can choose to logically denormalize the data using scripts, information views, and stored procedures. You can also leverage SAP Data Services to denormalize the data before it's physically stored in SAP HANA. In either case, careful consideration should be given to determine the best option to support the reporting and analytic needs of the organization.

### 6.3.2 Data Modeling versus Analytic Modeling

We just addressed the differences between logical denormalization and physical denormalization. To the same regard, there is also a difference between data modeling and analytic modeling. Although the SAP HANA modeling components are often referred to as data modeling tools, it's more appropriate to describe them as *analytic modeling* tools. Analytic modeling tools create logical views and semantics that presenting data in an intuitive format that facilitates analysis and reporting. In contrast, data modeling is a process where a new multidimensional optimized database schema is devised and subsequently loaded using ETL tools such as SAP Data Services. Because the data isn't physical moved into a new schema, the capabilities of the SAP HANA information views are best described as analytic modeling.

When discussing the capabilities of SAP HANA, it's important to understand the difference. There are three main reasons this distinction is important:

- **Performance**
  The performance of SAP HANA can be negatively affected if the solution relies predominantly on the analytic modeling and scripting capabilities of SAP HANA to transform the data. It's better to use SAP Data Services to transform the source data into a star schema that is optimal for multidimensional analysis. This simplifies the analytic modeling processes and increases the overall performance of the SAP HANA information views. Admittedly, the SAP HANA platform is incredibly efficient and powerful regardless of the state of the data. In many cases, this recommendation might only yield response times that are just a few seconds faster. With that said, if your goal is to maximize the performance of your queries, transforming your data into a physical star schema while loading data into SAP HANA will result in the best possible performance.

- **Manageability**
  It's very difficult to develop and subsequently manage stored procedures and scripts to achieve transformation. In addition, impact analysis, lineage, and business logic are very costly and difficult to manage when layers of code

are imbedded in the SAP HANA system. In contrast, SAP Data Services relies predominantly on graphical data flows and metadata to transform the data. Impact analysis and lineage are automatically generated with each data flow. In addition, relationships and dependencies between coding elements are easily visualized. Future versions of SAP HANA might include some of these same features, but at the moment, it doesn't contain any tools to help manage metadata.

▶ **Capabilities**
Developers need to be realistic about the capabilities of SAP HANA to manage the common and complex transformations that are needed when working with normalized data. SAP HANA's information views are limited to a basic set of native transformations. When complex transformations are needed, stored procedures are required. However, stored procedures aren't easily developed and maintained. In addition, stored procedures can lead to performance degradations. In contrast, SAP Data Services has a well-established set of transformations that were created to address the common needs associated with creating star schemas, data marts, data warehouses, and multidimensional models.

Being able to distinguish between the analytic model and data modeling is important when developing solutions based on the SAP HANA standalone appliance. SAP HANA offers several technological benefits that can easily disguise bad solution design. This might be acceptable for some organizations because the performance of the SAP HANA solution will likely be superior to solutions based on their legacy RDBMS. However, it's our opinion that a developer should always follow best practices when designing solutions on SAP HANA to maximize the organization's investment. If your source data requires significant transformation, it's wise to leverage SAP Data Services and an optimal data model for your solution. If your source data requires little or no transformation or real-time access to data, SAP HANA's information views will likely be able to manage and facilitate the multidimensional analytic modeling without consequence.

### 6.3.3 Solutions for Normalized Data in SAP HANA

While we've largely focused on the challenges associated with creating multidimensional models on normalized data, we now explore the areas where SAP HANA can natively transform normalized data. Table 6.18 outlines the main transformation options available in SAP HANA and provides a description of each option and the areas where they can be implemented.

| Option | Description | Implemented Within |
|---|---|---|
| Table joins | Joining tables in SAP HANA information views and stored procedures is a fundamental component of modeling. Assuming that there are no cardinality issues attributed to joining the tables, joining tables is an appropriate technique for managing normalized data in the SAP HANA information views. | ▸ Attribute view<br>▸ Analytic views<br>▸ Calculation views<br>▸ Stored procedures |
| Static filtering | Creating static filters is also a fundamental component of modeling. In situations where tables need to be filtered to denormalize the results, SAP HANA accommodates static filters in all information views and stored procedures. | ▸ Attribute view<br>▸ Analytic views<br>▸ Calculation views<br>▸ Stored procedures |
| Dynamic filtering | Dynamic filters are similar to static filters. However, dynamic filtering change based on input parameters. They are supported in analytic views and calculation views as variables. In stored procedures, input parameters can be created to provide dynamic filtering. | ▸ Analytic views<br>▸ Calculation views<br>▸ Stored procedures |
| Derived columns | Derived columns are instrumental in transforming columns in a table. They support type conversions, concatenations, string functions, date functions, and many other types of columnar transformations. | ▸ Attribute view<br>▸ Analytic views<br>▸ Calculation views<br>▸ Stored procedures |
| Aggregation | SAP HANA supports aggregations using the SUM, MIN, and MAX functions in analytic views. In addition to these, calculation views also support counters or count distinct aggregations. Stored procedures support the full array of aggregation functions as well. Aggregations aren't directly used to denormalize data, but they are the basis for measures in a multidimensional model. | ▸ Analytic views<br>▸ Calculation views<br>▸ Stored procedures |

**Table 6.18**  Options for Managing Normalized Data in the SAP HANA System

| Option | Description | Implemented Within |
|---|---|---|
| Union | The union function can be used to merge data sets into a single comprehensive set. There are several denormalization and calculation techniques that benefit from the union transformation. Calculation views and stored procedures support the use of a union function. | ▶ Calculation views<br>▶ Stored procedures |
| SQL functions | Generically speaking, functions are implemented in derived columns, calculation views, or stored procedures. Functions provide a variety of capabilities that are useful in transforming or denormalizing data. | ▶ Attribute view<br>▶ Analytic views<br>▶ Calculation views<br>▶ Stored procedures |
| Stored procedures | Stored procedures can be embedded directly into calculation views or executed directly from reporting tools. Stored procedures offer the most flexibility in managing normalized data, but they can also introduce performance and scalability penalties. | ▶ Calculation views |
| SQLScript | SQLScript code can be used in calculation views and stored procedures. SQLScript provides several options for managing normalized data. Assuming that the CE_ functions are used for the SQLScript, the performance will be exceptional. However, when mixed with SQL statements or recursive procedure logic, their performance will likely be degraded. | ▶ Calculation views<br>▶ Stored procedures |
| SQL statements | SQL statement code can be used in calculation views and stored procedures. It provides several options for managing normalized data. Compared to using SQLScript and CE_ functions, it generally results in slower performance. | ▶ Calculation views<br>▶ Stored procedures |

**Table 6.18** Options for Managing Normalized Data in the SAP HANA System (Cont.)

You should now have a better understanding of the components, methodologies, and techniques used in SAP HANA to produce analytic models. To gain further insight into these capabilities, let's review two case studies. The first case study guides you through the creation of a simple analytic view. The second case study guides you through a more complex scenario where a calculation view is required to produce the desired result.

## 6.4  Case Study 1: Modeling Sales Data to Produce Robust Analytics

The AdventureWorks Cycle Company has recently implemented a new BI platform based on SAP HANA, SAP Data Services, and SAP BusinessObjects. Using SAP Data Services, the company's BI resources were able to successfully extract, translate, and load the supporting Internet sales dimension and fact tables into an SAP HANA schema using a best practices approach.

Now that the required data is available, the Internet sales management team has requested access to this data. The sales management team's requirements were that the solution be simple and easy to use. In the past, the Internet sales team had to rely on multiple IT resources to compile data into reports and analytics. Given the capabilities of its SAP BusinessObjects Business Intelligence 4.0 platform, the team is requesting that IT develop a solution that grants the Internet sales manager access to the data without having to engage IT resources on a daily basis.

The BI team at AdventureWorks Cycle Company has determined that SAP Business-Objects Explorer and SAP BusinessObjects Analysis edition for Microsoft Office are the best end-user tools to accommodate the requirements. However, they must first develop an SAP HANA analytic view to support access to the requested data. The sales managers have requested the ability to analyze Internet sales transactions by customer, order date, and product.

Based on these requirements, let's walk through the processes of creating the attribute views and analytic views required to facilitate the requirements of the Internet sales managers.

## 6.4.1 Creating the Supporting Attribute Views

The first step is to produce four attribute views based on the SAP HANA tables listed in Table 6.19. These tables exist in the BOOK_USER schema in our example.

| Schemas and Tables |
|---|
| "BOOK_USER"."DIM_CUSTOMER" |
| "BOOK_USER"."DIM_PRODUCT" |
| "BOOK_USER"."DIM_DATE" |

**Table 6.19** Schemas and Tables Used in This Case Study

To design attribute views, you must first open SAP HANA Studio and configure an SAP HANA system.

### Defining an SAP HANA System

If your SAP HANA system is already defined, proceed to the next step. If not, perform these steps to configure a system in SAP HANA Studio.

1. Launch the SAP HANA Studio application.

2. Switch to the Modeler perspective. From the FILE menu bar, choose WINDOW • OPEN PERSPECTIVE • MODELER.

3. On the left side is the NAVIGATOR WINDOW. Right-click in the NAVIGATOR window, and choose ADD SYSTEM.

4. In the SYSTEM window, fill in the following fields, as shown in Figure 6.30:

   ▶ HOSTNAME: Enter the fully qualified domain name of the SAP HANA server.

   ▶ INSTANCE NUMBER: Enter the instance number of your SAP HANA system.

   ▶ DESCRIPTION: Enter a description as needed.

   ▶ LOCALE: Select your design-time language.

5. Click the NEXT button to proceed to the next step.

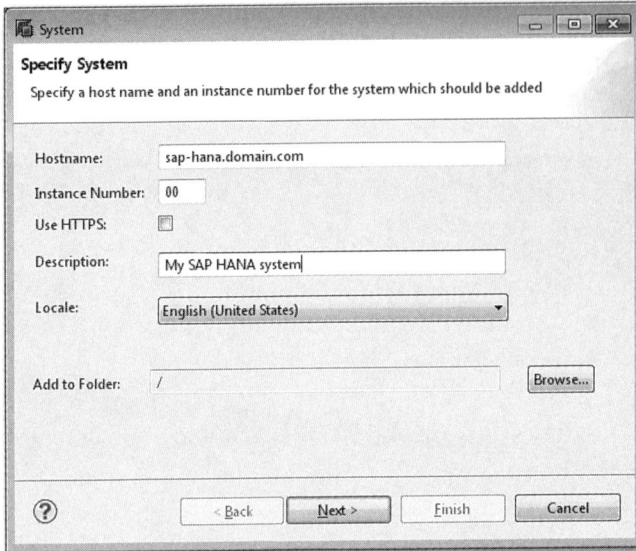

**Figure 6.30**  Configuring Properties in an SAP HANA System

6. In the CONNECTION PROPERTIES window, enter the database USER NAME and PASSWORD assigned by your SAP HANA administrator, as shown in Figure 6.31.

7. Click the FINISH button.

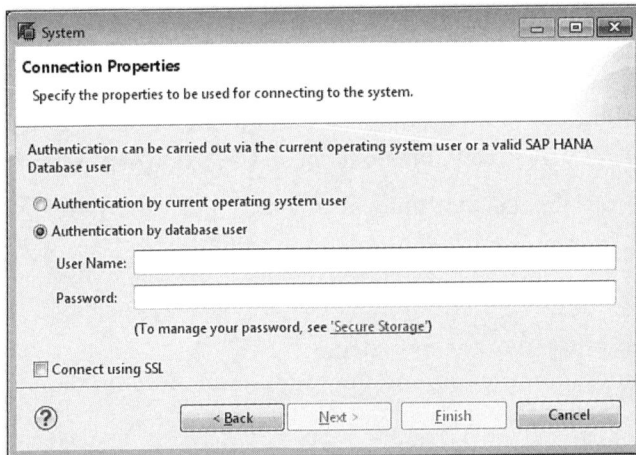

**Figure 6.31**  The Authentication Options When Defining a System Connection in SAP HANA Studio

Before you create an attribute view, you must create the root package ("saphana") and its subpackages ("commonattributes" and "internetsales") to store or common attributes and Internet sales modeling components.

### Creating the Root Package

Because AdventureWorks Cycle Company will develop multiple models over time, start by creating a root package ("saphana") and two subpackages to better organize the information views.

Follow these steps to create the root packages:

1. Using the Modeler perspective, expand the system listed in the NAVIGATOR window located on the left side by clicking the arrow next to the system name.

2. In the system hierarchy, expand the CONTENT node.

3. Right-click the CONTENT node, and choose NEW • PACKAGE.

4. In the NAME field, enter the package name "saphana".

5. In the DESCRIPTION field, enter a description of the package.

6. Specify the person responsible. This should be your SAP HANA database user account.

7. Choose the package's ORIGINAL LANGUAGE. This language should match the locale specified in the screen shown in Figure 6.30.

8. Click OK to save the package.

9. Right-click the SAPHANA package, and choose EDIT.

10. Change the STRUCTURAL option from NO to YES to prevent any modeling content from being creating directly in the root package.

### Creating the Subpackages

You now need to create two subpackages in the saphana root package. The subpackage "commonattributes" will store attributes that are reusable across multiple information views, and the subpackage "internetsales" will be used to store analytic views and calculation views pertaining to Internet sales. Follow these steps to create the two subpackages:

1. Right-click the SAPHANA root package, and select NEW • PACKAGE.

2. Enter the subpackage name "commonattributes". The subpackage name should be prefixed with "saphana." to indicate that it's a child of the saphana root package.

3. Enter the requested information for the remaining fields.

4. Right-click the SAPHANA root package, and select NEW • PACKAGE.

5. Enter the subpackage name "internetsales". The subpackage name should be prefixed with "saphana." to indicate that it's a child of the saphana root package.

**Creating Attribute Views**

Now that you've created the desired package hierarchy, you can begin the process of developing the attributes. To better organize and identify your attributes, adopt a standard attribute view naming convention in which standard attribute views are prefixed with ATBV_ and derived attribute views are prefixed with DATBV_.

*Defining the ATBV_BASE_DATE Attribute View*

Follow these steps to create the first attribute view:

1. Right-click the COMMONATTRIBUTES subpackage, and choose NEW • ATTRIBUTE VIEW.

2. Using Table 6.20 and Figure 6.32 as a reference, define the properties for the attribute view.

| Property | Value |
|---|---|
| NAME | ATBV_BASE_DATE |
| DESCRIPTION | The base date attribute view |
| PACKAGE | SAPHANA.COMMONATTRIBUTES |
| VIEW TYPE | ATTRIBUTE VIEW |
| COPY FROM | Unchecked |
| SUBTYPE | STANDARD |

**Table 6.20** Properties for the ATBV_BASE_DATE Attribute View

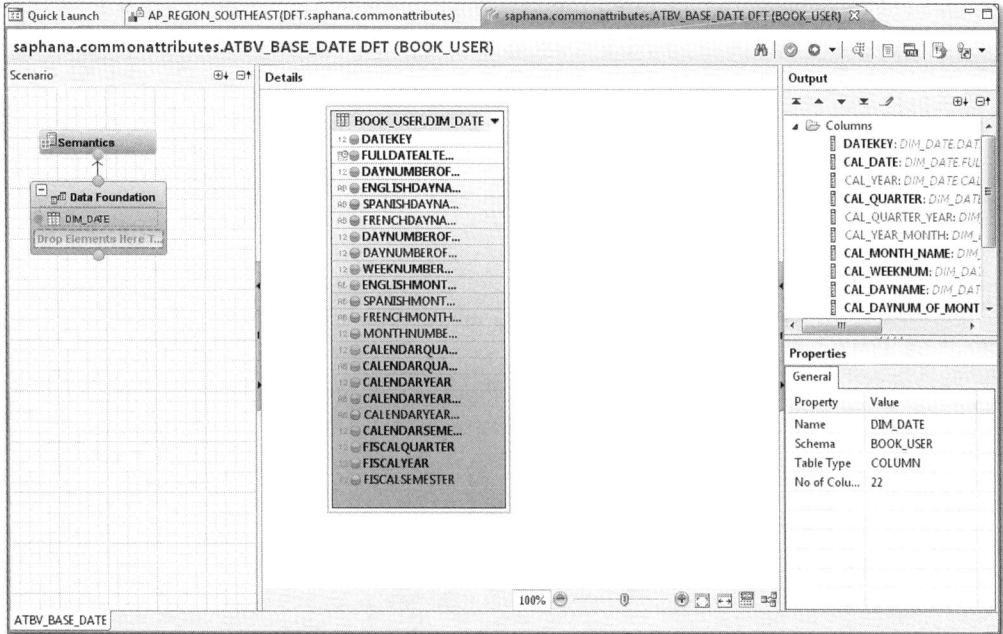

**Figure 6.32** The ATBV_BASE_DATE Attribute Design Window

3. Click the DATA FOUNDATION node located on the left side of the attribute view design window.

4. In the DETAILS pane, right-click the white space and choose ADD.

5. Using the provided search field, enter "DIM_DATE". Once found, click the DIM_DATE object listed in the MATCHING ITEMS window. Click OK to add the table to the DETAILS pane.

6. Highlight the columns, using Table 6.21 as reference. To select multiple columns, hold down the Ctrl key and click each column.

7. Right-click the highlighted columns, and choose ADD TO OUTPUT.

8. Using the OUTPUT pane on the far-right side of the attribute design window, click each column and update its name and label using the mapping values listed in Table 6.21. To update the attribute name and label, click each OUTPUT column. Using the PROPERTIES pane located below the OUTPUT pane, edit the NAME and LABEL fields.

| Database Column Name | Attribute Name | Attribute Label |
|---|---|---|
| DATEKEY | DATEKEY | CAL_DATE_KEY |
| FULLDATEALTERNATEKEY | CAL_DATE | CAL_DATE |
| CALENDARYEAR | CAL_YEAR | CAL_YEAR |
| CALENDARQUARTER | CAL_QUARTER | CAL_QUARTER |
| CALENDARQUARTERYEAR | CAL_QUARTER_YEAR | CAL_QUARTER_YEAR |
| CALENDARYEARMONTH | CAL_YEAR_MONTH | CAL_YEAR_MONTH |
| ENGLISHMONTHNAME | CAL_MONTH_NAME | CAL_MONTH_NAME |
| WEEKNUMBEROFYEAR | CAL_WEEKNUM | CAL_WEEKNUM |
| ENGLISHDAYNAMEOFWEEK | CAL_DAYNAME | CAL_DAYNAME |
| DAYNUMBEROFMONTH | CAL_DAYNUM_OF_MONTH | CAL_DAYNUM_OF_MONTH |
| DAYNUMBEROFWEEK | DAYNUMBEROFWEEK | CAL_DAY_OF_WEEK |
| FISCALQUARTER | FISCAL_QTR | FISCAL_QTR |
| FISCALYEAR | FISCAL_YEAR | FISCAL_YEAR |

**Table 6.21** Column Mappings for ATBV_BASE_DATE

9. On the left side of the attribute design window, click the SEMANTICS node located in the SCENARIO pane.

10. In the COLUMN pane, locate the CAL_YEAR, CAL_QUARTER_YEAR, and CAL_YEAR_MONTH columns. In the HIDDEN properties column, check the box to hide each column. We'll design a separate attribute view for these columns at a later time.

11. In the COLUMN pane, click the DATE_KEY column. Using the TYPE column on the far left, set the DATE_KEY to the type KEY ATTRIBUTE.

12. When complete, save and activate the attribute view by clicking the SAVE AND ACTIVATE button on the top-right side toolbar as shown in Figure 6.33.

In the toolbar, locate the green icon containing a right-pointing arrow. Each icon in the toolbar produces hover text when you place your mouse pointer over the icon. You can use this hover text to also identify the SAVE AND ACTIVATE icon.

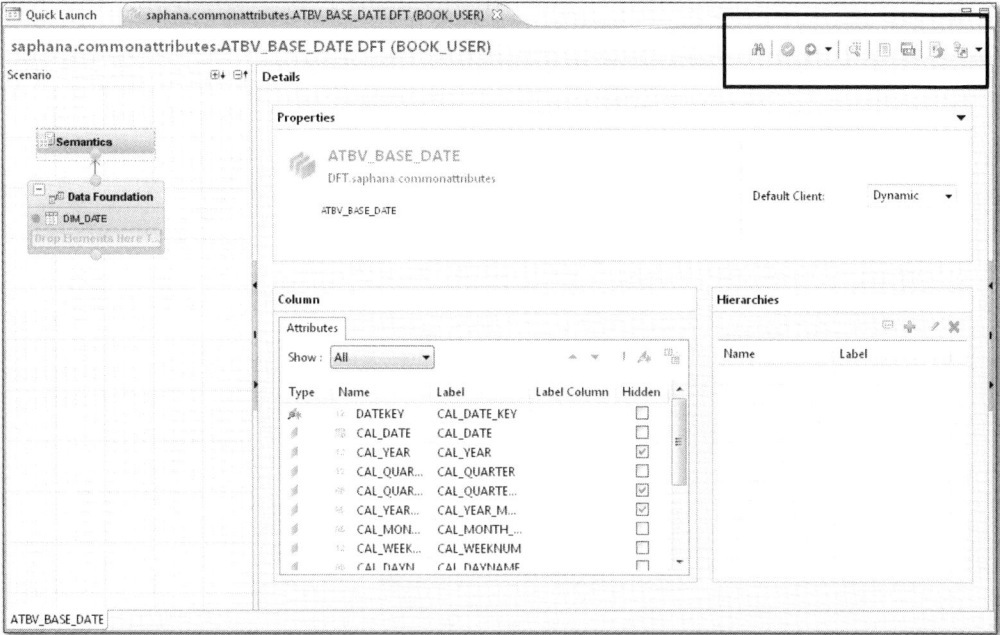

**Figure 6.33** The Location of the Save and Activate, Save and Validate, and Save and Activate All Icons

### Defining the ATBV_PRODUCT Attribute View

Follow these steps to create this attribute view:

1. Right-click the COMMONATTRIBUTES subpackage, and choose NEW • ATTRIBUTE VIEW.

2. Using Table 6.22 as a reference, define the properties for the attribute view.

| Property | Value |
|---|---|
| NAME | ATBV_PRODUCT |
| DESCRIPTION | The products attribute view |
| PACKAGE | SAPHANA.COMMONATTRIBUTES |
| VIEW TYPE | ATTRIBUTE VIEW |
| COPY FROM | Unchecked |
| SUBTYPE | STANDARD |

**Table 6.22** Properties for the ATBV_PRODUCT Attribute View

3. Click the DATA FOUNDATION node on the left side of attribute view design window.

4. In the DETAILS pane, right-click the white space, and choose ADD.

5. Using the provided search field, search for the tables listed in Table 6.23. Once found, add each table to the MATCHING ITEMS pane. Click OK to add the tables to the DETAILS pane.

| Tables Used in the Attribute View |
| --- |
| DIM_PRODUCT_CATEGORY |
| DIM_PRODUCT_SUBCATEGORY |
| DIM_PRODUCT |

**Table 6.23**  Tables Used in the ATBV_PRODUCT Attribute View

6. In the DETAILS pane, join the three tables using the information listed in Table 6.24, which contains two distinct join configurations. To create each join, right-click the white space in the DETAILS pane and choose CREATE JOIN. Once completed, the DETAILS pane should appear similar to the example in Figure 6.34. As an alternative, you can also join the tables graphically using the drag-and-drop method.

| Join | Property | Option |
| --- | --- | --- |
| JOIN 1 | Left Table | DIM_PRODUCT_SUBCATEGORY |
| | Left Column | PRODUCTSUBCATEGORYKEY |
| | Right Table | DIM_PRODUCT |
| | Right Column | PRODUCTSUBCATEGORYKEY |
| | Join Cardinality | (1:N) |
| | Join Type | Referential |
| JOIN 2 | Left Table | DIM_PRODUCT_CATEGORY |
| | Left Column | PRODUCTCATEGORYKEY |
| | Right Table | DIM_PRODUCT_SUBCATEGORY |
| | Left Column | PRODUCTCATEGORYKEY |
| | Join Cardinality | (1:N) |
| | Join Type | Referential |

**Table 6.24**  Join Conditions for the ATBV_PRODUCT Attribute View

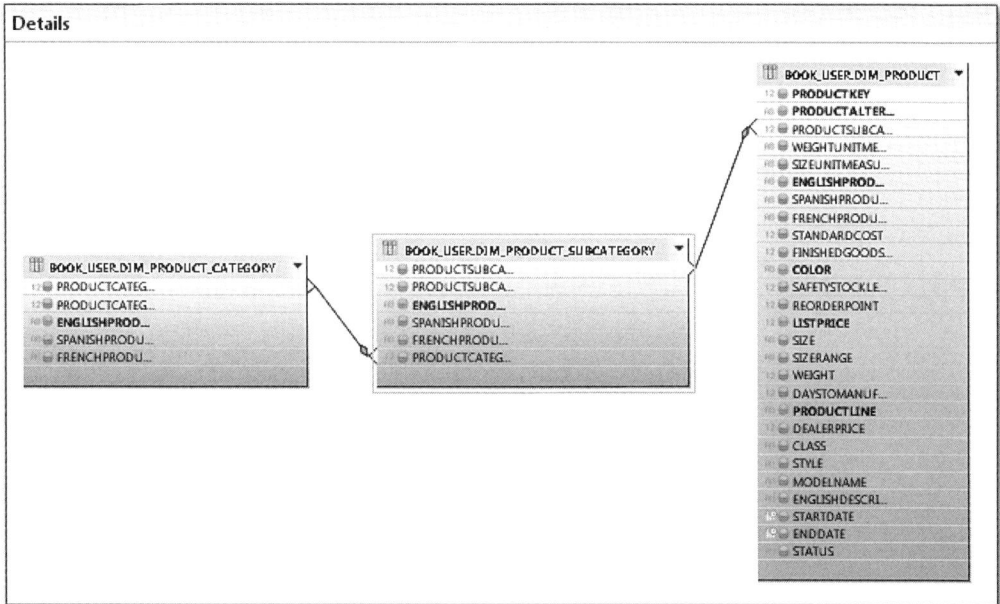

**Figure 6.34** Example Join Diagram for the ATBV_PRODUCT Attribute View

7. Highlight the columns, using Table 6.25 as reference. To select multiple columns, hold down the `Ctrl` key and click each column.

8. Right-click the highlighted columns, and choose ADD TO OUTPUT.

9. Using the OUTPUT pane on the right side of the attribute design window, click each column and update its name and label using the mapping values listed in Table 6.25. To update the attribute name and label, click each output column. Using the PROPERTIES pane located below the OUTPUT pane, edit the NAME and LABEL fields.

10. Create a calculated column for the product line attribute. Right-click the CALCULATED COLUMN node in the OUTPUT pane. Choose NEW.

11. In the data, the product line field is sometime `NULL`. You need to create a calculated measure to convert the `NULL` vales into a static alpha value X.

    Define the PRODUCT_LINE calculated column using the options listed in Figure 6.35 using the formula: `if(isnull("PRODUCTLINE"),'X',"PRODUCTLINE")`.

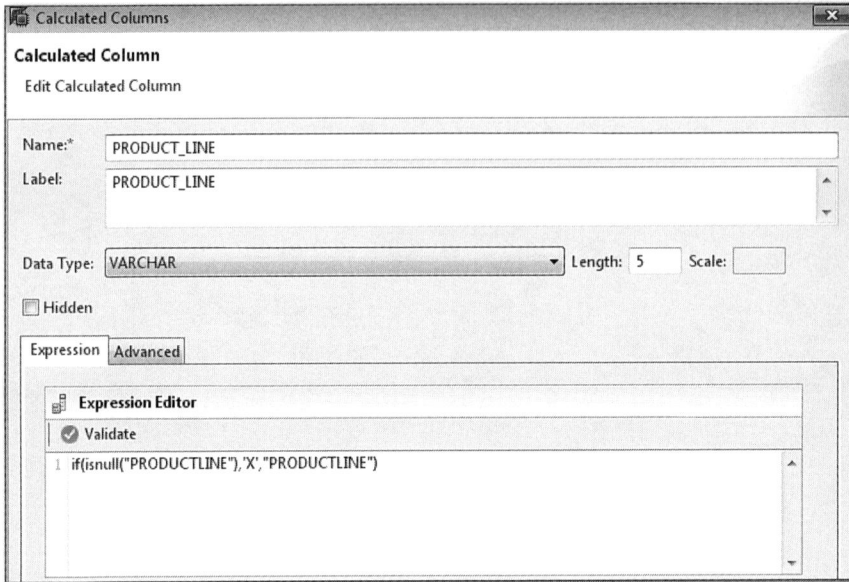

**Figure 6.35** The PRODUCT_LINE Calculated Column

| Column Name | Attribute Name | Attribute Label |
|---|---|---|
| DIM_PRODUCT.PRODUCTKEY | PRODUCT_KEY | PRODUCT_KEY |
| DIM_PRODUCT.PRODUCTALTERNATEKEY | PRODUCTAL TERNATEKEY | PRODUCT_ALTKEY |
| DIM_PRODUCT.ENGLISHPRODUCTNAME | PRODUCT_NAME | PRODUCT_NAME |
| DIM_PRODUCT.COLOR | PRODUCT_COLOR | PRODUCT_COLOR |
| DIM_PRODUCT.LISTPRICE | PRODUCT_LISTPRICE | PRODUCT_LISTPRICE |
| DIM_PRODUCT.PRODUCTLINE | PRODUCTLINE | PRODUCTLINE |
| DIM_PRODUCT_SUBCATEGORY.ENGLISHPRODUCTSUBCATEGORYNAME | PRODUCT_SUBCATEGORY | PRODUCT_SUBCATEGORY |
| DIM_PRODUCT_CATEGORY.ENGLISHPRODUCTCATEGORYNAME | PRODUCT_CATEGORY | PRODUCT_CATEGORY |

**Table 6.25** Column Mappings for ATBV_PRODUCT

12. On the left side of the attribute design window, click the SEMANTICS node located in the SCENARIO pane.

13. In the COLUMN pane, locate the PRODUCT_LINE column. In the HIDDEN properties column, check the box to hide the column.

14. In the COLUMN pane, click the PRODUCT_KEY column. Using the TYPE column, set the PRODUCT_KEY to the type KEY ATTRIBUTE.

15. In the HIERARCHY pane, select the green plus sign to create a products hierarchy. Define the hierarchy using the options listed in Figure 6.36.

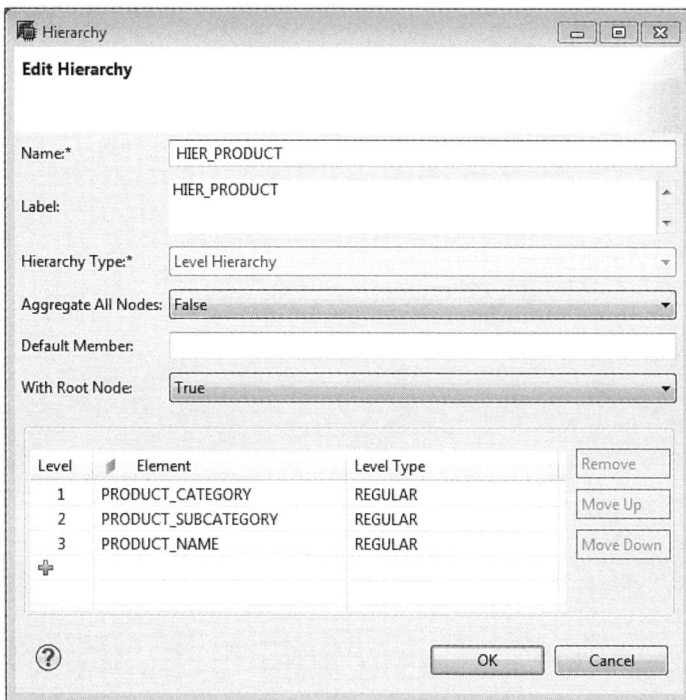

**Figure 6.36**  The Product Hierarchy in the ATBV_PRODUCT Attribute View

16. Define the properties for the product hierarchy. When defining each level of the hierarchy, use the green plus sign to add each level.

17. When complete, save and activate the attribute view by clicking the SAVE AND ACTIVATE button in the toolbar.

### Defining the ATBV_ORDERED_DATE_HIER Attribute View

Next we'll outline the steps for creating this attribute view. This attribute view will be used to define the specific elements required for the ordered date hierarchy. While we could have used the ATBV_BASE_DATE attribute view to manage this hierarchy, in subsequent steps, we use the ATBV_BASE_DATE attribute view as the basis for creating a derived attribute. In our testing, we've found that hierarchies in a derived attribute aren't compatible in some of the SAP BusinessObjects tools. As a result, we've decided to develop dedicated ordered data attribute views to manage each date hierarchy. To do so, follow these steps:

1. Right-click the COMMONATTRIBUTES subpackage, and choose NEW • ATTRIBUTE VIEW.

2. Using Table 6.26 as a reference, define the properties for the attribute view.

| Property | Value |
|---|---|
| NAME | ATBV_ORDERED_DATE_HIER |
| DESCRIPTION | The Ordered Date Hierarchy |
| PACKAGE | SAPHANA.COMMONATTRIBUTES |
| VIEW TYPE | ATTRIBUTE VIEW |
| COPY FROM | Unchecked |
| SUBTYPE | STANDARD |

**Table 6.26**  Properties for the ATBV_ORDERED_DATE_HIER Attribute View

3. Using Table 6.27 as a guide, develop the attribute view.

| Column Name | Attribute Name | Attribute Label |
|---|---|---|
| DIM_DATE.DATEKEY | ORDERED_DATEKEY | ORDERED_DATEKEY |
| DIM_DATE.CALENDARYEAR | ORDERED_YEAR | ORDERED_YEAR |
| DIM_DATE.CALENDARYEARMONTH | ORDERED_YEAR_MONTH | ORDERED_YEAR_MONTH |

**Table 6.27**  Column Mappings for ATBV_ORDERED_DATE_HIER

| Column Name | Attribute Name | Attribute Label |
|---|---|---|
| DIM_DATE. CALENDARQUARTERYEAR | ORDERED_YEAR_ QUARTER | ORDERED_YEAR_ QUARTER |
| DIM_DATE. CALENDARYEARWEEK | ORDERED_YEAR_WEEK | ORDERED_YEAR_WEEK |

**Table 6.27**  Column Mappings for ATBV_ORDERED_DATE_HIER (Cont.)

4. In the SEMANTICS node, configure the ORDERED_DATEKEY as a HIDDEN column.

5. In the COLUMN pane, click the ORDERED_DATEKEY column. Using the TYPE column on the far left, set the ORDERED_DATEKEY to the type KEY ATTRIBUTE.

6. Using Figure 6.37 as a guide, develop the ORDERED_DATE_HIER hierarchy.

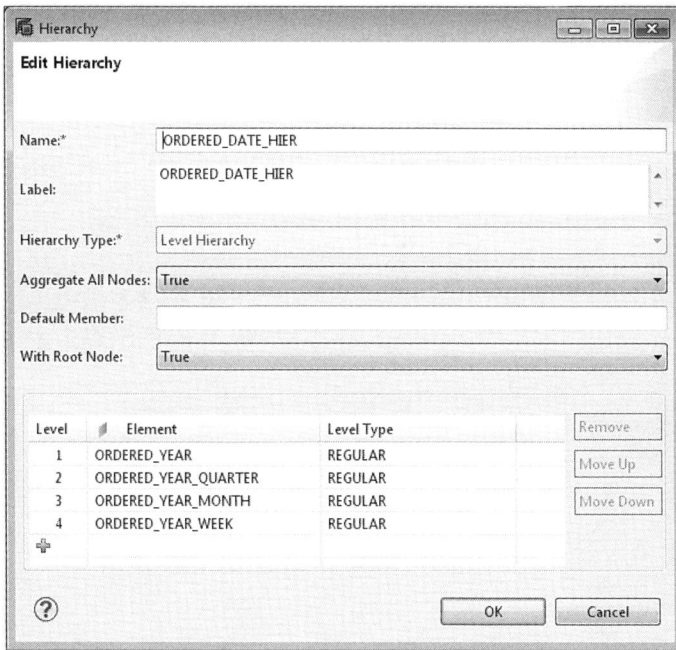

**Figure 6.37**  The Ordered Date Hierarchy in the ATBV_ORDERED_DATE_HIER Attribute View

7. When complete, save and activate the attribute view by clicking the SAVE AND ACTIVATE button on the toolbar.

### Defining the ATBV_CUSTOMER Attribute View

Follow these steps to create this attribute view:

1. Right-click the COMMONATTRIBUTES subpackage, and choose NEW • ATTRIBUTE VIEW.

2. Using Table 6.28 as a reference, define the properties for the attribute view.

| Property | Value |
|---|---|
| NAME | ATBV_CUSTOMER |
| DESCRIPTION | The products attribute view |
| PACKAGE | SAPHANA.COMMONATTRIBUTES |
| VIEW TYPE | ATTRIBUTE VIEW |
| COPY FROM | unchecked |
| SUBTYPE | STANDARD |

**Table 6.28**  Properties for the ATBV_CUSTOMER Attribute View

3. Click the DATA FOUNDATION node on the left side of the attribute view design window.

4. In the DETAILS pane, right-click the white space, and choose ADD.

5. Using the provided SEARCH field, search for the tables listed in Table 6.29. Once found, add each table to the MATCHING ITEMS pane. Click OK to add the tables to the DETAILS pane.

| Tables Used in the Attribute View |
|---|
| DIM_CUSTOMER |
| DIM_SALES_TERRITORY |
| DIM_GEOGRAPHY |

**Table 6.29**  Tables Used in the ATBV_PRODUCT Attribute View

6. In the DETAILS pane, join the three tables using the information listed in Table 6.30, which contains two distinct join configurations. To create each join, right-click the white space in the DETAILS pane, and choose CREATE JOIN.

| Join | Property | Option |
|------|----------|--------|
| JOIN 1 | Left Table | DIM_GEOGRAPHY |
| | Left Column | GEOGRAPHYKEY |
| | Right Table | DIM_CUSTOMER |
| | Right Column | GEOGRAPHYKEY |
| | Join Cardinality | (1:N) |
| | Join Type | Referential |
| JOIN 2 | Left Table | DIM_SALES_TERRITORY |
| | Left Column | SALESTERRITORYKEY |
| | Right Table | DIM_GEOGRAPHY |
| | Left Column | SALESTERRITORYKEY |
| | Join Cardinality | (1:N) |
| | Join Type | Referential |

**Table 6.30**  Join Conditions for the ATBV_CUSTOMER Attribute View

7. Using Table 6.31 as a guide, develop the attribute view.

| Column Name | Attribute Name | Attribute Label |
|-------------|----------------|-----------------|
| DIM_CUSTOMER. ADDRESSLINE1 | CUSTOMER_ADDRESSLINE1 | CUSTOMER_ADDRESSLINE1 |
| DIM_CUSTOMER. ADDRESSLINE2 | CUSTOMER_ADDRESSLINE2 | CUSTOMER_ADDRESSLINE2 |
| DIM_CUSTOMER. BIRTHDATE | CUSTOMER_BIRTHDATE | CUSTOMER_BIRTHDATE |
| DIM_CUSTOMER. COMMUTEDISTANCE | CUSTOMER_ COMMUTEDISTANCE | CUSTOMER_ COMMUTEDISTANCE |
| DIM_CUSTOMER. CUSTOMERALTERNATEKEY | CUSTOMERALTERNATEKEY | CUSTOMERALTERNATEKEY |

**Table 6.31**  Column Mappings for ATBV_CUSTOMER

| Column Name | Attribute Name | Attribute Label |
|---|---|---|
| DIM_CUSTOMER. CUSTOMERKEY | CUSTOMER_KEY | CUSTOMER_KEY |
| DIM_CUSTOMER. DATEFIRSTPURCHASE | CUSTOMER_ DATEFIRSTPURCHASE | CUSTOMER_ DATEFIRSTPURCHASE |
| DIM_CUSTOMER. EMAILADDRESS | CUSTOMER_EMAILADDRESS | CUSTOMER_EMAILADDRESS |
| DIM_CUSTOMER. ENGLISHEDUCATION | CUSTOMER_EDUCATION | CUSTOMER_EDUCATION |
| DIM_CUSTOMER. FIRSTNAME | CUSTOMER_FIRSTNAME | CUSTOMER_FIRSTNAME |
| DIM_CUSTOMER.GENDER | CUSTOMER_GENDER | CUSTOMER_GENDER |
| DIM_CUSTOMER. HOUSEOWNERFLAG | CUSTOMER_ HOUSEOWNERFLAG | CUSTOMER_ HOUSEOWNERFLAG |
| DIM_CUSTOMER. LASTNAME | CUSTOMER_LASTNAME | CUSTOMER_LASTNAME |
| DIM_CUSTOMER. MARITALSTATUS | CUSTOMER_ MARITALSTATUS | CUSTOMER_ MARITALSTATUS |
| DIM_CUSTOMER. MIDDLENAME | CUSTOMER_MIDDLENAME | CUSTOMER_MIDDLENAME |
| DIM_CUSTOMER. NAMESTYLE | NAMESTYLE | NAMESTYLE |
| DIM_CUSTOMER. NUMBERCARSOWNED | CUSTOMER_ NUMBERCARSOWNED | CUSTOMER_ NUMBERCARSOWNED |
| DIM_CUSTOMER. NUMBERCHILDRENATHOME | CUSTOMER_NUMCHILD_ AT_HOME | CUSTOMER_NUMCHILD_ AT_HOME |
| DIM_CUSTOMER.PHONE | CUSTOMER_PHONE | CUSTOMER_PHONE |
| DIM_CUSTOMER.TITLE | CUSTOMER_TITLE | CUSTOMER_TITLE |
| DIM_CUSTOMER. TOTALCHILDREN | CUSTOMER_ TOTALCHILDREN | CUSTOMER_ TOTALCHILDREN |

**Table 6.31** Column Mappings for ATBV_CUSTOMER (Cont.)

| Column Name | Attribute Name | Attribute Label |
|---|---|---|
| DIM_CUSTOMER. YEARLYINCOME | CUSTOMER_ YEARLYINCOME | CUSTOMER_ YEARLYINCOME |
| DIM_GEOGRAPHY. | CUSTOMER_COUNTRY | CUSTOMER_COUNTRY |
| DIM_GEOGRAPHY.CITY | CUSTOMER_CITY | CUSTOMER_CITY |
| DIM_GEOGRAPHY. POSTALCODE | CUSTOMER_POSTALCODE | CUSTOMER_POSTALCODE |
| DIM_GEOGRAPHY. STATEPROVINCECODE | CUSTOMER_STATECODE | CUSTOMER_STATECODE |
| DIM_GEOGRAPHY. STATEPROVINCENAME | CUSTOMER_STATENAME | CUSTOMER_STATENAME |
| DIM_SALES_TERRITORY. SALESTERRITORYCOUNTRY | CUSTOMER_ SALESTERRITORYCOUNTRY | CUSTOMER_ SALESTERRITORYCOUNTRY |
| DIM_SALES_TERRITORY. SALESTERRITORYGROUP | CUSTOMER_ SALESTERRITORYGROUP | CUSTOMER_ SALESTERRITORYGROUP |
| DIM_SALES_TERRITORY. SALESTERRITORYREGION | CUSTOMER_ SALESTERRITORYREGION | CUSTOMER_ SALESTERRITORYREGION |

**Table 6.31** Column Mappings for ATBV_CUSTOMER (Cont.)

8. In the SEMANTICS node, configure the NAMESTYLE as a HIDDEN column.

9. In the COLUMN pane, click the CUSTOMER_KEY column. Using the TYPE column on the far left, and set the CUSTOMER_KEY to the type KEY ATTRIBUTE.

10. Define the CUSTOMERF_FULL_NAME calculated column as a `varchar(250)` type using this formula:

   ```
   "CUSTOMER_LASTNAME" + ', ' + "CUSTOMER_FIRSTNAME" + ' ' + "CUSTOMER_
   MIDDLENAME"
   ```

11. Define the properties for the customer location hierarchy using Figure 6.38 as a reference.

433

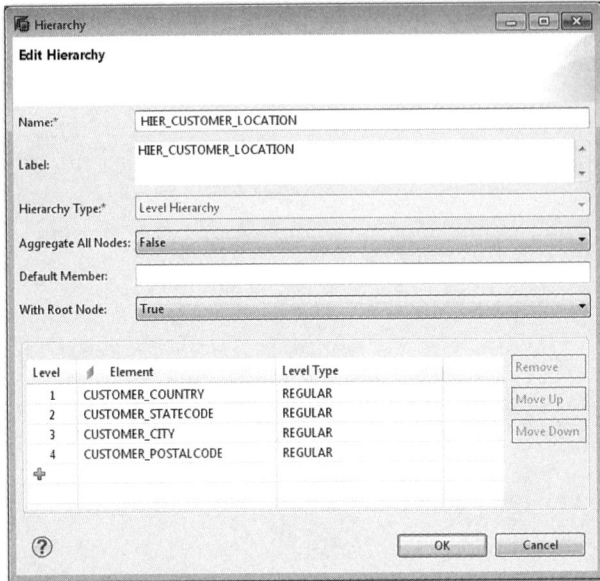

**Figure 6.38** The Customer Location Hierarchy

12. Define the properties for the product hierarchy using Figure 6.39 as a reference.

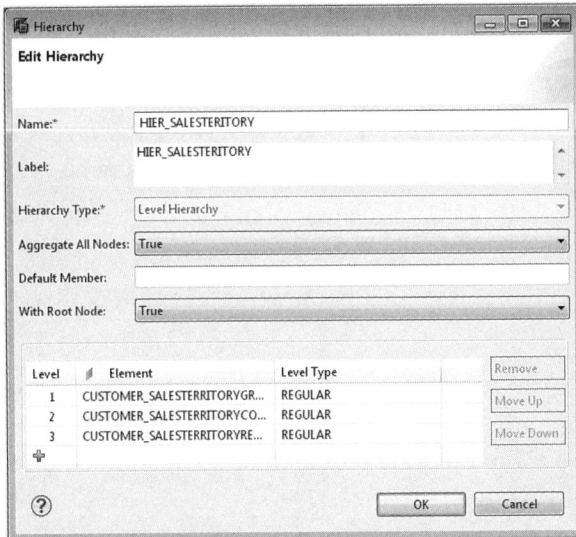

**Figure 6.39** The Customer Sales Territory Hierarchy

13. When complete, save and activate the attribute view by clicking the SAVE AND ACTIVATE button on the toolbar.

### *Creating the Derived Attribute View DATBV_ORDERED_DATE*

This section outlines the steps required to create a derived attribute view based on the ATBV_BASE_DATE attribute view.

1. Right-click the COMMONATTRIBUTES subpackage, and choose NEW • ATTRIBUTE VIEW.

2. Using Table 6.32 as a reference, define the properties for the attribute view. When complete, click OK.

| Property | Value |
|---|---|
| NAME | DATBV_ORDERED_DATE |
| DESCRIPTION | The derived ordered date attribute |
| PACKAGE | SAPHANA.COMMONATTRIBUTES |
| VIEW TYPE | ATTRIBUTE VIEW |
| COPY FROM | Unchecked |
| SUBTYPE | DERIVED |
| DERIVED FROM | Select the BROWSE button and search for saphana.commonattributes.ATBV_BASE_DATE |

**Table 6.32** Properties for the DATBV_ORDERED_DATE Derived Attribute View

3. No additional changes are required. With the derived attribute design window open, save and activate the derived attribute view by clicking the SAVE AND ACTIVATE button on the toolbar.

## 6.4.2 Creating Analytic Views

Now that you've developed and activated the required attribute views, you can now begin the process of designing an analytic view. In the analytic view, you'll define the foundation table, join the foundation to attributes, and define measures to facilitate the aggregation of the results.

## Designing the Data Foundation

Follow these steps to create an analytic view and define the DATA FOUNDATION node:

1. Right-click the INTERNETSALES subpackage, and choose NEW • ANALYTIC VIEW.

2. Using Table 6.33 as a reference, define the properties for the attribute view.

| Property | Value |
|---|---|
| NAME | AV_INTERNETSALES |
| DESCRIPTION | The Internet Sales Analytic View |
| PACKAGE | SAPHANA.COMMONATTRIBUTES |
| VIEW TYPE | ANALYTIC VIEW |
| COPY FROM | Unchecked |
| SUBTYPE | N/A |

**Table 6.33**  Properties for the ATBV_BASE_DATE Attribute View

3. Click the DATA FOUNDATION node located on the left side of analytic view design window, as shown in Figure 6.40.

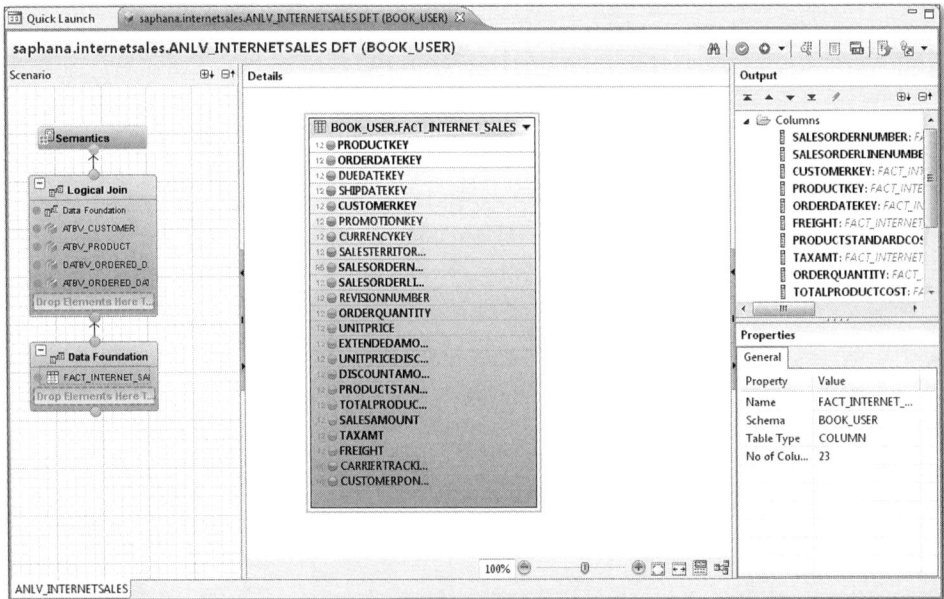

**Figure 6.40**  An Example Analytic View Design Window

4. In the DETAILS pane, right-click the white space, and choose ADD.

5. Using the provided SEARCH field, enter "FACT_INTERNET_SALES". Once found, click the FACT_INTERNET_SALES object listed in the MATCHING ITEMS pane. Click OK to add the table to the DETAILS pane.

6. Highlight the columns using Table 6.34 as reference. To select multiple columns, hold down the `Ctrl` key, and click each column.

7. Right-click the highlighted columns, and choose ADD TO OUTPUT.

| Column Name |
| --- |
| FACT_INTERNET_SALES.SALESORDERNUMBER |
| FACT_INTERNET_SALES.SALESORDERLINENUMBER |
| FACT_INTERNET_SALES.CUSTOMERKEY |
| FACT_INTERNET_SALES.PRODUCTKEY |
| FACT_INTERNET_SALES.ORDERDATEKEY |
| FACT_INTERNET_SALES.FREIGHT |
| FACT_INTERNET_SALES.PRODUCTSTANDARDCOST |
| FACT_INTERNET_SALES.TAXAMT |
| FACT_INTERNET_SALES.ORDERQUANTITY |
| FACT_INTERNET_SALES.TOTALPRODUCTCOST |
| FACT_INTERNET_SALES.EXTENDEDAMOUNT |
| FACT_INTERNET_SALES.UNITPRICEDISCOUNTPCT |
| FACT_INTERNET_SALES.DISCOUNTAMOUNT |
| FACT_INTERNET_SALES.SALESAMOUNT |
| FACT_INTERNET_SALES.UNITPRICE |

**Table 6.34**  The Internet Sales Data Foundation Columns

### Designing the Logic Joins

Follow these steps to define the logical joins between an analytic view and existing attribute views:

1. Click the LOGIC JOIN node located on the left side of analytic view design window.

2. In the DETAILS pane, right-click the white space, and choose ADD.

3. Using the provided SEARCH box, search for the following attribute views:
   ▶ ATBV_CUSTOMER
   ▶ ATBV_PRODUCT
   ▶ ATBV_ORDERED_DATE_HIER
   ▶ DATBV_ORDERED_DATE

   Click OK to add each attribute view to the LOGICAL JOIN pane.

4. Join each attribute view to the DATA FOUNDATION table by right-clicking the white space in the DETAILS pane and selecting CREATE JOIN.

5. Using Figure 6.41 as a reference, create the join between the DATA FOUNDATION table and the ATBV_CUSTOMER attribute view.

**Figure 6.41** The Join between the Data Foundation Table and the Customer Attribute View

6. Using Figure 6.42 as a reference, create the join between the DATA FOUNDATION table and the ATBV_PRODUCT attribute view.

**Figure 6.42**   The Join between the Data Foundation Table and the Product Attribute View

7. Using Figure 6.43 as a reference, create the join between the DATA FOUNDATION table and the ATBV_ORDERED_DATE_HIER attribute view.

**Figure 6.43**   The Join between the Data Foundation Table and the Ordered Date Hierarchy Attribute View

8. Using Figure 6.44 as a reference, create the join between the DATA FOUNDATION table and the DATBV_ORDERED_DATE derived attribute view.

**Figure 6.44** The Join between the Data Foundation Table and the Ordered Date Derived Attribute View

9. Update the alias name for the columns in the derived attribute view ordered date. Because a derived attribute acts as an alias of an existing attribute view, it's recommended that each of the columns in a referenced derived attribute view be aliased as well.

10. In the LOGICAL JOIN node, locate the OUTPUT pane on the right side. Expand the ATTRIBUTE VIEW • DATBV_ORDERED_DATE node.

11. Click each column in this node, and locate the PROPERTIES pane.

12. In the PROPERTIES pane, locate the ALIAS NAME and ALIAS LABEL fields. Using Table 6.35 as a reference, update both alias fields with the same value.

| Attribute View Column Name | Alias |
| --- | --- |
| DATEKEY | ORDERED_DATE_KEY |
| FULLDATEALTERNATEKEY | ORDERED_DATETIME |
| CALENDARYEAR | |
| CALENDARQUARTER | ORDERED_CAL_QTR |
| CALENDARQUARTERYEAR | |
| CALENDARYEARMONTH | |

**Table 6.35** The Alias Name and Alias Label Cross Reference Table

| Attribute View Column Name | Alias |
|---|---|
| ENGLISHMONTHNAME | ORDERED_CAL_MONTH |
| WEEKNUMBEROFYEAR | ORDERED_CAL_WEEKNUM |
| ENGLISHDAYNAMEOFWEEK | ORDERED_CAL_DAYNAME |
| DAYNUMBEROFMONTH | ORDERED_CAL_DOM |
| DAYNUMBEROFWEEK | ORDERED_CAL_DOM |
| FISCALQUARTER | ORDERED_FISCAL_QTR |
| FISCALYEAR | ORDERED_FISCAL_YEAR |

**Table 6.35** The Alias Name and Alias Label Cross Reference Table (Cont.)

Note that for CALENDARQUARTERYEAR and CALENDARYEARMONTH, the columns don't need an alias because they are hidden.

**Designing the Semantic**

In the SEMANTICS node we'll finalize the configuration of the analytic view by defining attributes and measures. We'll also hide columns.

1. Click the SEMANTICS node located on the left side of analytic view design window. Figure 6.45 contains an example of the window you should now see.

2. Locate the COLUMNS pane located just below the DETAILS pane.

3. Click the LOCAL tab in the COLUMN pane.

4. Configure the SALES ORDER NUMBER and SALES ORDER LINE NUMBER output columns as attributes. Using the [Ctrl] key, highlight both columns. In the COLUMNS pane, locate the ATTRIBUTE icon located on the right side header. Click the icon to convert the highlighted columns into attributes.

5. Configure the remaining columns as measures. Using the [Ctrl] key, highlight the remaining columns. In the COLUMNS pane, locate the MEASURE ICON located on the right side header. Click the icon to convert the highlighted columns into measures.

6. Click the SHARED tab in the COLUMN pane. This pane allows you to manage the columns returned from the connected attribute views.

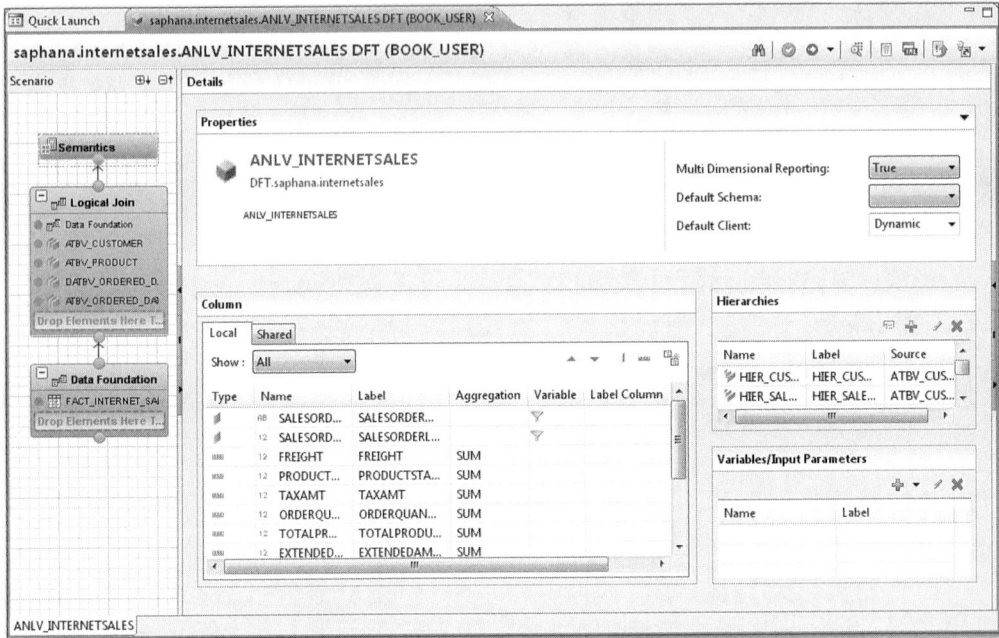

**Figure 6.45** Semantics Node Window

7. Locate the NAMESTYLE, PRODUCTLINE, CAL YEAR, CAL QUARTER YEAR, and CAL YEAR MONTH columns. To the right of each column locate the HIDDEN column. Place a checkmark in the provided box to hide these columns.

8. When complete, save and activate the analytic view by clicking the SAVE AND ACTIVATE button on the toolbar.

9. Preview the analytic view using the DATA PREVIEW (small magnifying glass image overlooking a table) icon located to the right of the SAVE AND ACTIVATE icon.

The analytic view and attribute views are now ready for consumption by the SAP BusinessObjects tools. In subsequent chapters, we'll examine how each SAP BusinessObjects tool connects; the analytic view will be the main connection point to the Internet sales data in SAP HANA. Users will be able to use this information view to analyze their Internet sales transactions by product, customer, and ordered date.

Let's consider another case study that better explains why you need calculation views to facilitate multidimensional analysis. In the next case study, we'll walk you through both the requirements and the solution for solving a common query issue using a calculation view.

## 6.5    Case Study 2: Building Complex Calculations for Executive-Level Analysis

The Internet sales managers at AdventureWorks Cycle Company have been using the self-services BI solution powered by SAP HANA, SAP Data Services, and SAP BusinessObjects Explorer 4.0 for a few weeks. They have found it to be a perfect self-service solution for analyzing their Internet sales transactions without waiting on IT developers to create reports.

AdventureWorks Cycle Company sells directly to customers via its website and directly to resellers or local bike shops. In their technical landscape, they use two different applications to manage these sales transactions: one system is hosted in the cloud and used to manage Internet sales, and the other system is based on a legacy ordering application that is hosted in the main office data center. The CEO needs to see the reseller sales transactions in the SAP HANA multidimensional models as well as the Internet sales. He also has a requirement to view both sources in a single comprehensive model. Having the transactions aggregated and combined into a single model will enable the CEO to analyze sales for the entire company.

The BI team at AdventureWorks Cycle Company has determined that they can incorporate the reseller sales information into their existing Internet sales SAP HANA landscape. Using SAP Data Services, they will add a new reseller sales fact table and update the existing dimension tables to include the relevant information for both Internet sales and reseller sales. In SAP HANA, they will build new attribute views, analytic views, and analytic privileges to support new analytic models. To directly address the requirements for the CEO, they will create a calculation view that intuitively combines the measures from the Internet sales analytic view and the reseller sales analytic view.

Based on these requirements, let's walk through the processes of creating the calculation view to support the requirements of the CEO. We'll assume that the reseller sales analytic view and supporting attribute views have already been created by IT. This case study will focus predominantly on the processes for creating the calculation view that combines both the Internet sales and reseller sales data.

### 6.5.1    Creating the Package

As with any information view, calculation views must also be stored in a package. We've decided to store the CEO's calculation view in a common package named "corporatemetrics." This package will be used to store any future information views that manage information across different business lines. This decision is purely subjective, meaning that there are no technical requirements for organizing information views this way. The IT department has simply decided that this will be the best way to organize the information views.

Follow these steps to create the package:

1. Launch the SAP HANA Studio application.

2. Switch to the Modeler perspective. From the FILE menu bar, choose WINDOW • OPEN PERSPECTIVE • MODELER.

3. Right-click the SAPHANA package, and choose NEW • PACKAGE.

4. Using Figure 6.46 as a guide, enter the name "corporatemetrics" following the "SAPHANA" package name. This creates a subpackage in the existing package.

5. Using Figure 6.46 as a guide, enter the remaining information. If your user account isn't BOOK_USER, choose the appropriate account as the owner of the package.

6. Click OK to save the package.

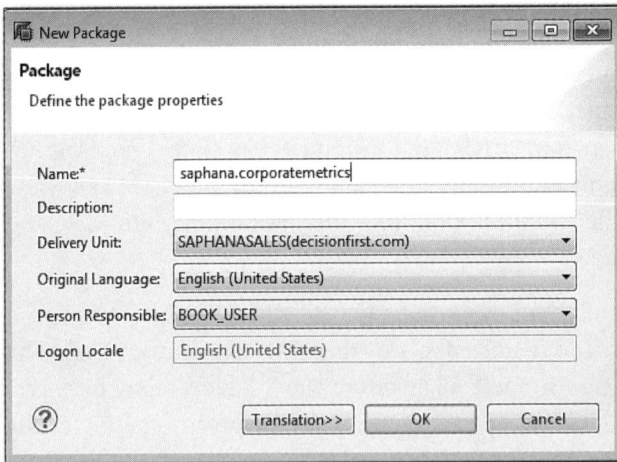

**Figure 6.46** Creating the "corporatemetrics" Package

## 6.5.2   Creating the Calculation View

Now let's create the calculation view. Because the process of combining the Internet sales and reseller sales is very basic, a graphical calculation view is sufficient to produce the desired results.

Follow these steps:

1. Launch the SAP HANA Studio application.

2. Switch to the Modeler perspective. From the FILE menu bar, choose WINDOW • OPEN PERSPECTIVE • MODELER.

3. Right-click the SAPHANA.CORPORATEMETRICS package, and choose NEW • CALCULATION VIEW.

4. Using Figure 6.47 as a guide, enter the calculation view name of "cv_corporate_product_sales". You're creating a new calculation view using the graphical view type.

5. Click FINISH because you'll define the remaining parts of the calculation view manually.

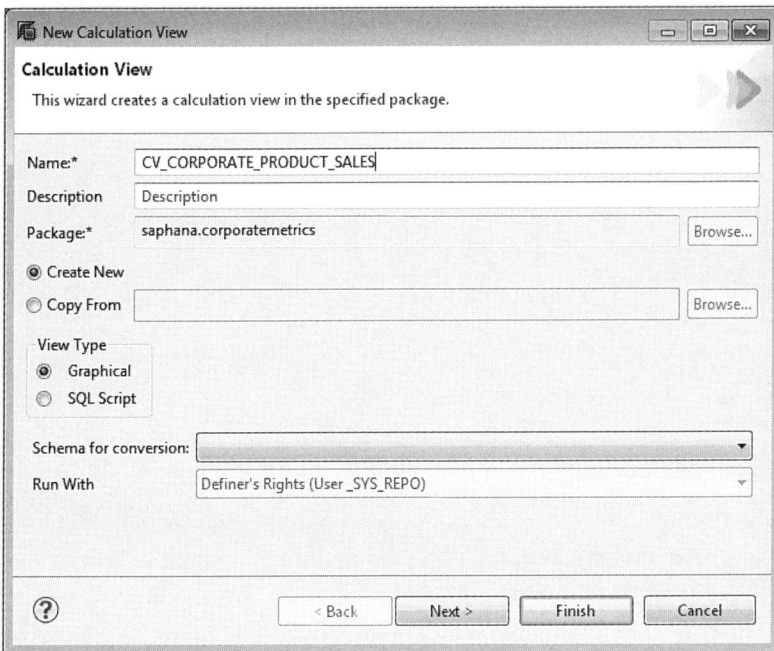

**Figure 6.47**   Creating the Calculation View

### Elements of the Calculation View Design Window

After clicking the FINISH button, you now see a blank calculation view design window like the one shown in Figure 6.48.

There are three main areas to focus on when designing a calculation view.

▶ **Tools Palette pane (far left)**
This pane is used when designing the graphical elements of the calculation view.

▶ **Details pane (center)**
This pane contains the details of any object that is highlighted in the TOOLS PALETTE pane.

▶ **Output columns (far right)**
This area is associated with any object that is highlighted in the TOOLS PALETTE pane.

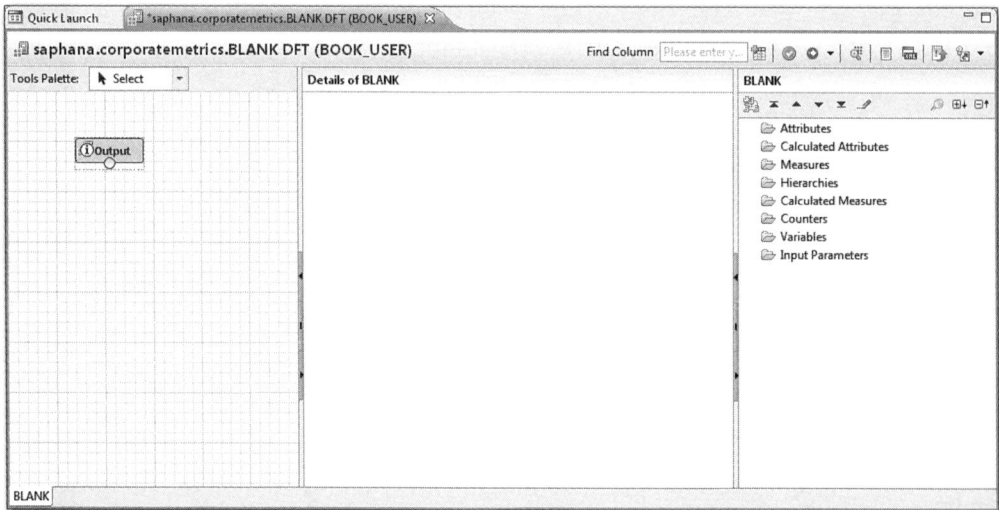

**Figure 6.48** An Undefined or Blank Calculation View

### Defining the Calculation View

We'll now walk through the processes of defining a graphical calculation view. At this point, you should have completed the case study in Section 6.4 and have imported the AdventureWorks sample content discussed in the appendix. The "resellersales" analytic view is assumed to already exist at this point.

### Adding the "internetsales" and "resellersales" Analytic Views

Starting with your bank calculation view design window, add the "internetsales" and "resellersales" views to the TOOLS PALETTE pane by following these steps:

1. In the SAP HANA Modeler perspective, expand the NAVIGATOR window on the far left side of Figure 6.49. Expand both the INTERNETSALES and RESELLERSALES packages to expose the ANLV_INTERNETSALES and ANLV_RESELLERSALES analytic views.

2. Drag and drop the ANLV_INTERNETSALES and ANLV_RESELLERSALES analytic views from the NAVIGATOR window to the TOOLS PALETTE pane.

   As shown in Figure 6.49, you now have two analytic views located below the OUTPUT transform in the TOOLS PALETTE pane.

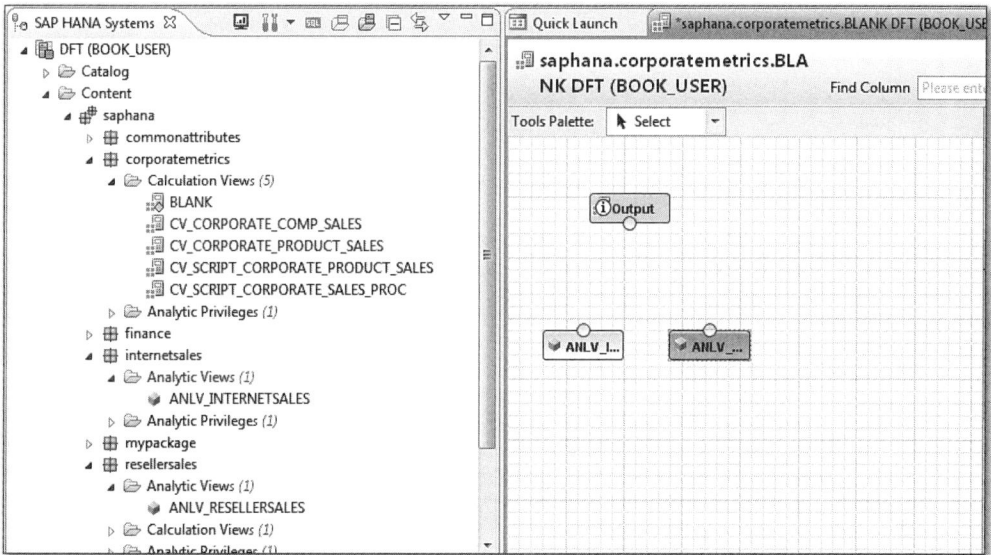

**Figure 6.49**  Adding the Existing Analytic View to the Calculation View Tools Palette

### Projecting the Analytic Views

Using the TOOLS PALETTE dropdown list, you'll add two projection transformations to the calculation view workflow. You'll then join each analytic view to its own project transform and select common columns from each analytic view. Follow these steps:

1. Select the PROJECTION transformation from the TOOLS PALETTE dropdown list shown in Figure 6.50. This will add the PROJECTION transformation to the TOOLS PALETTE pane.

2. Drag the first projection transform and drop it just above the ANLV_INTER-NETSALES analytic view. Use drag-and-drop techniques to join the analytic view to the projection transformation by joining the dot on the top of the analytic view to the dot located on the bottom of the projection transform, as shown in Figure 6.50.

3. As in the previous step, drag the second projection transform and drop it just above the ANLV_RESELLERSALES analytic view.

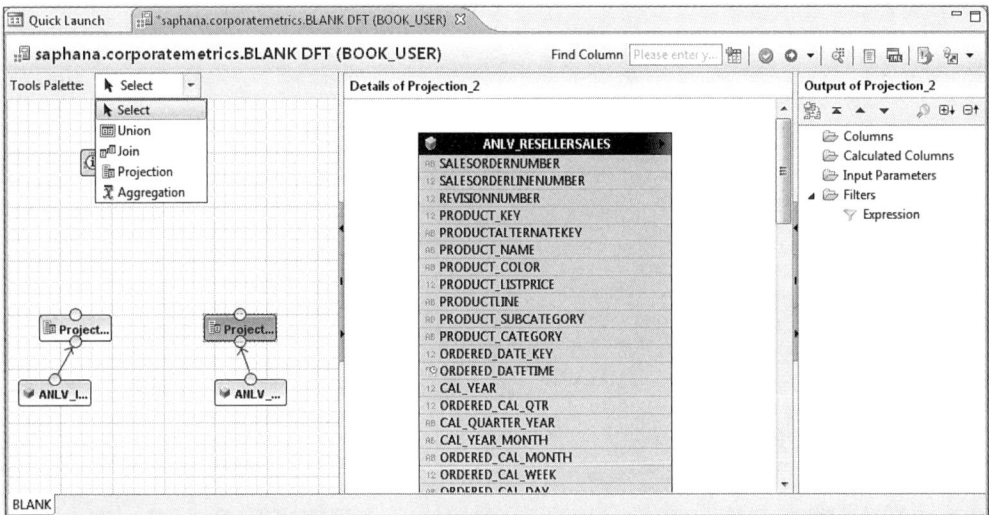

**Figure 6.50** Adding the Projection Transform to the Tools Palette

4. Highlight the projection transformation located above the ANLV_INTERNET-SALES analytic view.

5. Right-click the PROJECTION transformation, and choose RENAME. Rename the projection to "PRJ_INTERNETSALES".

6. Using the DETAILS pane, as shown in the middle of Figure 6.50, right-click the columns listed in Table 6.36, and choose ADD TO OUTPUT

| Column Name |
| --- |
| PRODUCT_CATEGORY |
| PRODUCT_SUBCATEGORY |
| PRODUCT_NAME |
| ORDERED_YEAR |
| ORDERED_YEAR_MONTH |
| SALESAMOUNT |
| ORDEREDQUANTITY |

**Table 6.36** Columns to Add to the Projection PRJ_INTERNETSALES

7. Using Figure 6.51 as a guide, create a calculated column by right-clicking the CALCULATED COLUMN folder in the OUTPUT pane, and choosing NEW.

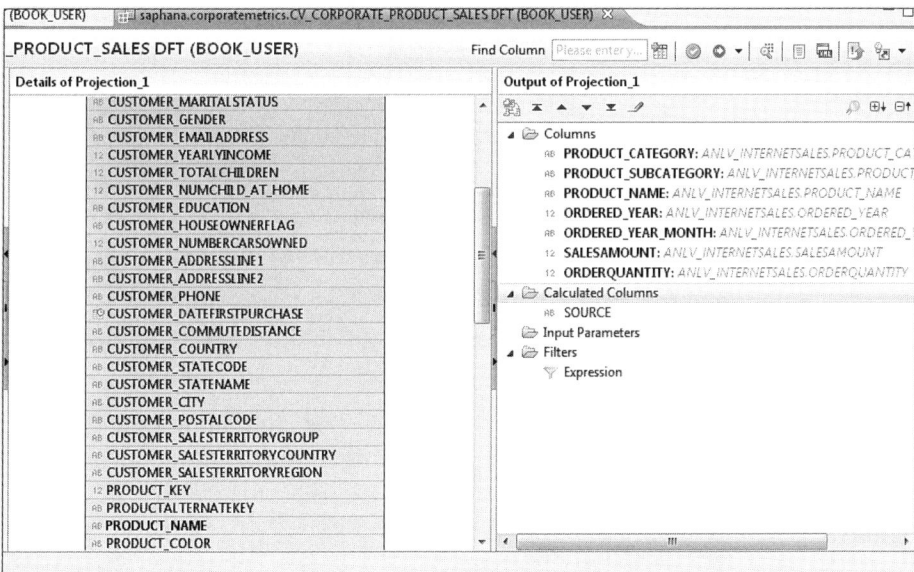

**Figure 6.51** Creating a Calculated Column

8. Using Figure 6.52 as a guide, create a calculated column named SOURCE. This column will be used in the final model to identify the source of the data. The formula is a string literal. Enter "INTERNET" surrounded by single quotes, as shown in the EXPRESSION EDITOR area of the screen.

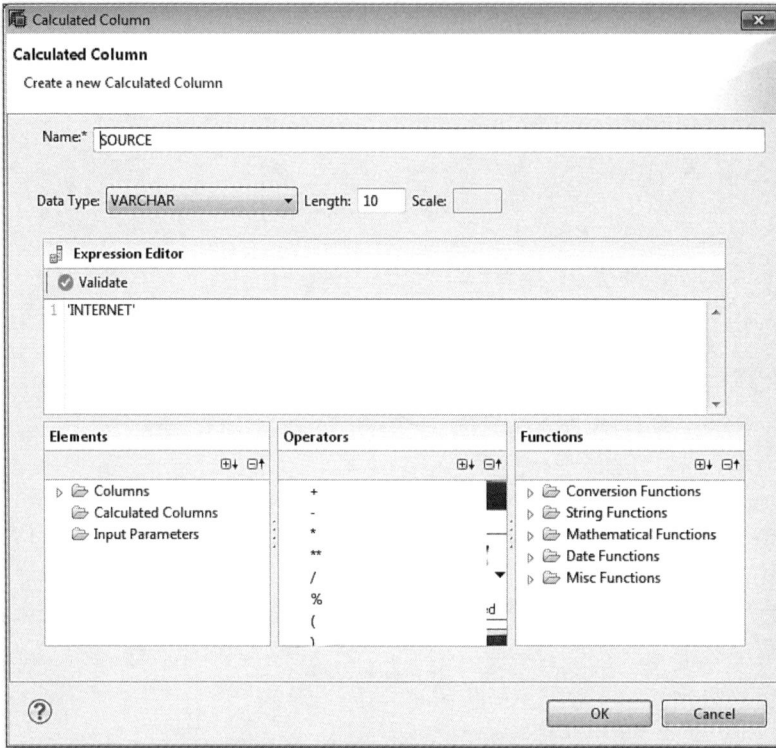

**Figure 6.52** Defining the Calculated Column SOURCE

9. Highlight the projection transformation located above the ANLV_RESELLER-SALES analytic view.

10. Right-click the projection transformation, and choose RENAME. Rename the projection to "PRJ_RESELLERSALES".

11. Using the DETAILS pane, right-click the columns listed in Table 6.37, and choose ADD TO OUTPUT.

| Column Name |
| --- |
| PRODUCT_CATEGORY |
| PRODUCT_SUBCATEGORY |
| PRODUCT_NAME |
| ORDERED_YEAR |

**Table 6.37** Columns to Add to the Projection PRJ_RESELLERSALES

| Column Name |
| --- |
| ORDERED_YEAR_MONTH |
| SALESAMOUNT |
| ORDEREDQUANTITY |

**Table 6.37**  Columns to Add to the Projection PRJ_RESELLERSALES (Cont.)

12. To create a calculated column, right-click the CALCULATED COLUMN folder, located in the OUTPUT pane, and choose NEW.

13. Using Figure 6.53 as a guide, create a calculated column named SOURCE. This column will be used in the final model to identify the source of the data. The formula used in the EXPRESSION EDITOR is a string literal. Enter "RESELLER" surrounded by single quotes.

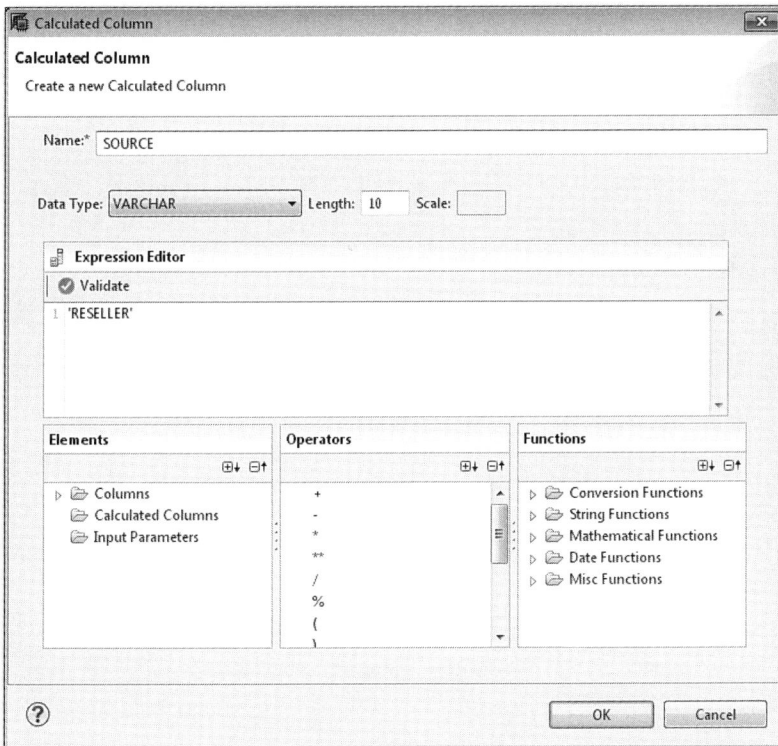

**Figure 6.53**  Defining the Calculated Column SOURCE

### Combining the Results with a Union

Now that you've selected or projected the appropriate columns from each analytic view, you must combine their results into a single logical data set using a union transformation. Follow these steps:

1. Using Figure 6.54 as a guide, select the UNION transformation from the TOOLS PALETTE dropdown list.

2. Place the UNION transformation above the PRJ_INTERNETSALES and PRJ_RESELLERSALES projections.

3. Using the drag-and-drop method, join PRJ_INTERNETSALES and PRJ_RESELLERSALES to the UNION transformation.

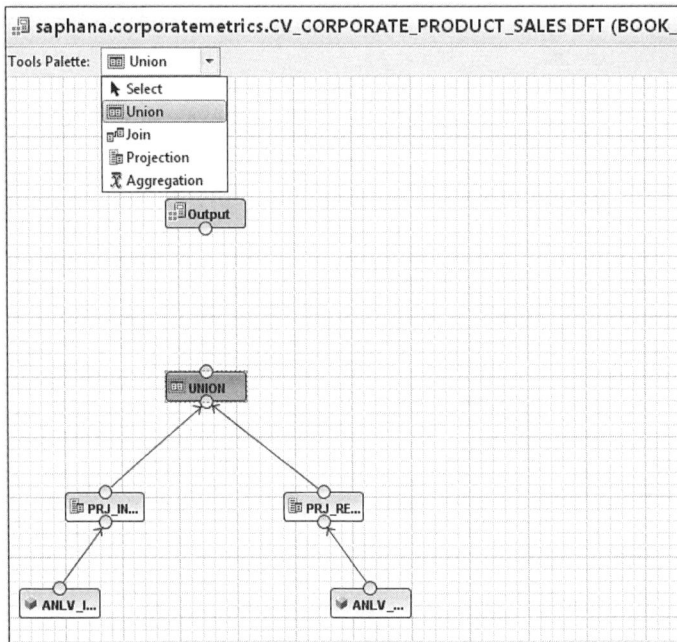

**Figure 6.54** Adding the UNION Transformation to the Tools Palette

4. After the objects are joined, highlight the UNION transform named UNION_3, right-click, and choose RENAME. Change the name to UNION.

5. With the UNION object highlighted, notice that the DETAILS pane contains two SOURCE items on the left side. On the right side of Figure 6.55, there is a TARGET(S) pane where you'll map the columns from each source.

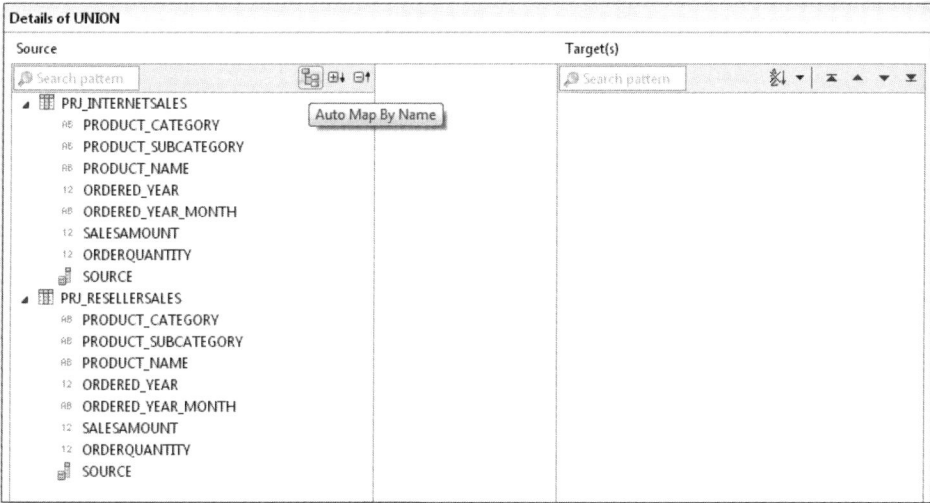

**Figure 6.55** The Source and Target Panes

6. There are two options for mapping the columns.

   ▸ You can manually drag and drop the columns from the PRJ_INTERNETSALES source and place them in the TARGET(S) pane. Then, using drag and drop again, you can map the same column from PRJ_RESELLERSALES to its equivalent output column in the TARGET(S) pane. Make sure to drop the source column over the existing TARGET(S) column to properly complete the mapping. A line appears depicting a connection between each merged column.

   ▸ You can allow the union design window to guess based on the column names from each source. Locate the AUTO MAP BY NAME icon located on the top right side of the source pane search box. This will generate an output similar to what is depicted in Figure 6.56.

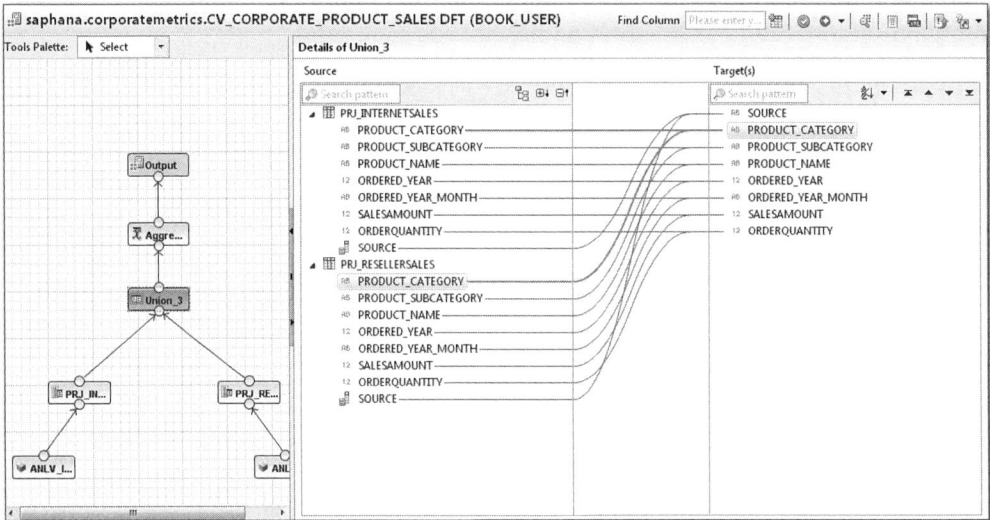

**Figure 6.56**  Mapping the Targets in the Union Transformation

### Aggregating the Results of the Union

Now that you've combined the projections of each analytic view, you need to aggregate the results on the UNION to produce a summary of sales by product and ordered year. The aggregation will effectively make the results appear as though they were produced from a single source. Follow these steps:

1. Using Figure 6.57 as a guide, select the AGGREGATION transformation from the TOOLS PALETTE dropdown list.

2. Place the AGGREGATION transformation above the UNION transformation, and then join the AGGREGATION to the UNION transformation using the drag-and-drop method.

3. After the objects are joined, highlight the AGGREGATION transform, named AGGREGATION_4, right-click it, and choose RENAME. Change the name to "Aggregation".

4. With the UNION object highlighted, notice that the DETAILS pane contains the output of the UNION transform. See Figure 6.57 for an example.

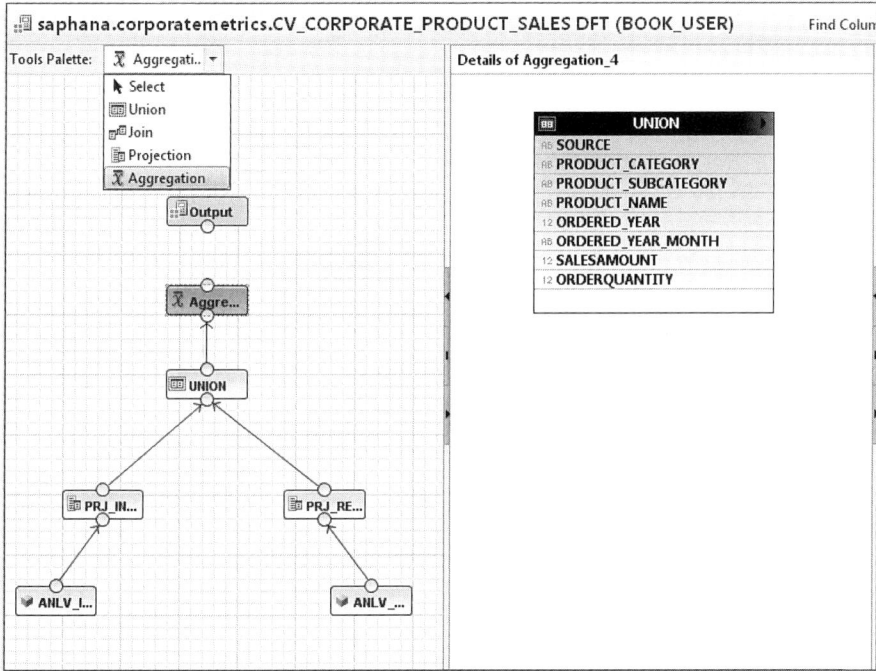

**Figure 6.57**  Adding the Aggregation Transformation to the Tools Palette

5. Right-click the columns listed in Table 6.38, and choose ADD TO OUTPUT. The columns defined as output only will be used as the GROUP BY columns in the aggregation engine.

| Column Name |
| --- |
| SOURCE |
| PRODUCT_CATEGORY |
| PRODUCT_SUBCATEGORY |
| PRODUCT_NAME |
| ORDERED_YEAR |
| ORDERED_YEAR_MONTH |

**Table 6.38**  Selecting the Output Columns

6. Right-click the SALESAMOUNT and ORDEREDQUANTITY columns, and choose ADD AS AGGREGATION COLUMN. These columns will be summarized based on the output columns listed in the table.

Once complete, the OUTPUT pane should look similar to the screen shown in Figure 6.58.

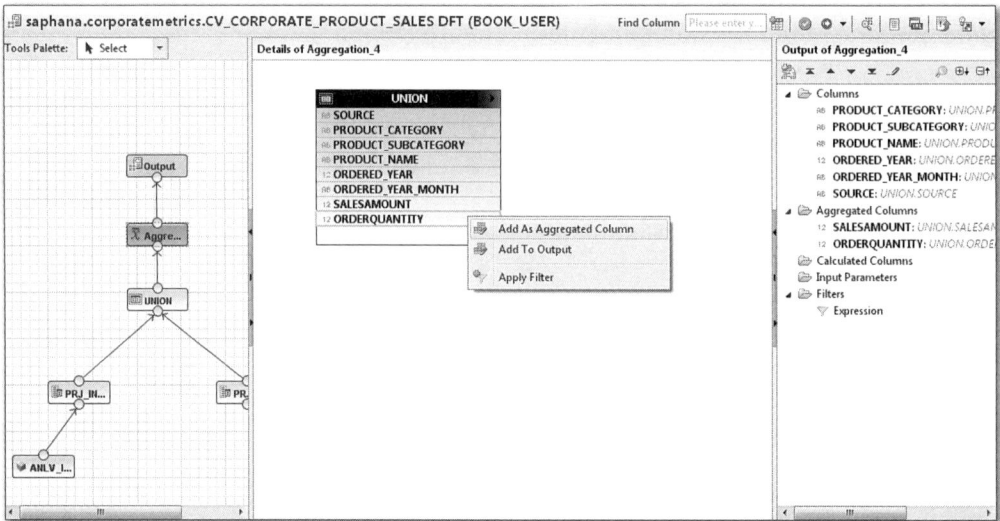

**Figure 6.58** Defining the Group By and Aggregate Columns

### Defining the Final Output of the Calculation View

In the final phase of the calculation view development processes, you'll link the output of the aggregation transformation to the output transformation. In the output transformation, you'll define attributes, measures, hierarchies, counters, calculated columns, calculated measures, variables, and input parameters. Follow these steps:

1. Using the drag-and-drop method, join the AGGREGATION to the OUTPUT transformation.

2. Using Figure 6.59 as a guide, select the OUTPUT transformation. Notice that the output of the aggregation transformation is now visible in the DETAILS pane.

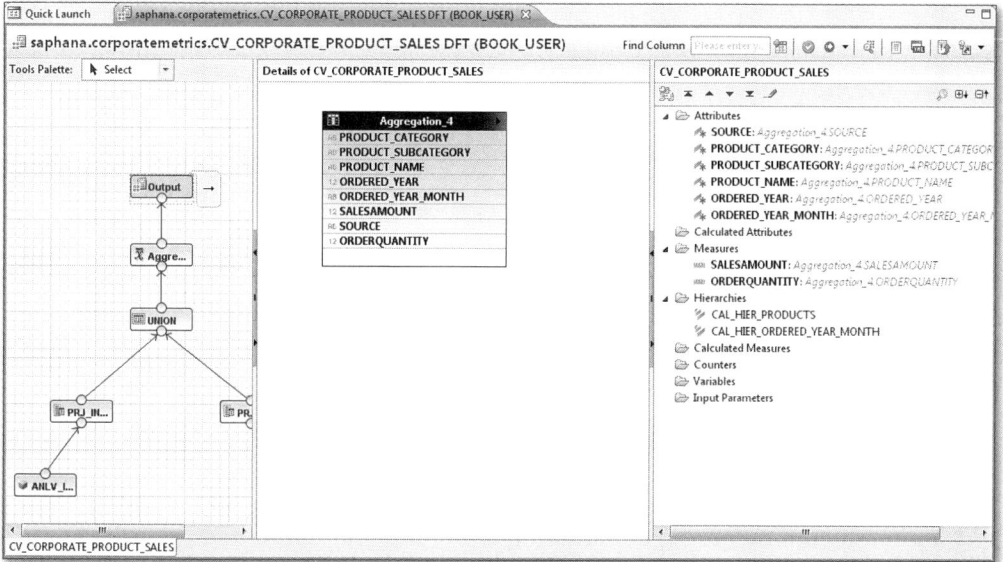

**Figure 6.59**  Defining the Final Output of the Calculation View

3. In the DETAILS pane, right-click the columns listed in Table 6.39, and choose ADD AS ATTRIBUTE.

| Column Name |
| --- |
| SOURCE |
| PRODUCT_CATEGORY |
| PRODUCT_SUBCATEGORY |
| PRODUCT_NAME |
| ORDERED_YEAR |
| ORDERED_YEAR_MONTH |

**Table 6.39**  Defining the Attributes for the Calculation View

4. In the DETAILS pane, right-click the SALESAMOUNT and ORDEREDQUANTITY columns, and select the option ADD AS MEASURE.

5. In the OUTPUT pane, right-click the HIERARCHIES section, and choose NEW LEVEL HIERARCHY.

6. Using Figure 6.60 as a guide, define the products hierarchy. To add levels to a hierarchy, click the green plus sign icon to add each level. Use the MOVE UP and MOVE DOWN buttons to arrange the order of the levels.

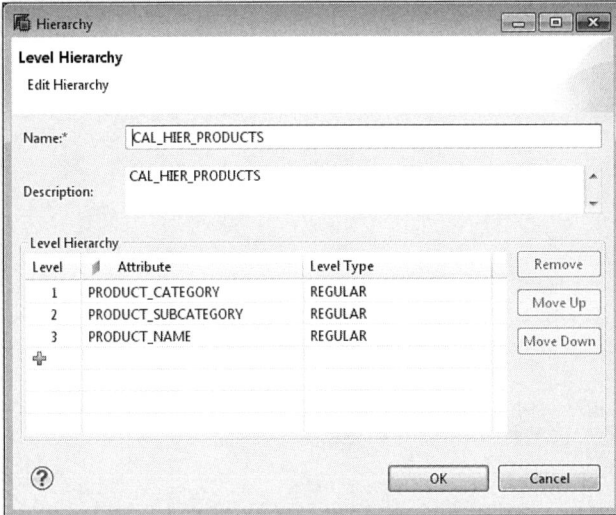

**Figure 6.60**  Defining the Products Level Hierarchy

7. Using Figure 6.61 as a guide, define the products hierarchy.

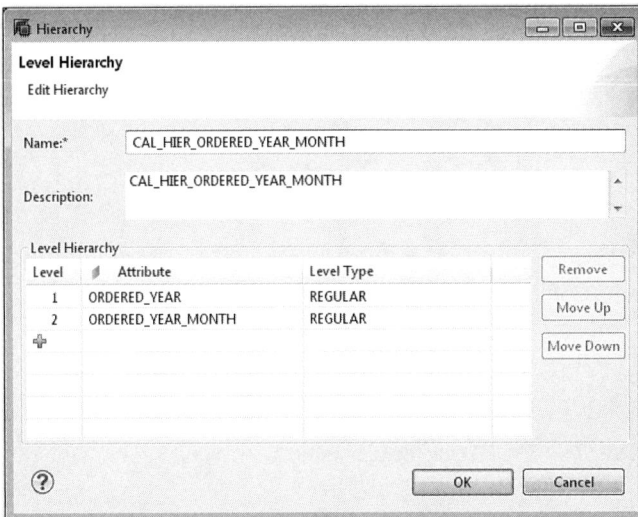

**Figure 6.61**  Defining the Ordered Date Hierarchy

8. Once completed, your output columns should be configured similar to what is depicted in Figure 6.62.

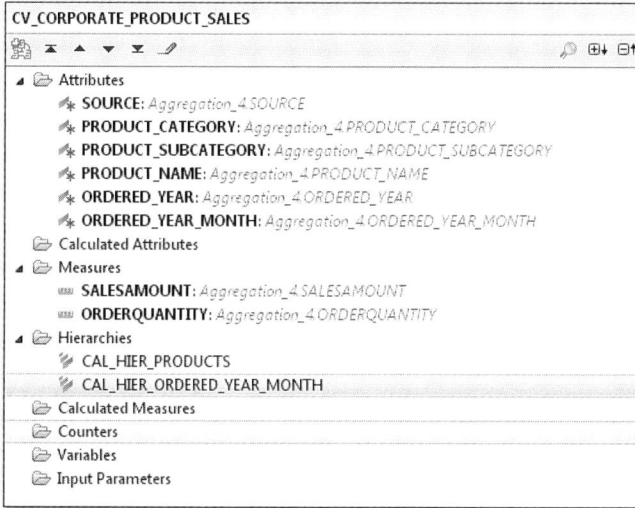

**Figure 6.62** The Calculation View Final Output Columns

9. When complete, save and activate the calculation view by clicking the green SAVE AND ACTIVATE button on the toolbar.

10. Preview the calculation view using the DATA PREVIEW (small magnifying glass image overlooking a table) icon located to the right of the SAVE AND ACTIVATE icon.

The calculation view should now be available for consumption by the SAP Business-Objects tools. Because the view was able to combine the Internet sales and reseller sales transactions by product and date, the CEO now has the means to produce a comprehensive metric. In addition, because the calculation view uses highly optimized SQLScript functions to combine the results, the view make the most use of the SAP HANA appliance hardware.

## 6.6   Summary

To truly assign value to data, that data must be structured and organized in a way that is intuitive and easy to understand. As you've seen in this chapter, you can transform complex data into intuitive data using the modeling components in SAP HANA.

Throughout this chapter, we've identified the main components of SAP HANA modeling. The models are developed using the SAP HANA Studio desktop client. Modeling components are organized in packages for purposes of security and organization. Attribute views, analytic views, and calculation views are the key information views stored in SAP HANA. They reference the SAP HANA columnar tables that are stored in schemas. Data-level security can be implemented through the use of analytic privileges. We also discussed how the modeling capability of SAP HANA, coupled with its robust and powerful platform, can be leveraged to benefit organizations of all types.

In terms of performance and manageability, we also discussed the differences between the processing of normalized and denormalized data in the SAP HANA system. We explored the differences between physically denormalizing the data using SAP Data Services verses logically denormalizing the data using the SAP HANA multidimensional modeling tools and components.

In subsequent chapters, we'll discuss how each of these components can be used by the SAP BusinessObjects platform to generate reports and analytics.

*Recognizing the need for organizations to tap into insights in their operational data, SAP has developed several tools that integrate with SAP HANA to run predictive algorithms on very large data sets.*

# 7  Integrating Predictive Analytics with SAP HANA

While previous chapters have focused on moving data into and transforming data within SAP HANA, we'll focus for the first time here on serving data to end users and the business community to synthesize operational data and make operational and strategic decisions.

In the past several years, the practice of business intelligence (BI) has begun a slow shift from reporting and visualizing to identifying insights and performing causation analysis. Users have traditionally often had the ability to drill down within traditional BI reports to derive the causes of trends, but an emerging need is the ability to use the rich historical data stored in an organization's data warehouse to determine what may happen in the future. Traditional statistical tools are often siloed and difficult to integrate into production environments, but SAP HANA has several features and companion tools that make the data manipulation, extraction, prediction, and model integration process more seamless than ever before.

The toolset for predictive analysis in SAP HANA includes three main components: predictive functions available in SAP HANA through the Predictive Analysis Library (PAL), the capability to integrate SAP HANA with an external Rserve host to run open source R algorithms efficiently, and the visualization and predictive user tool SAP Predictive Analysis, which incorporates all of the functionality of the SAP Lumira visualization tool and includes predictive functionality to run R and PAL predictive functions on SAP HANA.

In addition to summarizing features, implementation, and architecture of the SAP HANA predictive analysis tools listed previously, this chapter includes an overview of the predictive analysis process itself and common business problems for which predictive tools can provide solutions (Section 7.1) and several integration scenarios for implementing predictive algorithms in an SAP BusinessObjects BI environment running on SAP HANA (Section 7.2 and Section 7.3). Finally, we'll include two use cases for our AdventureWorks retail firm to integrate predictive models into their operational practices (Section 7.4 and Section 7.5).

## 7.1    Predictive Analytics Platform

Prior to discussing SAP HANA tools for predictive analysis, we'll include a brief overview of motivations for implementing predictive analytics in an organization and a discussion of the predictive analysis development process.

### 7.1.1    Introducing Predictive Analysis

At the most basic level, *predictive analysis* is focused on developing a way to determine the expected future result of some action or decision. This allows the business to evaluate alternative paths and select the most profitable option. A *predictive model* is an algorithm, or set of rules, used by an organization to generate this expected outcome based on known input characteristics. The predictive model can simply be a collection of existing business rules or management decisions, but to develop the most accurate and statistically valid predictions, organizations are now often relying on statistical techniques to develop the predictive model equation and values based on error-minimization techniques.

After the predictive model has been developed, an organization can use the prediction algorithm to evaluate the expected results of alternative business strategies and determine how best to allocate scarce resources, such as marketing funds, research and development budget, or labor hours.

Predictive algorithms can be used in many areas of an organization, including advertising, marketing, product development, customer service, operations, and human resources. Consider a few common applications of predictive analytics in an organization:

▸ Marketing response or uplift models that predict the likelihood of response (or incremental response) for customers reacting to a specific marketing stimulus (e.g., email, direct mail, text message, promotional offer)

▸ Product suggestion models to influence customers to increase their purchase size by cross-selling or up-selling complementary products

- Customer segmentation methodologies to categorize customers that behave or transact similarly and therefore may continue to transact or respond similarly in the future

- Fraud models for transactions, interactions, or claims to predict which events are most likely to merit further investigation or require confirmation prior to processing

Let's break this list down. One common source of confusion is differentiating between the common business applications in the preceding list and the actual predictive algorithms used to solve them. This list includes some common business applications for predictive solutions, but for each of these business problems, a number of different algorithms can be used. For example, a firm wanting to estimate the likelihood of a binary outcome (e.g., will a customer churn use of a service) could use a number of different algorithms, including a decision tree model, a logistic regression model, a Naive Bayes classifier, or even an unsupervised learning algorithm such as clustering. Selecting the most accurate and appropriate algorithm (or combination of several algorithms) for the business problem requires a balance of analytics experience, business knowledge, and trial and error; this is where predictive analytics is more art than science.

In this chapter, we use the term predictive analysis to include a broad set of analytical methods and tools for extracting insights and implementing better decision making in a BI environment. However, there are many related terms that you may be familiar with as well. Many of these overlap or are used interchangeably with each other and the broader predictive analysis term. Let's define and differentiate several popular terms used within the analytics industry:

- **Predictive analytics**
  This is one of the most popular analytics-related terms that is often used to refer to both predictive and descriptive analysis and is often used interchangeably with data mining and advanced analytics.

- **Data mining**
  This is a broader term that covers any method of extracting insights from large data sets. Data mining includes the discovery of both descriptive and predictive insights based on either statistical or machine learning methods.

- **Advanced analytics**
  Largely a marketing term, this phrase is typically used to distinguish any analysis that uses statistical or machine learning algorithms from analyses relying

only on simple database queries and manual examination of different slices of data. Advanced analytics also often refers to the analysis of unstructured data and text analysis.

▶ **Descriptive analytics**
Often bundled into the predictive analytics umbrella term, descriptive analytics focuses on exploring or profiling existing relationships and characteristics of the data, rather than predicting future outcomes like predictive analytics. Descriptive analytic techniques are often used to prepare or explore data prior to developing predictive models.

▶ **Business analytics**
This refers to the application of analytic methods to business environments. Common subclassifications include marketing, risk, fraud, customer, operations, and HR analytics. Business analytics may refer to the use of predictive or advanced analytical techniques or more straightforward reporting-type analysis.

▶ **Statistical models**
Statistical models are formal mathematical equations showing the relationship between input variables and results (e.g., linear regression), which are differentiated from models built on business rules, knowledge, or machine learning algorithms.

▶ **Knowledge discovery**
Synonymous with data mining, knowledge discovery is simply the process of uncovering patterns, trends, or relationships in large data sets.

▶ **Machine learning**
As a specific set of algorithms based on artificial intelligence principles, machine learning algorithms use data to learn about relationships. Popular tools that fall into the machine learning category include neural networks and support vector machines.

Predictive algorithms and statistical learning methods are often employed to synthesize, better understand, and extract actionable insights from large data sets. These tools have become especially attractive to organizations that are amassing vast repositories of data, including transaction history, web browsing patterns, sensor readings, and even social media chatter. Predictive models are already in use in many customer-serving organizations, influencing items suggested to customers, determining what types of promotional offers are extended, and even specifying how quickly a customer may be connected to a call center representative. Predictive models help organizations realize a return on the investment of collecting and maintaining their data repositories; extracting actionable insights from this data helps organizations better understand and serve their customers, and ensure that scarce resources are used to target customers most effectively.

At its core, a predictive model determines a mapping between input data (e.g., demographic information such as age, gender, household information, or purchase history) and a predicted output, such as whether customers will respond to an offer, make a transaction, or discontinue their relationship with the company.

Predictive models can be divided into the following two categories:

▶ **Supervised learning algorithms**
These models that have two sets of input data: inputs and outputs. Supervised algorithms attempt to determine the effect of the inputs on the related outputs for each input scenario. The inputs are assumed to be at the beginning of the causal chain and the outputs at the end. While supervised learning has the advantage of defining a model based on the actual output prediction that is desired, it does require that a sufficient quantity of accurate output data is available. For example, if an organization wants to predict which customers are most likely to respond to a particular marketing offer, it must have a sample of response records from a representative portion of their customer base. This might mean running a preliminary pilot program to gather response data or using data from a similar prior marketing campaign to build the model. Well-known and commonly used supervised learning algorithms include classification algorithms such as decision trees, all regression models (including linear, logarithmic, logistic, and exponential regression), time series models, neural networks, linear discriminant analyses, support vector machines, and association algorithms.

▶ **Unsupervised learning algorithms**
These models have only one set of input data and assume that the input observations are at the end of a causal chain of latent variables. Unsupervised learning algorithms can typically develop into larger, more complex models than supervised algorithms because the complexity of trying to find a connection between two sets of observations increases exponentially with each increase in the number of steps between the observations, while the complexity of an unsupervised learning algorithm increases only proportionally with each intermediate step. Popular unsupervised learning algorithms include clustering and some types of neural network learning algorithms.

The main difference between supervised and unsupervised learning is how the classifications are determined. In supervised learning, the known output class value (e.g., did customer respond to offer) for each input scenario is already determined prior to modeling, whereas one of the outputs of the unsupervised algorithm is actually the classification for each input observation.

To further explain, in the example of trying to determine whether a customer responded, the supervised learning method takes in the customer input characteristics (e.g., how long has it been since the customer's last transaction, where does the customer live, customer demographic characteristics) as well as the output (e.g., customer 1 responded, customer 2 did not, etc.) and extracts a mathematical relationship between the inputs and outputs. The unsupervised learning method takes in only the inputs and divides the customers into some number of similar groups based on these input characteristics. The unsupervised learning algorithm effectively creates groups of like customers, under the assumption that if demographically similar customers have similar behaviors, the groups determined by the clustering algorithm will have different response rates.

One consideration in determining which algorithm to use is the availability and reliability of data. Because unsupervised learning methods don't require known result data, they may be more attractive; however, there is no way to know if they are effectively differentiating customers. It's still necessary to have known output data to validate the effectiveness of the unsupervised algorithm model.

After you have fitted and validated a predictive model, your organization can effectively accept that the insights extracted from the historical data can be generalized to predict the future.

### 7.1.2 The Predictive Analysis Process

Developing a predictive model includes many different steps, including strategic planning (e.g., What predicted output would help my business? What data do I have to build this model?), technical execution in obtaining the modeling data set, and the statistical and analytical process to iterate through possible models and evaluate each one. Finally, the best model must be implemented and made available for business processes and decisions to take action on the results.

Here we've broken the modeling process down into six steps, some of which may be repeated more than once:

1. Identify the modeling strategy.

2. Select an appropriate modeling tool.

3. Perform data discovery and develop the modeling data set.

4. Develop the model.

5. Implement the selected model.

6. Maintain and update the model as needed.

Each of these steps may be performed by different teams of resources that include stakeholders from several business units and technical resources. Steps 1, 2, 3, and 6 may require budgeting and strategic approval from an executive team and the commitment of a team of cross-functional resources from the business, analytic, and IT departments to develop the modeling data set and implement the final model.

Let's walk through each of these steps in more detail.

**Step 1: Identifying the Modeling Strategy**

While it may seem straightforward, setting the strategy for an analytic project is critical to ensuring that the project finishes in a timely fashion and all parties receive the output they expect.

Too often, analytical projects start with unrealistic expectations and too broad of a focus, causing analysts to become overwhelmed with summarizing and examining the vast amounts of data available. Further, the timeline for analytical projects can easily be extended if each time the analyst brings a presentation of the findings to date, the team comes back with additional suggestions, such as "Why didn't you look at factor $X$ or break results down by customer group $Y$?" While this is often unavoidable, having all of the stakeholders in the room at the beginning of the project can help identify all of the angles for analysis upfront, and there should be general agreement on the dimensions and scope (including detail, complexity, and depth) of the analysis at the beginning of the project to ensure that the timeline is met.

To avoid this "analysis paralysis" and the never-ending cycle of re-analysis, a team that includes both the analysts completing the work and the managerial team should develop a few goals for the analysis with actionable results and quantifiable business benefits. Rather than asking broad, open-ended questions, this analytical and executive team should drill down to the most pressing questions. Table 7.1

shows examples of how extremely broad questions might be shaped into analytical projects with actionable results.

| Business Goal or Question | Analytical Project Goals | Actionable Implementation |
|---|---|---|
| Why are my customers leaving? | ▶ Which customers are most likely to defect?<br>▶ Is there a preceding event that occurs commonly immediately before a customer defects? | ▶ Customer outreach: Evaluate the impact of an outreach campaign in decreasing the defect rate. Alternatively, reduce investment into customers most likely to defect.<br>▶ Business process evaluation: If there are transactions that are likely causing defection, examine them for friction points or gaps that lead to defection. |
| How can I increase my sales? | ▶ Which customers are most likely to respond to the sales offer?<br>▶ Which product offering is most likely to result in the highest purchase amount/ profit/lifetime value? | ▶ Reduce marketing costs by contacting only customers most likely to respond.<br>▶ Optimize product offerings to suggest the goal-maximizing product for each sales opportunity. |
| How can I reduce the cost of fraud to my business? | ▶ Which transactions are most likely to be fraudulent?<br>▶ Which transactions are likely to result in the highest recoverable fraud amount? | ▶ Reduce fraud investigation costs by targeting investigations to only those transactions above a fraud value threshold. |

**Table 7.1**  Sample Analytical Project Scoping

A final consideration during the strategic planning process for an analytics project is considering the data available. While it's not necessary to dive deep into specifics at this point, the strategic discussion should include team members familiar enough with the organization's data to know whether there is data available for performing the analysis. For example, an organization that wants to build models to select customers for marketing campaigns but has never kept records of its previous marketing efforts may have to limit its initial analytic goals because the company won't have specific data available to train a response model, for example. The company may still be able to perform some basic customer segmentation, but it will have no basis for training response models. Unfortunately, this portion of the strategic planning is often skipped, and time and effort are wasted with the ultimate revelation that there is insufficient data to build the agreed-upon models.

### Step 2: Select an Appropriate Modeling Tool

After the analytical goals have been determined at a high level, the analytic team must select the appropriate statistical tool or tools for the project. To select a tool, the analytic team must consider its needs across seven key areas of the tool. Table 7.2 includes a summary of several key features users should consider when selecting a predictive modeling tool.

| Feature | Questions to Ask |
|---|---|
| Data access | ▶ How is data imported into the tool?<br>▶ Where is my data coming from, and can the tool access it directly?<br>▶ How can data be extracted from the modeling tool? Can it write data directly back to the database? |
| Data manipulation | ▶ Can the tool facilitate simple data manipulations (e.g., grouping values, calculations, and value changes for minor cleansing)?<br>▶ How much manipulation of the data do I want to do in the tool? |
| Capacity and processing power | ▶ How much data will be processed by the tool?<br>▶ What runtime for predictive algorithms am I willing to accept? |
| User interface and skill level | ▶ What is the skill level (technical and statistical) of the users for this software?<br>▶ Will the users be able to work in a code-based tool, or do they require a graphical user interface?<br>▶ How much support and explanation of statistical terms do the users require? |
| Predictive algorithms available | ▶ Based on the long-term goals of the organization, what is the breadth of algorithms that may be needed in the long term?<br>▶ Specifically, which algorithms are most likely to be important to the organization? |

**Table 7.2**  Tool Evaluation Dimensions

469

| Feature | Questions to Ask |
|---|---|
| Model evaluation | ▶ What automated visualizations and model accuracy comparison metrics are built-in to the tool? |
| Model implementation and maintenance | ▶ How will models developed by the tool be integrated back into the operational systems?<br>▶ What maintenance features are available (e.g., version control, archival, shared objects between users)? |

**Table 7.2** Tool Evaluation Dimensions (Cont.)

Because predictive tools are generally expensive and require an investment in infrastructure, talent, training, and integration, in addition to the software costs, selecting a tool is most likely a rare event in an organization and should be undertaken with great care. Prior to selecting a tool, the organization should think about its long term analytics strategy and what type of tool will fit these needs.

For example, an organization that expects to need very complicated predictive models for a variety of different operational areas might want to consider a full-function tool that has a wide variety of highly configurable statistical algorithms that can be employed. However, these tools are often quite expensive and require a technically savvy analyst with statistical experience to operate. In contrast, an organization that just wants to experiment with one particular approach such as customer clustering might select a tool that is specialized to that one area, lower cost, and has built-in visualizations or model-evaluation tools specific to that particular model or business area.

> **Evaluating SAP Predictive Analysis**
>
> So how does SAP's new predictive tool SAP Predictive Analysis rate in each of these tool assessment categories? We've assign a letter grade based on the current and expected functionality as described in the following list:
>
> ▶ **Data access: A**
> SAP Predictive Analysis can access data directly from SAP HANA and many other popular databases, as well as flat files and SAP BusinessObjects universes. Combined with SAP Data Services, data from nearly any source can be ported to SAP HANA for use in SAP Predictive Analysis.

▶ **Data manipulation: B**
In SAP HANA online mode, data can be manipulated in SAP HANA information views or during loading with SAP Data Services, but the data must be fully manipulated and assigned as an attribute or measure outside the predictive tool. In offline mode, SAP Predictive Analysis has tools for basic data manipulation such as calculation, grouping, and joining multiple data sets.

▶ **Capacity and processing power: A**
When paired with SAP HANA, SAP Predictive Analysis can handle extremely large data sets with impressively fast processing times.

▶ **User interface and skill level: A+**
The SAP Predictive Analysis interface is easy to understand, and even an inexperienced user can easily construct a predictive workflow. This is likely to be improved upon further through modules that help guide business users though the predictive process.

▶ **Predictive algorithm availability: B**
The current PAL and included R algorithms cover basic popular statistical algorithms. SAP recently introduced the ability to create custom R transforms in SAP Predictive Analysis. This allows a technical user to program any algorithm in the tool and share the custom transform with a wider audience.

▶ **Model evaluation: C**
Currently, model evaluation is limited; while some algorithms have fit statistics in the raw result printout, there are currently few fit visualizations, and many of those don't support large data sets.

▶ **Model implementation and maintenance: A (implementation)/C (maintenance)**
Current and expected features allow easy integration of predictive results and scoring algorithms, including exporting PAL-based models directly to SAP HANA and the ability to write predictive data directly back to the SAP HANA database. However, model versioning, archival, and comparison features don't currently exist.

## Step 3: Perform Data Discovery and Develop the Modeling Data Set

Data discovery is the process of evaluating all available data elements and determining which elements should be included in the analysis. This includes inspecting all elements for completeness and accuracy, and evaluating the likelihood and validity of a relationship between the modeled outcome and each potential predictor. This initial data discovery should reveal which predictors are correlated with the desired outcome and narrow down the list of predictors that will be considered during the modeling process.

This process is often iterative because insights gleaned from the initial data discovery push the analyst back to the data source to pull other data that might reveal additional trends or to change the data to increase or decrease complexity. The result of the data discovery process should be a finalized modeling data set and an understanding of all of the potential predictors.

### Step 4: Develop the Model

After completing the data discovery process and constructing the modeling data set, you'll test different predictive algorithms and variables to determine the best fit and result for the organization.

To accurately and independently evaluate a model, you need to divide the initial modeling data set into two sets: one used to fit or train the model, and another as an independent validation set. This data division ensures that the model that is developed accurately reflects the impact of the true influencing factors within the environment and not simply compensating for the specific random variation in one single data set, which is called over-fitting.

While evaluating different models, analysts must consider not only the accuracy of the prediction but also the complexity of the model and the impact on implementation. To rerun or score the model later and generate predicted results for new records, the same fields that were used during fitting must be pulled, generated, or calculated. Minimizing the number of predictors in the model not only reduces complexity in terms of data preparation for rescoring but also reduces the variance in the predicted values. Balancing complexity with accuracy is a difficult process that requires the modeler to evaluate the organization's needs, costs, and technical capabilities.

### Step 5: Implement the Selected Model

After the final model has been selected and approved for implementation, the analytical team must work with the systems team to make either model scores or the procedure for generating a model score for a given set of inputs. Simply writing calculated scores from the modeling engine back to a database is the easiest method of model implementation. However, to have immediate real-time scoring of new records, the modeling algorithm must be available within the database. The organization's use of the predictive model dictates the implementation process and determines whether implementation consists of only scores written back to a database from the modeling tool or whether the model algorithm is implemented within a database or application.

**Step 6: Maintain and Update the Model as Needed**

Predictive models require maintenance just like any other business rules, targets, and operational procedures. Model predictions may degrade with time due to either operational or technical changes that change the quality or meaning of input data or even environmental shifts, such as economic changes, product changes, competitive marketplace changes, or changes in consumer trends. Therefore, a model must be monitored regularly to ensure that predictions are still accurate and that the input data remains relevant and accurate.

If the accuracy of the model begins to degrade, you should either refit (recalculate new coefficients based on a more recent set of data) or rebuild (reconsider the list of predictor variables included in the model) the model. Rebuilding a model is a longer process, but it can allow an organization to add new predictors that may not have been available when the original model was developed. A general rule of thumb is that model maintenance should be performed whenever accuracy begins to degrade as well as any time there has been a significant change to the input data, in terms of quality, composition, or availability.

### 7.1.3    When to Use Predictive Analytics

Because predictive analytics is often used in areas with major revenue streams, the business case for developing better insight into trends and customer behavior is often quite strong. In this section, we'll first discuss the general foundation for typical business cases around predictive analytics and then walk through a brief example of calculating the financial impact of implementing a presales selection model to decrease the acquisition cost of prospective leads.

Predictive analytics is typically focused on generating more accurate predictions, so the savings is generated through reduction in waste or increasing the likelihood of sales. In addition, applying statistical algorithms to develop these models allows the development of more accurate predictive methods without the extensive manual analysis that would be required to identify these trends without predictive models. Finally, predictive models provide an objective and consistent evaluation methodology, rather than allowing inspectors or marketers to make their own judgments, which tend to be biased by past outliers.

Let's revisit some common business benefits and metrics that are impacted when you implement popular predictive models:

▶ **Product suggestion**
A model to suggest which product customers are most likely to purchase results in an increased purchase amount, manifesting as either an increase in the basket or purchase size during the initial purchase, or an increase in the number of purchases for each customer, depending on when the suggestion is made.

Even a small increase in the purchase basket has direct impact on profitability; for example, when an online retailer immediately suggests another product to be added to the purchase basket prior to completion of the order, the additional cost of sales is essentially zero. Increasing the purchase rate on these suggestions not only increases the purchase basket amount but also improves customer satisfaction by displaying products the customer is interested in.

▶ **Customer clustering or segmentation**
A clustering model allows customers to be divided into groups that are expected to act similarly. Therefore, if you have a model that divides customers into three segments and you've determined the lifetime value of the three segments to be different, you may invest more in attracting or acquiring the most valuable customer group than the less valuable customer groups.

Over time, this strategy can lead to a more valuable customer population, effectively increasing the value of the organization. Metrics for this improvement might include increased customer tenure, decreased customer defection, larger purchase or profit margins per customer, and other related impacts.

▶ **Marketing response model**
The ability to better predict which customers are most likely to respond to a marketing offer allows you to target only customers most likely to respond with expensive sales calls, mail pieces, or promotional offers. With this additional predictive intelligence, customer acquisition cost should decrease, as well as the response rate on marketing campaigns. This decrease in acquisition cost allows a reallocation of the marketing budget savings to other programs and ideally results in higher overall sales levels with the same marketing budget.

▶ **Retention or churn model**
Identifying customers who are most likely to churn (or defect) from an organization allows customer-saving resources to be allocated to customers most likely to need them and enables organizations to react proactively and prevent defection rather than retroactively trying to reacquire defected customers. With

predictive models identifying those most likely to defect and strategic programs to mitigate these defections, organizations can realize significant reduction in churn rates and related increases in tenure and customer value metrics.

▶ **Fraud likelihood prediction**
Organizations that implement fraud models can realize benefits in two main ways: fraud avoidance and fraud cost reduction. As a proactive technique, *fraud models* can be used prior to processing a transaction, and require additional identification or authorization to be processed. Retroactively, identifying likely fraudulent transactions or claims allows investigation resources to be deployed efficiently to the transactions most likely to results in a denial or recovery. A successful fraud model results in a lower rate of fraud within the organization as well as reduced fraud prevention and investigation costs.

▶ **Clinical decision support models**
Decision support models result in an automated suggestion or likelihood of diagnosis based on input data. These can help caregivers review the likelihood of diagnosis or suggested treatment based on symptom and diagnostic inputs. These models are also often used to identify patients most likely to be stricken with debilitating conditions and suggest preventative treatment. Used in these two ways, clinical models should reduce the time to diagnosis, improve treatment outcomes, and reduce occurrence of many preventable conditions, such as heart disease and diabetes. Often the preventative care and speed of diagnosis leads to a reduction in hospital stays and medical expenses, such as prescriptions.

Finally, let's walk through the actual financial impact of one case, which can be used as an example of how to approach the financial impact of predictive modeling for a marketing acquisition model.

Let's say you work in the marketing department at a large financial-services company that is promoting a new loan product. The sales force has a large prospect database, but the cost of contacting each prospect and going through the sales process is quite high, and only a portion of prospects are eligible for the loan product.

The executive management team has requested a methodology to identify prospects most likely to be eligible for the loan product so the marketing team can focus limited resources on customers most likely to be eligible.

The following details become apparent:

▶ Total prospect database: 1.2 million prospects available

▶ Experience: 36.6% eligible for product, with seven known demographic variables

▶ Cost per contact: $15

▶ Current effective cost per eligible prospect: $15/36.6% = $41

▶ Value per eligible prospect: $45

A decision tree model was built that is able to identify a portion of the database that has 71% eligibility. The full impact of expending marketing expenses on this portion of the prospect base is shown in Table 7.3.

| | No Model | Decision Tree |
|---|---|---|
| Prospects to contact | 1,200,000 | 495,000 |
| % eligible | 36.6% | 70.7% |
| Total marketing cost | $18,000,000 | $7,400,000 |
| Cost per eligible prospect | $41 | $21 |
| Total prospect value | $19,764,000 | $15,748,411 |
| Net prospect value | $1,764,000 | $8,323,639 |
| % improvement | | 371.9% |

**Table 7.3**  Business Case for Eligibility Decision Tree Model

Now that we've discussed the process for creating predictive models, let's take a look at the specific predictive tools available for use with SAP HANA.

### 7.1.4    Predictive Tools Available in SAP HANA

SAP HANA has three tools available to run predictive algorithms. The first two (the SAP HANA Application Function Libraries and SAP HANA-R integration) allow SAP HANA users to run predictive algorithms in the SAP HANA environment through code written and executed in SAP HANA Studio. The last, a companion product from SAP installed on the user's workstation, allows users to visualize data stored on SAP HANA and access the first two predictive toolsets through a graphical user interface (GUI).

Let's take a closer look at these tools.

**SAP HANA Application Function Libraries**

The SAP HANA *Application Function Libraries* (AFL) are collections of algorithms available to users and applications that run on SAP HANA. These libraries are linked dynamically to the SAP HANA database kernel, offering excellent performance. In the AFL, functions are grouped by topic into individual libraries. The AFL includes two libraries that are useful for predictive analytics: the BFL and the PAL.

The *Business Function Library* (BFL) contains functions implemented in C++, and makes available common business functions that are fully compliant with the SAP HANA calculation engine. The BFL enables significant performance improvement and application programming simplification by leveraging the calculation engine for complex functionality and allowing the use of SQLScript to call these complex, predefined functions. The BFL includes many financial functions, such as depreciation, cash flow discounting, present value and rate of return calculations, and forecasting, as well as several averaging algorithms. These functions are particularly useful for predictive analyses that require time series forecasting, such as budget setting by month, or financial analysis, such as discounting cash flows.

The *Predictive Analysis Library* (PAL) also includes functions that can be called using SQLScript, however, the PAL includes commonly used data mining algorithms. As of SP05 (which was released in March 2013), six categories of algorithms are available in the PAL, with a total of 23 algorithms represented:

▶ **Clustering**
Unsupervised learning algorithms that accept only numerical data to group similar observations or detect anomalies and divide a data set into discrete groups.

▶ **Classification**
Supervised learning algorithms that accept categorical or numeric data, including the popular decision tree, regression (linear, logistic and other forms), and Nearest Neighbor algorithms.

▶ **Association**
Includes the Apriori algorithm for determining correlations, patterns, and causal structures within a set of items, such as within transactions.

▶ **Preprocessing**
Commonly used in conjunction with the other categories to manipulate or adjust the data prior to modeling, including grouping, scaling, and sampling, as well as others.

▶ **Time series**
Used for forecasting time-dependent data series and includes only Exponential Smoothing algorithms (single, double, and triple).

▶ **Miscellaneous**
Includes two algorithms for grouping observations based on user-defined weights, which allows organizations to quickly apply business rules to their existing inventory or customer data.

**SAP HANA R Integration**

In addition to the PAL algorithms, SAP HANA also includes an integrated R client in the calculation engine. This allows SAP HANA to submit R code to an Rserve instance on an affiliated Linux host.

R is an open-source programming language that is very popular with mathematicians and statisticians. Originally used primarily within the academic community, R has surged in popularity for business users in the past few years. R stores all data, objects, and definitions in memory and performs its own memory management to ensure the workspace is appropriately sized.

Typically, R is run using a command-line interface; however, several editors and Integrated Development Environments (IDEs), such as R Studio, are available. One of the main benefits of R is the wide range of predictive algorithms available. R's predictive functionality is available in packages that are submitted by users to the Comprehensive R Archive Network (CRAN). These packages are subject to some review and testing prior to submission, but much of the functionality is user-tested. Popular packages are well-tested and reliable; more obscure algorithms may be less reliable. No formal support is available for R packages.

R was a natural choice for integration with SAP HANA both because it complements the in-memory architecture of SAP HANA and also because it's freely available and has extensive predictive functionality, essentially allowing SAP HANA to run thousands of predictive algorithms. Rserve is a TCP/IP server that supports remote connection, authentication, and file transfer and allows integration of R functionality in other applications. Rserve is called by the R client in the SAP HANA calculation engine. While there is some cost to marshaling data between the SAP HANA server and the Rserve host, this is minimal because both systems hold data in memory, eliminating the need for writing to disk, and also because the SAP HANA calculation engine's matrix primitives are similar to R's data frame structure. The transfer between R and SAP HANA is in binary format, minimizing the quantity of data transferred across the network. While Rserve is supported on most operating systems, SAP currently only officially supports an Rserve instance running on a separate supported Linux host for integration with SAP HANA.

The Rserve integration allows users to submit R code in SAP HANA Studio, which is processed by the integrated R Linux host. All packages called in R code must be installed and active on the R host.

### SAP Lumira and SAP Predictive Analysis

In 2012, SAP introduced a companion product called SAP Predictive Analysis that provides a frontend tool for visualization and calling both PAL and SAP HANA-R algorithms. SAP Predictive Analysis also includes all of the functionality of the SAP Lumira visualization tool. This tool provides a point-and-click interface to generate, save, and store various visualizations, including bar charts, line charts, pie charts, and even word clouds and geographic pie and choropleth charts. This visualization tool allows users to interact with data stored in SAP HANA information views and create presentation-ready exhibits directly from data in SAP HANA. Figure 7.1 shows several different visualizations available in SAP Lumira.

SAP Predictive Analysis includes the same PREPARE pane from SAP Lumira shown in Figure 7.2 but also includes the addition of the PREDICT pane shown in Figure 7.3, which holds all of the predictive functionality. (Notice the toggle functionality at the top of both figures to move between panes.)

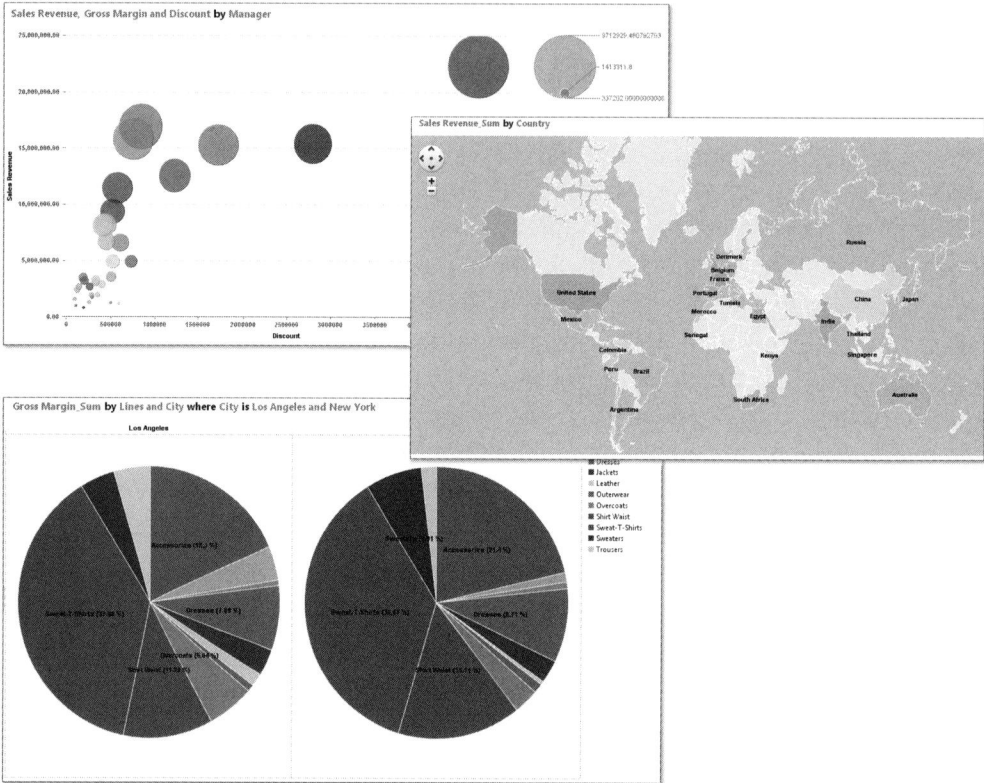

**Figure 7.1** Sample Visualizations from SAP Lumira

On the PREDICT pane, you can build a predictive workflow by dragging and dropping predictive algorithm modules from the ALGORITHM tab on the top half of the screen into the predictive workflow designer on the lower half of the screen. Each predictive module requires configurations specific to the algorithm prior to running, including selecting predictors and dependent variables. After configuration, you click the RUN ANALYSIS button, and you are notified after the analysis has been run. Upon completion, the RESULTS tab in the PREDICT pane is available and holds the result data and visualizations for all predictive modules that were run in the predictive workflow. In addition to predictive algorithms, there is also a module available to write the predictive result data set back to a table in SAP HANA.

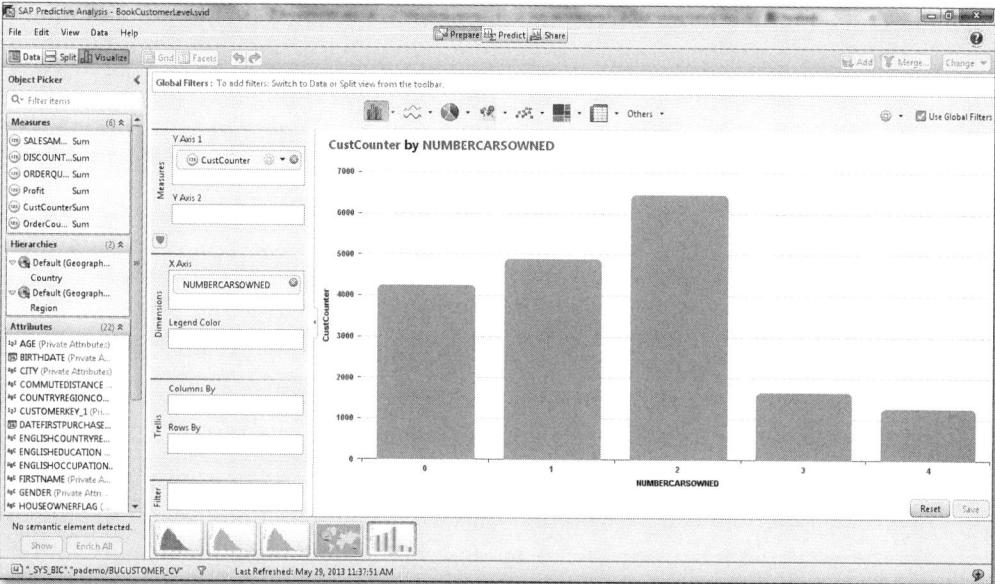

**Figure 7.2** SAP Predictive Analysis: Prepare Pane

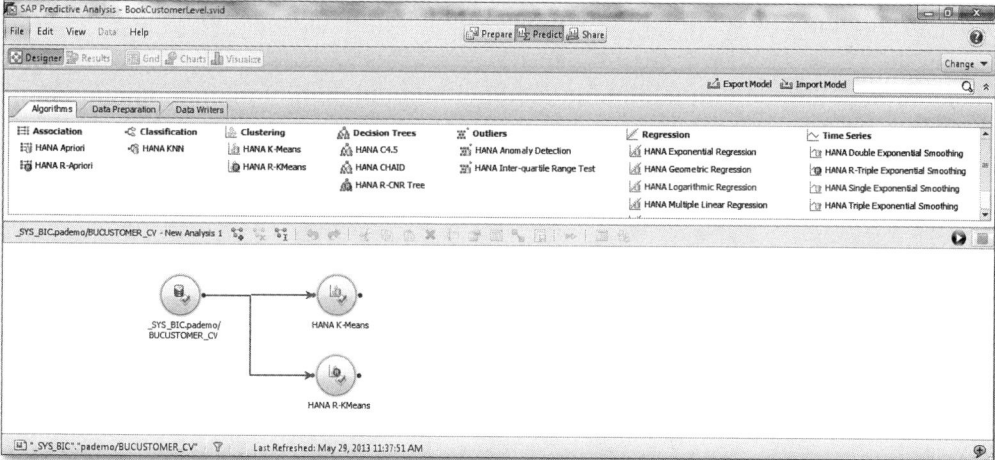

**Figure 7.3** SAP Predictive Analysis: Predict Pane

Now we'll walk through an overview of the installation and configuration of each of these predictive tools that integrate with SAP HANA.

## 7.2    Integrating with SAP HANA

R integration and AFL are available for any SAP HANA implementation, but you'll need to install and configure these pieces before users can access the predictive content.

### 7.2.1    Installing the Application Function Libraries

After you've installed SAP HANA SP05, next install the AFL using the Unified Installer, and start the scripting server so users can access PAL functions.

### 7.2.2    Deploying RServe

To install the SAP HANA-R integration components, the R Linux host must be configured. If the Linux host is running SUSE Linux with an active support agreement, R and Rserve can be downloaded and installed via the update repository. In this situation, there is no need to compile the R code. If the Linux host must be configured manually, the Java Developer Connection (JDC) (version 1.5.0_18 or higher) must be installed and configured. After Java is configured, R must be installed and compiled from its source code. SAP recommends R version 2.15 or higher.

Next, install Rserve on the R Linux host and all R packages for the algorithms that will be used for predictive analysis in SAP HANA. After the Linux host is configured, SAP HANA must be configured to interact with the R host. In SAP HANA Studio, the R server IP addresses and ports must be entered.

> **Additional Resources**
>
> Instructions for installing the AFL (which includes both the PAL and BFL functions) are included in the SAP HANA Installation Guide with SAP HANA Unified Installer (SP05), available at *http://help.sap.com/hana/SAP_HANA_Server_Installation_Guide_en.pdf*.
>
> Installation and user instructions for HANA-R integration are found in the *SAP HANA R Integration Guide (SP05)*, available at *http://help.sap.com/hana/SAP_HANA_R_Integration_Guide_en.pdf*.

### 7.2.3    Leveraging R and PAL to Produce Predictive Results

You can run R code in SAP HANA Studio by creating a procedure with R code wrapped by `LANGUAGE RLANG AS BEGIN <R Code> END;`. In the R code, the return data must be a data frame object, so it's common for the output to be converted using `as.data.frame(<output data matrix>)` in the R code. An R procedure can also be called from another procedure, for example one written in SQLScript.

To use PAL algorithms in SAP HANA Studio, the `afl_wrapper_generator` procedure must be created. This function is used each time a PAL procedure is built and takes in the procedure name, PAL function name specifying the algorithm and function to be used, and a table referencing the input and output table types. After the PAL procedure has been created, it can be called using a simple `CALL _SYS_AFL.<procedure name>(<procedure inputs and outputs>);` statement. In addition to the predictive functions, the PAL includes some scoring and diagnostic functions that may be called more regularly using the PAL procedures.

Using the SAP Predictive Analysis application with an SAP HANA online data source automatically generates the table types, formats, tables, and procedures required for either PAL or R algorithms. We've included examples of R and PAL algorithms using both the SAP HANA Studio and SAP Predictive Analysis methods in the case studies in this chapter.

---

**Additional Resources**

For additional details on syntax, specific function availability, and usage, SAP has provided user guides with examples for calling R, PAL, and BFL functions:

▶ SAP HANA R guide: *http://help.sap.com/hana/SAP_HANA_R_Integration_Guide_en.pdf*
▶ SAP HANA PAL reference: *http://help.sap.com/hana/SAP_HANA_Predictive_Analysis_Library_PAL_en.pdf*
▶ SAP HANA BFL reference: *http://help.sap.com/hana/SAP_HANA_Business_Function_Library_BFL_en.pdf*

---

### 7.2.4 Installing SAP Predictive Analysis

Installation of the SAP Predictive Analysis client tool is straightforward and easy. After downloading the installation file from the SAP site, you simply click through the wizard, which has no configurations required except for entering the license key. There is no additional configuration required to run algorithms on data located on SAP HANA using either the PAL or SAP HANA-R; you must simply enter the database and connection information as shown in Figure 7.4 to connect to the SAP HANA server and select analytic content.

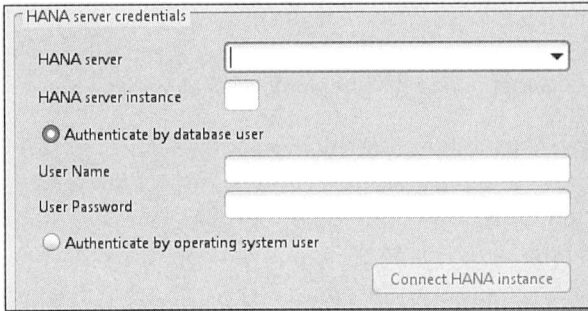

**Figure 7.4** SAP HANA Server Credentials in SAP Predictive Analysis

In addition to running predictive algorithms on SAP HANA, SAP Predictive Analysis can operate on data stored locally on the user's workstation, using a local installation of R. To be used in this SAP HANA offline or local mode, a local installation of R must be on the same workstation, and SAP Predictive Analysis must be directed to look for it in the correct installation folder.

### 7.2.5 User Privileges and Security with SAP Predictive Analysis

In addition to having SELECT, EXECUTE, and WRITE permissions on any analytic content, tables, and schemas that will be used for predictive analyses, you'll need special privileges for both PAL and SAP HANA-R execution access. To manage this access with minimal manual configuration for new users, one best practice is to create a predictive user security role that is allocated to any users that need to access predictive content. Table 7.4 and Figure 7.5 show the security settings required to execute algorithms in each of the different predictive toolsets available in SAP HANA.

| Predictive Functions | Permissions Required |
|---|---|
| BFL | ▸ AFL_SYS_AFL_AFLBFL_EXECUTE system privilege must be granted. |
| PAL | ▸ AFL__SYS_AFL_AFLPAL_EXECUTE system privilege must be granted.<br>▸ AFL_WRAPPER_GENERATOR(SYSTEM) stored procedure must be created. |

**Table 7.4** Security Provisioning for Predictive User Role

| Predictive Functions | Permissions Required |
|---|---|
|  | ▸ AFL_WRAPPER_GENERATOR(SYSTEM) SQL privilege execute must be granted. ▸ _SYS_REPO must have SELECT privileges with ability to grant to others on predictive users' schema. |
| SAP HANA-R Integration | ▸ CREATE R SCRIPT system privilege must be granted. |

**Table 7.4**  Security Provisioning for Predictive User Role (Cont.)

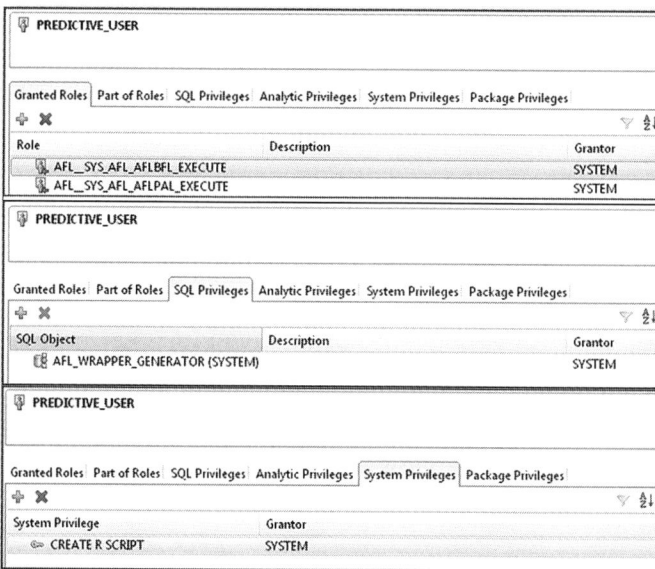

**Figure 7.5**  Predictive User Role Security Settings

**Note on PAL AFL_WRAPPER_GENERATOR(SYSTEM) Function**

Any time the SAP HANA server or scripting server is restarted, the AFL_WRAPPER_GENERATOR(SYSTEM) stored procedure must be re-created, and the associated SQL privileges for predictive users must be granted again to the predictive user role.

In addition to creating the predictive role with all access required to run predictive algorithms, we recommend that a limited number of users run predictive algorithms, especially those run through SAP Predictive Analysis. Some of the access privileges granted to predictive users have far-reaching effects, so we recommend minimizing the use of these privileges outside of predictive functions.

In addition, supporting tables for many algorithms are created in the user schema that runs predictive algorithms. These tables can accumulate over time, and while their size isn't typically an issue, the presence of dozens or hundreds of tables, stored procedures, and views can make the predictive user's schema difficult to navigate. Therefore, we recommend that you store any data used for predictive algorithms in schemas separate from the predictive user's schema, which you should clean out on a regular basis to minimize the accumulation of these support tables.

We'll now move on to discuss several methods of implementing predictive models created using any of the SAP HANA predictive tools in an SAP HANA Business-Objects environment.

## 7.3    Integrating with SAP BusinessObjects

Integrating predictive models back into the business process is often a stumbling block as organizations attempt to make predictive insights operationally actionable. This section discusses several ways to implement models in an existing BI environment.

### 7.3.1    Exporting Scored Data Back to Databases

The most straightforward method of implementing predictive models is to score the data in the predictive software and then write the scores back to a table in the database. For predictive models run in SAP HANA Studio using PAL or SAP HANA-R algorithms, this simply means taking the result set from the PAL or SAP HANA-R algorithm, and storing it in the BI environment. Using SAP Predictive Analysis, predictive model result data can be written back to the SAP HANA database using the HANA WRITER transform. This result table written back to SAP HANA can be used as a source for an analytical view or SAP BusinessObjects universe, which makes the predictive results available to users. SAP Predictive Analysis stores the predictive workflow, so each time new data must be scored, the SAP Predictive Analysis document can simply be reopened and rerun, replacing the original score table.

This method of writing predictive algorithm result scores back to the database has the advantage of being one of the fastest ways to implement predictive results and make predictive information available to everyone across the organization. Essentially, as soon as a model is approved by the executive team, scores can be written back to the database and integrated into BI environments. This also ensures that predictive results are relatively stable, and all scores are refreshed at the same time.

However, the drawback of this method of implementation is that scores can't be calculated on demand in a business application; predictive results are essentially calculated and written on a batch basis (either automated or manually triggered). This means that scores aren't immediately available on new records added to the database and that scores can't be calculated in real time and used for immediate decision support.

This type of implementation is sufficient and effective for many applications. If new data can be scored regularly (e.g., weekly), the delay may be sufficiently small for many applications, such as batch marketing, where marketing prospects for solicitations are selected based on model scores.

## 7.3.2 Exporting Algorithms

If simply exporting the scores for a predictive model is insufficient, the scoring algorithm, or method of assigning the predictive value must be exported from the modeling tool and integrated in a business application or database. This is necessary in situations where real-time scoring is required, for example, insurance or financial risk models, where customers are applying for an insurance or financial product and expect an immediate answer on whether they are accepted and what their rate will be. In these cases, batch processing won't suffice because customers expect results in a few seconds when contacting companies via web or phone. Similarly, customers expect that a change in their input data should result in an immediate impact on their return decision of acceptance or price level. To provide this type of response, the model scoring equation must be available either within an application or as a service that can be called by the application. This can be implemented as a web service or the function can be made available in the database or application.

There are a few ways to program a predictive algorithm in a database or application on SAP HANA:

▶ **Code the algorithm logic**

The first option is to extract and understand the actual modeling equation or logic of the fitted predictive model, and code it into a function available to the target application, such as a stored procedure in SAP HANA. The complexity of the final predictive model determines how complex the scoring algorithm is. For example, a simple decision tree can be coded in a few nested if-then statements, which is relatively easy to implement in almost any language. However, more complex algorithms such as clustering and neural networks may be very difficult to code. This method of implementation is one of the most labor-intensive because the algorithm must be coded and tested fully prior to implementation. Additionally, the SAP HANA scoring algorithm must also be updated any time the model is refitted or changed.

▶ **Predictive Model Markup Language export**

Predictive Model Markup Language (PMML) is an XML-based modeling format developed by data mining industry groups in an attempt to standardize predictive model representations. PMML defines both the predictive model and some limited preprocessing algorithms and supports the most common predictive models, including clustering, association, regression, time series, and decision trees.

While most predictive modeling tools (including R, PAL, and SAP Predictive Analysis) can export PMML models, very few databases or applications can accept and execute them. SAP HANA is slated with a future release to be able to accept PMML model formats. After this feature is available, the PMML method may be the best way to create a predictive algorithm in the SAP HANA database. The PMML file is exported directly from the modeling software to the database with no manual interventions, minimizing development and testing resource requirements.

▶ **Call the predictive scoring function**

In predictive software, there is typically stored model scoring functionality available for most algorithms. This allows a model to be fitted and saved in a proprietary format that can be scored only by the predictive software. Therefore, the model can effectively be scored by writing a stored procedure to call the predictive software from the target application or database.

For SAP HANA, this could mean creating a stored procedure that calls an R or PAL scoring process on a saved model object. While this doesn't require that the actual model function be coded in SAP HANA, it does require some effort to create the stored procedure; however, future updates would require minimal changes, as no details of the actual model (such as coefficients or weights) are included in the stored procedure. As of version 1.0.11 of SAP Predictive Analysis, a stored procedure that calls a PAL model scoring function can be exported directly from the SAP Predictive Analysis predictive workflow for any saved models from PAL algorithms.

To illustrate some of these predictive concepts, we'll build and implement predictive models to assist with customer relationship management for the AdventureWorks Cycle Company. These models will use the data that was provisioned using SAP Data Services and modeled using SAP HANA Studio.

## 7.4 Case Study 1: Clustering Analysis

To increase Internet sales, the AdventureWorks marketing team has requested an in-depth analysis of its customers to understand common customer profiles and how to identify valuable customers early in their lifecycle. Based on this request from the marketing team, we'll first run a customer clustering analysis to better understand and segment customers.

Clustering is one of the most popular customer segmentation algorithms; it creates groups of similar customers based on numeric characteristics. While any numeric characteristic can be used to build the cluster, if you restrict the clustering algorithm to using only demographic (i.e., non-purchase-related characteristics), you may be able to evaluate a customer's potential lifetime value prior to the customer establishing a purchase history.

Therefore, for this initial analysis, we'll restrict the clustering algorithm to demographic characteristics, in an effort to allow the model to predict valuable customers without the benefit of transaction history. We'll use the R KMeans clustering algorithm to create our clusters in both SAP Predictive Analysis and through SAP HANA-R integration within SAP HANA Studio.

### 7.4.1 Preparing the Data

The first step to customer clustering is to ensure that the data is at the customer level prior to modeling. This means that there must be only one record per customer going into the modeling algorithm. In this case, we've created a calculation view on top of the Internet sales analytic view (ANLV_INTERNETSALES) created in Chapter 6. This calculation view simply aggregates order and sales metrics up to the customer level, creating customer-level aggregate data of total number of orders per customer and total sales. While these sales aggregates aren't used in generating the cluster assignments, we'll evaluate the clusters based on these aggregated measures after they are created.

**Create the First Customer Calculation View**

First, create an initial calculation view with customer and order counters that are used in the clustering process by following these steps:

1. Launch the SAP HANA Studio application.

2. Right-click the SAPHANA.INTERNETSALES package, and choose NEW • CALCULATION VIEW.

3. Enter the calculation view name "cv_internet_sales_order". You're creating a new calculation view using the graphical view type.

4. Add the analytic view ANLV_INTERNETSALES created in prior steps in the SELECT OBJECTS dialog shown in Figure 7.6.

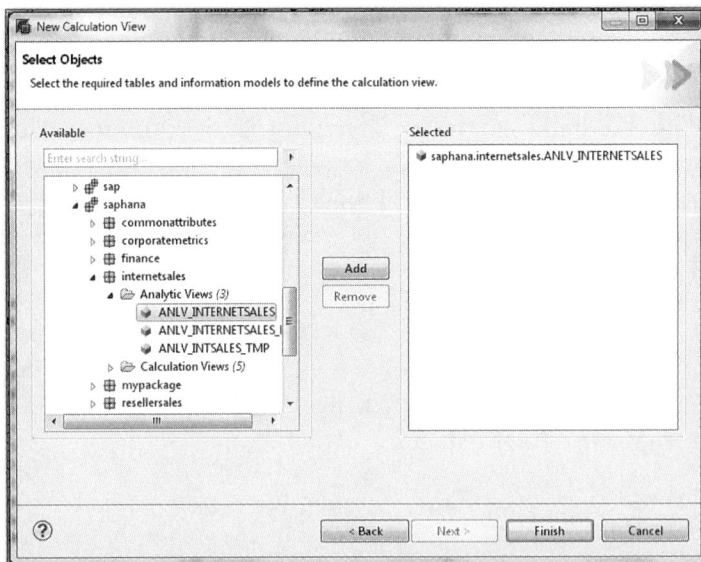

**Figure 7.6** Add Existing Internet Sales Analytic View to the Calculation View

5. Click FINISH, and define the rest of the calculation view manually.

6. In the TOOLS PALETTE dropdown box, select the AGGREGATION transform, as shown in Figure 7.7. This adds the AGGREGATION transform to the TOOLS PALETTE window. Connect the AGGREGATION transform from the ANLV_INTERNETSALES input element to the OUTPUT object.

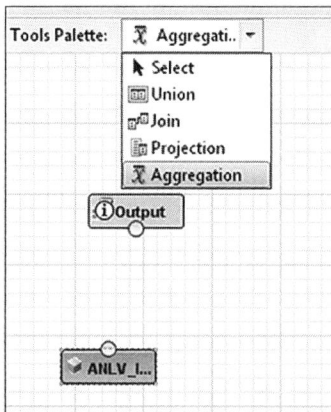

**Figure 7.7**  Selecting the Aggregation Transform

7. Click on the AGGREGATION transform, right-click on each element shown under COLUMNS in Figure 7.8, and click ADD TO OUTPUT to add the elements to the COLUMNS portion of OUTPUT OF AGGREGATION_1.

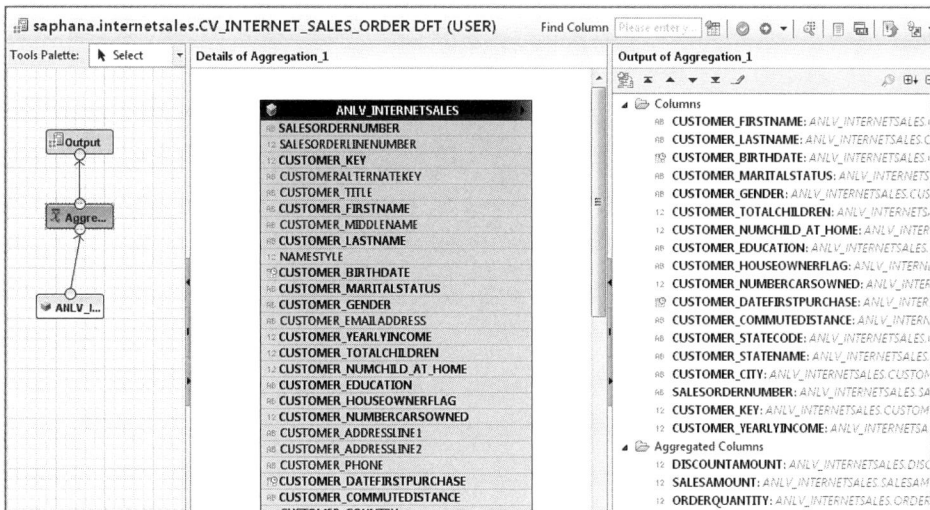

**Figure 7.8**  Configure Output Fields

491

8. Click on the DISCOUNTAMOUNT and SALESAMOUNT columns, right-click, and select ADD AS AGGREGATED COLUMN.

9. Right-click on CALCULATED COLUMNS and select NEW to create a calculated column for AGE, configured as shown in Figure 7.9.

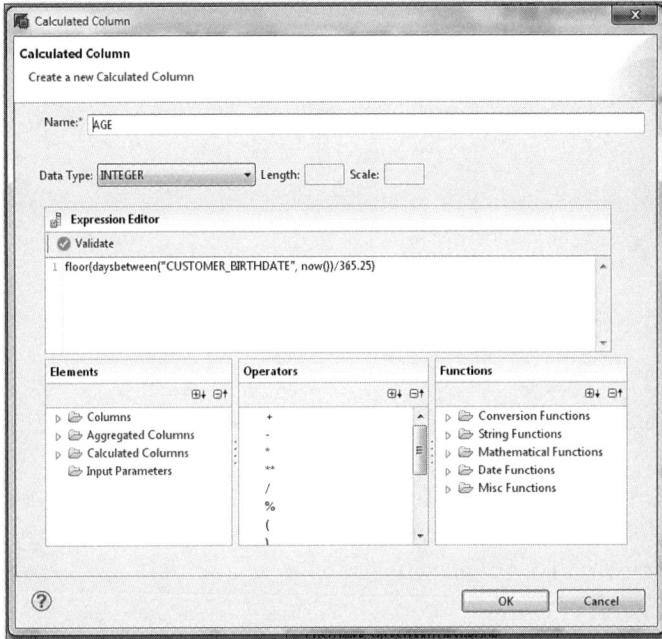

**Figure 7.9** Create Calculated Age Column

10. Click on the OUTPUT transform, right-click, and select ADD AS ATTRIBUTE for the list of variables shown under COLUMNS in Figure 7.9 as well as the new calculated AGE column. Right-click on the SALESAMOUNT and DISCOUNTA-MOUNT variables, and select ADD AS MEASURE.

11. Add counters for customers and orders by right-clicking on COUNTERS and choosing NEW. Configure each counter as shown in Figure 7.10.

12. Click SAVE AND VALIDATE the save the view, and then click on SAVE AND ACTI-VATE to active it.

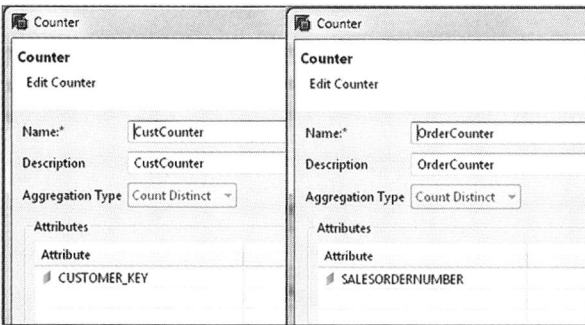

**Figure 7.10** Create Counters for Customers and Orders

### Create the Second Customer Calculation View

Follow these steps to create a second calculation view with a single record per customer using the order-level calculation view created just before that will be used to fit the clustering model.

1. Right-click the SAPHANA.INTERNETSALES package, and choose NEW • CALCULATION VIEW.

2. Enter the calculation view name "cv_internet_sales_customer". You're creating a new calculation view using the graphical view type.

3. Add the calculation view CV_INTERNET_SALES_ORDER created in prior steps in the SELECT OBJECTS dialog box shown previously in Figure 7.7.

4. Click FINISH, and define the rest of the calculation view manually.

5. Add and connect an AGGREGATION transform between the INPUT and OUTPUT transforms. In the AGGREGATION transform, add all customer fields, including AGE, to the COLUMNS output by right-clicking and selecting ADD TO OUTPUT. SALESORDERNUMBER should not be in the output of the AGGREGATION transform. Add SALESAMOUNT, DISCOUNTAMOUNT, CUSTCOUNTER, and ORDERCOUNTER as aggregated column outputs.

6. Click on the OUTPUT transform, select all customer fields, right-click, and select ADD AS ATTRIBUTES. Select the sales and discount amounts and counters. Right-click and select ADD AS MEASURE.

### 7.4.2 Performing Clustering Analysis

Now that the data has been prepared, you'll create the clustering model first in SAP Predictive Analysis and then later create the same model in SAP HANA Studio using the SAP HANA-R integration.

**Perform Cluster Analysis in SAP Predictive Analysis**

The SAP Predictive Analysis tool has an intuitive user interface and visualizations, where you'll create the predictive workflow and then visualize the cluster results. Although you're visualizing the data and creating the predictive workflow in the SAP Predictive Analysis tool on the user's local machine, the data is stored on SAP HANA, and the predictive algorithms are run on the configured Rserve instance. Follow these steps:

1. Open SAP Predictive Analysis, and click NEW DOCUMENT. Select a source type of HANA ONLINE. Enter the SAP HANA server address, instance name, and user name and password in the NEW DOCUMENT FROM HANA ONLINE dialog box, and click CONNECT HANA INSTANCE to open the content.

2. Navigate to the SAPHANA.INTERNETSALES package, and select the customer-level calculation view CV_INTERNET_SALES_CUSTOMER. Click SELECT to open the data set in SAP Predictive Analysis.

3. The document opens to the PREPARE pane, with the attributes and measures from the calculation view visible on the left in the OBJECT PICKER. Click on the PREDICT button at the top of the application screen to move to the PREDICT pane. In the top half of the PREDICT pane, on the ALGORITHMS tab, locate the HANA R-KMEANS algorithm under the CLUSTERING category. Double-click on the HANA R-KMEANS algorithm so that it's added to the predictive workflow, on the bottom half of the PREDICT pane, as shown in Figure 7.11.

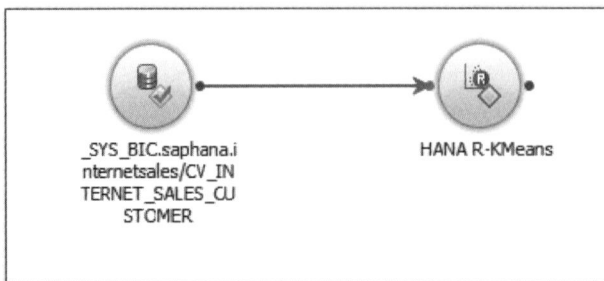

**Figure 7.11** Predictive Workflow for Clustering

4. Right-click on the HANA R-KMEANS module in the predictive workflow, and select CONFIGURE PROPERTIES. In the INDEPENDENT COLUMNS area, select the following fields: CUSTOMER_TOTALCHILDREN, CUSTOMER_NUMCHILD_AT_HOME, CUSTOMER_NUMBERCARSOWNED, AGE, and CUSTOMER_YEARLYINCOME.

Enter "3" for NUMBER OF CLUSTERS. The configurations should match Figure 7.12. Click SAVE AND CLOSE to return to the predictive workflow.

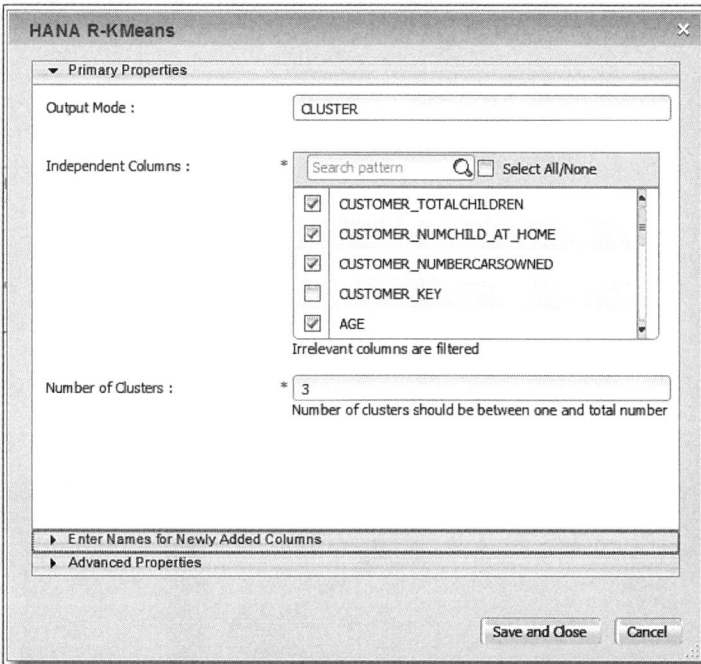

**Figure 7.12** SAP HANA R-KMeans Configuration

5. Right-click on the HANA R-KMEANS module in the predictive workflow and select RUN ANALYSIS. Upon completion, a success message will appear. Click YES to navigate to the predictive RESULTS pane.

6. On the RESULTS pane shown in Figure 7.13, review the result data, which should have the new CLUSTERNUMBER field included, and navigate to the RESULT CHARTS area to view the automated algorithm visualizations, shown in Figure 7.14.

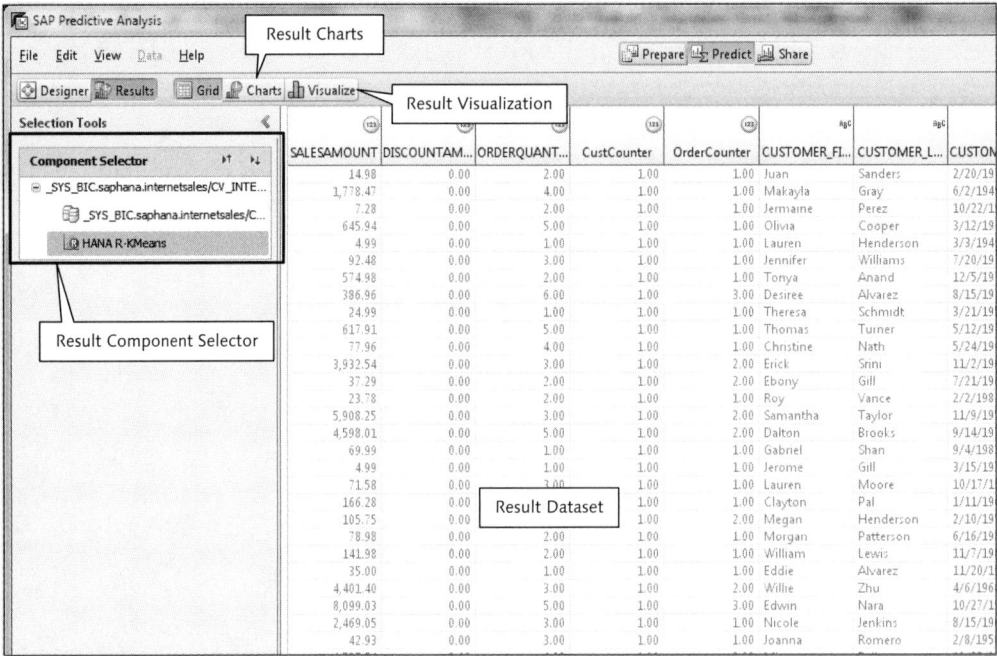

**Figure 7.13** Prediction Result Pane

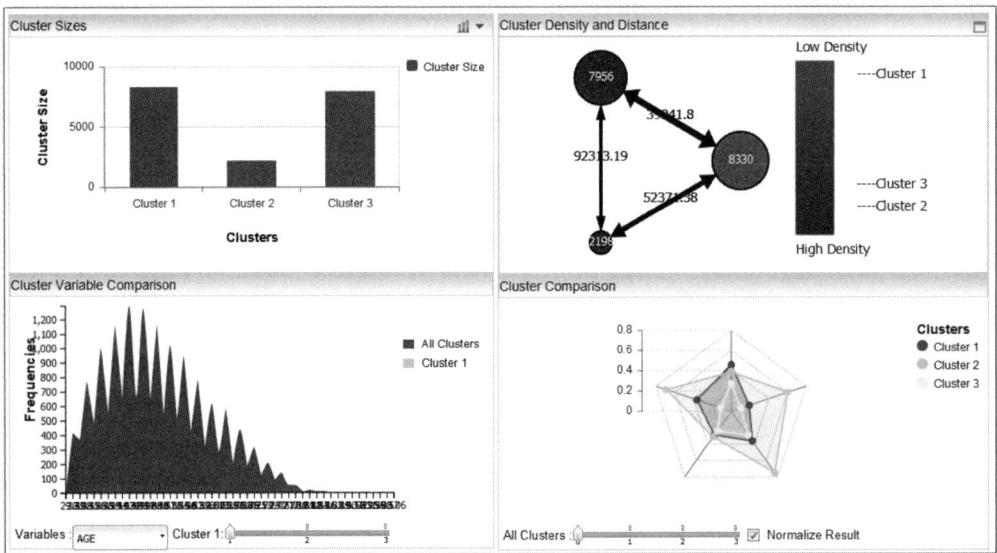

**Figure 7.14** SAP Predictive Analysis Clustering Visualization

> **Cluster Model Evaluation**
>
> After you've fit clusters to the AdventureWorks customer data, you should evaluate these clusters using both the automated output visualizations and by comparing key business metrics against the clustered customer groups. In Figure 7.14, the clusters are summarized, and you can see that there are two approximately equally sized larger clusters (1 and 3) and a single much smaller cluster. However, on the radar chart in the bottom-right area of the cluster visualization, you can see that while cluster 2 is the smallest in terms of customer volume, the cluster 2 customers are very different demographically from clusters 1 and 3. Cluster 2 customers have on average a higher income, almost twice as many cars, and are slightly older than customers in cluster 1 and 3.
>
> The true test of the segmentation model is evaluating how well it segments customers' shopping habits. After reviewing the cluster segmentation compared to key metrics, including sales and orders, you can see that cluster 2 also spends significantly more than clusters 1 and 3. This higher spending is driven primarily by a higher average order amount, but cluster 2 also shops more frequently than clusters 1 and 3. Therefore, internal customer group names will be assigned according to the spending habits of each group—cluster 2 will be "Gold" level customers, cluster 3 is "Silver," and cluster 1 is "Bronze," as in Table 7.6.

7. After reviewing the cluster visualizations, note the R output shown in Figure 7.15 by clicking on the center icon at the top of the predictive RESULTS CHARTS pane. While this text output may not look useful, it contains important information to re-create the cluster scoring algorithm in a database or other application. The data labeled CENTERS in the R output contains the center point for each cluster, and is used in the scoring algorithm later.

**Perform Cluster Analysis in SAP HANA Studio**

In the absence of the SAP Predictive Analysis client, the same clustering analysis can be performed by running R code in SAP HANA Studio. This process effectively runs the same predictive process as SAP Predictive Analysis, with predictive algorithms run on the configured Rserve instance. Because this data is being transferred between servers, it's critical to transfer only the data that will be run through the algorithm to the R server, and not include any extraneous fields. Follow these steps:

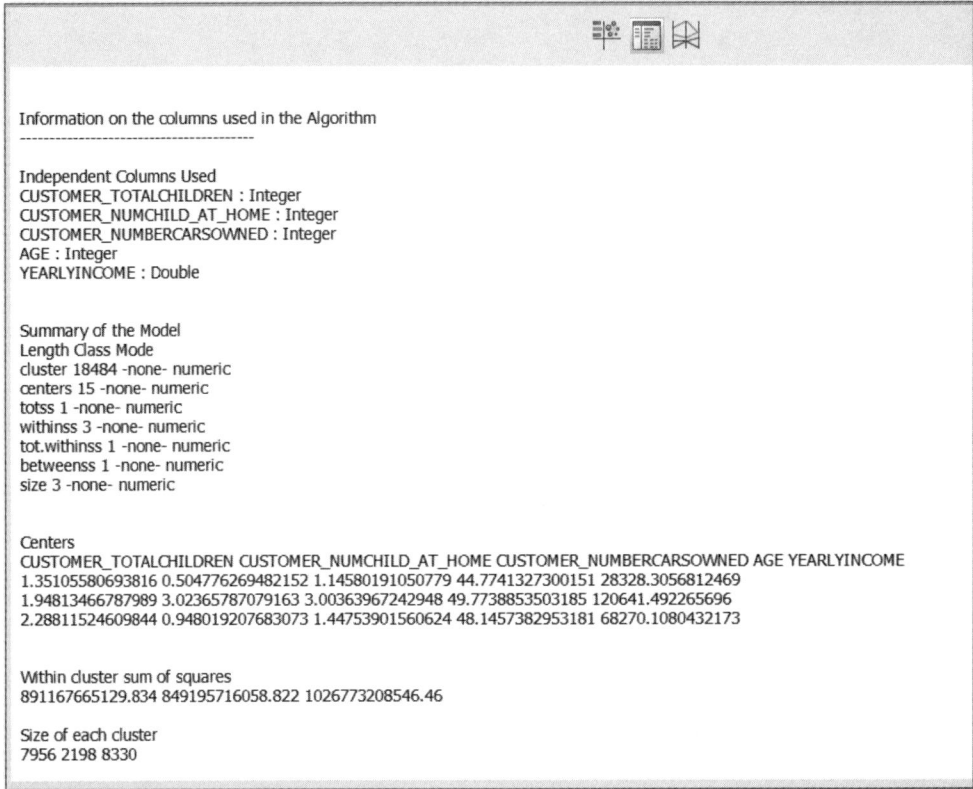

**Figure 7.15** SAP Predictive Analysis Clustering R Output

1. Open SAP HANA Studio, and create three new tables to hold the modeling input data and output data with structures as shown in Figure 7.16.

   Note that these tables need to be created in a separate schema called PA with the Predictive User role to isolate the predictive content generated by predictive algorithms. Table 7.5 offers a summary of these tables and the purpose for each.

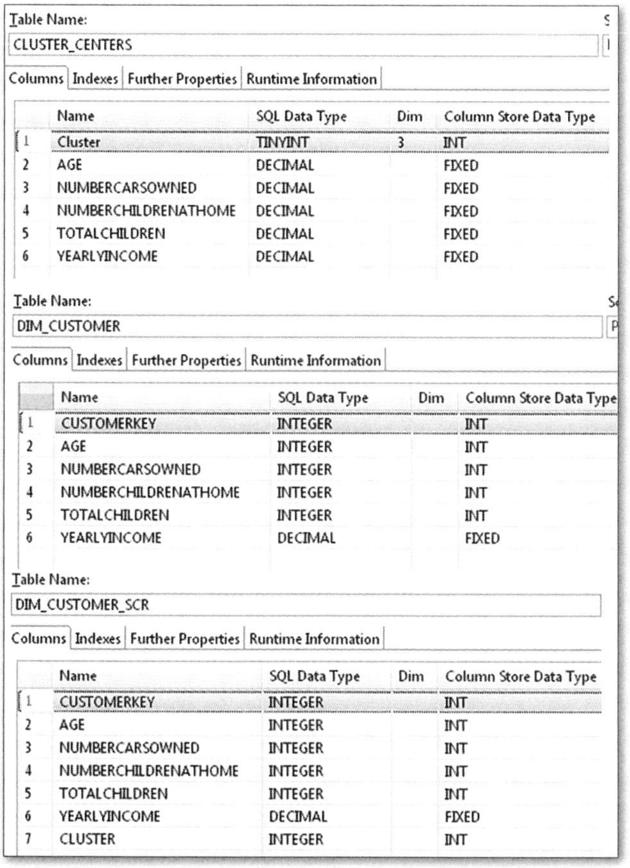

**Figure 7.16** Input and Output Tables for R Clustering in SAP HANA Studio

| Table | Purpose |
|---|---|
| CLUSTER_CENTERS | A model output table with the centers for each customer cluster. It's used in scoring new customers against the existing clustering model at a later time. |
| DIM_CUSTOMER | The model input table, which is a slimmed down copy of the DIM_CUSTOMER table from the BOOK_USER schema with only the five clustering variables and the CUSTOMER_KEY field. |
| DIM_CUSTOMER_SCR | The model output table, which has the same fields as the model input table with one additional column for the predicted cluster. |

**Table 7.5** Input and Output Tables for R Clustering in SAP HANA Studio

2. Populate the DIM_CUSTOMER modeling input table with the data required to build the clustering model in R, shown in Listing 7.1.

```
INSERT INTO "PA"."DIM_CUSTOMER"
select
  "CUSTOMERKEY",
  floor(days_between("BIRTHDATE", now())/365.25),
  "NUMBERCARSOWNED",
  "NUMBERCHILDRENATHOME",
  "TOTALCHILDREN",
  "YEARLYINCOME"
from "BOOK_USER"."DIM_CUSTOMER";
```

**Listing 7.1** SQL to Populate the Modeling Input Table

3. As shown in Listing 7.2, create the R procedure ClustScr to cluster the input table customers and return the customer scores as well as the cluster center information.

```
delete from "PA"."CLUSTER_CENTERS";
delete from "PA"."DIM_CUSTOMER_SCR";
DROP PROCEDURE ClustScr;
CREATE PROCEDURE
  ClustScr(
      IN train "PA"."DIM_CUSTOMER",
      OUT resulta "PA"."DIM_CUSTOMER_SCR",
      OUT resultb "PA"."RCLUSTER_CENTERS"
)
LANGUAGE RLANG AS
BEGIN
 custclust <- kmeans(train[,2:6], centers=3, nstart=1000);

 resultb <- as.data.frame(cbind(Cluster=1:dim(custclust$centers)[1],
custclust$centers));

 resulta <- as.data.frame(cbind(train, CLUSTER=custclust$cluster));
END;

CALL ClustScr(
      "PA"."DIM_CUSTOMER",
      "PA"."DIM_CUSTOMER_SCR",
      "PA"."RCLUSTER_CENTERS"
) WITH OVERVIEW;
```

**Listing 7.2** R Code to Run Cluster Analysis

4. Review the cluster distributions either by running the SQL in Listing 7.3, or by opening the data preview for the DIM_CUSTOMER_SCR table, which should return the results shown in Figure 7.17.

```
select
    CLUSTER, count(*)
from "PA"."DIM_CUSTOMER_SCR"
    group by CLUSTER;
```

**Listing 7.3** SQL to View Distribution by Cluster

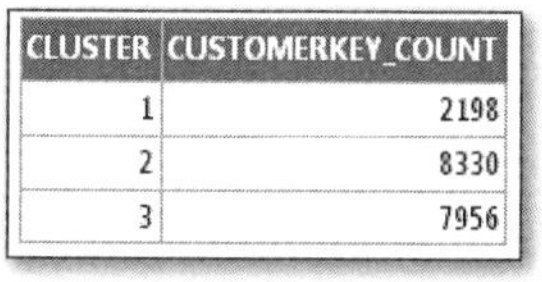

| CLUSTER | CUSTOMERKEY_COUNT |
|---------|-------------------|
| 1 | 2198 |
| 2 | 8330 |
| 3 | 7956 |

**Figure 7.17** Cluster Data Preview Results

Cluster numbers generated by the clustering algorithm are randomly assigned, so although the clusters were named differently between the SAP Predictive Analysis run and the SAP HANA Studio run, the clusters are constructed identically. After the clustering algorithm is accepted in the organization, the cluster names 1, 2, and 3 should be altered to reflect organizationally-accepted names.

To evaluate the value of the cluster algorithm you've created, let's review key metrics against the cluster breakdowns. Table 7.6 shows sales and orders per customer for each of the three clusters. While the clustering algorithm doesn't take into account any of these purchase-based metrics, it does effectively differentiate customers by purchase levels, with cluster 2 identifying a relatively small group of customers with a much higher than average order size and frequency. This analysis could be extended further to evaluate profitability per customer, and then be used to drive investment in acquiring and retaining these customers.

| Cluster | Customers | Sales/Customer | Orders/Customer | Sales/Order |
|---------|-----------|----------------|-----------------|-------------|
| 1 – Bronze | 7,956 | 1,327 | 1.42 | $935 |
| 2 – Gold | 2,198 | 2,195 | 1.65 | $1,330 |
| 3 – Silver | 8,330 | 1,678 | 1.53 | $1,097 |
| Overall | 18,484 | 1,588 | 1.50 | $1,061 |

**Table 7.6** Key Metrics by Cluster

### 7.4.3 Implementing the Model

Because this model is built using only demographic characteristics, a customer's cluster can be assigned immediately when the customer is added to the customer database. Therefore, you can implement a scoring algorithm in the database that allows you to assign new records to the appropriate cluster. For some R algorithms, there are R functions that consume a saved R model object created during the fitting process, as well as new observations, and score them in R; for these algorithms, one implementation option is to call the R fitting algorithm to score new observations. However, the KMeans clustering algorithm doesn't have a scoring procedure, so you have program your own scoring algorithm in SAP HANA.

To score a clustering model, you must calculate the Euclidian distance between a customer observation and the centers of each of the three clusters developed in the model. Euclidian distance is the straight-line distance between two points in n-space; in this case, there are five dimensional vectors for the customer and each of the cluster centers. An example calculation for the Euclidian distance between a customer observation o, and cluster 1 center is shown in Figure 7.18.

**Euclidian Distance Definition**

$$d(o, 1) = \sqrt{(o_1 - 1_1)^2 + (o_2 - 1_2)^2 + (o_3 - 1_3)^2 + (o_4 - 1_4)^2 + (o_5 - 1_5)^2}$$

**Example Observations**

| | Age | Number Cars Owned | Number Children at Home | Total Children | Yearly Income |
|---|---|---|---|---|---|
| Cluster Center 1 | 45 | 1.15 | 0.50 | 1.35 | $ 28,328.30 |
| Customer Observation O | 27 | 0 | 0 | 0 | $ 75,000.00 |

**Example Distance Calculation**

$$d(o, 1) = \sqrt{(45 - 27)^2 + (1.15 - 0)^2 + (0.5 - 0)^2 + (1.35 - 0)^2 + (28328.3 - 75000)^2} = 46{,}671.7$$

**Figure 7.18** Euclidian Distance between Observation o and Cluster 1

The Euclidian distance calculation is repeated for each cluster, and the new observation is assigned to the cluster with the minimum Euclidian distance from the observation.

Now you can implement the process just described to assign new observations to clusters in the SAP HANA database using the following steps:

1. Create a score table to hold the cluster scores, which will be keyed on the CUS-TOMERKEY field. An example creation statement for this table is given in Listing 7.4.

```
CREATE COLUMN TABLE "PA"."DIM_CUSTOMER_CLUSTER_SCORE"
("CUSTOMERKEY" INTEGER CS_INT NOT NULL ,
  "CLUSTER" INTEGER CS_INT,
  "SCORE_DATE" date CS_DATE,
  PRIMARY KEY ("CUSTOMERKEY")
  );
```

**Listing 7.4** SQL to Create a Cluster Score Dimension Table

2. Create a table in SAP HANA with the cluster center information. This can either be the PA.RCLUSTER_CENTERS table that was created with the HANA-R KMeans clustering output generated previously or entered manually using the R output from SAP Predictive Analysis shown earlier in Figure 7.15.

3. Create a view to calculate the Euclidian distance between each observation in the customer table and each of the three clusters. An example of this calculation is included in Listing 7.5. Although there are several ways to perform this calculation, this solution attaches the cluster center information for each of the three customer clusters to each customer record, calculates the Euclidian distance for each cluster, and returns the cluster number for the cluster with the minimum distance.

```
create view "PA"."CLUSTER_SCORE" as
select
a.CUSTOMERKEY, a.AGE, a.NUMBERCARSOWNED, NUMBERCHILDRENATHOME,
TOTALCHILDREN, YEARLYINCOME,
SQRT(age1diffsq+cars1diffsq+cah1diffsq+totchild1diffsq+inc1diffsq)
clust1dist,
SQRT(age2diffsq+cars2diffsq+cah2diffsq+totchild2diffsq+inc2diffsq)
clust2dist,
SQRT(age3diffsq+cars3diffsq+cah3diffsq+totchild3diffsq+inc3diffsq)
clust3dist

  ,

  case when SQRT(age1diffsq+cars1diffsq+cah1diffsq+totchild1diffsq+in
  c1diffsq) <SQRT(age2diffsq+cars2diffsq+cah2diffsq+totchild2diffsq+in
  c2diffsq)
    and SQRT(age1diffsq+cars1diffsq+cah1diffsq+totchild1diffsq+inc1dif
```

```
fsq)<SQRT(age3diffsq+cars3diffsq+cah3diffsq+totchild3diffsq+inc3diff
sq) then 1
 when
  SQRT(age2diffsq+cars2diffsq+cah2diffsq+totchild2diffsq+inc2diffsq)<
SQRT(age1diffsq+cars1diffsq+cah1diffsq+totchild1diffsq+inc1diffsq)
  and SQRT(age2diffsq+cars2diffsq+cah2diffsq+totchild2diffsq+inc2dif
fsq)<SQRT(age3diffsq+cars3diffsq+cah3diffsq+totchild3diffsq+inc3diff
sq) then 2
  else 3
   end Cluster
 from

 (
 select
cust.*,
c1."AGE" as AGE1,
c1."NUMBERCARSOWNED" as NUMBERCARSOWNED1,
c1."NUMBERCHILDRENATHOME" as NUMBERCHILDRENATHOME1,
c1."TOTALCHILDREN" as TOTALCHILDREN1,
c1."YEARLYINCOME" as YEARLYINCOME1,

c2."AGE" as AGE2,
c2."NUMBERCARSOWNED" as NUMBERCARSOWNED2,
c2."NUMBERCHILDRENATHOME" as NUMBERCHILDRENATHOME2,
c2."TOTALCHILDREN" as TOTALCHILDREN2,
c2."YEARLYINCOME" as YEARLYINCOME2,

c3."AGE" as AGE3,
c3."NUMBERCARSOWNED" as NUMBERCARSOWNED3,
c3."NUMBERCHILDRENATHOME" as NUMBERCHILDRENATHOME3,
c3."TOTALCHILDREN" as TOTALCHILDREN3,
c3."YEARLYINCOME" as YEARLYINCOME3,

POWER((cust.AGE-c1.AGE), 2) as age1diffsq,
POWER((cust.NUMBERCARSOWNED-c1.NUMBERCARSOWNED), 2) cars1diffsq,
POWER((cust.NUMBERCHILDRENATHOME-c1.NUMBERCHILDRENATHOME), 2)
cah1diffsq,
POWER((cust.TOTALCHILDREN-c1.TOTALCHILDREN), 2) totchild1diffsq,
POWER((cust.YEARLYINCOME-c1.YEARLYINCOME), 2) inc1diffsq,

POWER((cust.AGE-c2.AGE), 2) age2diffsq,
POWER((cust.NUMBERCARSOWNED-c2.NUMBERCARSOWNED), 2) cars2diffsq,
```

```
POWER((cust.NUMBERCHILDRENATHOME-c2.NUMBERCHILDRENATHOME), 2)
cah2diffsq,
POWER((cust.TOTALCHILDREN-c2.TOTALCHILDREN), 2) totchild2diffsq,
POWER((cust.YEARLYINCOME-c2.YEARLYINCOME), 2) inc2diffsq,

POWER((cust.AGE-c3.AGE), 2) age3diffsq,
POWER((cust.NUMBERCARSOWNED-c3.NUMBERCARSOWNED), 2) cars3diffsq,
POWER((cust.NUMBERCHILDRENATHOME-c3.NUMBERCHILDRENATHOME), 2)
cah3diffsq,
POWER((cust.TOTALCHILDREN-c3.TOTALCHILDREN), 2) totchild3diffsq,
POWER((cust.YEARLYINCOME-c3.YEARLYINCOME), 2) inc3diffsq

from
 (select
CUSTOMERKEY,
floor(days_between(BIRTHDATE, now()))/365.25) AGE,
NUMBERCARSOWNED,
NUMBERCHILDRENATHOME,
TOTALCHILDREN,
YEARLYINCOME

  from "BOOK_USER"."DIM_CUSTOMER") cust cross join
  (select * from "PA"."RCLUSTER_CENTERS" where "Cluster"=1) c1 cross
join
  (select * from "PA"."RCLUSTER_CENTERS" where "Cluster"=2) c2 cross
join
  (select * from "PA"."RCLUSTER_CENTERS" where "Cluster"=3) c3
) a
```

**Listing 7.5** SQL Query to Score DIM_CUSTOMER against the Clustering Model

4. Update or replace the score history table with the results of the view as appropriate for the implementation of the cluster score dimension. This view can be used in an SAP Data Services extract, transform, and load (ETL) job or SQLscript such as the one in Listing 7.6 to insert new values. In this case, truncate the DIM_CUSTOMER_CLUSTER_SCORE table and keep only the most recent score.

```
delete from "BOOK_USER"."DIM_CUSTOMER_CLUSTER_SCORE";
insert into
  "BOOK_USER"."DIM_CUSTOMER_CLUSTER_SCORE"
select
  CUSTOMERKEY,
```

```
CLUSTER,
now()
from "PA"."CLUSTER_SCORE";
```

**Listing 7.6** SQL to Populate the Cluster Score Dimension Table

5. Repeat the previous step only when the organization has determined that clusters should be recalculated on each customer.

6. Include the new DIM_CUSTOMER_CLUSTER_SCORE table in the existing customer attribute view in SAP HANA Studio by navigating to the saphana.commonattributes content package and double-clicking on ATVB_CUSTOMER. Drag and drop the new table DIM_CUSTOMER_CLUSTER_SCORE into the DATA FOUNDATION area, as shown in Figure 7.19.

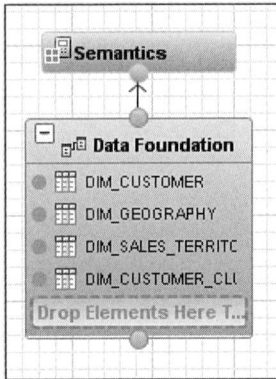

**Figure 7.19** Customer Attribute View with Clustering Score Added

7. Drag a connection between DIM_CUSTOMER.CUSTOMERKEY and DIM_CUSTOMER_CLUSTER_SCORE.CUSTOMERKEY to connect the new table to the existing dimension tables. Click on the CLUSTER field in the DIM_CUSTOMER_CLUSTER_SCORE table to add it to the attribute view.

8. Create a calculated column by right-clicking on CALCULATED COLUMNS in the OUTPUT area of the DATA_FOUNDATION object and click NEW. Use a case statement to translate the cluster numbers into organizationally accepted names for each customer group, as shown in Figure 7.20.

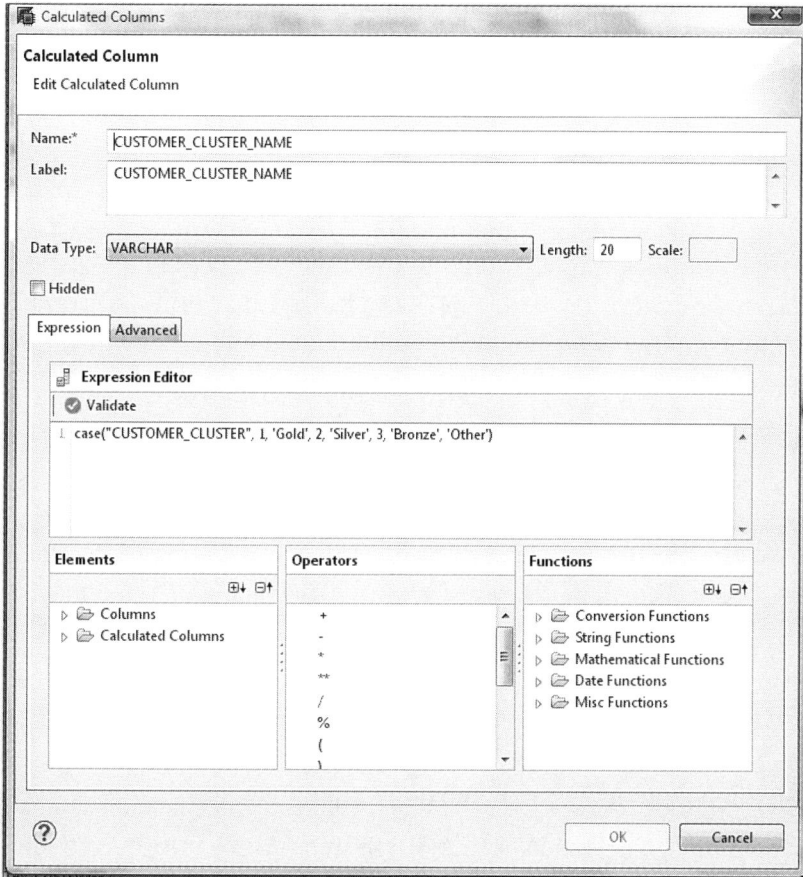

**Figure 7.20**  Calculated Field for Cluster Name

The clustering scores are now available in the common customer attribute view and can be added to dependent analytic views, SAP BusinessObjects universes, and end-user reports as necessary. The scoring algorithm you just developed can also be created as a stored procedure to score new records in the database.

## 7.5    Case Study 2: Product Recommendation Rules

AdventureWorks Cycle Company has also requested a method to identify likely companion purchases based on items already in a customer's online purchase basket. To determine which products to suggest, we'll develop an association model to suggest companion products to show on the website during the purchase process. These product suggestions should be prioritized to include items the customer is most likely to purchase, with a target of increasing average purchase size.

### 7.5.1 Preparing the Data

Unlike for the clustering model, the data from the existing Internet sales analytic view can be used for the Apriori algorithm that will suggest associations between items. Therefore, we'll access the ANLV_INTERNETSALES analytical view created in previous chapters as the input for this algorithm.

### 7.5.2 Performing Apriori Analysis

The Apriori algorithm examines correlations and patterns within groups of items and is commonly used to develop item sets that are selected with high frequency; therefore, if a customer has already expressed interest in a portion of that item set, suggesting the remaining items may result in a high likelihood of acceptance.

In this case, we'll perform this Apriori analysis in both SAP Predictive Analysis and SAP HANA Studio, with both processes using the same Apriori algorithm from the PAL.

**Perform Apriori Analysis Using SAP Predictive Analysis**

Follow these steps to first devise the Apriori suggestion rules by using SAP Predictive Analysis to run the PAL Apriori algorithm and review the visualization results:

1. Open SAP Predictive Analysis, and click NEW DOCUMENT. Select a source type of HANA ONLINE. Enter the SAP HANA server address, instance name, and user name and password in the NEW DOCUMENT FROM HANA ONLINE dialog box, and click CONNECT HANA INSTANCE to open content.

2. Navigate to the SAPHANA.INTERNETSALES package, and select the analytic view ANLV_INTERNETSALES. Click the PREVIEW AND SELECT DATA checkbox, and then click ACQUIRE to open the data set in SAP Predictive Analysis. In the field selection window, select only product-related fields (PRODUCT_KEY, PRODUCT_NAME, at a minimum) and the SALESORDERNUMBER transaction key. Optionally, include a measure such as SALESAMOUNT, if you want to perform any visualizations in SAP Predictive Analysis. Click OK to create the new SAP Predictive Analysis document.

3. Proceed to the PREDICT pane, and add the HANA APRIORI transform in the ASSOCIATION category of the ALGORITHMS tab to the predictive workflow. Right-click on the HANA APRIORI transform in the workflow, and select CONFIGURE PROPERTIES. Adjust the configurations for the transform to match those shown in Figure 7.21.

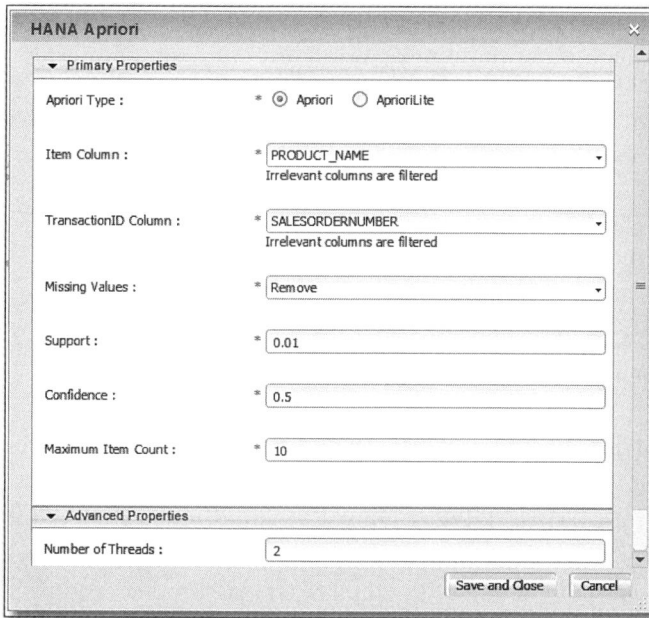

**Figure 7.21** SAP HANA Apriori Transform Configuration Settings

4. Navigate to the DATA WRITERS tab, and double-click on the HANA WRITER transform to add it to the predictive workflow. Right-click on the new transform, and select CONFIGURE PROPERTIES. Enter the target table schema name ("BOOK_USER") and table name ("APRIORI_RESULT"), and select the OVERWRITE check-box.

5. Click on the RUN ANALYSIS button to run the predictive workflow. When the success message is received, click YES to proceed to the RESULTS pane, and then click CHARTS to view the automated visualization output, shown in Figure 7.22.

6. Reopen the configuration window for the SAP HANA APRIORI transform, and enter "PRODUCT_KEY" in the ITEM COLUMN prompt. Rerun the analysis to generate the output table with keys rather than names for integration with the e-commerce application.

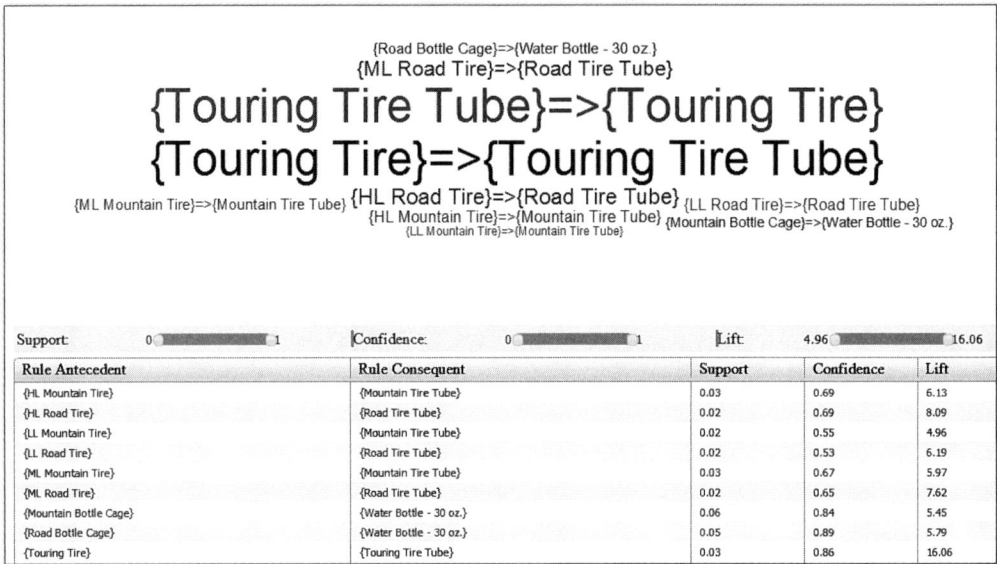

{Road Bottle Cage}=>{Water Bottle - 30 oz.}
{ML Road Tire}=>{Road Tire Tube}

# {Touring Tire Tube}=>{Touring Tire}
# {Touring Tire}=>{Touring Tire Tube}

{ML Mountain Tire}=>{Mountain Tire Tube} {HL Road Tire}=>{Road Tire Tube} {LL Road Tire}=>{Road Tire Tube}
{HL Mountain Tire}=>{Mountain Tire Tube} {Mountain Bottle Cage}=>{Water Bottle - 30 oz.}
{LL Mountain Tire}=>{Mountain Tire Tube}

| Support: | 0 | 1 | Confidence: | 0 | 1 | Lift: | 4.96 | 16.06 |

| Rule Antecedent | Rule Consequent | Support | Confidence | Lift |
| --- | --- | --- | --- | --- |
| {HL Mountain Tire} | {Mountain Tire Tube} | 0.03 | 0.69 | 6.13 |
| {HL Road Tire} | {Road Tire Tube} | 0.02 | 0.69 | 8.09 |
| {LL Mountain Tire} | {Mountain Tire Tube} | 0.02 | 0.55 | 4.96 |
| {LL Road Tire} | {Road Tire Tube} | 0.02 | 0.53 | 6.19 |
| {ML Mountain Tire} | {Mountain Tire Tube} | 0.03 | 0.67 | 5.97 |
| {ML Road Tire} | {Road Tire Tube} | 0.02 | 0.65 | 7.62 |
| {Mountain Bottle Cage} | {Water Bottle - 30 oz.} | 0.06 | 0.84 | 5.45 |
| {Road Bottle Cage} | {Water Bottle - 30 oz.} | 0.05 | 0.89 | 5.79 |
| {Touring Tire} | {Touring Tire Tube} | 0.03 | 0.86 | 16.06 |

**Figure 7.22**  SAP HANA Apriori Transform Charts Output

In reviewing the results of this analysis, you'll see several pairings that make sense; for example, there are several tube and tire combinations, where customers purchasing a tire are also purchasing a corresponding type of tire tube with a confidence of 60% or higher. This may seem like common sense, but simply making this suggestion available prior to the completion of the Internet transaction to customers who purchase only a tube or only a tire could drive significant sales at little to no cost to AdventureWorks. You can also review the output table that was created as a part of this process, as shown in Figure 7.23.

| A8 Rules | 12 Support | 12 Confidence | 12 Lift |
| --- | --- | --- | --- |
| {535} => {528} | 0.01728189739325355 | 0.5545243619489559 | 4.955602367413949 |
| {540} => {529} | 0.02154813984598142 | 0.6946386946386947 | 8.086284366587396 |
| {539} => {529} | 0.02190968581655157 | 0.6544276457883369 | 7.618187817701856 |
| {538} => {529} | 0.02006580136664377 | 0.5316091954022989 | 6.18845906381826 |
| {541} => {530} | 0.02921291442206876 | 0.8641711229946524 | 16.06324535679374 |
| {530} => {541} | 0.02921291442206876 | 0.543010752688172 | 16.06324535679374 |
| {536} => {528} | 0.02805596731624426 | 0.6683893195521102 | 5.97317615169364 |
| {537} => {528} | 0.03459994938356412 | 0.6855300859598854 | 6.126357559794659 |
| {479} => {477} | 0.05499114212372103 | 0.8884345794392523 | 5.790106511006192 |
| {478} => {477} | 0.06117357822047073 | 0.8355555555555556 | 5.445483296680282 |
| {478,485} => {477} | 0.01182255323764417 | 0.8341836734693877 | 5.436542465713901 |
| {477,485} => {478} | 0.01182255323764417 | 1.0 | 13.65876543209876 |

**Figure 7.23**  BOOK_USER.APRIORI_OUT Table

### Perform Apriori Analysis Using SAP HANA Studio

You can perform the same Apriori analysis from the SAP HANA Studio client by calling the PAL Apriori procedure via code using the following steps. These steps will create the Apriori function and then run it to retrieve the same Apriori rules output table generated by SAP Predictive Analysis.

1. Open SAP HANA Studio, and then open a new SQL window to run the table type creation and function generation scripts included in Listing 7.7.

```
SET SCHEMA PA;

DROP TYPE PAL_DATA_T;
CREATE TYPE PAL_DATA_T AS TABLE(
"CUSTOMER" VARCHAR(20),
"ITEM" INTEGER
);

DROP TYPE PAL_RESULT_T;
CREATE TYPE PAL_RESULT_T AS TABLE(
"PRERULE" VARCHAR(500),
"POSTRULE" VARCHAR(500),
"SUPPORT" DOUBLE,
"CONFIDENCE" DOUBLE,
"LIFT" DOUBLE
);

DROP TYPE PAL_PMMLMODEL_T;
CREATE TYPE PAL_PMMLMODEL_T AS TABLE(
"ID" INT,
"PMMLMODEL" VARCHAR(5000)
);

DROP TYPE PAL_CONTROL_T;
CREATE TYPE PAL_CONTROL_T AS TABLE(
"NAME" VARCHAR (50),
"INTARGS" INTEGER,
"DOUBLEARGS" DOUBLE,
"STRINGARGS" VARCHAR (100)
);

DROP TABLE PDATA;
CREATE COLUMN TABLE PDATA(
"ID" INT,
```

```
"TYPENAME" VARCHAR(100),
"DIRECTION" VARCHAR(100) );
INSERT INTO PDATA VALUES (1, 'PA_DEMO.PAL_DATA_T', 'in');
INSERT INTO PDATA VALUES (2, 'PA_DEMO.PAL_CONTROL_T', 'in');
INSERT INTO PDATA VALUES (3, 'PA_DEMO.PAL_RESULT_T', 'out');
INSERT INTO PDATA VALUES (4, 'PA_DEMO.PAL_PMMLMODEL_T', 'out');

GRANT SELECT ON PA_DEMO.PDATA to SYSTEM;

call SYSTEM.afl_wrapper_generator('PAL_APRIORI_RULE', 'AFLPAL',
'APRIORIRULE', PDATA);
```

**Listing 7.7** PAL Apriori Function Creation

2. After the `PAL_APRIORI_RULE` function has been created, you must create a table with the transaction and product information, as well as shell tables for the function output results. Finally, call the `PAL_APRIORI_RULE` function to populate the `PAL_RESULT_TAB` with the result table. The table creation and function script is found in Listing 7.8.

```
DROP TABLE PAL_TRANS_TAB;
CREATE COLUMN TABLE PAL_TRANS_TAB(
"CUSTOMER" VARCHAR(20),
"ITEM" INTEGER );
insert into PAL_TRANS_TAB
   (select SALESORDERNUMBER, PRODUCT_KEY from "_SYS_BIC"."saphana.
internetsales/ANLV_INTERNETSALES");

DROP TABLE PAL_CONTROL_TAB;
CREATE COLUMN TABLE PAL_CONTROL_TAB(
"NAME" VARCHAR (50),
"INTARGS" INTEGER,
"DOUBLEARGS" DOUBLE,
"STRINGARGS" VARCHAR (100)
);
INSERT INTO PAL_CONTROL_TAB VALUES ('THREAD_NUMBER', 2, null, null);
INSERT INTO PAL_CONTROL_TAB VALUES ('MIN_SUPPORT', null, 0.01, null);
INSERT INTO PAL_CONTROL_TAB VALUES ('MIN_CONFIDENCE', null, 0.5,
null);
DROP TABLE PAL_RESULT_TAB;
CREATE COLUMN TABLE PAL_RESULT_TAB(
"PRERULE" VARCHAR(500),
"POSTRULE" VARCHAR(500),
```

```
"SUPPORT" Double,
"CONFIDENCE" Double,
"LIFT" DOUBLE
);

DROP TABLE PAL_PMMLMODEL_TAB;
CREATE COLUMN TABLE PAL_PMMLMODEL_TAB(
"ID" INT,
"PMMLMODEL" VARCHAR(5000)
);

CALL _SYS_AFL.PAL_APRIORI_RULE(PAL_TRANS_TAB, PAL_CONTROL_TAB,
PAL_RESULT_TAB, PAL_PMMLMODEL_TAB) WITH overview;
```

**Listing 7.8** PAL Apriori Table Creation and Function Call

3. Review the results in PAL_RESULT_TAB, as shown in Figure 7.24.

| | PRERULE | POSTRULE | SUPPORT | CONFIDENCE | LIFT |
|---|---|---|---|---|---|
| 1 | 478 | 477 | 0.06117357686161995 | 0.8355555534362793 | 5.445483684539795 |
| 2 | 479 | 477 | 0.0549911409661647034 | 0.8884345293045044 | 5.790106296539307 |
| 3 | 535 | 528 | 0.017281897366046906 | 0.5545243620872498 | 4.955602645874023 |
| 4 | 536 | 528 | 0.028055967763066292 | 0.6683893203735352 | 5.9731764793396 |
| 5 | 537 | 528 | 0.034599948674440384 | 0.6855300664901733 | 6.126357555389404 |
| 6 | 538 | 529 | 0.0200658012181520046 | 0.5316092371940613 | 6.188459396362305 |
| 7 | 539 | 529 | 0.02190968580543995 | 0.6544276475906372 | 7.61818790435791 |
| 8 | 540 | 529 | 0.021548138931393623 | 0.6946386694908142 | 8.086283683776855 |
| 9 | 530 | 541 | 0.029212914407253265 | 0.5430107116699219 | 16.063243865966... |
| 10 | 541 | 530 | 0.029212914407253265 | 0.8641711473464966 | 16.06324577331543 |
| 11 | 478&485 | 477 | 0.011822553351521492 | 0.8341836333274841 | 5.436542510986328 |
| 12 | 477&485 | 478 | 0.011822553351521492 | 1.0 | 13.65876579284668 |

**Figure 7.24** PAL Apriori Function Output

### 7.5.3 Implementing the Model

To make the suggested products available to the web application, the Internet team requested the ability to send one or more product keys and be returned with a list of items that should be displayed to the customer.

There are three possible ways to execute this using SAP HANA:

1. Employ the SAP HANA XS Engine to develop a web service that returns data from an SAP HANA table.

2. Connect from the e-commerce application directly to the SAP HANA database over a JDBC connection or other appropriate database connection configuration to access the table directly.

3. Create a Query as a Service (QaaS) web service through SAP BusinessObjects Web Intelligence using the product table created by the Apriori algorithm.

Because the SAP BusinessObjects Web Intelligence web service uses SAP Business-Objects tools that already exist in the system, we'll employ this third method. This web service will be passed in one or more item keys that are currently in the customer's e-commerce basket and return the Apriori output table records for any suggested products for those input product keys. In this case, use the PAL_RESULT_TAB output table created previously, and execute the following steps:

1. Create an SAP BusinessObjects universe with only the Apriori result table PAL_RESULT_TAB and all fields from this table included as attributes, as shown in Figure 7.25.

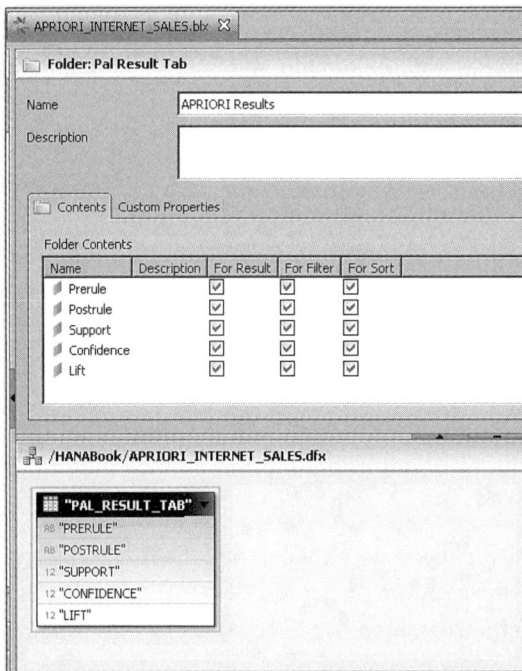

**Figure 7.25** Apriori Product Suggestion Universe

2. After the universe has been created, create a new SAP BusinessObjects Web Intelligence report using this universe, which returns all of the fields in the universe and uses a prompt for the PRERULE field, as shown in Figure 7.26.

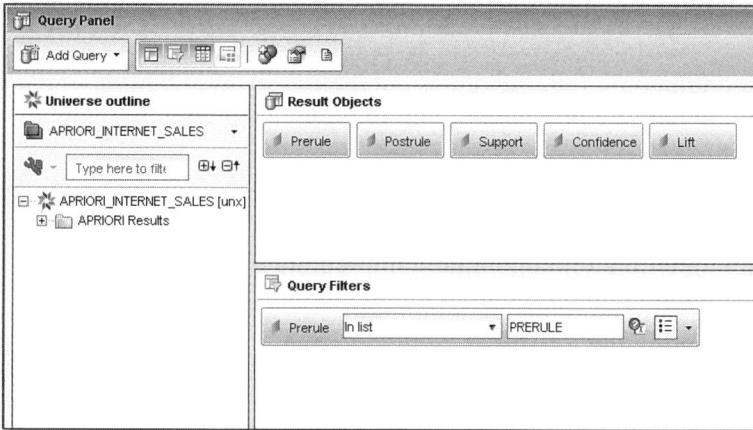

**Figure 7.26**   Apriori Product Suggestion Query

3. Click RUN, select any input from the list, and view the query results. After the report has generated as shown in Figure 7.27, select the entire report table, right-click, and select PUBLISH AS WEB SERVICE.

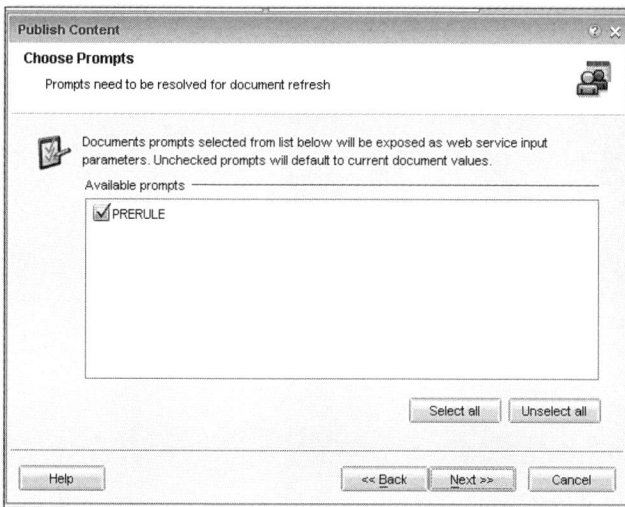

**Figure 7.27**   Product Suggestion Report

4. Click through the web service creation dialog, selecting the PRERULE prompt (see Figure 7.28), adding a name and description for the new web service (see Figure 7.29), and creating the service on the appropriate server. Finally, click PUBLISH.

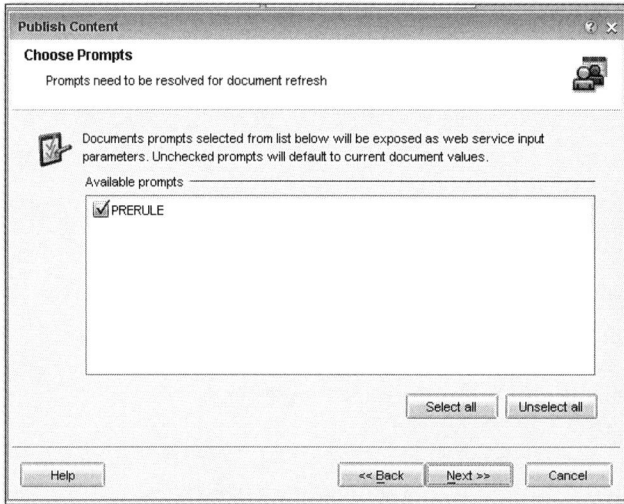

**Figure 7.28**  Apriori Product Suggestion Query

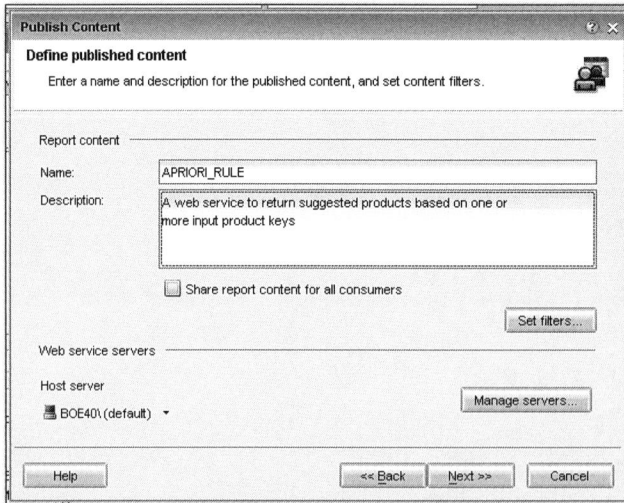

**Figure 7.29**  Web Service Name and Description

5. Test the web service by clicking on the TEST button in the WEB SERVICE PUBLISHER pane, shown in Figure 7.30. In the APRIORI_RULE web service testing interface, enter in the values "539" and "540", as shown in Figure 7.31, and click SEND to review the web service functionality.

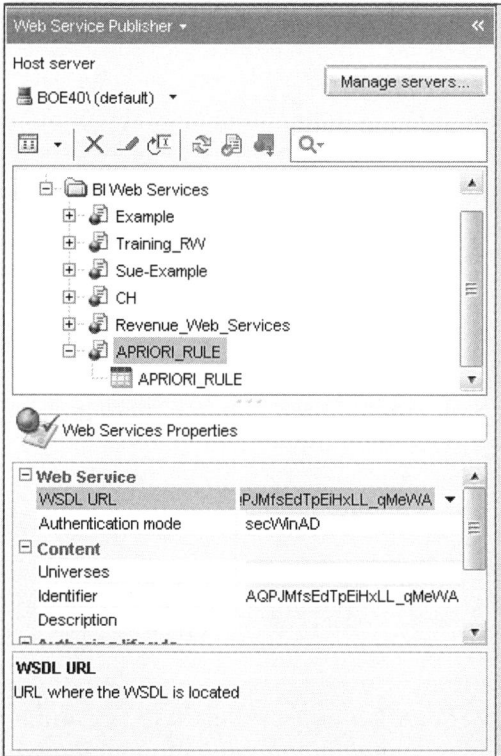

**Figure 7.30**  Web Service Publisher Pane

This web service can then be exposed to the e-commerce application and return a list of potential products to display to customers. The web service can use the returned keys to link to existing product information, including images, descriptions, and names, and prioritize these suggestions by the Confidence metric that is also returned to decide which items should be displayed first.

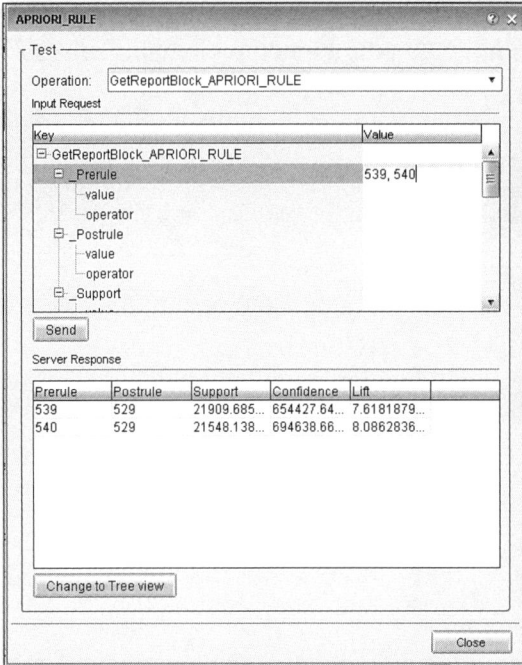

**Figure 7.31** Web Service Testing Interface

## 7.6 Summary

This chapter explored the tools available for performing predictive analysis in the SAP HANA database. By leveraging SAP HANA-R integration and PAL algorithms, you leverage the processing power of SAP HANA and existing BI infrastructure without the need to waste staff and system resources to transfer data between and maintain a separate predictive tool.

While there are powerful tools that can be accessed directly in SAP HANA Studio, SAP has provided a powerful visualization tool with a user interface that allows easier access to the SAP HANA predictive tools, enabling business and statistical users access to tools typically reserved for highly specialized technical resources. Furthermore, these predictive tools allow unparalleled integration with the SAP BusinessObjects toolset, which allows predictive models to be accessed and acted on by business users and executives quickly. Predictive models can often yield significant improvement on key business metrics such as acquisition rates and marketing expenses, so implementing models in days or weeks rather than months can impact revenue by tens or hundreds of thousands of dollars.

In the next chapter, we'll begin to discuss best practices surrounding allocating access to data stored on SAP HANA and discuss security and access management for SAP HANA.

*Deploying a comprehensive security model with SAP BusinessObjects 4.0 on SAP HANA is a key step in delivering an end-to-end solution that satisfies end users' needs to the fullest.*

# 8    Security in SAP Business-Objects BI and SAP HANA

One of the first concerns that arise when setting up a business intelligence (BI) solution—whether it's based on SAP HANA or not—is how to ensure that the right users get access to the right data, and the wrong users don't. Unfortunately, the solution is often more complex than we would like it to be. In this chapter, we'll look at the various security options available to you when implementing an SAP BusinessObjects Business Intelligence (SAP BusinessObjects BI) solution with SAP HANA, and we'll examine the pros and cons of different approaches.

We'll begin in Section 8.1 by reviewing some key terms and concepts that will show up throughout the rest of this chapter, such as authentication, authorization, provisioning, and maintaining user accounts. We'll include in our discussions review of various methods for performing authentication such as manual authentication or Single Sign-On (SSO), solutions such as Kerberos, and SAML. Finally, we'll discuss the different types of authorization, functional versus data, and the different tiers at which these authorizations can be applied, in SAP BusinessObjects or in SAP HANA.

After the conceptual groundwork has been laid, Section 8.2 looks at the specific features offered by the SAP BusinessObjects platform and SAP HANA that provide you with the tools to implement your security solution. We'll look at how you can provision users in both SAP BusinessObjects and SAP HANA, how you can manage different authentication scenarios, and how to manage and assign authorizations to users.

Tying all of the pieces together in Section 8.3, we'll walk through an end-to-end implementation of a security solution for a sales reporting structure that provides SSO from users' desktops into the SAP BusinessObjects platform and passes that authentication information all of the way to the SAP HANA database, so you can leverage SAP HANA data authorizations to ensure that each sales person has access to the appropriate data.

## 8.1 Security Solution Concepts

The primary information security concern for a BI solution is *access control*, which is the set of processes and procedures that ensures only those users specifically authorized to do so have "access" to information resources. There are two primary aspects to access control: *authentication* and *authorization*. *Authentication* is the process by which a user proves that he is who he says he is, and *authorization* is the process by which an information system determines if that person is allowed to perform a specific action or access a specific piece of data. Both elements are important pieces of an access control solution.

Many public standards are available for managing authentication and authorization, some of which are supported by the SAP BusinessObjects platform and SAP HANA. We'll look at two of the most important ones, Kerberos and SAML, in some detail later in Section 8.1.

### 8.1.1 Authentication

Just because you've authorized a particular user to access a specific information resource doesn't mean you should allow anyone who walks up and claims to be that user to have access. You must first verify that the user requesting access really is the person he says he is by using authentication. This proof of identity is typically handled by the exchange of a *security credential*—a form of proof that the provider is who he claims to be.

Authentication credentials come in many forms, but the most common is of course the combination of user name and a password. This "proves" the user's identity because only the real user should know what the password is, having never shared the password with anyone or written it down somewhere where others might find it. To verify that the provided credential is valid, you must have some kind of datastore where you keep a list of users and their valid security credentials. Adding users to the list of valid users is often referred to as *user provisioning*.

You must also establish a secure mechanism for users to provide their security credentials so that no one attempting to snoop on the connection can gain access to the credentials and thus masquerade as those users in the future. In the modern computing world, users must access many different systems. As we all know, keeping track of a unique set of credentials for every single system that we need to access for our day-to-day business is a substantial inconvenience. This often leads to insecure practices such as writing down passwords and leaving them in plain sight or using the same password for every system we access. A common solution to this complexity is the implementation of a Single Sign-On (SSO) system where users can prove their identity once to a centralized identity management system and that verified identity can then be passed around, in a secure fashion, to each of the business systems a user must access.

The combination of all of these elements just to prove a user's identity is sufficiently complex that there are numerous detailed computing standards that outline how a software system should go about implementing one or more of these aspects. The SAP BusinessObjects platform and SAP HANA both implement support for several different standards in this area, as listed in Table 8.1. Where support overlaps, you have opportunities for end-to-end security solutions. You should expect this table to grow and fill in with more supported methods as time moves on.

| Authentication Methods | SAP BusinessObjects Platform | SAP HANA |
| --- | --- | --- |
| Manual user name/ password | Supported | Supported |
| Kerberos | Supported | Supported |
| SAML | Supported (4.1) | Supported |
| X509 | Not supported | Supported |
| SAP Logon Tickets | Supported | Not supported as of writing, likely to be supported in near future |

**Table 8.1** Authentication Methods Supported by SAP BusinessObjects and SAP HANA

## 8.1.2 Authorization

After authentication of a user is complete, the information system now knows the identity of the incoming user. With this identity in hand, the system can determine what the user is authorized to do, completing the access control process.

Authorizations typically fall into two broad categories: functional authorizations that allow a user to perform certain types of actions, and data authorizations that allow users to access specific subsets of data.

Within the combined stack of SAP BusinessObjects and SAP HANA, these authorizations can take place in either or both of the systems layers. An example of authorization checks in a combined solution might look like the following.

1. Is the user allowed to log in to the SAP BusinessObjects BI Launchpad?

2. Is the user allowed to use SAP BusinessObjects Web Intelligence?

3. Is the user allowed to create a new SAP BusinessObjects Web Intelligence document?

4. Is the user allowed to create a query against the selected SAP HANA datasource?

5. Is the user allowed to log in to SAP HANA?

6. Is the user allowed to query the specific tables requested?

7. Is the user allowed to query for the specific rows requested?

> **Best Practices for Managing Authorizations**
>
> Because of the complexity of managing the assignment of the many required authorizations for even a simple task, it's always a best practice to develop a set of groups/roles to which authorizations are assigned, instead of attempting to assign them to individual users. During user provisioning, users are assigned to existing authorization groups/roles so that the setup process doesn't have to be repeated for each new user. Both SAP BusinessObjects and SAP HANA support this concept.

### 8.1.3  Authentication Methods

Now that we've covered some of the basic concepts, we can drill in to some of the technical details behind some of the most commonly implemented authentication strategies.

#### Direct Authentication

The simplest form of authentication in any software system is the direct storage of user accounts and passwords by the application itself. Most software systems support this type of authentication, and SAP HANA and SAP BusinessObjects are no different. You can create user accounts directly in SAP HANA as well as the

SAP BusinessObjects BI platform. Each account is stored with its password for future authentication. SAP BusinessObjects refers to this type of authentication as *enterprise authentication*; SAP HANA simply refers to it as *password authentication*.

This type of authentication is simple to set up but can be tedious to maintain in the long term, especially when scaled up for large organizations. Setup simply involves creating users using each application's built in user interface (UI) for managing accounts and credentials.

One problem with this approach is that there is no systematic integration between SAP HANA and SAP BusinessObjects when using this method. Each user account has to be maintained individually in each system, and depending on the tools used to access data, users may be required to log in twice, or some external mechanism for assigning database credentials back to SAP BusinessObjects accounts must be configured. Additionally there is no out-of-the-box mechanism to achieve an SSO solution when using directly authenticated accounts.

This method can be perfectly valid for the SAP HANA system if you don't require any row-level control of data, or you're implementing all row-level control within the BI application tier, such as using an SAP BusinessObjects universe or SAP BusinessObjects Explorer with Personalization. There are many BI solutions that get by with exactly this type of scenario. However, it does limit your BI tool selection somewhat if you want to include row-level security of data. For example, neither analysis for OLAP or Microsoft Office leverages the SAP BusinessObjects universe and thus can't take advantage of row-level security defined at that layer.

### Kerberos

Kerberos is a network authentication protocol that comes out of work done at MIT dating back to the early days of networked computing. It's designed to be a robust protocol that protects against many forms of attack and is based on strong cryptography. Because MIT released publicly available implementations of the protocol, and due to its robustness, Kerberos has been integrated in many computing systems over the years. One of the key integrations of Kerberos that has propelled its usage far and wide was the inclusion of the protocol in Microsoft's very popular Active Directory solution. This means that in almost every business environment, when you log on to your desktop, you're using Kerberos.

Kerberos uses a number of components and some peculiar nomenclature that is specific to its protocol, so let's review some of those components before we discuss how they interact with each other to achieve a secure authentication process:

▶ **Key Distribution Center**

The Key Distribution Center (KDC) is the heart of the Kerberos system. This central server process is responsible for managing the authentication of all users and mediating the authentication process between users and other computing services that users want to interact with. KDC has two subcomponents: Kerberos Authentication Service and a Ticket Granting Service.

▶ **Authentication Service**

The Authentication Service (AS) is the portion of the KDC responsible for validating authentication credentials that are provided by end users to establish network sessions.

▶ **Ticket Granting Service**

The Ticket Granting Service (TGS) is the portion of the KDC responsible for creating and managing encrypted tickets that are exchanged between parties in the Kerberos protocol to validate identities. It's also responsible for generating session keys that are used to encrypt traffic between a user and an application service on the network.

▶ **Ticket Granting Ticket**

A Ticket Granting Ticket (TGT) is provided to a user after the user authenticates himself to the Authentication Service in the KDC. The TGT serves to identify the user to the KDC on all subsequent conversations. The TGT is encrypted with a secret key known only to the KDC so it can't be forged. It contains details about the user, including the user's name, network address, and a session key that will also be shared with the user allowing the user to encrypt data so that only the TGS can decrypt it.

▶ **Session key**

A session key is shared between parties in a Kerberos exchange so that each party can encrypt values so that only the desired party on the other end of the connection can decrypt it. Session keys are shared between the KDC and a user as well as between a user and a target application.

▶ **Authenticator**

An authenticator is a small amount of information that is encrypted by a user using a session key, including the user's name, network address, and a time stamp. The KDC or other application service that receives an authenticator decrypts it with its copy of the session key and compares the contained values against known values. This essentially proves that the user is in possession of a valid session key and therefore must have gotten it from an authenticated session with the KDC. The encrypted time stamp ensures that a hacker isn't using a prerecorded authenticator to replay old network traffic.

▶ **Service ticket**
A service ticket is issued by the KDC when a user requests access to an application service on the network. Service tickets are encrypted using a long-term secret key that is known only to the KDC and the application service that is the target of the service ticket. Service tickets contain information about the user that requested the ticket as well as the session key that will also be given to the user so that the user and service can encrypt traffic to one another.

▶ **Service Principal Name**
For a KDC to generate service tickets for an application, the application must be known to the KDC. Each application is given a unique ID in the KDC known as a Service Principal Name (SPN). The KDC generates and stores a long-term key for the SPN just like it does for a regular user

▶ **KeyTab**
A KeyTab is a file that stores the long-term key for an SPN. This is given to an application so that it can use the key to decrypt any service tickets sent to it.

You should have noticed a strong emphasis on encryption in the various components involved in the Kerberos process. The storage and exchange of encryption keys is at the core of Kerberos's capability to authenticate users and ensure that malicious parties can't masquerade as a valid user. This key management requires that all users and all applications that users connect to are known to the KDC. The provisioning of users and applications in the KDC is one of the more complex aspects of configuring a Kerberos solution.

Now that we've introduced you to the various components of the Kerberos protocol, we can discuss the interaction between those components that achieve a secure authentication process. The process in essence involves a user authenticating himself to the KDC via the Authentication Service, obtaining a Ticket Granting Ticket (TGT) in response and then using the TGT to obtain a session key and service ticket for a target application. The process is somewhat more complex when the target application needs to access additional network applications on the user's behalf.

This is exactly the scenario that occurs when SAP BusinessObjects accesses SAP HANA using a user's identity. In this expanded scenario, the application in the middle (SAP BusinessObjects) must be authorized by the KDC to perform delegation. If authorized, the middle application requests a service ticket for the final target application (SAP HANA) on behalf of the user, using information taken from the user's initial request to the middle application. The complete authentication process proceeds as follows and is further mapped out in Figure 8.1.

❶ The client sends an Authentication Service request (AS_REQ) to the KDC, which includes the user's credentials. The Authentication Service in the KDC authenticates the user, and a TGT is returned to the client (AS_REP) along with a session key encrypted using the user's long-term key, which is derived from the user's password. The user is able to decrypt the message using his long-term key and can obtain the session key for further communication with the TGS.

❷ The client sends a Ticket Granting Service request (TGS_REQ) to the TGS to get a service ticket for Application 1. The request includes a copy of the TGT and an authenticator encrypted with the initial session key obtained in step 1. The TGS decrypts the TGT using its long-term key and extracts its copy of the session key from it. It then validates the authenticator using the session key and sends back a Ticket Granting Service Response (TGS_REP) encrypted with the initial session key. The TGS_REP contains a new session key for the user to communicate with the target service and a service ticket that is encrypted with the long-term key for the target service, known only to the KDC and the target service. The service ticket also contains a copy of the new session key for use by the target service.

❸ The client sends the service ticket and an authenticator to Application 1 as an Application Request (AP_REQ). The application decrypts the service ticket using its long-term key validating that it came from the KDC. From the ticket, it extracts the session key and uses that to decrypt the authenticator, ensuring that it came from the correct user, and finally it sends back an acknowledgement Application Response (AP_REP) to the user encrypted with the user's now shared session key.

❹ Application 1 sends a TGS_REQ to the KDC on behalf of the client, "impersonating" the client, which is allowed because the service account is "Authorized for Delegation" by the KDC. The KDC sends back the service ticket for Application 2 as a TGS_REP.

❺ Application 1 sends an AP_REQ to Application 2 with the service ticket received from KDC. Application 2 responds with AP_REP granting Application 1 access to Application 2 with the authorization levels granted to the client.

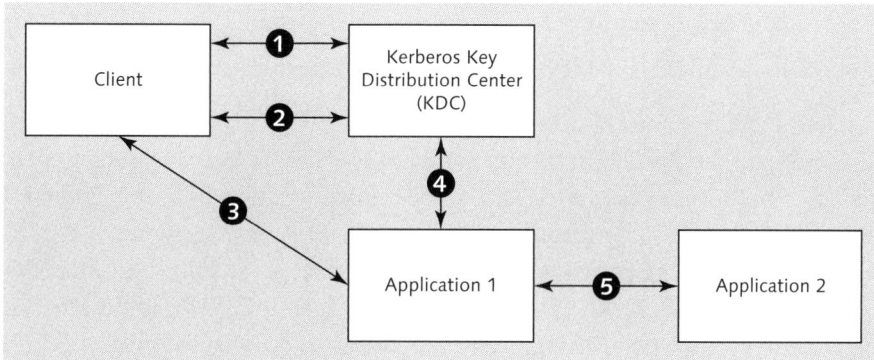

**Figure 8.1**  Kerberos Authentication Process

**Additional Resources**

For more technical details on Kerberos, we recommend the following resources:

▶ MIT's Kerberos Project Page (*http://web.mit.edu/kerberos/*)

▶ The Kerberos Consortium (*http://www.kerberos.org/*)

### SAML

Security Assertion Markup Language (SAML) is a relatively new authentication standard that comes from an open-source standards body called OASIS. One of its key benefits is that the transport of authentication and security data is done via simple XML messages. This makes implementing SAML support in applications rather straightforward.

SAML is somewhat different from Kerberos in that it has a much more decentralized architecture. This style of authentication solution is often referred to as a Federated Identity System. Though SAML isn't the only solution in this space, it's the only one adopted by SAP HANA and SAP BusinessObjects. The solution is called "federated" because there is a loose coupling of multiple systems that have agreed to cooperate with each other for the purpose of exchanging authentication and authorization data. Instead of a single central system that manages all identity information (as with Kerberos), SAML can support multiple *identify providers* that manage authentication of users for various parties.

SAML is a very complete standard that offers mechanisms for the exchange of identity information, authorization data, as well as general authentication and SSO scenarios. SAP BusinessObjects and SAP HANA don't yet support the full gamut of features offered by SAML, but they can leverage the authentication and SSO portions.

The relative simplicity and feature completeness of SAML has caused a rapid uptake of the solution in the cloud hosting and Software as a Service (SaaS) solution space. The most common use case for SAML is the implementation of web-based SSO solutions that allow SaaS companies to delegate identity management to a third party or back to their clients' internal identity management solutions. The SAP BusinessObjects to SAP HANA SSO solution is similar to this scenario despite not taking place over the web or using traditional web-based transport protocols.

The most basic SAML architecture involves three main entities: a user, an identity provider, and a service provider. Each entity has a relationship with the other two. The user's credentials and identity information are stored with the identity provider, meanwhile the user intends to consume the services offered by the service provider. The identify provider is responsible for authenticating the user whenever the user attempts to access a service provider, and the identify provider trusts a set of known service providers with whom it will share identity information if asked for it. The service provider has a service that the user wants to consume, and the service provider trusts that if the identity provider says a user is authenticated, then the user should be allowed to access the service.

These relationships can be used to achieve two primary authentication and SSO scenarios. The first is service provider-initiated SSO. In this scenario, the user attempts to access the service provider, who then redirects the user to the identify provider for authentication, after which the user is allowed to access the service. Second, but more pertinent to the SAP BusinessObjects with SAP HANA solution, is identity provider-initiated SSO. In this scenario, the user requests access to the service provider from the identity provider, who first authenticates the user and then forwards the user on to the service provider and passing along authentication details that the service provider can verify as coming from the identity provider due to their prearranged trust relationship.

An important concept with all SAML-based authentication scenarios is the trust relationship between the identify provider and service provider. This trust is validated with each received SAML message, whether it comes from the identity provider or service provider. The validation of the trust is based on digital signatures in the XML messages that prove the message came from a known and trusted source. These signatures are based on the exchange of keys between the parties so that the signatures can be decrypted and verified.

Let's look at the SAML process in detail in the following steps for the identity provider-initiated SSO, as shown in Figure 8.2.

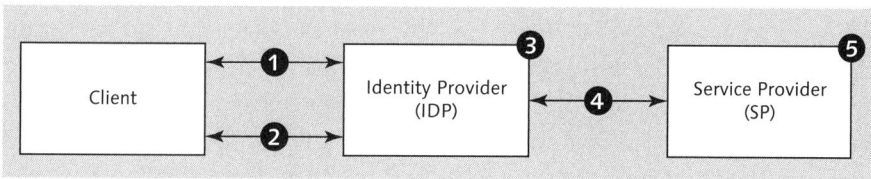

**Figure 8.2** SAML Authentication Process

❶ The user authenticates with the identity provider using any established authentication scheme.

❷ The user submits a request to access the service provider.

❸ The identify provider generates a SAML assertion with information about the user as well as the identify provider, and then signs the assertion with a digital signature using a key previously shared with the service provider.

❹ The identity provider then forwards the user to the service provider along with the SAML assertion or, in the case of SAP BusinessObjects to SAP HANA, submits a request to the service provider on behalf of the user with the SAML assertion.

❺ The service provider verifies that the signature in the assertion comes from a trusted source and then reads the user's identity from the assertion and allows the access to proceed.

**Additional Resources**

For more technical details on SAML, visit the following pages hosted by the OASIS standards group that created SAML:

▶ A technical overview of SAML at *https://www.oasis-open.org/committees/download. php/27819/sstc-saml-tech-overview-2.0-cd-02.pdf*

▶ The complete SAML specification at *http://saml.xml.org/saml-specifications*

Now that we've covered access control in general and discussed some of the underlying technologies used by SAP BusinessObjects and SAP HANA, we can start to examine some of the specific steps required to configure an access control strategy for a combined SAP BusinessObjects and SAP HANA solution.

## 8.2 Implementing an Access Control Strategy with SAP BusinessObjects BI 4.0 and SAP HANA

To configure an access control strategy, you'll need to set up the authentication solution, provision users, and establish authorizations for those users. There are a number of options for each of these steps, and they differ for both SAP HANA and SAP BusinessObjects. We'll examine each step of the process by working our way up from the bottom of the stack with SAP HANA to the user-facing layer in SAP BusinessObjects.

> **Note**
>
> We've separated Section 8.2 into its constituent parts because you can mix and match pieces from the different areas to form a total solution. For example, you could implement Kerberos to SAP BusinessObjects but use only password authentication to SAP HANA. Or, you might implement password authentication to SAP BusinessObjects but use SAML to SAP HANA. You might not implement a complex authorization solution in SAP HANA with roles depending on your row-level security needs but still implement an authorization solution in SAP BusinessObjects.

### 8.2.1 Configuring Authentication in SAP HANA

As we discussed in Table 8.1 earlier in this chapter, multiple authentication methods are supported by SAP HANA, and more are coming in the future. However, not all of them are supported by the SAP BusinessObjects platform. We'll only discuss the configurations that work with SAP BusinessObjects, with the exception of SAML integration between SAP BusinessObjects and SAP HANA. (This isn't officially generally available [GA] at this point, but the 4.1 ramp-up has made an early release version of the solution available.) This restricted set leaves you with the following authentication methods.

- Manual authentication (user name/password)
- Kerberos authentication
- SAML authentication

In the next few sections, we'll review the configuration steps necessary to implement each of these authentication solutions.

## Manual Authentication

Manual authentication requires essentially zero configurations on the SAP HANA system. When you stand up your SAP HANA server, this is the authentication method you'll use to access and administer the system from the start. We mentioned earlier that this is a valid authentication scenario if you don't need the user's unique identity at the database tier to enforce row-level security. It can also be a valid solution if you're using SAP BusinessObjects database credentials fields to store the SAP HANA credentials for each user. Of course, such a solution can be complex to maintain from a user provisioning perspective, but if done with a scripted approach so that it's not reliant on administrators manually keeping credentials up to date between systems, it can be a valid approach.

## Kerberos Authentication

Kerberos authentication is probably the most complex to set up of all of the authentication scenarios. There are a number of operating system libraries that must be available on the SAP HANA server, and there are a number of configurations that must be made to both the Windows Active Directory server and the Linux server hosting the SAP HANA database. It's also important to remember that configuration of Kerberos authentication will likely require significant involvement from your Active Directory administration team. You'll want to plan accordingly, making sure you leave enough time to loop in the additional parties and make them aware of the planned solution. It's also quite likely that the network security team will need to be involved to ensure the proper communication pathways are open between the SAP HANA servers and any KDCs that will be used.

> **Additional Resources**
>
> The complete detailed steps for configuring Kerberos authentication on the SAP HANA server has been well documented by the SAP Support team in a pair of SAP notes:

▶ Note 1837331: Detailed Instructions for Kerberos Configuration (*https://service.sap.com/sap/support/notes/1837331*)

▶ Note 1813724: Automation Tools to Assist with Kerberos Configuration (*https://service.sap.com/sap/support/notes/1813724*)

Though you should go to the SAP notes for detailed instructions, the following list provides an overview of the configuration steps. We encourage you to always refer back to the SAP notes before an actual implementation because new service packs may alter these steps slightly.

1. **Confirm/install the Kerberos client on the SAP HANA server.**
   Before you can integrate SAP HANA with your Kerberos environment, you need to make sure that the Kerberos client tools are available on the Linux server hosting your SAP HANA environment. If you have a multinode server environment, you need to make sure all nodes have the client tools. If you're missing any of the components, you need to patch your Linux system to include them.

2. **Create a service account and generate a KeyTab for the account.**
   For a service to accept Kerberos authentication information and interact with the KDC, it must establish a relationship with the KDC. This is done by creating an account in the KDC that will represent the service and assigning a Service Principal Name (SPN) to the account to mark it as an account that represents a service. This will be used during the Kerberos negotiation to identify the account that represents the target service. Secondly you have to create a KeyTab file for the account that will store the long-term keys used to authenticate and encrypt traffic targeted at this account. In total, this is a three-step process: create account, assign SPN, and generate KeyTab.

3. **Configure KeyTab and Kerberos configuration files on the SAP HANA server**.
   After a KeyTab file is created, it needs to be made available to the Kerberos client tools installed on the SAP HANA host machine. You'll also need to create a *krb5.ini* file that describes the Kerberos environment the system will operate in. The details for deploying the KeyTab file and configuring the *krb5.ini* file can all be found in SAP Note 1837331.

4. **Provision a test user in SAP HANA and assign Kerberos credentials.**
   Before you can move on to testing authentication using the SAP HANA client tools, you need to provision at least one test user in the SAP HANA database. (We'll talk about user provisioning in more detail in Section 8.2.6.) For now, you can simply create one user manually and assign the user a Kerberos identity,

as shown in Figure 8.3. That identity should be a real user in your Active Directory domain.

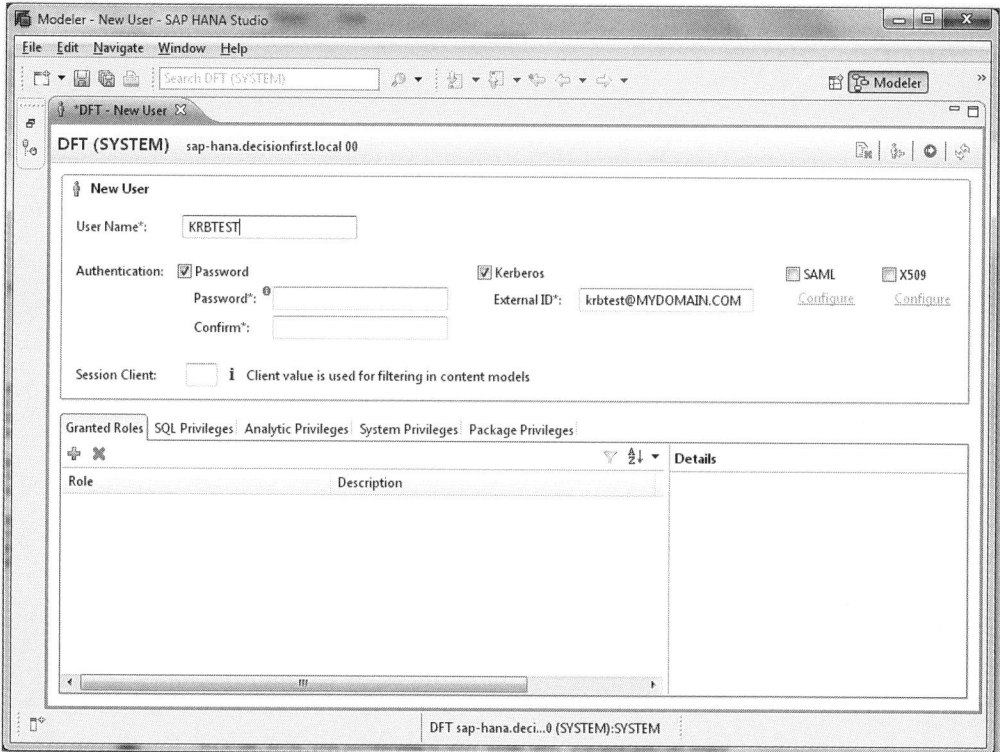

**Figure 8.3** Assigning a Kerberos Identity to a User

5. **Test SSO to the database using SAP HANA Studio or the hdbsql client.**
   Finally you can test your configuration with one or both of the client tools. You can test the client directly on the SAP HANA server by running `hdbsql` from the command line. You'll need to establish a Kerberos ticket for your test user first, however, using the `kinit` tools. An example scenario looks like this:

```
#> kinit krbtest@MYDOMAIN.COM
#> hdbsql -i 00 -n hanaserver.mydomain.com
```

If connections are working properly locally from the SAP HANA server, you can proceed to test connections from the SAP HANA Studio tool. To configure SAP HANA Studio for Kerberos authentication you simply need to add a new system reference and select the AUTHENTICATION BY CURRENT OPERATING SYSTEM USER option shown in Figure 8.4.

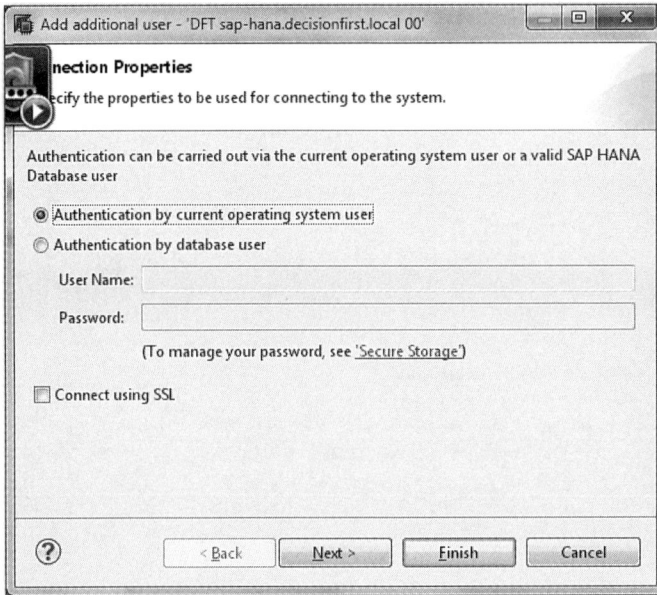

**Figure 8.4** Adding an SAP HANA Studio Connection with Kerberos Authentication

### SAML Authentication

In comparison to Kerberos authentication, SAML authentication is relatively straightforward to configure, but it doesn't have as much usage or documentation backing it up as the Kerberos method. This is due to the fact that the SAP BusinessObjects platform is only adding support for SAML authentication to SAP HANA in the new 4.1 release that is currently in ramp-up as of this writing. We expect the documentation and support for the SAML scenario to improve as the 4.1 ramp-up comes to a close and the product reaches general availability. It also appears that this area of the SAP HANA administration tools is being actively worked on, so we'll stick to a high-level overview of the process and refer you to the latest SAP HANA documentation from SAP for exact configuration steps.

There are two main configuration steps that must be performed within the SAP HANA server to support participation in a SAML authentication scenario. First is the enablement of Secure Sockets Layer (SSL) for the SAP HANA platform. SAML relies on digital signatures to verify the authenticity of the SAML identity assertions that are passed between the identity provider and the service provider (SAP HANA, in this case). These signatures use SSL certificates as part of the encryption routine. The second configuration step is the definition of the identity provider in the SAP HANA system and the storage of its public certificate in the SSL key stores just configured in the first step. Creation of the identity provider public certificate isn't part of this configuration, but it will be discussed later in Section 8.2.4 for the specific scenario using the SAP BusinessObjects platform as the identity provider. It's important to note that SAP HANA could interact with any SAML identity provider, not just SAP BusinessObjects, but SAP BusinessObjects is only configured to work with SAP HANA as the service provider.

Let's take a closer look at these steps to configure SAML authentication on the SAP HANA server:

1. **Enable SSL on the SAP HANA server host.**
   This step is performed at the operating system level on the SAP HANA host machine and is typically done using the <SID>adm OS user that runs SAP HANA. There are two supported SSL libraries for SAP HANA: OpenSSL and SAP Cryptographic Library. OpenSSL is the recommended choice because it's typically installed by default on the SAP HANA host and requires no further installation.

   Assuming the supported SSL library is available, you must generate and store a secret key for the server and then generate and sign an SSL certificate request for the server. You can refer to documentation for the SSL library being used for the steps to generate and sign the SSL certificate.

   After you have a key and signed certificate as well as the CA public certificate for the signing authority, you must store them in the SSL key store in the PEM file format. This is really just a specially formatted text file stored in the *.ssl* subdirectory in the home of the <SID>adm user (i.e., *$HOME/.ssl/key.pem*).

   You'll also need an SSL trust store. This is also just a text file in PEM format. In this file, you'll place the public certificates of the identity providers that you're accepting authentication messages from. This file is typically named *trust.pem* and is stored in the same directory as the *key.pem* (i.e., *$HOME/.ssl/trust.pem*).

   The identify provider gives you the certificate to store in this file. However, it's not always provided in PEM format. There are many different formats for exchanging SSL certificates between parties. You can use the SSL library tools to convert the provided value into PEM format, or you may have to manually format the value in PEM format and add it to your *trust.pem* file.

Finally, tell SAP HANA that SSL is enabled and the location of the key and trust stores using a number of INDEXSERVER.INI settings. You can set these using the SAP HANA Studio application as shown in the Figure 8.5. The settings are in the COMMUNICATION subsection on the CONFIGURATION tab, and are listed in Table 8.2. You need to restart the SAP HANA server for all of these changes to take effect.

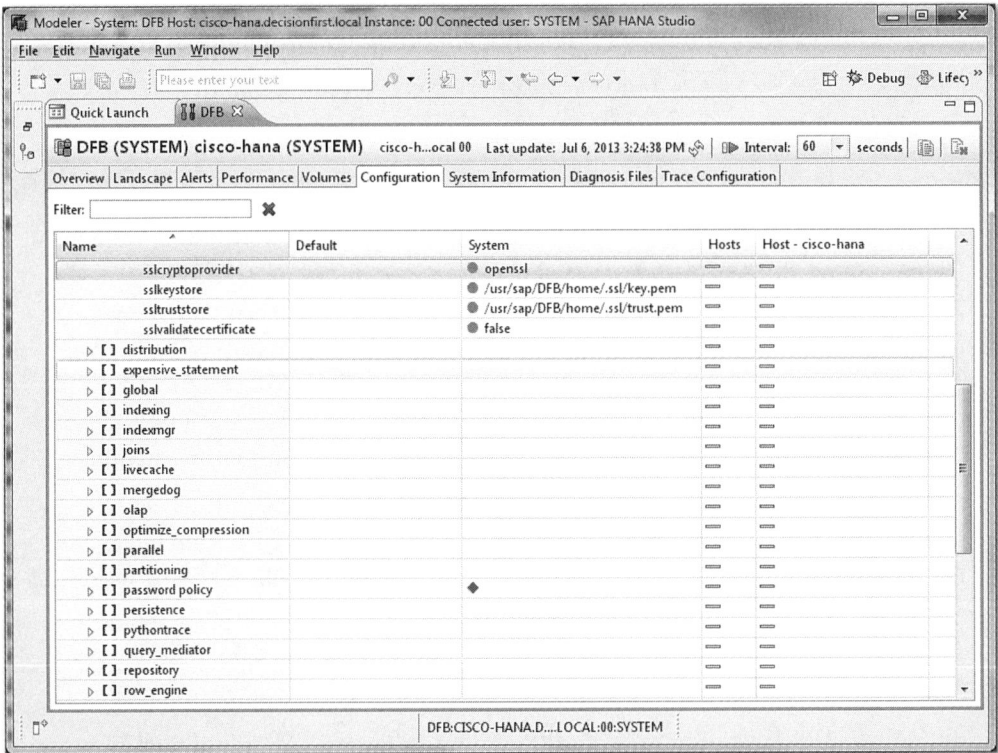

**Figure 8.5** Configuration of SSL Options

| SSL Setting | Description |
| --- | --- |
| SSLCRYPTOPROVIDER | The name of the SSL library to use, either openssl or sapcrypto. |
| SSLKEYSTORE | The path to the SSL key store (i.e., *$HOME/.ssl/key.pem*) |
| SSLTRUSTSTORE | The path to the SSL trust store (i.e., *$HOME/.ssl/trust.pem*) |
| SSLVALIDATECERTIFICATE | To validate the certificate or not; false if using self-signed certificates |

**Table 8.2** SSL Option Details

2. **Create an identify provider entry in the SAP HANA system.**

   SAML identity providers are defined as a specific type of entity in the SAP HANA system. These entries give the identity provider a name and the necessary metadata to look up the identity provider's public certificate in the trust store. The name and metadata should all be provided by the identify provider you're configuring. You can create the identity provider using SQL statements, or you can use the SAP HANA Studio application, which has a GUI dedicated to configuring SAML identity providers. For simplicity, we'll examine the GUI-based method.

To configure the identity provider, you'll need a connection to the SAP HANA database as the SYSTEM user. To access the SAML configuration GUI, open the properties for the SYSTEM connection, and select SECURITY • SAML CONFIGURATION. After you get to the SAML configuration page, you can click ADD to create the new identity provider. After you click ADD, the CREATE SAML IDENTITY PROVIDER screen appears where you can enter the details for the identity provider, as shown in Figure 8.6.

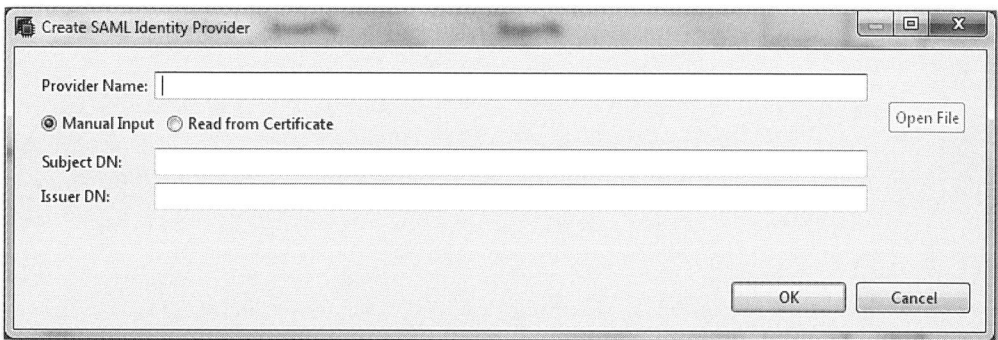

**Figure 8.6** Identity Provider Configuration

The values to enter on this screen all come from the identity provider system. The PROVIDER NAME is the unique ID for the identity provider, and the SUBJECT DN and ISSUER DN help describe this provider's public certificate. It's possible to read the latter two values from the certificate itself, but we had the most success just entering the values manually.

Testing SAML Authentication is a bit more complex than testing Kerberos because you must have a valid SAML assertion signed by the identity provider. Therefore, you really need the end-to-end solution in place before you can test the connectivity. You also need one or more users provisioned in the SAP HANA system with

SAML credentials mapped to the account. We'll see more of this in the next section on user provisioning.

### 8.2.2 Configuring Authorization in SAP HANA

In this section, we'll look at the tools used to configure authorization in SAP HANA. Developing a complete security model that allows for developer, administrator, and end-user access to the system is a very involved process. We'll focus primarily on the concerns of configuring end-user authorization in this section.

Authorization in SAP HANA is controlled by granting privileges to users or roles. Privileges represent a granular entitlement that allows a user or role to access one specific feature or aspect of the SAP HANA system. Privileges come in the following categories:

▶ **SQL privileges**
These typical rights give the ability to SELECT, UPDATE, INSERT, DELETE, CREATE, ALTER, and DROP content within a specific database schema. A common example that is granted to almost every end user is the privilege to SELECT and EXECUTE on _SYS_BIC.

▶ **Analytic privileges**
These privileges, which are covered in more detail in Chapter 7, control access to data within information views and form the basis of row-level security implementation within the SAP HANA system. In SP6 of SAP HANA, the ability to create analytic privileges driven by a stored procedure that can leverage arbitrary tables of data that describe the mapping of users to data is being improved with new UI elements. This should significantly improve the capacity for SAP HANA to drive row-level security.

- ▶ **System privileges**
  System privileges grant access to core system functionality. Note that in most end-user scenarios, system privileges won't be necessary.

- ▶ **Package privileges**
  Package privileges grant access to the content repository of the SAP HANA system. This is where developers define and model information views and construct applications with the XS Engine. Like system privileges, these privileges are typically reserved for developer and administrator scenarios.

- ▶ **Application privileges**
  Application privileges allow developers of XS Engine applications to define custom privileges that can be granted to users and roles that allow access to the features of those applications. These were first introduced in SP5 of SAP HANA, but there was no UI access to them via SAP HANA Studio. In SP6, integration into the SAP HANA Studio UI and developer tools should make these a more integral part of future SAP HANA development.

**Role-Based Security**

Although authorization in SAP HANA is driven by the granting of privileges to users and roles, you don't want to have to assign specific privileges every time a new user is provisioned, or even to have to think about privileges in most scenarios. The best practice approach is to identify the complete set of usage scenarios planned for the system. Each scenario is mapped to an SAP HANA role, and the specific privileges necessary to enable that role are granted to that role. Your population of users is then categorized by the one or more scenarios they will be able to perform, and they are then provisioned with those roles assigned. This system ensures that if new privileges are deemed necessary for a given scenario, a change to a single role object can implement that change.

The number of roles you'll need and the specific rights to grant each one will depend on your specific business requirements. However, there are some general guidelines you can consider:

- ▶ Grant the necessary rights to access analytic content in the _SYS_BIC schema, and ensure that all users who will consume information views have this access.

- ▶ If users will access plain database tables and procedures, grant access to the necessary schemas.

- ▶ Consider how analytic privileges will be mapped to users and how many roles will be necessary to cover all scenarios for row-level security.

- ▶ Consider leveraging the ability for one role to include the rights of another to avoid repeating common rights across multiple roles.

### 8.2.3 Provisioning Users in SAP HANA

In this section, we'll look at some of the methods for provisioning users in SAP HANA to support SSO scenarios. Unfortunately, this is one of the areas where SAP HANA is most lacking in features. We hope to see the tooling surrounding user management improve in future SAP HANA service pack versions. For now, you're primarily left with two solutions: manual provisioning using SAP HANA Studio, and custom-scripted solutions using SQL commands and possibly other programming languages.

#### Manual User Provisioning

Manual provisioning of users in SAP HANA Studio is only practical for scenarios in which small numbers of users are involved or where database access is handled by a single service account and security is predominantly enforced in the reporting tier.

However, if you do have a small number of users, you can conceivably manage the process using SAP HANA Studio. The following steps walk through the process of creating a user. Note that we're assuming the creation of an end user that will merely consume data and whose rights are all defined by roles. Configuration of users that will own data in the system is outside the scope of this chapter.

1. Connect to the SAP HANA database as the SYSTEM user.

> **User Provisioning Requires Elevated Privileges**
>
> User provisioning processes should be executed by the SYSTEM user or users with the necessary system privileges to manage users and roles.

2. Open the SECURITY folder within the connection. Right-click on the USERS entry, and select NEW USER. The result is shown in Figure 8.7.

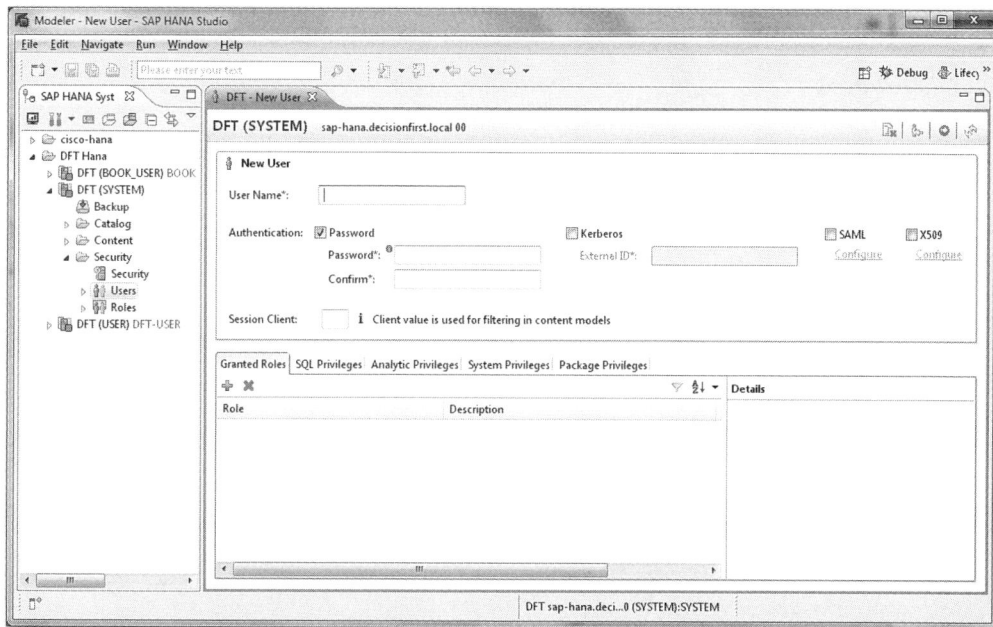

**Figure 8.7** Creating a New User

3. Assign the user a unique user name. User names in SAP HANA can be any string consisting of all capital letters. The specific value isn't important, but it should give some indication as to whom the user represents.

4. Depending on the authentication scenarios you plan to configure, you may need to assign the user one or more credentials. The options are PASSWORD, KERBEROS, SAML, and X509, which we won't cover here.

   ▶ Password credentials simply require the entry of a password that satisfies the password polices for the system. If you only plan to use Kerberos or SAML, uncheck the PASSWORD checkbox.

   ▶ To enable Kerberos credentials for a user, check the KERBEROS box and enter the external Kerberos ID in user@DOMAIN format.

   ▶ To enable SAML credentials, check the SAML box and then click the CONFIGURE link. This opens the CONFIGURE EXTERNAL SAML IDENTITIES configuration page shown in Figure 8.8. From here, you can assign a user name for a specific identity provider that will be mapped to this user account at logon.

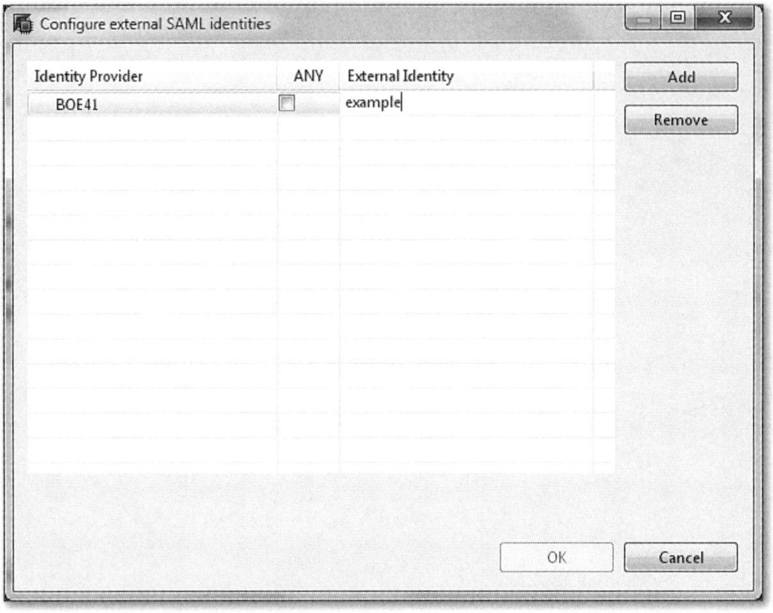

**Figure 8.8** Mapping SAML Identities to a User

5. Use the plus (+) icon on the GRANTED ROLES tab to assign the appropriate roles to the new user.

6. Deploy the new user by clicking the green DEPLOY icon or pressing the ⌗F8⌗ key.

**Scripted User Provisioning**

In an ideal world, you could attach the SAP HANA system to a third-party credential store such as LDAP, Active Directory, or an SAP system and map groups/roles from that external system into SAP HANA Roles directly. Unfortunately, this isn't an option. However, the creation of a user and assignment of external credentials can all be performed with a series of SQL statements, so you can achieve the same result although it requires some extra effort.

If you intend to implement an SSO solution where you need to map in large numbers of users, it's likely that you're using Kerberos or SAML, so in this section, we'll only examine these two scenarios. In both of these cases, you'll have a well-defined store of existing identities that you want to map into the SAP HANA server. For a

Kerberos scenario, this will be Active Directory. For SAML, it will be the identity provider system, although that system may itself be reading user identities from another source such as LDAP or Active Directory that are easier to query directly. In either case, the concept is to write a small program that connects to the external source of identities queries for a list of users and then executes the necessary SQL statements to create or maintain the users and credentials in SAP HANA.

The details of how to connect to an external identity source and programmatically retrieve a list of users is beyond the scope of this book; however, in the highly probable scenario that the external identity store can be queried by the LDAP protocol, there are a number of relatively simple solutions. LDAP query tools are likely available on the operating system hosting your SAP HANA system already, and SAP HANA ships with the Python programming language, which has easy to use APIs for querying an LDAP store. The Java programming language is also a good choice if controlling the process from an SAP BusinessObjects server, which has built in support for scheduling and hosting custom Java programs. Determining how to map groups of users from the external store to roles in SAP HANA is an exercise we leave up to you as well, but something as simple as a text-based configuration file will work.

After a set of users to provision is identified, the execution of the necessary SQL commands is no different from executing a SELECT statement. Table 8.3 lists some SQL statements that are pertinent to the process. For complete details, refer to the SAP HANA SQL Reference Guide.

| Action | SQL |
|---|---|
| Create and enable a Kerberos user | CREATE USER EXAMPLE WITH IDENTITY 'example@EXAMPLE.COM' FOR KERBEROS;<br>ALTER USER EXAMPLE ENABLE KERBEROS; |
| Create and enable a SAML user | CREATE USER EXAMPLE WITH IDENTITY 'example' FOR SAML PROVIDER BOE41;<br>ALTER USER EXAMPLE ENABLE SAML; |
| Drop a user that is no longer needed | DROP USER EXAMPLE; |

**Table 8.3** User Provisioning SQL Statements

### 8.2.4 Configuring Authentication in SAP BusinessObjects BI 4.0

In this section, we discuss the general structure of user authentication management in the SAP BusinessObjects platform, as well some of the specific details necessary to configure some of the authentication methods available.

One of the strengths of the SAP BusinessObjects platform is its highly flexible support for multiple authentication methods. We can't go into detail with every possible method supported by SAP BusinessObjects, so we'll focus on those methods that enable end-to-end solutions with SAP HANA. This includes traditional enterprise authentication, Kerberos authentication, and the coming support for SAML authentication in 4.1.

Authentication is generally managed in the AUTHENTICATION section of the CMC web application of the SAP BusinessObjects platform. However, SAML authentication in SAP BusinessObjects BI 4.1 is unusual in that it's configured in the APPLICATION section of the CMC. This makes some sense because SAML authentication is the only one that doesn't provide a built-in mechanism for provisioning users into the SAP BusinessObjects platform. This is an important point when considering how to provision users for an end-to-end solution.

In much the same way that SAP HANA allows you to store more than one set of credentials for a user account, SAP BusinessObjects provides a similar mechanism. SAP BusinessObjects refers to this concept as *aliases*. Each user object can have one or more aliases. An alias has a particular authentication type associated with it. For example, a user can have a Kerberos alias (i.e., secWinAD in SAP BusinessObjects terminology), an enterprise alias, and an SAP alias. When you authenticate to the SAP BusinessObjects platform, you choose which authentication type you want to use, which will determine which alias is used to confirm your credentials. In some scenarios, the choice of authentication method is made for you. Notice that because SAML doesn't provide a mechanism for provisioning users, it also doesn't provide for SAML aliases on accounts. To use SAML authentication to SAP HANA, you must use an alternate authentication method to first access SAP BusinessObjects.

#### Enterprise Authentication

Enterprise authentication is essentially equivalent to the manual user name and password configuration available in SAP HANA. This authentication method doesn't rely on any third-party systems or identity stores to configure users. This means that all identity information for a user exists solely in the SAP BusinessObjects platform and that all configurations and provisioning of accounts takes place in the CMC.

Enterprise authentication is important because it can work in conjunction with SAML authentication for connection to SAP HANA. Recall that SAML authentication doesn't provide a user provisioning mechanism, so a user must be created using another system. Enterprise authentication is one of those options.

Additionally there is the option of directly storing additional database credentials on SAP BusinessObjects user accounts. This option can work if the creation of accounts is managed and synchronized between the SAP BusinessObjects and SAP HANA platforms either using scripts to create the accounts or manually configuring the accounts in both systems. Once mapped together in this fashion, SSO to the database is possible. Obviously, this method has some significant maintenance overhead costs and is therefore seldom used. However, the initial configuration is rather straightforward because both SAP HANA and SAP BusinessObjects require no additional configuration or setup post-install to enable this type of scenario. You can start provisioning users immediately.

**SAML Authentication**

The implementation of SAML authentication to SAP HANA from SAP Business-Objects is unusual when compared to other SAP BusinessObjects authentication methods. In fact, SAML doesn't provide an authentication method for the SAP BusinessObjects platform; it only allows the passing of an already authenticated identity to the SAP HANA system. This means that users must authenticate to the SAP BusinessObjects platform first via some other traditional authentication method such as Enterprise, Kerberos, LDAP or SAP authentication. The key for making this solution work with the SAP HANA system is that the SAP Business-Objects user name must match the configured SAML identity for a target user in the SAP HANA system.

Configuring the SAP BusinessObjects platform to act as identify provider for the SAP HANA system is relatively straightforward. We mentioned in Section 8.2.1 that the information necessary to configure an identity provider in SAP HANA is provided by the identity provider system. Generating this information is the gist of the configuration steps in SAP BusinessObjects to support the SAML process.

Let's walk through the steps for configuring SAML in SAP BusinessObjects:

1. **Create a definition for the SAP HANA connection in the SAP HANA authentication application in the** APPLICATIONS **area of the** CMC.
   You'll find the configuration page for SAML authentication to SAP HANA in the APPLICATIONS section of the CMC. From this application configuration page, you'll create a connection to the SAP HANA server, as shown in Figure 8.9. It's important to distinguish this connection from the OLAP and relational connection objects created elsewhere in the SAP BusinessObjects system. This connection is really just metadata that will be used during authentication to the SAP HANA system for generating SAML assertions.

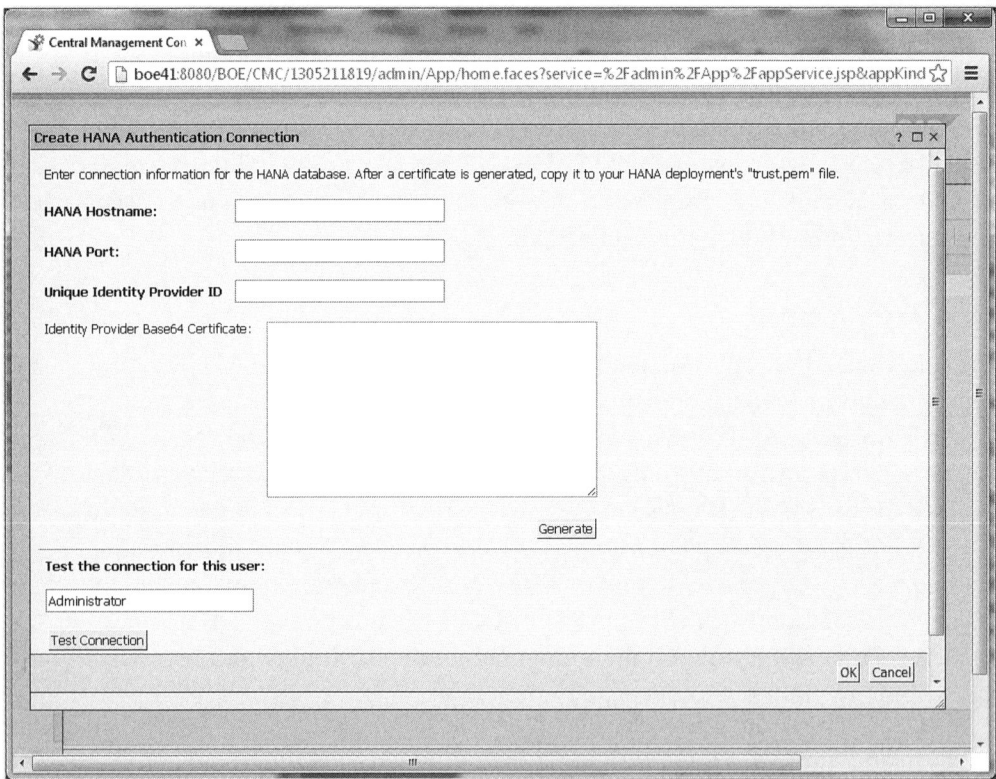

**Figure 8.9**  Configuration Page for a SAML Connection to SAP HANA

2. **Enter the SAP HANA host name and port.**
   You should enter the fully qualified DNS HANA HOSTNAME and HANA PORT for the SAP HANA server. This will be used when authentication is required to

determine which connection object in SAP BusinessObjects has the applicable SAML configuration data.

3. **Assign a unique identity provider ID.**
The UNIQUE IDENTITY PROVIDER ID field serves as the name that is passed to the SAP HANA system in the SAML assertion. This will be used in SAP HANA to determine which user mappings to apply. When you're configuring the identity provider in SAP HANA, this name must match the identity provider ID used there.

4. **Generate the public certificate used to sign SAML assertions.**
After you've entered the key values for this connection, click the GENERATE button. This creates the public certificate that will be used to sign the SAML assertions. This certificate also contains the subject and issuer distinguished names that you'll need when you configure the identity provider in SAP HANA. You can get SAP HANA to read these values from the certificate, but you can also simply deduce them based on the values you've entered on the screen so far, as they always follow the same format. The first few portions of the distinguished name never change. Only the final CN component changes and that is always equal to what you entered in the UNIQUE IDENTITY PROVIDER ID field on the screen. The SUBJECT and ISSUER values are also always the same. An example value for a system with the UNIQUE IDENTITY PROVIDER ID equal to "BOE41" is the following:

```
C=CA, ST=BC, O=SAP, OU=BOE, CN=BOE41
```

5. **Copy the generated certificate, and add it to the SSL trust.pem file on the SAP HANA server.**
As discussed in the section on configuring SAP HANA for SAML authentication, the SAP HANA server must trust the public certificate for the identity provider. The certificate generated here is the public certificate for this SAP BusinessObjects to SAP HANA connection.

From our perspective, there is no indication of which format the certificate is in with the current implementation as of the version 4.1 ramp-up. Testing seems to suggest that the file is in a partially configured PEM format—that is, it has the certificate data properly Base64 encoded according to PEM standards, but it's missing the required PEM header and footer lines and isn't line wrapped at the typical line length for PEM files. Manually adding the required headers and footers and establishing standard PEM line length results in a working PEM file. Working with SAP Support, we were able to locate a convenient website that reads the raw version of the Base64 string and returns the nicely formatted PEM form.

---

**Converting Certificate Data to PEM Format**

The website *www.redkestrel.co.uk/cgi/decodeCert.cgi* successfully parsed the raw data and gave back a PEM file output. Although we don't recommend sharing a production certificate with an external party, you can use the website to get a good idea of what a valid PEM file should look like and then manually correct your own PEM file.

---

At this point, your configuration of SAML authentication to SAP HANA in the SAP BusinessObjects platform is complete. Assuming you've made all of the configurations on the SAP HANA server as well, you can test the connection by entering a user name in the connection management screen and then clicking the TEST CONNECTION button. The process of generating the SAML assertion for connecting to SAP HANA in this way leverages the Security Token Service, so you'll need at least one of these functioning in your system for the test to work.

### Kerberos Authentication

Much like the configuration of Kerberos on the SAP HANA server, configuration of Kerberos for the SAP BusinessObjects platform is a complex process involving the setup of service accounts, SPNs, and KeyTab files. The concepts are all similar to the setup of the SAP HANA server discussed earlier, except SAP BusinessObjects acts as the middle service and performs the delegated authentication to the SAP HANA server.

Fortunately, the configuration of Kerberos at the SAP BusinessObjects tier has been an integral part of the SAP BusinessObjects platform for a long time and is very well documented. See the reference to the excellent white paper on this subject in the following box. Here, we'll stick to discussing those areas of the configuration that will differ from the documentation provided for the standard SAP Business-Objects solution.

---

**Additional Resources**

For more information on configuring Kerberos on SAP BusinessObjects, we recommend the SAP White Paper "Configuring Active Directory Manual Authentication and SSO for BI4" at *http://service.sap.com/sap/support/notes/1631734*.

---

There are two main deviations from the standard SAP BusinessObjects Kerberos configuration when configuring end-to-end access to the database with SAP HANA. First is the content of the *bscLogin.conf* file, and second is the necessity of referencing the *bscLogin.conf* and *Krb5.ini* files in a number of different locations in the SAP BusinessObjects platform.

Let's examine the necessary configuration differences.

### Configure bscLogin.conf

The standard bscLogin.conf for the SAP BusinessObjects platform is quite simple. It contains just one definition. However, to support an end-to-end connection to SAP HANA, this file needs an additional entry.

The normal bscLogin.conf looks as follows.

```
com.businessobjects.security.jgss.initiate { com.sun.security.auth.
module.Krb5LoginModule required debug=true;
};
```

For end-to-end Kerberos sign-on, bscLogin.conf must include the following additional entry, which points to a copy of the KeyTab file for the Kerberos service account. You can store that KeyTab file anywhere on the SAP BusinessObjects server and reference its complete path in this configuration file entry. You'll also need to reference the principal SPN you used to create the KeyTab.

In this example, we use placeholders for both KeyTab and principal, which you'll need to replace with the appropriate values for your environment:

```
com.businessobjects.security.jgss.accept { com.sun.security.auth.
module.Krb5LoginModule required
storeKey=true
useKeyTab=true
keyTab="C:/PATHTOKEYTAB/KEYTABFILE.keytab"
principal=" BICMS/boe40.mydomain.com@MYDOMAIN.COM"
debug = true;
};
```

### Configure SAP BusinessObjects Server Startup Parameters

Now that you've configured bscLogin.conf and Krb5.ini and stored the KeyTab file on the SAP BusinessObjects server, you need to let a number of key services within the SAP BusinessObjects platform know about these configuration files so they can use them to connect to SAP HANA. The simple rule is, if the service initiates any kind of database connection, it will need a reference to these files. This includes the adaptive processing servers, adaptive job servers, Explorer servers, connection Servers, and Java-based client tools such as IDT.

For any Java-based processes, these parameters are specified as part of the JVM startup arguments. This is the same type of startup arguments we specify for Tomcat under normal SAP BusinessObjects Kerberos configurations. These settings tell the JVM where to find the bscLogin.conf and Krb5.ini, as shown in this example.

```
-Djava.security.auth.login.config=C:\WINNT\bscLogin.conf
-Djava.security.krb5.conf=C:\WINNT\krb5.ini
```

Figure 8.10 shows an example of setting these parameters on the adaptive processing server.

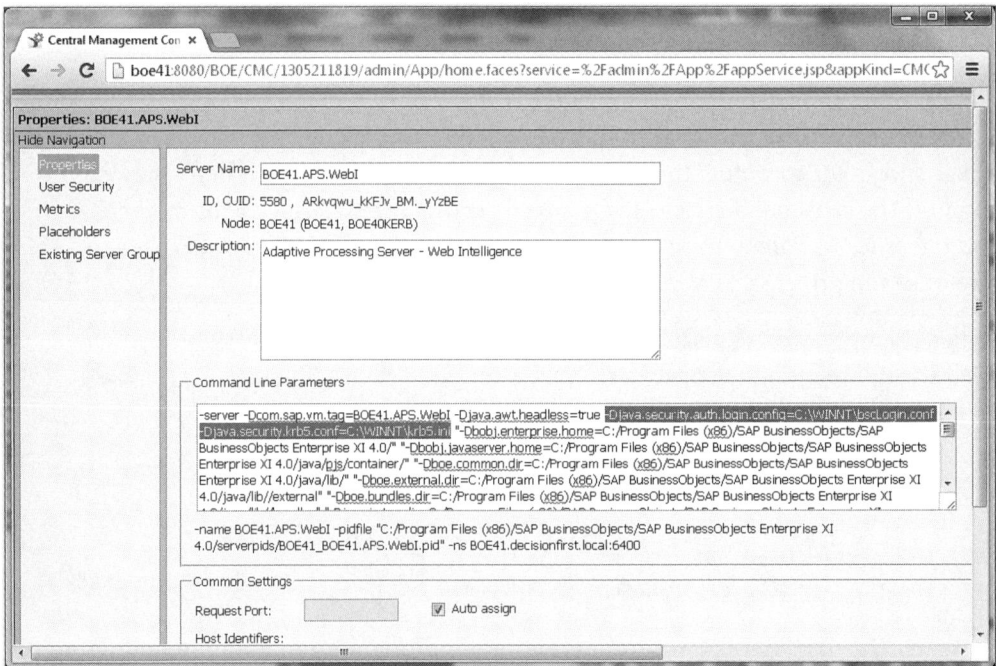

**Figure 8.10**  Configuring Startup Options for an Adaptive Processing Server

Configuring the connection server used by SAP BusinessObjects Web Intelligence and other processes is a bit more complicated. This service reads an XML configuration file from the SAP BusinessObjects environment. You need to place similar entries in that file. The file is named *cs.cfg* and is located in the following directory:

```
SAP BusinessObjects\BusinessObjects\SAP BusinessObjects Enterprise XI
4.0\dataAccess\connectionServer
```

Within that file, locate the `<JavaVM>` section, and then add the references to the two key files by adding `<Option>` entries to the `<Options>` section, as shown in Figure 8.11.

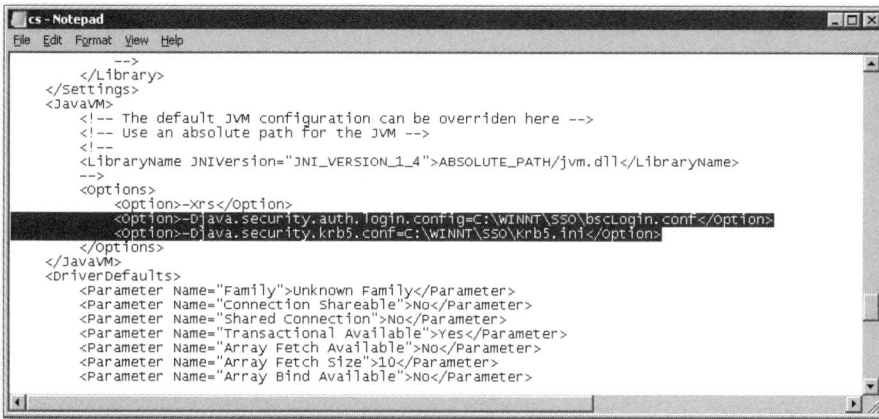

**Figure 8.11** Example Configuration of the Connection Server cs.cfg File

With these changes in place, and assuming you've provisioned equivalent users in SAP HANA, you should be able to test end-to-end SSO. You'll need to ensure that your relational JDBC connections to SAP HANA are set to use SSO and not a configured identity.

### 8.2.5 Configuring Authorization in SAP BusinessObjects BI 4.0

At the most granular level, configuration of authorization in SAP BusinessObjects is based on a concept of a *right*, or the ability to access a specific feature or portion of the system. Rights can be grouped together into a set of related rights for a given functional scenario and given a name. This is referred to as an *access level*. Users or groups in SAP BusinessObjects can be assigned a given access level to a specific piece of content.

For example, a group of users in a particular department might be given an access level on their departmental folder that grants them the necessary rights to view the content in the folder, refresh the data in reports, and schedule the reports to run.

In general, the configuration of a typical end-user security scenario in SAP Business-Objects involves granting users access to a number of objects:

► Authorization to log on and use the reporting tools of the SAP BusinessObjects system (possibly including access to SAP BusinessObjects Web Intelligence, SAP Crystal Reports, SAP BusinessObjects Explorer, etc.)

► Authorization to access and refresh data from the relational connections and universes that provide connections to the reporting data

► Authorization to access public folders containing reports on the connections and universes

► Authorization to view and possibly refresh and schedule reports in those folders

The fact that SAP BusinessObjects sees SAP HANA as just another database means that, for the purposes of authorization configuration, there is nothing special to do for SAP HANA. The same authorization strategy that would work for any database will work with SAP HANA.

### 8.2.6 Provisioning Users in SAP BusinessObjects BI 4.0

Unlike SAP HANA, provisioning users in the SAP BusinessObjects platform is generally straightforward. The platform has strong integration with most third-party identity stores such as Active Directory and LDAP. From these stores, you can automatically map externally defined groups of users into SAP BusinessObjects groups and then use those groups in the assignment of authorizations.

If you want to establish an end-to-end SSO scenario, the key is simply to ensure that you've mapped the same users into SAP BusinessObjects that have been mapped into SAP HANA. In a Kerberos scenario, you can simply map the same set of users from the Active Directory store into SAP BusinessObjects and SAP HANA. If you're implementing SAML, you have some flexibility. Your SAP BusinessObjects users can come from any supported identity store or be created manually, and as long as users with equivalent identities have been created in SAP HANA either manually or via script, the SAML process should be able to map them together.

### 8.2.7 SAP BusinessObjects BI 4.0 End User Tools and Support for SAP HANA Authentication Methods

Not every SAP BusinessObjects reporting tool has equal support for every end-to-end authentication method. Table 8.4 lists the SAP BusinessObjects tools we've had the opportunity to test and their support for end-to-end authentication scenarios in the current GA products as well as what is planned for SAP BusinessObjects 4.1.

| Tool | Current GA (4.0) | Ramp-Up (4.1) |
|---|---|---|
| SAP BusinessObjects Web Intelligence | Supports all authentication types. | Supports all authentication types. |
| SAP Crystal Reports | Supports all authentication types. | Supports all authentication types. |
| Analysis for OLAP | No end-to-end SSO; password authentication only. | Kerberos and SAML ostensibly supported, but we've not had an opportunity to test yet. |
| SAP BusinessObjects Explorer | There is an issue with Kerberos and the index server. Manually mapped SAP BusinessObjects database credentials (i.e., password authentication) does work. | We hope to see a fix for the SAP BusinessObjects Explorer on Kerberos issue as well as full support of SAML, but we haven't had a chance to test a corrected version of SAP BusinessObjects Explorer over Kerberos. |

**Table 8.4**  Authentication Support by SAP BusinessObjects Tools

We've now introduced you to many of the various options for configuring a security solution with SAP HANA and SAP BusinessObjects. In your own implementations, you have a great deal of flexibility to mix and match the various options together to form a complete solution. In the next sections, we'll combine a few of these options to show an example of an end-to-end implementation.

## 8.3 Case Study: Implementing an End-to-end Security Solution for Access to Sales Data

The rollout of the new BI solution based on SAP HANA and SAP BusinessObjects at AdventureWorks Cycle Company has been going well. In preparation for a broader role out, the IT team has been tasked with laying out a security plan for end-user access to content. The target audience for the next phase of the rollout is the group of regional sales managers and their subordinates. The following business requirements must be met by the rollout:

▶ It should integrate with existing Active Directory structures within the corporate network. Provisioning of users should be driven by changes made in Active Directory without the need for additional manual intervention. Real-time synchronization isn't a requirement; a modest delay between user creation/change and provisioning out to all platforms is acceptable.

▶ Users logged in to the corporate network should be able to access the SAP BusinessObjects BI Launchpad without providing additional authentication credentials.

▶ Sales data must be secured to each sales territory so that only users in a given region can access data for that region. Assignment to a region is managed by existing Active Directory groups that model the sales organization.

▶ The first phase of the rollout will support canned SAP BusinessObjects Web Intelligence reports as well as ad hoc query and analysis with SAP BusinessObjects Web Intelligence. However, the intentions are to continue rolling out additional reporting tools from the SAP BusinessObjects platform over time. Therefore, it's desirable that user data security exist in the database platform to better support future SAP HANA tools.

Based on these requirements, the team developed the following rollout plan:

1. Implement Kerberos authentication and SSO in the SAP BusinessObjects platform.

2. Implement Kerberos authentication in the SAP HANA server.

3. Implement analytic privileges limiting content to each sales territory and assign privileges to matched database roles.

4. Develop a script to query active directory via LDAP to retrieve users belonging to the sales territory groups and assign users to the matched database roles.

## 8.3.1 Implementing Kerberos Authentication in the SAP Business-Objects Platform

Using the SAP Guides for Kerberos-based authentication and SSO in SAP Business-Objects platform, the team successfully got Kerberos SSO working in the platform. The AdventureWorks SAP BusinessObjects environment currently consists of one large server hosting the main SAP BusinessObjects platform as well as the web application tier in Tomcat. The SAP BusinessObjects server name is *boe40.adventureworks.com*. However, a friendly DNS alias (*bi.adventureworks.com*) has been set aside for the system so that if the environment is expanded in the future, it can be hidden from end users.

Let's walk through the key steps alongside the team.

### Define a Kerberos Service Account in Active Directory

1. Create a service account named "BOE40KERB" within the ADVENTUREWORKS Windows domain.

2. Assign the account the following SPNs to mark it as the service account for SAP BusinessObjects and to enable HTTP SSO for Kerberos:

   ▶ `BICMS/boe40.adventureworks.com`

   ▶ `HTTP/boe40.adventureworks.com`

   ▶ `HTTP/boe40`

   ▶ `HTTP/bi.adventureworks.com`

   ▶ `HTTP/bi`

3. Create a KeyTab for the account with `ktpass`:

   ```
   ktpass -out c:\boe40kerb.keytab -princ BICMS/boe40.adventureworks.
   com -mapuser boe40kerb@ADVENTUREWORKS.COM -pass *** -ptype KRB5_NT_
   PRINCIPAL -crypto RC4-HMAC-NT
   ```

4. Using Active Directory tools, verify that the account is trusted for Kerberos delegation.

### Set Up Kerberos Configuration Files on the SAP BusinessObjects Server

1. Copy the KeyTab file to the SAP BusinessObjects server, and place it in the directory *C:/WINNT*.

2. Create and store a *krb5.ini* file in *C:/WINNT*, as shown:

```
[domain_realm]
.ADVENTUREWORKS.COM = ADVENTUREWORKS.COM
ADVENTUREWORKS.COM = ADVENTUREWORKS.COM

[libdefaults]
forwardable = true
default_realm = ADVENTUREWORKS.COM
dns_lookup_kdc = true
dns_lookup_realm = true
default_tkt_enctypes = RC4-HMAC
default_tgs_enctypes = RC4-HMAC

[realms]
ADVENTUREWORKS.COM = {
kdc = ADVENTUREWORKS.COM
default_domain = ADVENTUREWORKS.COM
}
```

3. Create and store a *bscLogin.conf* in *C:/WINNT*, as shown:

```
com.businessobjects.security.jgss.initiate {
com.sun.security.auth.module.Krb5LoginModule required
debug=true;
};
com.businessobjects.security.jgss.accept {
com.sun.security.auth.module.Krb5LoginModule required
storeKey=true
useKeyTab=true
keyTab="c:/WINNT/boe40kerb.keytab"
principal="BICMS/boe40.adventureworks.com"
debug = true;
};
```

**Configure the Service Account to Run the SIA**

1. Make BOE40KERB a member of the Administrators group on the SAP Business-Objects server.

2. Give BOE40KERB the necessary local security polices to run a service (ACT AS PART OF THE OPERATING SYSTEM, LOG ON AS A BATCH JOB, LOG ON AS A SERVICE, and REPLACE A PROCESS LEVEL TOKEN).

3. Configure the SIA to run as BOE40KERB instead of the local system.

**Configure Windows Active Directory Authentication in the CMC**

1. Enable Windows Active Directory authentication.

2. Enter "boe40kerb@adventureworks.com" as the AD ADMINISTRATION NAME.

3. Enter "ADVENTUREWORKS.COM" as the DEFAULT AD DOMAIN.

4. Map the Active Directory groups representing sales territories.

5. Enable use of Kerberos authentication, and set the SPN to match the service account:

```
BICMS/boe40.adventureworks.com
```

**Configure Tomcat for Kerberos SSO**

1. Update the Tomcat startup parameters with Kerberos configuration files:

   ▶ `-Djava.security.auth.login.config=C:\WINNT\bscLogin.conf`

   ▶ `-Djava.security.krb5.conf=C:\WINNT\krb5.ini`

2. Update `BILaunchpad.properties` with default authentication set to secWinAD.

3. Update `Global.properties` with sso.enabled set to true, and configure Vintela properties, as shown:

```
sso.enabled=true
siteminder.enabled=false
vintela.enabled=true
idm.realm=ADVENTUREWORKS.COM
idm.princ=BICMS/boe40.adventureworks.com
idm.allowUnsecured=true
idm.allowNTLM=false
idm.logger.name=simple
idm.logger.props=error-log.properties
idm.keytab=C:/WINNT/boe40kerb.keytab
```

**Configure Application Services in SAP BusinessObjects
Platform with Startup Parameters for Kerberos**

1. Add bscLogin.conf and krb5.ini to the startup parameters of the adaptive processing server, adaptive job server, and Explorer servers:

```
-Djava.security.auth.login.config=C:\WINNT\bscLogin.conf
-Djava.security.krb5.conf=C:\WINNT\krb5.ini
```

2. Add the same references to the *cs.cfg* file for the connection servers:

```
<Option>-Djava.security.auth.login.config=C:\WINNT\bscLogin.conf </
Option>
<Option>-Djava.security.krb5.conf=C:\WINNT\krb5.ini </Option>
```

### 8.3.2   Implementing Kerberos Authentication in the SAP HANA Server

The team can successfully get Kerberos working on the database by using the SAP guides for Kerberos authentication in SAP HANA. The AdventureWorks SAP HANA environment consists of one HANA system: *hana.adventureworks.com*.

These are the key steps performed by the team.

**Define a Kerberos Service Account in Active Directory**

1. Create a service account named HANAKERB within the ADVENTUREWORKS Windows domain.

2. Assign the account the following SPN to mark it as the service account for SAP HANA:

```
hdb/hana.adventureworks.com hanakerb
```

3. The team created a KeyTab for the account with the following `ktpass`:

```
ktpass -out c:\hanakerb.keytab -princ hdb/hana.adventureworks.com
hanakerb -mapuser hanakerb@ADVENTUREWORKS.COM -pass *** -ptype KRB5_
NT_PRINCIPAL -crypto RC4-HMAC-NT
```

**Set Up Kerberos Configuration Files on the SAP HANA Server**

1. Copy Hanakerb.keytab to /etc/krb5.keytab.

2. Reuse and copy krb5.ini from the SAP BusinessObjects configuration to /etc/krb5.conf.

3. Restart the SAP HANA database, and confirm that a test user account was successful.

### 8.3.3 Implementing Analytic Privileges and Roles

To support the requirement that each sales territory only receives access to its respective data, the implementation team develops a set of analytic privileges mapped to each logical sales territory. The team hopes to replace their multiple analytic privileges with a single table-driven dynamic analytic privilege when SAP HANA SP6 comes out.

The implementation of each privilege is straightforward. The sales team will have access to the ANLV_RESELLER_SALES and CV_CORPORATE_COMP_RESELLER_SALES analytic and calculation views. Each of these views contains the necessary SALESTERRITORY attribute to drive security. Following are the steps to configure the security.

1. One analytic privilege was created for each of the ten territories, granting access to only the data in that territory. Figure 8.12 shows an example of the analytic privilege for France.

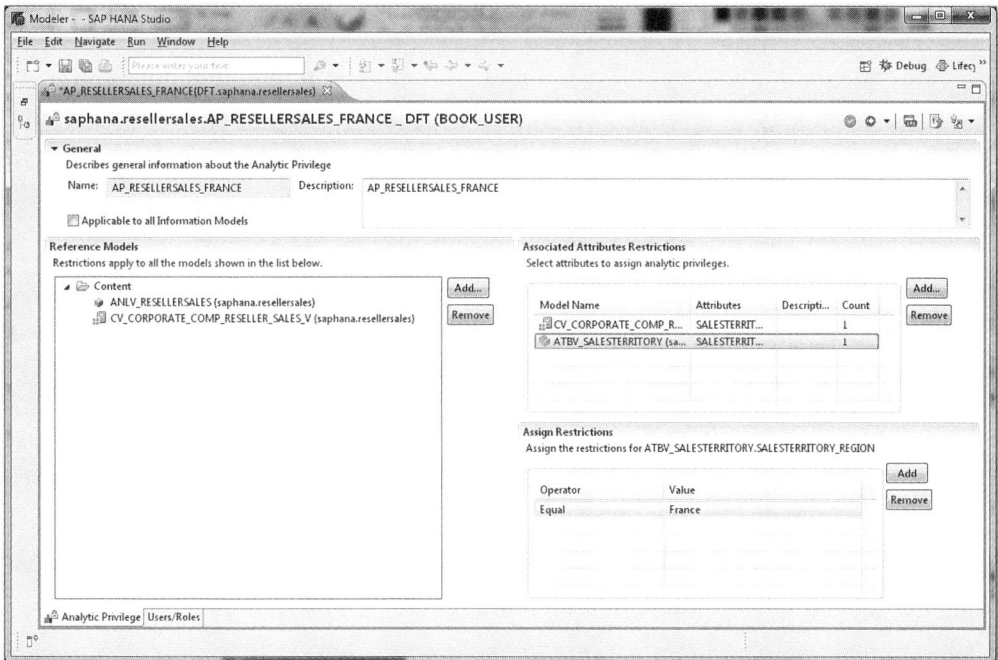

**Figure 8.12**   Creating the Analytic Privilege for the French Region

2. For each of the analytic privileges, a role was defined that grants that analytic privilege along with the necessary privileges to access the analytic content in _SYS_BIC. Figure 8.13 shows an example of the role for the French region.

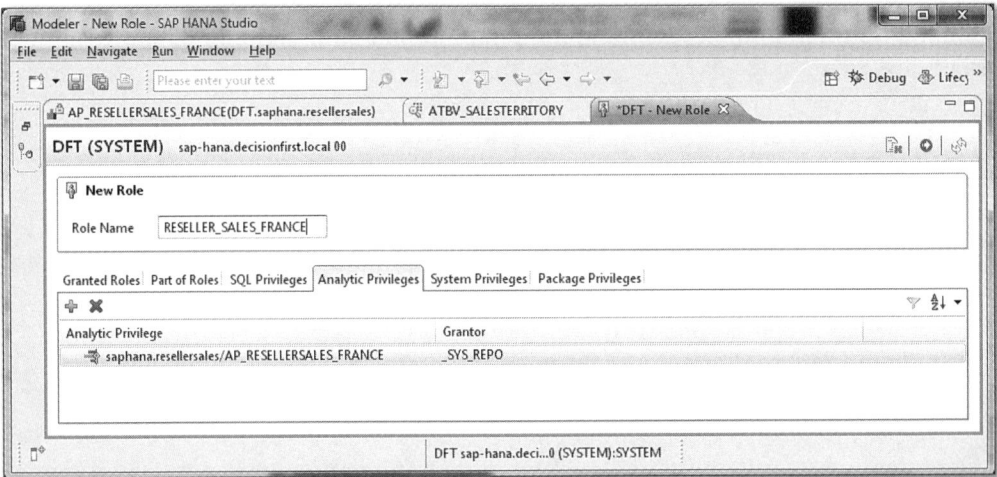

**Figure 8.13**  Creating the Role for the French Region

### 8.3.4  Developing Script to Provision Users to SAP HANA

Because SAP HANA doesn't currently provide for automatic provisioning of users from third-party sources such as Active Directory at this time, the team has to find a workaround. With fairly extensive knowledge of the Java programming language and the fact that Java has many libraries that support querying LDAP structures like Active Directory, the team decides to implement a script in Java that connects to Active Directory and provisions users from the target groups into mapped roles in SAP HANA. The script uses a simple Java properties file to determine which LDAP groups to collect users from, and each group is mapped to a role which users were assigned to. For each user found, the script executes the necessary CREATE USER statements.

## 8.4  Summary

This chapter offered a solid foundation in the technologies and processes needed to configure an access control strategy in a combined SAP BusinessObjects and SAP

HANA environment. Although this is a complex and involved topic with reliance on many third-party technologies, we hope the introduction here provides enough of a kick start to help you configure your own solutions.

It's important to remember that the SAP HANA system is still somewhat new, and the area of access control and integration with SAP BusinessObjects is still undergoing significant change. You have a number of options for configuring an end-to-end solution today, even if those solutions don't cover every tool or feature in the SAP BusinessObjects suite. Even as we write this (summer 2013), we're hearing of new features planned for future service packs of SAP HANA that will improve on the security integration features, and new patches for SAP BusinessObjects that should tighten the integration between the BI tools and the SAP HANA backend.

The important takeaway from this chapter should be the need to plan your security implementation carefully. It's a complex process with a number of moving pieces. It's likely an implementation that will involve team members from multiple areas of IT collaborating together, such as the Active Directory administrator, SAP HANA administrators, SAP BusinessObjects administrators, and network administrators, to get all of the systems talking to each other successfully.

At this point, you should have a solid idea of how to provision data to an SAP HANA system using SAP Data Services, prepare that data for consumption with analytic models, enrich the data further with predictive analysis, and now secure that data in preparation for consumption by end users. In the next chapter, you'll learn how to further prepare the data for consumption by using SAP BusinessObjects reporting tools and by creating rich semantic layers with the SAP BusinessObjects universe design tools.

# PART III
# Integrating SAP Business-Objects BI with SAP HANA

*This chapter provides an overview of the two universes or semantic layers built into SAP BusinessObjects 4.0 and how they are used to provide access to data within SAP HANA. The case study walks you through the processes of developing a universe on SAP HANA tables and analytic views.*

# 9    SAP BusinessObjects Universe Design

In many ways, the capabilities of the multidimensional models in SAP HANA and in an SAP BusinessObjects *universe* are very similar. The intent of both semantic layers is to provide consumers an intuitive or easy-to-understand multidimensional representation of their data. Both tools act as a *semantic layer* that shields the consumer from the complexities of the underlying data model and database coding languages. Data objects and semantics are represented as graphical business objects. This is all achieved while providing organizations with a central layer that adds metadata, applies data security, and centralizes business logic. Much like the SAP HANA multidimensional models, data objects in a universe are represented as attributes and measures. However, in a universe, the terms *dimensions* and *measures* are used to describe these same objects. Universes also contain other objects such as *details* and *conditions* that can also be used to further simplify access to the underlying data model. There are several other features of the SAP HANA multidimensional models and the SAP BusinessObjects universe that are similar as well. For example, derived columns, calculated measures, runtime filters, and hierarchies are supported in both tools.

There are also several profound differences between these tools. To list a few, the SAP BusinessObjects universe is designed to support multiple vendor-specific relational database management systems (RDBMS) and not just the columnar tables in SAP HANA. Universes support the coding languages of their source RDBMS, while the SAP HANA models only support the coding languages embedded within the SAP HANA platform. Universes can federate multiple disparate data sources into a single semantic layer while each SAP HANA model can only access a single instance of SAP HANA. SAP HANA models are configured to leverage the powerful hardware specifications of the SAP HANA appliance while the universe relies

567

on the performance capabilities of its source RDBMS. SAP HANA models can take advantage of coding libraries such as SQLScript, Predictive Analysis Library (PAL), R language, and Business Function Library (BFL) while the universe is limited to SQL or, in some cases, multidimensional expressions (MDX).

It can also be argued that some of the more power features of the universe are only enacted in the SAP BusinessObjects Web Intelligence reporting engines. In contrast, the SAP HANA calculation views can perform complex calculations directly in the SAP HANA Calculation Engine. Take, for example, cross-fact aggregation and data synchronization. Based on definitions in the universe, SAP BusinessObjects Web Intelligence executes multiple SQL statements and then synchronizes the results in its engine to create a merged view of the dimensions and measures. The SAP HANA calculation views can produce the same results without needing an external reporting tool engine.

Because the SAP HANA calculation view is embedded directly in the SAP platform, all supported tools can access these calculation views. Table 9.1 provides an outline of the major feature comparisons between an SAP BusinessObjects universe and the SAP HANA multidimensional models. Please note that there are additional similarities or differences; this table focuses on the high-level comparison.

| Major Feature Comparison | SAP BusinessObjects Universe | SAP HANA Information View |
|---|---|---|
| Acts as a semantic layer? | Yes. Developers can define dimensions, measures, business friendly names, descriptions, hierarchies, and so on. | Yes. Developers can define attributes, measures, business friendly names, descriptions, hierarchies, and so on. |
| Supports complex calculations? | Yes. Complex calculations might require reporting tool engines. Features may vary by underlying database. | Yes. Information views can produce complex calculations while directly leveraging the SAP HANA appliance engines. Complex calculations are reporting tool agnostic. |
| Supports calculated columns? | Yes. Using the coding syntax of the underlying data source, universe dimensions and measures can be designed to manipulate the source data. | Yes. Using the SAP HANA SQL syntax, developers can produce calculated columns and measures in information views. |

**Table 9.1** High-Level Feature Comparison between a Universe and SAP HANA Model

| Major Feature Comparison | SAP BusinessObjects Universe | SAP HANA Information View |
|---|---|---|
| Directly access data from multiple sources? | Yes. Using the data federator plugin, an IDT universe can access data from multiple supported data sources. | No. Data must first be loaded into SAP HANA using SAP Data Services or other supported provisioning methods. In SAP HANA SPS6, there is a new option to allow data to be federated from multiple sources. However, this feature was not available in SAP HANA SPS5. |
| Leverages Relational OLAP? | Yes. Application data is never stored in a universe. The universe and reporting tools only generate SQL or MDX code, and data is retrieved from the underlying data source. | Yes. Application data is never stored in an information view. Code is executed to retrieve the data from the underlying columnar store tables. |
| Provides a row-level surety layer | Yes. There are multiple ways to implement row-level security in a universe. | Yes. Information views can be configured with analytic privileges to implement row-level security. |
| Column-level security? | Yes. Columns can be restricted or suppressed based on logon credentials. | No. Information views are currently limited to the view and row level via analytic privileges. |
| Dynamic filters? | Yes. Universes support dynamic runtime filtering using prompts. | Yes. Analytic views and calculation views support dynamic runtime filters using variables. |
| Native support for R, PAL, and BAL libraries? | No. Universes only support the SQL and MDX languages based on their underlying data source. | Yes. Calculation views and stored procedures support the R, PAL, and BAL libraries. |
| Supports hierarchies? | Yes. Hierarchies are based on one or more dimensions. Used predominantly for SAP BusinessObjects Web Intelligence drilldown analysis. | Yes. Hierarchies can be defined from flat sources or parent-child sources. Predominantly used for expand and collapse functionality in pure play OLAP or MDX-based reporting tools. |

**Table 9.1** High-Level Feature Comparison between a Universe and SAP HANA Model (Cont.)

| Major Feature Comparison | SAP BusinessObjects Universe | SAP HANA Information View |
|---|---|---|
| Native support for currency conversion? | No. This can be achieved using complex prompt functions and custom currency tables but it's not a native feature of the universe. Functionality is limited. | Yes. Leverages tables and fields from the SAP Business Suite applications to easily and seamlessly convert currencies. |
| Native support for application data translation? | No. This can be achieved using complex prompts and custom language tables, but it's not a native feature of the universe. Functionality is limited. | Yes. Leverages tables and fields from the SAP Business Suite applications to easily and seamlessly display application data in the appropriate user locale. |
| Provides a dedicated object that acts as predefined filter? | Yes. The universe supports the creation of *conditions* or reusable filters that can be subjectively applied to reporting tool queries. | No. Filters are hardcoded into the information view as either static filters or variables. |
| Delegated measures or smart measures? | Yes. Measures that calculate averages and ratios can be flagged as delegated. This informs the reporting tool that the database must aggregate and calculate the column to prevent the report engine from producing incorrect results. | No. Measures can't be delegated or flagged to prevent the reporting tools from producing incorrect results. |

**Table 9.1** High-Level Feature Comparison between a Universe and SAP HANA Model (Cont.)

In this chapter, we'll discuss the basic concepts of the SAP BusinessObjects UNX universe and discuss why you need a universe to access data in SAP HANA. We'll explore in detail the new UNX universe and then briefly discuss the legacy UNV universe in the context of SAP HANA implementations. Because the legacy UNV universe concepts are very similar to that of the UNX universe, we don't go into the details, but the concepts you find in Section 9.2 also applies to Section 9.3. In conclusion, we'll walk you through a case study to demonstrate the processes of creating a universe to access SAP HANA.

## 9.1    Overview of the Universe in SAP BusinessObjects

Before SAP acquired Business Objects, the universe was the center point for many of the Business Objects reporting and analysis tools. In recent years, SAP has devised alternatives to support its own legacy reporting and analysis tools that don't require a developer to define universes for native SAP application data sources.

With that said, many organizations design the universe to provide an intuitive, central, and secure point of access to their third-party data sources. As we discussed earlier, universes are designed to make the report design process easy for the average business users when accessing data in an RDBMS. It shields report designers from the complexities of designing SQL statements, identifying database objects, and resolving complex SQL traps. As opposed to writing SQL statements, consumers can design queries against the universe, using a graphical user interface (GUI). Database objects such as tables, fields, joins, filters, and aggregates are embedded in the universe. They are then presented to the consumer in a graphical, object-oriented, multidimensional format that is rich in metadata. With a universe, users don't need to consult a data dictionary or have intimate knowledge of the data model to work with and to identify database objects. Universe objects can be defined with full text names and descriptions to help users quickly identify the object's purpose. In addition, the universe can be configured with technical metadata that provides the reporting tools information necessary to properly process complex queries.

Once completed, the universe effectively serves as a multidimensional model much like the SAP HANA information views. In the introduction to this chapter, we briefly discussed the similarities and differences between these multidimensional modeling layers. Some may argue that the SAP models effectively replace the universe, but you'll discover that this isn't always the case. There are specific instances where a universe is required when accessing SAP HANA with the SAP BusinessObjects tools.

In addition, you'll discover that SAP BusinessObjects 4.0 contains two types of universes. Because there are multiple universes, we'll also discuss the reasons for this specific functionality overlap. In the conclusion of this section, we'll discuss the technical requirements for connecting the universe to SAP HANA using the SAP HANA client software.

### 9.1.1 Using a Universe to Access SAP HANA Data

As mentioned previously, there is a degree of functionality overlap between the SAP HANA multidimensional models and the SAP BusinessObjects universe. Regardless of their similarities or differences, a universe is still required for many of the tools in the SAP BusinessObjects platform when connecting to SAP HANA. We do expect future enhancements to the SAP BusinessObjects tools to allow developers to automatically create a universe on an SAP HANA information view or to direct bind to an SAP HANA information view without the use of a universe. However, until that functionality is incorporated into all of the toolsets, a standard universe is required to accommodate many of the legacy reporting tools in the SAP BusinessObjects suite. In Section 9.1.2, we'll outline the different options for connecting the SAP BusinessObjects tools to SAP HANA and a universe.

So why do we currently require a universe to connect to SAP HANA, and when might the universe be a better option based on the end user's requirements? The following list outlines the primary reasons the universe is currently relevant even though SAP HANA has built-in models that function like a universe.

▶ Because the full integration between the SAP BusinessObjects tools and the SAP HANA information views hasn't been developed yet, a universe is currently required to support SAP HANA access for some of the SAP BusinessObjects reporting and analysis tools. Tools such as SAP BusinessObjects Explorer 4.0, SAP BusinessObjects Analysis for OLAP, SAP BusinessObjects Analysis for Microsoft Office, SAP BusinessObjects Design Studio, and SAP Lumira can all currently directly bind to the SAP HANA information views. Other tools such as SAP BusinessObjects Web Intelligence and SAP BusinessObjects Dashboards 4.0 currently use a universe to access data in SAP HANA. In addition, tools such as SAP Crystal Reports can connect directly using a universe, Open Database Connectivity (ODBC), or Java Database Connectivity (JDBC).

▶ Sometimes you need to use a universe to support the requirements of the users based on the functionality of the SAP BusinessObjects tools. Accounting for the fact that many of the SAP BusinessObjects tools were originally developed to support legacy third-party RDBMSs and that they are efficient in generating standard SQL statements based on metadata in the universe, some of the SAP BusinessObjects tools currently have more available options when using a universe.

▶ Organizations can have diverse reporting needs, so having the ability to choose between the functionality of a universe and the functionality of the SAP HANA multidimensional model can be an advantage. While there are several overlapping features between the two sources, there are also a few items that are very different. For example, the universe contains delegated measures, predefined conditions, and detail objects. These objects aren't currently available in SAP HANA models. With this in mind, the universe might be a better choice depending on the organization's requirements.

▶ Universes can be easily converted to support SAP HANA as a source, so customers that are already running SAP BusinessObjects on a third-party RDBMS will find it easier to adopt SAP HANA. From the perspective of the developers and the users, little will change because they will continue to support and use a universe.

### 9.1.2 The Two Universes in SAP BusinessObjects 4.0

If you're familiar with the new SAP BusinessObjects 4.0 environment, you've likely noticed that there are two types of universes and universe design tools available in the platform. This can sometimes be confusing for both legacy and new adopters of the SAP BusinessObjects platform.

However, SAP's choice to include both the legacy format and the new format was a wise decision; it allows an organization to easily adopt the SAP BusinessObjects 4.0 platform without having to make radical changes to their development processes. Throughout this section, we'll discuss the differences between the two universes and discuss their support options for SAP HANA as a source.

For the purposes of this conversation, it's important that we briefly review the product history of the SAP BusinessObjects universe. In SAP BusinessObjects version 3.1 and in earlier versions of Business Objects, there was only one universe type available. These universes (UNV), when saved to a disk, use the file extension .unv. They were created with a client tool called *Designer*. Starting with SAP Business-Objects 4.0, two universe design tools are available. The first is the traditional universe Designer we just mentioned. In the SAP BusinessObjects 4.0 platform, it works the same as the universe Designer that is found in version 3.1 or earlier. The second designer and universe (UNX) is called the *Information Design Tool* (IDT). When an IDT universe is saved to disk, its file extension is .unx. Both tools have a distinct user interface (UI), but they generally share the same principles with a few exceptions. Table 9.2 outlines the major feature comparison between the two different styles of universes in SAP BusinessObjects 4.0.

| Feature | Traditional UNV Universe | New UNX IDT Universe | Notes |
|---|---|---|---|
| Universe objects | Supports the creation of dimension, measure, condition and detail objects. Objects are created in the same design window where the table joins and logical schema are created. | Supports the creation of dimension, measure, condition, and detail objects. However, these objects are now defined in a distinct layer called the business layer. In addition, the list of values and prompts can now be defined as reusable objects. | While the principles are the same between each universe type, there a several distinct differences in both the UI and the design workflows. |
| Table joins or logical schema design | The table join design window is embedded in the same design window where objects are created. It can't be independently shared with other universes. | Tables are joined or the logical schema is defined in the data foundation layer. This layer is used to define tables, joins, filters, contexts, aliases, list of values, and prompts. The data foundation layer is separate from the business layer just mentioned. It's reusable between universes because it's a separate layer. Developers can also define reusable list of values and prompts in this layer. | While the principles are the same between each universe type, there are several distinct differences in both the UI and the design workflows. |

**Table 9.2**  Comparing Traditional Universe Features with the New IDT Universe

| Feature | Traditional UNV Universe | New UNX IDT Universe | Notes |
|---|---|---|---|
| Data sources | Only supports a single data source or database connection object per universe. | Through the use of the embedded SAP BusinessObjects Data Federator engine, the IDT universe supports multiple disparate data sources or connection objects in a single data foundation. Multisource universes use the common Data Federator SQL syntax. | The ability to manage multiple data sources in the IDT universe is a significant and long awaited enhancement to the universe. |
| User interface | The universe can be designed in a single design window. | The universe is predominantly designed in two distinct design windows or layers. The first layer is the data foundation mentioned earlier. The second is the business layer, also mentioned earlier. | Overall, the UI is significantly different in the aspects of both appearance and design workflow. For developers, the transition from the UNV Designer to the UNX Designer will require some time to adjust. |
| Prompts and list of values | Prompts are defined as functions that are embedded in objects or derived tables. Their list of values is defined with each dimension object. In either case, they aren't independent or reusable objects. | Both prompts and list of values can be defined as reusable or separate objects. These objects can be referenced in objects and derived tables. | Because they are independent and reusable objects in the IDT universe, developers need only update the central prompt or list of values object. The list of values object now natively supports the use of custom SQL without the need to override the SQL statement. |

**Table 9.2** Comparing Traditional Universe Features with the New IDT Universe (Cont.)

The presence of two universes and also multiple reporting and analysis tools in the SAP BusinessObjects 4.0 platform can cause confusion for adopters; how can they know which universe to use when connecting to SAP HANA sources?

It's our opinion that SAP BusinessObjects 4.0 was designed by SAP to aid organizations in the transition from their legacy universe content to the new enhanced universe content. However, there is still room for confusion for organizations that need the universe to connect to SAP HANA sources. There is also multiple reporting and analysis tools in the SAP BusinessObjects 4.0 suite to further add to the confusion. Each tool has a unique dependency on the type of universe that can be used. In addition, some tools have the ability to completely bypass the universe when connecting to SAP HANA information views. Table 9.3 contains a listing of the SAP BusinessObjects 4.0 tools and the universe types they support when accessing SAP HANA. Those tools that can access SAP HANA information views directly are marked with an asterisk character.

| SAP BusinessObjects Tool | Support for IDT Universe (UNX) | Support for Traditional Universe (UNV) |
|---|---|---|
| Web Intelligence 4.0 | Yes | Yes |
| Dashboards 4.0 | Yes | No |
| SAP Crystal Reports 2011 | No | Yes |
| SAP Crystal Reports for Enterprise 4.0 | Yes | No |
| Explorer 4.0 | Yes (*) | No (**) |
| SAP Lumira 1.0 | Yes (*) | Yes (*) |
| Analysis for OLAP | No | No |
| Analysis for Microsoft Office | No | No |
| Live Office 4.0 | No | Yes |

*It's better to use the direct binding to SAP HANA information views. The direct binding fully leverages the SAP HANA engines and hardware when processing queries.

** We expect SAP BusinessObjects 4.1 Explorer to support both UNV and UNX universes.

**Table 9.3** SAP BusinessObjects Tools that Use the Universe to Access SAP HANA

A universe isn't required for SAP BusinessObjects 4.0 Explorer, SAP Lumira, and SAP BusinessObjects Analysis for OLAP. These tools can directly connect to either an analytic view or calculation view that has been activated in the SAP HANA platform. When they connect directly to SAP HANA, they are able to leverage the power of its platform because only summarized data and metadata is exchanged between the visualizations and SAP HANA engines. This isn't to say that same can't be accomplished when using a universe. However, based on the diversity of how each tools works, direct binding to SAP HANA has proven to be the most direct option for leveraging the power of SAP HANA.

> **Note**
>
> As of the writing of this book, the remaining SAP BusinessObjects tools either require a universe or the SAP HANA client ODBC/JDBC connectivity to interact with SAP HANA data. As mentioned earlier in this section, it's our understanding that future releases of SAP BusinessObjects will provide support for direct binding using SAP Crystal Reports for Enterprise or automatic universe creation using IDT. However, until that is available, a manually developed universe will be needed for these tools when accessing SAP HANA. As we mentioned earlier, there are also cases where the universe can be advantageous because the SAP BusinessObjects tools currently provide more features when connecting to SAP HANA through a universe.

### 9.1.3  Using the SAP HANA Client as Middleware

On their own, the SAP BusinessObjects tools can't connect to the SAP HANA appliance without the use of database *middleware*. Middleware is software developed to provide an application access to (e.g., an RDBMS). It helps to ensure that both the application and database speak the same language. Practically every RDBMS today requires the use of middleware or software code to provide access to the database. The same is true for any application that requires access to SAP HANA. The special piece of software or middleware is called the *SAP HANA client*. The SAP HANA client must be installed on both the SAP BusinessObjects server and an SAP BusinessObjects developer workstation to provide the reporting and analysis tools access to the SAP HANA appliance.

The SAP HANA client provides industry-standard drivers such as ODBC, JDBC, and OLE DB for OLAP. The SAP BusinessObjects tools primarily use either ODBC or JDBC to access the SAP HANA appliance. The SAP HANA client is available in both 32-bit and 64-bit distributions. It currently supports the operating systems (OSs) listed in Table 9.4.

| Operating System | CPU Support | OS Versions |
|---|---|---|
| IBM AIX | RS/6000 64 bit | 5.2, 5.3, 6.1, 7.1 |
| HP UNIX | Intel Itanium 64 bit | 11.31 |
| Linux Redhat | x86 64 bit | EL5, EL6 |
| Linux SUSE 11 | x86 64 bit | SLES10, SLES11 |
| Linux SUSE 11 | x86 32 bit | SLES11 |
| IBM OS/400 | POWER | V7R1 |
| Solaris | SPARC 64 bit | 10, 11 |
| Solaris | x86 64 bit | 10, 11 |
| Microsoft Windows | x86 32 bit | Win7, XP, VISTA, 2008 |
| Microsoft Windows | x86 64 bit | Win7, VISTA, 2008, 2008 R2 |

**Table 9.4** Operating Systems Supported by the SAP HANA Client

**Additional Information**

The installation of the SAP client is beyond the scope of this book. In many cases, the installation of the SAP HANA client varies by OS. For complete instructions on the installation of the SAP HANA client, please review the information available at *http://help.sap.com/hana_appliance*. Look for the *SAP HANA Client Installation Guide*.

### Configuring ODBC Support

After the SAP HANA client is installed, you'll need to configure either the ODBC or JDBC clients to support the SAP BusinessObjects universe. Most OSs can be configured to recognize a data source name (DSN) using a configuration file or ODBC utility. This section walks you through the processes of configuring the ODBC DSN on the Microsoft Windows OS. Please note that the IDT requires the use of a DSN configured using the 32-bit ODBC Data Source Administrator. However, the SAP BusinessObjects Enterprise server requires the use of a DSN configured using the 64-bit ODBC manager.

To configure a 32-bit ODBC to support the SAP BusinessObjects client tools, follow these steps:

1. If you're running a supported 32-bit or 64-bit Windows OS, download and install the 32 bit SAP HANA client to support the SAP BusinessObjects IDT or other SAP BusinessObjects client tools. The SAP BusinessObjects client tools are compiled with 32-bit binaries.

2. If you're configuring the ODBC DSN for SAP BusinessObjects IDT, launch the 32-bit ODBC Data Source Administrator to configure the DSN. For Windows 64-bit OSs, this can typically be launched using the *C:\Windows\SysWOW64\ odbcad32.exe* executable. For native 32-bit OSs, this can typically be launched using the *C:\Windows\System32\odbcad32.exe* executable or the ODBC manager found in the Control Panel.

3. Figure 9.1 shows an example of what you should see after launching the ODBC Data Source Administrator. Click the ADD button to create an ODBC DSN.

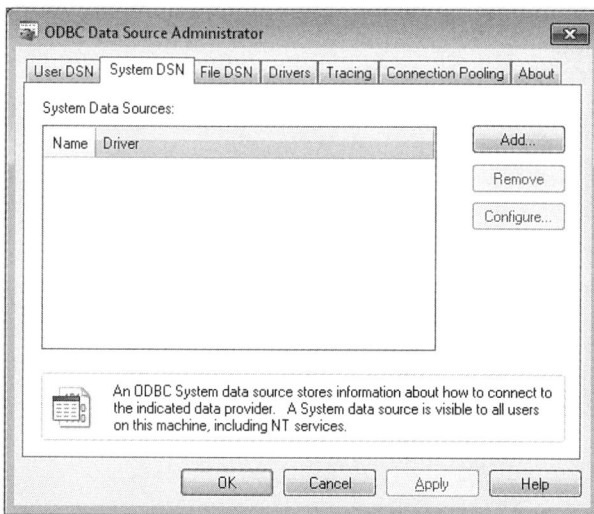

**Figure 9.1** The ODBC Data Source Administrator

4. As shown in Figure 9.2, select the SAP HANA ODBC driver. The driver name is HDBODBC. The driver version should match that of your SAP HANA server. The COMPANY column contains the name SAP AG.

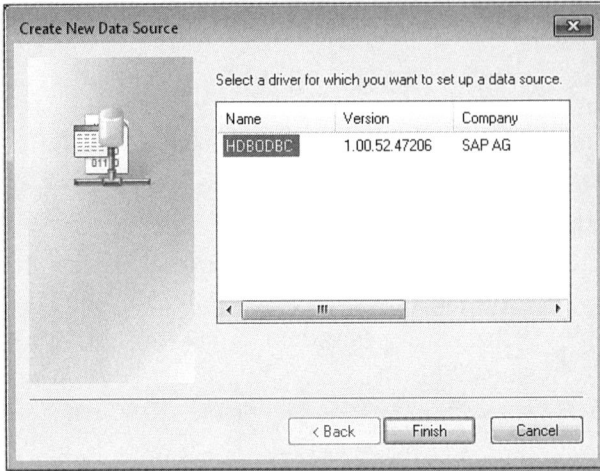

**Figure 9.2**  The SAP HANA ODBC Driver When Creating a New Data Source

5. After selecting the HDBODBC driver, you must configure the data source name, description, fully qualified hostname, and TCP/IP port of the SAP HANA appliance.

The data source name and description can be anything you prefer, but they should be defined so that the DSN is easily identified. In the SERVER:PORT field, the hostname you enter must resolve to the SAP HANA appliance's client network IP address. The port number is in the format of the 3<INSTANCE>15 where <INSTANCE> is the two-digit instance number of your SAP HANA instance. As shown in Figure 9.3, the value you enter for the SERVER:PORT field should be a concatenation of the SAP HANA host and port number.

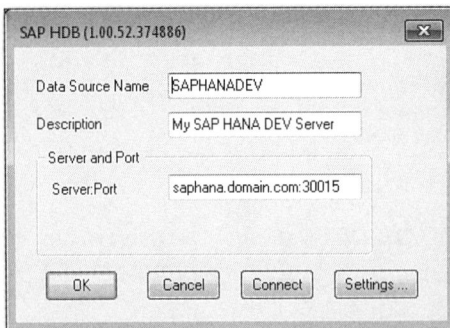

**Figure 9.3**  Configuring the SAP HANA and Port in an ODBC DNS

6. To configure SSL or other special properties for the connection, click the SET-TINGS button shown in Figure 9.3.

7. Click the CONNECT button to validate and test the connection details.

8. Using Figure 9.4 as a guide, enter your SAP HANA USER name and PASSWORD. Select the CONNECT USING SSL checkbox if your connection requires SSL encryption.

**Figure 9.4**  Testing the SAP HANA Connection while Creating the ODBC DSN

Assuming that your information was entered correctly, you'll receive a CONNEC-TION SUCCESSFUL! message as depicted in Figure 9.5.

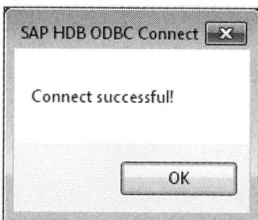

**Figure 9.5**  Connection Successful Message

9.  Click OK to close the message.

10. Click OK to save your ODBC DSN.

11. If you receive an error during the connection test, please contact your SAP HANA DBA.

To configure a 32-bit and 64-bit ODBC to support the SAP BusinessObjects Enterprise server, when you create an ODBC DSN on your workstation and subsequently configure a universe and universe connection based on an ODBC DSN, it's assumed that the same ODBC DSN will also exist on the SAP BusinessObjects Enterprise server. In short, you must also create a matching ODBC DSN on the SAP BusinessObjects Enterprise servers. Because there are multiple services that can interact with the SAP HANA appliance on the SAP BusinessObjects Enterprise platform, we recommend that you configure the same ODBC DNS on all SAP BusinessObjects Enterprise nodes used for report processing.

The process of configuring the ODBC DNS on the Windows servers is similar to that of the Windows workstation. However, there are a few items to note. The following instructions will guide you in configuring the ODBC DNS on a Windows 2008 R2 server and provide special notes when appropriate.

1.  The SAP BusinessObjects Enterprise 4.0 platform is a mix of 64-bit and 32-bit services, so download and install both the SAP HANA 64-bit Client and SAP HANA 32-bit Client for Windows on each SAP BusinessObjects Enterprise node.

2.  If you're configuring the ODBC DSN for SAP BusinessObjects 32-bit processes, launch the 32-bit ODBC Data Source Administrator to configure the DSN. For the Windows 2008 R2 server OS, this can typically be found in the *C:\Windows\ SysWOW64\odbcad32.exe* executable.

3.  If you're configuring the ODBC DSN for the SAP BusinessObjects 64-bit processes, launch the 64-bit ODBC manager, which is typically located in *C:\Windows\System32\odbcad32.exe* or in the Windows 2008 R2 Control Panel.

    We recommend that you configure both the 32-bit and 64-bit ODBC each time a new DSN is created. This will make the management processes easier in the long term. From this point forward, the process of configuring an ODBC DNS is the same as what is listed earlier.

4.  After you launch the ODBC Data Source Administrator, click the ADD button to create an ODBC DSN.

5. Select the SAP HANA ODBC driver. The driver name will be HDBODBC. The driver VERSION should match that of your SAP HANA server. The COMPANY column will contain the name SAP AG.

6. After selecting the HDBODBC driver, you must configure the data source name, description, fully qualified hostname, and TCP/IP port of the SAP HANA appliance. The data source name and description can be anything you prefer, but they should be entered so that the DSN is easily identified. In the SERVER:PORT field, the hostname you enter must resolve to the SAP HANA appliance's client network IP address. The port number is in the format of the 3<INSTANCE>15 where <INSTANCE> is the two-digit instance number of your SAP HANA host. The value you enter for the SERVER:PORT field should be a concatenation of the SAP HANA host and port number. Again, make sure your corporate firewall allows access from your client PC to the SAP HANA host and port.

7. To configure SSL or other special properties for the connection, click the SETTINGS button.

8. Click the CONNECT button to validate and test the connection details.

9. Enter your SAP HANA USER name and PASSWORD. Select the CONNECT USING SSL checkbox if your connection requires SSL encryption.

10. Assuming that your information was entered correctly, you'll receive a CONNECTION SUCCESSFUL! message.

11. Click OK to close the message.

12. Click OK to save your ODBC DSN.

13. If you receive an error during the connection test, please contact your SAP HANA DBA.

Let's turn our attention from configuring ODBC to configuring JDBC.

### Configuring JDBC

As an alternative to using ODBC, developers and administrators can configure their SAP BusinessObjects platform and its client tools to support the SAP HANA JDBC driver. JDBC is an industry standard Java-based driver that allows applications running under a Java Virtual Machine (JVM) to interact with an RDBMS. For SAP HANA, the installation of the SAP HANA client includes the JDBC library file. Unlike ODBC, JDBC doesn't have a central configuration GUI or configuration file. Each connecting application must be made aware of the connection information for SAP

HANA and the path to the SAP HANA JDBC library file. The SAP HANA library file is named *ngdbc.jar*. It's located in the SAP HANA client root installation directory. On a 64-bit Windows OS this is typically located under *C:\Program Files\sap\hdbclient*. The installation path under UNIX or Linux will vary based on the installation path information provided during the UNIX SAP HANA client installation.

In many cases, the JDBC client is easier to manage in environments that are using UNIX or Linux to run their SAP BusinessObjects Enterprise environment. With JDBC, there is no need for the SAP BusinessObjects administrator to create an identical ODBC DSN on server nodes. The JDBC connection details are read directly from the SAP BusinessObjects universe connection objects. The administrator needs only update a few configuration files, one time, on each SAP BusinessObjects Enterprise server node to indicate the path to the *ngdbc.jar* file. In addition, there are no special considerations for 32-bit verses 64-bit OSs. Many of the SAP BusinessObjects tools are preconfigured with either a 32-bit or 64-bit JVM. Because the *ngdbc.jar* is compiled to support the JVM, it's effectively OS and CPU independent.

To configure JDBC support for the SAP BusinessObjects universe, follow these steps. These directions apply to both the client workstation and the SAP BusinessObjects Enterprise server.

1. Install SAP HANA client. We recommend that you install 32-bit SAP HANA client on your workstation in the event you need ODBC support, but technically the ngdbc.jar can be obtained from either installation. For the server, we recommend that you install both the 32-bit and 64-bit SAP HANA client.

2. Locate the installation directory of your SAP HANA client. The 32-bit client installation directory is typically located under *C:\Program Files (x86)\sap\hdb client*. Likewise, the 64-bit client installation directory is located under *C:\Program Files\sap\hdbclient*.

3. Copy the *ngdbc.jar* file to the following path: *[BusinessObjects Install Path]\SAP BusinessObjects Enterprise XI 4.0\dataAccess\connectionServer\jdbc\drivers\newdb\*.

4. Note that the NEWDB folder might not exist. If the folder isn't available, create it.

5. Each time you update your SAP HANA client version, you'll need to copy the *ngdbc.jar* file from the client installation directory to the *newdb* directory. The JDBC driver version number should match that of your SAP HANA appliance.

These same steps will need to be followed on each SAP BusinessObjects Enterprise server node. No additional configuration is required to support JDBC.

## 9.2 Building UNX Universes with the Information Design Tool

To this point, we've discussed why a universe is sometimes required to provide the SAP BusinessObjects tools access to SAP HANA data despite their overlap in functionality. We discussed the reasons that there are two universe formats in the SAP BusinessObjects 4.0 platform to help you make the best implementation choice, and then the reasons that you need the SAP HANA client middleware to support both the developer and the SAP BusinessObjects server.

We'll now turn our attention to the process of building a UNX universe to support access to data in SAP HANA. Pay close attention to the concepts that are discussed in Section 9.2 and keep in mind that they also apply to the legacy UNV universe discussed in Section 9.3. As mentioned before, we'll only briefly discuss the role of the UNV universe in this chapter.

Recall that there are two types of universes in the SAP BusinessObjects Enterprise 4.0 platform. Accordingly, there are also two client tools available to manage each universe type. The IDT was first introduced in the SAP BusinessObjects 4.0 suite. It possesses several new capabilities and a new interface when compared to the legacy Universe Designer found in previous version of SAP BusinessObjects.

The IDT is included in the SAP BusinessObjects platform client tool installation package. When installing the SAP BusinessObjects platform client tools, it's important that the version and patches installed match that of your SAP BusinessObjects Enterprise platform. If you're unsure how to install SAP BusinessObjects 4.0 client tools, refer to the installation guide for Windows found on the SAP Help portal at *http://help.sap.com/bobip*. The installation guide for Windows contains instruction and information for installing the client tools on the Windows platform.

Once installed, the IDT can be found in the Windows START menu under the path START • ALL PROGRAMS • SAP BUSINESS INTELLIGENCE • SAP BUSINESSOBJECTS BI PLATFORM 4 CLIENT TOOLS • INFORMATION DESIGN TOOL. The IDT runs as a 32-bit process, but it can be installed on a supported 64-bit Windows OS. Because it's compiled in 32 bit, it will only work with locally installed middleware that is also complied in 32 bit. This is important for developers who want to construct and test a universe using their locally installed database drivers or middleware. Because it's a 32-bit application, it will only work with 32-bit middleware. There is an option in IDT to also use the SAP BusinessObjects Enterprise server's middleware, which we'll discuss in more detail later in this chapter.

> **Configuring the Information Design Tool to Support Windows Active Directory Authentication**
>
> By default, the IDT doesn't support Windows authentication unless the *krb5.ini* and *bsclogon.conf* files have been installed and configured on your Windows OS. For instructions for configuring Windows Active Directory authentication support for the IDT, please refer to SAP Note 1621106.

In this section, we'll provide you with the basic information and best practices for configuring an SAP BusinessObjects IDT universe based on SAP HANA as a data source. We'll discuss the steps required to create a relational connection to SAP HANA, and then the steps required to create an OLAP connection to SAP HANA and why this type of connection isn't used by the universe. We'll then discuss the steps required to create a project, data foundation, and business layer. To help you understand the design concepts specific to SAP HANA, we'll highlight both the data foundation and business layer options specific to SAP HANA. However we won't walk through all aspects of creating an IDT universe. We recommend that you attend the SAP training course BOID10 and BOID20 to gain a thorough understanding of universe design. If you already have experience in designing universes, this section will help supplement your knowledge.

> **Additional Universe Design Guides**
>
> As we stated, the goal of this chapter is to introduce you to universe design concepts specific to SAP HANA. SAP provides several excellent guides at *http://help.sap.com/ bobip#section5*. Here you'll find the *Information Design Tool User Guide* and the *Universe Design Tool User Guide*.

### 9.2.1 Creating Relational Connections

The first step in designing an SAP BusinessObjects IDT universe requires that you create a relational connection to your SAP HANA data source. However, you must also first install the SAP HANA client that was discussed in Section 9.1.3. The relational connection is used by the majority of the SAP BusinessObjects tools when accessing SAP HANA. Relational connections are created in the REPOSITORY RESOURCES window visible in the default IDT workspace, as shown in Figure 9.6.

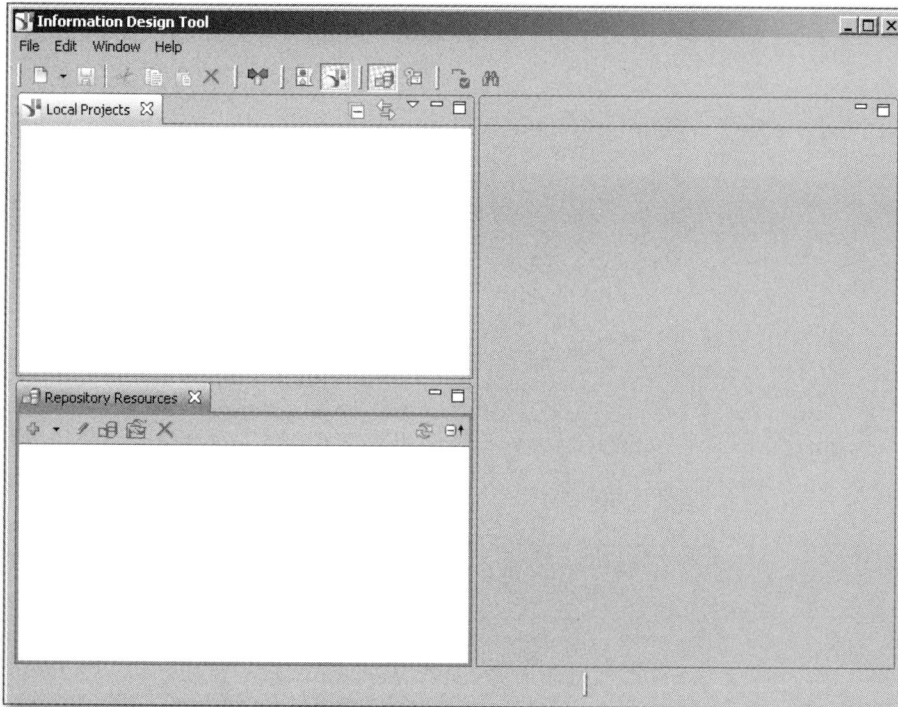

**Figure 9.6**  The Information Design Tool Default Workspace and Windows

Before creating a repository relational connection, you must first authenticate with the SAP BusinessObjects Enterprise platform and generate a session. To create a session, click the green plus sign located on the top-right side of the REPOSITORY RESOURCES window or the windows depicted in Figure 9.7, and choose INSERT SESSION.

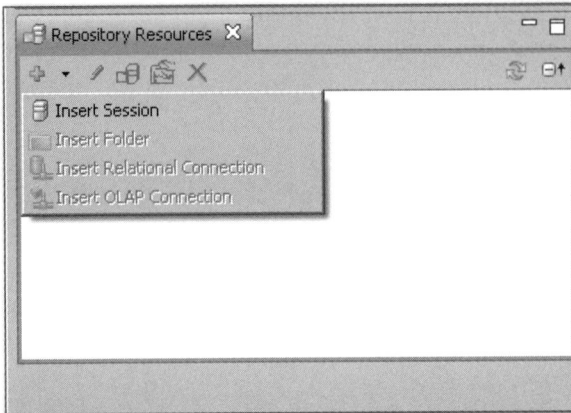

**Figure 9.7**  Inserting or Creating an SAP BusinessObjects Session

The OPEN SESSION window appears, allowing you to authenticate with your SAP BusinessObjects Enterprise platform. As shown in Figure 9.8, enter the host or cluster name of your SAP BusinessObjects system in the SYSTEM field. You can then enter your SAP BusinessObjects USER NAME, PASSWORD, and AUTHENTICATION type to create the session.

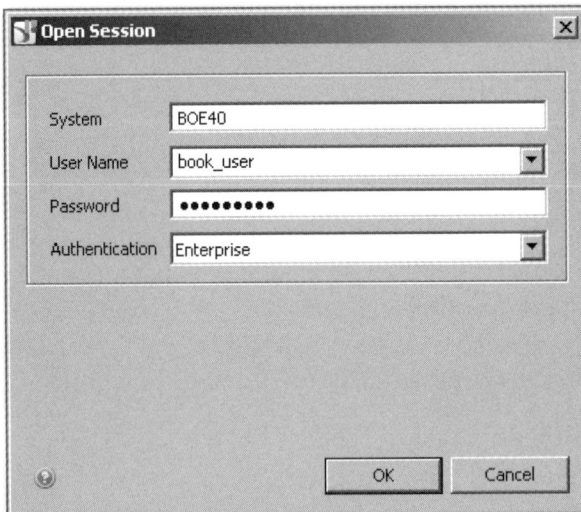

**Figure 9.8**  Authenticating with SAP BusinessObjects Enterprise

After successfully authenticating, you should now have a session in the REPOSITORY RESOURCES window. Expanding the session object reveals all existing connections and universes available to the authenticated user. Figure 9.9 shows the expanded session in the REPOSITORY RESOURCES window.

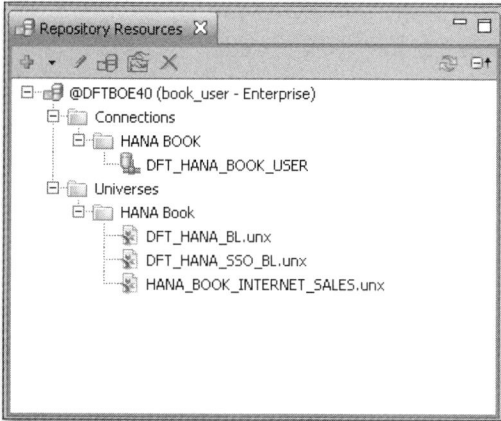

**Figure 9.9**   Viewing Universes and Connections in the Repository Resources Window

To create a relational connection, use Figure 9.10 as a guide, and right-click a location under the CONNECTIONS folder where your user account has the appropriate rights to create a connection. Choose INSERT RELATIONAL CONNECTION from the context menu.

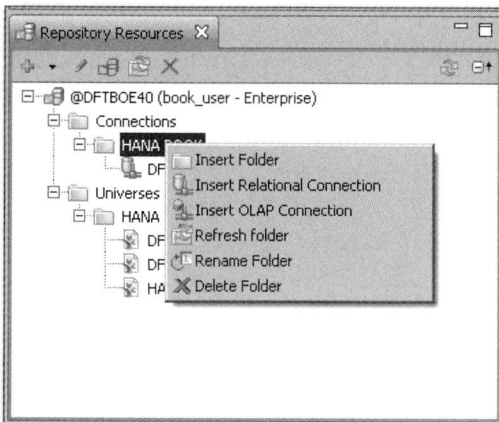

**Figure 9.10**   Creating a Relational Connection

The NEW RELATIONAL CONNECTION wizard appears, as shown in Figure 9.11. Enter the desired relation connection name in the RESOURCE NAME field and the desired description in the DESCRIPTION field. Because relational connections can be reused by multiple universes, we recommend you create a name that is generic and appropriate for use in multiple universes. We also recommend that you add a description to indicate the system and appropriate use of the connection. After you've entered the desired name and description, click the NEXT button.

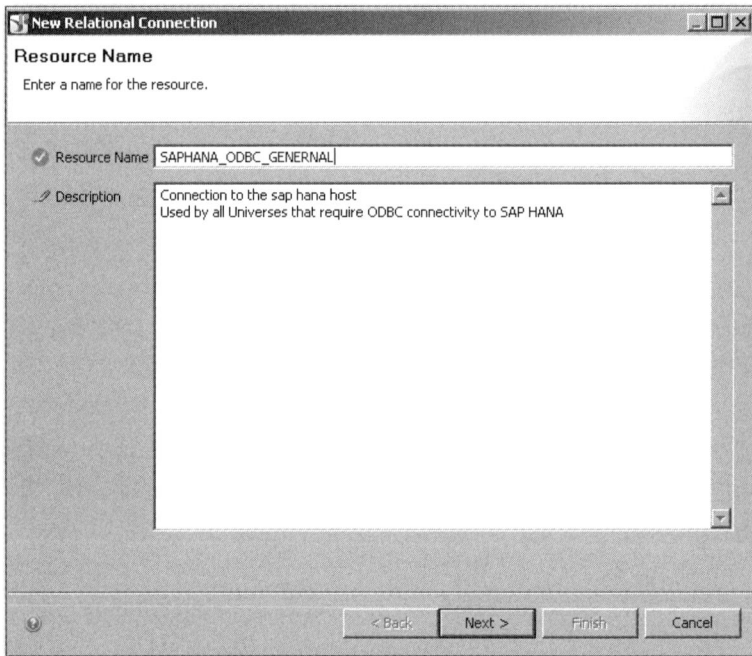

**Figure 9.11** The New Relational Connection Wizard

In the DATABASE MIDDLEWARE DRIVER SELECTION screen shown in Figure 9.12, expand the SAP node, and then expand the SAP HANA DATABASE 1.0 node. Choose the ODBC DRIVERS option, and click NEXT. You can also choose the JDBC DRIVERS option if you want to use JDBC. For the purposes of this section, first configure the connection using the ODBC middleware driver.

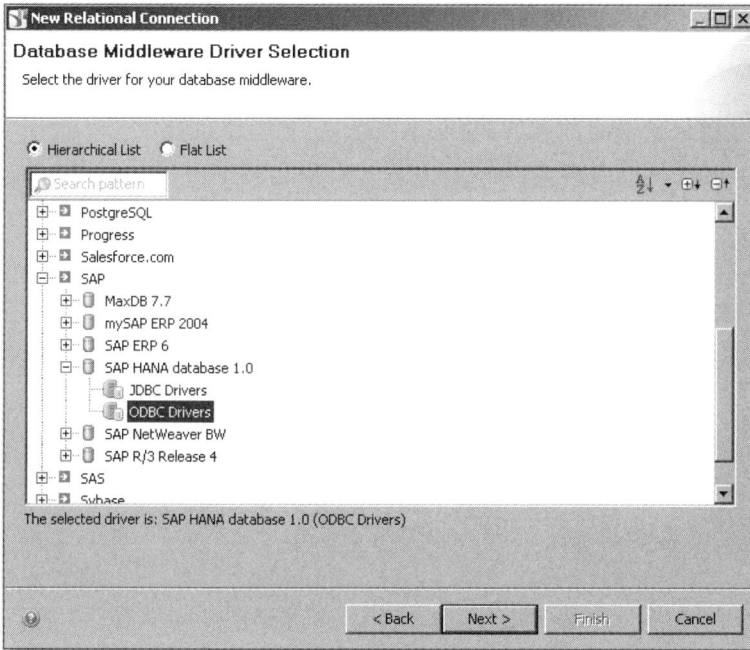

**Figure 9.12** Choosing the SAP HANA Middleware and Driver

In the parameters for the SAP HANA database 1.0 connection window shown in Figure 9.13, specify the Authentication Mode, User Name, Password, and ODBC DNS Data Source Name.

There are two authentication modes available for SAP HANA ODBC connections. The first option is labeled Use Specified Username and Password. With this option the user name and password are coded and stored with the connection option. Tools that access universes based on this connection will always send these credentials to the SAP HANA appliance to authenticate the connection.

As an alternative, you can also choose the Use BusinessObjects Credential Mapping option. With this option, tools that access the universes based on this connection will send the alternative credentials that are stored with each SAP BusinessObjects user account. With this option, individual credentials will be sent to the SAP HANA system based on those mapped to the SAP BusinessObjects user account. The second option is best used when analytic privileges are used in SAP HANA information views to restrict access to specific data. However, credential mapping requires that the SAP BusinessObjects administrator maintain alternative database credentials for each SAP BusinessObjects user.

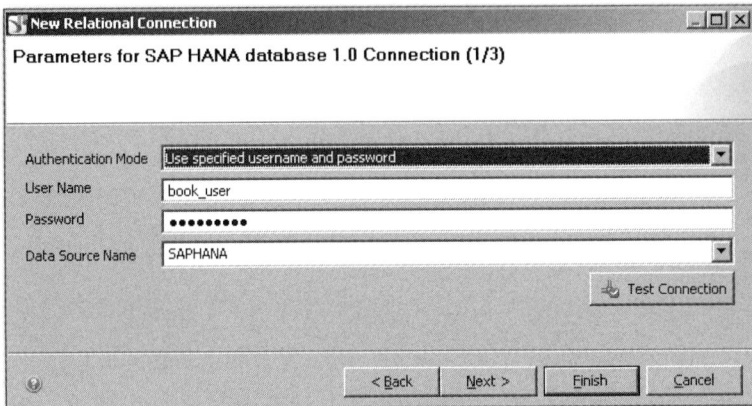

**Figure 9.13**  ODBC Parameters for the SAP HANA Database 1.0 Connection

When configuring the JDBC parameters for the SAP HANA database 1.0 connection there are only two main differences. The AUTHENTICATION MODE, USER NAME, and PASSWORD options are similar, but as opposed to choosing an existing ODBC DSN, with JDBC, you must specify the fully qualified SAP HANA hostname and TCP/IP port in the SERVER (HOST:PORT) field. The hostname and port should be separated with a colon.

There is also an additional AUTHENTICATION MODE option called USE SINGLE SIGN ON WHEN REFRESHING REPORTS AT VIEW TIME. With this option, the SAP HANA Kerberos and SAP BusinessObjects Kerberos configuration will be leveraged, and Kerberos tickets will be transferred between the SAP BusinessObjects system and the SAP HANA system to authenticate the user. For implementations where Single Sign-On (SSO) to the SAP HANA database is required, this option should be selected. This option also allows the solution to leverage individual SAP HANA user rights when analytic privileges are set up to restrict access to data in SAP HANA information views. Unlike the USE BUSINESSOBJECTS CREDENTIAL MAPPING option, there is no need for the SAP BusinessObjects administrator to manage alternative credentials for each SAP BusinessObjects user account.

As shown in Figure 9.14, click the TEST CONNECTION button to verify that your SAP HANA credentials and parameters are set up properly. If configured correctly, a TEST RESULT window appears as shown in Figure 9.15. Click the SHOW DETAILS button to expose the details view. This window and view provide details about the SAP HANA client build and the location of the various SAP BusinessObjects connection configuration files. If the connection test fails, double-check your connection parameters, network access to the SAP HANA host, or the configuration of your SAP HANA client. Click CLOSE to exit the TEST RESULT window and return to the screen shown in Figure 9.14. Click NEXT to proceed to the next step.

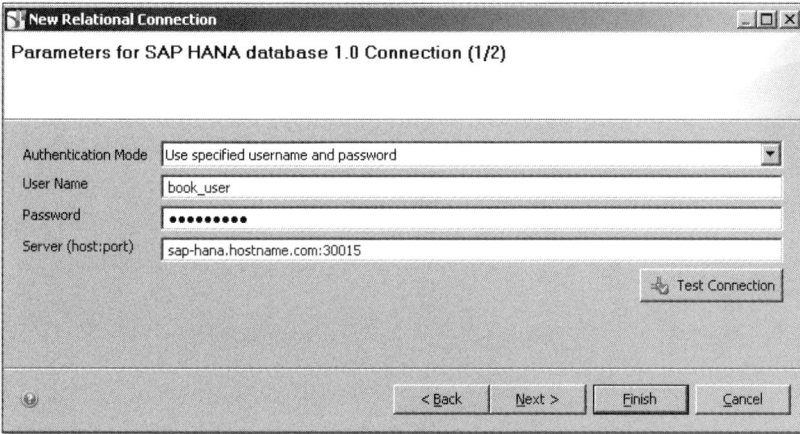

**Figure 9.14** JDBC Parameters for the SAP HANA Database 1.0 Connection

**Figure 9.15** The IDT Universe Connection Test Result Window

An additional parameters window appears as shown in Figure 9.16, which lets you configure additional connections pool options. In most cases, the default values are acceptable for most implementations and solutions. However, it's possible to manipulate these connection pool options to increase or decrease the overall reporting performance under specific scenarios. Connection pool options aren't unique to SAP HANA connections, but a basic understanding of these options is important as it relates to performance. In general terms, the creation of a database connection, in the SAP BusinessObjects platform, is an expensive process. If the pool settings are too aggressive, a user's reporting experience can be slowed. Table 9.5 outlines the various connection pool options and provides a description of how each option affects reporting users.

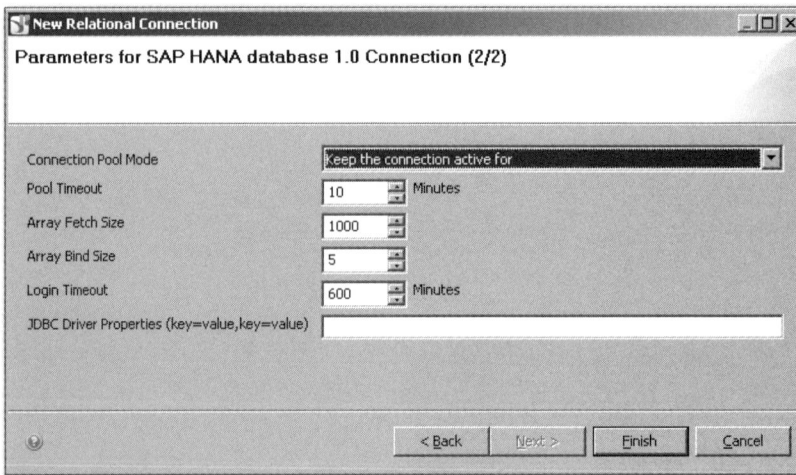

**Figure 9.16** Additional SAP HANA Connection Options

| Option | Description |
| --- | --- |
| CONNECTION POOL MODE • KEEP THE CONNECTION ACTIVE FOR | This is the default connection pool mode and should be used in most use cases. Each database connection is maintained for the specified timeout in anticipation that a subsequent request for a connection will be issued. Setting the value too low negatively affects users because new connections have to be created more often. Setting the value too high results in excess connection on the SAP HANA database. In most cases, 10 minutes is sufficient. |

**Table 9.5** Connection Pool Options for SAP HANA

| Option | Description |
|---|---|
| CONNECTION POOL MODE • DISCONNECT AFTER EACH TRANSACTION | This connection pool mode isn't recommended for normal reporting use. A new connection is created for each report transaction. If there are list of values and multiple queries in your reports, this option results in poor overall report performance. Traditionally, this option is only used with an RDBMS that is limited in its support of connections based on security or software licensing. SAP HANA isn't licensed by connection or user. Therefore, there is no need to use this option. |
| CONNECTION POOL MODE • KEEP THE CONNECTION ACTIVE DURING THE WHOLE SESSION (LOCAL MODE ONLY) | This connection pool mode is only applicable for local mode universe usage or use with client tools. The connection to the database remains open until the client tool is closed. This should only be used if the developer is frequently querying the SAP HANA system and doesn't want to create a connection for each attempt. |
| POOL TIMEOUT | When the KEEP THE CONNECTION ACTIVE FOR option is selected, this parameter specifies the desired timeout before the connection is closed. It's only closed when the connection has been idle for the specified time. |
| ARRAY FETCH SIZE | This option specifies the number of records that are retrieved from an SQL query per request. If the value is set to 1,000, and the query returns 10,000 records, the processing server will request 1,000 records from the database 10 times until the total number of records are transferred. Setting this value too low slows the performance of the query because there are too many requests and round trips required to process the records set. Setting the value too high results in network latency or saturation. In addition, setting the value too high can increase the CPU and RAM use on the SAP BusinessObjects platform. Ironically, setting the value too high can also result in slower report performance. In most cases, the default value is acceptable. However if you have the resources to manage a larger number of records concurrently, increasing the value might result in faster processing times. |

**Table 9.5**  Connection Pool Options for SAP HANA (Cont.)

| Option | Description |
|---|---|
| ARRAY BIND SIZE | This option specifies the size of the bind array before it's sent in a single request to the SAP HANA database. This option is most often used for inserting data with `INSERT` statements but it can also apply to `SELECT` statements. The default value of "5" is acceptable for universes based on SAP HANA. |
| LOGIN TIMEOUT | The amount of time that can pass before a connection is closed. If you query runs for longer than the specified time, in minutes, the query fails. |

**Table 9.5**  Connection Pool Options for SAP HANA (Cont.)

In general, customizations to these connection pool settings should be tested thoroughly when changed from the default. An important component of your testing should include the testing of the settings under high concurrent load and not just testing them with one user or request. The default settings are a well-balanced combination that addresses both individual user and multiple user concurrencies. After you've established these connection pool settings, click the FINISH button to save the connection to the SAP BusinessObjects repository.

After successfully creating the connection objects and saving it in the SAP Business-Objects Enterprise repository, you're now ready to move on to the next step. However, before we discuss the next steps, we want to provide you with additional information pertaining to SAP HANA connections and the SAP BusinessObjects platform.

### 9.2.2  Creating OLAP Connections

There are two types of connections in the SAP BusinessObjects repository. The *relational connection* is used to provide access to standard relational database sources. There is also an *OLAP connection* that can be used to access traditional OLAP sources such as SAP NetWeaver Business Warehouse (SAP NetWeaver BW) or Microsoft's SQL Server Analysis Services. In most cases, the relational connection manages the issuing of SQL statements to the RDBMS. OLAP connections manage the issuing of MDX statements to the OLAP source.

For those familiar with the capabilities of SAP HANA, this might be confusing. SAP HANA provides SQL access and MDX access to its information views, and its information views mimic the capabilities of OLAP in several ways. However, when establishing SAP HANA connectivity to the SAP BusinessObjects tools, you'll use the relation connection in almost all instances. The one exception is the use of the SAP BusinessObjects Analysis for OLAP client tool. For the SAP BusinessObjects Analysis for OLAP tool to access SAP HANA as an OLAP source, you must create an OLAP connection and store it in the SAP BusinessObjects Enterprise repository. The IDT allows you to create an OLAP connection and save it to the repository for most OLAP sources. However, you can't use the IDT to create an SAP HANA OLAP connection. As an alternative, you can use the SAP BusinessObjects Central Management Console (CMC) to create an SAP HANA OLAP connection.

To create an SAP HANA OLAP connection, you must have access to the CMC and the rights to create a connection, and then follow these steps:

1. Open your browser and access the CMC using the URL provided by your SAP BusinessObjects administrator. Typically the URL is constructed as follows: *http://<SAP BusinessObjects Host>:8080/BOE/CMC*.

2. Log on to the CMC using the appropriate credentials.

3. On the CMC home page, locate the OLAP CONNECTIONS link found at the bottom of the ORGANIZE list.

4. In the SAP BusinessObjects CMC OLAP connections manager, locate the folder you want to save the connection in and highlight it.

5. Click the green connection icon (third icon from the left) on the toolbar to create a new OLAP connection, as shown in Figure 9.17.

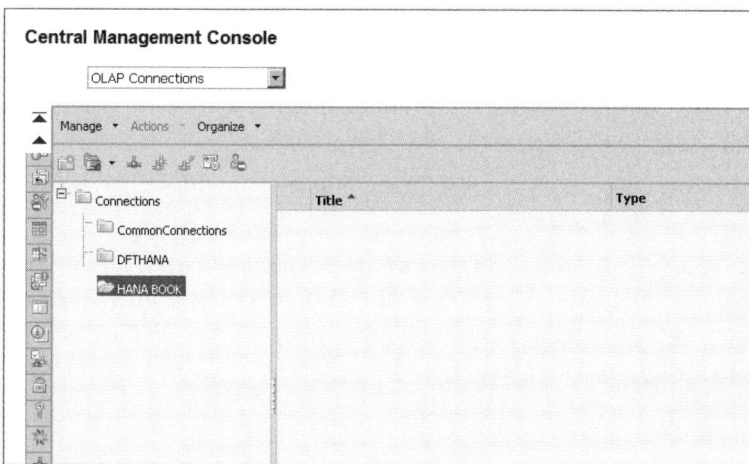

**Figure 9.17** The SAP BusinessObjects CMC OLAP Connections Manager

6. Select the SAP HANA provider first to enable the remaining fields that need to be completed, as shown in Figure 9.18.

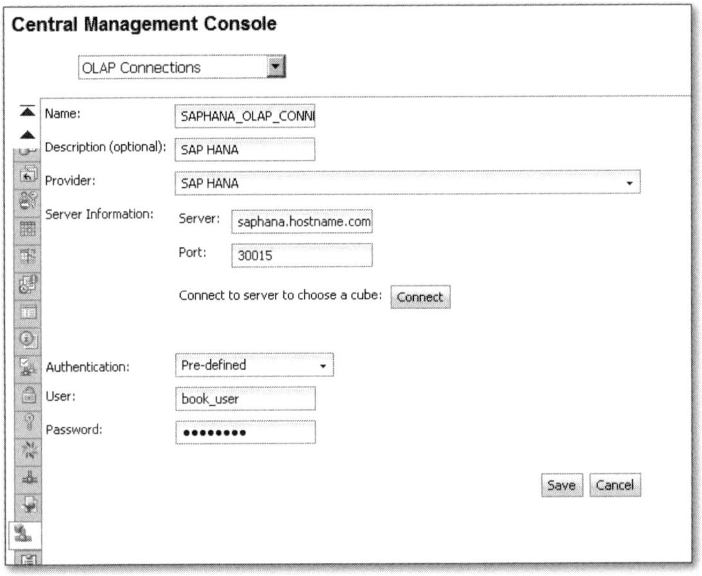

**Figure 9.18** Configuring an OLAP Connection to Access SAP HANA

7. In the NAME field, enter the desired name of the connection.

8. In the DESCRIPTION (OPTIONAL) field, enter the desired connection description. Note that the DESCRIPTION field is optional.

9. In the SERVER INFORMATION field, enter the hostname of the SAP HANA SERVER and the TCP/IP PORT that represents the instance of SAP HANA.

10. Click the CONNECT button to select a specific information view to act as the desired OLAP source. This is also optional. If you choose to bypass this step, the user can choose a desired information view when creating an SAP Business-Objects analysis for OLAP report.

11. In the AUTHENTICATION dropdown list, select the desired authentication option. The PRE-DEFINED option allows you to hard-code the SAP HANA user name and password. The PROMPT option forces the SAP BusinessObjects Analysis for OLAP users to specify their SAP HANA credentials when accessing the SAP HANA source.

12. Click the SAVE button to save and close the connection window and return to the OLAP Connection manager in the CMC.

### 9.2.3 Testing Connections Using the Local or Server Middleware

Another key option of the SAP BusinessObjects IDT is the ability to choose between the preference of testing connections and accessing data using either locally installed middleware or the middleware that is installed on the SAP BusinessObjects Enterprise server.

With most organizations, installing and maintaining database middleware on client workstations are time-consuming tasks. With IDT, users have the option to use the middleware installed on the SAP BusinessObjects Enterprise server. When this option is chosen, the IDT communicates all connection attempts through the SAP BusinessObjects Enterprise platform by using its connection libraries to access the desired data source. To change this preference, you need to access the IDT preferences by choosing WINDOW • PREFERENCES in the IDT FILE menu bar. In the PREFERENCES window, locate the option by expanding the INFORMATION DESIGN TOOL • SECURED CONNECTIONS option.

Figure 9.19 shows the two available options. Choose SERVER MIDDLEWARE to leverage the SAP BusinessObjects server for all SAP HANA connection attempts. Choose LOCAL MIDDLEWARE to leverage the middleware installed on your local workstation.

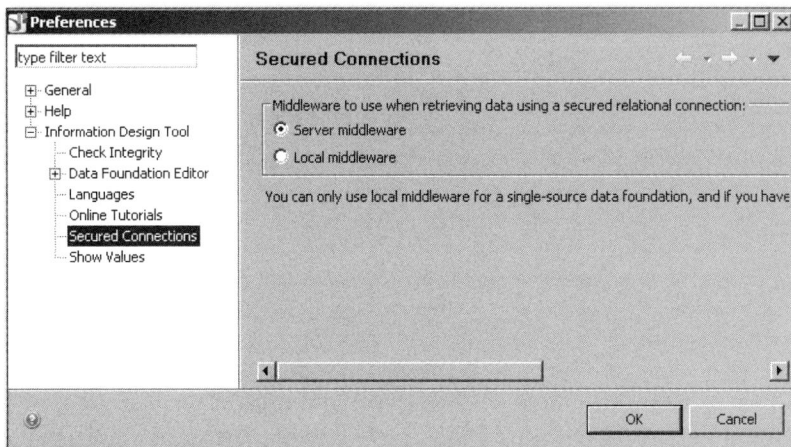

**Figure 9.19**  Choosing between the Local or Server Middleware

Server middleware can be useful in many ways (for example, when you need to ensure that the server's middleware is set up properly or when you need to ensure that the SAP HANA connections work when executed from the server). If connection attempts fail using this option, then they will likely also fail when interacting with SAP BusinessObjects reports and web-based tools. This option is also useful when you're unable to obtain or install the SAP HANA client on your local workstation.

### 9.2.4 Creating Projects

After creating a relational connection to an SAP HANA system, you're now ready to start the processes of designing a universe. However, before you can begin designing a universe, you must define a local *project* in the IDT. Projects are used to organize the local versions and individual components of an IDT universe. This is a new universe design concept that was first implemented with the IDT. Projects are only stored and maintained on the developer's workstation. They aren't stored with universes published to the SAP BusinessObjects repository.

While projects are represented as logical folders in the IDT, they are also physically stored on the developer's workstation in their OS user profile directory. To access your local IDT project files, outside of the IDT, browse to *%userprofile%\.business objects\bimodeler_14\workspace*. Remembering this path's location is useful when you need to recover project files from another user's profile or when you need to manage the project files independent of the IDT.

Follow these steps to create a project in the IDT:

1. Launch the IDT from the Windows START menu.

2. Ensure that you're using the IDT default display. If you're unsure, locate the RESET option under the FILE menu by selecting WINDOW • RESET TO DEFAULT DISPLAY.

3. Locate the NEW icon on the icon toolbar (first icon on the left). Click the arrow to the right of the NEW icon to activate the dropdown menu, as shown in Figure 9.20.

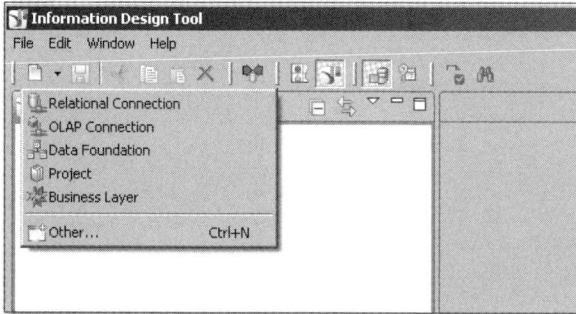

**Figure 9.20**   Activating the New Item Dropdown Menu

4. Choose PROJECT from the dropdown to create a new project and display the NEW PROJECT window.

5. Enter the desired name for your project, as shown in Figure 9.21. Remember that projects are only used to store the local components of the IDT universe. The name of your project won't be visible to other users or stored in the SAP BusinessObjects repository.

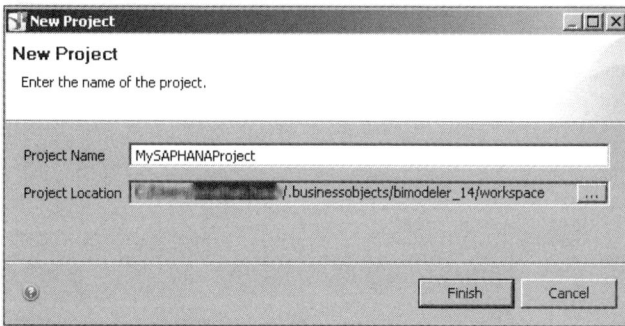

**Figure 9.21**   Configuring the Project Name

6. Click the FINISH button to save and create the project. Your project is now listed in the LOCAL PROJECTS window, as shown in Figure 9.22.

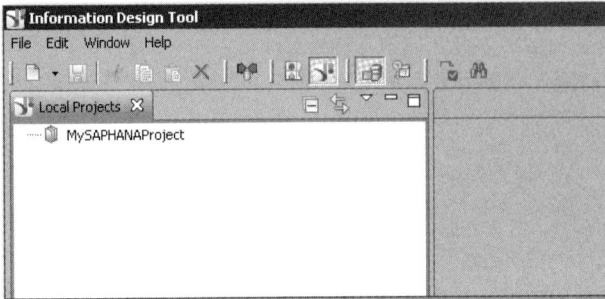

**Figure 9.22** Viewing Your Project in the Local Projects Window

## 9.2.5 Creating a Relational Connection in Your Project

All universes require a connection object to properly interact with schema information and data stored in an RDBMS. The first step in creating a universe requires that you define a connection object in your project. There are two types of connection objects that can be assigned to a project: *local connection* objects and *repository connection* objects.

Local connections are intended to only be available in the local project library. They can't be published to the SAP BusinessObjects library and shared with other users. We recommend that you only use local connections to test connectivity to a database or to design a universe for local use or unsecured use.

Repository connections are first created in the SAP BusinessObjects repository to represent the connection you created in Section 9.2.1 earlier in this chapter. They should be used in a local project when the universe is intended to be published to the SAP BusinessObjects repository for standard use with reporting and analytic tools.

However, when using a repository connection in a local project, you must define the connection as a *relational connection shortcut*. This means that the repository connection won't physically exist in the local project but rather logically exists as a shortcut.

To create a local connection in your project, right-click your project in the LOCAL PROJECTS window, and choose NEW • RELATIONAL CONNECTION, as shown in Figure 9.23.

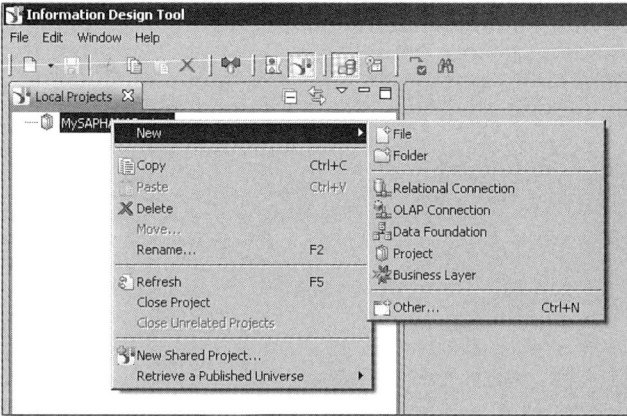

**Figure 9.23** Creating a Local Connection

From this point forward, the instructions are the same as those listed in Section 9.2.1.

To create a repository connection shortcut in your project, follow these steps:

1. In the REPOSITORY RESOURCES window, create a session, or log on to an existing session.

2. Locate the repository connection object that you want to use in your project.

3. Right-click the connection, and choose the CREATE RELATIONAL CONNECTION SHORTCUT option, as shown in Figure 9.24.

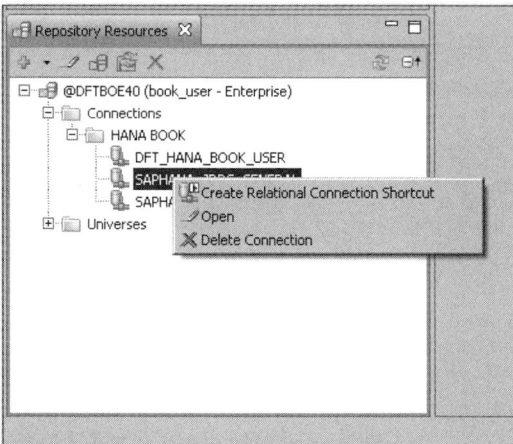

**Figure 9.24** Selecting a Relational Connection Shortcut for Use in a Local Project

4. The SELECT A LOCAL PROJECT window appears. Select a local project to store the relational connection shortcut, as shown in Figure 9.25. Click OK to save the shortcut. Accept the message to commit the shortcut to your local project.

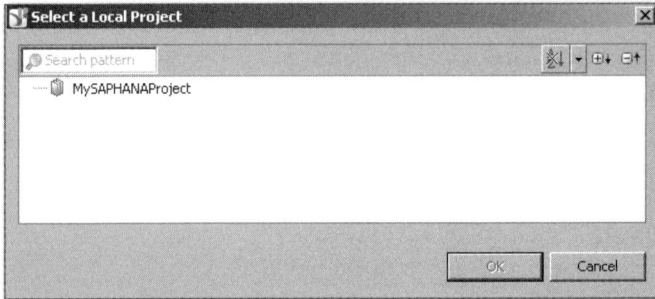

**Figure 9.25**  Selecting a Local Project

You now have instructions for creating either a local connection to your SAP HANA appliance or assigning an existing repository connection to your local project as a connection shortcut. In the next two sections of this chapter, we'll discuss both the data foundation and business layer components of the IDT universe. In addition, we'll discuss concepts relevant to designing those components when SAP HANA is the source RDBMS.

### 9.2.6  Designing the Data Foundation

Before we discuss the concepts of the data foundation that are unique to SAP HANA, you must first understand the basics of the data foundation and how they are created.

The *data foundation* is the next logical component of the IDT universe. Data foundations rely on one or more connection objects that reside in a local project. Data foundations can be designed using either a single source or multiple sources. Single-source connections use the database middleware associated with the connection object. For example, a single-source universe uses the SAP HANA client to interact with the SAP HANA appliance. Multisource data foundations use the SAP BusinessObjects Data Federator engine that is built-in to the SAP BusinessObjects platform to interact with one or more RDBMSs. For example, a multisource data foundation can be used to merge data from SAP HANA with data found in a flat file.

The data foundation component is used to describe the relationship between tables and their adjoining columns. Much like the data foundations found in an SAP HANA attribute view or analytic view, the defined relationships should be configured to produce the elements of a multidimensional model. However, the universe foundation is used to describe all of the possible joins and relationships that might exist between tables in a database or between databases. This includes both tables that contain transactions and tables that describe those transactions.

Figure 9.26 contains an example IDT universe data foundation. The left side of the figure contains the schemas and tables that reside in the assigned connection object. The right side contains a canvas where you define the join relationships between tables to produce a multidimensional model.

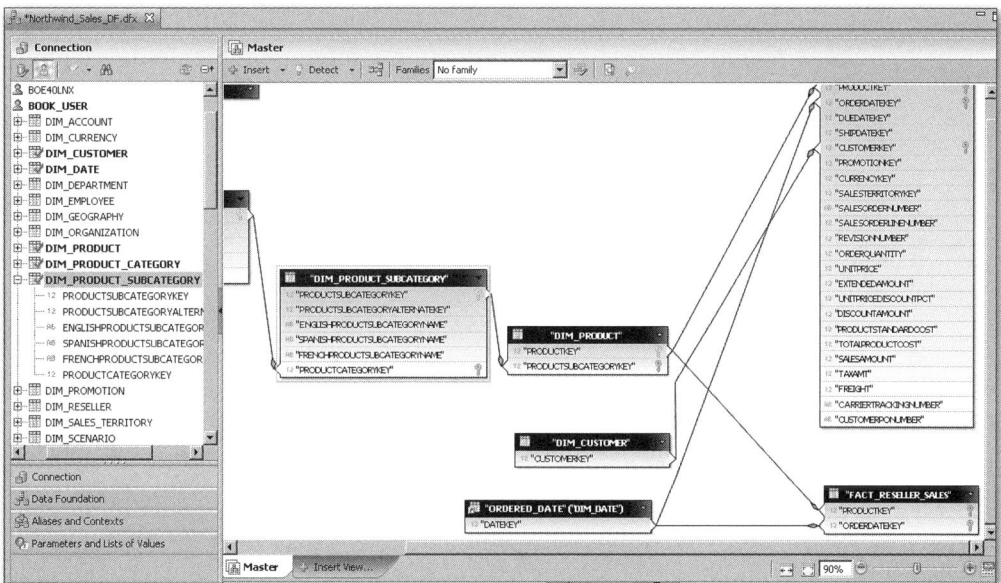

**Figure 9.26** An Example IDT Universe Data Foundation

The universe foundation includes other features, such as the concepts of an alias and context. Aliases are used to create alternative representations of physical tables. This is useful when a single table needs to be joined to a related table multiple times. Contexts can be used to define a series of joins that can be executed in a single SQL statement. Joins that exists in other contexts are considered incompatible and must be executed in a separate SQL statement. Though a complete explanation of these features is beyond the scope of this book, it's important to understand the basic concepts of a data foundation as it relates to working with SAP HANA.

Next we'll explorer the steps required to create a data foundation in a local project, where it's both created and stored.

To create a data foundation, follow these steps:

1. Right-click your project, as shown in Figure 9.27. Choose NEW • DATA FOUNDA-TION.

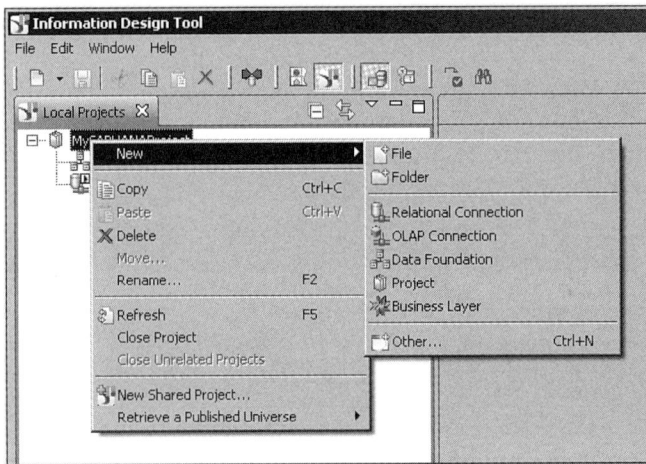

**Figure 9.27** Creating a Data Foundation

2. In the NEW DATA FOUNDATION window, enter the name of the data foundation and a description (see Figure 9.28). Click the NEXT button to continue.

3. Using Figure 9.29 as a guide, select the data foundation option of SINGLE SOURCE if you intend to only connect to a single RDBMS, or choose MULTISOURCE-ENABLED if you intend to build a single data foundation on two or more data sources. In this case, click SINGLE SOURCE and the NEXT button to continue.

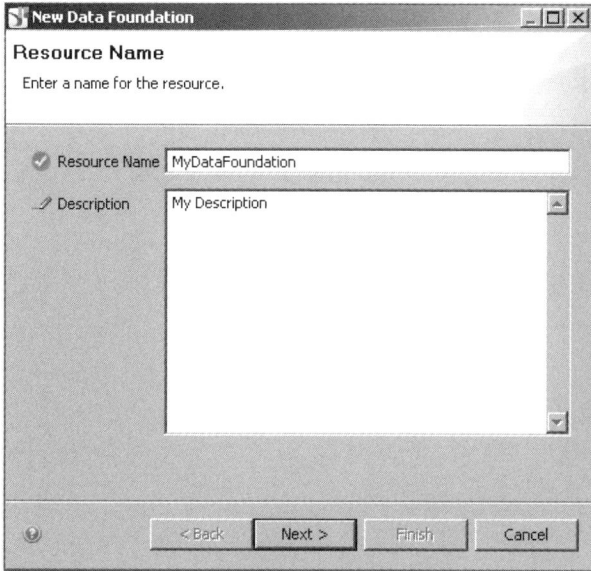

**Figure 9.28**   The New Data Foundation Window

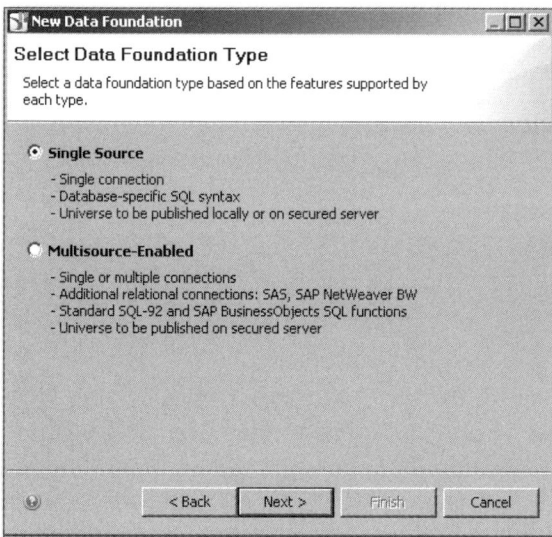

**Figure 9.29**   The Data Foundation Type

4. Place a check mark beside the connection that is configured to access SAP HANA, as shown in Figure 9.30. Click the FINISH button to complete the process.

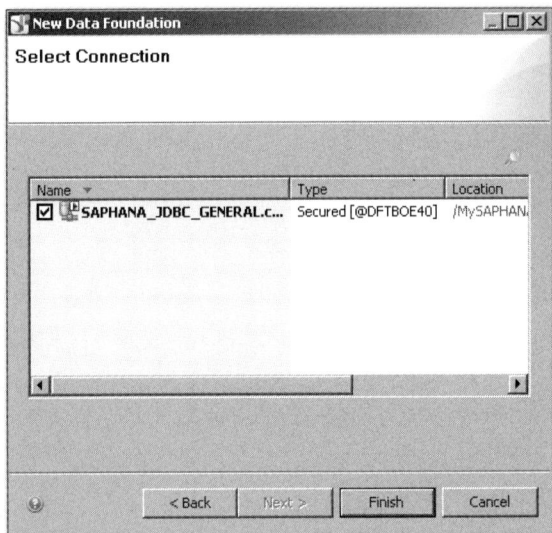

**Figure 9.30**  Selecting a Connection for a Single Source Data Foundation

Now that we've discussed the basic concepts of a data foundation and the steps required to create a data foundation, we'll discuss design concepts that are specific to SAP HANA. As stated before, the goal of this chapter isn't to make you an expert IDT universe designer. However, this chapter *is* designed to give experienced IDT universe designers information relevant to building a universe on SAP HANA.

### Information Views

As we discussed in Chapter 6, SAP HANA has built in multidimensional models that are developed and then published to the SAP HANA repository for consumption by reporting and analysis tools such as those found in SAP BusinessObjects. In many cases, those tools require the use of a universe to interact with the SAP HANA data. When you activate an SAP HANA information view, a column view is created in the _SYS_BIC schema. These column views then become a possible source for the IDT universe data foundation.

When designing a universe data foundation on an SAP HANA, you can choose to leverage the information views in the _SYS_BIC schema. To locate the _SYS_BIC schema, expand the connection object located in your data foundation. Figure 9.31 contains an example of a _SYS_BIC schema and the paginated list of column views that are available for use in the data foundation. From the perspective of an IDT universe designer, these column views appear as a typical table and can be used as such in the data foundation.

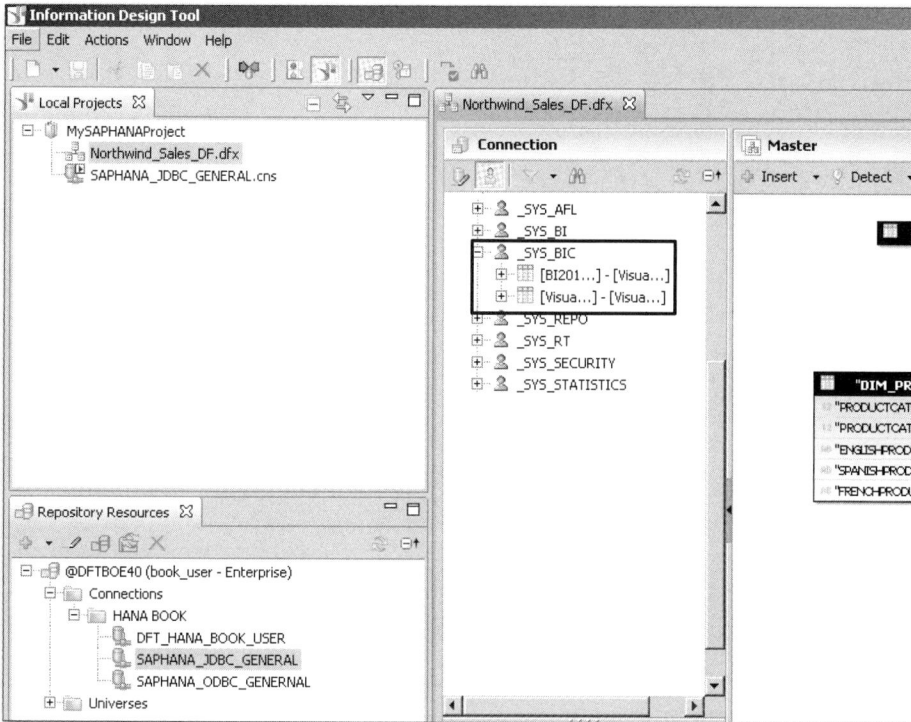

Figure 9.31 The _SYS_BIC Schema Available in an SAP HANA Connection

Figure 9.32 contains an example of how these information views are presented to the IDT developer in the data foundation. Each column view is named in the PACK-AGE.SUBPACKAGE/INFORMATION_VIEW format. For example, if you have a package named SAPHANA, a subpackage named INTERNETSALES, and an analytic view named ANLV_INTERNETSALES, then the full name would be SAPHANA.INTERNETSALES/ ANLV_INTERNETSALES/OLAP.

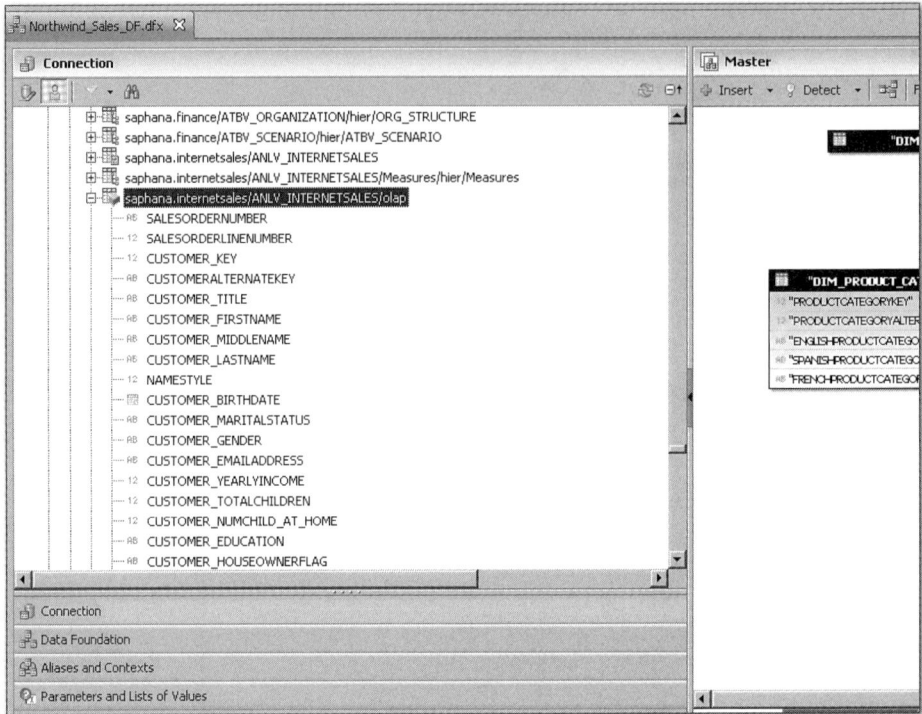

**Figure 9.32** The SAP Information Views Available as Tables in the IDT Data Foundation

There are four reasons to use an information view as the basis of a data foundation:

▶ Information views effectively perform similar functions when compared to a universe data foundation. You can either re-create the concepts of the information view in the data foundation or leverage the work that was completed in SAP HANA Studio to reduce the design cost of the universe. In short, it's quicker to use an information view as opposed to redefining the table and join relationships.

▶ The organization is using SAP BusinessObjects tools that directly access the SAP HANA information views without the need for a universe. In this case, the organization might not want to maintain both a standard model universe data foundation and an information view. For these organizations, it's better to leverage the information view as the central source of analytic modeling.

▶ Using an analytic view can result in better query performance compared to using the underlying columnar tables. This will be discussed in more detail when we address the various SAP HANA processing engines that are found in the SAP HANA index server.

▶ If you need to leverage the analytic privilege, applied to an information view, you have to define the universe using the information views, represented as columns views, in the _SYS_BIC schema. This is an appropriate design consideration when SSO to the SAP HANA appliance has been set up in the SAP BusinessObjects environment.

In addition to these reasons, there are also four types of information views that you can select from the _SYS_BIC schema: analytic, calculation, hierarchy, and attribute views. Proper identification of the different column views is important when defining an IDT universe data foundation on SAP HANA. Let's outline the types of information views that can be selected from the _SYS_BIC schema and the rules applicable to their use in the IDT data foundation.

### Analytic Views

An analytic view is a specific type of column view in the _SYS_BIC schema. Fortunately, an IDT universe data foundation configured with an SAP HANA connection depicts each column view type with a different icon. Analytic views can be identified by their icon that portrays an image of a table with a small cube in the bottom-right corner. The icon is very small but can be identified by the distinct orange color of the cube. Figure 9.33 shows an example image containing analytic views and their associated icons. The analytic views are depicted in both the listing windows and search results window below. Analytic views adhere to one of the two following standard naming conventions: either PACKAGE.SUBPACKAGE/ANALYTIC_VIEW_NAME OR PACKAGE.SUBPACKAGE/ANALYTIC_VIEW_NAME/OLAP.

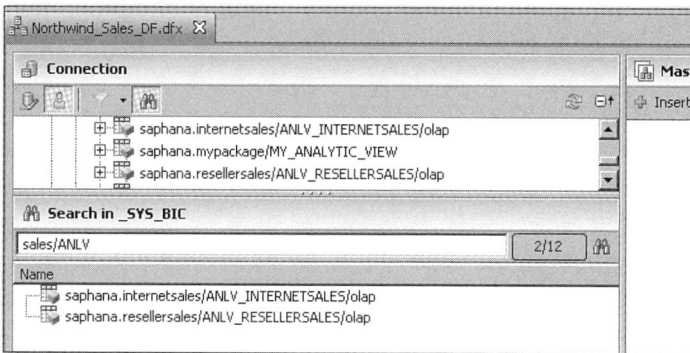

**Figure 9.33**  Identifying Analytic Views in the _SYS_BIC Schema

There is a good reason that the _SYS_BIC schema contains two different naming conventions for analytic views. If an analytic view contains a calculated column, the system will automatically generate two information views. The first is the base analytic view; it will have the /OLAP appended to the end. The second is a calculation view. The reasons for this will become clearer when we discuss calculation views in the next section. However, an analytic view will always have the distinct orange cube icon.

When choosing a column view from the _SYS_BIC schema, analytic views are the best overall choice. Analytic views should never be joined to other tables or information views as it relates to performance and best practices. Analytic views have strict rules as to how they can be queried. Every query that is produced from the IDT data foundation, based solely on an analytic view, must contain either a SELECT DISTINCT or GROUP BY and an aggregate function. Although they do typically result in the best overall performance, it can be difficult to automatically force a SELECT DISTINCT or GROUP BY statement into the queries that a report developer will likely produce. Later in this section, we'll discuss how aggregate awareness can be used to mitigate these problems.

### Calculation Views

A calculation view produces a column view in the _SYS_BIC schema that contains a distinct icon as well. This icon will be depicted as a table with a small calculator in the bottom-right corner. Figure 9.34 shows an example image containing calculation views and their associated icons.

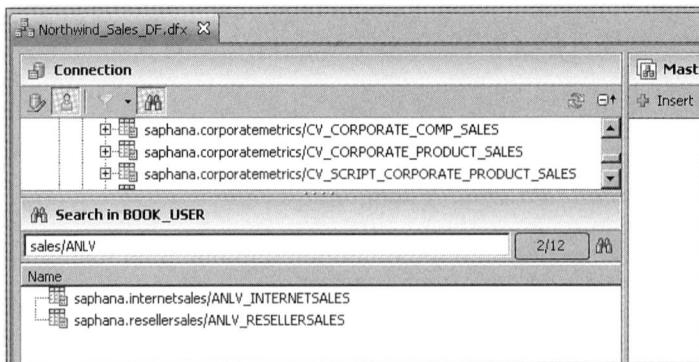

**Figure 9.34**  Identifying Calculation Views in the _SYS_BIC Schema

Calculation view can exist in two forms. The first form is the result of a user-defined calculation view. These calculation views are deliberately developed in SAP HANA Studio as calculation views. The second are those automatically generated by the system. When activating an analytic view that contains calculated columns, the system automatically creates two types of information views: the analytic view mentioned earlier and the calculation view based on that analytic view. Because calculated columns require the use of the SAP HANA Calculation Engine, the SAP HANA system automatically produces both the analytic view to manage the base star schema processing and a calculation view to manage the calculated columns. Those generated by the developer have the following naming convention: PACK-AGE.SUBPACKAGE/CALCULATION_VIEW_NAME. Those automatically generated by the system to support calculated columns in an analytic view have the following naming convention: PACKAGE.SUBPACKAGE/ANALYTIC_VIEW_NAME. In either case, the icon is exactly the same.

Calculation views are also acceptable to use in the IDT universe data foundation. As with analytic views, they should not be joined to other tables or information views in the data foundation. Again this is based on both performance and best practices. With that said, calculation views are necessary when the universe needs to be based on a calculation view, developed in SAP HANA Studio. In other cases, they are necessary when you need to access the calculated columns that are defined in an analytic view. Calculation views don't require the use of a SELECT DISTINCT or GROUP BY in their SQL query. As a result, they are easier to incorporate into the data foundation and overall universe design.

Calculation views are also important when the universe foundation needs to leverage the statistical and predictive scripting languages embedded in the SAP HANA platform. Script-based calculation views can use these languages and then be presented to the IDT data foundation for consumption.

Calculation views often impose additional layers of processing in the SAP HANA engines. These additional layers can slow performance, but they are often necessary to facilitate an organization's requirements. Calculation views can invoke multiple SAP HANA engines depending on the design techniques used in their development. For example, a script-based calculation view that uses a mixture of standard SQL statements, columnar tables, analytic views, and CE_ functions invokes the SAP HANA Join Engine, SAP HANA OLAP Engine, and SAP HANA Calculation Engine. Therefore, it's important to study the execution plans of a calculation view to ensure that an alternative or less costly option isn't available. These alternatives might include redevelopment of the calculation view or the use of columnar tables in the foundation. These concepts will become more apparent when we discuss the various engines used to process queries in the SAP HANA system.

### Hierarchy Views

A hierarchy view produces a column view in the _SYS_BIC schema that contains a distinct icon as well. Its icon portrays a table with a hierarchical folder structure in the bottom-right corner. Figure 9.35 contains an example listing of these information views in the IDT data foundation.

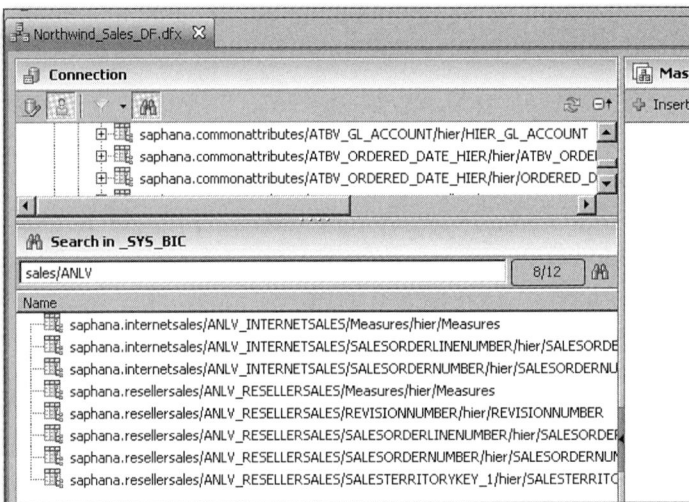

**Figure 9.35**   Identifying the Hierarchy Views

They can be identified by the use of the term "hier" in their name. Hierarchy views have the following naming convention: PACKAGE.SUBPACKAGE/INFORMATION_VIEW_NAME/HIER/COLUMN.

Hierarchy views have limited use in an IDT data foundation. They typically only return metadata specific to the creation of hierarchy groupings in supported reporting and analysis tools. Future functionality might use these information views in the universe, but at this time, they aren't useful in the data foundation or universe.

### Attribute Views

An attribute view produces a column view in the _SYS_BIC schema and contains a distinct icon as well. Its icon portrays a table with a series of joined tables covering the base of the icon. Figure 9.36 contains an example listing of these information views in the IDT data foundation.

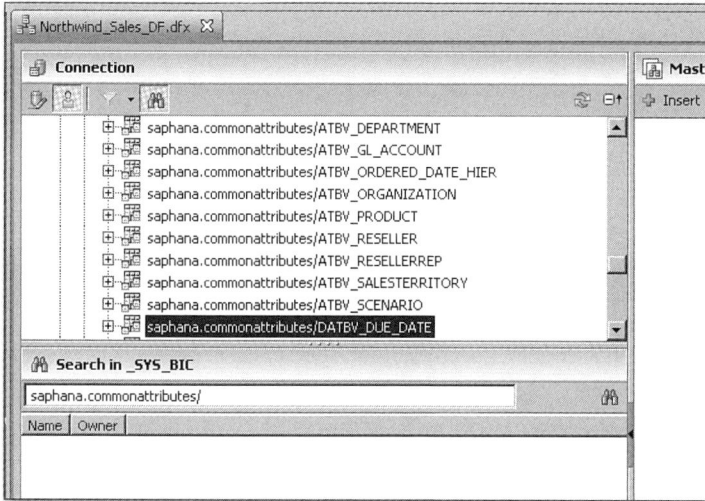

**Figure 9.36** Identifying Attribute Views

Attribute views have the following naming convention: PACKAGE.SUBPACKAGE/ ATTRIBUTE_VIEW_NAME.

Attribute views should have limited use in an IDT universe. It's not recommended that you join an information view to other tables or column views. Because only a single information view should be designed in the data foundation, advanced universe design concepts are no longer applicable. For example, contexts require that there are one or more tables joined in the data foundation. Without joins, there is no means to create contexts. Index awareness, aliases, and join paths are also not applicable when best practices are followed.

You should now have a greater understanding of the four types of column views that exist in the _SYS_BIC schema. Recall that the column views are representative of the various information views that are developed in SAP HANA Studio. The analytic view and calculation view representatives are the most appropriate for use in the IDT data foundation. Analytic views represent the best performing option but must be accessed using specific SQL statements. Next we'll explorer the development of the IDT data foundation using standard SAP HANA columnar tables.

### Columnar Tables

As an alternative to using the column views in the _SYS_BIC schema, you can also leverage columnar tables located in any schema. Recall from Chapter 6 when we used columnar tables to define the foundation of each information view. If you choose to define your universe data foundation using columnar tables, you could argue that you're performing a similar task. For those experienced with universe design based on a traditional RDBMS, this process will be very familiar. When using columnar tables, all standard universe design techniques are applicable.

There are five situations when it's appropriate to choose to develop your IDT foundation on columnar tables:

► The universe will be predominantly used for operational reporting needs. Universes used in this capacity make little use of measures and are most often used to list information based on strict filter criteria. Because analytic views require the use of GROUP BY statements and aggregate functions, it's difficult to force users to include a measure in every query.

► Some organizations will find it easier to adopt SAP HANA as a data mart solution if their existing universes can be quickly converted to use SAP HANA as a source. This is because the use of columnar tables in the data foundation is fundamentally the same as using row tables from a traditional RDBMS.

► If the organization needs to take advantage of traditional universe features, building the universe on columnar tables allows these features to be easily implemented. Take, for example, the use of contexts, index awareness, derived tables, aggregate awareness, access restrictions, and row-level security. When an information view is used in the data foundation, some of these features will be obsolete, incompatible, or difficult to implement.

► The organization doesn't have the skillset to create information views using SAP HANA Studio. If we assume they have adequate skillsets to design universes, this will likely be the easiest path for implementing SAP HANA with SAP Business-Objects.

► The use of columnar tables outperforms the use of calculation views in the data foundation. In some circumstances, querying a calculation view might require excessive processing and result in slower response times. This is especially true when the calculation view returns more columns than what is necessary to satisfy a user's ad hoc query. Universes based on columnar tables only request columns used in the reporting tool queries. This is particularly important because of the nature of the SAP HANA in-memory columnar store database.

While there are legitimate reasons to use columnar tables as the basis for the data foundation, there are also reasons that this is less than optimal. When using columnar tables as the basis, the reporting tools effectively issue standard ANSI SQL92 statements to the SAP HANA system. These types of statements predominantly use the SAP HANA Join Engine to processes queries. In many cases, this engine is slower than the engines that are invoked with the use of analytic views. With that said, the performance differences are often negligible in real-world testing. This is especially true when comparing the performance of calculation views to column tables used in the IDT data foundation.

**Optimization Tips**

When developing a universe on SAP HANA, there are a few optimization strategies that can be implemented to increase the performance of queries and the SAP HANA reporting tools. The following list outlines these optimization tips and provides a description of their use:

▶ Use mandatory filters on information views and column tables to increase the performance of queries. These filters can be implemented through the use of filters, conditions, and prompts. In future releases of SAP BusinessObjects, we expect SAP to provide support for information view variables in the data foundation. At this time, only information view parameters are supported through the use of derived tables and special SAP HANA statements.

▶ Avoid joining information view or column views in the _SYS_BIC schema to columnar tables or other column views. This process will likely invoke multiple SAP HANA engines and slow the performance. As an alternative, push the joins back into the information view by designing more complete models in SAP HANA Studio.

▶ When using information views as the basis of your data foundation, try to use analytic views as opposed to calculation views. Analytic views are processed by the SAP HANA OLAP Engine, which offers the best overall processing performance. Later in this chapter, we'll discuss the use of aggregate awareness as a solution to automatically force the use of GROUP BY and aggregate functions. Without this automation, users need to always include a measure in queries based on a universe that uses an analytic view in its data foundation.

▶ When establishing your SAP HANA connection, experiment with larger array fetch sizes to determine the best overall fetch size for your environment. In some cases, increasing the array fetch size can increase the response times of reports and queries.

▶ Use columnar tables when defining the data foundation. Avoid the use of row tables and joins between row tables and other SAP HANA tables or information views.

▶ The use of index awareness can result in fewer joins between tables when defining a traditional data foundation using columnar tables. It can also enable filtering on key columns verses large `varchar` columns.

**Aggregate Awareness**

Aggregate awareness is a feature of the SAP BusinessObjects universe that allows you to define alternative query paths against preaggregated tables. Historically, this technique required that special preaggregated tables be created in the source RDBMS schema. These preaggregated tables were designed as a smaller and better optimized source for aggregate queries. The process is dynamic and automatic, meaning that the queries are rewritten automatically to leverage the most aggregated table depending on the objects used in the report query panel.

As we established in Chapter 6, there is no need to create aggregate tables when using SAP HANA. This is because its architecture can produce fast results without the need to preaggregate data. With that said, SAP HANA offers a unique opportunity to take advantage of its different engines with the use of aggregate awareness. If you substitute the use of preaggregated tables with that of analytic views in the _SYS_BIC schema, you can design a universe that takes advantage of both the underlying columnar tables and the well-optimized information views at the same time. In many ways, this technique provides an opportunity to leverage the features of building a standard universe with the performance optimizations of an analytic view. As we mentioned before, querying an analytic view in the _SYS_BIC schema requires the use of the GROUP BY statement or an aggregate function. Given how aggregate awareness works, designing your universe with this functionality automatically rewrites queries to access an analytic view properly.

When defining an analytic view to support this functionality, we recommend that you keep a few items in mind:

▶ To define aggregate awareness, you must create an analytic view that contains the same underlying columnar tables as those defined in your universe data foundation. This is recommended to ensure that no discrepancies exist between the two foundations.

▶ The analytic view should be modeled to return the same results as those defined using columnar tables in the IDT data foundation. Make sure your joins are set up the same between the tables in the IDT data foundation and the tables in the analytic view foundations. This is also true for any attribute view used in the analytic view.

▶ You don't need to include every possible column from your columnar tables in the analytic view. In short, design your analytic view as if you were developing an aggregate table. Define only the columns that are commonly used in aggregate queries.

▶ Use the aggregate awareness function on both measures and dimensions. The mixture of both dimensions and measures in queries is key to properly leveraging this functionality.

▶ Make sure to establish aggregate incompatibilities using the Aggregate Navigation wizard. Dimensions and measure that don't incorporate the `@Aggregate_Aware` function should be marked as incompatible with the analytic view's column view.

▶ Be mindful that a query that uses only dimensions can fail if all of the dimensions are aggregate aware, and the query contains no other objects. This is because aggregate awareness will try to query the analytic view without the use of an aggregate function or `GROUP BY` function.

▶ Test your queries thoroughly, and view the generated SQL to make sure aggregate awareness is working properly.

**Additional Information**

A complete description of the implementation of aggregate awareness is beyond the scope of this book. For additional information, please review the *Information Design Tool User Guide* or the *Universe Design Tool User Guide* (*http://help.sap.com/bobip#section5*) or the DATA ACCESS AND SEMANTIC LAYER section.

The case study located at the end of this chapter will walk you through a few basic examples in the context of designing the universe against SAP HANA, but they don't outline every possible aspect of aggregate awareness.

When designing an IDT data foundation and using SAP HANA as the source, there are several considerations that are unique when compared to standard universe design. You can choose to use information views or columnar tables in your design. Each option has its advantages and disadvantages. Using aggregate awareness might provide an alternative that captures the advantages of both design considerations. In subsequent sections, we'll explore SAP HANA concepts specific to the business layer of the IDT universe.

### 9.2.7 Designing the Business Layer

The *business layer* is the next logical layer of the IDT universe to develop after the data foundation is complete. The business layer is the layer visible to both SAP BusinessObjects developers and ad hoc report developers that use the universe. In the business layer, classes, dimensions, measures, conditions, and detail objects are created. The objects should be named and organized so that users can easily identify the object in business terms. This is similar to the design considerations we discussed in Chapter 6.

To create a business layer, right-click your project folder, and choose NEW • BUSINESS LAYER. Choose the RELATIONAL DATA FOUNDATION option as the universe type, and click NEXT. Enter the desired name of the business layer, and choose NEXT again. Select the corresponding data foundation by clicking the three dots to the right of the DATA FOUNDATION field. In the SELECT A DATA FOUNDATION window, select the desired data foundation. Check the AUTOMATICALLY CREATE FOLDERS AND OBJECTS option if you want to have the IDT automatically generate the business layer and objects. Click FINISH to complete the process.

Regardless of the types of columnar tables or information views used in the data foundation, the business layer setup is the same. Dimensions should be organized into common classes, and measures should be developed using SAP HANA aggregate functions. Figure 9.37 shows an example of the various objects that are created in the IDT business layer. The objects are listed on the left side of the workbench.

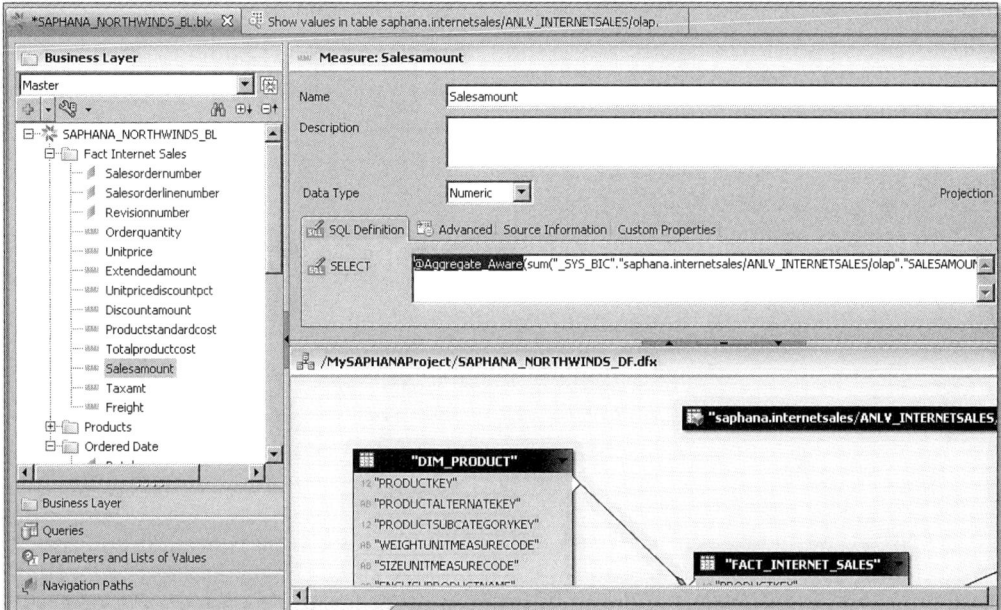

**Figure 9.37** The IDT Universe Business Layer

## Organizing Objects

Five types of objects can be defined in the business layer:

▶ **Dimension**
Dimensions are used for grouping, sorting, filtering, and displaying information. Each dimension represents a column in a table or a formula based on one or more table columns. When combined with a measure, dimensions are used to group the measures at both the query and possibly the reporting tool level.

▶ **Detail**
Details are used for grouping, sorting, filtering, and displaying information. At the query level, they perform the same function as the dimension. In some reporting tools, they act as detail objects that disable the report-level aggregation.

▶ **Measure**
Measures are objects that are used to aggregate columns. Measures should be defined with both a query-level aggregate and a report-level aggregate.

▸ **Condition**

Conditions are objects used to house predefined filters. Typically, they are created to perform complex filters that aren't easily developed by the user. They aren't mandatory in a query, but they can be set up as mandatory in any query that uses specific objects.

▸ **Class**

Classes are folders that are used to organize like objects into easy-to-identify groupings. For example, a customer class contains objects that return a customer's information and measures specific to customers.

When organizing the objects, it's best that dimensions of the same type are placed into the same class. When creating the business layer, the IDT offers to automatically create the objects and classes for you. Each table is converted into a class, and the columns in that table are converted into objects.

This is an efficient option when a traditional data foundation is designed. However, when creating a business layer on a data foundation that uses an information view, there will likely be only one table. When this type of data foundation is used to generate the business layer, only a single class, containing all columns as objects, is generated. If you're following best practices, these objects should be reorganized into classes that represent a common set of objects. For example, if your information view contains customer, date, and product columns, it's best to create a customer, date, and product class and then move related objects into each class. There are no technical requirements to perform this extra step, but it's advisable to help users locate the objects in a universe.

### Naming Objects

When naming objects, it's best to represent them using a convention that is easy for the average business user to understand. In addition, it's important to add descriptions to the objects to help communicate the use of the objects to all types of report developers. When you allow the IDT to automatically add objects to the business layer, they are created in their native column-naming convention. In short, the name of the column in the table is used when the object is automatically generated. In most cases, this naming convention is abbreviated or concatenated to support the requirements of the database naming convention. Often this convention is difficult for the average business user to identify, so we recommend renaming the objects and adding a description.

## Setting Query Options

When designing a business layer, there are a few query options that you must establish to ensure the proper function of the final universe. Query options are located on the right side of the business layer after selecting the topmost node of the object hierarchy. The top node represents the entire universe and is located just above the top-level classes.

Figure 9.38 contains an example business layer in the IDT. On the left side, you'll find the object hierarchy. Click the universe object in the object hierarchy to activate the universe properties on the right. Click the QUERY OPTIONS tab to display the options depicted on the right side of Figure 9.38.

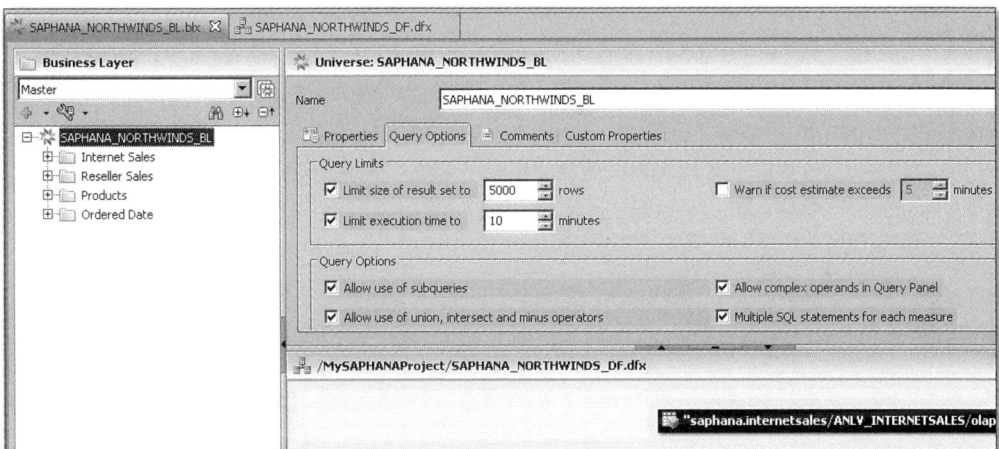

**Figure 9.38**   Setting the Query Options in the Business Layer

By default, these options might be set lower than expected, or they might produce unexpected results. In the QUERY LIMITS section, you should generally disable the LIMIT SIZE OF RESULT SET TO checkbox. The LIMIT EXECUTION TIME TO option is often set to the default limit of 10 minutes. This prevents long-running queries from being executed with the reporting tools. However, if your reports are scheduled, a high value might be appropriate. There are also specific query options that can be enabled or disabled based on the intended use of the universe. For example, you can prevent users from defining subqueries in the reporting tool QUERY PANEL.

### Creating Measures

When defining a business layer, you'll likely have several objects that can be converted into measures. Measure objects are used to aggregate columns. For example, you can create a measure for total sales, tax, or quantity sold. In addition to defining the object as a measure, it's important that you also add an SAP HANA aggregate function to the object definition. For example, if the column is ORDERS.SALES, you should update the definition to SUM(ODERS.SALES).

Placing the aggregate function around the measure definition is extremely important. Failure to define the objects with an aggregate function will significantly degrade the performance of reports that use the universe. Properly defined measures invoke an aggregation at the query level. If the measure object definition doesn't contain an aggregate function, then the resulting query won't contain a GROUP BY statement. The GROUP BY statement is critical to reducing the number of records transferred between the SAP HANA system and the SAP BusinessObjects reporting tool. Take, for example, a query that returns YEAR and TOTAL SALES. If you define the measure correctly using an aggregate function, the generated SQL statement looks like this:

```
SELECT YEAR, SUM(TOTAL SALES)
FROM TABLE
GROUP BY YEAR
```

Table 9.6 contains the example output of query that uses a properly defined measure. This query only returns a record for each year and a summary of all records making up that year.

| YEAR | TOTAL SALES |
|------|-------------|
| 2009 | 56,456,345  |
| 2010 | 65,657,123  |
| 2012 | 66,890,234  |
| 2013 | 59,345.134  |

**Table 9.6**  Correct Query Results

When the measure isn't properly defined, the following SQL query is generated:

```
SELECT YEAR, TOTAL SALES
FROM TABLE
```

Table 9.7 contains an example of the results when the measure object is incorrectly defined. This query returns all records from the source database and causes the reporting tool to manage the result set.

| YEAR | TOTAL SALES |
|------|-------------|
| 2009 | 6,456 |
| 2009 | 5,657 |
| 2009 | 6,890 |
| 2010 | 9,345 |
| 2010 | 9,345 |
| 2010 | 9,345 |

**Table 9.7**  Incorrect Query Results

With this in mind, it's important that you convert all measurable columns into measure objects defined with the proper aggregate function. This is especially important when using an information view as the data foundation source. Analytic views can only be queried if a GROUP BY aggregate function or SELECT DISTINCT operation is used in the query. Failure to define the measures with an aggregate function prevents the use of analytic views as a possible data foundation source.

**Optimization Tips**

Consider the following tips for optimizing a universe based on SAP HANA:

▶ As mentioned in the previous section, it's important that a measures definition contains an aggregate function to reduce the number of records transferred between the SAP HANA appliance and the SAP BusinessObjects reporting tool.

▶ Use aggregate awareness functions in the business layer objects when the data foundation contains both columnar tables and information views.

▶ Use the universe parameter JOIN_BY_SQL to push SAP BusinessObjects Web Intelligence data synchronization to the SAP HANA appliance for processing. When this parameter is enabled, SAP BusinessObjects Web Intelligence will generate a single SQL statement that queries each source as an inline view. It then performs a full outer join to merge the results. This too can increase the performance of reports by moving data synchronization to the SAP HANA appliance for processing.

▶ Avoid defining dimensions with formulas. When a calculated column is used in a GROUP BY statement, the performance of the query can be significantly degraded. In the context of this book, it's best to perform these types of operations using SAP Data Services before loading the data into SAP HANA. This recommendation will help when defining both the universe and the SAP HANA information views.

▶ Always check the integrity of your objects before publishing the universe to the SAP BusinessObjects repository. Keep in mind that analytic views might not parse correctly because the integrity checker doesn't know to use a GROUP BY, aggregate function, or SELECT DISTINCT when validating these objects. For other column views or tables, this is important because it will identify any potential issues with the design of the universe.

▶ The tasks performed in the universe business layer can have an impact on how SAP HANA performs, so it's also important to organize your universe objects in a fashion that is easy for ad hoc users to identify these data elements.

### 9.2.8 Publishing the Universe

After completing the design of the business layer and checking the integrity of the objects, you're ready to publish the universe to the SAP BusinessObjects repository. Before the reporting tools can access the universe, the universe must be published to the repository. When publishing the universe to the repository, the IDT offers to perform an integrity check on each object. Ordinarily this is a proper course of action. However, as mentioned in the previous section, objects-based analytic views might not parse correctly.

To publish a universe to the repository, follow these steps:

1. In the LOCAL PROJECTS area, locate the business layer object.
2. Right-click the business layer object, and choose PUBLISH • TO A REPOSITORY, as shown in Figure 9.39.

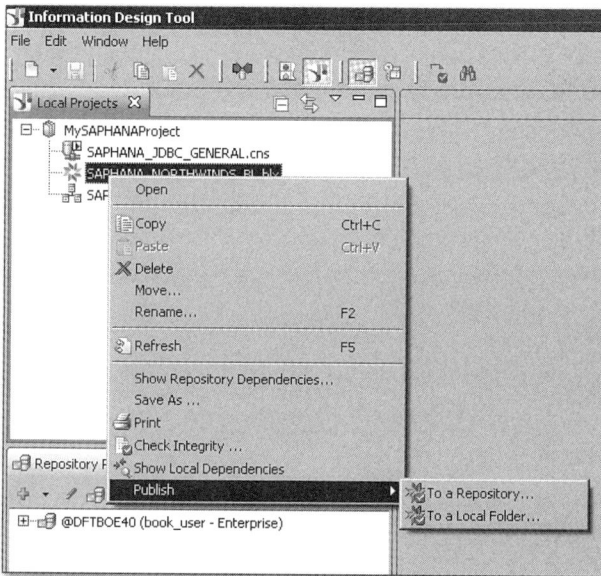

**Figure 9.39**   Publishing the Universe to the Repository

3. As shown in Figure 9.40, the CHECK UNIVERSE INTEGRITY wizard appears. Select the elements you want to validate, and click the CHECK INTEGRITY button. To skip the integrity check, click NEXT.

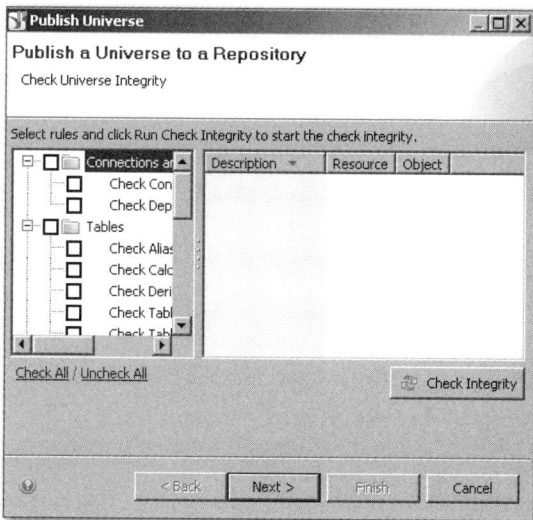

**Figure 9.40**   Checking the Integrity of the Universe before Publishing to the Repository

627

4. In the next window shown in Figure 9.41, select an existing universe repository folder, or create a new folder to store your universe. Select the desired folder, and click FINISH to publish the universe.

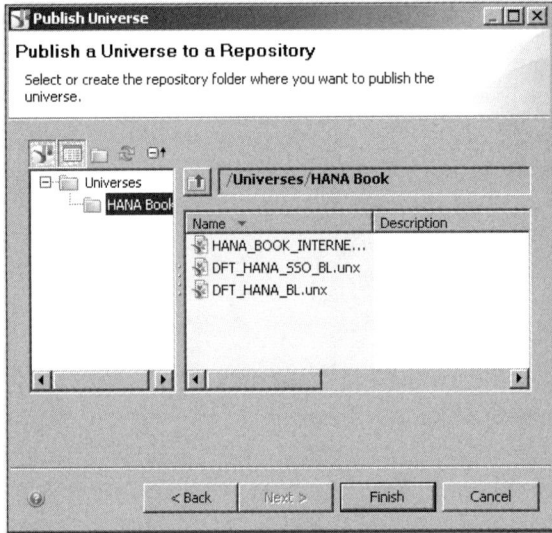

**Figure 9.41** Choosing the Repository Folder to Store the Universe

Because the SAP BusinessObjects 4.0 platform supports the use of both UNV and UNX universes, we need to briefly discuss how the information in this chapter applies to UNV universes. However, we won't go into the same level of detail as in Section 9.2.

## 9.3 Building UNV Universes with Universe Designer

In general, the principles in this chapter apply to both UNX and UNV universes. The compelling differences are that the UNV universe doesn't have a separate data foundation layer or a business layer. Instead, the UNV Universe Designer combines these layers into a single design canvas. In addition, the UNV universe doesn't support multiple connection or multiple data sources.

The SAP HANA-specific principles we discussed in the IDT data foundation section of this chapter apply to the UNV universe as well. You can either define the universe using columnar tables or column views in the _SYS_BIC schema. As with the IDT data foundation, you shouldn't join information views in the _SYS_BIC schema to other database objects. You can also leverage aggregate awareness with the UNV universe.

The SAP HANA-specific principles we discussed in the IDT business layer section apply to the UNV universe as well. Objects should be organized and named in a meaningful way. You should also avoid using nonaggregate functions in dimension definitions, and measures should be defined using an aggregate function.

The connection you created for SAP HANA in the IDT is backward-compatible with the UNV universe. The same can be said of connections created in the UNV universe. There are no functional differences when creating connections, but the workflow and interfaces are distinctly different when compared closely.

As with the IDT universe, the goal of this chapter isn't to fully discuss all aspects of universe design. However, this chapter will give you an understanding of specific universe design techniques that facilitate proper universe design where SAP HANA is the source.

> **Additional References**
>
> As we stated, the goal of this chapter is to introduce you to universe design concepts specific to SAP HANA. For more information, we recommend the *Information Design Tool User Guide* and the *Universe Design Tool User Guide* at *http://help.sap.com/bobip#section5*.

## 9.4    Understanding the SAP HANA Engines

When it comes to universe design, there are several ways to query the data that is stored in SAP HANA. As with any universe, you can define the relationships between the standard columnar tables that are defined in an SAP HANA schema. However, you can also define your universe on information views. Recall from previous sections of this chapter that there are different engines in the SAP HANA index server that are used to processes queries depending on the information views or SQL queries that are executed. When you design a universe—or even when you define an SAP HANA information view—it's important that you understand the capabilities of each engine and the circumstances in when each engine is used.

In SAP HANA Studio, you can use the plan visualization tool found in the SQL query console to identify the engines that are invoked with the queries generated by the universe. Simply copy and paste your generated SQL statements into SAP HANA Studio's SQL query console, highlight the contents of the statement, right-click the highlighted text, and choose VISUALIZE PLAN. The initial plan visualization provides a high-level overview of the processing workflow. Figure 9.42 is an example of the initial VISUALIZATION PLAN window that will appear.

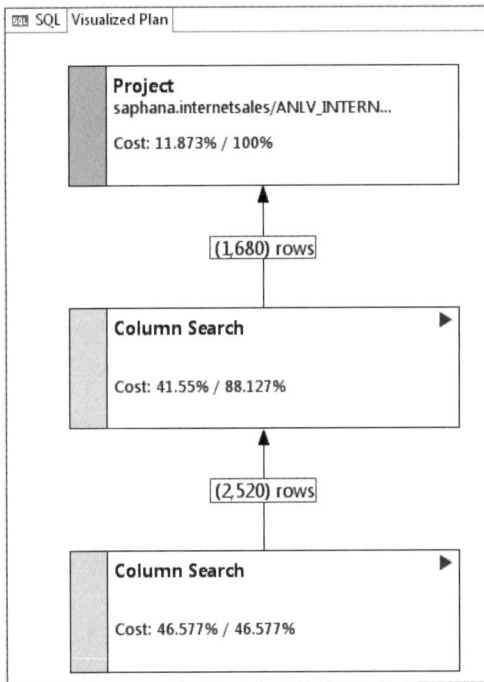

**Figure 9.42** The Initial Visualization Plan Window

To view the details of each node, right-click the visual blocks and choose EXECUTE to calculate the full execution plan. Figure 9.43 contains an example of the detail that can be seen after executing the plan and expanding the visual blocks.

In the SAP HANA index server, there are three main engines that are used to processes analytical queries. The Join Engine, OLAP Engine, and Calculation Engine are used to processes queries produced by a universe and the SAP BusinessObjects tools. When reviewing the VISUAL PLAN details, items that are prefixed with "JE" indicate processing with the Join Engine, items that are prefixed with "BW" indicate processing with the OLAP Engine, and items prefixed with "CE" indicate processing with the Calculation Engine. We'll now discuss these engines in more detail and provide information as how different universe design techniques will invoke the different engines.

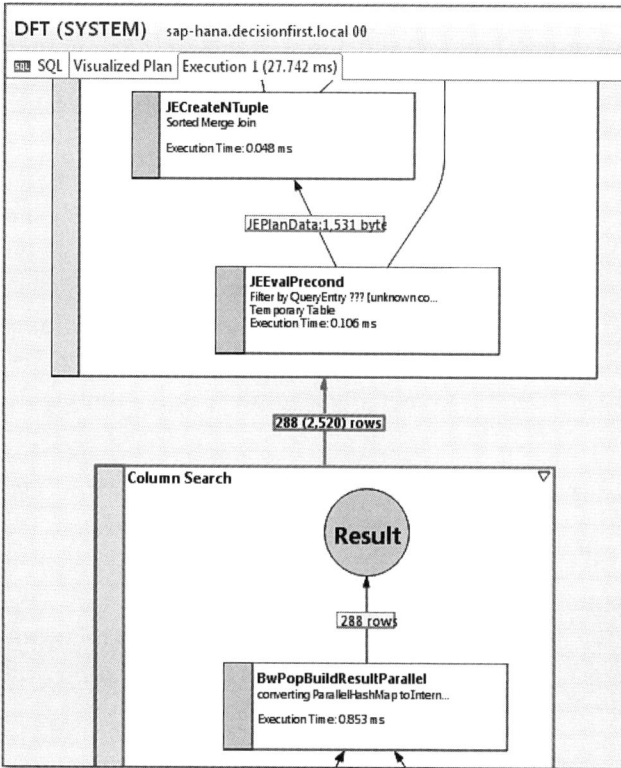

**Figure 9.43**  Details of the Visualization Plan

## 9.4.1   SAP HANA Join Engine

The Join Engine is used to processes standard SQL queries. These are the queries that follow the ANSI standard by incorporating the use of the SELECT, FROM, WHERE, GROUP BY, or ORDER BY statements. If your SQL statement contains joins between two or more columnar tables, the Join Engine is used to process the query. In addition, if you query an attribute view's column view in the _SYS_BIC schema, the Join Engine is also used. However, the Join Engine can also be invoked in a script-based calculation view that uses ANSI SQL, stored procedures, or joined multiple information views in the universe data foundation.

In most cases, the Join Engine's performance is superior to that of a traditional RDBMS. This is because the engine is able to leverage the in-memory and column store features of SAP HANA. However, the Join Engine isn't as well optimized as the OLAP Engine and, in some cases, the Calculation Engine. In real-world testing, the Join Engine experiences performance degradation when processing multiple concurrent joins or joins between large tables. With that said, its performance is still superior to that of a traditional disk-based RDBMS.

When developing a universe, it's important to understand that the use of columnar tables in the data foundation will likely be processed by the Join Engine. The Join Engine can also be invoked when you join a columnar table to an information view, when you use nonaggregate functions when querying an information view, or when you join an information view to another information view. When joining information views to other items, it's important to understand that the Join Engine is used at the tail end of the processing to merge the results of the information view to the other items.

The same is true when you use nonaggregate functions when querying an information view. From a processing standpoint, this can add significant overhead to the index server as it manages the temporary results of each information view and then attempts to join them or manipulate their results. In most cases, it's best to make sure your queries are processed by only one engine. In the case of the Join Engine, this can be achieved if you use only columnar tables in the data foundation or if your queries use a single information view in the SQL FROM clause.

### 9.4.2 SAP HANA OLAP Engine

The OLAP Engine is the most optimized engine in the SAP HANA index server. It's designed to processes star schema queries or queries with one or more attribute tables that have a one-to-many relationship with a transaction or fact table. The OLAP Engine is able to process joins and calculations in parallel to better leverage the hardware platform of SAP HANA. In terms of multidimensional processing, this is the optimal engine to use.

Analytic views are designed to use the OLAP Engine. When you define an analytic view in SAP HANA Studio, you're effectively designing a logical star schema by joining attribute views to an analytic foundation table. When developed correctly, this produces the required one-to-many joins that are efficiently processed in the OLAP Engine.

Not all analytic views are processed entirely by the OLAP Engine. Analytic views that contain calculated columns can invoke the use of the Calculation Engine during the processing of related queries. This includes the use of attribute views with calculated columns in the analytic view.

In reality, this process isn't automatic. The process occurs outside the query execution plan. When you activate an analytic view that contains calculated columns, two information views or column views are created in the _SYS_BIC schema. One information view is the pure analytic view version. The second is the calculation view version of the analytic view. The calculation view version must be used to process the calculated columns defined in the analytic view. The pure analytic view versions represent the base logical star schema, which will be processed in the OLAP Engine. The calculation view is built upon the analytic view to process the calculated columns. In short, it's up to the universe designer to determine which view is chosen when defining the data foundation of the universe. If the designer chooses the analytic view, the calculate columns will be absent from its column view in the _SYS_BIC schema.

In terms of universe design, avoid invoking nonaggregate functions in SQL queries based on an analytic view. For example, if your SELECT statement uses the function substr() on an attribute in the analytic view, the Join Engine will also be used to processes this extra calculation. To translate this in universe design terms, this means you should avoid using functions in the definition of dimensions. Functions used in measures don't have this effect, assuming that the universe measure is defined on a column that is also defined as a measure in the analytic view. In these situations, it's best to move these functions to the SAP Data Services ETL process to optimize both the analytic view and universe.

### 9.4.3 SAP HANA Calculation Engine

The Calculation Engine is used to process calculation views. Calculation views can use several different types of objects as their source. When defining a calculation view, using only analytic views as the source, the OLAP Engine is used to process each analytic view in the calculation view definition. After each analytic view has been processed in the OLAP Engine, the results are sent to the Calculation Engine to perform the additional calculations and transformations.

You can also use columnar tables as the source of the calculation view. In this instance, portions of the query leverage the OLAP engine if the query optimizer determines that it's possible to enhance performance. In addition, the Calculation Engine and Join Engine will also be used. With script-based calculation views, you can leverage columnar tables, stored procedures, and other information views. Because the developer has free range to define the script as needed, script-based calculation views have the potential to invoke multiple engines. If the script is defined using only CE_ functions and analytic views, only the OLAP Engine and Calculation Engine are used. However, if the script uses ANSI SQL statements or stored procedures, the Join Engine can also be invoked. To fully understand the engines used in a calculation view, it's best to analyze SQL statements using the plan visualization tool in SAP HANA Studio. While the examples just described are correct for the stated scenario, each calculation view should be analyzed to fully understand the engines that are invoked. For the purposes of this section, understand that calculation views often invoke the Calculation Engine and other engines when processing related queries.

As with analytic views, if you define additional function in universe objects, additional layers of processing are invoked to facilitate the complete execution plan. Again, avoid using functions in universe business layer objects to avoid this extra processing. In the context of this book, it's best to push this process back to SAP Data Services. However, don't assume that every calculation can be pushed back to SAP Data Services. In many cases, the calculation view is used to processes queries and calculations that can only be expressed at runtime. This is why the Calculation Engine and calculation views are needed in most SAP HANA BI solutions.

In terms of calculation view performance, analytic views are faster at processing data then calculation views. However, in the context of this book, the performance difference can be negligible. This is mostly due to the fact that SAP Data Services is performing the majority of the data denormalization and transmutation before SAP HANA is provisioned. However, calculation views can sometime perform much slower than an analytic view depending on their design and the structure of the data. In terms of the Join Engine, there is no set rule as to which is faster at processing multidimensional queries. The performance of a calculation view depends greatly on the way in which it's designed. The same is true of standard ANSI SQL queries executed in the Join Engine. From a universe design standpoint, you need to understand the impact of your design as it relates to the various options for configuring a universe against SAP HANA.

## 9.5 Case Study: Designing a Universe to Support Internet Sales Data

The AdventureWorks Cycle Company has recently implemented SAP HANA and has decided to use SAP Data Services to extract, transform, load, and cleanse data from multiple sources while provisioning columnar tables in SAP HANA. The company recently created several multidimensional models using SAP HANA Studio to support analysis of the Internet sales data. The views are now fully tested and ready for use with the SAP BusinessObjects 4.0 platform.

The IT department at AdventureWorks Cycle Company has received a request to create several dashboards and to provide ad hoc reporting access to the business users. To facilitate this request, the IT department needs to develop an SAP Business-Objects universe. Because they are new to the SAP BusinessObjects platform and they need to support direct binding queries in SAP BusinessObjects Dashboards 4.0, they have decided to design their universe in the IDT universes or UNX universes.

The lead universe developer has studied the Internet sales multidimensional models and has determined that he needs to develop a universe that leverages both the columnar tables, provisioned with SAP Data Services and the information views produced by the SAP HANA multidimensional models. To implement this universe correctly, the lead developer will use aggregate awareness to allow the universe to automatically switch between the universe modeled columnar tables and the Internet sales analytic view. This is an important design technique that allows the universe to supports both operational reporting and analytical reporting in a single solution.

### 9.5.1 Creating the Universe Connection and Project

The steps in this section leverage the existing step-by-step instructions already outlined in the beginning of this chapter in Section 9.2. Here we supply additional information and object names.

1. Using Section 9.2.1 as a guide, create a JDBC relation connection named "SAPHANA_JDBC_DEV". This connection will be used to connect to the SAP HANA system. Connections are typically named in reference to their system and environment.

2. Using Section 9.2.4 as a guide, create a project named "InternetSales" in the IDT.

3. Using Section 9.2.5 as a guide, create a relational connection shortcut in the InternetSales project.

## 9.5.2 Designing the Data Foundation

You must now create a data foundation that facilitates the use of both columnar tables and the column views found in the _SYS_BIC schema. Specifically you're going to add the column view that represents the Internet sales analytic view. This view was created in SAP HANA Studio and published to SAP HANA in Chapter 6. Follow these steps to create this data foundation:

1. Create a data foundation in your local project.

2. Right-click the local project named INTERNETSALES, and choose NEW • DATA FOUNDATION (see Figure 9.44).

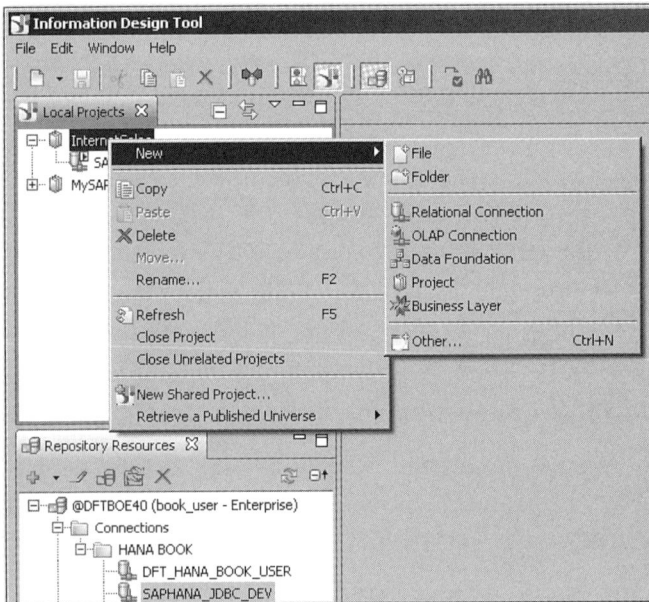

**Figure 9.44** Creating the Internet Sales Data Foundation

3. As shown in Figure 9.45, name the data foundation "INTERNETSALES_DF" and include a description to help others identify the data foundation. Click NEXT to proceed to the next window.

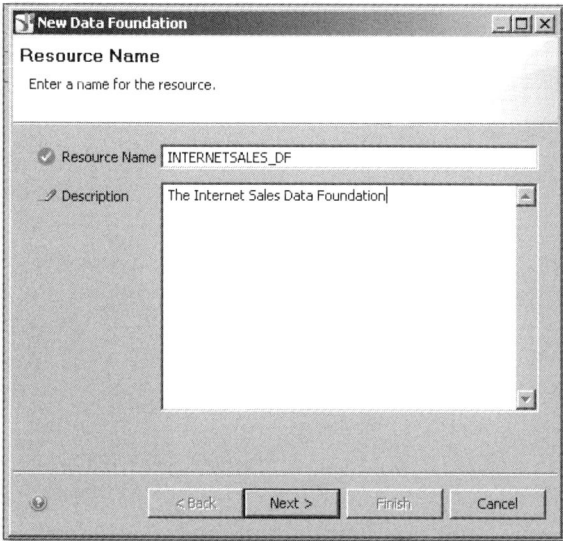

**Figure 9.45** Naming the INTERNETSALES_DF Data Foundation

4. Select Single Source as the data foundation type, as shown in Figure 9.46. In this example, you're only connecting to a single instance of SAP HANA. Click Next to proceed to the next window.

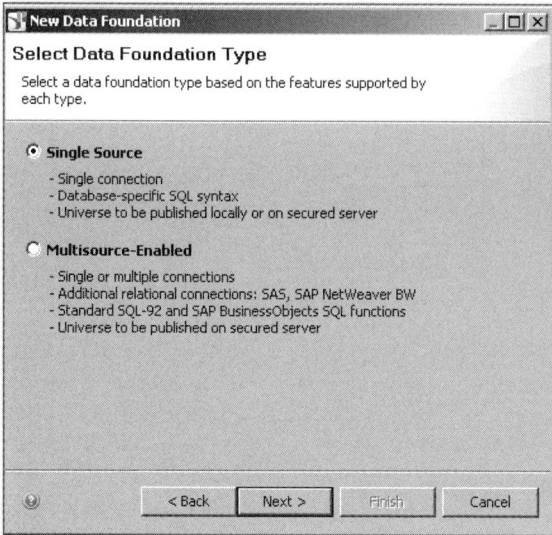

**Figure 9.46** Select the Data Foundation Type

5. As shown in Figure 9.47, select the connection name SAPHANA_JDBC_DEV, and choose FINISH. An undefined data foundation window appears.

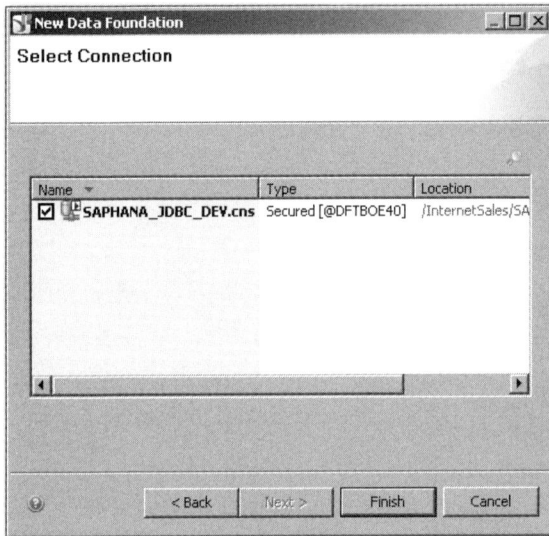

**Figure 9.47** Selecting a Connection for the Data Foundation

6. In the INTERNETSALES_DF.dfx DATA FOUNDATION tab, add the following tables to the MASTER design window located on the right side of Figure 9.48:

   ▶ DIM_CUSTOMER

   ▶ DIM_PRODUCT

   ▶ DIM_PRODUCTSUBCATEGORY

   ▶ DIM_PRODUCTCATEGORY

   ▶ DIM_DATE

   ▶ INTERNETSALES_FACT

7. To add tables to the master design window, expand the connection named SAPHANA_JDBC_DEV located in the leftmost CONNECTION window shown in Figure 9.48. Expand the BOOK_USER schema containing the listed columnar

tables. One at a time, highlight the listed tables and move them to the MASTER design window using the standard drag-and-drop technique.

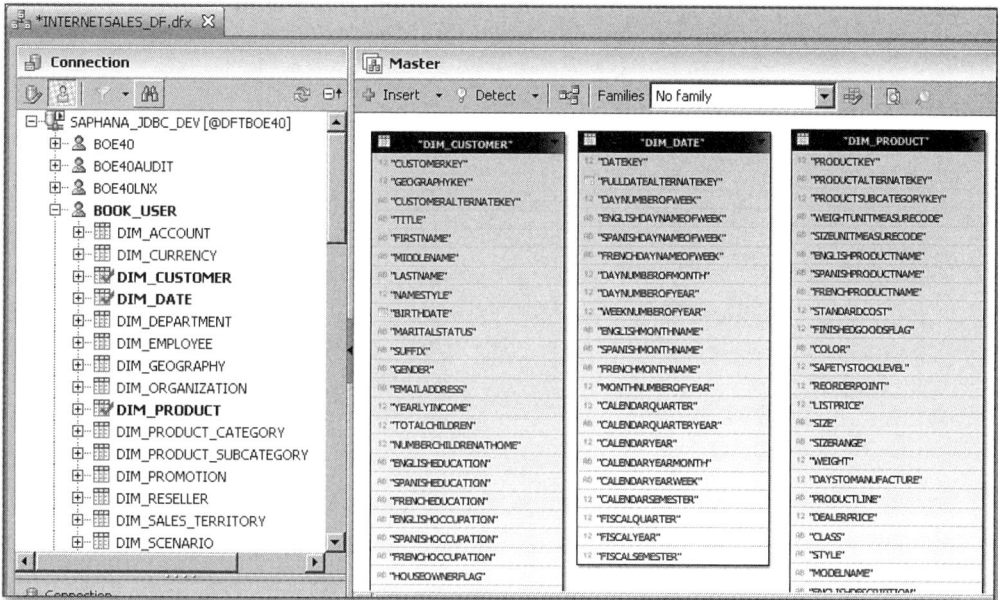

**Figure 9.48**  Adding Tables to the Data Foundation

8.  Join the table to produce a multidimensional data foundation. This is a foundation where the tables prefixed with "DIM_" (short for "dimension") are each joined to the FACT_INTERNET_SALES table. The relationship between each "DIM_" table and the FACT_INTERNET_SALES table must be one-to-many.

9.  To join a table, choose INSERT • INSERT JOIN from the dropdown menu in the MASTER window (see Figure 9.49).

    The join definition window should now appear.

10. As shown in the left side of Figure 9.50, choose the DIM_CUSTOMER table from the dropdown list. In the center of the screen, choose the = option. On the right side of the screen, choose FACT_INTERNET_SALES. Located near the bottom, set the CARDINALITY option to 1,N. Click OK to save the join definition.

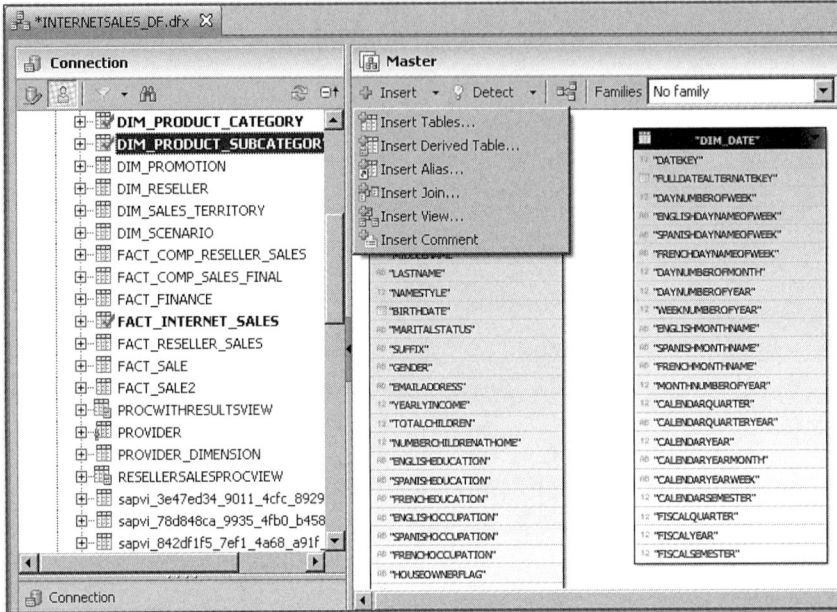

**Figure 9.49** Locating the Insert Join Wizard Launch Screen

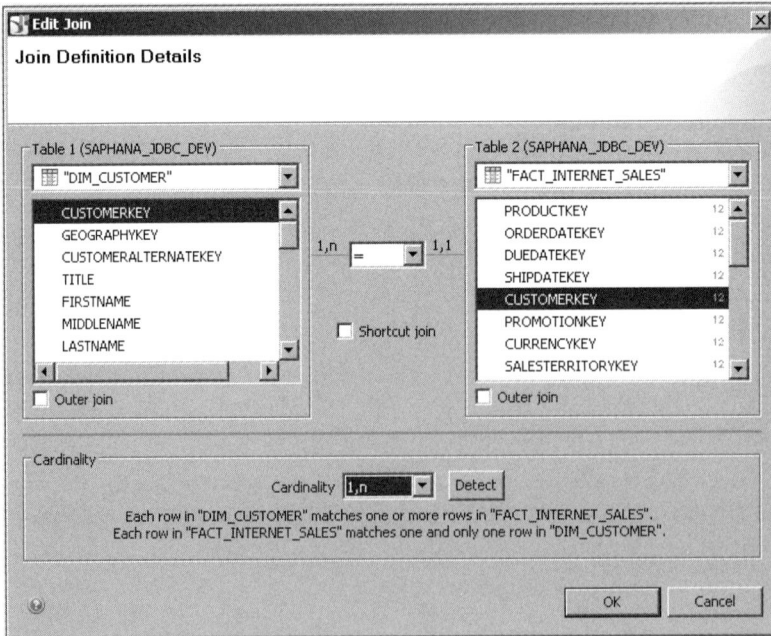

**Figure 9.50** The Join Definition for the DIM_CUSTOMER and FACT_INTERNET_SALES Tables

11. Define the join definition between DIM_DATE and FACT_INTERNET_SALES, as shown in Figure 9.51.

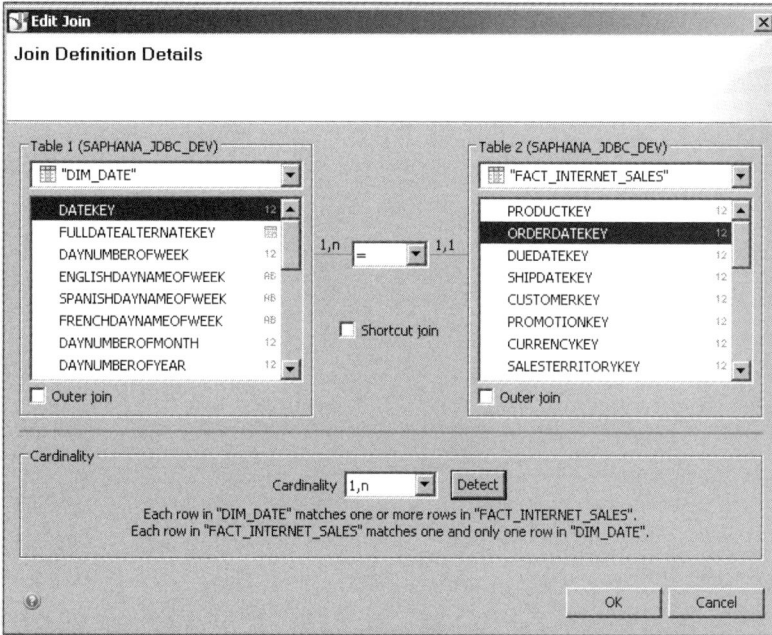

**Figure 9.51** The Join Definition for the DIM_DATE and FACT_INTERNET_SALES Tables

12. Using Figure 9.52 as a guide, define the join definition between DIM_PROD-UCT and FACT_INTERNET_SALES.

13. Define the join definition between DIM_PRODUCT and DIM_PRODUCT_SUB-CATEGORY, as shown in Figure 9.53. In this join definition, you're not joining to the FACT_INTERNET_SALES. This join is required to provide a product subcategory for each product. Notice that you're still maintaining a one-to-many join relationship between the two tables.

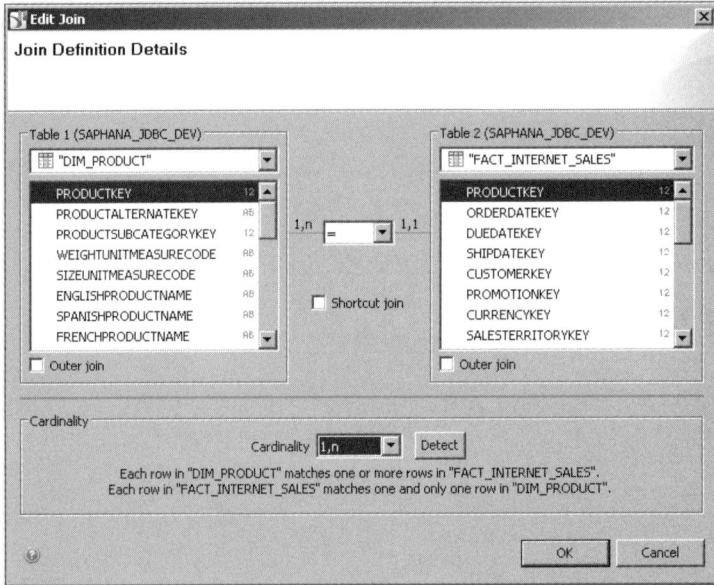

**Figure 9.52** The Join Definition for the DIM_PRODUCT and FACT_INTERNET_SALES Tables

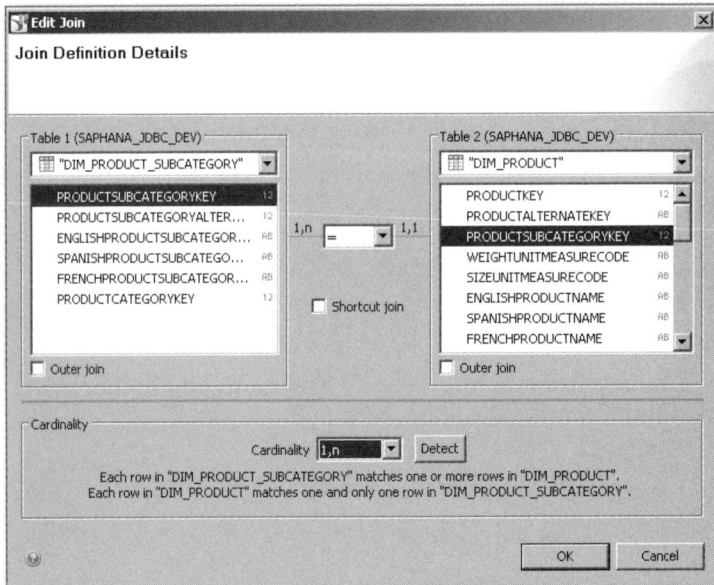

**Figure 9.53** The Join Definition for the DIM_PRODUCT and DIM_PRODUCT_SUBCATEGORY Tables

14. Using Figure 9.54 as a guide, define the join definition between DIM_PROD-UCT_CATEGORY and DIM_PRODUCT_SUBCATEGORY.

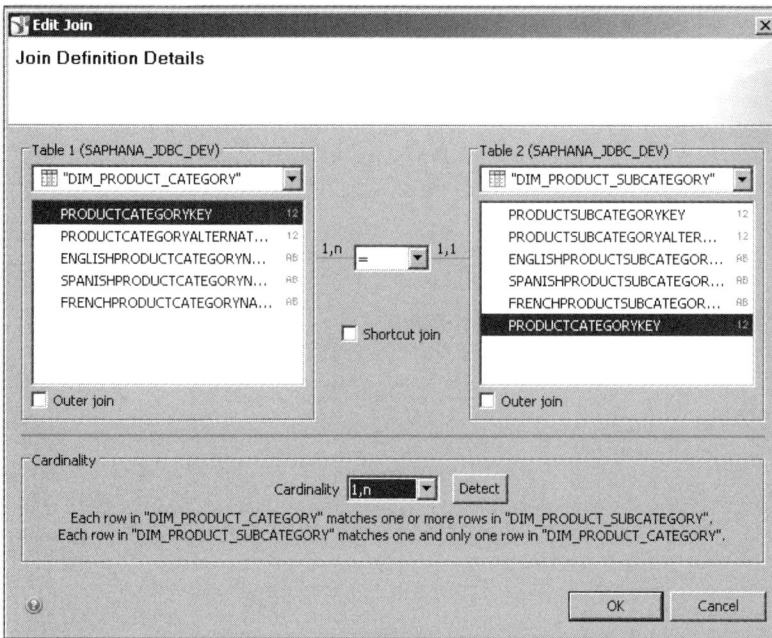

**Figure 9.54** The Join Definition for the DIM_PRODUCT_SUBCATEGORY and DIM_PRODUCT_CATEGORY Tables

15. To automatically arrange your table in the MASTER design window, click the AUTO-ARRANGE button on the MASTER design window icon bar, which is boxed in Figure 9.55.

16. Add the Internet sales analytic view to the data foundation but don't join it to any tables. Later you'll reference this column view in the business layer where you define @aggregrate_aware functions. Figure 9.56 shows an example of this analytic view in the CONNECTION window under the _SYS_BIC schema.

17. Drag the table named SAPHANA.INTERNETSALES/ANLV_INTERNETSALES/OLAP to the MASTER design window canvas just below the tables that are joined.

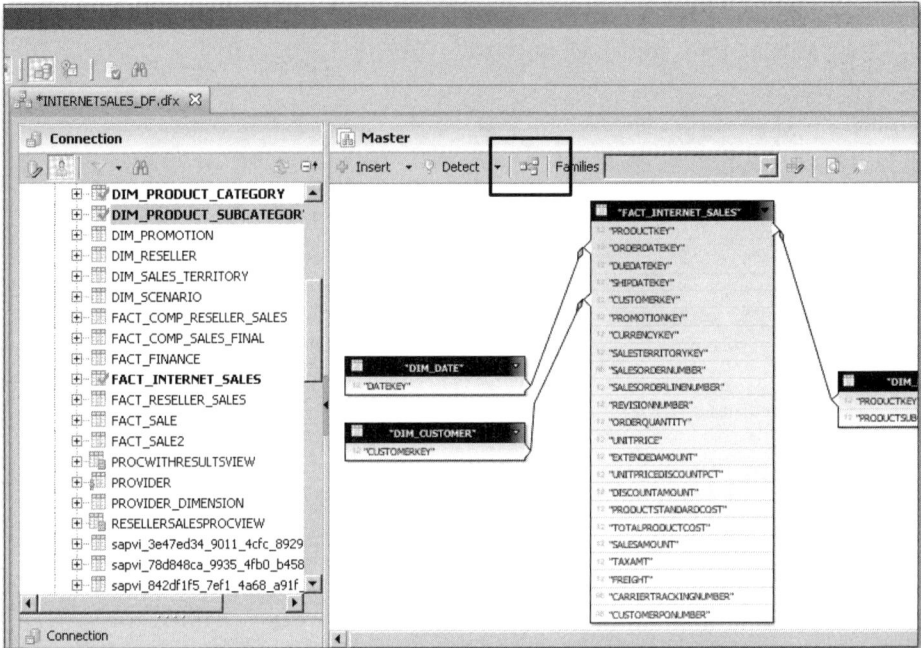

**Figure 9.55**  Using the Auto-Arrange Button to Better Organize the Tables

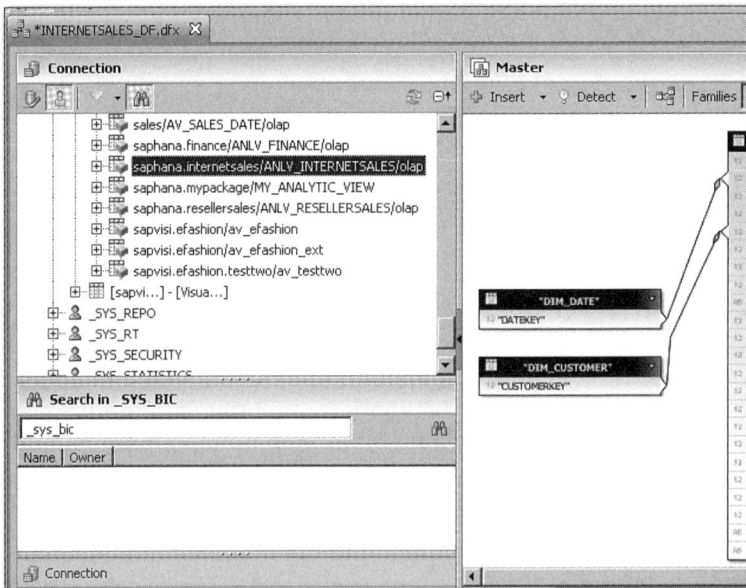

**Figure 9.56**  Adding the Internet Sales Column View from the _SYS_BIC Schema to the Data Foundation Master Design Window

18. Save the data foundation in the local project workspace by pressing $\boxed{\text{Ctrl}}$+$\boxed{\text{S}}$.

### 9.5.3 Designing the Business Layer

The next step in the design processes is the definition of the business layer. In this layer, you'll define the dimensions, measures, and classes using the columnar tables and Internet sales analytic view. In some cases, you'll delete objects, rename objects, or reorganize them to help simplify the universe.

Because the Internet sales analytic view isn't joined to the columnar tables, you'll define some of the universe objects with aggregate awareness. This allows the universe to automatically switch between querying an analytic view or the columnar tables based on the definition of reporting tools queries. To create the business layer, follow these steps:

1. Right-click the project named INTERNETSALES, and choose NEW • BUSINESS LAYER, as shown in Figure 9.57.

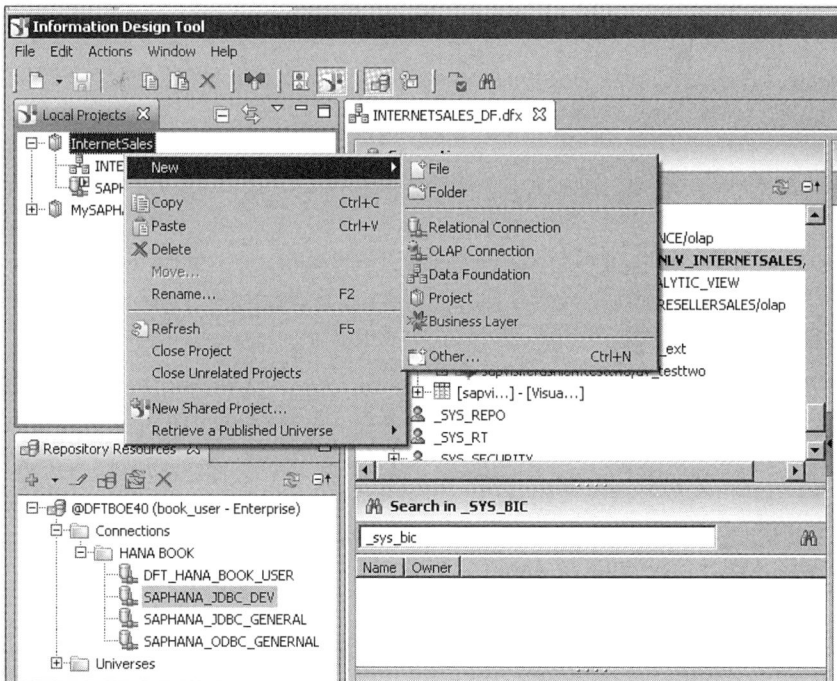

**Figure 9.57**  Creating the Business Layer in Your Local Project

2. When the NEW BUSINESS LAYER wizard appears, choose the RELATIONAL DATA FOUNDATION option, and click NEXT (see Figure 9.58).

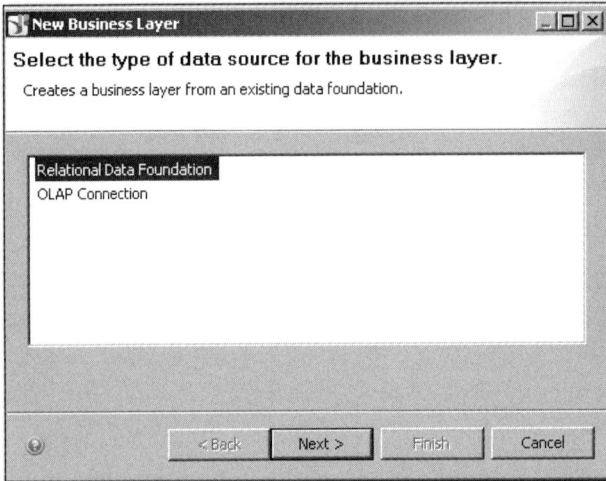

**Figure 9.58**  Selecting the Relational Data Foundation Option

3. When the RESOURCE NAME window appears, enter the name "INTERNETSALES_ BL", and click NEXT to continue, as shown in Figure 9.59.

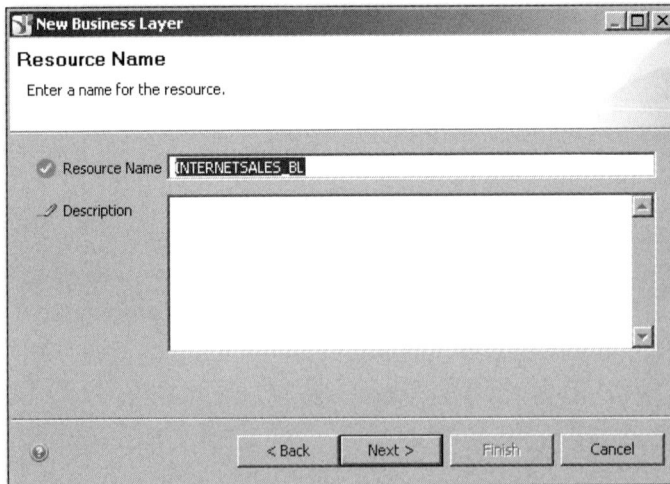

**Figure 9.59**  Naming the Business Layer in the New Business Layer Wizard

4. When the SELECT DATA FOUNDATION window appears, click the ellipsis, and select the INTERNETSALES_DF.DFX data foundation that is stored in the INTERNETSALES local project. Make sure the option AUTOMATICALLY CREATE FOLDERS AND OBJECTS is selected as shown in Figure 9.60. Although you'll change the auto-generated objects later, selecting this option saves time compared to creating them individually. Click FINISH to close the wizard.

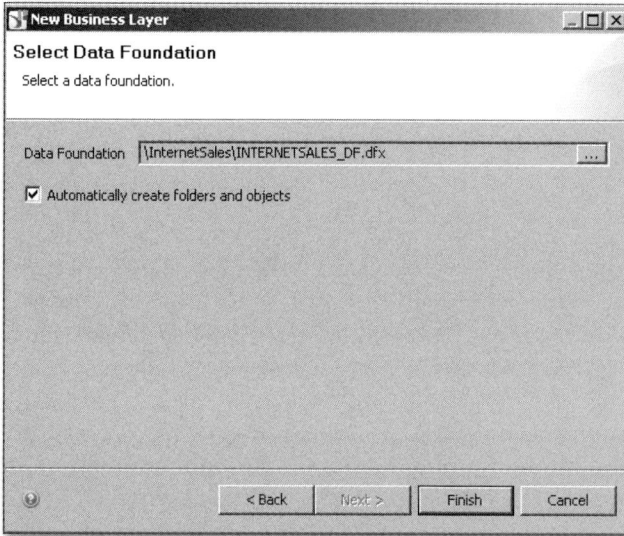

**Figure 9.60** Selecting the Data Foundation to Support the Business Layer

5. The business layer should not be visible in the IDT workspace. Figure 9.61 contains an example of this business layer. On the left side is the BUSINESS LAYER design window, in which the objects and classes that were automatically generated by the NEW BUSINESS LAYER wizard appear. The right side contains two windows. The top of the rightmost window contains the options for any highlighted object. The bottom side contains an image of the referenced data foundation.

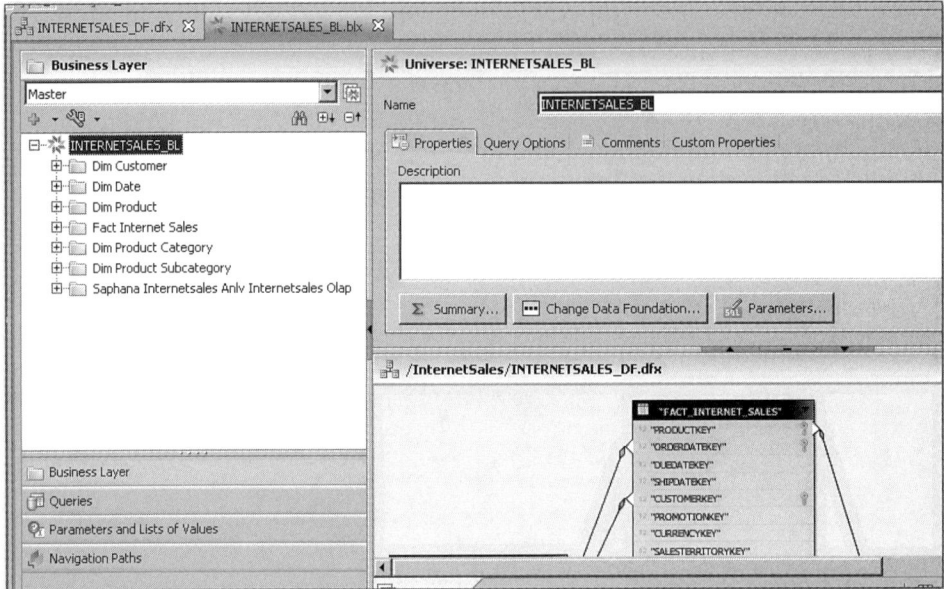

**Figure 9.61** The Internet Sales Business Layer

6. Because you chose to have the business layer automatically generate folders and objects, you must now remove or rename objects to make the universe more user friendly.

### Renaming Objects

Follow these steps to rename objects in the BUSINESS LAYER windows:

1. Locate the object and highlight it to activate the options window on the right side. In the options window for the selected object (see the fields boxed in Figure 9.62), locate the NAME field.

2. Expand each class or folder, and rename the objects to be more user friendly. The process of renaming the objects is the same as the one described for renaming classes earlier. Later, figures are provided to help you create the suggested object names.

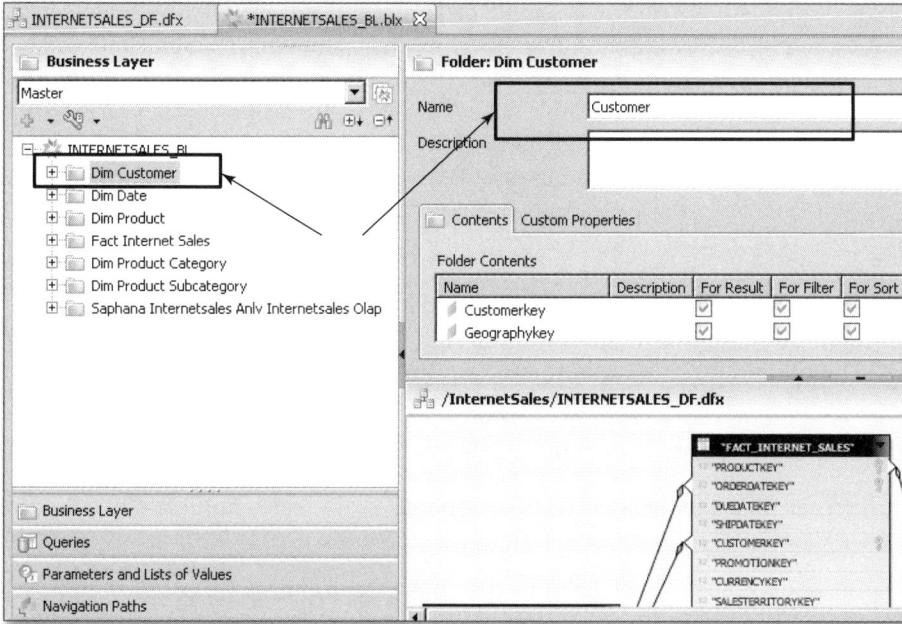

**Figure 9.62** Changing Object Names in the Business Layer

3. Rename each folder or class as listed in Table 9.8.

| Auto-Generated Class Name | New Class Name |
|---|---|
| Dim Customer | Customer |
| Dim Date | Ordered Date |
| Dim Product | Products |
| Fact Internet Sales | Internet Sales Transactions and Measures |
| Dim Product Category | Product Category |
| Dim Product Subcategory | Product Subcategory |

**Table 9.8** Renaming the Internet Sales Business Layer Classes

### Deleting Objects

Delete the Saphana Internetsales Anlv Internetsales Olap class and objects from the business layer. These objects can't be referenced directly in the business layer without generating a database Cartesian product. To delete this class and its objects, right-click the class and choose DELETE. Confirm the deletion by selecting the option YES. Later, you'll define existing objects to reference the underlying Internet sales analytic view using aggregate awareness.

Delete objects that won't be used by users or the universe designer. To delete an object, right-click the object and choose DELETE.

### Hiding Objects

Hide objects that should not be made available to users but need to remain available to the universe designer. The outputs of these objects don't have any meaning to a user because they are used by the database for joining or for other purposes in the data model. However, the universe designer might find them useful when designing the universe. Follow these steps to hide objects:

1. Click each object in the BUSINESS LAYER window. To select multiple objects, hold down the [Shift] key while selecting each.

2. Once selected, right-click the object or objects, and choose CHANGE STATE • HIDDEN, as shown in Figure 9.63. Figures are provided later to suggest objects to hide.

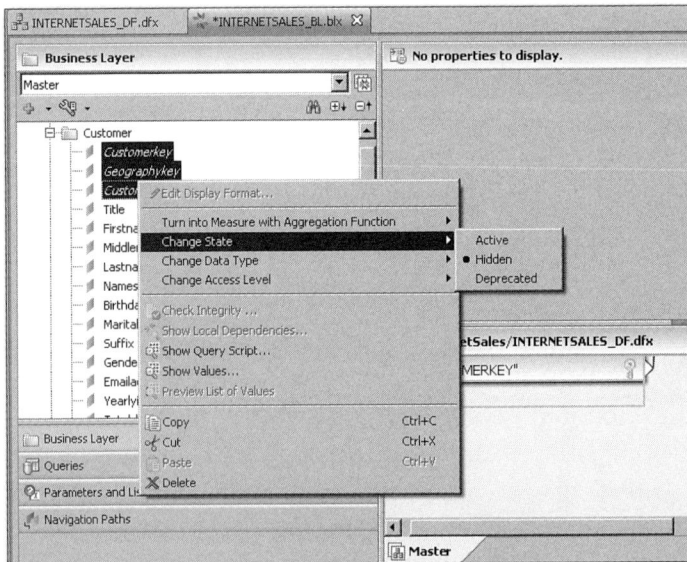

**Figure 9.63**  Hiding Objects from Users in the Business Layer

## Moving Objects

You can move an object from the top level so that it's nested in existing classes. Because the product subcategory and product category are effectively attributes of the product class, follow these steps to move them to the product class to help the user easily identify them:

1. Highlight the Product Subcategory class, and place it in the Product class using the drag-and-drop method. This can be a tricky process at first.

2. To ensure that you're dropping the class into the correct location, hover your mouse over the Products class until it expands.

3. Release the mouse button to move the product subcategory class and its objects. Once complete, move the Product Category class into the Products class as well.

## Adding Objects

Add objects or classes to the business layer to enhance the user experience. In some cases, you'll want to create subclasses or folders to organize your objects. To add an object, follow these steps:

1. To add an object, right-click the parent class or folder, and choose New, as shown in Figure 9.64.

2. A window appears allowing you to choose from various object types. To create a subclass, choose the Folder option.

## Defining Dimensions and Measures

The next part of the business layer design process is to define the relevant dimensions and business measures. Follow these steps to do so:

1. Ensure that your Customer class, subclasses, and objects appear as depicted in Figure 9.65. Rename the objects and create the subclasses shown. Note that the Customer Number references the Customerkey field.

> **Note**
>
> In cases where English, Spanish, or French language columns appear, choose the column appropriate to the users of the universe throughout this section. In this example, we chose the English version.

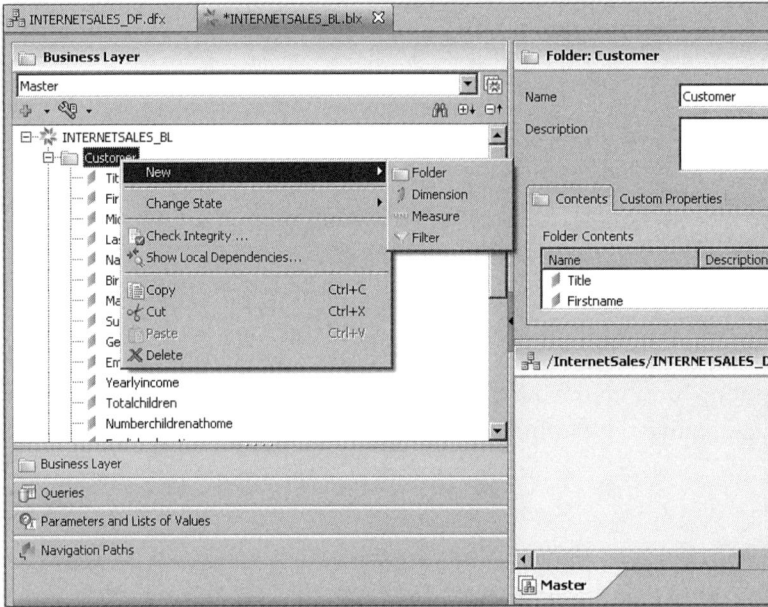

**Figure 9.64** Adding New Objects in the Business Layer

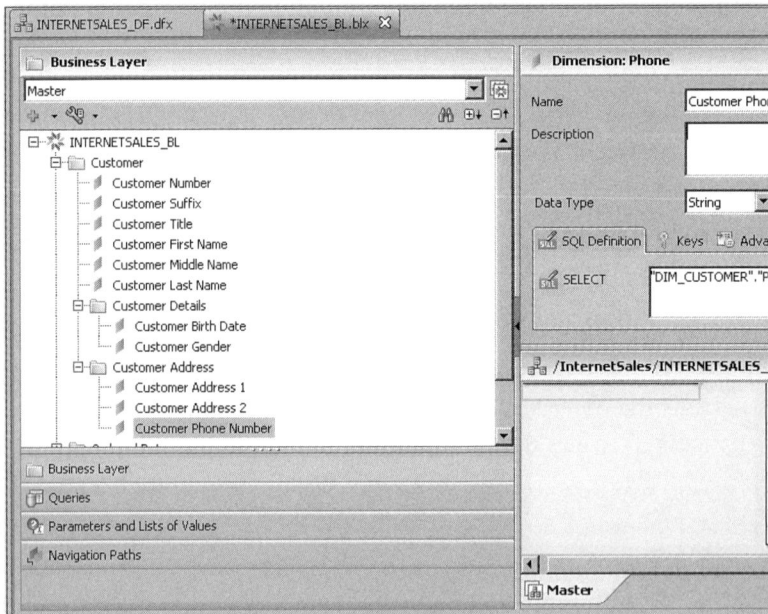

**Figure 9.65** The Customer Class and its Objects

2. Ensure that the ORDERED DATE class appears as depicted in Figure 9.66. Notice that the DATEKEY field is hidden.

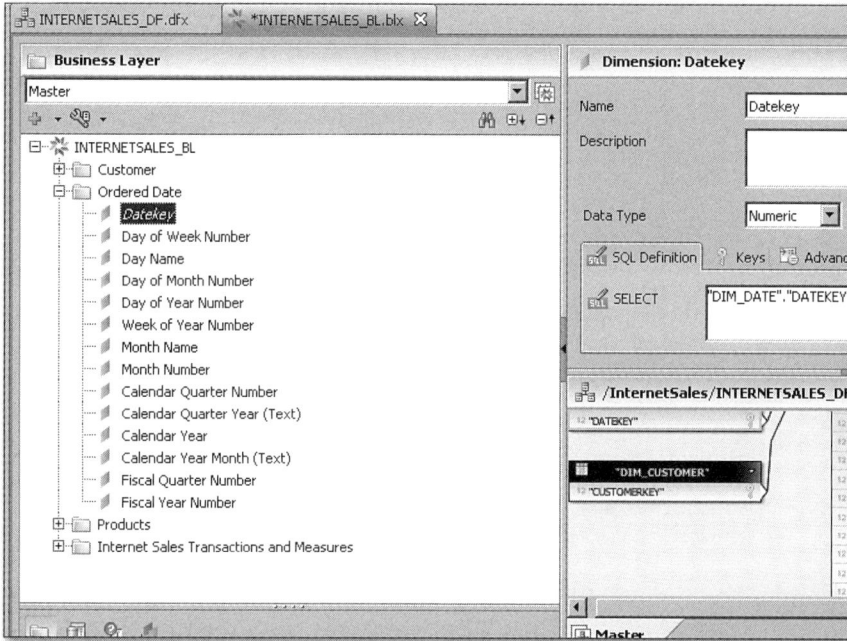

**Figure 9.66** The Ordered Date Class and its Objects

3. Ensure that the PRODUCTS class appears as depicted in Figure 9.67.

4. Convert dimensions into measures and add the SUM() function to the object's definition. To convert an object or objects, highlight the dimensions. To select multiple dimensions, use the Shift key while highlighting. Right-click the highlighted measures, and choose TURN INTO MEASURE WITH AGGREGATION FUNCTION • SUM, as shown in Figure 9.68.

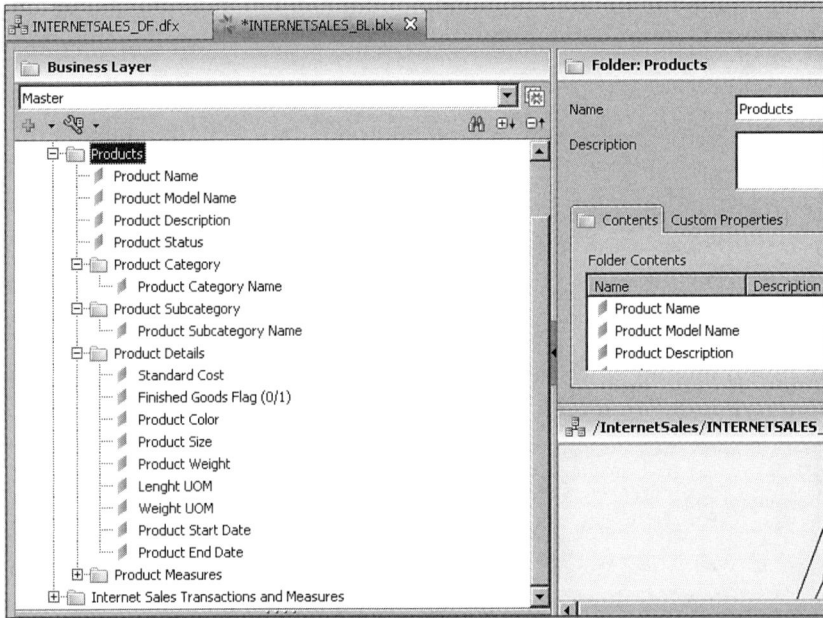

**Figure 9.67**  The Products Class and its Objects

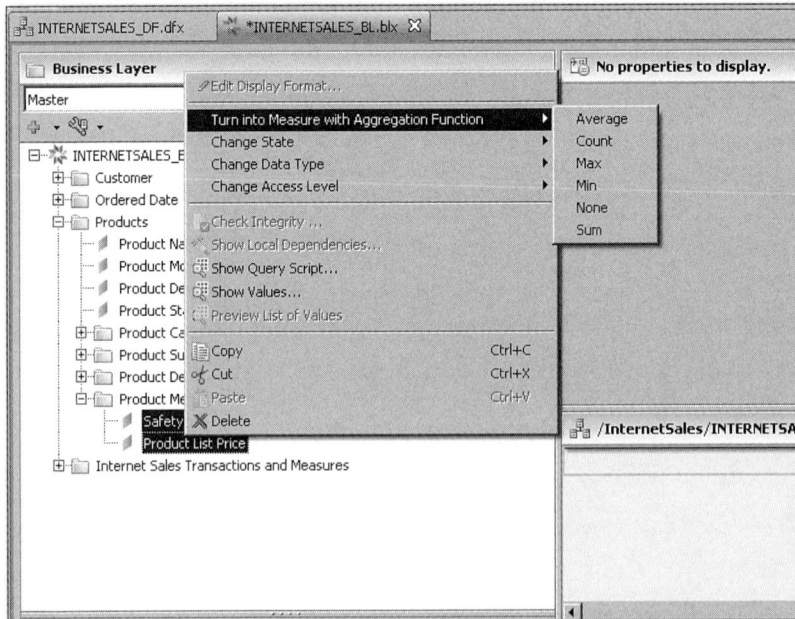

**Figure 9.68**  Converting Dimensions into Measures

5. Create the PRODUCT MEASURES class, move the objects listed in Figure 9.69 into the class, and convert them to measures with a SUM() function.

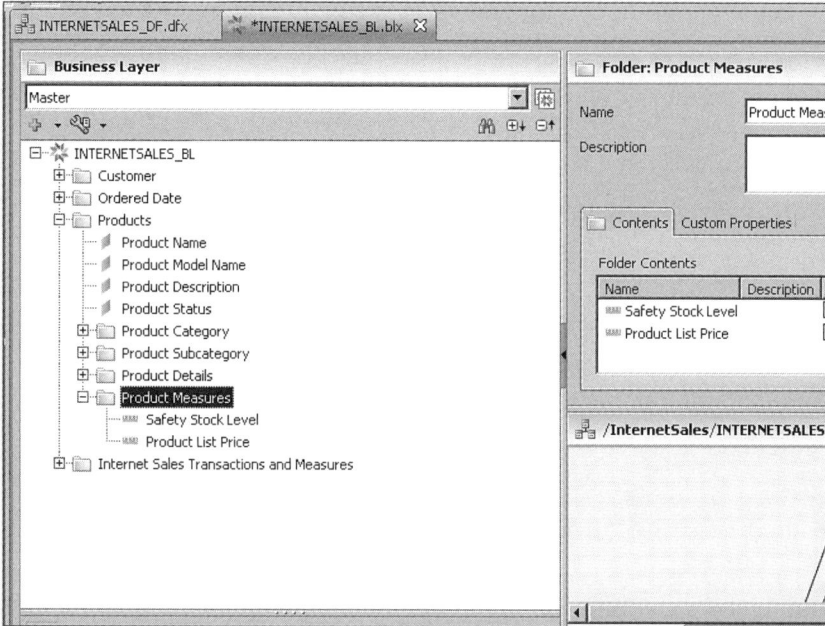

**Figure 9.69** The Product Measures Class and its Objects

6. Define the INTERNET SALES TRANSACTIONS AND MEASURES class as depicted in Figure 9.70. Convert the DIMENSIONS into MEASURES with the SUM() function as shown, and delete any objects not defined in the screen.

7. Review the definition of each measure. Highlight each measure and look at its definition in the rightmost windows. Notice the SELECT field. In this field, the underlying columnar table column appears. The syntax of this field is the SQL syntax of SAP HANA. Notice that the standard SUM() function has been added to each object. Later when you define aggregate awareness, you'll include additional universe specific syntax to the SELECT field.

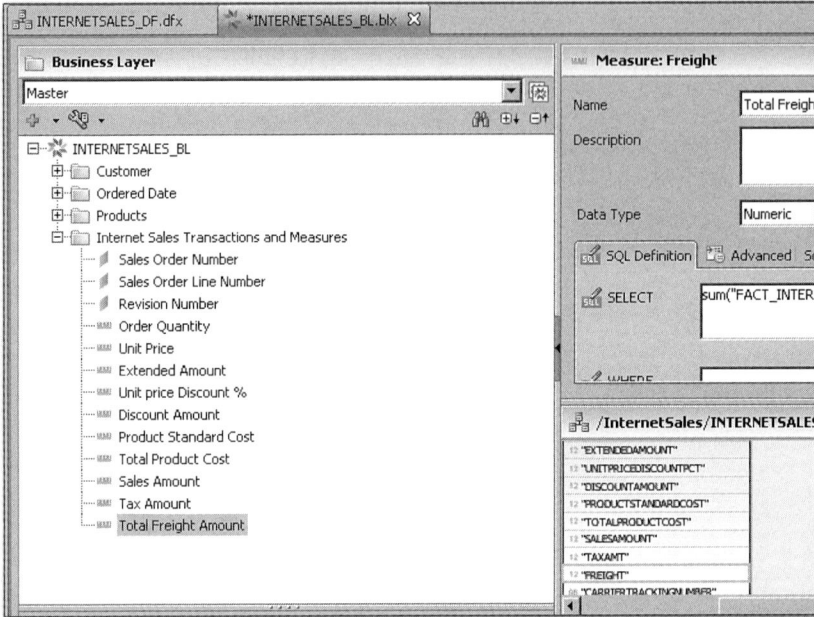

**Figure 9.70**  The Internet Sales Transactions and Measures Class and Its Objects

**Configuring Aggregate Awareness**

In this section, we walk you through the processes of implementing aggregate awareness, which involves modifying dimensions and measures by incorporating the universe function `@Aggregate_Aware()` in the object definition. This function must have a minimum of two input parameters, each separated by a comma. In the classical universe based on a legacy RDBMS, there can be multiple aggregate tables defined in the source schema. With SAP HANA, we only expect there to be one aggregate table or analytic view. In the context of using this method with SAP HANA, each input parameter represents one object in the columnar tables and a corresponding object in the analytic view.

The objects should be defined in the input parameters working from left to right as follows: The corresponding analytic view column should be defined as the first input parameter. If the object is a measure make sure to wrap the function `SUM()` around the column. The second input parameter should be the corresponding column in the columnar table. Again, make sure to wrap the column in the function `SUM()` if it's a measure.

The same process is true for each dimension object. However, with dimension objects, aggregate functions should not be included in the object definition. Figure 9.71 contains an example of how this function is defined on the ORDER QUANTITY measure. Figure 9.72 contains a closer view of the syntax.

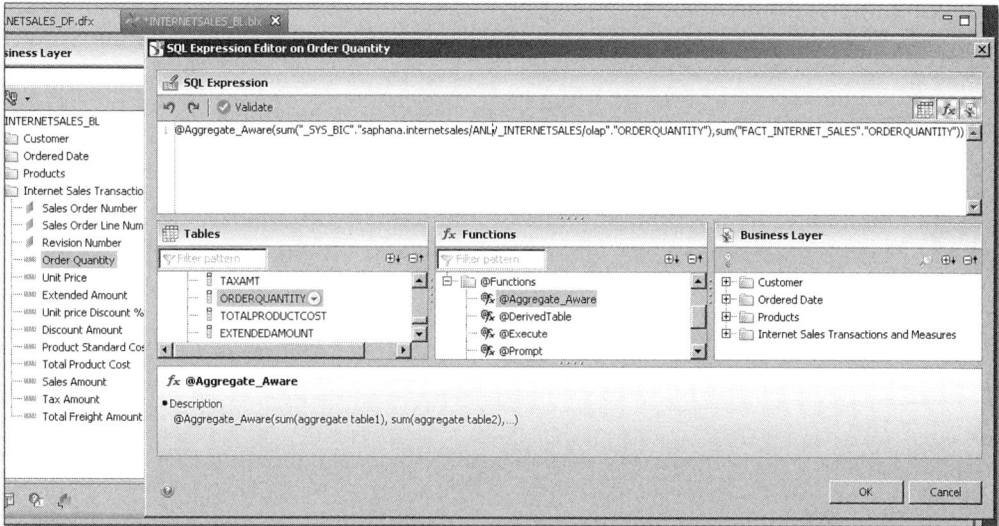

**Figure 9.71** Updating Objects to Use Aggregate Awareness

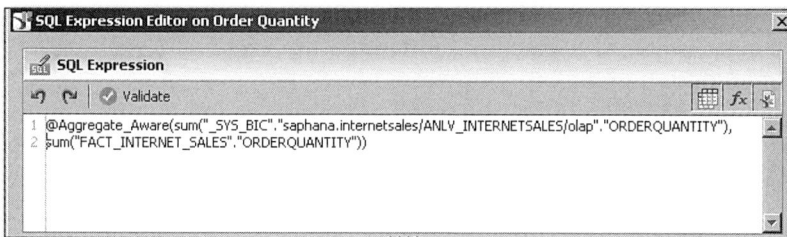

**Figure 9.72** Defining Aggregate Awareness on a Measure

Update the objects outlined here to incorporate aggregate awareness into the case study universe. The instructions will contain screenshots of each object's SELECT field located in the rightmost window of the BUSINESS LAYER tab.

1. Update the ORDER QUANTITY measure using the syntax shown previously in Figure 9.72. Click the SQL ASSISTANT button to the right of the SELECT field to activate the editor that is shown.

2. Update the SALES AMOUNT measure using the syntax shown in Figure 9.73.

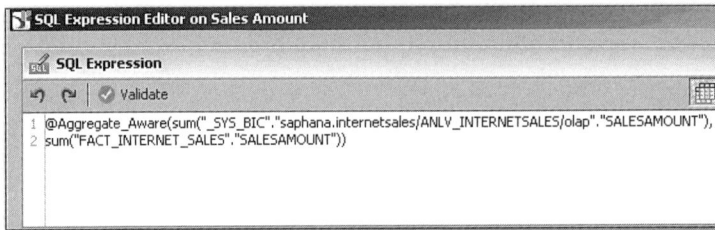

**Figure 9.73** Defining Aggregate Awareness on the Sales Amount Measure

3. Repeat the process on the remaining measures. In each case, define the column from the Internet sales analytic view as the first parameter and the column from the columnar table as the second. Because they are measures, each input parameter column should contain the SUM() function.

4. Update dimensions to include aggregate awareness. Dimensions defined in the analytic view and columnar tables must also be made aggregate aware.

5. Update the calendar year dimension in the ordered date class to include the aggregate aware function. Figure 9.74 contains the syntax that is required. Notice that the analytic view column is in the first parameter, and the columnar table column is in the second parameter. In addition, notice that the SUM() function isn't included with the dimension objects.

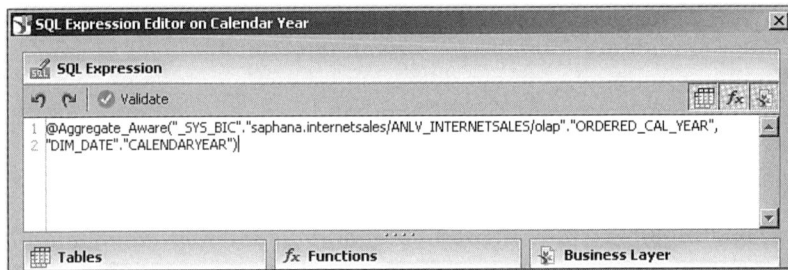

**Figure 9.74** Updating the Calendar Year Dimension in the Ordered Date Class

6. Update the remaining dimensions to use aggregate awareness. Note that only dimensions that exist in both the analytic view and the defined dimension list should be included. In addition, this process is only necessary for objects that

are commonly used in analytical queries. Please also note that with SAP HANA, dimension objects will fail validation. The IDT validation engine doesn't take into account that the analytic view objects must be tested with a measure to meet the minimum requirements of querying an analytic view.

7. Save the business layer.

8. Set aggregate incompatibilities using aggregate navigation. The AGGREGATE NAVIGATION wizard is located under ACTIONS • SET AGGREGATE NAVIGATIONS.

9. In this wizard, select DETECT INCOMPATIBILITIES at the bottom of the screen. This is a vital step that informs the universe concerning which combination of objects can be combined and used against the analytic view and which objects are incompatible with aggregate awareness. If an incompatible object is used in a universe query, the SQL syntax is updated to use only the columnar tables and joins. Failure to complete this step will result in a Cartesian product for most queries. Therefore, it's extremely important that aggregate incompatibilities are defined.

10. Save the business layer.

### Setting Query Options

Before publishing the universe to the SAP BusinessObjects repository, you need to review and establish a few options for the universe. These options control several important features of the universe and should be reviewed. The following steps outline the processes of accessing these options and changing the critical options to facilitate a properly designed universe.

1. To access the query options in the IDT business layer, locate the topmost node of the universe class and object hierarchy located in the left side of the business layer. Highlight the top node, which represents the entire universe. On the right side, a new window appears that contains four tabs. Click the QUERY OPTIONS tab. Figure 9.75 contains an example of the expected view, found in the IDT business layer.

2. Take note of the QUERY LIMITS and QUERY OPTIONS areas.

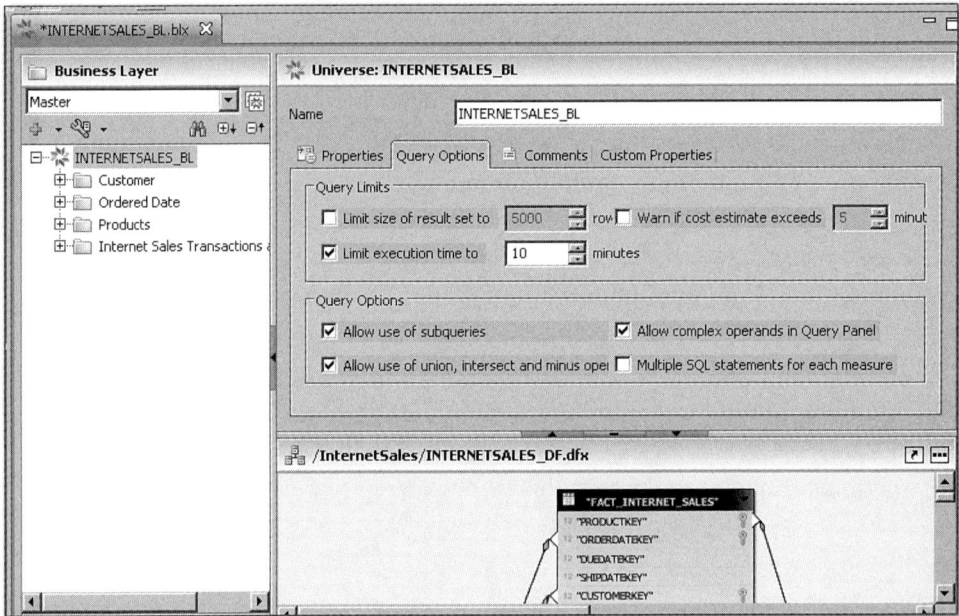

**Figure 9.75** Setting the Query Options for a Universe

3. Change the option Limit size of result set to. By default, the business layer options restrict the universe to 5,000 rows. For most organizations, this number is too low and should be either disabled or increased. To disable this option, uncheck it. To increase the number of rows, change the value to a more suitable number. Note that restricting to a specific number of rows might result in partial results in reports. Based on firsthand experience, this can lead user to incorrect conclusions. Granted the reporting tool will indicate partial results, but the warning isn't apparent to most users. Query limits should be restricted by time and not by number of records.

4. Change the option Multiple SQL statements for each measure. When enabled, a separate SQL query is generated by the reporting tool to facilitate each measure. This can lead to access queries and slow performance. It's best to disable this option when dealing with star schemas in the data foundation.

## Setting Universe Parameters

In addition to setting the query parameters, you can also establish or change parameters that affect the way SQL statements are generated by following these steps:

1. To access the query options in the IDT business layer, highlight the top node, and a new window appear. Click the PROPERTIES tab. Figure 9.76 contains an example of the expected view found in the IDT business layer.

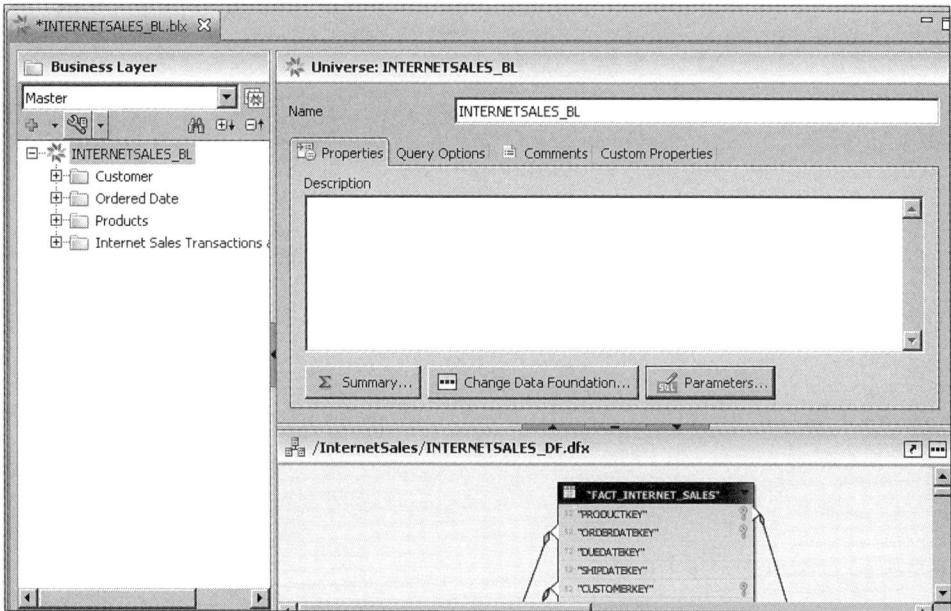

**Figure 9.76**   Setting the Properties and Parameters for a Universe

2. Click the PARAMETERS button to launch the universe properties window. Figure 9.77 contains an example of the EDIT QUERY SCRIPT PARAMETERS window.

3. To change a parameter, highlight the parameter in the list. Click the VALUE column to enable the dropdown list. In the dropdown list, select the desired value for the parameter.

4. To add an additional parameter, locate the dropdown at the bottom of the window. This dropdown contains the ADD, DELETE, and DEFAULT VALUE buttons.

5. In the dropdown, locate the JOIN_BY_SQL parameter. Click the ADD button to add this parameter to the list. The JOIN_BY_SQL parameter moves SAP

BusinessObjects Web Intelligence data synchronization from the report engine to SAP HANA for processing. In most cases, this option results in increased performance.

6. Change its value from the default No to Yes. Click OK to save your changes.

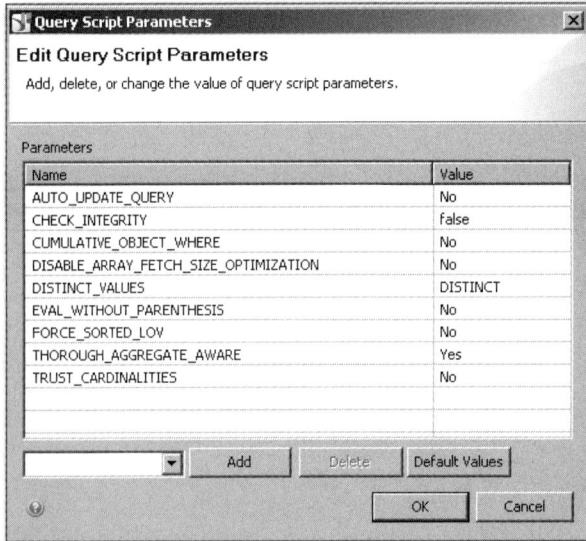

**Query Script Parameters**

**Edit Query Script Parameters**

Add, delete, or change the value of query script parameters.

Parameters

| Name | Value |
| --- | --- |
| AUTO_UPDATE_QUERY | No |
| CHECK_INTEGRITY | false |
| CUMULATIVE_OBJECT_WHERE | No |
| DISABLE_ARRAY_FETCH_SIZE_OPTIMIZATION | No |
| DISTINCT_VALUES | DISTINCT |
| EVAL_WITHOUT_PARENTHESIS | No |
| FORCE_SORTED_LOV | No |
| THOROUGH_AGGREGATE_AWARE | Yes |
| TRUST_CARDINALITIES | No |

Add   Delete   Default Values

OK   Cancel

**Figure 9.77**  The Edit Query Script Parameters Window

### 9.5.4   Publish the Universe

After all objects have been updated, you can now publish the universe to the SAP BusinessObjects 4.0 repository. This step, which is outlined in Section 9.2.8, is required to allow the SAP BusinessObjects reporting tools to access the universe.

Now that the design process is complete, AdventureWorks Cycle Company has a universe that can support many of the SAP BusinessObjects tools. This universe was designed to support all types of queries. The universe foundation is designed with both columnar tables and analytic views to facilitate both operational and analytic reporting. This design decision will help facilitate features that are unique to both the universe semantic layer and features that are unique to SAP HANA's multidimensional models. The business layer is organized and contains named objects to help users identify their use. In addition, aggregate awareness is incorporated into the definition of objects. Aggregate awareness automatically rewrites queries to use the most efficient SAP HANA object.

## 9.6   Summary

Since the inception of Business Objects, the universe has played a key role in providing report developers and ad hoc report designers a business-centric representation of their organization's data. SAP HANA too shares this concept in the form of its multidimensional models. Although there is functional overlap between these two layers, you must still use the universe to fully integrate SAP HANA and SAP BusinessObjects. This isn't to say that every tool in the SAP BusinessObjects portfolio requires the use of a universe to access data in SAP HANA, but rather it's an indication that the universe continues to play a role in these implementations.

The SAP BusinessObjects 4.0 platform contains two types of universes as a means to help organizations transition from the traditional UNV universe to the new IDT UNX universe. Some of the tools in the SAP BusinessObjects platform support both universe types, while others only support one or the other. When you implement SAP HANA with SAP BusinessObjects, understanding the role each universe type plays as it relates to delivering the correct solution is important.

When designing a universe against an SAP HANA source, you need to pay close attention to the different options you can use to access data in SAP HANA. Depending on the options you choose, different engines are used to process universe-generated SQL queries. Each engine has different capabilities in terms of performance and scalability. To fully analyze queries and to understand the engines they invoke, SAP HANA Studio provides a utility to visually analyze the execution plan of queries.

You should now have a better understanding of the rules and concepts that are specific to creating a universe against SAP HANA. In subsequent chapters, we'll explore the different SAP BusinessObjects tools and how they leverage either the universe or the SAP HANA multidimensional models directly. Regardless of the requirements, the SAP BusinessObjects tools are able to deliver unparalleled flexibility, speed, and performance.

*Harnessing the transactional power of SAP HANA with the functionality of a well-designed dashboard can provide unique and attractive insight into key performance indicators as businesses have never before seen in tabular analytics.*

# 10  Professionally Authored Dashboards Powered by SAP HANA

There is beauty and simplicity in a good design. Analytics used by businesses to gain insight into their metrics are usually very cold and pragmatic in their development and use, but time and experience have shown that businesses are excited by graphics that are simple and elegant while effective and powerful.

Conceptually, we have two types of dashboards. The first type of dashboard, those considered "self-service," are built to suit a user's needs at design time. When using self-service dashboards, a user understands the requirements of the dashboard and the business questions to which he seek answers. Further, these dashboards provide an ongoing resource by which the users can continue to receive answers to their business questions. Self-service dashboards are discussed in Chapter 11 of this book.

Meanwhile, dashboards of the second type—professionally authored dashboards (PADs)—are built by trained designers who are familiar with the tools that are used to create such dashboards. PADs go through a full project management process, which includes a requirements gathering session, a prototyping phase, and a time to adjust the dashboard so that it conforms closer to the intended requirements of the project.

In this chapter, we discuss PADs, where they fit in the grand scheme of reporting and analytics, how SAP HANA changes the concept of summarized data, and finally whether these types of dashboards are needed at all (Section 10.1). In Section 10.2, we describe the tools that are used to develop these dashboards and the methods by which you can connect to data. We focus on the connectivity to SAP HANA by various methods. Section 10.3 wraps it all up with a case study that goes through the typical process and implementation of a PAD in the solutions presented.

## 10.1    Introduction to Professionally Authored Dashboards

The phrase "professionally authored dashboard" is a relatively new term that describes an old concept. Historically, dashboards were developed by trained professionals with knowledge and experience in developing visualizations of this type.

Projects of this type follow a specific pattern. The original process was to gather specific requirements and developing a dashboard based on them. As requirements changed, these dashboards sometimes didn't reflect the most up-to-date requirements, and the dashboard projects usually failed as a result. A newer, more agile methodology called Scrum then became the popular design methodology. The major difference is that the requirements are gathered in a series of iterations (usually three) rather than one all-encompassing iteration. After the requirements are gathered, the dashboarding professionals then build a prototype to display to the end-user team. Any changes that are made to the dashboard would be made by the dashboarding professionals until a final design is achieved, agreed upon, and signed off.

These professional processes can take anywhere from weeks to months, depending on the complexity of the dashboard and the location within the project pipeline at which the dashboarding project falls. The amount of time that it typically takes for a PAD project lends a major disadvantage to these types of dashboards. This is because at the end of the dashboard project, business processes may have changed, and the business questions answered by the dashboarding project may no longer be required.

So if project duration is a major disadvantage of a PAD project, why should you undertake a PAD process to start with? One reason is aesthetics. Consider the use case where an executive is a stickler for design and envisions the dashboard being released to the shareholders of the company to monitor the state of the business at a glance. It's apparent that the look of the dashboard is extraordinarily important, so the executive may need to request a PAD due to the tight design constraints.

Also consider the case where the business has decided to implement increased transparency of the company to its employees. As part of this initiative, the company has installed multiple large screens around the office. These screens will rotate a series of dashboards containing metrics describing the performance of the company overall. In an effort to provide a polished look to the visualizations, the company requests a PAD. Figure 10.1 provides you with an idea of a PAD that, at a glance, gives information on the sales in a company while allowing for a drillable experience into sales rep performance. Meanwhile, Figure 10.2 gives information on the top ten customers and a focus on the key performance indicators (KPIs) of each one.

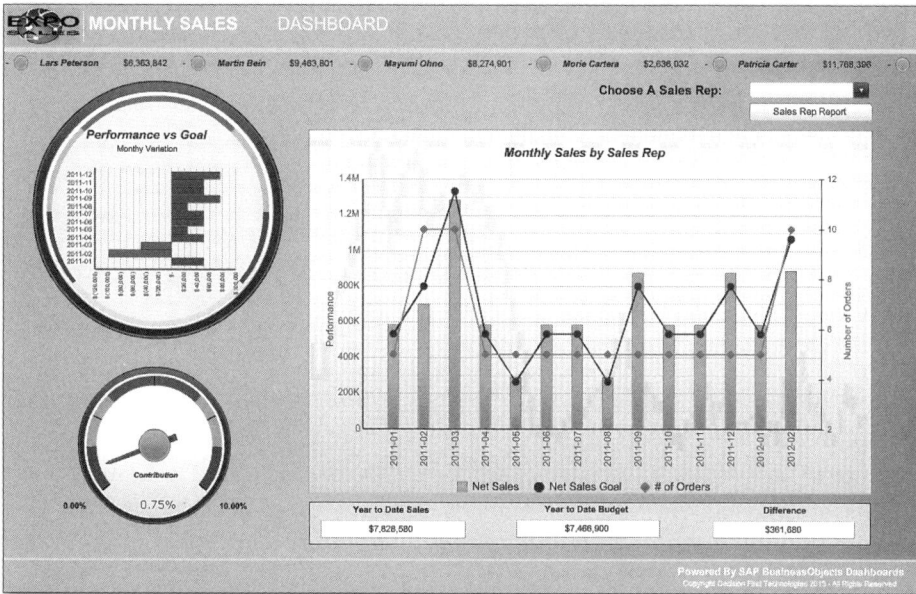

**Figure 10.1** Sales Rep Performance Dashboard

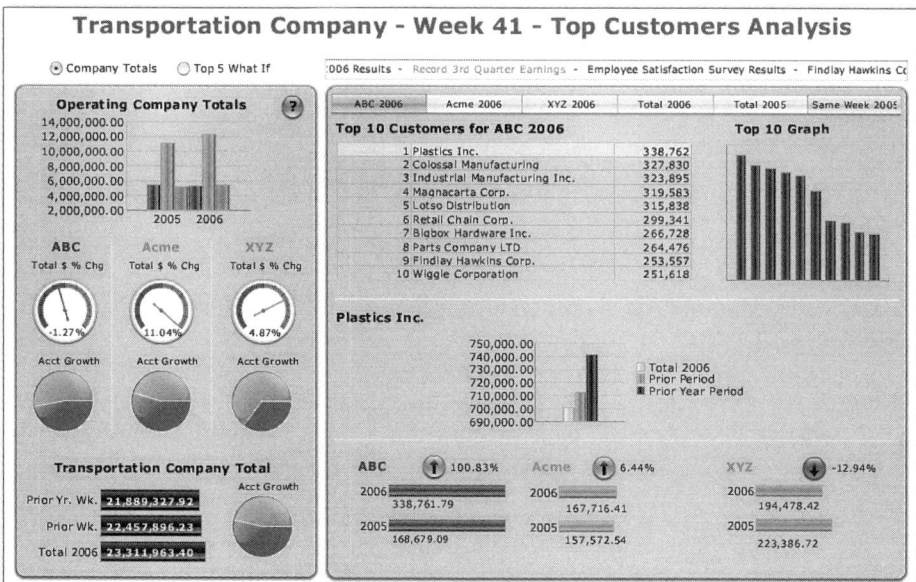

**Figure 10.2** Top Customers and KPIs

### 10.1.1 Comparing Dashboards

Now let's compare PADs and self-service dashboards. First of all, PADs are professionally designed by trained developers, typically in the IT department, and anything that is professionally designed by knowledgeable professionals may take time to complete. Waiting for a professional to complete this type of project can consume a lot of time and money, and there is no guarantee that the end result will meet the needs of the end users. The dashboards then need to go back to the design team for updating to meet any new requirements.

Self-service dashboards, on the other hand, take advantage of tools that put the power of the design back in the user's hands, but the results of a self-service dashboard are typically pragmatic and boring. Of course, the answers that the users require are right there in front of them.

But what if these same users have further questions that their current self-service dashboard doesn't handle? This process is as simple as the end user opening the dashboard in the design tool of their choice and making the modifications. The result is an immediately available, infinitely changeable, useful dashboard that does exactly what the user needs when he needs it.

So when choosing between a PAD and a self-authored dashboard, consider the desired end result of your dashboarding project. Do you need a dashboard that is highly polished yet doesn't change very often? This is an ideal case for a dashboard that is designed by a professional. Do you need to gather quick answers or create a dashboard that changes slightly each week or two regardless of slickness of design? This is more geared toward a self-service dashboard. As you can see, self-service dashboards and PADs each serve a purpose. It all comes down to the choice between slick design with a professional appearance versus quick and easily changed dashboards.

### 10.1.2 Why Use a PAD Rather Than a Report or Self-Service Dashboard?

Because a dashboard provides the user with the ability to quickly view data and make decisions based on the data without the need for lengthy analyses, above all, the purpose of a dashboard must be clear. A dashboard provides an interface by which a user can access information on a summary level and view specific KPIs that are optionally represented with colors and icons, so these need to be explained and easily understood by the readers. The key metrics tracked by the dashboard should be applicable to the subject on which the dashboard was built.

Reports, on the other hand, are typically built to contain both summary and detailed data. A designer can build a report to display data in a summary table such as the year-after-year sales figures. The designer can also generate a report within the same document that provides more detail on the transactional elements that compose the summary figures.

This type of approach, while functional, doesn't provide the professional appearance that a dashboard can provide. One course of action is to generate a PAD that displays the necessary summary information along with symbols and icons that allow the user to immediately derive answers to his most important business questions. If the user needs to drill further down into the data to provide insight into the summary data, then the dashboard designers can provide a hyperlink to a detail report that serves that purpose.

Dashboards were never intended to be reports. Some dashboarding users have trouble determining the best way to handle large amounts of data even if the dashboarding tool does support larger quantities. A best practice in good dashboard design is to limit the amount of drilling that is required within the dashboard. To immediately drive business value, the dashboard should summarize detail data according to requirements derived from the end users. The dashboard designer may provide the ability to drill down by one more level to see a further level of detail, but it's typically better to link to a report to provide this detail rather than dealing with the overhead of importing the data into the dashboarding tool and handling it on the presentation layer.

### 10.1.3    Professionally Authored Dashboards Process

The type of methodology whereby the requirements are gathered, prototyped, and presented is typically used to handle a dashboard design project but can also be applied to any sort of design project where a deliverable must be reconciled against requirements.

**Requirements Gathering**

When undertaking a new dashboard design project, we typically start with a requirements elicitation discussion. This session for end users and knowledge experts is meant to determine which questions the dashboard should answer and how those should be represented. Different sets of data lend themselves to different types of display. For instance, if you have a small number of dimensions in a data set such as five categories, you may consider using a pie chart to represent this data. The designer might also add a small scorecard to the left of the pie chart to represent the data in a tabular method along with a scorecard to show whether the data is good, bad, or moving in a positive or negative direction.

### Iterative Approach

Next we begin the first of three iterations of the design project. During this process, we discuss with the database administrators the sourcing of the data required by the dashboard. While the data is being sourced, the dashboard designer can begin prototyping the dashboard in the design tool, even though the data may not be available yet. The designer is welcome to develop "dummy data" so that the design of the prototype can be completed. In later phases, the data can be finalized and incorporated into the dashboard.

In a standard dashboard design project, we conduct three iterations. In the first iteration, we take the requirements and storyboards elicited during the initial meetings and design the dashboard in the design tool. We place the components from the storyboards on the dashboard to get a "feel" of how the dashboard will function. At this point, the prototype can be updated and carried into phase 2 or can be completely thrown out and a new dashboard created in the next phase.

The second phase begins after the initial prototype is reviewed and a sign off is received. The designer takes the marked up prototype from phase 1 and provides an update to the prototype. During this phase, the database administrators should be working to complete the data feeds required by the database. The dashboard designer should be able to bring in a first pass at the data to integrate into the dashboard. The second prototype should be nearly production ready. The end users provide their feedback and sign off. When sign-off is achieved, the third and final prototype phase can begin.

The third phase begins in the same manner as the second phase. The requested modifications are taken from the phase 2 sign-off, and the dashboard designer updates the prototype with the recommendations. At this point, the database administrator should have the data sets finalized and ready for consumption by the dashboard. The dashboard designer then connects the dashboard to the finalized data sets. After the third prototype is completed, a quality assurance (QA) process should commence to ensure correct design, adherence to corporate standards and accuracy of data. When the dashboard has been properly tested and verified to be valid, it can be released for use by the end user.

### 10.1.4  Professionally Authored Dashboards Outlook

With the introduction of self-service dashboarding tools such as SAP Business-Objects Explorer and SAP Lumira, the question remains: Are professionally authored dashboards dead?

Let's look at it from this perspective. When Crystal Decisions was acquired by Business Objects in 2003, the question arose whether there was a real need for Crystal Reports alongside the self-service Web Intelligence tool. The verdict was clear: Crystal Reports was well known as a pixel-perfect reporting tool that provides professional looking reports, while Web Intelligence, on the other hand, was ideal for providing users with the ability to answer business questions and analyze data sets with relative ease. The tool was not intended to provide highly formatted reports, rather it provided the ability to get quick answers. As time went on, Web Intelligence received advanced features that provided advanced formatting capabilities for reports. A dichotomy still exists between the two reporting systems.

The relationship between SAP Crystal Reports and SAP BusinessObjects Web Intelligence is analogous to the relationship between SAP BusinessObjects Explorer/SAP Lumira and SAP BusinessObjects Dashboards/SAP BusinessObjects Design Studio. SAP BusinessObjects Explorer and SAP Lumira allow end users to build what are essentially self-service dashboards. Users are able to connect to their data, extract only the data that is required for the analysis under study, and then represent the data in ways that make the most sense to their application. The interface can be configured and reconfigured as required.

SAP BusinessObjects Dashboards and SAP BusinessObjects Design Studio are two applications for specially trained professional dashboard designers. Because these dashboards adhere to the standard dashboard project we've already defined, modifications to these dashboards must be made by the dashboard designers and presented to the end user for approval and distribution.

It's true that self-service dashboards are extraordinarily useful to put the power of the tools back in the hands of the users. Users can update and change the visualizations on the fly without requiring assistance from any other user or IT. These dashboards are typically used by the end user to answer their own business questions.

PADs, on the other hand, are typically used to convey information to executives, shareholders, the general public, or everyone in the company. Some requirements for dashboards are too complex to be rendered using a self-service dashboarding tool in their current form. The resulting PAD dashboards can be distributed in many different formats for consumption by these groups: on a company portal, external website, or overhead, screen among others. When the dashboards are distributed in these ways, the dashboards should represent the best design that the company can offer in an effort to project a more professional and reliable image. With this in mind, the answer to the original question—"Are PADs dead?"—is a solid "no."

## 10.2    Tools for Designing Dashboards with SAP HANA

SAP BusinessObjects provides two tools for designing PADs: SAP BusinessObjects Dashboards and SAP BusinessObjects Design Studio. Both tools are client-side installations that are separate from the core SAP BusinessObjects client/server installation. Each tool requires its own unique skill set in designing the dashboard; however, the overall graphical design of the dashboard requires a set of skills common to both tools.

In this section, we introduce the two tools that allow for the design of PADs and compare and contrast them to provide you with more information on how to select the right tool for the job.

### 10.2.1    SAP BusinessObjects Dashboards

What has become the current version of SAP BusinessObjects Dashboards was launched in 2003 by Infommersion, Inc. After SAP acquired Business Objects and eventually released the SAP BusinessObjects 4.1 platform, SAP renamed many of the tools in an effort to "bring more clarity to [its] business intelligence (BI) portfolio naming and use names that reflect the capabilities of [its] solutions." Of course, like other tools that were renamed, SAP BusinessObjects Dashboards is still popularly known by its legacy name, Xcelsius.

SAP BusinessObjects Dashboards is a fully featured dashboarding tool that allows experienced designers to develop polished, professional looking dashboards with little more than a drag-and-drop motion. Dashboards works in conjunction with Microsoft Excel to provide interactivity across multiple components that, together, form the dashboard and leverages Adobe Flash technology as the rendering engine to present the content to the users. It's the interactivity of these components and the data that they represent that changes available insight into data in ways that are immediately recognized and usable.

When the SAP BusinessObjects Dashboards application was initially designed, the only way to pull data into a dashboard was to embed the data directly within an instance of Excel with which the application worked. As the application was developed further, Excel was eventually embedded within the SAP BusinessObjects application itself, as shown in Figure 10.3. As the development cycles passed and newer versions of SAP BusinessObjects were released, the Data Manager was introduced to multiply the ways in which dashboard designers could connect to their data, as shown in Figure 10.4.

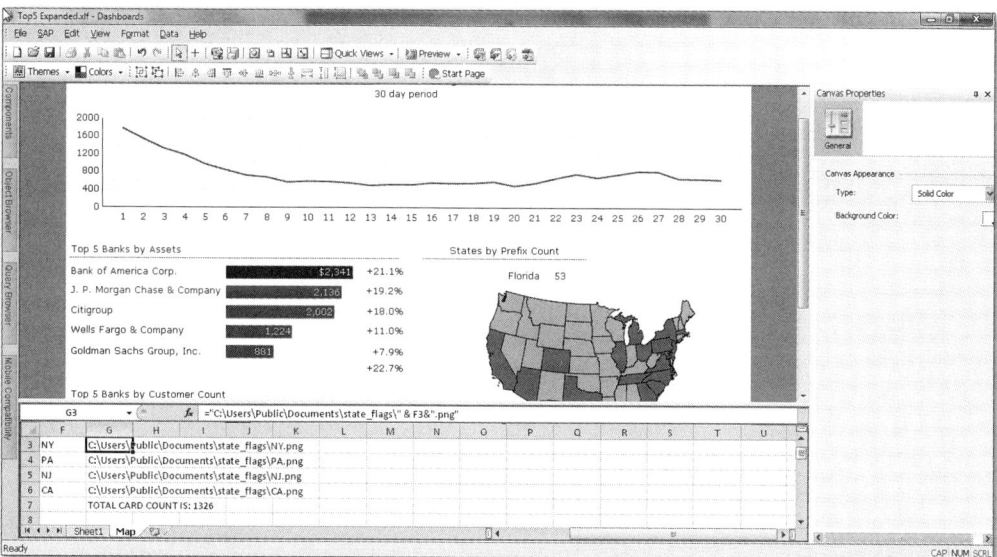

**Figure 10.3** The SAP BusinessObjects Dashboards Interface

In versions prior to SAP BusinessObjects 4.1, a new method of connecting to data was introduced. A new panel was revealed in the SAP BusinessObjects Dashboards application called the Query Browser. The Query Browser panel made available the ability to connect directly to a UNX universe or an SAP Business Explorer (hereafter, BEx) query in SAP BusinessObjects.

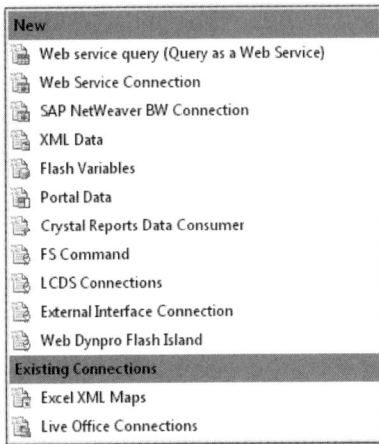

**Figure 10.4** Connection Methods Currently Available from SAP BusinessObjects Dashboards

### SAP HANA as a Dashboard Data Source

Let's transition from discussing SAP BusinessObjects Dashboards applications and the methods by which you pull data into the application, and continue with its natural progression into the types of data and sources that you can pull into the dashboard. Recall the semantic layer from Chapter 9. The semantic layer can connect to nearly any data source: relational, OLAP, SAP ERP, and so on.

#### Accessing SAP HANA Using Universes

You've seen in Chapter 9 that you can build a semantic layer on top of an SAP HANA instance. This semantic layer can take advantage of the calculation views and analytics views as well as tap directly into the relational tables that are loaded into the SAP HANA database.

From a dashboards perspective, SAP HANA is just another data source and requires no special consideration apart from understanding the structure of the required database. Connecting data from SAP HANA into your SAP BusinessObjects Dashboards application is as simple as building a semantic layer on SAP HANA and then adding a query in the Query Panel within SAP BusinessObjects Dashboards to connect to that data. Finally, you design the dashboards as you typically would by employing the same project management skills and design approaches.

Upon selecting the Query Browser panel, the designer is presented with a dialog that asks the user to log in to an SAP BusinessObjects 4.1 platform. After logging in, the designer is shown a listing of universes or BEx queries that have been published to the platform, as shown in Figure 10.5. It's important to note that the listing of universes presented doesn't include the legacy universe files (.unv).

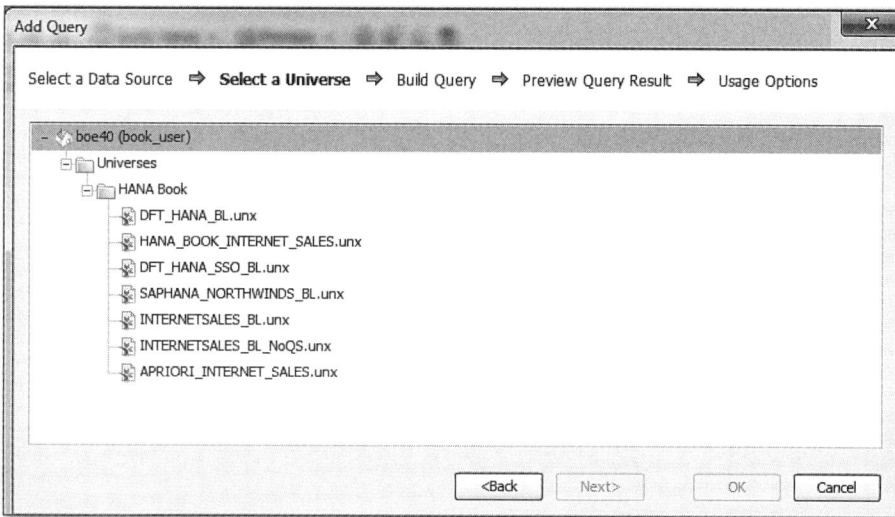

**Figure 10.5**   Listing of Universes on the SAP BusinessObjects Platform

After the designer selects the appropriate semantic layer, a dialog is presented that allows the user to build a query like the one shown in Figure 10.6. The design of the dialog shows the objects from the business layer of the semantic layer on the left side. The right side contains three panels: RESULTS OBJECTS, FILTERS, and RESULT SETS. The designer pulls objects from the business layer listing to the RESULTS SET panel. These objects will be available within the dashboard for projection into the dashboard components. To filter the data, the designer pulls the objects from the business layer listing to the FILTER panel. To perform a filter, the designer must select an operator and an operand (i.e., OBJECT: YEAR OPENED, OPERATOR: EQUAL TO, or OPERAND: 2001). The data is filtered out on the database level and only the matching records are returned. Finally, the designer can click the PREVIEW window to pull back 200 records (default) to see how the data set will appear before committing to the creation of the query.

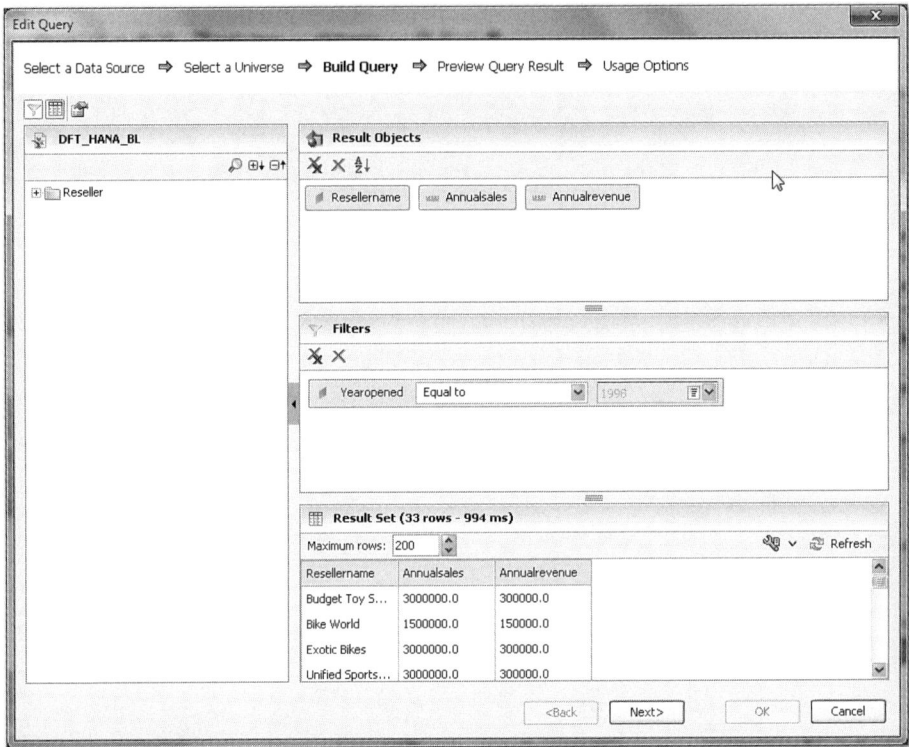

**Figure 10.6** The Edit Query Dialog

When the designer completes the query and continues on, two other screens are presented: a full window preview and the query options.

Finishing up the Query Browser process, the designer is left with a query that can be used to "direct bind" to various components in the SAP BusinessObjects Dashboards application. Introduced in SAP BusinessObjects 4.1 is a dual mode button that allows a designer to bind data directly to a range of cells with Excel. Figure 10.7 gives an example of the dual mode binding button. This has been the traditional method of interacting with data within the dashboard. The other, newer method is direct binding to a query that is built in the Query Browser. When binding a component to a query in the Query Browser, the designer effectively removes the instance of Excel from the binding path in the dashboard. Data is executed directly against the data source through the objects referenced in the query. The data is returned and displayed in the appropriate areas in the bound component. Figure 10.8 shows an example of the dashboard at design time after the data is bound.

Notice that the data associated with the direct bind is automatically displayed within the component. The result is an increase in performance and a decrease in the potential of error with binding to ranges of cells within Excel.

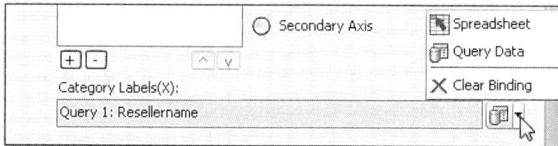

**Figure 10.7** The Binding Menu: Spreadsheet or Query Data

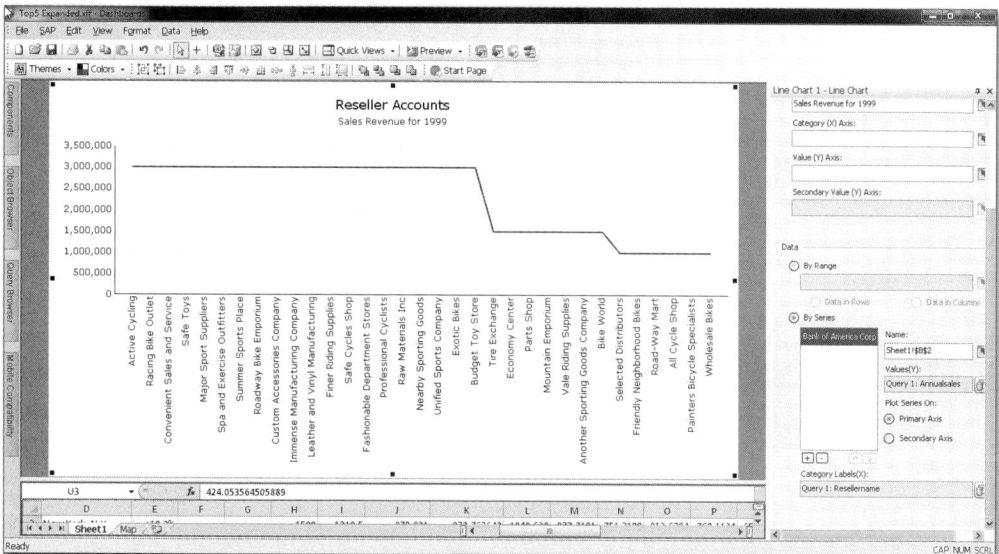

**Figure 10.8** A Dashboard that Has Been Directly Bound to a Query on SAP HANA

### Accessing SAP HANA Using Query as a Web Service

Another method to connect SAP BusinessObjects Dashboards to SAP HANA is through Query as a Web Service (QaaWS). *Web services* are methods by which applications can connect to data sources using a standard URL. Data is accessed by referencing a specially created URL that optionally accepts input parameters. The output of such a web service is determined by the developer of the web service, such as the calculation of values passed into the input parameters, a table of data returned by a method in the web service, or even no output at all if the function of the web service is to simply accept input and provide no output.

The SAP BusinessObjects version of these web services is QaaWS. SAP Business-Objects has developed the web services so that a block of data is created in a reporting tool and then published as an accessible web service on the SAP BusinessObjects platform. The web service is then provided to dashboard designers to use within the SAP BusinessObjects Dashboards application to access data.

Let's consider how this is accomplished. First of all, a QaaWS query must be generated. This query starts with the creation of an SAP BusinessObjects Web Intelligence report. The SAP BusinessObjects Web Intelligence report process is described later in Chapter 12. Following standard development procedures, the SAP BusinessObjects Web Intelligence developer generates a report on an SAP HANA data source. Because the dashboard is only concerned with tables of data, the layout of the report is inconsequential to the dashboard. The SAP BusinessObjects Web Intelligence developer creates one or more tables of data, then right-clicks on the table to be used within the dashboard, and chooses PUBLISH AS A WEB SERVICE from the context menu. The user is then prompted for the location and name of the web service to publish. The output of this process is a URL that contains multiple methods, which accept input (user credentials, filters, prompt values, etc.) and outputs tables of data (cross tabs, vertical tables, etc.).

After the URL is passed to the dashboard developer, the dashboard developer generates a dashboard using standard dashboard design methodologies. To use a web service that was previously created, go to the DATA • CONNECTIONS menu in the Dashboards application. The DATA MANAGER (see Figure 10.9) screen displays and provides a listing of connections that can be used to pull data into the dashboard. Select WEB SERVICE QUERY (QUERY AS A WEB SERVICE). The web service query is added to the listing of available data connections, and the options for a QaaWS query are shown on the right side of the interface. Provide a descriptive name, and paste the URL that was generated when the QaaWS query was published in SAP BusinessObjects Web Intelligence. Click the IMPORT button, and select the name of the method that was specified when the web service was published. The Web Service URL is automatically generated and requires no interaction from you as a designer.

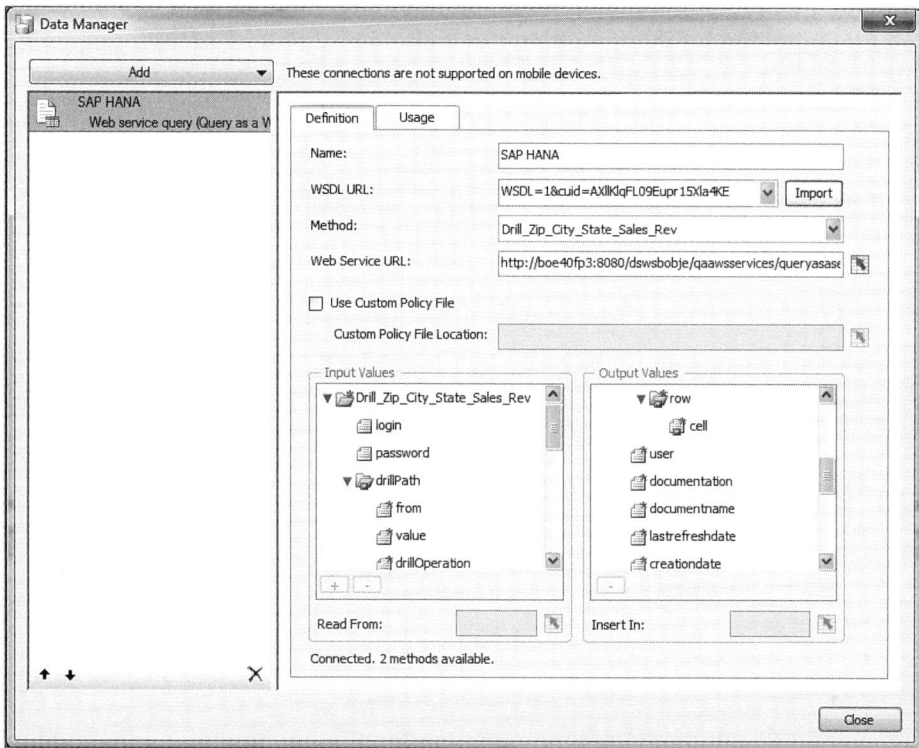

**Figure 10.9** The Dashboards Data Manager Interface—Definition Tab

The next step is to bind the INPUT VALUES and OUTPUT VALUES to control the behavior of the QaaWS query. Remember that a QaaWS query is a specialized web service that contains a "wrapper" developed by SAP. The web service standard is used for communication, but when a web service is created in SAP BusinessObjects Web Intelligence, other functions are added that make the web service a QaaWS query, such as username and password for SAP BusinessObjects authentication, prompt input, filter values, and so on. These values can be passed into the query and thus are found in the INPUT VALUES section of the query. The OUTPUT VALUES section contains the data that is passed out from the QaaWS query into the dashboard. These items include header, body, and footer data, as well as metadata elements such as refresh date, document name, creator name, and so on. These data elements are most useful to your end users when developing the dashboard to provide information on the backend data source.

The last step is to provide usage information so that the SAP BusinessObjects Dashboards application can refresh the data at the right time. In this interface, set the REFRESH BEFORE COMPONENTS ARE LOADED option shown in Figure 10.10 so that the data is imported before the components are drawn on the SAP BusinessObjects Dashboards canvas. Other options exist to refresh the data on a time interval and/or when the value of a specified cell either changes or the value becomes a specific value. For instance, if a component writes a value to cell C1 and the USAGE tab is set to update the data when the trigger cell (C1) changes, any modifications to the value in C1 will cause the data to refresh. Alternatively, if you set the USAGE settings to only update the data when cell C1 becomes the value January, then the data isn't refreshed until that value is written in C1 regardless of the other values that are written to the cell.

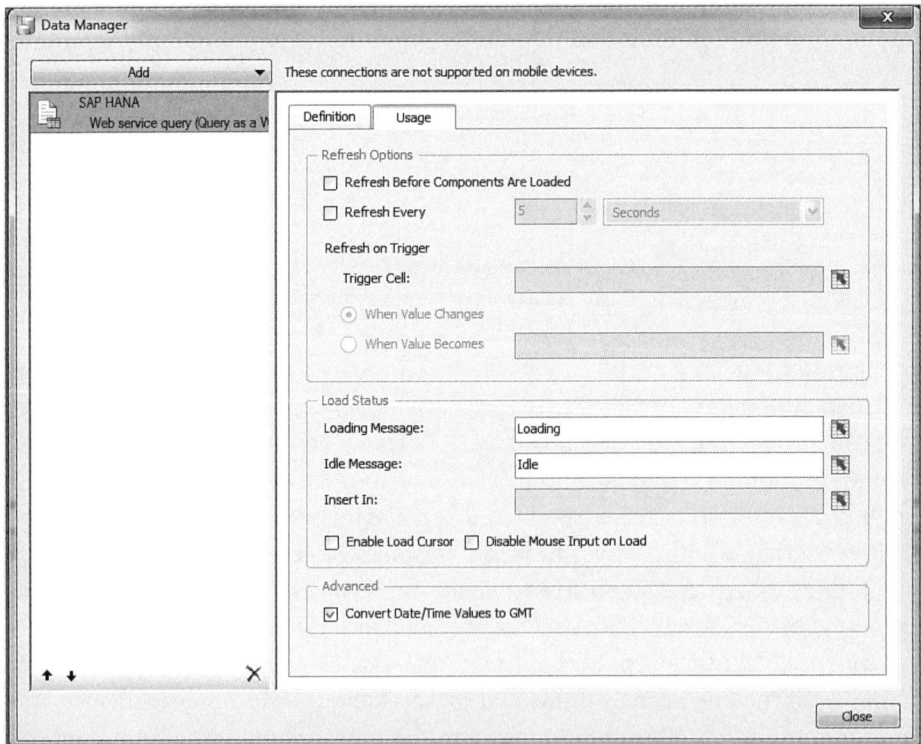

**Figure 10.10** The Dashboards Data Manager Interface—Usage Tab

*Choosing between Universes or QaaWS*

Data source selection is a part of the overall design considerations that must be handled before the development of the dashboard can start. These two methods of data access have their own advantages and disadvantages. When deciding what data source to use in a dashboarding project, consider the current inventory of data sources. Does your company currently have a large inventory of universes that should be used rather than generating a set of SAP BusinessObjects Web Intelligence reports or web service queries? On the other hand, does your company have a range of existing QaaWS queries that must be used rather than connecting directly to universes? QaaWS provides a distinct advantage of data manipulation on the SAP BusinessObjects Web Intelligence level before the data is imported into SAP BusinessObjects Dashboards. Calculations can be performed on the report level that may not be accomplished in the universe level. If this is the case, consider using QaaWS.

However, the biggest advantage in terms of performance goes to the universe queries because they can be bound directly to the dashboard. The one aspect that sets a QaaWS query apart from a direct bind to a universe is the fact that data *must* be bound to a range of cells with Excel inside of the SAP BusinessObjects Dashboards application. You should minimize the number of cells used within Excel in the dashboard due to performance reasons. Direct binding of a universe to a dashboard removes the requirement of binding a data set to a range of spreadsheet cells, eliminating the performance hit of this extra layer. Keep this in mind when planning the dashboarding project.

**Performance Note**

QaaWS requires that the designer bind data to a range of cells in Excel with the dashboard. The more Excel cells that are used, the more the performance of the dashboard is impacted. Consider direct binding using the Query Builder over the QaaWS approach to enhance performance.

## Sharing SAP BusinessObjects Dashboards

After a dashboard has been designed, it can be shared with others. The definition of "others" can vary from system to system—that is, from certain members of an organization, to the entire organization, to the general public. Designers must understand how the dashboards will be shared so they can provide an adequate picture of the various methods of sharing.

### Browser-Based Sharing

A basic feature of website design is the ability to embed various file types within a web page. A web designer can create special code that allows for the display and usage of a Flash file. Using this capability, you can take advantage of web pages, portals, widgets, and other applications that support such embedded file types. Go to File • Export • Flash (SWF) within the SAP BusinessObjects Dashboards application, and provide a location where the file will be stored. You can then embed this file within the portal of your choice.

Most often, these files are embedded into portals such as SharePoint. Other times, however, these dashboards can be embedded into web pages on corporate websites and made available to the public. Special attention must be paid in cases such as these as live refreshing of data in a dashboard against a data source will consume an SAP BusinessObjects license. Remember that you're still connecting to a semantic layer published into the SAP BusinessObjects 4.1 repository. The user must be validated and have access to the system before any data is retrieved and displayed.

The most effective and robust method of sharing a dashboard is through the SAP BusinessObjects portal, called the SAP BusinessObjects BI Launchpad. To share a completed dashboard via SAP BusinessObjects BI Launchpad, choose File • Save to Platform. Several options appear. Choosing Mobile Only publishes the dashboard as a mobile dashboard; choosing Desktop Only saves the dashboard on the platform so that it's visible only on the desktop through the SAP BusinessObjects BI Launchpad; and choosing Desktop and Mobile publishes the dashboard so that it's available on both the desktop and mobile devices.

### Mobile Sharing

Let's consider the differences between the Desktop Only and Mobile Only options. SAP BusinessObjects Dashboards is a Flash-based application. Flash is a technology that enables rich animation within sites across the web. Xcelsius was originally created as a Flash-based application to take advantage of these rich features. When the Xcelsius dashboards were published to the repository in BusinessObjects XI R2 or SAP BusinessObjects 3.1, they were published as Flash files, denoted by a .swf file extension. The original source dashboard file was stored in an Xcelsius file type, denoted by an .xlf file extension. The biggest disadvantage to this scenario was that dashboards could be published and used within the portal, but if the original files were lost, then any changes to the dashboard required a complete rebuild because the .swf file could not be edited by the Xcelsius application.

In SAP BusinessObjects 4.0, a new combined file type fixed this by including both the original source file and the compiled .swf file within the same file. When you edit the file in the SAP BusinessObjects 4.1 Dashboards application, use the .xlf original stored within the combined file. When you execute the dashboard in the SAP BusinessObjects BI Launchpad, you reference the original .xlf file, but the portal serves up the embedded .swf file.

> **Dashboards and Adobe Flash**
>
> Most mobile devices don't support Adobe Flash. SAP BusinessObjects Dashboards and SAP BusinessObjects Design Studio can export dashboards in HTML5 for usage on non-Flash mobile devices.

As of SAP BusinessObjects 4.0 SP5, Dashboards can export dashboards as HTML5, which can be executed on any mobile device that supports the standard. When you select FILE • SAVE TO PLATFORM • MOBILE ONLY or DESKTOP AND MOBILE, the application creates an HTML5 version of the dashboard stored within the original .xlf file type. Figure 10.11 shows the options available in the SAVE TO PLATFORM menu option in SAP BusinessObjects Dashboards. If the dashboard is saved as MOBILE ONLY, the user can see the dashboard on the platform, but if the user tries to execute the dashboard, a message appears that reads "Warning: This dashboard is only supported in mobile device. Please try to view it on your mobile device." The dashboard should be opened on the mobile device to be properly viewed. SAP has updated the SAP BusinessObjects BI Mobile application to allow the viewing of SAP BusinessObjects Dashboards on mobile devices. With this update, any device that can download and run the app and can connect to an SAP BusinessObjects 4.0 SP5 or higher environment can view the HTML 5 version of SAP BusinessObjects Dashboards.

> **Warning!**
>
> Not all of the components traditionally associated with SAP BusinessObjects Dashboards are available for mobile devices. Refer to the new COMPONENTS panel in the application to view a dropdown that shows the difference between ALL components and MOBILE ONLY components.

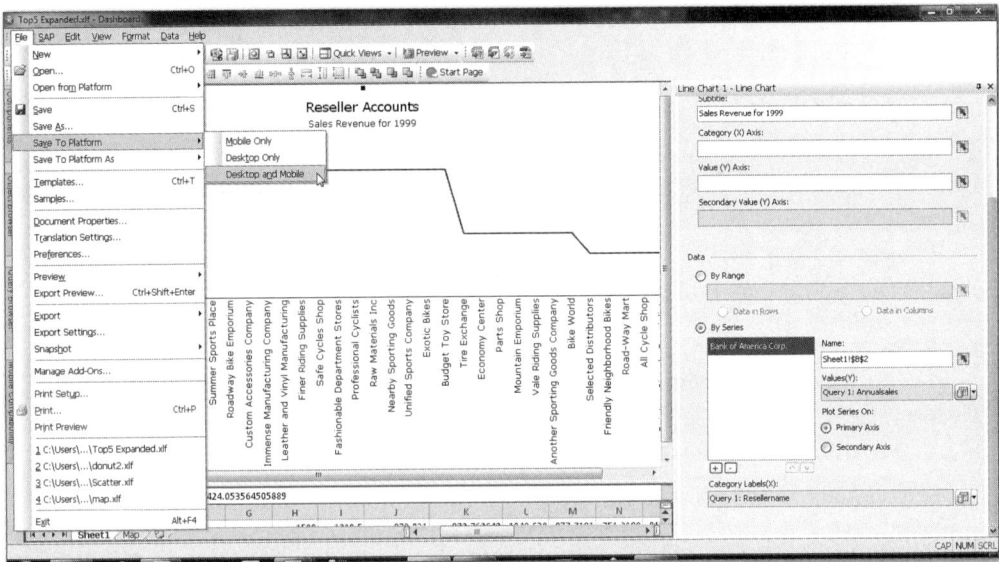

**Figure 10.11** The Save to Platform Options Available in SAP BusinessObjects Dashboards

### 10.2.2 SAP BusinessObjects Design Studio

SAP BusinessObjects Design Studio is a tool by which designers can develop dashboards with a polished, professional look. Design Studio was developed by SAP under the code name "Zen." It was released in an initial version in 2012 and officially changed its name to Design Studio. The application is based on the open source Eclipse integrated development environment (IDE).

> **Note**
>
> Eclipse allows for industrious developers to modify the code to develop a customized environment to their own specifications.

This is the case with SAP BusinessObjects Design Studio as well as the Information Design Tool (IDT) installed with the client tools for the SAP BusinessObjects BI platform.

Users familiar with the BEx Web Application Designer will notice a similarity between the familiar Web Application Designer and the new SAP BusinessObjects Design Studio. SAP BusinessObjects Design Studio is considered the next release of the application, and SAP will eventually encourage existing users to migrate to the new application. You can see how the SAP BusinessObjects Design Studio currently looks in Figure 10.12.

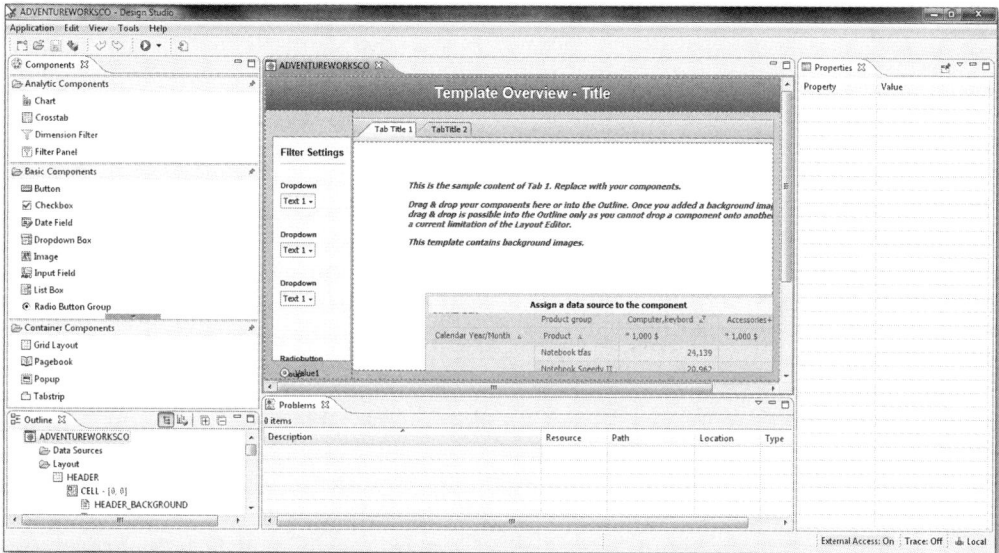

**Figure 10.12** A Typical SAP BusinessObjects Design Studio Designer Interface

## Connecting SAP BusinessObjects Design Studio to SAP HANA Data Sources

SAP BusinessObjects Design Studio allows you to connect to both SAP NetWeaver BW on SAP HANA queries as well as directly to SAP HANA systems. Using these connectivity methods, you can achieve better performance over the traditional Excel/Flash-based SAP BusinessObjects Dashboards 4.1.

### Connecting to SAP NetWeaver BW on SAP HANA

Upon launching SAP BusinessObjects Design Studio, go to the TOOLS • PREFERENCES menu item. In the PREFERENCES dialog, the choose BACKEND CONNECTIONS. The BACKEND CONNECTIONS option lists the available SAP NetWeaver BW systems as well as the existing SAP HANA sources (see Figure 10.13 in the next subsection for a look at this dialog box).

To add a new SAP NetWeaver BW system, you must have the SAP GUI installed on your local machine. On entering the SAP logon interface, you add a new system. After the system is added, SAP BusinessObjects Design Studio picks up on the new addition and adds it to the listing of available systems. When a new SAP

BusinessObjects Design Studio application is created, SAP BusinessObjects Design Studio uses one or more data sources that will be used within the application. Right-click the DATA SOURCES in the OUTLINE area in the bottom-left part of the screen, and choose NEW. Enter the connection information by clicking BROWSE and selecting the appropriate SAP NetWeaver BW system. The interface asks for credentials to access the system, and then you can select a specific data source. Finally, after the data source is added to the application, you can apply the new data source to one or more existing components.

### Connecting Directly to SAP HANA

This process can also be applied to SAP HANA data sources. The first step is to install the SAP HANA middleware on the local machine. After the middleware is installed, an Open Database Connectivity (ODBC) source is created that connects the local machine to the SAP HANA instance. In Windows, go to the ODBC Data Source Administrator. See Figure 10.13 to see how the ODBC data source looks after the SAP HANA middleware has been added. The SAP HANA middleware has been discussed in Chapter 9.

> **Tip**
>
> Open the PREFERENCES dialog in the SAP BusinessObjects Design Studio application and click the gears icon on the BACKEND CONNECTIONS dialog to open the 32-bit ODBC Data Source Administrator.

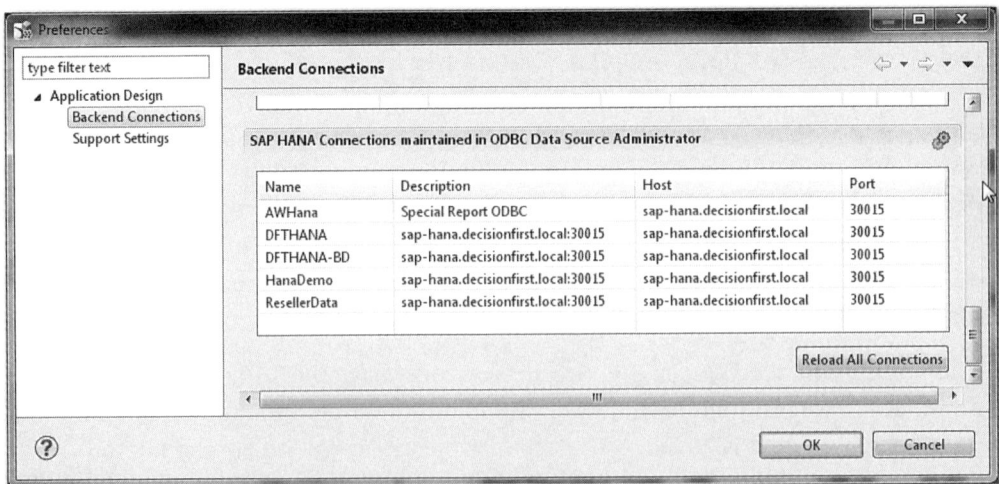

**Figure 10.13** The Backend Connections Dialog Box after ODBC is Added

### Consuming the SAP HANA Connections

After the ODBC data source has been created or the SAP NetWeaver BW on SAP HANA entry has been added in the SAP GUI, check the Preferences dialog in SAP BusinessObjects Design Studio to make sure that the data source is available. If SAP BusinessObjects Design Studio was open when the data source was created, simply click the Reload All Connections button on the Backend Connections dialog.

After the connection is created and is visible in SAP BusinessObjects Design Studio, right-click Data Sources in the Outline panel, and then select New. Click Browse beside the Connection box, and select the proper SAP HANA connection. When the connection is selected, the application prompts you for credentials—user ID, password, and language—to log in to the system. Once validated, click the Browse button beside the Data Source box, and select the desired Analytic View or Calculation View. After the data source to SAP HANA has been added, the available connection appears as shown in Figure 10.14.

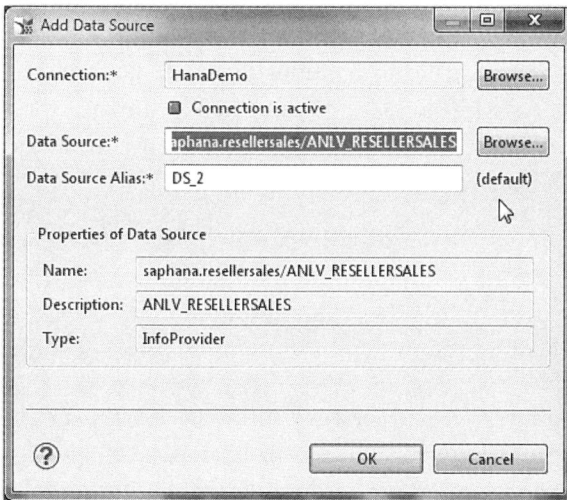

**Figure 10.14** A Completed Add Data Source Dialog

### Interactivity across Components

Typical dashboard design methodology includes multiple components within a window that tell a story. The story can range from showing which regions within the world are doing well, signified by the red/yellow/green color-coding standard, to displaying tabular information that provides summaries that executives can pick

687

up to make better informed decisions on corporate direction and policy. Regardless of the tool being used, the methodology remains the same: individual components are linked together to provide the story.

SAP BusinessObjects Design Studio adopts a new paradigm to connecting components to which traditional SAP Business Objects Dashboards designers aren't accustomed. When the dashboard is launched in SAP BusinessObjects Design Studio, the canvas is drawn and the components are added to the canvas. A series of scripts are fired off that populate the data, set the initial state of the dashboard, and finalize the drawing of the canvas so that you can begin using the dashboard. You then review the components on the canvas. Ideally, you should be able to get quick insight into the metrics being related by the dashboard without having to interact with the components at all. However, the power of the dashboard comes in its interactivity. To create the interactivity that is desired, simply select the component that will react to a click, and find the appropriate interactivity option.

There are two types of connectivity (scripted events) on the dashboard: project and components. When SAP BusinessObjects Design Studio initially loads, you can designate a series of scripts that execute to manipulate the dashboard. For instance, building a new SAP BusinessObjects Design Studio application based on an iPad template provides a series of startup scripts that populates rows from the data providers. The default lines appear as such:

```
// You can use moveDimension API methods to change the initial drill-
down of data sources
//DS_1.moveDimensionToRows("ZSALES_REGION");
//DS_1.moveDimensionToColumns("ZSALES_CHANNEL", 1);
//DS_2.moveDimensionToRows("ZCALMONTH");
```

To view this code, select the top level of the hierarchy in the OUTLINE panel in SAP BusinessObjects Design Studio. Then in the PROPERTIES panel, locate the ON STARTUP property in the EVENTS section. Clicking on the value of the ON STARTUP property makes a button available that will reveal the Script Editor.

This level of coding gives you unprecedented access and control to the components and canvas in SAP BusinessObjects Design Studio. For this reason alone, SAP BusinessObjects Design Studio qualifies as a professionally authored dashboarding tool. You can take advantage of the New Statement Wizard by pressing $\boxed{\text{Ctrl}}$+$\boxed{\text{space}}$ within the SCRIPT EDITOR dialog (Figure 10.15) to assist with the creation of a new script. If you're unfamiliar with coding in SAP BusinessObjects

Design Studio, this method can help you learn to develop more sophisticated dashboards.

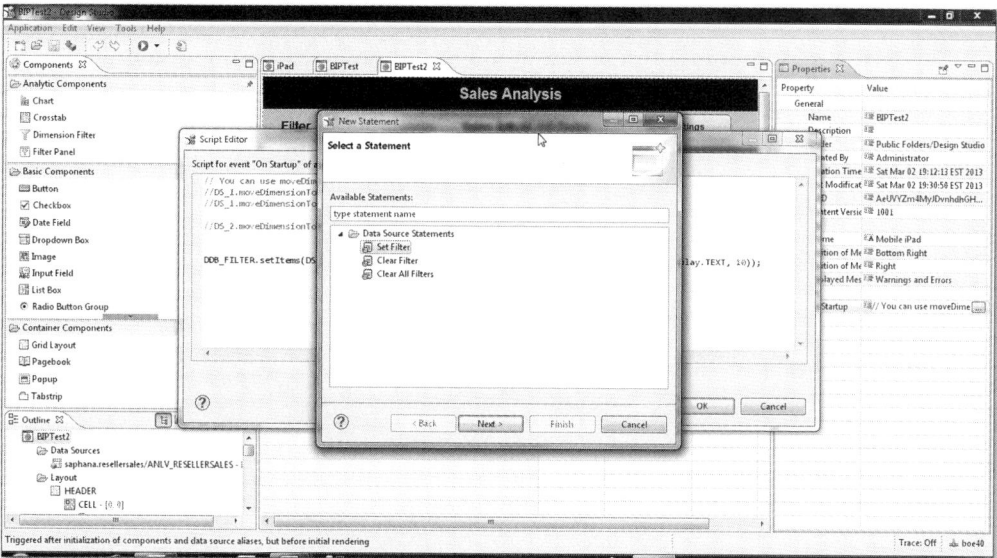

**Figure 10.15** An Example of a Script Wizard

The second type of scripted event is the component-level events. When the dashboard loads, the On Startup event assists in setting the initial view of the dashboard. You then begin interacting with the dashboard by clicking on the various components. The On Select or On Click event handles the interaction based on the type of component clicked. For instance, on the iPad template previously described, there is a SHOW SETTINGS button. Selecting the button on the canvas reveals the properties for the button. An On Click event available, so when you click the button, the script defined in this property is executed. The function of this button is to toggle a dialog that allows further interaction with the dashboard.

Executing this script methodically runs through the code line by line and executes it sequentially. First it tests to see if a specific component is showing. If the test evaluates to true, then it executes the first portion of the script; otherwise, it executes the second. The first portion of the script (when the popup is visible) hides the popup panel and then sets the text of the button to "Show Settings". An example of the SHOW SETTINGS dialog is given in Figure 10.16. The second portion of the script (when the popup is hidden) shows the popup and then sets the text of the button to "Hide Settings". This script provides interactivity on the dashboard that lends to a neat and clean interface and a more professional view for users.

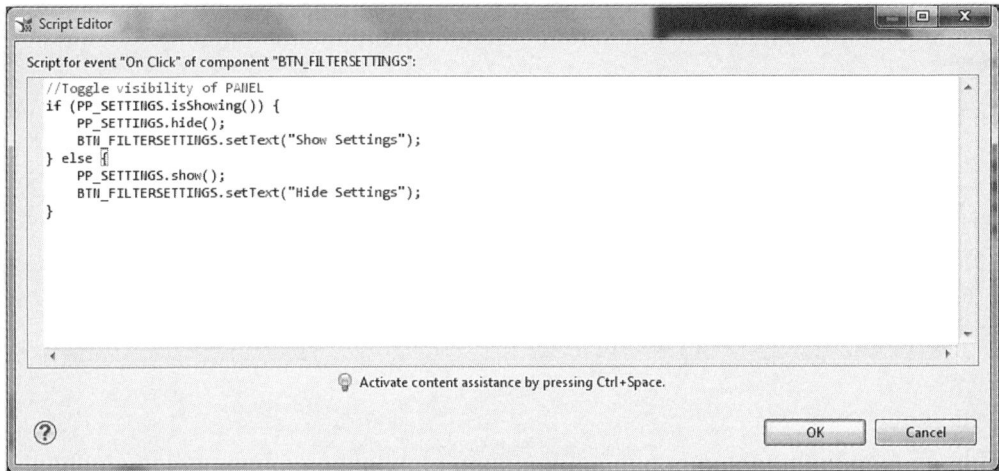

```
Script Editor

Script for event "On Click" of component "BTN_FILTERSETTINGS":

//Toggle visibility of PANEL
if (PP_SETTINGS.isShowing()) {
    PP_SETTINGS.hide();
    BTN_FILTERSETTINGS.setText("Show Settings");
} else {
    PP_SETTINGS.show();
    BTN_FILTERSETTINGS.setText("Hide Settings");
}

Activate content assistance by pressing Ctrl+Space.

OK    Cancel
```

**Figure 10.16**  The Script Editor for the Show Settings Button

### Sharing SAP BusinessObjects Design Studio Dashboards

The great news is that SAP BusinessObjects Design Studio was built from the ground up for mobile! When you design your dashboards in SAP BusinessObjects Design Studio, the output—whether it was built using a Desktop or an iPad template—is a dashboard created in HTML5. Any device, regardless of form factor, that can render web pages in HTML5 will be able to render dashboards built in SAP BusinessObjects Design Studio. No longer do you need to worry about Flash and what devices support it or about third-party applications that provide the appearance of running Flash on noncompliant devices, no matter their ease of use or simplicity.

#### Browser-Based Sharing

Figure 10.17 shows a small dashboard built in SAP BusinessObjects Design Studio against the SAP HANA Reseller data source. It simply shows a table with the year and the sales amount alongside the same data represented in a pie chart. If you click the EXECUTE LOCALLY button on the toolbar, the dashboard is then rendered in the default browser. When SAP BusinessObjects Design Studio is installed, it runs its own embedded version of Tomcat. When the browser launches, analyze the URL. You'll notice that the name of the local server is colon-delimited with the port on which Tomcat is listening. The dashboard is rendered in the browser, and you can view the source to see that it is indeed using HTML5. To share the dashboard, simply share the URL with others who require the functionality.

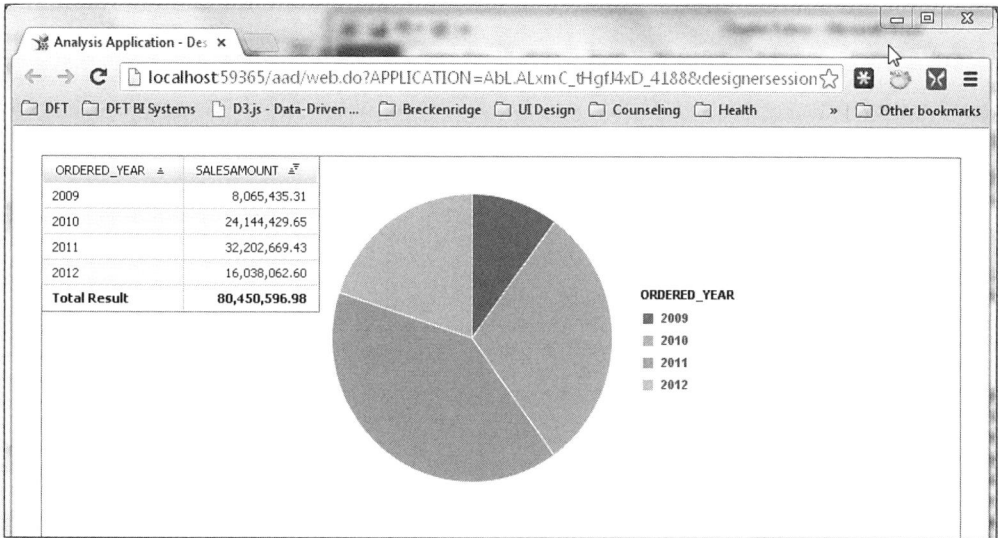

**Figure 10.17**  The HTML5 Dashboard Displayed in Google Chrome

You can also publish dashboards to the SAP BusinessObjects 4.1 platform. To do this, you must install the platform add-on for SAP BusinessObjects Design Studio. The add-on can be found in the SAP Service Marketplace alongside the installation for SAP BusinessObjects Design Studio. This adds a new Analysis Processing Server to the listing of servers in the SAP BusinessObjects Central Management Console (CMC). It also enables you to save the dashboards to the repository. You must also ensure that SAP BusinessObjects Design Studio is at SP1 at the bare minimum.

In SAP BusinessObjects Design Studio, choose TOOLS • APPLICATION DESIGN, and then select CONNECT TO BI PLATFORM in the STARTUP MODE line in the GENERAL section. This option displays a dialog when opening SAP BusinessObjects Design Studio to allow you to connect to the platform. The dialog also offers the ability to skip the logon if the dashboard will be developed locally.

To publish a dashboard to the SAP BusinessObjects BI platform, open SAP Business-Objects Design Studio and connect to the platform where the SAP BusinessObjects Design Studio add-on was installed. Either open an existing dashboard or develop a new dashboard to meet your requirements. Save the dashboard by choosing APPLICATION • SAVE AS. A dialog appears giving you the option to store the application

691

on either your FAVORITES or in the PUBLIC FOLDERS on the platform. Select the location on the platform, and then click SAVE. See Figure 10.18 for an example of the SAVE AS dialog.

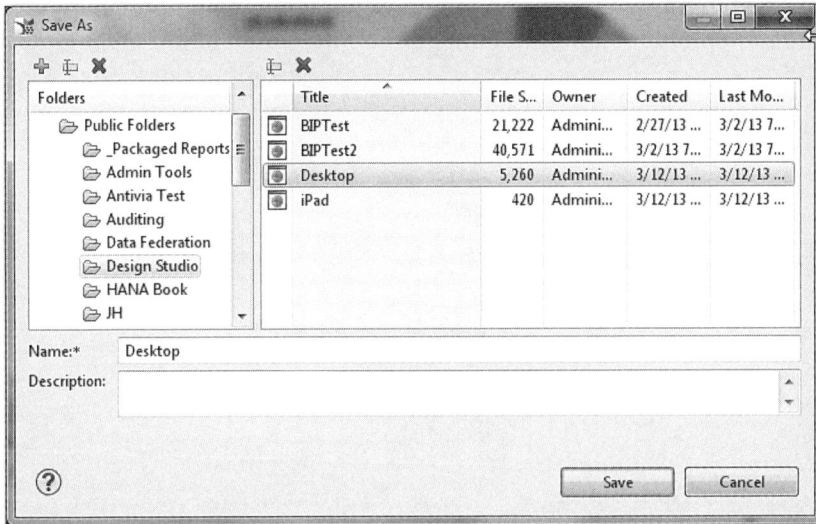

**Figure 10.18**  The Save As Dialog in SAP BusinessObjects Design Studio

You may now navigate to the BI LAUNCH PAD screen and execute the dashboard in the browser. Notice that the URL is now referencing your SAP BusinessObjects BI platform instead of the locally installed and running instance of Tomcat. Figure 10.19 shows an example of the dashboard in preview mode within the browser.

### Mobile Sharing
Now let's take this one step further. Let's assign the newly published DESKTOP application to the MOBILE category.

To do this, navigate to the DESKTOP application in the proper folder, right-click, and select CATEGORIES. Select the MOBILE category in CORPORATE CATEGORIES, and click OK. If this category doesn't exist, contact your SAP BusinessObjects BI 4.1 administrator to ensure that you're on the latest version of the SAP Business-Objects 4.1 platform. Connect to your instance of SAP BusinessObjects using the SAP BusinessObjects BI Mobile application on the mobile device of your choice. You'll see the new DESKTOP application as an option in the SAP BusinessObjects BI Mobile application. Executing the DESKTOP application will display the same visualization on your mobile device. Going mobile has never been so easy!

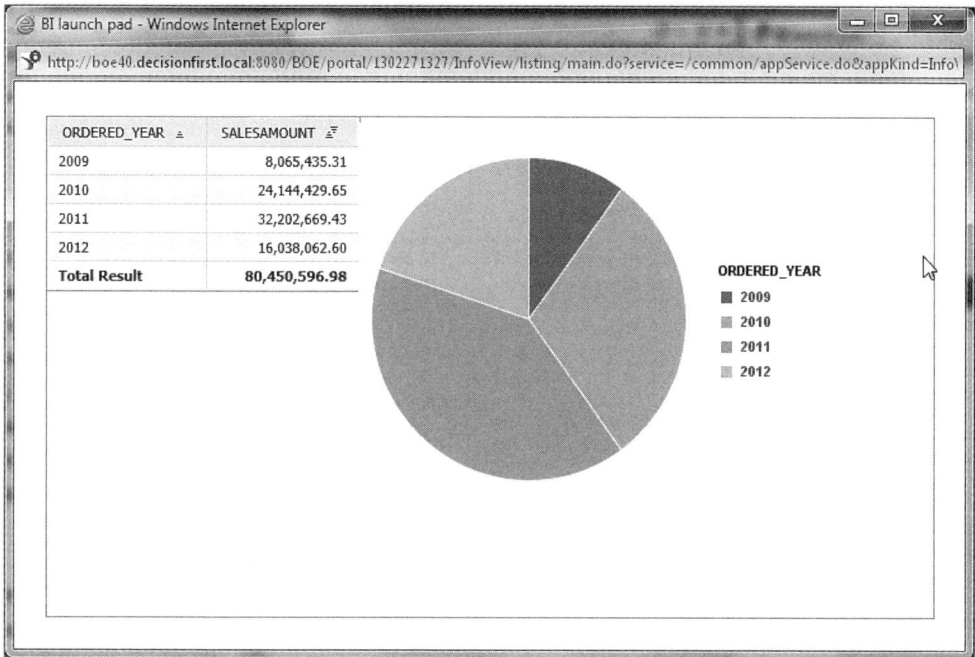

**Figure 10.19** A Dashboard Preview in Internet Explorer

## 10.2.3 Bringing It All Together

We've covered two very powerful dashboarding tools used by professionals to deliver dashboards that provide business value in a polished interface. The two tools each have their own strengths and weaknesses, but they both fill a need.

But how do you decide which tool to use? If the outcome is so similar, then there must be a way to decide which application can best answer predetermined questions.

First of all, consider your data source. Does your data come from a source other than SAP NetWeaver BW on SAP HANA or SAP HANA itself? If so, you can only use SAP BusinessObjects Dashboards because SAP BusinessObjects Design Studio only supports SAP NetWeaver BW and SAP HANA. Other data sources must be implemented through SAP BusinessObjects Dashboards.

Second, do you need to take your dashboards mobile? The answer to this question isn't as cut and dried as it used to be. SAP BusinessObjects Dashboards has always been Flash-based application that required third-party tools to render dashboards on noncompatible devices. This is no longer the case in SAP BusinessObjects 4.0 SP5 and higher due to the implementation of HTML5 dashboards. The biggest caveat is the number of components that are compatible with HTML5. Check the types of available components to ensure that they meet your requirements before choosing your tool. SAP BusinessObjects Design Studio is built natively for mobile, but the visualizations may not be as robust as you desire. This is very quickly changing due to the fact that SAP BusinessObjects Design Studio is still a very new application and is growing day by day.

Next, evaluate the audience that will use the dashboard and the user requirements. If the dashboards will be viewed by the general public (external customers) or by C-level executives, chances are the design of the dashboard needs to be as professional as possible. This attribute typically requires a more polished dashboard that is associated with dashboards built in the SAP BusinessObjects Dashboards application. SAP BusinessObjects Design Studio dashboards are still graphically evolving and will eventually become the cornerstone of PADs.

Finally, consider the experience that the resources in your company currently possess. Do you have in-house resources that are knowledgeable in SAP BusinessObjects Dashboards? Do you not have any experience in-house?

Find the answers to these questions, and you should have a better understanding of which tool should be used for your dashboarding project.

## 10.3 Case Study: Creating a Dashboard

AdventureWorks Cycle Company is in the business of building and distributing bicycles. The bicycles are created by the company and distributed via multiple regional distributorships, each managed by a regional manager. The company wants to monitor the system to determine overall sales figures and to proactively respond to fluctuations in specific KPIs. The company isn't sure of what tools are available or how to even start such a project. The resulting dashboard will be made available to the regional managers and executives.

### 10.3.1 Gathering Requirements

The requirements-gathering phase begins with standard questions, which will in turn prompt others. The objective is to create a discussion that is influenced by varying viewpoints to elicit the necessary information.

The first thing to consider is the project as a whole. The main requirement is to monitor sales data and provide input back to the regional managers and executives on the performance of the company. Which metrics are most important to the business? What sort of visualizations can be used to represent these metrics? Are there any trending analyses involved? Is it more than just charts and tables? Does the dashboard need some color-coding or trending icons that provide instantaneous feedback?

In our case study, a project manager, a dashboarding/visualization expert, two expert users/end users, and a database administrator are gathered in a conference room with a whiteboard to take notes. The project manager begins by opening the meeting and outlining the purpose of the meeting. He then asks everyone in the room to introduce themselves and talk about what they want to get out of the project. After the introductions are complete, the dashboarding/visualization expert then leads off the meeting and asks the initial question: "What are we trying to track?"

The two experts state that the sales figures for the entire country have dipped over the past year. They want to use a dashboard to track sales revenues for the entire country along with the regional breakdowns of the same data. They want to include month-over-month trending to determine if there are any regions that are trending negatively (sales are decreasing).

The leader then captures that data on a whiteboard and continues listening to the conversations in the room. With a simple metric to be captured, they can then begin visualizing the data on a whiteboard, considering how the data will be used. The AdventureWorks team wants the initial view of the data to include a visual of a map of the continental United States with a range of color codes (a choropleth map) showing the different sales figures for the various states. Regional icons can also be toggled to show the appropriate sales numbers.

## 10.3.2 Storyboarding

After the requirements are gathered, the storyboarding process can begin. Storyboarding is a process where the overall flow of a visualization is determined. It begins with the initial state of the dashboard. When the dashboard first loads, what is displayed? Ideally, the end users should be able to view the dashboard and derive some sort of value from the initial view. The dashboard can also provide a bit of drill down so that more information can be determined from the initial view.

Figure 10.20 shows a first view of the potential solution. It identifies metrics (Sales Revenue) and the divisions used (State, Region, and Country). The AdventureWorks team also brainstormed that they need to see the refresh date on the dashboard to inform users of the "freshness" of the data.

The design includes a placeholder for the corporate logo. This also starts the conversation about the required branding and other logos on the dashboard.

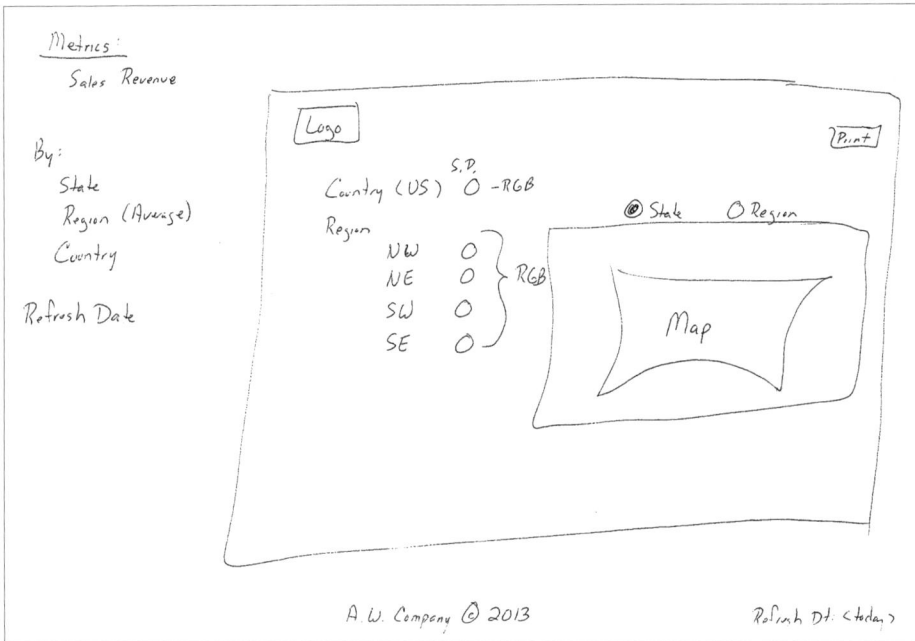

**Figure 10.20**   A Storyboarding Process Using a Whiteboard

### 10.3.3   Iterative Process

Now that the team has an understanding of the outcome of the dashboarding project along with a first iteration of the dashboard drawn on a whiteboard, the dashboard designer begins with an initial iteration of the dashboard.

**Iteration 1**

First, the designer must decide what tool to use to build the dashboard by considering the requirements (slicing data, graphical map, and color-coded icons) and the capabilities of the dashboarding tools available from SAP. SAP BusinessObjects

Design Studio is a new product currently in its 1.0 release. SAP BusinessObjects Design Studio can project tables and a range of charts and has the native capability of going mobile on non-Flash mobile devices, but currently it has no ability to use score cards, symbology, or geographic components. The ideal application for this type of visualization is SAP BusinessObjects Dashboards due to the rich set of components available to render the data as required.

So the designer opens the SAP BusinessObjects Dashboards application and begins laying out the components according to the sketches derived from the requirements phase. The designer also works with the database administrators to understand the data that is required and the form it will take for the most effective use in the dashboard. Because mobility is a requirement, the dashboard designer plans the development of the dashboard using only the set of components that are available for usage on mobile devices.

The result of this session is a dashboard that can be presented back to the original group for discussion and improvement (see Figure 10.21). The designer can also continue the discussion with the database administrators on the structure of the data. The designer has an initial understanding of what the data should look like (see Figure 10.22) and can provide the database admins with this picture.

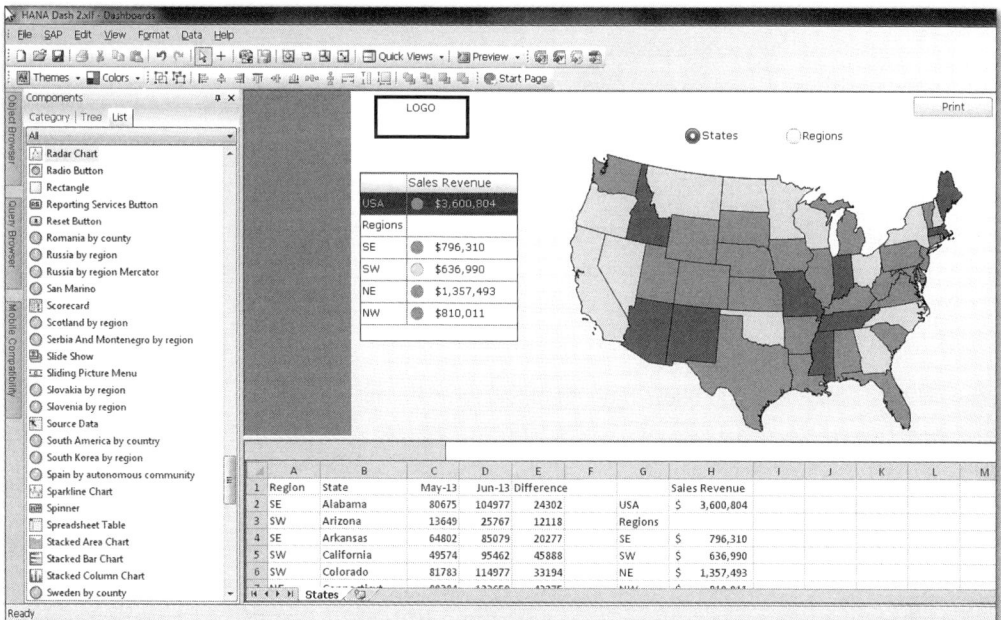

**Figure 10.21** The Dashboard Result of the First Iteration

| ◢ | A | B | C | D | E | F | G |
|---|---|---|---|---|---|---|---|
| 1 | Region | State | May-13 | Jun-13 | Difference | | |
| 2 | SE | Alabama | 84507 | 80580 | -3927 | | |
| 3 | SW | Arizona | 13955 | 21215 | 7260 | | |
| 4 | SE | Arkansas | 30203 | 45703 | 15500 | | |
| 5 | SW | California | 74169 | 19499 | -54670 | | |
| 6 | SW | Colorado | 19762 | 96349 | 76587 | | |
| 7 | NE | Connecticut | 99105 | 42167 | -56938 | | |
| 8 | NE | Delaware | 62188 | 18007 | -44181 | | |
| 9 | SE | Florida | 27372 | 65120 | 37748 | | |
| 10 | SE | Georgia | 28912 | 39110 | 10198 | | |
| 11 | NE | Idaho | 11058 | 62306 | 51248 | | |
| 12 | NE | Illinois | 44056 | 40563 | -3493 | | |
| 13 | NE | Indiana | 20143 | 32993 | 12850 | | |
| 14 | NE | Iowa | 25201 | 79773 | 54572 | | |
| 15 | SW | Kansas | 13648 | 15120 | 1472 | | |
| 16 | SE | Kentucky | 90974 | 93205 | 2231 | | |
| 17 | SE | Louisiana | 41411 | 40992 | -419 | | |
| 18 | NE | Maine | 27988 | 41749 | 13761 | | |
| 19 | NE | Maryland | 58600 | 67171 | 8571 | | |
| 20 | NE | Massachusetts | 79140 | 36609 | -42531 | | |
| 21 | NE | Michigan | 38143 | 98015 | 59872 | | |
| 22 | NW | Minnesota | 87608 | 49816 | -37792 | | |
| 23 | SE | Mississippi | 70502 | 52776 | -17726 | | |
| 24 | SE | Missouri | 60331 | 85428 | 25097 | | |

| ◄ ◄ ► ►| | Sales Revenue | **States** | 🖑 |

**Figure 10.22**  An Initial View of the Data from the First Iteration

The discussion then proceeds with the original team to review the first iteration of the dashboard and data. At this point, the team should have a better understanding of the overall flow of the dashboard and how the users can interact. Feedback is gathered from the users on what works and what doesn't work. If the users see that the components are easy to read and understand, the designer can then proceed to the second iteration if the group agrees with the design. However, since this is the first iteration, the team can completely throw out this design and start again. The first iteration is for discovery and doesn't necessarily mean that any of the results will come across into the next iteration.

In this meeting, the users have decided that the dashboard design is good, and the designer can proceed with the second phase using the first iteration as a design. The designer can then work with the database administrators to begin finalizing the data and determine how the data will be linked into the dashboard. Branding, colors, and logos for the next iteration of the dashboard are also discussed. As a last step in the process, the designer receives sign-off (either verbal or written) that the first iteration is complete and that the second can begin.

### Iteration 2

Once again, the designer can begin from scratch to rebuild a new prototype or can continue with the results from iteration 1. In this case study, the project team has decided to continue working with the prototype that was presented to them.

The designer sets up time with the database team to receive the results from the database pull and expose the data so that it's available to the dashboard. The database team builds an SAP HANA analysis view that provides the data for the designer to use in the dashboard. If one isn't already built, a semantic layer is constructed on top of the SAP HANA database. This semantic layer can be used to pull the data into the dashboard. The designer would bind the summary data directly to the scorecard, but he must write the state data to a range of cells in the spreadsheet to bind it to the map. This is due to the fact that some components aren't designed to use direct query binding.

The designer applies the branding and logos to the dashboard and binds all of the data to the components and spreadsheet. Any of the issues that were uncovered in the iteration 1 design review are handled, and the dashboard is updated. The original design team is then called back together to review the second iteration. This iteration should be nearly production ready with few, if any, outstanding issues. The dashboard shown in Figure 10.23 as the result from iteration 2 is presented to the original project team. The designer and team discuss the dashboard and address any outstanding issues. After the issues are addressed, the designer receives the official sign-off to begin iteration 3.

### Iteration 3

In this final iteration, the designer handles any of the outstanding issues that were discovered in the review phase of iteration 2. At this point, the designer should have a final decision on graphical, functional, and data design. The dashboard is cleaned up, and all aspects of its design are finalized. The designer also opens the SAP BusinessObjects BI Mobile application on supported Apple and Android devices to verify that the connectivity and functionality works as expected. At the end of iteration 3, a production-ready dashboard should be ready to use by the end users. It's highly recommended that the dashboard go through a quality assurance (QA) phase at the end of the third iteration to ensure that the dashboard fully meets the users' requirements and expectations.

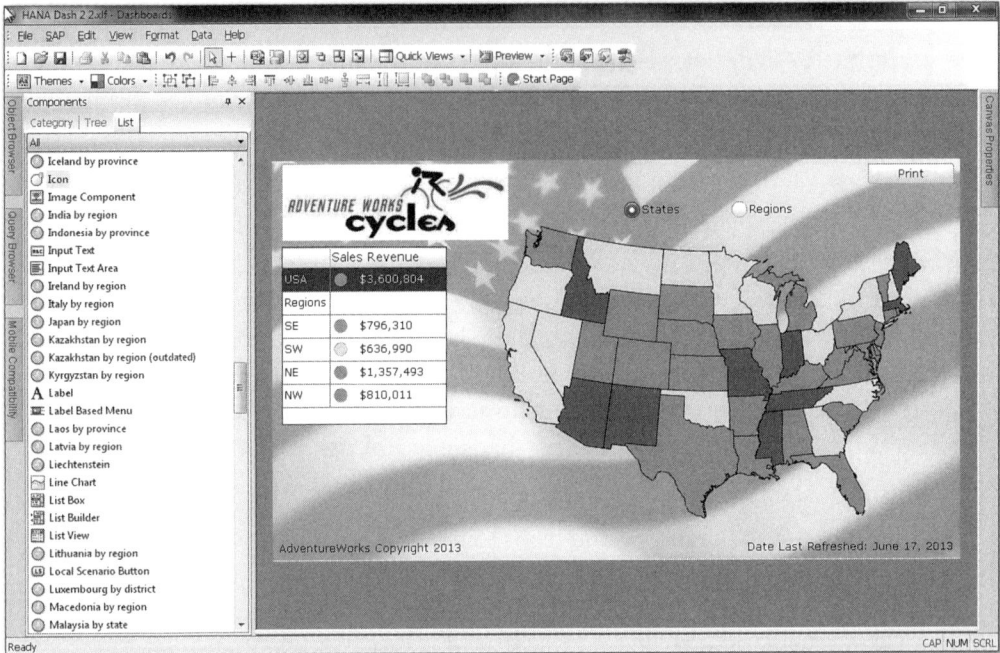

**Figure 10.23**  The Result of Iteration 2

## 10.4  Summary

In this chapter, we introduced the concept of professionally authored dashboards (PADs). As visualization requirements and available technologies evolve, various methods of generating required analytics will become more robust and useful. As professionals, we must understand the capabilities of the self-service dashboarding tools and the tools that are intended to deliver content via trained and experienced developers.

Consider the two tools that we've discussed in this chapter—SAP BusinessObjects Design Studio and SAP BusinessObjects Dashboards (formerly Xcelsius)—and how these two tools are similar to one another. They both provide robust, interactive dashboarding experiences that quickly and efficiently allow end users to derive valuable business knowledge with little or no interactivity.

The SAP BusinessObjects Dashboards application has been around for about 10 years now and has been put through its paces in the business world. The application has its own reputation in the industry. Books have been written and conferences have been solely on the topic of SAP BusinessObjects Dashboards. It's a well-established dashboarding standard.

SAP BusinessObjects Design Studio has been available for less than a year now and has extraordinary potential to initially complement SAP BusinessObjects Dashboards and eventually combine and even take over for the dashboarding application. According to the SAP Product Roadmap, SAP BusinessObjects Dashboards and SAP BusinessObjects Design Studio are on nearly parallel yet converging paths. SAP BusinessObjects Dashboards will continue to be available and supported, but SAP BusinessObjects Design Studio is just starting to hit the market and will grow very quickly.

When code name "Zen" (renamed to Design Studio) hit the market, a rumor circulated that it would be the "new Xcelsius," and many wondered whether it was wise to invest the time and money into the development of Xcelsius dashboards with Zen on the horizon. From our perspective, the answer at the time was an emphatic "yes." It's important to remember that SAP BusinessObjects Dashboards (Xcelsius) is still a supported tool by SAP and if your corporation has a need for dashboards generated by this type of tool, by all means start or continue development on the project with the SAP BusinessObjects Dashboards tool.

Keep in mind, however, that if your company has a mobile strategy, you must understand which components in SAP BusinessObjects Dashboards support mobility. SAP BusinessObjects Dashboards is still a Flash-based tool, but with the new HTML5 export option, not all of the components have been designed for HTML5. If the components that aren't supported on HTML5 are still required by your corporate dashboards, you'll have no choice than to go with a third-party tool that provides the ability to view Flash content on devices that don't support Flash (i.e., iPad, iPhone). There are several tools on the market, each with their strengths and weaknesses and varying price points.

Also remember that SAP BusinessObjects Design Studio is going to continually grow and expand and provide more capabilities in terms of design and functionality of dashboards. SAP BusinessObjects Design Studio dashboards are natively generated in HTML5 and supported within any web browser on any device that supports the HTML5 standard. Eventually, the two applications will converge, but that is well into the future, and there is no need to postpone current requirements just because of these timelines.

Regardless of the tool that you select to generate these dashboards, the processes and the iterative steps that we've outlined in this chapter can apply to the design of the dashboard. A knowledgeable dashboard designer must understand the difference between the two design tools and be prepared to advise the end users on the advantages and disadvantages of each. The well-informed dashboard designer may even determine that the requirements can be fulfilled using self-service dashboarding without the need for a professionally authored dashboarding project at all! Using this approach, we can be assured that the correct tool will be used, and the dashboard will be designed according to proven practices. The combination of these skills and communications will ensure that your dashboard is well designed, warmly received, and highly successful.

In the next chapter, we turn our attention to using a self-service business intelligence solution powered by SAP HANA.

*Unleash the power and flexibility of a self-service business intelligence solution powered by SAP HANA for easy access to massive data sets in real time.*

# 11 Data Exploration and Self-Service Analytics with SAP HANA

So far in this book, we've addressed how you can load, cleanse, model, and secure your data with SAP HANA. In this chapter, we discuss the role that self-service data exploration and visualization tools play in delivering analysis and visualization of your data to a broad audience of users—both sophisticated data analysts and general business consumers. To accomplish this, we'll introduce you to two key tools in the SAP BusinessObjects product portfolio: SAP BusinessObjects Explorer 4.x (Section 11.2) and SAP Lumira 1.x (Section 11.3).

This chapter begins with a discussion of data exploration and the role that self-service analytics play (Section 11.1). We then discuss the technical aspects of these two SAP BusinessObjects product portfolio tools—and how to leverage them in conjunction with an SAP HANA appliance, including how this scenario provides significant benefits over the use of these tools in a standalone configuration. In Section 11.4, we address how these tools can be leveraged in a mobile environment to provide on-demand data to a modern mobile workforce. Finally, the chapter concludes with a case study where we walk through the complete implementation of a solution delivering mobilized analytics on corporate sales data, including the secured delivery of relevant data to different members of the workforce (Section 11.5).

## 11.1 What Is Data Exploration and Self-Service Analytics?

Throughout most of the history of business intelligence (BI), end users and data analysts were beholden to IT or a dedicated data warehousing BI department to provide them with information. This usually resulted in users specifying report definitions to IT, followed by IT spending possibly weeks implementing these requests with a traditional reporting tool such as SAP Crystal Reports.

In later years, ad hoc query and analysis tools such as Web Intelligence came on the market. These tools allowed some sophisticated data analysts to do their own reporting and querying of the data warehouse environment. However, these tools still required a high level of end user training to leverage them fully, and the time it took to answer relatively straightforward business questions was still too high.

Roughly parallel with the development of ad hoc query and analysis tools was the introduction of online analytical processing (OLAP) tools. These tools offered relatively good user experience for slicing and dicing data and performing analysis, but they required extensive precalculation of results and didn't allow for the easy addition of new data into the analysis. They too suffered from a fairly steep learning curve.

This situation left a hole in the BI toolbox, a hole which is filled today by a class of tools that provides users the ability to easily explore and filter data, perform analysis and visualization on that data, and rapidly expand and integrate additional data into the analysis when necessary, without the need to go back to IT for additional resources.

Within the SAP BusinessObjects portfolio, this need is satisfied by two tools: SAP BusinessObjects Explorer, a tool aimed at the general business consumer, and SAP Lumira, a tool aimed at the dedicated data analyst or power user. We'll examine each of these tools in detail in the later sections of this chapter.

### 11.1.1 Self-Service Access for General Business and Power Users

Let's examine the self-service use case for the general business user in more detail. These users often have a variety of ad hoc questions that need to be answered with corporate data, such as the following: What were the total sales for my product line last month? Are we on track to meet our quarterly goal? What about a regional breakdown of those sales to see if we need to focus our efforts more in a particular region?

You can obviously build a report on behalf of this user that answers these questions and more, but by the time you finish that report, the interest of the business will likely have changed, and you'll need to produce an entirely new report. Over time, this scenario has traditionally led to a proliferation of many distinct reports, leaving business users the unpleasant task of sifting through the many reports available to find the one that answers the current question—or giving up in frustration.

Users need an interface that allows them to easily and visually pick the content they are interested in at the moment from the vast array of data available to the business and add some basic visualization to that data so that it's in a form that is easily consumed and interpreted. In this example, the user simply wants to see the summation of sales for a specific product line for a specific date range and then break that down by a sales region dimension.

Given an appropriate tool, users won't need the help of IT to produce this answer, and it will take them no more than a few minutes to access this information. In fact, users can access the information on the fly in the midst of a meeting where the question about the data came up in the first place using a mobile tablet device or laptop. This is the scenario end users can experience with SAP BusinessObjects Explorer on SAP HANA.

## 11.1.2  Comparing Self-Service and Professionally Authored Content

It's important that we make a distinction between the use cases described in the previous section and the use cases for professionally authored dashboards. It's true that both business scenarios lead to the delivery of visualized information—that is, charts and graphs—but there are significant differences in the consumption scenarios.

In the self-service case that we are addressing here, the user is typically looking for a very specific piece of information pertinent to an active business question. This is more likely to be an operational concern than a strategic question about the business. Tomorrow, the user may have a totally different question, thus the ad hoc nature of the consumption.

The alternative scenario we are examining here of a data analyst exploring a data set looking for patterns of strategic interest is unique in that the value of the output is unknown at the start of the analysis. If the user can't identify a useful pattern, he must reexamine the hypotheses and go back to do further analysis.

These examples contrast heavily with the business case for professionally authored dashboards. Professionally authored content is typically reserved for operational dashboards reporting on data that has a well-established value and pattern of usage. In these cases, the user isn't going to ask a different question tomorrow. The user has a well-defined set of data that he needs access to in the same way every time. In this case, taking the time and resources necessary to craft a custom delivery mechanism is worthwhile because it will be paid back in time savings from the user community throughout the life of the tool's consumption.

For data of strategic interest, the same theory applies. After a data analyst has successfully identified data of strategic value, and possibly after it has first been shared with others via a self-service solution to prove its value, it then becomes worthwhile to invest the additional effort in the delivery of a professionally authored solution dedicated to that data set with a tool that offers a level of flexibility and design choice beyond what can be accomplished with a self-service focused tool.

## 11.2   Introduction to SAP BusinessObjects Explorer

Now that we've established the business scenarios in which a tool like SAP Business-Objects Explorer can be used, we'll introduce you to the technical and functional details of the tool. We'll discuss the development background of the product, which helps place the tool in context with the rest of the SAP BusinessObjects suite, its system architecture, and the functional components that make up the user interface (UI) and interaction scenarios with the product. We'll particularly focus on the distinction between using SAP BusinessObjects Explorer with SAP HANA and using it with data extracted from a traditional database.

Explorer was first introduced to the Business Objects product suite near the end of the XI R2 product line. The tool was acquired by Business Objects, prior to the acquisition of Business Objects by SAP, and was originally referred to as Polestar. You may still see some documentation and files reference the Polestar name. Initially, the tool was designed as its own standalone BI tool, but Business Objects later integrated it into the broader Business Objects platform and added support to the tool for accessing Business Objects universes. In the most recent editions of the tool, support has been added for direct access to SAP HANA and SAP NetWeaver BW Accelerator (BWA) systems. The addition of support for SAP HANA vastly increased the amount of data that the product can access and the speed with which that information can be delivered to end users.

The SAP BusinessObjects Explorer application uses a number of terms and concepts that aren't seen in other BI tools:

▶ **Information Space**
As one of the two main content types produced with the SAP BusinessObjects Explorer tool, it represents a set of data consisting of measures and dimensions. End users "explore" an Information Space using SAP BusinessObjects Explorer. You can think of an Information Space as simply the results of a large query presented to the user in an accessible manner.

▶ **Exploration View Set**
The second of the two main content types produced using the SAP Business-Objects Explorer tool consists of a set of visualizations that are based on one or more Information Spaces. The visualizations are organized into individual pages called Views.

▶ **Facet**
This is a synonym for a dimension in other BI tools. The reason for the unusual name is historical and comes from one of the underlying technologies that SAP BusinessObjects Explorer is based on: Apache Lucene.

▶ **Index**
This refers to the collection of the index files generated by SAP BusinessObjects Explorer for each Information Space. The index stores metadata describing the structure and content of the Information Space, such as the list of facets and their values. For the non-SAP HANA scenario, the index also stores a cached version of the data set for the Information Space. Indexing is the process by which an index is generated and is performed by the index server.

Let's apply these terms to the SAP BusinessObjects Explorer architecture and workflows.

## 11.2.1 SAP BusinessObjects Explorer System Architecture

Architecturally, SAP BusinessObjects Explorer consists of several backend services, which we'll detail later; a web application that mediates client access to those services; and a UI created using the Adobe Flex programming environment. The Flex environment results in a UI that leverages the Flash player found in most modern browsers. In addition, SAP has added an Apple iPad version of the UI that runs natively on that device. This allows users of those devices to access SAP Business-Objects Explorer in a mobile environment due to the lack of Flash on iPads.

Together, these components interact to provide the highly interactive user experience that is the cornerstone of the self-service usage model. In the next few sections, we examine the functions of the various components and how they interact, and make note of where those functions deviate in an SAP HANA-supported scenario.

### SAP BusinessObjects Explorer Backend Services

Four backend services perform the actual work of the SAP BusinessObjects Explorer application. These components cooperate with each other to generate the indexed data structures used by SAP BusinessObjects Explorer and to respond to incoming requests for information from the web application tier. They sit at the heart of the application, as shown in Figure 11.1, and are described in the following list:

▶ **Explorer Master Server**
This service is similar to the SAP BusinessObjects Central Management Service (CMS) in that it's responsible for managing and coordinating the activities of the other SAP BusinessObjects Explorer services.

▶ **Explorer Indexing Server**
This service is responsible for generating the local indexes that describe the data sets served by SAP BusinessObjects Explorer to end users. In an SAP HANA-supported scenario, the work of this component is greatly reduced. You'll see this in more detail later.

▶ **Explorer Exploration Server**
This service is responsible for dealing with the interactive requests made by end users as they view and consume SAP BusinessObjects Explorer content. The Exploration server consumes the indexes generated by the Indexing server.

▶ **Explorer Search Server**
This service handles requests by end users to search for content in the SAP BusinessObjects Explorer index. This server also consumes the index produced by the Indexing server.

These server applications run in and are managed by the broader SAP BusinessObjects platform architecture. This is similar to the way that SAP Crystal Reports, SAP BusinessObjects Web Intelligence, and other SAP BusinessObjects components function in the SAP BusinessObjects landscape. The *services* are implemented as Java applications with each service running in it its own Java Virtual Machine (JVM). The services communicate with each other and the rest of the platform over the network.

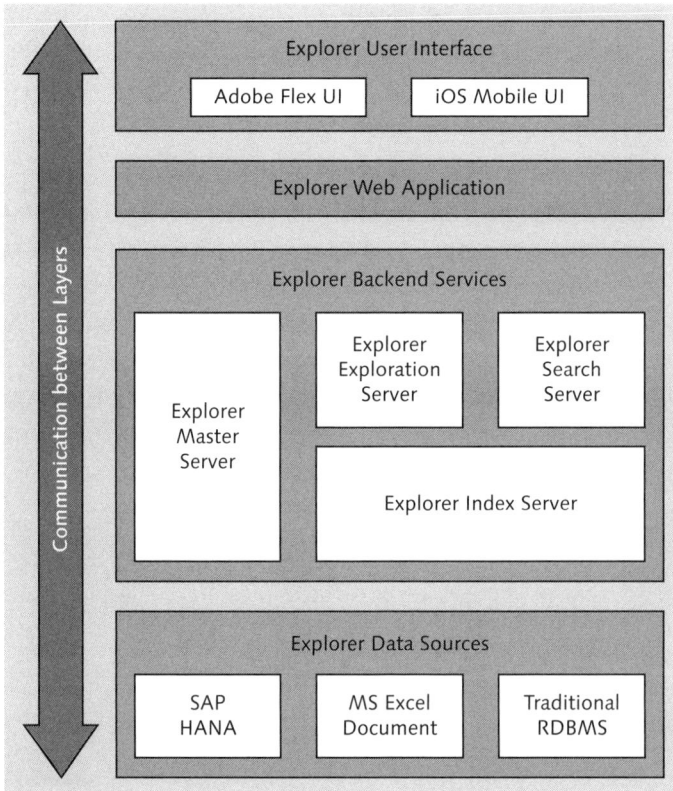

**Figure 11.1** SAP BusinessObjects Explorer Application Components

### SAP BusinessObjects Explorer Web Application

The interactions of end users with the backend SAP BusinessObjects Explorer services are mediated by a Java web application. This ensures that all communication between clients and the services can be transported over HTTP, which makes deployment and security of the communication in a modern networked environment simple and convenient, as opposed to old-fashioned client-server architecture. This web application is most often deployed to the same web application server hosting the rest of the SAP BusinessObjects platform UI, such as the SAP BusinessObjects BI Launchpad and Central Management Console (CMC). If deployed to the Apache Tomcat web application server shipped with SAP BusinessObjects, the installer will handle all of the web application deployment for you automatically.

The web application component of SAP BusinessObjects Explorer doesn't directly define the UI in the way that a more traditional web application might. Instead it's primarily a service interface that is consumed by the Flex-based or iPad-based UIs.

### SAP BusinessObjects Explorer UI

Recall from earlier that the SAP BusinessObjects Explorer UI comes in two flavors: the Flex version (what you see when using SAP BusinessObjects Explorer from a web browser) and the native iPad version. Both versions offer full access to the information served by SAP BusinessObjects Explorer although interactions differ due to the smaller screen size and touch interface on the mobile device. When you initiate an interaction in the UI, a command is sent to the web application server, which is then processed by either the Explorer Exploration Server or Explorer Search Server, depending on the nature of the interaction.

---

**Additional References**

For more information about the SAP BusinessObjects platform architecture and how services are controlled and interact, see the *SAP BusinessObjects Business Intelligence Platform Administrators Guide* at *http://help.sap.com/businessobject/product_guides/boexir4/ en/xi4sp5_bip_admin_en.pdf.*

For information about deploying and managing an SAP BusinessObjects Explorer system, see the *SAP BusinessObjects Explorer Administrators Guide* at the same place.

---

Now that you're familiar with the basic concepts of the SAP BusinessObjects Explorer tool, let's dive in to the details of the SAP BusinessObjects Explorer on SAP HANA scenario.

### 11.2.2 SAP BusinessObjects Explorer Workflows and How They Differ in an SAP HANA Solution

In this section, we'll discuss the indexing and user exploration processes in more detail and see how those processes differ between standalone SAP BusinessObjects Explorer and SAP BusinessObjects Explorer with SAP HANA. We'll also look at the necessary system configurations that must be made to establish a connection between SAP BusinessObjects Explorer and SAP HANA, the Information Space creation process when using SAP HANA, and finally some of the benefits of the SAP HANA scenario for end user experience.

**Exploring and Indexing**

Recall that whenever users interact with the SAP BusinessObjects Explorer application, they are consuming data from an Information Space. The metadata describing that Information Space—and in the case of a non-SAP HANA scenario, the data itself—is stored in an SAP BusinessObjects Explorer index that was generated by the Indexing Server. Note that the distinction between metadata describing the Information Space and the data itself is important. It's what separates the SAP BusinessObjects Explorer on SAP HANA scenario from the standalone SAP BusinessObjects Explorer scenario.

When you consume an Information Space built on an SAP HANA data source, the Exploration Service prepares and executes calls to the SAP HANA appliance to provide all of the necessary data instead of consuming local data from the index. When exploring an Information Space created from a traditional database, the database can't typically respond fast enough to support the style of interaction necessary for the SAP BusinessObjects Explorer UI. Therefore the Index Server must cache all of the data ahead of time and store it locally on the Explorer Server. This is in contrast to the SAP HANA-supported scenario in which the Index Server merely stores the description of the Information Space (i.e., it's a list of facets and measures.) Using SAP HANA as the live data source for the Exploration Service significantly reduces the load on the SAP BusinessObjects server hosting the Exploration Services and allows for the consumption of Information Spaces that are orders of magnitude larger than what is physically possible without SAP HANA. This method also supports near instant feedback to the user, thus providing a superior user experience. Figure 11.2 walks you through the process of retrieving data from an Information Space backed by an SAP HANA data source.

Another significant benefit of the SAP BusinessObjects Explorer on SAP HANA scenario is that the data presented to the user is always as current as the data in the SAP HANA appliance. If you're using a real-time or near real-time data load strategy, then users have access to the most current records. Because the non-SAP HANA scenario requires an extra indexing step and local storage of data in the

Index Server, the user only receives data that is as fresh as the most recent indexing. Although this can be kept fresh by regular re-indexing, it adds an extra layer and complicates the data management process.

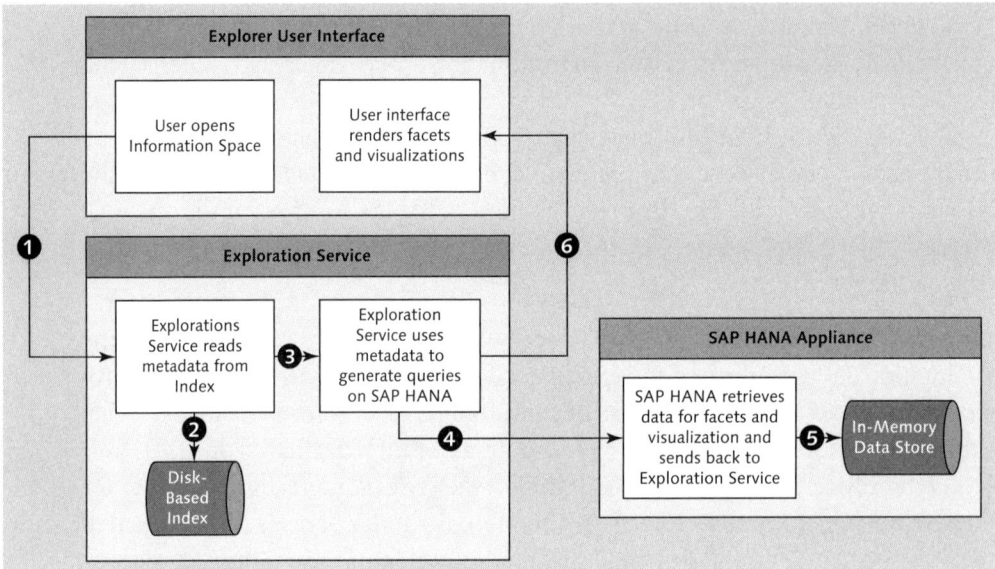

**Figure 11.2** Exploring an Information Space on SAP HANA

If you look at the server hosting the Index Service, you can actually locate the constituent files that make up an index. On a typical Windows installation of SAP BusinessObjects Explorer, the indexes are stored in the following path:

*<SAP_BUSINESS_OBJECTS_ROOT>\SAP BusinessObjects Enterprise XI 4.0\Data\Polestar\ index\<SIANODE_NAME>.ExplorerIndexingServer\Published\ExplorationIndexes*

Inside this folder, you'll find one or more cryptically named folders. Each folder stores one index. The cryptic name is the internal ID of the index. At the next layer down, you'll find a date- and time-stamped folder representing a specific version of the index. Finally, inside that folder, you'll find the actual index files. Figure 11.3 shows an index based on a non-SAP HANA source.

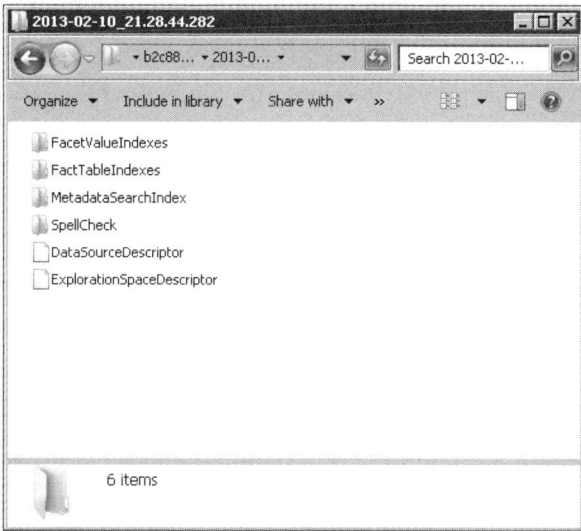

**Figure 11.3** SAP BusinessObjects Explorer Index on a Non-SAP HANA Data Source

Notice that this index contains folders to store values for the fact and facet values. As shown in Figure 11.4, these elements are missing from an SAP HANA-based index.

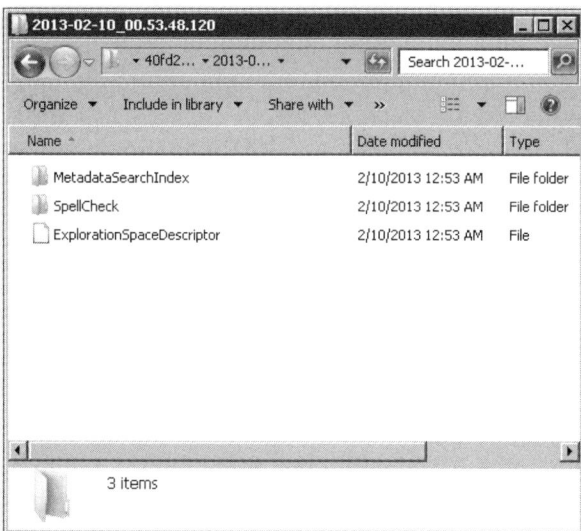

**Figure 11.4** SAP BusinessObjects Explorer Index on an SAP HANA Data Source

If you look at the space required to store an SAP HANA Explorer index, you'll see that it's a very small amount of data, no more than a few kilobytes. On the other hand, an index on a non-SAP HANA data source can easily run in to the hundreds of megabytes. When you consider that the Exploration Service must load and process the index into memory, it's evident how much faster it is for the system to process the SAP HANA index.

This physical storage of the index on disk and the loading and unloading of the data from memory on the Exploration Server is one of the main limiting factors of the standalone SAP BusinessObjects Explorer solution. As a general rule of thumb, an Information Space of average complexity (10-20 facets) should have no more than one to two million rows of data. That may sound like a lot, but in the age of big data, when information accumulates by terabytes and petabytes, it's easy to devise scenarios that exceed this limit even for medium-sized businesses.

Meanwhile, the SAP HANA Information Space can easily process a billion rows of data and do it with better overall performance to the end user. It's important not to underestimate the value of end-user performance in scenarios like this. Even if the data presented to users is of high value, if they have to wait very long to access it or they feel the UI is unresponsive, that data will likely go unused.

### Connecting SAP BusinessObjects Explorer to SAP HANA

To take advantage of the SAP BusinessObjects Explorer on SAP HANA scenario, you must make some initial configurations to the SAP BusinessObjects platform to allow the Explorer Services to connect with the SAP HANA appliance. In the non-SAP HANA scenario, the Information Spaces are generated either from static Excel documents or against queries generated from an SAP BusinessObjects universe. In the SAP HANA scenario, the Information Spaces are designed based on either analytic views or calculation views in the SAP HANA appliance. To access these data elements, the SAP BusinessObjects Explorer system must know how to communicate with the SAP HANA appliance.

There are two methods for defining the connection information: one uses the advanced configuration properties for SAP BusinessObjects Explorer in the Central Management Console (CMC), and the other uses connection objects defined using the Information Design Tool (IDT). Of the two methods available, the latter is preferred; the former is primarily a legacy option, so we'll only detail the solution using IDT.

To define the connection information, follow these steps:

1. Open IDT by choosing START • ALL PROGRAMS • SAP BUSINESSOBJECTS BI PLAT-FORM 4 • SAP BUSINESSOBJECTS BI platform CLIENT TOOLS • INFORMATION DESIGN TOOL.

2. Open the REPOSITORY RESOURCES window by choosing WINDOW • REPOSITORY RESOURCES.

3. Connect to the SAP BusinessObjects platform by opening a session. You'll need to authenticate to the platform as a user that has the rights to create connections.

4. Select and then right-click the folder you plan to store the SAP HANA connection in. Choose INSERT RELATIONAL CONNECTION.

5. At this point, the NEW RELATIONAL CONNECTION wizard appears. Walk through the wizard, giving your connection a name and description and providing the necessary connection values, as listed in Table 11.1. Figure 11.5 shows an example of the connection configuration process.

| DATABASE MIDDLEWARE DRIVER SELECTION | Select either JDBC (choose SAP • SAP HANA DATABASE 1.0 • JDBC DRIVERS) or ODBC (SAP • SAP HANA DATABASE 1.0 • ODBC DRIVERS). |
|---|---|
| AUTHENTICATION MODE | ▶ Use specified user name and password. <br> ▶ Provide values for a hard-coded system account that will be used for all communication with the database. <br> ▶ Use SAP BusinessObjects Credential Mapping. <br> ▶ Use credentials mapped to individual SAP BusinessObjects user accounts to connect to the SAP HANA appliance. <br> ▶ Use Single Sign-On (SSO) when refreshing reports at view time. <br> ▶ Use SSO to the database to pass through credentials. <br> Note that Single Sign-On for SAP BusinessObjects Explorer isn't fully functional in the current GA release of SAP BusinessObjects on SAP HANA. The Indexing process fails to work with the SSO layer. SAP Support suggests this will be resolved in a later patch for SP6 and or 4.1 |
| USER NAME | The name of the database user account if using a specified user name and password. |

**Table 11.1** New Relational Connection Values

| PASSWORD | The password of the database user account if using a specified user name and password. |
|---|---|
| SERVER (HOST:PORT) | The server host name and port number that the SAP HANA appliance is listening on. The port number can be found using the SAP HANA Studio. |

**Table 11.1** New Relational Connection Values (Cont.)

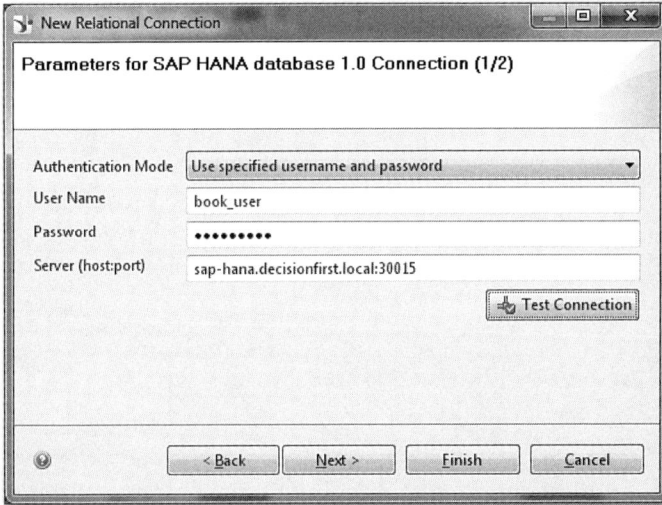

**Figure 11.5** Example of an SAP HANA Connection Configuration Screen

**Additional Information**

For more information on using the IDT, consult the *Information Design Tool User Guide* at *http://help.sap.com/businessobject/product_guides/boexir4/en/xi4sp5_info_design_tool_en.pdf*.

### Creating an Information Space on SAP HANA

After you've established a connection to SAP HANA, you can begin construction of your Information Spaces. As mentioned, the content types within SAP HANA that you can access using SAP BusinessObjects Explorer are analytic and calculation views. These appear in the SAP BusinessObjects Explorer interface inside their respective packages. This is the same structure in which you organize the content within SAP HANA Studio.

Information Spaces are created using the MANAGE SPACES view in the SAP Business-Objects Explorer UI. In the SOURCES area, you'll find the SAP HANA appliance node as shown in Figure 11.6. If this is expanded, you should see the connection name that you defined with the IDT. Finally, inside that node, you should find the list of views you can access. Unfortunately, all views are displayed at the same level in the tree with their full path, including package and view name concatenated together. We can only hope that future versions of SAP BusinessObjects Explorer will improve on this small UI element to make navigation easier.

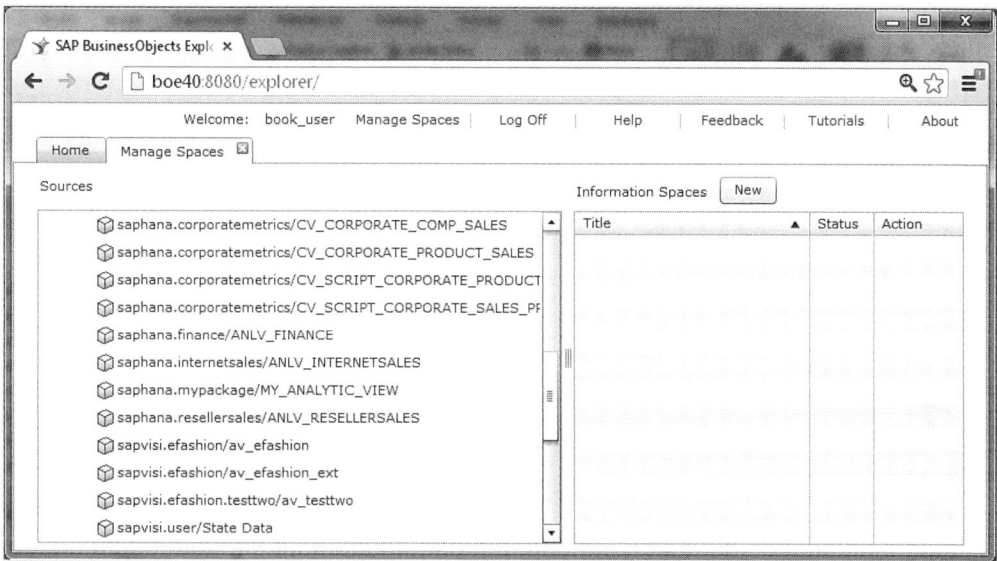

**Figure 11.6** List of SAP HANA Views in SAP BusinessObjects Explorer

To create the new Information Space you need, select the appropriate source view, and then click the NEW button at the top of the screen. This takes you to the Information Space Creation Wizard. As you proceed through the wizard, you'll give your Information Space a name and description, and select a location to store the Information Space in the SAP BusinessObjects repository. The location in which the space is stored affects which users have access to view the Information Space.

The majority of the work to create an Information Space is carried out on the OBJECTS tab. Here you'll select which dimensions and measures from the SAP HANA view you want to make available to end users. Facets are organized on this screen by the attribute view or hierarchy they were created from, while measures are simply listed at the root of the object tree.

Adding objects to the Information Space is as simple as dragging and dropping into the central panel of the screen. After you've selected a number of facets, you have the option of organizing them into facet groups. This doesn't have a significant impact on the user experience at this time, but it can make managing a larger Information Space clearer. For each facet, you can define the default sort order and classify it as a geographic facet if necessary. For each measure, you can define the qualitative description as being positive either when increasing or decreasing.

In some cases, you may need to create calculated measures that go beyond what the SAP HANA view provides. This is typical for measures that don't have a simple aggregation, such as a percent change between periods. This measure is derived from two other measures after aggregation has been applied and can't be simply aggregated on its own. This formula must therefore be defined based on the constituent elements from the SAP HANA view. Unfortunately, at this time, SAP BusinessObjects Explorer can only handle very simple definitions for calculated measures consisting of just two constituent values and one operator. Often this means you need to define at least some of the formula in your SAP HANA views. For example, to construct a percentage change over time, follow this equation: *(Current Period – Prior Period) Prior Period*. Because you can only do one operation in SAP BusinessObjects Explorer, and you don't want to do the division ahead of time to ensure proper aggregation, you need to precalculate the subtraction operation and expose it on the SAP HANA view as a period Delta. Then you can define the percentage change calculation as *delta prior period*.

**Calculated Measures in Calculation Views**

Although you can define sophisticated calculated measures in calculation views that have arrived at postaggregation, SAP BusinessObjects Explorer doesn't currently handle these measures correctly. For now, you have to use SAP BusinessObjects Explorer's internally calculated measures. We hope to see SAP resolve this limitation in the future.

The last steps to create your Information Space are to validate the definition on the OBJECT tab and click the OK button to save the Information Space, with the final step being to index the Information Space one time so that the metadata describing the Information Space can be stored. The other two tabs in the Information Space creation screen, SCHEDULING and PERSONALIZATION, aren't really pertinent to an Information Space created on SAP HANA. SCHEDULING is unnecessary because the Information Space only needs to be indexed once, and PERSONALIZATION is unnecessary because row-level security of data can be handled by the SAP HANA appliance using analytic privileges. Recall that SSO to the database isn't quite working with SAP BusinessObjects Explorer yet, so for the time being, you have to use the SAP BusinessObjects Credential Mapping to leverage the row-level security via analytic privileges. We expect this to be resolved in the near future with additional patches.

---

**Additional Resources**

We've definitely not covered every nuance and best practice in Information Space design, nor have we covered exploration views. Many of these elements are general to all SAP BusinessObjects Explorer scenarios and not just SAP BusinessObjects Explorer on SAP HANA. For more information on designing content with SAP BusinessObjects Explorer, see the *SAP BusinessObjects Explorer User Guide* at *http://help.sap.com/businessobject/ product_guides/boexir4/en/xi4_exp_user_en.pdf*.

---

## 11.3 Introduction to SAP Lumira

SAP Lumira is a desktop-based application that provides powerful analytic and predictive capabilities. SAP Lumira connects to a variety of data sources, including CSV files, Freehand SQL across different databases, Excel spreadsheets, universes (UNV), semantic layers (UNX), and SAP HANA. Each of the connectivity methods has its own advantages and disadvantages. Although you can use any of the connectivity methods for analysis and visualization, our discussion is primarily concerned with connectivity to SAP HANA.

As one of the newer applications in the SAP collection of products, SAP Lumira has been developed from the ground up using the Eclipse Integrated Development Environment (IDE). Eclipse is an open-source, extensible IDE that provides windowing and utilities commonly used by today's developers. Because it's an open-source application, users can modify the source code to manipulate the interface and add all new functionality. SAP has taken advantage of this by building SAP Lumira within this framework. This is becoming a familiar pattern; Eclipse has also been used to form the framework of SAP BusinessObjects Design Studio, SAP Predictive Analysis, and SAP HANA Studio.

With the ability to analyze data in new and different ways, SAP Lumira puts power back in the hands of users to quickly derive business value by connecting directly to data that matters most to the user. After users connect to this data, they can calculate, sort, filter, and share data and visualizations to provide insights into business data in new and different ways. Users can manipulate data sets by adding new calculations, changing the representation of the attributes and measures, and building geographic and time hierarchies on various attributes.

### 11.3.1 Why Use SAP Lumira?

SAP Lumira provides capabilities that have, in the past, been associated with SAP BusinessObjects Explorer. The SAP BusinessObjects Explorer application is a web-based application that provides quick and easy access to data. SAP Lumira takes similar functionality in a familiar interface and provides a desktop application within which you perform analysis and visualizations. It represents the data that is stored in a data source. Like all of the other visualization and analysis tools, SAP Lumira doesn't require changes to the underlying data. The data stored in the data source is simply queried and represented within the interface. Manipulation tools are presented within SAP Lumira to provide for the modification of the data, but the changes only live within the SAP Lumira session and aren't written back to the data source.

SAP Lumira also provides a series of more advanced computational and visualization tools for use on the various data sources. When a new visualization is created on a data source, all of the fields within the system are linked into the visualization as measures, hierarchies, and attributes. The measures and hierarchies that are displayed are derived from the multidimensional views created in SAP HANA Studio (see Chapter 6). Creating the measures and hierarchies in SAP HANA Studio provides a unified view of the data with a single version of the truth as opposed to providing a more loosely defined view that can be manipulated by the author of the visualization.

After the objects are imported from the data source, you have advanced tools available for use. First of all, the aggregation of measures can be modified. The default is SUM, but, you can select MIN, MAX, AVERAGE, COUNT, and COUNT DISTINCT. You can also create measure objects that take advantage of running SUM, running COUNT, and running AVERAGE. Dimensions that contain a geographical component such as county, state, and city can be mapped into a geographic hierarchy like the one shown in Figure 11.7. The creation of a geographic hierarchy enables you to analyze data in the form of a map. In addition, if you've created a measure based on a numeric field and also created a time-based hierarchy, a visualization showing the projected values for a time in the future can also be displayed as shown in Figure 11.8. For instance, if you have five years' worth of sales revenue on a monthly basis, you can use forecast or linear regression to calculate the next six months' worth of sales revenues. These powerful tools provide a wide range of analytic, visualization, and predictive functions for you to take advantage of while working with the data directly within an application on your desktop.

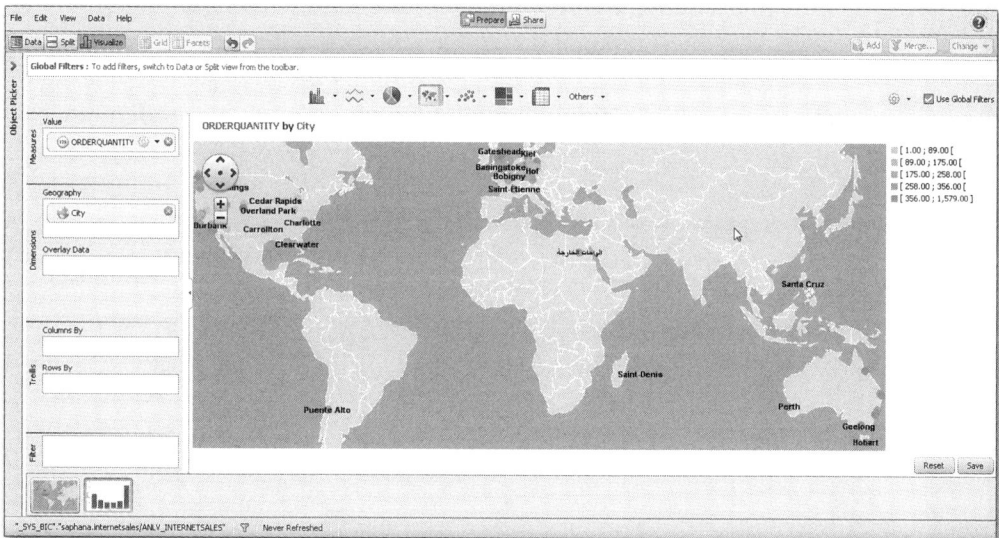

**Figure 11.7** A Geographic Visualization of Tabular Data

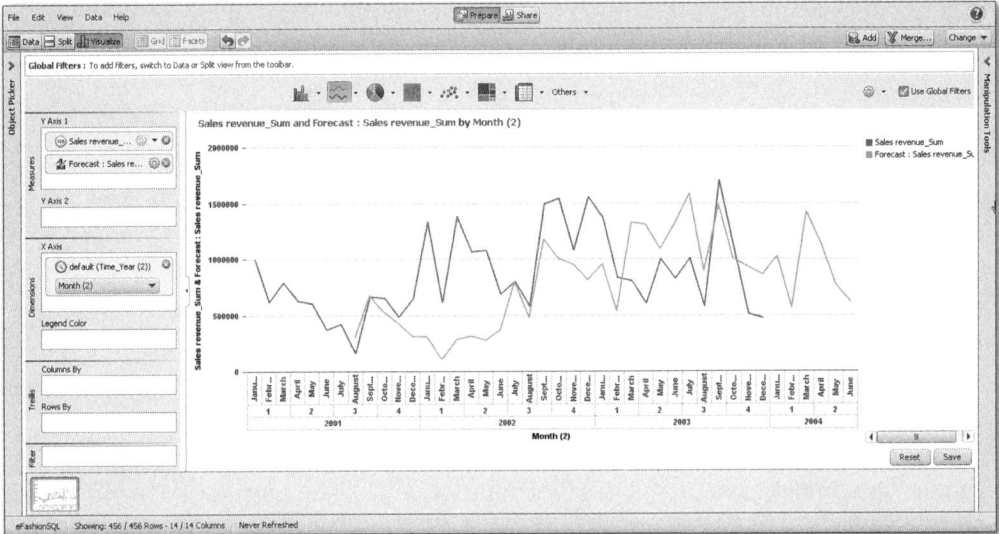

**Figure 11.8**  A Two Series Line Chart by Month, Quarter, and Year

## 11.3.2  Connecting SAP Lumira to SAP HANA

SAP Lumira provides the ability to connect to SAP HANA in two different ways: online and offline. Let's take a look at each of the methods, as shown in Figure 11.9.

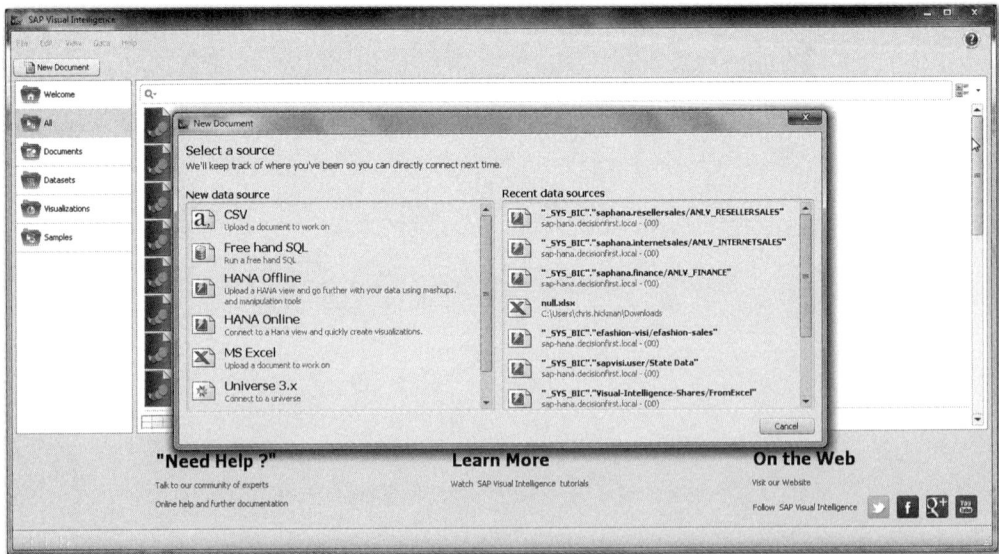

**Figure 11.9**  Options for Connecting to Various Data Sources

**Online Connectivity**

The most popular method of connectivity is connecting to data online. Connecting to online data sources enables you to take advantage of the speed and capacity of the SAP HANA system. You can connect to SAP HANA online to analyze thousands to millions of records of data in seconds.

The only disadvantage to the online connectivity method is that you must be online and have the ability to connect to the SAP HANA server. Connecting to SAP HANA online provides access to calculation views and analytic views that were created in SAP HANA Studio. We described these two types of views earlier in the book.

To connect to SAP HANA online, follow these steps:

1. Start by opening SAP Lumira.

2. Click NEW DOCUMENT, and then select SAP HANA ONLINE.

3. Enter the credentials that correspond to the SAP HANA installation to which you're connecting.

4. Click CONNECT HANA INSTANCE. A listing of analytic and calculation views appears (see Figure 11.10).

5. Select a desired view and click ACQUIRE.

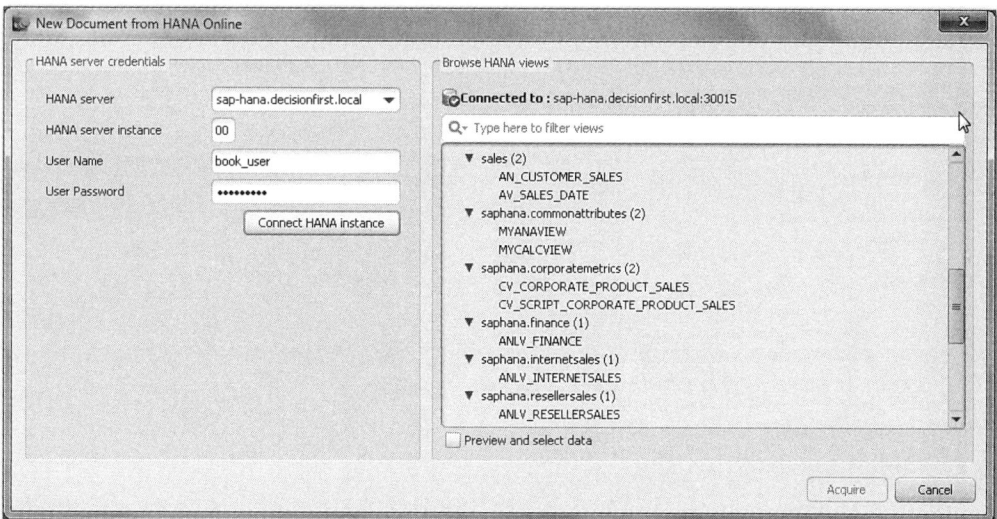

**Figure 11.10** Connecting to SAP HANA Online

The data is read into the SAP Lumira interface, and you are immediately forwarded to a visualization interface that allows for visualization of the data source.

One option you have when selecting a view in the New Document dialog is to preview the data prior to acquiring the data set from the SAP HANA instance. Click the Preview and select data checkbox. The Acquire button then changes into a Select button. After you click the Select button, the application reads a sample of the data from SAP HANA into the SAP Lumira interface. This dialog enables you to remove measures and facets that aren't required by the analysis to be developed. You then toggle the checkboxes beside the needed measures and facets, filter any appropriate fields, and then click OK. The fields and filters are applied to the query performed against the SAP HANA data source (see Figure 11.11). In this case, the dimensions and facets that were not selected as well as the items that were filtered out aren't pulled from SAP HANA. This provides the ability to filter data and objects before they are pulled in from the data source, reducing the overall size of the data set.

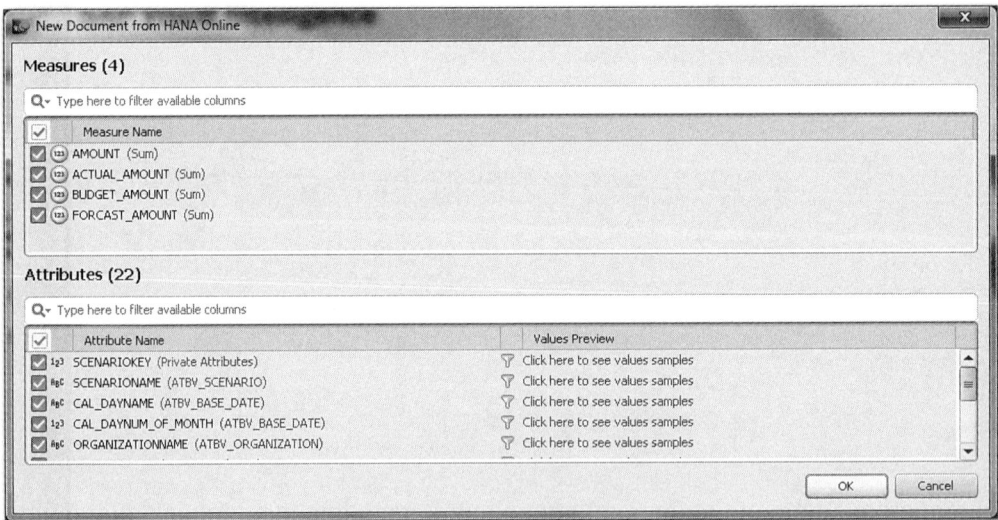

**Figure 11.11** Users May Filter Data Directly from the Source

**Offline Connectivity**

Alternatively, you can also connect to SAP HANA data sources as an offline data source (see Figure 11.12). At design time, you are connected to the SAP HANA system and can take advantage of the speed and resources of such a server. However, when the visualization is saved, the data is saved in a local instance of a Sybase database. The index of the data is stored along with the definition of the visualization.

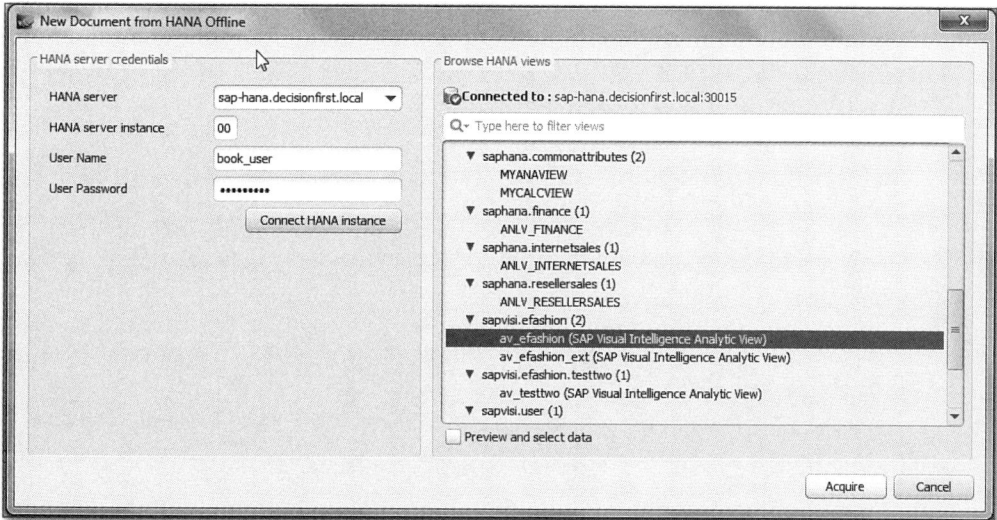

**Figure 11.12** Connecting to SAP HANA Offline

On launching an instance of SAP Lumira, you are presented with six options for connecting to data:

- CSV
- Freehand SQL
- SAP HANA Offline
- SAP HANA Online
- Universe 3.x
- Universe 4.x

To connect to SAP HANA, follows these steps:

1. Select SAP HANA Offline from the list of available connections.
2. Provide the SAP HANA server name, instance number, username, and password, and click Connect SAP HANA Instance.
3. Select the desired data source from SAP HANA from the right side of the dialog.
4. Click the Acquire button.

5. Behind the scenes, an instance of the Sybase IQ Network Server is launched on your machine. This service (iqsrv15.exe) is a local instance of the Sybase IQ database server that will be used to store the offline data retrieved from SAP HANA.

6. After the iqsrv15.exe instance is launched, SAP Lumira scans the SAP HANA data source for the overall size of the data. If the number of cells in the SAP HANA source number more than 30 million, a warning is displayed with that information (see Figure 11.13). You can then continue or cancel the request.

7. If you continue, the full record set is then downloaded from the SAP HANA data source into the local instance of Sybase IQ, and the visualization in SAP Lumira can begin.

**Cell Size Warning from SAP HANA**

The maximum number of cells limitation was increased from 15 million cells to 30 million cells in SAP Lumira version 1.0.7.

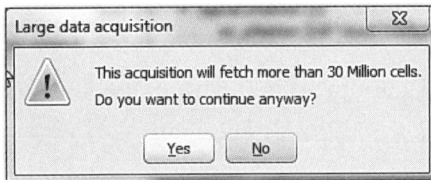

**Figure 11.13** A Warning If More Than 30M Cells Are to Be Imported Offline

The SAP HANA offline connectivity method is typically used when the data sets are relatively small. The speed at which the data is downloaded can vary with the overall bandwidth between the SAP HANA system and the local machine that is downloading the data. In our benchmark tests, it took approximately 10 minutes to download 10 million rows of data from SAP HANA.

This results in a SVID file that can be potentially huge. This also eliminates the advantage that SAP HANA brings to big data analysis. When the visualization is saved locally, the resulting SVID file is essentially a renamed ZIP file. If you rename this file as .zip, the file can be opened, and the data component can be extracted. If this extracted data file is given the .csv extension, it can be opened in any application that supports a CSV.

SAP HANA is synonymous with big data—a CSV file isn't. An SAP Lumira file that is stored using the SAP HANA Offline connectivity method eliminates the speed, and the result is a visualization that performs poorly. The advantage to an offline dashboard is the ability to analyze the data while disconnected from the SAP HANA data server. You should be aware of the differences between online and offline data connectivity. If the visualization is filtered to the point where just a few hundred thousand records of data (or fewer) are imported, then an offline method is acceptable. If there are any more records than this, then the SAP HANA online method should be used, and the dashboard won't have the capability of being disconnected.

When the data is downloaded from SAP HANA using offline connectivity, the data is brought down and written to a temporary file stored in <DIRECTORY> (HILO.DB). After all of the data is retrieved to the temporary file space, it's then loaded into the local instance of the Sybase IQ database, which we'll describe momentarily. The user can then disconnect and continue working with the data set seamlessly, clicking the SAVE button upon finishing the session. The data is persisted within the saved SVID file, so keep the overall size of the data set in mind when determining which sets should be downloaded for offline analysis. The offline method is best used for record sets that are smaller relative to the sets typically associated with SAP HANA.

After the visualization is saved and the offline record set is persisted with the SVID file, you can open the SVID file directly from the save location. When the file is opened, an instance of the Sybase IQ database is launched. Next, the contents of the file are analyzed, the component that contains the data (i.e., data_stream_0) is opened, and the data is imported into the in-memory instance of Sybase IQ. After the data is loaded, the data is then made available in the SAP Lumira interface for offline in-memory analysis.

### Sybase IQ

Let's take moment to zoom in on Sybase IQ. Sybase IQ is a columnar datastore that has the capability to handle large amounts of data in a compact database management system. Sybase IQ is installed alongside SAP Lumira to facilitate SAP HANA offline data visualization capabilities. The Sybase IQ system uses a database called HILO.DB. Hilo is the developmental code name for the SAP Visualization Project (i.e., SAP Design Studio was once referred to as "Zen"). The databases are stored on the directory *C:\Users\<username>\AppData\Local\SAP\SAP Visual Intelligence* and can be deleted at any time to free up drive space or to clear out issues with any inconsistencies in the databases. The database will be reinitialized when the SAP Lumira application is loaded. It's important to remember that the data sets aren't actually stored within the Hilo database. The data sets are persisted within the SVID files and are loaded into the Sybase IQ in memory database on the fly when the SVID file is loaded into SAP Lumira.

### 11.3.3 Analyzing Data with SAP Lumira

Keeping a visualization stored locally opens a wide range of offline capabilities to data visualization when connections back to the server aren't possible. You can open a new visualization disconnected from scratch. The data is streamed from the SVID file and loaded into the Sybase in-memory database, and the visualization opens in SAP Lumira. If you then decide to open a new visualization, the data is retained in the in-memory Sybase database for faster retrieval in case you decide to reopen the SAP HANA offline file.

### 11.3.4 Merging Data Sets

Similar to other BI tools, SAP Lumira provides the means of merging different data sources into a single visualization on the presentation layer without the need for lengthy ETL planning processes. When two or more data sets are merged on a common dimension, all of the columns of each data source are merged into a single data set and presented in a unified view in the tool.

A few rules govern merging data sets:

▶ The two data sources being merged together must have a primary key specified.

▶ Columns of the same data type can only be merged together. Numeric columns can only be matched with numeric columns while text columns can only match text columns.

▶ All of the columns from each data set are merged. You can't select which columns to merge.

Many data sets can be merged together in SAP Lumira. For instance, a data set from a universe can be acquired into SAP Lumira. You can then connect to a local instance of an Excel spreadsheet and merge the data on a common dimension (e.g., an account number). After the two data sets are merged together, the columns from each data set become one large data set. Visualizations can then be completed that contain representations of data from both data sources but appear within the application as a single data source.

This limitation doesn't, however, preclude you from using SAP HANA in a merged data scenario. You can certainly create visualizations based on SAP HANA online. You can also create SAP Lumira visualizations based on other sources of data. To merge SAP HANA data with your own data sources, you must upload your alternate source of data into SAP HANA using the sharing techniques described in the following section. You then work in conjunction with the SAP HANA administration team to merge this data with the SAP HANA data already in existence. This allows processing to happen on the SAP HANA side that provides the benefit of an in-memory data system while allowing you to use your own data sources. While it's true that this method doesn't allow for instantaneous merging of data, it does allow you to take advantage of merged data sources from multiple locations into a single, memory-optimized database management system.

### 11.3.5    Sharing SAP Lumira Visualizations

After you've achieved visualization of data within SAP Lumira, you'll likely need to share your findings with others either within the application or outside the system. SAP Lumira makes this process simple and easy.

First of all, SAP Lumira operates in two modes: PREPARE and SHARE. You can toggle between modes at the top center of the SAP Lumira application (Figure 11.14).

The design and visualization phase of the SAP Lumira application occurs in the Prepare mode, which is when you can import data, manipulate the data sets, merge data, and add visualizations that assist in the business decision process. After this process has produced analyses or visualizations that can be of use to others, you switch to Share mode by clicking the SHARE button.

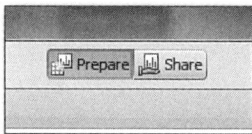

**Figure 11.14**    The Prepare-Share Toggle

Share mode offers several methods by which you can share your data sets and visualizations. When you switch into Share mode, the screen is split into two different types of sharable content: DATASETS and VISUALIZATIONS (see Figure 11.15). Visualizations allow you to share all saved visualizations by email or through SAP StreamWork, a social networking platform developed by SAP to facilitate teamwork on projects.

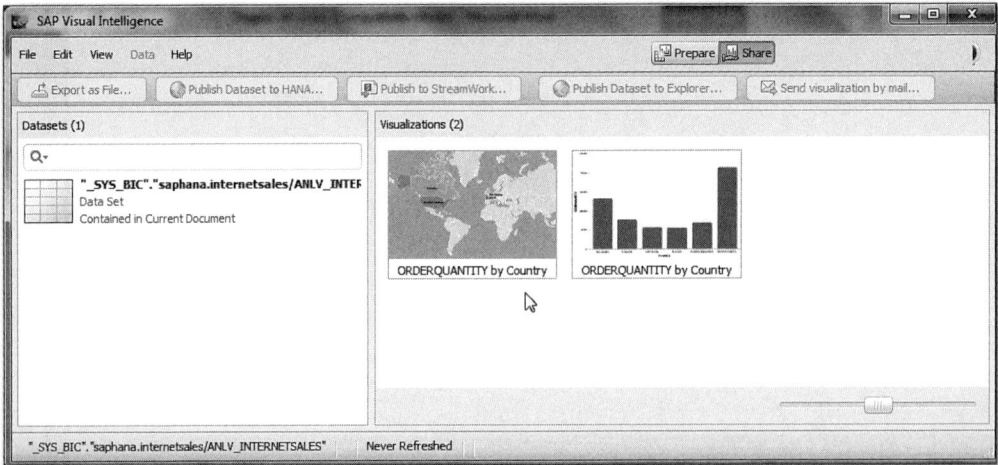

**Figure 11.15**   The Share Screen with Datasets and Visualizations Panes

Sharing visualizations by email prompts you to select a size of the image to be inserted into an email, as shown in Figure 11.16. On selecting the image size, you are presented with a new email message within your locally installed default email client, as shown in Figure 11.17. You can then complete the email and send the visualization to the recipients.

**Figure 11.16**   Exporting an Image to Email and Providing a Resolution Selection

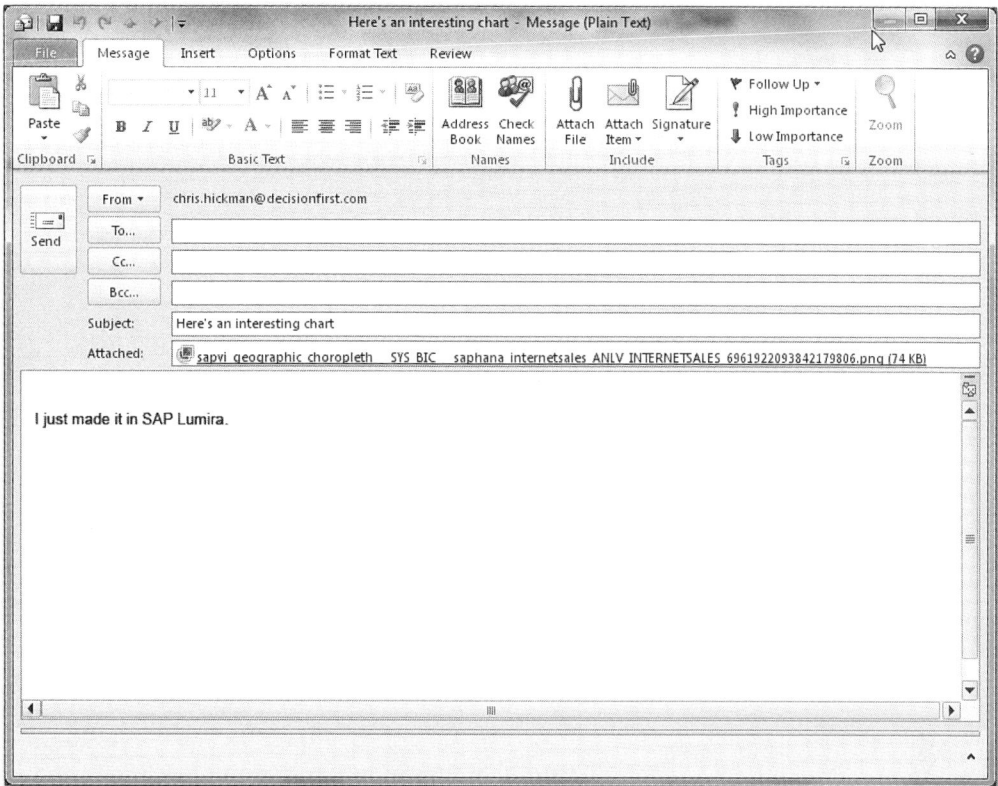

**Figure 11.17** Sharing a Visualization by Email

The second type of sharing in SAP Lumira is through data sets. Within the DATASETS window on the left side of the interface, you can select one of the data sets within the current SAP Lumira session. After the data set is chosen, an applicable listing of export options will highlight in the share bar above the selected data set. In this example, select the first data set in the left side listing of data sets <INSERT DATASET NAME>. Four buttons are enabled at the top of the screen: EXPORT AS FILE, PUBLISH DATASET TO HANA, PUBLISH TO STREAMWORK, and PUBLISH DATASET TO EXPLORER. Let's quickly look at the non-SAP HANA options first.

The first option, EXPORT AS FILE, is self-explanatory. Clicking this button provides options to export the current data set as a CSV file or as an Excel file (.xlsx), as shown in Figure 11.18. Remember that these two file-based datastores were not intended to store tens to hundreds of thousands of record sets. Keep this in mind when trying to export your data to a file. Exporting more than this limit will result in long-running export processes or file-based datastores that are too large to open in calling applications.

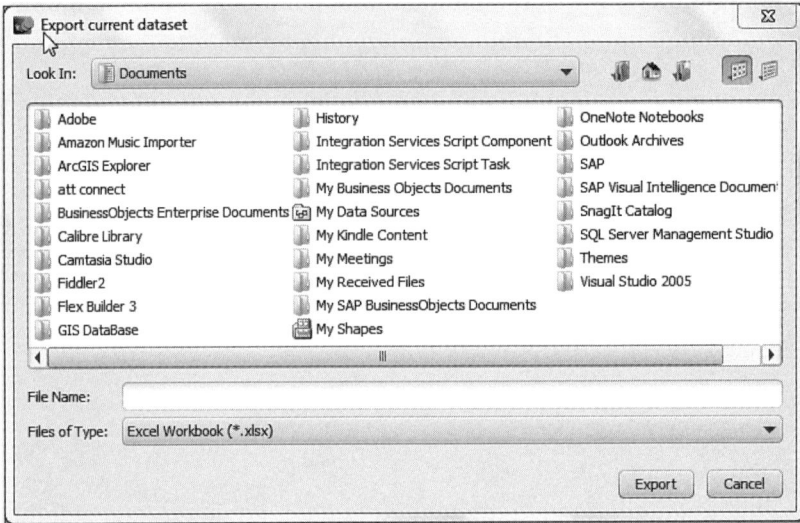

**Figure 11.18** Exporting the Current Data Set to an Excel Spreadsheet

The second option, PUBLISH TO STREAMWORK, is similar to the VISUALIZATION EXPORT option. The PUBLISH TO STREAMWORK option shown in Figure 11.19 enables you to save the data set on the SAP StreamWork website for other users to view and consume. Again, the data sets should remain small due to the file-based nature of the storage device in SAP StreamWork. SAP StreamWork stores its data as CSV or XLSX, similar to the way that the EXPORT TO FILE process stores its data.

The third option, PUBLISH TO EXPLORER, enables you to publish the data set as an Information Space that can be used within an SAP BusinessObjects Explorer session to analyze via SAP BusinessObjects BI Launchpad. Clicking on the PUBLISH TO EXPLORER button opens a dialog that asks you to log in to an SAP BusinessObjects 4 CMS. On successful login, you then select a folder where the data set will be published as an Information Space.

Two things happen when a data set is published as an Information Space. First, an Excel spreadsheet is generated and uploaded to the target directory that you've specified. Next, an Information Space is generated in the same directory as the Excel spreadsheet. The Information Space is generated based on the Excel spreadsheet that was published, and then the Information Space is automatically indexed.

After the publication is complete, you can log in to SAP BusinessObjects Explorer and analyze the Information Space as usual. This also extends natively to a mobile device, which is discussed in a later section.

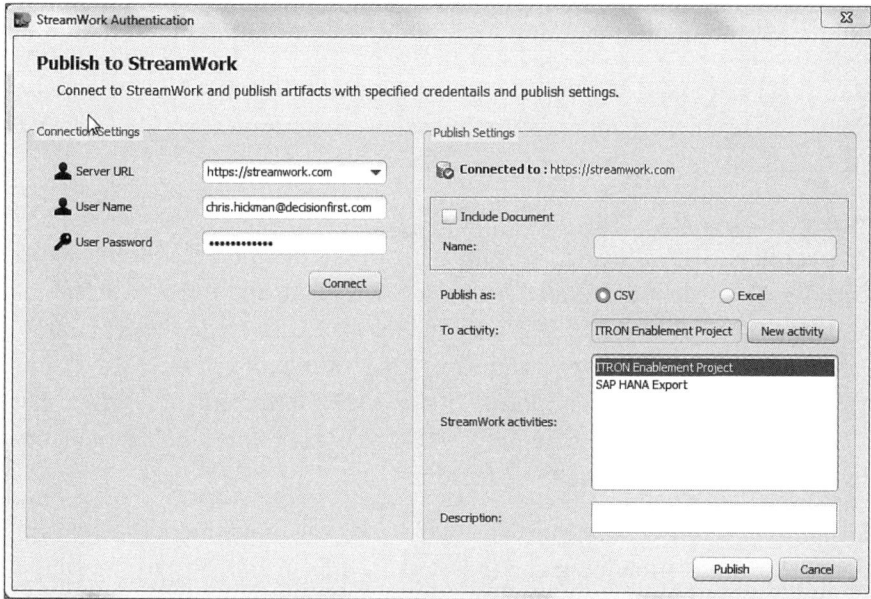

**Figure 11.19** A Dialog to Publish the Data Set to SAP StreamWork

The fourth and final option for sharing data, PUBLISH DATA SET TO HANA, is the most powerful because it allows you to publish the current data set up to an instance of SAP HANA as an analytic view. To publish to SAP HANA, click the PUBLISH button, and then enter valid credentials for the SAP HANA system with rights to create analytic views. Next, create and/or select a package within which SAP Lumira will publish the new analytic view. Click the CREATE VIEW button, and provide a name for the new analytic view. Make sure the new view is selected, and then click OK. After the process is complete, you can then create a new visualization to consume the new analytic view or use another of the SAP tools that can connect to and consume analytic views from SAP HANA (e.g., SAP BusinessObjects Explorer, SAP BusinessObjects Design Studio, etc.).

When the data set is published, the user account with which you made the connection must have the appropriate rights on the SAP HANA system. You must have the Development role privilege to the package.

## 11.4 Mobilizing Content with SAP BusinessObjects Explorer and SAP Lumira Based on SAP HANA Data

SAP Lumira provides a robust desktop application by which you manipulate, analyze, and visualize data. SAP Lumira also provides various methods by which you can share the data with other users in various ways. However, the tool doesn't provide a direct method to take the visualizations mobile. The most direct method of visualizing data from SAP Lumira is to publish the visualization as an SAP Business-Objects Explorer Information Space.

To take SAP HANA data within SAP Lumira and make it mobile, first take the SAP HANA data offline. This offloads the data from SAP HANA into the local instance of Sybase IQ. Next, click the SHARE button to switch into Share mode. Select the data provider to be published to SAP BusinessObjects Explorer, and select PUBLISH DATASET to EXPLORER. Remember that the resulting Information Space will be based on an Excel spreadsheet that is published alongside the Information Space. The spreadsheet can take no more than 10,000,000 cells, therefore, the data must be filtered prior to importing it into SAP Lumira.

SAP BusinessObjects Explorer, on the other hand, was born mobile. After you complete the process of building and indexing an Information Space, you simply open the SAP BusinessObjects Explorer app on your iPad or iPhone and connect to your CMS. After connecting, you see a listing of Information Spaces that your user ID has access to view. Simply tap one of the Information Spaces and begin viewing the space in real time on your mobile device.

Now that we've discussed the abilities of SAP BusinessObjects Explorer and SAP Lumira to harness the capabilities of SAP HANA and take it mobile, imagine the power that this now puts in the hands of the user in the field or simply walking around the office. Data sets as large as tens to hundreds of millions of records can be consumed within both tools. Building an Information Space on an SAP HANA data set that runs this large has traditionally posed a huge performance problem. However, using the lightning fast speeds of in-memory processing, users can now tap their data in real time and aggregate through all of those millions of records of data. SAP BusinessObjects Explorer even shows you at the top-right side of the screen how many records were returned and how long it took to render. It's impressive to see 70 *million* records of data returned in just 1.5 seconds. With big data capabilities such as these, users will flock to this type of solution to answer their questions, which leads to increased user adoption and greater return on investment overall due to the high usage level. Let's take a practical look at all of these topics in a case study in the next section.

## 11.5    Case Study: Exploring Sales Data with SAP Lumira and SAP BusinessObjects Explorer

The Sales Management Team at AdventureWorks Cycle Company has been tapped as the pilot business unit to leverage the new BI platform based on SAP HANA. As part of the pilot project, the BI team has modeled and loaded the company's sales data into the SAP HANA appliance and provided access to the SAP BusinessObjects platform tools. In previous chapters, we've covered the initial phases of the project where data was loaded and modeled in SAP HANA. Now we'll examine the specific business analytic options using SAP Lumira and SAP BusinessObjects Explorer.

### 11.5.1    Business Requirements

AdventureWorks Cycle Company operates two sales distribution channels: a direct to customer sales channel via the company's website, and a traditional retail reseller channel. Resellers are all independent retail operations spread throughout North America, Europe, and the Pacific. Resellers are organized into sales territories with a reseller representative assigned to manage the relationship. Most resellers have relationships with multiple brand manufacturers, so the reseller representative relationship is important to driving product sales.

As part of the pilot program, the North American Reseller Sales team wants to construct a better sales tracking and performance management solution. To date, the team only gets periodic updates on total sales metrics at the close of each month. Their ability to react to shifts in the market or downward trends is limited by the delay in data access. They want access to daily updates of sales trends and the ability to make comparisons to prior periods.

The reseller sales team is also a highly mobile workforce. They want the primary delivery mechanism for content to be supported on a tablet device. Currently, they receive static reports as PDF.

Finally, the sales team is sensitive to the sharing of data across different sales territories and reseller representatives. Therefore, they want to leverage the security features of the platform to ensure that each user only sees data appropriate to his role.

### 11.5.2 Planned Solution

To satisfy the pilot program's requirements the BI team plans to leverage SAP Lumira to do the deeper analysis of data, look for trends and patterns, and help identify areas of interest for the end users to focus on. The BI team will work with a business analyst from the sales team to conduct a number of working sessions where they will explore the data together. In these sessions, the business analyst will get an opportunity to become familiar with the SAP Lumira tool, hopefully leading to a point where the analyst can transition to a self-service model.

It's Monday afternoon, and AdventureWorks employee Bob is about to leave for the day. He knows that there is some analysis work that is required for tomorrow's 10am meeting, but he must leave for a dinner party with his friends this evening. (We all wish we were Bob, right?) He opens SAP Lumira and creates an offline connection to the SAP HANA system, as shown in Figure 11.20.

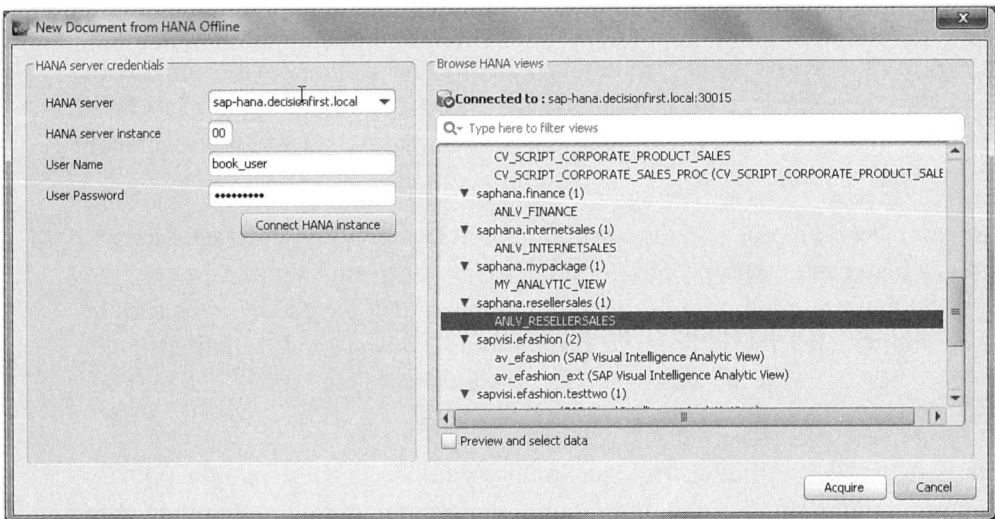

**Figure 11.20** Offline Connection to the SAP HANA System

Bob enters credentials to connect to the SAP HANA system. After he connects, he selects the analytic view that the administrators have made available to him. By clicking the ACQUIRE button, he sees that all of the latest data is included in the data set. Because the data are displayed in descending order, he can see that the order data dates are loaded as of June 2012 from the record highlighted in Figure 11.21.

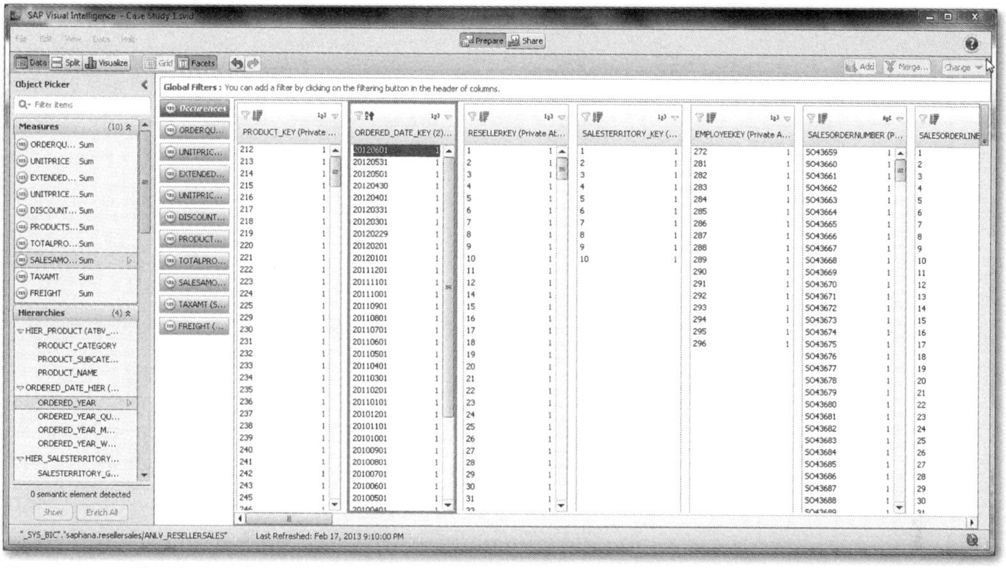

**Figure 11.21**  The Ordered Date Showing the Latest Data

Now that Bob has been able to connect to the data and has been able to import the data into SAP Lumira using an offline connection, he can save the visualization to a local file and disconnect to leave the office for the day. Because the data is saving to a local database in Sybase IQ, the visualization takes a little time for the save to complete.

After the data loads within the application, Bob is able to start his analysis of the data from the train on his commute home. First, he begins by analyzing the total sales and order quantities by region for all years. It's very easy to see in Figure 11.22 that the Southwest region has had the highest sales by all regions. This could be attributed to multiple factors, such as a milder winter season, which allows people to engage in outside activities for more days out of the year.

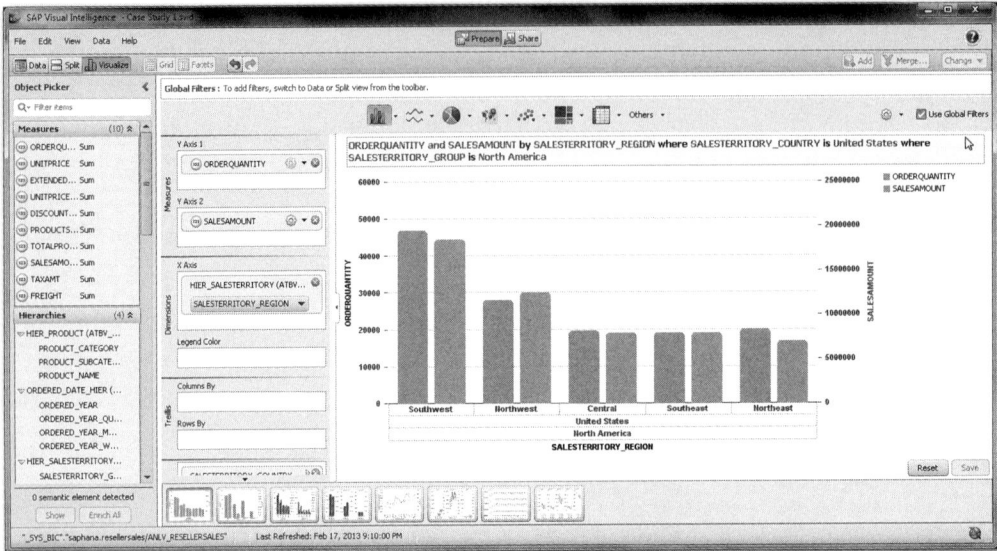

**Figure 11.22** A View of All Sales and Orders by Region in the United States

Bob already knows that bikes constitute a large portion of the corporate sales. However, comparing the total sales amount by the total number of orders can reveal interesting facts. First of all, when looking at the chart in Figure 11.22, Bob sees that the total sales amount per quantity ordered is actually higher for only one region: the Northwest. All other regions are showing nearly equivalent or lower sales per order. It appears that the Northwest region spends more per order than anywhere else in the country. Bob could then drill into the reasons why. However, this could mean that Bob can tell the regional sales manager about this fact to potentially run marketing ads to increase the total sales on bigger ticket items. If he looks at the overall sales and order quantities, he can clearly see which items constitute a higher sales price per order. Bob stores both of the visualizations that he has generated for future use.

Next, Bob throws in a time-related hierarchy so that he can analyze the data over a range of periods. Because he can see that the Bikes category is providing the bulk of the sales revenue, he'll focus on that category (see Figure 11.23).

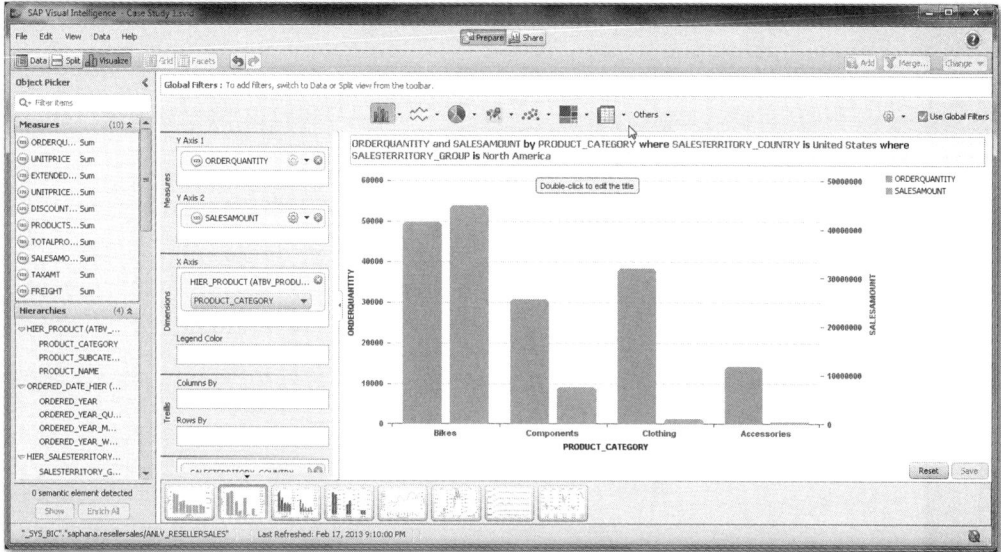

**Figure 11.23**   Sales and Orders by Category

Projecting the sales amount and order quantity on two different vertical axes, and then changing the horizontal axis to the date hierarchy and selecting Year-Quarter, Bob can see a trend in total sales amounts from one quarter to the next as he moves through the years (see Figure 11.24). He begins seeing trends in the data as the weather warms in the United States. Bob can also see that the sales and order quantities fluctuate depending on the time of year. However, he can't adequately see an overall trend, whether positive or negative. In this case, Bob can add a running average to show the quarter-to-quarter average that displays a more precise overall trend. The overall trend is shown to be moving slightly positive over the four-year study period from $2.3M in 2009 to $3.7M in 2012.

Bob can even provide a bit of predictive analytics capabilities. To do this, he first must create a time hierarchy based on a valid time field. SAP Lumira provides recommendations for attributes to be enriched as actual time hierarchies. After the hierarchies are created, Bob then replaces the existing time hierarchy dimension with the new dimension. Bob can then select the menu for the SALES AMOUNT in the Y AXIS 1 field and choose PREDICTIVE CALCULATION. He can provide any number of quarters in the future as recommendations. Using a linear regression analysis and predicting for the next two quarters shows continued growth for the remainder of the year (see this visualization in Figure 11.25). The Q3 numbers are at $8.45M, and the Q4 numbers are at $8.89M. Bob saves the visualization, closes his laptop, and leaves the train.

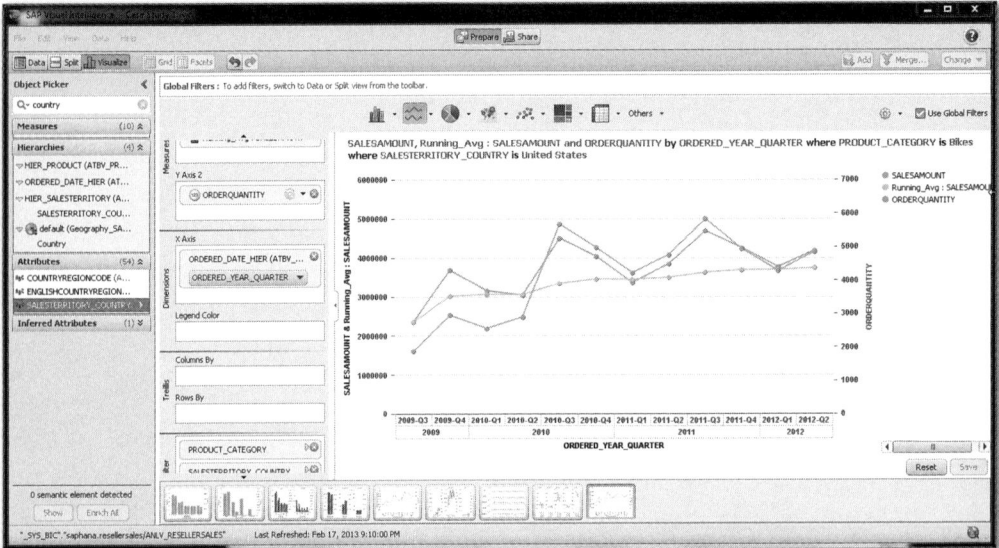

**Figure 11.24** Quarter-to-Quarter Trends for Bike Sales in the United States

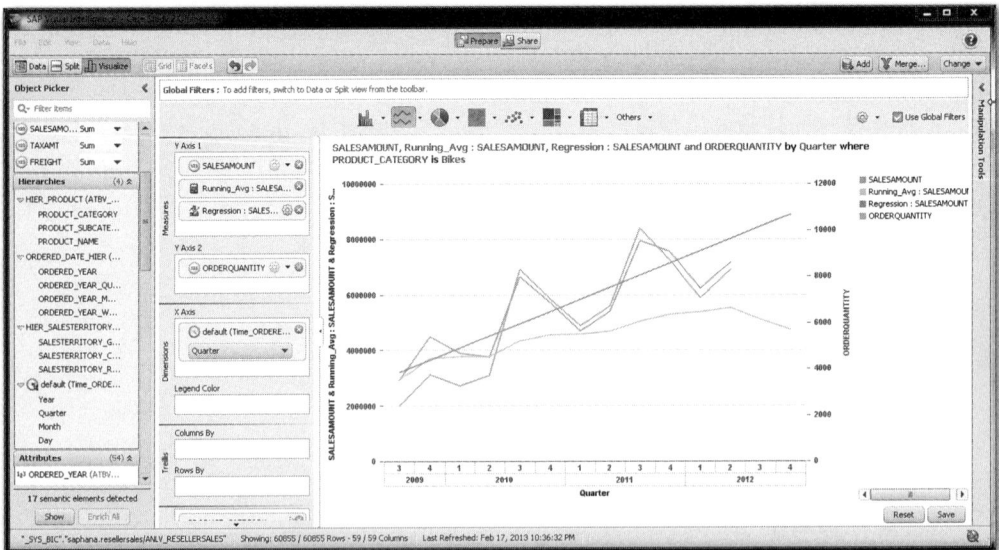

**Figure 11.25** A Quarterly Study Showing a Linear Regression Trending Upward

Bob returns to the office the next day a little groggy from the late-night dinner party but ready to share what he has found. He opens the saved visualization from the day before. While he does have the ability to refresh the data against the data source, he wants to share what he has found with this data intact. Inside SAP Lumira, he switches to the SHARE mode at the top of the application. Selecting the visualizations that we've seen in this case study, he can email them to his colleagues. Finally, he can take the data set as he worked with it and publish it back to SAP HANA for further analysis, or he can publish it up to SAP BusinessObjects Explorer for further exploration.

### 11.5.3  Delivering Data to End Users with SAP BusinessObjects Explorer

We identified in the analysis phase the key elements the organization wants to track. Obviously, the primary figure to be tracked is the sales by month for each sales representative. In addition, the team wants to compare sales to the equivalent period in the prior year to eliminate seasonality from comparisons (e.g., compare August sales for the current year to August of the prior year). Finally, the data needs to be filterable and sliceable by the pertinent dimensions of the Sales Territory, Time, and Reseller Geography. To facilitate this delivery, the BI team has created an SAP HANA calculation view that provides the necessary values with comparison to prior period values.

**Implementing the Information Space**

The first task to deliver the information to the Sales Team via SAP BusinessObjects Explorer is to design the Information Space on top of the calculation view created by the Modeling team.

1. Locate the calculation view to be used under the SAP HANA connection in the SAP BusinessObjects Explorer MANAGE SPACES view, as shown in Figure 11.26. The view name is CV_CORPORATE_COMP_RESELLER_SALES. Once located, click NEW to start the Information Space creation process.

2. In the Information Space creation wizard, select a meaningful name and add a description for the Information Space and the target folder to save the space in, as shown in Figure 11.27. Because all users in the Sales organization need to access this Information Space, place it in a folder they can access—in this case, the Sales folder.

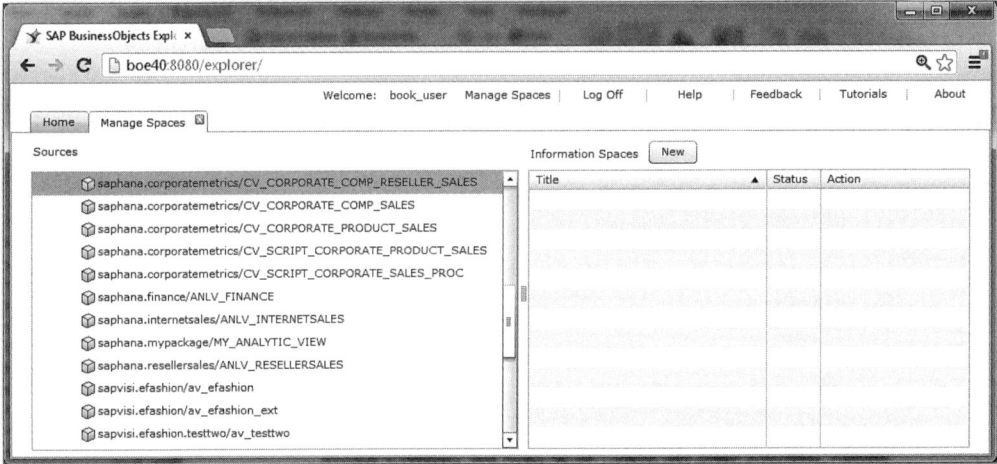

**Figure 11.26** Selecting the Calculation View

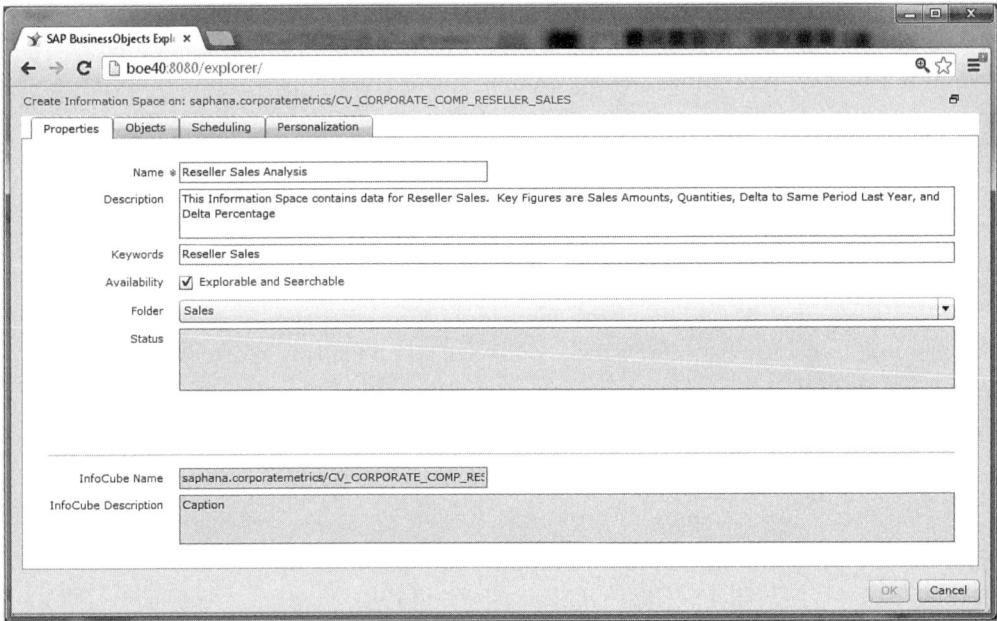

**Figure 11.27** Defining Information Space Properties

3. Add the desired attributes and measures to the Information Space on the OBJECTS tab of the Information Space wizard shown in Figure 11.28. Because this

calculation view was created specifically for this use case, select all of the objects. You can then organize the facets into meaningful facet groups.

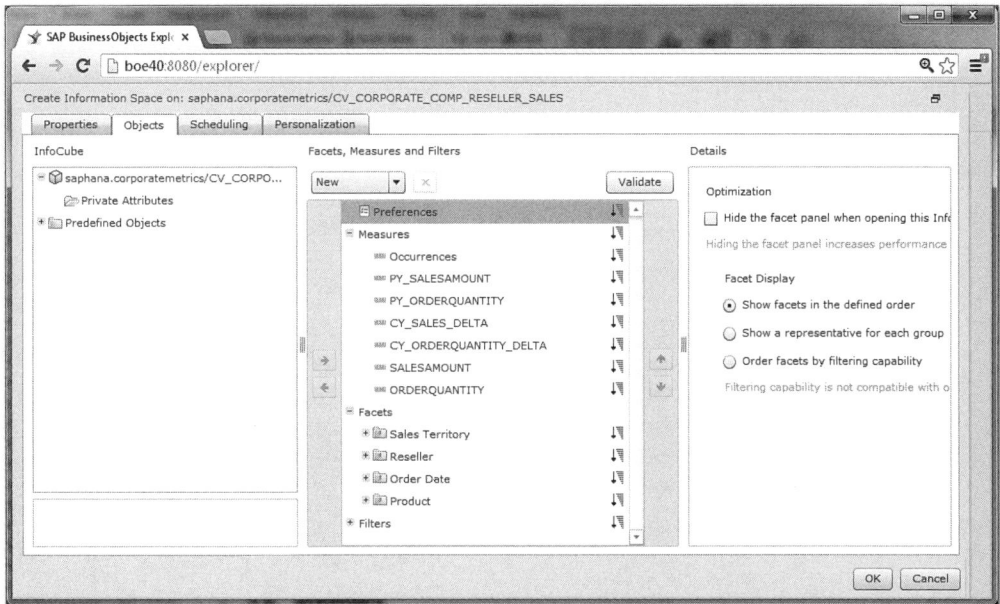

**Figure 11.28**  Selecting Objects

### SAP BusinessObjects Explorer and Calculation Views

Because we are using a calculation view, all of the attributes of the view are considered private attributes. This is a quirk of how SAP BusinessObjects Explorer perceives calculation views. We hope this will be improved in a later edition of SAP BusinessObjects Explorer.

4. After all of the core elements are added, you can add the calculated measures for the scenario, as shown in Figure 11.29. In this case, it's the percentage change calculations for sales amount and order quantity. The constituent elements are in the space already, so you just need to do the final division operation in SAP BusinessObjects Explorer. You can also take this opportunity to give the rest of the metrics more user-friendly names.

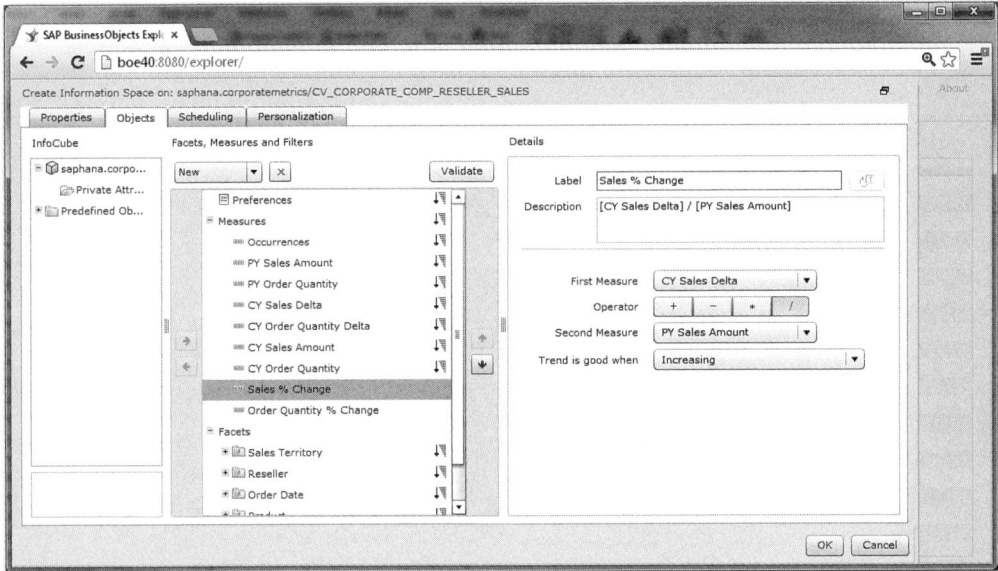

**Figure 11.29**  Adding Calculated Measures

**Formatting Measures in SAP BusinessObjects Explorer**

Unfortunately, there is no method in the current version of SAP BusinessObjects Explorer to format a calculated measure. This means the percentage change values in our case study are displayed in decimal format. There are open issues at SAP Ideas Place to address this, however.

5. The final step to preparing the Information Space for consumption by end users is creating the Information Space index. After closing the wizard, click the INDEX Now button. This process should only take a few seconds. Once complete, navigate to the HOME tab, and click REFRESH LIST to see the new Information Space and start exploring.

**Exploring the Information Space**

With the Information Space created, you can start testing and confirm that the design will provide the desired user experience—that is, allowing users to answer their key questions.

When users first open the Information Space, they are presented with the standard SAP BusinessObjects Explorer UI. The facets are displayed across the top in the order you defined, grouped by their facet groups with a bar chart showing the first measure by the first facet in the VISUALIZATIONS panel. At this point, you can filter the data using the facets and change the visualized facet if necessary.

**Creating the Exploration View Set**

To give users a quick entry to the data without them having to always start from the basic Information Space, you can create an Exploration View Set with a few predefined visualizations by following these steps:

1. Open the Information Space, and click CREATE VIEW SET.

2. A new view set (see Figure 11.30) opens with the current visualization displayed. At this point, you can tailor the visualization to your needs. The desired entry point for this example is a comparison of sales to prior period values for each sliced by ordered date year and month. To achieve this visualization, enable the visualization toolbar by clicking the icon that looks like a wrench and box. With the toolbar displayed, select the measures and facets as shown in Table 11.2.

| Measures | CY Sales Amount, PY Sales Amount |
|---|---|
| Facet | Ordered Year Month |
| Facet Sort Type | Sort; Ordered Year Month A-Z; Show Other False |

**Table 11.2** Create View Set Values

3. With the visualization defined, you can see that by default it will show a lot of data. This is probably more information than the user can really absorb. To give them an easy mechanism to filter the view to a more meaningful set but still give them the freedom to navigate through the data, you can add a facet selector to the visualization. Drag this in from the VISUAL ELEMENTS area. Make the following facets available for filtering; ORDERED YEAR, PRODUCT CATEGORY, and PRODUCT SUBCATEGORY. This provides the users the filtering they need without having to open the complete facet list. In Figure 11.30, you can see the completed view set ready for consumption by an end user.

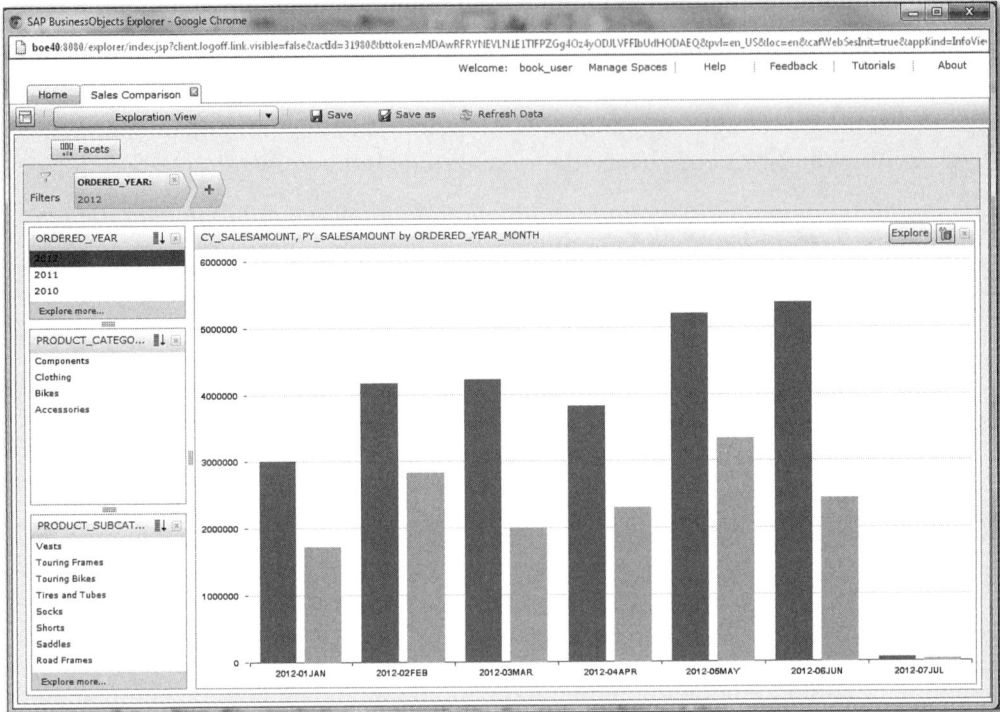

**Figure 11.30** Opening an Exploration View Set

### Mobilizing the Content

Now that you've created the Information Space and Exploration View Sets to deliver information to the end users, let's make the information available to the mobile workforce, leveraging the built-in mobility features of SAP BusinessObjects Explorer. The advantage to this approach is there is no additional work to be done to the content to make it available. You simply need to connect your iPad tablet to the server's URL and begin using the tool.

The configuration of the iPad is straightforward; the user follows these steps:

1. The user must enter an application password to protect any locally cached data.

2. Once in the application, the user configures a new connection, providing the URL of the server, the authentication mode, and the user name and password.

3. The user can now access the Information Space and Exploration View Set (created earlier) on their iPad, as shown in Figure 11.31.

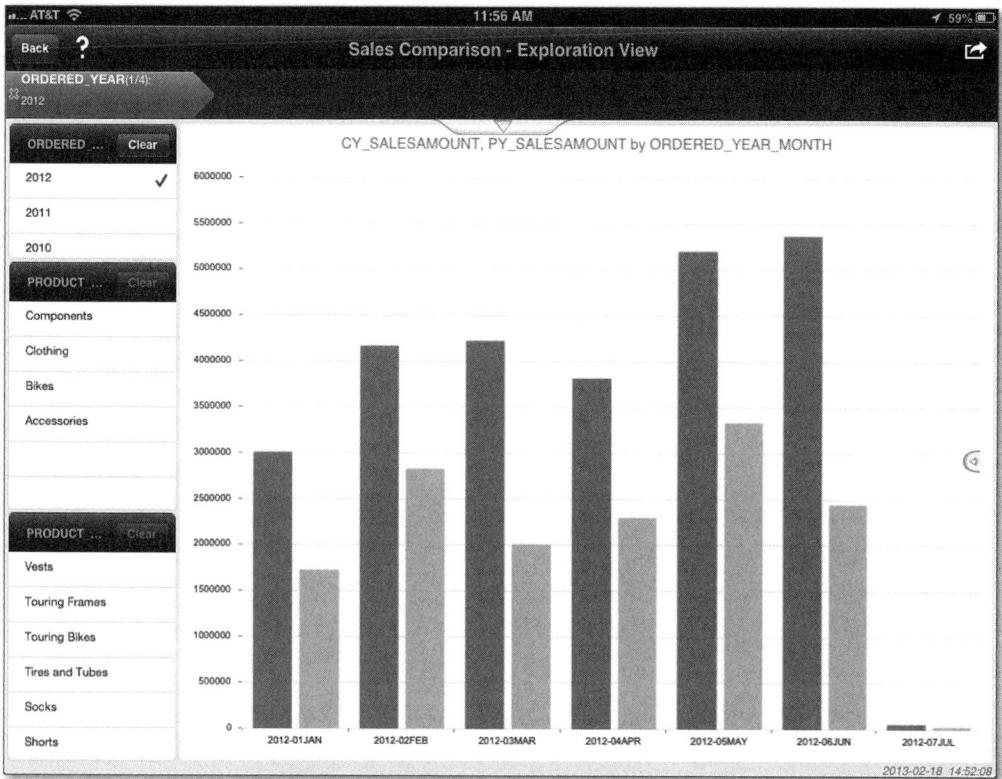

**Figure 11.31** Exploration View Set on an iPad

## 11.6    Summary

As you've seen throughout this chapter, the combination of SAP BusinessObjects Explorer, SAP Lumira, and SAP HANA provides a powerful toolkit to deliver information to a variety of user populations. The speed and power of the SAP HANA device delivers one of the key features of the solution. In this mobile era, users expect a solution that provides responsiveness in seconds. Combined with the user-friendly interface of SAP BusinessObjects Explorer and SAP Lumira, you can deliver a compelling user experience.

In the next chapter, we'll introduce SAP BusinessObjects Web Intelligence. We'll discuss methods of connecting to SAP HANA and reveal several optimization methods that can be implemented on the report and universe to enhance the performance of the reports. We'll cover several methods of sharing the SAP BusinessObjects Web Intelligence reports and will conclude with a real-world use case tying all of the topics together.

*Ad hoc reporting with SAP BusinessObjects Web Intelligence puts the power of SAP HANA into the hands of the users who need it most.*

# 12    SAP BusinessObjects Web Intelligence Powered by SAP HANA

The concept of reporting has inherent advantages and disadvantages. Reporting technologies provide access to data allowing a wide range of viewers to make informed decisions from thoughtful and timely access to that data. Reporting allows users to build their own analytics and visualizations for quick access in addition to the ability to request highly formatted reports that project a more professional image.

In this chapter, we introduce SAP BusinessObjects Web Intelligence (Section 12.1). We provide a comparison between SAP BusinessObjects Web Intelligence and SAP Crystal Reports (Section 12.2) and give information on the construction and manipulation of SQL statements within the tool (Section 12.3). Next we cover how connect SAP BusinessObjects Web Intelligence to SAP HANA (Section 12.4). We continue with a discussion of features that can be applied on the universe level and within SAP HANA to optimize queries and performance (Section 12.5). We conclude the chapter in Section 12.6 with a discussion on sharing reports developed within SAP BusinessObjects Web Intelligence and provide a use case outlining each of the elements that were covered within the chapter (Section 12.7).

## 12.1    The Road to SAP BusinessObjects Web Intelligence

SAP BusinessObjects Web Intelligence is a reporting tool that allows for quick and easy access to data that provides pragmatic benefits to the user. This reporting tool is a fully featured enterprise tool that provides both a web-based and desktop-based interface. The resulting reports are hosted on the SAP BusinessObjects platform or shared via Microsoft Excel spreadsheet, Adobe Acrobat (PDF), or Comma-Separated Value (CSV) file.

Since the tool was created, SAP BusinessObjects Web Intelligence reports have provided connections to data only through a universe. Introduced in the Business Objects XI R2 (pre-SAP acquisition), Web Intelligence started out as a browser-based application that provided access to data in terminology that made sense to the user. The users needed no knowledge of databases, their syntax, or any connectivity concepts—the users simply selected specific "business objects" from a listing of available objects. On the backend, Web Intelligence would build an SQL statement specifically for the database to which it was connected. This feature was discrete yet powerful because users no longer needed technical knowledge.

With the next version of SAP BusinessObjects (3.0/3.1), a desktop version of Web Intelligence was introduced. This version was called SAP BusinessObjects Web Intelligence Rich Client. The Rich Client provided all of the same functionality of the original Web Intelligence online, with some major differences. The biggest difference was the ability to connect to local data sources. Web Intelligence Rich Client provided the ability to connect these text and spreadsheet files called personal data sources, to the Web Intelligence application for analysis and visualization using familiar Web Intelligence tools. It also provided the ability to merge these data sources together with online data sources using the concept of merged dimensions. These provided users unprecedented access to integrate and analyze data from multiple online and local data sources. Rich Client reports based on universes could be published back to the platform to be shared with other users, scheduled, or even edited using the online version of Web Intelligence. Web Intelligence reports built on personal data sources are primarily designed to work on the user's desktop. These reports can be published to the repository if the data source is referenced by UNC path and the SIA is running under and account that has access to the UNC path. Server-based personal data sources are limited to a Windows server and become more difficult on non-Windows environments such as Linux and Solaris.

The current version of SAP BusinessObjects, which is 4.1, builds on this same web client/desktop client model by keeping the same look and feel of both clients consistent through the ground-up rebuild of SAP BusinessObjects Web Intelligence. The Rich Client still has the ability to connect to personal data sources as well as universes hosted on the platform. Reports can still be published to the platform and shared via the same methods. However, SAP BusinessObjects Web Intelligence on SAP BusinessObjects 4 improves upon the reporting model by more fully integrating data sources such as SAP NetWeaver Business Warehouse (BW) queries. Direct connectivity to SAP Business Explorer (BEx) queries and the hierarchies built within provides a greater return on investment by not requiring that the same queries be rebuilt within a universe. Users connect directly to these queries from SAP NetWeaver and generate reports without requiring a new middle layer.

SAP BusinessObjects Web Intelligence at SAP BusinessObjects 4 was rewritten from the ground up to include enhanced workflows through a completely redesigned interface. The same concepts of the original Web Intelligence are still there, but the methods by which you put these concepts into practice have been updated to make them easier to discover and implement. For instance, the context-sensitive PROPERTIES tab that was available in SAP BusinessObjects Web Intelligence at the SAP BusinessObjects 3.x release has been replaced by a combination of tabs and subtabs at the top of the interface as well as an enhanced context menu available after right-clicking an element of the report.

The combination of the new connectivity methods along with the newly redesigned SAP BusinessObjects Web Intelligence interface has helped the tool become one of the easiest and best integrated enterprise reporting tools available. The acquisition of BusinessObjects by SAP has taken both companies in a direction that provides both a wider and more diverse audience as well as a more fully featured set of reporting and analytic tools.

## 12.2 Comparing SAP BusinessObjects Web Intelligence and SAP Crystal Reports

The idea of reporting has always been central to business intelligence (BI). We've discussed the SAP BusinessObjects Web Intelligence tool and how it has become one of the most used reporting tools available today. However, we need to discuss how SAP BusinessObjects Web Intelligence fits into the reporting tools that are available in the SAP BusinessObjects suite. We'll discuss this relationship in an effort to understand how SAP HANA fits with the tools and what advantage SAP BusinessObjects Web Intelligence can bring that other tools can't.

In the beginning of the tools, Web Intelligence (see Figure 12.1) and its sibling Full Client (renamed to Desktop Intelligence or "Deski" at XIR2) worked together to provide both an online, ad hoc reporting system as well as a desktop-based reporting tool. The de facto standard for professional reporting was (and still is) Crystal Reports. After Business Objects purchased Crystal Reports, the internal dynamics among the reporting tools began to shift. Desktop Intelligence became overshadowed as a reporting tool due to the wide usage of Crystal Reports and was retired as a reporting tool as of SAP BusinessObjects 4. This introduced an issue to clients who used Deski reports within their organization. While there are migration paths to convert Deski reports to SAP BusinessObjects Web Intelligence, some clients have hundreds or thousands of Deski reports that would take time to convert and test for accuracy. At SAP BusinessObjects 4.1, SAP introduces a new Desktop Intelligence Compatibility Kit to address this concern.

With the deprecation of Desktop Intelligence, we now have two reporting tools available: SAP BusinessObjects Web Intelligence and SAP Crystal Reports. While the two reports provide the same conceptual outcome (actionable reports), there are two very different paradigms, tools, and audiences for each tool. Actionable reports are those that provide data in a real and concise manner on which viewers can either immediately take action or use as input into other processes that provide business value. Both SAP BusinessObjects Web Intelligence and SAP Crystal Reports provide this capability. However, let's look at how the two tools are different.

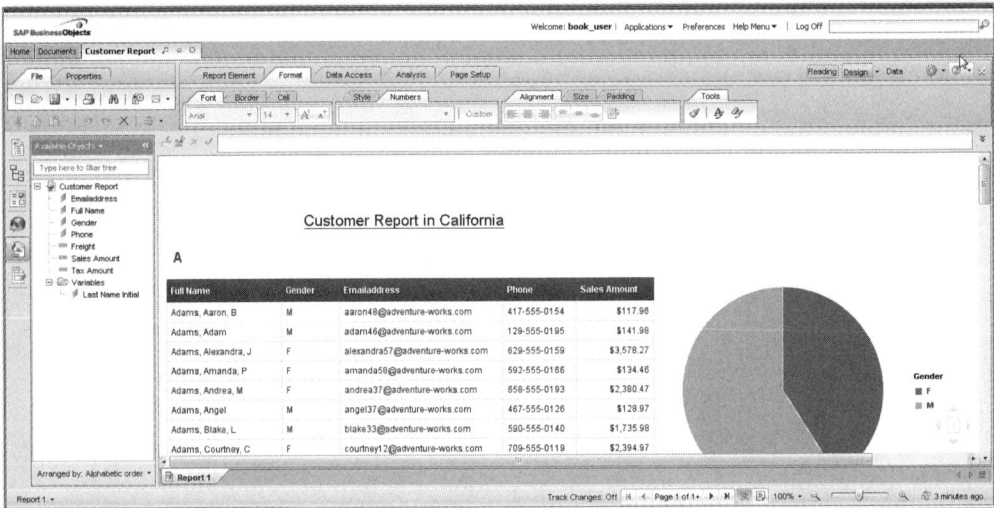

**Figure 12.1** A Standard SAP BusinessObjects Web Intelligence Interface

## 12.3 Manual Construction of an SQL Statement

Building SQL statements can be a daunting task to some business users. SAP BusinessObjects Web Intelligence was built to provide nontechnical users a way to connect to their data regardless of the location or type of the database. Let's have a look at what is involved in building a simple SQL statement.

Let's take the case of a report that uses sales revenue. The sales revenue column may be contained in a table called EAS_XLS_SLS_DATA inside of a column called SLS_RVE. At the bare minimum, a user needs to build an SQL statement such as:

```
SELECT SLS_RVE
FROM EAS_XLS_SLS_DATA
```

However an SQL statement is rarely, if ever, this simple. The Sales Revenue figure must be projected with a descriptive column to make it more useful. Consider the case where the sales revenue needs to be projected with Fiscal Year. The Fiscal Year can be in the same EAS_XLS_SLS_DATA table but kept in a text field called FISCAL_YR. If you project the Fiscal Year alongside the Sales Revenue figure, your SQL statement must be expanded to something like this:

```
SELECT FISCAL_YR, SLS_RVE
FROM EAS_XLS_SLS_DATA
```

Good universe design dictates that you enhance the SQL statement to include aggregate functions. Aggregate functions push the calculation of fields back down to the database level because database servers are typically much more powerful than application servers such as the SAP BusinessObjects server. Enhancing the SQL statement with this best practice, the SQL statement now reads:

```
SELECT FISCAL_YR, SUM(SLS_RVE )
FROM EAS_XLS_SLS_DATA
GROUP BY FISCAL_YR
```

Time and practice provide a user the ability to swiftly create such SQL statements. However, the more complex the reporting requirements become, the more complex the SQL statements can be. It's a better use of a person's time to analyze data rather than build SQL statements. SAP BusinessObjects Web Intelligence solves this problem through the use of a universe. The *universe* is the semantic layer that provides mapping of real-world terminology (Sales Revenue) to underlying database tables and fields (EAS_XLS_SLS_DATA.SLS_RVE). Web Intelligence uses the structure of the universe to create what's known as inferred SQL, as shown in Figure 12.2.

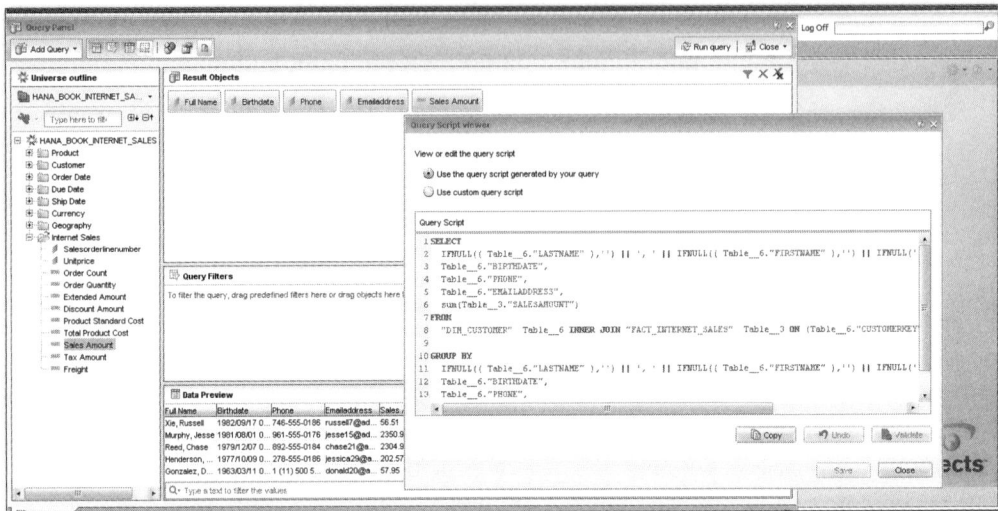

**Figure 12.2** SAP BusinessObjects Web Intelligence's Query Panel and Inferred SQL

## 12.4 Connecting SAP BusinessObjects Web Intelligence to SAP HANA

Now that we've talked about SAP BusinessObjects Web Intelligence, its history, and how it fits into business as a true ad hoc reporting and analytic tool, let's talk about how SAP BusinessObjects Web Intelligence connects to SAP HANA. With the on-the-fly nature of data within SAP BusinessObjects Web Intelligence, you can see the obvious advantage of having real-time data available when and where you need it. But there are things to consider when you build reports in SAP BusinessObjects Web Intelligence against such large (and fast!) data sources.

First of all, you need to connect SAP BusinessObjects Web Intelligence to SAP HANA. In other chapters, we've discussed ways to connect to SAP HANA. In SAP BusinessObjects Web Intelligence, you connect to SAP HANA via a universe by installing the client middleware. Recall from Chapter 9 that after the client middleware is installed, you can create either an Open Database Connectivity (ODBC) or Java Database Connectivity (JDBC) connection to the SAP HANA system. The administrator of the SAP HANA system should provide you with a server name, port number, user name, and password with which you can log in to the system, as shown in Figure 12.3.

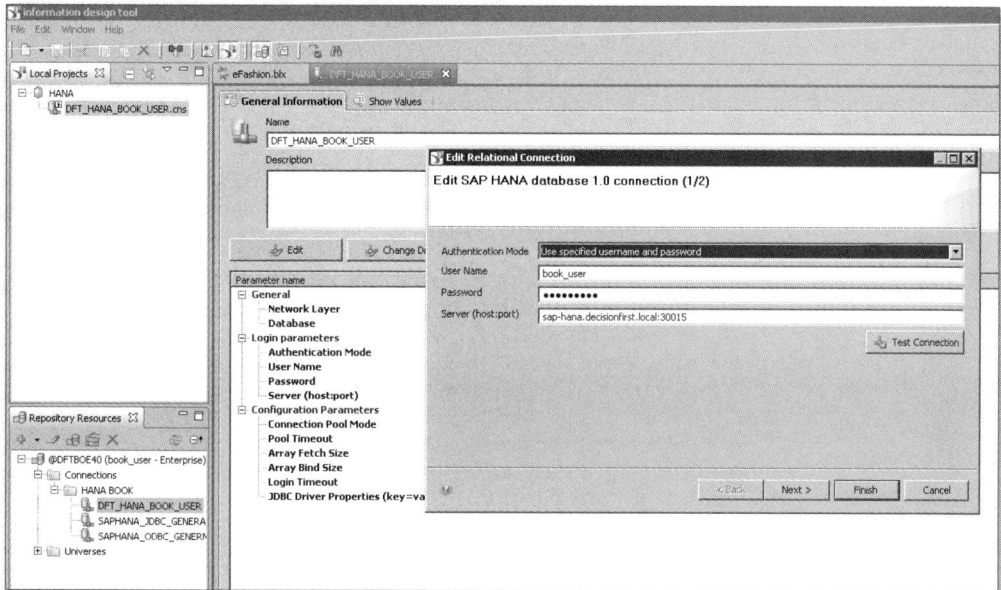

**Figure 12.3**  Creating a Connection to an SAP HANA Instance from the Information Design Tool

After the ODBC/JDBC source has been created, you now create the connection to the SAP HANA system using the Information Design Tool (IDT). We discussed these steps in Chapter 9. Next you determine whether you'll allow your users to connect to the raw tables in the user's schema or if views will be implemented. The two types of views are analytic views and calculation views, which are available in the _SYS_BIC schema. After the raw tables and/or views are discovered, simply lay them out in a data foundation and create the associated objects in the business layer. Ensure that the objects from the SAP HANA system have appropriate names. For instance, we previously used the topic of Sales Revenue. If the Sales Revenue measure is kept in a raw data table called HANA_SALES_DATA in a field called SLS_REV, simply drag the SLS_REV field to the appropriate class in the business layer and provide a name that is descriptive of what is contained within the field (i.e., sales revenue). Finally, you systematically move from object to object and qualify each as a dimension, detail, or measure, as defined here:

► **Dimensions**

Fields that contains data represented as text (e.g., street names, customer names, product categories).

▶ **Details**
Fields that provide more information about a dimension. A detail is typically attached to a dimension (e.g., street number, telephone area code).

▶ **Measures**
Fields that can be aggregated (e.g., sales revenue, taxes paid, quantity).

Now that you've created the connection to the SAP HANA system and have generated a universe in the IDT, the universe should be published to an SAP BusinessObjects 4.1 repository. The act of publishing a universe makes the objects available to the various tools available with the suite, of which SAP BusinessObjects Web Intelligence is one.

The SAP BusinessObjects Web Intelligence application, as mentioned earlier, has two forms: online and Rich Client. To access the universe-based on SAP HANA in SAP BusinessObjects Web Intelligence online, simply log in to the platform via a compatible browser such as Internet Explorer 9. The standard URL follows this format: *http://<servername>:<port>/BOE/BI*.

Given proper permissions, SAP BusinessObjects Web Intelligence will display within the portal. Click the SAP BusinessObjects Web Intelligence icon on the applications window in the HOME screen to launch the application. A report can be created in either Web mode (no download required) or in the Rich Internet Application. The Web mode is a HTML-based creation tool that provides a full range of features from the SAP BusinessObjects Web Intelligence application. The Rich Internet Application is a Java-based application that provides similar features. The Web editor or Rich Internet Application can be selected in the SAP BusinessObjects Web Intelligence section of the PREFERENCES window in the SAP BusinessObjects BI Launchpad.

After the application is launched, click the NEW REPORT button. A listing of available data providers is presented. The web client can be built without a data source (that is, be used as a template) or connect to a universe. The Rich Internet Application can use no data source, universe, BEx queries, or analysis views. The desktop-based Rich Client can take advantage of the same data providers as the Rich Internet Application plus personal data providers. Personal data providers are local files such as CSVs or Excel spreadsheets. At this point, you click UNIVERSE, and navigate through the listing of universes built in both the Universe Designer and the IDT. SAP BusinessObjects Web Intelligence reports can be built from this point against SAP HANA tables and views as with any other data source available through a universe.

It may come as a surprise that, from an SAP BusinessObjects Web Intelligence perspective, there are no special skills needed to build reports against data loaded into SAP HANA. However, there are many known features of SAP BusinessObjects Web Intelligence that you can take advantage of to optimize the performance of SAP BusinessObjects Web Intelligence with larger data volumes. Let's turn our attention to these next.

## 12.5    Report Optimization Features with SAP HANA

The elements that you should consider are data synchronization using multiple queries, query drilling, and query stripping. The combination of these topics and standard reporting best practices can provide reports that are concise, useful, and expedient.

The creation of a report requires the construction of a query, which is built using the QUERY PANEL in SAP BusinessObjects Web Intelligence that connects to a data source through a universe. Objects are selected from the universe and dropped into the results objects as well as objects selected to be used as filters. As the objects are selected, SAP BusinessObjects Web Intelligence builds an SQL statement that is formatted properly for the type of data source that is being queried.

In the previous section, we discussed connectivity from SAP BusinessObjects Web Intelligence to SAP HANA. We described the methods by which you create a universe to access calculation views and analytic views as well as raw data stored in SAP HANA. In this section, we talk about several features of the semantic layer and SAP BusinessObjects Web Intelligence that can be used to optimize performance within SAP BusinessObjects Web Intelligence reports. Let's take a closer look at each of these features.

### 12.5.1    Usage of JOIN_BY_SQL

On the universe level, a feature is available that has existed since the very early versions of pre-SAP Business Objects. Recall that running multiple queries is expensive on the reporting engine side, so it's recommended that the designer move as much processing to the database server as possible. For this reason, we don't recommend using merged dimensions on an SAP HANA data source.

So when using two or more queries returning large sets of data, one feature to consider is the JOIN_BY_SQL parameter in the Universe Designer and IDT, which is shown in Figure 12.4.

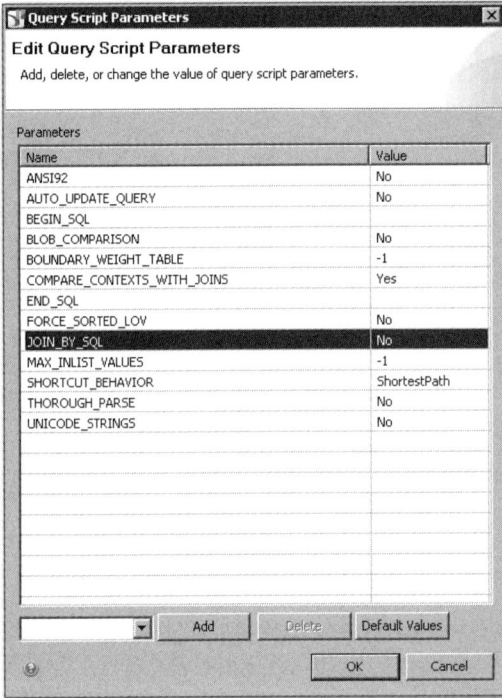

**Figure 12.4** Query Script Parameters Used to Set JOIN_BY_SQL

Let's start with a description of the JOIN_BY_SQL parameter and then conclude with information on how to set the connection and prove its operation. The JOIN_BY_SQL function is a parameter that instructs the middleware to execute a report using multiple queries on the database level rather than in the report engine. By setting this parameter, the universe designer is making the decision that all queries generated by the reporting application are to be pushed down on the database level. This is advantageous in cases where you have large data volumes—such as when you use SAP HANA.

For instance, look at the queries in Listing 12.1 and Listing 12.2.

```
SELECT
    Table__7."PRODUCT_NAME",
```

```
  sum(Table__7."SALESAMOUNT")
FROM
  "_SYS_BIC"."saphana.internetsales/ANLV_INTERNETSALES/olap"  Table__7
GROUP BY
  Table__7."PRODUCT_NAME"
```

**Listing 12.1** SQL Statement Returning Sales Amounts for Internet Sales

```
SELECT
  Table__7."PRODUCT_NAME",
  sum(Table__8."SALESAMOUNT")
FROM
  "_SYS_BIC"."saphana.internetsales/ANLV_INTERNETSALES/olap"  Table__7,
  "FACT_RESELLER_SALES"  Table__8
GROUP BY
  Table__7."PRODUCT_NAME"
```

**Listing 12.2** SQL Statement Returning Sales Amounts for Reseller Sales

Using merged dimensions, these two queries would be executed independently on the database server and the results sent back to the reporting engine to be merged together into a single result set. This approach introduces latency delays because of the slower speeds of the reporting engine. We do, however, take advantage of the speeds of in-memory database processing because of the speed at which the result sets of the two queries are returned. The bottleneck in this case is the merging step required on the database level.

Now let's have a look at the same query when using the JOIN_BY_SQL statement as shown in Listing 12.3.

```
SELECT
  COALESCE(F__1.Axis__1,F__2.Axis_1),
  F__1.M__1,
  F__2.M__1
FROM
  (
SELECT
  Table__3."ENGLISHPRODUCTNAME" AS Axis__1,
  sum(Table__4."SALESAMOUNT") AS M__1
FROM
  "DIM_CUSTOMER"  Table__1 INNER JOIN "FACT_INTERNET_SALES"  Table__4
ON (Table__1."CUSTOMERKEY"=Table__4."CUSTOMERKEY")
  INNER JOIN "DIM_PRODUCT"  Table__3 ON (Table__3."PRODUCTKEY"=Table__
```

```
4."PRODUCTKEY")

GROUP BY
  Table__3."ENGLISHPRODUCTNAME",
  Table__1."CUSTOMERKEY",
  Table__1."SUFFIX",
  Table__1."TITLE"
)
F__1
FULL OUTER JOIN
(
SELECT
  Table__7."PRODUCT_NAME" AS Axis__1,
  sum(Table__8."SALESAMOUNT") AS M__1
FROM
  "_SYS_BIC"."saphana.internetsales/ANLV_INTERNETSALES/olap"  Table__7,
  "FACT_RESELLER_SALES"  Table__8
GROUP BY
  Table__7."PRODUCT_NAME"
)
F__2
)
```

**Listing 12.3** A Combined SQL Statement from JOIN_BY_SQL

You can see that the two SQL statements are still generated by creating the same two queries on the reporting level. However, when the SQL is created, it's immediately generated as a combined SQL statement taking advantage of an outer join. The single SQL statement is then passed to the database for processing. The result set is then sent back to the report for display.

With this definition, we'll now show how to set the JOIN_BY_SQL parameter in the universe level. Begin by following the steps provided in Chapter 9 to generate a semantic layer on an SAP HANA data source. These steps remain the same. After the connection, connection shortcut, and the data foundation layers are created, you select the data foundation in the project explorer. Ensure that the properties for the data foundation can be viewed on the bottom-right corner of the screen. If not, click the "dash button" underneath the layout of the data foundation. Click the PARAMETER button. You'll see a dialog with a listing of parameters available to your database. One of these parameters is JOIN_BY_SQL. Simply change the value from No to YES by clicking the arrow beside the value. Save the data foundation and continue with the development of the universe. If you forget to set the JOIN_BY_SQL parameter before creating your business layer, just go back into the data foundation and set the parameter. It doesn't need to be set at any specific point in time during the development of the semantic layer; just remember to publish or republish your universe after setting the parameter.

### 12.5.2  Merged Dimensions versus Analytic/Calculation Views

When building queries, data requirements sometimes dictate that you use multiple queries to pull data into the report. When multiple queries are required, you have two choices of locations for the queries to be built and executed: either on the report server or on the database server. Typically when a query is created, you try to put as much processing on the database server as possible because database servers are usually resourced to have many more processors and more memory than a typical report server. The database handles the query and returns the data set.

When a report generates two or more queries based on the selection of objects, the reporting engine is responsible for stitching the results of the multiple queries together. This is usually the slowest route because one data set for each query is pulled. There is at least one common dimension that ties each of the queries together so that the report engine can match the resulting data sets. The data is then made available to be used in the report. The common dimension(s) in SAP BusinessObjects Web Intelligence is called a merged dimension.

The concept of merged dimensions as they relate to every data source is the same as the relationship to SAP HANA. The queries built on the data sources on SAP HANA are built in the same manner as any other data sources. However, consider where the queries are being stitched together. When the multiple queries are executed, each query pulls back a data set and holds it in memory. Each data set has its own location in memory. Now consider the fact that SAP HANA systems are attributed to very large and very fast data sets. When working with an SAP HANA data source, it's typically a best practice to build views in SAP HANA, and then access those views in the universe as opposed to manipulating separate queries and merging the data together.

> **Note**
>
> Minimize or eliminate the usage of merged dimensions on SAP HANA data sources. Build views that serve the data through the universe to SAP BusinessObjects Web Intelligence to maximize performance.

### 12.5.3   Implementing Query Drill for SAP HANA

Another feature of SAP BusinessObjects Web Intelligence that is discretely enhanced by using SAP HANA is *query drill*. Query drill is used when drilling into data that doesn't exist in memory in SAP BusinessObjects Web Intelligence. When creating a query in SAP BusinessObjects Web Intelligence, you specify a listing of dimensions and measures that are to be used in the report by adding them to the RESULT OBJECTS section of the QUERY PANEL. The inferred SQL is generated by SAP BusinessObjects Web Intelligence and passed to the database level when the query is executed. The data that is returned by the database server is held in memory and is available to the SAP BusinessObjects Web Intelligence report. Remember that not all of the objects in the RESULTS OBJECTS section may necessarily be used in the report.

To enable query drill for the current document, you access the properties of the document. Simply click the PROPERTIES tab on the top-left corner of the report designer, and then click DOCUMENT. A listing of properties appears that are available for the current document, including QUERY STRIPPING, AUTO MERGE DIMENSIONS, and QUERY DRILL. Click the checkbox beside QUERY DRILL to enable the setting. Leaving this unchecked will prevent a query drill from occurring in a report. This setting should be considered during the standard report design process due to the potential of increased traffic on the SAP HANA server. If drilling isn't required by the document, turn off QUERY DRILLING so that unnecessary (and potentially incorrect) queries aren't required of the SAP HANA database.

When building the query, you can open a fourth panel in the QUERY PANEL called SCOPE OF ANALYSIS. The SCOPE OF ANALYSIS panel allows you to pull extra data into the report without using the objects in the report until the report is drilled. With conventional data sources and smaller amounts of data, this is advantageous because data is held in memory until it's needed. However, this data is held in memory at the SAP BusinessObjects server, which isn't necessarily provisioned as strongly as a database server is. You can specify different levels in SCOPE OF ANALYSIS: NONE, ONE, TWO, THREE, or CUSTOM. These settings determine the depth of drillable data that will be pulled into the report.

When drilling is enabled in a report, you click on the underlined text to drill down into more detail. Hovering over the underlined text displays what happens when you click on the text. However, if you click on text that drills into an object that doesn't exist in the RESULTS OBJECTS area, you'll see (NEW QUERY) appended to the end of the tooltip. This means that SAP BusinessObjects Web Intelligence doesn't have enough data to provide the required level of drilling and must create a new query to pull the data into memory. Depending on the data source being used and the volume of data, this can run quickly, or it can take a long time.

Consider this same scenario when using SAP HANA as a data source. SAP HANA with its in-memory capabilities can be very quickly queried and data can be returned much faster than a conventional database. The idea here is that query drill is used without any scope of analysis (i.e., SCOPE OF ANALYSIS is NONE). When designing the query for the report, don't bring any objects into the report that aren't needed. This reduces the amount of memory required by the report on the SAP Business-Objects server. Because the data is available within a second or so on demand, take advantage of query drill for all drilling requirements.

Let's have a look at an example scenario of creating a report that uses a time hierarchy. You start on the YEAR level and show the total sales by YEAR. The requirements for this example dictate that you drill into QUARTER, MONTH, and WEEK. When you design the query, the only objects requested are YEAR and SALES AMOUNT. Leave the QUERY FILTERS blank because you don't want any data filtered out of the query. Click the SCOPE OF ANALYSIS button and ensure that SCOPE OF ANALYSIS is set to NONE. You'll see YEAR in the SCOPE OF ANALYSIS window, but you shouldn't see any of the other drillable dimensions. Click RUN QUERIES, and view the report.

Now turn on drilling and hover over YEAR. A tooltip displays with the text DRILL TO MONTH (NEW QUERY). When you click on YEAR, a new query is generated that pulls the Sales Amount aggregated by Month. The report is then redrawn to replace the YEAR column with MONTH. Using a conventional data source such as SQL Server or Oracle could take seconds, minutes, or hours to return this data depending on the amount of data being aggregated. This example isn't using summary tables or aggregate awareness that is generally attributed to drilling scenarios. With the optimizations of the SAP HANA data source, the transactional data is queried on demand. The transactional data is queried, and the appropriate result is returned to the report in real time.

The advantages here are twofold. First of all, the design of the report is simpler. Only the data that is required by the report is pulled into the reporting engine. The data volumes typically associated with an SAP HANA implementation are possible because data that isn't immediately required by the report isn't queried.

Second, the depth of drilling is dictated only by the requirements of the report, not by the resources available to the SAP BusinessObjects server. Because the data held in the SAP HANA data source is queried and returned almost immediately, the data held by the reporting server is reduced or made available to handle larger sets of data that are immediately required.

### 12.5.4 Implementing Query Stripping for SAP HANA

The cardinal rule when designing a report in any tool is that if the data isn't required, don't pull it into the report. Pulling too much unnecessary data into a report not only increases the memory use on the report server responsible for generating the report but also increases the load on the database server that is responsible for providing data to the report server. A feature of SAP BusinessObjects Web Intelligence that has, in the past, applied only to online analytic processing (OLAP) data sources is *query stripping*. This feature existed for OLAP data sources only. For SAP BusinessObjects 4.1, released in late 2013, query stripping was added for SAP HANA data sources to automatically reduce the number of data cells returned by all database queries.

The concept of query stripping in a report means that you shouldn't request an object's data from the database if that object isn't used in the report. The SQL statement is rewritten so that the unused objects aren't included, and the data isn't retrieved.

Query stripping can be enabled in the Document Properties section of an SAP BusinessObjects Web Intelligence report. Click on the Properties tab on the top-left corner of the reporting interface, and click Document. Select the Query Stripping checkbox to enable the functionality.

Let's look at an example of query stripping in an SAP BusinessObjects Web Intelligence document. Enabling the Query Stripping checkbox in an SAP BusinessObjects Web Intelligence document tells the report engine that if an object isn't used in the report, don't request it from the database server. For instance, consider the case in which you bring in Full Name, Address 1, Address 2, Email Address, and Sales Amount. In the report, you build a block that displays Full Name, Email Address, and Sales Amount. In a standard query without query stripping, all of the objects in the query results window are used to build the inferred SQL statement. That query is shown here:

```
SELECT full_name, Address_1, Address_2, Email_Address, Sales Amount
FROM INTERNET_SALES
```

The SQL statement is passed to the database server, and the full set of data is returned. The result is a block with 3,500 records and 5 columns resulting in approximately 17,500 cells of data.

But with QUERY STRIPPING enabled, the SQL statement is modified to only pull the objects that are referenced in the report. The resulting SQL statement with the unnecessary fields stripped away appears like this:

```
SELECT full_name, Email_Address, Sales Amount
FROM INTERNET_SALES
```

The result of this SQL statement is 3,500 records of data, but this time with only 3 columns of data. This SQL call results in 10,500 cells of data, which is just over half of the original request.

While these smaller results sets won't mean a lot of savings in total data consumed by enabling query stripping, consider cases when your queries return hundreds of thousands to millions of records of data. If you were to multiply the returned rows in the example that we just gave by 1,000, the benefit of query stripping becomes obvious. It's much better to return 10.5 million cells of data than 17.5 million cells. The memory savings on the reporting side is considerably less if the data isn't needed and isn't retrieved.

Let's modify the report once again. This time, add the ADDRESS1 field that you added in the query results pane of the QUERY PANEL. It doesn't matter where the ADDRESS1 field is added in the report; it can be a field in one or more tables, an axis in a chart, or even referenced in a report filter. Because the dimension is referenced in the report, the SQL is updated to include the ADDRESS1 field with QUERY STRIPPING enabled, as follows:

```
SELECT full_name, Address1, Email_Address, Sales Amount
FROM INTERNET_SALES
```

This results in the number of cells returned increases by the number of rows returned by the query. The benefit to query stripping is that it returns smaller result sets if they aren't used within the report. This is done automatically after QUERY STRIPPING is set in the DOCUMENT PROPERTIES. No other intervention is required by the user.

## 12.6    Sharing Reports within SAP BusinessObjects 4.1

Development of SAP BusinessObjects Web Intelligence reports is a process by which you can derive real and actionable data from transactional systems via in-memory database technology such as SAP HANA. When connecting to SAP HANA via a universe, the development of these reports follows typical report design methodology. After the reports are developed and are verified as accurate, they can then be shared with other users within the organization or outside of the SAP BusinessObjects system. Sharing reports isn't a process that is specific to those that are developed for SAP HANA. After a report is published, the data connection is inconsequential to the sharing method. There are several methods by which you can share SAP BusinessObjects Web Intelligence reports. In the following sections, we'll divide the sharing of reports into two sections: internal users and external users.

### 12.6.1    Sharing Reports for Internal Users

Internal users are defined as users who have access to the internal network and are able to log in to the SAP BusinessObjects system. These users can access the reports within the repository and execute the reports themselves without any sort of distribution plan—for example, someone within the enterprise who has been explicitly granted an SAP BusinessObjects license or the URL for the SAP Business-Objects system.

#### Storing Documents for Internal Users

The easiest and most secure method of distributing reports is to internal users. To distribute a report based on an SAP HANA universe, the only thing that you need to consider is the length of the report. The number of records that are typically associated with an SAP HANA data source are usually very high; a large data set can extend the length of a report to tens or hundreds of pages. Distributing a report that is this large can be cumbersome and can actually fail in email systems that have limitations on the size of email attachments, and distributing large reports to FTP sites can also be troublesome due to potential issues in upload bandwidth.

The application that is used to build the report has an impact on how it's shared. Using desktop-based tools such as Web Intelligence Rich Client and SAP Crystal Reports 2011 provide different distribution options and processes than tools such as the server-based SAP BusinessObjects Web Intelligence application. A report developed in a server-based environment is saved in the repository and has many options for sharing as do reports developed in a desktop-based application. However, the server-based environment can take advantage of publications and sharing by scheduling reports.

### Repository Access for Internal Users

Let's walk through an example of developing a report in SAP BusinessObjects Web Intelligence in a server-based environment. As developer, you log into the SAP BusinessObjects BI Launchpad via any supported browser and develop the report as usual, creating it against a universe (i.e., the semantic layer UNX, not the legacy universe UNV) and saving it to a folder in the repository. Clicking SAVE when working with a report presents options of places to save the report within the repository. You can save the report in SAP BusinessObjects Web Intelligence format in both the FAVORITES folders and the PUBLIC FOLDERS. In the FAVORITES folders, only the user for whom the FAVORITES folder was created can access the reports. If the user saves the document in the PUBLIC FOLDERS, any user who has access to the target folder will be able to view the saved report.

### Accessing Documents Using OpenDocument

When the report is saved to a public folder, you can share the report in a secure method using a protocol called OpenDocument. To get started with OpenDocument, right-click a report and choose DOCUMENT LINK, as shown in Figure 12.5.

The browser is updated to display a full hyperlink that can be distributed to internal users of the system. When this hyperlink is sent to other users by direct email, embedded in a document, included in a custom corporate portal, or by other means, the user can click on the link or paste it in a browser. This action immediately forwards the browser to the SAP BusinessObjects system and request credentials. On entering the proper credentials, the user is taken directly to the report without needing to navigate through the SAP BusinessObjects BI Launchpad. This is particularly advantageous when users have not been trained on the system, yet need quick and secure access to their documents.

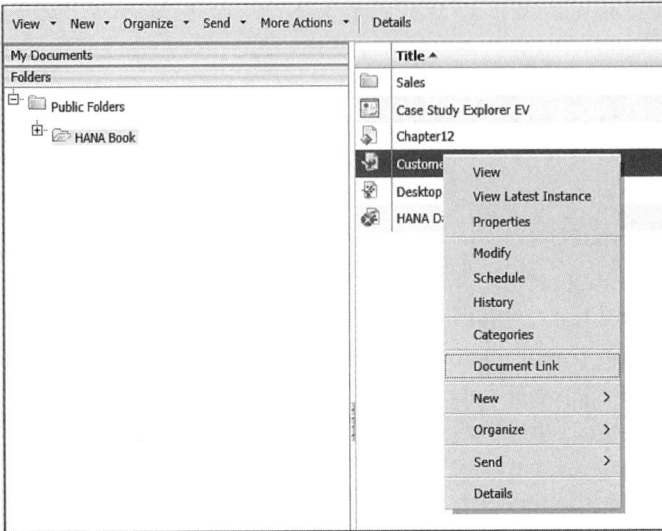

**Figure 12.5**  The Document Link Option for the Customer Report

---

**Note**

A typical OpenDocument hyperlink has this format: *http://BOESystem40/BOE/OpenDocument/opendoc/openDocument.jsp?sIDType=CUID&iDocID=AWvattjQqXNFgl9Ln0iUToI*.

See the *OpenDocument User's Guide* for more information at *http://help.sap.com/businessobject/product_guides/sbo41/en/sbo41_opendocument_en.pdf*.

---

### My Favorites Folders

Another option for internal users is to save the report to their FAVORITES folder. They can continue to manipulate the folder in the FAVORITES folder for as long as necessary. However, if the report needs to be accessed by another user, the report can be moved or copied to PUBLIC FOLDERS. Moving a report from a FAVORITES folder to the PUBLIC FOLDERS removes the original from the FAVORITES folder and relocates it to the PUBLIC FOLDERS.

Technically, an ID and a CUID are generated when a file is created in SAP Business-Objects. When moving the report, the same ID and CUID are maintained, thereby keeping any links to the report intact. If a report is copied, the original report is kept in the FAVORITES folder, and a complete copy is created in the target folder. A brand new ID and CUID are generated for the report.

**Saving Reports for Mobile Access**

Another secure method of distributing reports provides for access of the reports on mobile devices such as Apple iPad. In SAP BusinessObjects 4 SP6, you can view SAP Crystal Reports, SAP BusinessObjects Web Intelligence, SAP BusinessObjects Dashboards, and SAP BusinessObjects Design Studio documents on the mobile device.

SAP Crystal Reports are displayed on the mobile device exactly as they appear on the desktop launchpad. The report can be refreshed on demand directly on the mobile device without the need to interact with the report in the launchpad. SAP BusinessObjects Web Intelligence reports are a bit different.

SAP BusinessObjects Web Intelligence reports are developed on the desktop with mobility in mind. However, there is a subset of tables, charts, and report elements that isn't supported on the mobile device. Also, specific layouts during the design of the reports will affect the layout of the report on the mobile device. Consult the document *Designing BI Documents for Mobile Users* on the SAP Product Guides website for further design information (*http://help.sap.com/businessobject/product_guides/boexir4/en/xi4_mobile_bi_rep_design_en.pdf*).

Several layers of security are built into the SAP BusinessObjects BI Mobile application. Printed reports can be quickly picked up and carried away as well as photocopied and distributed. Email can be easily intercepted, and sensitive information can be compromised very quickly.

As a result, the SAP BusinessObjects BI Mobile application requires two levels of security. First of all, an application password is required to allow access to the app itself. If the mobile device is lost or otherwise intercepted, the user must have the password before accessing the system. After the app password is entered, the user must then connect to the SAP BusinessObjects platform to access reports. Reports can be secured so that they can't be saved to the mobile device or emailed from the mobile application.

## 12.6.2　Sharing Reports for External Users

External users are defined as users who don't have access to an account in the SAP BusinessObjects system. These users typically receive their reports via email, file share, or FTP. Examples of these users include customers, franchise managers, contractors, or anyone who won't have access to the internal network and won't have a license to use SAP BusinessObjects.

While in the report editor, the user can immediately share the document by clicking the EXPORT button in the toolbar. The EXPORT button at the top of Figure 12.6 exposes three options: EXPORT DOCUMENT AS (exports the entire document, including the report tabs), EXPORT CURRENT REPORT AS (exports only the currently selected REPORT tab), and EXPORT DATA TO CSV (exports only the data to a CSV file).

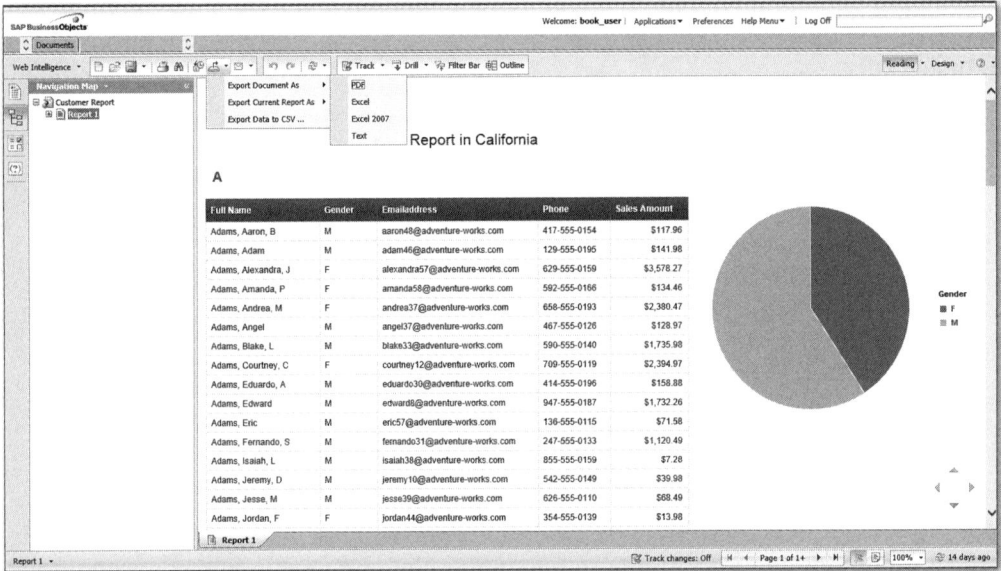

**Figure 12.6**  Export Options Available in SAP BusinessObjects Web Intelligence

The third option (EXPORT DATA TO CSV) directly saves the data as a file. (The other two options present the same listing of options that must be selected prior to generating a local file.) When you're choosing a file type, selecting the PDF option directly exports the document or specific report as a PDF file. This resulting PDF is then a file that can be emailed, copied, printed, or otherwise distributed as any local file can be distributed. Selecting either EXCEL or EXCEL 2007 prompts the user to save an .xls or .xlsx file, respectively.

Saving a document as an Excel file as illustrated in Figure 12.7 provides the user with the layout and data of the original report. However, this format is limited to the standard 65,535 rows and 256 columns, which can be easily exceeded by a data source such as SAP HANA. Exporting the report using the EXCEL 2007 option greatly increases these limits. An Excel 2007 or higher file (.xlsx) can hold up to 1,048,576 rows and 16,384 columns.

While this is only a fraction of the cells that an SAP HANA system can serve, it still provides enough data for an individual to use to make business decisions. If more data is required, the user should connect directly to the SAP HANA data source rather than exporting the data to another format.

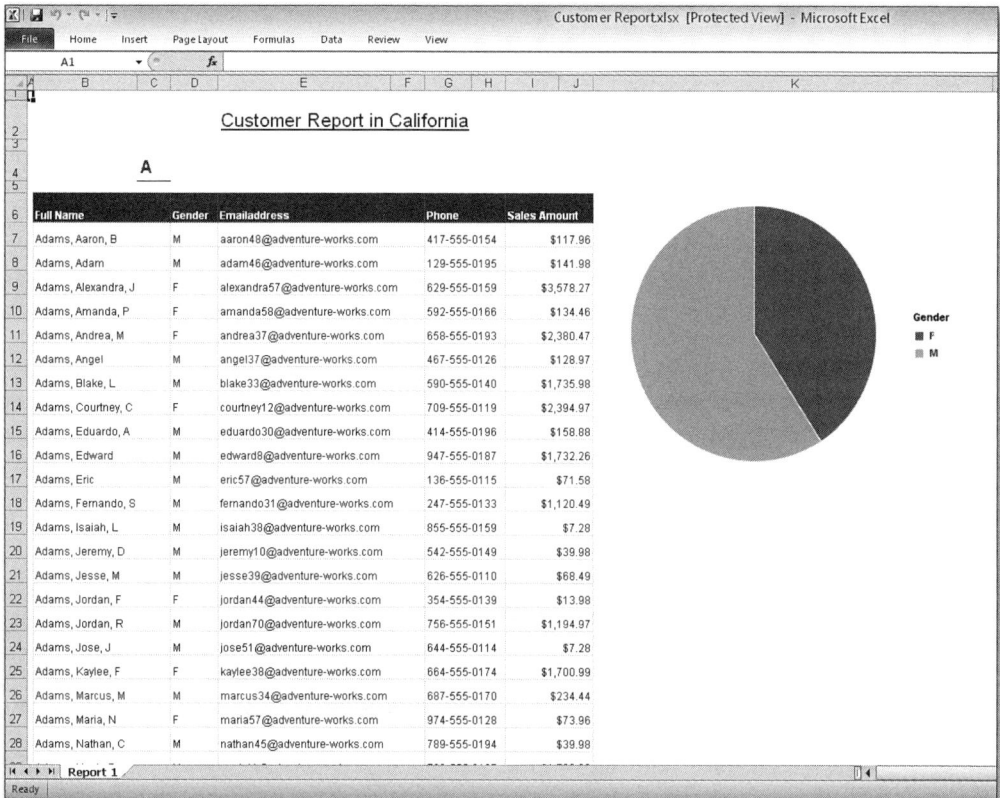

**Figure 12.7** The Report Exported as Excel 2007

The last option in the secondary dropdown is TEXT. When selecting this option, the file that results is a simple text file that is stripped of all formatting and contains all header, title, body, and footer text on separate lines, as shown in Figure 12.8. The tabular data is displayed as tab-separated text. The tabular data also retains the same format as displayed in the source report. In the text format, all charts and graphical elements are ignored.

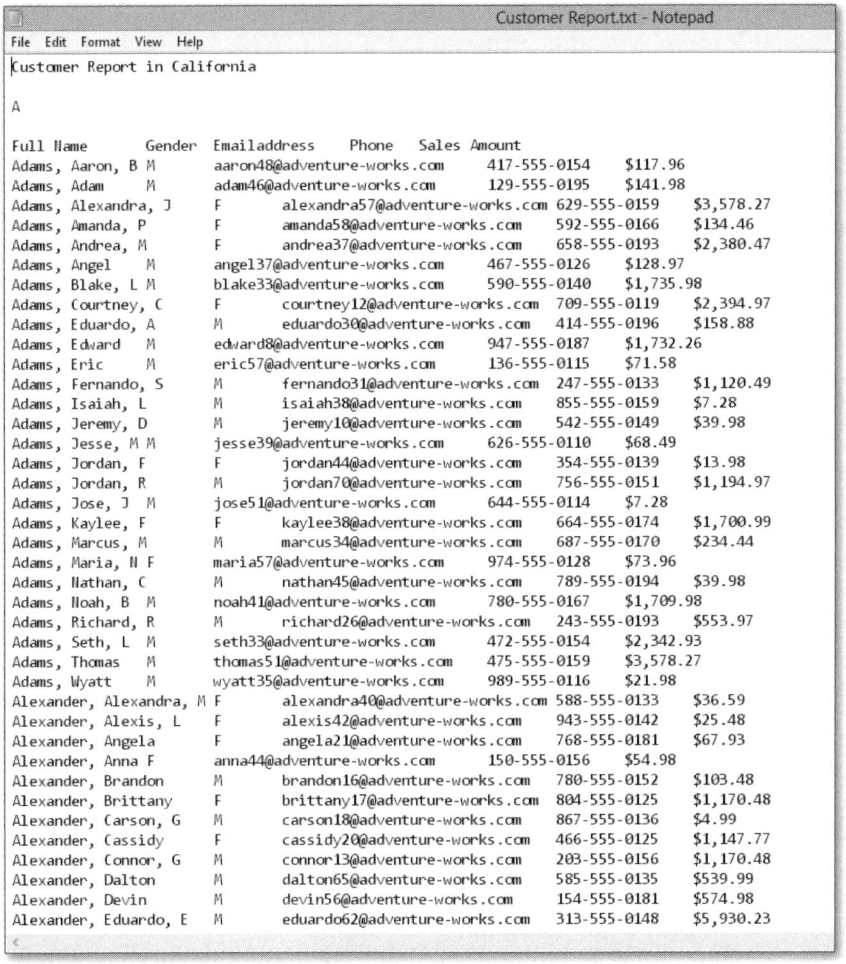


```
Customer Report in California

A

Full Name       Gender  Emailaddress    Phone   Sales Amount
Adams, Aaron, B M       aaron48@adventure-works.com     417-555-0154    $117.96
Adams, Adam     M       adam46@adventure-works.com      129-555-0195    $141.98
Adams, Alexandra, J     F       alexandra57@adventure-works.com 629-555-0159    $3,578.27
Adams, Amanda, P        F       amanda58@adventure-works.com    592-555-0166    $134.46
Adams, Andrea, M        F       andrea37@adventure-works.com    658-555-0193    $2,380.47
Adams, Angel    M       angel37@adventure-works.com     467-555-0126    $128.97
Adams, Blake, L M       blake33@adventure-works.com     590-555-0140    $1,735.98
Adams, Courtney, C      F       courtney12@adventure-works.com  709-555-0119    $2,394.97
Adams, Eduardo, A       M       eduardo30@adventure-works.com   414-555-0196    $158.88
Adams, Edward   M       edward8@adventure-works.com     947-555-0187    $1,732.26
Adams, Eric     M       eric57@adventure-works.com      136-555-0115    $71.58
Adams, Fernando, S      M       fernando31@adventure-works.com  247-555-0133    $1,120.49
Adams, Isaiah, L        M       isaiah38@adventure-works.com    855-555-0159    $7.28
Adams, Jeremy, D        M       jeremy10@adventure-works.com    542-555-0149    $39.98
Adams, Jesse, M M       jesse39@adventure-works.com     626-555-0110    $68.49
Adams, Jordan, F        F       jordan44@adventure-works.com    354-555-0139    $13.98
Adams, Jordan, R        M       jordan70@adventure-works.com    756-555-0151    $1,194.97
Adams, Jose, J  M       jose51@adventure-works.com      644-555-0114    $7.28
Adams, Kaylee, F        F       kaylee38@adventure-works.com    664-555-0174    $1,700.99
Adams, Marcus, M        M       marcus34@adventure-works.com    687-555-0170    $234.44
Adams, Maria, N F       maria57@adventure-works.com     974-555-0128    $73.96
Adams, Nathan, C        M       nathan45@adventure-works.com    789-555-0194    $39.98
Adams, Noah, B  M       noah41@adventure-works.com      780-555-0167    $1,709.98
Adams, Richard, R       M       richard26@adventure-works.com   243-555-0193    $553.97
Adams, Seth, L  M       seth33@adventure-works.com      472-555-0154    $2,342.93
Adams, Thomas   M       thomas51@adventure-works.com    475-555-0159    $3,578.27
Adams, Wyatt    M       wyatt35@adventure-works.com     989-555-0116    $21.98
Alexander, Alexandra, M F       alexandra40@adventure-works.com 588-555-0133    $36.59
Alexander, Alexis, L    F       alexis42@adventure-works.com    943-555-0142    $25.48
Alexander, Angela       F       angela21@adventure-works.com    768-555-0181    $67.93
Alexander, Anna F       anna44@adventure-works.com      150-555-0156    $54.98
Alexander, Brandon      M       brandon16@adventure-works.com   780-555-0152    $103.48
Alexander, Brittany     F       brittany17@adventure-works.com  804-555-0125    $1,170.48
Alexander, Carson, G    M       carson18@adventure-works.com    867-555-0136    $4.99
Alexander, Cassidy      F       cassidy20@adventure-works.com   466-555-0125    $1,147.77
Alexander, Connor, G    M       connor13@adventure-works.com    203-555-0156    $1,170.48
Alexander, Dalton       M       dalton65@adventure-works.com    585-555-0135    $539.99
Alexander, Devin        M       devin56@adventure-works.com     154-555-0181    $574.98
Alexander, Eduardo, E   M       eduardo62@adventure-works.com   313-555-0148    $5,930.23
```

**Figure 12.8** Text Document Exported from an SAP BusinessObjects Web Intelligence Report

We touched on the subject of data security in the section on the SAP BusinessObjects BI Mobile app for the iPad, but it bears repeating here as the concept of big data takes hold and ubiquitous access to data becomes more prevalent with SAP HANA. When reports are generated and exported to any format, whether it's PDF, CSV, TXT, XLS, XLSX, or any other exportable format, the data is decoupled from the system and can no longer be controlled by the SAP BusinessObjects security. If reports are saved onto a drive, the drive location can be compromised and the reports can be stolen. If reports are emailed to any email address, the email can be intercepted, and the data compromised. Consider the nature of the data being generated in the exported reports and the ramifications should the reports be intercepted. The built-in distribution methods of the SAP BusinessObjects platform optimize data security and accessibility while providing an easy access to data for those who need it when they need it.

Let's walk through a case study to build an SAP BusinessObjects Web Intelligence report that uses SAP HANA as a data source. We'll follow the use case of the Global Sales Manager from AdventureWorks to provide reporting on sales figures stored in SAP HANA.

## 12.7 Case Study: Exploring Sales Data with SAP Business-Objects Web Intelligence

The AdventureWorks Global Sales Manager, Dave, is interested in learning more about the company's sales figures. Although Dave can request that the reporting team handle the creation of the report for him, he knows that that the reporting team is overtasked, and he might wind up waiting a long time before his report is created and returned to him.

Rather than waiting for the reporting team, Dave decides to take advantage of SAP BusinessObjects Web Intelligence to get quick answers to his questions. As a manager, he's savvy enough to know how to log in to the SAP BusinessObjects Web Intelligence application but has no knowledge of databases and doesn't want to learn. Although he doesn't know that the industrious BI team has invested in SAP HANA, he has heard that there have been "phenomenal" response times reported.

Dave wants to begin by building a report showing the various products that were sold in both the Internet sales and reseller sales. He doesn't know anything about the location or type of the database. All that he knows is that a universe called InternetSales has been created.

So he opens the SAP BusinessObjects portal and launches an instance of SAP BusinessObjects Web Intelligence. On creating a new report, he is presented with options of data source connections: No Data Source, Universe, BEx, and Analysis View. He selects Universe and receives the list of universes stored on the system, as shown in Figure 12.9.

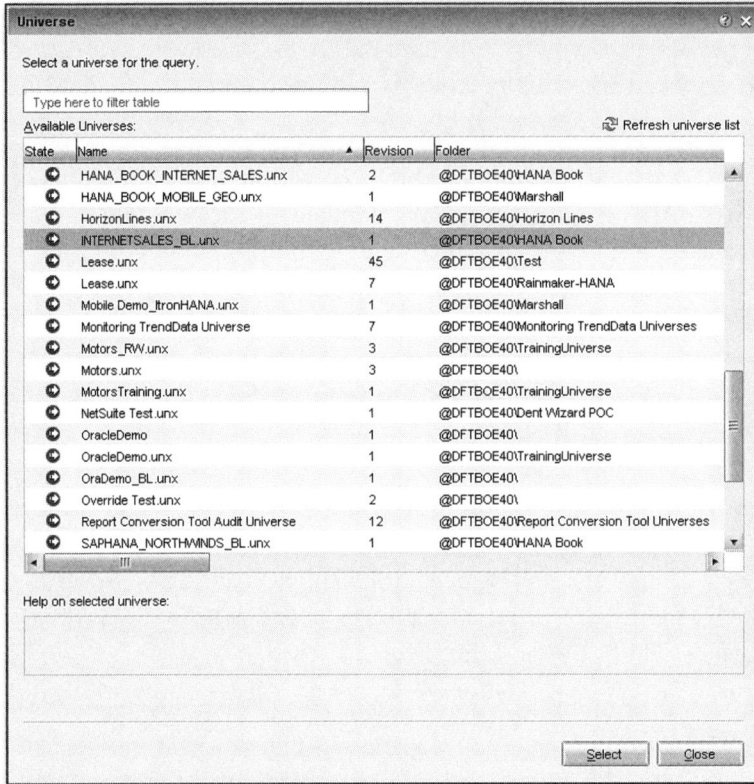

**Figure 12.9**   A Listing of Available Universes

Dave sees the INTERNETSALES_BL.unx and assumes that this is the correct Internet-Sales universe that the BI team told him about. When he picks the universe, he sees familiar objects organized into classes named in terms that he understands. Dave navigates through the classes and objects and pulls a few of the objects out into the RESULTS OBJECTS area, as shown in Figure 12.10.

Dave can now run this report. He starts by performing a query showing the different product names by sales amount and quantity for both the Internet sales and reseller channels. When he runs the report, the results of the query populate the body of the report as expected. He can then analyze and share the report as he sees fit.

Note that Dave simply selected a universe for InternetSales—that is, he didn't need to know about the location, format, or structure of the underlying database. He simply ran the report and received the data.

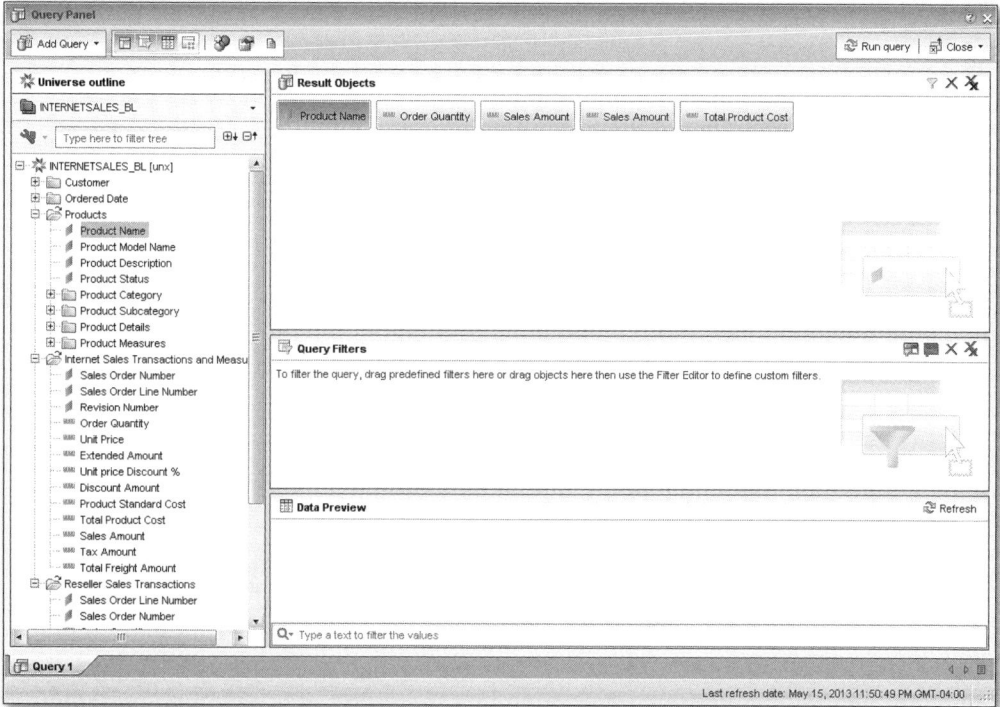

**Figure 12.10** The Resulting Query Panel

With the query that Dave executed, the sales information for both the Internet sales and reseller channels consists of two different contexts in the universe. He could have viewed the SQL and seen that the result set is generated by the union of two different queries and different SQL statements, as shown in Figure 12.11. These two statements are executed independently, and the results are returned to the reporting engine. It's then the reporting engine's responsibility to bring the two queries together and deliver the results.

For smaller result sets from the two queries, this would be difficult because the resulting query would return data relatively quickly. The load on the report server is higher because the two SQL statements must be stitched together. On queries where the result set is much larger, there is a much larger load placed on the reporting engine as it attempts to union the queries together. It's better to push the processing down to the database server in cases such as these.

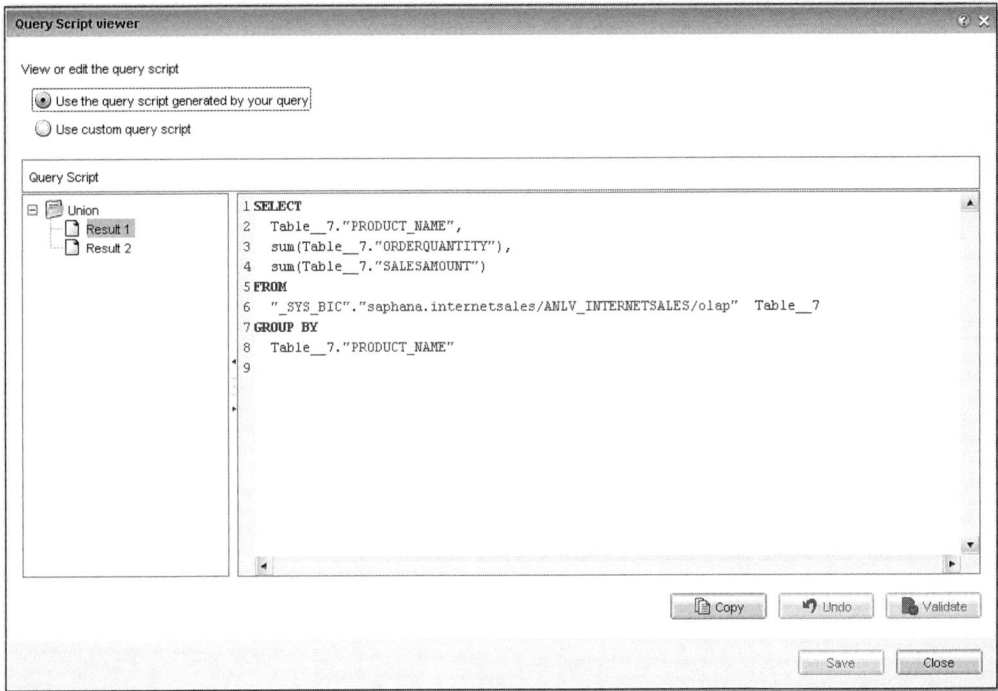

**Figure 12.11** Two Separate Queries in the Query Script Viewer

Because the database being used is SAP HANA, the universe designer can take steps to ensure that the queries are processed on the database server as much as possible. These two queries are executed, then unioned together on the reporting engine level. In the universe, the universe developer understands that this sort of query can occur due to the sort of contexts that are available. The universe designer sets a parameter in the universe that unions the two queries together on the universe. The parameter is called JOIN_BY_SQL, and it's set on the data foundation in the semantic layer. After the JOIN_BY_SQL parameter is set, the query is then reformulated, as shown in Figure 12.12.

Given this statement, the two individual queries are executed and then unioned together on the database server, as opposed to the two different queries being unioned on the report server. This results in much faster query times due to the extreme speeds possible from an SAP HANA data source.

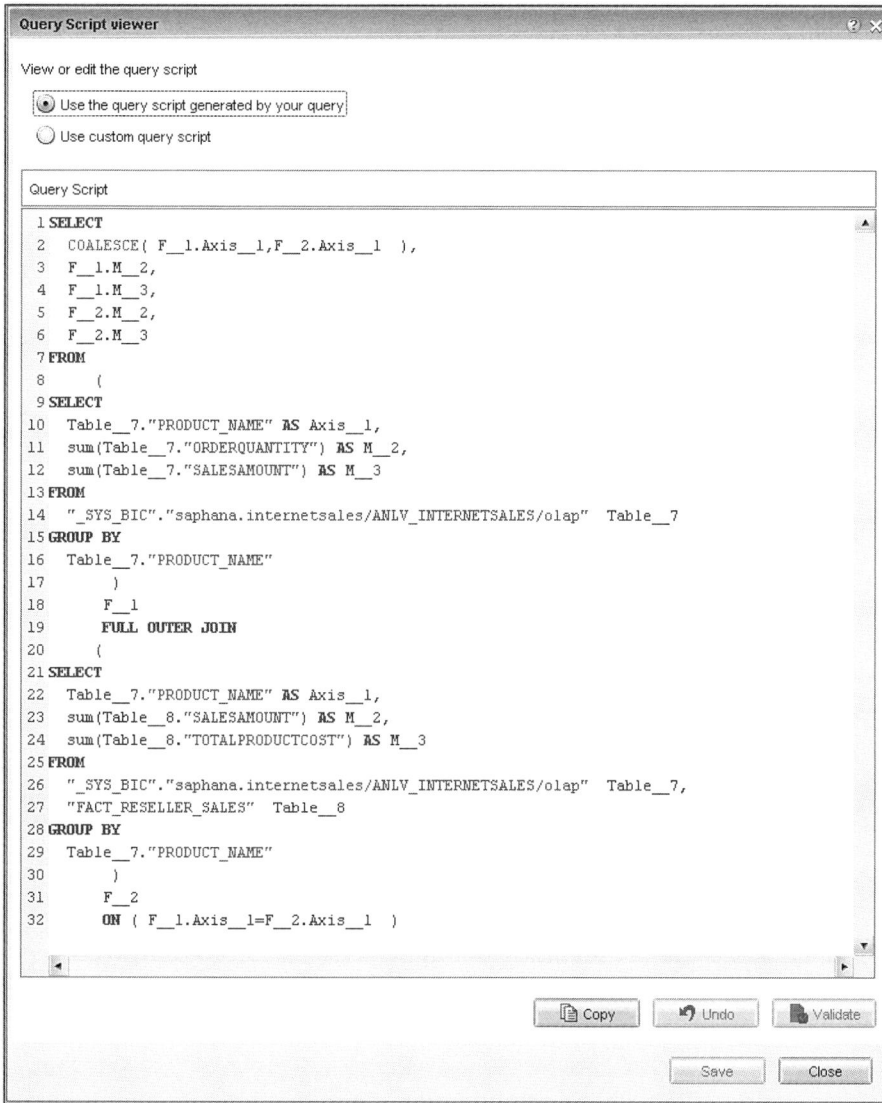

**Figure 12.12** The Same Query Joined Together in the Query Script Viewer

Dave has been chatting with some SAP BusinessObjects Web Intelligence developers. He has heard of an SAP BusinessObjects Web Intelligence feature that can further enhance the query performance by removing objects from a query if they aren't used in the report. He's been told that the feature is called Query Stripping, which can be found in the DOCUMENT PROPERTIES of a document on which he is currently working. He opens the DOCUMENT PROPERTIES and finds the QUERY STRIPPING checkbox. He ensures that the checkbox is enabled and runs his query again. There isn't a visual indicator that the setting is working other than query times being decreased even more.

Finally, Dave will be drilling in the report. In the existing Product report that he has developed, he can currently drill down into the next level of detail, which is product model name. He can open the Query Panel and set the scope of analysis as he typically would by opening the SCOPE OF ANALYSIS panel and selecting the levels. These will bring more data into the microcube in the server memory to make it available for the report to use as soon as he clicks on the next drill level.

Because he is using an SAP HANA data source, he can take advantage of query drilling to modify the underlying query to directly pull data from the SAP HANA database rather than the microcube in server memory. Query drilling is traditionally used when there are calculations on the report that can't be easily recalculated when the report is drilled into such as database delegated averages, ranking, statistical functions, and the like. Query drilling passes the calculation of these measures back down to the database so that the correct context can be derived, and the calculations can be accurately completed by the database server. You can take that one step further here by taking advantage of the increased speed of the SAP HANA data source to quickly request the next level of data that is required by the report. Coupled with query stripping, query drilling can provide your system with an SQL statement that is quick and concise and that returns the necessary data within a very short interval while minimizing the amount of memory used on the SAP BusinessObjects Server.

The combination of the techniques given in this case study can provide the end user with a report that not only takes advantage of best reporting practices when using an SAP HANA database but also minimizes the execution time while also minimizing the amount of data required on the server. An SAP BusinessObjects Web Intelligence designer has no control over the JOIN_BY_SQL parameter, but a well-informed designer can have a look at the inferred SQL in the QUERY PANEL to determine if multiple SQL statements are used. He can then question the universe designer to determine if the JOIN_BY_SQL parameter should be used. The other two techniques, query drilling and query stripping, are controlled by the developer in the DOCUMENT PROPERTIES panel of the SAP BusinessObjects Web Intelligence report. The utilization of all three of these items will push as much of the processing back to the database server as possible while ensuring that the reports run as quickly as possible for the end users.

## 12.8    Summary

SAP BusinessObjects Web Intelligence is an extraordinarily powerful tool that puts data into the hands of those that need to use it, when they need to have it, and how they need to see it. The tool provides enterprise-level reporting and analytics capabilities so that everyone from seasoned report writers to quickly trained executives are able to access the reports and manipulate the data. SAP HANA takes the power of SAP BusinessObjects Web Intelligence and shoves it into overdrive by allowing for superfast queries and quick and easy analysis of the resulting data sets.

On the universe level, the designer can enable the JOIN_BY_SQL parameter so that queries that normally run separately are joined together via a union and executed on the database level. This sort of query executes much more quickly than the individual queries, and the results are merged together at the database level instead of the reporting level.

Document and query options that are known within the SAP BusinessObjects Web Intelligence application can be manipulated to optimize reports that are built on an SAP HANA data source. First of all, it should be noted that all data synchronization should be pushed back to the database level as much as possible. This means reducing or eliminating the need for merged dimensions in SAP BusinessObjects Web Intelligence. Merged dimensions run two or more queries and then merge the data sets on the report engine level. Because the reporting engine isn't as powerful as the SAP HANA system, it shouldn't be tasked with this sort of load.

On the reporting level, you can use two document properties to help enhance the performance of the reports. Query drill can be used for reports that use drilling. Turning on QUERY DRILL and reducing the number of objects in the Scope of Analysis forces the initial query to bring back a minimal number of records for the report. When you drill into the report, each drill level executes a new query against the SAP HANA data source, which returns the data very quickly rather than holding large amounts of data in memory on the SAP BusinessObjects server.

The other document property that can be set is QUERY STRIPPING, which, when enabled, removes objects from the query that aren't actively used within the report.

Query stripping has been historically used by OLAP data sources, but this has been extended to reports based on SAP HANA. By removing objects from the query, the execution time and scope can be reduced by eliminating objects that won't be used in a report. If the objects are added to the report after the execution of the query, the query will be re-run against the SAP HANA database so that the data is made available to the report.

Finally, after the reports are generated, there are various methods available for sharing the results. Reports can be published to the SAP BusinessObjects repository so that only users who have an SAP BusinessObjects license can access the reports. Users can access these reports by navigating through the SAP BusinessObjects BI Launchpad or accessed directly by an OpenDocument link. Reports can also be securely shared in the SAP BusinessObjects BI Mobile app on an Android or Apple iPad mobile device. This mobile app is secured by an app password as well as SAP BusinessObjects security. Reports can be refreshed, annotated, and shared depending on security settings within the system. Regardless of how users access reports, the reports and the data that they contain will remain securely stored within the SAP BusinessObjects system.

Reports and their data can also be shared outside of the SAP BusinessObjects system. SAP BusinessObjects Web Intelligence provides multiple methods and formats of exporting reports and data into different file formats. The formats that are currently supported are PDF, TXT, CSV, XLS, and XLSX. After the reports are exported, the resulting files can be copied to network share locations, sent via email, or posted in an internal portal, among other distribution methods. Reports in these formats are no longer controlled by the SAP BusinessObjects system, and data security can be compromised by the interception of these files by unauthorized users. Careful planning and attention to detail can keep data safe while also making it available to users when and where they need it.

In the next chapter, we'll provide an overview of how SAP Crystal Reports can interact with data from SAP HANA. We'll discuss the SAP BusinessObjects BI landscape and how SAP Crystal Reports still plays an important role. We'll review the different versions of SAP Crystal Reports that are available in SAP BusinessObjects BI 4.0, and where each tool fits within an organization. Finally, we'll conclude with an example scenario showing how SAP Crystal Reports can be used to deliver externally facing reports for marketing and sales analysis.

*Delivering operational and external reports in the age of big data can be a significant challenge. SAP Crystal Reports powered by SAP HANA can help bring things under control.*

# 13  SAP Crystal Reports Powered by SAP HANA

Throughout this book, we've examined the many advantages that SAP HANA's in-memory solutions bring to highly interactive visualizations and analytic business intelligence (BI) content. As exciting as these new delivery mechanisms are, substantial portions of the world's BI content and usage scenarios still require traditional operational reporting content as well as the external delivery of highly formatted reports. Although these use cases may not be as exciting and "sexy" as newer interactive delivery mechanisms, they still form the backbone of many information delivery solutions.

So with the advent of SAP HANA and highly interactive and visual information delivery tools, is there still a need for traditional reporting solutions? The answer is yes. It's true that some use cases that have been traditionally handled with reports may move entirely to newer, more visual and interactive interfaces; however, there are still many use cases that are best suited to a traditional report delivery mechanism. There are also cases where the newer interactive visualizations may simply serve to augment and enhance, but not replace, the traditional reports.

We find these use cases in almost every industry—in health care, in the delivery of lab results to patients, and in manufacturing or wholesale, in the performance reports sent to out to resellers. Cash flow is an excellent example of a scenario where newer interactive visualizations can serve to augment but not replace a traditional report. Cash flow monitoring dashboards are a common use case for newer dashboard development tools, but traditional cash flow statement reports aren't going anywhere.

Because traditional reports aren't going to disappear, is there any value brought by the SAP HANA platform to this type of reporting, or is this a case where SAP

HANA is just another database? Here, too, the answer to the first part of this question is yes. SAP HANA brings a number of features that enable new innovations in the area of traditional report delivery.

The first of these is raw speed. Delivery of externally facing reports is often a very time-consuming process in the BI landscape; the generation of possibly thousands of documents for clients or partners can take hours in large overnight batch jobs. A significant portion of the execution time for these jobs is often the backend query execution. This may be queries implemented in the reports themselves or large batch SQL procedures that prepare the data for the reports. Both of these can be greatly enhanced by a solution such as SAP HANA where it may be possible to execute reports in real time as requested by end users without the need to manage a complex scheduling system, or at minimum reduce the total execution time of scheduled jobs if reports must still be sent out ahead of time.

Second, and more specific to operational reporting, is the direct implementation of application databases on SAP HANA. Operational reports typically need access to transactional details in real time. These reports therefore often run directly against application databases. In traditional systems, this can cause a number of problems—negative performance impacts to the application caused by reporting, the need to run reports against a replicated copy of the application database, and/ or the requirement that the reports wait for the data to move into a warehouse solution via extract, transform, and load (ETL)—causing them to lag behind real time. With the move by SAP to implement its entire suite of business applications on the SAP HANA platform, as well as the option to load in real-time operation tables via tools such as SAP Landscape Transformation (SLT), operational report authors will now have the ability to access application data directly without as many performance concerns.

This scenario is still in its infancy at this point, so we still see a strong need for traditional data warehousing solutions or replication of data from operational systems into platforms such as SAP HANA in the medium term. However, it looks to be an exciting time for changes in how and where we access data for operational reporting, and SAP Crystal Reports is an excellent tool for taking advantage of this scenario going forward.

In this chapter, we'll provide an overview of how SAP Crystal Reports can interact with data from SAP HANA. We'll discuss the BI landscape and how SAP Crystal Reports still plays an important role. In Section 13.1, we'll review the different versions of SAP Crystal Reports that are available in SAP BusinessObjects BI 4.0, and where each tool fits within an organization. We'll also discuss the various ways that users can access and share reports and analytics created within SAP Crystal Reports in Section 13.2. Section 13.3 offers a look at the upcoming roadmap and discusses what new features are on their way for the SAP Crystal Reports product line. Finally, we'll conclude with an example scenario in Section 13.4 that shows how SAP Crystal Reports can be used to deliver externally facing reports for marketing and sales analysis.

## 13.1 Implementing Solutions with SAP Crystal Reports

In this section, we examine the specific implementation choices and procedures for delivering content with SAP Crystal Reports on top of SAP HANA. One of the more significant issues we need to clarify is the difference between the two distinct "flavors" of SAP Crystal Reports: SAP Crystal Reports 2011 and SAP Crystal Reports for Enterprise. We then cover the key elements in connecting both SAP Crystal Reports types to SAP HANA and offer best practices for you to follow.

> **SAP Crystal Reports Version Name Changes**
>
> With the advent of SAP BusinessObjects BI Platform 4.1, SAP Crystal Reports 2011 is now being updated to SAP Crystal Reports 2013. Because this chapter was predominantly written using the 2011 version of SAP Crystal Reports, we use that naming convention throughout. The same features will also apply to SAP Crystal Reports 2013.

### 13.1.1 A Tale of Two SAP Crystal Reports

The very first question that comes up when looking at the SAP Crystal Reports landscape in SAP BusinessObjects 4.0 is why there are two different versions of SAP Crystal Reports, and which one should be used when. Here we seek to answer these questions through the lens of SAP HANA because it will be used in conjunction with SAP Crystal Reports.

When SAP started work on the BusinessObjects 4.0 platform, one major goal was to harmonize the user interface (UI) and functionality across the various BI tools. SAP BusinessObjects 4.0 attempted to rectify something that SAP BusinessObjects is sometimes criticized for—being a collection of unrelated tools with significant product overlap instead of being a tightly integrated suite of complementary products.

783

However, making a significant UI and functionality change doesn't come without cost. SAP Crystal Reports has been one of the most popular reporting tools for a generation. Because SAP didn't want to rush in to rolling out a radically altered SAP Crystal Reports solution and risk alienating the substantial customer base that exists today—as well as cause complex migration paths from prior versions to SAP BusinessObjects 4.0—as a compromise, the decision was made to offer up two flavors of SAP Crystal Reports.

The first flavor is SAP Crystal Reports 2011. This is the tool offered to the existing user community with essentially no UI changes and an attempt to make the migration path as smooth as possible. Although it doesn't offer much of anything in the way of new or enhanced features, it does offer a stable and safe path forward for users with heavy existing investments. SAP Crystal Reports 2011 is sometimes referred to using the shorthand CR2011.

The second flavor is SAP Crystal Reports for Enterprise. This is the tool offered to new adopters of SAP Crystal Reports. It has a significantly reworked UI that was the product of usability studies attempting to make SAP Crystal Reports into a more user-friendly tool. SAP Crystal Reports for Enterprise also received the new platform enhancements that SAP Crystal Reports 2011 lacked, such as 64-bit support and tighter coupling to the SAP BusinessObjects BI Platform semantic layers. The development client has also been completely rewritten as a Java desktop application. SAP Crystal Reports for Enterprise is sometimes referred to as CR4E.

It's beyond the scope of this book to address every distinction between SAP Crystal Reports 2011 and SAP Crystal Reports for Enterprise, but we do want to compare a few important differences, as listed in Table 13.1, to help put things in perspective.

| | SAP Crystal Reports 2011 | SAP Crystal Reports for Enterprise |
| --- | --- | --- |
| User Interface | Traditional SAP Crystal Reports interface, familiar to existing users, implemented as a traditional windows desktop application | Revised UI, harmonized with the rest of the SAP Business-Objects BI Platform, designed for improved usability for new users, implemented as a Java desktop application |

**Table 13.1** Comparison of SAP Crystal Reports 2011 to SAP Crystal Reports for Enterprise

| | SAP Crystal Reports 2011 | SAP Crystal Reports for Enterprise |
|---|---|---|
| **Processing Architecture** | 32 bit. Hosted in essentially the same processing servers from the 3.1 version of Business Objects, minimizing possible migration issues | 64 bit. Provides improved performance and scalability, new Java architecture provides better support for non-Windows platforms |
| **Data Connectivity** | Emphasizes direct data connection via query, has the largest selection of connection options | Emphasizes connection via semantic layer (IDT Universe, BW BEX query); not as large a selection of connection options at this time but gradually more are being added |

**Table 13.1** Comparison of SAP Crystal Reports 2011 to SAP Crystal Reports for Enterprise (Cont.)

| SAP Crystal Reports Outlook |
|---|
| Although we expect the separation to continue for some time, SAP has communicated that it will work to bring the tools together after SAP Crystal Reports for Enterprise has had time to mature and the current feature gaps have been closed. We don't expect this to be a short-term solution, however, so you should expect continued support for traditional SAP Crystal Reports for some time to come. |

Finally, given that you have two tools to choose from, which should you use to construct reports with when using SAP HANA data sources? The answer is generally going to be SAP Crystal Reports for Enterprise. It will receive the focus of new development and enhancements; its new UI, although possibly requiring a transition stage for older SAP Crystal Reports developers, is an overall improvement on usability; and it has the 64-bit architecture necessary to function in the modern era of big data. That said, we'll still cover the basic techniques and options for connecting SAP Crystal Reports 2011 to SAP HANA in this chapter.

> **Additional Resources**
>
> Refer to the following external resources for more information on SAP Crystal Reports:
> - SAP Crystal Reports for Enterprise: *http://help.sap.com/bocre*
> - SAP Crystal Reports 2013: *http://help.sap.com/bocr*
> - Comparing SAP Crystal Reports for Enterprise to SAP Crystal Reports 2011: *http://scn.sap.com/docs/DOC-21819*

Let's begin our deep dive on SAP Crystal Reports 2011, before transitioning into using SAP Crystal Reports for Enterprise.

### 13.1.2 Using SAP Crystal Reports 2011

In this section, we review the specific features of SAP Crystal Reports 2011 related to connecting to and working with SAP HANA data. We look at how connections are established, the types of content that can be accessed, and key elements that are specific to SAP HANA.

Before we begin, let's examine some of the key UI elements you'll interact with in SAP Crystal Reports 2011. Recall that the SAP Crystal Reports 2011 UI should be familiar to anyone who has worked with SAP Crystal Reports in the past; as shown in Figure 13.1, the toolbar and menus across the top are still present, and a main work area fills the majority of the screen. By default, you are presented with a START PAGE that provides quick links to start new reports either from a template/wizard or a blank report. For our examples, we'll always start with a blank report.

SAP Crystal Reports is a substantial and sophisticated reporting tool, and reviewing every aspect of its UI is beyond the scope of this book. We'll limit our coverage to those portions of the UI directly related to connecting to and working with SAP HANA. This means you'll need to use one of the following UI elements, which are called out in Figure 13.2.

- DATABASE EXPERT
  This tool is used to create and manage connections to data sources (accessed from the toolbar or the DATABASE menu).

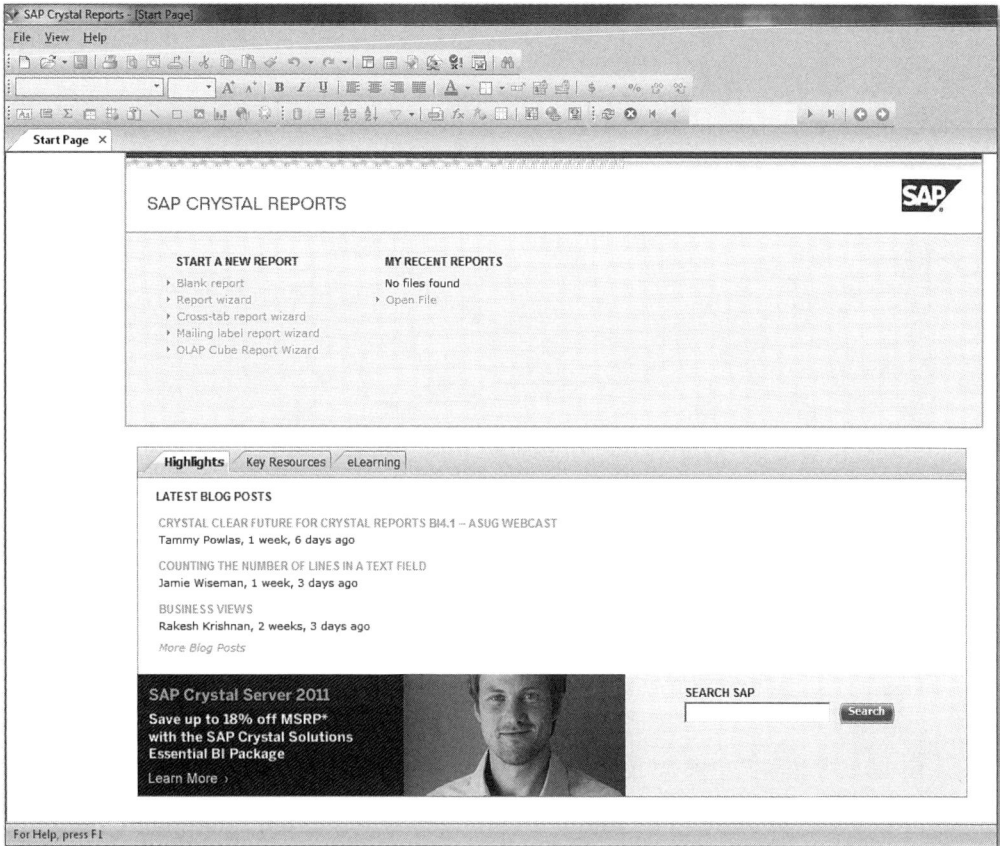

**Figure 13.1** Crystal Reports 2011 Start Page

- ▶ FIELD EXPLORER
  This tool is used to add fields from the data source to the report. By default, this window is docked to the right-hand side of the main work space. If closed, it can be reactivated from the VIEW menu.

- ▶ SHOW SQL QUERY
  This menu option allows you to verify the SQL being sent to the database. It can be accessed from the DATABASE menu. It's only available after you create at least one database connection and query in your report.

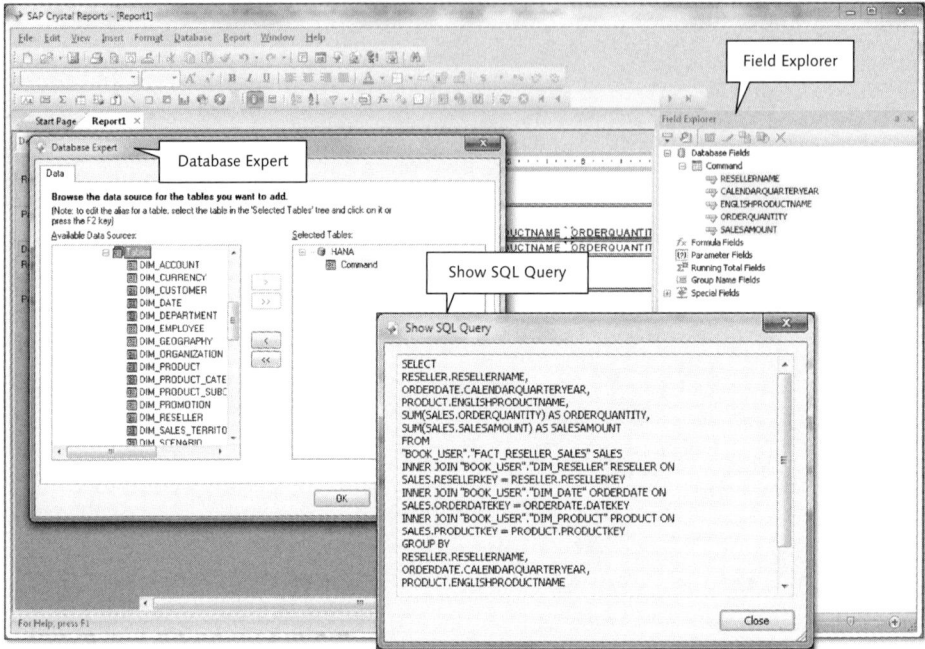

**Figure 13.2** SAP Crystal Reports UI Elements Used in Database Connections

### Connecting SAP Crystal Reports 2011 to SAP HANA

To leverage SAP Crystal Reports 2011 with SAP HANA data, you must create a connection to the database. From the perspective of SAP Crystal Reports, SAP HANA is just another database. That means the process you go through to connect is really no different from connecting to Oracle or SQL Server or any other vendor's database product.

Like all database connections you need a set of database driver middleware to mediate the connection between the SAP Crystal Reports developer client and the database. For SAP HANA, there are two driver options to select from for use with SAP Crystal Reports: JDBC and ODBC.

---

**Driver Versions and 32-Bit versus 64-Bit**

It's important to remember that SAP Crystal Reports 2011 is a 32-bit product and can therefore only reference 32-bit database drivers. The SAP HANA database client software comes in both 32-bit and 64-bit flavors. (Other tools you interact with may work best with the 64-bit options, but for SAP Crystal Reports 2011, you must have the 32-bit version installed.)

---

Luckily there is no problem having both the 32-bit and 64-bit versions of the SAP HANA client installed on the same machine. In fact, it's probably best for developers to go ahead and keep both versions up to date on their workstations at all times.

At development time, it doesn't really matter if you choose Open Database Connectivity (ODBC) or Java Database Connectivity (JDBC), but when it comes time to deploy your report to be processed on the server, this choice does matter. Windows server environments are typically best served by ODBC driver configurations, whereas UNIX server environments are best served by JDBC driver configurations. If you're unsure of the deployment architecture for your environment, check with your SAP BusinessObjects server administrators before committing to one driver or the other.

One advantage to ODBC configurations is that they externalize configuration details, such as server addresses, from the report definitions and BI applications. This generally makes dealing with migration of content between development, test, and production server regions easier. Something similar can be achieved with JDBC by using a host name alias in the JDBC URL and then using the operating system's HOST file to configure connections to an appropriate database server for the current region, but it requires more manual work on the server.

### Setting Up ODBC Connections
To use an ODBC connection in your SAP Crystal Report, you first need to define the connection as an ODBC system connection in the 32-bit ODBC configuration panel. Only then can you create a connection in SAP Crystal Reports 2011 by following these steps:

1. Ensure that the 32-bit SAP HANA database client is installed, as done in Chapter 9.

2. Configure a 32-bit SAP HANA connection in the ODBC configuration panel accessed from either the Control Panel on 32-bit Windows or from the SysWOW64 directory on 64-bit Windows (*C:\Windows\SysWOW64\odbcad32.exe*).

3. Provide the data source a NAME and DESCRIPTION, as shown in Figure 13.3. The SERVER:PORT field entry should be the same value that you used when configuring SAP HANA Studio. Remember that SAP HANA listening ports are configured as 3<*Installation Number*>15. So for a typical SAP HANA installation on instance 00, the port would be "30015".

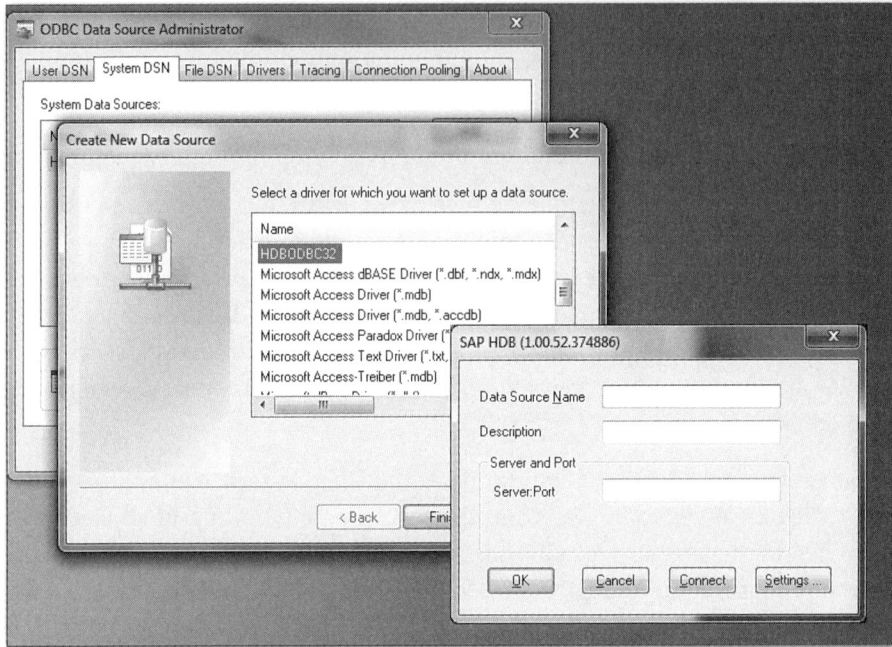

**Figure 13.3** Creating ODBC Connections

Now you have everything in place to configure a connection from SAP Crystal Reports 2011 to SAP HANA. To do that, you need to open SAP Crystal Reports 2011, create a new blank report, and then use the Database Expert to configure your connection by following these steps:

1. From the DATABASE EXPERT, expand the CREATE NEW CONNECTION folder and choose ODBC.

2. Click MAKE NEW CONNECTION, and select the connection name you created previously. Enter a user ID and password to connect to SAP HANA. Figure 13.4 shows an example of this process

You can now start selecting objects based on the connection to construct your report. We'll discuss the types of content that can be selected in a later section.

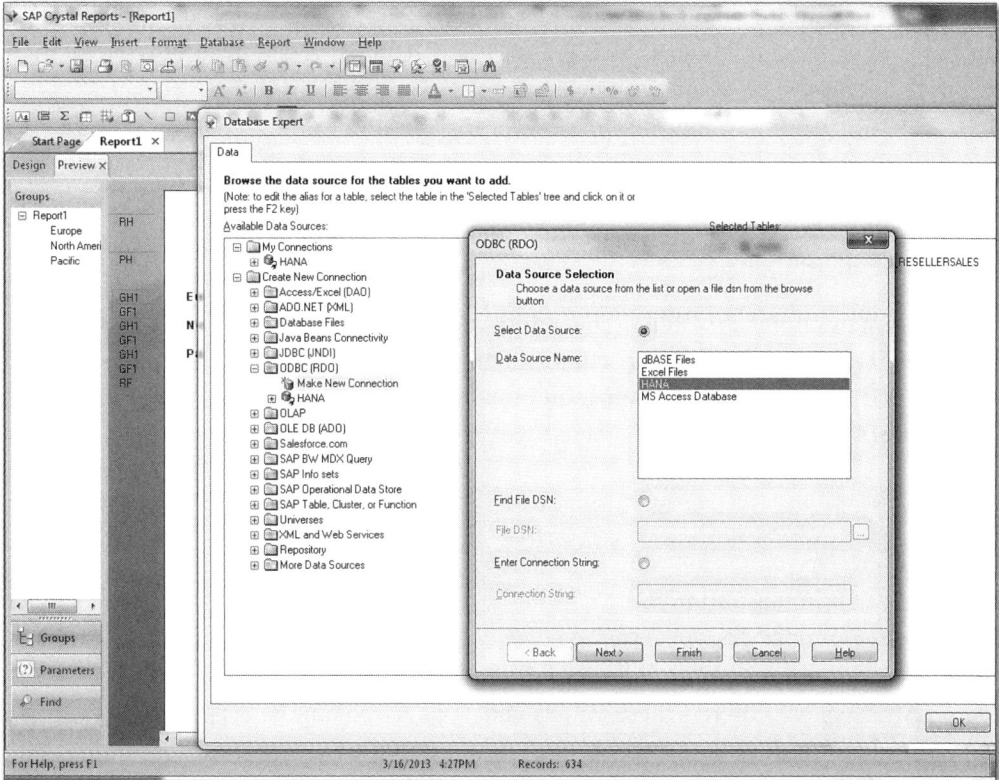

**Figure 13.4** Configuring the ODBC Connection in SAP Crystal Reports

### Setting Up JDBC Connections

Unlike ODBC connections, JDBC connections don't require any OS-level preconfiguration. However, you need to make some changes to your SAP Crystal Report 2011 application configuration files before you can access SAP HANA via JDBC. SAP Crystal Reports doesn't know where you installed the SAP HANA database client, and it doesn't ship with a JDBC driver for SAP HANA, so you need to tell SAP Crystal Reports where the JAR file containing your JDBC driver is located. This is true for most SAP Crystal Reports JDBC connections, not just SAP HANA. Follow these steps:

1. The jar file configuration must be added to the file, *C:\Program Files (x86)\SAP BusinessObjects\SAP BusinessObjects Enterprise XI 4.0\java\CRConfig.xml.*

2. Open this file and locate the `<classpath></classpath>` entry. At the end of that entry, append the path to the SAP HANA JDBC jar file in the following location in the default Windows environment:

*C:\Program Files (x86)\sap\hdbclient\ngdbc.jar*

3. Make sure to put a semicolon between any existing entries and your new entry.

4. After these steps are complete, restart SAP Crystal Reports 2011 if it was currently running.

From this point, creating a JDBC connection in SAP Crystal Reports 2011 starts just like creating an ODBC connection, but this time, of course, you choose JDBC instead of ODBC. The configuration values for JDBC are also slightly different; instead of selecting an ODBC DATA SOURCE NAME, you'll enter the values listed in Table 13.2.

| JDBC URL | jdbc:sap://your-hana-server-name:3<INSTALLTION NUMBER>15 |
|---|---|
| DATABASE CLASSNAME | com.sap.db.jdbc.Driver |

**Table 13.2**   JDBC Connection Properties

After you've entered these values and your user name and password, you'll be ready to retrieve data from the SAP HANA system. From this point forward there is no distinction between JDBC and ODBC connections.

### Retrieving Data from SAP HANA

After you've established the connection to SAP HANA, you are presented with a view of the database catalog, not unlike any other database system you would use with SAP Crystal Reports. At the top of the list, you're likely to see a number of system schemas, depending on your configured security and which optional components are installed on your SAP HANA system. At minimum, you should see the _SYS_BIC schema, as shown in Figure 13.5.

In addition to the system schemas—and depending on your authorizations within the SAP HANA system—you should see one or more user schemas that belong to users of the SAP HANA system.

Within a schema, you'll see up to three subcategories of items, TABLES, VIEWS, and STORED PROCEDURES. Within a user schema, these items map to the traditional relational database content types. To access this content with SAP Crystal Reports, simply drag an item from the left panel over to the right to make it part of the active query. This is exactly like querying a traditional database. From here, you can use the LINKS tab to configure any joins between the objects you selected.

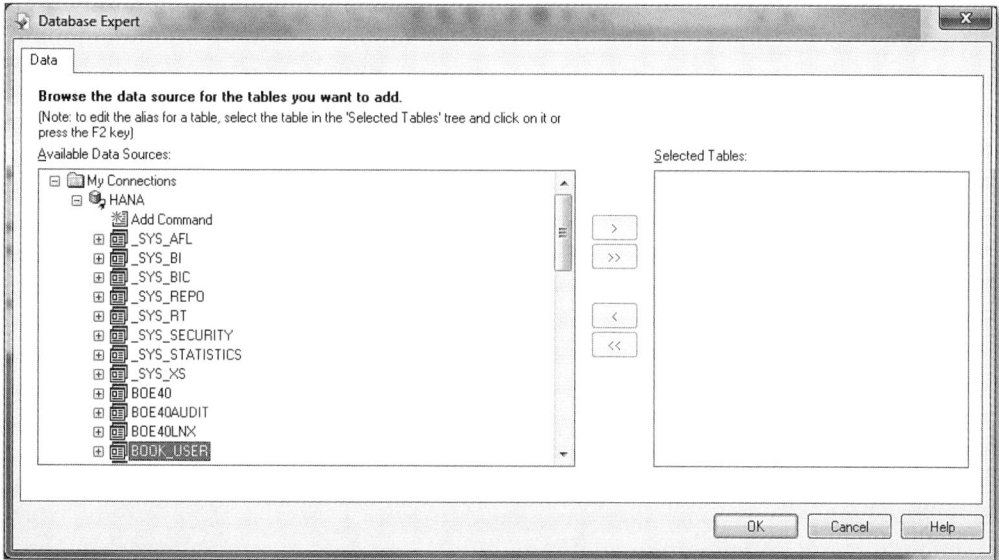

**Figure 13.5**  Browsing an SAP HANA Data Source

As an alternative to selecting objects and then using the LINKS tab to graphically define a query, you can use the ADD COMMAND option at the top of the catalog to handcraft your query using any arbitrary SQL statement. In most cases, creating commands with SQL gives you the best control over your query design.

### Organizing Data in the Report

After you've selected the database content you plan to access, you can move on to crafting your report. The selected content is available in the FIELD EXPLORER. From here, you can drag fields into your report layout. If you aren't using a command object, the selections you make affect the generated SQL statement. You can verify the SQL statement produced is doing what you want by using the SHOW SQL option.

Another important option to consider when using base tables instead of command objects is the PERFORM GROUPING ON THE SERVER option, which is also located in the DATABASE menu. If the view you're querying contains details at a lower granularity than what is shown in the report, this option can help reduce unnecessary record retrieval. This is another reason why command objects are a good idea; you have more exact control over this type of scenario.

### 13.1.3  Using SAP Crystal Reports for Enterprise

In this section we look at the options for connecting SAP Crystal Reports for Enterprise to SAP HANA data. We cover essentially the same workflows that were discussed with SAP Crystal Reports 2011 but highlight those areas where SAP Crystal Reports for Enterprise deviates.

The first UI element that sticks out is the ribbon interface that is common to many of the tools in SAP BusinessObjects Enterprise 4.0. This interface, similar to the ribbon interface in current versions of Microsoft Office, categorizes the different application functions into groups. In theory, this makes elements easier to find for beginners because the ribbon headers use plain text labels instead of cryptic icons. Some long-time SAP Crystal Reports users may find that it takes a few more clicks to reach functions that were merely one click away in the old UI.

The second major interface convention of SAP Crystal Reports for Enterprise is the dock on the left side of the screen. Many of the wizards and so called "experts" from SAP Crystal Reports 2011 have their counterparts located here. This interface is very similar to the dock of panels in SAP BusinessObjects Web Intelligence 4.0. The most significant of these panels for our purposes is the DATA EXPLORER panel, which is at the top of the list of items (see Figure 13.6). From here, you can establish connections and create queries as well as add results from queries to the report layout.

The rest of the SAP Crystal Reports for Enterprise UI should be more familiar. The main report layout still uses the same grouping structure as SAP Crystal Reports 2011, and most of the report layout concepts are the same. The STRUCTURE and PAGE view modes are equivalent to the DESIGN and PREVIEW modes in SAP Crystal Reports 2011.

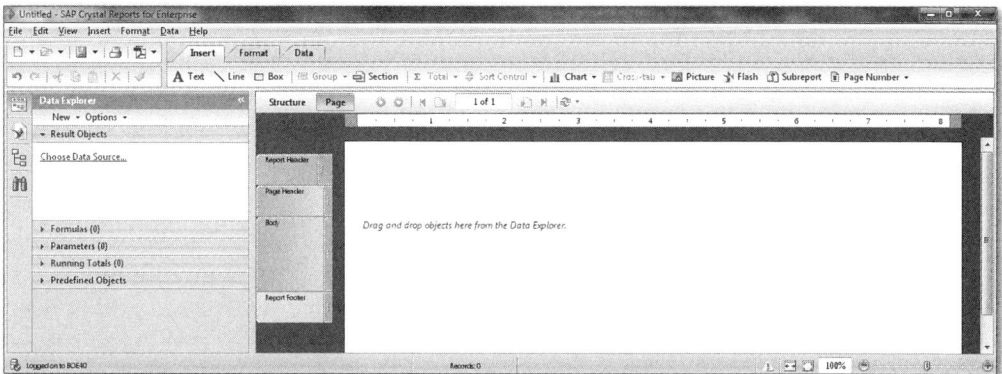

**Figure 13.6**  SAP Crystal Reports for Enterprise User Interface

### Connecting SAP Crystal Reports for Enterprise to SAP HANA

SAP Crystal Reports for Enterprise has several additional methods for connecting to SAP HANA beyond traditional ODBC and JDBC support. In fact, ODBC and JDBC support were only recently added to SAP Crystal Reports for Enterprise. Instead, the emphasis by SAP has been on the use of connections managed by the SAP BusinessObjects Platform, as well as modeled semantic layers such as the new Information Design Tool (IDT) universes and SAP NetWeaver Business Warehouse (SAP NetWeaver BW) BEx queries.

The complete list of connection options for SAP HANA is as follows:

▶ ODBC

▶ JDBC

▶ IDT universe

▶ Relational connection from SAP BusinessObjects Platform

Creating connections in a report is done using a wizard accessed via the DATA EXPLORER panel or is initiated at report creation time. The wizard categorizes connections into three groups: PREVIOUS CONNECTIONS, SAP BUSINESSOBJECTS BUSINESS INTELLIGENCE PLATFORM, and CONNECTIONS BY VENDOR. The latter is where you'll find direct connections to databases by vendor middleware. For SAP HANA, this refers to the same ODBC and JDBC options available in SAP Crystal Reports 2011.

The SAP BUSINESSOBJECTS BUSINESS INTELLIGENCE PLATFORM category is where you'll find the two additional connection choices available to SAP Crystal Reports for Enterprise. Selecting this option requires you to authenticate to the SAP BusinessObjects platform. From there, you have the option of selecting Universes, BEx Queries, or Relational Connections. For connecting to SAP HANA, you can use the Universe or Relational Connection option.

### Configuring ODBC and JDBC Connections

Because we've already discussed ODBC and JDBC setup for SAP Crystal Reports 2011, we'll merely give a brief set of highlights for these connections. The essential nature of the connections isn't changed in SAP Crystal Reports for Enterprise. You still need to configure your ODBC connections in Windows, but you don't need to configure the *CRConfig.xml* file for JDBC connections; it appears that SAP Crystal Reports for Enterprise has the necessary JDBC drivers included.

Beyond this point, the selection of content via these methods is essentially the same as it was for SAP Crystal Reports 2011.

### Using SAP BusinessObjects Enterprise Relational Connections

A major advantage that SAP Crystal Reports for Enterprise offers is the ability to let the SAP BusinessObjects platform manage connection metadata instead of configuring and storing this data in each and every report. This vastly improves the manageability of SAP Crystal Reports and facilitates migrations of content between environments. Therefore, instead of directly configuring a connection to SAP HANA using ODBC or JDBC in your report, you can instead configure the connection just once using the Information Design Tool (IDT) and storing the connection in the SAP BusinessObjects repository. Behind the scenes, this connection still uses either the ODBC or JDBC SAP HANA drivers, but the report authors can be abstracted from this detail.

To create a report using a platform-managed connection using SAP Crystal Reports for Enterprise, you must first create the connection object with IDT (covered in Chapter 9, Section 1.2.1). After you have a connection object in place, follow these steps.

1. Either start a new report From Data Source or click Choose Data Source from the Data Explorer.

2. From the Choose a Data Source Connection wizard, select the SAP Business-Objects Business Intelligence Platform • Browse Repository link, as shown in Figure 13.7.

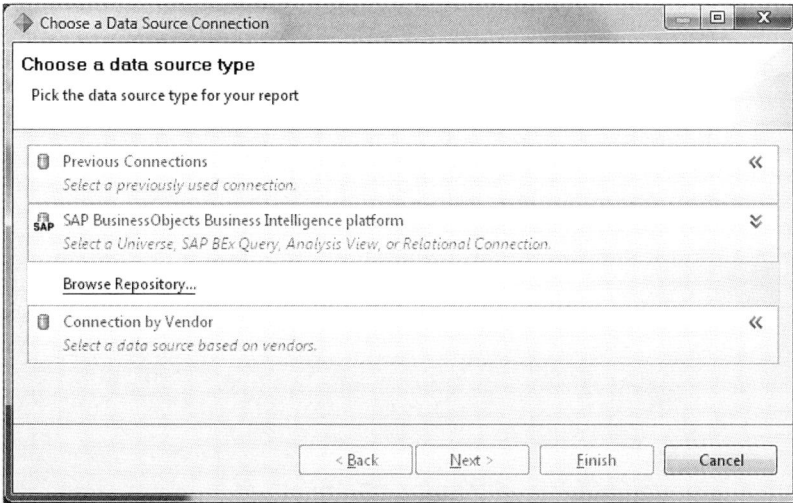

**Figure 13.7** Selecting Platform Connections

3. Authenticate to the platform.

4. Select DATA SOURCE TYPE • RELATIONAL CONNECTION, as shown in Figure 13.8.

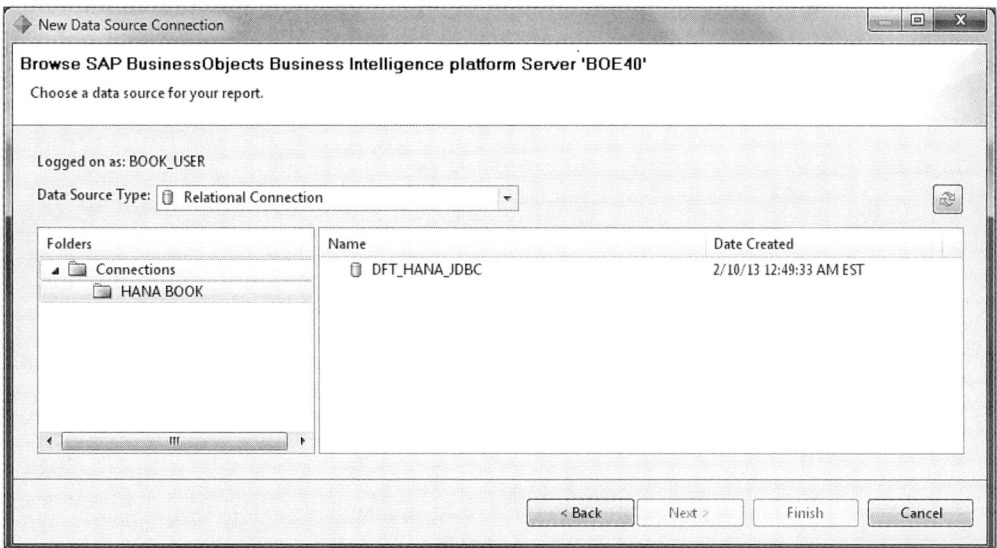

**Figure 13.8** Selecting a Relational Connection

5. Navigate to the REPOSITORY, and choose the connection you created with IDT.

6. The connection is opened, and you're presented with the same view of the SAP HANA catalog that you would see if you had created the connection directly against ODBC or JDBC (see Figure 13.9).

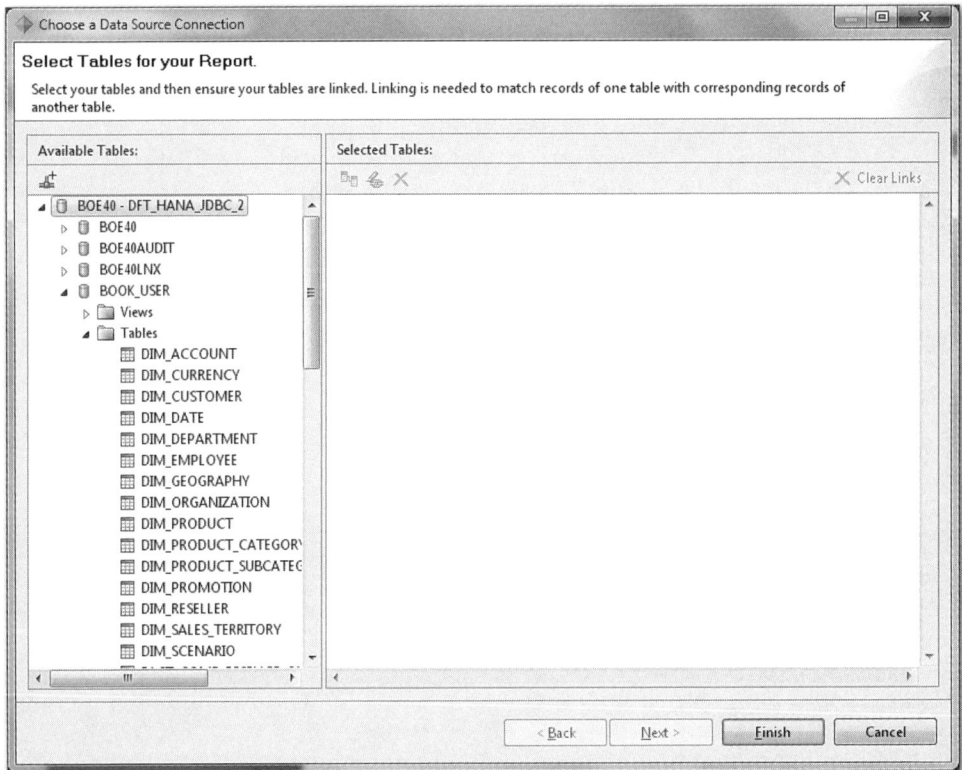

**Figure 13.9**  Selecting Tables from a Connection

After you've connected to the catalog, the selection of tables, views, or content from analytic/calculation views is really no different from the choices made when selecting content with SAP Crystal Reports 2011.

**Sorting Content in SAP HANA Catalog**

A subtle difference when locating content from an SAP HANA connection, whether direct or platform-managed, is the sorting of objects in the catalog. The sorting isn't necessarily alphabetical, so the object you're looking for may be further down the list than you expect. This is especially true when selecting analytic and calculation views.

### Using SAP BusinessObjects IDT Universes

In addition to using a platform-managed connection to SAP HANA directly, SAP Crystal Reports for Enterprise can leverage IDT-based universes constructed on top of SAP HANA. This approach is mostly appropriate when connecting to base column tables as opposed to connecting to information models, that is, analytic and column views.

If you're leveraging base tables directly, then using a universe (as opposed to crafting SQL statements by hand) is generally considered the best practice. The universe layer offers the BI team the opportunity to construct reusable business definitions instead of recreating the wheel in each report. Because SAP Crystal Reports for Enterprise was designed from the start to work with universes, you don't have the drawbacks that older versions of SAP Crystal had when working with universes, where the integration between the two tools was more of an afterthought.

The question of whether to use base tables or information models configured in SAP HANA is more ambiguous when considering SAP Crystal Reports for Enterprise. We addressed some of those questions in Chapter 9, where we compared the options of constructing models in SAP HANA versus universes.

The steps to establish a report connection to a universe in SAP Crystal Reports for Enterprise are nearly identical to the steps for connecting to a platform-managed relational connection, until you connect to the repository and choose the type of object to connect to. From that point forward, follow these steps:

1. Select DATA SOURCE TYPE • UNIVERSE, and then choose the universe from the repository.

2. You are presented with the EDIT QUERY panel, which is shown in Figure 13.10. This is the same panel you would be presented with for querying any type of universe, not just SAP HANA. Its UI is common across all SAP BusinessObjects BI 4.0 products that support universe queries.

3. Craft your query by dragging and dropping universe objects into the RESULT and FILTER areas.

4. At this point, you can construct your report just like any other data source.

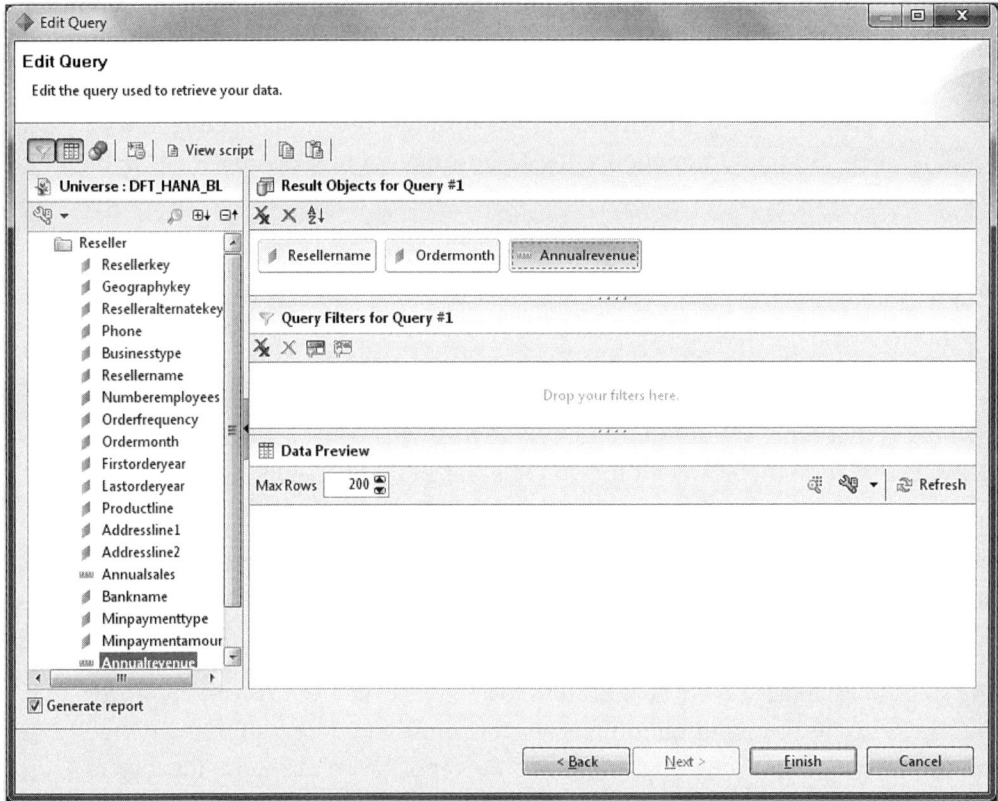

**Figure 13.10** Universe Query on SAP HANA

### 13.1.4 Accessing Analytic Content via ODBC/JDBC and Enterprise Relational Connections

One area where SAP HANA differs significantly from other database platforms is, of course, in its embedded calculation engine and semantic modeling layers (analytic and calculation views). This content can be used within either SAP Crystal Report 2011 or SAP Crystal Report for Enterprise, but accessing it isn't entirely obvious. Because these data types are virtual, there is no physical table to query; instead, these content types are expressed as views in the _SYS_BIC catalog.

Accessing these views is additionally complicated by the fact that a given analytic or calculation view may generate more than one view object in the _SYS_BIC schema. The possible combinations of analytic content and the resulting views that will be created is complex. We'll clarify what the different views are and which one should be used if you're creating SAP Crystal Reports on these content types in a moment.

It's important to understand the basic naming scheme that these views follow. Each piece of analytic content exists in a package. These packages are visible in the Modeling perspective of SAP HANA Studio. Behind the scenes, these content types are manifested as column views and procedures in the _SYS_BIC schema. These views follow a specific naming scheme. For each level of the package hierarchy, the package name is included in the final view name with each level separated by a period (.). At the end of the package name, a forward slash (/) is used to separate the package name from the base object name—for example, _SYS_BIC"."SAPHANA. INTERNETSALES/ANLV_INTERNETSALES.

Specialized versions of the view object used to represent OLAP hierarchies, measures, and different access models have suffixes appended to the end of the base view name also separated by forward slashes (/). Of particular note are the versions of the view that have /HIER/ and /MEASURES as the suffix followed by a named hierarchy. These views represent the hierarchical structures for OLAP access to content. These views are essentially internal structures that should be ignored. They aren't appropriate for use by SAP Crystal Reports directly, so you can safely ignore them from now on.

We covered the view types and their naming conventions inside the _SYS_BIC schema in detail in Chapter 9. The same rules for accessing these items via universes apply to SAP Crystal Reports:

▶ **Attribute view**
These views are only useful for constructing lists of master data. You can just as easily query the underlying dimension tables, and in most cases, that is the recommended approach.

▶ **Analytic view**
These views equate to a star schema for a specific fact table. Remember that you must select either distinct values or include a group by clause with aggregation on all selected measures.

▶ **Calculation view**
These views can represent a more complicated query, such as a comparison of values across multiple star schemas.

Now that you understand the different views and the naming conventions within the _SYS_BIC schema, you can add this type of content to your report. The steps are essentially the same as adding any other table to a report, except you select the table from the _SYS_BIC schema. One key thing to remember when reporting on analytic or calculation views is that the views already model all of the necessary joins, and you should never add more than one of these objects to your report. Figure 13.11 shows an example of selecting analytic content from the _SYS_BIC schema.

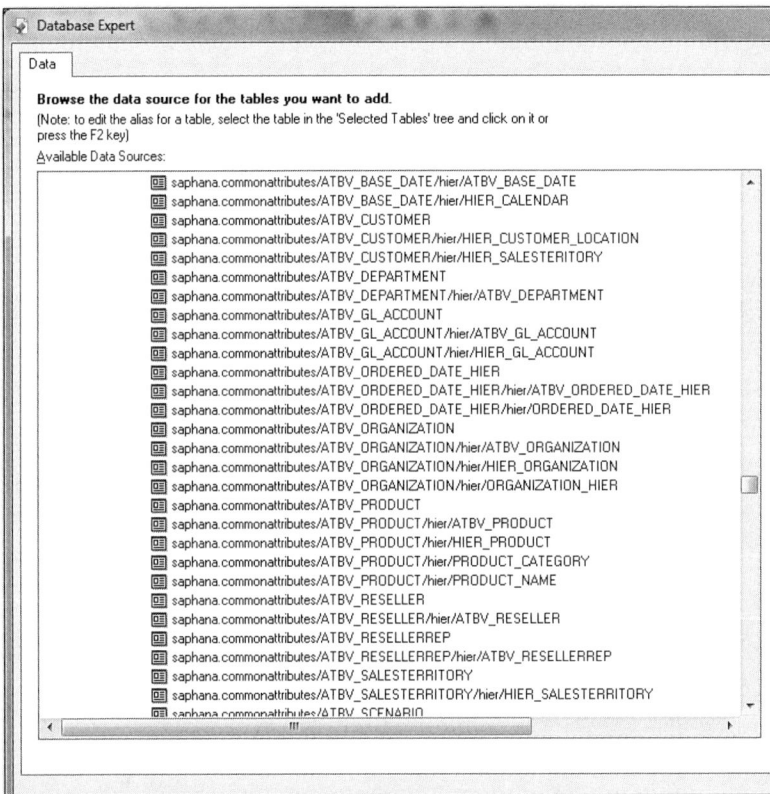

**Figure 13.11** Browsing Semantic Content in _SYS_BIC

---

**Importance of Naming Conventions**

We can't overstate the significance of good naming conventions when designing your semantic layer content with SAP HANA. This screen should reinforce that argument. As you can see, it would be very easy to select the wrong object for your query if you haven't followed a well-defined naming pattern.

---

## 13.2 Sharing SAP Crystal Reports with SAP BusinessObjects Enterprise

An important aspect of operational reporting is the delivery of information to end users. The SAP BusinessObjects platform offers a number of ways to share content from SAP Crystal Reports 2011 and SAP Crystal Reports for Enterprise, with both internal and external users. In this section, we examine some of the different options available for distributing and integrating SAP Crystal Reports content.

Note that, for years, SAP Crystal Reports has been one of the most integrated SAP BusinessObjects products, with a large number of clients embedding its content in their own applications. Custom integration options using the Software Development Kit (SDK) are still available and are in fact enhanced in SAP BusinessObjects 4.0, but there are too many methods available to cover them all in this book. Instead we cover more of the standard off-the-shelf solutions for sharing content.

### End User Viewing from Browser Clients in SAP BusinessObjects BI Launchpad

The most common method of distributing SAP Crystal Reports content is, of course, the traditional SAP BusinessObjects BI Launchpad. From this web application, users can both access scheduled instances of reports and interactively view and refresh reports against live data.

It's in the latter scenario where reports constructed on SAP HANA really have the opportunity to shine. Complex reports probably required scheduled output in the past, but with SAP HANA, it's highly likely that the reports can be viewed interactively. The on-demand scenario allows for several advantages over scheduled report output: easier implementation and maintenance of row-level security by pushing all filtering down to the database, removal of complex scheduling scenarios, and the removal of the need to monitor the schedules for completion.

### Embedding Content in Third-Party Portals

Like all SAP BusinessObjects Platform content, SAP Crystal Reports can be directly embedded into other portal- and web-based business applications besides the SAP BusinessObjects BI Launchpad. This is done using the SAP BusinessObjects OpenDocument API or one of the various SAP Crystal Viewer APIs. The scenarios in which this solution can work are greatly enhanced with SAP Crystal Reports on SAP HANA, especially for business applications.

This enhancement comes from the speed improvements offered by SAP HANA. In the past, many use cases of this sort would have simply taken too long to run, and you would have had to break the user's workflow by scheduling the report content from the source application to be retrieved later. With the combination of real-time ETL or direct storage of application data in SAP HANA, as is done with SAP ERP on SAP HANA, users can access reports pertinent to their current business workflow immediately.

> **Additional Resources**
>
> For more information on the OpenDocument API, refer to the OpenDocument Developers guide (*http://help.sap.com/businessobject/product_guides/boexir4/en/xi4_opendocument_en.pdf*).

### Publishing and Scheduling Content for External Delivery

For internal users, the advantages offered by directly refreshing content on demand offer a compelling advantage over traditional scheduled reports. However, there are numerous use cases where scheduled output is still required. In these cases, you still have access to the traditional scheduling tools of the SAP BusinessObjects platform as well as the improved publication system within SAP BusinessObjects 4.0. Both of these solutions allow you to schedule the refreshing of SAP Crystal Reports as a background process and then deliver the output to external destinations such as email, FTP, or network file locations.

Publications specifically offer advantages for bursting large quantities of reports to many external recipients while applying filters to the data per recipient. You can use one report to gather a list of external recipients and use that list to drive the distribution of another report with filtered data per recipient.

> **Additional Resources**
>
> For more information on managing publications, refer to Chapter 10 of the *SAP Business-Objects BI Launchpad User Guide* (*http://help.sap.com/businessobject/product_guides/boexir4/en/xi4sp5_bip_iv_en.pdf*).

### End User Viewing from Mobile Clients via SAP BusinessObjects Mobile

An important enhancement to the delivery of SAP Crystal Reports content and SAP BusinessObjects content in general is the use of SAP BusinessObjects Mobile to deliver content to users in the field or users who simply don't want to be tied down to a desk. SAP Crystal Reports—whether implemented on SAP HANA or not—is deployable via the SAP BusinessObjects mobile application.

When deployed on a mobile device SAP Crystal Reports has the advantage over some other content types, such as SAP BusinessObjects Web Intelligence, of maintaining the what-you-see-is-what-you-get design experience. This means that however the report looks at design time is how it will look on the mobile device. With the newer client devices sporting very high resolution screens, this content can remain very legible even when rendered on relatively small screens.

**Additional Resources**

For more information on using mobile clients, refer to the *SAP BusinessObjects BI Mobile User Guide* at *http://help.sap.com/businessobject/product_guides/boexir4/en/xi4sp5_mobile_user_en.pdf*.

### Custom Integration Options

In addition to all of the options discussed so far, SAP Crystal Reports offers a number of custom SDK-driven integration options for those clients that want to exercise precision control over the report delivery experience. SAP Crystal Reports can be embedded into desktop applications, web applications, and even mobile-friendly web applications via embedded browsers and JavaScript-based report viewers.

## 13.3 Product Roadmap

At the time of writing (summer 2013), the current generally available version of SAP BusinessObjects and SAP Crystal Reports was SP5. However, some information is available about the upcoming release of the SAP BusinessObjects platform, version 4.1. As with any comment on unreleased software, the following forward-looking sections can only be as accurate as the information that was available at the time and is subject to change by SAP. That said, there are a number of interesting announcements coming from SAP regarding BusinessObjects 4.1 specific to SAP Crystal Reports and especially for SAP Crystal Reports on SAP HANA. We touch on a few of those here.

### 13.3.1 Improved SAP HANA Connection Options

The most significant change coming for SAP Crystal Reports on SAP HANA is better support for querying information models (analytic and calculation views) with SAP Crystal Reports for Enterprise. Early tests of 4.1 show an improved navigation interface that recognizes the package structure and allows for easier selection of information models. This should result in a much smoother and more intuitive development process for these data sources going forward.

Version 4.1 also brings the option to develop *command objects* against published relational data sources in the same way that you could write your own command objects against traditional data source connections in SAP Crystal Reports 2011. This removes one of the roadblocks for migrating older reports from SAP Crystal Reports 2011 to SAP Crystal Reports for Enterprise.

### 13.3.2 Other Miscellaneous Improvements

Numerous additional improvements are coming to SAP Crystal Reports for Enterprise. Some are minor UI improvements to better streamline the report design workflows, and others are focused on end user experience.

## 13.4 Case Study: Delivering Targeted Marketing with SAP Crystal Reports for Enterprise on SAP HANA

AdventureWorks Cycle Company offers its products through two primary channels: a self-hosted Internet sales channel that is direct to customers, and a reseller sales channel that works with independent sports retailers throughout the world. Competition for access to reseller floor space within the cycling sports industry is very high. Therefore, reseller relations are a key strategic initiative at AdventureWorks.

To help maintain positive relationships with its dealer network, AdventureWorks engages in multiple forms of outreach. One of these methods is providing marketing data and analysis to resellers based on AdventureWorks own direct-to-customer sales. Currently, this data is delivered as a set of scheduled reports that are mailed out on a monthly basis.

The reseller relations team wants to achieve a higher level of engagement with the resellers. To help achieve this goal, they have started an initiative to construct a reseller access portal that brings together all of the interactions that AdventureWorks has with its resellers into a single one-stop shop. The hope is to provide live data content to resellers leveraging the enhanced performance that the newly implemented SAP HANA data warehouse provides. One of the first pieces of content to be delivered on the new platform will be a new version of the Reseller Marketing Report that is currently delivered as static content.

The new report will be implemented as an SAP Crystal Reports for Enterprise document. The marketing team doesn't want to expose the resellers to the complexity of the SAP BusinessObjects BI Launchpad as a UI, so they take advantage of the OpenDocument API to embed report output directly into the reseller portal in context with other marketing content. In addition, the portal will pass through the reseller region of the logged-in user so that data can be dynamically filtered to suit the current user.

### 13.4.1  Report Design

The information delivered to the resellers will consist of product sales trends tailored to the geographic region the reseller operates in. Product sales in the cycling industry are highly regional due to different materials and riding styles popular in more rugged areas versus flatter geographies.

The report header will consist of overview charts showing recent order volumes by product category/subcategory in the region. The rest of the report will focus in on the details of what products sold in the region by month.

### 13.4.2  Building the Report

For this implementation, we opted to construct the report on top of a relational universe that queries the base column tables in SAP HANA. As discussed earlier, the relational universe is the easiest of the possible SAP HANA sources to consume—at least until SAP Crystal Reports for Enterprise 4.1 comes out. Our universe offers data about our sales history by product, time, and geographic dimensions—all of which will be used in the construction of the report.

#### Connecting to Data

The first stage of development is to connect to the data source. Because you're building the report off a universe, select the SAP BusinessObjects BI platform source to choose the data connection from. After you authenticate to the repository, select the DATA SOURCE TYPE of the universe and then navigate to the folder where the

Universe is stored. In this example, the universe is stored in HANA Book, and the universe is named HANA_BOOK_INTERNET_SALES.unx, as shown in Figure 13.12.

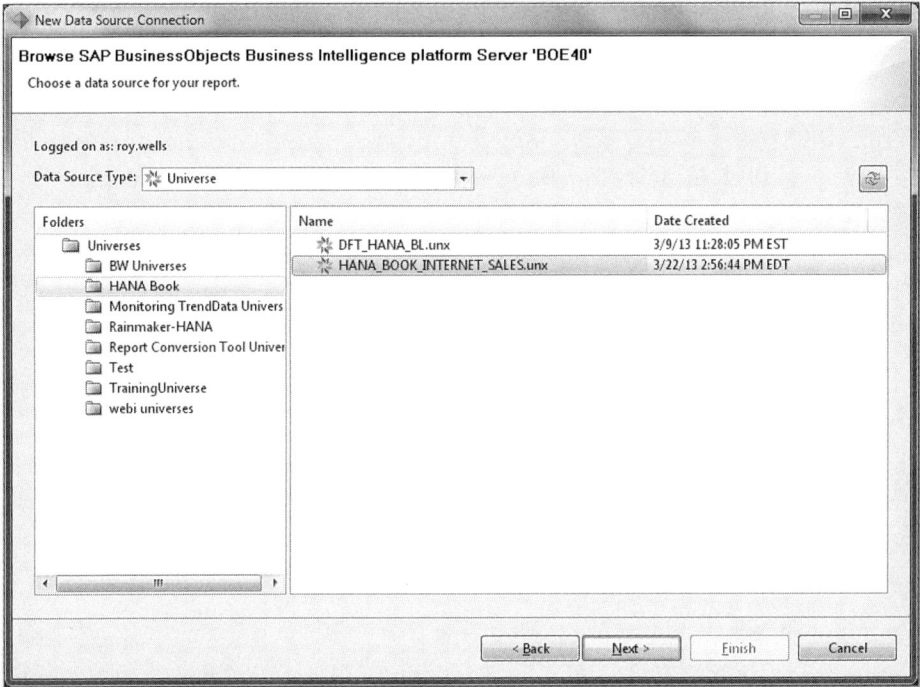

**Figure 13.12**   Selecting the Report Data Source

### Designing the Query

After you've selected a source, you need to construct the query. You're presented with the Universe Query panel where you can select the Dimensions and Measures for the result set and choose appropriate filters to limit the data. In this example report, make the selections listed in Table 13.3.

| Dimension/Measures | Values |
| --- | --- |
| Product | Product Category Name, Product Subcategory Name, Product Name |
| Order Date | Calendar Year-Month |
| Internet Sales | Order Count, Sales Amount |

**Table 13.3**   Selected Values

### Limiting Query Results with Filter

As you can see in Figure 13.13, several predefined filters from the universe are used to limit the values returned. You can, of course, define additional filters in your report query, but whenever possible, it's a good practice to use predefined filters in the universe. These greatly improve the reuse of code. The filter on GEOGRAPHY also contains a predefined prompt. This provides the runtime filtering necessary to connect the reseller portal to the report, allowing you to show just the data appropriate for the current resellers region. Make the selections shown in Table 13.4.

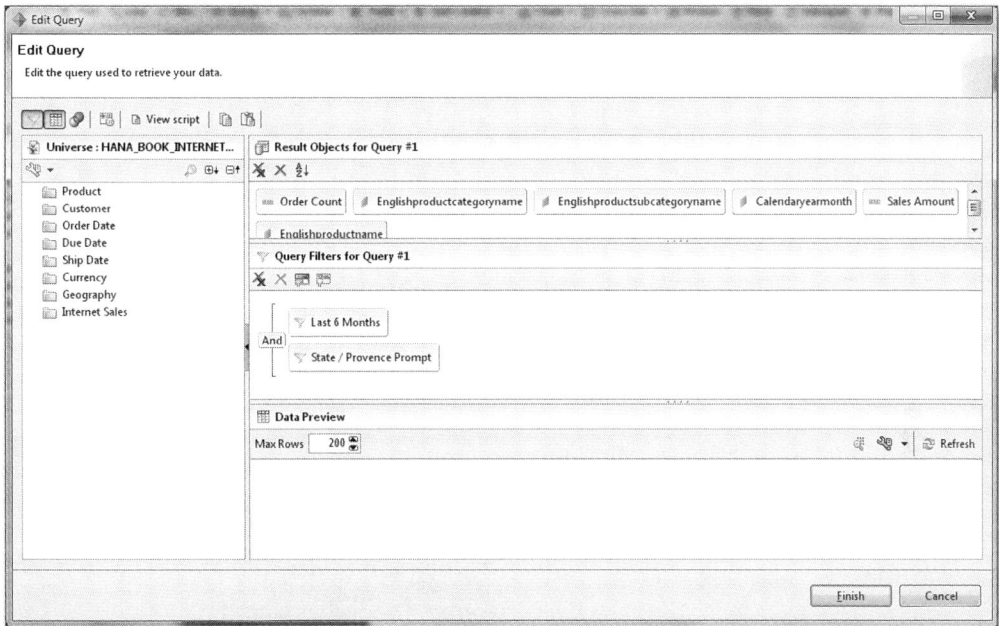

**Figure 13.13**  Constructing the Report Query

| Dimension/Measure | Values |
| --- | --- |
| ORDER DATE | LAST 6 MONTHS |
| GEOGRAPHY | STATE/PROVENCE PROMPT |

**Table 13.4**  Selected Filters

### Formatting the Report Display

After the data is selected, you can lay out the report as described earlier. Place a report title in the REPORT HEADER section, and use some of the drawing tools to provide visual separation. You can then set up the report grouping structure to prepare for adding charts and data. To show an overview of data by product category on the first page, make that the first group. Inside that group, add a chart showing the top five products sold by order count. Use the SAP Crystal Reports TOP N sorting feature to limit the results in the charts. The final page layout is shown in Figure 13.14.

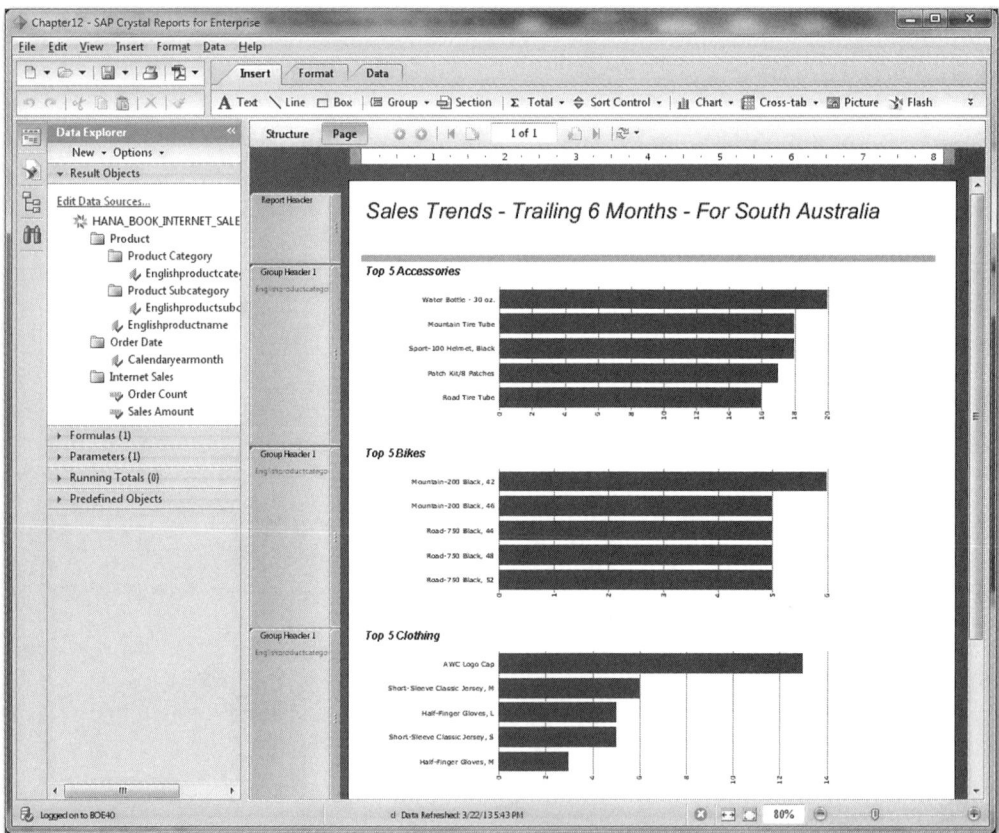

**Figure 13.14** Layout of Sales Trend Report

## Enabling Drill Down

You can take advantage of some of the SAP Crystal Reports guided navigation features that allow users to drill down to detail sections in a report when they double-click on a group header. To take advantage of this, hide the body and other group footers but flag them as available for drill down. Then, add detailed values in the body of the report to show order counts and sales amounts by product and month. Now when users drill down, they will be taken to the details for the given category. You can see what this would look like to an end user in Figure 13.15.

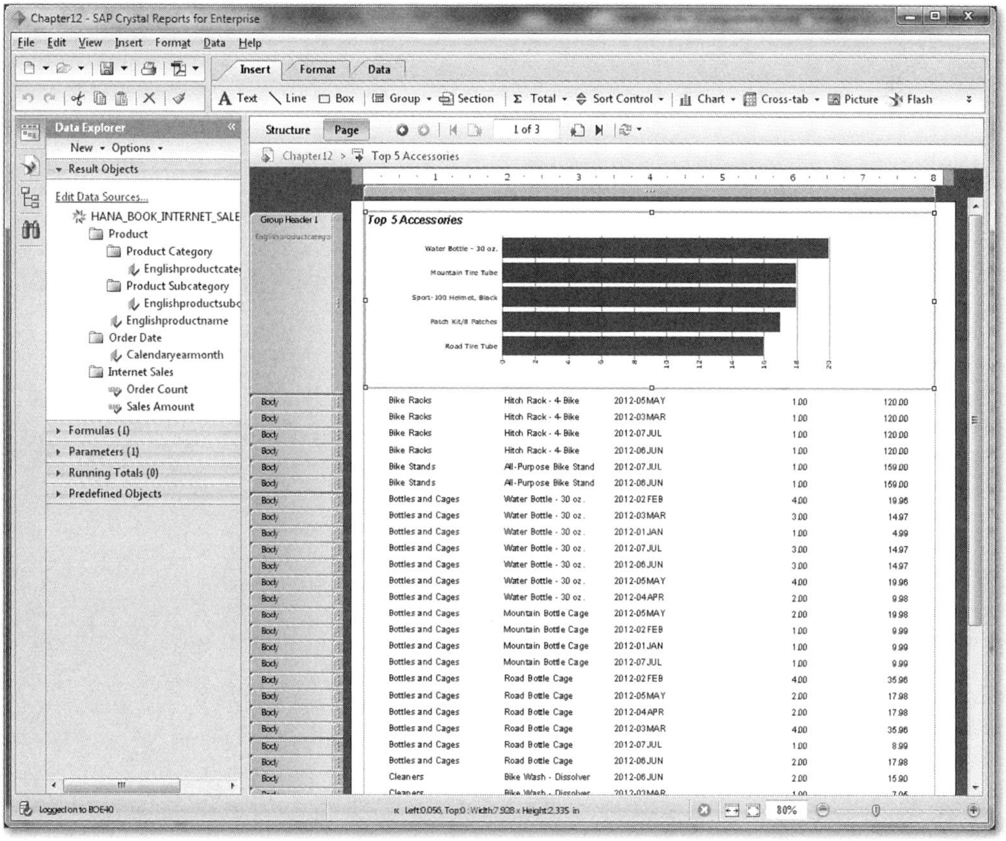

**Figure 13.15**  Drilling into a Report Section

## Deploying Report via OpenDocument

You can come back later to do more formatting, but for now, you should get the report deployed to the platform and locate the OpenDocument link to be used in the reseller portal so that you can test the integration. Saving the document is a simple matter of clicking the SAVE toolbar button and then navigating to the appropriate location in the repository structure.

From there, you can log in to the SAP BusinessObjects BI Launchpad and navigate to the same folder. Once there, you simply have to right-click on the report and choose the DOCUMENT LINK option shown in Figure 13.16 to find the link for the portal application.

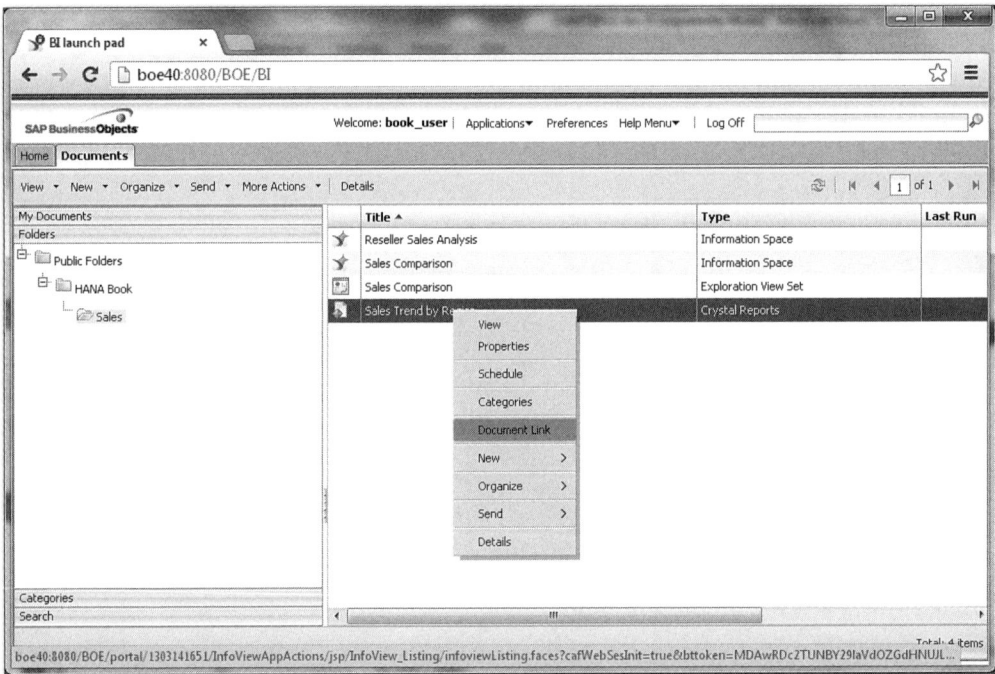

**Figure 13.16**   Locating the Document Link for Opening a Report

**Testing the Complete Solution**

With the link in hand, you can test the report in a web browser to see what resellers will see from the portal (see Figure 13.17). Because a prompt was defined on the STATE/PROVINCE, you're first presented with a prompt screen and then you're taken to the report itself. Resellers won't have to fill in the prompt value because the portal will have the opportunity to pass the report prompt on the URL. Because it's perfectly OK for resellers to see data in other regions, you can safely pass this value on the URL. If you needed to protect the data, you could implement row-level security in the universe or in SAP HANA.

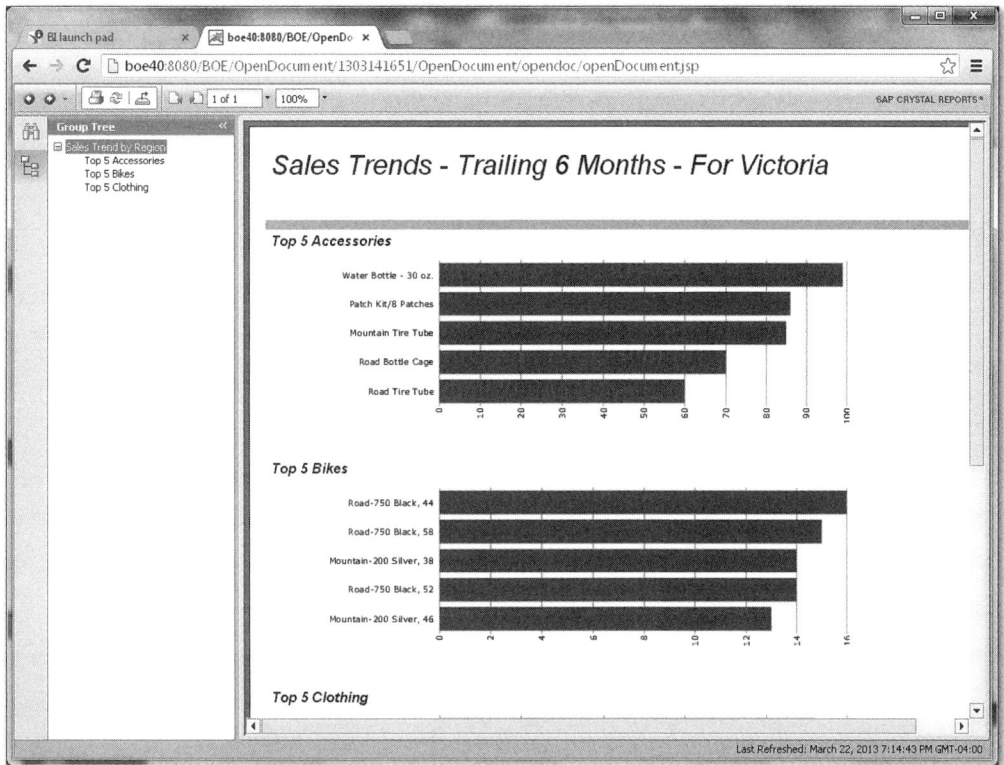

**Figure 13.17** Viewing the Final Report in the Browser

## 13.5 Summary

You've seen in this chapter that there are still uses for traditional reporting tools despite the move to in-memory computing and interactive data visualization. SAP Crystal Reports has been near the top of the BI toolbox for a generation, and its latest rendition in SAP Crystal Reports for Enterprise still brings value to the table. This value should increase even further in the upcoming 4.1 edition, where the native support for analytic and calculation views will provide a more seamless reporting environment.

In the meantime, you do have the option of reporting off of SAP HANA analytic content using column views, but the process is less than seamless. For that reason, reporting on universes for SAP Crystal Reports for Enterprise and/or direct queries on column tables in SAP Crystal Reports 2011 is the recommended approach for the time being.

*As an extension of Chapter 3, this appendix focuses on predata provisioning with SAP Information Steward.*

# A   Source System Analysis with SAP Information Steward

In Chapter 3, we discussed the predata provisioning steps to take before you provision data into SAP HANA, including why you should perform source system analysis (SSA), what could be achieved with analyzing a source, what the all-important principle of data quality is, and how to avoid "fast trash" in SAP HANA.

These topics were all discussed around the context of what SAP Data Services offers as a profiling tool. SAP Data Services has two primary profiling mechanisms: column and relationship. These are great because they are shipped with SAP Data Services, and a runtime license of SAP Data Services is included with SAP HANA, but profiling and SSA are not the primary focus of SAP Data Services. However, SAP has a solution that *is* designed around the concept of data quality monitoring: SAP Information Steward.

> **Note**
>
> This content has been included as an appendix instead of a chapter because not all companies who implement SAP HANA will necessarily have SAP Information Steward installed.

SAP Information Steward is a business user-targeted tool that is focused on being the central hub of organization for data quality, metadata, and data cleansing activities. For example, you can create business rules to render scores on data quality dimensions such as completeness or accuracy, as shown in Figure A.1.

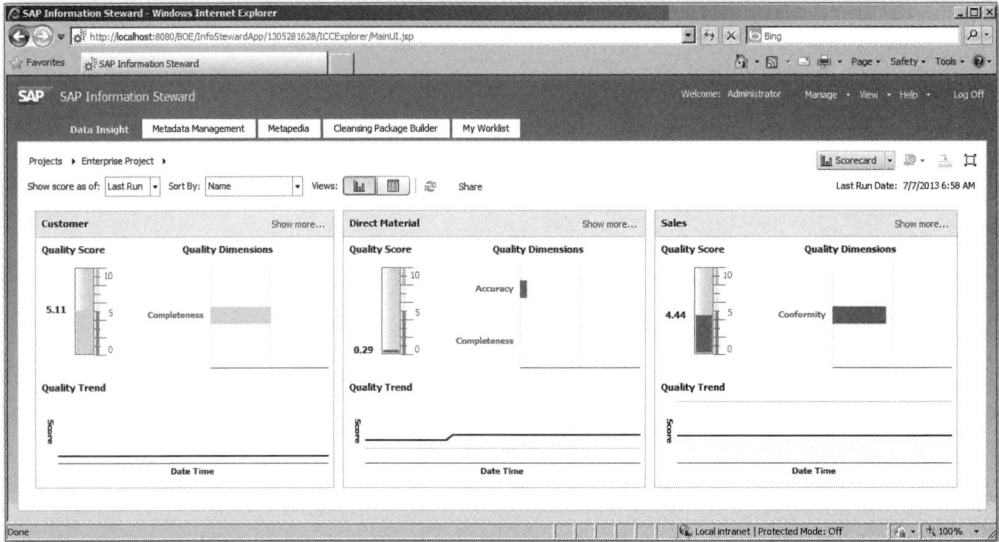

**Figure A.1**  SAP Information Steward's Data Quality Monitoring

However, you can also perform complex data profiles, collect metadata, organize a data dictionary, or create cleansing packages to fix data issues with SAP Data Services and SAP Data Quality Management. SAP Information Steward is a flexible application with many purposes and five distinct modules (shown as tabs in Figure A.1):

▶ **Data Insight**
This robust module offers complex data profiling and data scorecarding capabilities. You can also implement validation rules created by business users that can be shared in SAP Data Services as custom validation functions for ETL developers.

▶ **Metadata Management**
This is the metadata hub for the organization. You can capture metadata from most SAP tools as well as SAP BusinessObjects BI and SAP Data Services. However, these capabilities can extend to practically any metadata-creating tool from other vendors if multisource integration licensing is procured.

▶ **Metapedia**
This is designed to house the corporate data dictionary by housing business terms and categories. A workflow process is enabled with user security so that proper approvals must be maintained before terms and categories are shared with the organization.

▶ **Cleansing Package Builder (CPB)**
This is the only module specifically designed to work with SAP Data Services. CPB is used to create and maintain custom data cleansing package contents (both logic as well as dictionary values) to provide a true organizationally specific data cleansing platform.

▶ **My Worklist**
This module is new for version 4.1 and is the central hub for the workflow approval process for all of the other modules containing workflow functionality. Business users may also use this module to review match results and fix errant matching data linkage results from SAP Data Services and SAP Data Quality Management data flows.

Because there are many different aspects to SAP Information Steward, in this appendix we limit the scope of our exploration to only the Data Insight module of SAP Information Steward. Data Insight contains many powerful tools for the data steward, but our goal for this appendix is to focus on SAP Information Steward elements that support SSA for implementing SAP HANA, as well as the five types of data profiling.

## A.1    SAP Information Steward Data Insight

SAP Information Steward's Data Insight module performs a variety of different tasks. Data quality scorecards are often the first capability of Data Insight that is highlighted and touted because they are so powerful. With Data Insight, business users can create customized validation rules for a metadata-driven connection, much like a datastore in SAP Data Services. These rules are then scored against that connection to provide a baseline index of the score of the rules. Then, the rules may be gathered together on a scorecard as shown in Figure A.1, which is really just a composite score value of all of the scores assembled in Data Insight on three different data domains: customer, sales, and direct materials. These data domains are completely customizable and are used to measure almost any facet in the enterprise. Companies are using this functionality to actively monitor data quality in systems ranging from SAP Business Suite to data warehousing systems. The performance is quite good against SAP systems, and customers are exploiting this to give a dramatic view of what is going on in their operation systems to provide data-driven key performance indicators (KPIs) on the quality of their data.

This powerful functionality makes for many attention-grabbing demonstrations with the product, but the complex data profiling capabilities are often overlooked. SAP Information Steward also has five means of profiling your data, and it's this functionality that is important for supporting our quest of SSA for the organization. We'll explore these five different types of profiling in detail in the next section to see what unique insights they shed on our data to save valuable coding and development time for procurement into SAP HANA.

## A.2   Profile Your Data

The five types of profiling in the Data Insight module are both unique to SAP Information Steward and very useful for SAP HANA data procurement. These profiling types go well beyond basic column and relationship profiling using SAP Data Services:

- **Column profiling**
  Column profiling profiles numerous attributes of a column's data. This is much like SAP Data Services, but there are many more options available.

- **Address profiling**
  Unique to SAP Information Steward, address profiling uses the SAP Data Quality Management engine to quickly tell a user if an address is valid, invalid, or correctable from a deliverability standpoint using certified postal service delivery supplementary data.

- **Dependency profiling**
  Dependency profiling is much like SAP Data Services profiling, but multiple columns may be used to show the dependency of any of the columns contained within two tables.

- **Redundancy profiling**
  Redundancy profiling can determine the degree of overlapping data values or duplication between two sets of columns.

- **Uniqueness profiling**
  The uniqueness profiling task returns the count and percentage of rows that contain nonunique data for the set of column(s) selected

So there are many data investigation tools that can be used to support and extend SSA activities for an SAP HANA data mart project, but there is also another feature of Data Insight that makes it uniquely suited to an SAP HANA project: Data Insight profiling can be scheduled over time. An SAP HANA project does not happen overnight, so multiple profile tasks must be run over time manually using SAP Data Services.

While this is not a difficult task, per se, it's another task that must be maintained and executed while in the midst of a complex project. SAP Information Steward takes care of that functionality for the developer, as it is designed to be set and scheduled. Then, whenever the developer needs to investigate a column's contents and metadata, he always has an up-to-date view. This allows the SAP HANA development to capture more scenarios, as more will be uncovered with constant and consistent data collection. This can be replicated with a regular "push of a button" in SAP Data Services profiling, but it's unrealistic that the manual run will be as consistent as a machine-scheduled task. This functionality, as well as the five types of data profiling, makes SAP Information Steward a great choice for an SAP HANA development project. Let's explore these profile types in more detail.

## A.2.1    Column Profiling

Column profiling, which is shown in Figure A.2, is the first of the profile task types and arguably the most useful profiling task to support SSA activities in an SAP HANA project.

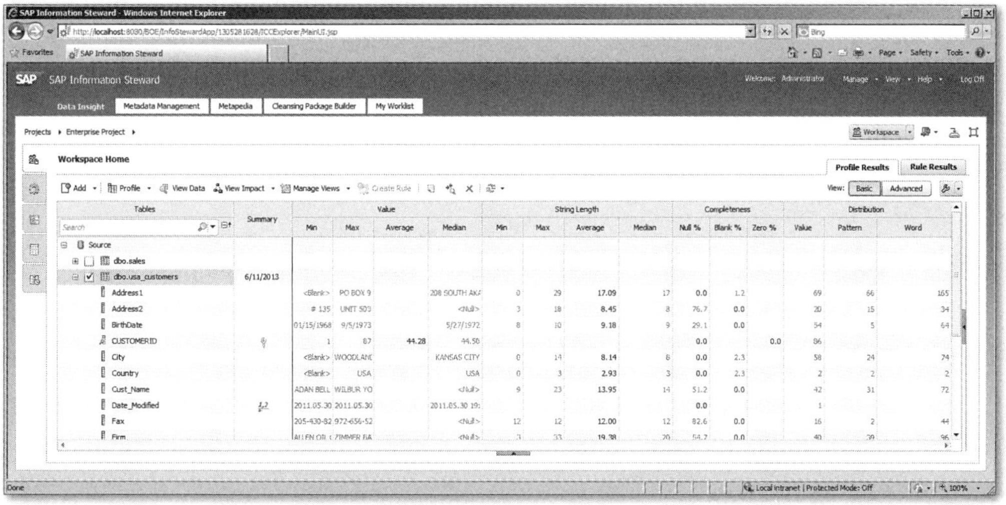

**Figure A.2**  Column Profiling Details in SAP Information Steward

You can use the columns profiling task to examine the values and characteristics of columns in a table. The profile task returns many characteristics of the attributes of a table, ranging from simple (e.g., properties) to complex (e.g., distribution). These attributes are shown in Table A.1 in increasing level of complexity.

| Column Profile Element | Category | Description |
|---|---|---|
| TYPE | Properties | Data type of the column |
| DESCRIPTION | Properties | Text metadata business description of the column if present in the source connection |
| MIN | Value | Minimum value present in the column |
| MAX | Value | Maximum value present in the column |
| AVERAGE | Value | Average value present in the column |
| MEDIAN | Value | Median value present in the column |
| MIN | String Length | Minimum string length in the column |
| MAX | String Length | Maximum string length in the column |
| AVERAGE | String Length | Average string length in the column |
| MEDIAN | String Length | Median string length in the column |
| NULL % | Completeness | Percentage of NULL values in the column |
| BLANK % | Completeness | Percentage of blank values in the column |
| ZERO % | Completeness | Percentage of zero values in the column |
| VALUE | Distribution | Number of distinct values present in a column |
| PATTERN | Distribution | Number of distinct patterns of data present in a column |
| WORD | Distribution | Number of distinct words present in a column |

**Table A.1** Column Profile Elements Available in Data Insight

You can see the usefulness of the WORD data profiling element exemplified in Figure A.3. Not only are the words broken out in an easy-to-see distribution and pattern, but you can click on the word percentages link and see the data in the pane below, which makes up the word count and distribution.

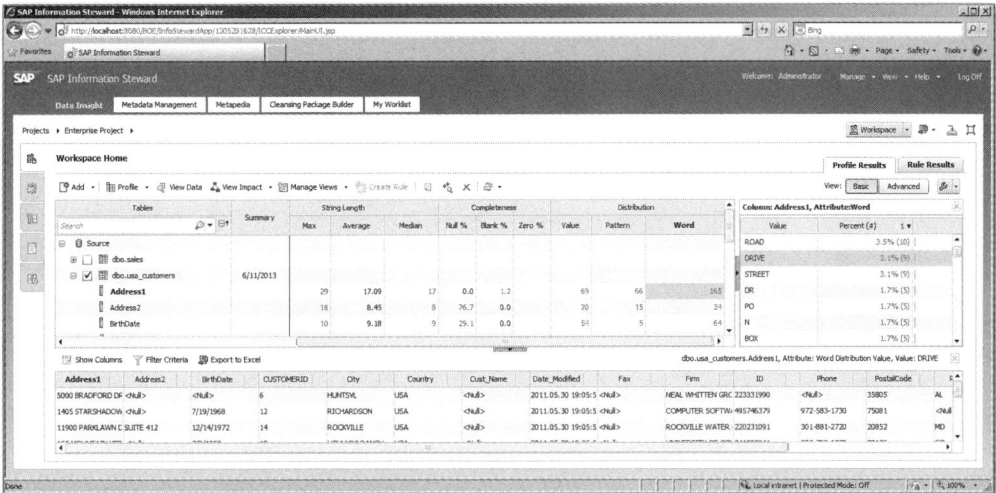

**Figure A.3** Distinct Words Shown against a varchar() Column

This is powerful functionality, but it's actually even more powerful than it seems. This isn't simply a white space break to separate words. The software is actually using data quality functionality that breaks down the words to their individual components. This is much like how data cleansing works, but that complexity is performed at the click of a button. This is much more than can be accomplished by simply profiling using SAP Data Services alone for your SAP HANA project.

## A.2.2 Address Profiling

Address profiling is a complex profiling task that quickly identifies whether address data within a record set is valid, invalid, or correctable for delivery, as described in the following list:

▶ Address data is *valid* if the address data in the record is a deliverable address.

▶ Address data is *invalid* if the address data in the record is a nondeliverable address.

▶ Address data is *correctible* when there are enough elements present in the address data that the SAP Data Quality Management software in SAP Data Services can fashion the incorrect address into a correct deliverable address.

This is possible because the address profiling task uses the SAP Data Quality Management engine to process the data and return accurate results via supplementary data from various postal services and agencies. After processing, the data is rendered into a graphical chart format with the details of all three results. As shown in Figure A.4, you can select anywhere on the chart to see detailed data for any of the three results.

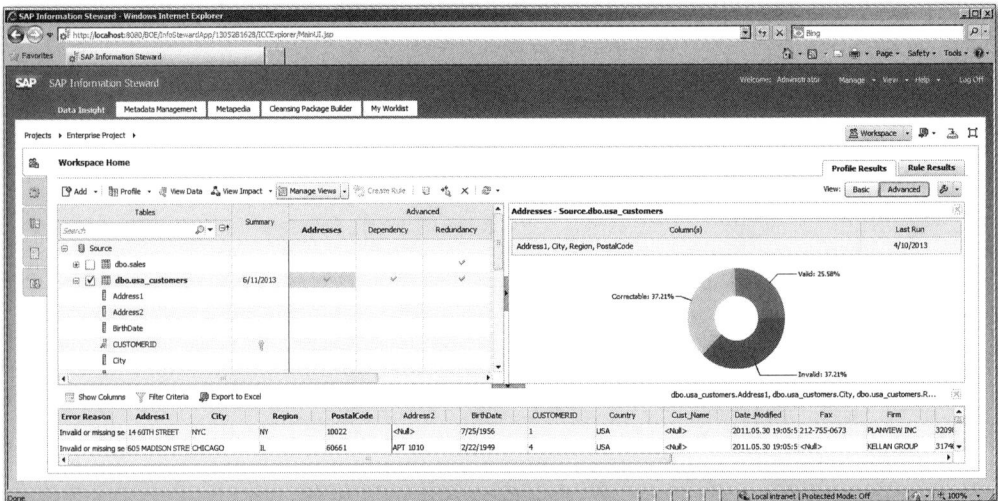

**Figure A.4** Address Profiling Showing Invalid Addresses in SAP Information Steward

Because this is a quite complex profiling task result that is being performed, it's sometimes assumed that the setup and running of the profiling task is difficult as well. Setting up data quality data flows and jobs in SAP Data Services isn't a trivial task, so it makes sense that this is the case in SAP Information Steward as well. However, this opposite is true. SAP Information Steward offers just a *single* input screen to map the address elements and a one-click execution, as shown in Figure A.5.

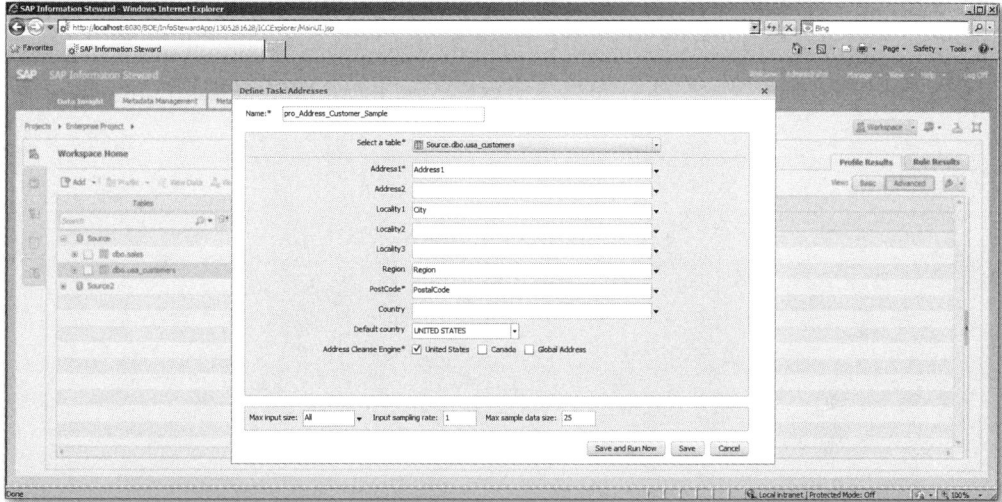

**Figure A.5**  Simplicity of the Input Screen for Address Profile Tasks

All you need to do is open the screen shown in Figure A.5, give the profiling task a name in the NAME field, and map all of the fields from the connection to the address fields. Then either save the task by clicking SAVE or execute the task by clicking SAVE AND RUN NOW.

### A.2.3  Dependency Profiling

The dependency profiling task is another powerful and complex profiling task for identifying attribute-level relationships in the data. The dependency profiling task shows true dependencies not just the relationship of one table.

The dependency profiling task finds the values in one or more dependent columns that rely on values in a primary column in another table. For example, for each state (primary column), you can find the corresponding city name (dependent column) and report on the number of related cities to states as well as the percentage of the relationship. Just as in SAP Data Services, these columns don't have to be related in the database or application. The tables and columns exist as metadata divorced from the source systems. You define the relationship as well as the connection. Figure A.6 illustrates this process with an example of a postal code to region dependency profile.

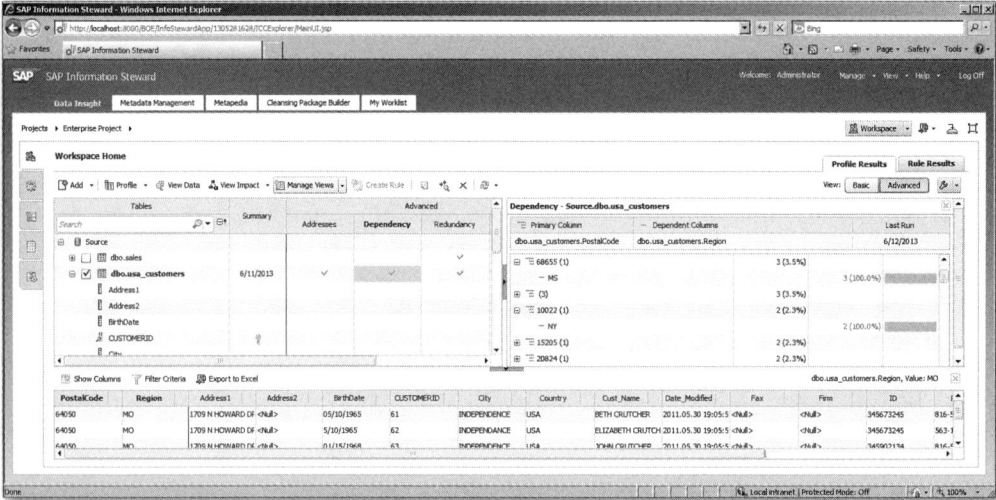

**Figure A.6** Dependency Profile Results in SAP Information Steward

## A.2.4 Redundancy Profiling

The redundancy profiling task is used to determine the degree of overlapping data values or duplication between two sets of columns in two different tables. The results will list all of the matching and nonmatching values between the set of columns. Each set can contain one or more columns to use as comparison columns, and as with all of the other SAP Information Steward profiling tasks, there is no relationship at the database level required on any of the columns. The databases can be on different platforms and of differing connection types, as this is all metadata driven.

This type of profiling aligns closest with relationship profiling in SAP Data Services, but it's more flexible because redundancy profiles show any types of related columns—not just one relationship per table noting orphan records, as in SAP Data Services. You have the concept of a main table and a comparison table, and you may select as many comparison columns as make sense between the two tables.

Figure A.7 shows redundancy profiling between a customer table (USA_CUSTOMERS) and a table containing sales information (SALES), comparing the primary key of the customer table CUSTOMERID with the foreign key CUSTOMERID from the SALES table.

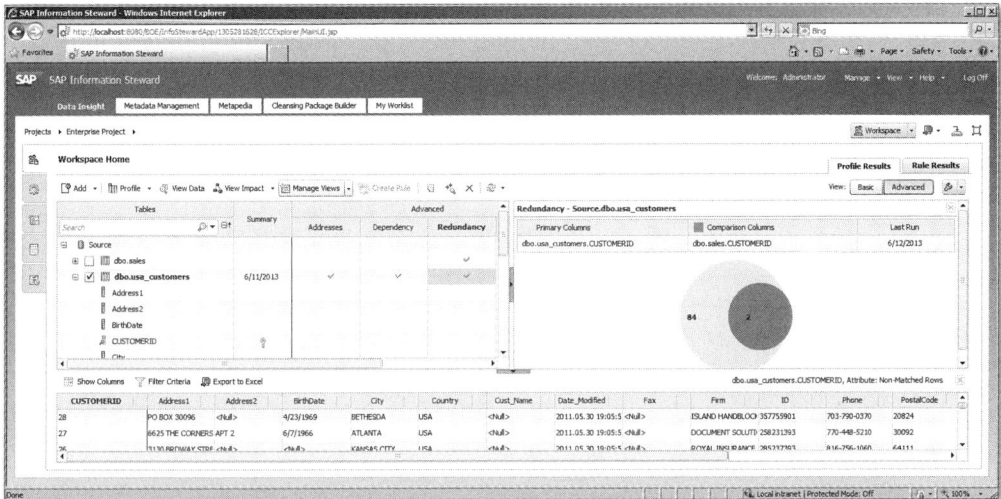

**Figure A.7** Redundancy Profile Results in SAP Information Steward

## A.2.5 Uniqueness Profiling

Uniqueness profiling is the final type of profiling task in SAP Information Steward; it returns the count and percentage of rows that contain nonunique data for the set of column(s) selected. For example, you can run a uniqueness profiling task on an employee ID column to ensure that each employee has a unique ID. An example of uniqueness profiling is shown in Figure A.8. The title column in the figure is mostly duplicated or nonunique with a representation of 89% of the columns row count. This tells you that the column doesn't have very many unique values.

Uniqueness profiling is particularly useful to determine the cardinality of columns (i.e., uniqueness of data) in a particular table. Because multiple columns may be run against the same table, it's easy to report on the relative cardinality of data in a number of columns. This is very useful to an SAP HANA initiative. Recall from Chapter 2 that cardinality is important for calculating join cost and determining the level of denormalization required when designing the data model for high performance in SAP HANA. This is just one example of another great SAP Information Steward profiling use case for SAP HANA.

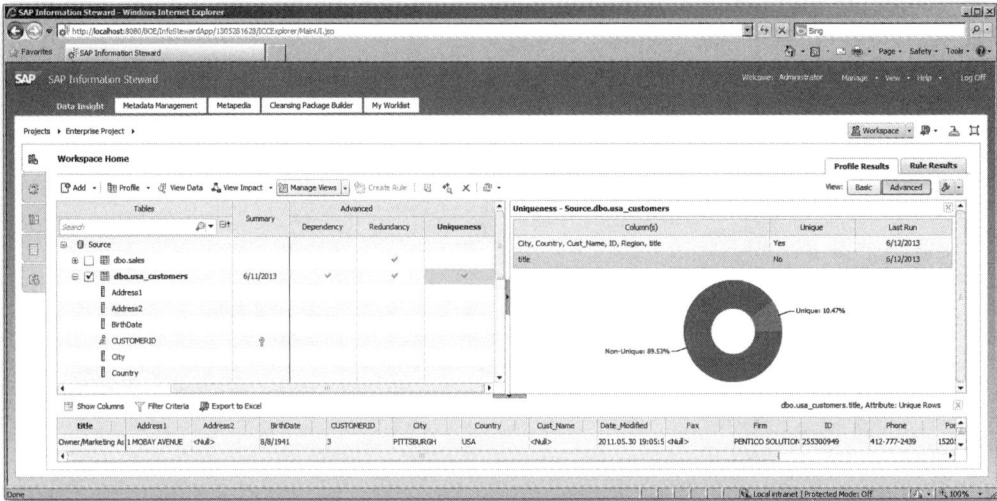

**Figure A.8** Uniqueness Profile Results in SAP Information Steward

## A.3 Summary

In this appendix, we discussed many options for profiling tasks in SAP Information Steward that are helpful to better understand your data before you provision that data into SAP HANA. SAP HANA is an immensely powerful platform, but it's only really useful with data that has high quality. Discovering the information quickly is only advantageous if the information is worth discovering and actionable.

Profiling your sources is important because it saves time and money. You can use SAP Data Services for your profiling tasks as you get a runtime license for an enterprise class data integration tool complete with enterprise class profiling and SSA capabilities. However, many more types of profiling are available with SAP Information Steward, which, even though a separate license is needed, may be quite valuable to your predata provisioning tasks.

Predata provisioning is one step in the process that you don't want to skip. Not performing proper source system analysis upfront in the process can lead to costly mistakes in your development cycle. Performing proper source system analysis shows you the real story behind your data, and makes sure that you aren't just loading "fast trash" into SAP HANA. It's only after this step that you're ready to begin the process to provision your data into SAP HANA.

# B    The Authors

**Jonathan Haun** currently serves as the lead SAP HANA consultant and consulting manager with Decision First Technologies. Over the past two years, he has had the opportunity to help several clients implement solutions using SAP HANA. In addition to being certified in multiple SAP BusinessObjects tools, he is also a SAP Certified Application Associate and SAP Certified Technology Associate for SAP HANA 1.0. Jonathan has worked in the field of business intelligence for more than 10 years. During this time, he has gained invaluable experience while helping customers implement solutions using the tools from the SAP BusinessObjects product line. Before working as a full-time business intelligence consultant, he worked in a variety of information technology management and administrative roles. His combination of experience and wealth of technical knowledge make him an ideal source of information pertaining to business intelligence solutions powered by SAP HANA. You can follow Jonathan on Twitter at *@jdh2n* or visit his blog at *http:// bobj.sapbiblog.com*.

**Chris Hickman** is a certified SAP BusinessObjects consultant and principal consultant at Decision First Technologies. His specific areas of expertise include reporting, analysis, dashboard development, and visualization techniques. Chris' software development background has enabled him to achieve proven effectiveness in architecting, developing, testing, and supporting both desktop-based and web-based applications for many customer engagements representing various industries. Chris also speaks globally at SAP and ASUG events.

**Don Loden** is a principal consultant at Decision First Technologies with full lifecycle data warehouse and information governance experience in multiple verticals. He is an SAP Certified Application Associate on SAP Business-Objects Data Integrator, and he is very active in the SAP community, speaking globally at numerous SAP and ASUG conferences and events. He has more than 14 years of information technology experience in the following areas: ETL architecture, development, and tuning; logical and physical data modeling; and mentoring on data warehouse, data quality, information governance, and ETL concepts. You can follow Don on Twitter at *@donloden*. You can contact Don by email at *don.loden@decisionfirst.com*.

**Roy Wells** is a principal consultant at Decision First Technologies, where he uses his 15 years of experience in system and application architecture to lead clients in the successful implementation of end to end BI solutions. He is particularly interested in delivering innovative visualization solutions and developing customized end user experiences that enable business transformation. He also enjoys mentoring and speaking publicly about BI, software development, and system integration solutions at conferences and venues worldwide. You can follow Roy on Twitter at *@rgwbobj* or contact him by email at *roy.wells@decisionfirst.com*.

### Contributor

**Hillary Bliss** is the analytics practice lead at Decision First Technologies and specializes in data warehouse design, ETL development, statistical analysis, and predictive modeling. She works with clients and vendors to integrate business analysis and predictive modeling solutions into the organizational data warehouse and business intelligence environments based on their specific operational and strategic business needs. She has a master's degree in statistics and an MBA from Georgia Tech. You can follow Hillary on Twitter at *@HillaryBlissDFT* or reach her by email at *hillary.bliss@decisionfirst.com*.

# Index

829

- For the executive: what SAP HANA is and how it can help you

- For the practitioner: details on data modeling, data provisioning, and the SAP HANA client tools

- For everyone: the latest and greatest developments—Suite on SAP HANA

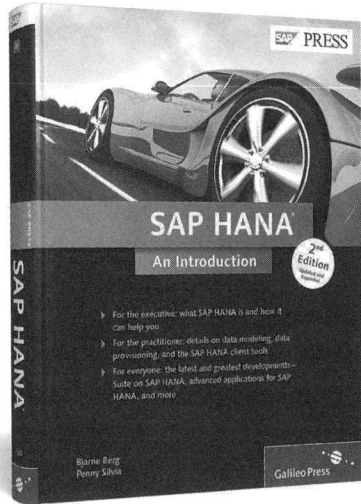

Bjarne Berg, Penny Silvia

# SAP HANA

## An Introduction

HANA is shifting SAP into high gear—don't get left in the dust. In this updated edition of our best-selling book, explore the what, why, when, and how of SAP HANA. From building a business strategy to administering a system—and all the pit stops in between—you'll get the big picture you need to get started. Buckle up!

527 pp., 2. edition 2013, 69,95 Euro / US$ 69.95
ISBN 978-1-59229-865-5
www.sap-press.com

**Interested in reading more?**

Please visit our website for all new
book and e-book releases from SAP PRESS.

**www.sap-press.com**